*The American
Immigration Collection*

International Migrations

Volume I: Statistics

IMRE FERENCZI

Arno Press and The New York Times

NEW YORK 1970

Reprint Edition 1970 by Arno Press Inc.

Reprinted from a copy in
The Kansas State University Library

LC# 77-129396
ISBN 0-405-00550-4

The American Immigration Collection—Series II
ISBN for complete set 0-405-00543-1

Manufactured in the United States of America

PUBLICATIONS OF THE NATIONAL BUREAU OF
ECONOMIC RESEARCH, INCORPORATED

No. 14

INTERNATIONAL MIGRATIONS

VOLUME I

National Bureau of Economic Research, Inc.

Incorporated under the Membership Corporation Laws of the State of New York, January 29, 1920

ITS ORGANIZATION AND PURPOSES

THE National Bureau of Economic Research was organized in 1920 in response to a growing demand for exact and impartial determinations of facts bearing on economic, social, and industrial problems.

It seeks not only to find facts and make them known, but to determine them in such manner and under such supervision as to make its findings carry conviction to Liberal and Conservative alike.

Entire control of the Bureau is vested in a Board of Directors, representing universities, learned and scientific societies, financial, industrial, agricultural, commercial, labor, and technical organizations.

Rigid provisions in the Charter and By-Laws guard the Bureau from becoming a source of profit to its members, directors, or officers and from becoming an agency for propaganda. No report of the Research Staff may be published without the approval of the Directors, and any Director who dissents from any finding approved by a majority of the Board may have such dissent published with the majority report.

The members of the Board of Directors are as follows:

DIRECTORS AT LARGE

H. W. LAIDLER, Executive Director, League for Industrial Democracy, *Vice President.*
T. W. LAMONT, Member of the firm of J. P. Morgan and Company, New York.
L. C. MARSHALL, Institute for the Study of Law, Johns Hopkins University.
GEORGE O. MAY, Member of the firm of Price, Waterhouse and Company, New York, *Chairman of the Board.*
ELWOOD MEAD, Commissioner of Reclamation, Washington, D. C.
GEORGE SOULE, Director, The Labor Bureau, Inc.
N. I. STONE, Industrial Consultant, New York.
MATTHEW WOLL, Vice President, American Federation of Labor.

DIRECTORS BY UNIVERSITY APPOINTMENT

THOMAS S. ADAMS, Professor of Political Economy, Yale University, *President.*
JOHN R. COMMONS, Professor of Economics, University of Wisconsin.
EDWIN F. GAY, Professor of Economic History, Harvard University, *Director of Research.*
WESLEY C. MITCHELL, Professor of Economics, Columbia University, *Director of Research.*
JOSEPH H. WILLITS, Professor of Industry, Wharton School of Finance and Commerce, University of Pennsylvania.

DIRECTORS BY APPOINTMENT OF OTHER REPRESENTATIVE ORGANIZATIONS

DAVID FRIDAY, American Economic Association.
M. C. RORTY, American Statistical Association.
GEORGE E. ROBERTS, American Bankers Association, *Treasurer.*
HUGH FRAYNE, American Federation of Labor.
A. W. SHAW, National Publishers' Association.
GRAY SILVER, American Farm Bureau Federation.
LEE GALLOWAY, American Management Association.
ROBERT B. WOLF, American Engineering Council.

O. W. KNAUTH, *Recording Secretary.*   G. R. STAHL, *Executive Secretary.*

RESEARCH STAFF

EDWIN F. GAY, *Director*
FREDERICK R. MACAULAY
HARRY JEROME
WILLFORD I. KING
WILLARD L. THORP

WESLEY C. MITCHELL, *Director*
FREDERICK C. MILLS
WALTER F. WILLCOX
LEO WOLMAN
SIMON KUZNETS

INTERNATIONAL MIGRATIONS

VOLUME I

STATISTICS

COMPILED ON BEHALF OF THE
INTERNATIONAL LABOUR OFFICE, GENEVA

WITH

INTRODUCTION AND NOTES

By

IMRE FERENCZI

AND EDITED ON BEHALF OF THE
NATIONAL BUREAU OF ECONOMIC RESEARCH

By

WALTER F. WILLCOX

NEW YORK
NATIONAL BUREAU OF ECONOMIC
RESEARCH, Inc.
1929

PRINTED IN THE UNITED STATES OF AMERICA BY
THE MESSENGER PRESS, ST. ALBANS, VT.

PREFACE

The present volume has grown out of the appointment in 1924 by the Social Science Research Council of a Committee on the scientific aspects of human migration, a subject of great and growing interest in the United States upon which further studies supported by an adequate subvention were thought to be needed. Previous American work in this field has been done mainly through official channels which have necessarily influenced its character and conclusions, or through private associations, often of a propagandist tendency, or by single scholars whose time and resources were narrowly limited.

This Committee approved an initial project for a statistical study of international migration and entrusted its preparation to the National Bureau of Economic Research which asked the writer to organize and direct the enquiry. It has fallen into two parts: first, the preparation of the present volume containing international migration statistics from the beginning of the record in each country through 1924 and, secondly, the preparation of a series of interpretative studies of migration statistics written by scholars in different countries. Both volumes aim to be international and objective in dealing with a problem upon which judgments, national and individual, differ widely.

To further the project by enlisting international co-operation, the writer visited Geneva where he fortunately obtained the support of the International Labour Office. That Office through its Migration Section ably headed by Professor Louis Varlez had already done important pioneer work in improving current migration statistics. Under authorization of the peace treaties it had established or was in a position quickly to establish direct and cordial relations with the offices in all countries responsible for migration statistics past or present, a matter the importance of which persons familiar with the leisurely and circumlocutory way in which routine correspondence between governments is often handled will be quick to appreciate. The International Labour Office was thus in a favorable position to push its researches back into the pre-war period.

The preparation of this volume was entrusted to that Office under an agreement that the net cost should be borne by the National

Bureau of Economic Research. The office at the request of the writer placed Dr. Imre Ferenczi in immediate charge of the work. While he had been acting chief of the Migration Section he had prepared and brought out the report on "Mouvements Migratoires 1920-23" which by a fortunate coincidence came from the press on the very day on which the writer arrived in Geneva and the excellence of which immediately roused his admiration. Dr. Ferenczi is to be regarded as the author of this book and particularly of the Introduction and Notes; the relation of the undersigned to it has been that of adviser, editor and liaison agent between the National Bureau of Economic Research in New York and the International Labour Office in Geneva. In that capacity he has carefully followed its progress and is glad to commend the conscientious care and expert knowledge shown in its preparation. It is far more than a mere compilation of known and available migration statistics. Much material hitherto unknown has been disinterred and much energy, persistance and organizing ability have gone into its preparation within a period of ten months. Evidence to support this conclusion will be found throughout the volume but especially in Dr. Ferenczi's introduction and notes.

WALTER F. WILLCOX.

RESOLUTION

INTERNATIONAL MIGRATIONS

CONTENTS

LIST OF TABLES

LIST OF INTERNATIONAL TABLES

NORTH AMERICA

NORTHERN

CANADA

MIQUELON AND SAINT PIERRE

NEWFOUNDLAND AND LABRADOR

UNITED STATES

IMMIGRATION

SOUTHERN

MEXICO

CENTRAL AMERICA
AND
WEST INDIES AND BERMUDAS

BRITISH WEST INDIES

RUSSIA

SOUTHWESTERN EUROPE

ITALY

PORT STATISTICS

STATISTICS OF CARPI

B

LIST OF DIAGRAMS

INTERNATIONAL MIGRATION STATISTICS

PART I

INTRODUCTION

INTRODUCTION

History and Conduct of the Inquiry.

The offer made to the International Labour Organization in 1925 by the National Bureau of Economic Research under the auspices of the Social Science Research Council to finance an historical inquiry into international migration statistics, if the former would undertake it, was cordially accepted, as such an inquiry fell entirely within its province.

The International Labour Office had already published a report on methods[1] and a first annual report[2] on migration drawn up in accordance with a recommendation adopted by the International Labour Conference of 1922.[3] The offer of the National Bureau of Economic Research thus afforded an opportunity of proceeding one step farther towards co-ordinating international migration statistics. An investigation of the development of these statistics from their introduction to the present day would render possible a more intelligent appreciation of their foundation and growth, and also of the necessity and feasibility of improving them. Such an historical study, it was felt, would tend likewise to facilitate international negotiations regarding uniformity in this field.

Acceptance of the proposal was recommended October 4, 1925, by the Director of the International Labour Office, M. Albert Thomas, to the Governing Body of the International Labour Organization in the following words:

> The Governing Body will be interested to learn of an important proposal made to it by Professor Willcox on behalf of the American National Bureau of Economic Research, which is undertaking an extensive inquiry into the past history of migration. Professor Willcox was very favourably impressed by the recent publication of the Office: "Migration Movements, 1920-1923," and has requested that the Office should undertake a comple-

[1] *Methods of compiling Statistics of Emigration and Immigration*, Geneva, 1922.
[2] *Migration Movements*, 1920-1923, Geneva, 1925.
[3] Section II of the Recommendation runs as follows:—
The General Conference recommends that each Member of the International Labour Organisation should make every effort to communicate to the International Labour Office, within six months of the end of the year to which they refer, and so far as information is available, the total figures of emigrants and immigrants, showing separately nationals and aliens, and specifying particularly, for nationals, and, as far as possible, for aliens: (1) sex, (2) age, (3) occupation, (4) nationality, (5) country of last residence, (6) country of proposed residence.

mentary work dealing with official migration statistics so far as they are available from the beginning in each country in which they have been issued. For this purpose the National Bureau of Economic Research is prepared to place a sum of 30,000 francs at the disposal of the Office for the purpose of making the necessary researches in the national archives and engaging the temporary assistance necessary.[1] It is proposed to place the investigation under the direction of Dr. Ferenczi, the author of the study already published; and the sum placed at our disposal by the American institution will make it possible to afford the necessary assistance to the Migration Service and avoid the ordinary work of the Office being interfered with by this new piece of work, which is within the general framework of its researches. The offer is interesting as showing the increasing appreciation of the scientific work of the Office in competent circles and the Governing Body will no doubt wish to approve of the arrangement proposed by Professor Willcox.

The proposal was adopted by the Governing Body. The first paragraph of the resulting contract reads:

The International Labour Office will assemble and publish in one volume the international statistics of human migration from the beginning of the record in each country to the present time. It is understood that the definitions, classifications and tabulations established by the International Labour Office in "Migration Movements, 1920-1923" will be adopted in the present document as far as the difference of the conditions permits.

The writer was designated for the task in the middle of September 1925 and, with the results of his earlier studies[2] and the aid of documents and books already available, he began at once upon preliminary plans. Two months later he submitted a detailed program of work which assumed that a purely scientific task had to be executed, and that the inquiry could be fruitful only if the collection of national statistics were made exhaustive and summarized, so far as possible, in international tables.

[1]As the material proved to be much more abundant than had been anticipated and the duration of the inquiry had to be extended from July 1, 1926 to April 15, 1927, the National Bureau allotted another $4,000 which, with the $6,500 already contributed, and an additional $2,000, made a total of $12,500 placed at the disposal of the inquiry.
[2]I. Ferenczi, *Unemployment and the International Migration of Workers:* Report to the International Committee of the International Association on Unemployment, Jena, 1913, page 31.

The accumulation of an unbroken series of statistics for particular countries from the beginning of the record, which in some cases goes back more than one hundred years and in many cases more than fifty, would not of itself have permitted an accurate review of the migratory movements recorded in the national tables. An international and historical tabulation and interpretation of the statistics thus became necessary, revising and extending as far as possible what earlier statisticians (Bodio, Sundbärg) had begun.

Moreover, migration statistics, even those of recent date, are very incomplete and, for not a few countries, are altogether wanting. This being so, it was planned at first to publish under each emigration country tables showing the number of emigrants from it to each country recording their arrival and also tables showing the number of immigrants returning to it from each country recording their departure ("indirect migration statistics"). This would give under each country a conspectus of all the statistical information about international migration affecting it, whether that country produced the statistics or not. Such tables were prepared but the unexpected wealth of material developed by the inquiry and the necessary limits of publishing costs and of pages for this volume led to their omission. Under the notes for each country, however, will be found, as a substitute, references to other parts of the volume where the information thus assembled can be gathered.

The inquiries into the origin of migration statistics went back to the discovery of America which really opened the modern period of inter-continental migrations. The colonial expansion of Europe, more than any preceding mass migration, has radically changed the face of the earth. The population, not only of the colonies, but also of Europe, grew to enormous dimensions. World commerce and industry arose and European languages and customs spread over the globe.

Inasmuch as the number of emigrants from Europe during three centuries was checked, first, by the emigrants from Africa as slaves and, later, by semi-voluntary or indentured emigrants from Africa, Asia and Polynesia, it was imperative to take account also of these currents of migration. Accordingly, the broadest possible definition of an emigrant has been adopted, a definition which includes not merely all persons changing their residence from one country to another but also all persons going from one continent to another with a view to residing there for over a year, even if the destination

was a colonial possession of the country to which the migrant belonged.[1]

While inter-continental migrations have occupied the foreground in the present study, continental migrations within Europe and in other parts of the world could not be disregarded. The two had their origin in much the same historical, economic and political conditions and involved approximately the same groups of persons. The continental migrations of the eighteenth century to Hungary, Galicia, Prussia and Russia are especially noteworthy. They were organized on a large scale by the far-sighted rulers of those countries and down to the close of the century they effectively competed with inter-continental migrations. Similarly, the second half of the nineteenth century saw the development within Europe and Asia of seasonal and temporary migrations of no mean importance. After the Great War the United States and France became the main centers for continental immigration.

The original intention was to limit the scope of the present work to international migration. This raised many problems. The emigration of Frenchmen to Algiers, or of Russians to Siberia, is not international migration. But it is inter-continental and analogous to the migration of English to Canada or Australia. So it was decided to include inter-continental as well as international migration for which records were obtainable.

Collection of the Materials.

The material here presented was procured by:

(1)   Correspondence between the International Labour Office and Member States.

(2)   Application to statistical offices and other competent authorities and experts.

(3)   Researches made in the leading archives and libraries of Europe.

(4)   The good offices of the editor of this work and the representative of the International Labour Office at Washington.[2]

As a consequence of its youth—it dates from 1920—the Inter-

[1]The definition of the term "emigrant" has varied incessantly since the advent of the inter-continental movement of emigration. Until the nineteenth century emigration was predominantly involuntary, including as it did numbers of delinquents, prisoners of war, rebels, slaves, serfs, and others wholly or partly unfree.

[2]In this way a complete collection of statistical reports of the United States and the advice of the Commissioner General of Immigration were obtained.

national Labour Office did not have in its library the earlier books and documents presenting figures on international migration. But the relations of that office to the Member States, relations that were to be utilized in the inquiry, were a guarantee that the investigation would be carried to a successful issue. A circular letter from it could count on a cordial reception from the Member States, but the exceptional material needed would not be readily available or easily secured. A circular letter, indeed, was sent to extra-European Governments with which the International Labour Office did not stand in active relations.[1] The author attended the session of the International Statistical Institute at Rome in October, 1925, where this inquiry was discussed, met many officials of statistical departments or of migration offices, and bespoke their interest. These contacts led in many cases to a direct correspondence. On the basis of previous international reports and printed national sources, historical outline tables were prepared and submitted to competent authorities for criticism. Needed volumes of statistics were obligingly loaned; historical tables were prepared with the utmost care and forwarded. Where still earlier data were shown to exist they were sooner or later forthcoming. Many discrepancies were explained and other obstacles removed.

Statistical departments, having to do only with the statistical period, could hardly be expected to know what records about migration were in the archives or the older literature. The connections of the International Labour Office with the Governments were therefore utilized to facilitate local studies in European archives and libraries. Furnished with introductions from the Director of the International Labour Office, the writer was able quickly to run through the material in archives and libraries and, with the help of his collaborators, to extract what was wanted. The branch offices of the International Labour Office were most helpful and the temporary staff engaged for the inquiry were devoted and zealous.

Eight study tours were made after full preparation by correspondence with Government Departments and experts, and the following archives and libraries of Europe were visited in order to examine their material:

London: British Museum Library, Public Record Office, Foreign Office, Home Office, Board of Trade, Colonial Office, Overseas Settlement Department, Offices of the High Commissioners for Australia,

[1]These were: Costa Rica, Salvador, Guatemala, Colombia, Peru, Nicaragua, Panama, Bolivia, Honduras, Haiti, Persia, Albania.

Canada, New Zealand, and South Africa, the Royal Statistical Society, the Royal Colonial Institute and the Imperial Institute. *Paris*: Archives Nationales, Bibliothèque nationale, Archives du Ministère des colonies, Ministère du commerce, Prèfecture de la Police, Statistique gènèrale de la France.

Strassburg: Archives du Departement du Bas Rhin.

Berlin: Preussisches Geheimes Staatsarchiv, Preussische Staatsbibliothek, Statistisches Reichsamt, Archiv des Ministeriums des Äussern.

Hamburg: Kommerzbibliothek, Staatsarchiv.

Bremen: Städtisches Archiv, Bibliothek der Handelskammer.

Vienna: Staatsarchiv, Staatsbibliothek, Universitätsbibliothek, Bibliothek des Bundesamtes für Statistik.

Budapest: M. kir. Központi statisztikai Hivatal könyvtára (Library of the National Statistical Office).

The researches in London where they began were promoted in every way by numerous Government departments. Some formal difficulties were promptly removed through the intervention of the British representative on the Governing Body of the International Labour Organization. With such friendly support, simultaneous researches were prosecuted in several libraries and archives. Personal connections were established which later continued to be helpful. The Ministry of Labour transmitted data about British possessions and for months replied to numerous questions. The statistical department of the Board of Trade prepared a valuable memorandum on the development of British migration statistics.[1]

The ready help given in England was paralleled in other nations. The French Colonial Ministry addressed a circular letter to all the French colonies which brought in a large mass of statistical material and ensured a number of improvements in their statistics for the future. Through the French Ministry of the Interior unpublished migration statistics of Morocco and Tunis were obtained. The publication by that Ministry of annual reports concerning emigration had been discontinued in 1881. Only one complete set of these reports from 1856 onward could be traced. It was found in the cellars of the Police Prefecture of Paris, and was courteously opened for examination. The old decrees on which these statistics were

[1]The recent official publications of the United Kingdom usually have not distinguished between emigration to Australia and that to New Zealand. Separate information for these colonies has been discovered and also statistics for the Cape of Good Hope, 1821-40. It has also been possible to establish statistics of emigration to the British Colonies in North America during the years 1842-67.

based were found in manuscript and examined in the room of the sub-prefect.[1]

The representative of the German Reich on the Governing Body of the International Labour Office requested the persons in charge of a number of German archives which could not be visited to forward rare documents to Geneva. In some cases this was done most generously; in others, special copies of the documents were forwarded.[2]

In Italy the General Emigration Office put its branch services at our disposal and instructed the emigration commissioner of Genoa to facilitate researches in the archives and libraries of that city.[3] The Emigration Office has also thoroughly revised the provisional statistics published for 1920-24.

In the State archives in Vienna officials had examined the earlier records before the arrival of the writer, enabling him to proceed at once to a close study of the documents.

In the Netherlands the Director of the Statistical Office arranged for a preliminary study of the earlier manuscript documents in his files, had extracts made from periodical and other publications, and secured contacts with other scientific institutions of the country.

The Swiss Emigration Office compiled statistical data from 1868 to the present day that are more complete than any foreign scholar could get from the Swiss archives. Thereby practically all contradictions in the tables have been eliminated.

The statistics for the United States have been compiled in European libraries supplemented by all the important American publications, including Bromwell, Young, the *Monthly Summary of Commerce and Finance* for the United States and the *Annual Reports of the Commissioner General of Immigration*. With the assistance of the numerous documents which have been collected, the present series of American migration statistics is probably more nearly complete than any heretofore published in the United States.

The Canadian Government has supplied statistics beginning with the first attempts at colonization in that country. These data for the period before 1848 have been supplemented by the examination of archives and annual statistics. Mention should be made of

[1]It thus became possible to distinguish early French port statistics from passport statistics, with which they had been confused.

[2]The seaport migration statistics by nationality are of special interest. For the important period 1837-54, it has been possible to determine that many more Germans left for America by foreign than by German ports.

[3]The Austrian statistics from 1819 were the first to show emigration from Venice and Lombardy, at that time parts of the Austrian Empire.

special assistance given by the Canadian archivists at Paris and in the Public Record Office at London.

For Australian colonies it was very difficult to construct a complete series from the widely scattered sources, but here also the present figures are probably more nearly complete and certainly date from earlier years than has hitherto been supposed possible. Some questions and contradictions remain unsolved, which the Government itself may be able later to elucidate.

The Japanese delegation at the International Labour Organisation actively collaborated in order that Japanese statistics derived from a variety of sources might be reduced to uniformity. Complete and up-to-date statistics relating to Japanese possessions are also published in this volume for the first time.

Government departments having active relations with the International Labour Office also persuaded numerous libraries to send to Geneva material found to be in their possession. In this way 60 rare volumes were made accessible for several months.

To each and all the authorities who rendered aid during the local visits, or by correspondence, hearty thanks are extended for their keen personal interest in the inquiry and the pains they took to further it.

* * *

An international phenomenon like migration could be thoroughly studied only when attacked at all points—countries of emigration, of transit, and of immigration. Hence the need of appealing to the sense of solidarity in all nations concerned.[1]

The Library of the British Museum offered not only rich materials on the migration statistics of the whole British Empire, but also publications about many other countries particularly those for which information could be procured elsewhere with difficulty or not at all. This Library also supplied statistics of certain States not Members of the International Labour Office (*e. g.* Russia).[2] The library of the Royal Statistical Society and certain libraries on the Continent contained not a little material, especially in conti-

---

[1] Thus in the National Statistical Office in Budapest was found a comprehensive official report of the Portuguese possession, Macao, relating to Chinese emigration through that port before 1872; another report dealing with Serbian, and a third dealing with early Bulgarian emigration. The publication of these reports had been discontinued and their existence was unknown in the countries to which the reports related.

[2] The Central Statistical Commission of the Union of Socialist Soviet Republics sent in September, 1927, six tables concerning the movement of passengers across the frontier with passports or short-dated cards during the former imperial régime, superseding, in the main, the tables which had been earlier compiled in the Library of the British Museum.

nental languages, and some relating to parts of the British Empire, which was unavailable at the Library of the British Museum.

The legislation and the administrative practice of a country was examined in order to ascertain the basis for the statistics. These researches revealed data previously unsuspected by archival authorities who were unaware that seaport passenger lists could be utilized for statistical purposes. This statistical method, which to-day is most reliable, appears to have been applied for centuries. The inquiries led to the discovery in the archives of Seville of an enormous number of lists of colonial emigrant permits dating as far back as 1509 and coming down to 1834, some of them arranged according to countries of destination. Unfortunately the late date of this discovery and limitations of time and means made it impracticable to utilize these lists.

Legislation concerning the control of travel by sea from England to Scotland was found dating back to 1389 and further developed in connection with the emigration of Nonconformists and Roman Catholics in the seventeenth century. This legislation accounts for the complete passenger lists of the Port of London for the year 1635 reproduced in Hotten's *Original Lists of Emigrants to America, 1600-1700*, a volume which has excited the interest of Americans in search of their immigrant ancestors.

The situation in France was not different. For about two hundred years the Colonial Ministry (formerly Marine Department) had had in its archives the lists of passengers (according to the ships' registers) who repaired to or returned from its colonies through French ports. The emigrants were registered upon the basis of a Royal Edict of 1779, which ordained that the lists should be carried back to the year 1749 and transmitted to the State Secretary of the Marine Department. These port lists, although with many gaps, are available down to 1830. A circular letter of about the same period from the English Lords of the Treasury caused the Customs authorities to collect for 1773 to 1776 the first national port statistics for England and Scotland. These reports in the Public Record Office in London are styled "lists of emigrants," but they appear not to have been utilized heretofore.[1]

Later port statistics in the United Kingdom and other European countries are based on the widely imitated Passengers Acts introduced by Great Britain in 1803 in order to afford some protection to emigrants. Statistical information, for instance, was collected in

[1]Public Record Office. *List and Indices, XXVI, Treasury.*

this manner after 1859 at Genoa—the only Italian emigration port at that time—and was based on a Sardinian Edict of February 11, 1859,[1] considerably earlier than the beginning of the current Italian statistics in 1876.

Not only have these port statistics, the existence of which was hardly suspected, been unearthed but other forms of migration statistics also have come to light. These include permit statistics such as those based on the emigration patent issued by the Emperor Joseph II on August 10, 1782, and containing ingeniously constructed statistical schedules to be filled in by the officials. This patent was found in the State Archives in Vienna. The annual statistics from 1819 onward resulting from it are in unpublished lithographic manuscripts and were discovered in the archives of the Austrian Federal Statistical Office. The first passport statistics relating to continental emigrants in transit may be said to be those of Vienna (from 1762 onward) for colonists emigrating from Germany and other countries to Hungary, and those of Strassburg (1663-64) for German emigrants to Cayenne and other French colonies. Passport permit lists are a transitional form between permit and passport statistics. Such lists for the first six months of 1817 and relating to four French Departments (Bas-Rhin, Haute-Rhin, Moselle and Meurthe) have been compiled from records in the French national archives.

It was known that during the years 1816-1817 a wave of emigrants which originated in Central Europe swept through the port of Rotterdam, but nothing in the Dutch archives shed light on this movement. In the archives of Bremen, however, was a theater poster announcing a benefit performance on behalf of emigrants stranded in that town. The hints on the poster led to the contemporary press and the archives of the countries of emigration (Vienna, etc.) where many details about the volume and conditions of migration in that important period were discovered.

All these sources provided a mass of materials which threw light upon the origin and development of current migration statistics. It is not advisable, however, to burden this volume, devoted to recording historically the statistics of modern migration, with a detailed presentation of the results.

The principal object of the enquiry was to discover and bring together the migration statistics of the nineteenth and twentieth centuries up to 1924 inclusive. For this purpose it was necessary to

[1]*Regolamento sul transporto di passagieri ne viaggi maritime.*

investigate the sources, which had never been studied and compared. The greatest difficulty was to determine from the official publications the definitions and statistical methods to be used as a basis for the tables.

The labor was sometimes superfluous or fruitless. A guide to the earlier British statistics in isolated Parliamentary Reports was found in "Papers concerning Emigration for the years 1812-1840" and the "General Accounts and Papers, etc., printed for the order of the House of Commons, etc., during the years 1801-1851, published in 1853 (Parliamentary Papers)." Later the Colonisation Circular of 1875 was found which contained the first complete collection of emigration statistics of the United Kingdom, 1815-75, with special tables showing the immigration into the West Indies, etc. There were numerous contradictions in official reports; for example, when the statistics published by the various colonies were compared with those published by the mother-country discrepancies appeared. There were contradictions also within the tables and these had to be cleared up by reference to later reports or other publications (Statistical Abstracts of the Colonies, Statistical Tables of the Colonies, Blue Books, Year Books, etc.).

The headings in the tables for different years, e. g. "Indian immigrants," "coolies," "indentured labourers," sometimes differed and this made definitions uncertain. Some reports were corrected by later official statistics, and in some countries, e. g. India, the figures were sometimes for calendar years and sometimes for fiscal years without any indication of the change. Other reports contained emigration data which were not continued in later years. Statistics of the occupations of emigrants were frequently shown in unexpected places, e. g. British Post Office Reports.

Expert officials often spent days in searching for isolated data, e. g. the sex and age of emigrants to Western Australia, and it was seldom that research failed to bring results.

Sometimes only a volume for a later year, or a few scattered figures for recent years could be found. Even when the whole series was obtained the data for later years had to be searched for time-saving comprehensive tables including several years, which could then be photographed. As annual figures were often corrected in subsequent volumes, preference was given to the latest statement. In cases like that of Japan where countries of destination were shown for a series of years, the consolidated figures were occasionally substituted for transcription. Preparing statistics from

original lists of emigrants was very difficult since frequently the sex, age, or occupation was not indicated. The returns were often in the form of separate sheets, written on both sides in an illegible hand. The notes to the tables compiled from these original lists reveal the technical difficulties which arose in arriving at complete and réliable statistics. All tables were collated on the spot or verified.

In view of the mass of material, the limited means and the need for haste, the original recommendations were fully carried out only for the principal countries; in the case of other countries the inquiry was pushed as far as possible. Statistics have also been established for special classes of migration such as State-assisted emigration or Chinese immigration.

The results of the investigation are set forth in statistical tables of migration for 116 countries or political divisions past or present, and references make it possible to construct tables for certain countries such as Poland, Serbia or Turkey which have no migration statistics at all—or none for the periods involved—from the figures given by other countries about immigration from them. The tables were definitely closed on February 15, 1927. The total number of tables relating to each continent and the number for each of the best represented countries on that continent are given in the following summary:

	Number of Tables for Countries Best Represented	Total Number of Tables
America..		150
Canada............................	11	
United States.......................	56	
Argentina..........................	8	
Brazil.............................	8	
Uruguay...........................	17	
Europe..		288
Austria..........................	17	
Belgium..........................	15	

British Isles........................	34
France............................	15
Germany...........................	15
Hungary...........................	31
Italy.............................	28

Asia...		57
	British India.......................	7
	China....:......................	8
	Japan............................	7
Oceania......................................		75
	Commonwealth of Australia..........	11
	New South Wales...................	9
	Queensland........................	9
	Victoria..........................	8
	New Zealand	13
Africa.......................................		73
	South Africa.......................	20
	Total...............	643

The sources utilized in this volume will enable future investigators to get an insight into various aspects of migration statistics outside its field. Such are the combined tables which are included as a rule, only in cases in which sex, age, or occupation is combined with nationality.

Historical statistics have thus been established for forty-two more states or political divisions than were represented in *Migration Movements, 1920-1924*, making a total of 116 political divisions.

Elaboration of the Materials.

The present volume as a whole falls into two parts. Part II contains official statistics in the narrower sense, that is, in the main the statistics of international migrations during the nineteenth century. Part I includes the same material in a descriptive form with historical commentaries.

Part II is not merely a collection of such statistics as were readily available in the different countries; on the contrary, an effort has been made to extend the study along the following lines:—

(1) To discover when the first annual statistics were available in the different countries;

(2) To find out what statistics are available in comparable sources, and, where these are lacking, to discover supplementary sources;

(3) To discover all statistics which refer to the same events and to explain their relative value;

(4) To discover the different legislative and technical bases on which the statistics of each country have been compiled, in order to estimate their value at various periods.

The statistics are presented in a national and an international form, and to these are annexed references to the sources and explanations of the methods, without which it would be impossible to estimate the significance of the data, and difficult for future students to interpret them. A general introduction to the tables and notes is given at this point in order to permit some insight into the system and principles by which the statistics have been arranged.

I. GENERAL INTRODUCTION TO THE NATIONAL TABLES.

In the national tables only current migration statistics are reproduced, that is, only statistics which record migrants at the time of their departure from the country of their last permanent residence, their arrival in the country of their future permanent residence, or in a third country during transit. Population statistics compiled periodically, and including foreigners residing in a country at a given moment, or industrial statistics like those of employment agencies which lead indirectly to conclusions about the volume of migration, are generally excluded. On the other hand, where there are current migration statistics arrived at by different methods, all the tables have been given (for example, port statistics, passport statistics, frontier statistics).

National migration statistics alone have been reproduced. But where emigrants are classified by country of destination, or immigrants by country of origin, the statistics refer to two countries, only one of which is directly responsible for them. For the other country these constitute indirect or unofficial statistics. In the notes about each country reference is made to all indirect statistics elsewhere in the volume which relate to it.[1]

Where important distinctions such as between citizens and aliens or between continental and intercontinental migrants were not indicated in the original headings of the tables, they were inserted in the new headings. The distinction between citizen and alien officially adopted by the country in question[2] has always been accepted. A migration is continental when it takes place between

[1]Indirect statistics regularly relate to countries (Germany, Belgium, etc.) but where data for a country have been lacking, the figures relating to nationality or race (Germans, Belgians) have been given. For Cuba the number of immigrants is indicated by nationality (citizenship) from 1902 onward. All the figures in the indirect statistics of the European countries concerning immigration to Argentina which are not found in the national tables of that country (1921-24) are reproduced from *Resumen Estadistico del Movimiento Migratorio en la Republica Argentina* and refer to the number of migrants. At the last moment we changed National Table IV by reproducing, according to Bodio, *Statistica della Emigrazione Italiana per l'Estero*, the number of emigrants by calendar years for 1901-1906 in place of fiscal years. It was, however, necessary to leave undisturbed the classification by fiscal years in the indirect statistics of European countries.

[2]For example: only those are regarded as citizens in Canada, who are (1) native-born, (2) naturalized, or (3) British domiciled. In Southern Rhodesia, pursuant to Ordinance 7 of 1914, the following British nationalities were distinguished: British home-born, South African British, South African Dutch, British (other Dominions). (Southern Rhodesia. *Report of the Commissioner of British S. African Police, for the year 1922.* Salisbury, 1923. page 11.)

territories of different countries on the same continent, and intercontinental when different continents are involved.

As a rule, we give the personal particulars specified in Recommendation 19 of the Conference of 1922, viz., sex, age, nationality, occupation, country of last permanent residence, and country of future permanent residence. In some cases, as for Palestine or Poland, the religion of the migrant is stated.

The arrangement of countries, colonies and continents in the tables, does not follow the same order as that in *Migration Movements*. The National Bureau of Economic Research, for which this inquiry was undertaken, proposed to adopt the order of countries followed by the Bureau of Foreign and Domestic Commerce in the United States Department of Commerce, and that was done with certain changes required by this work.

The classification of countries in the American list was designed for commercial purposes and is exclusively geographical, disregarding citizenship. In migration studies the reader should know to what State a territory belongs if he is to distinguish between citizens and aliens. So, after the name of a colony, possession or mandated territory, an abbreviated indication of the State to which it belongs has been placed. A commercial classification gives little attention to history, but for this study historical relations are important. For instance, British Guiana and British Honduras appear under West Indies in our historical tables. It is misleading today to speak of the "United Kingdom," the meaning of which changed with the establishment of the Irish Free State, so the recognized expression "British Isles" has been used. It includes the United Kingdom as it stood before the establishment of the Irish Free State. Where an historical territory has undergone a change of boundary, the new territory is given as a main heading and the older territory is placed under it, *e. g.* Hungary (pre-war and post-war), Austria (pre-war and post-war), Serb-Croat-Slovene State (Serbia, etc.), Irish Free State (Ireland). Where a former territory has ceased to have an independent political or administrative unity, it is classified under the former predominant country, *e. g.* Bosnia and Herzegovina are placed under Austria.

The national tables of each country are preceded by a list giving the headings of the tables. Where statistics for the same migratory movement have been compiled according to several methods, the tables have been grouped under special headings, as port statistics

or passport statistics. The national tables are numbered in Roman figures, and the international tables in Arabic.

In all the tables the migrants are shown, where possible, in twelve-month periods. Fiscal years have not been distinguished from calendar years, but information about the exact period is given in the notes. When the fiscal year ends on March 31 or before, the figures have been classed as of the previous year and when it ends after that date, generally June 30, the figures were carried to the succeeding year. This procedure appears to us justified by the fact that migration is at its maximum in the spring.

Where statistics were found only for decennial or quinquennial periods, the actual data were sought in the original records. Sometimes the migration for a period of several years has been given, but only where it was so recorded in the sources and seemed likely to be useful to the student. For example, figures for five or ten years have been retained, even if they did not agree with the periods of the international tables.[1] In fact, it was necessary to reproduce such figures when others were lacking. On the other hand, statistics for less than a whole year are not considered except in dealing with continental seasonal migrations.

The notes for the tables are of three kinds: I. General Notes, II. Sources, III. Explanatory Notes (footnotes); but the first kind were not required for every country.

Only statistics from official sources have been used; secondary sources being seldom resorted to, and then only where they quote official matter (authentic letters with date, etc., or other official communications). Official statistics, of course, include those recognized and adopted by official authorities such as statistics of shipping companies or travel agencies or furnished in manuscript for the purposes of this inquiry.

Preference has usually been given to documents of latest date. National sources are given first, then foreign sources. The national sources have been arranged in approximately the same order as the tables; where this was not possible, in the chronological order of the first years of the source. First come the printed sources and those taken from archives, and subsequently tables in Government communications; then come the more general sources and the complementary sources (which help to complete isolated data); literary sources were the last to be quoted. The years for which

[1]We also retained the percentage figures of the original tables when they conduced to a better understanding of them (Hungary, Uruguay, etc.)

each source is utilized, when it does not comprise the whole period of the table, have been indicated in parentheses.

The General Notes give the origin of the information, the method of its preparation and the definitions of terms. They also contain other observations useful for understanding and appreciating the figures; and indicate important alterations which have arisen in the course of time, such as changes in relation to definitions, method, territory covered (changes as the result of war, or of peace treaties), and period covered (calendar year or fiscal year, etc.).

The Explanatory Notes explain minor difficulties; for example, absence of statistics for one or more years, changes in classification. These notes carry Arabic numerals and are arranged by sets, one for each country.

The national tables showing occupations usually reproduce the classification in the source, but where the original subdivision is minute the occupations have been grouped either according to the system in the national statistics or according to the six classes adopted for international comparison, namely, (1) agriculture; (2) industry and mining; (3) transport and commerce; (4) domestic service and general labor; (5) liberal professions and public service; (6) other occupations, no occupation, or occupation unknown.

Members of families having no occupation, unless otherwise indicated, are included in group 6. It was planned at first to print in an appendix the detailed lists of occupations under each of the foregoing main groups in each country, but considerations of space (the lists occupy 25 type-written pages) and a conviction that certain returns were gathered so hurriedly and loosely that they have little scientific value, turned the scales to the side of omitting them.

In the national tables immigrants have been shown by the country of last residence or by nationality, the classification used in the source being usually retained. The classification used by the United States has been adopted as the basis. If the national statistics are subdivided more minutely than those of the United States, the smaller groups have usually been assigned to the larger ones including them. Where it was difficult to assign territory to a continent, the classification used by the Permanent Office of the International Statistical Institute has been adopted. In other cases nationalities or races have been classified from the geographical or political point of view. Thus Jews (unspecified) have been assigned to the heading "other Europeans;" Jews (Polish) to the heading "Poles;" Turks (unspecified) to the heading "Turkey in Asia." Syria and

Iraq (Mesopotamia) have been combined with Palestine, and Negroes usually included in "unknown" or "other countries."

In certain tables and diagrams, as well as occasionally in the text, immigrants to the United States have been classified into five groups: (1) Northern and Western Europe; (2) Southern and Eastern Europe; (3) Canada; (4) Mexico; and (5) Other countries. The first two of these five groups include the following countries:

Northern and Western Europe	*Southern and Eastern Europe.*
Belgium	Albania
Danzig	Armenia
Denmark	Austria
Finland	Bulgaria
France	Czechoslovakia
Germany	Greece
Luxemburg	Hungary
Netherlands	Italy
Norway	Poland
Sweden	Portugal
Great Britain	Rumania
Irish Free State	Russia
Switzerland	Estonia
	Lithuania
	Serb, Croat and Slovene State
	Spain
	Turkey
	Other countries

II. GENERAL INTRODUCTION TO THE INTERNATIONAL TABLES. (Nos. 1 to 36.)[1]

The international tables have for their objects:

(a) To give through international comparisons a clear picture of the waves of migration in different countries;

(b) To reveal the growth and spread of the methods and definitions of migration statistics and of the collection of information about immigrants;

(c) To facilitate the future development of uniform statistical methods in all countries.

The national methods of statistical registration (port statistics, passport statistics, local registers, labor contracts, etc.) and the definitions underlying them, differ appreciably from one country to another. Moreover, there are differences in the exactness and reliability of the figures. The effort has been made to get the most accurate and most comparable figures. The personal description of the migrant (sex, age, race, nationality, country of last or future residence, occupation) has been organized into the fewest practicable groups.

For the tables, eight homogeneous groups of migrants have been assumed, a classification taken from the introduction to *Migration Movements, 1920-1923.*[2] For each of these groups not only the aggregate figures, but also the particulars mentioned concerning the migrants have been given.

Historical tables were prepared only when information was available for at least two countries in relatively similar conditions[3] and figures for at least two quinquennial periods.[4]

[1]The principles followed in the compilation of these international tables are summed up in this Introduction. The notes to the basic national tables also should be read in order to learn how far the data are comparable. But the explanatory notes to the international tables attempt to make of the latter an integral whole which is comprehensible apart from the national tables and their notes. Data which are not in complete accord with the headings of the tables are explained in the notes.

[2]The eight groups are: (1) overseas emigration of citizens: (2) continental emigration of citizens: (3) overseas immigration of citizens; (repatriation); (4) continental immigration of citizens; (repatriation); (5) overseas emigration of aliens (generally returning to their country of origin); (6) continental emigration of aliens (generally returning to their country of origin); (7) overseas immigration of aliens; (8) continental immigration of aliens.

[3]In very important cases the principle of only utilizing data when these are available for the first or the last quinquennial period has been disregarded; for example, in table 28 where the United States has figures only for 1906-10, or in table 7, where in the first two quinquennial periods the United States figures beside Brazil and the latter does not give the last country of residence of the immigrants; or lastly in table 21, where Norway appears by itself as it was inadvisable to sacrifice, in this instance, the comparison between the several quinquennial periods.

[4]In respect of the number of years, each case was considered on its merits. Fewer

In view of the lengthy periods covered by the statistics of some countries it has seemed best to use quinquennial figures and annual averages, thus facilitating a rapid survey and emphasizing what is typical in the movement.

The comparability of the figures was increased by selecting one particular method, where there were several. The most accurate statistics were chosen as a rule and, accordingly, port statistics were selected generally for overseas migrations, even when the statistics were collected in foreign ports as in the case of Austria. However, where the less accurate statistics comprise a much greater number of years, or where they afford the possibility of calculating net emigration and immigration because the two types of figures have the same basis (*e. g.* the passenger statistics of Great Britain until 1924) these inferior figures were given the preference. In some cases the two sets of statistics have been reproduced in parallel columns. This was done because a comparison of the results of the two sets in the later period made it possible to judge the results of the earlier period.

It was a specially delicate matter to link up the older statistics which had been discontinued with more recent statistics having a different basis, *e. g.* to connect permit statistics with port statistics based on a correct definition of an emigrant, or to connect passport statistics with those of transport companies (Hungary). Naturally, where the differences in the value of older and later statistics were great this could not be done. For instance, prior to 1908 only "passengers departed" were reported in the United States, without distinguishing between citizens and aliens, while after 1908 "alien emigrants departed" were shown. In these circumstances, "passengers departed" have not been entered in the international tables. In cases where the same statistics indicated very heterogeneous data for a series of quinquennial periods, the procedure has been the same. Thus, for 1881-85 the United States published fairly reliable figures concerning the continental immigration of aliens, while later, until 1907, the figures were manifestly incomplete.

Broadly speaking, in deciding whether to prepare a certain table or to include a certain country in a table, no strict rule was followed. To illustrate, it was not deemed advisable to prepare a table for countries of intercontinental immigration showing the emigration of aliens by countries of destination, because these countries of desti-

than two quinquennial periods were shown when there was a special interest in the country for purposes of comparison (*e. g.* Australian table 2; Hungary in tables 27 and 28.

nation and the years for which the figures exist are too diversified
to admit of international comparisons.   For the period 1871-1907
Argentina and Queensland gave countries of destination.   For the
period 1879-1903 Uruguay gave the same.   But the figures for
Argentina refer to European countries exclusively; those for Uruguay
to South American countries also, and those for Queensland only
to the United Kingdom.   Nor did it appear advisable to include
Queensland after 1900 in such international tables, seeing that the
Australian Commonwealth was founded in that year.   Lastly, the
figures relating to the immigration of citizens (repatriation) view
the same current from the other end and offer quite reliable data
for the most important European countries.

British statistics relating to the occupations of emigrants were
not used because the data were collected for only $1\frac{3}{4}$ years before
the world war, and differ from the post-war grouping to such an
extent that they cannot be readily compared.

In several tables particular countries have been omitted when it
appeared that their statistics were not comparable with those of
other countries.   Thus, the statistics of the communal registers of
the Netherlands lump together citizens and aliens, inter-continental
and continental migrants.

Guided by the widely prevailing practice in national statistics
(United States, Germany, Argentina, Belgium, Sweden, Norway,
the Philippines) the quinquennial periods adopted have been 1851-5,
1856-60, etc.   If there were no statistics for certain years, the
aggregate number of migrants in the years for which data were
available was not divided by the number of years but by five, in
order to prevent the movement appearing larger than it actually
was (Mauritius).   In doubtful cases the average was found by
dividing the total by the number of years reported.

* * *

When the statistics in an international table do not correspond
exactly to the heading or do not conform to the above-mentioned
principles, a note of explanation is introduced.   This occurs (a)
when a figure does not cover five years, or (b) when the heading
refers to the overseas emigration of citizens, while the figures for
certain countries include also alien emigrants or emigrants for continental destinations; or (c) when the heading refers to emigrants
in general while the figures for certain countries are limited to a
certain type of emigrants (e. g. family head alone, or adults over 15
years of age, or males over 15 years of age, or Indian indentured

laborers). When the method on which a certain figure was based seemed doubtful that method was stated.

The notes for the first 18 tables are more detailed and contain references to certain national tables (indicated in Roman figures). The notes to the later tables are given in condensed form. In tables showing the age of the migrants, introductory notes state the general rule for age groups in the several countries, and explain that exceptions will be set forth in special notes.

The reference numbers prefixed to the notes correspond to the reference numbers affixed to the figures of the quinquennial periods. Should the note refer to only one quinquennial period, it is not generally connected with the country concerned. The collective heading "other countries" differs in meaning according to its position.

* * *

The meaning of the fiscal years is to be derived from the notes to the national tables. But it may be said here that the statistics of the immigration countries of the Philippines, Natal, Canada, United States, Portugal, Hawaii and Fiji, are based on fiscal years. The United States frequently altered its method of calculating the year and since 1920 its migration figures have been given by both fiscal and calendar years. For Canada the fiscal-year figures are given in the tables up to 1920 only, but they are quoted in the Introduction for all years for purposes of comparison.

* * *

The international tables (see table on page 76) comprise 348 particulars for 51 countries and territories. They date back to different initial years: those relating to statistics of immigration to 1821 and those to statistics of emigration to 1846.

LIST OF COUNTRIES INCLUDED IN THE INTERNATIONAL TABLES

#	Country	1	2	3	4	5	6	7	8	9	10	11	12	13	14	15	16	17	18	Total
		1846	1846	1876	1846	1886	1821	1901	1886	1876	1886	1866	1866	1821	1821	1876	1876	1876	1876	
1	Canada	*					*	*						*						4
2	Newfoundland and Labrador						*	*												2
3	United States of America	*			*		*	*				*		*	*					7
4	Mexico				*		*	*	*					*	*					6
5	West Indies	*			*		*							*						4
6	Cuba	*					*	*						*	*					5
7	Guadeloupe						*													1
8	Dutch Guiana						*							*						2
9	Argentina	*	*	*			*	*												5
10	Brazil	*	*				*					*	*							5
11	Paraguay		*				*					*	*							4
12	Uruguay	*	*				*					*	*							5
13	Austria	*	*	*				*	*	*		*	*	*	*	*	*			14
14	Belgium	*	*							*		*	*			*	*			7
15	British Isles	*	*									*	*							4
16	Denmark											*	*							2
17	France	*	*									*	*					*	*	6
18	Germany	*	*						*	*		*	*							6
19	Hungary	*	*									*	*							4
20	Irish Free State	*	*							*		*	*							5
21	Netherlands	*	*									*	*							4
22	Norway	*	*						*	*	*	*	*	*	*	*	*			11
23	Sweden		*	*	*							*	*							5
24	Switzerland		*									*	*				*			4
25	Finland		*		*							*	*							4
26	Poland		*		*		*			*		*	*	*	*	*	*			10
27	Russia				*		*					*	*							4
28	Italy	*			*		*		*	*		*	*							7
29	Portugal				*		*		*			*								4
30	Spain				*		*					*	*							4
31	Malta				*		*													2
32	British India				*		*													2
33	Straits Settlements				*		*			*		*	*	*	*					7
34	Ceylon				*		*							*	*					4
35	Philippine Islands (U. S. A.)						*							*						2
36	Japan						*			*				*	*					4
37	Commonwealth of Australia													*	*					2
38	New South Wales				*					*				*	*					4
39	Queensland													*	*					2
40	Victoria				*					*				*	*					4
41	New Zealand													*	*					2
42	Fiji						*							*						2
43	New Caledonia (Fr.)						*							*						2
44	Hawaii (U. S. A.)						*							*						2
45	Mauritius						*							*						2
46	St. Helena	*					*													2
47	Seychelles						*							*						2
48	Natal						*													1
49	Cape of Good Hope				*		*													2
50	Union of South Africa				*		*													2
51	Cape Verde Islands				*		*													1
	Total	22	17	7	19	6	26	11	8	11	3	20	20	13	13	6	6	3	3	214

Number of International Table and First Year of Statistics therein

LIST OF COUNTRIES INCLUDED IN THE INTERNATIONAL TABLES (Concluded).

No.	Country	\multicolumn{19}{c}{Number of International Table and first year of statistics therein.}																	
		19	20	21	22	23	24	25	26	27	28	29	30	31	32	33	34	35	36	Total
		1851	1851	1851	1851	1841	1841	1876	1876	1871	1871	1891	1891	1856	1856	1906	1906	1856	1856	
1	Canada																			
2	Newfoundland and Labrador																			
3	United States of America			*	*	*	*							*	*	*	*			8
4	Mexico			*	*	*	*													4
5	West Indies			*	*	*	*													4
6	Cuba			*	*	*	*							*	*					6
7	Guadeloupe			*	*	*	*													4
8	Dutch Guiana																			
9	Argentina	*	*			*	*	*	*	*	*	*	*							10
10	Brazil	*	*			*	*	*	*	*	*									8
11	Paraguay									*	*	*	*							4
12	Uruguay	*	*							*	*	*	*							6
13	Austria	*	*			*	*			*	*									6
14	Belgium	*	*					*	*	*	*							*	*	8
15	British Isles	*	*																	2
16	Denmark	*	*							*	*							*	*	6
17	France	*	*							*	*							*	*	6
18	Germany	*	*					*	*	*	*							*	*	8
19	Hungary	*	*							*	*									4
20	Irish Free State	*	*							*	*									4
21	Netherlands	*	*															*	*	4
22	Norway	*	*																	2
23	Switzerland	*	*					*	*											4
24	Finland																			
25	Poland																			
26	Russia																			
27	Italy	*	*	*	*			*	*	*	*									8
28	Portugal	*	*																	2
29	Spain	*	*			*	*													4
30	Malta																			
31	British India																			
32	Straits Settlements																			
33	Ceylon					*	*							*	*					4
34	Philippine Islands (U. S. A.)																			
35	Japan													*	*	*	*			4
36	Commonwealth of Australia			*	*									*	*					4
37	New South Wales																			
38	Queensland																			
39	Victoria																			
40	New Zealand																			
41	Fiji																			
42	New Caledonia (Fr.)																			
43	Hawaii (U. S. A.)																			
44	Mauritius																			
45	St. Helena																			
46	Seychelles																			
47	Natal																			
48	Cape of Good Hope																			
49	Union of South Africa																			
50	Cape Verde Islands																			
	Total	17	17	7	7	10	10	6	6	12	12	3	3	5	5	2	2	5	5	134

III. GENERAL INTRODUCTION TO THE HISTORICAL SURVEY.

Prior to the establishment of current systems of migration statistics in the nineteenth century (Great Britain, 1815; United States, 1820) records and lists of emigrants were frequently kept. These more or less official data have survived in archives or been drawn upon by writers on history and colonisation.[1] They indicate the number, sex, age, and occupation of the citizen settlers and frequently also of the aliens. Their existence suggested that an attempt should be made to digest and co-ordinate these scattered data. They might throw light upon the significance of the mass migrations of the nineteenth century. The direction of recent migratory currents is in part explained by settlements made by fellow-citizens in earlier days.

These scattered early data have not been arranged by countries of emigration and immigration, but according to the character or type of the migration. One type is represented by Portuguese and Spanish migration. The French and the Dutch represent an intermediate type. The inter-continental group migrations of Anglo-Saxons and Germans in the seventeenth and eighteenth centuries belong to a different type. These diverse types rose to prominence at different epochs and characterize more or less the several centuries. Among them they cover the settlement of well nigh the whole globe by European peoples and their discussion must be supplemented by a survey of the migration movements of other races.

The type of these early migrations was not determined by the geographical position of the territory where they originated, but by the migrating people themselves. Before the nineteenth century migration among the first type of peoples was State-regulated. In other countries migration, as a rule, was the act of fellow-citizens bound to a common lot who, frequently in despite of their Government and notwithstanding the difficulties likely to be encountered in the country of reception, determined to settle in another country. The great migration movements of the various peoples were hardly affected by political frontiers and their modifications.

[1] In the footnotes the sources are indicated by giving the author's name, with initials. The titles of the works referred to will be found in the Bibliography, p. 1085. Where, however, we have occasion to refer to more than one work by an author, we have given both author and work.

Neither totals nor even reliable estimates of the total migration during the earlier centuries can be secured. But it does appear that the movement of peoples belonging to the Spanish-Portuguese type was slight; that this movement was not justified on the whole by the population conditions and economic circumstances of the participating countries in the sixteenth and seventeenth centuries; and that what movement there was had to be kept alive by artificial means right down to the close of the colonial period. The fruitless efforts on the part of France to create vast colonial settlements overseas and the large volume, the steadiness and the natural increase of the Anglo-Saxon and the German migrations can be readily understood by the reader, without studying the details of contemporary legislation or of economic and political incentives.

The most important migration waves during these centuries and their immediate causes have received especial attention. This appeared reasonably possible, especially as the colonization period was almost free from the national and international complications of the contemporary movement. The main determining factors could be roughly ascertained, and the statistics reinforced the conclusions. Such a detailed historical survey of migrations in the sixteenth to eighteenth centuries lies outside the scope of the present work, but a few tables concerning these periods are included as examples of early precise current statistics and methods.

The statistics of national migrations from the sixteenth to the nineteenth century, may be discussed elsewhere; the present volume discusses those of the nineteenth century.

The procedure of sketching the conditions which influenced migrations in the various countries has been used only for the first half of the nineteenth century. In this earlier period the conditions were not as involved as they became later. Since national statistics form the basis of the work for the nineteenth century, national migrations have been treated separately by the countries to which they belong and not by peoples. In that century, also, the leading incentives to European emigrations are the industrial and the agricultural conditions prevailing in the countries of immigration.[1] The statistics of immigration are more international, more complete, and more reliable than those of the countries of emigration, even the port statistics which are far the best. In order to avoid repetition the description of the national statistics of the emigration

---

[1] *See* H. Jerome, *Migration and Business Cycles*, p. 186, New York, 1926 (Nat. Bur. Econ. Research, No. 9).

countries has been limited to stating the volume and direction of the currents. The general migrations of the nineteenth century have been sketched in the light of the international tables of the immigration countries, and statistics of the emigration countries have been utilized only for the purpose of supplementing and controlling the other data. By means of sixteen tables in the text and of sixteen diagrams based on them, the descriptions have been made as brief and vivid as possible.

PART I

PROLETARIAN MASS MIGRATION, XIXTH AND XXTH CENTURIES

1. Introduction

International migration as measured by current official statistics began soon after the end of the Napoleonic Wars. The longest series in the following national tables commence, for the countries of immigration, with Canada (1816), United States (1820), Brazil (1820), and New South Wales (1825); and for the countries of emigration with the British Isles (1815), Austria (1819) and Norway (1821). Thus, within a decade after Waterloo national emigration statistics had been set up in several countries of Europe and national or colonial immigration statistics in parts of North America, South America and Australia. The roots of these mass movements, which began to be systematically recorded about a century ago, run far back into the earlier period of colonization but the present study does not demand a survey of migration in that pre-statistical period.

The account starts, then, with the Treaty of Paris which had settled the colonial possessions of the European Powers, and although there were subsequent discoveries and subsequent changes in the ownership of colonies, the colonial period may be regarded as then closed. The settlement of North America, from the first English colony in Virginia in 1607 and the first French, Dutch, and other agricultural colonies, was carried out by separate groups formed or organized for each attempt, although frequently assisted by the authorities at home or abroad, and was quite different from the migration movement of modern times.

The latter has been a regular mass movement, composed of disconnected individuals or families not forming a coherent association on either side of the ocean.

Modern emigration is not due to Governmental policy and is not a national undertaking, but results from the spontaneous decision of individuals on the ground of personal motives. Even when the current appears to be a collective whole, it is seen on closer investigation to be only a very loose association of interested individuals. The typical modern emigrant goes overseas with certain hopes, often without a definite plan, and takes his place among previous

emigrants with little regard for ties of relationship, national peculiarities or his own previous occupation. The typical representative of mass emigration in the nineteenth and twentieth centuries is the proletarian—an industrial or agricultural worker without means, though previously in many cases a small holder of land. Among the mass are also to be found now and then, as the occupational statistics show, capitalists and intellectuals as well as shipwrecked lives and persons without occupation.

The total number of international emigrants to all countries since the beginning of the nineteenth century cannot be precisely determined, since the statistics do not as a rule begin until the migration movement has assumed significant proportions.[1] The statistics of European intercontinental emigration and the immigration statistics of overseas countries show about the same totals. For the years 1820-1924 the latter figure is about 55½ millions, while the total recorded emigration from Europe for 1846-1924 amounts to 50 millions. When one remembers that immigration as a rule is more completely recorded than emigration, these totals indicate that no important series of figures are missing.

In the first half of the nineteenth century the largest emigration was from Great Britain and Germany, while that from other countries, notably France, Scandinavia and Switzerland, was a small part of the whole, although large perhaps in comparison with their own populations.

During that period emigration continued to be directed principally towards territories where the emigrant found racial connections, language, religion and institutions similar to those of his mother country. It was in such places that he might hope for the most rapid accomplishment of his plans. The citizens of the United Kingdom thus went in large numbers to the United States or to British possessions. But other considerations, such as economic conditions, forms of government, legislation or mere curiosity, strongly influenced the decisions of individuals. For example, during the years 1820-1840, Germans migrated to Brazil, Argentina and Australia, in larger numbers than to the United States; emigration to the United States did not assume its importance again until the 40's. The world movement thus took on an international character.

The economic motives and political causes of this great movement

[1] Friedrich Kapp states in his *European Emigration to the United States*, New York, 1869, p. 4, that even for the United States from 1777 to 1815 immigration had been very slight. See also p. 374f, United States: General Notes.

of migration are partly to be found in the conditions of the countries of emigration and immigration, and partly in the improvement of transportation.

Until about 1850 the movement was determined mainly by conditions in European countries. Emigration was practically confined to persons who were driven to it by economic, political or religious circumstances in the mother country. The new lands beyond the sea were not well known or attractive, and no one knew what fate awaited him there. Moreover, the high cost of the journey and grievous conditions in the emigration ports and on board ship were added deterrents, while transportation by land was extremely troublesome, so that many persons never reached the port of embarkation. The emigrants were exposed on a long voyage to starvation and disease. It was not uncommon for 1 to 10 per cent of the emigrants to perish either on board ship or soon after landing.

Nevertheless, at the beginning of the nineteenth century there was a fairly large movement, but not until the 40's did it become a mass movement of European populations and that principally because the legal obstacles to emigration had been gradually removed.

Everywhere serfdom was coming to an end. One of the results of the French Revolution was the freedom of the individual to migrate within and from his country. Increased capitalistic production through the use of machinery and cheap raw material from overseas involved everywhere an increase in population which provided labor for overseas territories. Industrial production was stimulated by technical improvements, and under favorable conditions it attracted from the land increasing numbers of unskilled workers. The recurring depressions of the economic cycle involved periodical unemployment. One relief measure was emigration, sometimes spontaneous but frequently assisted by the authorities.

The number of emigrants was increased by the impoverishment of agriculture. Countries where large estates and a tenant system prevailed suffered severely from the periodical depressions. This appeared in Ireland and Germany, whence numerous agricultural workers went to the United States and Canada, particularly in the years between 1840 and 1860 as the result of depressions and bad harvests. Agricultural emigration was also increased by the introduction of free trade. In countries where small holdings prevailed, as in southern Germany and Switzerland, the progressive subdivision of the land frequently led to considerable emigration. Certain political disturbances, such as the despotism in Germany

after the Napoleonic period and the democratic revolution in 1848, induced large sections of the middle classes to seek a livelihood in the New World.

In earlier centuries overseas production was determined mainly by the needs of the home population, but in the nineteenth century a change took place which may be attributed to the improvement of transportation. The natural wealth of the overseas countries came to be exploited without limit and this called for the introduction of a large supply of labor which was available in Europe.[1]   Since the slave trade in African Negroes had been abolished as the result of the growth of civilization reinforced by the unproductive nature of compulsory labor under modern technical conditions (coolie labor, introduced to replace the Negro slaves, was found equally unsatisfactory), the interests of the new overseas states and of the European colonial powers concentrated on population problems. The United States were in the most favorable position for bringing in an unlimited number of European immigrants.   They had at their disposal a tremendous amount of land, liberal agrarian legislation, and capitalistic industry which started during the Napoleonic Wars and continually offered more and better possibilities of employment.   A large westward movement from the Atlantic seaboard took place and expanded the possibilities of employment.   The laws for the protection of passengers on board ship, beginning with the statutes of 1819, also encouraged immigration.

The British colonies adjusted their political and economic life to serve the permanent interests of the settlers.   The theoretical views of Gibbon Wakefield concerning the settlement and self-government of the colonies were realized in the Dominions, particularly in Australia.   Wakefield opposed the free distribution of Crown lands among settlers without capital.   He expressed the view that settlers must not only possess capital before they became independent landowners, but also should have acquired knowledge of the local needs of overseas agriculture.   He therefore called for the immigration of masses of workers who were to take employment in the colonies for a period, until they had saved some money.   They should then pay for land.   The sums paid for the land were to go to a fund for paying the expenses of transportation of other workers.   Previously, this system had often been approximately realized in the form of "indentured servants."   In Canada, up to the end of the nineteenth

[1]The first year in which more than 100,000 immigrants arrived in the United States was 1842; in 1854 the number reached 425,000.

century, the policy of free land prevented its adoption. In the Australian colonies, however, it was introduced with such results that the deportation of convicts became superfluous. As soon as these colonies had a sufficient free population, self-government based on the English parliamentary system could be introduced. This had been proposed for Canada by Wakefield and Lord Durham (1837) and was completely realized in 1867. Just as Upper and Lower Canada, New Brunswick, Newfoundland, and Prince Edward Island were then united in a federation, so the South African possessions were made into a union after the Boer War and the Australian States into a commonwealth in 1900. In the course of further developments, the Dominions gradually became autonomous States co-ordinate with the mother country in a personal union under the King of England (1926). Great Britain thus succeeded in retaining these territories and uniting them into a commonwealth which offers the British extraordinary opportunities for migration and livelihood (Empire settlement).

The predominance of the British among emigrants of the nineteenth and twentieth centuries is easily understood from the causes of emigration already set forth and because the movement was to some extent assisted by the State. Protection of emigration by the state was also first established among the British. The number of emigrants from Great Britain between 1815 and 1924 was about 19,000,000, according to the passenger statistics, which after 1860 included about one-fifth more than the number of actual emigrants; Germany was next with about 6,000,000.

While English emigration has continued up to the present time except for brief intervals to be the most extensive, German emigration in the second half of the nineteenth century was reduced to a minimum by the strengthening of the economic position of the country and the lack of German colonies. Scandinavian and Swiss emigration also reached their peak in the 80's.

Certain investigators have claimed that the Germanic races are particularly inclined to emigrate. Calvo remarks: "The south of Europe appears as a whole less inclined to expatriation than the centre and the north, that is to say, with the exception of Austria, perhaps more apparent than real, the races of Germanic stock are, when the climate is suitable, more migratory than the Latin races."[1] But as soon as the same causes of emigration began to press on the countries of southern and eastern Europe as had for-

[1] Calvo, *Etude sur l'émigration et la colonisation*, Paris, 1875.

merly influenced the northwestern peoples, a great movement of emigration from them set in, encouraged by the extraordinary demand for labor in overseas countries.

The center of gravity of emigration, during the last two decades, has moved away from the industrial western States to the southern and eastern agricultural States of Europe, notably Italy, Austria, Hungary, and Russia.

This was greatly assisted by the multiplication of steamships and the changed technique of navigation. After 1870 sailing vessels practically ceased to be used for transporting emigrants.[1] Several groups of commercial interests in the carrying trade arose which, by an elaborate and complicated system of agencies, drew the attention of peoples who hitherto had known little of emigration to the attractive conditions in overseas countries. As soon as German emigration declined, the great steamship companies were keenly interested in drawing the high wages in America to the attention of the agricultural proletariat of European countries in which the system of large estates had brought about unsatisfactory conditions of wages and life (Italy, Hungary, Galicia, Russia).[2] Satisfactory terms of transportation offered them the prospect of realizing within a few years their ideal, the possession of a small piece of land free from rent.

After one generation had migrated, the further current was affected by the same causes as had formerly appeared in the countries of northwestern Europe: relations between those who had remained at home and those who were prospering abroad (letters, remittances, etc.). In spite of the defence measures adopted by the countries of emigration, the movement soon amounted to hundreds of thousands annually.

More recent emigration was affected of course, apart from the recruiting devices of those commercially interested (steamship companies and agents), by the prospect of a better livelihood and a higher standard of living (economic, political and moral), and by

[1]According to the statistics of the port of New York, the proportion of sailing vessels was 96.4 per cent in 1856 and 3.2 per cent in 1873.

[2]I. Ferenczi. *Unemployment and International Migrations of Workers* (Report to the International Committee of the International Association on Unemployment), Jena, 1913, p. 31.

The prevalence of large estates and the splitting-up of small holdings had brought about a bad state of affairs in agriculture in those countries, just as they had in Ireland and Germany. The number of agricultural wage workers had been swollen by the decrease of the peasantry and by the large number of employees dismissed by the owners of medium and large estates. The extension of the use of machinery in agriculture and the disappearance of cattle had greatly limited the possibility of employment and more intensive types of cultivation appeared only to a moderate extent.

the attractive reports of persons who had already emigrated—imponderable psychological factors. But all these causes of agricultural emigration are insignificant compared with the fundamental fact that the peasant population could not find employment either in agriculture or in industry, adequate to assure them an annual income which would satisfy their standards.

It was not so much the difference between money wages or real wages at the start which induced hundreds of thousands of agricultural workers to cross the frontiers every year, but the possibility of a permanent livelihood, an increased annual income and considerable savings afforded by foreign agricultural or industrial areas.

Earlier legislation (Passenger Acts) actually encouraged emigration or immigration, but the influx of aliens on a lower cultural and economic level aroused in the older elements of the population in immigration countries fears for their own standard of living, and in the Governments fears about their assimilation. This brought about in the United States after 1882 an increasingly strict selective legislation (exclusion of persons incapable of earning a living). Then came the political experiences of the War, after which drastically restrictive immigration laws were passed. This legislation not only limited the scope of international migration throughout the world, but also changed its direction except in so far as it was likewise checked in other immigration countries where similar tendencies prevailed. This anti-migration tendency has also recently appeared in the European countries of emigration and immigration, notably in Italy.

In spite of post-war conditions, which were inimical to emigration and immigration, in spite of the disappointment of hopes that emigration might be a general measure of relief in Europe,[1] and in spite of the legislation hostile to migration on both sides of the ocean, the fact that there is on one side a thickly populated territory with an intensive economic regime, and on the other side whole continents with small populations and great economic possibilities is bound to lead to increased migration. The more orderly conditions become in the new countries, the more widespread the knowledge of their circumstances, the more rapid, secure and safe the means of communication, and the closer the relations between the inhabitants of the old and the new countries, the more complicated and fluctuating will be the whole migration movement. A survey of modern inter-

[1] *Idem, Assistenza ai Disoccupati ed il Problema dell' Emigrazione*, Nuova Antologia, Roma, 16 luglio, 1924.

national migrations is rendered difficult by the fact that most countries are to an increasing extent countries both of emigration and of immigration. A rational international regulation of this phenomenon, serving the interests of all alike, will be possible only on the basis of precise and comprehensive international statistics. The national and international tables together with our historical sketch of migration movements show to what extent this task has been accomplished with respect to the intercontinental and continental currents, and how much still remains to be done.

The picture of nineteenth-century migration would be incomplete if it were confined to the movement of European races. One of the characteristics of modern migration is the participation of the colored races in overseas movements and the increasing exchange of workers between the countries and continents inhabited by them. The Spanish colonies in America after the proclamation of their independence, as well as the English and French colonies after the emancipation of their Negro slaves, were compelled to make up for the lack of labor by calling in cheap workers from all parts of the world. Laborers were required who were suited for working in tropical climates. Resort was had to the system of "indentured laborers," which had already served in the sixteenth and seventeenth centuries. This system of labor contracts for long periods brought workers from four principal areas: the Spanish and Portuguese islands of the Atlantic Ocean, African islands and the African continent, India and China. This type of semi-slavery was seen, in the course of time, to be unsatisfactory and it led to social disturbances and racial antagonisms. The British colonial world and the United States at the end of the nineteenth century closed their doors more and more to the immigration of alien races, and a strong movement also arose in the Asiatic countries of emigration against the exportation of "indentured laborers," so that this current was practically limited to movements within the continent of Asia.

2. INTERCONTINENTAL EMIGRATION ACCORDING TO NATIONAL STATISTICS

EUROPE

AUSTRIA-HUNGARY [1]

(a) Austria

The people in the Southern Tyrol showed a tendency towards emigration in quite early times, particularly under pressure of the high cost of living after the Napoleonic Wars. The mere rumor that recruiting agents for settlers in Spain and America were in Genoa guaranteeing free passage, was enough to bring about a considerable exodus from the Southern Tyrol in 1816 and 1817.[2] The very incomplete statistics of permits recorded only slight emigration until 1851. In the first year, 1819, they showed 1,323 intercontinental and continental emigrants; in 1821, 2,656; but in 1826, only 794. In the later years of this period the number exceeded 1,000 only four times. An increase began in 1852 and reached its height in 1854 with 7,223 and 1867 with 9,299. The principal centers of emigration were Bohemia and Tyrol.[3]

For precise data for the years before 1871 it is necessary to consult the statistics of the overseas countries of immigration. To the United States the number of Austrian immigrants increased from 49 in 1861 to 4,424 in 1870. In Argentina 1,112 Austro-Hungarian subjects arrived between 1857 and 1870. According to the port statistics (Table VI), overseas emigration began in 1871 with 9,205 emigrants. From 1879 to 1880 the number rose from 7,366 to 20,993, and the following decades showed an enormous increase but with considerable breaks, until the War. In 1891, 53,778 Austrians sailed from European ports; in 1903 the number was 102,316; and in 1913, 194,462. The years of relatively small emigration were 1897

---

[1] Table 1 shows emigration figures from 1871 to 1924 for the whole territory of the former Austria-Hungary, and diagram 3 gives the curve of the same total. These figures are considered in connection with the international tables. Only the national tables for Austria and Hungary are discussed here.

[2] Note of Police Minister Sedluitzky, dated 28-5-1817, in the Vienna State Archives.

[3] There are data for immigration into Austria from 1819 to 1854 (Table IV). In 1819, 4,860 immigrants settled in Austria; from 1820 to 1822, about 5,000 to 6,000; in 1823, nearly 3,000. During these years the immigration shown by the statistics is considerably more than the emigration. From 1825 to 1851, the number of immigrants was almost constantly less than 1,000. In 1853 it rose again to 3,338, but did not remain at that high level.

(25,104); 1908 (58,932); and 1911 (91,868). Austria has been since 1900 one of the most important European countries of emigration, and its outflow, like that of Germany, was directed almost exclusively towards America.

According to the European port statistics, over 90 per cent of the Austrian emigrants between 1876 and 1885 went to the United States (Table VII). In the following years the proportion for the United States declined to some extent; in 1906 to 1910 it amounted to 80.3 per cent. From 1901 to 1910 Canada received over 11 per cent of the Austrian emigrants. Argentina received only 412 from 1876 to 1880, but 44,145 or 6.8 per cent from 1906 to 1910. Brazil received a fairly large number from 1891 to 1900: during these ten years 37,229 Austrian emigrants gave Brazil as their destination, but for 1901 to 1910 only 9,271.

The repatriation of Austrian subjects can be determined from the statistics of some overseas countries of immigration. The figures for immigration and repatriation of Austro-Hungarian subjects in Argentina may be tabulated as follows:

1857-1920.

Austrian immigrants into Argentina	87,266	100 per cent
Austrian emigrants from Argentina	36,726	42 per cent
Net immigration	50,540	58 per cent

The United States give the following figures for 1908 to 1913:

Austrian immigrants into the United States	604,857	100 per cent
Austrian emigrants from the United States	238,870	40 per cent
Net immigration	365,987	60 per cent

These data show that about three-fifths of the Austrian emigration to the western hemisphere is permanent.

There was also a considerable continental seasonal emigration from Austria before the War, but very few data are available. According to the records of the Frontier Police, the number of continental emigrants for the years 1906 to 1911 was 1,394,539 (Table XI). In 1911, 343,224 persons passed the boundaries to take work, mainly of an agricultural nature, in European states; in 1912 and 1913 the number was probably not smaller. The majority of these emigrants went to Germany. According to the *Reports* of the German Central Agency for Agricultural Labourers from Austria-

Hungary (Deutsche Feldarbeiterzentrale), Germany received between 200,000 and 250,000 seasonal workers, mostly Poles and Ruthenians, in each of the years 1907-08 to 1909-10.

Overseas emigration from the Austrian Republic rose from 5,176 in 1921 to 15,497 in 1923, but sank to 2,650 in 1924 (Table XIV). In the post-war period the United States continued to exert the strongest attraction upon Austrian emigrants; Brazil and Argentina played a measurable part in 1923.

(b) Hungary

Apart from the immigration statistics for the period 1760 to 1787, emigration statistics for Hungary are available from 1871 based on the records of various European ports (Table V). In 1871, according to these sources, overseas emigration from Hungary amounted to 294. The number remained insignificant until 1879 (1,759) but rose to 17,520 in 1882. In the following years the number of emigrants varied mostly between 10,000 and 25,000, rose to 35,125 in 1892, and fell to 8,044 in 1894. Towards the end of the century emigration revived and increased, with a single relapse, from 22,802 in 1898 to 209,169 in 1907. In the following year it fell to 49,365. It then rose again, but continued less than 130,000 up to 1913. So far as there are available data regarding the destination of Hungarian overseas emigrants (Table VI) they went almost exclusively to the United States.

For the repatriation of overseas emigrants the following data are available. In 1901, 6,801 emigrants returned from America. The number increased to 50,801 in 1908, but in the following year fell to 14,867. In 1913 there were 20,302 repatriations.

In tabulating the figures, these statistics of repatriation must be compared with the emigration movement according to the passport statistics (Table VIII). The figures are as follows:

1901-1913

Emigrants	1,139,140	100.0 per cent
Repatriates	298,435	26.2 per cent
Net emigration	840,705	73.8 per cent

The statistics of the United States for 1908 to 1913 show a stronger movement of repatriation:

Hungarian immigrants into the U. S.	585,344	100.0 per cent
Hungarian emigrants from the U. S.	221,596	37.9 per cent
Net immigration	363,748	62.1 per cent

Continental emigration was principally directed to Rumania and Germany (Table VIII). Emigration for the years 1899 to 1913 was:

To Rumania	102,378
To Germany	41,585
To other countries, including emigration to overseas countries other than America	49,815
Total	193,778

Repatriations from the same countries for 1901 to 1913 were as follows (Table XXI):

Rumania	13,816
Germany	8,469
Other countries	6,411
Total	28,696

It thus appears that only a small proportion of the continental emigrants returned to Hungary. Transport companies' statistics for post-War Hungary give 6,004 persons emigrated to overseas countries in 1921 (Table XXIX). The number then declined, remaining over 5,000 in 1923 and falling to 1,710 in 1924. From 1921 to 1923 emigration was almost exclusively to the United States; in 1924 Canada took nearly two-thirds of the emigrants and the United States less than one-third.

BALKAN STATES[1]

Greece, Turkey in Europe, Rumania and Bulgaria, Serbia and Montenegro

Among the Balkan States, Greece has furnished the largest number of emigrants. According to the statistics of the United States, 410,568 Greeks entered that country between 1820 and 1924. Turkey in Europe occupies the second place with 153,752 immigrants to the United States; then comes Rumania with 144,621, and next Bulgaria, Servia and Montenegro with 81,441.

Until the 80's immigration from the Balkans was insignificant. Turkey and Greece appear in the statistics of the United States with isolated figures, generally only a few individuals. The two countries together did not in any of those years send as many as 100 emigrants. In the later period immigration from the Balkans became more considerable.

Greece sent more than 100 first in 1882, and 1,000 in 1891; in 1900 she sent 3,771. At the beginning of the twentieth century the increase became more rapid. The maximum, 36,580, was reached in 1907. After a decrease to 14,111 in 1909 the number of immigrants from Greece again rose, and reached a second peak in 1914 with 35,832. In the post-War period, 1921 brought a considerable number of immigrants, namely 28,502, but the following years less than 5,000.

Greek migration to other countries has been very small compared with that to the United States. Greeks are not shown in statistics before 1900. Canada received over 1,000 annually in 1907 and 1912-1914. Australia received more than 200 Greeks each year after 1902 and 2,028 in 1924. To Brazil and Cuba the number is generally less than 100.

The only information about the repatriation of Greeks comes from the statistics of the United States. Emigration of Greeks from the United States was less than 10,000 in most years. This number was exceeded, however, in 1912-1914 and in 1919-1921; in 1913 there were 30,603 and in 1920, 20,314.

The total Greek immigration into the United States between 1908 and 1923 was 366,454, with 168,847 repatriations. The net gain by the United States for these sixteen years was thus 197,607, or 54 per cent of the immigration.

[1]Based on the statistics of the overseas countries of immigration.

Immigration from Turkey in Europe to the United States exceeded 100 for the first time in 1884 and remained less than 1,000 until 1903, except for the year 1892. As in the case of the other Balkan States, a high point was reached in 1907 when Turkish immigrants to the United States were 20,767; in the following years the movement remained considerable, almost always exceeding 10,000. The post-War period, however, showed a considerable decline. In 1921 the United States statistics reported 6,391 immigrants from European Turkey; in 1922, less than 2,000; and after being doubled in 1923 the number fell to 1,481 in 1924.

A considerable number of Turks have emigrated to Argentina and Brazil. The statistics for these countries include Turkey in Asia. In the ten years 1891-1900 Turkish immigration to Argentina was 11,583; in 1901-1910 it was 66,558, and in 1911-1920, 59,272. After the War, Turkish immigration was much smaller. Brazil showed isolated figures after 1871 and an unbroken series from 1897. Between 1904 and 1907 the number varied between 1,000 and 1,500 and then rose to 10,886 in 1913. For the post-war period the maximum was reached in 1923 with 4,829. Turkish immigration to Canada and Cuba is insignificant.

Repatriation statistics for Turkey are published by the United States and Argentina. From the United States repatriations amounted to between one-ninth and one-third of the immigrants in the years 1908-1913; in the post-war period it was very small. In Argentina between 1901 and 1910 the repatriations amounted to almost half of the immigrants and from 1911-1920 to one-third.

For Bulgaria, Serbia[1] and Montenegro the immigration statistics of the United States do not give any data before 1899. In that year there were 52 immigrants. The number rapidly increased to 1,761 in 1903 and 11,359 in 1907. In 1908 there were over 10,000, but in the following year only 1,054. In 1914 a high point, 9,189, was reached in comparison with the years immediately preceding and following. In 1921, after a fall to 19 in 1918, it was in turn exceeded with 9,999. Post-War figures are for Bulgaria and Yugoslavia.

[1]According to the statistics of the Serb-Croat-Slovene State, overseas emigration for 1920 amounted to 5,988. The number rose to 12,965 in 1921 and fell to 6,086 in 1922. An increasing tendency appeared in the following two years; in 1924 the number amounted to 17,238. Until 1922 the emigration was directed almost exclusively to the United States. In 1923 Argentina and Brazil received almost half, in 1924 Brazil more than one-third and Argentina more than one-fifth, the United States one-eighth and Canada and Australia one-tenth each. The year 1920 saw the greatest number of repatriations; no less than 18,980 persons returned from overseas countries in this year. The movement then showed a decreasing tendency. In 1923 the statistics show only 1,981 repatriations and in 1924, 5,159.

After 1900 Canada recorded the arrival of a few Serbian immigrants. Their number varied between 209 and 366 from 1911 to 1914. During the two years 1923 and 1924 other countries show a larger Yugoslav intercontinental immigration. In the course of the latter year, 7,889 arrived in Brazil, 3,959 in Argentina, 1,933 in Australia, and 1,620 in Canada. Yugoslav immigration into Cuba has been small, 365 marking the maximum in 1924.

From 1908 to 1923 the United States received 104,808 Bulgarian, Serbian and Montenegrin immigrants, with 92,886 repatriations, giving a net gain of only 11,922 or 11 per cent of the immigration.

Immigration to the United States from Rumania was not recorded before 1880. The number remained less than 80 until 1883 and less than 1,000 until 1898, except for the years 1887 and 1888 when it amounted to 2,045 and 1,186 respectively.

Toward the end of the century there was a considerable increase in Rumanian immigration. In 1900 there were over 6,000 and in 1903, 9,310. The number then decreased, but did not fall below 4,000 until 1908. From 1909-1913 it varied between 1,500 and 2,500 and in 1914 again exceeded 4,000.

During the War Rumania acquired new territories which more than doubled its population. This explains in part the fact that the largest movement of migration from Rumania to the United States appeared after the War. In 1921 there were 25,817 and from 1922-1924 the number varied around 11,000.

Canadian statistics show a few hundred Rumanian immigrants each year from 1900 to the outbreak of the War; in 1913 there were 1,504. This figure was exceeded in 1924 with 2,056.

A few Rumanian immigrants arrived in Brazil and Cuba before the war but the number was not significant. In 1924 Rumanian immigration to Brazil was 6,340 and to Cuba 951; but for that year only 3 immigrants to Cuba gave Rumania as the country of last residence. Finally, Argentina and Palestine should be mentioned since their statistics show Rumanian immigration for the post-War period. The number entering Palestine was 990 in 1922 and 593 in 1924; the number entering Argentina was 1,500 in 1923 and the same in 1924.

According to the statistics of the United States the repatriation of Rumanians from 1908 to 1923 was smaller than in the case of Bulgars, Serbs or Montenegrins; for this period there was a net gain of 34 per cent of the immigrants.

BELGIUM

The statistics of Belgian emigration through Antwerp, the principal port of embarkation, begin with 1885.

Some idea of the emigration for the earlier years of the nineteenth century may be formed from the statistics of the countries of immigration.

The United States received a few Belgian immigrants annually from 1820 on. The figures are discontinuous until 1840. For 1820 only one immigrant was reported; 14 was the highest figure in any of the first twenty years.

From 1841 when 106 arrivals were reported, Belgian immigration began to assume larger proportions. The maximum for the period 1820-1884 was 1,982 in 1856.[1] In 1884 the statistics show 1,576 arrivals. Between 1820 and 1884, the United States received 30,040 Belgians, an annual average of 462.

Belgian emigration to Argentina is reported from 1857, when 17 arrivals were recorded. The maximum until 1885 was 383 in 1883.

Brazil reports Belgian immigration in 1847. The number for 1862 (376) is the maximum; the movement then declines, and in 1884 there were only 19 arrivals.[2]

The Antwerp emigration statistics (Table XIII) for 1885 show 1,286 departures. The movement increased during the following years and reached a first maximum in 1889 with 8,406. It then declined to a minimum in 1897 with 923. At the beginning of the twentieth century it began to revive; in 1907 the statistics show 6,423 emigrants, and in 1913, just before the War, 7,590. For the war period, figures are completely lacking. The United States immigration statistics show 73 Belgians for 1918. In 1919 the records give 1,967 departures from Antwerp. The emigration in 1920 was the culminating point of the whole movement with 9,384 departures; this was followed by a decline to only 2,923 in 1924. The reported emigration from 1885 to 1924 was 127,843, and the United States alone registered the arrival of 111,864 Belgians.

[1]On February 23, 1848, the Belgian Government presented to the Chamber of Representatives a Bill providing 500,000 francs to finance a scheme of emigration and colonization of Flemish paupers, in either the western parts of the United States, Central America, or Algeria.

The Government decided in 1849 and 1850 to encourage a two-fold scheme of settlement, one in the State of Pennsylvania, the other in the State of Missouri. Various families from Flanders and other provinces left for North America in this way. After ten years the colony of "New Flanders (Sainte Marie of Pennsylvania)" numbered only 200 inhabitants. (Duval, L'Emigration, p. 117 et seq., 120 f.)

[2]These indirect statistics show numerous gaps during the period 1847-1884.

The emigration to Canada is not so great. The minimum is 77 in 1899 and the maximum 2,072 in 1913. The immigration statistics do not show any large figures. In 1913, which marks the culmination of the movement, 2,651 arrivals were recorded.

Certain emigration statistics concerning the number of aliens in transit for the port of Antwerp, discovered at the National Library in 1912 and attributable to M. Royers, former Secretary of the Port, provide figures for the period 1843-1901. Some of the figures agree with the official statistics; others, however, show considerable discrepancies. The figures conform to the official data only from 1852. While 3,179 emigrants were officially registered for the year 1843, M. Royers' table shows only 3,130 departures. Apart from these differences the statistics have the advantage of giving figures for the years 1855-1859, for which official statistics are lacking.

1843.. 3,130	1849..10,260	1855.. 7,589
1844.. 2,961	1850.. 6,831	1856..10,010
1845.. 5,241	1851.. 8,375	1857..13,445
1846..13,178	1852..14,463	1858.. 4,080
1847..15,800	1853..15,197	1859.. 1,300
1848..11,513	1854..25,709	1860.. 2,507 (2,442 according to the official statistics.)

Although these figures should be used with caution, they show a noticeable decline during this period, which continued until 1871 when no departures were recorded. From then on the movement rose continuously until 1903 (72,486), as shown by the official statistics.

BRITISH ISLES

The Napoleonic Wars reduced intercontinental emigration, except to Canada, to insignificant proportions. But after the Peace of 1815 emigration came to be widely regarded as a panacea for social ills.[1] The Peace threw thousands either altogether or in a great measure out of employment.[2]

During the early decades of the nineteenth century Great Britain, from being mainly agricultural, became pre-eminently industrial.[3]

[1]A. Redford, p. 148.
[2]J. M'Gregor, *British America*, Edinburgh, 1883, II; quoted by E. Abbott, *Historical*, p. 82.
[3]In 1811 the industrial and commercial population was 44.2 per cent and in 1900, 68.7 per cent.

This economic change which replaced workers by machinery plunged large sections of the working classes into misery and pauperism. By adopting the policy of free trade, England obtained agricultural produce more cheaply than by growing all of it at home, but the agricultural population suffered. As a consequence, Great Britain and Ireland became countries of large estates and extensive pastures, and the small farmers turned to the colonies for a livelihood.

In 1824 the interdiction of emigration of skilled workers was definitely abolished; in 1825 and 1826 acute distress prevailed among the workers, and in 1827 there was a marked increase in the working class emigration. The immense growth of this movement becomes manifest when we learn that there were 2,081 passengers in 1815 (the beginning of the statistical era) and in 1832, seventeen years later, 103,140 passengers (British and aliens).

Here are two illustrations of the economic condition of the country and its effect on those who were not entirely without resources. "High rents and heavy taxation, exorbitant tithes and grinding leases, are driving the small farmers out of the country," states *Niles' Weekly Register* on July 31, 1830, p. 402;[1] and the *Edinburgh Review*, in an article on "The Irish Crisis," wrote in January, 1848: "The emigrants generally belonged to that class of small holders who, being somewhat above the level of the prevailing destitution, had sufficient resources left to enable them to make the effort required to effect their removal to a foreign land... Large remittances, estimated to amount to £200,000 in the year ending on the 30th March 1847, were also made by the Irish emigrants settled in the United States and the British North American provinces, to enable their relations in Ireland to follow them."[2] Cobbett, writing in 1830 to an advocate of State-aided emigration, says: "The industrious people of England....are going of their own accord, and at their own expense. From Kent and Sussex, about 2,000; from Yarmouth, 400; from Boston, about 200; from Yorkshire and Lancashire, 1,500 or thereabouts; from Hull, gone this year and going, about 7,000; from Scotland, about 2,000."[3]

The introduction about 1840 of certain automatic devices in the textile industry greatly increased its production, giving rise to an economic crisis and unemployment, and contributed to swell the number of emigrants as well as to increase the endeavor to get rid

[1]Quoted in E. Abbott, *Historical*, p. 75.
[2]E. Abbott, *Historical*, pp. 112-113.
[3]Cobbett, quoted in *Niles' Weekly Register*, 12 June 1830, p. 296; quoted in E. Abbott, *Historical*, p. 74.

of them by assisting emigration. The current grew from 62,527 passengers in 1833 to 128,344 passengers in 1842, followed after an inconsiderable fall by a further rise.

British emigration from 1815 to 1834 may be subdivided as follows:

English	110,000
Scotch	30,000
Irish	420,000
Total	560,000

So, too, for the subsequent period 1835-1850:

English	320,000
Scotch	80,000
Irish	1,409,000
Total	1,809,000[1]

Separating Irish emigration from the total we obtain the following figures for the former during the critical period 1845-1850:

1845	77,686
1846	109,624
1847	217,512
1848	187,803
1849	218,842
1850	213,649[2]

Irish emigration in the first half of the nineteenth century supplied the largest contingent of emigrants from the British Isles. In fact, Ireland, which is eminently an agricultural country, suffered most from England's adoption of free trade. Unable to withstand the competition which ensued, many of its fields were converted into hunting preserves and pastures. The landlords expelled their tenants. The country's fate was the more distressing as in the seventeenth century almost every trace of industry except the linen industry had been rooted out by English competition and legislation. Hence, the inhabitants of Ireland expatriated themselves in mass. This was emphasized by the hopeless condition of the Irish during 1846 and 1847, when the potato crops almost completely failed.

[1]M. G. Mulhall, p. 248a.
[2]E. Philippovich, article "Auswanderung," p. 291.

A series of misfortunes and of waves of emigration caused the population of Ireland to fall by about half, from more than 8 million souls in 1841 to 4,456,000 in 1901, and to 4,230,000 in 1926.

An important factor in enabling intending emigrants to realize their plan, was the monetary assistance rendered by the Government. Financial support of emigration began with the £50,000 voted in 1819 by Parliament to assist emigration to the Cape, and between 1821 and 1827 there were four more appropriations. In 1826 a Committee on Emigration recommended the colonization of the oversea possessions. Soon afterwards the local authorities were authorized to assist emigration.[1]

The Commissioner-General of Emigration during 1837-1839 assisted 13,550 emigrants, and the Emigration Office during 1840-1846 assisted 30,854 emigrants and during 1847-1851, 60,194 emigrants. These are large figures, but of the total emigration they form only a small percentage. From the earliest years up to 1924 almost one million (964,299) immigrants arriving in Australia received State assistance.[2]

With the year 1853 British statistics began to distinguish between citizen and alien passengers, but the number of aliens who embarked in British ports was inconsiderable. In the same year, 278,129 departures of citizens were registered, Ireland supplying the largest contingent. After this date the pendulum swung back and in 1861 reached its lowest point with 65,197 departures.

During the next period the stream of emigration broadened. Thus for 1873 the statistics show 228,345 British passengers, but after the crisis four years later this number dropped to 95,195. Then there was a fresh upward movement, culminating with 320,118 departures in 1883. Towards the close of the century the movement slackened, and 140,644 British passengers departed in 1898.

From the opening of the twentieth century, the emigration movement showed a pronounced upward tendency, reaching the peak in 1913, with 469,640 British passengers. Naturally, the War arrested the efflux of emigrants, only 17,319 passengers leaving in 1918. With the return of peace and under the influence of the Empire Settlement legislation the numbers began to approach the earlier pre-war figures, 263,480 passengers leaving in 1924 (Table IV).

For emigration proper, figures are available since April 1, 1912. In 1912 there were 326,959 emigrants. The following year the

[1]C. Stanley Johnson, p. 86-91.
[2]*Official Year-Book of the Commonwealth of Australia*, 1926, p. 895.

figure rose to 389,394. The minimum was reached in 1917—during the War—with 10,004. In 1924, 155,374 emigrants were recorded. For this entire period the number of emigrants (2,298,976) was about three-fourths (74 per cent) the number of passengers.[1] Until near the close of the eighteenth century, the goal of British emigrants was North America. Then the stream of emigration branched out in two further principal directions, South Africa and Australia.

The passenger statistics make it clear that during the nineteenth century and the first decade of the twentieth, the majority of British intercontinental passengers left for the United States. Perhaps three-fifths of them sailed for that country where they knew that they would find not only high wages, but much the same customs as prevailed in their home land. From 1910 onward the statistics show a considerable shift in the destination of the emigrants, the stream flowing more strongly toward the British colonies and leaving less than half the aggregate number of emigrants for the United States.

The movement of emigrants to the United States is predominantly permanent. According to the emigration statistics of the United States a little over one-third of the British emigrants return to their home country.

From 1815 onward the movement to Canada[2] became gradually more pronounced. It started with 680 passengers, citizen and alien, in 1815, and rose to 109,680 passengers in 1847. In 1853, 31,779 passengers sailed for Canada, the number dropping to 2,469 in 1859. Then emigration to Canada recovered until in 1913 there were 196,278 departures. Those for 1924 were 99,717.

The number of British citizens returning from Canada is considerably smaller than the number emigrating. However, the divergence markedly decreased between 1910 and 1924.

Emigration to other American countries may be said to be relatively unimportant. Approximately half of those emigrating to these countries return.

For Australia and New Zealand combined figures are available since 1825.[3] In that year 485 passengers sailed for that destination.

[1] The ratio net departures/population has nearly doubled since 1851-1913.

[2] Canada here also includes other British possessions in North America, but the emigration to those is comparatively insignificant.

[3] For the two countries separately for 1840-1875 and 1906-1924. Accordingly, in the text the more comprehensive figures are given as they cover the whole period from 1825 to date. Taking the separate periods, it appears that from 1840 to 1875, 908,341 passengers embarked for Australia, 194,556 for New Zealand, and from 1906 to 1924, 615,750 for the former destination and 168,659 for the latter.

But in consequence of state-aid to emigrants the movement speedily assumed considerable proportions. Thus, in 1853, 54,818 departed, while in the following year, owing to the discovery of gold in Australia, the number of departures rose to 77,526. Then there was a decline, reaching 11,695 in 1871, followed by an ascent culminating in 96,800 passengers in 1912. For the year 1924 the figure was 58,500.

The number of returning British citizens during the period 1871-1886 was inconsiderable. Thus, in 1871 there were 11,695 departures against 1,994 returning. But from 1887 the relative proportions change. In that year, for instance, 34,183 departures and 10,258 returning are recorded. In general, however the departures far exceed the arrivals.[1]

At first Australia was regarded by the British Government as primarily a penal colony. Accordingly, a stream of convicts was poured into the country. Before 1836 those who had come out to Australia of their own accord could not have exceeded 40,000. Meanwhile, from 1787 (New South Wales, Botany Bay) to 1836, about 103,000 criminals had been transported to New South Wales and Tasmania.[2][3]

Summing up the matter of convict shipments to Australia,[4] it has been calculated that from 1793 to 1860, England sent there 131,450 convicts, excluding Irish convicts prior to 1860.[5] The rate at which they were deported has an interest of its own. Thus while for 1844-46 there were 681 annually sentenced to deportation, during the succeeding three years this number rose to an average of 2,658 because

[1]With regard to emigration to Australasia, it is helpful to bear in mind the date of the creation of the colonies: New South Wales, 1786; Tasmania, 1825; Western Australia, 1829; South Australia, 1834; New Zealand, 1841; Victoria, 1851; Queensland, 1859; and the Northern Territory, 1863.

[2]H. Merivale, p. 351. From 1788 to 1806, convicts, soldiers, officers, and some clerks were about the only Europeans in Australia.

[3]According to the Proceedings of the Land Committee of 1836 (question 1879), the following were the arrivals in New South Wales from 1829 to 1834:

	Deported	Voluntary emigrants
1829	3,664	564
1830	3,225	309
1831	2,633	457
1832	3,119	2,006
1833	4,151	2,885
1834	3,161	1,564

Extending the period to 10 years, from 1825 to 1834, the total number of emigrants arriving in New South Wales was 28,983, of whom only 4,141 were females.—K. Rathgen, p. 17f.

[4]The penal colonies under the British Government were four in number: New South Wales, Tasmania, Bermuda, and Norfolk Island.

[5]A. Legoyt, p. 15.

of the famine which raged in Ireland.[1] A universal outcry then was raised in the Colonies against receiving criminals, and finally about the middle of the nineteenth century, the British Government reluctantly consented to deport no more convicts. The deportation of females had previously been abolished by the Act of November 19, 1839.

The number of emigrants to New South Wales can be approximately gauged by noting that the number of its inhabitants was about 50,000 in 1832, 97,512 in 1838, and 265,503 in 1850.[2] In the twenty-five years 1832-1856 the number of immigrants was 151,394, of whom 109,286 were assisted.[3]

Official regulations defining the desirable types of emigrants to be recruited for New South Wales and South Australia were published in 1849. These included the following suggestions: The emigrants should be mainly married couples, not over 40 years of age, fit for work and wage-earners. Preference was to be given to newly married couples without children (as suggested by Wakefield). Persons who intended to purchase land or wished to establish an industrial undertaking in the Colony and persons in receipt of poor relief were not granted free passage. No one was to be accepted without good testimonials regarding character and efficiency. The cost of traveling to the port of embarkation was to be borne by the emigrant.[4]

New Zealand was colonized almost entirely through the activity of certain colonization companies,[5] the principal one being the New Zealand Colonization Company. In the first year, in September 1839, over 1,200 British emigrants sailed for New Zealand.[6] Among these were 168 adults and 48 children of the educated classes and 583 adults and 320 children of the working classes.[7] By 1850, eleven years later, New Zealand had 26,700 inhabitants.[8] The creation of this colony is first and foremost owing to the determination of the emigration reformer, E. G. Wakefield, who influenced British and colonial emigration legislation to a vital extent.[9]

[1] K. Rathgen, pp. 164-165.
[2] To Tasmania til 1853 and West Australia til the 60's.
[3] K. Rathgen, p. 52.
[4] *Ibid.*, p. 40.
[5] *Ibid.*, p. 25.
[6] *Ibid.*, p. 23.
[7] Beit, p. 11.
[8] K. Rathgen, p. 63.
[9] At the Public Record Office is correspondence of the New Zealand Colonization Company which throws an interesting light on various aspects of emigration. Thus, it is stated in parts of the correspondence relating to 1840-1841 (Letter-book No. 4, Letter 1522) that "the fact of a family including more than two children under 7 years of age

The British statistics of passengers for South Africa go back to the year 1821. For the following twenty years the annual number did not generally exceed 500. The net immigration, 1824-61, was 470,000 persons. From 1841 to 1876 the statistics comprise citizens and aliens in one figure; but it may be said that for this period the annual figure doubled. Then from 1877 to 1924—when citizens and aliens were separately recorded again—809,476 British sailed for South Africa. However, something like three-fourths of the passengers to the Cape and to Natal returned. In fact, from 1882 to 1924 no fewer than 610,825 British subjects returned to the British Isles.

Examining now the immigration statistics of the country of arrival, we find that 321,792 British immigrants arrived at the Cape during the period 1900-1912, and 238,639 or 74 per cent of that number departed. Natal recorded 12,270 British arrivals for 1911 and 1912, as against 13,448 British departures.

During 1820 and 1821 some 5,000 British settlers arrived at the Cape,[1] Parliament having voted £50,000 in 1819 for sending 4,000 persons to South Africa.[2] In response to the Government's announcement, no less than 90,000 applicants clamored to be taken with their families. However, only 3,659 people embarked and arrived at the Cape between March and October, 1820. Of these, 1,020 were men; 607, women; and 2,032, children. The occupations of the settlers were various: doctors, artists, printers, wine-dealers, rope-makers, bakers and woodcutters, were mixed with a few agricultural laborers.[3] At the close of 1822 Mr. Ingram, the head of one of the Irish Parties, obtained the financial assistance of the Government and transported a shipload of 347 emigrants (laborers, with women and children) to the same destination.[4] In 1844 Cape Colony began to assist the immigration of maids, farm hands, and certain manual workers, such as smiths and building operatives, by providing bounties, while under the supervision of the Emigration Office, during the period 1848 to 1850, 3,690 persons

renders the whole family ineligible to receive a free passage"; (Letter 2585) that "single women can only receive a passage in one of the Company's ships in the event of their going under the protection of a near married relative"; that single men were not granted free passages to New Zealand; that "we have already a very much larger proportion of young children to the number of adults than is sanctioned by the Directors," and that therefore such applications must be discouraged; and, lastly, "the price of a steerage passage in the Company's ships averages from £17 to £20."

[1]*Official Year-Book of South Africa.*
[2]K. Rathgen, p. 8.
[3]A. Redford, pp. 228-229.
[4]G. E. Cory, II.

were sent over.[1] Lastly, as the result of a stirring propaganda by Byrne, 3,792 emigrants departed for Natal between 1848 and 1850.[2] As we see from the preceding figures and from the official statistics given above, the efflux to South Africa was intermittent and, in the first half of the nineteenth century, decidedly restricted. By 1849 there were some 34,000 white inhabitants in the eastern districts of the Cape.[3] The presence of the Dutch in various parts of South Africa, the existence of an enormous native population, and the climate, accounted for the relatively insignificant number of British emigrants to that part of the world.

FRANCE

At the beginning of the nineteenth century French colonial emigration was confined to refractory persons wishing to escape military conscription due to the great wars of the Empire. Napoleon I (1804) carried out a policy of complete abandonment of the colonies, which were left to fend for themselves. This policy paved the way for the loss of the French possessions. By the Treaty of Paris in 1814, however, France recovered Réunion, Guadeloupe, Martinique, Guiana and Madagascar.

The heavy taxation and other burdens of France during and after the Napoleonic wars led to extensive emigration, both continental and intercontinental. The north-eastern Departments of France, the Moselle, the Meurthe, the Lower and Upper Rhine were principally affected. Since the strict prohibition of emigration to foreign countries had by this time been abandoned, there was nothing to stop the movement. Late in 1816 and 1817 simultaneously with a continental emigration, many Frenchmen went to America. Agents for America, commissioned by Amsterdam firms, offered the poor wretches the possibility of becoming landowners and promised them their passage.[4] There are hardly any numerical data for this overseas emigration. Many of the unfortunates did not reach their destination; it was necessary to return them for lack of means of subsistence.

Requests for foreign passports had to be sent to the Ministry of the Interior and were required for all countries, without distinction.

[1] K. Rathgen, p. 9.
[2] G. E. Cory, IV, p. 393.
[3] K. Rathgen, p. 9.
[4] A letter of March 28, 1817 to the Ministry of War states that unknown agents were endeavoring to bring about emigration to the United States from the French provinces on the Rhine.

The scanty numerical data which it has been possible to compile for this first half of the nineteenth century are furnished by the statistics of these requests. Even these statistics are not complete for 1817 for the Departments concerned. Many persons attempted to leave without passports or with simple passports for travel within France. Others left France with passports for Switzerland and Germany, and consequently did not appear in the records as emigrants to America or Russia.

It is impossible to determine precisely the extent of the continental and overseas emigration; but according to the requests for passports received by the Prefects of the Departments of the Meurthe, the Moselle and the Lower and Upper Rhine, the available figures for the first half of 1817 have been collected. From January to May 1817, 940 applications are recorded for the Department of the Meurthe, most of them for Russia.[1] From October 1816 to the middle of April 1817, 3,222 persons left the Moselle;[2] their destination is not known. The Department of the Lower Rhine provided the largest contingent of emigrants. For the first half of 1817 (January to June) 4,858 persons proposed to leave their country for a more hospitable land.[3] From January 29, 1817, to June 21 of the same year, the passport statistics of the Upper Rhine show 3,996 applications.[4]

In a letter of March 23, 1817, to the Ministry of General Police the Prefect of the Lower Rhine states that the majority of the emigrants are day-laborers and asks for authority to check this emigration by refusing passports, at least to farmers and day-laborers without sufficient means to undertake a long journey. According to this document emigrants were encouraged to emigrate to the East. Indeed, five Amsterdam houses undertook to pay the passage of the emigrants in this direction.[5]

Mention should be made of an attempt at colonization in 1817. Three hundred officers and soldiers on half pay left under the command of General Lallemand and founded the colony of Champ d'Asile in what is now Texas. But in 1819 the Viceroy of Mexico had the settlement destroyed.[6]

In spite of the obstacles which the Prefects attempted to put in the way of emigration to America in the following years, they did

[1] 18 applications were recived on May 18, 1816.
[2] National Archives of France, F. 7, 6138[9].
[3] National Archives of France, F. 7, 6138[9].
[4] National Archives of France, F. 7, 6138[10].
[5] National Archives of France, F. 7, 6138[8].
[6] G. Chandèze, p. 98.

not succeed in stopping the movement. They were often compelled to assist many of these emigrants who departed with great hopes but soon returned poorer than when they left.

Direct statistics showing that emigration to America still continued, though greatly diminished, are preserved in the Archives of the Department of the Lower Rhine; for the 10 years 1828-1837, 14,365 inhabitants of the Lower Rhine left for the New World.[1] Since the other three Departments mentioned above were subject to the same economic conditions, it is probable that their emigration was as extensive as that of the Department of the Lower Rhine.

For the years 1820-1836 a precise notion of French emigration can be derived from the figures of the United States. The French Trans-Atlantic Steamship Commission in 1840 expressed the desire to know the number of French and foreign passengers annually embarking at French ports for the two Americas, and the Ministry of the Interior instructed the Prefects of the maritime Departments to report the total number of embarkations during the past three years.[2]

The Prefects of the maritime Departments report the departure of 35,721 emigrants during these three years: 12,028 in 1837; 9,610 in 1838; 14,083 in 1839.

The port statistics from 1837 to 1839 are neither complete nor precise, since the Prefects as a rule did not distinguish between French citizens and aliens and omitted to record the servants and children who appeared on collective passports. It may be presumed,

[1] They were distributed among the districts of this Department as follows:

Saverne	4,620
Schlestadt	385
Strasburg	2,711
Wissenburg	6,649
	14,365

(Archives of the Lower Rhine: Record of persons emigrating to America from 1828 to 1837 inclusive.)

[2] The Havre statistics, by countries of destination up to 1875, do not distinguish French citizens from citizens of other nations. But for the years 1837 to 1839, when the maritime Prefects were requested by the Ministry of the Interior to give the total number of French emigrants, it has been possible to arrive at the following figures for that port— the destinations are unknown:

	French	American	German
1837	1,376	503	5.527
1838	744	444	2,677
1839	1,216	580	7,800
	3,336	1,427	16,004

(Arch. Nat. F. 7, 12,337.)

therefore, that the figures presented by the marine registers are less than the truth. The largest numbers of emigrants to America sailed from Havre and Bordeaux. Regular departures from these ports took place every month and ships were run specially for the passenger service.

Many travellers who did not find an opportunity for sailing from France proceeded to embark at ports of neighboring countries, particularly England, where there were regular and frequent services for North America.

The immigration statistics of the United States for these three years show the arrival in 1837 of 5,074 French immigrants, of 3,675 in 1838, and 7,198 in 1839.

The port register of Bordeaux distinguishes only emigration to South and Central America.[1] It may be presumed that French emigration was fairly large by reference to that of later years. The Basque population, which still figures most largely in the movement, was the first to form a regular stream of emigration. Their presence in Argentina is indicated from 1825. Departures of Basques from France were 1,575 in 1840 and 2,827 in 1841. These figures do not include the numerous clandestine departures through Spain.[2] After the discovery of gold in California or about 1850 French emigration to the United States increased, especially through recruiting agents, but numerous agencies abused their privileges. The Government was therefore obliged to follow the example of the English and German ports. On January 15, 1855, a Decree was promulgated regulating French emigration. Special commissioners were appointed for the protection of emigrants and measures taken to obtain more accurate statistics.

While French statistics start with the year 1857, the statistics of other countries show French emigration for earlier years. The arrival of French immigrants began to be recorded in the United States in 1820. The number was then unimportant, only 371; but from 1827 there was an upward tendency. In 1840 French immigration reached its first peak, with 7,419 arrivals. Then the movement slowed down for a time, after which it began to rise until in 1851, as the result of the political and economic crisis of 1848 in France,

[1]The figures are:

	North America	Central America	South America
1837	512	929	728
1838	464	703	432
1839	539	672	392

(Archives, F. 7, 12,337).

[2]G. Chandèze, p. 98.

it reached the maximum of 20,126. The total number of French arrivals in the United States for the period 1820-1856 was 195,971.

For Brazil we possess only some discontinuous figures of French immigration prior to 1857, and these are insignificant. In fact, only 345 arrivals in all are recorded for the years 1842-1843, 1846, and 1850-1852.

According to the statistical evidence, French overseas emigration in 1857 amounted to 5,721, a figure which is negligible in relation to the population of France. The movement steadily diminished during the following years. In 1862, only 2,334 Frenchmen emigrated; the movement had thus decreased by half. This fall in emigration, which was already so slight in 1857, is explained by favorable economic circumstances.

From 1863, however, emigration increased. It rose from 2,384 in that year to 7,898 in 1869. During this period emigration agents were trying to induce Frenchmen to settle in the South American states; this is probably the explanation of the increase. In the two following years, 1870-1871, the movement decreased considerably because of the Franco-Prussian war and the insurrection of Sept. 4, 1871, in which all classes of the population took part, and also the repression of May 1871; but it revived in 1872 when it amounted to 15,829, almost three times as many as the 5,947 in the preceding year. Emigration thus assumed proportions previously unknown, but only for a moment. By 1873 the movement had decreased appreciably and reached its lowest level in 1877 with 2,116. Beginning with 1878, when there were 2,316 emigrants, there was a gradual increase until 1886 (7,314), when the number was about three times as great as in 1877.

During the four following years the increase was accentuated. In 1887 the number reached 11,170. In 1888 it rose to 23,339 and in 1889 it was highest of all, 31,354. The following year saw a decrease to 20,560 and in 1891 there were only 6,217 emigrants. From that point the movement continued to decline. The statistics for 1894 show only 4,000. During the period 1895-1902 there was no great change. From 1903 a slight increase appeared. The curve rose to a peak in 1907 with 8,000 or much less than the previous maximum. Emigration then continued to decrease, rapidly at first and with great variations until the beginning of the War (1914-1918). In 1914 the figure was relatively large (3,057). From 1915 to 1918 the figures are insignificant; French emigration was checked by the political events which were overwhelming Europe. As in the

period after 1870, the post-war period showed an increase: 5,439 for 1919; 4,012 for 1920. From 1921 to 1924 French emigration continued to decrease; from 1,762 in 1921, it reached 1,568 in 1924. (Tables I and VI).

Direction of French Emigration

During the second half of the nineteenth century French emigrants turned in the main to South America.

The statistics are incomplete, since only departures from the most important French ports (Bayonne, Bordeaux, Marseilles from 1865 to 1874, and also Havre from 1875) were registered; they indicate the countries of destination of French emigration.[1] From 1865 to 1891 (figures are lacking for the years 1886-1889) there were 54,605 departures of citizens for Montevideo and Buenos Aires, 3,941 for Brazil and 28,288 for the United States and Canada. Chile and Peru attracted only a few hundred. These are the only destinations which figure to any extent in the statistics. The other continents—Africa and Australia—received only a few.

Canadian statistics indicate the arrival of an increasing number of Frenchmen up to the eve of the war; the number rose from 360 in 1900 to 2,755 in 1912. During and after the war the number decreased; in 1924 it was less than in 1900 (326). The total number of arrivals 1900-24 was 29,428.

Beginning with 1911 Cuba reported immigrants from France and in 1924 the number became considerable. From 264 in 1901, with an interval during the war, the number departing from France rose to 504 in 1920.

Argentina has received considerable numbers of French immigrants since 1857; up to the war there was a steady increase in the numbers. From 1857 to 1924 the total was 226,894. French emigration to Brazil has been much less. The total from 1842 to 1924 was 33,304. Mexico received only 10,986 French immigrants between 1909 and 1924. There was a steady movement to Uruguay from 1879 to 1904, which was resumed after an interval from 1913 to 1921. The annual figure was generally under 1,000. Between 1867 and 1921

[1] In the national tables the data relating to the countries of destination of the French emigrants have not been included. They cover only a small proportion of the emigrants and do not even permit one to judge of the shares of the different countries of destination in French emigration as a whole. The figures which follow in the text are taken, for the period down to 1881, from the *Rapports à S. E. le Ministre de l'Intérieur sur l'Émigration* and for the years 1882–1885 and 1890–1891 from the *Statistica dell' Emigrazione italiana* (Rome).

Uruguay received 24,114 French immigrants. Paraguay received only 1,736 from 1883 to 1906. Of the other continents Australia has received the largest number. Its total from 1902 to 1924 was 24,615. South Africa received only 844 from 1913 to 1924.

There are serious discrepancies between the French emigration statistics and the immigration statistics of the countries of destination. From 1857 to 1890, for example, French statistics show 237,218 departures for all countries. But the United States, Argentina and Brazil alone received a hundred thousand more than that number of French immigrants. During the period 1857-1890 the arrivals from France were:

$$
\begin{array}{lr}
\text{United States} & 170,748 \\
\text{Argentina} & 136,036 \\
\text{Brazil} & 12,532 \\
\hline
& 319,316
\end{array}
$$

or one-third more than the recorded departures from France for all countries. For the period 1910-1924, the French statistics show 43,450 departures of French citizens. The indirect statistics of the American countries (United States, Canada, Cuba, Argentina, Mexico, Uruguay, Paraguay) and of Australia and South Africa show the arrival during the same period of 199,868 French citizens or nearly five times as many.

French emigration to French colonies in the nineteenth century was insignificant. The government therefore sought to bring in— besides colored labor—other European immigrants by granting privileges to colonists.

By decree of March 27, 1852, it authorized labor contracts and allowed free passage, defrayed out of the immigration fund to European workers engaged by colonial employers, on condition that the undertakings needing such support were of value to the public.[1] In spite of this decree, no current of European emigration to French colonies has been observed. Officials and soldiers are the chief white immigrants. Indians and Africans seem to possess the necessary qualifications for laboring on large agricultural estates in a climate such as that of the French colonies. The Government therefore, during the nineteenth century, called for colored labor in order to exploit its colonies.[2]

Guiana and New Caledonia, however, received white convict im-

[1]Brunel, p. 181.
[2]See Indian and Chinese emigration.

migrants.[1] The transportation of European convicts injures a colony by checking free colonization. In 1870 there were in New Caledonia 1,562 colonists, 289 officials, 754 soldiers, 1,176 Asiatic or African immigrants and 2,302 non-political prisoners. Three thousand to 4,000 persons were deported there for taking part in the insurrection of 1871 in Paris.[2] From 1879 to 1883 New Caledonia received only 751 immigrants of various nationalities, including 330 French. From 1897 to 1924 continuous statistics are available. During this period the registers show 15,013 immigrants, including 6,658 French and 1,347 English. The rest were mostly Chinese and Japanese. Repatriations for the same period number 14,488 including 6,633 French and 1,301 English. The French population is thus unstable.

The French Government was at first uncertain about measures for the colonization of Algeria. It prohibited immigration of such aliens as could not show adequate means of subsistence. In spite of the steps taken to encourage French emigration, that current never assumed large proportions, not even when the Constituent Assembly voted 50 millions of credits to people Algeria from the streets of Paris. After the revolution of 1848, however, 13,500 unemployed workers were sent to Algeria.[3] This was an exceptional measure. The decree of April 26, 1851, opened a new period by granting property in land from the first day of occupation. The population of Algeria thenceforward increased rapidly, in spite of the decree of April 23, 1852, which required colonists to show proof of sufficient resources to carry on exploitation.[4] From 1853 to 1864 French statistics show continuous emigration to the Mediterranean colony. During this period 55,352 French emigrants landed in Algeria.[5]

[1]The State transported to New Caledonia from Mar. 27, 1852, to Dec. 31, 1867, 18,078 convicts including 292 women, an annual average of 1,205. From 1867 to 1879, 3,656 more arrived. (French Colonial Ministry, 135, cf. Lagneau, p. 519.)

[2]Leroy-Beaulieu, pp. 285-286.

[3]Deslinières, p. 33.

[4]Increase in the population according to Chandèze, p. 139—

Year	French	Total European population
1833	3,748	7,812
1836	5,485	14,561
1839	11,000	25,000
1841	16,677	37,374
1845	46,339	95,321
1851	66,050	131,283
1856	92,750	167,670

[5]By Decree of April 26, 1853 the State granted a Genevese company lands in the vicinity of Sètif. But the colonists exploited by the company were expropriated by it and left the country. The population of the Genevese estates on January 1868 was only 308. The indigenous population in these white colonies on the same date numbered 3,242. (Chandèze, pp. 138-9).

After the war of 1870 emigration was organized from Alsace-Lorraine to Algeria, amounting to 11,000 in 1871.[1] From 1877 to 1881 Algeria received 2,992 French immigrants, as shown below.[2]

In Morocco 39,896 French immigrants were registered from 1916 to 1924. But 15,304 Frenchmen left the colony during the four years 1920-1924 alone.

In the sugar colonies of Martinique, Guadeloupe, and Réunion, accountants, mechanics, commercial and industrial agents, officials, troops and priests are to be found, but they go with the intention of returning. The French Antilles receive principally colored immigrants. From 1857 to 1862 the house of Regis at Marseilles settled 10,000 free negroes in Guadeloupe, Réunion and Martinique.[3] In 1923-24 Martinique received only 29 European immigrants (English, French and Dutch) and 6 Venezuelans.

St. Pierre and Miquelon receive a few immigrants; although their stay is temporary, the movement is renewed each year with such regularity that this element of the population is almost as fixed in its numbers as the permanent inhabitants. Some fishermen pass the winter there with their wives and children. The number varies from year to year between two and three thousand.

Madagascar receives only a few French immigrants. From 1921 to 1924 the arrivals numbered 2,598, an annual average of 650. Repatriations for the same years were 616.

French emigration to Tonkin shows a slight increase. But a comparison of the figures for immigration with those for repatriation shows that the French emigration is temporary.

[1]Johnston, A., p. 137.

[2]French emigration to Algeria, 1877-1881;

Year	Number
1877	890
1878	870
1879	649
1880	352
1881	231
Total,	2,992

(Lagneau, p. 516f).

For movements during 1893-1924 see National Tables, Algeria Tables I-III, and Tunis Tables I and II.

[3]In 1833 there were still 79,760 slaves in Martinique out of 114,260 inhabitants. In 1848 the population was 120,350. In the same year the population of Guadeloupe was 124,850 including 99,040 slaves. (Zimmermann, *Kolonialpolitik Frankreichs*, p. 35f.)

Year	French[1]	
	Immigrants	Emigrants
1920	480	375
1921	510	406
1922	512	410
1923	472	424
1924	518	417

Foreign immigration is slight:

Year	Foreign	
	Immigrants	Emigrants
1920	80	69
1921	91	83
1922	75	72
1923	82	74
1924	76	72

Foreign immigration into Cochin-China is not large. According to a communication received from the Minister of the Colonies arrivals and departures for the years 1920-1924 were as follows:

Year	Foreign	
	Immigrants	Emigrants
1920	635	503
1921	614	442
1922	551	583
1923	572	518
1924	533	475

While this study was passing through the press additional tables for a number of French colonies in America and Africa came to hand.

GERMANY

With the end of the Napoleonic wars, a new period of German emigration began. It changed from a series of separate movements to a continuous flow. Checked for years by the wars, German emigration in 1816 and 1817 began to assume proportions previously unknown.[2] The immediate cause was the bad harvests of those two

[1] Communication from the Tonkin police.

[2] On August 7, 1816, the Oberpräsident of Cologne, Count von Solms-Laubach, reported to Berlin "that frequently nowadays persons not provided with passports float down the Rhine on rafts towards Holland. Almost every day people arrive here both by land and by water with similar intentions." (Prussian State Archives, A. A., *Acta generalia*, No. 73.68)

years; in Baden, for example, in January 1817, provisions had to be distributed at public expense.

In 1815 only three persons were recorded as leaving Württemberg for North America; in 1816, the number was 443 (in addition to the continental emigration, which was considerably greater); and in 1817, about 6,000 had emigrated to America by July, 1,070 in March alone.[1] The emigration from Württemberg was estimated by the government at Cleve at one-fifteenth of the population of the kingdom.[2] The *Amsterdamsche Courant* on April 24, 1817, was informed from Stuttgart that 12,000 had emigrated from Württemberg since the first of the year.

In the southern parts of Baden everyone was eager to go to America. The Government did not hamper the movement but rather encouraged it, as appears from the following letter of the Austrian ambassador at Carlsruhe, dated May 22, 1817: "The Grand-Ducal Ministry has hitherto done everything possible to encourage emigration from this country. This would seem to be due to over-population and it may be hoped that the removal of so many families will lead to better conditions... The Grand-Ducal authorities soon had their hands full with the task of satisfying the desire to emigrate."[3] Up to the middle of May 1817, according to the reports of the Ministry, over 20,000 persons had applied for permission to emigrate. Permission was granted to about 16,000 persons, of whom a few thousand were compelled by poverty to return home from Holland.[4] From 1816 onward the Dutch ports were crowded with German emigrants.

In confirmation of this, the contemporary sources agree that the principal roads on both banks of the Rhine were crowded with such unfortunates. The *Maynzer Zeitung* on May 3, 1817, reports the passage of 839 families comprising 3,312 persons from April 13-30; 5,517 persons (1,739 men, 1,235 women, 2,543 children) from May 1-15; and 3,041 persons from May 16-31, or 11,870 persons in a month and a half.[5]

[1] E. V. Philippovich, p. 236.
[2] Letter from Oberpräsident von Solms to Hardenberg, May 19, 1817; Prussian State Archives, *Acta generalia*, Rep. I.
[3] Vienna State Archives.
[4] E. V. Philippovich, p. 113, 117.
[5] "During this spring the number of persons who passed by water was over 10,000; this does not include those who, in considerable numbers, drove through with a starved horse and a wagon full of children. Only the numbers of emigrants passing down the Rhine during the second half of April will be quoted:
13 April 369 families 1,344 persons from Baden, Alsace, Switzerland.

| 22 | 16 | 93 | Alsace |
| 22 | 18 | 60 | Württemberg |

(Footnote continued on next page.)

Many emigrants got no further than Holland. They either came without funds or spent them during the long delay in the ports and so could not pay for transportation and were forced to beg their way home. Others turned back when they heard from the returning mobs of the wretched state of affairs in Holland. Many then turned eastward to Prussia and Russia, which at that period exercised a strong attraction.

How many emigrants actually reached America is unknown. Freiherr von Gagern, in his work, expresses the opinion that 6,000 persons in 19 ships arrived in Philadelphia between July 12, 1816, and the beginning of 1817. Since the principal movement took place in the first half of 1817, it may be estimated that in the two years at least 15,000-20,000 Germans arrived in America. A rather old but not unreliable writer[1] estimates the emigration at 30,000 for each of these two years. Incomplete official American statistics make the total immigration 22,000 for 1817.

In the autumn of 1817 emigration rapidly declined   The Prussian envoy at Stuttgart reported to Berlin on September 3, 1817, that emigration from Württemberg to America had practically ceased and that to Poland entirely, since the Russian legation would grant no more passports.[2]   In 1818 emigration to the United States was almost nil. The following years brought good harvests, which acted as a brake on emigration, particularly to countries where it was not specially encouraged, as in the United States.

This improvement did not last long.   The liberation of the peasants with the abolition of tithes and ground-rents had a bad effect, since the taxation involved money payments. This induced the peasants to sell land, which brought about a further reduction in earnings. The economic position of purely agricultural parishes from 1830 on was very difficult. In many districts the margin of food supply could no longer be maintained. "In the southern parts of Baden," says Philippovich, "for a long time a proportion of the population, corresponding to the excess of births, had to leave the country or seek employment in nearby industries. The latter could not offer much of a livelihood."[3]   Certain industries, especially

22 April   59 families   235 persons from Württemberg (Quakers, etc.)
23   33   257   Alsace
27   131   538   Baden and Alsace
29   64   241   Baden, Alsace, Switzerland.
30   149   544   Baden
Total = 839 families, 3,312 persons."
    [1]Löher, p. 254.
    [2]Prussian State Archives, Emigration Office, *Acta generalia*, Rep. II, Vol. 1-2.
    [3]E. V. Philippovich, p. 130.

house industries such as weaving and spinning, were depressed by the competition of new mechanical processes The agricultural depression was thus aggravated by an industrial crisis.

From 1820 on the United States immigration statistics record the arrival of German subjects. From 1820 to 1831 the number was 10,142. The figures for this period vary between a minimum of 148 in 1822 and a maximum of 2,413 in 1831. In 1828 and 1829 Brazil received 1,984 German immigrants. For the following years emigration statistics are available for Bremen from 1832 to 1836, and for Bremen and Hamburg for the subsequent period. The number of emigrants leaving the port of Bremen was 10,344 in 1832 and 6,185 in 1835. The number of German emigrants through the ports of Bremen, Hamburg and Havre for the years 1836 to 1840 was:

	Total	Bremen and Hamburg[1]	Havre
1836	17,007	17,007	. . . . .
1837	23,041	17,514	5,527
1838	12,944	10,267	2,677
1839	21,781	13,981	7,800
1840	33,874	14,526	19,348

For the same years (1836 to 1840) the United States statistics[2] show the arrival of the following numbers of Germans:

1836	20,707
1837	23,740
1838	11,683
1839	21,028
1840	29,704

The statistics of German emigrants are those for all destinations. It should be added that the records of the United States for this period are incomplete. On the other hand, the death rate on the voyage during this period considerably diminished. From 1841 to 1844 only the statistics of the two German ports mentioned above are available for emigration; there is no important change in the movement during these three years.

The depression became more intense after 1844. The interna-

[1]The German emigration statistics for the ports of Bremen (from 1832) and Hamburg (from 1836) did not distinguish between nationals and aliens until 1846 and 1871, respectively. It may be assumed, however, that during this period there were few non-Germans. Swiss Germans were departing via Havre also.

[2]The statistics of the United States show 152,454 arrivals for the years 1831 to 1840, an annual average of 15,245 German immigrants.

tional widening of markets was equally ruinous for small enterprises in agriculture and the crafts. The years 1846 and 1847 were particularly serious, partly because of the potato disease. The whole agriculture of southwestern Germany centered around the potato crop. Further inadequate harvests in the early 'fifties and several bad years for the wine industry completed the economic depression of agriculture, and involved the craftsmen of the towns in equal disaster. The immediate result was a rapid increase in emigration.

Figures are available for German emigration from 1844 to 1854 for national and foreign ports. The number rose from 45,655 in 1844 to a maximum of 108,457 in 1847: after decreasing to 78,549 in 1850, it again rapidly increased and reached its culmination in 1854 with 240,427 departures of German citizens (116,190 through German ports and 124,237 through foreign ports).

For the year 1840 and the period 1844 to 1854, the total German emigration through the ports of Hamburg and Bremen together with that through foreign ports amounted to 1,239,900. German immigration in the United States for the same years was 989,283. A decrease began in 1855. The American Civil War (1861 to 1865) closed the principal outlet for emigration, the United States, considerably checking the exodus. After the end of that war, the movement increased and reached a level higher than before with 102,400 departures in 1868 (Hamburg, Bremen and French ports). The volume of emigration increased in 1870 and 1871, but diminished after the depression of 1873 until 1877 when it fell to 22,898. (From 1870 onward foreign ports are included.) But this falling off was followed during subsequent years by a considerable increase. The year 1881 marks the culmination of the whole movement with 220,902 German emigrants. The economic depression which is bound to result from the economic transformation of a country passing suddenly from agricultural to industrial economy is undoubtedly a leading cause of the acceleration of this movement of emigration.

The large numbers of 1881, 1882 and 1883, did not continue but for the next ten years the totals remained high. In 1898 the number of emigrants fell to a very low level; only 22,221 departures were recorded for that year, one-tenth of the number in 1881. German emigration up to this time had been principally drawn from the rural population; but in the Germany of our own time, which instead of an agricultural power had become above all an industrial power, the agricultural population decreased; the growth of the

cities and the development of industries brought peasant workers into the towns and thus provided an alternative remedy for their wretched situation. Until the World War, during which the movement absolutely ceased, emigration decreased steadily. After the War, the movement was resumed. The general position of Germany after the War was responsible for this exodus which in 1923 amounted to 115,416 and in 1924 decreased to 58,328.[1]

It is interesting to observe that one of the characteristics of German emigration is that it moves in masses. Comparison of the movement with emigration as a whole to the United States shows that the one current which cannot be compared with any other in volume is that from Germany to the United States. Apart from the exceptional years of the War, about 90 per cent of German emigrants go to the United States to join relatives and compatriots who send for them and often provide them with funds for the journey. From 1836 to 1870 direct statistics are available only for Hamburg and even these include departures both of aliens and of German citizens. The number of aliens embarking at this port during the period in question, however, was probably very small.[2] From 1836 to 1870 the immigration statistics of the United States record the arrival of 2,280,323 Germans. The Hamburg figure represents hardly more than one quarter of the German immigration into the United States. For the subsequent period 1871 to 1924 the German port statistics provide figures for the total emigration of German citizens. The movement to the United States maintained its volume during this period. In 1871 departures from German ports amounted to 73,816. The movement increased rapidly and culminated in 1881 with 206,189 departures.

During the first twenty years of the present century German emigration to the United States did not exceed 30,000 annually except in 1903 with 33,649; during the War it practically ceased. After the War it revived. In 1923, 92,808 Germans left for the United States; in 1924, only 22,475.

[1] Table II up to 1870; Table VIII, 1871 to 1924.

[2] In 1836 the direct statistics showed 2,870 departures for the United States. The movement decreased during the following years to a minimum of 484 in 1838, and then rose, culminating in 1868 with 37,274. In 1870 the movement was checked; only 24,874 German and alien emigrants through the port of Hamburg were recorded.

From 1836 to 1870 German statistics also showed the indirect emigration to the United States through that port. These figures are not without importance. In 1854 there were 18,509 indirect departures. The minimum was reached in 1861 with 675. In 1870 the statistics show 5,114 departures for the United States.

The total emigration from Hamburg to the United States from 1836 to 1870 was 513,364 (direct and indirect departures of German emigrants).

The statistics of the United States show that from 1820 to 1924, 5,643,793 German immigrants arrived. The German emigration to the United States may be regarded as permanent migration. During the years 1908 to 1924 arrivals numbered 381,179, and departures only 57,241, or one-seventh of the arrivals.

The other countries of North America received very few German immigrants.[1]

Canada attracts only a small number of Germans, about 1 per cent. According to her statistics, the arrivals from 1831 to 1924 were 223,376. This small proportion is probably due to the fact that many emigrants to Canada come from Germany indirectly, either embarking for other destinations and passing on to British North America or departing through other European countries.

The statistics of Mexico show the current of German emigration from 1910 to 1924. During this period Mexico[2] received 12,916 German immigrants; but from 1911 to 1924 Mexico lost 8,602, leaving a net immigration of 4,314, or about two-fifths.

Direct statistics show 5,861 departures of German subjects for Central America and the West Indies from 1871 to 1924. According to the indirect statistics Cuba received only 1,186 German immigrants from 1911 to 1924.[3]

After North America, Brazil has received the largest number of immigrants.[4] Altogether 32,448 German and foreign emigrants left Hamburg for Brazil 1838-70.

German emigration to Brazil was 6,872 in 1921, and 21,016 in

[1]During the years 1846 to 1870 several thousand Germans and foreigners left for the other countries of North America. The number shown by the Hamburg statistics rose from 399 in 1846 to 4,208 in 1857. In 1870 only 97 persons left Hamburg for other North American countries. The total number of emigrants leaving Hamburg for North America (exclusive of the United States), from 1846 to 1870, was 43,219.

[2]German emigration to Mexico began in 1832 (Berlin Archives, Vol. II, Acta VI, March 1829-November 1833); to British Guiana in 1838 (Vol. II, Acta VIII, February 1837 to September 1840). In 1835 there was German emigration to Jamaica and in 1840 to Central America.

[3]There is documentary evidence of German emigration to Cuba in 1819. (Archives of Munich, 419-41.)

[4]Documents have been discovered in the Berlin Archives relating to emigration to Brazil from 1819. In 1828 Austrian movement of emigration to Brazil paralleled that of Germans. A communication from Vice-President Fritsche of Coblenz mentions in 1828 the departure of 313 persons for Brazil (Berlin Archives, Vol. II, Acta V, June 1827, December, 1828). Documents discovered in the Archives of Munich show that there was a movement of emigration to Brazil from 1822 to 1824 (Archives of Munich, 614-624). A document in the Bremen Archives (C. 12. E) shows that free passage was granted to German emigrants to Brazil. Hamburg statistics show only a few disconnected figures for 1836 to 1848; but from 1849 the figures show a marked increase from year to year. From 37 emigrants in 1849, the number reaches its maximum in 1858 with 3,431 departures. The movement then decreased and again rose. From 414 departures in 1865, it passed to 3,475 in 1869.

1924. The indirect statistics, which are rather incomplete, indicate the arrival of 174,816 Germans for the period 1828 to 1924.

Emigration to Argentina from 1871 up to the War was fairly regular but generally less than 1,500 each year. Here also there was an increase after the end of the War. Argentina received 9,640 Germans in 1923 and 8,125 in 1924. The Argentine statistics for the period 1857 to 1924 show the arrival of 100,699 Germans; departures for the same period number only 49,252.[1]

Peru, Chile, and Uruguay receive few Germans.[1] For the other countries of America, Central and South America, there were only a few emigrants from the port of Hamburg between 1836 and 1870; only a few hundred are shown annually for these countries.

Chile has encouraged foreign immigration since 1846.[2] In 1850 two convoys arrived with 185 Germans. According to the report of an Inspector of Colonisation the foreign colonies in the south, mostly German, numbered about 600 in 1851. In 1856, 1,822 Germans were counted in Chile. Between 1871 and 1924, 6,050 Germans left for Chile from German ports and 1,096 for Peru, which received about 1,000 Germans in 1851.[3] Between 1886 and 1924, 857 German emigrants left for Uruguay.

In Venezuela the Government favors foreign immigration. In 1843 a model colony was founded at Torar under the management of Colonel Codazzi, who introduced a section of 600 Germans.[4] On Oct. 31, 1853 the colony numbered only 469 inhabitants—253 men and 216 women.

The discovery of gold in Australia in the middle of the nineteenth century attracted European emigrants.[5] Until 1848 the statistics give only a few disconnected figures. After that date a continuous current of emigration was set up between Hamburg and Australia. In 1848 1,069 emigrants embarked. The movement reached its maximum in 1854 with 4,880 departures. During the second half

[1]Traces have been found, however, in the Munich Archives, of emigration to Argentina in 1835. A document of 1855 refers to the operations of an agent who solicited emigrants for Buenos Aires. (Munich Archives, Act. Mo. 955.)

[2]F. Duval, pp. 242 ff.

[3]From 1851 documents are found in the Berlin Archives referring to German emigration to Peru. A document of 1853 speaks of the steps taken to encourage colonization. On April 14, 1857, 300 Germans left for Callao (Berlin Archives, 18, acts referring to the supervision of emigration from Germany to the West Coast of America, October 1852-August 1863). From 1847, there was German emigration to Chile (Berlin Archives, Vol. XI, Acta IV, July-December 1847).

[4]Emigration from Baden to Venezuela is reported in 1844 (Berlin Archives, Vol. 1).

[5]German emigrants embarked for Australia as early as 1836 (Berlin Archives, Vol. II, Acta 7, April 1834-December 1836.) Other documents of 1841 refer to further departures in the same direction (Vol. II, Acta 9, January 1841-December 1842).

of the nineteenth century, the movement decreased. In 1869 it was reduced to 73; in 1870 emigration to Australia amounted to 1,259. From 1836 to 1870 direct emigration from Hamburg to Australia numbered 30,318. Emigration to Australia became fairly extensive from 1871 to 1883. A maximum was reached in 1883 with 2,104. After that date emigration amounted only to a few hundreds and ceased completely from 1914 to 1922.

The other continents, Asia and Africa, have not attracted many German emigrants. Only 3,063 Germans embarked for Asia between 1871 and 1924, an annual average of only 57 emigrants.

ITALY

Emigration Before 1876[1]

For the first half of the nineteenth century there is no official statistical record of emigration from Italy, but there was an overseas movement as well as emigration to European countries. From 1820 to 1850, the United States received 4,561 passengers from Italy. The number of immigrants into South America was larger. From 1835 to 1842, 7,945 Italians migrated into Uruguay. The Brazilian records show 180 Italian immigrants for 1836. These numbers are not important; but they indicate a regular movement of emigration from Italy to South America. From 1856 on the statistics of French ports give the number of Italians departing, mostly to South America. Before 1865 the annual number remained less than 1,000; in 1873 it rose to 21,727. The number of emigrants via Genoa, 1861-73, is also known. Before 1866 it varied between 4,287 and 8,790; during 1867-73, between 10,651 and 26,183. In 1873 the total via Genoa and the French ports was 47,910.

The United States received 24,000 Italian immigrants from 1851 to 1875; 209,000 arrived in Argentina from 1857 to 1875. However, the repatriation . from Argentina for the same period amounted to 127,000 or more than three-fifths of the immigration. According to Duval there were 15,000 Italians in the province of Buenos Aires in 1859; and 2,738 Sardinians are said to have emigrated to that province in 1856 through Italian, French, and Spanish ports. In 1852 as many as 674 Italians also arrived in Montevideo.[2] The General

[1]See General Notes, Italy.
[2]J. Duval, pp. 157, 247f.

Commissioner of Immigration in Montevideo received 4,929 applications for work from newly arrived Italians between 1867 and 1875. From 1862 to 1875 9,533 Italian subjects immigrated into Brazil. Correnti estimated the number of Italians living in South America in 1858 at 30,000.[1]

In addition to the La Plata states, Algiers attracted numerous Italian emigrants. Its Italian population in June 1860 was 12,755. The importance of the emigration to other parts of North Africa and to European States is indicated by the fact that in 1861 there were 12,000 Italians settled in Alexandria; 6,000 in Tunis; 78,000 in France; 14,000 in Germany, an equal number in Switzerland, and 4,500 in England.[2]

According to the statistics of Carpi, which are incomplete,[3] from 100,000 to 150,000 persons left Italy annually 1869-1875, and, as far as there is any information· about their destinations, from one-fifth to one-third went overseas, principally to America.

Migrations Since 1876

According to the official statistics the total number of emigrants in 1876 amounted to 108,771. In 1887 it exceeded 200,000 and in 1896, 300,000. In the twentieth century the numbers became even greater, increasing from 533,245 in 1901 to 787,977 in 1906, and reaching the maximum of 872,598 in 1913. The statistics for 1920 show 614,611 emigrants but those for 1921 only 201,291; for 1924, 364,614. Italy stands at the head of European countries of emigration. Before the War it often held the first place in overseas emigration.

The Italian statistics distinguish between emigrants to European countries and the Mediterranean area and those to overseas countries.

The overseas emigration was at first considerably less than that to European countries and the Mediterranean area. From 1887 on, however, it exceeded the latter and in the years 1905 to 1913 it was sometimes almost twice as great. The movement began in 1876 with 19,848 emigrants and in 1886 had reached 82,877. In the following year, as a result of the increased demand for labor in the

[1]Quoted by R. F. Foerster, *The Italian Emigration of our Times*, Cambridge, 1919, p. 5.
[2]General Commissioner of Emigration, *Les statistiques de l'émigration italienne* (1876-1924), Rome, 1925, p. 8.
[3]Tables II-VI; cf. also General Notes. It appears from the text, (*Delle Colonie*, etc., p. 31) that the figures given for 1871 refer only to adult emigrants.

American market, it rose to 130,302 and in 1888 to 204,700. The volume of this emigration then declined; but in 1901 it again exceeded 200,000, reaching 511,935 in 1906. The American depression decreased Italian emigration to 238,573 in 1908, but in 1913 it reached its maximum with 559,566. By 1918 the number of emigrants had diminished to 4,010, but the post-war period saw a considerable increase. The passport statistics for 1920 show 409,239, which obviously exceeds the actual number of emigrants.[1] In 1921, as a result of the limitation of emigration and the depression in the United States, the overseas emigration amounted only to 198,891, and then fell to 186,192 in 1923 and to 137,517 in 1924.

Continental emigration is much less variable than the overseas movement. Up to 1896 it ranged between 75,065 (1878) and 113,425 (1894). After that there was an increase reaching 253,571 in 1901, 308,140 in 1912, and 313,032 in 1913. Continental emigration also reached its minimum in 1918 with 24,301. By 1924 it had risen again to 271,089.

Before 1921 statistics of repatriation exist only in the case of overseas emigrants, and before 1902 these figures make no distinction between Italian subjects and aliens. The total repatriation for 1884 was 12,908; in 1900 it reached 80,570. The proportion of aliens in these totals is obviously very small. In 1902 the repatriated included 92,707 Italians. The maximum was reached in 1908 with 300,834. In 1918, however, there were only 9,025; in 1920, 78,498. The number for 1924 was 65,390. By comparing the number of intercontinental emigrants with the number of repatriations, the following result is obtained:

	1902-1924		
Emigration	4,782,134	100	per cent
Repatriations	3,004,950	62.8	per cent
Net emigration	1,777,184	37.2	per cent

Continental emigration for 1921 to 1924 is tabulated as follows:—

Emigration	759,593	100	per cent
Repatriations	272,643	35.9	per cent
Net emigration	486,950	64.1	per cent

[1]It appears by reference to the statistics of actual emigrants that these figures are too high. The statistics for 1920 show 211,227 emigrants as against 409,239 shown by the passport statistics. The passport statistics have, however, been given in the international tables, first because they give continuous figures from 1876 to 1920, and secondly because they show the countries of destination in such detail that we are able to distinguish overseas emigrants from emigrants to other parts of the world.

It thus appears that since the War continental emigration has become much less seasonal than in the past.

THE NETHERLANDS

For the period before Dutch emigration statistics began to be compiled, some idea of the movement from the Netherlands may be formed from the immigration statistics of the United States. The latter show 49 Dutch immigrants in 1820. Until 1844, the annual movement remained less than 350. But in 1847, it reached a first peak with 2,631; in the following years it declined and then increased until 1873 with its 3,811 arrivals. The movement for this period culminated in 1881 with 8,597.

The port statistics of emigration from the Netherlands began in 1882. The figures are incomplete, however, and do not include emigration to the Dutch colonies.

In 1882 the port statistics recorded 7,304 departures for intercontinental destinations. The movement decreased; in 1886 there were only 2,024. After rising to its culminating point in 1889 with 9,111, it fell to a minimum in 1897 with 792. It rose to 4,393 in 1907 and then diminished year by year, reaching another low point of 867 in 1917. After the war it resumed its importance, but did not attain the proportions reached at the end of the nineteenth century. In 1920 emigration from Holland was 5,978; in 1923, 5,648; in 1924, only 3,137.

The United States attracted the majority of Dutch immigrants, receiving 9,517 in 1882. The movement then declined to 767 in 1898 and increased during the following years; in 1907 the indirect statistics show 6,637. In 1911 the number of immigrants reported as entering other countries rose to 8,358, while the Dutch statistics of emigration for that year, including all intercontinental destinations (except Dutch colonies), show only 2,638 emigrants.

The War caused a decline in emigration; in 1917 only 2,235 arrivals from the Netherlands are recorded, and in 1918 only 944. After the war it revived; in 1920 such arrivals numbered 5,187; in 1921, 6,493. The movement then rapidly declined; in 1923 the United States received only 3,150 immigrants and in 1924 only 3,783. While the Dutch statistics for the period 1882-1924 show 130,222 departures, the American statistics show 179,258 arrivals from the Netherlands.

After the United States, Canada receives the majority of the

Dutch immigrants.   In 1900 only 25 are reported.   The first peak was reached in 1912 with 1,524 and the movement culminated in 1924 with 1,637 arrivals.

Since 1913 South Africa has received a few hundred Dutch immigrants.   In 1913 there were 225.   The movement culminated in 1920 with 431; in 1924 there were only 136.

POLAND

Polish immigration to the United States began between 1820 and 1830.   The annual number before 1831 was never above 5 and until 1851 it was always less than 100.   A relatively large immigration took place in the three years 1872-1874 (1,647; 3,338; and 1,795). Apart from these years the number before 1879 never exceeded 1,000.   From 1880 to 1889 it stood between 2,000 and 6,000.   The curve then rose very sharply and in 1892 reached 40,536, falling again in 1894 to less than 2,000 and in 1895 to less than 1,000.

For the years 1899-1919 immigrants from Poland were not separately shown in the statistics of the United States, but were classed under Austria-Hungary, the German Empire and the Russian Empire.   Statistics were published, however, showing immigrants of Polish race.   The number rose from 28,466 in 1899 to 138,033 in 1907; during the next five years it fluctuated between 68,105 and 128,348, rising in 1913 to 174,365.

Canada has also received a considerable number of immigrants of Polish race, 162 in 1900 and 2,177 in 1910, but nearly 10,000 in 1912 and 1913.   In the United States statistics Jews arriving from Poland have been classed as "Jews" since 1899; in Canada since 1905 they have been separated as far as possible into "Hebrew Polish" and "Hebrew, N. E. S."[1]

Moreover, the statistics of Congress Poland give certain data for this period.   The "permanent" emigration for 1901 was 11,439.   The emigration for 1904 is given as 17,239, of which 14,573 went to North America.   In 1908, a total of 20,817 Poles emigrated to the United States; in the following years, up to the outbreak of the war, the number varied between 15,000 and 22,000, to which, for example, should be added for 1913, 25,074 temporary emigrants. The majority of these emigrants went to the United States; in certain years there was also a considerable emigration to South America.

After the war the overseas emigration from the Polish Republic

[1]Canada Sessional Papers, v. XLI, No. 10, "Immigration".

rose from 74,121 in 1920 to 87,334 in 1921. The next year it fell to less than half, rising slightly in 1923 and falling in 1924 to 22,511. It should be noted that the proportion going to the United States has continuously decreased during these years. In 1921 about four-fifths of the Polish emigration went to the States, but in 1924 only one-fifth. In the latter year Argentina and Palestine received more than the United States. Brazil and Canada each received about one-tenth.

During the fiscal year 1920 the statistics of the United States show the immigration from Poland as 4,813, and that of 1921 as 95,089. This unusually large number of immigrants did not continue. In the following years 1922-1924 the number varied between 27,000 and 29,000.

Argentina in 1921 registered 2,407 Polish immigrants. The number rose to 9,938 in 1923 and fell to 6,637 in 1924.

Polish immigration to other immigration countries, so far as statistics have been published, is of less importance than to Argentina. In Canada the numbers for the years after the war range from 2,700 to 4,200, and in Palestine for 1922-1924 from 2,252 to 5,702. Still smaller numbers are recorded in Brazil and Cuba, where the number exceeded 1,000 for the first time in 1923 and 2,000 in 1924.

Repatriations are not recorded in the Polish statistics. It appears from the statistics of the United States that 788,957 Poles entered the country during 1908-1923 and 318,210 left it. This shows a net immigration for these years of 470,747 Poles or 60 per cent of the Polish immigration.

The annual number of repatriates from the United States, 1908-14, varied between 46,727 in 1908 and 16,884 in 1910. In the fiscal year 1921, 42,207 Poles left the United States and 31,004 in 1922; in 1923 and 1924 the number of repatriates was very small (3,361 and 2,590).

Far more important than permanent emigration was temporary emigration, principally to Germany. In 1903 and 1904, there were 150,000 "temporary" emigrants from Congress Poland to European countries and America. The number rose from 254,895 in 1908 to 377,674 in 1913. In the latter year 343,415 of these emigrants went to Germany.

Continental emigration from the Polish Republic decreased from 26,846 in 1920 to 12,129 in 1921, rose to 72,020 in 1923, and fell to 52,082 in 1924. In 1922 and 1923, for which years the countries of destination are known, practically all the continental emigration

was directed to France, but it may be assumed that there was considerable clandestine emigration to Germany.

PORTUGAL

For the period prior to 1855, when the emigration statistics of Portugal began, the United States and Brazil give a few insignificant immigration figures. In 1820 the United States registered 35 arrivals, and in 1833 the maximum for this period, 633. Between 1820 and 1854 the United States received 1,844 Portuguese immigrants. Brazil attracted the majority. In 1837 the statistics show 120. The figures are discontinuous until 1849. After 1851 there was a pronounced increase. For the period 1837-1854 the maximum was 8,329 in 1853, and the total was 16,927.

From 1855 to 1865 the Portuguese emigration statistics show 80,821 departures, an annual average of 7,347. In 1872 the movement reached 17,284; it then declined until 1878 (9,926) and increased again, reaching another peak in 1895 with 44,746. The numbers decreased slightly until the end of the century with 17,776 in 1899, but in the twentieth century rose to a very high level, reaching 88,920 in 1912. The War brought about a slight decrease in emigration. In 1918 there were only 11,672, but it recovered in 1920 with 64,651. In 1921 it diminished to 24,523 but rose in 1924.

Between 1855 and 1921 Portugal lost 1,484,763 by emigration. The immigration statistics of Brazil show that during the same period 1,058,208 Portuguese immigrants, or more than seven-tenths of the outflow, arrived in that country.

For the years 1922 to 1924 we have also the emigration figures relating to third class passengers for the ports of Oporto and Lisbon. In 1922 embarkations numbered 31,601. In 1923 there were 36,311 and 25,742 in 1924.

Practically all these emigrants proceeded overseas. The annual number of passport departures for European countries did not exceed 500 except for the years 1885 and 1916 to 1924.

On the average, during the period 1872 to 1921, 95 per cent of the emigrants left for America. For earlier years the statistics do not show destination, but it is probable that America received the majority of the emigrants recorded. The movement to America underwent much the same fluctuations as the total emigration.

The immigration statistics are more instructive, enabling us to see which American countries attract the majority of Portuguese emigrants.

Until 1891 the annual figures for the United States, with one exception, were less than 1,000. In 1892 the number was 3,400; increasing until 1913 with 14,171 and diminishing during the War to only 1,222 in 1919, it rose in 1921 to 19,195. It did not remain at that level for in 1924 only 2,769 arrivals were reported. From 1820 to 1924 the United States received in all 221,759 Portuguese immigrants.

A continuous stream of Portuguese immigrants arrived in Argentina from 1857 on. Though insignificant at first the movement gradually increased and in 1912 culminated with 4,959. During the War immigration declined, with only 197 in 1917, but increased again as soon as the War was over. In 1923 2,873 immigrants arrived, and 1,742 in 1924. Between 1857 and 1924 Argentina received altogether 38,196 immigrants.

Portuguese immigration into Brazil rose from 120 in 1837 to 12,918 in 1872. After diminishing to 3,692 in 1875, it reached a higher peak in 1891 with 32,349. The movement increased, particularly in the twentieth century. The culminating point was in 1913 when arrivals numbered 76,701. The movement diminished during the War to only 6,817 in 1917 but after the War again increased. In 1923 it amounted to 31,866, and in 1924 to 23,267. Between 1837 and 1924 Brazil received 1,158,890 Portuguese immigrants.

Between 1867 and 1924 a few Portuguese immigrants arrived in Uruguay. The number was insignificant, seldom exceeding 300 annually.

Portuguese emigration to the other continents is very slight. After America, Africa is the principal destination; but the annual figures never amount to as much as 2,500 departures.

RUSSIA

Overseas emigration from Russia before the 'seventies was very small. According to the statistics of the United States, the annual immigration from Russia through the period before 1868 never exceeded 300 and was frequently less than 10. Into Argentina the immigration of Russians was also very slight, not exceeding 78 in any year between 1857 and 1870. In later years it was different. Russian emigration through German ports increased from 2,480 in 1871 to 11,400 in 1882 and 109,515 in 1891. It did not continue on this scale, but decreased to 17,792 in 1894. Towards the end of the

century it again rapidly increased; in 1904 the number was 105,554 and in 1906, 129,184. After great variations (46,376 in 1908), it reached 127,747 in 1912 and 208,719 in 1913. In the post-War period Russia ceased to play a part as a country of emigration; the maximum was reached in 1923 with 4,233.

The principal destination of Russian emigrants was America, especially the United States. In most years more than four-fifths of these emigrants went to that country. To this number has been added the considerable number of Jews and Poles from Russia, who since 1899 can be distinguished (as in Canada) from the total numbers of Jews and Poles. The United States continued in the post-War period to be the most important destination for Russian emigration, although at times Canada, Brazil, and Argentina have figured to some extent. In 1890 and 1891 Russian emigration to Brazil was 29,226 and 10,051 respectively. In 1911 the number again exceeded 10,000. In that same year 3,001 Russians emigrated to Canada and 17,433 in 1913. Russian emigration to Argentina from 1905 to 1913 fluctuated between 4,503 in 1911 and 15,274 in 1912.

There are no European statistics for the repatriation of Russians,[1] but the statistics for Argentina and the United States provide some information:

Immigration and emigration of Russians in Argentina, 1857 to 1924.

Immigration	169,257	100	per cent
Emigration	70,899	41.9	per cent
Net immigration	98,358	58.1	per cent

Immigration and emigration of Russians in the United States, 1908 to 1924.

Immigration	1,438,861	100	per cent
Emigration	273,885	19	per cent
Net immigration	1,164,976	81	per cent

The seasonal emigration of Russian agricultural workers to Germany has been even more important than overseas emigration.

[1]The volume of the Jewish emigration dating from the Russo-Turkish War, 1856, is not exactly known. Most of the Jewish emigrants were but temporarily in the British Isles, leaving later for America. Pre-war statistics by the Home Office and the Board of Trade were unsatisfactory. Alien statistics by the Home Office show an insignificant number of Russians admitted by permit as laborers since 1921.

According to the Russian short-dated passport statistics, this seasonal emigration amounted to 71,428 in 1898; followed by an almost unbroken increase to 283,536 in 1902; 493,260 in 1906; 636,826 in 1910; 849,792 in 1913.

SCANDINAVIA

(Sweden, Norway and Denmark)

Overseas emigration from Scandinavia is directed almost exclusively towards North America, and here again the United States receives a preponderant number. This current may be considered therefore on the basis of the figures of the United States.

Between 1820 and 1924 Scandinavian immigration into the United States was as follows:

From Sweden	1,168,260
From Norway	768,030
From Denmark	318,809
From Scandinavia	2,255,099

The population of these three countries in 1910-1911 amounted to 10,637,000. It thus appears that emigration has been very great relative to population. The principal reason for it is unfavorable natural conditions in the country of origin, but religious and political circumstances have also contributed to it.

Scandinavian emigration to the United States may be divided into five periods.[1]

Up to 1865 there was a slow increase. From 1820 to 1830 the number remained less than 100; after that there was a more rapid increase, but before 1865 the number exceeded 4,000 in only one year.

In the second period, 1865 to 1877, emigration increased to 43,941 in 1869 and then declined to 11,274.

The third period, 1877 to 1898, was marked by the largest volume of emigration. From 1880 to 1893 the annual number was over 40,000; in 1882 it reached 105,326. During the twenty years 1879 to 1898, the total number was 1,062,139, or 47 per cent of the emigration for the 105 years.

[1]See *Annual Report of the Commissioner General of Emigration to the Secretary of Labor, fiscal year ended June 30, 1920.* Chart 2: "Immigration into the United States from the different countries."

The fourth period, began in 1898 with 19,282 arrivals. The number rose to 77,647 in 1903, and the period ended in 1919 with 5,590.

In the post-War period the movement seems to be increasing; in 1924 the number of emigrants from the Scandinavian States to the United States was 35,577.

The following comparison of immigration and emigration of Scandinavians for the years 1908 to 1923 shows that Scandinavians are for the most part permanent settlers.[1]

Immigration	448,846	100 per cent.
Emigration	97,920	22 per cent
Net gain	350,926	78 per cent

The Swedish immigration and emigration statistics for 1876 to 1924 confirm this conclusion. (Diagram 11, p. 199.)

As far as it is possible to conclude from national statistics the migration of Scandinavians within Europe, apart from migration from one Scandinavian country to another, seems to be very slight. What there is, takes place between Finland, Russia and Scandinavia.

SPAIN

Spanish passenger statistics did not begin until 1882. For previous years the only figures available are the immigration statistics of the United States, Argentina and Brazil.

The United States has not received any considerable current of Spaniards. From 139 persons recorded in 1820, the number reached a maximum in 1854 with 1,433. The movement then declined to only 484 in 1881. Between 1820 and 1881 the United States received 28,695 Spaniards. From 1857 on Argentina shows larger figures. Beginning with 854 emigrants in 1857 the number rose to a maximum in 1873 with 9,185. Between 1857 and 1881 emigration to Argentina was 73,967.

Brazilian immigration statistics record the arrival of 10 Spaniards in 1841, but continuous statistics are available only from 1868. From 218 in that year the number rose to 727 in 1872. Figures are lacking for 1873 and 1874; in 1875 only 39 Spaniards are reported. But the movement soon became more extensive. In 1881 2,677 Spaniards arrived. Between 1841 and 1881 Brazil received 8,716.

The insignificance of the movement is probably a reflection of the

[1]"A Century of Immigration," *Monthly Labor Review*, Washington, January, 1924. p. 13.

relative incompleteness of Spanish statistics. Spanish passenger statistics began in 1882. In that year 71,806 departures were recorded. In 1885 the movement decreased to 40,316 and then increased. In 1889 there were 125,807 passengers registered. During the following years the volume decreased; in 1890 only 65,860 passengers were recorded. It again increased to 166,269 departures in 1896, decreased in the following years with 51,593 passengers in 1902, then increased and culminated in 1912 with 257,264. During the War the movement decreased: the year 1918 marked the minimum of emigration with 36,254. In 1920 it revived with 189,517. For 1921 and 1922 the number of departures was less than 100,000 and in 1923 there were 123,804. The total number of passengers leaving Spain during the period 1882 to 1923 was 4,262,594.

Repatriations for the same period number 3,318,343, showing a net loss of 944,251 (Spain, Table I).

In 1924 the number of emigrants proper from Spain to non-European countries was 86,920. More than half of the Spanish emigrants were destined for South America.

The passenger statistics show a few departures for the United States between 1882 and 1899, but the figures are insignificant. The number 278 in 1899 is the culminating point; from 1882 to 1899 only 1,132 passengers left for the United States. No more departures for the United States are indicated by the statistics until 1914. In 1914 the movement revived to an extent hitherto unknown. In that year 3,017 passengers left for the United States. In 1920 the movement culminated with 18,575 and decreased to 185 in 1923.

Concerning indirect statistics, those of the imigration countries based on ethnical character included in certain cases Spanish immigrants arriving from other regions as well as from Spain. This explains certain discrepancies with the corresponding figures of Spain.

The indirect statistics of the United States show the arrivals of Spanish emigrants since 1820. During the nineteenth century the movement was very slight, but in the twentieth century it increased. From 1820 to 1900 the United States received 41,361 Spaniards; 12,311 arrived between 1882 and 1899. Although the Spanish passenger statistics show no departures between 1901 and 1913, the immigration statistics of the United States record 45,503, possibly from Spanish possessions. Between 1914 and 1923, 76,367 Spanish immigrants landed in the United States, but Spanish emigration statistics show only 40,855 departures for that destination.

Numbers of Spaniards go to Mexico.   In 1882 there were 414 passengers; the movement increased and culminated in 1907 with 4,766.   During the following years it decreased to 3,758 in 1909. In 1913 we find 3,136 departures.   During the War the movement continued to decrease (2,030 in 1914) and in 1918 reached 413 passengers, a level lower than in the first year.   In 1921 there were 4,617 passengers, and 3,279 in 1923.   Mexican immigration statistics before 1909 do not show the arrival of foreigners.   In that year they record 5,635 Spanish.   A decrease appeared in 1913 (4,487) and the minimum was reached in 1914 with 1,393.   Immigration then increased and culminated in 1921 with 8,364 arrivals. In 1923 and 1924 the movement declined with 5,904 and 3,869 respectively.   The total Spanish emigration to Mexico between 1909 and 1924 was 71,084.   Between 1911 and 1924 the number of Spaniards leaving Mexico was 51,699, as compared with 65,449 arrivals, showing a net gain of 13,750 or 21 per cent for that period. If we compare the statistics of emigration with those of immigration, a considerable discrepancy appears.   The direct statistics show 41,936 departures from Spain for Mexico between 1909 and 1923; the indirect statistics show 67,215 "Spanish" arrivals in Mexico during the same period.

The largest number of Spanish passengers give Cuba as their destination.   Direct statistics give 30,730 for 1882; the movement then declined to 8,319 in 1885 but revived during the following years, reaching 90,527 in 1896.   It decreased to 10,323 in 1902 and then rose to 37,544 in 1913.   In 1918 emigration to Cuba amounted to 15,460.   Two years later the movement culminated with 99,487 departures.   In 1923 it decreased to 47,689.   The total Spanish emigration to Cuba from 1882 to 1923 was 1,252,500.   Indirect statistics are available only from 1901.   From 17,330 in that year the number reached its culminating point in 1920 with 94,294; in 1923, 46,439 Spaniards landed in Cuba and 41,070 in 1924.   While the direct statistics for the period 1902 to 1923 show 693,516 departures, the indirect statistics for the same years show 663,478 arrivals.

Departures from Spain for Argentina rose from 3,245 in 1882 to 58,135 in 1889.   The movement declined to 3,821 in 1891 and then rose to its culmination in 1912 with 154,720 departures.   It decreased to 11,278 in 1918 and then revived.   In 1923 Spanish emigration to Argentina was 41,720.   The number of Spaniards arriving in Argentina passed from 854 in 1857 to 71,151 in 1889.   In 1891 there were only 4,290, but in 1912 the maximum number was

reached with 165,662. In 1918 only 9,188 Spaniards entered the country. In 1923 the indirect statistics recorded 48,428, and 45,691 in 1924. From 1857 to 1924, the total Spanish emigration to Argentina was 1,780,295. While the emigration statistics from 1882 to 1923 show 1,362,272 departures for Argentina, the indirect statistics for the same period show 1,660,637 arrivals.

In 1882 Spain sent 2,247 passengers to Brazil. This movement decreased to 332 departures in 1886 but recovered in the following years with 11,993 departures in 1896; and diminished again until 1902. From then it increased, culminating in 1906 with 19,748 departures. In 1913, just before the War, the number was 10,857. In 1918 the movement decreased to 909; in 1920 it amounted to 3,127 and in 1923 to 1,533. The indirect statistics however show higher figures. In 1882 Brazil received 3,961 Spanish immigrants. The movement rapidly increased, reaching the maximum for the nineteenth century in 1893 with 38,998 arrivals. In 1894 there were only 5,986, but in 1896 the number was 24,154. From then on to the end of the century immigration decreased. After falling to 3,588 in 1902, it increased again and culminated in 1913 with 41,064 arrivals. The War checked immigration, which fell to 5,895 in 1915. After the signing of the Peace Treaty the movement still remained less than before the War. In 1923 arrivals numbered only 10,140 and in 1924 but 7,238. Between 1901 and 1924 Spanish immigration for Brazil was 343,327. While the Spanish statistics show the departure of 226,037 Spaniards for Brazil the Brazilian statistics register 530,330 "Spaniards" arriving for the period 1882 to 1923.

Among the other countries of Latin America, Spanish emigration has been directed principally to Uruguay and Porto Rico. In 1882 992 passengers embarked for Uruguay; the minimum was reached in 1899 with 557, and the maximum was 3,442 in 1913. The movement decreased towards the end of the War with 832 in 1918, but in 1923 again rose to 3,081 departures. The indirect statistics of Uruguay give the figures from 1867 and are noticeably higher than the Spanish emigration statistics. In 1882 recorded arrivals were 2,487; in 1899, 3,110; and in 1913, 5,751. The indirect statistics however, are defective.

Several thousand Spaniards annually emigrated to the Pacific, particularly to the Philippines during the period 1882 to 1895. In 1896 an extraordinary number was reached (24,681). In the subsequent years, until 1923, the movement decreased; except for the

year 1907 when there were 2,672, the annual figures are less than 1,000.

The emigration to Africa has been more considerable. The movement began with 17,621 in 1882 and culminated in 1913 with 37,111. In 1918 there were only 5,133 passengers but in 1923 they increased to 12,629.

SWITZERLAND

Wherever German emigrations took place in earlier centuries, Swiss were to be found among them, as a rule, and the maxima of German emigration coincided with those of the Swiss. The parallelism between the two movements is to be seen, for instance, in the years 1816 to 1817 when emigration was very extensive, for Switzerland continuing into 1819.[1]

In the first half of the nineteenth century emigration to the United States frequently took the form of founding Swiss settlements. The American immigration statistics long confused Swiss with Germans or French. In 1842, for example, Swiss were reported as landing at New York only; this was remarked upon by the Swiss consul at Alexandria, Va., as very improbable.[2] In 1820 the American returns showed only 31 Swiss immigrants and in the following years until 1851 the numbers were less than 500, and in only two years exceeded 1,000.

About 1850 emigration revived considerably, often exhibiting a character typical of pauper emigration; numerous complaints were made of the shipping out of paupers, convicts, and persons unable to work.[3]

In 1852 and 1853 over 2,700 Swiss arrived in the United States; in 1854 there were 7,953, a number which was not equalled until 1881; in 1855 there were 4,433. After 1855 emigration to the United

[1]*The Amsterdamsche Courant* of April 10, 1816, reported that several ships with 300 to 400 Swiss were proceeding down the Rhine to Holland about to embark for America. On May 31 it was informed from Zurich that a large ship with about 300 Swiss of all ages had left Basle to proceed to the United States by way of Holland. On June 24 the same paper reported further Swiss emigration. On August 6, it mentioned the departure of a ship from Basle in the direction of Holland with about 300 Swiss. In 1817 emigration from Switzerland continued in even larger numbers, so that the Swiss Consul in Amsterdam asked for instructions from his Government concerning the numerous Swiss emigrants to America. On March 9 the departure of 200 Swiss and on April 25 of 1,400 from Basle was reported. Many returned for lack of accommodation in the ships; others halted halfway, as for example 105 Swiss who went from Holland to Lisbon, where they lived in dire need and supported by charity.

[2]*Emigration suisse*, p. 52.

[3]Karrer, p. 14 ff.

States declined considerably and did not recover until after the Civil War. In 1867 there were 4,168 immigrants.

The number of Swiss emigrants to North America (based on passport visas) via Havre according to the Administrative Reports of the Federal Council (A), and according to Legoyt,[1] based on the reports of the Swiss consul at Havre (B) was as follows:

	(A)	(B)
1852	. . . . .	6,675
1853	5,881	5,273
1854	12,098	12,098
1855	3,451	. . . . .
1856	2,367	. . . . .
1857	·about 4,000	3,856
1858	1,401	1,402

For the years 1860 and 1861 the total of Swiss emigration to North America was given by the Federal Council as 1,727 and 1,587 respectively.

The first great movement of Swiss emigration to South America began in 1819. John VI of Brazil in 1818 officially applied to Switzerland for colonists. The proposal was taken up by various Swiss authorities in order to get rid of their paupers. The undertakings which the Brazilian Government was willing to make were very favorable. It was prepared to transport at its own expense such Catholic families as were provided with legal evidence of former respectability, to settle them, and support them until they were able to live by their own harvests. The agent who was appointed for this purpose carried out his recruiting without special attention to the conditions, having regard merely to his bonus for each emigrant, and instead of about 1,500 persons as anticipated, sent over 2,000 poor and even disreputable individuals, including many Protestants. In 1819 there were 2,003 persons emigrated from western and central Switzerland; and in Holland they were packed into a few ships without sufficient space. Their subsistence was also poor in quality and quantity so that 316 persons, or 15.5 per cent, perished on the voyage.[2] The place of settlement, also badly

[1]Cf. Legoyt, p. 71 ff.

According to Legoyt, Swiss emigration also passed through German and Dutch ports:—

	1857	1858
Via Antwerp	695	80
Via Hamburg	94	45

[2]Karrer, p. 3; Lehmann, p. 37.

chosen, was in the primeval forest and without any modern means of transportation, so that the Novo-Friborgo colony did not succeed.

The Brazilian immigration statistics for 1820 give the population of Novo-Friborgo as 1,682 among the immigration figures (cf. Explanatory note to National Table I for Brazil).[1]

Emigration to Brazil from Switzerland after the Novo-Friborgo experiment continued to a slighter extent and as a movement of individuals.[2]

In the 'forties Brazil again developed intensive propaganda in Switzerland. Numerous agents advertised the metayer system as offering the poor the possibility of rapid prosperity.[3] Hundreds of Swiss emigrated to Brazil in the following years. Many Swiss communes granted those who desired to emigrate advances to facilitate their settlement, in order to get rid of these possible paupers. The anticipated prosperity, however, proved to an appalling will-o'-the-wisp. From the beginning the colonists were indebted to their landlords and it was practically impossible for them to work out of this oppressive condition.[4]

For 1847 the Brazilian statistics show 17 Swiss immigrants. The number rose to 604 in 1854, but did not exceed 500 for any year up to 1922; frequently it was under 50. In the 'fifties settlement by Swiss took place in the La Plata countries, particularly in Santa Fe, where in 1858 the Basle Company formed a Swiss settlement and granted advances. In 1861 New Helvetia was founded in Rosarioa Oriental (Uruguay) and in 1864 we find 600 persons settled there.[5]

Argentina reported very little Swiss immigration during this period. Between 1857 and 1870 the number rose from 68 to 499.

In Chile 60 Swiss settled in 1858. The active propaganda of the Chilian Government induced 1,311 Swiss to emigrate there in 1884

[1]Many deserted it and sought land elsewhere, settled in the towns or entered the Foreign Legion. In 1825 about 100 Swiss families are said to have been still there, together with a few hundred new German settlers, who did not, however, contribute to the development of the colony. (cf. Lienau, *Darstellung meines Schicksals in Brasilien*, Schleswig, 1826, quoted by Brauns, p. 545; Lehman, p. 38,)

[2]The Swiss consul in Bahia (*Émigration suisse*, p. 85) reported that from 1830 to 1850 Swiss individuals provided with small capital had established coffee plantations and worked them with slaves, and had also brought artisans from Europe for their business.

[3]The inventor of this system was Senator Vergueiro, who in 1847 founded a colony of metayers with about 400 Swiss on his property in the province of São Paulo. (Lehman, p. 53; cf. also Handelman, pp. 569-571.)

[4]"There could no longer be any doubt about the matter. Two thousand Swiss in Brazil were reduced to a state resembling slavery from which they were unable to free themselves." (Karrer, p. 70). The bad situation could only be remedied by relief from the Federation and a cancellation of the repayment of the advances made by the communes.

[5]Karrar, p. 78 f.

and several hundred more followed in the next year.[1] The failure of the settlement led to a prohibition of emigration to Chile.

For the emigration to Algiers a few figures are available, based on the passport visas issued to Swiss in Marseilles. The number was:[2]

1838	76
1839	73
1840	173
1841	156
1842	392

The majority of these emigrants were from Tessin (building operatives, plasterers, smiths, etc.) and their emigration appears to have been of a seasonal nature, including hardly any families. In 1843, for the first time, about 50 families emigrated to settle as agriculturalists. In 1854 a highly capitalized colonization company was organized in Geneva and settled two villages and a huge farm in Sètif in the province of Constantine where settled 361 Swiss. But climatic conditions made any significant emigration impossible.

The statistics of Switzerland, which are very incomplete for the first years, show 5,007 emigrants for 1868, Swiss and foreigners settled in Switzerland. The number of emigrants then declined almost continuously, including those to overseas territories, to 1,691 in 1877, the smallest number before the War. This minimum was followed by a rapid increase to the maximum of 13,502 in 1883. Since then there have never been as many as 10,000. Until 1893 the movement remained relatively great, always exceeding 6,000; it then decreased, reaching a second minimum of 2,288 in 1898: but soon recovered and in 1913 again exceeded 6,000. During the War only a few inhabitants of Switzerland could emigrate overseas; only 304 in 1918. After the War the frontiers were opened and the number of emigrants reached its highest point since 1884. In 1920, 9,276 persons left Switzerland. The number diminished to 5,787 in 1922, but increased again to over 8,000 in 1923, decreasing by half in 1924.

In the statistics after 1882 the emigration of Swiss citizens alone is recorded separately. They form the great majority of the totals given above. The proportion represented by aliens settled in Switzerland for the years 1902 to 1913 was usually about one-quarter. The number of Swiss citizens among the emigrants rose

[1]Karrer, p. 87.
[2]*Emigration suisse*, p. 21 f.

from 10,896 in 1882 to 12,758 in 1883, and decreased to 1,694 in 1898, reaching 4,705 in 1913. In the years 1920 to 1924, following the curve of the total emigration, an average of 5,918 Swiss citizens emigrated, more than in any five individual years between 1886 and 1890.

The majority of the emigrants from Switzerland have gone to the United States, over 80 per cent from 1881 to 1910, and 90.7 per cent from 1891 to 1895. South America comes next, particularly Argentina. In 1871 to 1880 over 20 per cent emigrated to South America and in 1906-1910 and 1911-1915, 11.4 per cent and 14.4 per cent respectively to Argentina. Before the War Canada and Brazil were receiving increasing numbers, and in the post-war period this tendency became more pronounced. In the years 1921 to 1924 the United States received only 58.4 per cent, while Canada received 10.4 per cent; Argentina, 9.6 per cent; Brazil, 7.8 per cent; and Africa, which played no part before 1919, 6.2 per cent.

Immigration to the United States from Switzerland during 1820-1924 amounted to 278,187; the total immigration of Swiss into Argentina for the years 1857 to 1924 was 37,017. During the same period 14,709 Swiss or 39.7 per cent of the immigrants left Argentina.

ASIA

BRITISH INDIA[1]

Indian emigration, aside from that to Ceylon and Mauritius, dates from the early decades of the nineteenth century.[1] It was intimately connected with the abolition of slavery throughout the British Empire in 1838, because this change gave rise to a demand for laborers in semi-tropical districts, such as India could supply. In fact, Indian emigrant labor being indentured labor, was of a type intermediate between slave and free labor.

A Parliamentary Committee investigated in 1842 the industrial depression which ensued on the abolition of slavery and concluded that "the principal causes of the diminished production [of sugar] and consequent distress are the great difficulty which has been experienced by the planters in obtaining steady and continuous labour."[2] This demand for labor naturally stimulated Indian emigration.

The Government of India assumed from the beginning the rôle

[1]The data here given upon Indian emigration are largely drawn from "Emigrant," *Indian Emigration* (London, 1924), published under the general editorship of the Director of the Central Bureau of Information of the Government of India.
[2]"Emigrant," p. 7.

of protector of East Indian emigrants and never relaxed control over emigration, suspending or prohibiting it in certain cases, although never actively encouraging it. Its only requirement before 1837 was that emigrants should present themselves before a magistrate and show that they went voluntarily and were acquainted with what was in store for them.[1]

In 1837 an Act was passed making provision "for the suitable treatment of the emigrant during the voyage," and a long series of enactments followed.

Act XIV of 1839 illustrates the general attitude of the Government of India. It "made the recruiting of a native of India for labour to be performed 'in any British or Foreign Colony without the territories of the East India Company' a penal offence, and the amending Act of 1844 recognised emigration only to the colonies of Jamaica, Trinidad, British Guiana and Mauritius. Recruitment of labour for Ceylon was consequently made illegal by the Act of 1839. An Act was passed in August 1847 which removed the legal disability in the case of Ceylon."

An Act of 1864, consolidating twenty-one preceding Acts, reinforced the earlier legislation and for the first time defined the duties of the Protectors of Emigrants, as comprising the care of the emigrant from the moment of his arrival at the port to his embarkation.

Act XIII of 1869 defined emigration as the "departure of any native of India out of British India for the purpose of labouring for hire in some other place."

The principal object of the next important Act, that of 1883, was to establish a more uniform and careful method of registration. It sought to minimize abuse (a) by confining recruiting to persons specially licensed for the purpose, and (b) by providing for the registration of recruits by a magistrate, or other person especially empowered.

In 1910 a new Act provided that the Government could prohibit emigration to any country, and extended protection to emigrants who paid their own passage and who emigrated for other reasons than that of labor.

The purpose of the emigration legislation of India, and the procedure under it may be summarized thus:

"At first," the author of *Indian Emigration* states, "recruitment was a purely personal venture, undertaken for profit, sometimes

[1] *Ibid.*, p. 15.

certain, and sometimes a mere speculation." Later a co-ordinating agency was created. "Recruiting was carried on by men specially engaged for the purpose who worked in the interior of the country. When a batch of emigrants was ready, it was sent to the port of embarkation where the emigration agent for the importing colony arranged for their accommodation before departure, and for shipment. On arrival at destination, they were distributed among the estates on which they were to work. This machinery was gradually supplemented, and its operation brought under legislative control, when the state intervened to regulate emigration."

"The main features of the new emigration were that it was for the purposes of labour, and that it was assisted. The emigrant undertook to work for a fixed term which varied from one month to three or five years in the different colonies and at different periods in the same colony, in consideration of a wage and the cost of his passage. On the expiration of that period he had three courses open to him: renewal of the contract, settlement in the country with freedom to follow the vocation of his choice, or, except in the case of Mauritius after 1857, return at the expense of the importing colony to his home. This was the essence of the system which has become famous under the name of Indenture.... Its achievements in the colonies varied, but nowhere gave complete satisfaction."

1.   Intercontinental Movement

Viewed comprehensively, Indian emigration for intercontinental destinations shows an upward trend from 1842 to 1918. In the earlier year it was in its infancy and included only 459 emigrants. The figures then mounted in irregular fashion until in 1858 the peak was reached, with 45,838 emigrants. Thereafter the movement slackened and fell to 7,614 in 1867, then began to gain in volume without, however, exceeding the highest figures of the earlier years. From 1870-71 to 1912-13, the movement was fairly steady, the figure of 29,243 emigrants for 1873-74 being the highest for this long period, and 6,559 for 1887-88, the lowest. The War led to a virtual arrest of Indian emigration, illustrated by the statement that the number of emigrants for 1912-13 was 12,658 and for 1919-20, 221. Latterly there has been a feeble revival, the figure for 1923-24 being 1,227. But another cause, the abolition of indentured emigrant labor, had an even greater effect in restricting emigration.

The counterpart to Indians emigrating is those returning to the

home country. On this aspect of the migration problem figures for the period 1878-79 to 1921-22 are available. They show that repatriation equals less than half of the emigration. For some years, however, the proportions are reversed. As the result of the abolition of indentured labor, 11,543 emigrants left India during 1916-17 to 1921-22, while 37,571 remigrants arrived. But if continental migration is included the number of emigrants for 1923-1924 (230,642) greatly exceeded the number of remigrants (12,316).

2. Intercontinental Destinations

To judge by direct and indirect statistics, it appears that British Indians emigrated in larger numbers to Africa than to America.

From 1904 to 1924 Canada received only 5,408 British Indians. After 1905 a decline in immigration set in, occasioned in the main by restrictive regulations. By 1919 the number of Indians in Canada had dwindled to 1,200. At present Indian merchants, students, and tourists can enter Canada, but solely for temporary residence.

The number of East Indian emigrants to the United States is hardly appreciable. For the period of 105 years, from 1820 to 1924, only 8,837 British Indians arrived, and between 1908 and 1924, 2,835 returned home.

The movement of East Indian emigrants to the West Indies is more important. Indirect statistics indicate the arrival of appreciable contingents between 1845 and 1872, the main current going to Trinidad, British Guiana, Jamaica, and the French Antilles.

Indian emigration to Jamaica has fluctuated not a little. In 1845 there were 1,047 departures and in the following year the maximum number of 2,390 was reached. Between 1845 and 1847 some 4,500 Indian laborers were introduced into Jamaica. This first experiment proved a failure. Between 1860 and 1863, another 4,680 Indian laborers were introduced. From 1869 to 1876 immigration was fairly brisk; but after 1879 large-scale immigration may be said to have ceased. It was renewed between 1891 and 1897; stopped in the latter year because of the plague in India; renewed once more in 1899 and 1900. Since 1911 immigration has ceased. Jamaica, by the census of 1921, had an East Indian population of 18,610.

The first British Indian emigrants for Trinidad left in 1844, and within four years 5,162 had arrived. From 1844 to 1891 no less than 88,000 British Indian immigrants arrived and only about 12,000 returned. By 1921 there were some 128,000 East Indians in

Trinidad.   Of this large number only 45 in 1924 were under indenture.

More striking is the movement of East Indians towards French colonies in the West Indies.   At an early date, on finding that after the slave trade had been stopped white labor was disinclined to emigrate to those colonies, the French Government decided to introduce British Indian laborers.   From 1852 to 1855 we find 1,191 were landed at Martinique and by 1861 between 1,200 and 1,500 more had arrived at Martinique and Guadeloupe.[1] Up to 1884 the French colony had received 26,000, of whom only 4,500 asked to be returned.   From 1884 onwards, however, organized immigration was suspended, and the number of those returning assumed large dimensions.   By 1893 the Indian population in the island had fallen to 7,210.[2] By 1858, 2,885 British Indians had arrived at Guadeloupe,[3] and for some years after 1865 annual contingents of about 1,300 arrived.   In 1888 the stream of immigrants was completely arrested by restrictive Indian regulations.   The movement of British Indians to French Guiana commenced in 1850, and 8,472 arrived between 1856 and 1877.[4] To this colony, likewise, the supply of immigrants was cut off by the Indian Government.

The direct tables show a wave-like movement of migration to the French West Indies.   In 1856 only 525 emigrants arrived; in 1866 the number reached 5,776; and in 1884-85 it was only 495.   Just as the abolition of the slave trade gave rise to an extensive movement of East Indian laborers to the British and French colonies, so decisions of the Government of India eventually prohibited the departure of indentured laborers to the French colonies.

In 1838 East Indian labor was introduced into British Guiana. From that time onwards, with a few interruptions, the flow of immigrants continued until 1911.   The figures rose from 1,591 in 1845 to 8,497 in 1873-74, and fell to 2,248 in 1914-15.   There are about 125,000 East Indians in the colony, nearly one-third of the population.

For Dutch Guiana the tables start with the year 1872-73.   From 410 East Indian emigrants in that year, the number rose to 3,523 in the following year, and fell to the lowest point in 1905-06 with 175 emigrants, after which it remained small.   However, in 1859 there were some 46,000 Indian laborers in the Dutch West Indies.

[1]R. Robin, p. 238.
[2]E. Zimmermann, *Kolonialpolitik*, p. 169.
[3]E. Roy, p. 28.
[4]République française, *Notices coloniales*, vol. III, p. 110.

Emigration to Surinam commenced in 1873, and virtually ceased in 1912. During this period there were 31,000 immigrants from British India of whom 8,800 returned.

Emigration to the Danish colonies was stopped in 1865, and to Cayenne in 1877.

The only direct emigration of Indian contract laborers to Australia occurred between November 1837 and July 1838. In 1839 there were 1,283 Indian indentured laborers obtained by 111 ranchmen.[1] After this date an unimportant stream of free Indians entered the dominion. Restrictions were placed on oriental immigration generally in 1901. The tables show that 3,738 British Indians arrived in the Australian commonwealth between 1902 and 1924. Altogether about 2,000 Indians have adopted Australia as their home.

East Indian emigration to New Zealand has been negligible, as is shown by the estimate that on March 31, 1925 the number residing there was 642.[2]

The East Indian population of Fiji numbers about 60,000, of whom 37,000 are males and 23,000 females. The total population of the island is about 160,000.

The largest number of East Indian emigrants proceeded to Africa, and from 1842 to 1865 almost the whole stream of emigrants flowed towards Mauritius. Emigration to Mauritius—which, like the West Indian islands, was a sugar-producing country—is said to have begun as early as 1819. More probably it started between 1826 and 1830. However, large-scale emigration to this colony did not commence until the abolition of slavery in 1834. From 1834 to 1837, 7,000 emigrants departed from Calcutta for Mauritius. From 459 emigrants in 1842, the number rose to 38,735 in 1858. Thereafter, there was a continuous drop. In fact, only 587 arrived in Mauritius in 1907-08. The proportion of emigrants from Mauritius is remarkably small for most of the period; amounting to scarcely one-fifth of the immigrants; but for the years 1906 to 1910, repatriation slightly exceeded immigration. Emigration to Mauritius was stopped in 1910. However, in 1924, exceptional permission was given for the emigration during that year of 1,500 laborers for employment on public works. In that year the Indian population of the island amounted to 255,000, of whom 23,000 were then still indentured.

[1] *Official Year-Book of the Commonwealth of Australia*, 1925, p. 951.
[2] *New Zealand Official Year-Book*, 1926, p. 88.

The number of British Indian emigrants to Natal has fluctuated greatly. In 1860 it was 1,226, but by 1874-75 it had risen to 6,025. In 1886-87 there were only 496; in 1906-07 as many as 10,049; and in 1910-11 there were 6,257.

About 6,000 East Indians reside in the Cape Province, some 10,000 in the Transvaal, and approximately 133,000 in Natal.

The Asiatic population of the Union of South Africa for the census years 1904, 1911 and 1921 was as follows, Asiatics being practically identical with East Indians:[1]

	Males	Females	Total
1904	82,809	39,925	122,734
1911	96,135	56,068	152,203
1921	97,336	68,395	165,731

Under the Union Immigrants Act, 1913, Asiatics, with the exception of wives and children of domiciled relatives, are prohibited from entering the Union.[2]

The Indians in East Africa number now about 25,000. Uganda has a considerable number of Indians, mainly traders, artisans, and skilled laborers.

Dr. Mouat is said to have found some 23,000 smuggled-in Indian laborers in Réunion (Fr.) as early as 1851. As a result of an agreement with the Government of India, 6,000 Bengalese landed in Réunion in 1861.[3]   Thereafter, immigration decreased, to revive somewhat in 1872. By the close of 1882 Réunion had received 86,905 British Indians, but in that year the Government of India stopped further recruiting.[4] The Indian population of the island was 4,631 in 1848[5] and 20,644 in 1892.[6]

Indian emigration was first and foremost a matter of indentured laborers leaving their country for colonial destinations. Unfortunately this form of labor lent itself only too readily to grave abuses, so that in 1916 the Government of India informed the Secretary of State for India that "the time had come for His Majesty's Government to assent to a total abolition of the system of indentured Indian labour in the four British Colonies where it still prevailed and in Surinam." The British Government concurred in

[1]*Official Year-Book of the Union of South Africa*, 1924, p. 133.
[2]*Ibid.*, p. 134.
[3]P. Guirre, p. 19.
[4]*Ibid.*, p. 130.
[5]République française, *Notices coloniales*, vol. II, p. 76.
[6]R. Robin, p. 228.

the decision arrived at by the Government of India so that indentured emigration, and with it intercontinental emigration on the part of East Indians, came to an end. Leaving aside the neighboring colonies of Ceylon and the Straits Settlements, to which Indians still emigrate in large numbers, the number of Indian laborers emigrating has fallen from some 25,000 in 1858 to some 500 in 1924.

Emigration from British India to the Malay Peninsula commenced early in the nineteenth century and continued unimpeded until 1857, when emigration was indirectly restricted by increasing the cost of the voyage. About 1870, three classes of East Indians migrated to the Straits Settlements: (a) those paying their own passage; (b) those who had been assisted but engaged themselves to repay; and (c) those under a definite labor contract. The Act of 1883 rendered emigration free from India to the Straits Settlements. Recruiting is now subject to the Controller of Labour, and the expenses are jointly met by the employers and the State. Since 1910 indentured emigration has ceased, and laborers are now engaged on monthly contract. The Indian population of Malaya was about 470,000 in 1924, and of these some 360,000 were working on estates. In the Straits Settlements this population was about 109,000, of whom some 39,000 were on estates.

One of the tables shows the number of East Indian indentured laborers arriving in the Straits Settlements between 1900 and 1910. From 7,615 immigrants in 1900, there is a fall to 572 in 1903, followed by a rise in 1907 to 5,449, and a decrease again to 2,523 in 1910. For East Indian indentured laborers leaving Penang, figures are available for the period 1900-1924. In the first of these years the number of emigrants was lowest, 11,251. By 1913 the maximum of 70,090 emigrants was reached. Then the movement slackened and in 1922 only 45,733 were recorded.

The tables furnish figures for East Indian immigration into Ceylon from 1878 to 1900. In 1878 the number of immigrants was 105,862. The movement then slackened, and in 1883 the number had fallen to 39,055; but afterwards it grew larger, and in 1892, 113,379 immigrants were recorded, only to fall by 1900 to 86,055.

From 1911 to 1924 the numbers were very high. Thus in 1911 there were 137,115 immigrants, and until 1916 there was a continuous rise, the number of immigrants reaching at this date 200,146. Thenceforward there was a certain falling off, the number being 106,598 in 1921.

But the return movement from Ceylon is scarcely less important. From 1878 to 1882 there was an excess of emigrants over immigrants and in the course of the immediately following years this excess was accentuated. In 1900 Ceylon received 86,055 British Indians and 52,067 departed. From 1911 to 1923 there was an excess of 224,158 immigrants, viz:

Immigrants	Emigrants	Excess of immigrants
2,052,731	1,828,573	224,158

The recent sharp rise in emigration is attributed to bad crops in British India, and the increasingly attractive conditions of Ceylon estates.[1] According to the 1921 census about 1,407,000 persons of Indian extraction inhabited this colony. The recruit for Ceylon has his expenses paid by the kangani or sirdar, whose sphere of selection includes neighbors, friends, and even strangers in his locality. Since 1822 the Indian laborer is expected to start free from debt.

The total number of Indians domiciled abroad amounts to 2,130,766 (1924), of whom 2,030,241 are living in the British Empire and 100,525 in foreign countries.[2]

In conclusion, it should be noted that there is a certain amount of immigration into British India. In 1921 the total number of persons not born in India, including the French and Portuguese possessions, was 603,526. Of these, 343,890 were from adjacent countries; 128,686 from other Asiatic countries; 115,606 from the United Kingdom; 10,587 from continental Europe, America, and Australasia; 4,757 were born in Africa or elsewhere, or at sea.

CHINA

Long before the nineteenth century the teeming population of the Chinese provinces flowed over into neighboring Asiatic countries, and during the last century this tendency was accentuated. Statistics of the movement are, of course, almost non-existent. After the abolition of African slavery between 1838 and 1850, Chinese laborers were recruited and transported at first by clandestine agencies in the most inhuman manner (mortality on shipboard reached 20 per cent). Chinese emigration pressed in practically every direction,

[1] *Indian Immigrant Labour*, 1924, p. 1.
[2] *The Indian Year-Book*, 1925, p. 392 (The Times of India, Bombay).

not excluding Europe, and Chinese emigrants did not confine themselves to agricultural labor; some became independent farmers, skilled workers, shopkeepers, traders, and the like. Many, finding it difficult to adopt the customs of the populations among which they had settled, ended by returning home. For various reasons their entry into many countries has now been restricted or barred, and Chinese emigration to other than Asiatic countries is at a very low ebb.

Overpopulation, with the economic distress it entailed, is said to have been the principal cause of Chinese emigration, but it is important to note that those who emigrated came largely from the provinces of Fukien and Kwantung. Moreover, owing to satisfactory experiences with officially organized emigration schemes, Chinese legislation tends to control or prohibit private recruiting.[1]

Although the number of emigrants cannot be derived from population statistics, yet a tolerable idea of the results may be thus obtained. Accordingly we here reproduce from Ta Chen a table giving the total numbers of Chinese residing abroad in 1922.[2]

Annam	197,300	Java	1,825,700
Australia	35,000	Korea	11,300
Brazil	20,000	Macao	74,560
Burma	134,600	Mexico	3,000
Canada	12,000	Peru	45,000
Cuba	90,000	Philippines	55,212
East Indies	1,023,500	Siam	1,500,000
Europe	1,760	Siberia	37,000
Formosa	2,258,650	Straits Settlements	432,764
Hawaii	23,507	South Africa	5,000
Hongkong	314,390	Continental United States	61,639
Japan	17,700		
			8,179,582

In dealing with Chinese emigration, the legislative aspect becomes of signal importance. In 1718 emigration was prohibited and all Chinese residing abroad were recalled. Ten years later a sentence of banishment was pronounced on all who had not returned, and

[1] Ta Chen, p. 20. A British Commissioner for coolies was stationed at Canton in 1858.
[2] With these figures may be compared the following established or estimated figures of Chinese abroad at the beginning of this century: Siam, 2,500,000; Malay Peninsula, 985,000; Sunda Archipelago, 600,000; Hongkong, 274,543; America, 272,829; Indo-China, 150,000; Philippines, 80,000; Macao, 74,568; Burma, 40,000; Australia, 30,000; Asiatic Russia, 25,000; Japan, 7,000; and Korea, 3,710. (E. Philippovitch, *Auswanderung*.)

those returning were treated as having committed a capital offence. These drastic measures did not exclude a certain leakage.

In 1842, when the Port of Amoy was opened by the Treaty of Nankin, the stream of emigrants began to swell rapidly. In 1859 the emigration of contract laborers was first legalized by Pehkwei, governor of Kwangtung, who permitted British and French authorities to recruit indentured Chinese laborers from the province. This process was rendered legal throughout China by Article V of the Treaty of 1860 between China and Great Britain which involved the annulment of the Chinese enactments against emigration. In 1865 a Convention to regulate the employment of Chinese emigrants by British and French subjects was signed at Peking by France, Great Britain, and China, and although not ratified by France or Great Britain was later proclaimed effective by the Chinese Government. The Treaty of 1877 between China and Spain prohibited Chinese laborers from emigrating under contract to Spanish possessions, and this prohibition the Chinese Government subsequently extended to all countries.[1] Owing to the protests of the Powers, the prohibition remained inoperative and emigration continued.[2] The latest Chinese legislation on the subject of emigration is contained in the Labour Emigration Law of China and the Labour Recruiting Agency Regulations of China (both promulgated April 21, 1918).

Volume of Emigration According to Chinese Port Statistics

There are no comprehensive Chinese statistics, the only available ones being those kept at certain foreign ports in China and at Chinese ports open to foreign trade. But these port statistics are not uniform and continuous.

Emigration took place between 1848 and 1873 on a considerable scale through several ports in the province of Canton (Amoy, Macao, Warupu, Caming, Hongkong). Although information about the destination of the emigrants as a rule is not available a large proportion doubtless sailed for distant overseas countries, such as the United States or Peru. While only 180 emigrants were recorded in 1845, the movement grew until in 1857 it culminated with 33,363 departures. After a steady fall for some years, the lowest point

---

[1] In regard to the restrictions imposed on Chinese immigration by the immigration countries, see the particulars in the General Notes following the national tables, and the remarks below in connection with the individual countries.

[2] Ta Chen, pp. 174-179.

being in 1862, the curve swept slowly upward until in 1873 the number of Chinese emigrants reached 13,016.

There are statistics also for intercontinental emigration from the Portuguese port of Macao during the two periods 1856-64 and 1868-73. The movement, which is much feebler than that from Hongkong, is marked by considerable fluctuations.

Taking the ports of the province of Canton separately, the statistics available for the period 1855-70 for Hongkong, the principal port of ·embarkation for intercontinental destinations, are more complete although they do not make it possible to distinguish clearly between continental and intercontinental emigration. Immigration statistics of some continental countries of destination, particularly those of the Straits Settlements, show that a considerable proportion of Chinese arrivals sailed from Hongkong.

If the figures indicating the destinations of the emigrants in 1857 are compared with the total for 1855-61, it appears that most Chinese emigrants were bound for an intercontinental destination.

For succeeding years to 1900 there are no official figures. But this does not mean that intercontinental emigration had ceased. According to a table given by Campbell, 18,077 emigrants left Hongkong in scattered years between 1856 and 1867.[1] In 1868 the number of emigrants reached 18,285.

Between 1900 and 1924 the main current flowed from Hongkong towards the Straits Settlements. In 1900 there emigrated thither 83,643, a figure markedly above that to be found in earlier years. In the next year there was a drop to 69,774, followed in 1907 by another peak with 105,976 emigrants. In 1908 and 1909, there was a return to the normal (71,081 and 77,430); but this was succeeded by a steady rise, reaching in 1913 a maximum of 142,759. The advent of the World War led to a 50 per cent drop in the figures for 1914 and 1915, only to be succeeded by a swift rise to 117,653 in 1916

[1]Here are the figures showing destinations:

Havana, 1856-58	4,991
British West Indies, 1859-62	6,630
Bombay, 1864	2,370
Tahiti, 1864	1,035
Dutch Guiana, 1856-57	1,609
Honolulu, 1865	780
Borneo, 1865	62
Labuan, 1866	164
Sarawak, 1866	436
Total	18,077

(P. C. Campbell, p. 150).

There were further falls until 1920; but in 1921 the figure leaped up to 156,011, a new high point.

For the Chinese ports open to international trade—Amoy, Kungchow, and Swatow—somewhat complete statistics for the period 1876-1901 were compiled by the Chinese Customs. Those emigrating from the south of China (Canton) to Asiatic destinations sail, as a rule, from the ports of Swatow and Amoy.[1] Kungchow is the port of embarkation for emigrants coming from the north of China.

From 1876 to 1901 there were 3,723,017 Chinese left their country through these three ports. Swatow is the most important and Kungchow the least. In 1876, only 67,902 emigrants left China. By 1883 the annual figure had grown to 129,955; by 1893, to 194,568; and by the last year on record (1901), to 206,811.

For the opening years of the present century we found no comprehensive statistics. For Amoy there are only intermittent records, but they show that the outward movement was not losing volume. The maximum number was 126,008 in 1912 and the minimum 66,907 in 1915.

The number of returning Chinese emigrants is also of interest. For the ports of Amoy, Kungchow, and Swatow the return movement during the period 1876-1901 was notable, but there was an appreciable balance on the side of emigration. During the period 1876-1901 there were 3,723,017 departures from these ports and 2,913,764 arrivals, a balance of 809,253 emigrants or more than one-fifth. The difference in the balance, however, greatly varied according to directions. The arrivals from the Straits Settlements were only one-fifth of the departures thither, but the two streams frequently approached equality.

Continental Destinations

Chinese sailing from the ports of Amoy, Swatow, and Kungchow go in much the same direction. Those sailing for the Straits Settlements leave mainly from Swatow. About half the departures are for that destination, and this ratio became more pronounced for the period 1883-89. Chinese immigrants arrived in the Straits Settlements in considerable numbers from 1881 to 1913. In the first of these years 89,803 arrived and in the last no less than 278,140.

Encouraged by the East India Company, 60 Chinese families

[1]For Amoy there are a few figures relating to an early period, but the countries of destination are not indicated. Altogether 5,588 emigrants left Amoy from 1845 to 1852.

had settled at Penang by 1787. In 1794 the number of Chinese residing there was officially estimated at 3,000.

In 1826, 5,513 Chinese arrived at Singapore direct from China.[1] In 1843 the number of Chinese immigrants into Singapore is stated to have been 7,000; in 1844, 1,600; in 1848, 10,475; for the year ending April 30, 1850, there arrived 10,928 (presumably Chinese); in 1852-3 the number was 11,434.[2]

Another source also contains a statement with regard to the same period. According to the figures in the *Journal of the Indian Archipelago,* "the total annual immigration of Chinese, free and indentured, increased from 5,063 during 1840-41 to 11,484 during 1852-53."[3] In the Straits Settlements 16,668 Chinese immigrants were examined in 1877.

Chinese emigration was often assisted. In 1823 the so-called "credit ticket system" was in operation, and emphasized the tendency to emigrate from the southern provinces of China to Singapore and Penang. However, compared with free emigration, this type of emigration was of minor importance.[4] In 1877, of the 9,776 immigrants arrived at Singapore, 2,653 were "unpaid" or "credit-ticket" passengers.[5] Of 136,001 Chinese emigrating to Singapore in 1905, only 12,144 did not pay their passage; in 1914, of 124,032 emigrants, only 2,648.[6]

Chinese contract labor in Malaya was terminated by the British Government in 1914-15 and thereafter no indentured Chinese were found in territories under British control, save Western Samoa and Nauru.[7] However, the provision for indentured labor remained effective until June 1916 for the Kelantan district.

For French Indo-China the statistics of immigration show that 57,209 Chinese arrived during 1879-83. Ratzel states that Indo-China has been the favored goal of Chinese emigrants, that millions of them have settled there, and that thousands enter every year.[8]

According to official information received from Hanoi, the number of Asiatic aliens in Tonkin arriving from or departing for China were as follows from 1920 to 1924:

[1]F. Ratzel, *Auswanderung,* pp. 200, 209.
[2]W. Makepeace, pp. 350-351.
[3]P. C. Campbell, p. 8.
[4]*Ibid.,* p. 1.
[5]*Ibid.,* p. 8.
[6]Ta Chen, p. 84. By 1850, out of 80,000 inhabitants of Singapore 50,000 were Chinese; by 1881 the respective numbers were 86,766 out of 139,208; and in 1911 no less than 219,577 out of 303,321. (W. Makepeace, p. 376.)
[7]P. C. Campbell, p. 217.
[8]F. Ratzel, p. 140.

Year	Immigration	Emigration
1920	19,320	19,280
1921	19,420	19,386
1922	19,110	19,080
1923	18,980	18,892
1924	19,412	19,383

As will be seen, the two columns practically balance.

According to the statistics of the Port of Amoy, there is a regular stream of emigrants to Manila.[1] The total for 1876-1901 was 228,294; but the number in the capital in 1918 was only 17,760. In 1898, after the Spanish-American war, the Chinese Exclusion Act in force in the United States was applied to the Philippines.[2]

Writing in 1828, Crawford spoke of Chinese immigrating into Siam at the rate of 7,000 per annum.[3] The movement has been growing since 1885. The number of Chinese domiciled there in 1922 was estimated at 1,500,000.

In the course of the 15th century some 25,000 Chinese emigrated to Formosa, and under Koxinga and his sons (1644-1688) about 40,000 went to colonize that island. It now contains some $2\frac{1}{2}$ million Chinese.[4]

A table, communicated by the Japanese Government, gives an estimate of the number of Chinese arriving (1912-15) in the Liaotung Peninsula. It does this by striking the balance between the recorded general increase of population and its natural annual increase. The figures are as follows:

1912	18,023
1913	46,599
1914	17,770
1915	37,060

The number of Chinese in Korea and in Japan proper is not large, 11,300 in the former and 17,700 in the latter being recorded in 1922.

[1]The Chinese were so numerous in 1580 that the Spanish Governor had a special quarter constructed for them. Historians speak of a rebellion in 1603, when some 25,000 Chinese were killed. (F. Ratzel, p. 130.) In the Philippines Chinese immigration has been alternately favored and prohibited during the last three centuries.

[2]Ta Chen, p. 103.

[3]Ratzel, F., p. 163.

[4]Ta Chen pp. 40, 42-3.

Intercontinental Destinations

The statistics of the countries receiving Chinese immigrants are of special interest.

From 1858 to 1864 the discovery of gold in Canada proved a potent incentive to Chinese immigration. In 1882 some 5,000 to 6,000 Chinese were shipped directly from Hongkong to Victoria under engagement to the contractors building the Canadian Pacific Railway, and 15,701 Chinese arrived in British Columbia between 1881 and 1884, either direct or from the United States.[1] The first Canadian head tax of 50 dollars was imposed upon Chinese in 1885. This amount was increased to 100 dollars on January 1, 1901, and to 500 dollars on January 1, 1904. The tax was abolished by the Chinese Immigration Act of 1923 and only merchants and students are now admitted.[2]

Large-scale immigration into Canada began after 1907. In that year 1,884 arrived. Then the number steadily rose until it reached 7,445 for 1912. Owing to restrictive legislation in succeeding years, the process was reversed. Altogether 43,462 Chinese arrived in Canada from 1906 to 1924, those registered for leave during 1912-13-1923-24 being 57,996.[3] In 1922 about 12,000 Chinese resided in Canada.

Mexico has attracted a number of Chinese, especially since 1909. From then to 1913 the numbers were large—3,487 in 1909 and 4,910 in 1913. There was a great drop during the War to 228 in 1916, and a decided rise (2,669) after the War. From 1909 to 1924 we find 27,950 arrivals recorded, but the fact that in 1922 only 3,000 Chinese remained in Mexico indicates that most of the immigrants had left the country.

In 1847, 800 Chinese came to Cuba under contract. It was calculated that by July 1852, agents had contracted for the shipment to Havana of between 8,000 and 15,000 Chinese laborers.[4] The number of Chinese emigrating to Cuba between 1847 and 1860 was 56,235; but only 48,167 arrived.[5] By 1862 there were over 60,000 Chinese in Cuba[6] and 90,000 in 1922.[7]

[1]P. C. Campbell, p. 37.
[2]Canada. *Report of the Department of Immigration and Colonisation for the fiscal year ended March 31, 1924*, p. 18.
[3]*Ibid.*, p. 18.
[4]P. C. Campbell, p. 94.
[5]F. Ratzel, p. 241.
[6]Leroy-Beaulieu, p. 255.
[7]Ta Chen, p. 15. The following table is taken from England, *Accounts and Papers, 1852-3*, p. 666:

(Footnote continued on next page.)

Immigration into Cuba has been considerable of recent years. During the four years 1918-1921, for which we have records, a total of 12,167 Chinese arrived.

From 1853 to 1879, 14,002, and from 1880 to 1913, 1,718 Chinese laborers entered British Guiana, altogether 13,485 men and 2,235 women.[1]   According to the Census of 1911, however, only 2,622 Chinese were domiciled there, of whom 1,481 were males and 1,141 females.[2]

The statistics of the United States record only 87 Chinese immigrants for the 33 years between 1820 and 1853. But from the later date the figures begin to climb rapidly.

In 1848 approximately 10 Chinese emigrated to California; 900 in 1849; 3,118, in 1850; 3,508, in 1851, and 15,000 during the first half of 1852.[3] In 1882 we find 39,579 arrived in the United States. These large and increasing numbers of arrivals caused alarm and led to drastic restrictive legislation.

In 1862 Congress prohibited United States citizens and vessels from participating in the traffic in Chinese laborers, but this prohibition did not extend to Chinese certified as free emigrants.   In 1880 a treaty regulated, limited, or suspended the arrival of Chinese laborers and their residence in the United States, and in 1894 a convention prohibited absolutely the immigration of Chinese laborers into the States, subject to certain exceptional conditions.[4]

As a consequence the numbers arriving diminished from 1884 to 1889, reaching the incredibly small figure of 10 in 1887. The current soon commenced to flow more freely, but without assuming conspicuously large dimensions. Still, there were 1,795 arrivals in 1918 and the figure for 1924 was 6,992. But the return current has been always of considerable importance. The statistics of the United States for the period 1908-1924 show that the arrivals of Chinese slightly exceeded the departures, so that in 1920 the total

(Continued from previous page.)

Emigration of Contract Laborers to Cuba.

Year	From	Number	Mortality
1847	Amoy	640	50
1852	Amoy	1,740	..
	Namoa	702	..
1853	Amoy	300	..
	Namoa	1,123	..

[1]C. P. Campbell, p. 160.
[2]Cecil Clementi, *The Chinese in British Guiana.* 1915, p. 1.
[3]*Relatorio*, etc.
[4]Ta Chen, p. 20.

number of Chinese in the United States was only 61,639. The historical aspect requires stressing. The number of Chinese in the States has varied from decade to decade, the figures being 34,933 for 1860; 63,199 for 1870; 105,465 for 1880; 107,488 for 1890; 89,863 for 1900; 71,531 for 1910; and 61,639 for 1920. It is important to note that the number of Chinese women in the States is only about 4,000.[1]

Of recent years few Chinese have entered Brazil. The statistics record only 673 arrivals for 1908-24. But the number of Chinese in Brazil in 1922 is given as about 20,000.[2]

The port statistics of Macao show a considerable emigration of Chinese to Peru.[3] In 1857 there were recorded 450 departures for this destination, while in 1872 there were no less than 13,809 such departures. From that date onward no official statistics are available. We learn, however, from Ratzel that during the decade 1860-1870, 38,648 arrived at Callao in Peru,[4] and in the early months of 1871, according to Hutchinson, as many as 9,021. At present 45,000 Chinese appear to be residing in Peru.

The States constituting the Australian Commonwealth have also attracted large numbers of Chinese, this being partly explicable by its proximity to China.

At first Chinese were brought to Australia under contract. In 1849 this traffic was carried on systematically. Here is a small table for the period 1848-53, relating to the emigration of Chinese contract laborers to Sydney:[5]

Year	From	Number	Mortality
1848	Amoy	120	. . .
1849	Amoy	150	. . .
1850	Amoy	406	19
1851	Amoy	1,478	106
1852	Amoy	717	20
. . . .	Namoa	260	. . .
1853	Amoy	254	. . .

New South Wales received 3,022 Chinese in 1859. The discovery of gold and the need for a considerable labor force explain

[1] Jenks and Lauck, p. 231.
[2] Ta Chen, p. 15.
[3] In 1852 and 1853 (according to *Accounts and Papers, 1852-3*, LXVIII, p. 666), 404 and 500 emigrants respectively left Amoy and Namoa for Peru.
[4] F. Ratzel, p. 246.
[5] England, *Accounts and Papers, 1852-3*, LXVIII, p. 677.

this movement. But the number of arrivals diminished to a minimum of 229 in 1872, only to resume its upward course and reach 4,465 in 1881. Soon there was another big drop, due to restrictive legislation.

Queensland arrivals included 7,254 Chinese in 1875, but only 891 in 1900.

In Victoria there were similar conditions. While 1,108 arrived in 1886, only 569 entered in 1900.

The number of Chinese received annually in the Australian Commonwealth varied little from 1901-1924, being 1,336 in 1901 and 1,917 in 1924.

In 1855 the first State restrictive act was passed, followed by several others which effectually checked Chinese immigration. After a protracted struggle, the Immigration Restriction Act of 1901 practically ended Chinese immigration into Australia.

The following are the Census figures of Chinese in Australia, indicating a progressive diminution and a startling disproportion of males and females:[1]

Year	Full-blood			Half-caste		
	Males	Females	Total	Males	Females	Total
1881	38,274	259	38,533	.....	.....	.....
1891	35,523	298	35,821	.....	.....	.....
1901	29,153	474	29,627	1,556	1,534	3,090
1911	21,856	897	22,753	1,518	1,501	3,019
1921	16,011	1,146	17,157	1,884	1,771	3,655

After 1871, when 1,596 arrived, Chinese emigrants began to settle in New Zealand. But because of restrictive measures, the arrivals rapidly fell and for a time practically ceased. In 1896 an Act was passed raising the poll-tax on Chinese immigrants to £100 per head and limiting the number of Chinese passengers that may be carried by vessels to New Zealand to one for every 200 tons burthen. It is estimated that 3,229 Chinese were living in New Zealand on March 31, 1925.[2]

Chinese immigration into Hawaii began in 1850 and a thin but steady stream found its way thither. In 1851 and 1852 respectively 199 and 101 entered from Amoy.[3] Legal restrictions came into

[1]Official Year-Book of the Commonwealth of Australia, 1925, p. 956.
[2]The New Zealand Official Year-Book, 1926, p. 88.
[3]Accounts and Papers, 1852-53, LXVIII, p. 666.

force in 1883 and were reinforced in 1884, the number allowed to disembark from any vessel in a Hawaiian port being limited to 25.[1] Chinese laborers leaving the islands were not permitted to return. In 1886 over 20,000 Chinese resided in Hawaii.[2] In 1889 and 1890, owing to the remonstrances of the planters, an arrangement was made whereby 10 Chinese farm laborers could be introduced for every European or American immigrant. Under this arrangement, 7,364 Chinese immigrated. With the annexation by the United States, the Exclusion Acts of the annexing country were applied.[3]

The estimated number of Chinese in Hawaii on June 30, 1924, was 24,522.

The number of Chinese employed by France during the World War was stated by the French Government to be as follows:

Laborers from North China	31,409
Laborers from South China	4,024
Skilled workers from Shanghai	1,066
Skilled workers from Hongkong	442
Total	36,941

Practically all the Chinese in France were repatriated at the conclusion of hostilities.

The British introduced about 100,000 Chinese for their armies in France.[4]

The number residing at present in Europe is estimated at less than 2,000.

The planters of Mauritius in 1843 introduced 1,000 Chinese from the Straits Settlements.

Chinese reached the Transvaal to the number of 178,197 from 1904 to 1910, the largest number in one year being 51,427 in 1906.[5] These immigrants were repatriated practically without exception. In 1922 there were about 5,000 Chinese in South Africa.

In the course of the nineteenth century a few Chinese emigrated to the French colonies, mainly as the result of the French Government being in search of laborers for its overseas possessions; but owing to the high cost of Chinese labor the number introduced was insignificant. In 1848 there were 590 Chinese counted in Réunion.

[1]Ta Chen, pp. 115-116.
[2]W. F. Blackman, pp. 194-195.
[3]Ta Chen, p. 118.
[4]*Ibid.*, p. 144.
[5]*Ibid.*, p. 131.

In 1859, at Shanghai 208 Chinese were recruited for Guadeloupe,[1] and 2,101 embarked in 1882 for Réunion.[2]

It should be added that Chinese immigration into French—as well as into Spanish and Dutch—colonies met with administrative obstacles, due to the presumed competition of Chinese with white labor.

JAPAN

From 1636 to 1866 emigration from Japan was a capital offense, and the stream did not begin to flow freely until the eighties of the last century.   Before that, however, emigration to China, Korea, and other neighboring lands, had begun, being tolerated rather than permitted.   Large scale intercontinental emigration of laborers was directed in the first instance to Hawaii whence the Japanese, until they were excluded, flowed towards the United States.   Eventually, emigration to Hawaii, as well as to Canada, was arrested by restrictive legislation and the stream turned to the Japanese colonies and the Asiatic continent, concentrating more particularly in Formosa, Sakhalin, Korea, and southern Manchuria.   This continental, even more than the intercontinental, migration is characterized by a heavy percentage of returning emigrants.   The figures below indicating the number of Japanese resident in foreign countries, furnish some notion of effective Japanese emigration.

As early as 1866 regulations were set up for issuing passports for foreign countries.   At that time all passports for emigrants were issued by the Bureau of Aliens under the Shogun Government. These passports bore the name of the ports (Kanafawa and other treaty ports) where they were issued, the date of issue, the name and age of the holder, and the statement requesting India and other countries to pass the holders freely and asking for their protection. Passport holders were forbidden to acquire the nationality of the country ·to which they emigrated; and required to observe the treaty provisions.

Later the passport regulations were amended so that passports were issued by the Secretary of State for Foreign Affairs.   All emigration statistics since 1868 have been based on the number of passports issued.

The passenger passport statistics testify to a continuous and ascending movement of Japanese emigration.   In its initial stages

[1]P. Guiral, p. 86.
[2]*Ibid.*, p. 130.

from 1868 to 1875 it averaged 580 departures per annum, but in 1875-90 it assumed noticeable proportions and then progressed by leaps until 58,851 persons left Japan in 1906. For the succeeding three years the curve dropped steeply, 15,502 passengers being recorded for 1909. Then it soared once more, recording 62,571 passengers for 1918, only to plunge again and register 26,932 Japanese leaving the country in 1924.

In addition to passenger passport statistics, there are passport statistics confined to emigrants proper and covering the period 1884-1924. However, for the fourteen years before 1898 only "labourers" and "Japanese employed in the service of aliens" were counted as emigrants proper. In the first year, 1884, the number of emigrant passports issued was only 291; but by 1899 it was 31,354 (26,161 men and 5,193 women). Then it fell two years later to 6,490 only to bound upwards and reach 36,124 by 1906. After this there was another plunge and the number of emigrants recorded for 1909 was 4,278. In the succeeding years the number of emigrants fluctuated and in 1924 stood at 13,098.

The figures for passengers and emigrants show that the latter are a considerable percentage of the former. Thus in 1884 there were 1,554 passengers and 291 emigrants and in 1909, when both classes reached the minimum, their respective numbers are 15,502 and 4,278. Taking the whole period, from 1884 to 1924, the proportion of emigrants proper steadily rises until at the last date it forms approximately one half of the number leaving the country, 13,098 out of 26,932 persons.

Intercontinental Destinations

A strong current of Japanese emigration flowed towards America.

There was an irregular and inconsiderable movement of Japanese migration to Canada. From 1,151 emigrants sailing for Canada in 1898 the number fell to 35 four years later. By 1907, however, the culminating point was reached with 2,753, and by 1924 the number of Japanese emigrants to Canada was nearly the same, 1,103, as in 1898. Approaching the matter though Canadian statistics, it appears that 22,205 Japanese arrived in Canada during the period 1900-1924.

To judge by the Japanese remigration statistics, Japanese immigrants do not, as a rule, settle permanently in Canada, immigration and remigration practically balancing. In 1908 there were 601

Japanese entering Canada and 393 returned; in 1914 the respective numbers were 1,284 and 1,244, but since 1919 those returning are in a majority. Thus while 7,071 left for Canada in 1919 to 1924, 9,111 returned to their home in Japan. Still, the Census of 1921 shows a Japanese population of 15,868 in Canada.

On the legislative side it should be noted that in 1908 an agreement was concluded between Canada and Japan. This provided that no more than 400 Japanese laborers may enter Canada in any one year. This number has been sometimes exceeded, as in 1918 when more than twice this number entered.[1]

The number of Japanese sailing for the United States has been appreciably larger than of those embarking for Canada. In 1898 only 170 Japanese left for the United States. By 1900 their number had risen to 7,585; but in the following year, because of restrictive regulations, it fell to 32. Then the movement accelerated, and after some violent fluctuations it reached in 1917 the highest figure, 6,457, to fall again to 4,064 by 1924.

The United States statistics cover the period 1861 to 1924, and show a considerable inflow after 1891. In that year 1,136 Japanese immigrants were recorded; in 1907 no less than 30,226 arrived; but by 1924 the number fell to 8,801.

The direct and indirect figures given above for the United States differ startlingly, suggesting that a special explanation should be forthcoming for the serious discrepancy. In this connection it should be noted that a considerable proportion of Japanese emigration to the United States was indirect.

Thus from January 1, 1902 to September 30, 1906, 29,417 persons left Hawaii for the continent of America, most of whom were Japanese.[2]

The table opposite[3] shows also the high percentage of Japanese non-immigrants arriving in the United States during the years 1909-1918.

To check the clandestine entry of Japanese into the United States, the President on March 14, 1907, issued a proclamation excluding from continental United States "Japanese or Korean laborers, skilled or unskilled, who have received passports to go to Mexico, Canada, or Hawaii, and come therefrom."[4] In this connection "an

[1] A. M. MacLean, p. 104.
[2] E. Grünfeld, p. 46.
[3] Quoted by Iyenaga and Sato.
[4] *Annual Report of the Commissioner General of Immigration for the fiscal year ended June 30, 1908*, p. 125.

Year	Total number admitted	Immigrants	Non-immigrants	
			Numbers	Percentages of total number admitted
1909	1,593	255	1,338	84.0
1910	1,552	116	1,436	92.5
1911	4,282	736	3,546	83.0
1912	5,358	894	4,464	83.3
1913	6,771	1,371	5,400	79.7
1914	8,462	1,762	6,700	79.1
1915	9,029	2,214	6,815	75.5
1916	9,100	2,958	6,142	67.5
1917	9,159	2,838	6,321	69.0
1918	11,143	2,604	8,539	76.6

understanding was reached with Japan that the Japanese Government shall issue passports to continental United States only to such of its subjects are as non-laborers or are laborers who, in coming to the continent, seek to resume a formerly acquired domicile, to join a parent, wife, or children residing there, or to assume active control of an already possessed interest in a farming enterprise" in the States.[1]

The number of Japanese returning from the United States during the period 1908 to 1924 markedly exceeded departures. Thus against 69,377 departures there were 113,817 returning. But according to the United States statistics, the numbers of Japanese re-migrants for the period is given as 42,906.

The United States Census of 1870 reported 55 Japanese residents. Ten years later the number was 148, which had increased to 2,039 in 1890, to 24,326 in 1900, to 72,157 in 1910, and to 111,010 in 1920.[2]

According to the indirect statistics 747 Japanese arrived in Cuba from 1911 to 1924.

The movement towards Mexico is, on the whole, negligible apart from the year 1906 when 5,068 emigrants left for that destination. However, the indirect statistics record the arrival of 4,362 Japanese between 1911 and 1924.

With the encouragement of the French Government, 493 Japanese were introduced into Guadeloupe in 1894.[3]

A strong current moved towards South America, Brazil and Peru

[1] *Ibid.*, pp. 125-6.
[2] E. M. Boddy, p. 27.
[3] R. Robin, p. 248.

being the favored destinations.   Japanese first arrived in Brazil in 1908, 799 being recorded for that year; but the movement gathered strength and 6,947 sailed for Brazil in 1913, falling to 3,689 in 1924. According to Sato, altogether some 20,000 Japanese have proceeded to Brazil.[1]   As regards Peru, there were 790 emigrants to this country in 1899, rising to 2,880 in 1908, falling then again to 651 in 1924.

Australia receives few Japanese immigrants.   In 1898 only 997 Japanese embarked for Australia; and this number diminished rapidly, only 2 sailing in 1906 for that continent.   The numbers then rose, reaching 112 in 1924.   According to the statistics of immigration 11,460 Japanese arrived in Australia from 1902 to 1924.   The Japanese population of Australia in 1921 is given by the census as 2,740.[2]

During the period 1897-1924 there were 2,515 Japanese emigrated to New Caledonia, and 2,633 returned from there.

In 1898 there were 10,145 Japanese emigrants to Hawaii.   In the following year this number was more than doubled.   The year after, in 1900, it fell to 1,529.   The number rose again until 1906; then fell to 1,717 in 1910; after which the movement grew slowly stronger, arriving in 1924 at 2,163 emigrants.   It is interesting to note that from 1913 onward, the main stream of Japanese emigrants turns to the United States.

The return movement from Hawaii is far from being inconsiderable.   In 1908, for example, there were 3,455 emigrants and 4,507 remigrants.   Only the years 1912, 1913, 1916, and 1917 show a slight excess of emigrants.

The two tables opposite indicate the remarkable increase in the number of Chinese and Japanese born abroad and living in the Hawaiian islands.[3]

Continental Destinations

Russia in Asia is the objective of not a few Japanese emigrants. In 1899 the number was only 543.   In 1904, for obvious reasons, the number fell to 8; but two years later it had risen to 1,642, and in 1922 the highest number, 3,249, was reached.   Two years later, in 1924, only 329 Japanese emigrants to Russia were recorded.

Emigrants have shown no strong predilection for Malaysia.   For

[1]Iyenaga and Sato, p. 69.
[2]*Official Year-Book of the Commonwealth of Australia*, 1926, p. 881.
[3]E. Grünfeld, p. 69.

Absolute figures

Year	Hawaiian	Mixed Hawaiian	Chinese born abroad	Japanese born abroad	Others	Total
1853	70,036	983	364	.....	1,755	73,138
1866	57,125	1,640	1,206	.....	2,988	62,959
1872	49,044	1,487	1,938	.....	4,428	56,897
1878	44,088	3,420	5,916	.....	4,561	57,985
1884	40,014	4,218	17,937	116	18,293	80,578
1890	34,436	6,186	15,301	12,360	21,707	89,990
1896	31,019	8,485	19,382	22,329	27,805	109,020
1900	29,799	7,857	21,746	56,230	38,369	154,001
1910	26,041	12,506	21,674	79,674	52,014	191,909

Percentages

Year	Hawaiian	Mixed Hawaiian	Chinese born abroad	Japanese born abroad	Others	Total
1853	95.76	1.34	0.50	.....	2.40	100
1866	90.73	2.60	1.92	.....	4.75	100
1872	86.20	2.61	3.41	.....	7.78	100
1878	76.03	5.90	10.20	.....	7.87	100
1884	49.66	5.24	22.26	0.14	22.70	100
1890	38.27	6.87	17.00	13.74	24.12	100
1896	28.45	7.78	17.78	20.48	25.51	100
1900	19.35	5.10	14.12	36.51	24.92	100
1910	13.57	6.52	11.29	41.52	27.10	100

1899, our tables record 32 emigrants and the highest point is reached in 1917 with 560 emigrants. Thereafter the numbers again diminish, the figure for 1924 being 152.

After 1902 an appreciable number of Japanese left for the Philippines. For that year only 77 emigrants were recorded; but two years later their number reached 2,923, only to fall to 71 in 1906. Thenceforward there was a considerable rise and 3,170 left for that destination in 1917. Seven years later, in 1924, the number had again fallen to 548.

Sex

Male emigration is considerably in excess of female, but there is a tendency for the proportion of females to increase. It is noteworthy that for the period 1910-1924 female emigration to Hawaii exceeded male.

The following figures are based on a census taken on October 1, 1920, and reproduced from the "Rapport de M. le Docteur Hatoyama," published in 1922. They throw light on the total effect of the Japanese emigration movement to foreign countries.

Aggregate number of Japanese residing outside Japan proper, 648,915

Japanese living in
   Liao-Tung Peninsula 79,307
   Territory of Tsing-Tao 23,557
   Territories under Japanese mandate 3,399   106,261

Difference 542,654

The 648,915 emigrants are distributed in the following manner among the different continents:

Asia 342,751
North America 135,325
Oceania 120,894
South America 46,947
Europe 2,925
Africa   73

Taking into consideration primarily the chief countries of destination, the Japanese emigrants are distributed as follows:[1]

	Males		Females		Total	
	1922	1909	1922	1909	1922	1909
China	114,841	46,260	85,899	35,019	200,740	81,279
United States (continental)	75,743	114,382	39,443	28,087	115,186	142,469
Hawaii	64,145	44,617	48,076	21,143	112,221	65,760
San Francisco	. . . . .	48,590	. . . . .	4,771	. . . . .	53,361
Brazil	19,885	474	14,373	131	34,258	605
Canada	11,886	7,717	5,830	1,137	17,716	8,854
Philippines	9,740	1,686	1,416	470	11,156	2,156
British Possessions	7,253	. . . . .	3,575	. . . . .	10,828	. . . . .
Peru	7,668	4,337	2,434	223	10,102	4,560
Asiatic Russia	3,823	1,808	3,205	1,792	7,028	3,600
Australia	4,998	3,791	276	169	5,274	3,960
Dutch Indies	2,883	344	1,603	436	4,436	781
Hongkong	2,309	1,173	774	2,291	3,083	3,464
Mexico	1,925	2,327	273	138	2,198	2,465
Argentina	1,571	27	387	. . . . .	1,958	27
Great Britain	1,500	. . . . .	138	. . . . .	1,638	. . . . .
British India	890	242	388	539	1,278	781
Siam	. . . . .	123	. . . . .	61	. . . . .	184
Chile	. . . . .	142	. . . . .	3	. . . . .	145

[1]The figures for 1909 are from E. Grünfeld, *Die Japanische Auswanderung*, p. 16.

3. MIGRATIONS ACCORDING TO INTERNATIONAL STATISTICS

A. INTERCONTINENTAL MOVEMENTS

I Volume and Direction

(a) Immigration Statistics

Modern world migrations grew out of the overseas migration of the European nations. Comprehensive and comparable data for the *total* movement over a lengthy period are not available, but on the basis of the immigration statistics of overseas countries it is possible to form a tolerably complete and accurate picture of intercontinental migrations.

In order to secure such statistics it would be desirable to combine the immigration figures for the several countries in the Americas with all other intercontinental statistics. As a matter of fact, fairly good statistics for intercontinental immigration exist only during the period 1911-24 for the Australian Commonwealth, New Zealand, Hawaii, the Philippines, the South African Union and Mauritius, Seychelles, New Caledonia, and Fiji. From International Table 6 the following general view of world migration may be obtained for each five years of the pre-War and post-War periods:

Annual average amount of intercontinental immigration			
	1911-15[1]	1921–24	Per cent of decrease
Into American countries	1,403,442	843,983	40
Into other countries	173,709	149,076	14
Total	1,577,151	993,059	37

In the nineteenth century the main streams of international migration flowed from Europe to America, and these oversea migrations

[1]Comparison with other quinquennial periods is impossible, although Table 6 gives besides the immigration into America since 1821, the immigration into Mauritius since 1836; into New Zealand since 1853; and into the Australian colonies since 1861. Figures for South Africa are available only since 1881. This does not permit us to conclude that no immigration was recorded into these territories before the dates mentioned. In Australia, more particularly, there was a regular stream of immigration, voluntary and involuntary, from the third decade of the nineteenth century onward, as shown by the national tables, but they could not be utilized except those for Victoria, in the international tables because they did not distinguish between continental and intercontinental migrations.

were first recorded in a complete and accurate manner in the American countries of largest immigration, notably the United States. To illustrate the growth of the immigration of aliens into America from 1821 to 1924, we subjoin Text Table 1 and Diagram 1, which give, on the basis of Table 6, the quinquennial averages for the whole period. These aggregate figures have been derived from the immigration statistics of countries or colonies which in the past, and even to-day, have not a few gaps and defects, and therefore they furnish only a rough picture of the total movement. Only port statistics have been used, and in the chief countries of immigration these began early: Canada in 1816, United States in 1820, Uruguay in 1835, and Argentina in 1857.[1]

TEXT TABLE 1.

INTERCONTINENTAL IMMIGRATION OF ALIENS INTO AMERICAN COUNTRIES IN ANNUAL AVERAGES, BY QUINQUENNIA, 1821-1924.

Period	Number of countries or colonies included	Number of Immigrants
1821–25	3	8,958
1826–30	3	38,822
1831–35	2	79,936
1836–40	5	89,009
1841–45	9	138,453
1846–50	8	298,660
1851–55	8	397,348
1856–60	11	212,898
1861–65	10	207,017
1866–70	8	405,324
1871–75	7	410,442
1876–80	8	259,913
1881–85	8	652,425
1886–90	8	709,036
1891–95	8	650,057
1896–1900	8	528,032
1901–05	10	1,039,774
1906–10	9	1,481,844
1911–15	11	1,403,442
1916–20	10	374,919
1921–24	12	843,983[2]

The curve representing immigration into America (Diagram 1) shows four waves whose crests and troughs, apart from the trough

[1]The other countries included in these figures are the following: Brazil (from 1820), Cuba (from 1901), Guadeloupe (1856-1883), Newfoundland (1842-1865, 1903-1913), British West Indies (from 1836), Mexico (from 1911), Dutch Guiana (from 1853), and Paraguay (from 1887).
[2]For Canada and the United States the figures are for fiscal years.

DIAGRAM 1

Intercontinental Immigration of Aliens into America and into the United
States alone from 1821 to 1924,
in Quinquennial Averages.

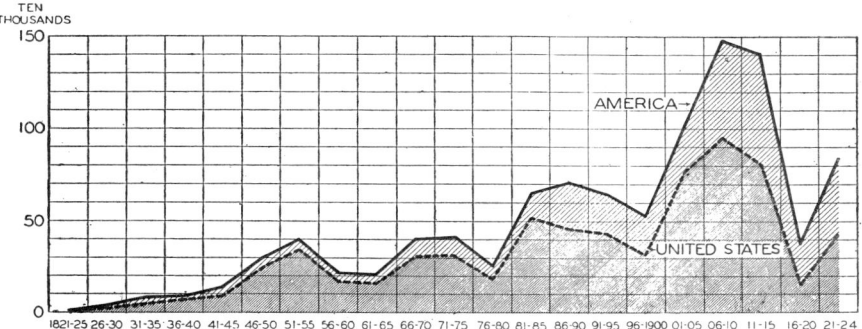

of 1916-20, steadily rose. Overseas immigration into America as a
whole grew from a recorded annual average of less than 9,000 in
1821-25 to 138,000 for 1841-45 and 400,000 for 1851-55. The annual
number of immigrants then fell to about 200,000 as a result of the
bad American harvests of 1854, the commercial crisis of 1857, the
activities of a party in the United States opposed to immigration,
and, at the same time, an improvement in German economic conditions. The war of 1861-5 postponed the revival of immigration
until the period 1866-70, during which the annual average was about
double that of the preceding five years. The increase in the succeeding quinquennial period was only about one per cent, probably
because of the disastrous financial and commercial crisis of 1873.
In the second half of the seventies, the movement was reduced by
about three eighths as a result of the long continued depression
following the panic of 1873. After that, owing to the extraordinary
increase in emigration from Germany and northwestern Europe, it
rose to 652,000, and in 1886-90 to 709,000. In the nineties a re-
gressive tendency is observable. This began in 1890-91 with the
grave economic and financial crisis in Argentina, followed by
commercial crises in the United States. On this account the annual
average of immigration fell in 1891-95 to 650,000, and in 1896-1900
to 528,000. At this point, the rapidly increasing emigration from
the southern and eastern European states, caused a phenome-
nal leap upward. The annual average reached 1,040,000 in
1901-05 and 1,482,000 in 1906-10, notwithstanding the acute crisis

of 1907. Then in the period 1911-15, the last two years of which were markedly influenced by the World War, there was a slight fall to 1,403,000. Until hostilities commenced immigration continued to increase; thus the average for the period 1911-13 exceeded that of the preceding quinquennium. From 1896-1900 to 1911-13 the average annual immigration trebled, increasing by roughly one million. During the war period, 1916-20, the immigrants into America annually were fewer by 375,000 than in the period 1851-55, but after the end of the War the numbers once more increased until in 1921-24 they reached 844,000.

Diagram 1 which gives besides the aggregate oversea immigration into America, also the curve for the immigration into the United States, shows that the latter was controlling for the whole movement. The two lines run almost parallel, but after 1880 and particularly for the period 1906-1924, when other American countries absorbed an appreciable proportion of the immigrants, there were considerable deviations.

The increasing difference between the two curves is indicated by the following figures for five peak periods:

Period	Average annual immigration of aliens		
	Into all American countries	Into the U. S.	Per cent to U. S.
1851–55	397,000	343,000	86
1871–75	410,000	308,000	75
1881–85	652,000	516,000	79
1906–10	1,482,000	949,000	64
1921–24	844,000	426,000	51

Diagram 2 shows that until the seventies Canada had the largest immigration after the United States, while later Argentina, and at times Brazil, became of the greatest importance.[1]

[1]The distribution of immigrants since 1856 among the four principal countries of immigration is indicated in Text Table 2 and Diagram 3. From these it appears, as already shown in commenting on Diagram 1, that during two thirds of a century the share of the United States diminished and the shares of other American countries of immigration increased. The proportion of the United States, 1856-1885, lay between 78.7 and 81.4 per cent, but in 1911-1924 between 56.5 and 61.9 per cent. The proportion of Argentina, 1856-1885, lay between 4.8 and 9.3 per cent but after 1885 there were only three of the eight quinquennial periods during which it was under 15 per cent, and it reached its maximum in 1921-24 with 20.4 per cent. Brazil had a comparatively large immigration, much of it probably subventioned, for 1886-1900 11.6 to 21.1 per cent, but the proportion for 1921-24 was only 8.5 per cent. The Canadian proportion for 1856-1870 lay between 8.6 and 11.1 per cent and for 1911-1924 between 13.1 and 15.2 per cent, a relatively high figure, but for half of the entire period it was under 8 per cent.

DIAGRAM 2

Quinquennial Averages of Intercontinental Immigration of Aliens to Argentina, Brazil, Canada, Cuba, United States and Victoria (Australia) from 1821 to 1924 as far as figures are available.

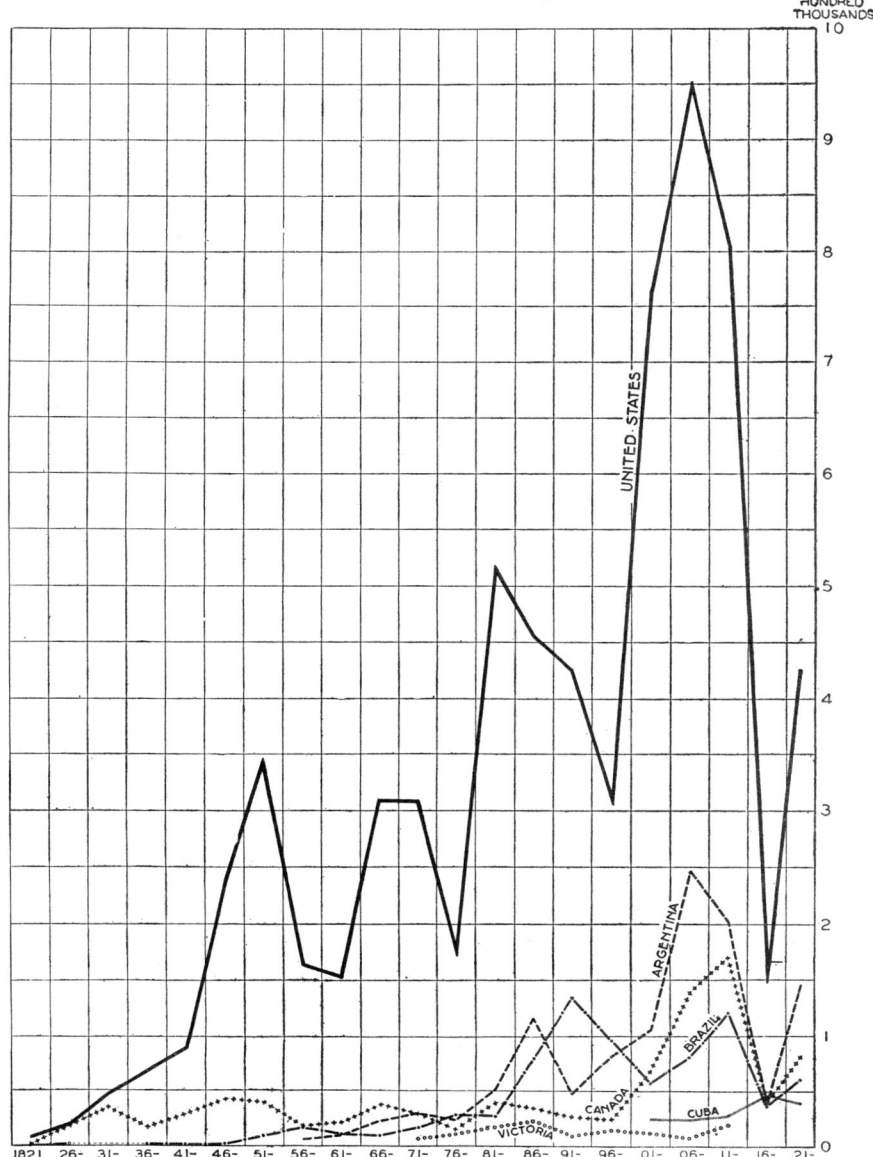

The percentage share of a large number of States in the immigration into America during the period 1901-1924 is shown in Table 7. It is singular that during 1916-20 Cuba and the British West Indies had a larger share than Brazil, Canada, or Argentina, and that in the post-War period their importance increased.

TEXT TABLE 2

INTERCONTINENTAL IMMIGRATION OF ALIENS INTO ARGENTINA, BRAZIL, CANADA, AND THE UNITED STATES, AS PERCENTAGE OF THE TOTAL IMMIGRATION INTO THESE COUNTRIES FROM 1856 TO 1924, IN QUINQUENNIAL AVERAGES.

Period	Total Immigration	Percentage entering			
		United States	Canada	Brazil	Argentina
1856–60	203,299	78.7	8.6	7.9	4.8
1861–65	193,362	78.9	11.1	5.2	4.8
1866–70	377,410	81.9	9.6	2.5	6.0
1871–75	384,138	80.4	7.7	4.2	7.7
1876–80	240,573	73.3	5.9	11.5	9.3
1881–85	633,321	81.4	6.2	4.3	8.1
1886–90	683,304	66.4	4.8	11.6	17.2
1891–95	631,146	67.3	4.1	21.1	7.5
1896–1900	513,730	60.8	4.6	18.6	16.0
1901–05	994,718	76.8	6.8	5.8	10.6
1906–10	1,415,077	67.1	9.7	5.7	17.5
1911–15	1,299,119	61.9	13.1	9.4	15.6
1916–20	266,202	56.5	15.2	13.8	14.5
1921–24	713,543	59.7	11.4	8.5	20.4

With regard to the curve of intercontinental immigration into several oversea countries during the post-War period, the following may be added. The figures below (for fiscal years) show the amount for the United States.

1920	1921	1922	1923	1924
287,615	702,153	243,195	342,140	416,870

The number of intercontinental immigrants had grown by 1921 to 702,153. The "Percentum Limit Act" or "Quota Act,"[1] which came into force in June 1921, led to a reduction to about one-third

[1] Under this Act the number of citizens of each country to be admitted to the United States under the immigration laws was limited to an annual maximum of 3 per cent of the total number of citizens of that country resident in the United States in 1910.

DIAGRAM 3

Intercontinental Immigration of Aliens into Argentina, Brazil, Canada and the United States as Percentage of the Total Immigration into these Countries from 1856 to 1924, in Quinquennial Averages.

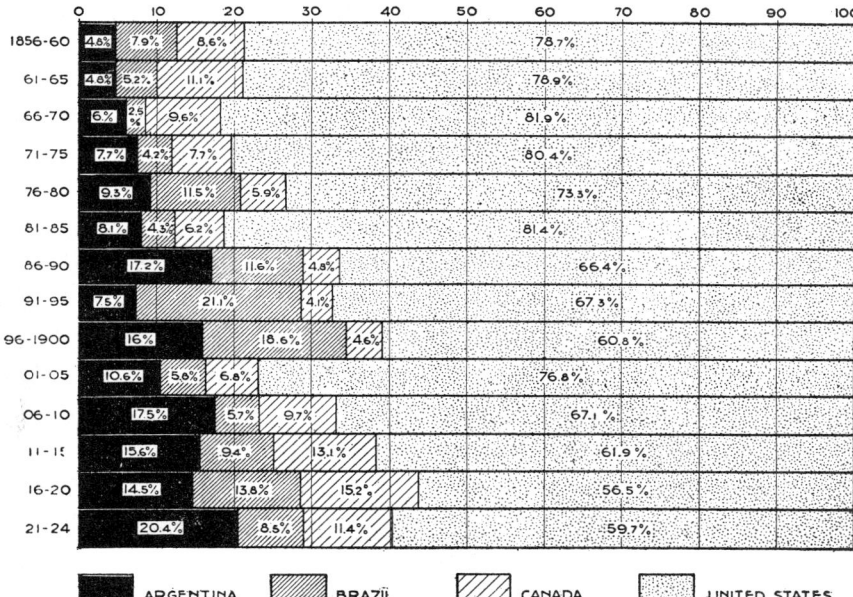

| | ARGENTINA | BRAZIL | CANADA | UNITED STATES |

in the following year.   Thereafter for two years an upward tendency was noticeable.

Canadian immigration during the last century underwent marked variations.   Early in that period Canada was not far behind the United States.   Thus from 1817-26 to 1831-35 the annual figures rose from 900 immigrants to 33,443.   Thereafter there were considerable fluctuations, the annual average for 1836-40 being 17,000.   This was followed by a steady rise reaching during 1846-1850 the maximum of 41,000 only to fall back in 1856-1860.   After this, the absolute figures fluctuated between 14,000 and 39,000.   In the twentieth century they bounded up, attaining 171,000 during 1911-15.   In the course of the war period Canada received annually a mean of 40,000 intercontinental immigrants but by 1921-24, in part as the result of the Empire Settlement Act, the annual mean rose to 82,000.

From 1821 down to the fifties the incomplete Brazilian statistics[1]

[1]See also the sections on emigration from Germany, Switzerland, and Portugal in the nineteenth century.

registered for one period, 1826-30, an annual mean of over 1,000 immigrants. From 1851-1860 to 1881-1885 immigration fluctuated between 8,000 and 28,000, thereafter, until the World War, between 133,000 in 1891-5 and 58,000 annually in 1901-05. In 1916-20 the immigration figure had sunk to 37,000, but in 1921-24 it had risen again to 60,000.

Immigration into Argentina,[1] where the statistics started with the year 1857, climbed from 5,000 in the first year to an annual average of 30,000 in 1871-75. During 1876-80 there was a fall to 22,000, followed during 1886-90 by an annual average of 117,000. The grave financial and economic crisis of 1890-91 checked the stream of immigration (1891-95 to 47,000), but this was succeeded by an intermittent rise until 1906-10 when the high figure of 248,000 was reached. During 1914 and 1915 the influence of the World War is clearly traceable. The annual average for 1911-15 fell to 202,000 and for 1916-20 to 39,000, but rose to 146,000 for 1921-24.

Immigration into Cuba during 1901-05 amounted to an average of 24,581 persons and remained near that figure until the War. It rose to 46,043 during 1916-20 and maintained itself during 1921-24 at about the same level, influenced no doubt by Spanish seasonal migration.

The annual average of immigrants into Uruguay for 1836-40 was 2,820 and for 1841-42 was 8,770. For two subsequent decades there were no statistics. Towards the close of the sixties and the opening of the seventies, the influx of immigrants was considerable. In certain years 20,000 "passengers" entered the port of Montevideo by foreign oversea commerce, but in 1875 the number had sunk to scarcely more than 5,000. During 1881-85 an average of 10,000 intercontinental passengers disembarked at Montevideo and during the succeeding quinquennium as many as 18,000. Later years show an average of less than 10,000, but there are no data for the years 1904-1912.

Diagram 2 shows only one non-American country, namely the Australian colony, Victoria, the figures for which are comparable. Intercontinental immigration fluctuated between 7,000 and 22,000.

The immigration figures for the Australian Commonwealth, beginning in 1902, relate in part to ordinary passengers. The number

[1]The legislature of Argentina in 1854 passed an Act authorizing the Government to constitute an honorary commission, consisting of from 9 to 15 persons of Argentine or foreign nationality, for dealing with all matters pertaining to immigration. The same Act exempted from harbor dues all vessels carrying more than 50 immigrants. Immigration on a great scale began two years later, in 1856.

of these rose from 46,000 in 1901-05 to 125,000 in 1911-15, only to fall to 60,000 during 1916-20 and to rise again to 95,000 in 1921-24.

* * * *

In order to characterize the immigration to the United States by region of origin,[1] the immigrants have been classified in the following Text Table 3 and Diagram 4 into five groups (Western and Northern Europe, Eastern and Southern Europe,[2] British North America, Mexico, Other countries) and the time into four periods (1821-1840, 1841-1890, 1891-1915, 1921-1924).

TEXT TABLE 3

DISTRIBUTION OF ALIEN IMMIGRANTS (UNITED STATES), BY REGION OF LAST RESIDENCE, FROM 1821 TO 1924.

Country of last residence[2]	1821–1840	1841–1890	1891–1915	1921–1924
Absolute figures				
1. Eastern and Southern Europe..	9,113	1,210,628	11,323,787	968,113
2. Western and Northern Europe.	585,391	11,916,400	4,343,427	591,631
3. British North America........	15,901	1,030,975	537,279	436,828
4. Mexico....................	11,416	15,615	132,620	203,413
5. Other countries and countries not stated...............	120,743	511,474	605,668	144,614
Total...............	742,564	14,685,092	16,942,781	2,344,599
Percentages				
1. Eastern and Southern Europe.	1.2	8.2	66.8	41.3
2. Western and Northern Europe	78.8	81.2	25.6	25.2
3. British North America.......	2.2	7.0	3.2	18.6
4. Mexico....................	1.5	0.1	0.8	8.7
5. Other countries and countries not stated...............	16.3	3.5	3.6	6.2
Total.............	100.0	100.0	100.0	100.0

A glance at this table confirms the common statement that there has been a remarkable shift among the countries of emigration.

[1]So far as the extra-European immigration countries classify the immigrants according to place of former permanent residence or according to their nationality, the data have been utilized in International Tables 13 and 14, which cover the total period 1821-25 to 1921-24. But here not only intercontinental immigration but the stream of immigration as a whole is examined.

[2]See p. 71 for the basis underlying the classification of European countries into two groups.

DIAGRAM 4

Distribution of Alien Immigrants (United States), by Regions of Last Residence (Eastern and Southern Europe, Western and Northern Europe, British North America, Mexico, Other Countries), from 1821 to 1924.

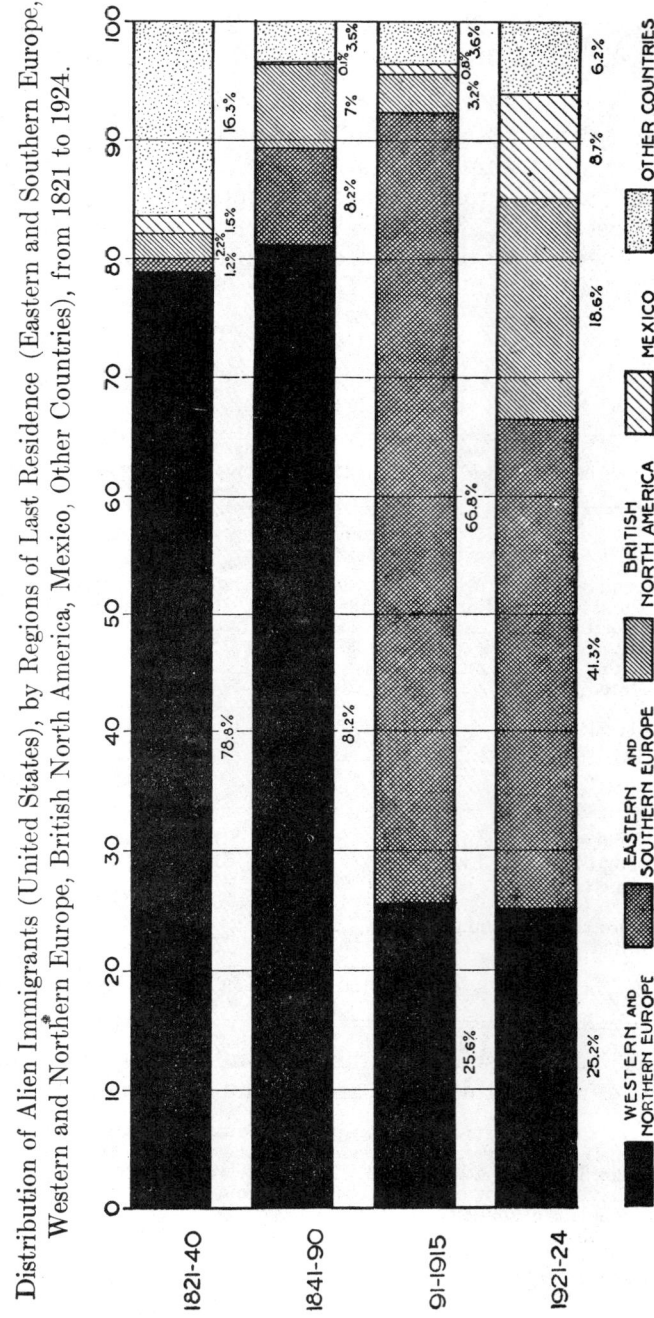

During the periods 1821-40,[1] and 1841-90, approximately four-fifths of the immigrants entering the United States came from Western and Northern Europe, but during 1891-1915 and 1921-24 only one-fourth. On the other hand the proportion of immigrants coming from Eastern and Southern Europe rose enormously until 1915: from 1.2 per cent in 1821-1840 to 8.2 per cent in 1841-1890 and 66.8 per cent in 1891-1915. Owing to the recent restrictive legislation, the proportion for these regions again fell to 41.3 per cent during 1921-24.[2]

Another noteworthy fact is the growth of continental immigration to the United States in the post-war period. Thus 27.3 per cent of the total immigrants in 1921-24 entered the United States from British North America and Mexico. Text Table 3 and Diagram 4, however, do not make it possible to draw a correct comparison between the post-War and the pre-War periods inasmuch as the statistics of continental immigration into the United States were incomplete (clandestine immigration since 1921 is estimated, officially, at over 100,000 annually).

Text Table 4 gives the alien immigration into the United States classified by country of origin. It shows that 8,500,000 or 23.6 per cent of the 36,000,000 immigrants from 1820 to 1924, came from the British Isles (4,400,000, or more than one-half of them, from Ireland); 5,600,000 or 15.7 per cent were Germans; Italy occupies the third place with 4,600,000 or 12.7 per cent. Next in order is Austria-Hungary with 4,200,000 or 11.8 per cent, and Russia and Finland with 3,400,000 or 9.3 per cent. In addition, although the record from Canada is incomplete, over 2 million persons came from British North America and over one million from Sweden.

Until 1875 the great majority of the immigrants came from the British Isles or Germany. The British share in this period oscillates between 38 and 63 per cent, that of Germany between 24 and 37 per cent. The term "British" includes Irish and these latter constituted in the first half of the nineteenth century from one-third to one-half of the immigrants into the United States, sometimes indeed over 50 per cent. Later the importance of British immigration diminished, but up to 1890 British and German immigration ac-

---

[1]During the period 1821-1840 the country of origin of the immigrants was not recorded in 16.3 per cent of the cases, and those concerned were almost exclusively from Western Europe. Hence, the number and proportion of the immigrants from Northern and Western Europe were even greater than the figures show.

[2]During the whole period, 1820-1924, the number of immigrants was:

    From western and northern Europe 17,600,000   49.0 per cent

    From eastern and southern Europe 13,900,000   38.6 per cent

counted for over one-half of the total. Text Table 5 will clarify the subsequent development.

TEXT TABLE 4.[1]

IMMIGRATION INTO THE UNITED STATES, 1820 TO 1924, BY COUNTRIES OF ORIGIN.

	Absolute figures	Per cent of im- migrants
Western and Northern Europe		
United Kingdom	8,507,378	23.6
France	557,304	1.6
Netherlands	235,077	0.6
German Empire	5,643,793	15.7
Denmark	318,809	0.9
Norway	768,030	2.1
Sweden	1,168,260	3.2
Switzerland	278,187	0.8
Belgium	148,904	0.4
Other western and northern Europe	16,598	0.1
Total	17,642,340	49.0
Eastern and Southern Europe		
Italy	4,561,379	12.7
Spain	164,163	0.5
Portugal	249,019	0.7
Austria-Hungary	4,239,895	11.8
Russian Empire and Finland	3,353,177	9.3
Poland	349,063	1.0
Bulgaria, Serbia, and Montenegro	81,441	0.2
Greece	410,568	1.1
Rumania	144,621	0.4
Turkey in Europe	153,752	0.4
Turkey in Asia	204,606	0.6
Total	13,901,682	38.6
British North American possessions	2,410,093	6.7
South America	1,034,986	2.9
China	373,731	1.0
Japan	271,385	0.8
India	8,802	0.0
Other specified countries	108,205	0.3
Countries not specified	254,066	0.7
Grand total	35,999,042	100.00

[1]The figures down to 1923 are taken from the *Monthly Labor Review* (Washington, January, 1924, "A Century of Immigration"). To these the data for 1924 have been added. Totalling the figures for the several countries, we have 36,005,290 immigrants, 6,248 too many. This discrepancy is in the source.

For 1920-24 the number reported by the Bureau of Immigration as from Czecho-slovakia, and 60 per cent of the number from Yugoslavia have been included with Austria-Hungary. The remaining 40 per cent of Yugoslavia and the total of Albania have been included with Bulgaria, Serbia, and Montenegro. The numbers for Estonia, Latvia, and Lithuania have been included with Russia.

TEXT TABLE 5.

PERCENTAGE SHARE OF IMMIGRANTS FROM THE BRITISH ISLES, ITALY, AUSTRIA-HUNGARY
AND RUSSIA, IN THE TOTAL IMMIGRATION INTO THE UNITED STATES,
1891-95 to 1911-15.

Years	British Isles	Italy	Austria-Hungary	Russia	Total per cent
1891–95	19.9	13.6	13.1	11.6	58.1
1896–1900	15.2	23.3	20.2	16.6	75.1
1901–05	10.1	25.0	24.6	17.2	76.9
1906–10	9.7	21.9	24.2	18.9	74.6
1911–15	8.7	21.1	19.9	20.0	69.7

From the above table it appears that Italy came into prominence after 1891 and that during ten years, 1896-1905, it occupied the first place but in the second five-year period it was nearly overtaken by Austria-Hungary. In 1906-10 the first place went to the latter[1] but in 1911-15 Italy again took the lead. Germany fell behind from the second half of the nineties and during 1896-1900 the British Isles were outdistanced not only by Austria-Hungary but also by Russia. During 1906-10 there were twice as many immigrants from Russia as from the British Isles, and for 1911-15 Russia took second place from Austria-Hungary. During 1916-20 among the European countries only Italy showed over 10 per cent of immigrants, but during the next period 1921-24, it had 15.6 per cent and the British Isles 10.8 per cent.

It was during the latest periods that continental immigration swelled to unusual proportions. In 1911-15 of the immigrants 437,000 or 9.8 per cent came from British North America and Mexico; in 1916-20 they were 524,000 or 31.1 per cent; 640,000 or 27.3 per cent in 1921-24. In these numbers British North America is much more strongly represented than Mexico. Among both currents were European emigrants who, after a brief stay in one of the two regions, proceeded to and entered the United States.

The figures relating to intercontinental immigration into the United States during 1920-24 will be found in the foregoing pages. But the total immigration curve pursues a markedly different path. In the post-War period the total immigration into the United States under the old legislative provisions was 430,001 during the fiscal year 1920, and 805,228 in 1921. As the result of the new legislation the number of immigrants dropped abruptly to 309,556 in 1922,

[1]International tables 13 and 14 give the figures for Austria and Hungary separately •

and rose again to 706,896 persons in 1924. The rise from 1920 to 1921 was chiefly due to an increase in European immigration, the number of continental immigrants falling. Among European countries the British Isles, the Austrian Republic, Germany, Denmark, Norway and Sweden showed a marked rise in 1922 and 1924; the other European countries merely maintained their numbers. The increase in the total immigration in this last period is to be ascribed mainly to the more rapid influx from other American States, in the first instance Canada and Mexico (66,361 in 1922, 290,026 in 1924) which is to be explained by American countries being exempt from the application of the Quota Act (but see p. 177).

Until 1907 the statistics of Brazil were incomplete and the utmost caution is required in judging the early growth of Brazilian immigration. Down to 1845 "other countries" accounted for over 50 per cent of the immigrants. This precludes the possibility of determining nationality. But it is clear that in the first half of the last century Germany, and at certain times Portugal, sent numbers of emigrants to Brazil. During 1846-50 Germans made up 43.5 per cent of the immigrants. Most of the remainder were Portuguese but until 1900 their proportions diminished: 1851-55 two-thirds of all immigrants; during 1856-70 approximately one half; 1871-75 two-fifths; 1876-85, under one-third; 1886-95 under one-fifth; and 1896-1900 one-seventh. From this last period the Portuguese share in Brazilian immigration rose steadily to 41.7 per cent in 1916-20, dropping to 34.1 per cent in 1921-24. The main contingent was supplied by Italy, 1876-1900: 40.2 per cent in 1876-80; 58.8 per cent in 1886-90; and 63.0 per cent in 1896-1900. Thereafter came a sharp turn dropping to 20.0 per cent in 1906-10 and further falling to 17.5 per cent in 1911-15, still sliding downwards to 14.5 per cent in 1916-20, but slightly recovering to 17.1 per cent in 1921-24.

The Spanish come next. In 1891-95 they formed 14.3 per cent of the immigrants; in 1901-05 they were 18.1 per cent; in 1906-20 21 to 22.2 per cent; and 11.8 per cent in 1921-24, In the last four years the proportion of Germans became again of some importance (14.3 per cent in 1924) after having fallen as low as 3.5 per cent in the years before the War.

The Succession States of Austria-Hungary differed much in importance. Owing to the Quota Act in the United States, Yugoslavia in 1924 accounted for 7,889 immigrants to Brazil, a number much above the preceding years. Only 760 Austrians arrived in 1921, but in 1923 their number had increased to 2,163, only to fall

below 1,000 in 1924. The immigration of Hungarians and Czecho-slovaks rose a little in these years, but in 1924 the number of the former was only 996, and of the latter, 610.[1]

From 1829 to 1850 immigrants into Canada came almost exclusively from the British Isles. From 1851 to 1870, German immigrants also were of some importance. The share of the former was 16.7 per cent in 1851-55, after which it fluctuated between 31 and 36 per cent. German immigrants were 8.5 per cent in 1871-75. For 1875-80 the statistics indicate only two groups: immigrants from the British Isles and those from other countries: in the following decades arrivals from the United States are also recorded. During 1881-90 the United States were represented by about 60 per cent and the British Isles by about 30 per cent. For 1891-95 their shares are 28.8 and 52.5 per cent respectively and for 1896-1900, 23.1 and 36.5 per cent. From 1900 onward the statistics record the nationalities of all immigrants. For 1901-05 immigrants from the British Isles and the United States were 35 per cent. These shares remained approximately constant until 1911-15. For 1916-20 immigrants from the United States were 56.8 per cent and from the British Isles 32.5 per cent, but by 1921-24 the proportions were altered, British immigrants representing 47.2 per cent and those for the United States only 20.8 per cent, the difference being largely due to the Empire Settlement Act.

For Argentine the proportion of immigrants for 1856-60 was 61.8 per cent from Italy, 16.9 from Spain, and 5.5 per cent from France. By 1866-70 the Italians made up 70.9, Spaniards 14.4 and French 5.9 per cent. After this period Italian immigration gradually decreased, while the Spanish increased.

Statistics began to be compiled in Uruguay during 1835-42. During this early period there arrived 13,765 French (41.5 per cent), 8,481 Spanish (25.6 per cent), and 7,945 Italians (24 per cent). The number of Brazilians, British and Germans at this period constituted 3 per cent, or less than 1,000 immigrants each. Among the arriving passengers through foreign overseas commerce, Spain and Italy were best represented. In no year did the number of Spanish immigrants reach 6,000, while the number of Italian immigrants was 8,805 in 1885 and twice above 12,000. The relative numbers for the two nationalities show a rising percentage of Spanish immigrants and a falling one for Italians.

[1]Magyars probably have been classified under their *political* citizenships (Rumanians, etc.)

	1881–85	1921–24
Spanish	23.3 per cent	41.7 per cent
Italians	47.0 per cent	17.1 per cent

Among immigrants into Cuba the Spanish predominate. Except for 1902 the numbers arriving annually from Spain were always above 10,000 and the figure frequently rose to between 20,000 and 30,000, sometimes even to 40,000, and in 1920 to 94,294 (mostly seasonal workers). There was also considerable immigration into Cuba from the West Indies, notably Haiti and Jamaica.

Of the extra-American countries of immigration only Australia, New Zealand and South Africa can be considered since these alone record the country of origin or the nationality of the immigrants for a number of years.

Among the immigrants into the former Australian colonies passengers from the British Isles predominate and Germans take second rank. Thus 10,569 Germans arrived in Queensland during the period 1870-79. The statistics of the Australian Commonwealth show that 80 to 90 per cent of the immigrants for 1902-1924 were British subjects, but a part of them came from British possessions, notably from New Zealand.

MOVEMENT OF BRITISH SUBJECTS TO AUSTRALIA

	1905	1912	1917	1924
Arrivals of British subjects (Table V)..	39,975	146,602	45,988	88,335
Arrivals from the United Kingdom. (Tables II and III)................	10,594	90,882	2,049	47,955

Among the passengers during 1902-1913 there were 2 to 2.5 per cent Germans and during the whole period (1902-24) 2 to 3 per cent. The remaining nationalities played no noticeable part.

Of the passengers arriving in New Zealand, over nine-tenths came from the United Kingdom and Australia. The relative importance of these two countries of origin was subject to strong fluctuations. In 1856-60 the United Kingdom accounted for 68.9 per cent and Australia for 27.6 per cent. In the following quinquennial period, 1861-65, the proportion was about reversed, 33.4 per cent and 66.1 per cent, and during 1871-75 the earlier percentage was reached, 68.7 per cent for the United Kingdom and 20.9 per cent for Australia. After 1886, Australian passengers were in a decided majority (over 80 per cent in 1891-1900).

In the Union of South Africa 70-80 per cent of the "new arrivals" during 1913-23 were British subjects and these did not reach 20,000 even in years when immigration was greatest.

(b) Emigration Statistics

The study of emigration from the various European countries scarcely modifies the results obtained from a study of the statistics of immigration.   Diagram 5 indicates the movement of the inter-

DIAGRAM 5

Total Intercontinental Emigration of Citizens from European Countries from 1846 to 1924, and Total Intercontinental Immigration of Citizens into European Countries (Repatriation) from 1886 to 1924, in Quinquennial Averages.

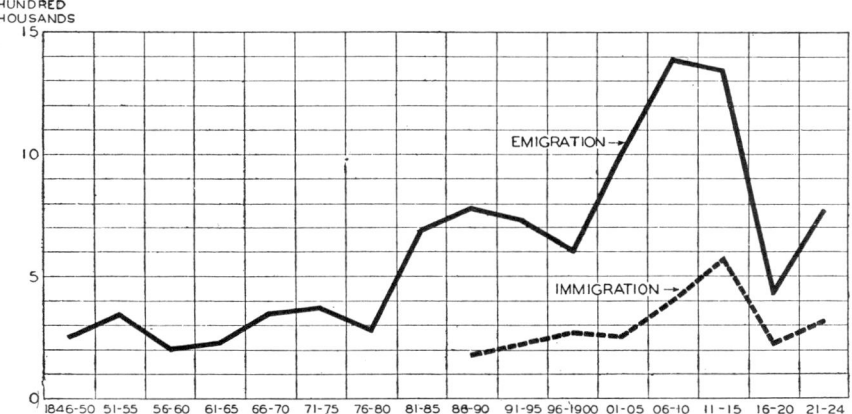

continental emigration from Europe, while Diagrams 6 and 7 show the movement from the several countries.

From 1846 onward quinquennial averages for European emigration have been computed, as from that date several European states (Germany, Austria, the Netherlands and Norway) possess emigration statistics.   These statistics are far less comparable among themselves than the immigration statistics of overseas countries, but they supplement effectively the data recorded by the latter. The number of emigration countries at the commencement of the period under review was limited (four countries as above) and slowly increased until 1910 (17 countries: Germany, Austria-Hun-

DIAGRAM 6

Intercontinental Emigration of Citizens from European Countries with
Over 50,000 Emigrants per Annum from 1846 to 1924,
as far as direct or indirect statistics are available,
in Quinquennial Averages.

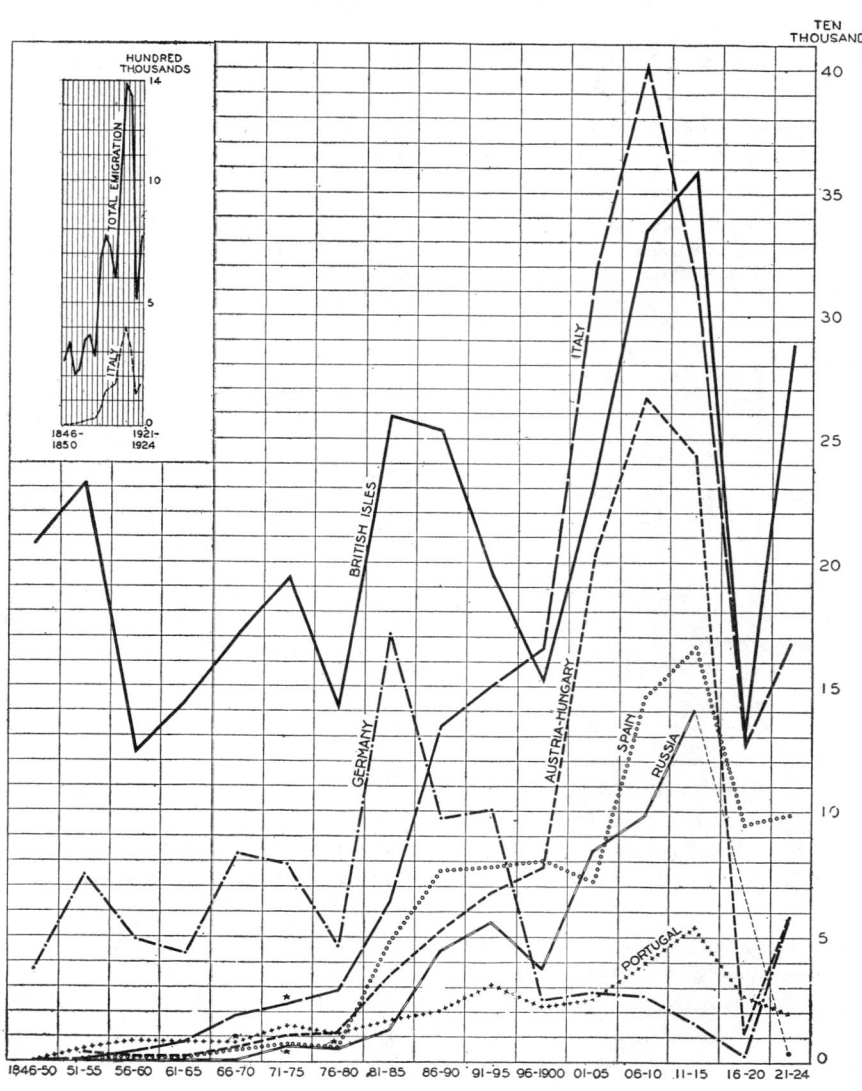

gary, Belgium, Denmark, Spain, Finland, France, British Isles, Malta, Italy, Norway, Netherlands, Portugal, Russia, Poland, Sweden and Switzerland). So these international tables have been completed as far as possible by the figures of immigration of the oversea countries which have been also included in the totals.[1] The statement of these quinquennial averages (see Diagram 5) therefore is far from being exactly correct, but still it conveys a clear impression of the general movement of European intercontinental emigration.

If the emigration curve of Europe is compared with the immigration curve of America, it must be borne in mind that European emigration does not go exclusively to America, and that intercontinental immigration into America includes emigrants from extra-European countries. It is also true that the figures for the same movement of migration derived from the country of origin and the country of destination show important differences because of the heterogeneity and defectiveness of the statistics, particularly in their early stages. One marked divergence between European emigration statistics and American immigration statistics springs from the fact that European emigration data are for calendar years and the corresponding immigration data for certain American countries are based on fiscal years for certain periods. This applies specially to the United States, the premier immigration country.

Notwithstanding these difficulties it appears that the recorded total 50,000,000 aliens who migrated 1846-1924 from overseas into America corresponds approximately to the total number of intercontinental emigrants leaving Europe. Moreover, the two curves resemble each other closely and when long periods are considered the differences appear to be compensating.

In comparing quinquennial averages the immigration figures for America until 1871-75 are higher, except for 1861-65, than the European emigration figures, and from 1876-80 onward the European emigration figures exceed the immigration figures of the United States save for the years 1906-10 to 1911-15 and 1921-24. However, after 1850 the former never exceed the latter by more than one-sixth. This difference is due partly to the fact that statistics of immigration are more exact than those of emigration, and that beginning with about 1870 the other overseas countries (which had no statistics) commenced to be of consequence as countries of destina-

[1]This total does not include the emigrants proper from the British Isles and from Spain (1911-24), the third-class passengers from Portugal (1921-24), Ireland (Irish port statistics), and Poland until 1915 (but figures for Poland after 1915 are included).

DIAGRAM 7

Intercontinental Emigration of Citizens from European Countries with
Under 50,000 Emigrants per Annum from 1846 to 1924 as far as
direct or indirect statistics are available,
in Quinquennial Averages.

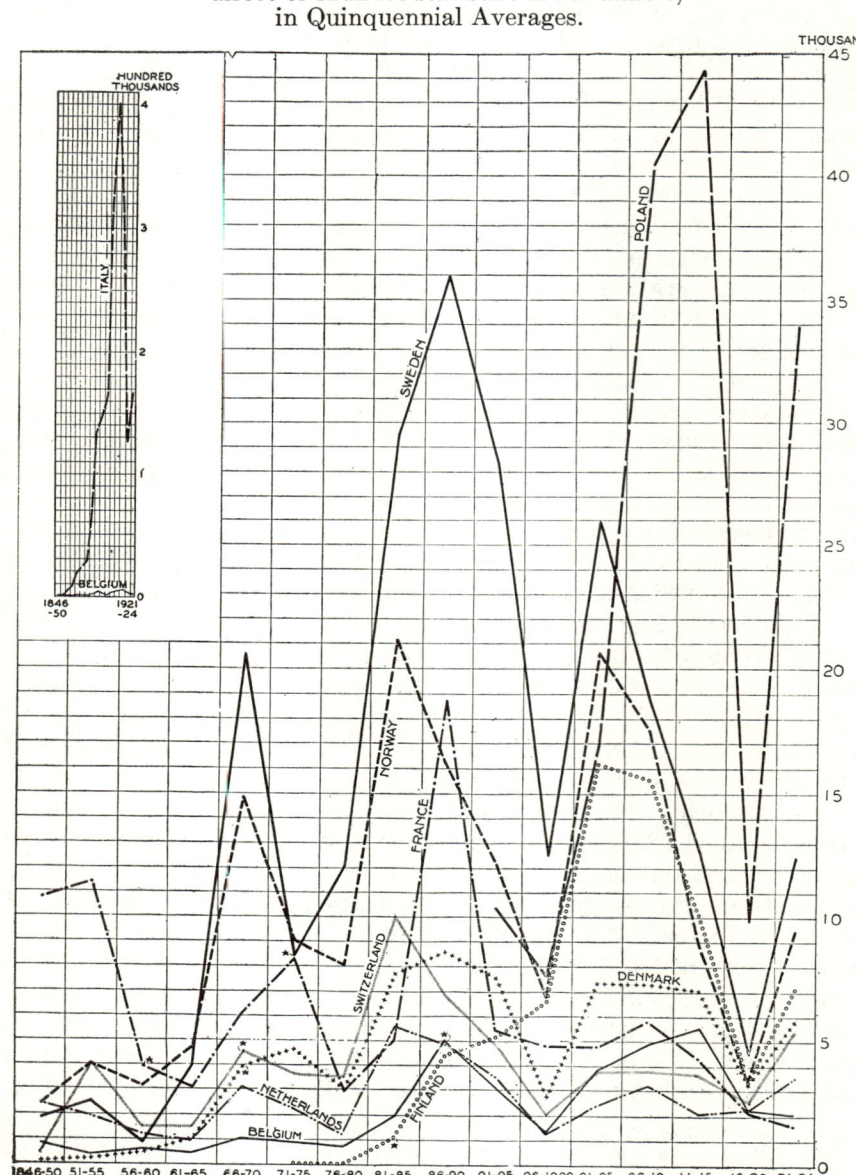

tion for European emigrants. It is true, also, that certain European passport statistics and communal registers are evidence of an intention to emigrate rather than of the emigration.

(c) The Significance of the Several Countries of Transit

International Tables 35 and 36 give the number of alien transients proceeding through certain European countries to oversea countries, as shown by available port statistics. The five countries included do not cover the whole transit traffic and the statistics are incomplete, e. g. frequently no distinction is drawn between aliens resident in the country and transients proper, and the statistics do not always relate to the whole period. Still, it has seemed worth while to compute the totals and give for each quinquennial period the percentage share of each transit country.

The totals reflect fairly accurately the cycles of European emigration.

In the period 1856-85, which included Germany, France, the British Isles, and the Netherlands after 1867, France at first showed the largest number of transients, but during 1861-65 she was overtaken by the British Isles, and during 1876-80 by Germany also. The British Isles led.

From 1891 to 1924 figures are available for Germany, Belgium, the British Isles and the Netherlands. By 1886-90 Germany was in the van and remained there until the outbreak of the War. The British Isles followed. Then came Belgium and next the Netherlands. The relative positions of these countries remained approximately the same until the World War. During 1911-15 Belgium was a little behind the Netherlands, but this was because the Belgian statistics give figures only down to 1913. During the next period, 1916-20, Germany ceased to be of any importance (0.9 per cent). The largest number of transients passed through ports in the British Isles (63.8 per cent). The Netherlands took second place with 23.7 and Belgium followed with 11.5 per cent.

During the post-War period the share of Belgium and the Netherlands was about the same (10 per cent) but the pre-War relation between the British Isles and Germany was inverted in favor of the former. There emigrated through the British Isles 61.3 per cent and only 18 per cent through Germany. The absolute figures show that the average number of emigrants through the ports of the British Isles during 1921-24 was half the number of those in 1906-10.

DIAGRAM 8

Intercontinental Emigration of Citizens, Percentage Distribution of the
Average Annual Emigration from Europe over the Various
Countries of Emigration from 1846 to 1924, in
Quinquennial Periods.

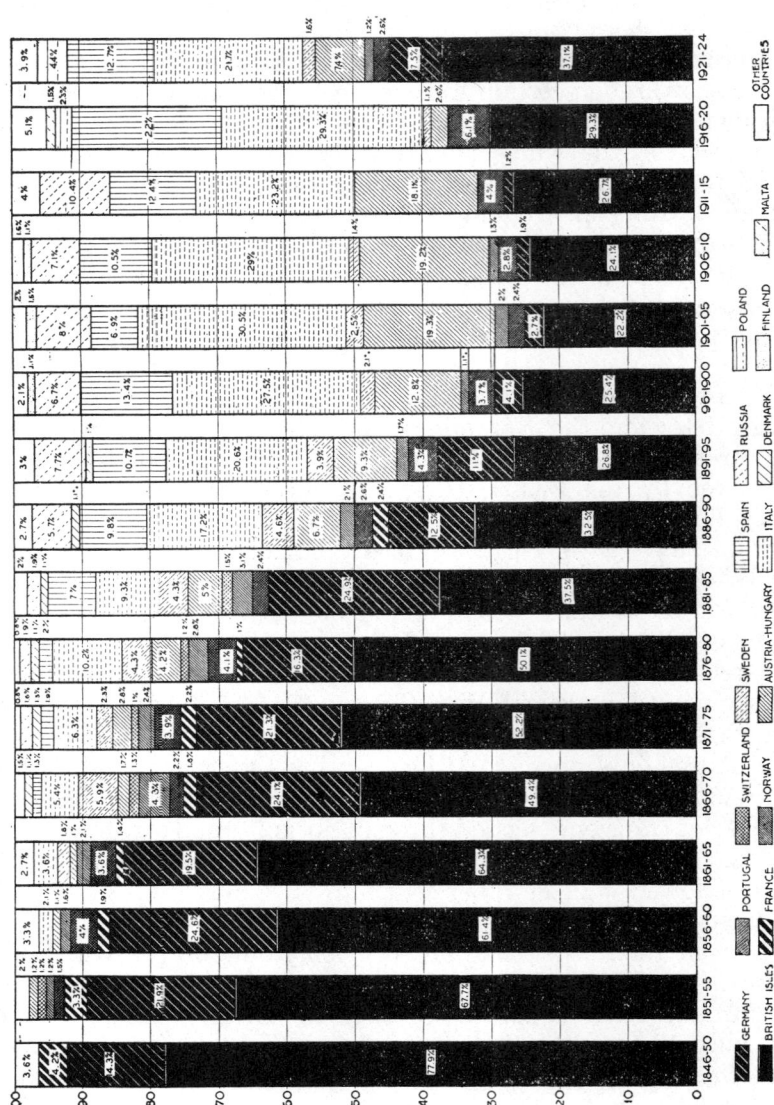

(d) Movement of Emigrants from the Most Important Countries of Emigration

With the aid of Diagrams 6 and 7 four periods in European pre-War emigration may be distinguished. The years 1820-40 showed a growth in British, German, and French emigration; during 1846-55 came the first crest in British (or Irish) emigration. At the same time oversea emigration from other northwestern European nations began to be of importance. The second crest of British and German emigration fell in the decade 1881 1890. Simultaneously, 'emigration from the Scandinavian countries, from France, and from Switzerland reached their crests, and emigration from southeastern Europe became of importance. Until the War emigration from Italy, Austria-Hungary, Russia, Portugal, Spain, Poland, and Finland increased; while emigration from northwestern Europe diminished.

Among the several emigration countries the British curve follows most closely the general European movement. Until 1876-80 the crests and troughs in the two curves practically coincide; German emigration, until the nineties, also followed the main curve. But the curves for the remaining countries deviate markedly from the curve of total emigration.

The following figures give the total number of oversea emigrants from Europe during the post-War period (in calendar years):[1]

1920	1921	1922	1923	1924
845,367	647,568	561,707	895,665	574,223

From these figures it appears that the outflow of emigrants diminished from 1920 to 1922, but reached the 1920 number again in 1923. From 1923 to 1924 there was a drop of over 300,000 emigrants, falling again nearly to the 1922 number.[2]

The emigration curves of the British Isles, Italy and Spain run almost parallel with the general curve, but the German curve turned upward from 1920 to 1923 (from 8,457 to 115,088), and dropped in 1924 (to 58,328). The Austro-Hungarian Succession States show scarcely any common tendencies, save that Austria and Czechoslovakia dip strongly. During the post-War period emigration from

[1]International Labour Office, *Migration Movements, 1920 to 1924*, Geneva, 1926, p. 9.

[2]This diminution is to be ascribed mainly to the new United States Immigration Act which came into force on July 1, 1924. The Act limits the number of citizens of each country to be admitted into the United States, to 2 per cent of the total number of citizens of that country resident in the United States in 1890.

three extra-European countries (India, China and Japan) to intercontinental destinations also fell.

International Table 2 and Diagram 8 show the share of the several countries in the aggregate European emigration 1846-50 to 1921-24. The shifting of the focus of emigration from western and northern European countries to eastern and southern European

DIAGRAM 9

Distribution of European Emigrant Citizens, by Countries of Future Residence, from 1891 to 1924

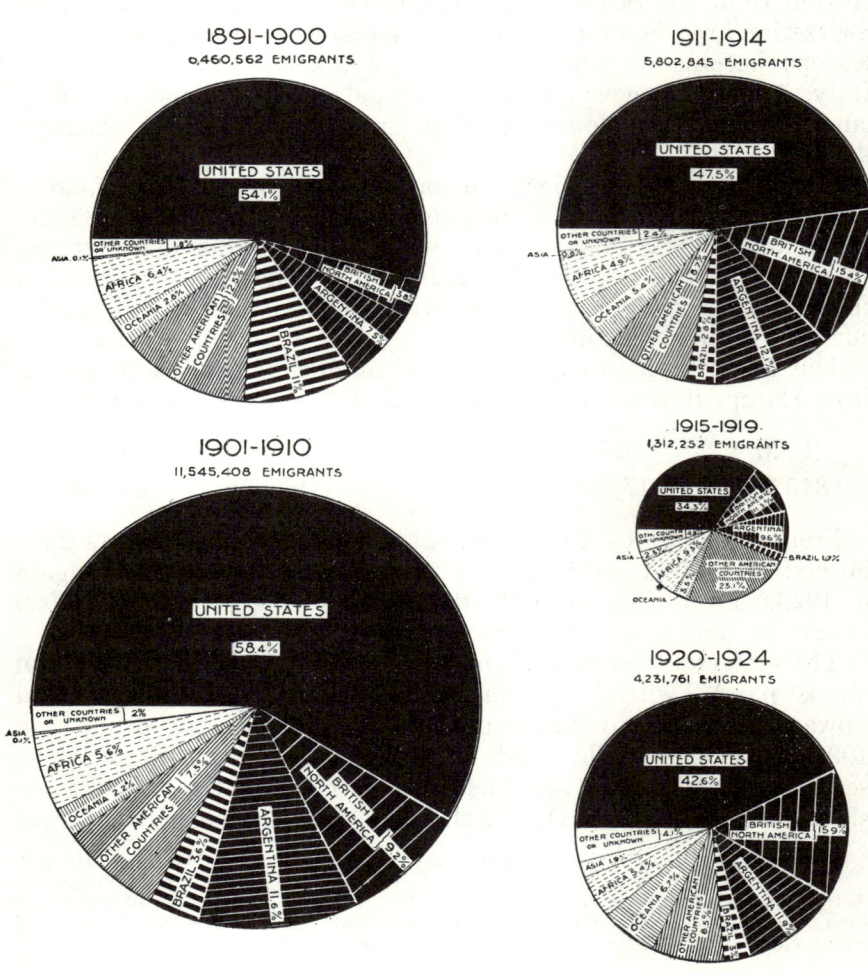

countries is presented in detail. In the initial stages of European emigration the United States was pre-eminently its goal.[1]

For the period starting with 1891 quinquennial totals have been compiled (Text Table 6) shown also in Diagram 9 for which approximately the same countries furnish figures. The years specially affected by the War, 1915-19, have been given separately thus clearly showing the distribution in the pre-War and post-War periods.

According to Text Table 6 and Diagram 9, America's share among the countries of future residence in the two decades 1891-1900 and 1901-10, was about nine-tenths, dropping slightly to 86.5 per cent in the four years 1911-14, going further down to 80 per cent during the War, and later recovering slightly.

Among American immigration countries the United States plays the most important part. Until 1910 they absorbed more than one-half of the European emigrants, 54.1 per cent in 1891-1900, and 58.4 per cent in 1901-1910. In the years immediately preceding the War its importance was slightly less (47.5 per cent) and during the War it dropped to 34.3 per cent. It rose during 1920-24 to 42.6 per cent, but the absolute number of emigrants during those five years went down to one-third of the four years 1911-1914. In the years following the War a downward tendency has been observable. In 1924 only one-fifth of the European emigrants went to the United States.

During the period here considered British North America and Argentina grew in importance. British North America figured for 1891-1900 at 3.8 per cent, and by 1911-14 mounted to 15.4 per cent, dropped during the War period, and during 1920-24 reached 15.9 per cent, a high figure principally due to increased emigration from the British Isles and Central Europe. Argentina was indicated, during 1891-1900, as future residence by 7.5 per cent of the emigrants. By 1911-14 this quota rose to 12.1 per cent, fell during the War period to 9.6 per cent, and rose again during the succeeding period to 11.9 per cent.

Brazil has lost in importance. During 1891-1900 its quota was 11.0 per cent. In the following decade, 1901-1910, it dropped to 3.6 per cent, and in 1911-14 to 2.8 per cent. A very slight gain to 3.0 per cent was registered for 1921-24.

[1]In Tables 11 and 12 the available data are given for the countries of future residence of European emigrants from 1866 onward. Seven countries or groups of countries of future residence are shown. These constitute the main immigration regions and are generally cited separately in the statistics of emigration. United States, British North America, Argentina, Brazil, other American countries, Australasia, Africa, Asia, Other countries or future residence unknown.

TEXT TABLE 6.

DISTRIBUTION OF EUROPEAN EMIGRANT CITIZENS BY COUNTRIES OF FUTURE RESIDENCE, FROM 1891 TO 1924.

Period	Countries of future residence									Total
	United States	British North America	Argentina	Brazil	Other American States	Oceania	Africa	Asia	Other countries or destination unknown	
	Absolute figures									
1891–1900	3,500,198	243,476	486,002	712,238	805,273	178,498	413,833	3,862	117,182	6,460,562
1901–1910	6,757,866	1,064,962	1,337,365	410,838	837,864	255,960	644,357	7,811	228,385	11,545,408
1911–1914	2,759,318	894,419	699,460	159,792	502,154	315,294	285,147	47,551	139,710	5,802,845
1915–1919	450,039	148,418	126,530	21,788	303,304	46,288	121,480	29,654	64,751	1,312,252
1920–1924	1,810,014	673,296	503,832	125,653	357,946	283,022	226,875	79,472	171,651	4,231,761
	Percentages									
1891–1900	54.1	3.8	7.5	11.0	12.5	2.8	6.4	0.1	1.8	100
1901–1910	58.4	9.2	11.6	3.6	7.3	2.2	5.6	0.1	2.0	100
1911–1914	47.5	15.4	12.1	2.8	8.7	5.4	4.9	0.8	2.4	100
1915–1919	34.3	11.3	9.6	1.7	23.1	3.5	9.3	2.3	4.9	100
1920–1924	42.7	15.9	11.9	3.0	8.5	6.7	5.4	1.9	4.1	100

The share of the "other American States" was about 8 per cent, except 1891-1900 when it was 12.5 per cent, and 1915-19 when it soared as high as 23.1 per cent. The extraordinary figure for the War years was due mainly to the large emigration from Spain to Cuba.

The extra-American countries of immigration have remained of comparatively minor importance, even in the post-War period. Nevertheless, Australasia and Asia have improved their position. Africa, apart from the increase during the War, has remained approximately on the same level.

Concerning the aggregate emigration from Europe during 1891-1924, it may be said that the share of the United States diminished after 1901-10, but that it has not lost its leading position. For 1891-1900 Brazil held the second place with 11 per cent and Argentina the third. Africa followed with 6.4 per cent and British North America with 3.8 per cent. The "other American States" were represented with 12.5 per cent, Australasia with 2.8 per cent, and Asia with as little as 0.1 per cent.

In the first five years of the post-War period British North America stood next to the United States with 15.9 per cent, Argentina followed with 11.9 per cent, Australasia with 6.7 per cent, Brazil with 3 per cent, "other American States" with 8.5 per cent, and Asia with 1.9 per cent.

In Text Table 7 and Diagram 10 a comparison has been made between emigration from European countries to the United States and immigration into the States from these countries. The first column under each country in the table shows the emigration reported by that country with the United States as its destination, and the second shows the immigration reported by the United States from that country. In the diagram the balance of the respective class of migrants is indicated by black spaces. The United States statistics are based on fiscal years, the European statistics on calendar years. Moreover, until 1898 the former records the immigrants according to country of origin or nationality and from 1899 according to country of last residence.

Norway shows the least difference in the comparison. Except for 1881-1895, the immigration statistics of the United States indicate a slightly larger current than do the statistics of Norway. The British statistics differ most from the American. For 1856-60 the United States figures are larger and thereafter smaller than those of Great Britain. Thus for 1891-95 British statistics indicate

DIAGRAM 10

Emigration from specified Country to the United States as reported by the specified country and by the United States (*i. e.* "immigration"), with excess of one figure over the other.

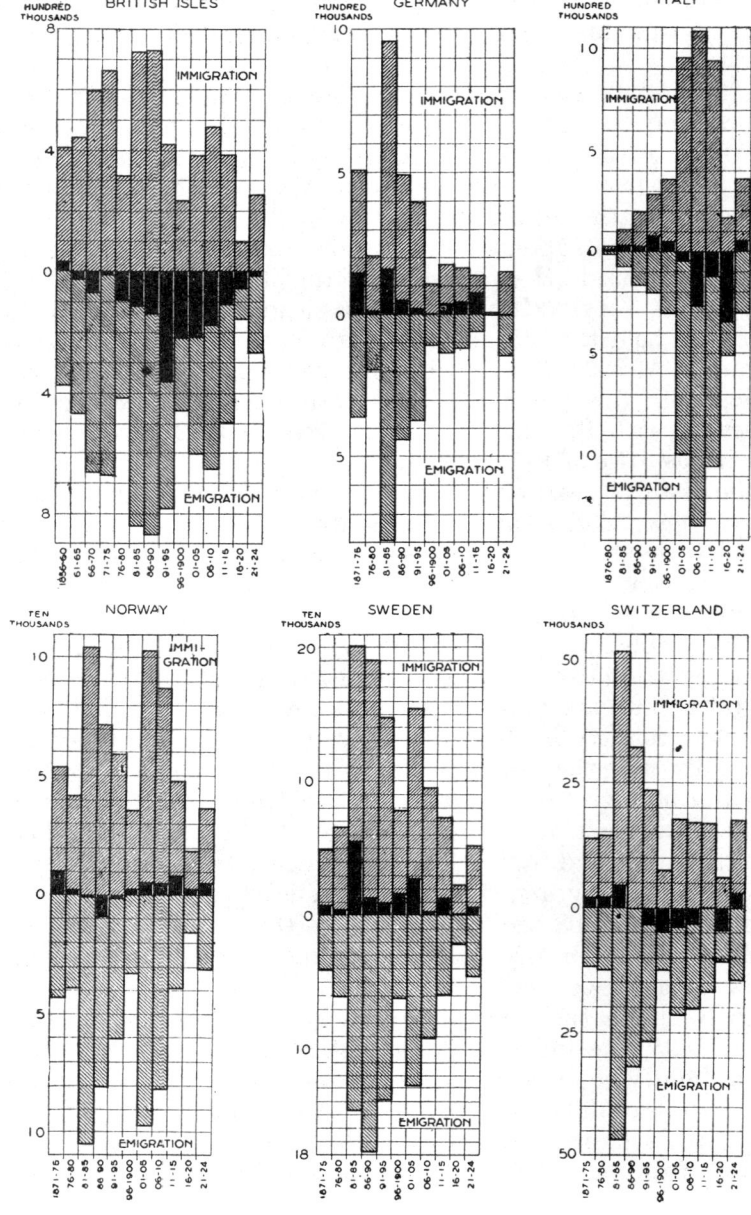

TEXT TABLE 7.

COMPARATIVE TABLE OF EMIGRATION AND IMMIGRATION STATISTICS CONCERNING MIGRATION BETWEEN CERTAIN COUNTRIES OF EUROPE AND THE UNITED STATES.

Year	British Isles		Germany		Italy		Norway		Sweden		Switzerland	
	Emigration	Immigration	Emigration	Immigration	Emigration	Immigration	Emigration	Immigration	Emigration	Immigration	Emigration	Immigration
1856–60	374,778	407,429										
1860–65	466,042	443,448										
1866–70	666,584	599,226										
1871–75	674,267	664,972	360,563	508,394			43,671	53,563	41,580[1]	49,751	11,976[2]	13,933
1876–80	413,105	319,942	195,303	209,788	13,235[3]	28,699	39,563	41,760	60,099[1]	66,171	12,396[2]	14,360
1881–85	842,547	730,035	797,019	960,020	74,758	109,504	105,633	104,534	146,744	201,444	46,977[2]	50,169
1886–90	871,406	732,804	440,117	492,950	170,472	197,805	80,665	72,052	177,835	190,332	31,958[2]	31,819
1891–95	685,886	422,564	371,506	397,640	206,596	288,235	60,497	59,100	138,995	148,082	26,879	23,585
1896–1900	460,018	237,390	107,424	107,512	307,731	363,658	33,090	35,915	61,568	78,184	12,424	7,594
1901–05	605,171	385,253	134,862	176,995	998,352	959,768	97,185	103,065	127,949	154,607	21,661	17,820
1906–10	653,842	479,762	120,311	164,503	1,331,099	1,086,109	81,512	87,440	91,300	94,927	20,279	17,102
1911–15	498,864	388,566	61,811	137,711	1,054,701	938,984	39,577	47,527	59,923	72,055	16,968	17,020
1916–20	159,886	99,023	1,939	6,234	512,081	170,540	15,891	18,868	21,614	23,019	10,817	6,071
1921–24	269,445	253,409	148,968	148,102	304,563	365,499	31,215	36,446	45,869	52,021	14,631	17,695

[1]Including a small number of emigrants to other American countries.
[2]North America.
[3]Including British North America, 1876-1878.

686,000 emigrants to the United States while the United States statistics record 422,000 British arriving. These differences are largely accounted for by the fact that the British statistics are of passengers and the United States statistics, after 1869, are of immigrants.

The European figures for Swedish and German emigration are throughout lower than the American. So far as Switzerland is concerned, the excess is sometimes in the Swiss and sometimes in the American figures. The differences for Germany, 1876-80 and 1891-1910, and for Switzerland 1886-90 are trifling. During the War the small emigration of Germans (1,939) to the United States was only through Switzerland.

For Italy the divergence is very great. During the period 1916-20, according to the passport statistics, 512,000 Italians received passports for the United States; but the latter country recorded only one-third as many or 171,000 Italian immigrants.

(e) Returning Emigrants; Net Emigration and Net Immigration; Migration in Relation to Population

The preceding analysis throws some light on European emigration to overseas countries. A balanced judgment, however, about the significance of this emigration can be reached only after examining the opposite form of migration, the number of emigrants returning, but only recently have data regarding them become available and for a few European countries of emigration (Table 9).[1] Of the more important immigration countries corresponding statistics exist only for New Zealand (since 1853), Argentina (since 1857), Australia (since 1904), and the United States (since 1908).

TEXT TABLE 8

TOTAL IMMIGRATION OF CITIZENS INTO EUROPEAN COUNTRIES (REPATRIATION), 1866-1924, IN QUINQUENNIAL AVERAGES[2]

1886–90	175,595
1891–95	220,875
1896–1900	269,013
1901–05	255,916
1906–10	400,572
1911–15	567,132
1916–20	223,973
1921–24	319,885

[1]During the quinquennial period 1876-80 only three countries, British Isles, Netherlands, and Sweden figure; in the following one Spain is added, and from 1886-90 Belgium and Italy are added. Later Finland and Hungary enter. For Spain and British Isles, the passengers, and not immigrants proper have been chosen for the total. The immigration curve in Diagram 5 is based on this total.

[2]To interpret these figures correctly, account should be taken of the hiatus in the Spanish statistics for 1901-10. As Spain contributed heavily to the totals in the other quinquennial periods, this gap appreciably affects the general curve.

From the above table it will be seen that the repatriation of citizens steadily mounted until it reached its peak in 1911-15. During the post-war period the number of remigrants was only a little over half (56 per cent) of the peak figure.

On comparing the general movement of citizens returning to their former European homes and European emigration, the two curves are found to differ. The immigration curve showed no downward bend during the quinquennial period 1896-1900, but before the War an upward tendency was common to the two.

In the different countries this immigration, as a rule, follows the curve of emigration. Especially noticeable is the volume of the re-migration movement to Spain, the British Isles, Italy and Hungary. For the remaining countries the figures are insignificant.

The average annual number of Spanish citizens who arrived in Spain as passengers from overseas countries rose from 36,999 for 1882-85 to 93,401 for 1896-99. During 1911-15 it was 138,783, and during 1921-24 it was 86,071.

The number of returning British passengers steadily rose from 1876-1880 to 1911-15, except for a slight set back during 1896-1900. In the interval the figure grew from 55,036 to 195,813. During the last period, that of 1921-24, the number of returning passengers averaged 156,390, of whom, however, only 66,673 were remigrants proper.

Italian remigration assumed even larger proportions, rising from an average of 31,194 during 1887-90 to 200,521 in 1906-10. For the following quinquennial period, 1911-15, it decreased a little, but during 1921-24 it fell far below the pre-War figures to 63,673.

Hungary has quinquennial figures for 1901-13. The average rose from 13,034 in 1901-1905 to 31,942 in the following quinquennial period, but fell to 24,519 in 1911-13. For this country, too, the return of citizens during the post-war period was insignificant.

It is not proposed to discuss here the causes of migration movements or their effects on population policy. All that is sought is as accurate an estimate as possible of their magnitude and a comparison of their relative volumes in the different countries. For this purpose the relation of emigration and immigration to population has been calculated from the decrease (number of emigrants per 100,000 inhabitants) or increase (number of immigrants and returning emigrants per 100,000 inhabitants) of the population.

In addition, a balance has been struck for the annual migration to or from countries which record not only intercontinental emi-

gration but also the repatriation of their citizens, by comparing the two figures of relative intensity calculated as above; the last part of Text Table 10 shows the net annual increase ($+$) or decrease ($-$) of the population per 100,000 inhabitants.

In Text Table 9 the annual emigration average per 100,000 inhabitants per decade is shown. For the period immediately preceding the World War the basis is the emigration figures for 1913. The emigration figures are derived from International Table 1.

The highest intensity of emigration was reached by Italy in 1913: 1,630 per 100,000 inhabitants. Then follow for the same year: Portugal with 1,296 passengers, Spain with 1,051 (of whom 757 were emigrants proper), and the British Isles with 1,035 (858 emigrants proper). The intensity was lowest for France, with 15; and Germany and the Netherlands with 40.

If these figures for 1913 are compared with those for 1881-90 and 1921-1924, considerable displacements will be observed. In the former period, leaving aside Ireland, Norway led with 952, followed by the British Isles (passengers) with 702 and Sweden with 701. Italy, Portugal, Spain and Denmark showed an intensity between 300 and 400, that of Germany being 287. The Belgian and French figures were negligible.

During 1921-24 apart from Malta with 767, the British Isles led with 607 passengers, of whom 432 were emigrants proper. Spain followed with 461 passengers, of whom 359 were emigrants proper, Norway with 357, and Portugal with 321. The lowest intensities were shown by France with 4, Belgium with 28, and the Netherlands with 52.

For the purpose of comprehending the movement of population in a country, it is more important to be acquainted with its gain or loss of population from migration than with the absolute or relative emigration figures. For this reason and on the basis of International Tables 1 and 9, the emigration and immigration figures of citizens for five countries (Sweden, Spain, Italy, British Isles, and Finland), for which comparable data are available, have been juxtaposed and the relation expressed in Diagram 11.[1]

[1]Tables 1 and 9 give figures also for Belgium and the Netherlands about migration in both directions. These have not been utilized for the diagram as they are in no way comparable (the basis for the emigration figures is port statistics, and that for the immigration figures communal registers statistics). Diagram 11 shows that for Spain (passengers) emigration is about balanced by remigration. Indeed, in the period 1896-1900, there was an excess of remigrants over emigrants pointing to the seasonal or temporary character of the emigration movement at that moment. Sweden and Finland show considerable emigration surpluses, remigration amounting sometimes to less than one-tenth of emigration. Italy and the British Isles have smaller emigration surpluses.

DIAGRAM 11

Intercontinental Emigration and Immigration of Citizens of Various
European Countries as Far as Figures for Both Movements
are Available in Quinquennial Averages.

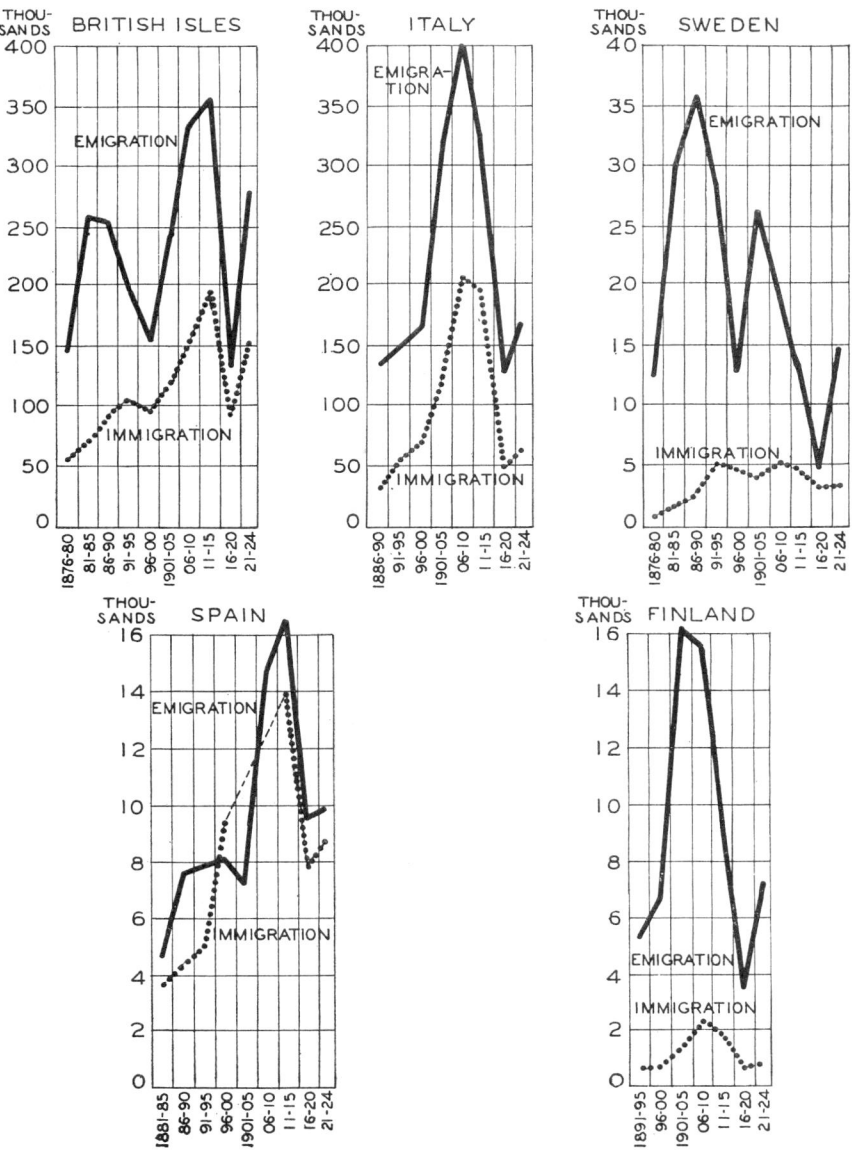

TEXT TABLE 9.

INTERCONTINENTAL EMIGRATION OF CITIZENS FROM EUROPEAN COUNTRIES, PER 100,000 INHABITANTS, 1851-1924.

Country	1851-1860 Mean population (thousands)	1851-1860 Avg annual emigration Absolute figures	1851-1860 per 100,000 inhabitants	1861-1870 Mean population (thousands)	1861-1870 Avg annual emigration Absolute figures	1861-1870 per 100,000 inhabitants	1871-1880 Mean population (thousands)	1871-1880 Avg annual emigration Absolute figures	1871-1880 per 100,000 inhabitants	1881-1890 Mean population (thousands)	1881-1890 Avg annual emigration Absolute figures	1881-1890 per 100,000 inhabitants
Austria-Hungary							38,052	11,122	29	40,957	43,572	106
Belgium										5,795	5,012	86
British Isles: Passengers	28,292	164,085¹	580	30,351	157,183	518	33,328	167,892	504	36,454	255,854	702
Denmark							1,877	3,860	206	2,071	8,162	394
France	36,039	3,893²	11	38,067	4,593	12	36,906	5,650	15	37,931	11,923	31
Germany							42,727	62,597	147	46,856	134,242	287
Ireland							5,294	35,009	661	4,940	69,992	1,417
Netherlands	3,183	1,584	50	3,444	2,047	59	3,796	1,749	46	4,262	5,244	123
Norway	1,490	3,607	242	1,702	9,795	576	1,807	8,539	473	1,961	18,669	952
Sweden	3,641	1,690	46	4,014	12,245	305	4,367	10,250	235	4,675	32,750	701
Switzerland							2,743	3,574	130	2,875	9,198⁴	320
Finland										2,220	2,941	132
Italy				4,193	7,976³	190	27,630	28,899	105	29,487	99,139	336
Portugal							4,533	13,107	289	4,875	18,536	380
Spain: Passengers										17,566	63,597⁴	362

¹1853-1860.
²1857-1860.
³1856-1870.
⁴1882-1890.

TEXT TABLE 9—continued

INTERCONTINENTAL EMIGRATION OF CITIZENS FROM EUROPEAN COUNTRIES, PER 100,000 INHABITANTS, 1851–1924.

Country	1891–1900 Mean population (thousands)	1891–1900 Absolute figures	1891–1900 per 100,000 inhabitants	1901–1910 Mean population (thousands)	1901–1910 Absolute figures	1901–1910 per 100,000 inhabitants	1913 Mean population (thousands)	1913 Absolute figures	1913 per 100,000 inhabitants	1921–1924 Mean population (thousands)	1921–1924 Absolute figures	1921–1924 per 100,000 inhabitants
Austria-Hungary	44,950	72,399	161	49,219	234,218	476	51,355	313,621	611	54,337	57,220	105
Belgium	6,381	2,205	35	7,059	4,321	61	7,424	7,590	102	7,466	2,078	28
British Isles: Passengers	39,745	174,279	438	43,490	284,146	653	45,371	469,640	1,035	47,359	287,517	607
Emigrants proper								389,394	858		204,426	432
Denmark	2,311	5,151	223	2,603	7,342	282	2,757	8,846	321	3,268	5,831	178
France	38,269	5,122	13	38,845	5,311	14	39,192	5,701	15	39,210	1,598	4
Germany	52,280	52,686	101	60,641	27,415	45	64,926	25,775	40	59,852	58,142	97
Ireland (Irish Free State)	4,582	40,557	885	4,425	30,888	698	4,390	29,818	679	4,439	13,248[6]	298
Netherlands	4,808	2,392	50	5,481	2,801	51	5,858	2,330	40	6,865	3,557	52
Norway	2,111	9,485	449	2,290	19,086	833	2,358	9,876	419	2,650	9,466	357
Sweden	4,961	20,451	412	5,329	22,404	420	5,522	17,224	312	5,904	12,457	211
Switzerland	3,117	4,408	141	3,534	4,907	139	3,753	6,191	165	3,880	6,265	161
Finland	2,546	5,905	232	2,914	15,883	545	3,115	20,057	644	3,365	7,056	210
Italy	31,495	157,959	502	33,573	361,520	1,077	34,671	564,971	1,630	38,756	167,887	433
Portugal	5,236	26,585	508	5,692	32,399	569	5,960	77,227	1,296	6,033	19,382[6]	321
Spain: Passengers	18,078	79,106	438	19,284	109,083	566	19,951	209,705	1,051	21,338	98,292[6]	461
Emigrants proper		.....	.....	.....	.....	.....		151,000	757		76,703	359
Malta		.....	.....	.....	.....	.....	212	1,568	740	225	1,725	767

5 1921 only.
6 1921-1923.

In Text Table 10 below the figures for intercontinental emigration and remigration, and the difference between them, that is, the migration intensity,[1] are given for the five countries which compile remigration statistics. In this connection continental migration has been left out of account.[2]

The years of most intense emigration also show the highest net loss in population. For instance, in the years of greatest emigration (1911-15 apart), 1881-85 and 1906-10, the British Isles showed emigration balances of 534 and 394 per 100,000 inhabitants, while during 1896-1900 when the emigration figures were relatively low there was an emigration balance of only 134 per 100,000 inhabitants. Sweden holds the record for net emigration with 702 per 100,000 for 1886-90. Then follows Italy, with 630 per 100,000 for 1901-1905, and Finland with 547 for the same quinquennial period.

In order to illustrate the comparative volume of returning aliens, or net immigration, the figures for the intercontinental emigrants and immigrants in Argentina, the United States, and Australia, have been given (see Tables 4 and 6).

From 1857 to 1924, Argentina received 5,481,276 persons and 2,562,790, or 46.8 per cent of them left the country. There was thus an excess of 2,918,486 immigrants, or 53.2 per cent. Until the outbreak of the War, emigration from Argentina rose almost without intermission, trebling both relatively and absolutely between 1901-1905 and 1911-1915; the years of greatest immigration (1886-90 and 1906-10) were also the years of greatest immigration balances. During the War the numbers emigrating exceeded those immigrating. In the post-War period, however, there was a net balance of some 100,000 immigrants (see Diagram 12 and Text Table 11, p. 206).

Since 1868 the United States statistics have recorded departing passengers, distinguishing the sex and the age of other than cabin

---

[1]The migration intensity has been calculated for quinquennial periods. The basis for calculating the intensity has been the population by the censuses taken at the close of each decade (e. g. population of 1880 for 1876-80 and 1881-85). The figures in the table do not accord with Diagram 11, for in the latter the data of the international tables have been utilized while in Table 10 only those years were taken into consideration for which there were both emigration and immigration figures. Spain shows how far these displacements may go. The Spanish mean emigration for 1911-15 was 27,476 above the mean remigration for 1914-15 (diagram), while for the middle of 1914 and 1915 remigration exceeded by 36,163 (table).

[2]Only Italy and Sweden compile continental migration statistics. Besides, continental migration, unlike intercontinental, seldom leads to a permanent loss of population.

DIAGRAM 12

Intercontinental Immigration and Emigration of Aliens
(United States, Australia and Argentina),
in Quinquennial Averages.

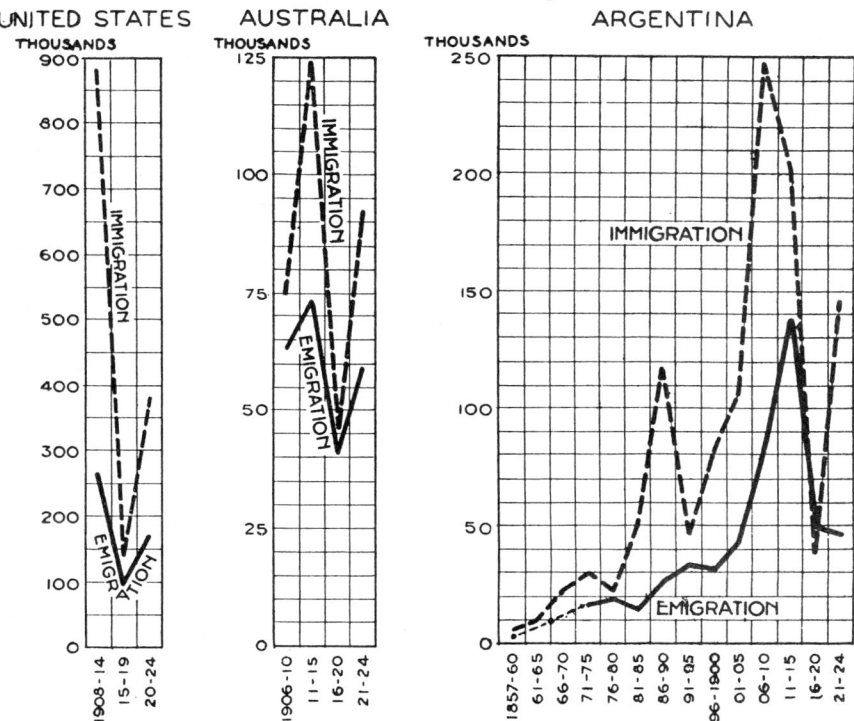

passengers, but emigrants proper have been distinguished only
since 1908.[1]

[1]On page 228 of the *Annual Report of the Commissioner General of Immigration* for
the fiscal year ended June 30, 1908 (Washington, 1908) is given an estimate of the total
alien departures and of the net immigration for the years 1899-1907. We reproduce
from that series the following figures:

Year	Net immigration (estimated)	Estimated ÷ Accepted immigration Per cent
1899	183,878	59
1900	307,856	69
1901	353,550	72
1902	510,695	79
1903	673,756	79
1904	508,695	63
1905	674,644	66
1906	810,096	74
1907	1,007,163	78

It should be noted that these data are not comparable with the above quoted figures
for the period 1908-1924, the one dealing with alien arrivals and departures, and the
other with the ratio between intercontinental immigrants and emigrants.

TEXT TABLE 10.

INTERCONTINENTAL EMIGRATION AND IMMIGRATION OF CITIZENS OF CERTAIN EUROPEAN COUNTRIES, WITH BALANCE, PER 100,000 INHABITANTS, 1876-1924.

1876-1880

Country	Absolute figures			Population 1880 (in thousands)	Annual averages, per 100,000 inhabitants		
	Emigration	Immigration	Balance		Emigration	Immigration	Balance
British Isles: Passengers	141,876	55,036	86,840	35,026	405	157	248
Sweden	12,089	578	11,511	4,566	265	13	252
Spain: Passengers	.....	.....	.....	16,634	...	...	...

1881-1885

Country	Absolute figures			Annual averages, per 100,000 inhabitants		
	Emigration	Immigration	Balance	Emigration	Immigration	Balance
British Isles: Passengers	258,462	71,609	186,853	738	204	534
Sweden	29,524	1,434	28,090	647	32	615
Spain: Passengers	47,892[1]	36,999[1]	10,893	288	222	66

1886-1890

Country	Absolute figures			Population 1890 (in thousands)	Annual averages, per 100,000 inhabitants		
	Emigration	Immigration	Balance		Emigration	Immigration	Balance
British Isles: Passengers	253,245	94,433	158,812	37,881	668	249	419
Sweden	35,977	2,406	33,571	4,785	752	50	702
Finland	.....	.....	.....	2,380	...	...	...
Italy	145,938[2]	31,194[2]	114,744	30,515	478	102	376
Spain: Passengers	76,161	44,338	31,823	17,566	434	253	181

1891-1895

Country	Absolute figures			Annual averages, per 100,000 inhabitants		
	Emigration	Immigration	Balance	Emigration	Immigration	Balance
British Isles: Passengers	195,715	106,133	89,582	517	280	237
Sweden	28,376	5,063	23,313	593	106	487
Finland	2,700[3]	638[3]	2,062	114	27	87
Italy	150,226	55,045	95,181	492	180	312
Spain: Passengers	77,904	50,776	27,128	443	289	154

1896-1900

Country	Absolute figures			Population 1900 (in thousands)	Annual averages, per 100,000 inhabitants		
	Emigration	Immigration	Balance		Emigration	Immigration	Balance
British Isles: Passengers	152,843	97,219	55,624	41,609	367	233	134
Sweden	12,327	4,561	7,966	5,136	244	89	155
Finland	6,608	699	5,909	2,713	244	26	218
Italy	165,692	68,840	96,852	32,475	510	212	298
Spain: Passengers	85,569[4]	93,401[4]	-7,832	18,618	460	502	-42

1901-1905

Country	Absolute figures			Annual averages, per 100,000 inhabitants		
	Emigration	Immigration	Balance	Emigration	Immigration	Balance
British Isles: Passengers	234,168	116,804	117,364	563	281	282
Sweden	25,949	3,891	22,058	505	76	429
Finland	16,211	1,362	14,849	597	50	547
Italy	320,604	115,831	204,773	987	357	630
Spain: Passengers	.....	.....	.....	...	...	...

TEXT TABLE 10 continued

INTERCONTINENTAL EMIGRATION AND IMMIGRATION OF CITIZENS OF CERTAIN EUROPEAN COUNTRIES, WITH BALANCE, PER 100,000 INHABITANTS, 1876-1924.

Country	1906–1910 Absolute figures Emigration	Immigration	Balance	1906–1910 Annual averages per 100,000 Emigration	Immigration	Balance	Population 1910 (in thousands)	1911–1915 Absolute figures Emigration	Immigration	Balance	1911–1915 Annual averages per 100,000 Emigration	Immigration	Balance
British Isles:													
Passengers	334,125	155,261	178,864	736	342	394	45,371	357,991	195,813	162,178	789	432	357
Emigrants proper								268,842[5]	91,264[5]	177,578	592	201	391
Sweden	18,859	5,107	13,752	342	93	249	5,522	12,672	4,549	8,123	229	82	147
Finland	15,555	2,362	13,193	499	76	423	3,115	10,134	1,794	8,340	325	57	268
Italy	402,436	200,521	201,915	1,160	578	582	34,671	312,246	195,614	116,632	900	564	336
Spain: Passengers	...	...	...	...	...	...	19,951	102,620[6]	138,783[6]	—36,163	514	695	—181

Country	1916–1920 Absolute figures Emigration	Immigration	Balance	1916–1920 Annual averages per 100,000 Emigration	Immigration	Balance	Population 1920 (in thousands)	1921–1924 Absolute figures Emigration	Immigration	Balance	1921–1924 Annual averages per 100,000 Emigration	Immigration	Balance
British Isles													
Passengers	129,484	90,878	38,606	273	192	81	47,359	287,517	156,390	131,127	607	330	277
Emigrants proper	101,118	51,607	49,511	214	109	105		204,426	66,673	137,753	432	141	291
Sweden	4,532	3,288	1,244	77	56	21	5,904	12,457	3,204	9,253	211	54	157
Finland	3,336	664	2,672	99	20	79	3,365	7,056	723	6,333	210	22	188
Italy	126,572	46,656	79,916	326	120	206	38,756	167,887	63,673	104,214	433	164	269
Spain: Passengers	94,901	77,180	17,721	445	362	83	21,338	98,292[7]	86,071[7]	12,221	460	403	57
Emigrants proper	69,101	41,248	27,853	324	193	131		76,703	47,673	29,030	359	223	136

[1] 1882–1885.
[2] 1887–1890.
[3] 1894–1895.
[4] 1896–1899.
[5] 1911–1913.
[6] 1914–1915.
[7] 1921–1923.

TEXT TABLE 11

ARGENTINA.

INTERCONTINENTAL IMMIGRATION AND EMIGRATION OF ALIENS INTO AND FROM ARGENTINA

Quinquennial averages from 1857 to 1924

Period	Immigration	Emigration
1857–1860	5,000	2,225
1861–1865	9,375	
1866–1870	22,539	8,298
1871–1875	29,739	16,999
1876–1880	22,438	18,154
1881–1885	51,037	13,927
1886–1890	117,187	26,764
1891–1895	47,250	33,861
1896–1900	82,415	31,828
1901–1905	105,206	43,131
1906–1910	247,615	85,645
1911–1915	202,367	137,588
1916–1920	38,617	49,577
1921–1924	145,588	45,887

The immigration and emigration figures for aliens were as follows for 1908-1924:

		Per cent
Immigrants	1,400,358	100.0
Emigrants	526,178	37.7
Net immigration	874,180	62.3

As shown by Text Table 12 and the accompanying Diagram 12, the net immigration, 1908-1914, was very high (621,265, or 70.4 per cent). During the War period 1915-1919, however, it was exceedingly low (43,884, or 31.5 per cent), rising to a certain extent during 1920-24 (209,031, or 55.2 per cent.)

The different national stocks differ widely in the balance between immigration into and emigration from the United States. In the *Monthly Labor Review* (January 1924, p. 13) is given a table of "immigration and emigration and net gain or loss, 1908 to 1923, by race." During these 16 years the total alien emigration, including continental, was 35.2 per cent of the immigration. The largest proportion of emigrants was among the Chinese, of whom 30 per cent more emigrated than immigrated. The percentage of emigrants in relation to immigrants was over 50 per cent in the following stocks: Bulgarians, Serbians and Montenegrins, 89 per cent, Tur-

kish, 86 per cent; Koreans, 73 per cent; Roumanians, 66 per cent; Magyars, 66 per cent; Italians (South), 60 per cent; Cubans, 58 per cent; Slovaks, 57 per cent, and Russians, 52 per cent. Moderate remigration (under 30 per cent) is shown by the following stocks: Hebrews, 5 per cent; Irish, 11 per cent; Scotch and Welsh, 13 per cent; Armenians, 15 per cent; Dutch and Flemish, 18 per cent; Mexican, 19 per cent; English, 21 per cent; French, 21 per cent; African, 22 per cent; Scandinavian, 22 per cent; Syrian, 24 per cent; Lithuanian, 25 per cent; and Finnish, 29 per cent.

TEXT TABLE 12

UNITED STATES

INTERCONTINENTAL IMMIGRATION AND EMIGRATION OF ALIENS INTO AND FROM UNITED STATES.

Averages from 1908-1914, 1915-1919, 1920-1924.

Periods	Immigration	Emigration
1908–1914	882,702	261,437
1915–1919	139,261	95,377
1920–1924	378,395	169,364

Among the other peoples remigration amounts to between 30 and 50 per cent. For Australia a special series of comparable immigration and emigration figures have been compiled from which the mean values of Text Table 13 and of Diagram 12 have been taken. The immigration and emigration curves follow the same direction, but the years of highest gross are also those of highest net immigration.

The summary for the years 1906-1924 gives the following figures:

Immigration	1,597,673	100 per cent
Emigration	1,119,099	70 per cent
Net immigration	478,574	30 per cent

The small net immigration indicates that much of this current consists of ordinary passengers.

* * *

Inasmuch as European emigrants go principally to a few immigration countries in America, most of which have a small population, it is clear that the intensity of immigration or the ratio of immi-

DIAGRAM 13

Distribution of Alien Immigrants to the United States by Sex from
1831 to 1924, in Quinquennial Averages.

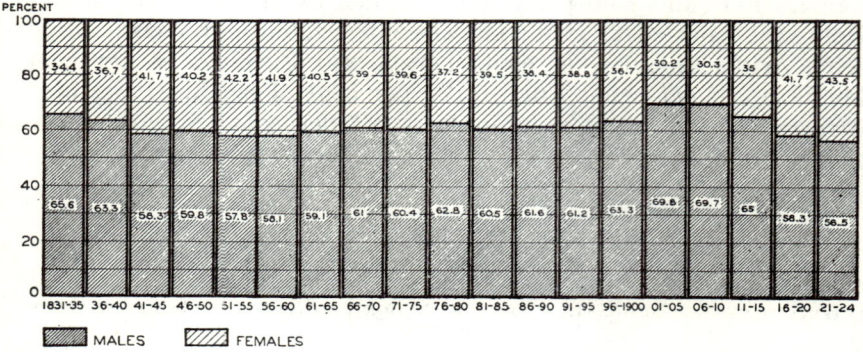

grants to population—is greater in them than the intensity of emigration is in the countries of emigration.   Text Table 14 shows that
among the American countries of immigration (Canada, United
States, Cuba, Argentina and Brazil) the United States occupies an
intermediate position.   In the twenties and thirties of the nine-

TEXT TABLE 13

AUSTRALIA.

INTERCONTINENTAL IMMIGRATION AND EMIGRATION OF ALIEN PASSENGERS
INTO AND FROM AUSTRALIA

Quinquennial averages from 1906 to 1924.

Periods	Immigration	Emigration
1906–1910	74,207	62,751
1911–1915	124,859	73,022
1916–1920	46,690	41,504
1921–1924	92,224	58,179

teenth century the stream of immigrants was small, and when in
the fifties some 250,000 intercontinental immigrants arrived annually, the population was relatively high (some 25,000,000).   At all
events, immigration increased in a greater ratio than population.
During the above period, 1820-1850, the population increased in
the ratio of 1 to 2½, and the immigration (between the decades
1821-1830 and 1851-1860) in the ratio of 1 to 19, while the intensity

TEXT TABLE 14.

INTERCONTINENTAL IMMIGRATION OF ALIENS INTO CERTAIN AMERICAN COUNTRIES, PER 100,000 INHABITANTS, 1821–1924.

Country	1821–1830 Mean population (in thousands)	1821–1830 Average annual immigration Absolute figures	per 100,000 inhabitants	1831–1840 Mean population (in thousands)	Absolute figures	per 100,000 inhabitants	1841–1850 Mean population (in thousands)	Absolute figures	per 100,000 inhabitants	1851–1860 Mean population (in thousands)	Absolute figures	per 100,000 inhabitants
Canada	.....	.....	.....	.....	.....	.....	.....	.....	.....	2,800	27,768	992
United States	11,252	13,635	121	14,968	56,478	377	20,131	166,826	829	27,318	253,583	928
Argentina	.....	.....	.....	.....	.....	.....	.....	.....	.....	.....	5,000[1]	385

Country	1861–1870 Mean population (in thousands)	1861–1870 Average annual immigration Absolute figures	per 100,000 inhabitants	1871–1880 Mean population (in thousands)	Absolute figures	per 100,000 inhabitants	1881–1890 Mean population (in thousands)	Absolute figures	per 100,000 inhabitants	1891–1900 Mean population (in thousands)	Absolute figures	per 100,000 inhabitants
Canada	3,445	28,331	832	4,007	21,978	548	4,579	35,920	784	5,102	24,923	488
United States	35,001	227,238	649	44,357	242,376	546	56,552	485,190	858	69,471	368,352	530
Argentina	1,610	15,957	991	2,230	26,089	1,170	3,794	84,112	2,217	3,955	64,833	1,639
Brazil	.....	.....	.....	10,788	21,913	204	12,903	53,091	411	15,826	114,390	723

Country	1901–1910 Mean population (in thousands)	1901–1910 Average annual immigration Absolute figures	per 100,000 inhabitants	1913 Population 1910 (in thousands)	1913 Immigration Absolute figures	per 100,000 inhabitants	1921–1924 Population 1920 (in thousands)	1921–1924 Average annual immigration Absolute figures	per 100,000 inhabitants
Canada	6,289	105,375	1,676	7,207	276,731	3,840	8,788	82,701	941
United States	83,983	856,652	1,020	91,972	1,117,727	1,215	105,711	349,623	331
Cuba	2,049	24,260	1,184	2,150	33,129	1,541	2,889	39,236	1,358
Argentina	6,046	176,410	2,918	7,885	302,047	3,831	9,548	145,588	1,525
Brazil	20,366	68,912	338	24,618	189,790	771	30,636	60,306	197

[1]1857–1860.

rose from 121 in the third decade to 928 in the sixth. In the succeeding 20 years immigration slightly abated, but the intensity fell
to 546 in 1871-1880, rose again to 858 in 1881-1890, only to sink to
530 during 1891-1900. After the opening of the new century the
figure exceeded 1,000, or 1 per cent, but in 1914 it had mounted to
1,215. In 1921-24 the intensity of immigration was equivalent
to only 331 persons per 100,000 inhabitants.

Aside from 1857-1860, Argentina has had the largest number of
immigrants in proportion to population;[1] 2,217 for 1881-1890
and 3,831 for 1913. Canada occupies, as a rule, a higher place than
the United States; Cuba also stands high (always above 1,000);
Brazil, on the contrary, always has had a low ratio.

2 Sex and Age

In temporary emigration, the proportion of females is regularly
very small. Frequently men seek a future in foreign countries,
leaving their families to follow later. Sometimes also single women
emigrate with the hope of marrying or of earning a living more
easily overseas.

The conditions of sex and age in the migration movement as a
whole can best be investigated by using the statistics of the extra-
European countries of immigration. For this purpose the United
States is the best since the majority of emigrants go there and its
statistics were established early. The distribution of emigration to
the United States according to sex since 1831 has been specially
shown in Text Table 15 and in Diagram 13.[2]

In all years the males were more numerous. In twelve of the
nineteen quinquennial periods the proportion of males exceeded 60
per cent. In the first period it was 65.6 per cent and in the second
slightly smaller. It then varied, from 1841-45 to 1891-95, between
57.8 per cent and 62.8 per cent. Between 1881-85 and 1901-05 the
proportion increased continuously from 60.5 per cent to 69.8 per
cent and remained at about the same height in 1906-10. The years
of greatest immigration show the largest proportion of males. Since
1906-10 the percentage has decreased. It appears from Diagram 4
that this development is closely connected with the proportion of
immigrants from the northwest and the southeast of Europe. The

[1]According to the table, the intensity in Canada was higher in 1913; but it should
be noted that for Argentina the basis is the population in 1914 and for Canada the
population in 1911.

[2]The year 1831 has been taken as the starting point because in the first ten years
the statistics of sex were very incomplete.

years 1921-24 are characterized by the nearest approach to equality in the numbers of the sexes; only 66.5 per cent of these immigrants came directly from Europe, as compared with 92.4 per cent in the years 1891-1915.

Immigrants to Argentina show a larger proportion of males than those to the United States. The figure varied between 80.5 in 1857-60 and 63.1 in 1916-20. Apart from the years of the War, the minimum was 67.4 per cent in 1891-95, whereas to the United States the maximum was 69.8 per cent. In most years the proportion of males lay between 70 per cent and 80 per cent; in only four of the fourteen periods did it fall below 70 per cent. The preponderant Italian and Spanish immigration, part of it seasonal, shows a considerable excess of males.

In the Cuban statistics (available since 1901) the immigration shows a very uneven sex distribution. The proportion of males has always been over 80 per cent and in 1916-20 it rose to 89.6 per cent (861 males to 100 females); the immigration is principally Spanish.

New Zealand is an example of a change in the proportion of the sexes resulting from deliberate family policy. In the earlier years

TEXT TABLE 15

DISTRIBUTION OF ALIEN IMMIGRANTS (UNITED STATES) BY SEX, FROM 1831 TO 1924 IN QUINQUENNIAL AVERAGES.

Years	Numbers			Percentage	
	Total	Males	Females	Males	Females
1831–35	248,214	162,734	85,480	65.6	34.4
1836–40	341,139	215,991	125,148	63.3	36.7
1841–45	428,535	249,874	178,661	58.3	41.7
1846–50	1,278,850	764,322	514,528	59.8	40.2
1851–55	1,746,845	1,009,092	737,753	57.8	42.2
1856–60[1]	649,354	377,283	272,071	58.1	41.9
1861–65	801,680	477,382	324,298	59.5	40.5
1866–70	1,644,948	1,003,264	641,684	61.0	39.0
1871–75	1,659,278	1,001,561	657,717	60.4	39.6
1876–80	1,285,432	806,667	478,765	62.8	37.2
1881–85	2,832,342	1,714,246	1,118,096	60.5	39.5
1886–90	2,361,795	1,455,591	906,204	61.6	38.4
1891–95	2,208,026	1,350,823	857,203	61.2	38.8
1896–1900	1,596,193	1,011,013	585,180	63.3	36.7
1901–05	4,061,932	2,834,315	1,227,617	69.8	30.2
1906–10	4,988,311	3,474,747	1,513,564	69.7	30.3
1911–15	4,143,396	2,691,732	1,451,664	65.0	35.0
1916–20	1,580,562	921,040	659,522	58.3	41.7
1921–24	2,050,892	1,158,188	892,704	56.5	43.5

[1]1857-60.

there was an excess of males: 75.6 per cent in 1861-65; 70.3 per cent in 1866-70. The ratio then varied until 1910 between 61.4 per cent in 1871-75 and 67.5 per cent in 1901-05. Since 1911 it has been under 60 per cent and decreasing; 59.3 per cent in 1911-15, 53.7 per cent in 1921-24. These figures include all intercontinental passengers and thus non-immigrants. The situation in Australia is similar to that in New Zealand. During the War the figures were considerably affected by the influx of military personnel (81.3 per cent males in 1916-20 and 60.9 per cent in 1921-24).

The statistics of Mauritius are for East Indian immigration, and owing to the partly temporary nature of the movement, the females are slightly more represented.

Discussion of the age of immigrants also may begin with the United States.[1] The proportion of children under 15 varied greatly before 1865; 5.2 per cent from 1821-25; 21.4 per cent to 27.4 per cent from 1826-30 to 1851-55; 18.5 per cent and 18.4 per cent in 1856-60 and 1861-65. From 1868 to 1895 (see Text Table 16 and Diagram 14)[2] the proportion of children (under 15) varied between 23.0 per cent and 13.9 per cent; from 1901 to 1915 (under 14) between 12.0 per cent and 13.2 per cent. During 1916-20 and 1921-24 the percentage rose to 17.6 and 18.5, partly because from 1918 on the figures include all persons under 16 years of age, but also because of the increased immigration of families, resulting from economic conditions and "quota" legislation.

The group between 15 and 40 years of age has varied, from 1868 to 1895, between 64.6 per cent in 1871-75 and 79.3 per cent in 1891-95. During these years it increased while both the other groups decreased. From 1901 to 1915 (14 to 44) it varied between 83.4 per cent and 80.9 per cent. From 1916-20 to 1921-24 (16 to 44 after 1918) the proportions are 71.8 per cent and 72.3 per cent. For persons over 40 years of age the maximum between 1868 and 1895 was 13.7 per cent in 1871-73, and the minimum 6.8 per cent in 1891-95; the maximum for immigrants 45 years of age and over between 1901 and 1924 was 10.6 in 1916-20, and the minimum 4.6 per cent in 1906-10. A comparison of changes in the two extreme groups shows a parallel development, although the variations are

[1]National Table VII shows the ages of immigrants in three groups from 1820 to 1924. Until 1867 the figures refer to all passengers including citizens of the United States, and until 1866 the age of a large number of passengers is not given. After 1841 these figures are contained in Tables 23 and 24.

[2]The age groups are not always the same (see footnotes to Text Table 16). The figures given here therefore are not altogether comparable.

DIAGRAM 14

Immigrants in Three Age Categories as Percentage of all Alien Immigrants to the United States from 1868 to 1924, in Quinquennial Averages.

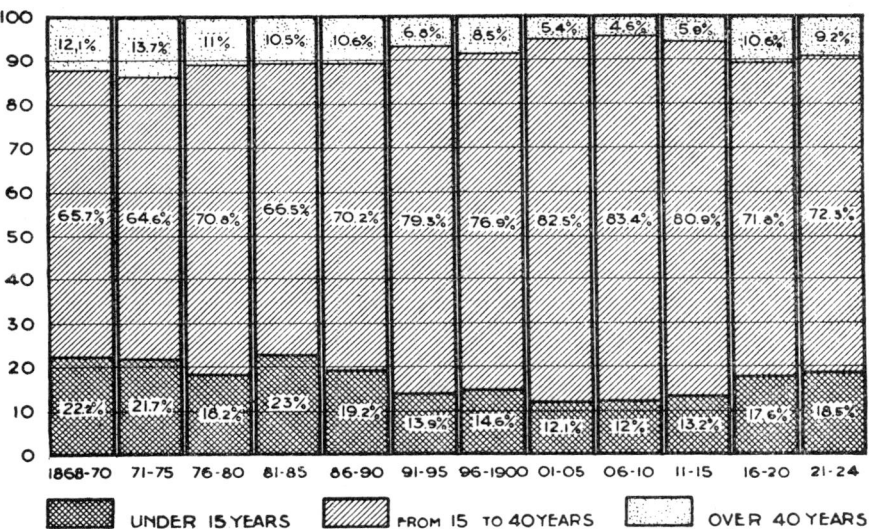

partly due to alteration in the limits of the groups. When Diagrams 13 and 14 are compared a certain parallelism between the age data and the sex data becomes apparent. A high proportion of young persons involves, as a rule, a high proportion of older persons and a high proportion of families. This parallelism cannot be clearly demonstrated for all periods, but roughly speaking it appears to hold. It indicates that at certain times there is a larger immigration of families than at other times. This also depends on the contribution of the different nations or territories of emigration to the general movement.

The Argentina statistics show the ages of immigrants by 10-year periods. In National Table II the absolute figures for eight age groups are given. In the international table only children under 13 are distinguished. The proportion of children from 1857 to 1924 varies between 17.4 per cent in 1857-60 and 7.6 per cent in 1861-70. Here, as in the United States, there is a decreasing proportion of child immigrants. Compared with the United States, the proportion of child immigrants appears to be higher. From 1901 to 1910 there

TEXT TABLE 16

ALIEN IMMIGRANTS TO THE UNITED STATES, CLASSED BY AGES, 1868 TO 1924.

Years	Numbers				Percentage		
	Total	Under 15 Years	15–40 Years	Over 40 Years	Under 15 Years	15–40 Years	Over 40 Years
1868–70	1,022,160	226,569	671,721	123,870	22.2	65.7	12.1
1871–75	1,726,796	374,162	1,116,312	236,322	21.7	64.6	13.7
1876–80	1,085,395	197,622	768,431	119,342	18.2	70.8	11.0
1881–85	2,975,683	684,808	1,978,701	312,174	23.0	66.5	10.5
1886–90	2,270,930	436,691	1,593,572	240,667	19.2	70.2	10.6
1891–95	2,280,735	317,482	1,809,088	154,165	13.9	79.3	6.8
1896–1900[1]	1,563,685	228,242	1,203,174	132,269	14.6	76.9	8.5
1901–05[1]	3,833,076	462,874	3,162,397	207,805	12.1	82.5	5.4
1906–10[1]	4,962,310	595,667	4,138,583	228,060	12.0	83.4	4.6
1911–15[1]	4,459,831	590,298	3,605,708	263,825	13.2	80.9	5.9
1916–20[2]	1,275,980	224,149	916,465	135,366	17.6	71.8	10.6
1921–24[2]	2,344,599	434,403	1,695,877	214,319	18.5	72.3	9.2

[1]Age groups during 1899-1917: under 14 years, 14 to 44 years, 45 years and over.
[2]Age groups during 1918-1924: under 16 years, 16 to 44 years, 45 years and over.

were 12.1 per cent and 12 per cent of children under 14 among the immigrants to the United States, and 15.9 per cent of children under 13 among the immigrants to Argentina.

In Australia immigrants under 12 are shown from 1904-1915. The proportion varies between 8.3 per cent and 13.3 per cent.

Finally Uruguay[3] calls for mention. Among the child immigrants before 1900 there were usually more boys than girls, e.g. in 1881-85 there are 7.6 per cent of boys and 3.9 per cent of girls, and in 1886-90 5.8 per cent boys and 2.8 per cent girls. Since the age limit is 15, this situation shows that some boys under 15 immigrated for the purpose of earning a living.

*   *   *

According to emigration statistics differences appear in the distribution by sex of citizen emigrants in different countries at the same period and the same country at different periods. With few exceptions the national statistics show a preponderance of males among emigrants. A very high percentage of males appears among the Portuguese and Italians. In Portugal, up to 1910, it varied between 72.6 per cent and 87.2 per cent; in Italy up to 1915 between 77.1 per cent and 85.3 per cent. In 1916-20 it decreased to 66.2 per cent in Italy and to 66.4 per cent in Portugal, but in 1921-

[3]The statistics include all passengers, both citizens and aliens.

24 it was higher again. It should be noted, however, that during this last period continental emigration was not included in the Italian statistics. In both countries the extraordinary excess of males is due to temporary emigration. British India and France, and in certain periods Japan, also show a large excess of males among emigrants.

In other countries the proportion of males varies between 51.0 per cent and 60 0 per cent, *i. e.* between 104 and 150 male to 100 female emigrants. At all periods for which figures are given in the tables the proportion of the sexes remains within these limits for Germany, Austria, and the British Isles and, for the most part, also for Norway.

An excess of females appears at certain periods in the emigration from Ireland, Sweden and Finland: in 1896-1900, from Ireland 54.7 per cent, Sweden 52.6 per cent females; in 1916-20, Ireland 64.7 per cent, Sweden 55.8 per cent, Finland 52.7 per cent females.

The age limits for children and young persons and adults are not the same in all countries and a precise comparison of the different countries is therefore impossible. Among emigrants from Finland, Ireland, and Italy, the proportion of adults is noticeably high. It varies in Finland (limit 16 years) between 84.1 per cent and 92.9 per cent; in Ireland (15 years) between 82.0 per cent and 92.4 per cent; in Italy (15 years) between 84.0 per cent and 90.7 per cent. Here also the cause is the return of many emigrants to their mother country. Emigrants from most countries show 80 per cent to 85 per cent adults. The large proportion of young persons in Austrian emigration up to 1880 is probably due to the high limit (17 years). A relatively large number of children emigrated from Norway and Denmark (20 per cent to 25 per cent), and in some periods from Germany (26.3 per cent to 23.9 per cent in 1881 to 1895).

It appears from these figures that among children and young persons the males slightly predominate. The great excess of males in the total figures is due to the numerical relation of the sexes among adults. With the exception of Ireland, Finland, and Sweden, the adult emigrants include more men than women, the proportion in many cases being 2 to 1, and in Finland 1886-1890, reaching 8 to 1.

3 Occupations

The occupations of immigrants are shown in the statistics of a few extra-European countries of immigration. The United States and Argentina show the distribution by occupations from the beginning

DIAGRAM 15

Distribution of Alien Immigrants (United States), by
Occupations, from 1821 to 1924.

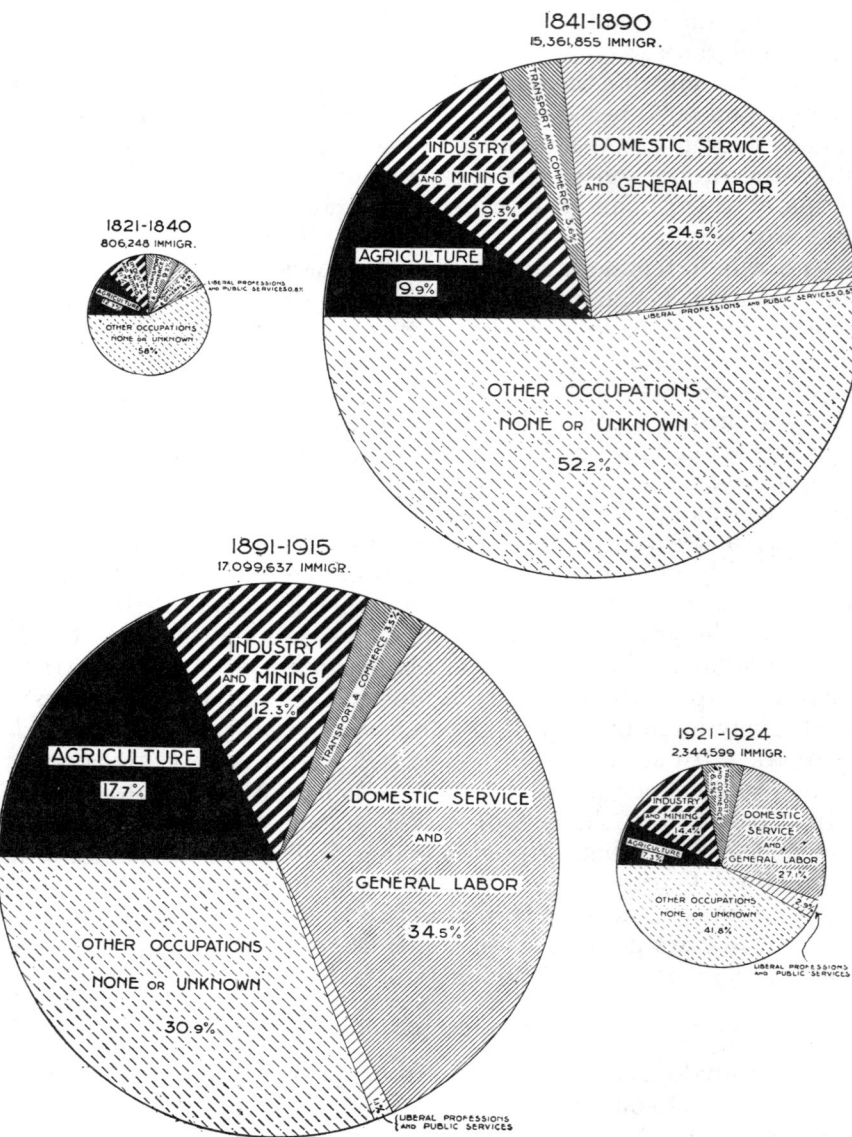

1841-1890
15,361,855 IMMIGR.

1821-1840
806,248 IMMIGR.

1891-1915
17,099,637 IMMIGR.

1921-1924
2,344,599 IMMIGR.

of their statistics (1820 and 1857 respectively). The same practice was later introduced in Uruguay, the Philippines and Cuba.[1] Only the United States and Argentina are of importance for this purpose; their data on occupations are shown only for decennial periods. Text Table 17 and Diagram 15 show the occupations of alien immigrants to the United States both absolutely and relatively during the four principal periods: 1821-40, 1841-90, 1891-1915, 1921-24.

TEXT TABLE 17

DISTRIBUTION OF ALIEN IMMIGRANTS TO THE UNITED STATES, BY OCCUPATIONS, FROM 1821 TO 1924.

Periods	Total	Agri-culture	Industry and Mining	Transport and Commerce	Domestic Service and General Labor	Liberal professions and Public Service	Other occupations, None or Unknown
Absolute figures							
1821–1840	806,248	102,371	88,688	74,507	66,874	6,480	467,328
1841–1890	15,361,855	1,517,778	1,433,724	552,978	3,762,919	77,115	8,017,341
1891–1915	17,099,637	3,037,206	2,098,565	597,407	5,898,453	181,587	5,286,419
1921–1924	2,344,599	169,881	338,457	152,937	635,755	66,867	980,702
Percentages							
1821–1840	100	12.7	11.0	9.2	8.3	0.8	58.0
1841–1890	100	9.9	9.3	3.6	24.5	0.5	52.2
1891–1915	100	17.7	12.3	3.5	34.5	1.1	30.9
1921–1924	100	7.3	14.4	6.5	27.1	2.9	41.8

The group "Other Occupations, No Occupation or Occupation Unknown" includes members of families accompanying the head; the other groups include only persons practising an occupation. The preponderance of "Other Occupations, No Occupation or Occupation Unknown" until 1890 should be ascribed mainly to defective reports. In 1891-1915 this group [comprises 30.9 per cent; in 1921-24 it has 41.8 per cent.

The proportion of persons engaged in agricultural occupations decreased from 12.7 per cent in 1821-40 to 7.3 per cent in 1921-24. The proportion engaged in industry or mining decreased from 11

[1]The figures available for comparison from 1856 on have been tabulated in International Tables 31 and 32 in six occupational groups.

per cent in 1821-40 to 9.3 per cent in 1841-90, and then rose to 12.3 per cent in 1891-1915 and 14.4 per cent in 1921-24. Those in transport and commerce decreased from 9.2 per cent in 1821-40 to 3.5 per cent in 1891-1915, but then rose to 6.5 per cent in 1921-24. There was considerable increase of those engaged in domestic service and general labour up to 1891-1915, 8.3 per cent to 34.5 per cent; in 1921-1924 this group comprised 27.1 per cent. Persons engaged in the liberal professions and public services also showed a considerable increase. At first they decreased from 0.8 per cent to 0.5 per cent, but in 1891-1915 rose to 1.1 per cent and in 1921-24 to 2.9 per cent. These fluctuations are mostly to be explained by changes in the countries of origin of the immigrants.

It has already been indicated that until 1890 the absolute majority of immigrants to the United States came from northern and western Europe, while from 1891 to 1915 the absolute majority and from 1921 to 1924 the relative majority came from eastern and southern Europe. From 1899 the statistics of the United States combined the occupations of immigrants with their "race or people". In Text Table 18 and Diagram 16 the distribution by occupation of immigrants from western and northern Europe has been shown on one side, and from eastern and southern Europe on the other side, for the years 1891-1915, and 1921-24. From this it appears that in 1899-1915 of the immigrants from eastern and southern Europe 24.6 per cent had been engaged in agriculture, while of the immigrants from western and northern Europe only 9.2 per cent had been so engaged; agriculture and industry together show the same percentage for western and northern Europe as agriculture alone for eastern and southern Europe (24.6 per cent). During this period there were about 2½ times as many immigrants from eastern and southern Europe as from northern and western, this is the explanation of the high figures for agriculture in Diagram 15 for the years 1891-1915. From Text Table 18 and Diagram 16 it also appears that both an absolute and a relative majority of those belonging to commerce and transport and to the professions have come from western and northern Europe. In 1921-24, for example, the proportions for transport and commerce were 8.3 per cent and 4.8 per cent, and for the liberal professions 4.2 per cent and 1.7 per cent; domestic service and general labor were better represented during 1921-24 in the emigration from eastern and southern Europe than in that from western and northern Europe (32.2 per cent and 19.4 per cent); other occupations are of equal importance, but

DIAGRAM 16

Distribution of Alien Immigrants (United States), by Occupations, from 1899 to 1924.

I. FROM EASTERN AND SOUTHERN EUROPE.

1899-1915
9,398,277 IMMIGR.

INDUSTRY AND MINING 12.2%

TRANSPORT & COMMERCE 2%

AGRICULTURE 24.6%

DOMESTIC SERVICE AND GENERAL LABOR 35.7%

OTHER OCCUPATIONS NONE OR UNKNOWN 25%

LIBERAL PROFESSIONS AND PUBLIC SERVICES 0.4%

1921-1924
1,007,929 IMMIGR.

TRANSPORT & COMMERCE

INDUSTRY AND MINING 15.1%

AGRICULTURE 8.8%

DOMESTIC SERVICE AND GENERAL LABOR 32.2%

OTHER OCCUPATIONS NONE OR UNKNOWN 41.3%

LIBERAL PROFESSIONS AND PUBLIC SERVICES

II. FROM WESTERN AND NORTHERN EUROPE.

1899-1915
3,916,828 IMMIGR.

INDUSTRY AND MINING 15.4%

TRANSPORT & COMMERCE 6%

AGRICULTURE 9.2%

DOMESTIC SERVICE AND GENERAL LABOR 34.7%

OTHER OCCUPATIONS NONE OR UNKNOWN 32%

LIBERAL PROFESSIONS AND PUBLIC SERVICES

1921-1924
1,018,079 IMMIGR.

INDUSTRY AND MINING 18.1%

TRANSPORT & COMMERCE

AGRICULTURE 9.5%

DOMESTIC SERVICE AND GENERAL LABOR 19.4%

OTHER OCCUPATIONS NONE OR UNKNOWN 41.3%

LIBERAL PROFESSIONS AND PUBLIC SERVICES

TEXT TABLE 18

DISTRIBUTION OF ALIEN IMMIGRANTS TO THE UNITED STATES, BY OCCUPATIONS,
FROM 1899 TO 1924.

Periods	Total	Agriculture	Industry and Mining	Transport and Commerce	Domestic Service and General Labor	Liberal professions and Public Service	Other occupations None or Unknown

I. Immigrants from eastern and southern Europe

Numbers

Periods	Total	Agriculture	Industry and Mining	Transport and Commerce	Domestic Service	Liberal professions	Other occupations
1899–1915	9,398,277	2,313,443	1,149,444	195,491	3,347,917	39,678	2,352,304
1921–1924	1,007,929	69,550	132,227	48,312	324,514	17,038	416,288

Percentages

Periods	Total	Agriculture	Industry and Mining	Transport and Commerce	Domestic Service	Liberal professions	Other occupations
1899–1915	100	24.6	12.2	2.1	35.7	0.4	25.0
1921–1924	100	6.9	13.1	4.8	32.2	1.7	41.3

II. Immigrants from western and northern Europe

Numbers

Periods	Total	Agriculture	Industry and Mining	Transport and Commerce	Domestic Service	Liberal professions	Other occupations
1899–1915	3,916,828	362,077	602,773	233,357	1,357,399	106,198	1,255,024
1921–1924	1,018,079	88,255	184,179	84,309	197,622	43,070	420,644

Percentages

Periods	Total	Agriculture	Industry and Mining	Transport and Commerce	Domestic Service	Liberal professions	Other occupations
1899–1915	100	9.2	15.4	6.0	34.7	2.7	32.0
1921–1924	100	8.7	18.1	8.3	19.4	4.2	41.3

in industry and mining, and agriculture, western and northern
Europe is in the majority.[1] It is important to note that the occupational distribution of eastern and southern Europeans from 1890
to 1915 corresponds with the occupational distribution of the total

[1] Since the statistics of occupations were defective during the first decades, the
figures can hardly be used for purposes of comparison. The proportion of Other Occupations decreased considerably from 1841-90 to 1891-1915, while the proportions in
Agriculture and Domestic service and general labor increased. It cannot be ascertained
whether the larger proportion for the latter group would not have appeared earlier if
the statistics had been more accurate.

immigration to the United States. This is the case in 1921-24 except for the intellectual and industrial groups which are smaller. It is explained by the fact that these immigrants may hope for more success in the country of immigration if classed as laborers.[1]

In Argentina the proportion of agricultural workers among immigrants has been much higher than in the United States; from 1857 to 1900 the proportion varied between 38.6 per cent in 1871-80 and 54.1 per cent in 1881-90. It then declined: 31.9 per cent in 1901-10; 17.5 per cent in 1911-20; 24.6 per cent in 1921-24. The second most important group, apart from other occupations, is that of domestic service and general labor; 9.3 per cent in 1857-60; 11.1 per cent in 1881-1890; 19.7 per cent in 1891-1900; and 37.3 per cent (exceeding agriculture) in 1916-20. In 1921-24 it again takes the second place with 21.5 per cent. Increases also appear in industry and mining, transport and commerce, and the liberal professions: they amounted to 12.2 per cent, 8.4 per cent, and 2.0 per cent in 1921-24, as compared with 3.0 per cent, 2.5 per cent and 0.3 per cent in 1861-70.

The occupational statistics of Uruguay include passengers of all classes and citizens. This explains the relatively great proportion of the transport and commerce group after 1901 (14.5 per cent to 16.6 per cent). At first the most important group was agriculture (11.5 per cent to 18.3 per cent in 1881-90). Subsequently the next principal group was domestic service and general labor (20.7 per cent to 43.2 per cent); after 1901 agriculture declined. Industry was represented by 10.4 per cent and 17.1 per cent in 1896-1900 and 1901-3; in other periods it was less than 6.0 per cent. From 1916-24 the liberal professions rose to 6.5 and 4.9 per cent.

Cuba from 1911 to 1924 received mostly persons engaged in domestic service or general labor (43.3 per cent to 68.2 per cent); in the Philippines the "Other Occupations" group represents a large proportion, 89.1 per cent for 1921-24. The remainder are principally agriculture, and transport and commerce.

For the distribution by occupations of the emigration from separate countries in the different periods reference must be made to the emigration statistics of the respective countries (International Tables 27 and 28). In the occupational tables of the British statistics all passengers are included. During all years the largest group is that of domestic service and general labor. Apart from the years

---

[1] In 1909-16 immigrants of unskilled labor responded more readily to cyclical fluctuations than did those of the skilled professions and agriculture (Jerome, p. 152).

1881-85 (37.2 per cent) the proportion of this group varies between 29.4 per cent in 1877-80 and 23.9 per cent in 1901-05. A decreasing movement can be observed. An increase appears in the industry and mining, and the transport and commerce groups:

	1881–85	1906–10
Industry and Mining.......	8.4 per cent	14.9 per cent
Transport and Commerce...	1.7 per cent	6.2 per cent

Agriculture and liberal professions show considerable variation; no general tendency can be discovered (agriculture 5.7 per cent in 1881-85; 11.1 per cent in 1886-90; liberal professions 8.9 per cent in 1896-1900; 0.7 per cent in 1906-10). The recent developments are partly to be attributed to the increasing proportion of ordinary passengers.[1]

Emigration from Italy belonged principally to the first two occupational groups, agriculture, and industry and mining. The figures refer to adult emigrants, over 14 until 1903 and over 15 for later years, including continental emigration; adult members of families practicing no occupation are placed in the groups of their respective heads of families. Up to 1910 the figures vary between the following limits:—

	1886–90	1906–10
Agriculture	56.9 per cent	34.1 per cent
Industry and Mining.......	35.4 "	52.9 "

Until the outbreak of the War the proportion in agriculture decreased and that in industry increased. From 1916 to 1924 there were further changes. Persons classified under Domestic Service and General Labor, who came principally from agricultural sources, increased considerably, with 24.4 per cent in 1916-20 and 22.0 per cent in 1921-24. Agriculture was represented by 28.8 per cent in 1921-24 and Industry by 41.9 per cent. The German statistics show the occupations of emigrants from 1899, when the movement had already lost its importance. During this period emigration was principally recruited from Agriculture and Industry; less important groups were Transport and Commerce, Domestic Service

[1]Emigrants proper, the figures for whom are shown in the national tables for 1912 and 1913, as well as for 1921-24, have not been considered in the international tables, principally because the classification was not the same before and after the War, and also because the pre-War period includes 1¾ years only during which the statistics are not so reliable as after the War. Moreover occupational figures are lacking for passengers from 1912 to 1924.

and General Labor, and Liberal Professions. From 1901-05 Agriculture was more important than Industry (36.4 per cent and 31.3 per cent); after the War Industry became predominant; the figures for 1921-24 are Agriculture 21.9 per cent; Industry and Mining 34.7 per cent; Transport and Commerce 14.0 per cent.

In French emigration, according to the port statistics for 1857-84, Industry declined and Agriculture increased. In Belgium (1886-1924) Agriculture was well represented; day laborers fairly numerous, Industry and Commerce insignificant. Emigration from Denmark (1872-1924) was at first principally Domestic Service and General Labor; the proportion later changed in favor of Agriculture, and Transport and Commerce, and at times also in favor of Industry and Mining. Sweden and Norway show a similar development. Finnish emigration 1893-1924 shows a preponderance of Agriculture throughout; it declines in later years, however, giving way to Domestic Service and General Labor, and to a smaller extent to Industry and Mining. In Sweden also (1886-1924) Agriculture furnishes the majority of emigrants almost throughout; the decline of this group in the course of the period is made up by an increase in Transport and Commerce, and the Liberal Professions. Austria shows principally Agriculture emigration (1896-1910). For Hungary the figures are only available for two biennial periods, 1905-07 and 1911-13. The majority of the emigrants are in Agriculture (67 per cent). Next come Domestic Service and General Labor (28.6 per cent and 25.9 per cent); Other Occupations is insignificant.

In the course of the period under review a general European displacement appears in as much as Agriculture, particularly in the post-War period, declined in importance while the proportion of industrial emigrants increased.

B. Continental Migrations

It should be mentioned at once that continental migrations in Asia, America, Oceania, and Africa cannot be compared with the European movements.[1] Asiatic overseas and continental migration is discussed in the National Section (Indian, Chinese and Japanese movements). The North American continental migration, which is at present unusually important having risen from 63,000 in 1908-

[1]Genuine migration statistics, distinguishing overseas from continental migrants and taking account of the more important movements of native labor, were introduced after the War.

10 to 160,000 in 1921-24, is considered in connection with immigration into the United States. South American internal movements have not been investigated sufficiently for definite treatment.

For Africa also only a few isolated statistics are available, *e. g.* for Basutoland and Kenya, and these are given in the National Tables. The present discussion will be limited to Europe. The statistics of continental emigration and repatriation of citizens may be supplemented by the statistics of immigration of aliens, particularly in France for the post-War period (International Table 8).

The available figures for continental emigration of citizens are collected in International Table 3. For the whole period 1876-1924 there are data for three countries, Italy, Ireland and Sweden, but the last two are insignificant. Italian emigration, however, during these years was considerable. The annual average for quinquennial periods increased from 80,000 to 249,000 in 1906-10. In 1911-15 emigration lessened somewhat (236,000) and in 1921-24 it reached only 185,000. Emigration from Ireland to Great Britain in 1876-80 was 17,000. This number rapidly declined to 4,900 in 1886-90; 1,800 in 1911-15, and 387 in 1921. Emigration from Sweden also declined from 5,000 in 1876-80, to 3,100 in 1911-15, and 2,700 in 1921-24.

Belgian statistics are not reliable, since they do not include seasonal emigration. According to the available figures there is a continuous increase in continental emigration from 9,300 in 1886-90. to 34,000 in 1916-20; in 1921-24 the number was 19,000, which is more than the largest volume of emigration before the War.

Figures for Hungary, 1898-1913, show annually 9,200 to 15,700; and for Austria 210,000 in 1906-10 to 343,000 in 1911. The seasonal emigration from Austria was principally to Germany.

A comparison of 1906-10 shows Italy leading with 249,000. Then come Austria with 210,000, Belgium and Hungary with 15,000 to 16,000, and Ireland and Sweden with 3,100 each.

For the direction of continental emigration, there is information only for Italy, Belgium, Ireland and Sweden (see International Tables 17 and 18). The Irish emigration figures contained in Table 3 refer exclusively to emigration to Great Britain. The Italian emigrants of 1876-85 went principally to France, 46.1 per cent and 49.4 per cent; Austria-Hungary, 24.0 per cent and 28.4 per cent; Switzerland, 16.6 per cent and 7.8 per cent; and Germany, 9.2 per cent and 7.7 per cent. In 1886-1900 Austria-Hungary took the first place with 38.9 per cent to 32.0 per cent. France decreased in importance from 34.5 per cent to 17.2 per cent, while Germany and

Switzerland increased. In 1901-15 Germany and France were about equal. Austria-Hungary fell, and Switzerland rose and in 1906-15 took first place. During the period 1916-20 three-fourths of the Italian emigrants went to France, and 16.7 per cent to Switzerland; 79.1 per cent to France and 5.5 per cent to Switzerland in 1921-24. Emigration to Germany ceased. Swedish emigration was mainly to Denmark and Norway; except for the years 1896-1900 Denmark is the more important until 1906-10, in other years Norway; a smaller number go to Finland. Belgian continental emigration is directed to France to the extent of 70.8 per cent in 1901-05 and 86.5 per cent in 1921-24. Next in importance are Holland with 10.7 per cent in 1896-1900 and 6.4 per cent in 1921-24, and Germany with 8.6 per cent in 1901-05 and 2.7 per cent in 1921-24.

Concerning the continental immigration of aliens (International Table 8), of European countries only Belgium, Hungary and Germany could be compared. Belgium was of some importance for the whole period 1886 to 1924. Immigration rose from 15,500 to 32,200 in 1911-13, and then fell to 29,000 in 1919-20, and 23,000 in 1921-24. At the same time there was a considerable continental emigration from Belgium. The immigration to Hungary 1907-10 was 13,900, and 1911-15, 8,800 (according to incomplete communal registers). Most significant was the continental immigration to Germany; according to the frontier statistics for foreign workers, the immigration was 434,000 in 1911-15; 174,000 in 1916-20; 28,000 in 1921-24.[1]

Comparison of International Tables 5 and 10 (Continental Emigration of Aliens and Continental Immigration of Citizens), shows that considerable continental repatriations take place. Continental emigration is mostly seasonal.

Since the figures at our disposal for long periods apply to only a few countries, some attention will be given to the post-War situation in certain states. After 1920 there are regular statistics of continental emigration from Belgium, Italy, Poland, Sweden and Czechoslovakia. The Belgian and Swedish statistics include only persons who have remained away from home for over a year.

A better idea of the scope of this movement may be obtained by supplementing the emigration statistics with figures published by France concerning immigration by nationalities; for many countries

[1]See J. Trzcinski, *Russisch-Polnische und Galizische Wanderarbeiter im Grossherzogtum Posen*, Stuttgart, 1905, p. 20 f.; Souchon, *La crise de la main-d'oeuvre agricole*, Paris, 1914.

France is since the War[1] the most important, indeed almost the exclusive, destination of emigrants. The following Text Table 19 shows these data.

TEXT TABLE 19

CONTINENTAL EMIGRATION (EUROPEAN FIGURES) 1920-1924

Country	1920	1921	1922	1923	1924
Belgium...............					
(Direct figures)........	32,135	18,086	21,991	18,969	17,142
(French figures)........	28,422	26,260	24,677	33,912	40,256
Czechoslovakia..........	16,000*	16,000*	31,558	24,334	29,371
Italy..................	153,717	88,295	170,155	229,854	271,089
Poland................	26,846	12,129	31,373	72,058	26,136
Portugal...............					
(French figures)........	6,741	45	6,771	11,767	6,715
Spain..................					
(French figures)........	53,306	28,310	45,392	36,497	38,960
Sweden.................	3,149	3,069	2,812	2,679	2,270
Other countries..........					
(French figures)........	2,889	2,585	21,828	19,873	28,915
Total (according to data supplied)............	323,205	194,779	356,557	449,943	460,854

*Exclusive of seasonal workers without passports.

According to the figures in this table it may be seen that continental emigration has followed closely the fluctuations of the labor market. Thus the economic crisis in 1921 caused a considerable drop, while the great demand for workers (particularly in France) during the period 1922-24 resulted in a considerable rise.

Continental immigration of aliens into France has become much more considerable since the War. Continental migrations in Europe as a whole, however, have declined.

In view of the unemployment prevailing throughout Europe, most countries—except France—have in recent years adopted severe restrictions amounting in certain cases to prohibition, upon the immigration of foreign workers. Germany, which before the War needed over a million foreign workers, introduced a system of permits that has reduced the number of seasonal immigrants to a minimum; and the United Kingdom has reduced its laborer immigrants to 3,000 annually.[2]

[1] I. Ferenczi, Die Regelung den kontinentalen Arbeiterwanderungen in Europa, *Arch. f. Weltwirtschaft*, 1924, p. 441 ff.

[2] Immigration from the Continent to the United Kingdom remained moderate throughout the 19th century and rarely alarmed public opinion. The absolute number

Movements between the different Central European countries, which were considerable during the first years after the War, have also declined. In so far as they continue, they take place clandestinely and are not susceptible of statistical treatment.

Statistics of repatriations are derived principally from the Italian and French statistics.

The statistics covering the years after the World War indicate that the European streams of continental migration which are often considered as temporary, are tending more and more to assume the character of migrations which end in definite settlement abroad, *e. g.* Italians and Poles as farmers and *métayers* in southern France, and as miners and industrial workers in northern France.

The character of continental emigration is thus approaching that of intercontinental emigration, which for a time was designated in official publications as "definitive" in contrast to "continental." Another cause of assimilation is to be found in the fact that during the last half-century overseas emigration has become more and more temporary.

of alien immigrants for England were 100,638 in 1871, and 118,031 in 1881—135,000 for the United Kingdom (E. Pépin, *L'Aliens Acte de 1905*, Paris, 1914, p. 128).

Between 1881 and 1905 immigration increased greatly while its social consequences and racial character alarmed the public. The immigrants were chiefly Russian and Polish Jews fleeing from repeated persecutions. When they were without means or subsidies to proceed direct to the United States, these peoples came first to England and settled there indefinitely. The problem was the subject of various inquiries and Parliamentary proceedings (W. H. Wilkins, *The Alien Invasion*, London 1892, p. 25; E. Pépin, *op. cit.*, p. 130-8.) The partial statistics by the Board of Trade for 1890 show 29,885 aliens arrived from Europe (Georg Halpern, *Die juedischen Arbeiter in London*, Stuttgart & Berlin, 1903, p. 13). The number increased to 62,505 in 1900 and to 82,845 in 1904 (*Statistical tables relating to emigration and immigration from and to the United Kingdom*, 1891-1905). Russians and Poles made up two-fifths of the whole at that time. New but perhaps exaggerated statistics by the Home Office from 1905 onward indicated a steady decrease of immigration to 19,820 in 1912. Of these only one-fifth were Russians, more than one-fifth were French, and the balance mainly Italians, Germans, and Scandinavians (Pépin, *op. cit.*, p. 474 f., Annex Tables IIIa, IIIb).

Some cases of group immigration admitted exceptionally to Soviet Russia did not succeed. The Russians, up to the War, migrated in larger numbers to Siberia than overseas. The movement in 1905-1914 amounted to about 3 million settlers, or 300,000 annually, but the numbers have decreased markedly since and in 1924 were but 73,400 (*Druk*, 28 Dec. 1926).

INTERNATIONAL MIGRATION STATISTICS

PART II

INTERNATIONAL TABLES

TABLE 1—INTERCONTINENTAL

Country of Emigration	1846–1850	1851–1855	1856–1860	1861—1865	1866–1870	1871–1875	1876–1880
EUROPE:							
1 Austria-Hungary[1]	**1,616**	**4,027**	**2,241**	**2,177**	**5,747**	**10,471**	**11,773**
(former territory)	*1,849*[2][3]	*20,137*[2]	*11,204*[2]	*10,886*[2]	*28,734*[2]	*52,357*	*58,864*
2 Belgium[6]	*817*	*376*	*601*	*485*	*1,060*	*910*	*720*
3 British Isles (Passengers)	*199,108*	**231,733**	**123,497**	**143,559**	**170,807**	**193,907**	**141,876**
(Emigrants)	.....	695,199[9]	617,484	717,796	854,033	969,537	709,382
	.....	.....	.....	.....	.....	.....	.....
4 Denmark	**73**	*254*	*496*	*1,049*	**3,942**	**4,682**	**3,038**
					7,884[11]	23,409	15,191
5 France	*10,740*	*11,418*	*3,893*	*3,045*	**6,141**	**8,325**	**2,974**
			15,572[12]	15,223	30,703	41,627	14,868
6 Germany	36,505\[13]	**74,926**	**49,386**	**43,535**	**83,356**	**78,963**	**46,231**
	182,526/[14]	374,629[14]	246,928[14]	217,673[14]	416,782[14]	394,814	231,154
7 Irish Free State (Ireland)[15]							**35,009**
							175,043
8 Netherlands	**2,418**	**1,943**	**1,225**	**987**	**3,107**	**2,250**	**1,248**
	12,089	9,714	6,123	4,937	15,534	11,250	6,242[17]
9 Norway[13]	**2,400**	**4,054**	**3,160**	**4,710**	**14,881**	**9,028**	**8,049**
	12,000	20,270	15,800	23,550	74,403	45,142	40,244
10 Sweden	*1,834*	**2,549**	**831**	**3,963**	**20,526**	**8,411**	**12,089**
		12,744[18]	4,156[18]	19,816[18]	102,641[18]	42,055	60,447
11 Switzerland	*377*	*4,019*	*1,534*	*1,539*	**4,569**[19]	**3,630**	**3,517**
					13,707[20]	18,152[20]	17,583[20]
12 Finland						57	44
13 Poland (Russian, pre-war)	.....	.....	.....	.....	.....	.....	.....
14 Russia[26]	*66*	*4*	*117*	*163*	*423*	**6,080**	**5,505**
						30,398	27,525
15 Italy	*240*	*738*	*4,202*	*8,027*	*18,714*	*23,329*	**28,899**
							144,495
16 Portugal (passport statistics) (port statistics)	*144*	*5,265*	8,082 / 80,821		**7,762** / 38,812	**14,649** / 73,245	**11,565** / 57,824
17 Spain (Passengers)	*255*	*865*	*1,850*	*1,878*	*4,622*	*7,109*	*5,758*
(Emigrants)	.....	.....	.....	.....	.....	.....	.....
18 Malta (Brit.)	.....	.....	.....	.....	.....	.....	.....
TOTAL EUROPE (averages)[32]	**255,593**	**342,171**	**201,115**	**223,199**	**345,657**	**371,801**	**283,286**
ASIA							
19 British India	**10,919**	**18,535**	**29,768**	**21,639**	**14,120**	**19,425**	**18,316**
	54,595	92,677	148,842	108,196	70,600	97,128	91,582
20 Japan	.....	.....	.....	.....	.....	.....	.....
AFRICA:							
21 St. Helena (Brit.)	.....	.....	.....	.....	.....	.....	.....
22 Cape Verde (Port.)	.....	.....	.....	.....	.....	.....	.....

For reference notes see page 349.

EMIGRATION OF CITIZENS, 1846-1924.

1881–1885	1886–1890	1891–1895	1896–1900	1901–1905	1906–1910	1911–1915	1916–1920	1921–1924
34,645	52,500	67,551	77,249	203,025	265,411	243,629	11,453	57,220
173,223	262,498	337,754	386,243	1,015,127	1,327,055	730,886[4]	57,265[5]	228,880
1,959	5,012	3,019	1,390	3,807	4,836	5,526	2,270	2,078
	25,058	15,096	6,951	19,033	24,178	16,578	11,351[7]	8,312
258,462	253,245	195,715	152,843	234,168	334,125	357,991	129,484	287,517
1,292,309	1,266,226	978,574	764,216	1,170,839	1,670,625	1,789,956	647,419	1,150,066[9]
......	......	......	.....	......	......	268,842	101,118	204,426
						1,008,157[10]	505,588	817,704
7,725	8,598	7,533	2,769	7,356	7,327	7,058	3,263	5,831
38,627	42,988	37,666	13,845	36,779	36,636	35,290	16,313	23,323
5,098	18,747	5,443	4,800	4,800	5,823	4,300	2,130	1,598
25,488	93,737	27,217	24,000	24,000	29,114	21,501	10,652	6,390
171,457	97,027	80,513	24,859	28,382	26,449	15,820	2,387	58,142
857,287	485,136	402,567	124,294	141,910	132,244	79,102	11,936	232,567
73,595	66,389	46,494	34,619	33,117	28,659	22,576	4,402	13,243
367,975	331,945	232,469	173,096	165,586	143,294	112,881	22,011	13,248[16]
5,627	4,001	3,529	1,255	2,375	3,226	2,074	2,271	3,557
28,134	24,307	17,645	6,276	11,875	16,130	10,371	11,355	14,229
21,141	16,197	12,203	6,767	20,639	17,533	8,910	3,394	9,466
105,704	80,984	61,017	33,837	103,195	87,663	44,552	16,969	37,862
29,524	35,977	28,376	12,527	25,949	18,859	12,672	4,532	12,457
147,619	179,886	141,879	62,634	129,746	94,297	63,361	22,658	49,826
10,098	6,835	4,870	2,053	3,752	3,764	3,640	2,506	5,400
50,492[20]	34,174	24,349	10,264	18,761	18,820	18,201	12,531	21,601
1,126	4,394	5,201	6,608	16,211	15,555	10,134	3,336	7,056
4,503[21]	21,968	26,006	33,040	81,056	77,776	50,668	16,678	28,221
......	......	10,431	7,637	16,854	40,431	44,386	9,883	33,960
		52,157[22]	38,187[22]	67,415[22][23]	121,293[24]	133,157[4]	49,414[25][5]	135,841[25]
12,879	44,650	55,852	40,349	84,083	98,058	140,215[27]	......	3,356
64,393	223,248	279,258	201,744[27]	420,417[27]	490,292[27]	420,646[4]		6,712[28]
64,043	134,235	150,226	165,692	320,604	402,436	312,246	126,572	167,887
320,213	671,175	751,131	828,461	1,603,021	2,012,178	1,561,228	632,859	671,548
16,576	20,497	31,035	22,135	25,371	39,428	53,948	26,407	19,382
82,881	102,483	155,175	110,676	126,855	197,138	269,742	132,035	19,382[16]
								25,006
								100,023
47,892	76,161	77,904	80,307	72,209	145,958	166,259	94,901	98,292
191,569[21]	380,803	389,521	401,536	361,043	729,789	831,295	474,503	294,875[29]
......	......	......	......	......	135,997	120,416	69,101	76,703
					271,994[30]	602,081	345,504	306,812
......	......	......	......	......	......	1,061	6,349	1,725
						5,306	9,524[31]	6,900
686,293	778,936	728,970	601,603	1,052,731	1,388,788	1,345,483	431,138	774,924
14,662	12,466	14,820	19,123	17,728	15,009	9,100	2,099	826
73,312	62,332	74,100	95,616	88,640	75,047	45,498	10,496	2,478[33]
......	......	.....	17,984	10,883	15,506	13,187	15,669	9,697
			53,951[34]	54,415	77,531	65,937	78,347	38,788
......	......	.....	.....	1,805	127	101	87	165
				7,219[35]	634	504	433	658
......	......	.....	.....	....	......	2,867	1,890	1,024
						11,469[36]	9,448[37]	5,123

The figures in italics represent the averages for the indirect statistics, those in block type, for the direct statistics.

TABLE 2.—INTERCONTINENTAL EMIGRATION OF CITIZENS. PERCENTAGE DISTRIBUTION OF THE AVERAGE ANNUAL EMIGRATION FROM EUROPE BY COUNTRIES OF EMIGRATION 1846-1924.

Country of Emigration	1846–1850	1851–1855	1856–1860	1861–1865	1866–1870	1871–1875	1876–1880	1881–1885
EUROPE:								
1 Territory of former Austria-Hungary	0.2	1.2	1.1	1.0	1.7	2.8	4.2	5.0
2 Belgium	0.3	0.1	0.3	0.2	0.3	0.2	0.3	0.3
3 British Isles (Passengers)	77.9	67.7	61.4	64.3	49.4	52.2	50.1	37.6
4 Denmark	0.0	0.1	0.2	0.5	1.1	1.3	1.1	1.1
5 France	4.2	3.3	1.9	1.4	1.8	2.2	1.0	0.7
6 Germany	14.3	21.9	24.6	19.5	24.1	21.3	16.3	24.9
7 Netherlands	0.9	0.6	0.6	0.4	0.9	0.6	0.4	0.8
8 Norway	0.9	1.2	1.6	2.1	4.3	2.4	2.8	3.1
9 Sweden	0.7	0.7	0.5	1.8	5.9	2.3	4.3	4.3
10 Switzerland	0.1	1.2	0.8	0.7	1.3	1.0	1.2	1.5
11 Finland	...	...	...	...	...	0.0	0.0	0.2
12 Poland (Russian before the war)	0.0	0.0	0.1	0.1	0.1	...	...	...
13 Russia	0.1	0.2	2.1	3.6	5.4	1.6	1.9	1.9
14 Italy	0.1	1.5	4.0	3.6	2.2	6.3	10.2	9.3
15 Portugal (Passengers)	0.1	0.3	0.9	0.8	1.3	3.9	4.1	2.4
16 Spain (Passengers)	...	...	...	...	...	1.9	2.0	7.0
17 Malta (Brit.)	...	...	...	...	...	...	...	...
Total Europe (averages)	100.0	100.0	100.0	100.0	100.0	100.0	100.0	100.0

Country of Emigration	1886–1890	1891–1895	1896–1900	1901–1905	1906–1910	1911–1915	1916–1920	1921–1924
EUROPE:								
1 Territory of former Austria-Hungary	6.7	9.3	12.8	19.3	19.1	18.1	2.6	7.4
2 Belgium	0.6	0.4	0.2	0.4	0.3	0.4	0.5	0.3
3 British Isles (Passengers)	32.5	26.8	25.4	22.2	24.1	26.6	30.0	37.1
4 Denmark	1.1	1.1	0.5	0.7	0.5	0.5	0.8	0.8
5 France	2.4	0.7	0.8	0.5	0.4	0.3	0.5	0.2
6 Germany	12.5	11.0	4.1	2.7	1.9	1.2	0.5	7.5
7 Netherlands	0.6	0.5	0.2	0.2	0.2	0.2	0.8	0.5
8 Norway	2.1	1.7	1.1	2.5	1.3	0.7	1.1	1.2
9 Sweden	4.6	3.9	2.1	0.4	1.4	0.7	0.6	1.6
10 Switzerland	0.9	0.7	0.3	1.5	0.3	0.3	0.8	0.7
11 Finland	0.6	0.7	1.1	...	1.1	0.8	2.3	0.9
12 Poland (Russian before the war)	...	...	...	...	...	...	...	4.4
13 Russia	5.7	7.7	6.7	8.	7.1	10.4	...	0.4
14 Italy	17.2	20.6	27.5	30.5	29.0	23.2	29.3	21.7
15 Portugal (passports)	2.6	4.3	3.7	2.4	2.8	4.	6.1	2.5
16 Spain (Passengers)	9.8	10.7	13.4	6.9	10.5	12.4	22.0	12.7
17 Malta (Brit.)	...	...	...	...	...	0.1	1.5	0.2
Total Europe (Averages)	100.0	100.0	100.0	100.0	100.0	100.0	100.0	100.0

The figures in italics represent the averages for the indirect statistics.

TABLE 3.—CONTINENTAL EMIGRATION OF CITIZENS, 1876-1924

Country of Emigration	1876–1880	1881–1885	1886–1890	1891–1895	1896–1900	1901–1905	1906–1910	1911–1915	1916–1920	1921–1924
EUROPE:										
1 Austria	.....	.....	.....	.....	.....	.....	**210,263**	**343,224**	.....	.....
							1,051,315	343,224[1]		
2 Belgium	.....	.....	**9,298**	**11,071**	**11,703**	**11,271**	**15,475**	**16,420**	**34,343**	**19,047**
			46,491	55,357	58,516	56,357	77,376	49,261[2]	68,685[3]	76,188
3 Hungary	.....	.....	.....	.....	**9,237**	**12,273**	**15,749**	**11,730**	.....	.....
					18,474[4]	61,366	78,747	35,191[2]		
4 Ireland	**16,951**	**9,240**	**4,917**	**2,153**	**3,439**	**4,317**	**3,112**	**1,795**	**1,378**	**387**
	84,753	46,199	24,587	10,766	17,195	21,584	15,560	8,976	6,888	387[5]
5 Sweden	**5,072**	**5,442**	**4,337**	**3,917**	**4,535**	**3,586**	**3,138**	**3,114**	**3,357**	**2,708**
	25,359	27,209	21,687	19,583	22,676	17,932	15,692	15,571	16,785	10,830
6 Italy	**79,898**	**90,098**	**87,742**	**106,284**	**144,742**	**233,446**	**248,852**	**236,366**	**90,429**	**184,744**
	399,489	450,492	438,711	531,422	723,712	1,167,231	1,244,260	1,181,831	452,147	738,974
ASIA										
7 China (Hongkong)	.....	.....	.....	.....	.....	**73,103**	**88,454**	**109,110**	**84,602**	**126,123**
						365,514	442,270	545,552	423,008	504,490
8 Japan	.....	.....	.....	.....	**397**	**1,538**	**1,038**	**1,679**	**2,802**	**1,905**
					1,192[6]	7,692	5,190	8,393	14,009	7,618

For reference notes see page 349.

TABLE 4.—INTERCONTINENTAL EMIGRATION OF ALIENS, 1846-1924.

Country of Emigration	1846–1850	1851–1855	1856–1860	1861–1865	1866–1870	1871–1875	1876–1880	1881–1885	1886–1890	1891–1895	1896–1900	1901–1905	1906–1910	1911–1915	1916–1920	1921–1924
AMERICA																
1 United States	..	..	..	..	..	..	...	...	....	....	....	.....	**251,688** 755,063[1]	**251,039** 1,255,193	**114,146** 570,729	**143,195** 572,781
2 Mexico	..	..	..	..	..	..	..	...	....	....	....	.....	.....	**10,015** 50,075	**6,381** 31,907	**11,300** 45,200
3 Argentina[2]	..	..	**2,225** 8,900[3]	**8,298** 82,976		**16,999** 84,993	**18,154** 90,770	**13,927** 69,633	**26,764** 133,822	**33,861** 169,304	**31,828** 159,140	**43,131** 215,657	**85,645** 428,224	**137,588** 687,941	**49,577** 247,884	**45,887** 183,546
4 Uruguay[4]	..	..	..	..	..	..	**6,167** 12,333[5]	**5,291** 26,457	**9,477** 47,387	**8,645** 43,226	**5,371** 26,857	**5,885** 17,655[6]	.....	**9,283** 27,849[7]	**3,859** 19,294	**3,802** 3,802[8]
EUROPE:																
5 Belgium	..	..	..	..	..	..	...	...	**384** 1,918	**239** 1,193	**366** 1,832	**332** 1,658	**580** 2,898	**703**[9] 2,108	**541** 1,081[10]	**476** 1,903
6 Switzerland	..	..	..	..	..	..	..	**775** 3,098[11]	**843** 4,214	**1,059** 5,296	**834** 4,171	**1,110** 5,551	**1,187** 5,935	**1,044** 5,218	**446** 2,232	**865** 3,461
ASIA:																
7 Philippines U. S. A.	..	..	..	..	..	..	...	...	....	....	....	.....	.....	**1,059** 5,295	**1,035** 5,176	**1,211** 4,844
OCEANIA																
8 Australia[12]	..	..	..	..	..	..	...	...	....	....	....	**50,648** 101,295[13]	**62,751** 313,756	**72,022** 365,108	**41,504** 207,519	**58,179** 232,716
9 New South Wales[14]	..	..	..	..	..	..	...	...	....	....	....	**15,613** 78,066	**18,570** 92,852	**31,156** 155,778	**16,696** 83,480	**21,236** 63,709[15]
10 Queensland[14]	..	..	..	..	..	**684** 3,418	**2,289** 11,447	**1,482** 7,412	**1,776** 8,882	**1,467** 7,333	**1,906** 9,528	**1,933** 9,666	**2,226** 11,131	**2,680** 13,399	**1,523** 7,613	**2,906** 11,624
11 Victoria[14]	..	..	..	..	**5,281** 26,407	**4,529** 22,647	**5,284** 26,420	**8,173** 40,867	**11,641** 58,207	**9,935** 49,673	**13,942** 69,711	**10,555** 52,774	**5,262** 26,312	**7,784** 38,920		
12 New Zealand (Passengers)[16]	..	..	..	..	..	**1,633** 8,164	**1,562** 7,812	**1,869** 9,347	**3,115** 15,577	**2,528** 12,640	**2,786** 13,929	**4,320** 21,599	**4,726** 23,631	**5,553** 27,767	**19,899** 99,493	**29,302** 117,209
(Emigrants)	..	..	..	..	..	..	...	...	....	....	....	.....	.....	.....	.....	**2,220** 8,326[17]
13 Fiji (Brit.)[18]	..	..	..	..	..	..	...	**989** 3,956[19]	**695** 3,476	**791** 3,957	**469** 2,345	**499** 2,496	**605** 3,024	**904** 4,520	**2,710** 5,419[20]	**2,095** 4,190[21]
14 New Caledonia (Fr.)	..	..	..	..	..	..	...	...	....	....	**246** 983	**465** 2,327	**396** 1,980	**555** 2,776	**500** 2,498	**658** 2,630
15 Hawaii (U. S.)	..	..	..	..	..	..	...	...	....	....	....	.....	.....	**7,134** 35,672	**7,789** 38,946	**10,249** 40,996
16 Mauritius[22] (Brit.)	**3,235** 16,176	**3,133** 15,665	**5,123** 25,615	**2,925** 14,623	**2,984** 14,919	**3,485** 17,426	**2,588** 12,940	**2,335** 11,674	**1,755** 8,775	**1,227** 6,135	**1,015** 5,077	**5,045** 25,224	**3,439** 17,195	**3,941** 19,703	**3,463** 17,316	**2,853** 11,410
17 Seychelles (Brit.)	..	..	..	..	..	..	...	...	....	....	....	**351** 1,753	**311** 1,556	**333** 1,667	**492** 2,458	**338** 1,353
AFRICA:																
18 Cape of Good Hope[14]	..	..	..	..	..	..	...	...	....	....	....	**28,187** 140,934	**33,854** 169,269	**30,320** 60,639[23]		
19 Union of South Africa[24]	..	..	..	..	..	..	...	...	....	....	....	.....	.....	.....	**9,885** 29,656[25]	**13,066** 52,262

For reference notes see page 349.

TABLE 5.—CONTINENTAL EMIGRATION OF ALIENS, 1886-1924.

Country of Emigration	1886–1890	1891–1895	1896–1900	1901–1905	1906–1910	1911–1915	1916–1920	1921–1924
AMERICA								
1 United States	.....	.....	.....	.....	**22,749** 68,248[1]	**37,867** 189,337	**26,347** 131,735	**7,972** 31,888
2 Mexico	.....	.....	.....	.....	.....	**12,790** 63,952	**4,628** 23,142	**16,177** 64,708
EUROPE								
3 Belgium	**7,971** 39,854	**7,211** 36,056	**9,791** 48,955	**11,087** 55,435	**14,980** 74,898	**15,934** 47,802[2]	**17,354** 34,707[3]	**9,265** 37,061
4 Germany	.....	.....	.....	.....	.....	**380,255** 1,901,276	**260,661** 1,042,642[4]	.....
ASIA								
5 Straits Settlements (Brit.)[5]	**50,770** 253,852	**23,077** 115,386	**19,879** 99,395	**18,304** 91,519	**30,755** 153,773	**59,094** 295,471	**53,288** 266,442	**46,847** 187,388[6]
6 Ceylon (Brit.)[7]	.....	.....	.....	**70,347** 351,734[8]	**65,603** 328,017[8]	**142,513** 712,565	**142,552** 712,758	**139,943** 559,773

For reference notes see page 350.

TABLE 6.—INTERCONTINENTAL IMMIGRATION OF ALIENS, 1821-1924.

	1821–1825	1826–1830	1831–1835	1836–1840	1841–1845	1846–1850	1851–1855	1856–1860	1861–1865	1866–1870
AMERICA										
1 Canada (fiscal years)	900 / 9,000[1]	18,126 / 72,504[2]	33,443 / 167,214	16,512 / 82,562	27,941 / 139,704	41,177 / 205,886	38,281 / 191,405	17,255 / 86,274	20,404 / 102,020	36,259 / 181,294
2 New Brunswick (Br.)[3]					4,639 / 18,564	6,584 / 32,922	2,884 / 14,420	419 / 2,095	719 / 3,594	
3 Nova Scotia (Br.)[3]					1,225 / 4,898[4]	662 / 3,310	222 / 1,112	151 / 754	358 / 1,790	
4 Newfoundland (Brit.)[3]					560 / 2,210[4]	501 / 2,505	180 / 902	248 / 1,240	73 / 365	
5 Prince Ed. Islands (Br.)[3]					611 / 2,445[4]	211 / 1,053	84 / 420	93 / 463	36 / 181	
6 United States[5] (fiscal years)	7,851 / 39,257	19,418 / 97,088	46,493 / 244,086[6]	66,963 / 334,814	87,829 / 417,186[7]	238,299 / 1,251,071[8]	342,655 / 1,713,277	164,510 / 822,550	153,389 / 766,945	309,292 / 1,391,816[9]
7 Mexico[10]										
8 British West Indies[10]				2,146 / 10,730	6,504 / 32,518	10,241 / 51,204	5,226 / 26,129	7,335 / 36,677	11,335 / 56,677	8,910 / 44,549
9 Cuba[11]								1,276 / 6,381	1,134 / 5,672	1,510 / 7,548
10 Guadeloupe (Fr.)[12]								770[13]		463
11 Dutch Guiana								77		4,625[14]
12 Argentina[15]								5,000 / 20,000[16]	9,375 / 46,874	22,539 / 112,696
13 Brazil[17]	207 / 1,035	1,278 / 6,388		568 / 2,838	374 / 1,870	985 / 4,925	7,816 / 39,078	16,534 / 82,669	10,194 / 50,970	9,320 / 46,601
14 Paraguay										
15 Uruguay[18]				2,820 / 14,102	8,770 / 17,540[19]					
ASIA										
16 Philippines (U. S. A.)										
OCEANIA										
17 Australia[20]										
18 New South Wales									6,663 / 33,316	3,231 / 16,157
19 Queensland[21]										
20 Victoria[21]										9,183 / 45,916
21 New Zealand (Passengers)[22] (Immigrants)							2,192 / 6,575[23][24]	5,316 / 26,580[23]	9,628 / 48,141[23]	4,071 / 20,357[23]
22 Fiji (Brit.)[25]										
23 New Caledonia (Fr.)										
24 Hawaii (U. S. A.)										
AFRICA										
25 Mauritius (Brit.)[26]				4,245[27] / 25,468	18,846 / 56,538[28]	6,985 / 34,926	13,941 / 69,705	22,979 / 114,895	11,575 / 57,876	3,022 / 15,111
26 Seychelles (Brit.)										
27 Natal										
28 Cape of Good Hope[21]										
29 Union of South Africa[10]										

For reference notes see page 350.

TABLE 6—INTERCONTINENTAL IMMIGRATION OF ALIENS, 1821-1924 (continued.)

	1871–1875	1876–1880	1881–1885	1886–1890	1891–1895	1896–1900	1901–1905	1906–1910	1911–1915	1916–1920	1921–1924
AMERICA											
Canada (fiscal years)	**29,719**	**14,237**	**38,994**	**32,846**	**25,979**	**23,749**[3]	**67,785**	**138,062**	**170,549**	**40,428**	**81,559**
	148,596	71,187	194,972[3]	164,231[3]	129,897[3]	106,870[30]	338,927	793,858[31]	852,744	202,140	326,236
(calendar years)	......	.....	......	......	......	......	......	......	......	.....	**82,701**
											330,803
Newfoundland[3]	......	.....	......	......	......	......	**784**[32]	**885**	**712**[33]	.....	......
							2,351[34]	4,426[32]	2,135[32]		
United States[5] (fiscal years)	**308,417**	**176,335**	**516,194**	**454,186**	**424,643**	**312,060**	**764,121**	**949,182**	**804,570**	**150,355**	**426,090**
	1,542,083	881,677	2,580,968	2,270,930	2,123,216	1,560,300	3,820,607	4,745,911	4,022,848	751,774	1,704,358
(calendar years)	......	.....	......	......	......	......	......	......	......	.....	**349,623**
											1,398,490
Mexico	......	.....	......	......	......	......	......	......	**13,013**	**8,393**	**18,492**
									65,067	41,964	73,967
British West Indies[10]	**10,769**	**8,802**	**6,857**	**6,284**	**7,585**	**4,563**	**11,202**	**39,019**	**50,979**	**46,760**	**63,593**
	53,843	44,008	34,286	31,421	37,924	22,813	48,388[35]	121,691[36]	225,837[37]	233,646[38]	128,850[39]
Cuba[11]	......	.....	......	......	......	......	**24,581**	**23,939**	**27,345**	**46,043**	**39,236**
							122,903	119,697	136,723	230,213	156,942
Guadeloupe[12]	**970**	**1,916**	**1,674**	......	......	......	......	......	......	.....	......
	4,852	9,578	5,023[40]								
Dutch Guiana	......	**696**	......	**881**	**1,498**	**1,057**	**1,054**	**1,954**	**1,587**	**1,670**	**1,256**
		6,964[41]		8,806[42]	4,495[43]	5,287	5,271	9,772	4,760	8,350	3,767
Argentina[15]	**29,719**	**22,438**	**51,037**	**117,187**	**47,250**	**82,415**	**105,206**	**247,615**	**202,367**	**38,617**	**145,588**
	148,694	112,191	255,185	585,937	236,252	412,074	526,030	1,238,073	1,011,833	193,086	582,351
Brazil[17]	**16,263**	**27,563**	**27,096**	**79,085**	**133,274**	**95,506**	**57,606**	**80,218**	**121,633**	**36,802**	**60,306**
	81,314	137,814	135,482	395,424	666,370	477,532	288,031	401,088	608,163	184,010	301,528
Paraguay	......	.....	**165**	**905**	**323**	**222**	**318**	**970**	**929**	**315**	**294**
			823	4,523	1,614	1,111	1,588	4,852[44]	4,644[44]	1,573[44]	882[45]
Uruguay[18]	**14,565**	**7,296**	**10,408**	**17,662**	**9,505**	**8,460**	**7,117**	......	**9,758**	**5,536**	**7,569**
	72,824	39,629	52,041	88,308	47,526	42,302	21,350[46]		29,274[33]	27,681	7,569[47]
ASIA											
Philippines	......	.....	......	......	......	......	......	......	**3,573**	**7,500**	**7,754**
									17,865	37,498	31,017
OCEANIA											
Australia[20] [21]	......	......	......	......	......	......	**46,478**	**76,632**	**124,880**	**59,596**	**95,465**
							185,911[48]	383,161	624,398	297,979	381,858
New South Wales [21]	......	......	......	......	......	......	**16,454**	**23,760**	**44,569**	**17,984**	**30,961**
							82,271	118,798	222,845	89,919	92,883[46]
Queensland[21]	**7,708**	**8,434**	**15,875**	**9,248**	**1,998**	**2,648**	**1,922**	**4,779**	**9,959**	**2,894**	**5,332**
	38,541	42,168	79,377	46,239	9,991	13,240	9,611	23,896	49,795	14,470	21,327
Victoria[21]	**6,622**	**10,022**	**16,964**	**22,219**	**9,286**	**13,707**	**11,328**	**7,205**	**19,118**	**4,125**[49]	......
	33,111	50,112	84,818	111,096	46,431	68,536	56,640	36,023	95,588	4,125	
New Zealand (Passengers) (22)	**17,411**	**11,732**	**7,699**	**5,223**	**3,551**	**3,455**	**6,400**	**11,459**	**13,235**	**6,242**	......
	87,055	58,659	38,495	26,113	17,754	17,276	32,000	57,296	66,173	24,968[50]	......
(Immigrants)	......	......	......	......	......	......	......	......	......	......	**11,651**
											43,690[51]

For reference notes see page 350.

TABLE 6—INTERCONTINENTAL IMMIGRATION OF ALIENS, 1821-1924 concluded).

	1871-1875	1876-1880	1881-1885	1886-1890	1891-1895	1896-1900	1901-1905	1906-1910	1911-1915	1916-1920	1921-1924
OCEANIA (continued)											
Fiji[26]			**2,262**[32] / 9,048	**903** / 4,515	**1,398** / 6,989	**1,316** / 6,578	**2,125** / 10,624	**2,890** / 14,448	**3,037** / 15,186	**351** / 1,756	**1,844** / 1,844[47]
New Caledonia						**413**	**541**	**267**	**652** / 3,258	**380** / 1,900	**811** / 3,242
Hawaii						1,653	2,707	1,334	**9,358** / 46,790	**7,733** / 38,667	**12,321** / 49,285
AFRICA											
Mauritius[26]	**5,365** / 26,827	**2,267** / 11,336	**1,981** / 9,903	**1,858** / 9,290	**847** / 4,236	**823** / 4,117	**5,148** / 20,590[53]	**3,659** / 18,703	**3,741** / 18,297	**2,100** / 10,501	**3,371** / 13,484
Seychelles							**394** / 1,970	**350** / 1,752	**340** / 1,698	**294** / 1,471	**304** / 1,214
Natal			**3,091** / 15,453	**1,558** / 7,790	**3,589** / 17,946	**4,741** / 23,707	**6,889** / 34,447[54]	**6,345** / 31,723[54]	**4,698**[54] / 9,395[55]		
Cape of Good Hope[21]							**43,568** / 217,839	**30,606** / 153,032	**34,073** / 68,146[56]		
Union of South Africa[10]									**9,485** / 28,456[56]	**8,439** / 42,193	**15,555** / 62,218

For reference notes see page 350.

TABLE 7.—INTERCONTINENTAL IMMIGRATION OF ALIENS. PERCENTAGE DISTRIBUTION OF THE AVERAGE ANNUAL IMMIGRATION INTO AMERICA BY COUNTRIES OF IMMIGRATION, 1901-1924.

Country of Immigration	1901–1905	1906–1910	1911–1915	1916–1920	1921–1924
AMERICA:					
1 Canada	6.5	9.3	12.2	10.8	9.7
2 Newfoundland	0.1	0.1	0.1	...	...
3 United States	73.5	64.1	57.3	40.1	50.5
4 Mexico	...	...	0.9	2.2	2.2
5 British West Indies	1.1	2.6	3.6	12.5	7.5
6 Cuba	2.4	1.6	1.9	12.3	4.6
7 Dutch Guiana	0.1	0.1	0.1	0.4	0.1
8 Argentina	10.1	16.7	14.4	10.3	17.3
9 Brazil	5.5	5.4	8.7	9.8	7.1
10 Paraguay	0.0	0.1	0.1	0.1	0.0
11 Uruguay	0.7	...	0.7	1.5	0.9
Total	100.–	100.–	100.–	100.–	100.–

TABLE 8.—CONTINENTAL IMMIGRATION OF ALIENS, 1886-1924.

Country of Immigration	1886–1890	1891–1895	1896–1900	1901–1905	1906–1910	1911–1915	1916–1920	1921–1924
AMERICA								
1 United States	......	......	......	......	62,672	87,397	104,841	160,060
	......	......	......	......	188,015[1]	436,983	524,206	640,241
2 Cuba[2]				2,362	8,942	8,368	34,807	22,187
				11,810	44,708	41,839	174,035	88,748
3 Brazil					583	639	475	......
					1,748[3]	3,197	2,377	2,556
EUROPE								
4 Belgium	15,506	15,794	18,671	24,239	29,943	32,188	28,993	23,048
	77,532	78,968	93,354	121,196	149,713	96,563[4]	57,985[6]	92,191
5 Germany						434,489	174,239	27,591
						2,172,444	871,196	110,364
6 Hungary					13,934	8,849		
					55,735[5]	44,246		
ASIA								
7 Straits Settlements[7] (Brit.)				269,743	299,399	351,532	232,190	220,102
				1,348,717	1,496,993	1,757,658	1,160,948	880,409
8 Ceylon (Brit.)[8]	62,301	91,461	76,225	101,839	85,906	172,817	147,563	150,258
	311,505	457,304	381,126	509,194[9]	429,528[9]	864,085	737,817	450,774[10]

For reference notes see page 351.

TABLE 9.—INTERCONTINENTAL IMMIGRATION OF CITIZENS, 1876-1924.

	1876-1880	1881-1885	1886-1890	1891-1895	1896-1900	1901-1905	1906-1910	1911-1915	1916-1920	1921-1924
EUROPE										
1 Belgium	......	......	**256** 1,281	**375** 1,873	**396** 1,980	**460** 2,302	**829** 4,144	**1,006** 3,019[1]	**1,135** 2,269[2]	**1,261** 5,043
2 British Isles (Passengers)	**55,036** 275,181	**71,609** 358,046	**34,433** 472,166	**106,133** 530,663	**97,219** 486,094	**116,804** 584,021	**155,261** 776,304	**195,813** 979,064	**90,878** 454,388	**156,390** 625,558[3]
(Immigrants)								**85,560** 342,240[4]	**51,607** 258,035	**66,673** 266,690
3 Hungary[5]	......	......				**13,034** 65,168	**31,942** 159,709	**24,519** 73,558[1]	......	**3,286** 822
4 Netherlands[6]	**2,497** 12,485	**3,292** 16,458	**2,968** 14,842	**2,845** 14,227	**3,895** 19,477	**4,534** 22,668	**4,550** 22,748	**5,054** 25,271	**4,853** 24,267	**7,741** 30,963
5 Sweden	**578** 2,891	**1,434** 7,172	**2,406** 12,031	**5,063** 25,316	**4,561** 22,805	**3,891** 19,456	**5,107** 25,536	**4,549** 22,743	**3,288** 16,441	**3,204** 12,814
6 Finland[7]	......	......		**638** 1,276[8]	**699** 3,493	**1,362** 6,812	**2,362** 11,810	**1,794** 8,968	**664** 3,318	**723** 2,893
7 Italy[9]			**31,194** 124,776[10]	**55,045** 275,226	**68,840** 344,198	**115,831** 579,156	**200,521** 1,002,607	**195,614** 978,069	**46,656** 233,280	**63,673** 254,691
8 Spain (Passengers)	......	**36,999** 147,997[11]	**44,338** 221,691	**50,776** 253,881	**93,401** 373,605[12]			**138,783** 277,566[13]	**77,180** 385,899	**86,071** 258,212[14]
(Immigrants)	......	......							**41,248** 206,239	**47,673** 190,690
ASIA										
9 British India	**6,611** 19,832[15]	**6,509** 32,546	**7,839** 39,194	**6,061** 30,304	**6,237** 31,186	**9,668** 48,339	**7,117** 35,586	**5,712** 28,560	**5,698** 28,490	**7,132** 21,397[16]
10 Japan							**8,404** 25,213[17]	**9,161** 45,807	**14,857** 74,287	**14,130** 56,520
AFRICA										
11 St. Helena (Brit.)[18]	......					**345** 1,380[19]	**47** 235	**72** 358	**51** 253	**100** 400

TABLE 10.—CONTINENTAL IMMIGRATION OF CITIZENS, 1886-1924.

	1886-1890	1891-1895	1896-1900	1901-1905	1906-1910	1911-1915	1916-1920	1921-1924
EUROPE								
1 Belgium	**4,742** 23,709	**5,914** 29,570	**7,463** 37,316	**7,944** 39,718	**8,333** 41,665	**9,073** 27,220[1]	**15,870** 31,740[2]	**9,907** 39,628
2 Hungary	......			**1,887** 9,436	**2,923** 14,616	**1,548** 4,644[1]		
3 Sweden	**2,838** 14,190	**2,728** 13,639	**3,410** 17,050	**4,089** 20,443	**3,798** 18,989	**3,341** 16,705	**3,933** 19,665	**3,452** 13,809

For reference notes see page 351.

TABLE 11.—INTERCONTINENTAL EMIGRATION OF CITIZENS BY COUNTRY OF FUTURE RESIDENCE, 1866-1924.

a. Absolute figures, 1866-1870.

Country of Future Residence / Country of Emigration	British North America	United States	Argentina	Brazil	Other American States	Asia	Oceania	Africa	Other countries or future residence unknown	Total
EUROPE										
1 British Isles[1]	82,569	666,584	....	....	....	....	81,020	....	23,860	854,033
2 Norway[2]	....	58,880	....	....	....	....	68	....	....	58,948
ASIA										
3 British India[3]	....	....	....	....	55,671	....	....	13,842	....	69,513

a. Absolute figures, 1871-1875.

Country of Future Residence / Country of Emigration	British North America	United States	Argentina	Brazil	Other American States	Asia	Oceania	Africa	Other countries or future residence unknown	Total
EUROPE:										
1 Austria[4]	19	33,723	8	1,192	487	....	242	....	....	35,671
2 British Isles[1]	11,415	674,267	....	....	....	....	139,411	....	44,444	969,537
3 Denmark[1]	456	19,037	....	....	164	5	3,723	6	....	23,391
4 Germany[4]	924	360,563	745	11,606	1,869	102	5,246	30	13,729	394,814
5 Hungary[4]	....	2,887	4	17	3	....	34	....	....	2,945
6 Norway[4]	....	43,671	....	....	....	....	1,471	....	....	45,142
7 Sweden	....	41,580[6]	....	....	....	....	475	....	....	42,055
8 Switzerland[7]	....	11,976[8]	{ 4,316[9] (Argentina + Brazil)		645[10]	52	413	543	207	18,152
9 Russia[11]	4,339	25,985	5	22	9	1	36	1	....	30,398
10 Portugal[12]	....	....	....	....	59,180	30	....	1,338	....	60,548
ASIA:										
11 British India[3]	....	....	....	....	60,741	....	....	36,156	....	96,897

For reference notes see page 351.

TABLE 11.—INTERCONTINENTAL EMIGRATION OF CITIZENS BY COUNTRY OF FUTURE RESIDENCE FOR 1866 UPWARDS (cont.)

a. Absolute figures, 1876-1880.

Country of Future Residence →

Country of Emigration	British North America	United States	Argentina	Brazil	Other American States	Asia	Oceania	Africa	Other countries or future residence unknown	Total
EUROPE										
1 Austria	6	42,184	412	3,005	351	1		117	183	46,259
2 British Isles[1]	66,561	413,105				1	163,956	378	65,760	709,382
3 Denmark	454	13,330	797		111		908	1,248	17,088	15,182
4 Germany	377	195,303	1	9,298	2,208	179	4,656	2		231,154
5 Hungary[5]	2	11,014		43			3			11,065
6 Ireland	6,501	139,622					27,836		1,084	175,043
7 Norway		39,563					679	2		40,244
8 Sweden		60,099[6]					348			60,447
9 Switzerland[7]	2,150	12,396[8]	2,970[9]	4,194	495[10]	94	535	771	322	17,583
10 Russia[11]	139[13]	20,056	953	6	6	2	5	159		27,525
11 Italy		13,235[14]	45,350[15]	18,612[16]	54,341[16]	89	126[17]	12,035	568	144,495
12 Portugal					56,119	55		1,650		57,824
ASIA:										
13 British India[3]					61,461		498	29,623		91,582

a. Absolute figures, 1881-1885.

Country of Future Residence →

Country of Emigration	British North America	United States	Argentina	Brazil	Other American States	Asia	Oceania	Africa	Other countries or future residence unknown	Total
EUROPE										
1 Austria	104	94,631	6,858	949	1,471		43	8		104,064
2 British Isles[1]	159,510	842,547		-			214,885	37,932	37,435	1,292,309
3 Denmark	538	37,848			64	3	140	34		38,627
4 Germany	2,680	797,019	3,047	7,937	3,133	232	5,366	1,945	35,928	857,287
5 Hungary[5][18]	72	45,728	12	48	4		3	9		45,876
6 Ireland	27,484	313,682					26,102		707	367,975
7 Netherlands[19]		17,803	23[9]				44	164		18,034
8 Norway	10	105,633			2		52	7		105,704
9 Sweden		146,744			99		776			147,619
10 Switzerland[7]		46,977[8]	6,055[9]		250[10]	10	136	116	46	53,590
11 Finland[19]					4,503					4,503
12 Russia[11]	184	63,815	60	52	33	2	38	209		64,393
13 Italy	1,059	74,758	132,660	41,857	41,577	315	534	27,453		320,213
14 Portugal					79,472	113	424[20]	2,872		82,881
15 Spain[19]		493	20,323	4,301	95,913	7	8,571	61,961		191,569
ASIA:										
16 British India[3]					45,678		6,304	20,189	1,141	73,312

For reference notes see page 351.

TABLE 11.—INTERCONTINENTAL EMIGRATION OF CITIZENS BY COUNTRY OF FUTURE RESIDENCE FROM 1866 UPWARDS (cont.)

a. Absolute figures, 1886-1890.

Country of Future Residence / Country of Emigration	British North America	United States	Argentina	Brazil	Other American States	Asia	Oceania	Africa	Other countries or future residence unknown	Total
EUROPE:										
1 Austria	679	128,158	9,918	5,406	326	16	64	267	....	144,834
2 Belgium	5,916				7,663	118	30	128	335	14,190
3 British Isles[1]	142,412	871,406					157,859	39,477	55,072	1,266,226
4 Denmark	994	39,806			1,793	25	363	7		42,988
5 Germany	1,194	440,117	5,322	10,855	2,726	1,000	2,543	1,717	19,672	485,136
6 Hungary	12,302	299,826					17,427		2,390	331,945
7 Ireland	19,650 (British North America & United States)		4,522[9] (Argentina & Brazil)				8	127		24,307
8 Netherlands	177	80,665			34	1	98	9		80,984
9 Norway		177,835			1,218		833			179,886
10 Sweden		31,958[8]	6,247[9] (Argentina & Brazil)		8[10]	14	107	54		38,388
11 Switzerland[7]					21,968					21,968
12 Finland										
13 Russia[11]	1,951	187,089	3,933	29,528	50	10	176	511		223,248
14 Italy	5,213	170,472	258,843	173,695	45,268	237	1,057	16,390		671,175
15 Portugal					97,137	38	741	4,567		102,483
16 Spain		97	111,187	16,209	139,617	19	9,072	104,602		380,803
ASIA:										
17 British India[3]					37,513		2,966	20,741	1,112	62,332

For reference notes see page 351.

TABLE 11.—INTERCONTINENTAL EMIGRATION OF CITIZENS BY COUNTRY OF FUTURE RESIDENCE FROM 1866 UPWARDS (cont.)

a. Absolute figures, 1891-1895.

Country of Emigration	British North America	United States	Argentina	Brazil	Other American States	Asia	Oceania	Africa	Other countries or future residence unknown	Total
EUROPE:										
1 Austria	4,699	181,874	4,538	19,424	1,850	8	302	36	......	212,731
2 Belgium		6,505	......	......	928	128	24	227	144	7,956
3 British Isles[1]	103,645	685,886	......	......	......	......	68,184	65,489	55,370	978,574
4 Denmark	1,597	35,109	......	......	539	30	235	156	......	37,666
5 Germany	11,279	371,506	3,594	8,441	2,281	648	1,511	3,307	......	402,567
6 Hungary[21,22]	499	56,214	65	408	8	......	2	7	......	57,203
7 Ireland	4,211	222,460	......	......	......	......	5,184	......	614	232,469
8 Netherlands		17,377			......	......	268	......	......	17,645
9 Norway	405	60,497	......	......	16	1	22	76	......	61,017
10 Sweden	......	138,995	......	......	2,351	......	533	......	......	141,879
11 Switzerland[7]	102[23]	26,879	1,712	439	278	26	118	91	......	29,645
12 Finland	......	......	......	......	26,006	......	......	......	......	26,006
13 Russia[11]	7,227	253,103	5,720	10,769	9	37	155	2,238	......	279,258
14 Italy	2,344	206,596	155,583	329,904	39,529	1,279	1,204	14,692	......	751,131
15 Portugal	......	......	......	......	147,855	19	643	6,658	......	155,175
16 Spain	......	235	30,014	39,682	215,860	17	9,840	93,873	......	389,521
ASIA:										
17 British India[3]	......	......	......	......	46,717	......	5,845	21,381	157	74,100

For reference notes see page 351.

TABLE 11.—INTERCONTINENTAL EMIGRATION OF CITIZENS BY COUNTRY OF FUTURE RESIDENCE FROM 1866 UPWARDS (cont.)

a. Absolute figures, 1896-1900.

Country of Future Residence / Country of Emigration	British North America	United States	Argentina	Brazil	Other American States	Asia	Oceania	Africa	Other countries or future residence unknown	Total
EUROPE:										
1 Austria	20,300	179,604	5,604	17,805	1,182	7	1,878	145	....	226,525
2 Belgium	2,053 [B.N.A. + U.S.]		....	....	463	109	24	318	203	3,170
3 British Isles	83,331	460,018	....	....	....	....	59,497	100,706	60,664	764,216
4 Denmark	457	12,379	....	....	459	77	179	294	....	13,845
5 Germany	1,651	107,424	2,812	4,018	2,398	691	998	4,302	....	124,294
6 Hungary	508	114,835	44	69	15	3	9	250	....	115,733
7 Ireland	2,376	165,029	....	....	....	....	4,191	....	1,500	173,096
8 Netherlands	201	5,175[24]	51[9][24]	....	21	....	....	258[24]	792	6,276
9 Norway	....	33,090	....	185	....	5	265	255	....	33,837
10 Sweden	....	61,568	....	....	422	....	644	....	....	62,634
11 Switzerland[7]	628	12,424	1,322	....	162	38	57	181	925	14,435
12 Finland	....	....	....	....	33,027	8	....	....	....	33,036
13 Russia[11]	1,594	162,814	4,991	1,070	36	703	97	3,304	....	173,914
14 Italy	3,571	307,731	211,237	250,320	32,187	16	2,236	20,476	....	828,461
15 Portugal	....	....	....	....	102,474	12	185	8,001	....	110,676
16 Spain	....	307	58,715	29,704	194,917	....	30,833	87,048	....	401,536
ASIA:										
17 British India[3]	....	....	....	....	28,319	....	6,563	60,445	289	95,616
18 Japan[26]	5,587	10,895	....	....	792	1,192	36,677	....	5,362	60,505

For reference notes see page 351.

TABLE 11.—INTERCONTINENTAL EMIGRATION OF CITIZENS BY COUNTRY OF FUTURE RESIDENCE FROM 1866 UPWARDS (cont.)

a. Absolute figures, 1901-1905.

Country of Emigration	British North America	United States	Argentina	Brazil	Other American States	Asia	Oceania	Africa	Other countries or future residence unknown	Total
EUROPE:										
1 Austria	52,363	385,624	22,572	1,585	407	40	847	236	503	464,177
2 Belgium	8,052				792	138	16	374	252	9,624
3 British Isles[1]	253,820	605,171					71,119	169,680	1,049	1,170,839
4 Denmark	1,562	33,708			889	96	225	299		36,779
5 Germany	1,249	134,862	1,765	2,590	118	10	786	530		141,910
6 Hungary	3,259	365,329	3,049	123	11		3	294		372,068
7 Ireland	7,237	153,840					2,481	1,954	74	165,586
8 Netherlands	8,878[27]							34[27]	2,963	11,875
9 Norway	5,411	97,185[27]			90	1	23	485		103,195
10 Sweden		127,949			1,254		543			129,746
11 Switzerland[7]	150[23]	21,661	1,483	225	209	122	292	170		24,312
12 Finland					80,693				363	81,056
13 Russia[11]	2,787	321,504	11,107	963	7		66	3,740		340,174
14 Italy	19,654	998,352	278,511	200,103	38,853	2,405	3,512	61,631		1,603,021
15 Portugal					116,884	35	94	9,842		126,855
16 Spain			97,860	29,049	119,342	520	3,641	110,631		361,043
ASIA:										
17 British India[3]					30,340		11,049	46,934	317	88,640
18 Japan	568	1,774			3,495	7,692	48,578		2,322	64,429

For reference notes see page 351.

TABLE 11.—INTERCONTINENTAL EMIGRATION OF CITIZENS BY COUNTRY OF FUTURE RESIDENCE FROM 1866 UPWARDS (cont.)

a. Absolute figures, 1906-1910.

Country of Emigration	British North America	United States	Argentina	Brazil	Other American States	Asia	Oceania	Africa	Other countries or future residence unknown	Total
EUROPE:										
1 Austria	73,762	519,307	44,145	7,686	698	33	785	376	....	646,792
2 Belgium		13,561			1,463	268	52	754	276	16,374
3 British Isles (Passengers)	590,273	653,842					160,988	112,611	152,911	1,670,625
4 Denmark	2,263	31,501			2,105	237	417	113		36,636
5 Germany	1,960	120,311	2,846	1,395	4,856	1	730	145		132,244
6 Hungary	1,153	349,376	3,767	54	12		2	2		354,366
7 Ireland	17,690	120,625					3,535	982	462	143,294
8 Netherlands		13,375	2,714[9]					41		16,130
9 Norway	5,969	81,512			73	3	33	73		87,663
10 Sweden	584	91,300			2,567	152	430			94,297
11 Switzerland[7]		20,279	2,830	279	311		213	107		24,755
12 Finland		77,708							68	77,776
13 Poland[28]		53,944	6,481						7,590	68,015
14 Russia[11]	3,292	424,128	35,644	8,232	38		87	550		471,971
15 Italy	45,451	1,331,099	456,086	103,258	23,680	3,205	4,026	45,373		2,012,178
16 Portugal				190,834		21	3,309	2,974		197,138
17 Spain			372,986	55,296	173,970	524	4,694	122,319		729,789
ASIA:										
18 British India[3]					32,276		11,151	30,870	750	75,047
19 Japan	4,615	7,715	4	1,714	14,740	5,190	48,740	3	139	82,860

For reference notes see page 351.

TABLE 11.—INTERCONTINENTAL EMIGRATION OF CITIZENS BY COUNTRY OF FUTURE RESIDENCE FROM 1866 UPWARDS (cont.)

a. Absolute figures, 1911-1915.

Country of Emigration	British North America	United States	Argentina	Brazil	Other American States	Asia	Oceania	Africa	Other countries or future residence unknown	Total
EUROPE:										
1 Belgium[29]	3,703		211	....	5,438	128	37	1,204	214	10,935
2 British Isles (Passengers)	681 201	498,864	....	....	....	....	318,424	117,661	173,806	1,789,956
(Emigrants)[30]	434,618	273,429	....	....	....	24,203	194,454	34,944	46,509	1,008,157
3 Denmark	3,344	27,737	....	....	3,275	178	624	132	....	35,290
4 Germany	3,288	61,811	3,634	805	8,343	....	1,159	62	....	79,102
5 Hungary[29]	2,094	174,365	815	92	....	....	10	5	....	177,381
6 Ireland	21,445	86,187	....	....	....	....	4,437	660	152	112,881
7 Netherlands	9,230		953[9]	....	....	....	....	11	177	10,371
8 Norway	4,816	39,577	....	....	51	17	32	59	....	44,552
9 Sweden		59,923	....	....	2,888	....	550	....	....	63,361
10 Switzerland[7]	1,090	16,968	3,363	812	364	200	404	218	....	23,419
11 Finland			....	....	50,570	....	....	....	98	50,668
12 Poland[29]	42,140		12,986	....	....	....	....	....	4,025	59 151
13 Russia[11,12]	24,693	330,377	31,939	21,559	19,838	2,012	117	1,009	....	409,911
14 Italy	71,134	1,054,701	259,957	107,422	268,910	6	6,248	39,916	....	1,561,228
15 Portugal		5,078	....	35,344	206,306	497	419	147,676	....	269,742
16 Spain (Passengers)	7,831		433,772	31,516	160,859	64	2,622	2,616[32]	....	831,295
(Emigrants)	1,238	6,481	403,083	....	....	....	1,452	....	....	602,081
17 Malta			....	....	....	....	....	....	....	5,306
ASIA:										
18 British India[3]	5,177	20,773	195	....	23,346	8.393	14,883	5,200	2,069	45,498
19 Japan			....	13,371	4,974		21,446	1	136	74,466

For reference notes see page 351.

TABLE 11.—INTERCONTINENTAL EMIGRATION OF CITIZENS BY COUNTRY OF FUTURE RESIDENCE FROM 1866 UPWARDS (cont.)

a. Absolute figures, 1916–1920.

Country of Emigration	British North America	United States	Argentina	Brazil	Other American States	Asia	Oceania	Africa	Other countries or future residence unknown	Total
EUROPE:										
1 Belgium[33]	1,111	3,740[34]	72		272	112	40	923	322	6,592
2 British Isles (Passengers)	251,767	159,886				24,777	78,995	49,853	106,918	647,419
(Emigrants)	215,685	127,893			760	5	70,839	25,837	40,557	505,588
3 Denmark	940	14,553	588				38	17		16,313
4 Germany		1,939		131	9,278			10	129	11,936
5 Irish Free State (Ireland)	3,674	17,443					664			22,011
6 Netherlands	973	10,272	543[9]					9	101	11,355
7 Norway		15,891			40	52		13		16,969
8 Sweden	224	21,614		916	747	552	297			22,658
9 Switzerland[7]		10,817	1,142		288	651	46	778		14,763
10 Italy		512,081	55,558	18,462	5,477	34	1,229	26,907		632,859
11 Portugal		33,671		10,391	126,313	319	9	5,679		132,035
12 Spain (Passengers)		27,287	113,311	8,066	266,573		1,757	48,481		474,503
(Emigrants)		4,806	88,350		220,801			3,660[32]		345,504
13 Malta[35]	736						322			9,524
ASIA:										
14 British India[3]					3,079		1,756	1,210	4,451	10,496
15 Japan	7,196	30,756	612	13,576	7,883	14,009	18,323	1	451	92,807

For reference notes see page 351.

TABLE 11.—INTERCONTINENTAL EMIGRATION OF CITIZENS BY COUNTRY OF FUTURE RESIDENCE FROM 1866 UPWARDS (cont.)

a. Absolute figures, 1921-1924.

Country of Emigration / Country of Future Residence	British North America	United States	Argentina	Brazil	Other American States	Asia	Oceania	Africa	Other countries or future residence unknown	Total
EUROPE:										
1 Belgium	1,021	3,025[31]	110		370	274	109	2,556	407	7,872
2 British Isles (Passengers)[36]	375,493	269,445					216,580	90,942	165,133	1,117,593
(Emigrants)[37]	270,657	231,312				29,858	190,969	36,872	48,059	807,727
3 Denmark	4,407	16,322			2,307	48	195	44		23,323
4 Germany	2,992	148,968	24,817	42,069	10,834	200	54	2,633		232,567
5 Ireland[39]	1,422	11,417					340	37	32	13,248
6 Netherlands		12,989	961[9]		112	68		163	116	14,229
7 Norway	6,394	31,215					36	37		37,862
8 Sweden		45,869			3,401		556			49,826
9 Switzerland[7]	2,600[9]	14,631	2,405	1,956	706	742	455	1,567		25,062
10 Italy	15,169	304,563	260,382	47,479	8,873	512[40]	10,041	20,382	4,147	671,548
11 Portugal[38]					18,375	22	3	982		19,382
12 Spain (Passengers)[41]		2,106	124,104	6,061	122,754	135	1,141	38,574		294,875
(Emigrants)[42]		671	157,381	7,353	138,124				3,283	306,812
13 Malta	396	430					2,027	4,047[32]		6,900
ASIA:										
14 British India[3]								1,397	1,575	2,972
15 Japan	3,936	14,560	229	6,441	2,242	7,618	11,380		273	46,679

For reference notes see page 351.

TABLE 12.—INTERCONTINENTAL EMIGRATION OF CITIZENS BY COUNTRY OF FUTURE RESIDENCE FROM 1866 UPWARDS (cont.)

b. Percentages

1886-1890

Country of Future Residence — Country of Emigration	British North America	United States	Argentina	Brazil	Other American States	Asia	Oceania	Africa	Other countries or future residence unknown	Total
EUROPE:										
1 Austria	0.5	88.5	6.8	3.7	0.2	0.0	0.0	0.2	...	100
2 Belgium	41.7 (BNA+US)		...	...	54.—	0.8	0.2	0.9	2.4	100
3 British Isles[1]	11.2	68.8	...	...	...	...	12.5	3.1	4.3	100
4 Denmark	2.3	92.6	...	...	4.2	0.1	0.8	0.0	...	100
5 Germany	0.2	90.7	1.1	2.2	0.6	0.2	0.5	0.4	4.1	100
6 Hungary	...	...	...	...	...	...	...	...	...	·100
7 Ireland	3.7	90.3	...	...	...	...	5.2	...	0.7	100
8 Netherlands	80.8 (BNA+US)		18.6[9] (Arg+Brazil)		0.0	0.0	0.0	0.5	...	100
9 Norway	0.2	99.6	...	...	...	0.0	0.1	0.0	...	100
10 Sweden	...	98.8	...	...	0.7	...	0.5	...	...	100
11 Switzerland[7]	...	83.3[8]	16.3[9] (Arg+Brazil)		0.0[10]	0.0	0.3	0.1	...	100
12 Finland	...	100.—	...	...	...	0.0	0.1	...	...	100
13 Russia	0.9	83.8	1.8	13.2	0.0	0.0	0.2	0.2	...	100
14 Italy	0.8	25.4	38.7	25.9	6.7	0.0	0.7	2.4	...	100
15 Portugal	...	...	...	...	94.8	0.0	2.4	4.5	...	100
16 Spain	...	0.0	29.2	4.3	36.7	0.0	...	27.5	...	100
ASIA:										
17 British India[2]	...	...	...	...	60.2	.	4.8	33.3	1.8	100

For reference notes see page 352.

TABLE 12.—INTERCONTINENTAL EMIGRATION OF CITIZENS BY COUNTRY OF FUTURE RESIDENCE FROM 1866 UPWARDS (cont.)

b. Percentages

1891-1895

Country of Emigration / Country of Future Residence	British North America	United States	Argentina	Brazil	Other American States	Asia	Oceania	Africa	Other countries or future residence unknown	Total
EUROPE:										
1 Austria	2.2	85.5	2.1	9.1	0.9	0.0	0.1	0.0	....	100
2 Belgium	{81.8		....	....	11.7	1.6	0.3	2.9	1.8	100
3 British Isles[1]	10.6	70.1	....	....	1.4	0.1	7.—	6.7	5.7	100
4 Denmark	4.2	93.2	0.9	2.1	0.6	....	0.6	0.4	....	100
5 Germany[21][22]	2.8	92.3	0.1	0.7	0.0	0.2	0.4	0.8	....	100
6 Hungary[21][22]	0.9	98.3	....	....	....	....	0.0	0.0	0.3	100
7 Ireland	1.8	95.7	....	....	....	....	2.2	....	....	100
8 Netherlands	{98.5		....	....	0.0	0.0	0.0	1.5	....	100
9 Norway	0.7	99.2	....	....	0.0	0.0	0.4	0.1	....	100
10 Sweden	....	98.—	....	....	1.6	0.1	....	0.3	....	100
11 Switzerland[7]	0.3[23]	90.7	5.8	1.5	0.9	0.1	....	0.4	....	100
12 Finland	....	....	....	....	100.—	....	....	....	....	100
13 Russia[11]	2.6	90.6	2.1	3.9	0.0	0.0	0.2	2.—	....	100
14 Italy	0.3	27.5	20.7	43.9	5.3	0.2	0.4	4.3	....	100
15 Portugal	....	....	7.7	10.2	95.3	....	2.5	24.1	....	100
16 Spain	....	0.1	....	....	55.4	0.0	....	....	0.2	100
ASIA:										
17 British India[3]	....	....	....	....	63.1	....	7.9	28.9	....	100

For reference notes see page 352.

TABLE 12.—INTERCONTINENTAL EMIGRATION OF CITIZENS BY COUNTRY OF FUTURE RESIDENCE FROM 1866 UPWARDS (cont.)

b. Percentages

1896-1900

Country of Emigration \ Country of Future Residence	British North America	United States	Argentina	Brazil	Other American States	Asia	Oceania	Africa	Other countries or future residence unknown	Total
EUROPE:										
1 Austria	9.—	79.3	2.5	7.5	0.5	0.0	0.8	0.1	...	100
2 Belgium	64.8 [a]		...	...	14.6	3.4	0.8	10.—	6.4	100
3 British Isles[4]	10.9	60.2	...	...	...	...	7.8	13.2	7.9	100
4 Denmark	3.3	89.4	...	...	3.3	0.6	1.3	2.1	...	100
5 Germany	1.3	86.4	2.3	3.2	1.9	0.6	0.8	3.5	...	100
6 Hungary	0.4	99.2	0.0	0.1	0.0	0.0	0.0	0.2	...	100
7 Ireland	1.4	95.3	...	...	...	...	2.4	...	0.9	100
8 Netherlands	...	82.5[24]	0.8[9][24] [b]		0.1	0.0	0.8 [c]	4.1[24]	12.6	100
9 Norway	0.6	97.8	...	...	...	0.0	0.8 [c]	0.8	...	100
10 Sweden	...	98.3	...	...	0.7	...	1.—	...	...	100
11 Switzerland[7]	0.5[23]	86.1	9.2	1.3	1.1	0.3	0.4	1.3	...	100
12 Finland	...	100.—	...	...	...	...	...	...	0.05[25]	100
13 Russia[11]	0.9	93.6	2.9	0.6	0.0	0.1	0.1	1.9	...	100
14 Italy	0.4	37.1	25.5	30.2	3.9	0.0	0.3	2.5	...	100
15 Portugal	...	...	...	92.6	...	...	...	7.2	...	100
16 Spain	...	0.1	14.6	7.4	48.5	...	7.7	21.7	...	100
ASIA:										
17 British India[3]	...	...	...	...	29.6	...	6.9	63.2	0.3	100
18 Japan[26]	9.2	18.—	...	...	1.3	2.—	60.6	...	8.9	100

[a] Belgium: the figure 64.8 (with brace) covers British North America and United States combined.
[b] Netherlands: the figure 0.8[9][24] (with brace) covers Argentina and Brazil combined.
[c] Netherlands and Norway: Oceania figure 0.8 covers both rows (brace).

For reference notes see page 352.

TABLE 12.—INTERCONTINENTAL EMIGRATION OF CITIZENS BY COUNTRY OF FUTURE RESIDENCE FROM 1866 UPWARDS (cont.)

b. Percentages

1901-1905

Country of Emigration	British North America	United States	Argentina	Brazil	Other American States	Asia	Oceania	Africa	Other countries or future residence unknown	Total
EUROPE:										
1 Austria	11.3	83.1	4.9	0.3	0.1	0.0	0.2	0.1	0.1	100
2 Belgium		83.7‡			8.2	1.4	0.2	3.9	2.6	100
3 British Isles[1]	21.7	51.7					6.1	14.5	6.1	100
4 Denmark	4.2	91.7			2.4	0.3	0.6	0.8		100
5 Germany	0.9	95.—	1.2	1.8	0.1		0.6	0.4		100
6 Hungary	0.9	98.2	0.8	0.0	0.0	0.1	0.0	0.1		100
7 Ireland	4.4	92.9					1.5	1.2	0.0	100
8 Netherlands		74.8‡[27]						0.3[27]	25.—	100
9 Norway	5.2	94.2			0.1	0.0	0.0	0.5		100
10 Sweden	0.6[23]	98.6			1.—		0.4			100
11 Switzerland[7]		89.1	6.1	0.9	0.9	0.5	1.2	0.7	0.5	100
12 Finland	0.8	94.5		0.3			0.0	1.1		100
13 Russia[21]	1.2	62.3	3.3		0.0		0.2	3.8		100
14 Italy			17.4	12.5	2.4	0.2	0.1	7.8		100
15 Portugal				92.1		0.0	1.0			100
16 Spain			27.1	8.1	33.1	0.1		30.6		100
ASIA:										
17 British India[3]					34.2		12.5	53.—	0.4	100
18 Japan	0.9	2.8			5.4	11.9	75.4		3.6	100

‡ In the original, for Belgium and Netherlands the figure shown under United States is joined by a brace combining British North America and the United States.

For reference notes see page 352.

TABLE 12.—INTERCONTINENTAL EMIGRATION OF CITIZENS BY COUNTRY OF FUTURE RESIDENCE FROM 1866 UPWARDS (cont.)

b. Percentages

1906-1910

Country of Emigration	British North America	United States	Argentina	Brazil	Other American States	Asia	Oceania	Africa	Other countries or future residence unknown	Total
EUROPE										
1 Austria............	11.4	80.3	6.8	1.2	0.1	0.0	0.1	0.1	....	100
2 Belgium...........	6.2	86.–	....	....	8.9	1.6	0.3	4.6	1.7	100
3 British Isles[1]...	35.3	39.1	....	....	5.7	....	9.6	6.7	9.2	100
4 Denmark..........	1.5	91.–	2.1	1.1	3.7	0.6	1.1	0.3	....	100
5 Germany..........	0.3	98.6	1.1	0.0	0.0	0.0	0.6	0.1	....	100
6 Hungary..........	82.8 (Brit. N. America + United States)		16.8[5] (Argentina + Brazil)		....	....	....	....	0.3	100
7 Ireland...........	12.3	84.2	....	....	0.0	....	2.5	0.7	....	100
8 Netherlands......	82.9 (Brit. N. America + United States)		....	....	0.1	0.0	....	0.3	....	100
9 Norway..........	6.8	93.–	....	....	2.7	....	0.0	0.1	....	100
10 Sweden.........	....	96.8	....	....	1.3	....	....	0.5	....	100
11 Switzerland[7]..	2.4	81.9	11.4	....	....	0.6	0.9	0.4	0.1	100
12 Finland.........	....	99.9	....	1.1	....	....	....	....	....	100
13 Poland[28]......	0.7	89.9	....	....	0.0	....	0.0	0.1	11.2	100
14 Russia[11]......	2.3	66.1	7.6	1.7	1.2	0.2	0.2	2.3	....	100
15 Italy...........	79.3 (Brit. N. America + United States)		9.5 (Argentina + Brazil)		0.0	0.2	1.7	1.5	....	100
16 Portugal........	....	....	22.7	5.1	96.8	0.0	1.7	16.8	....	100
17 Spain...........	....	....	51.1	7.6	23.8	0.1	0.6	0.0	0.2	100
ASIA:										
18 British India[3].	....	....	....	....	43.0	6.3	14.9	41.1	1.–	100
19 Japan...........	5.6	9.3	0.0	2.1	17.8	....	58.8	0.0	0.2	100

For reference notes see page 352.

TABLE 12—INTERCONTINENTAL EMIGRATION OF CITIZENS BY COUNTRY OF FUTURE RESIDENCE FROM 1866 UPWARDS (cont.)

b. Percentages

1911-1915

Country of Emigration \ Country of Future Residence	British North America	United States	Argentina	Brazil	Other American States	Asia	Oceania	Africa	Other countries or future residence unknown	Total
EUROPE:										
1 Belgium[29]	33.9 (British North America and United States)		1.9	....	49.7	1.2	0.3	11.–	2.–	100
2 British Isles (Passengers)	38.1	27.9	....	....	....	....	17.8	6.6	9.7	100
(Emigrants)[30]	43.1	27.1	....	....	....	2.4	19.3	3.5	4.6	100
3 Denmark	9.5	78.6	....	....	9.3	0.5	1.8	0.4	....	100
4 Germany	4.2	78.1	4.6	1.–	10.5	....	1.5	0.1	....	100
5 Hungary[29]	1.2	98.3	0.5	0.1	....	....	0.0	0.0	....	100
6 Ireland	19.–	76.4	....	....	....	....	3.9	0.6	0.1	100
7 Netherlands	89.– (British North America and United States)		9.2[9] (Argentina and Brazil)		....	....	....	0.1	1.7	100
8 Norway	10.8	88.8	....	....	0.1	0.0	0.1	0.1	....	100
9 Sweden	....	94.6	....	....	4.5	....	....	0.9	....	100
10 Switzerland[7]	4.7	72.5	14.4	3.5	1.6	0.9	1.7	0.9	....	100
11 Finland	....	....	....	....	99.8	....	....	....	0.2	100
12 Poland[29]	71.2 (British North America and United States)		22.– (Argentina and Brazil)		....	....	....	...	6.8	100
13 Russia[11 29]	6.0	80.6	7.8	5.3	0.1	....	0.0	0.3	....	100
14 Italy	4.5	67.5	16.7	6.9	1.3	0.1	0.4	2.6	....	100
15 Portugal	....	....	....	....	99.7	0.0	0.2	0.2	....	100
16 Spain (Passengers)	....	0.6	52.2	4.3	24.8	0.1	0.3	17.8	....	100
(Emigrants)	0.0[31]	1.1	66.9	5.2	26.7	0.0	....	....	....	100
17 Malta	23.3	....	....	....	....	....	27.4	49.3[32]	....	100
ASIA:										
18 British India[3]	....	....	....	....	51.3	....	32.7	11.4	4.6	100
19 Japan	7.–	27.9	0.3	18.–	6.7	11.3	28.8	0.0	0.2	100

For reference notes see page 352.

TABLE 12.—INTERCONTINENTAL EMIGRATION OF CITIZENS BY COUNTRY OF FUTURE RESIDENCE FROM 1866 UPWARD (cont.)

b. Percentages

1916-1920

Country of Future Residence → / Country of Emigration ↓	British North America	United States	Argentina	Brazil	Other American States	Asia	Oceania	Africa	Other countries or future residence unknown	Total
EUROPE:										
1 Belgium[33]	16.9	56.7[34]	1.1	....	4.1	1.7	0.6	14.—	4.9	100
2 British Isles (Passengers)	38.9	24.7	....	....	....	....	12.2	7.7	16.5	100
(Emigrants)	42.7	25.3	....	....	....	4.9	14.—	5.1	8.—	100
3 Denmark	5.8	89.2	....	....	4.7	0.0	0.2	0.1	....	100
4 Germany	....	16.2	4.9	1.1	77.7	....	....	....	....	100
5 Ireland	16.7	79.2	....	....	....	....	3.—	0.5	0.6	100
6 Netherlands	94.2 (BNA + US combined)		4.8[9] (Argentina + Brazil combined)		0.2	....	....	0.1	0.9	100
7 Norway	5.7	93.7	....	....	....	0.3	....	0.1	....	100
8 Sweden	....	95.4	....	....	3.3	....	1.3	....	....	100
9 Switzerland[7]	1.5	73.3	7.7	6.2	2.—	3.7	0.3	5.3	....	100
10 Italy	2.—	80.9	8.8	2.9	0.9	0.1	0.2	4.3	....	100
11 Portugal	....	7.1	23.9	2.2	95.7	0.1	0.0	10.2	....	100
12 Spain (Passengers)	....	7.9	25.6	2.3	56.2	....	0.4	....	....	100
(Emigrants)	7.7	50.5	....	....	64.2	....	....	....	....	100
13 Malta[35]	....	....	....	....	....	....	3.4	38.4[32]	....	
ASIA:										
14 British India[3]	....	....	....	....	29.3	....	16.7	11.5	42.4	100
15 Japan	7.8	33.1	0.7	14.6	8.5	15.1	19.7	0.0	0.5	100

For reference notes see page 352.

TABLE 12—INTERCONTINENTAL EMIGRATION OF CITIZENS BY COUNTRY OF FUTURE RESIDENCE FROM 1866 UPWARDS (cont)

b. Percentages

1921-1924

Country of Emigration	British North America	United States	Argentina	Brazil	Other American States	Asia	Oceania	Africa	Other countries or future residence unknown	Total
EUROPE:										
1 Belgium	13.—	38.4[4]	1.4		4.7	3.5	1.4	32.5	5.2	100
2 British Isles[36] (Passengers)	33.6	24.1					19.4	8.1	14.8	100
(Emigrants)[37]	33.5	28.6				3.7	23.6	4.6	5.9	100
3 Denmark	18.9	70.—			9.9	0.2	0.8	0.2		100
4 Germany[38]	1.3	64.1	10.7	18.1	4.7	0.2	0.0	1.1	0.2	100
5 Ireland[38]	10.7	86.2				0.1	2.6	0.3	0.2	100
6 Netherlands	91.3		6.8[9]					1.1	0.8	100
7 Norway	16.9	82.4			0.3	0.2	0.1	0.1		100
8 Sweden		92.1			6.8		1.1			100
9 Switzerland[7]	10.4[39]	58.4	9.6	7.8	2.8	3.—[40]	1.8	6.2	0.6	100
10 Italy	2.3	45.4	38.8	7.1	1.3	0.1[40]	1.5	3.0		100
11 Portugal[38]					94.8	0.1	0.0	5.1	0.6	100
12 Spain[41] (Passengers)		0.7	42.1	2.1	41.6		0.4	13.1		100
(Emigrants)[42]		0.2	51.3	2.4	45.—				1.1	100
13 Malta[42]	5.7	6.2					29.4	58.7[23]		100
ASIA:										
14 British India[3]								47.0	53.0	100
15 Japan	8.4	31.2	0.5	13.8	4.8	16.3	24.4		0.6	100

For reference notes see page 352.

TABLE 13.—IMMIGRATION OF ALIENS, BY COUNTRY OF LAST RESIDENCE OR NATIONALITY[1], 1821–1924.

a.   Absolute figures

Country of Last Residence or Nationality	1821–1825 United States[2]	1821–1825 Brazil[3]	1826–1830 United States[2]	1826–1830 Brazil[3]	1831–1835 Canada	1831–1835 United States[2]	1831–1835 Brazil[3]	1836–1840 Canada	1836–1840 United States[2]	1836–1840 West Indies	1836–1840 Brazil
Germany	1,394	……	5,367	1,984	15[4]	45,592	……	485[2]	106,862	561	270
Belgium	16	……	11	……	……	5	……	……	17	……	……
Denmark	61	……	108	……	……	278	……	……	785	……	……
Spain	1,195	……	1,282	……	……	949	……	……	1,176	……	……
France	2,073	……	6,424	……	……	17,766	……	……	27,809	8	……
Greece	5	……	15	……	……	9	……	……	40	……	……
Italy	250	……	158	……	—[4]	1,895	……	—[4]	358	……	180
Norway	36[6]	……	55[6]	……	……	415[6]	……	……	786[6]	……	……
Poland	12	……	4	……	……	143	……	……	226	……	……
Portugal	96	……	49	……	……	711	……	……	118	……	467
Netherlands	203	……	875	……	……	630	……	……	782	……	……
Russia	41[6][7]	……	34[6][7]	……	……	236[6][7]	……	……	416[6][7]	1,027	……
British Isles	21,816	……	53,987	……	165,320	104,439	……	80,808	178,752	……	……
Sweden	—[6]	……	—[6]	……	……	—[5]	……	……	—[5]	……	……
Switzerland	669	……	2,557	……	……	2,763	……	……	2,058	……	……
Turkey in Europe	8	……	1	……	……	2	……	……	5	……	……
Other European Countries	2	……	1	……	……	7	……	……	33	……	……
China	1	……	6	……	……	8	……	……	……	……	……
India	2	……	……	……	……	22	……	……	17	406	……
Other Asiatic countries	……	……	13	……	……	1	……	……	……	……	……
Africa	3	……	……	……	……	20	……	……	32	67	……
United States	……	……	……	……	……	……	……	……	……	1,294	……
British North America	1,024	……	1,253	……	……	4,191	……	……	9,433	……	……
Central America	21	……	84	……	……	40	……	……	4	……	……
Mexico	222	……	4,595	……	……	4,215	……	……	2,384	……	……
West Indies	1,074	……	2,760	……	……	5,530	……	……	6,771	6,143	……
South America	127	……	404	……	……	462	……	……	394	405	……
Oceania	2[8]	……	…[8]	……	……	4[8]	……	……	5[8]	……	……
Atlantic Islands	19	……	333	……	……	65	……	……	38	……	……
Other Countries	10,131	1,035	22,548	4,404	1,879	62,096	……	1,269	7,705	819	1,921
Total	40,503	1,035	102,936	6,388	167,214	252,494	……	82,562	346,631	10,730	2,83…

For reference notes see page 353.

TABLE 13.—IMMIGRATION OF ALIENS BY COUNTRY OF LAST RESIDENCE OR NATIONALITY FROM 1821 UPWARDS (cont.)

a. Absolute figures

Country of Immigration — Country of Last Residence or Nationality	1841–1845				1846–1850				1851–1855				
	Canada (8 bis)	United States[2]	West Indies	Brazil[3]	Canada (8 bis)	United States[3]	West Indies	Brazil[3]	Canada	United States[2]	West Indies	Brazil[3]	New Zealand[9][10]
Germany		105,188		576	3,764[4]	329,438		2,143	31,983[4]	647,273		5,213	
Belgium		991				4,083		2		1,867		13	
Denmark		174				365				1,268			
Spain		1,056	23	10		1,153		122		4,301		22	
France		23,674		159		53,588		114		57,020		72	
Greece		10				6				23			
Italy		674			—[4]	1,196			—[4]	3,668		24	
Norway		4,735[5]				9,168[8]		5		14,243[6]			
Poland		84				21				823			
Portugal		84				466		256		490		25,836	
Netherlands		1,849		207		6,402				6,793			
Russia		222[7]				329[6]						123	
British Isles	136,557	267,280	1,365		199,611	780,482		292	155,088	930,664	21		4,145
Sweden		3,097				1,547		338		18,349		1,746	
Switzerland		26				33				36			
Turkey in Europe		75				4				2			
Other European countries		18				17				16,668			
China		6	1,302			30	20,497			17	2,107		
India		9								8	14,163		
Other Asiatic countries		41				14				25			
Africa			14,060				29,297				9,596		
United States		11,302	265			30,421	32			33,866			
British North America		34	170			334				121			
Central America						1,423				1,281			
Mexico		1,848				8,184				5,490			
West Indies		5,344	13,145			3,055	820			463	129		
South America		524	1,821			218	558			43[8]	113		
Oceania		8[8]				290							7,454[11]
Atlantic Islands		47								1,007			
Other countries		1,934	367	918	2,511	50,843		1,653	4,334	2,594		6,029	2,430
Total	139,704	430,335	32,518	1,870	205,886	1,282,915	51,204	4,925	191,405	1,748,424	26,129	39,078	14,029

For reference notes see page 353.

TABLE 13.—IMMIGRATION OF ALIENS BY COUNTRY OF LAST RESIDENCE OR NATIONALITY FROM 1821 UPWARDS (cont.)

a. Absolute figures

Country of Last Residence or Nationality	1856–1860						1861–1865					
	Canada	United States[2]	West Indies	Argentina[3 12 13]	Brazil[3]	New Zealand[9]	Canada	United States[2]	West Indies	Argentina[3 12]	Brazil[3]	New Zealand[9]
Germany	27,325[4]	304,394		240	13,707		34,751[4]	233,052		426	7,124	
Austria				297[14]	13			490		370[14]		
Belgium		2,871		95				1,753		251	420	
Denmark		2,481			37			5,245			83	
Spain		4,997		3,370	69			2,905		6,401		
France		19,338		1,105				14,017		1,687	1,414	
Finland								22				
Greece		8		—[14]				409				
Hungary								3,448		—[14]	3,023	
Italy	—[4]	5,563		12,355			—[4]	11,493[5]		33,664		
Norway		6,688						898				
Poland		341						810		91	25,386	
Portugal		565			43,082			2,618		39		
Netherlands		3,996		156						185		
Russia		436[6]		42				629[6]		864		
British Isles	58,450	407,429[7]	1	120	324	25,301	67,204	443,448[7]			236	47,555
Sweden				518	649						304	
Switzerland		6,662		286				6,625		548	522	
Turkey in Europe		47						57				
Other European countries		3						5				
China		24,729	2,641					24,282	10,088			
India		26	26,549					23	33,665			
Japan								1				
Turkey in Asia												
Other Asiatic countries		7						7				
United States												
Africa		185	7,448					148	4,942			
British North America		25,443						34,030				
Central America		328						52				
Mexico		1,797						748				
West Indies		5,170	38					3,003	7,982			
South America		761						637				
Oceania		115[8]				10,125[11]		163[8]				94,065[11]
Atlantic Islands		2,083		1,416	24,788	1,279		1,694		2,348	12,458	586
Other countries	499	23,327					65	9,011				
Total	86,274	849,790	36,677	20,000	82,669	36,705	102,020	801,723	56,677	46,874	50,970	142,206

For reference notes see page 353.

TABLE 13.—IMMIGRATION OF ALIENS BY COUNTRY OF LAST RESIDENCE OR NATIONALITY FROM 1821 UPWARDS (cont.)

a. Absolute figures

Country of Immigration / Country of Last Residence or Nationality	1866–1870						1871–1875						
	Canada	United States[2]	West Indies	Argentina[3,12]	Brazil[3]	New Zealand[9]	West Indies [16 bis]	United States[2]	Canada	Argentina[3,12]	Brazil[3]	Queensland[9]	New Zealand[9]
Germany	66,040[1]	554,416		872	5,648			508,394	12,672[4]	1,963	5,224	6,578	
Austria		6,826[7]		445[14]	104			29,601[7]		548[4]	321		
Belgium		4,981		268	53			4,120		291	138		
Denmark		11,849						16,374					
Spain		3,792		16,226	588			2,780[5]		28,458	1,276		
France		21,969		6,684	1,152			45,218		22,308	2,153		
Finland		—[6]						226					
Greece		50						107					
Hungary		75		—[14]				3,316		—[14]			
Italy		8,277		79,890	1,900			27,060		82,851	4,610		
Norway	—[4]	97,805[5]						53,563	—[4]				
Poland		1,129						8,299					
Portugal		986		327	24,776			1,553[15]		344	32,688		
Netherlands		6,484		72				10,394		18			
Russia		1,883[6][7]		234				15,169[7]		222	145		
British Isles	115,227	599,226		3,033	2,689	18,556		664,972	133,864	5,898	1,038	22,770	75,617
Sweden					141			49,751			2,076		
Switzerland		16,661		1,446	311			13,933		3,742	926		
Turkey in Europe		72						185					
Other European countries		865	1,386					5,570					
China		40,019	36,620				14,845	65,428				7,254[16]	
India		46						77					
Japan		185						128					
Turkey in Asia		2						14			31		
Other Asiatic countries		65	497				260	80					
United States													
Africa		164	1,428					205					
British North America		119,842						182,140					
Central America		43						85					
Mexico		1,443	4,618					2,573					
West Indies		6,049					591	7,916					
South America		760				32,412[11]		640				41,933[17]	23,027[18]
Oceania		51						6,312					
Atlantic Islands	27	749[16]						—[14]				1,939	11,438
Other countries		6,337		3,199	9,239	1,801		613	2,060	2,051[19]	30,688		
Total	181,294	1,513,101	44,549	112,696	46,601	52,769	15,696	1,726,796	148,596	148,694	81,314	80,474	110,082

For reference notes see page 353.

TABLE 13.—IMMIGRATION OF ALIENS BY COUNTRY OF LAST RESIDENCE OR NATIONALITY FROM 1821 UPWARDS (cont.)

a. Absolute figures

Country of Last Residence or Nationality	1876-1880						1881-1885							
	Canada	United States[2]	Argentina[3 12]	Brazil[3]	Queensland[9]	New Zealand[9]	Canada	United States[2]	Argentina[3 12]	Brazil[3]	Paraguay[3]	Uruguay[3 21]	Queensland[9]	New Zealand[9]
Germany		209,788	1,856	11,782				960,020	5,914	10,570	607	2,095		
Austria		33,408[7]	3,713[14]	7,551				97,414[7]	5,529[4]	1,603	7	377[14]		
Belgium		3,101	367	132				7,876	1,854	64	17	111		
Denmark		15,397						46,356			3			
Spain		2,486[5]	16,068	3,901				1,774[15]	23,133	10,960		13,088		
France		26,988	10,409	2,284				23,155	20,763	1,071	80	4,663		
Finland		220						2,886						
Greece		103						427						
Hungary		6,644	—[14]					51,176	—[14]					
Italy		28,699	69,210	55,419				109,504	182,620	62,724	7	26,473		
Norway		41,760						104,534						
Poland		4,671						19,918						
Portugal		3,074[5]	359	42,564				1,530[15]	643	42,568	1	643		
Netherlands		6,147	76					30,250	113	1,066	2			
Russia		23,669[7]	190	7,463				58,829[7]	120		8			
Rumania		11						1,213						
British Isles	68,576	319,942	3,803	967	23,033	53,225	154,133	730,035	4,991	617	1	2,488	71,063	34,211
Sweden		66,171		176				201,444		69	2			
Switzerland		14,360	2,544	813				50,169	5,294	307	89	237		
Turkey in Europe		152						515						
Other European countries		4,886						7,062					6,308[16]	
China		57,773			14,794[16]			59,801						
India		86						98						
Japan		21						112						
Turkey in Asia		53						5						
Other Asiatic countries		163						416						
Africa		153						331						
United States				21			282,094[20]			103		133		
British North America		201,129						392,802						
Central America		125						105						
Mexico		2,589						1,913						
West Indies		6,359						8,770						
South America														
Argentina		488						387				317		
Brazil												3,730		
Uruguay														
Other countries												181[22]		
Oceania		4,602			45,622[18]	28,116[19]		4,406					81,393[17]	37,573[18]
Other countries	2,611	177	3,596[19]	4,741	687	5,434	40,839	450	4,211[19]	3,760		1,733	2,006	4,284
Total	71,187	1,085,395	112,191	137,814	87,790	86,775	477,066[20]	2,975,683	255,185	135,482	881	56,271	160,770	76,068

For reference notes see page 353.

TABLE 13.—IMMIGRATION OF ALIENS BY COUNTRY OF LAST RESIDENCE OR NATIONALITY FROM 1821 UPWARDS (cont.)

a. Absolute figures

Country of Last Residence or Nationality	Canada[20]	United States[2]	Argentina[3][12]	Brazil[3]	Paraguay[3]	Uruguay[2][21]	Queensland[9]	New Zealand[9]
				1886–1890				
Germany		492,950	8,270	11,058	691	1,773		
Austria		128,624[7]	10,989[4]	4,954	249[4]	774		
Belgium		12,301	13,947	2,090	98	146		
Denmark		41,776			24			
Spain		2,645[15]	135,631	28,839	718	19,583		
France		27,309	73,080	4,389	795	4,779		
Finland		9,022						
Greece		1,881			2			
Hungary		76,505	—[14]	2				
Italy		197,805	311,265	232,339	1,542	45,523		
Norway		72,052						
Poland		31,888			4			
Portugal		586[16]	1,227	75,195	22	608		
Netherlands		23,451	4,585		5			
Russia		142,545[19]	4,035	27,271	1			
Rumania		5,135		1				
British Isles	126,640	732,804	11,221	563	103	2,263	43,216	22,024
Sweden		190,332		354	17			
Switzerland		31,819	6,713	701	184	349		
Turkey in Europe		1,047						
Other European countries		8,482					1,398[16]	
China		1,910					432[23]	
India		171						
Japan		2,158						
Turkey in Asia		2,215						
Other Asiatic countries		1,494					1,069[24]	
Africa		526						
United States	244,880[20]				67	160		
British North America		357						
Central America								
Mexico		20,716			1[25]			
West Indies								
South America								
Argentina						368		
Brazil		1,917			214	3,328		
Uruguay								
Other countries						103[22]		
Oceania	37,591	8,168					123,730[17]	47,703[18]
Other countries		339	4,974[19]	7,671		12,350	124	4,089
Total	409,111	2,270,930	585,937	395,424	4,737	92,107	169,969	73,816

For reference notes see page 353.

TABLE 13.—IMMIGRATION OF ALIENS BY COUNTRY OF LAST RESIDENCE OR NATIONALITY FROM 1821 UPWARDS (cont.)

a. Absolute figures

Country of Immigration / Country of Last Residence or Nationality	1891—1895							
	Canada[20]	United States[9]	Argentina[3][12]	Brazil[3]	Paraguay[3]	Uruguay[3][21]	Queensland[9]	New Zealand[9]
Germany	……	397,640	4,403	9,216	338	1,152	……	……
Austria	……	277,438[7][14]	2,489[14]	18,461	271[14]	745[14]	……	……
Belgium	……	13,154	1,079	569	8	116	……	……
Denmark	……	37,417	……	……	2	……	……	……
Spain	……	6,615[18]	36,450	95,242	161	9,774	……	……
France	……	20,777	11,197	3,707	566	2,641	……	……
Finland	……	—[6]	……	……	……	……	……	……
Greece	……	……	—[14]	……	……	……	……	……
Hungary	……	4,790[14]	……	……	……	……	……	……
Italy	……	288,235	160,240	378,143	237	20,231	……	……
Norway	……	59,100	……	……	……	……	……	……
Poland	……	87,138	……	……	……	……	……	……
Portugal	……	12,782[15]	707	132,228	……	362	……	……
Netherlands	……	20,754	111	……	……	……	……	……
Russia	……	246,432[8][10]	11,010	12,462	22	……	……	……
Rumania	……	2,209	……	2,245	2	……	……	……
British Isles	95,709	422,564	1,483	2,053	87	1,356	5,355	13,130
Sweden	……	148,082	……	410	4	……	……	……
Switzerland	……	23,585	2,243	……	136	214	……	……
Turkey in Europe	……	2,764	……	……	……	……	……	……
Other European countries	……	2,203	……	……	……	……	……	……
China	……	5,017	……	……	……	……	2,271[16]	……
India	……	42	……	……	……	……	41	……
Japan	……	5,597	……	3	……	……	375	……
Turkey in Asia	……	3,344	……	……	……	……	……	……
Other Asiatic countries	……	163	……	……	……	……	882[24]	……
Africa	52,516[21][26]	……	……	……	……	……	……	……
United States	……	……	……	……	14	146	……	……
British North America	……	438	……	……	……	……	……	……
Central America	……	333	……	……	……	……	……	……
Mexico	……	225	……	……	2[25]	……	……	……
West Indies	……	12,999	……	……	……	……	……	……
South America	……	……	……	……	……	……	……	……
Argentina	……	739	……	……	185	441	……	……
Brazil	……	……	……	……	……	5,254	……	……
Uruguay	……	……	……	……	8	……	……	……
(Other countries)	……	……	……	……	……	9[22]	……	……
Oceania	……	2,215	……	……	……	……	119,022[17]	88,033[18]
Other countries	34,188	13,833	4,840[19]	11,631	……	10,789	1,067	4,624
Total	182,413[26]	2,123,879	236,252	666,370	1,799	53,313	129,013	105,787

For reference notes see page 353.

TABLE 13.—IMMIGRATION OF ALIENS BY COUNTRY OF LAST RESIDENCE OR NATIONALITY FROM 1821 UPWARDS (cont.)

a. Absolute figures

Country of Last Residence or Nationality	Canada [20][27]	United States[2]	Argentina [3][12]	Brazil[3]	Paraguay[3]	Uruguay [3][31]	Queensland[9]	New Zealand[9]
				1896–1900				
Germany		107,512	4,290	3,273	94	1,433		
Austria		315,269[7][14]	6,298[4]	19,869	15	554[14]		
Belgium		5,013	930	87	3	253		
Bulgaria		160[28][29]						
Denmark		12,814						
Spain		2,116[15]	95,264	61,877	122	14,317		
France		9,993	14,403	1,257	124	2,833		
Finland		—[6]						
Greece		11,189	—[14]					
Hungary		—[14]						
Italy		363,658	264,453	300,618	535	18,021		
Norway		35,915						
Poland		9,582[30]						
Portugal		12,645[16]	991	70,201		308		
Netherlands		6,004	212		4			
Russia		258,858[6][7]	6,456	1,978	0			
Rumania		10,541						
British Isles	50,741	237,390	2,521	539	155	1,301	6,062	11,510
Sweden		78,184		39				
Switzerland		7,594	2,028	415	41	339		
Serbia and Montenegro								
Turkey in Europe		862						
Other European countries								
China		9,782					3,077[12]	
India		26					487	
Japan		20,345					2,645	
Syria								
Turkey in Asia		21,544		4,323				
Other Asiatic countries		284					252[24]	
Africa		187						
United States	32,019[31]	—		7	139			
British North America		2,639						
Central America		223						
Mexico		746						
West Indies		20,294						
South America								
Argentina						273		
Brazil		336			115	3,044		
Uruguay								
Other countries		1,049				142[22]		
Oceania								
Pacific Islands		701					154,100[17]	73,987[18]
Atlantic Islands								
Other countries	56,129	230	14,228[19]	13,056	2	2,804	717	5,766
Total	138,889[31]	1,563,685	412,074	477,532	1,226	45,761	167,340	91,263

For reference notes see page 353.

TABLE 13.—IMMIGRATION OF ALIENS BY COUNTRY OF LAST RESIDENCE OR NATIONALITY FROM 1821 UPWARDS (cont.)

a. Absolute figures

1901–1905

Country of Last Residence or Nationality	Canada[3]	United States[2]	Argentina[2,12]	Brazil[3]	Paraguay[3]	Uruguay[3,21,32]	Australia[2,9,33]	New Zealand[9]
Germany	9,663	176,995	5,852	3,109	222	802	3,939	
Austria	48,570[4]	944,239[14]	13,838[14]	2,495	46	400[14]	3,069	
Belgium	2,312	16,884	908	94	13	105	79	
Bulgaria		6,637[28]						
Denmark	4,335	33,968			8		374	
Spain	37	10,243[15]	146,774	52,013	335	6,801	147	
France	5,005	31,419	14,034	1,117	107	1,347	5,879	
Finland	5,876	—[6]						
Greece	724[14]	49,962[14]					793	
Hungary	19,827	959,768	—[14]					
Italy	5,662	103,065	289,534	135,167	662	9,561	3,522	
Norway	2,080							
Poland	1	—[30]					10	
Portugal		30,532[15]	1,691	71,744	2	309	38	
Netherlands	733	18,501	432	1,861	9		11	
Russia	12,995	658,735[6]	19,739		18		144	
Rumania	2,030	35,185					527	
British Isles	186,594	385,253	3,506	652	69	743	149,392	19,791
Sweden	7,973	154,607		43	3		1,204[4]	
Switzerland	398	17,820	1,817	244	24	176	217	
Serbia and Montenegro	42							
Turkey in Europe	—[34]	10,989						
Other European countries	17,290[5]	216					28	
China	9	12,792					1,145	
India	45	660					4,438	
Japan	360	64,102					730	
Syria	3,696[26]	30,515		4,577			1,792	
Turkey in Asia	60[24]	7,872					187[37]	
Other Asiatic countries	59	1,829					3	
Africa	66						2,080	
United States	182,870				47	88	2,198	
British North America	1,044	7,239					7[38]	
Central America		3,042						
Mexico		5,230						
West Indies	155	42,891			29[1]			
South America								
Argentina	3					137		
Brazil					647	1,387	28	
Uruguay					21			
Other countries	404	5,372				81[22]		
Oceania							12	119,579[18]
Pacific Islands		5,411					2,566	
Atlantic Islands		723						
Other countries	5[39]	380	27,905[19]	14,915		1,018	1,352[40]	12,209
Total	521,489	3,833,076	526,030	288,031	2,235	22,955	185,911	151,579

For reference notes see page 353.

TABLE 13.—IMMIGRATION OF ALIENS BY COUNTRY OF LAST RESIDENCE OR NATIONALITY FROM 1821 UPWARDS (cont.)

a. Absolute figures

Country of Last Residence or Nationality	1906-1910						
	Canada [3][41]	United States [2]	Cuba	Argentina [3][12]	Brazil [3]	Australian Commonwealth [3][9]	New Zealand [9]
Germany	11,482	164,503	194	13,452	14,424	9,717	
Austria	72,431[14]	556,219		23,952[14]	13,495	3,789	
Belgium	6,271	24,751		1,366	310	227	
Bulgaria	4,460	32,643[28]					
Denmark	2,747	31,317				1,307	
Spain	373	17,692[26]	116,394	505,884	85,600	280	
France	11,231	41,960	1,631	20,146	3,678	7,604	
Finland	7,622	—[6]					
Greece	3,273	117,557				1,445	
Hungary	—[14]	644,808		—[14]			
Italy	43,990	1,086,109	217	506,656	80,719	4,694	
Norway	8,136	87,440					
Poland	7,311	—[30]				68	
Portugal	27	38,617[16]		8,585	146,449	27	
Netherlands	4,162	29,761		1,147	15,360	667	
Russia	26,337	938,571[6]		64,754		2,231	
Rumania	2,858	17,823				26	
British Isles	498,473	479,762	417	9,079	3,166	324,600	47,641
Sweden	11,376	94,927			487	4,875[4]	
Switzerland	1,089	17,102		3,124	882	464	
Turkey in Europe	—[34]	68,987				42	
Serbia and Montenegro	228						
Other European countries	31,387[35]	449	839			197	
China	11,315	7,813				7,875	
India	5,155	4,053				564	
Japan	12,768	65,695				2,551	
Syria, Mesopotamia, Palestine	1,974[36]		5[42]			350[37]	
Turkey in Asia	3,327[34]	46,878					
Other Asiatic countries	70	3,187			15,127	2,170	
Africa	424	5,539	13,599			12[38]	
United States	436,676						
British North America	12,452	171,987	96			3,881	
Central America		5,150	7,520				
Mexico		44,412	22,795				
West Indies	1,379	64,657				55	
South America		11,908					
Argentina	25		698			64	
Brazil							
Uruguay							
Other countries							
Oceania		6,564					137,434[19]
Pacific Islands	1,779	326				514	
Other countries	378[9]	33,143				2,865[40]	9,655
Total	1,242,986	4,962,310	164,405	1,238,073	402,836	383,161	194,730

For reference notes see page 353.

TABLE 13.—IMMIGRATION OF ALIENS BY COUNTRY OF LAST RESIDENCE OR NATIONALITY FROM 1821 UPWARDS (cont.)

a. Absolute figures

Country of Immigration	1911–1915									
Country of Last Residence or Nationality	Canada[3]	United States[2]	Mexico[2]	Cuba	Argentina[3,12]	Brazil[3]	Uruguay[3,21,43]	Australian Commonwealth[3,9]	New Zealand[9]	Hawaii[3]
Germany	17,653	137,711	3,848	173	15,191	20,968	845	13,458		
Austria	79,014[14]	449,274		12	17,807[14]	9,727		3,536		
Belgium	7,399	25,447		11	1,735	1,010		410		
Bulgaria	13,836[44]	21,487[28]								
Denmark	3,678	29,798	42			259		1,991		
Spain	2,391	27,921[15]	18,326	133,827	484,092	128,537	11,351	737		4,290
France	8,918	40,432	3,764	952	18,635	5,548	982	5,677		
Finland	7,818	—[6]								
Greece	4,477	118,916		33		1,453		2,932		
Hungary	—[14]	440,153			—[14]	1,327				
Italy	55,529	938,984	2,101	107	300,451	106,906	7,155	7,247		
Norway	6,191	47,527		25				72		
Poland	26,782	—[30]		31				53		
Portugal	81	48,580[15]		7	13,409	243,777				2,145
Netherlands	4,898	31,344			841	910		1,499		
Russia	58,290	894,003[6]			55,308	35,055		5,649		404
Rumania	3,778	11,187				244		86		
British Isles	483,225	388,566	12,546	332	9,003	3,832	1,238	546,747	51,108	
Sweden	8,399	72,055		1		1,216		6,663[4]		
Switzerland	996	17,020		20	3,512	1,071		825		
Turkey in Europe	—[34]	52,254		537				41		
Serbia and Montenegro	1,052									
Other European countries	27,693[35]	3,138		3		125	1,144	10,807		113[46]
China	20,550	10,942	5,877			365		981		2,618
India	97	1,260						2,789		20
Japan	3,338	36,457	15,218			13,799		288[37]		18,595[46]
Syria, Mesopotamia, Palestine	764[36]	72,231	1,123	601		28,477		1,901		
Turkey in Asia	1,957[34]	3,279	1,427	14[2]				198[8]		
Other Asiatic countries	68	5,847		2						15,439[42]
Africa	268							6,608		
United States	477,406		53,205	13,005	91,849[10]	1,196	319			8[47]
British North America	4,723	354,976	643	56						
Central America		6,782	2,973[26]	2,301						
Mexico	21	82,007		5,344						
West Indies	2,055	64,377		19,652				25		
South America										
Argentina	14	19,956	837	1,475[48]		3,197	223	104		
Brazil							1,549			
Uruguay		5,625								
Other countries										
Oceania										
Pacific Islands	642	501		2				404	127,661[18]	3,158
Other countries	21	244		4		2,361	7,384	1,705[10]	15,065	
Other countries	851[39]			6						
Total	1,334,873	4,459,831	121,888	178,562	1,011,853	611,360	31,046	624,398	193,834	46,790

For reference notes see page 353

TABLE 13.—IMMIGRATION OF ALIENS BY COUNTRY OF LAST RESIDENCE OR NATIONALITY FROM 1821 UPWARDS (cont.)

a. Absolute figures

Country of Last Residence or Nationality	1916-1920									
	Canada[3]	United States[2]	Mexico[3]	Cuba	Argentina[3 12]	Brazil[3]	Uruguay[3 21]	Australian Commonwealth[3 9]	New Zealand[9 49]	Hawaii[2]
Germany	160	6,234	2,063	105	6,967	5,152	667	715		
Austria	368[14]	4,375		20	991[14]	1,479		38		
Belgium	3,370	8,299		11	458	426	275	260		
Bulgaria	5	1,046[28]				10				
Denmark	1,092	12,185				123		733		
Spain	333	40,690[15]	17,080	209,804	105,001	41,407	15,065	185		20
France	2,980	21,465	2,846	6,324	6,623	2,319	1,582	3,363		
Finland	1,809	750[60]				2				
Greece	700	65,285		594	—[14]	359				
Hungary	—[14]	2,540				111		937		
Italy	6,041	170,540	1,201	352	46,937	27,104	2,976	1,043		
Norway	1,237	18,868		80		40		33		
Poland	4,153	4,813[50]		17		576		33		
Portugal	9	41,152[15]		302	2,199	77,730	1,089			399
Netherlands	1,053	12,374		27	423	305		1,738		
Russia	1,728	27,198[6]		21	1,489	1,930	621	1,300		26
Rumania	994	2,124		7		898		46		
British Isles	155,242	99,023	5,299	538	4,557	1,583	2,090	261,705	12,169	
Sweden	1,545	23,019		2		66		2,716[4]		
Switzerland	388	6,071		88	1,066	763		220		
Czechoslovakia		3,426[50]				92				
Turkey in Europe	—[24]	2,423		10				2		
Serbia and Montenegro	104	1,888[50]		514						
Other European countries	3,887[25]	4,973	4,210	643		50				2,054
China	8,474	10,786	5,199	10,310		15		845		187[46]
India	10	822		12		102		9,276		2
Japan	3,952	47,380	2,255	27		47		790		19,707[48]
Syria, Mesopotamia, Palestine	171[36]	7,158		43		13,698		3,274		
Turkey in Asia	62[24]	2,694	895	246[42]		6,313		98[37]		
Other Asiatic countries	5	2,596		4		103				13,591[48]
Africa	459							5,469		
United States	271,373		31,295	10,449		771	1,130	1,520		
British North America	4,440	387,209		151		3		5[38]		
Central America		10,377	2,367	6,512		25				
Mexico	4	136,997		3,104		9				
West Indies	1,053	59,047	2,067[25]	151,166						
South America										
Argentina	6	21,943				2,377	1,092	76		
Brazil							3,815			
Uruguay										
Other countries										
Oceania	366	6,723		2					45,317	
Pacific Islands		578		110				213		
Atlantic Islands		903	916	2,651[48]		396	2,186	1,328[40]	12,799	2,681
Other countries	380[99]			2	16,375[19]			18		
Total	477,953	1,275,980	77,693	404,248	193,086	186,384	32,588	297,979	70,285	38,667

For reference notes see page 353.

a. Absolute figures

Country of Immigration / Country of Last Residence	1921-1924								
	Canada[3]	United States[2]	Mexico[3]	Cuba	Argentina[3][12]	Brazil[3]	Uruguay[3][21][51]	Australian Commonwealth[8][9]	Hawaii[3]
Albania		250[92]							
Germany	4,383	148,102	5,734	908	31,003	43,375	237	487	
Austria	6,788[14]	25,574		16	4,603[14]	4,650		24	
Belgium	3,787	11,362		20	593	414	71	298	
Bulgaria	382	1,824				83			
Denmark	4,236	18,773		12	2,252	361		741	
Estonia		765[82]							
Spain	63	26,256[15]	24,116	129,825	177,543	35,770	3,443	327	19
France	1,294	24,539	3,453	16,047	5,820	2,601	400	2,092	
Finland	13,219	13,868				75			
Greece	877	40,163		237	[11]	345		3,680	
Hungary	[14]	25,178				2,082			
Italy	13,215	365,499	5,172	2,371	262,903	51,739	1,409	10,924	
Latvia		1,473[82]						[4]	
Lithuania		2,369[82]				126			
Norway	5,961	36,446		68	24,029	4,522	183	265	295
Poland	12,573	179,068	10,946	155	7,467	103,736		14	
Portugal	5	26,298[15]	4,046	541	640	490		1,021	34
Netherlands	3,097	15,416		1,259		3,984	90	784	
Russia	10,122	53,697	1,984	1,010	5,395	9,770		60	
Rumania	4,673	59,193		355	3,949	2,145			
British Isles	199,663	253,409	11,367	1,509	441	153	513	334,556	
Sweden	7,064	52,021			2,654	1,935		1,722[4]	
Switzerland	2,605	17,695		61		1,677		755	
Czechoslovakia	[32]	13,275							
Turkey in Europe	3,242	80,819		238		8,758		6	
Serb, Croat and Slovene Kingdom		41,599		44		44			
Other European countries	20,953[82]	6,077		93	7,497	2,274			
China	3,131	20,393		1,857		175		5,251	
India	120	1,311		107		44		7,688	
Japan	1,879	29,204		148		5,633		674	16,266[47]
Syria, Palestine, Mesopotamia	711[34]	2,946		16				1,134	
Turkey in Asia	975[82]	18,736		23	15,563	13,050		581[37]	
Other Asiatic countries	41	2,477	4,246	2[72]		81		1,229	25,805[42]
Africa	239	3,269			961	206			[6]
United States	88,020			4,493		1,032	267		
British North America	8,552	436,828		702		8		5,819	
Central America		6,499		1,659		67			
Mexico		203,413				16			
West Indies	1	51,963		78,302				18	737[47]
South America									
Argentina	235	21,690	1,816	1,345[48]		2,596	172	89	
Brazil	15						510		
Uruguay						8			
Other countries									
Oceania									
Pacific Islands	614	4,392		1				186	
Atlantic Islands		242		18					
Other countries	163[35]	228	1,087	2,247	29,038[19]	103	956	1,433[40]	1,760
Total	422,808	2,344,599	155,244	245,690	582,351	304,084	8,251	381,858	49,285

For reference notes see page 353.

TABLE 14.—IMMIGRATION OF ALIENS BY COUNTRY OF LAST RESIDENCE OR NATIONALITY[1] FROM 1821 UPWARDS

b. Percentages

Country of Last Residence or Nationality	1821–1825		1826–1830		1831–1835		
	United States[2]	Brazil[3]	United States[2]	Brazil[3]	Canada	United States[2]	Brazil[3]
Germany	3.44	......	5.21	31.06	0.01[4]	18.05	......
Belgium	0.03	......	0.01	......	......	0.00	......
Denmark	0.15	......	0.10	......	......	0.11	......
Spain	2.95	......	1.24	......	......	0.37	......
France	5.11	......	6.24	......	......	7.03	......
Greece	0.01	......	0.01	......	......	0.00	......
Italy	0.61	......	0.15	......	......	0.75	......
Norway	0.08[5]	......	0.05[5]	......	—[5]	0.16[5]	......
Poland	0.02	......	0.00	......	......	0.05	......
Portugal	0.23	......	0.04	......	......	0.28	......
Netherlands	0.50	......	0.85	......	......	0.24	......
Russia	0.10[6][7]	......	0.03[6][7]	......	......	0.09[6][7]	......
British Isles	53.86	......	52.44	......	98.87	41.36	......
Sweden	—[5]	......	—[5]	......	......	—[5]	......
Switzerland	1.65	......	2.48	......	......	1.09	......
Turkey in Europe	0.01	......	0.01	......	......	0.00	......
Other European countries	0.00	......	0.00	......	......	0.00	......
China	0.00	......	0.00	......	......	0.00	......
India	0.00	......	0.00	......	......	0.01	......
Other Asiatic countries	......	......	0.01	......	......	0.00	......
Africa	0.07	......	......	......	......	0.01	......
United States	......	......	......	......	......	......	......
British North America	2.52	......	1.21	......	......	1.65	......
Central America	0.05	......	0.08	......	......	0.01	......
Mexico	0.54	......	4.46	......	......	1.66	......
West Indies	2.65	......	2.68	......	......	2.19	......
South America	0.31	......	0.39	......	......	0.18	......
Oceania	0.00[8]	......	—[8]	......	......	0.00[8]	......
Atlantic Islands	0.04	......	0.32	......	......	0.02	......
Other countries	25.01	100	21.90	68.94	1.12	24.59	......
Total	100.	100.	100.	100.	100.	100.	100.

For reference notes see page 353.

TABLE 14.—IMMIGRATION OF ALIENS BY COUNTRY OF LAST RESIDENCE OR NATIONALITY[1] FROM 1821 UPWARDS (cont.)

b. Percentages

Country of Last Residence or Nationality	1836-1840				1841-1845			
	Canada	United States[2]	West Indies	Brazil[3]	Canada[8bis]	United States[2]	West Indies	Brazil[3]
Germany	0.59[4]	30.82	5.23	9.51		24.44		30.80
Belgium		0.00				0.23		
Denmark		0.22				0.04		
Spain		0.33				0.24		
France		8.02	0.07			5.50	0.07	0.53
Greece		0.01				0.00		8.50
Italy	—[4]	0.10		6.34		0.16		
Norway		0.22[5]				1.10[5]		
Poland		0.06				0.02		
Portugal		0.03		16.46		0.02		11.07
Netherlands		0.22				0.43		
Russia		0.01[6][7]				0.05[6][7]	4.20	
British Isles	97.98*	51.56	9.57		98.79	62.11		
Sweden		—[5]				—[5]		
Switzerland		0.59				0.71		
Turkey in Europe		0.00				0.01		
Other European countries		0.09				0.02		
China						0.00		
India		0.00	3.78			0.00	4.	
Other Asiatic countries						0.00		
Africa		0.01	0.62			0.01	43.24	
United States			12.06				0.81	
British North America		2.72				2.62	0.52	
Central America		0.00				0.01		
Mexico		0.68				0.42		
West Indies		1.95	57.25			1.24	40.42	
South America		0.11	3.77			0.12	5.60	
Oceania		0.00[8]				0.00[8]		
Atlantic Islands		0.01				0.01		
Other countries	1.54	2.22	7.63	67.69	1.21	0.44	1.13	49.09
Total	100.	100.	100.	100.	100.	100.	100.	100.

For reference notes see page 353.

TABLE 14.—IMMIGRATION OF ALIENS BY COUNTRY OF LAST RESIDENCE OR NATIONALITY[1] FROM 1821 UPWARDS (cont).

b. Percentages

Country of Last Residence or Nationality	1846-1850				1851-1855				
	Canada[8bis]	United States[2]	West Indies	Brazil[3]	Canada	United States[2]	West Indies	Brazil[3]	New Zealand[9,10]
Germany	1.70[4]	25.67		43.51	16.71[4]	37.02		13.34	
Belgium		0.31		0.04		0.10		0.03	
Denmark		0.02				0.07			
Spain		0.08		2.48		0.24		0.06	
France		4.17		2.31		3.26		0.18	
Greece		0.00				0.00			
Italy		0.09		0.10		0.20		0.06	
Norway		0.71[5]				0.81[5]			
Poland	—[4]	0.00			—[4]	0.04			
Portugal		0.03		5.20		0.02		66.11	
Netherlands		0.49				0.38			
Russia		0.02[6,7]				0.00[7]			
British Isles	97.16	60.83		5.93	81.03	53.22	0.08	0.31	29.5
Sweden		—[5]				—[6]			
Switzerland		0.12		6.86		1.04		4.48	
Turkey in Europe		0.00				0.00			
Other European countries		0.00				0.00			
China		0.00				0.95	8.06		
India		0.00	40.03			0.00	54.20		
Other Asiatic countries		0.00				0.00			
Africa		0.00	57.22			0.00	36.73		
United States		2.37				1.93			
British North America		0.02				0.01			
Central America		0.11				0.07			
Mexico		0.63				0.31			
West Indies		0.23	1.60			0.02	0.49		
South America		0.008	1.09			0.008	0.43		
Oceania		0.02				0.05			
Atlantic Islands									53.1[11]
Other Countries	1.14	3.96		33.56	2.26	0.14		15.43	17.3
Total	100.	100.	100.	100.	100.	100.	100.	100.	100.

For reference notes see page 353.

TABLE 14.—IMMIGRATION OF ALIENS BY COUNTRY OF LAST RESIDENCE OR NATIONALITY[1] FROM 1821 UPWARDS (cont.)

b. Percentages

Country of Last Residence or Nationality	1856–1860						1861–1865					
	Canada	United States[2]	West Indies	Argentina[3,12,13]	Brazil[3]	New Zealand[9]	Canada	United States[2]	West Indies	Argentina[3,12]	Brazil[3]	New Zealand[9]
Germany	31.67[4]	35.82		.20	16.58		34.06[4]	29.06		0.91	13.98	
Austria				1.49[11]				0.06[7]		0.79[14]		
Belgium		0.34		0.48	0.02			0.21		0.54	0.82	
Denmark		0.29						0.65				
Spain		0.59		16.85	0.04			0.36		13.66	0.16	
France		2.28		5.53	0.08			1.74		3.60	2.77	
Finland												
Greece		0.00						0.00				
Hungary				—[14]				0.05		—[14]		
Italy	—[4]	0.65		61.78	52.11		—[4]	1.43[5]		71.82	5.93	
Norway		0.79						0.11				
Poland		0.04						0.10				
Portugal		0.07		0.78				0.32		0.19	49.81	
Netherlands		0.47		0.21						0.08		
Russia		0.05[6,7]		0.60				0.07[6,7]		0.39		
British Isles	67.75	47.94	0.00	2.59	0.39	68.9	65.87	55.31		1.84	0.46	33.4
Sweden					0.79			0.82			0.60	
Switzerland		0.78		1.43				0.01		1.17	1.02	
Turkey in Europe		0.01						0.00				
Other European countries		0.00						3.02				
China		2.91	7.20					0.00	17.80			
India		0.00	72.39					0.00	59.40			
Japan								0.00				
Other Asiatic countries		0.00	20.31					0.01	8.72			
Africa		0.02						4.24				
British North America		2.99						0.01				
Central America		0.04						0.09				
Mexico		0.21	0.10					0.37	14.08			
West Indies		0.61						0.07				
South America		0.09										
Oceania		0.01[8]				27.6[11]		0.02[8]				66.1[11]
Atlantic Islands		0.25						0.21				
Other countries	0.58	2.75		7.08	29.98	3.5	0.06	1.12		5.01	24.44	0.4
Total	100.	100.	100.	100.	100.	100.	100.	100.	100.	100.	100.	100.

TABLE 14.—IMMIGRATION OF ALIENS BY COUNTRY OF LAST RESIDENCE OR NATIONALITY[1] FROM 1821 UPWARDS (cont.)

b. Percentages

Country of Last Residence or Nationality	1866–1870						1871–1875						
	Canada	United States[2]	West Indies	Argentina[3][12]	Brazil[3]	New Zealand[9]	Canada	United States[2]	West Indies[10bis]	Argentina[3][12]	Brazil[3]	Queensland[9]	New Zealand[9]
Germany	36.43[4]	36.64		0.77	12.12		8.53[4]	29.44		1.32	6.42	8.17	
Austria		0.45[7]		0.39[14]	0.22			1.71[7]		0.37[14]	0.39		
Belgium		0.32		0.24	0.11			0.23		0.20	0.17		
Denmark		0.78						0.94					
Spain		0.25		14.40	1.26			0.16[15]		19.14	1.57		
France		1.45		5.93	2.47			2.61		15.	2.65		
Finland		—[6]						0.01					
Greece		0.00						0.01					
Hungary		0.54		—[14]			—[1]	0.19		—[14]			
Italy		6.46[6]		70.89	4.08			1.56		55.72	5.67		
Norway	—[4]	0.07						3.10					
Poland		0.06						0.48					
Portugal		0.42		0.29	53.17			0.08[16]		0.23	40.20		
Netherlands		0.12[6][7]		0.06				0.60		0.01			
Russia				0.21	5.77			0.87		0.15	1.28		
Sweden				2.69	0.30			2.88		3.97	2.55		
British Isles	63.56	39.60[5]				35.2	90.09	38.50				28.29	68.7
Switzerland		1.10		1.28	0.67			0.80		2.52	0.18		
Turkey in Europe		0.00						0.01					
Other European countries		0.05						0.32			1.14	9.01[16]	
China		2.64	3.11					3.78					
India		0.00	82.20					0.01	94.58				
Japan		0.00						0.00					
Turkey in Asia		0.00						0.00					
Other Asiatic countries													
United States													
Africa		0.01	1.12					0.01	1.66				
British North America		7.92	3.21					10.54					
Central America		0.00						0.00					
Mexico		0.09						0.14					
West Indies		0.39	10.37					0.45					
South America		0.05						0.03	3.77		0.04		
Oceania		0.00						0.36					
Atlantic Islands		0.04[15]				61.4[11]		—[18]				52.11[17]	20.9[18]
Other countries	0.01	0.41		2.84	19.83	3.4	1.39	0.03		1.38[19]	37.74	2.41	10.4
Total	100.	100.	100.	100.	100.	100.	100.	100.	100.	100.	100.	100.	100.

For reference notes see page 353.

TABLE 14.—IMMIGRATION OF ALIENS BY COUNTRY OF LAST RESIDENCE OR NATIONALITY[1] FROM 1821 UPWARDS (cont.)

b. Percentages[2]

Country of Immigration → Country of Last Residence or Nationality	1876–1880						1881–1885							
	Canada	United States[2]	Argentina[3][12]	Brazil[3]	Queensland[9]	New Zealand[9]	Canada	United States[2]	Argentina[3][12]	Brazil[3]	Paraguay[3]	Uruguay[3][21]	Queensland[9]	New Zealand[9]
Germany		19.32	1.65	8.55	4.16			32.26	2.32	7.80	68.90	3.7		
Austria		3.07	3.31[14]	5.48				3.27	3.17[14]	1.18	0.79	0.7[14]		
Belgium		0.28	0.33	0.10				0.26	0.73	0.05	1.93	0.2		
Denmark		1.41						1.55			0.23			
Spain		0.22[15]	14.32	2.83				0.05[15]	9.07	8.09	9.10	23.3		
France		2.48	9.28	1.66				0.77	8.14	0.79		8.3		
Finland		0.02						0.09						
Greece		0.01						0.01						
Hungary		0.61	—[14]					1.71	—[14]					
Italy		2.64	61.69	40.21				3.67	71.56	46.30	0.79	47.		
Norway		3.84						3.51						
Poland		0.43[16]						0.66						
Portugal		0.28	0.32	30.89				0.05[16]	0.25	31.42	0.11	1.1		
Netherlands		0.56	0.07	5.42				1.01	0.04	0.79	0.23			
Russia		2.18[7]	0.17					1.97[7]	0.05		0.91			
Rumania		0.00						0.04						
British Isles	96.33	29.47	3.39	0.70	26.24	61.3	32.31	24.53	1.96	0.46	0.11	4.4	44.20	45.0
Sweden		6.09		0.13				6.76		0.05	0.23			
Switzerland		1.32	2.27	0.59				1.68	2.07	0.23	10.10	0.4		
Turkey in Europe		0.01						0.01						
Other European countries		0.45	3.21[19]					0.23	1.65[19]					
China		1.32		0.02	16.85[16]			2.		0.08			3.92[16]	
India		0.01						0.00						
Japan		0.00						0.00						
Turkey in Asia		0.00						0.01						
Other Asiatic countries		0.01						0.01						
Africa		0.01												
United States							59.13[20]							
British North America		18.53						13.20						
Central America		0.01						0.00						
Mexico		0.23						0.06						
West Indies		0.58						0.29						
South America														
Argentina												0.6		
Brazil		0.04						0.01			6.58	6.6		
Uruguay														
Other countries												0.3[22]		
Oceania		0.42			51.97[17]	32.4[18]		0.14					50.63[17]	49.4[18]
Other countries	3.67	0.01		3.44	0.78	6.3	8.56	0.01		2.78		3.1	1.25	5.6
Total	100.	100.	100.	100.	100.	100.	100.	100.	100.	100.	100.	100.	100.	100.

For reference notes see page 353.

TABLE 14.—IMMIGRATION OF ALIENS BY COUNTRY OF LAST RESIDENCE OR NATIONALITY[1] FROM 1821 UPWARDS (cont.)

b. Percentages

Country of Last Residence or Nationality	1886–1890							
	Canada[20]	United States[2]	Argentina[3][12]	Brazil[3]	Paraguay[3]	Uruguay[2][21]	Queensland[9]	New Zealand[9]
Germany		21.70	1.41	2.80	14.60	1.9		
Austria		5.66[7]	1.88[14]	1.25	5.26[14]	0.8		
Belgium		0.54	2.38	0.53	2.10	0.2		
Denmark		1.83			0.51			
Spain		0.11[15]	23.15	7.29	15.16	21.3		
France		1.20	12.47	1.11	16.80	5.2		
Finland		0.39						
Greece		0.08			0.04			
Hungary		3.36	—[14]					
Italy		8.71	53.12	58.76	32.60	49.4		
Norway		3.17						
Poland		1.40						
Portugal		0.02[15]	0.21	19.02	0.08	0.7		
Netherlands		1.03	0.78		0.46			
Russia		6.27[7]	0.69	6.90	0.11			
Rumania		0.22			0.02			
British Isles	30.95	32.26	1.92	0.14	2.17	2.5	25.43	29.8
Sweden		8.38		0.09	0.36			
Switzerland		1.40	1.15	0.18	3.90	0.4		
Turkey in Europe		0.04						
Other European countries		0.37						
China		0.08					0.82[16]	
India		0.01					0.25[23]	
Japan		0.09						
Turkey in Asia		0.09						
Other Asiatic countries		0.06					0.63[24]	
Africa		0.02						
United States	59.86[20]				1.41	0.2		
British North America		0.01						
Central America								
Mexico		0.01						
West Indies		0.91			0.02[25]			
South America								
Argentina						0.4		
Brazil					4.52	3.6		
Uruguay		0.08						
Other countries						0.11[22]		
Oceania		0.35					72.80[17]	64.6[18]
Other countries	9.19	0.01	0.85[19]	1.94		13.4	0.07	5.5
Total	100.	100.	100.	100.	100.	100.	100.	100.

For reference notes see page 353.

TABLE 14.—IMMIGRATION OF ALIENS BY COUNTRY OF LAST RESIDENCE OR NATIONALITY[1] FROM 1821 UPWARDS (cont.)

b. Percentages

Country of Immigration

"1891–1895" spans the Argentina, Brazil, Paraguay, Uruguay, Queensland, and New Zealand columns.

Country of Last Residence or Nationality	Canada[20]	United States[2]	Argentina[3,12]	Brazil[3]	Paraguay[3]	Uruguay[3,21]	Queensland[9]	New Zealand[9]
Germany		18.72	1.86	1.33	18.79	2.2		
Austria		13.06[7,14]	1.05[14]	2.77	1.50[14]	1.4[14]		
Belgium		0.6[3]	0.46	0.09	0.44	0.2		
Bulgaria					0.11			
Denmark		1.76			8.5			
Spain		0.31[16]	15.43	14.29	31.46	18.3		
France		0.98	4.74	0.56		5.		
Finland		—[6]						
Greece		0.23						
Hungary		—[14]	—[14]					
Italy		13.57	67.83	56.75	13.17	37.9		
Norway		2.78						
Poland		4.10						
Portugal		0.60[5]	0.30	19.84	1.22	0.7		
Netherlands		0.98	0.05	1.87	0.11			
Russia		11.60[6,7]	4.66	0.34	4.84			
Rumania		0.10		0.31	0.22			
British Isles	52.47	19.90	0.63	0.06	7.56	2.5	4.15	12.4
Sweden		6.97						
Switzerland		1.11	0.95			0.4		
Turkey in Europe		0.13						
Serbia and Montenegro								
Other European countries		0.10						
China		0.23					1.76[16]	
India		0.00					0.03	
Japan		0.26					0.29	
Syria								
Turkey in Asia		0.25						
Other Asiatic countries		0.16						
Africa		0.01		0.00	0.78	0.3		
United States	28.79[20,26]				0.11[25]			
British North America		0.02						
Central America		0.02						
Mexico		0.01						
West Indies		0.61						
South America								
Argentina					10.28	0.8		
Brazil		0.03				9.9		
Uruguay								
Other countries		0.10				0.2[22]		
Oceania							0.68[24]	
Pacific Islands							92.26[17]	83.2[18]
Other countries	18.74	0.65	2.05[19]	1.75	0.44	20.2	0.83	4.4
Total	100.[26]	100.	100.	100.	100.	100.	100	100.

For reference notes see page 353.

TABLE 14.—IMMIGRATION OF ALIENS BY COUNTRY OF LAST RESIDENCE OR NATIONALITY[1] FROM 1821 UPWARDS (cont.)

b. Percentages

1896–1900

Country of Last Residence or Nationality	Canada[20][27]	United States[2]	Argentina[3][12]	Brazil[3]	Paraguay[3]	Uruguay[3][21]	Queensland[9]	New Zealand[9]
Germany		6.87	1.04	0.69	7.67	3.1		
Austria		20.16[14]	1.53[14]	4.16	1.22	1.2[14]		
Belgium		0.32	0.23	0.02	0.24	0.6		
Bulgaria		0.01[8][29]						
Denmark		0.81						
Spain		0.13[15]	23.12	12.96	9.95	31.3		
France		0.63	3.50	0.26	10.11	6.2		
Finland		—[0]						
Greece		0.71						
Hungary			—[14]					
Italy		23.25	64.18	62.95	43.64	39.4		
Norway		2.29						
Poland		0.61[30]						
Portugal		0.80[5]	0.24	14.70	0.33	0.7		
Netherlands		0.38	0.05	0.41	0.73			
Russia		16.55[6][7]	1.57					
Rumania		0.67						
British Isles	36.53	15.18	0.61	0.11	12.64	2.8	3.62	12.6
Sweden		4.99		0.01				
Switzerland		0.48	0.49	0.09	3.34	0.7		
Turkey in Europe		0.05						
Serbia and Montenegro								
Other European countries		0.62						
China		0.00					1.84[16]	
India							0.29	
Japan		1.30					1.58	
Syria		1.37		0.91				
Turkey in Asia		0.01						
Other Asiatic countries		0.01					0.15[24]	
Africa								
United States	23.05[31]				0.57	0.3		
British North America		0.16						
Central America		0.01						
Mexico		0.04						
West Indies		1.29						
South America								
Argentina						0.6		
Brazil		0.02			9.38	6.7		
Uruguay								
Other countries						0.3[22]		
Oceania		0.06			0.16			
Pacific Islands		0.04					92.09[17]	81.1[18]
Other countries	40.41	0.01	3.45[19]	2.73		6.1	0.43	6.3
Total	100[31]	100	100	100	100	100	100	100

For reference notes see page 353

TABLE 14.—IMMIGRATION OF ALIENS BY COUNTRY OF LAST RESIDENCE OR NATIONALITY[1] FROM 1821 UPWARDS (cont.)

b. Percentages

_1901–1905_

Country of Immigration / Country of Last Residence or Nationality	Canada[3]	United States[2]	Argentina[3,12]	Brazil[3]	Paraguay[3]	Uruguay[3,31,32]	Australian Commonwealth[2,9,33]	New Zealand[9]
Germany	1.85	4.61	1.11	1.08	9.93	3.5	2.12	
Austria	9.31[14]	24.63[14]	2.63[14]	0.87	2.06	1.7[14]	1.65	
Belgium	0.44	0.44	0.17	0.03	0.58	0.5	0.04	
Bulgaria	0.00	0.17[28]						
Denmark	0.83	0.89			0.36		0.20	
Spain	0.01	0.26[5]	27.90	18.06	14.99	29.6	0.08	
France	0.96	0.81	2.67	0.39	4.79	5.9	3.16	
Finland	1.13	—[6]						
Greece	0.14[5]	1.30					0.43	
Hungary	—[5]	—[14]	—[14]					
Italy	3.80	25.03	55.04	46.93	29.62	41.7	1.89	
Norway	1.09	2.68						
Poland	0.40	—[30]					0.02	
Portugal	0.00	0.79[15]	0.32	24.91	0.09	1.3	0.01	
Netherlands	0.14	0.48	0.08		0.40		0.08	
Russia	2.49	17.18[6]	3.75	0.65	0.81		0.28	
Rumania	0.39	0.91					0.01	
British Isles	35.78	10.05	0.67	0.23	3.09	3.2	80.36	13.1
Sweden	1.53	4.03		0.01	0.13		0.65[4]	
Switzerland	0.08	0.46	0.35	0.08	1.07	0.8	0.12	
Turkey in Europe	—[34]	0.28					0.02	
Serbia and Montenegro	0.01							
Other European countries	3.32[35]	0.01					0.62	
China	0.00	0.33					2.39	
India	0.01	0.01					0.39	
Japan	0.07	1.67					0.96	
Syria	0.71[36]			1.59			0.10[7]	
Turkey in Asia	0.12[34]	0.79					0.00	
Other Asiatic countries	0.01	0.20					1.12	
Africa	0.01	0.04					0.00[38]	
United States	35.07				2.10	0.4	1.18	
British North America	0.2	0.18						
Central America		0.07						
Mexico		0.13			0.09[45]			
West Indies	0.03	1.11					0.02	
South America: Argentina						0.6		
Brazil	0.00	0.14			28.95	6.	0.01	
Uruguay								
Other countries	0.08				0.94	0.4[22]		
Oceania		0.14					1.38	78.9[18]
Pacific Islands	0.01	0.01					0.73[40]	
Other countries	0.00[29]	0.01	5.30[19]	5.18		4.4		8.1
Total	100.	100.	100.	100.	100.	100.	100.	100.

For reference notes see page 353.

TABLE 14.—IMMIGRATION OF ALIENS BY COUNTRY OF LAST RESIDENCE OR NATIONALITY[1] FROM 1821 UPWARDS (cont.)

b. Percentages

Country of Last Residence or Nationality	1906–1910						
	Canada [3][41]	United States [2]	Cuba	Argentina [3][12]	Brazil [3]	Australian Commonwealth [3][9]	New Zealand [9]
Germany	0.92	3.31	0.11	1.09	3.58	2.54	
Austria	5.83[14]	11.20		1.93[14]	3.35	0.99	
Belgium	0.5	0.49		0.11	0.08	0.06	
Bulgaria	0.35	0.65[5,8]					
Denmark	0.22	0.63				0.34	
Spain	0.03	0.35[15]	70.80	40.86	21.25	0.07	
France	0.90	0.84	0.99	1.63	0.91	1.98	
Finland	0.61	—[6]					
Greece	0.26	2.36				0.38	
Hungary	—[14]	12.99		—[14]			
Italy	3.46	21.88	0.13	40.92	20.04	1.23	
Norway	0.65	1.76					
Poland	0.59	—[30]				0.02	
Portugal	0.00	0.77[15]		0.69	36.35	0.01	
Netherlands	0.33	0.59		0.09		0.17	
Russia	2.12	18.91[6]		5.23	3.81	0.58	
Rumania	0.23	0.35				0.01	
British Isles	40.10	9.66	0.25	0.73	0.79	84.72	24.5
Sweden	0.92	1.91			0.12	1.27[4]	
Switzerland	0.09	0.34		0.25	0.22	0.12	
Turkey in Europe	—[34]	1.39				0.01	
Serbia and Montenegro	0.02						
Other European countries	2.53[35]	0.01	0.51			0.05	
China	0.91	0.15				2.06	
India	0.41	0.08				0.15	
Japan	1.03	1.32				0.67	
Syria, Mesopotamia, Palestine	0.16[36]	0.94				0.09[37]	
Turkey in Asia	0.27[34]						
Other Asiatic countries	0.01	0.06	0.00[42]		3.76	0.57	
Africa	0.03	0.11				0.00[38]	
United States	35.13		8.27			1.01	
British North America	1.00	3.46					
Central America		0.10	0.06				
Mexico		0.89	4.57				
West Indies	0.11	1.30	13.87			0.01	
South America							
Argentina							
Brazil							
Uruguay	0.00	0.23	0.42			0.02	
Other countries	0.14	0.13					
Oceania							
Pacific Islands		0.01				0.13	70.6[18]
Other countries	0.03[39]	0.66		6.46[19]	5.74	0.75[40]	5.
Total	100.	100.	100.	100.	100.	100.	100.

For reference notes see page 353.

TABLE 14.—IMMIGRATION OF ALIENS BY COUNTRY OF LAST RESIDENCE OR NATIONALITY[1] FROM 1812 UPWARDS (cont.)

b. Percentages

Country of Last Residence or Nationality	1911–1915									
	Canada[3]	United States[2]	Mexico[3]	Cuba	Argentina[3][21]	Brazil[3]	Uruguay[3][21][43]	Australian Commonwealth[3][9]	New Zealand[9]	Hawaii[3]
Germany	1.32	3.08	3.16	0.10	1.50	3.43	2.7	2.16		
Austria	5.92[14]	10.07		0.01	1.76[14]	1.59		0.57		
Belgium	0.55	0.57		0.01	0.17	0.17		0.07		
Bulgaria	1.04[44]	0.48[8]								
Denmark	0.28	0.66	0.02	0.02		0.04		0.32		
Spain	0.18	0.62[15]	15.04	74.95	47.84	21.02	36.6	0.12		9.17
France	0.67	0.90	3.09	0.53	1.84	0.91	3.2	0.91		
Finland	0.59	[6]								
Greece	0.34	2.66		0.02		0.24		0.47		
Hungary	[14]	9.86			—[14]	0.22				
Italy	4.16	21.05	1.72	0.06	29.69	17.49	23.	1.16		
Norway	0.46	1.06		0.01						
Poland	2.01	[30]						0.01		
Portugal	0.01	1.08[15]		0.02	1.33	0.15		0.01		4.58
Netherlands	0.37	0.70		0.00	0.08	5.73		0.24		
Russia	4.37	20.04[6]			5.47	0.04		0.90		0.86
Rumania	0.28					0.63		0.01		
British Isles	36.20	8.71	10.3	0.19	0.89	0.20	4.	87.56	26.4	
Sweden	0.63	1.61		0.00		0.18		1.07[8]		
Switzerland	0.07	0.38		0.01	0.35			0.13		
Turkey in Europe	—[34]	1.17		0.30		0.02		0.01		
Serbia and Montenegro	0.08	0.07								
Other European countries	2.07[35]	0.23	4.82			0.06		0.18		0.24[45]
China	1.54	0.02	12.49	0.00				1.73		5.60
India	0.01	0.81						0.16		0.04
Japan	0.06[56]		0.92			2.26		0.45		39.74[46]
Syria, Mesopotamia, Palestine	0.15[34]	1.61		0.34				0.05[37]		
Turkey in Asia	0.01	0.07	1.17	—[42]		4.66				
Other Asiatic countries	0.02	0.13		0.00				0.30		33.[41]
Africa								0.008[38]		
United States	35.76		43.65	7.28		0.20				
British North America	0.35	7.95	0.53	0.03			1.	1.06		
Central America		0.15	2.44[25]	1.29						
Mexico		1.83		2.99						
West Indies	0.00	1.44		11.01			0.7	0.00		—[47]
South America	0.15	0.44	0.69	0.83[48]	9.08[19]	0.52	5.			
Argentina							23.8			
Brazil										
Uruguay	0.00									
Other countries										
Oceania	0.05	0.12		0.00		0.39		0.02		
Pacific Islands	0.00	0.01		0.00				0.06	65.9[18]	
Other countries	0.06[69]	0.01		0.00				0.27[40]	7.8	6.75
Total	100.	100.	100.	100.	100.	100.	100.	100.	100.	100.

For reference notes see page 353.

TABLE 14.—IMMIGRATION OF ALIENS BY COUNTRY OF LAST RESIDENCE OR NATIONALITY[1] FROM 1821 UPWARDS (cont.)

b. Percentages

Country of Immigration — 1916–1920

Country of Last Residence or Nationality	Canada[3]	United States[2]	Mexico[3]	Cuba	Argentina[3,12]	Brazil[3]	Uruguay[3,21]	Australian Commonwealth[3,9]	New Zealand[9,9]	Hawaii[2]
Germany	0.03	0.48	2.66	0.03	3.61	2.76	2.	0.24		
Austria	0.01[14]	0.34		0.00	0.51[14]	0.79		0.01		
Belgium	0.71	0.65		0.00	0.24	0.23	0.8	0.09		
Bulgaria	0.00	0.08[28]				0.01				
Denmark	0.23	0.95		1.56		0.07		0.25		
Spain	0.07	3.18[15]	21.98	51.90	54.38	22.22	46.2	0.06		0.05
France	0.62	1.68	3.66	0.15	3.43	1.24	4.9	1.13		
Finland	0.38	0.06[49]				0.00				
Greece	0.15	5.11		0.02		0.19		0.31		
Hungary	—[14]	0.19			[14]	0.06				
Italy	1.26	13.36	1.55	0.09	24.31	14.54	9.1	0.35		
Norway	0.26	1.47		0.00		0.02				
Poland	0.87	0.37[40]				0.31		0.01		
Portugal	0.00	3.22[15]		0.07	1.14	41.70	3.3	0.01		1.03
Netherlands	0.22	0.96		0.01	0.22	0.16		0.58		
Russia	0.36	2.13[6]		0.01	0.77	1.04	1.9	0.44		0.07
Rumania	0.21	0.16		0.00		0.48		0.02		
British Isles	32.48	7.76	6.82	0.13	2.36	0.85	6.4	87.83		
Sweden	0.32	1.80		0.00		0.04		0.91[4]		
Switzerland	0.08	0.47		0.02	0.55	0.41		0.07		
Czechoslovakia		0.26[50]				0.05				
Turkey in Europe	—[34]	0.18		0.16		0.03		0.00		
Serbia and Montenegro	0.02	0.14[50]		0.00		0.01				
Other European countries	0.81[35]	0.38	5.42	0.13		0.05		0.28		0.48[45]
China	1.77	0.84	6.69	2.55		0.03		3.11		5.31
India	0.00	0.06		0.00		0.05		0.27		0.01
Japan	0.83	3.71	2.90	0.01		7.35		1.10		50.97[48]
Syria, Mesopotamia, Palestine	0.04[36]							0.03[37]		
Turkey in Asia	0.01[34]	0.56		0.06[42]		3.39		0.51		
Other Asiatic countries	0.00	0.21		0.00				0.00[38]		35.15[42]
Africa	0.01	0.20	1.15			0.06				
United States	56.78		40.28	2.58		0.41		0.01		
British North America	0.93	30.34	3.05	0.04		0.00	3.5	1.84		
Central America		0.81		1.61		0.00				
Mexico		0.73		0.77						
West Indies	0.00	4.62	2.66[25]	37.39				0.03		
South America										
Argentina	0.00	1.71	1.18	0.66[48]		1.28	3.4			
Brazil							11.7			
Uruguay				0.00						
Other countries	0.08				8.48[19]	0.21	6.7			
Oceania										
Pacific Islands	0.08[39]	0.52		0.03				0.07		
Other countries	0.22	0.04		0.00				0.44[40]		6.93
Total	100.	100.	100.	100.	100.	100.	100.	100.	100.	100.

For reference notes see page 353.

TABLE 14.—IMMIGRATION OF ALIENS BY COUNTRY OF LAST RESIDENCE OR NATIONALITY[1] FROM 1821 UPWARDS (cont.)

b. Percentages

Country of Last Residence or Nationality	1921–1924								
	Canada[3]	United States[2]	Mexico[3]	Cuba	Argentina[3,12]	Brazil[3]	Uruguay[3,21,51]	Australian Commonwealth[3,9]	Hawaii[3]
Albania		0.01[82]						0.13	
Germany	1.04	6.32	3.69	0.37	5.32	14.26	2.9	0.01	
Austria	1.61[14]	1.09		0.01	0.79[14]	1.53		0.08	
Belgium	0.90	0.48		0.01	0.10	0.14	0.9	0.19	
Bulgaria	0.09	0.08				0.03			
Denmark	1.	0.80		70.00	0.39	0.12		0.09	0.04
Estonia	0.01	0.03[82]							
Spain	0.31	1.12[15]	15.53	52.84	30.49	11.76	41.7	0.55	
France	3.13	1.05	2.22	6.53	1.	0.86	4.8	0.96	
Finland	0.21	0.59				0.02			
Greece	—[14]	1.71		0.10	—[14]	0.11		2.86	
Hungary	3.13	1.07	3.33	0.97		0.68			
Italy		15.59			45.15	17.01	17.1	—[4]	
Latvia		0.06[82]		0.26					
Lithuania	1.41	0.10[82]		0.03	4.13	0.04		0.07	
Norway	2.97	1.55		0.06	1.28	1.49	2.2	0.00	0.60
Poland	0.00	7.64		0.22	0.11	34.11		0.27	
Portugal	0.73	1.12[15]		0.51	0.93	0.16	1.1	0.21	0.07
Netherlands	2.39	0.66		0.41		1.31		0.02	
Russia	1.11	2.29		0.14		3.21		87.61	
Rumania	47.22	2.52	7.32	0.61	0.68	0.71	6.2	0.45[4]	
United Kingdom	1.67	10.81		0.00	0.08	0.05		0.20	
Sweden	0.62	2.22		0.02	0.46	0.64			
Switzerland		0.75				0.55		0.00	
Czechoslovakia	—[34]	3.45		0.10					
Turkey in Europe	0.77	0.57	7.05	0.02	1.29	2.88		1.38	
Serb, Croat and Slovene Kingdom	4.95[35]	1.77	2.61	0.04		0.75		2.01	
Other European countries	0.74	0.26		0.76		0.06		0.18	
China	0.03	0.87	1.28	0.04		0.01		0.30	8.86
India	0.42	0.06		0.06		1.85		0.15[37]	0.00
Japan	0.17[36]	1.24		0.01					33.00[46]
Syria, Mesopotamia, Palestine	0.80	0.13	2.74	0.00[42]	2.67	4.29		0.32	
Turkey in Asia	0.23[34]	0.80				0.03			
Other Asiatic countries	0.01	0.10				0.07			
Africa	0.06	0.14			0.17			1.52	
United States	20.82		48.40	1.83		0.34	3.2		
British North America	2.02	18.63	3.96	0.29		0.00			
Central America		0.28		0.68		0.02			
Mexico		8.68		31.87		0.01	2.1	0.00	
West India	0.00	2.22							
Argentina (South America)	0.16					0.85	6.2		
Brazil (South America)		0.93	1.17	0.55[58]					
Uruguay (South America)	0.00					0.00			
Other countries (South America)		0.19						0.05	
Oceania	0.15	0.01		0.00					
Pacific Islands				0.01					52.36[42]
Atlantic Islands								0.33[40]	0.50[47]
Other countries	0.04[39]	0.01	0.7	0.91	4.99[19]	0.03	11.6		3.57
Total	100.	100.	100.	100.	100.	100.	100.	100.	100.

For reference notes see page 353

TABLE 15.—INTERCONTINENTAL IMMIGRATION OF CITIZENS BY COUNTRY OF LAST RESIDENCE, 1876-1924

a. Absolute figures

Country of Immigration / Country of Last Residence	United States	British North America	Argentina	Brazil	Other American States	Oceania	Africa	Asia	Other countries or unknown	Total
1876-1880										
EUROPE:										
British Isles (Passengers)	180,181	2 6,705				22,300			45,995	275,181
Sweden					2,828		63			2,891
Spain										
1881-1885										
EUROPE:										
British Isles (Passengers)	224,022	37,061				35,850			61,113	358,046
Sweden	7,051				37	5,459[1]	84			7,172
Spain	214[1]		4,815[1]	302[1]	69,631[1]		67,560[1]	16[1]		147,997[1]
1886-1890										
EUROPE:										
Belgium	475				600	3	20	69	114	1,281
British Isles (Passengers)	321,415	40,999				50,286	21,785		37,681	472,166
Sweden	11,802				89		140			12,031
Italy	16,687[2]		101,116[2]	6,566[2]	318[2]				89[2]	124,776[2]
Spain	257		19,154	2,335	84,369	9,725	105,850	1		221,691
1891-1895										
EUROPE:										
Belgium	1,122				605	5	55	68	18	1,873
British Isles (Passengers)	353,516	48,396				49,230	33,561		45,960	530,663
Sweden	24,834				273					25,316
Italy	89,661		140,739	43,009	1,817		209	6		275,226
Spain	280		25,425	5,751	108,752	9,883	103,784			253,881
1896-1900										
EUROPE:										
Belgium	1,367				424	6	86	56	41	1,980
British Isles (Passengers)	272,037	48,308				40,154	77,223		48,372	486,094
Sweden	22,321				164					22,805
Italy	131,167		126,099	81,180	4,989		320			344,198
Spain	1,793[3]		24,014[3]	5,761[3]	240,738[3]	30,742[3]	70,474[3]	83[3]	763	373,605[3]

For reference notes see page 354.

TABLE 15.—INTERCONTINENTAL IMMIGRATION OF CITIZENS BY COUNTRY OF LAST RESIDENCE, 1876-1924 (cont.)

a. Absolute figures

Country of Last Residence (Country of Immigration)	United States	British North America	Argentina	Brazil	Other American States	Oceania	Africa	Asia	Other countries or unknown	Total
1901–1905										
EUROPE:										
Belgium	1,605				362	13	164	95	63	2,302
British Isles (Passengers)	314,492	72,316				43,999	102,294		50,920	584,021
Sweden	19,070				142		244			19,456
Italy	361,994		123,486	116,317					8,524	610,321
Spain										
ASIA:										
Japan	12,671[4]	1,494[4]				11,048[4]				25,213[4]
1906–1910										
EUROPE:										
Belgium	3,196				488	18	230	157	55	4,144
British Isles (Passengers)	306,560	171,971				58,822	114,546		124,405	776,304
Sweden	24,959				292		285			25,536
Italy	707,373	326	212,576	77,511	4,299				522	1,002,607
Spain										
ASIA:										
Japan										45,807
1911–1915										
EUROPE:										
Belgium	893[5]				1,539[5]	11[5]	428[5]	97[5]	51[5]	3,019[5]
British Isles (Passengers)	345,056	267,475				86,260	112,360		167,913	979,064
(Immigrants)	67,927[6]	115,443[6]				49,521[6]	38,964[6]	23,919[6]	46,466[6]	342,240[6]
Sweden	21,478				900		365			22,743
Italy	668,982	1,673	245,962	56,695	3,669				1,088	978,069
Spain	5,576[7]		111,174[7]	15,328[7]	65,542[7]	998[7]	78,867[7]	81[7]		277,566[7]
ASIA:										
Japan	23,958	4,615				17,234				45,807
1916–1920										
EUROPE:										
Belgium	1,127[8][9]	362[9]	73[9]		148[9]	8[9]	430[9]	58[9]	63[9]	2,269[9]
British Isles (Passengers)	123,207	144,686				40,195	47,470	29,426	98,830	454,388
(Immigrants)	52,164	86,247				34,010	22,288		33,900	258,035
Sweden	15,675				449		317			16,441
Italy	160,385	5,317	54,708	11,065	342				1,463	233,280
Spain	18,000		135,114	14,930	149,805	1,683	66,096	271		385,899
ASIA:										
Japan	43,180	8,215				22,892				74,287

For reference notes see page 354.

TABLE 15.—INTERCONTINENTAL IMMIGRATION OF CITIZENS BY COUNTRY OF LAST RESIDENCE, 1876-1924 (cont.)

a. Absolute figures

Country of Immigration / Country of Last Residence	United States	British North America	Argentina	Brazil	Other American States	Oceania	Africa	Asia	Other countries or unknown	Total
						1921–1924				
EUROPE:										
Belgium	2,260[8]	827	99	......	292	33	1,358	160	14	5,043
British Isles (Passengers)	133,901[10]	177,392[10]	......	......	......	69,971[10]	79,140[10]	—[10]	159,575[10]	619,979[10]
(Immigrants)	|46,267[11]	65,899[11]	......	......	......	42,410[11]	27,425[11]	36,686[11]	45,460[11]	264,147[11]
Sweden	12,044				442		328			12,814
Italy	177,107	..3,779	53,910	15,858	2,247	681	292		817	254,691
Spain	24,043[12]		54,181[12]	7,177[12]	124,673[12]	1,199[12]	46,885[12]	54[12]	......	258,212[12]
ASIA:										
Japan	34,008	5,225	......	......	......	17,287	......	......	......	56,520

For reference notes see page 354.

TABLE 16.—INTERCONTINENTAL IMMIGRATION OF CITIZENS BY COUNTRY OF LAST RESIDENCE, 1876-1924.

b. Percentages

Country of Immigration \ Country of Last Residence	United States	British North America	Argentina	Brazil	Other American States	Oceania	Africa	Asia	Other countries or unknown	Total
1876–1880										
EUROPE										
British Isles (Passengers).....	65.5	9.7				8.1			16.7	100
Sweden.........										100
Spain.........					97.8		2.2			..
1881–1885										
EUROPE:										
British Isles.....	62.6	10.3				10.			17.1	100
Sweden.........	98.3				0.5		1.2			100
Spain.........	0.1[1]		3.3[1]	0.2[1]	47.1[1]	3.7	45.7[1]	0.0[1]		100[1]
1886–1890										
EUROPE										
Belgium.........	37.1				46.8	0.2	1.6	5.4	8.9	100
British Isles (Passengers).....	68.	8.7				10.7	4.6		8.	100
Sweden.........	98.1				0.7		1.2			100
Italy.........	13.4[2]		81.0[2]	5.3[2]	0.3[2]				0.1[2]	100[2]
Spain.........	0.1		8.6	1.1	38.1	4.4	47.8	0.01		100
1891–1895										
EUROPE:										
Belgium.........	59.9				32.3	0.3	2.9	3.6	1.	100
British Isles (Passengers).....	66.6	9.1				9.3	6.3	8.7		100
Sweden.........	98.1				1.1		0.8			100
Italy.........	32.6		51.1	15.6	0.7					100
Spain.........	0.1		10.	2.3	42.8	3.9	4.9	0.0		100
1896–1900										
EUROPE:										
Belgium.........	69.0				21.4	0.3	4.3	2.8	2.1	100
British Isles (Passengers).....	56.	9.9				8.3	15.9		9.9	100
Sweden.........	97.9				0.7		1.4		0.2	100
Italy.........	38.1		36.6	23.6	1.4					100
Spain.........	0.5[3]		6.4[3]	1.5[3]	64.4[3]	8.2[3]	18.9[3]	0.0[3]		100[3]

For reference notes see page 354.

TABLE 16.—INTERCONTINENTAL IMMIGRATION OF CITIZENS BY COUNTRY OF LAST RESIDENCE, 1876-1924 (cont.)

b. Percentages

Country of Last Residence / Country of Immigration	United States	British North America	Argentina	Brazil	Other American States	Oceania	Africa	Asia	Other countries or unknown	Total
1901–1905										
EUROPE:										
Belgium..........	53.8				15.7	0.6	7.1	4.1	2.7	100
British Isles (Passengers).....	{69.7	12.4			....	7.6	17.5	....	8.7	100
Sweden..........	98.0	....	....	....	0.7		1.3		....	100
Italy..........	59.3	....	20.2	19.1	....				1.4	100
Spain..........	....	....	....	....	....				....	....
ASIA:										
Japan..........	50.3[4]	5.9[4]	....	....	....	43.8[4]	....	....	....	100[4]
1906–1910										
EUROPE:										
Belgium..........	39.5				11.8	0.4	5.6	3.8	1.3	100
British Isles (Passengers).....	{77.1	22.1			....	7.6	14.8	....	16.0	100
Sweden..........	97.7	....	....	....	1.1		1.1		0.1	100
Italy..........	70.6	....	21.2	7.7	0.4				....	100
Spain..........	....	....	....	....	....				....	....
ASIA:										
Japan..........	52.3	10.1	....	....	....	37.6	....	....	....	100
1911–1915										
EUROPE:										
Belgium..........	35.2				51.0[8]	0.4[5]	14.2[5]	3.2[5]	1.7[5]	100[5]
British Isles (passengers).....	19.8[8]	27.3			....	8.8	11.5		17.2	100
(Immigrants)..........	{29.6[5]	33.7[6]			....	14.5[6]	11.4[6]	.7[6]	13.6[6]	100[8]
Sweden..........	94.4	....	25.1	5.8	4.0		1.6		....	100
Italy..........	68.4	0.2	40.1[7]	.5[7]	0.4	0.4[7]	28.4[7]		0.1	100
Spain..........	2.0[7]	....	....	....	23.6[7]	....	....		....	100[7]
ASIA:										
Japan..........	52.3	10.1	....	....	....	37.6	....	0.0[7]	....	100
1916–1920										
EUROPE:										
Belgium..........	49.7[8][9]	16.0[9]	3.2[9]		6.5[9]	0.4[9]	19.0[9]	2.6[9]	2.8[9]	100[9]
British Isles (Passengers).....	27.1	31.8	....		....	8.9	10.4	....	21.8	100
(Immigrants)..........	20.2	33.4	....		....	13.2	8.6	11.4	13.2	100
Sweden..........	95.3	2.3	23.5	4.7	2.7	0.4	1.9		0.6	100
Italy..........	68.8	....	35.0	3.9	0.1		17.1	0.1	....	100
Spain..........	4.7	....	....	....	38.8				....	100
ASIA:										
Japan..........	58.1	11.1	....	....	....	30.8	....	....	....	100

For reference notes see page 354.

TABLE 16.—INTERCONTINENTAL IMMIGRATION OF CITIZENS BY COUNTRY OF LAST RESIDENCE, 1876-1924 (cont.)

b. Percentages

Country of Immigration \ Country of Last Residence	United States	British North America	Argentina	Brazil	Other American States	Oceania	Africa	Asia	Other countries or unknown	Total
					1921–1924					
EUROPE:										
Belgium	44.8	16.4	2.0	....	5.8	0.7	26.9	3.2	0.3	100
British Isles (Passengers)	21.6[10]	28.6[10]	....	....	....	11.3[10]	12.8[10]	13.9[11]	25.7[10]	100[10]
(Immigrants)	17.5[11]	25.0[11]	....	....	....	16.1[11]	10.4[11]		17.2[11]	100[11]
Sweden	94.0	....	....	....	3.4	0.3	2.6	....	....	100
Italy	69.5	1.5	21.2	6.2	0.9	....	0.1	....	0.3	100
Spain	9.3[12]	....	21.0[12]	2.8[12]	48.3[12]	0.5[12]	18.2[12]	0.0[12]	....	100[12]
ASIA:										
Japan	60.2	9.2	....	....	....	30.6	....	....	....	100

For reference notes see page 354.

TABLE 17.—CONTINENTAL EMIGRATION OF CITIZENS BY COUNTRY OF FUTURE RESIDENCE, 1876-1924.

a. Absolute figures

Country of Emigration

Country of Future Residence	Germany	Austria-Hungary	Denmark	Spain and Portugal	Finland	France	British Isles	Italy	Luxemburg	Norway	Netherlands and Belgium	Russia	Serbia and Balkan States	Sweden	Switzerland	Other countries	Total
1876-1880																	
Sweden			10,425		2,217[7]					8,654						4,063	25,359
Italy	36,574	95,979		3,162		184,279	2,612				949[2]	1,647[3]	6,703	118[4]	66,410	1,056	399,489
1881-1885																	
Sweden			13,734		1,460					7,453		345				4,217	27,209
Italy	34,634	128,122		4,385		222,501	2,807				2,575[2]	1,452[3]	15,371	187[4]	35,161	3,297	450,492
1886-1890																	
Belgium	2,299	54		217		37,111	966	220	456		4,695[4]	76			96	301	46,491
Sweden			9,759		1,809					6,020		288				3,811	21,687
Italy	51,758	170,589		3,600		151,570	2,942				1,185[2]	1,496[3]	12,935	195[1]	36,014	6,427	438,711
1891-1895																	
Belgium	2,752	119		346		44,217	623	200	674	622	5,873[5]	215			581	205	55,357
Sweden			7,652		1,554					6,965		204				3,208	19,583
Italy	76,228	181,724		2,847		134,484	2,949				868[2]	1,707[3]	60,731	631[4]	60,829	8,424	531,422
1896-1900																	
Belgium	4,542	268		300		41,563	1,008	284	919		6,254[5]	3,132			167	324	58,516
Sweden			8,356		1,775					8,782		255				3,508	22,676
Italy	154,703	231,335		3,182		124,799	4,717				1,761[2]	6,530[3]	54,292	197[4]	128,233	13,963	723,712
1901-1905																	
Belgium	4,867	125		428		39,900	1,159	398	1,109		6,852[5]	1,151			235	323	56,357
Sweden			6,656		1,477					5,658		219				3,922	17,932
Italy	280,045	272,268		3,584		271,493	18,810				6,460[2]	7,166[3]	14,207	783[4]	269,141	23,274	1,161,231
1906-1910																	
Belgium	5,532	157		378		57,836	1,498	726			7,956[5]	1,258			343	583	77,376
Sweden			5,254		1,713					4,286		325				4,114	15,692
Italy	310,999	185,694		3,135		301,123	20,847				12,072[2]	6,042[3]	16,376	772[4]	386,527	673	1,244,260
1911-1915																	
Belgium	2,957[6]	140[6]		235[6]		37,606[6]	837[6]	268[8]	619[6]		5,097[5,6]	790[6]			347[6]	365[6]	49,261[6]
Sweden			4,741		1,509					4,932		378				4,011	15,571
Italy	280,906	159,416		3,676		325,317	16,915				11,619[2]	5,449[3]	17,649	1,111[4]	357,977	1,796	1,181,831
1916-1920																	
Belgium	2,949[7]	317[8]		183[7]		55,385[7]	2,426[7]	246[7]	864[7]		6,063[5,7]	66[7]			239[7]	233[7]	68,685[7]
Sweden			6,530		946					7,069		184				2,056	16,785
Italy	4,167	5,071		1,836		339,170	14,699				4,669[2]	255[3]	6,001	165[4]	75,525	589	452,147
1921-1924																	
Belgium	2,058			283		65,940	1,134	313	854		4,913[8]	37			211	445	76,188
Sweden			2,993		1,260					3,381		63				3,133	10,830
Italy	5,366	16,245[9]		2,063		584,803	5,785		12,248		50,777[10]	205[11]	19,074	364[4]	40,496	1,548	738,974

For reference notes see page 354.

TABLE 18.—CONTINENTAL EMIGRATION OF CITIZENS BY COUNTRY OF FUTURE RESIDENCE, 1876-1924.

b. Percentages

Country of Future Residence / Country of Emigration	Germany	Austria-Hungary	Denmark	Spain and Portugal	Finland	France	British Isles	Italy	Luxemburg	Norway	Netherlands and Belgium	Russia	Serbia and Balkan States	Sweden	Switzerland	Other countries	Total
Country of Emigration																	
1876–1880																	
Sweden	9.2		41.1	0.8	8.7[1]					34.1						16.1	100
Italy	7.7	24.0				46.1	0.7				0.2[2]	0.4[3]	1.7	0.03[4]	16.6	0.3	100
1881–1885																	
Sweden	4.9		50.5	1.0	5.4					27.4						15.5	100
Italy	11.8	28.4				49.4	0.6				0.6[2]	0.3[3]	3.4	0.04[4]	7.8	0.7	100
1886–1890																	
Belgium	5.0	0.1		0.5		79.8	2.1	0.5	1.0		10.1[5]	0.2			0.2	0.7	100
Sweden			45		8.3					27.8		1.3				17.6	100
Italy	14.3	38.9		0.8		34.5	0.7				0.3[2]	0.3[3]	2.9	0.04[4]	8.2	1.5	100
1891–1895																	
Belgium	7.8	0.2		0.6		79.9	1.1	0.4	1.1		10.6[5]	0.4			0.3	0.4	100
Sweden			39.1		7.9					35.6		1.0				16.4	100
Italy	21.4	34.2		0.5		25.3	0.6				0.2[2]	0.3[3]	11.4	0.12[4]	11.4	1.6	100
1896–1900																	
Belgium	8.6	0.5		0.5		71.00	1.7	0.5	1.2		10.7[5]	5.4			0.3	0.6	100
Sweden			36.8		7.8					38.7		1.1				15.5	100
Italy	24.0	32.0		0.4		17.2	0.7				0.2[2]	0.9[3]	7.5	0.03[4]	17.7	1.9	100
1901–1905																	
Belgium	7.1	0.2		0.8		70.8	2.1	0.7	1.6		12.2[5]	2.0			0.4	0.6	100
Sweden			37.1		8.2					31.6		1.2				21.9	100
Italy	25.0	23.3		0.3		23.3	1.6				0.6[2]	0.6[3]	1.2	0.07[4]	23.1	2.0	100
1906–1910																	
Belgium		0.2		0.5		74.7	1.9	0.9	1.4		10.3[5]	1.6			0.4	0.8	100
Sweden			33.5		10.9					27.3		2.1				26.2	100
Italy	23.8	14.9		0.3		24.2	1.7				1.0[2]	0.5[3]	1.3	0.06[4]	31.1	0.05	100
1911–1915																	
Belgium	6.0[6]	0.3[6]		0.5[6]		76.3[6]	1.7[6]	0.5[6]	1.3[6]		10.3[5,6]	1.6[6]			0.7[6]	0.7[6]	100
Sweden			30.4		9.7					31.7		2.4				25.8	100
Italy		13.5		0.3		27.5	1.4				1.0[2]	0.5[3]	1.5	0.09[4]	30.3	0.15	100
1916–1920																	
Belgium	4.3[7]	0.04[8]		0.3[7]		80.6[7]	3.5[7]	0.4[7]	1.37[7]		8.8[5]	0.1[7]			0.3[7]	0.7[7]	100
Sweden			38.9		5.6					42.1		1.1				12.2	100
Italy	0.9	1.1		0.4		75.0	3.3				1.0[2]	0.067	1.3	0.04[4]	16.7	01.3	100
1921–1924																	
Belgium	2.7			0.4		86.5	1.5	0.4	1.7		6.4[5]	0.05			0.3	0.6	100
Sweden			27.6		11.6					31.2		0.6				28.9	100
Italy	0.7	2.2[9]		0.3		79.1	0.8				6.9[10]	0.02[11]	2.6	0.04[3]	5.5	0.2	100

For reference notes see page 354.

TABLE 19.—DISTRIBUTION OF EMIGRANT CITIZENS, BY SEX AND AGE, 1851-1924[1]

a. Absolute figures

Country of Emigration	Children or young persons			Adults			Total		
	Males	Females	Total	Males	Females	Total	Males	Females	Total
1851–1855									
EUROPE:									
Austria[2]			7,787[j]			10,086	9,222	8,651	17,873
France[3]	......	......	......	......	......	......	......	......	......
Ireland[4]	......	......	4,054	......	......	8,690	7,380	5,364	12,744
Sweden	......	......	......	......	......	......	......	......	......
ASIA:									
British India			10,444	67,953	14,280	82,233	......	......	92,677
1856–1860									
EUROPE:									
Austria[2]	1,527[5]	......	4,625	......	......	6,579	6,026	5,178	11,204
France[3]	......	1,425[5]	2,952[5]	21,653[5]	9,445[5]	31,098[5]	23,180[5]	10,870[5]	34,050[5]
Ireland[4]	......	......	64,520	......	......	350,035	221,323	194,096	415,419
Sweden	......	......	1,372	......	......	2,784	2,339	1,817	4,156
ASIA:									
British India			23,563	90,463	34,816	125,279	......	......	148,842
1861–1865									
EUROPE:									
Austria[2]	695[6]	......	4,511	......	......	6,375	5,983	4,903	10,886
France[3]	......	663[6]	1,358[6]	13,073[6]	5,281[5]	18,354[6]	13,768[6]	5,944[6]	19,712[6]
Ireland[4]	......	......	79,405	......	......	361,433	246,131	221,173	467,304
Norway	......	......	4,382	......	......	15,434	11,485	8,331	19,816
Sweden	......	......	......	......	......	......	......	......	......
Portugal	......	......	......	......	......	......	......	......	......
ASIA:									
British India			3,315	73,197	21,684	94,881	......	......	108,196
1866–1870									
EUROPE:									
Austria[2]	......	......	11,859	......	......	16,875	15,057	13,677	28,734
France[3]	......	......	1,400[7]	......	......	21,805[7]	......	......	23,205[7]
Ireland[4]	......	......	48,439	......	......	336,188	223,686	158,846	382,532
Norway	12,397	11,197	23,594	29,572	21,182	50,754	41,969	32,379	74,348
Sweden	......	......	24,487	......	......	78,144	59,054	43,577	102,631
Portugal	......	......	......	......	......	......	45,196[8]	6,313[8]	51,509[8]
ASIA:									
British India			9,229	43,632	17,739	61,371	......	......	70,600

For reference notes see page 354.

TABLE 19.—DISTRIBUTION OF EMIGRANT CITIZENS, BY SEX AND AGE, 1851-1924[1] (cont.)

a. Absolute figures

Country of Emigration	Children or young persons			Adults			Total		
	Males	Females	Total	Males	Females	Total	Males	Females	Total
1871–1875									
EUROPE:									
Austria[2]	......	......	......	......	......	......	......	......	......
British Isles	......	......	......	......	......	......	......	......	......
Denmark	......	......	4,376[9]	......	......	15,127[9]	14,389	9,020	23,409
France[3]	......	......	2,408[10]	......	......	32,402[10]	......	......	34,810[10]
Germany[11]	36,389	34,546[9]	70,935[9]	132,727[9]	102,350[9]	235,077[9]	210,291	170,794	381,085
Ireland[4]	......	......	51,242	......	......	316,306	204,693	160,444	365,137
Norway	6,204	5,742	11,946	17,103	13,939	31,042	24,546	20,596	45,142
Sweden	......	......	12,625	......	......	51,838	34,928	29,535	64,463
Italy[12]	......	......	......	......	......	......	......	......	......
Portugal	......	......	10,171[9]	......	......	50,377[9]	52,815[9]	7,733[9]	60,548[9]
ASIA:									
British India	......	......	......	......	......	......	......	......	......
1876–1880									
EUROPE:									
Austria[2]	51,297[14]	......	29,549[13]	......	......	42,136[13]	38,772[13]	32,913[13]	71,685[13]
British Isles	......	47,733[14]	99,030[14]	308,256[14]	192,627[14]	500,883[14]	359,553[14]	240,360[14]	599,913[14]
Denmark	......	......	3,547	......	......	11,641	9,453	5,738	15,191
France[3]	......	......	2,324[15]	......	......	21,077[15]	11,835[16]	5,112[16]	23,401[15]
Germany	24,164	23,104	47,268	103,310	63,535	166,845	127,232	86,545	213,777
Ireland[4]	......	......	39,931	......	......	224,401	137,584	122,212	259,796
Norway	4,642	4,401	9,043	19,131	12,043	31,174	23,785	16,459	40,244
Sweden	......	......	15,357	......	......	70,449	48,560	37,246	85,806
Italy[12]	......	......	53,346	......	......	490,638	463,794	80,190	543,984
Portugal	......	......	9,076	......	......	48,717	47,774	10,049	57,823
ASIA:									
British India	......	......	......	......	......	......	34,958[17]	14,610[17]	49,568[17]

For reference notes see page 354.

TABLE 19.—DISTRIBUTION OF EMIGRANT CITIZENS, BY SEX AND AGE, 1851–1924 (cont.)

a. Absolute figures

Country of Emigration	Children or young persons			Adults			Total		
	Males	Females	Total	Males	Females	Total	Males	Females	Total
1881–1885									
EUROPE:									
Austria[4]	......	......	13,590[18]	......	......	22,091[18]	19,767	15,914	35,681
Belgium[19]	124,613	115,255	239,868	634,904	417,537	1,052,441	759,517	532,792	1,292,309
British Isles	......	......	9,270	......	......	29,357	23,078	15,549	38,627
Denmark	......	......	1,870[20]	......	......	11,779[20]	......	......	13,649[20]
France[5]	111,202	103,576	214,778	352,849	249,136	601,985	464,603	352,978	817,581
Germany[11]	......	......	68,032	......	......	347,318	211,275	202,899	414,174
Ireland[4]	......	......	5,103[21]	7,911[21]	5,041[21]	12,952[21]	......	......	18,055[21]
Norway	13,884	12,828	26,712	45,218	33,741	78,959	59,122	46,582	105,704
Sweden	......	......	35,159	......	......	139,669	94,887	79,941	174,828
Switzerland	......	......	......	......	......	......	......	......	......
Finland[12]	143[21]	149[21]	292[21]	3,377[21]	464[21]	3,841[21]	3,611[21]	892[21]	4,503[21]
Italy[12]	......	......	71,679	......	......	699,026	654,191	116,514	770,705
Portugal	......	......	13,129	......	......	71,553	66,948	17,734	84,682
ASIA:									
British India	......	......	......	......	......	......	45,683	18,757	64,440
1886–1890									
EUROPE:									
Austria[2]	4,488	3,703	8,191	12,014	4,853	16,867	16,502	8,556	25,058
Belgium[19]	104,415	95,505	199,920	648,923	417,383	1,066,306	753,338	512,888	1,266,226
British Isles	......	......	8,134	......	......	34,854	26,159	16,829	42,988
Denmark	......	......	......	......	......	......	......	......	......
France[5]	55,671	53,351	109,022	194,675	151,631	346,306	250,849	205,520	456,369
Germany[11]	......	......	38,336	......	......	319,005	184,023	172,509	356,532
Ireland[4]	......	......	7,032	10,955	6,320	17,275	......	......	24,307
Netherlands	7,627	7,128	14,755	39,770	26,412	66,182	47,417	33,567	80,984
Norway	......	......	30,733	......	......	170,840	112,101	89,472	201,573
Sweden	3,152[22]	2,832[22]	5,984[22]	17,005[22]	9,057[22]	26,062[22]	20,157[22]	11,889[22]	32,046[22]
Switzerland	676	592	1,268	11,269	1,446	12,715	16,772	5,196	21,968
Finland[12]	......	......	157,833	......	......	950,663	869,708	238,788	1,108,496
Italy[12]	......	......	20,407	......	......	84,539	80,420	24,526	104,946
ASIA:									
British India	......	......	......	......	......	......	42,326	18,973	61,299

For reference notes see page 354.

TABLE 19—DISTRIBUTION OF EMIGRANT CITIZENS, BY SEX AND AGE, 1851-1924[1] (cont.)

a. Absolute figures

Country of Emigration	Children or young persons			Adults			Total		
	Males	Females	Total	Males	Females	Total	Males	Females	Total
1891-1895									
EUROPE:									
Austria[2]	......	......	6,721[23]	......	......	22,397[23]	15,676[23]	13,442[23]	29,118[23]
Belgium[19]	2,065	1,804	3,869	8,112	3,115	11,227	10,177	4,919	15,096
British Isles	63,586	57,723	121,309	501,504	355,761	857,265	565,090	413,484	978,574
Denmark	......	......	7,280	......	......	30,386	21,628	16,038	37,666
Germany[11]	45,555	43,296	88,851	165,922	129,971	295,893	211,549	173,296	384,845
Ireland[4]	......	......	20,244	......	......	223,721	115,301	127,934	243,235
Netherlands	......	......	4,572	8,069	5,004	13,073	......	......	17,645
Norway	4,838	4,478	9,316	30,503	21,143	51,646	35,370	25,647	61,017
Sweden	......	......	26,318	......	......	135,144	84,861	76,601	161,462
Switzerland	2,577	2,408	4,985	15,421	9,239	24,660	17,998	11,647	29,645
Finland	2,052	1,791	3,843	13,736	6,656	20,392	16,887	9,119	26,006
Italy[10]	......	......	199,746	......	......	1,082,807	989,055	293,498	1,282,553
Portugal	......	......	33,299	......	......	123,400	117,143	39,556	156,699
ASIA:									
British India	......	......	......	......	......	......	50,718	23,382	74,100
1896-1900									
EUROPE:									
Austria[2]	......	......	29,802	......	......	114,176	33,951[24]	25,728[24]	59,679[24]
Belgium[19]	799	736	1,535	3,744	1,672	5,416	4,543	2,408	6,951
British Isles	42,275	39,002	81,277	394,610	288,329	682,939	436,885	327,331	764,216
Denmark	......	......	1,872	......	......	11,973	7,971	5,874	13,845
Germany[11]	9,780	9,719	19,499	56,403	43,680	100,083	66,201	53,403	119,604
Ireland[4]	......	......	15,029	......	......	181,816	86,269	104,022	190,291
Netherlands	......	......	1,511	3,133	1,632	4,765	......	......	6,276
Norway	1,921	1,855	3,776	18,712	11,323	30,035	20,643	13,194	33,837
Sweden	......	......	10,235	......	......	75,075	40,420	44,890	85,310
Switzerland	1,050	1,006	2,056	7,814	4,565	12,379	8,864	5,571	14,435
Finland	2,016	2,030	4,046	17,485	11,048	28,533	19,809	13,231	33,040
Italy[12]	......	......	209,797	......	......	1,342,376	1,240,093	312,080	1,552,173
Portugal	......	......	26,079	......	......	86,105	81,488	30,696	112,184
ASIA:									
British India	......	......	......	......	......	......	75,758	19,858	95,616

For reference notes see page 354.

TABLE 19.—DISTRIBUTION OF EMIGRANT CITIZENS, BY SEX AND AGE, 1851-1924[1] (cont.)

a. Absolute figures

Country of Emigration	Children or young persons			Adults			Total		
	Males	Females	Total	Males	Females	Total	Males	Females	Total
1901–1905									
EUROPE:									
Austria[2]	....	....	44,555	....	....	302,043	90,105[24]	43,032[24]	133,137[24]
Belgium[19]	2,258	2,051	4,309	10,672	4,052	14,724	12,930	6,103	19,033
British Isles	77,968	70,261	148,229	612,544	410,066	1,022,610	690,512	480,327	1,170,839
Denmark	....	....	5,252	....	....	31,527	23,241	13,538	36,779
Germany[21]	14,485	14,044	28,529	64,839	43,438	108,277	79,391	57,493	136,884
Hungary[25]	....	....	....	....	....	....	223,783	85,222	309,005
Ireland[4]	....	....	17,290	....	....	172,157	88,810	98,360	187,170
Netherlands	....	....	3,090	5,776	3,009	8,785	....	....	11,875
Norway	7,153	6,668	13,821	58,390	30,911	89,301	65,599	37,596	103,195
Sweden	....	....	18,855	....	....	128,823	82,833	64,845	147,678
Switzerland	1,733	1,613	3,346	14,091	6,875	20,966	15,824	8,488	24,312
Finland	4,563	4,724	9,287	48,123	23,039	71,162	52,920	28,136	81,056
Italy[22]	....	....	277,760	....	....	2,492,492	2,286,848	483,404	2,770,252
Portugal	....	....	26,214	....	....	102,146	94,356	34,004	128,360
ASIA:									
British India	....	....	....	....	....	....	61,704	26,936	88,640
Japan[26]	....	....	....	....	....	....	52,196	10,382	62,578
1906–1910									
EUROPE:									
Austria[2]	....	....	51,507	....	....	360,878	125,517[24]	64,415[24]	189,932[24]
Belgium[19]	2,665	2,299	4,964	14,318	4,896	19,214	16,983	7,195	24,178
British Isles	124,630	113,289	237,919	861,636	571,070	1,432,706	986,266	684,359	1,670,625
Denmark	2,438	2,223	4,661	20,585	11,390	31,975	23,023	13,613	36,636
Germany[21]	11,811	11,204	23,015	59,513	39,482	98,995	73,316	52,022	125,338
Hungary[25]	....	....	82,675[27][28]	....	....	256,747[27][28]	327,968	145,255	473,223
Ireland[4]	....	....	14,367	....	....	147,211	83,487	75,367	158,854
Netherlands	....	....	4,254	7,958	3,918	11,876	....	....	16,130
Norway	4,662	4,451	9,113	49,730	28,800	78,530	54,403	33,260	87,663
Sweden	....	....	14,875	....	....	95,114	62,790	47,199	109,989
Switzerland	1,682	1,682	3,364	14,261	7,130	21,391	15,943	8,812	24,755
Finland	3,676	3,682	7,358	46,646	23,007	69,653	50,657	27,119	77,776
Italy[22]	....	....	338,138	....	....	2,918,300	2,658,627	597,811	3,256,438
Portugal	....	....	34,805	....	....	163,004	152,827	44,982	197,809
ASIA:									
British India	....	....	....	....	....	....	52,773	22,274	75,047
Japan[26]	....	....	....	....	....	....	66,367	16,493	82,860

For reference notes see page 354.

TABLE 19.—DISTRIBUTION OF EMIGRANT CITIZENS, BY SEX AND AGE, 1851-1924 (cont.)

a. Absolute figures

Country of Emigration	Children or young persons			Adults			Total		
	Males	Females	Total	Males	Females	Total	Males	Females	Total
1911-1915									
EUROPE:									
Belgium[19]	1,574[29]	1,444[29]	3,018[29]	10,037[29]	3,523[29]	13,560[29]	11,611[29]	4,967[29]	16,578[29]
British Isles (Passengers)	76,789[30]	73,476[30]	150,265[30]	446,970[30]	324,958[30]	771,928[30]	523,759[30]	398,434[30]	922,193[30]
(Emigrants)			181,343[31]	453,309[31]	385,540[31]	838,849[31]			1,020,192[31]
Denmark	2,026	2,051	4,077	20,176	11,037	31,213	22,202	13,088	35,290
Germany[11]	6,156	6,025	12,181	33,729	19,817	53,546	43,346	28,115	71,461
Hungary[25]			25,195[28][29]			120,530[28][29]	102,905[29]	93,975[29]	196,880[29]
Ireland[4]			9,432			114,133	65,675	56,182	121,857
Netherlands			2,361	5,564	2,446	8,010			10,371
Norway	2,112	1,996	4,108	23,598	16,833	40,431	25,716	18,836	44,552
Sweden			11,230			67,702	42,791	36,141	78,932
Switzerland	1,488	1,399	2,887	13,670	6,862	20,532	15,158	8,261	23,419
Finland	2,831	2,815	5,646	26,665	18,097	44,762	29,626	21,042	50,668
Italy[12]			303,013			2,440,046	2,197,626	545,433	2,743,059
Portugal			57,837			213,388	185,614	85,611	271,225
ASIA:									
British India							32,755	12,743	45,498
Japan[26]							42,317	30,902	73,219
1916-1920									
EUROPE:									
Belgium[19]	1,486[32]	1,380[32]	2,866[32]	4,702[32]	3,783[32]	8,485[32]	6,188[32]	5,163[32]	11,351[32]
British Isles (Passengers)									
(Emigrants)									
Denmark	921	935	1,856	8,809	5,648	14,457	9,730	6,583	16,313
Germany[11]	97	92	189	412	268	680	4,434	2,527	6,961
Hungary[25]									
Ireland[4]			4,497			24,680	10,204	18,695	28,899
Netherlands			1,963	5,652	3,740	9,392			11,355
Norway	1,177	1,152	2,329	7,195	7,418	14,613	8,393	8,576	16,969
Sweden			6,644			32,799	17,436	22,007	39,443
Switzerland	828	804	1,632	8,461	4,670	13,131	9,290	5,473	14,763
Finland	1,668	1,749	3,417	6,214	6,943	13,157	7,892	8,786	16,678
Italy[12]	67,747	59,012	126,759	650,457	307,790	958,247	718,204	366,802	1,085,006
Portugal			22,330			131,304	101,946	51,688	153,634
ASIA:									
British India							8,894	1,602	10,496
Japan[28]							57,500	35,307	92,807

For reference notes see page 354.

TABLE 19.—DISTRIBUTION OF EMIGRANT CITIZENS, BY SEX AND AGE, 1851-1924[1] (cont.)

a. Absolute figures

Country of Emigration	Children or young persons			Adults			Total		
	Males	Females	Total	Males	Females	Total	Males	Females	Total
				1921–1924					
EUROPE:									
Belgium[19]	919	879	1,798	3,793	2,721	6,514	4,712	3,600	8,312
British Isles[23] (Passengers)	.....	.....	122,654	359,201	302,235	661,436	.....	.....	784,090
(Emigrants)	.....	.....	.....	.....	.....	.....	.....	.....	.....
Denmark	1,241	1,266	2,507	14,144	6,672	20,816	15,385	7,938	23,323
Germany[11]	14,697	14,465	29,162	114,618	80,334	194,952	133,285	96,746	230,031
Ireland[4]	.....	.....	2,330	7,665	4,234	11,899	5,308[34]	8,327[34]	13,635[34]
Netherlands	1,677	1,673	3,350	23,909	10,600	34,509	25,588	12,274	37,862
Norway	.....	.....	6,913	.....	.....	53,743	37,277	23,379	60,656
Sweden	1,436	1,294	2,730	14,218	8,114	22,332	15,654	9,408	25,062
Switzerland	.....	.....	.....	.....	.....	.....	16,916	11,620	28,536
Finland	.....	.....	.....	.....	.....	.....	.....	.....	14,229
Italy[12]	56,865	47,011	103,876	415,617	131,636	547,253	472,482	178,647	651,129
Portugal	.....	.....	2,013[34]	.....	.....	22,510[34]	17,937[34]	6,586[34]	24,523[34]
ASIA:									
British India[25]	.....	.....	.....	.....	.....	.....	2,157	321	2,478
Japan[26]	.....	.....	.....	.....	.....	.....	29,412	17,267	46,679

For **reference** notes see page 354.

TABLE 20.—DISTRIBUTION OF EMIGRANT CITIZENS, BY SEX AND AGE, 1851-1924[1]

b. Percentages

Country of Emigration	Children or young persons			Adults			Total		
	Males	Females	Total	Males	Females	Total	Males	Females	Total
1851–1855									
EUROPE:									
Austria[2]	....	....	43.6	....	....	56.4	51.6	48.4	100
France[3]	....	....	....	....	....	....	....	....	....
Ireland[4]	....	....	31.8	....	....	68.2	57.9	42.1	100
Sweden	....	....	....	....	....	....	....	....	....
ASIA:									
British India	....	....	11.3	....	....	88.7	73.3	15.4	100
1856–1860									
EUROPE:									
Austria[2]	4.5[5]	....	41.3	63.6[5]	....	58.7	53.8	46.2	100
France[3]	....	4.2[5]	8.7[5]	....	27.7[5]	91.3[5]	68.1[5]	31.9[5]	100[5]
Ireland[4]	....	....	15.6	....	....	84.4	53.3	46.7	100
Sweden	....	....	33.0	....	....	67.0	56.3	43.7	100
ASIA:									
British India	....	....	15.8	....	....	84.2	60.8	23.4	100
1861–1865									
EUROPE:									
Austria[2]	3.5[6]	....	41.4	66.3[6]	....	58.6	55.	45.	100
France[3]	....	3.4[6]	6.9[6]	....	26.8[6]	93.1[6]	69.8[6]	30.2[6]	100[6]
Ireland[4]	....	....	18.0	....	....	82.0	52.7	47.3	100
Norway	....	....	....	....	....	....	....	....	....
Sweden	....	....	22.1	....	....	77.9	58.0	42.0	100
Portugal	....	....	....	....	....	....	....	....	....
ASIA:									
British India	....	....	12.3	....	....	87.7	67.7	20.0	100

For reference notes see page 354.

TABLE 20.—DISTRIBUTION OF EMIGRANT CITIZENS BY SEX AND AGE, 1851-1924[1] (cont.)

b. Percentages

Country of Emigration	Children or young persons			Adults			Total		
	Males	Females	Total	Males	Females	Total	Males	Females	Total
1866–1870									
EUROPE:									
Austria[2]	....	....	41.3	....	....	58.7	52.4	47.6	100
Denmark	....	....	....	....	....	....	64.3	35.7	100
France[3]	....	....	6.0[7]	....	....	94.0[7]	....	....	100[7]
Ireland[4]	....	....	12.6	....	....	87.4	58.5	41.5	100
Norway	16.7	15.1	31.7	39.8	28.5	68.3	56.4	43.6	100
Sweden	....	....	23.8	....	....	76.2	57.5	42.5	100
Portugal	....	....	....	....	....	....	87.7[8]	12.3[8]	100[8]
ASIA:									
British India	....	....	13.1	....	....	86.9	61.8	25.1	100
1871–1875									
EUROPE:									
Austria[2]	....	....	....	....	....	....	....	....	....
British Isles	....	....	....	....	....	....	....	....	....
Denmark	....	....	22.4[9]	....	....	77.6[9]	61.5	38.5	100
France[3]	....	....	6.9[10]	....	....	93.1[10]	....	....	100[10]
Germany[11]	11.9[9]	11.3[9]	23.2[9]	43.4[9]	33.4[9]	76.8[9]	55.2	44.8	100
Ireland[4]	....	....	13.9	....	....	86.1	56.1	43.9	100
Norway	14.4	13.4	27.8	39.8	32.4	72.2	54.2	45.8	100
Sweden	....	....	19.6	....	....	80.4	54.1	45.9	100
Italy[12]	....	....	....	....	....	....	....	....	....
Portugal	....	....	16.8[9]	....	....	83.2[9]	87.2[9]	12.8[9]	100[9]
ASIA:									
British India	....	....	....	....	....	....	....	....	....
1876–1880									
EUROPE:									
Austria[2]	....	....	41.2[13]	....	....	58.8[13]	54.1[13]	45.9[13]	100[13]
British Isles	8.6[14]	7.9[14]	16.5[14]	51.4[14]	32.1[14]	83.5[14]	59.9[14]	40.1[14]	100[14]
Denmark	....	....	23.3	....	....	76.7	62.2	37.8	100
France[3]	....	....	9.9[15]	....	....	90.1[15]	69.8[16]	30.2[16]	100[16]
Germany[11]	11.3	10.8	22.1	48.3	29.6	77.9	59.5	40.5	100
Ireland[4]	11.5	10.9	15.1	47.6	29.9	84.9	53.0	47.0	100
Norway	....	....	22.5	....	....	77.5	59.1	40.9	100
Sweden	....	....	17.9	....	....	82.1	56.6	43.4	100
Italy[12]	....	....	9.8	....	....	90.2	85.3	14.7	100
Portugal	....	....	15.7	....	....	84.3	82.6	17.4	100
ASIA:									
British India	....	....	....	....	....	....	70.5[17]	29.5[17]	100[17]

For reference notes see page 354.

TABLE 20.—DISTRIBUTION OF EMIGRANT CITIZENS BY SEX AND AGE, 1851–1924 (cont.)

b. Percentages

Country of Emigration	Children or young persons			Adults			Total		
	Males	Females	Total	Males	Females	Total	Males	Females	Total
1881–1885									
EUROPE:									
Austria[2]	....	....	38.1[18]	....	....	61.9[18]	55.4	44.6	100
Belgium[19]	9.6	8.9	18.5	49.1	32.3	81.4	58.8	41.2	....
British Isles	....	....	24.0	....	....	76.	59.7	40.3	100
Denmark	....	....	13.0[20]	....	....	86.3[20]	....	....	100[20]
France[3]	13.6	12.7	26.3	43.2	30.5	73.7	56.8	43.2	100
Germany[11]	....	....	16.4	....	....	83.6	51.0	49.0	100
Ireland[4]	....	....	28.3[2]	43.8[21]	27.9[21]	71.7[21]	....	44.1	100[21]
Netherlands	13.1	12.1	25.3	42.8	31.9	74.7	55.9	44.1	100
Norway	....	....	20.1	....	....	79.9	54.3	45.7	100
Sweden	....	....	....	....	....	....	....	....	....
Switzerland	....	....	....	....	....	....	....	....	....
Finland[21]	3.5[21]	3.6[21]	7.1[21]	81.7[21]	11.2[21]	92.9[21]	80.2[21]	19.8[21]	100[21]
Italy[12]	....	....	9.3	....	....	90.7	84.9	15.1	100
Portugal	....	....	15.5	....	....	84.5	79.1	20.9	100
ASIA:									
British India	....	....	....	....	....	....	70.9	29.1	100
Japan	....	....	....	....	....	....	....	....	....
1886–1890									
EUROPE:									
Austria[2]	17.9	14.8	32.7	47.9	19.3	67.2	65.9	34.1	....
Belgium[19]	8.2	7.5	15.8	51.2	33.	84.2	59.5	40.5	100
British Isles	....	....	18.9	....	....	81.1	60.9	39.1	100
Denmark	....	....	....	....	....	....	....	....	....
France[3]	....	....	....	....	....	....	....	....	....
Germany[11]	12.2	11.7	23.9	42.8	33.3	76.	55.	45.	100
Ireland[4]	....	....	10.7	45.1	26.	89.3	51.6	48.4	100
Netherlands	....	8.8	28.9	49.1	32.6	71.1	58.6	41.4	100
Norway	9.4	....	18.2	....	....	81.8	55.6	44.4	100
Sweden	....	....	15.2	....	....	84.8	55.6	44.4	100
Switzerland	9.8[22]	8.8[22]	18.7[22]	53.1[22]	28.3[22]	81.3[22]	62.9[22]	37.1[22]	100[22]
Finland	4.8	4.2	9.1	80.6	10.3	90.9	76.3	23.7	100
Italy[12]	....	....	14.2	....	....	85.8	78.5	21.5	100
Portugal	....	....	19.5	....	....	80.6	76.6	23.4	100
ASIA:									
British India	....	....	....	....	....	....	69.0	31.0	100
Japan	....	....	....	....	....	....	....	....	....

For reference notes see page 354.

TABLE 20.—DISTRIBUTION OF EMIGRANT CITIZENS BY SEX AND AGE, 1851-1924[1] (cont.)

b. Percentages

1891–1895

Country of Emigration	Children or young persons			Adults			Total		
	Males	Females	Total	Males	Females	Total	Males	Females	Total
EUROPE:									
Austria[2]	...	...	23.1[23]	...	...	76.9[23]	53.8[23]	46.2[23]	100[23]
Belgium[19]	13.7	12.0	25.7	53.8	20.6	74.4	67.4	32.6	100
British Isles	6.5	5.9	12.4	51.2	36.4	87.6	57.7	42.3	100
Denmark	...	...	19.3	...	...	80.7	57.4	42.6	100
France	...	...	...	...	...	...	...	...	...
Germany[11]	11.8	11.3	23.1	43.1	33.8	76.9	55.0	45.0	100
Ireland[4]	...	...	8.3	...	...	91.7	47.4	52.6	100
Netherlands	...	...	25.9	45.7	28.4	74.1	58.0	42.0	100
Norway	7.9	7.3	15.3	50.0	34.7	84.7	52.5	47.5	100
Sweden	...	...	16.3	...	...	83.7	...	...	100
Switzerland	8.7	8.1	16.8	52.0	31.2	83.2	60.7	39.3	100
Finland	8.5	7.4	15.9	56.7	27.5	84.1	64.9	35.1	100
Italy[12]	...	...	15.6	...	...	84.4	77.1	22.9	100
Portugal	...	...	21.3	...	...	78.8	74.8	25.2	100
ASIA:									
British India	...	...	...	...	...	...	68.4	31.6	100
Japan	...	...	...	...	...	...	...	...	...

1896–1900

Country of Emigration	Children or young persons			Adults			Total		
	Males	Females	Total	Males	Females	Total	Males	Females	Total
EUROPE									
Austria[2]	...	...	20.7	...	...	79.3	56.9[24]	43.1[24]	100[24]
Belgium[19]	11.5	10.6	22.1	53.9	24.0	77.9	65.4	34.6	100
British Isles	5.5	5.1	10.6	51.6	37.7	89.4	57.2	42.8	100
Denmark	...	...	13.5	...	...	86.5	57.6	42.4	100
Germany[11]	8.2	8.1	16.3	47.2	36.5	83.7	55.4	44.6	100
Hungary[25]	...	...	7.6	...	...	92.4	45.3	54.7	100
Ireland[4]	...	...	24.1	49.9	26.0	75.9	61.0	39.0	100
Netherlands	5.7	5.5	11.2	55.3	33.4	88.8	47.4	52.6	100
Norway	...	...	12.0	...	...	88.0	61.4	38.6	100
Sweden	7.3	7.0	14.2	54.1	31.6	85.8	60.0	40.0	100
Switzerland	...	...	12.4	...	...	87.6	61.4	38.6	100
Finland	6.2	6.2	13.5	53.7	33.9	86.5	79.9	20.1	100
Italy[12]	...	...	23.3	...	...	76.8	72.6	27.4	100
Portugal	...	...	...	...	...	...	...	...	...
ASIA:									
British India	...	...	...	...	...	...	79.2	20.8	100
Japan[26]	...	...	...	...	...	...	...	...	...

For reference notes see page 354.

TABLE 20.—DISTRIBUTION OF EMIGRANT CITIZENS, BY SEX AND AGE, 1851-1924[1] (cont.)

b. Percentages

Country of Emigration	Children or young persons			Adults			Total		
	Males	Females	Total	Males	Females	Total	Males	Females	Total
1901–1905									
EUROPE:									
Austria[2]	....	....	12.8	....	....	87.2	67.7[24]	32.3[24]	100[24]
Belgium[19]	11.9	10.8	22.6	56.1	21.3	77.4	67.9	32.1	100
British Isles	6.7	6.0	12.7	52.3	35.0	87.3	59.0	41.0	100
Denmark	....	....	14.3	....	....	85.7	63.2	36.8	100
Germany[11]	10.6	10.3	20.9	47.4	31.7	79.1	58.0	42.0	100
Hungary[23]	....	....	....	....	....	....	72.4	27.6	100
Ireland[4]	....	....	9.1	....	....	91.9	47.4	52.6	100
Netherlands	....	....	26.0	48.7	25.3	74.0	....	....	100
Norway	6.9	6.5	13.4	56.6	30.0	86.6	63.6	36.4	100
Sweden	....	....	12.8	....	....	87.2	56.1	43.9	100
Switzerland	7.1	6.6	13.8	58.0	28.3	86.2	65.1	34.9	100
Finland	5.7	5.9	11.5	59.8	28.6	88.5	65.3	34.7	100
Italy[12]	....	....	10.0	....	....	90.0	82.6	17.4	100
Portugal	....	....	20.4	....	....	79.6	73.5	26.5	100
ASIA:									
British India	....	....	....	....	....	....	69.6	30.4	100
Japan[26]	....	....	....	....	....	....	83.4	16.6	100
1906–1910									
EUROPE:									
Austria[2]	....	....	12.5	....	....	87.5	66.1[24]	33.9[24]	100[24]
Belgium[19] (Passengers)	11.0	9.5	20.5	59.2	20.2	79.4	70.2	29.8	100
British Isles (Emigrants)	7.4	6.8	14.2	51.6	34.2	85.8	59.0	41.0	100
Denmark	6.7	6.1	12.7	56.2	31.1	87.3	62.8	37.2	100
Germany[11]	9.7	9.2	18.9	48.8	32.3	81.1	58.5	41.5	100
Hungary[25]	....	....	24.4[27][28]	....	....	75.6[27][28]	69.3	30.7	100
Ireland[4]	....	....	8.9	....	....	91.1	52.6	47.4	100
Netherlands	....	....	26.4	49.3	24.3	73.6	....	....	100
Norway	5.3	5.1	10.4	56.7	32.9	89.6	62.1	37.9	100
Sweden	....	....	13.5	....	....	86.5	57.0	43.0	100
Switzerland	6.8	6.8	13.6	57.6	28.8	86.4	64.4	35.6	100
Finland	4.8	4.8	9.6	60.6	29.9	90.4	65.1	34.9	100
Italy[12]	....	....	10.4	....	....	89.6	81.6	18.4	100
Portugal	....	....	17.6	....	....	82.4	77.3	22.7	100
ASIA:									
British India	....	....	....	....	....	....	70.3	29.7	100
Japan[26]	....	....	....	....	....	....	80.1	19.9	100

For reference notes see page 354.

TABLE 20.—DISTRIBUTION OF EMIGRANT CITIZENS, BY SEX AND AGE, 1851-1924[1] (cont.)

b. Percentages

Country of Emigration	Children or young persons			Adults			Total		
	Males	Females	Total	Males	Females	Total	Males	Females	Total
1911-1915									
EUROPE:									
Austria	...	...	...	...	...	...	...	...	...
Belgium[19]	9.5[29]	8.7[29]	18.2[29]	60.5[29]	21.3[29]	81.8[29]	70.0[29]	30.0[29]	100[29]
British Isles (Passengers)	8.3[30]	8.0[30]	16.3[30]	48.5[30]	35.2[30]	83.7[30]	56.8[30]	43.2[30]	100[30]
British Isles (Emigrants)	...	...	17.8[31]	44.4[31]	37.8	82.2[31]	...	...	100[31]
Denmark	5.7	5.8	11.6	57.2	31.3	88.4	62.9	37.1	100
Germany[11]	9.4	9.2	18.6	51.3	30.2	81.5	60.7	39.3	100
Hungary[25]	...	...	17.3[28][29]	...	...	82.7[28][29]	52.3[29]	47.7[29]	100[29]
Ireland[4]	...	...	7.6	...	...	92.4	53.9	46.1	100
Netherlands[4]	...	...	22.8	53.6	23.6	77.2	...	...	100
Norway	4.7	4.5	9.2	53.0	37.8	90.8	57.7	42.3	100
Sweden	...	...	14.2	...	...	85.8	54.2	45.8	100
Switzerland	6.4	6.0	12.3	58.4	29.3	87.7	64.7	35.3	100
Finland	5.6	5.6	11.2	52.9	35.9	88.8	58.5	41.5	100
Italy[12]	...	...	11.0	...	...	89.0	68.4	31.6	100
Portugal	...	...	21.3	...	...	78.7	80.1	19.9	**100**
ASIA:									
British India	...	...	...	...	...	...	...	...	100
Japan[26]	...	...	...	...	...	...	...	...	100
1916-1920									
EUROPE:									
Belgium[19]	...	...	...	...	...	...	...	...	...
British Isles[33] (Passengers)	13.1[22]	12.2[22]	25.2[22]	41.4[22]	33.3[22]	74.7[22]	54.5[22]	45.5[22]	100[22]
British Isles (Emigrants)	...	...	...	...	...	...	...	...	...
Denmark	11.2	10.6	21.8	47.4	30.9	78.3	...	...	100
Germany[11]	...	...	...	...	...	...	59.6	40.4	100
Hungary[25]	5.6	5.7	11.4	54.0	34.6	88.6	...	...	...
Ireland[4]	...	...	15.4	...	...	84.6	35.3	64.7	100
Netherlands[4]	...	...	17.3	49.8	32.9	82.7	63.7	36.3	100
Norway	6.9	6.8	13.7	42.5	43.8	86.3	49.5	50.5	100
Sweden	...	...	17.0	...	...	83.0	44.2	55.8	100
Switzerland	5.6	5.4	11.1	57.3	31.6	88.9	62.9	37.1	100
Finland	10.1	10.6	20.6	37.5	41.9	79.4	47.3	52.7	100
Italy[12]	6.2	5.4	11.7	59.9	28.4	88.3	66.2	33.8	100
Portugal	...	...	14.5	...	...	85.5	66.4	33.6	100
ASIA:									
British India[35]	...	...	...	...	...	...	84.7	15.3	100
Japan[26]	...	...	...	...	...	...	62.0	38.0	100

For reference notes see page 354.

TABLE 20—DISTRIBUTION OF EMIGRANT CITIZENS, BY SEX AND AGE, 1851-1924[1] (cont.)

b. Percentages

1921–1924

Country of Emigration	Children or young persons			Adults			Total		
	Males	Females	Total	Males	Females	Total	Males	Females	Total
EUROPE:									
Belgium[19]	11.1	10.6	21.6	45.6	32.7	78.4	56.7	43.3	100
British Isles[33] (Passengers)	...	...	15.6	45.8	38.6	84.4	...	...	100
(Emigrants)	...	...	...	...	...	...	...	...	...
Denmark	5.3	5.4	10.7	60.6	28.6	89.2	66.0	34.0	100
Germany[21]	6.6	6.5	13.0	51.1	35.8	87.0	57.9	42.1	100
Hungary[25]	...	...	...	...	...	...	...	...	...
Ireland[4]	...	...	11.4	...	...	88.6	38.9[34]	61.1[34]	100[34]
Netherlands	4.4	4.4	8.8	63.1	28.0	91.2	67.6	32.4	100
Norway	...	...	16.4	53.9	29.8	83.7	61.4	38.6	100
Sweden	...	...	...	...	...	...	...	...	...
Switzerland	5.7	5.2	10.9	56.7	32.4	89.1	62.5	37.5	100
Finland[22]	...	...	...	...	...	...	59.3	40.7	100
Italy[22]	8.7	7.2	16.0	63.8	20.2	84.0	72.6	27.4	100
Portugal	...	...	8.2[34]	...	...	91.8[34]	73.1[34]	26.9[34]	100[34]
ASIA:									
British India[35]	...	...	...	...	...	...	87.0	13.0	100
Japan[36]	...	...	...	...	...	...	63.0	37.0	100

For reference notes see page 354.

TABLE 21.—DISTRIBUTION OF EMIGRANT ALIENS, BY SEX AND AGE, 1851-1924

a.   Absolute figures

Country of Emigration	Children or young persons			Adults			Total		
	Males	Females	Total	Males	Females	Total	Males	Females	Total
1851-1855									
OCEANIA: New Zealand[1]	.....	.....	931[2]	4,425[2]	1,373[2]	5,798[2]	.....	.....	6,729[2]
AFRICA: Mauritius[3]	.....	.....	.....	.....	.....	.....	13,564	2,101	15,665
1856-1860									
OCEANIA: New Zealand[1]	.....	.....	1,337	7,683	2,169	9,852	.....	.....	11,189
AFRICA: Mauritius[3]	.....	.....	.....	.....	.....	.....	21,157	4,458	25,615
1861-1865									
OCEANIA: New Zealand[1]	1,361	1,124	2,485	42,880	3,672	46,552	44,241	4,796	49,037
AFRICA: Mauritius[3]	959	905	1,864	10,678	2,181	12,859	11,637	3,086	14,723
1866-1870									
OCEANIA: New Zealand[1]	1,941	1,518	3,459	23,977	4,797	28,774	25,918	6,315	32,233
AFRICA: Mauritius[3]	1,168	1,092	2,260	10,064	2,595	12,659	11,232	3,687	14,919
1871-1875									
OCEANIA: New Zealand[1]	2,084	1,739	3,823	18,975	5,338	24,313	21,059	7,077	28,136
AFRICA: Mauritius[3]	1,465	1,531	2,996	11,094	3,386	14,480	12,559	4,917	17,476
1876-1880									
OCEANIA: New Zealand[1]	2,338	1,915	4,253	20,841	6,894	27,745	23,179	8,809	31,988
AFRICA: Mauritius[3]	1,031	977	2,008	8,599	2,361	10,960	9,630	3,338	12,968

For reference notes see page 355.

TABLE 21.—DISTRIBUTION OF EMIGRANT ALIENS, BY SEX AND AGE, 1851-1924 (cont.)

a. Absolute figures

Country of Emigration	Children or young persons			Adults			Total		
	Males	Females	Total	Males	Females	Total	Males	Females	Total
1881–1885									
AMERICA: Uruguay[4]	2,502	713	3,215	23,470	4,691	28,161	25,972	5,404	31,376
OCEANIA: New Zealand[1]	3,545	3,163	6,708	28,641	11,760	40,401	32,186	14,923	47,109
AFRICA: Mauritius[3]	717	715	1,432	7,948	2,324	10,272	8,665	3,039	11,704
1886–1890									
AMERICA: Uruguay[4]	2,466	1,284	3,750	39,518	7,637	47,155	41,984	8,921	50,905
OCEANIA: New Zealand[1]	6,603	6,178	12,781	47,623	22,114	69,737	54,226	28,292	82,518
AFRICA: Mauritius[3]	518	465	983	5,953	1,852	7,805	6,471	2,317	8,788
1891–1895									
AMERICA: Uruguay[4]	2,243	985	3,228	37,267	6,883	44,150	39,510	7,868	47,378
OCEANIA: New Zealand[1]	5,154	4,701	9,855	54,428	26,184	80,612	59,582	30,885	90,467
AFRICA: Mauritius[3]	377	300	677	4,264	1,178	5,442	4,641	1,478	6,119
1896–1900									
AMERICA: Uruguay[4]	1,583	886	2,469	25,187	3,997	29,184	26,770	4,883	31,653
OCEANIA: New Zealand[1]	3,833	3,645	7,478	48,497	24,650	73,147	52,330	28,295	80,625
AFRICA: Mauritius[3]	315[5]	240[5]	555[5]	2,794[5]	803[5]	3,597[5]	3,109[5]	1,043[5]	4,152[5]

For reference notes see page 355.

TABLE 21.—DISTRIBUTION OF EMIGRANT ALIENS, BY SEX AND AGE, 1851-1924 (cont.)

a. Absolute figures

Country of Emigration	Children or young persons			Adults			Total		
	Males	Females	Total	Males	Females	Total	Males	Females	Total
1901-1905									
AMERICA:									
United States[6]	.....	.....	.....	.....	.....	.....	.....	.....	.....
Uruguay[4]	355[7]	203[7]	558[7]	5,287[7]	819[7]	6,106[7]	5,642[7]	1,022[7]	6,664[7]
OCEANIA:									
Australian Commonwealth[8]	4,224[9]	3,514[9]	7,738[9]	57,104[9]	26,791[9]	83,895[9]	61,328[9]	30,305[9]	91,633[9]
New Zealand[1]	4,302	3,556	7,858	66,768	31,507	98,275	71,070	35,063	106,133
AFRICA:									
Mauritius[3]	136	80	216	1,295	412	1,707	1,431	492	1,923
1906-1910									
AMERICA:									
United States[6]	.....	.....	37,556[10]	.....	.....	756,047[10]	656,734[10]	136,869[10]	793,603[10]
Uruguay[4]	.....	.....	.....	.....	.....	.....	.....	.....	.....
OCEANIA:									
Australian Commonwealth[3]	10,211	9,654	19,865	177,588	81,849	259,437	187,799	91,503	279,302
New Zealand[1]	6,764	6,155	12,919	92,159	48,686	140,845	93,923	54,841	153,764
AFRICA:									
Mauritius[3]	146[11]	133[11]	279[11]	1,816[11]	570[11]	2,386[11]	1,962[11]	703[11]	2,665[11]
1911-1915									
AMERICA:									
United States[5]	.....	.....	65,730	.....	.....	1,378,800	1,176,980	267,550	1,444,530
Uruguay[4]	1,153[12]	837[12]	1,990[12]	24,421[12]	4,416[12]	28,837[12]	25,574[12]	5,253[12]	30,827[12]
ASIA:									
Philippines[13]	.....	.....	616	.....	.....	4,679	4,213	1,082	5,295
OCEANIA:									
Australian Commonwealth[8]	11,607	10,735	22,342	237,326	96,667	333,993	248,933	107,402	356,335
New Zealand[1]	7,599	6,453	14,052	89,757	54,464	144,221	97,356	60,917	158,273
Hawaii[14]	.....	.....	6,757[15]	16,918[15]	5,211[15]	22,129[15]	.....	.....	28,886[15]
1916-1920									
AMERICA:									
United States[5]	.....	.....	39,135	.....	.....	663,329	565,319	137,145	702,464
Uruguay[4]	1,582	1,506	3,088	17,236	5,884	23,120	18,818	7,390	26,208
ASIA:									
Philippines[13]	.....	.....	507	.....	.....	4,669	4,033	1,143	5,176
OCEANIA:									
Australian Commonwealth[8]	3,827[16]	3,152[16]	6,979[16]	33,176[16]	26,414[16]	59,590[16]	390,238	78,286	468,524
New Zealand[1]	.....	.....	9,771	21,705	7,470	29,175	54,954	44,539	99,493
Hawaii[14]	.....	.....	.....	.....	.....	.....	.....	.....	38,946

For reference notes see page 355.

TABLE 21.—DISTRIBUTION OF EMIGRANT ALIENS, BY SEX AND AGE, 1851-1924 (cont.)

a. Absolute figures

Country of Emigration	Children or young persons			Adults			Total		
	Males	Females	Total	Males	Females	Total	Males	Females	Total
					1921-1924				
AMERICA:									
United States[6]			28,575			576,094	444,422	160,247	604,669
Uruguay[4]	324[17]	285[17]	609[17]	3,280[17]	1,408[17]	4,688[17]	3,604[17]	1,693[17]	5,297[17]
ASIA:									
Philippines[13]			575			4,269	3,925	919	4,844
OCEANIA:									
Australian Commonwealth[8]							141,139	101,872	243,011
New Zealand[1]							64,188	53,021	117,209
Hawaii[14]			8,861	23,737	8,398	32,135			40,996

For reference notes see page 355.

TABLE 22—DISTRIBUTION OF EMIGRANT ALIENS, BY SEX AND AGE, 1851-1924

b. Percentages

Country of Emigration	Children or young persons			Adults			Total		
	Males	Females	Total	Males	Females	Total	Males	Females	Total
1851–1855									
OCEANIA: New Zealand[1]	....	....	13.8[2]	65.8[2]	20.4[2]	86.2[2]	....	....	100[2]
AFRICA: Mauritius[3]	....	....	....	....	....	....	86.6	13.4	100
1856–1860									
OCEANIA: New Zealand[1]	....	....	11.9	68.7	19.4	88.1	....	....	100
AFRICA: Mauritius[3]	....	....	....	....	....	....	82.6	17.4	100
1861–1865									
OCEANIA: New Zealand[1]	2.8	2.3	5.1	87.4	7.5	94.9	90.2	9.8	1C0
AFRICA: Mauritius[3]	6.5	6.2	12.7	72.5	14.8	87.3	79.0	21.0	100
1866–1870									
OCEANIA: New Zealand[1]	6.0	4.7	10.7	74.4	14.9	89.3	80.4	19.6	100
AFRICA: Mauritius[3]	7.8	5.4	15.2	67.5	17.4	84.9	75.3	24.7	100
1871–1875									
OCEANIA: New Zealand[1]	7.4	6.2	13.6	67.4	19.0	86.4	74.8	25.2	100
AFRICA: Mauritius[3]	8.4	8.8	17.1	63.5	19.4	82.9	71.9	28.1	100
1876–1880									
OCEANIA: New Zealand[1]	7.3	6.0	13.3	65.2	21.6	86.7	72.5	27.5	100
AFRICA: Mauritius[3]	8.0	7.5	15.5	66.3	18.2	84.5	74.3	25.7	100

For reference notes see page 355.

TABLE 22—DISTRIBUTION OF EMIGRANT ALIENS, BY SEX AND AGE, 1851-1924 (cont.)

b. Percentages

Country of Emigration	Children or young persons			Adults			Total		
	Males	Females	Total	Males	Females	Total	Males	Females	Total
1881–1885									
AMERICA:									
Uruguay[4]	8.0	2.3	10.2	74.8	15.0	89.8	82.8	17.2	100
OCEANIA:									
New Zealand[1]	7.5	6.7	14.2	60.8	25.0	85.8	68.3	31.7	100
AFRICA:									
Mauritius[3]	6.1	6.1	12.2	67.9	19.9	87.8	74.0	26.0	100
1886–1890									
AMERICA:									
Uruguay[4]	4.8	2.5	7.4	77.6	15.0	92.6	82.5	17.5	100
OCEANIA:									
New Zealand[1]	8.0	7.5	15.5	57.7	26.8	84.5	65.7	34.3	100
AFRICA:									
Mauritius[3]	5.9	5.3	11.2	67.7	21.1	88.8	73.6	26.4	100
1891–1895									
AMERICA:									
Uruguay[4]	4.7	2.1	6.8	78.7	14.5	93.2	83.4	16.6	100
OCEANIA:									
New Zealand[1]	5.7	5.2	10.9	60.2	28.9	89.1	65.9	34.1	100
AFRICA:									
Mauritius[3]	6.2	4.9	11.1	69.7	19.3	88.9	75.8	24.2	100
1896–1900									
AMERICA:									
United States[6]	….	….	….	….	….	….	….	….	….
Uruguay[4]	5.0	2.8	7.8	79.6	12.6	92.2	84.6	15.4	100
OCEANIA:									
New Zealand[1]	4.8	4.5	9.3	60.2	30.6	90.7	64.9	35.1	100
AFRICA:									
Mauritius[3]	7.6[5]	5.8[5]	13.4[5]	67.3[5]	19.3[5]	86.6[5]	74.9[5]	25.1[5]	100[5]

For reference notes see page 355.

TABLE 22.—DISTRIBUTION OF EMIGRANT ALIENS, BY SEX AND AGE, 1851-1924 (cont.)

b. Percentages

Country of Emigration	Children or young persons			Adults			Total		
	Males	Females	Total	Males	Females	Total	Males	Females	Total
1901–1905									
AMERICA:									
United States[6]	5.3[7]	3.0[7]	8.4[7]	79.3[7]	12.3[7]	91.6[7]	84.7[7]	15.3[7]	100[7]
Uruguay[4]	....	....	....	....	....	....	....	....	....
OCEANIA:									
Australian Commonwealth[8]	4.6[9]	3.8[9]	8.4[9]	62.3[9]	29.2[9]	91.5[9]	66.9[9]	33.1[9]	100[9]
New Zealand[1]	4.1	3.4	7.4	62.9	29.7	92.6	67.0	33.0	100
AFRICA:									
Mauritius[3]	7.1	4.2	11.3	67.3	21.4	88.7	74.4	25.6	100
1906–1910									
AMERICA:									
United States[6]	....	....	4.7[10]	....	....	95.3[10]	82.8[10]	17.2[10]	100[10]
Uruguay[4]	....	....	....	....	....	....	....	....	....
OCEANIA:									
Australian Commonwealth[8]	3.7	3.5	7.2	63.6	29.3	92.9	67.2	32.8	100
New Zealand[1]	4.4	4.0	8.4	59.9	31.7	91.6	64.3	35.7	100
AFRICA:									
Mauritius[3]	5.0[11]	5.0[11]	10.5[11]	68.1[11]	21.4[11]	89.5[11]	73.6[11]	26.4[11]	100[11]
1911–1915									
AMERICA:									
United States[6]	....	....	4.6	....	....	95.4	81.5	18.5	100
Uruguay[4]	3.7[12]	2.7[12]	6.5[12]	79.2[12]	14.3[12]	93.5[12]	83.0[12]	17.0[12]	100[12]
ASIA:									
Philippines[13]	....	....	11.6	....	....	88.4	79.6	20.4	100
OCEANIA:									
Australian Commonwealth[8]	3.3	3.0	6.3	66.6	27.1	93.7	69.9	30.1	100
New Zealand[1]	4.8	4.1	8.9	56.7	34.4	91.1	61.5	38.5	100
Hawaii[14]	....	....	23.4[15]	58.6[15]	18.0[15]	76.6[15]	....	....	100[15]

For reference notes see page 355.

TABLE 22.—DISTRIBUTION OF EMIGRANT ALIENS, BY SEX AND AGE, 1851-1924 (cont.)

b. Percentages

Country of Emigration	Children or young persons			Adults			Total		
	Males	Females	Total	Males	Females	Total	Males	Females	Total
1916-1920									
AMERICA:									
United States[5]	....	....	5.6	....	....	94.4	80.5	19.5	100
Uruguay[4]	6.0	5.7	11.8	65.8	22.5	88.2	71.8	28.2	100
ASIA:									
Philippines[13]	....	....	9.8	....	....	90.2	77.9	22.1	100
OCEANIA:									
Australian Commonwealth[9]	5.7[16]	4.7[16]	10.5[16]	49.8[16]	39.7[16]	89.5[16]	83.3	16.7	100
New Zealand[1]	....	....	....	....	....	....	55.2	44.8	100
Hawaii[14]	....	....	25.1	55.7	19.2	74.9	....	....	100
1921-1924									
AMERICA:									
United States[5]	6.1[17]	....	4.7	....	....	95.3	73.5	26.5	100
Uruguay[4]	....	5.4[17]	11.5[17]	61.9[17]	26.6[17]	88.5[17]	68.0[17]	32.0[17]	100[17]
ASIA:									
Philippines[13]	....	....	11.9	....	....	88.1	81.0	19.0	100
OCEANIA:									
Australian Commonwealth[8]	....	....	....	....	....	....	58.1	41.9	100
New Zealand[1]	....	....	....	....	....	....	54.8	45.2	100
Hawaii[14]	....	....	21.6	57.9	20.5	78.4	....	....	100

For reference notes see page 355.

TABLE 23.—DISTRIBUTION OF IMMIGRANT ALIENS BY SEX AND AGE, 1841-1924[1]

a. Absolute figures

Country of Immigration	Children or young persons			Adults			Total		
	Males	Females	Total	Males	Females	Total	Males	Females	Total
1841–1845									
AMERICA:									
United States[2] (age known)......	.....	.....	106,273	.....	.....	346,372			452,645
(sex known)......	.....	.....	.....	.....	.....		249,874	178,661	428,535
OCEANIA:									
New Zealand[3]........	.....	.....	.....	.....	.....	.....	.....	.....	.....
AFRICA:									
Mauritius[4]........	.....	.....	.....	.....	.....	.....	49,417	8,253	57,670
1846–1850									
AMERICA:									
United States[2] (age known)......	.....	.....	290,951	.....	.....	962,425			1,253,376
(sex known)......	.....	.....	.....	.....	.....		764,322	514,528	1,278,850
OCEANIA:									
New Zealand[3]........	.....	.....	.....	.....	.....	.....	.....	.....	.....
AFRICA:									
Mauritius[4]........	.....	.....	.....	.....	.....	.....	30,445	5,574	36,019
1851–1855									
AMERICA:									
United States[2] (age known)......	.....	.....	419,904	.....	.....	1,456,608			1,876,512
(sex known)......	.....	.....	.....	.....	.....		1,009,092	737,753	1,746,845
OCEANIA:									
New Zealand[3]........	.....	.....	1,791[6]	8,502[5]	3,319[5]	11,821[5]	.....	.....	13,612[5]
AFRICA:									
Mauritius[4]........	.....	.....	.....	.....	.....	.....	56,445	14,603	71,048
1856–1860									
AMERICA:									
United States[2] (fiscal years)......	.....	.....	172,484	.....	.....	761,197	398,555[6]	286,647[6]	685,202[6]
(calendar years)..	.....	.....	.....	.....	.....		377,283[6]	272,071[6]	649,354[6]
Argentina[7]........	.....	.....	3,476[6]	.....	.....	16,524[6]	16,102[6]	3,898[6]	20,000[6]
OCEANIA:									
New Zealand[3]........	.....	.....	8,309	19,336	9,873	29,209	.....	.....	37,518
AFRICA:									
Mauritius[4]........	.....	.....	.....	.....	.....	.....	79,415	33,592	113,007

For reference notes see page 355.

TABLE 23.—DISTRIBUTION OF IMMIGRANT ALIENS BY SEX AND AGE, 1841-1924[1] (cont.)

a. Absolute figures

Country of Immigration	Children or young persons			Adults			Total		
	Males	Females	Total	Males	Females	Total	Males	Females	Total
1861–1865									
AMERICA: United States[2] (fiscal years)	.....	.....	165,388	.....	.....	735,646	425,374	294,064	719,438
(calendar years)							477,382	324,298	801,680
Argentina[7]	.....	.....	.....	.....	.....	.....	36,635	10,239	46,874
OCEANIA: New Zealand[3]	10,044	9,285	19,329	97,482	25,305	122,877	107,526	34,680	142,206
AFRICA: Mauritius[4]	4,084	3,407	7,491	37,814	10,896	48,710	41,898	14,303	56,201
1866–1870									
AMERICA: United States[2] (fiscal years)	.....	.....	318,915	.....	.....	1,203,144	1,010,371	647,470	1,657,841
(calendar years)							1,003,264	641,684	1,644,948
Argentina[7]	.....	.....	12,185[8]	.....	.....	147,385[8]	85,354	27,342	112,696
OCEANIA: New Zealand[3]	3,552	2,921	6,473	33,533	12,763	46,296	37,085	15,684	52,769
AFRICA: Mauritius[4]	1,250	1,027	2,277	8,750	3,285	12,035	10,000	4,312	14,312
1871–1875									
AMERICA: United States[2] (fiscal years)	.....	.....	374,162	.....	.....	1,352,634	1,035,565	691,231	1,726,796
(calendar years)							1,001,561	657,717	1,659,278
Argentina[7]	.....	.....	.....	.....	.....	.....	105,951	42,743	148,694
OCEANIA: New Zealand[3]	13,404	12,323	25,727	54,156	30,199	84,355	67,560	42,522	110,082
AFRICA: Mauritius[4]	2,164	1,685	3,849	16,209	6,588	22,797	18,373	8,273	26,646
1876–1880									
AMERICA: United States[2] (fiscal years)	.....	.....	197,622	.....	.....	887,773	689,583	395,812	1,085,395
(calendar years)							806,667	478,765	1,285,432
Argentina[7]	.....	.....	42,295[9]	.....	.....	218,590[9]	77,596	34,595	112,191
OCEANIA: New Zealand[3]	8,138	7,258	15,396	46,911	24,468	71,379	55,049	31,726	86,775
AFRICA: Mauritius[4]	951	838	1,789	6,485	2,900	9,385	7,436	3,738	11,174

For reference notes see page 355.

TABLE 23.—DISTRIBUTION OF IMMIGRANT ALIENS BY SEX AND AGE, 1841-1924[1] (cont.)

a. Absolute figures.

Country of Immigration	Children or young persons			Adults			Total		
	Males	Females	Total	Males	Females	Total	Males	Females	Total
1881–1885									
AMERICA: United States[2] (fiscal years)	.....	.....	684,808	.....	.....	2,290,875	1,808,297	1,167,386	2,975,683
(calendar years)						.....	1,714,246	1,118,096	2,832,342
Argentina[7]	4,322	2,225	6,547	40,692	9,932	50,624	174,917	80,268	255,185
Uruguay[10]							45,014	12,157	57,171
OCEANIA: New Zealand[3]	6,327	5,601	11,928	41,817	22,323	64,140	48,144	27,924	76,068
AFRICA: Mauritius[4]	709[11]	652[11]	1,361[11]	6,075[11]	2,464[11]	8,539[11]	6,784[11]	3,116[11]	9,900[11]
1886–1890									
AMERICA: United States[2] (fiscal years)	.....	.....	436,691	.....	.....	1,834,239	1,397,614	873,316	2,270,930
(calendar years)						.....	1,455,591	906,204	2,361,795
Argentina[7]	5,44	2,574	129,660[12]	69,176	16,014	711,462[12]	410,270	175,667	585,937
Uruguay[10]			8,015			85,190	74,617	18,588	93,205
OCEANIA: New Zealand[3]	4,518	4,267	8,785	44,797	20,234	65,031	49,315	24,501	73,816
AFRICA: Mauritius[4]	751	667	1,418	5,825	2,046	7,871	6,576	2,713	9,289
1891–1895									
AMERICA: United States[2] (fiscal years)	.....	.....	317,482	.....	.....	1,963,253	1,401,856	878,879	2,280,735
(calendar years)						.....	1,350,823	857,203	2,208,026
Argentina[7]	3,026	1,459	4,485	41,670	8,208	49,878	159,155	77,097	236,252
Uruguay[10]							44,696	9,667	54,363
OCEANIA: New Zealand[3]	6,395	6,129	12,524	63,104	30,159	93,263	69,499	36,288	105,787
AFRICA: Mauritius[4]	239[13]	208[13]	447[13]	2,833[13]	942[13]	3,775[13]	3,072[23]	1,150[13]	4,222[13]
1896–1900									
AMERICA: United States[2] (fiscal years)	.....	.....	228,242	.....	.....	1,335,443	982,773	580,912	1,563,685
(calendar years)						.....	1,011,013	585,180	1,596,193
Argentina[7]	2,929	1,859	102,433[14]	35,933	6,289	545,893[14]	298,396	113,678	412,074
Uruguay[10]			4,788			42,222	38,862	8,148	47,010
OCEANIA: New Zealand[3]	5,040	4,753	9,793	54,610	26,860	81,470	59,650	31,613	91,263
AFRICA: Mauritius[4]	241[15]	235[15]	476[15]	2,771[15]	959[15]	3,730[15]	3,012[15]	1,194[15]	4,206[15]

For reference notes see page 355.

TABLE 23—DISTRIBUTION OF IMMIGRANT ALIENS BY SEX AND AGE, 1841-1924[1] (cont.)

a. Absolute figures

1901–1905

Country of Immigration	Children or young persons			Adults			Total		
	Males	Females	Total	Males	Females	Total	Males	Females	Total
AMERICA:									
United States[2] (fiscal years)	......	......	462,874	......	......	3,370,202	2,684,584	1,148,492	3,833,076
(calendar years)	......	......	......	......	......	......	2,834,315	1,227,617	4,061,932
Cuba	......	......	......	......	......	......	113,805	22,464	136,269
Argentina[7]	......	......	......	......	......	......	380,016	146,014	326,030
Uruguay[10]	767[16]	518[16]	1,285[16]	6,711[16]	1,624[16]	8,335[16]	7,478[16]	2,142[16]	9,620[16]
ASIA:									
Philippines	......	......	......	......	......	......	......	......	......
OCEANIA:									
Australian Commonwealth[17]	4,047[18]	3,851[18]	7,898[18]	61,513[18]	25,761[18]	87,274[18]	65,560[18]	29,612[18]	95,172[18]
New Zealand[3]	8,253	7,721	15,974	94,040	41,565	135,605	102,293	49,286	151,579
Hawaii	......	......	......	......	......	......	......	......	......
AFRICA:									
Mauritius[4]	579	497	1,076	6,981	2,379	9,360	7,560	2,876	10,436

1906–1910

Country of Immigration	Children or young persons			Adults			Total		
	Males	Females	Total	Males	Females	Total	Males	Females	Total
AMERICA:									
United States[2] (fiscal years)	......	......	595,667	......	......	4,366,643	3,457,358	1,504,952	4,962,310
(calendar years)	......	......	......	......	......	......	3,474,747	1,513,564	4,988,311
Cuba	......	......	......	......	......	......	133,710	30,331	164,041
Argentina[7]	......	......	280,009[19]	......	......	1,484,092[19]	901,228	336,845	1,238,073
Uruguay[10]	......	......	......	......	......	......	......	......	......
ASIA:									
Philippines	......	......	......	......	......	......	......	......	......
OCEANIA:									
Australian Commonwealth[17]	20,583	20,360	40,943	233,393	99,975	333,368	253,976	120,335	374,311
New Zealand[3]	11,149	10,041	21,190	113,228	60,312	173,540	124,377	70,353	194,730
Hawaii	......	......	......	......	......	......	......	......	......
AFRICA:									
Mauritius[4]	33[20]	16[20]	49[20]	869[20]	286[20]	1,155[20]	902[20]	302[20]	1,204[20]

1911–1915

Country of Immigration	Children or young persons			Adults			Total		
	Males	Females	Total	Males	Females	Total	Males	Females	Total
AMERICA:									
United States[2] (fiscal years)	......	......	590,298	......	......	3,869,533	2,893,900	1,565,931	4,459,831
(calendar years)	......	......	......	......	......	......	2,691,732	1,451,664	4,143,396
Cuba	......	......	15,545	......	......	163,017	143,825	34,737	178,562
Argentina[7]	......	1,068[21]	2,482[21]	......	......	30,207[21]	720,041	291,792	1,011,833
Uruguay[10]	1,414[21]	......	......	24,965[21]	5,242[21]	......	26,379[21]	6,310[21]	32,689[21]
ASIA:									
Philippines	......	......	4,065	......	......	13,800	......	2,433	17,865
OCEANIA:									
Australian Commonwealth[17]	42,584	40,458	83,042	371,940	169,333	541,273	414,524	209,791	624,315
New Zealand[3]	11,880	11,017	22,897	103,132	67,805	170,937	115,012	78,822	193,834
Hawaii	......	......	4,537[22]	22,896[22]	12,592[22]	35,488[22]	......	......	40,025[22]
AFRICA:									
Mauritius[4]	......	......	......	......	......	......	......	......	......

For reference notes see page 355.

TABLE 23—DISTRIBUTION OF IMMIGRANT ALIENS BY SEX AND AGE, 1841-1924[1] (cont.)

a. Absolute figures

Country of Immigration	Children or young persons			Adults			Total		
	Males	Females	Total	Males	Females	Total	Males	Females	Total
1916–1920									
AMERICA:									
United States[2] (fiscal years)...	......	......	224,149	......	......	1,051,831	749,485	526,495	1,275,980
(calendar years)...							921,040	659,522	1,580,562
Cuba...			12,366			391,882	362,359	41,889	404,248
Argentina[7]...			176,733[23]			1,028,188[23]	121,813	71,273	193,086
Uruguay[10]...	3,043	2,874	5,917	19,805	9,969	29,774	22,848	12,843	35,691
EUROPE:									
Norway[24]...	665[25]	628[25]	1,293[25]	23,250[25]	8,957[25]	32,207[25]	24,320[25]	9,786[25]	34,106[25]
ASIA:									
Philippines...			8,843			28,655	32,391	5,107	37,498
OCEANIA:									
Australian Commonwealth[17]...	4,229[26]	4,386[26]	8,615[26]	34,017[26]	27,653[26]	61,670[26]	438,720	100,764	539,484
New Zealand[3]...				23,915	11,757	35,672	61,933	52,414	114,347
Hawaii...			2,995						38,667
1921–1924									
AMERICA:									
United States[2] (fiscal years)...			434,403			1,910,196	1,329,871	1,014,728	2,344,599
(calendar years)...							1,158,188	892,704	2,050,892
Cuba...			8,852			236,838	208,077	37,613	245,690
Argentina[7]...			59,563			522,788	408,872	173,479	582,351
Uruguay[10]...									
EUROPE:									
Norway[24]...	254	278	532	7,488	5,635	13,123	7,780	5,949	13,729
ASIA:									
Philippines...			8,975			22,042	25,692	5,325	31,017
OCEANIA:									
Australian Commonwealth[17]...			21,904			131,514	230,093	147,884	377,977
New Zealand[3]...							82,421	70,997	153,418
Hawaii...			4,601	32,729	11,955	44,684			49,285

For reference notes see page 355.

TABLE 24.—DISTRIBUTION OF IMMIGRANT ALIENS BY SEX AND AGE, 1841-1924[1]

b. Percentages

Country of Immigration	Children or young persons			Adults			Total		
	Males	Females	Total	Males	Females	Total	Males	Females	Total
1841-1845									
AMERICA:									
United States[2] (fiscal years).....	....	....	23.5	....	....	76.5	....	....	100
(calendar years)..	....	....	....	....	....	....	58.3	41.7	100
OCEANIA:									
New Zealand[3]...............	....	....	....	....	....	....	....	....	....
AFRICA:									
Mauritius[4]................	....	....	....	....	....	....	85.7	14.3	100
1846-1850									
AMERICA:									
United States[2] (fiscal years).....	....	....	23.2	....	....	76.8	....	....	100
(calendar years)..	....	....	....	....	....	....	59.8	40.2	100
OCEANIA:									
New Zealand[3]...............	....	....	....	....	....	....	....	....	....
AFRICA:									
Mauritius[4]................	....	....	....	....	....	....	84.5	15.5	100
1851-1855									
AMERICA:									
United States[2] (fiscal years)...	....	....	22.4	....	....	77.6	....	....	100
(calendar years)..	....	....	....	....	....	....	57.8	42.2	100
Argentina................	....	....	....	....	....	....	....	....	....
OCEANIA:									
New Zealand[3]...............	....	....	13.2[5]	62.5[5]	24.4[5]	86.8[5]	....	....	100
AFRICA:									
Mauritius[4]................	....	....	....	....	....	....	79.4	20.6	100
1856-1860									
AMERICA:									
United States[2] (fiscal years)...	....	....	18.5	....	....	81.5	58.2[6]	41.8[6]	100[6]
(calendar years)..	....	....	....	....	....	....	58.1[6]	41.9[6]	100[6]
Argentina[7]............	....	....	17.4[6]	....	....	82.6[6]	80.5[6]	19.5[6]	100[6]
OCEANIA:									
New Zealand[3]...............	....	....	....	....	....	....	....	....	....
AFRICA:									
Mauritius[4]................	....	....	22.1	51.5	26.3	77.9	70.3	29.7	100

For reference notes see page 355.

TABLE 24.—DISTRIBUTION OF IMMIGRANT ALIENS BY SEX AND AGE, 1841-1924[1] (cont.)

b. Percentages

Country of Immigration	Children or young persons			Adults			Total		
	Males	Females	Total	Males	Females	Total	Males	Females	Total
1861–1865									
AMERICA:									
United States[2] (fiscal years)....	....	....	18.4	....	....	81.6	59.1	40.9	100
(calendar years)....	....	....	....	....	....	....	59.5	40.5	100
Argentina[7]......							78.2	21.8	100
OCEANIA									
New Zealand[3].......	7.1	6.5	13.6	68.5	17.9	86.4	75.6	24.4	100
AFRICA:									
Mauritius[4]........	7.3	6.1	13.3	67.3	19.4	86.7	74.6	25.4	100
1866–1870									
AMERICA:									
United States[2] (fiscal years)....	....	....	21.0	....	....	79.0	60.9	39.1	100
(calendar years)....	....	....	....	....	....	....	61.0	39.0	100
Argentina[7]......	....	....	7.6[8]	....	....	92.4[8]	75.7	24.3	100
OCEANIA:									
New Zealand[3].......	6.7	5.5	12.3	63.5	24.2	87.7	70.3	29.7	100
AFRICA:									
Mauritius[4]........	8.7	7.2	15.9	61.1	23.0	84.1	69.9	30.1	100
1871–1875									
AMERICA:									
United States[2] (fiscal years)....	....	....	21.7	....	....	78.3	60.0	40.0	100
(calendar years)....	....	....	....	....	....	....	60.4	39.6	100
Argentina[7]......							71.3	28.7	100
OCEANIA:									
New Zealand[3].......	12.2	11.2	23.4	49.2	27.4	76.6	61.4	38.6	100
AFRICA:									
Mauritius[4]........	8.1	6.3	14.4	60.8	24.7	85.6	69.0	31.0	100
1876–1880									
AMERICA:									
United States[2] (fiscal years)....	....	....	18.2	....	....	81.8	63.5	36.5	100
(calendar years)....	....	....	16.2[9]	....	....	83.8[9]	62.8	37.2	100
Argentina[7]......							69.2	30.8	100
OCEANIA:									
New Zealand[3].......	9.4	8.4	17.7	54.1	28.2	82.3	63.4	36.6	100
AFRICA:									
Mauritius[4]........	8.5	7.5	16.0	58.0	26.0	84.0	66.5	33.5	100

For reference notes see page 355.

TABLE 24.—DISTRIBUTION OF IMMIGRANT ALIENS BY SEX AND AGE, 1841-1924[1] (cont.)

b. Percentages

Country of Immigration	Children or young persons			Adults			Total		
	Males	Females	Total	Males	Females	Total	Males	Females	Total
1881–1885									
AMERICA:									
United States[2] (fiscal years)...	....	....	23.0	....	....	77.0	60.8	39.2	100
(calendar years)...	....	....	....	....	....	....	60.5	39.5	100
Argentina[7]...	....	....	....	....	....	....	68.5	31.5	100
Uruguay[10]...	7.6	3.9	11.5	71.2	17.4	88.6	78.7	21.3	100
OCEANIA:									
New Zealand[3]...	8.3	7.4	15.7	55.0	29.3	84.3	63.3	36.7	100
AFRICA:									
Mauritius[4]...	7.2[11]	6.6[11]	13.8[11]	61.4[11]	24.9[11]	86.3[11]	68.5[11]	31.5[11]	100[11]
1886–1890									
AMERICA:									
United States[2] (fiscal years)...	....	....	19.2	....	....	80.8	61.5	38.5	100
(calendar years)...	....	....	....	....	....	....	61.6	38.4	100
Argentina[7]...	....	....	15.4[12]	....	....	84.6[12]	70.0	30.0	100
Uruguay[10]...	....	2.8	8.6	74.2	17.2	91.4	80.1	19.9	100
OCEANIA:									
New Zealand[3]...	6.1	5.8	11.9	60.7	27.4	88.1	66.8	33.2	100
AFRICA:									
Mauritius[4]...	8.1	7.2	15.3	62.7	22.0	84.7	70.8	29.2	100
1891–1895									
AMERICA:									
United States[2] (fiscal years)...	....	....	13.9	....	....	86.1	61.5	38.5	100
(calendar years)...	....	....	....	....	....	....	61.2	38.8	100
Argentina[7]...	....	....	8.3	....	....	91.7	67.4	32.6	100
Uruguay[10]...	5.6	2.7	....	76.7	15.1	....	82.2	17.8	100
OCEANIA:									
New Zealand[3]...	6.0	5.8	11.8	59.7	28.5	88.2	65.7	34.3	100
AFRICA:									
Mauritius[4]...	5.7[12]	4.9[12]	10.6[13]	67.1[13]	22.3[13]	89.4[13]	72.8[13]	27.2[13]	100[13]
1896–1900									
AMERICA:									
United States[2] (fiscal years)...	....	....	14.6	....	....	85.4	62.8	37.2	100
(calendar years)...	....	....	15.8[14]	....	....	84.2[14]	63.3	36.7	100
Argentina[7]...	....	....	10.2	....	....	89.8	72.4	27.6	100
Uruguay[10]...	6.2	4.0	....	76.4	13.4	....	82.7	17.3	100
OCEANIA:									
New Zealand[3]...	5.5	5.2	10.7	59.8	29.3	89.3	65.4	34.6	100
AFRICA:									
Mauritius[4]...	5.7[15]	5.6[15]	11.3[15]	65.9[15]	22.8[15]	88.7[15]	71.6[15]	28.4[15]	100[16]

For reference notes see page 355.

TABLE 24.—DISTRIBUTION OF IMMIGRANT ALIENS BY SEX AND AGE, 1841-1924[1] (cont.)

b. Percentages

Country of Immigration	Children or young persons			Adults			Total		
	Males	Females	Total	Males	Females	Total	Males	Females	Total
1901–1905									
AMERICA:									
United States[2] (fiscal years)	....	....	12.1	....	....	87.9	70.0	30.0	100
(calendar years)							69.8	30.2	100
Cuba							83.5	16.5	100
Argentina[7]							72.2	27.8	100
Uruguay[10]	8.0[16]	5.4[16]	13.4[16]	69.8[16]	16.9[16]	86.6[16]	77.7[16]	22.3[16]	100[16]
ASIA:									
Philippines	....	....	....	....	....	....	....	....	....
OCEANIA:									
Australian Commonwealth[17]	4.3[18]	4.0[18]	8.3[18]	64.6[18]	27.1[18]	91.7[18]	68.9[18]	31.1[18]	100[18]
New Zealand[3]	5.4	5.1	10.5	62.0	27.4	89.5	67.5	32.5	100
Hawaii									
AFRICA:									
Mauritius[4]	5.6	4.8	10.3	66.9	22.8	89.7	72.4	27.6	100
1906–1910									
AMERICA:									
United States[2] (fiscal years)	....	....	12.0	....	....	88.0	69.7	30.3	100
(calendar years)							69.7	30.3	100
Cuba							81.5	18.5	100
Argentina[7]	....	....	15.9[19]	....	....	84.1[19]	72.8	27.2	100
Uruguay	....	....	....	....	....	....	....	....	....
ASIA:									
Philippines	....	....	....	....	....	....	....	....	....
OCEANIA:									
Australian Commonwealth[17]	5.5	5.4	10.9	62.4	26.7	89.1	67.9	32.1	100
New Zealand[3]	5.7	5.2	10.9	58.1	31.0	89.1	63.9	36.1	100
Hawaii									
AFRICA:									
Mauritius[4]	2.7[20]	1.3[20]	4.1[20]	72.2[20]	23.8[20]	96.0[20]	74.9[20]	25.1[20]	100[20]
1911–1915									
AMERICA:									
United States[2] (fiscal years)	....	....	13.2	....	....	86.8	64.9	35.1	100
(calendar years)							65.0	35.0	100
Cuba	....	....	8.7	....	....	91.3	80.5	19.5	100
Argentina[7]							71.2	28.8	100
Uruguay[10]	4.3[21]	3.3[21]	7.6[21]	76.4[21]	16.0[21]	92.4[21]	80.7[21]	19.3[21]	100[21]
ASIA:									
Philippines	....	....	....	....	....	....	....	....	....
OCEANIA:									
Australian Commonwealth[17]	6.8	6.5	13.3	59.6	27.1	86.7	66.4	33.6	100
New Zealand[3]	6.1	5.7	11.8	53.2	35.0	88.2	59.3	40.7	100
Hawaii	....	....	11.3[22]	57.2[22]	31.5[22]	88.7[22]	....	....	100[22]
AFRICA:									
Mauritius[4]	....	....	22.8	....	....	77.2	86.4	13.6	100

For reference notes see page 355.

TABLE 24—DISTRIBUTION OF IMMIGRANT ALIENS BY SEX AND AGE, 1841-1924[1] (cont.)

b. Percentages

Country of Immigration	Children or young persons			Adults			Total		
	Males	Females	Total	Males	Females	Total	Males	Females	Total
1916–1920									
AMERICA:									
United States[2] (fiscal years)	....	....	17.6	....	....	82.4	58.7	41.3	100
(calendar years)	....	....	....	....	....	....	58.3	41.7	100
Cuba	....	....	3.1	....	....	96.9	89.6	10.4	100
Argentina[7]	....	....	14.7[23]	....	....	85.3[23]	63.1	36.9	100
Uruguay[10]	8.5	8.1	16.6	55.5	27.9	83.4	64.0	36.0	100
EUROPE:									
Norway[24]	2.0[26]	1.9[26]	3.9[26]	69.4[26]	26.7[26]	96.1[26]	71.3[26]	28.7[26]	100[25]
ASIA:									
Philippines	....	....	23.6	....	....	76.4	86.4	13.6	100
OCEANIA:									
Australian Commonwealth[17]	6.0[26]	6.2[26]	12.3[26]	48.3[26]	39.3[26]	87.7[26]	81.3	18.7	100
New Zealand[3]	....	....	7.8	61.8	30.4	92.2	54.2	45.8	100
Hawaii	....	....	....	....	....	....	....	....	100
1921–1924									
AMERICA:									
United States[2] (fiscal years)	....	....	18.5	....	....	81.5	56.7	43.3	100
(calendar years)	....	....	....	....	....	....	56.5	43.5	100
Cuba	....	....	3.6	....	....	96.4	84.7	15.3	100
Argentina[7]	....	....	10.2	....	....	89.8	70.2	29.8	100
Uruguay[10]	....	....	....	....	....	....	....	....	....
EUROPE:									
Norway[24]	1.9	2.0	3.9	54.8	41.3	96.1	56.7	43.3	100
ASIA:									
Philippines	....	....	28.9	....	....	71.1	82.8	17.2	100
OCEANIA:									
Australian Commonwealth[17]	....	....	....	....	....	....	60.9	39.1	100
New Zealand[3]	....	....	14.3	....	....	85.7	53.7	46.3	100
Hawaii	....	....	9.3	66.4	24.3	90.7	....	....	100

For reference notes see page 355.

TABLE 25.—DISTRIBUTION OF IMMIGRANT CITIZENS BY SEX AND AGE, 1876-1924[1]

a.   Absolute figures

Country of Immigration	Children or young persons			Adults			Total		
	Males	Females	Total	Males	Females	Total	Males	Females	Total
1876-1880									
EUROPE:									
Belgium[2]	.....	.....	29,635[4]	113,790[4]	60,352	174,142[4]	.....	.....	203,777[4]
British Isles (Passengers)[3]	.....	.....	.....	.....	.....	.....	9,390	3,095	12,485
Netherlands[5]	.....	.....	2,690	.....	.....	12,252	8,605	6,337	14,942
Sweden[6]	.....	.....	.....	.....	.....	.....	.....	.....	.....
ASIA:									
British India	.....	.....	.....	.....	.....	.....	13,823[7]	4,960[7]	18,783[7]
1881-1885									
EUROPE:									
Belgium[2]	.....	.....	46,601	210,913	100,532	311,445	.....	.....	358,046
British Isles (Passengers)[3]	.....	.....	.....	.....	.....	.....	95[8]	36[8]	131[8]
Netherlands[5]	.....	.....	3,853	.....	.....	17,527	12,573	8,807	21,380
Sweden[6]	.....	.....	.....	.....	.....	.....	13,089	3,369	16,458
ASIA:									
British India	.....	.....	.....	.....	.....	.....	21,585	9,219	30,804
1886-1890									
EUROPE:									
Belgium[2]	.....	.....	59,374	272,937	139,855	412,792	.....	.....	472,166
British Isles (Passengers)[3]	.....	.....	.....	.....	.....	.....	818	463	1,281
Netherlands[5]	.....	.....	4,711	.....	.....	21,510	15,306	10,915	26,221
Sweden[6]	.....	.....	.....	.....	.....	.....	11,576	3,266	14,842
ASIA:									
British India	.....	.....	.....	.....	.....	.....	25,361	11,818	37,179
1891-1895									
EUROPE:									
Belgium[2]	.....	.....	71,637	285,332	173,694	459,026	.....	.....	530,663
British Isles (Passengers)[3]	.....	.....	.....	.....	.....	.....	1,290	583	1,873
Netherlands[5]	.....	.....	6,722	.....	.....	32,233	23,542	15,413	38,955
Sweden[6]	.....	.....	.....	.....	.....	.....	10,671	3,556	14,227
ASIA:									
British India	.....	.....	.....	.....	.....	.....	20,668	9,636	30,304

For reference notes see page 355.

TABLE 25.—DISTRIBUTION OF IMMIGRANT CITIZENS BY SEX AND AGE, 1876-1924[1] (cont.)

a. Absolute figures

Country of Immigration	Children or young persons			Adults			Total		
	Males	Females	Total	Males	Females	Total	Males	Females	Total
1896–1900									
EUROPE:									
Belgium[2]	.....	.....	.....	.....	.....	.....	1,238	742	1,980
British Isles (Passengers)[3]	.....	.....	67,441	250,643	168,010	418,653	.....	.....	486,094
Netherlands[4]	.....	.....	.....	.....	.....	.....	15,597	3,880	19,477
Sweden[6]	.....	.....	7,468	.....	.....	32,387	21,584	18,271	39,855
ASIA:									
British India	.....	.....	.....	.....	.....	.....	24,633	6,305	30,938
1901–1905									
EUROPE:									
Belgium[2]	.....	.....	.....	.....	.....	.....	1,533	769	2,302
British Isles (Passengers)[3]	.....	.....	69,400	308,116	206,505	514,621	.....	.....	584,021
Netherlands[4]	.....	.....	.....	.....	.....	.....	17,468	5,200	22,668
Sweden[6]	.....	.....	7,920	.....	.....	31,979	21,403	18,496	39,899
ASIA:									
British India	.....	.....	.....	.....	.....	.....	39,092	9,247	48,339
1906–1910									
EUROPE:									
Belgium[2]	.....	.....	.....	.....	.....	.....	2,819	1,325	4,144
British Isles (Passengers)[3]	.....	.....	95,272	417,173	263,859	681,032	.....	.....	776,304
(Immigrants)	.....	.....	.....	.....	.....	.....	.....	.....	.....
Hungary	.....	.....	4,571[9][10]	.....	.....	88,241[9][10]	146,624	27,701	174,325
Netherlands[4]	.....	.....	.....	.....	.....	.....	16,366	6,382	22,748
Sweden[6]	.....	.....	8,171	.....	.....	36,354	24,254	20,271	44,525
ASIA:									
British India	.....	.....	.....	.....	.....	.....	25,037	10,549	35,586
1911–1915									
EUROPE:									
Belgium[2]	.....	.....	.....	.....	.....	.....	2,096[11]	923[11]	3,019[11]
British Isles (Passengers)[3]	.....	.....	79,088[11]	327,248[11]	213,206[11]	540,454[11]	.....	.....	619,542[11]
(Immigrants)	.....	.....	59,804[12]	176,568[12]	113,216[12]	289,784[12]	.....	.....	349,588[12]
Hungary	.....	.....	1,239[9][11]	.....	.....	62,750[9][11]	62,826	15,376	78,202
Netherlands[5]	.....	.....	.....	.....	.....	.....	16,283	8,988	25,271
Sweden[6]	.....	.....	7,012	.....	.....	32,436	21,683	17,765	39,448
ASIA:									
British India	.....	.....	.....	.....	.....	.....	20,482	8,078	28,560

For reference notes see page 355.

TABLE 25—DISTRIBUTION OF IMMIGRANT CITIZENS BY SEX AND AGE, 1876-1924[1] (cont.)

a. Absolute figures

Country of Immigration	Children or young persons			Adults			Total		
	Males	Females	Total	Males	Females	Total	Males	Females	Total
				1916-1920					
EUROPE:									
Belgium[2]	.....	.....	.....	.....	.....	.....	1,421[13]	848[13]	2,269[13]
British Isles (Passengers)[3] (Immigrants)	.....	.....	.....	.....	.....	.....	.....	.....	.....
Netherlands[5]	.....	.....	.....	.....	.....	.....	15,269	8,998	24,267
Sweden[6]	.....	.....	6,148	.....	.....	29,958	18,386	17,720	36,106
ASIA:									
British India	.....	.....	.....	.....	.....	.....	12,068[14]	4,847[14]	16,915[14]
				1921-1924					
EUROPE:									
Belgium[2]	.....	.....	.....	.....	.....	.....	3,066	1,977	5,043
British Isles (Passengers)[3] (Immigrants)	.....	.....	47,315[16]	105,537[16]	107,548[16]	213,085[16]	.....	.....	2 60,400[16]
Netherlands[5]	.....	.....	.....	.....	.....	.....	17,995	12,968	30,963
Sweden[6]	.....	.....	4,531	.....	.....	22,092	12,880	13,743	26,623
ASIA:									
British India	.....	.....	.....	.....	.....	.....	.....	.....	.....

For reference notes see page 355.

TABLE 26.—DISTRIBUTION OF IMMIGRANT CITIZENS BY SEX AND AGE, 1876-1924[1]

b. Percentages

Country of Immigration	Children or young persons			Adults			Total		
	Males	Females	Total	Males	Females	Total	Males	Females	Total
1876–1880									
EUROPE:									
Belgium[2]	...	...	14.5[4]	55.8[4]	29.6[4]	85.5[4]	...	...	100[4]
British Isles (Passengers)[3]	...	...	...	...	...	...	75.2	24.8	100
Netherlands[5]	...	...	18.0	...	...	82.0	57.6	42.4	100
Sweden[6]	...	...	...	...	...	...	...	...	
ASIA:									
British India	...	...	...	...	...	...	73.6[7]	26.4[7]	100[7]
1881–1885									
EUROPE:									
Belgium[2]	...	...	13.0	58.9	28.1	87.0	72.5[8]	27.5[8]	100[8]
British Isles (Passengers)[3]	...	...	...	...	...	...	79.5	20.5	100
Netherlands[5]	...	...	18.0	...	...	82.0	58.8	41.2	100
Sweden[6]	...	...	...	...	...	...	...	...	100
ASIA:									
British India	...	...	...	...	...	...	70.1	29.9	100
1886–1890									
EUROPE:									
Belgium[2]	...	...	12.6	57.8	29.6	87.4	63.9	36.1	100
British Isles (Passengers)[3]	...	...	...	...	...	...	78.0	22.0	100
Netherlands[5]	...	...	18.0	...	...	82.0	58.4	41.6	100
Sweden[6]	...	...	...	...	...	...	...	...	100
ASIA:									
British India	...	...	...	...	...	...	68.2	31.8	100
1891–1895									
EUROPE:									
Belgium[2]	...	...	13.5	53.8	32.7	86.5	68.9	31.1	100
British Isles (Passengers)[3]	...	...	...	...	...	...	75.0	25.0	100
Netherlands[5]	...	...	17.3	...	...	82.7	60.4	39.6	100
Sweden[6]	...	...	...	...	...	...	...	...	100
ASIA:									
British India	...	...	...	...	...	...	68.2	31.8	100

For **reference notes** see page 355.

TABLE 26.—DISTRIBUTION OF IMMIGRANT CITIZENS BY SEX AND AGE, 1876-1924[1] (cont.)

b. Percentages

Country of Immigration	Children or young persons			Adults			Total		
	Males	Females	Total	Males	Females	Total	Males	Females	Total
1896–1900									
EUROPE:									
Belgium[2]							62.5	37.5	100
British Isles (Passengers)[3]			13.9	51.6	34.6	86.1	80.1	19.9	100
Netherlands[5]							54.2	45.8	100
Sweden[6]			18.7			81.3			100
ASIA:									
British India							79.6	20.4	100
1901–1905									
EUROPE:									
Belgium[2]							66.6	33.4	100
British Isles (Passengers)[3]			11.9	52.8	35.4	88.1	77.1	22.9	100
Netherlands[5]							53.6	46.4	100
Sweden[6]			19.9			80.1			100
ASIA:									
British India							80.9	19.1	100
1906–1910									
EUROPE:									
Belgium			12.3	53.7	34.0	87.7	68.0	32.0	100
British Isles (Passengers)[3]									
(Immigrants)									
Hungary			4.9[9][10]			95.1[9][10]	84.1	15.9	100
Netherlands[6]			18.4			81.6	71.9	28.1	100
Sweden[6]							54.5	45.5	100
ASIA:									
British India							70.4	29.6	100
1911–1915									
EUROPE:									
Belgium[2]							69.4[11]	30.6[11]	100[11]
British Isles (Passengers)[3]			12.8[11]	52.8[11]	34.4[11]	87.2[11]			100[11]
(Immigrants)			17.1[12]	50.5[12]	32.4[12]	82.9[12]			100[12]
Hungary			1.9[11]			98.1[11]	80.3	19.7	100
Netherlands[6]			17.8			82.2	64.4	35.6	100
Sweden[6]							55.0	45.0	100
ASIA:									
British India							71.7	28.3	100

For reference notes see page 355.

TABLE 26.—DISTRIBUTION OF IMMIGRANT CITIZENS BY SEX AND AGE, 1876-1924[1] (cont.)

b. Percentages

Country of Immigration	Children or young persons			Adults			Total		
	Males	Females	Total	Males	Females	Total	Males	Females	Total
1916—1920									
EUROPE:									
Belgium[2]	....	....	....	....	....	....	62.6[13]	37.4[13]	100[13]
British Isles (Passengers)[3]	....	....	....	....	....	....	62.9	37.1	100
(Immigrants)	....	....	....	....	....	....	....	....	....
Hungary	....	....	....	....	....	....	....	....	....
Netherlands[5]	....	....	17.0	....	....	83.0	50.9	49.1	100
Sweden[6]	....	....	....	....	....	....	....	....	....
ASIA:									
British India	....	....	....	....	....	....	71.3[14]	28.7[14]	100[14]
1921—1924									
EUROPE:									
Belgium[2]	....	....	....	....	....	....	60.8	39.2	100
British Isles (Passengers)[3]	....	....	....	....	....	....	58.1	41.9	100
(Immigrants)	....	....	18.2[16]	40.5[15]	41.3[15]	81.8[15]	....	....	100[16]
Netherlands[5]	....	....	17.0	....	....	83.0	48.4	51.6	100
Sweden[6]	....	....	....	....	....	....	....	....	....
ASIA:									
British India	....	....	....	....	....	....	....	....	....

For reference notes see page 355.

TABLE 27.—DISTRIBUTION OF INTERCONTINENTAL EMIGRANT CITIZENS BY OCCUPATION, 1871-1924[1]

a. Absolute figures

Country of Emigration	Agriculture	Industry and mining	Transport and commerce	Domestic service and general labor	Liberal professions and public services	Other occupations, none or unknown	Total
1871–1875							
EUROPE:							
British Isles[2]	......	......	......	......	......	......	......
Denmark[8]	286[5]	1,529[4]	178[4]	7,162[4][5]	......	466[4]	9,621[4]
France[6]	11,553	10,032	......	......	......	12,743	34,328
Norway[9]	4,794	2,444	1,158	8,403[8]	252	44	17,095
Italy[9]	......	......	......	......	......	......	......
1876–1880							
EUROPE:							
British Isles[2]	36,562[10]	54,076[10]	11,031[10]	147,390[10]	44,098[10]	207,726[10]	500,883[10]
Denmark[8]	961	1,736	222	3,990	......	606	7,515
France[6]	5,944	5,064	......	......	......	5,891	16,899
Norway[7]	1,524	2,840	1,198	11,700	359	1,523	19,144
Italy[9]	200,721	239,163	19,943	7,492	6,510	16,809	490,638
1881–1885							
EUROPE:							
Belgium	......	......	......	......	......	......	......
British Isles[2]	59,851	88,395	18,068	391,485	63,296	431,346	1,052,441
Denmark[8]	2,976	4,582	789	8,775	......	1,223	18,345
France[4]	8,072[11]	3,467[11]	......	......	......	7,886[11]	19,425[11]
Norway[7]	3,810	6,053	4,817	27,995	747	1,816	45,238
Switzerland[12]	......	......	......	......	......	......	......
Italy[9]	333,329	313,704	17,969	8,461	7,372	18,191	699,026
1886–1890							
EUROPE:							
Belgium	4,706	......	298	2,494	......	9,366	16,864
British Isles[2]	118,750	124,092	27,234	305,681	62,080	428,469	1,066,306
Denmark[8]	2,372	6,038	1,451	10,751	......	1,351	21,963
France[6]	......	......	......	......	......	......	......
Norway[7]	4,523	5,011	7,773	21,221	614	648	39,790
Switzerland[12]	12,726	7,422	2,176	2,910	528	12,626	38,388
Italy[9]	540,655	336,909	22,815	11,847	10,075	28,362	950,663

For reference notes see page 356.

TABLE 27.—DISTRIBUTION OF INTERCONTINENTAL EMIGRANT CITIZENS BY OCCUPATION, 1871-1924 (cont.)

a. Absolute figures

Country of Emigration	Agriculture	Industry and mining	Transport and commerce	Domestic service and general labor	Liberal professions and public services	Other occupations, none or unknown	Total
1891–1895							
EUROPE: Austria......	2,291[13]	3,255[13]	1,195[13]	11,635[13]	134[8]	10,608[13]	29,118[13]
Belgium[14]	4,518	146		2,463	.....	4,100	11,227
British Isles[2]	65,781	91,218	31,553	236,600	57,058	375,045	857,255
Denmark[3]	1,659	5,037	1,153	8,302	212	1,872	18,023
Norway[7]	6,311	3,877	6,628	13,053	.....	332	30,413
Sweden[15]	30,879	23,823	5,219	86,128	.....	15,313	161,362
Switzerland[12]	8,450	6,088	2,859	2,603	557	9,088	29,645
Finland[16]	11,191[17]	760[17]	491[17]	1,708[17]	74[17]	293[17]	14,517[17]
Italy[9]	512,582	483,425	25,616	14,714	12,590	33,880	1,082,807
1896–1900							
EUROPE: Austria......	69,839	12,363	5,325	14,967	644	40,840	143,978
Belgium[14]	1,377	128		378	.....	3,533	5,416
British Isles[2]	40,686	81,185	33,240	176,495	60,665	290,668	682,939
Denmark[3]	780	1,810	820	2,972	.....	634	7,016
Norway[7]	4,425	2,440	4,359	7,034	113	351	18,722
Sweden[15]	23,654	14,157	3,196	37,816	.....	6,487	85,310
Switzerland[12]	3,547	2,701	1,715	1,172	458	4,842	14,435
Finland[16]	26,569	946	595	4,163	160	607	33,040
Italy[9]	589,561	633,103	33,297	14,772	16,883	54,760	1,342,376
1901–1905							
EUROPE: Austria......	242,265	37,613	8,813	2,144	1,225	55,138	347,198
Belgium[14]	5,258	172		1,046	.....	8,248	14,724
British Isles[2]	80,514	146,596	60,078	244,176	21,315	469,431	1,022,610
Denmark[3]	2,415	6,455	2,061	8,630	.....	1,079	20,640
Germany[18]	53,344	45,810	18,160	13,965	2,705	12,556	146,540
Hungary[19]	14,105	13,032	12,132	17,199	335	1,643	58,446
Norway[7]	43,724	32,699	5,718	55,860	.....	9,677	147,678
Sweden[15]							
Switzerland[12]	6,604	5,299	2,436	1,657	472	7,844	24,312
Finland[16]	55,030	5,780	2,461	15,261	779	1,745	81,056
Italy[9]	984,620	1,272,218	53,790	77,331	24,994	79,539	2,492,492

For reference notes see page 356.

TABLE 27.—DISTRIBUTION OF INTERCONTINENTAL EMIGRANT CITIZENS BY OCCUPATION, 1871-1924[1] (cont.)

a. Absolute figures

Country of Emigration	Agriculture	Industry and mining	Transport and commerce	Domestic service and general labor	Liberal professions and public services	Other occupations, none or unknown	Total
1906–1910							
EUROPE:							
Austria	258,805	55,906	12,502	734	3,144	80,894	412,385
Belgium[14]	7,812	134		2,095		9,169	19,214
British Isles[2]	112,405	213,920	89,450	355,250	10,627	651,054	1,432,706
Denmark[3]	3,117	5,664	2,117	8,113		1,574	20,585
Germany[18]	40,652	42,169	18,072	12,452	4,389	15,371	133,105
Hungary[19]	225,447[20]	11,080[20]	635[20]	96,962[20]	1,041[20]	4,257[20]	339,422[20]
Norway[7]	19,091	12,978	10,560	4,941	347	1,824	49,741
Sweden[18]	34,155	30,814	5,748	32,244		7,028	109,989
Switzerland[12]	5,787	5,397	3,090	1,764	797	7,920	24,755
Finland[16]	53,331	4,819	1,916	14,533	820	2,357	77,776
Italy[9]	995,485	1,545,018	83,817	200,195	28,223	65,562	2,918,300
1911–1915							
EUROPE:							
Belgium[14]	5,336[21]	110[21]		4,029[21]		4,085[21]	13,560[21]
British Isles							
Denmark[3]	4,501	4,794	2,135	7,351		1,395	20,176
Germany[18]	20,582	24,547	9,345	7,134	2,110	15,691	79,409
Hungary[19]	97,619[21]	5,899[21]	601[21]	37,769[21]	586[21]	3,251[21]	145,725[21]
Norway[7]	10,800	5,812	5,339	1,145	196	312	23,604
Sweden[18]	25,651	25,023	4,944	15,360		7,954	78,932
Switzerland[12]	5,293	5,672	3,041	1,443	1,207	6,763	23,419
Finland[16]	31,359	3,963	1,564	11,010	578	2,194	50,668
Italy[9]	730,466	1,345,095	86,607	189,952	26,163	61,763	2,440,046
1916–1920							
EUROPE:							
Belgium[14]	2,117[22]	100[22]		2,179[22]		4,091[22]	8,487[22]
British Isles							
Denmark[3]	1,526	1,851	2,132	2,131		1,169	8,809
Germany[18]	354	212	138	71	62	11,100	11,937
Hungary[19]							
Norway[7]	1,852	1,888	2,764	210	132	371	7,217
Sweden[18]	9,192	13,229	3,000	8,761		5,261	39,443
Switzerland[12]	2,797	2,721	2,809	824	1,192	4,420	14,763
Finland[16]	9,589	1,368	588	3,165	296	1,672	16,678
Italy[4]	215,479	404,428	44,918	233,948	37,351	22,123	958,247

For reference notes see page 356.

TABLE 27.—DISTRIBUTION OF INTERCONTINENTAL EMIGRANT CITIZENS BY OCCUPATION, 1871-1924[1] (cont.)

a. Absolute figures

1921–1924

Country of Emigration	Agriculture	Industry and mining	Transport and commerce	Domestic service and general labor	Liberal professions and public services	Other occupations none or unknown	Total
EUROPE:							
Belgium[14]........	2,123	186 (industry & transport, braced)		531	......	3,674	6,514
Denmark[8]........	3,794	3,215	2,256	3,778	......	1,101	14,144
Germany[18].......	51,169	81,009	32,694	23,064	9,233	36,553	233,722
Norway[7].........	8,564	8,386	4,672	278	193	1,818	23,911
Sweden[15]........	17,921	20,497	5,244	9,983	......	7,011	60,656
Switzerland[12]....	5,393	4,995	3,973	2,051	1,807	6,843	25,062
Finland[16]........	14,003	3,400	1,075	5,961	366	3,731	28,536
Italy[9]...........	301,261	438,648	24,159	230,662	22,473	29,865	1,047,068

For reference notes see page 356.

TABLE 28.—DISTRIBUTION OF INTERCONTINENTAL EMIGRANT CITIZENS BY OCCUPATION, 1871-1924[1]

b. Percentages

1871–1875

Country of Emigration	Agriculture	Industry and mining	Transport and commerce	Domestic service and general labor	Liberal professions and public services	Other occupations, none or unknown	Total
EUROPE:							
British Isles[2]	3.0[1][5]	15.9[4]	1.9[4]	74.4[1][5]	....	4.8[4]	100[4]
Denmark[3]	33.7	29.2	....	....	....	37.1	100
France[6]	28.0	14.3	6.8	49.2[8]	1.5	0.3	100
Norway[7]	....	....	....	....	....	....	....
Italy[9]	....	....	....	....	....	....	....

(brace annotation: {1.8})

1876–1880

Country of Emigration	Agriculture	Industry and mining	Transport and commerce	Domestic service and general labor	Liberal professions and public services	Other occupations, none or unknown	Total
EUROPE:							
British Isles[2]	7.3[1]	10.8[10]	2.2[10]	29.4[10]	8.8[10]	41.5[10]	100[10]
Denmark[3]	12.8	23.1	3.0	53.1	....	8.1	100
France[6]	35.2	30.0	....	....	....	34.9	100
Norway[7]	8.0	14.8	6.3	61.1	1.9	8.0	100
Italy[9]	40.9	48.7	4.1	1.5	1.3	3.4	100

1881–1885

Country of Emigration	Agriculture	Industry and mining	Transport and commerce	Domestic service and general labor	Liberal professions and public services	Other occupations, none or unknown	Total
EUROPE:							
British Isles[2]	5.7	8.4	1.7	37.2	6.0	41.0	100
Denmark[3]	16.2	25.0	4.3	47.8	....	6.7	100
France[6]	41.6[11]	17.9[11]	....	....	....	40.6[11]	100[11]
Norway[7]	8.4	13.4	10.7	61.9	1.7	4.0	100
Italy[9]	47.7	44.9	2.6	1.2	1.1	2.6	100

1886–1890

Country of Emigration	Agriculture	Industry and mining	Transport and commerce	Domestic service and general labor	Liberal professions and public services	Other occupations, none or unknown	Total
EUROPE:							
Austria	27.9	{1.8}		14.8	....	55.5	....
Belgium[14]	11.1	11.6	2.6	28.7	5.8	40.2	100
British Isles[2]	10.8	27.5	6.6	48.9	1.5	6.1	100
Denmark[3]	11.4	12.6	19.5	53.3	1.4	1.6	100
Norway[7]	....	....	....	....	....	....	....
Sweden[15]	....	....	....	....	....	....	....
Switzerland[13]	33.2	19.3	5.7	7.6	1.4	32.9	100
Finland[16]	....	....	....	....	....	....	....
Italy[9]	56.9	35.4	2.4	1.2	1.1	3.0	100

1891–1895

Country of Emigration	Agriculture	Industry and mining	Transport and commerce	Domestic service and general labor	Liberal professions and public services	Other occupations, none or unknown	Total
EUROPE:							
Austria	7.9[13]	11.2[13] {1.3}	4.1[13]	40.0[13]	0.5[13]	36.4[13]	100[13]
Belgium[14]	40.2	10.6	3.7	21.9	....	36.5	100
British Isles[2]	7.7	27.9	6.4	27.6	6.7	43.7	100
Denmark[3]	9.2	12.8	21.8	46.1	0.7	10.4	100
Norway[7]	20.8	14.8	3.2	42.9	....	1.1	100
Sweden[15]	19.1	20.5	9.6	53.4	1.9	9.5	100
Switzerland[13]	28.5	5.2[17]	3.4[17]	8.8	0.5[17]	30.7	100[17]
Finland[16]	77.0[17]	....	....	11.8[17]	....	2.0[17]	....
Italy[9]	47.3	44.6	2.4	1.4	1.2	3.1	100

1896–1900

Country of Emigration	Agriculture	Industry and mining	Transport and commerce	Domestic service and general labor	Liberal professions and public services	Other occupations, none or unknown	Total
EUROPE:							
Austria	48.5	8.6 {2.4}	3.7	10.4	0.4	28.4	100
Belgium[14]	25.4	11.9	4.9	7.0	8.9	42.6	100
British Isles[2]	6.0	25.8	11.7	25.8	0.6	42.6	100
Denmark[3]	11.1	13.0	23.3	42.4	....	9.0	100
Norway[7]	23.6	16.6	33.7	37.6	....	1.9	100
Sweden[16]	27.8	18.7	11.9	44.3	3.2	7.6	100
Switzerland[13]	24.6	16.6	....	8.1	0.5	33.5	100
Finland[16]	80.4	2.9	1.8	12.6	....	1.7	100
Italy[9]	43.9	47.2	2.5	1.1	1.3	4.1	100

For reference notes see page 356.

TABLE 28.—DISTRIBUTION OF INTERCONTINENTAL EMIGRANT CITIZENS BY OCCUPATION, 1871-1924[1] (cont.)

b. Percentages

1901-1905

Country of Emigration	Agriculture	Industry and mining	Transport and commerce	Domestic service and general labor	Liberal professions and public services	Other occupations, none or unknown	Total
EUROPE:							
Austria	69.8	10.8	2.5	0.6	0.4	15.9	100
Belgium[14]	35.7	{1.2}		7.1	....	56.0	100
British Isles[2]	7.9	14.3	5.9	23.9	2.1	45.9	100
Denmark[8]	11.7	31.3	10.0	41.8	....	5.2	100
Germany[18]	36.4	31.3	12.4	9.5	1.9	8.6	100
Hungary[19]	....	....	....	....	....	....	....
Norway[7]	24.1	22.3	20.8	29.4	0.6	2.8	100
Sweden[15]	29.6	22.1	3.9	37.8	6.6	....	100
Switzerland[17]	27.2	21.8	10.0	6.8	0.9	32.3	100
Finland[16]	67.9	7.1	3.0	18.8	1.0	2.2	100
Italy[9]	39.5	51.0	2.2	3.1	1.0	3.2	100

1906-1910

Country of Emigration	Agriculture	Industry and mining	Transport and commerce	Domestic service and general labor	Liberal professions and public services	Other occupations, none or unknown	Total
EUROPE:							
Austria	62.8	13.6	3.1	0.2	0.8	19.6	100
Belgium[14]	40.7	{0.7}		10.9	....	47.7	100
British Isles[2]	7.8	14.9	6.2	24.8	0.7	45.4	100
Denmark[4]	15.1	27.5	10.3	39.4	....	7.6	100
Germany[18]	30.5	31.7	13.6	9.4	3.3	11.5	100
Hungary[19]	66.5[20]	3.2[20]	0.2[20]	28.6[20]	0.3[20]	1.2[20]	100[20c]
Norway[7]	38.4	26.1	21.2	9.9	0.7	3.7	100
Sweden[5]	31.1	28.0	5.2	29.3	....	6.4	100
Switzerland[12]	23.4	21.8	12.5	7.1	3.2	32.0	100
Finland[16]	68.6	6.2	2.5	18.7	1.1	3.0	100
Italy[9]	34.1	52.9	2.9	6.9	1.0	2.2	100

1911-1915

Country of Emigration	Agriculture	Industry and mining	Transport and commerce	Domestic service and general labor	Liberal professions and public services	Other occupations, none or unknown	Total
EUROPE:							
Austria	39.4[21]	{0.8[21]}		29.7[21]	....	30.1[21]	100[21]
Belgium[14]	22.3	23.8	10.6	36.4	....	6.9	100
British Isles[2]	25.9	30.9	11.8	9.0	2.7	19.8	100
Denmark[8]	....	....	....	....	0.4[21]	2.2[21]	100[21]
Germany[18]	67.1[21]	4.0[21]	0.4[21]	25.9[21]	....	....	....
Hungary[19]	....	....	....	....	....	....	....
Norway[7]	45.8	24.6	6.3	4.9	0.8	1.3	100
Sweden[15]	32.5	31.7	13.0	19.4	5.2	10.1	100
Switzerland[17]	22.6	24.2	3.1	6.2	1.1	28.9	100
Finland[16]	61.9	7.8	3.1	21.7	1.1	4.3	100
Italy[9]	29.9	55.1	3.5	7.8	1.1	2.5	100

1916-1920

Country of Emigration	Agriculture	Industry and mining	Transport and commerce	Domestic service and general labor	Liberal professions and public services	Other occupations, none or unknown	Total
EUROPE:							
Austria	24.9[21]	{1.2[22]}		25.7[22]	....	48.2[22]	100[22]
Belgium[14]	17.3	21.0	24.2	24.2	....	13.3	100
British Isles[2]	3.0	1.8	1.2	0.6	0.5	93.0	100
Denmark[4]	....	....	....	....	....	....	....
Germany[18]	....	....	....	....	....	....	....
Hungary[19]	....	....	....	....	....	....	....
Norway[7]	25.7	26.2	38.3	2.9	1.8	5.1	100
Sweden[5]	23.3	33.5	7.6	22.2	....	13.3	100
Switzerland[12]	18.9	18.4	19.0	5.6	8.1	29.9	100
Finland[16]	57.5	8.2	....	19.0	....	10.0	100
Italy[9]	22.5	42.2	4.7	24.4	3.9	2.3	100

1921-1924

Country of Emigration	Agriculture	Industry and mining	Transport and commerce	Domestic service and general labor	Liberal professions and public services	Other occupations, none or unknown	Total
EUROPE:							
Belgium[14]	32.6	{2.9}		8.2	....	56.4	100
Denmark[4]	26.8	22.7	15.9	26.7	....	7.8	100
Germany[18]	21.9	34.7	14.0	9.9	4.0	15.7	100
Norway[7]	35.8	35.1	19.5	1.2	0.8	7.6	100
Sweden[15]	29.5	33.8	8.6	16.5	....	11.6	100
Switzerland[12]	21.5	19.9	15.9	8.2	7.2	27.3	100
Finland[16]	49.0	11.9	3.7	20.9	1.3	13.1	100
Italy[9]	28.8	41.9	2.3	22.	2.1	2.9	100

For reference **notes see page 356.**

TABLE 29.—DISTRIBUTION OF INTERCONTINENTAL IMMIGRANT CITIZENS BY OCCUPATION, 1891-1924

a. Absolute figures

Country of Immigration	Agriculture	Industry and mining	Transport and commerce	Domestic service and general labor	Liberal professions and public services	Other occupations, none or unknown	Total
1891-1895							
EUROPE: Belgium[1]	465	713			51	644	1,873
Sweden[2]	8,377	8,233	1,814	16,122	......	4,409	38,955
1896-1900							
EUROPE: Belgium[1]	393	862			89	636	1,980
Sweden[2]	8,699	10,127	2,319	14,380	......	4,330	39,855
1901-1905							
EUROPE: Belgium[1]	467	1,021			115	699	2,302
Hungary[3]	......	......	......	......	......	......	......
Sweden[2]	8,558	12,018	2,678	12,979	......	3,666	39,899
1906-1910							
EUROPE: Belgium[1]	777	1,796			178	1,393	4,144
Hungary[3]	20,181[4]	11,113[4]	111[4]	60,145[4]	146[4]	1,116[4]	92,812[4]
Sweden[2]	10,858	14,102	3,225	12,581	......	3,759	44,525
1911-1915							
EUROPE: Belgium[1]	599[5]	1,293[5]			182[5]	945[5]	3,019[5]
Hungary[3]	11,940[5]	8,834[5]	87[5]	41,851[5]	137[5]	1,140[5]	63,989[5]
Sweden[2]	10,461	12,718	3,130	7,598	......	5,541	39,448
1916-1920							
EUROPE: Belgium[1]	376[6]	896[6]			142[6]	855[6]	2,269[6]
Sweden[2]	8,163	11,442	4,136	6,652	......	5,713	36,106
1921-1924							
EUROPE: Belgium[1]	726	2,068			304	1,945	5,043
Sweden[2]	5,465	7,423	2,928	5,873	......	4,934	26,623

For reference notes see page 356.

TABLE 30.—DISTRIBUTION OF INTERCONTINENTAL IMMIGRANT CITIZENS, BY OCCUPATION: 1891-1924

b. Percentages

Country of Immigration	Agriculture	Industry and mining	Transport and commerce	Domestic service and general labor	Liberal professions and public services	Other occupations, none or unknown	Total
1891-1895							
EUROPE: Belgium[1]	24.8	{ 38.1	}	......	2.7	34.4	100
Sweden[2]	21.5	21.1	4.6	41.4	...	11.4	100
1896-1900							
EUROPE: Belgium[1]	19.8	{ 43.5	}	.....	4.5	32.1	100
Sweden[2]	21.8	25.4	5.8	36.1	...	10.9	100
1901-1905							
EUROPE: Belgium[1]	20.3	{ 44.4	}	.....	5.0	30.4	100
Sweden[2]	21.4	30.1	5.7	32.6	...	9.2	100
1906-1910							
EUROPE: Belgium[1]	18.8	{ 43.3	}	.....	4.3	33.6	100
Hungary[3]	21.8[1]	11.9[1]	0.1[1]	64.8[1]	0.2[1]	1.2[1]	100[4]
Sweden[2]	24.4	31.7	7.2	28.3	...	8.4	100
1911-1915							
EUROPE: Belgium[1]	19.8[5]	{ 42.8[5]	}	......	6.0[5]	31.3[5]	100[5]
Hungary[3]	18.7[5]	13.8[5]	0.1[5]	65.4[5]	0.2[5]	1.8[5]	100[5]
Sweden[2]	26.5	32.2	7.9	19.3	...	14.1	100
1916-1920							
EUROPE: Belgium[1]	16.6[6]	{ 39.5[5]	}	.....	6.3[5]	37.7[6]	100[6]
Sweden[2]	22.6	31.7	11.4	18.4	...	15.8	100
1921-1924							
EUROPE: Belgium[1]	14.4	{ 41.0	}	......	6.0	38.6	100
Sweden[2]	20.5	27.9	11.0	22.0	....	18.5	100

For reference notes see page 356.

TABLE 31.—DISTRIBUTION OF IMMIGRANTS (ALIENS), BY OCCUPATION, 1856-1924.

a. Absolute figures

Country of Immigration	Agriculture	Industry and mining	Transport and commerce	Domestic service and general labor	Liberal professions and public services	Other occupations, none or unknown	Total
1856-1860							
AMERICA:							
United States[1]	117,995	101,674	63,031	162,457	3,344	528,083	976,584
Argentina[2]	9,421[3]	1,105[3]	823[3]	1,850[3]	124[3]	6,677[3]	20,000[3]
1861-1865							
AMERICA:							
United States[1]	67,190	95,286	60,688	215,088	5,492	492,166	935,910
Argentina[2]							
1866-1870							
AMERICA:							
United States[1]	149,998	165,101	76,208	396,240	9,459	927,273	1,724,279
Argentina[2]	77,671[4]	4,699[4]	4,053[4]	16,373[4]	5,544	56,220[4]	159,570[4]
1871-1875							
AMERICA:							
United States[1]	150,122	179,981	48,680	434,231	12,034	901,748	1,726,796
Argentina[2]							
1876-1880							
AMERICA:							
United States[1]	111,513	116,467	42,156	277,161	9,207	528,891	1,085,395
Argentina[2]	100,701[5]	18,319[5]	8,653[5]	24,780[5]	2,064[5]	106,368[5]	260,885[5]
Uruguay[6]							
1881-1885							
AMERICA:							
United States[1]	234,223	265,812	68,502	799,846	12,635	1,594,665	2,975,683
Argentina[2]							
Uruguay[6]	6,565	2,070	2,841	6,551	1,264	37,880	57,171
1886-1890							
AMERICA:							
United States[1]	143,140	210,367	66,810	785,889	14,371	1,050,353	2,270,930
Argentina[2]	454,919[7]	67,686[7]	26,217[7]	93,115[7]	5,288[7]	193,897[7]	841,122[7]
Uruguay[6]	17,103	2,636	2,809	9,164	1,092	60,401	93,205
1891-1895							
AMERICA:							
United States[1]	125,920	188,232	71,114	754,100	12,378	1,128,991	2,280,735
Argentina[2]							
Uruguay[6]	7,385	1,685	2,749	8,352	1,796	32,396	54,363

For reference notes see page 356.

TABLE 31.—DISTRIBUTION OF IMMIGRANTS (ALIENS), BY OCCUPATION, 1856-1924 (cont.)

a. Absolute figures

Country of Immigration	Agriculture	Industry and mining	Transport and commerce	Domestic service and general labor	Liberal professions and public services	Other occupations, none or unknown	Total
1896–1900							
AMERICA:							
United States[1]	129,511	186,368	60,174	609,251	9,767	568,614	1,563,685
Argentina[2]	288,429[8]	50,613[8]	29,068[8]	127,415[8]	4,364[8]	148,437[8]	648,326[8]
Uruguay[6]	11,180	4,870	3,712	14,635	3,210	9,403	47,010
1901–1905							
United States[1]	495,649	520,524	149,526	1,658,171	39,509	969,697	3,833,076
Argentina[2]	......	......	......	......	......	......	......
Uruguay[6]	1,480[9]	4,055[9]	3,899[9]	8,539[9]	206[9]	5,592[9]	23,771[9]
1906–1910							
United States[1]	1,230,420	630,788	155,830	1,541,376	55,864	1,348,032	4,962,310
Argentina[2]	562,884[10]	161,092[10]	107,983[10]	493,685[10]	14,248[10]	424,211[10]	1,764,103[10]
Uruguay[6]	......	......	......	......	......	......	......
ASIA: Philippines	......	......	......	......	......	......	......
1911–1915							
AMERICA:							
United States[1]	1,055,706	572,663	160,763	1,335,555	64,069	1,271,085	4,459,831
Cuba	31,574	8,459	16,354	77,358	2,264	42,553	178,562
Argentina[2]	......	......	......	......	......	......	......
Uruguay[6]	1,840[11]	1,807[11]	4,748[11]	14,134[11]	658[11]	9,501[11]	32,688[11]
ASIA: Philippines	2,803	1,482	2,468	445	761	9,906	17,865
1916–1920							
AMERICA:							
United States[1]	111,247	148,063	100,257	334,006	41,471	540,936	1,275,980
Cuba	96,345	16,574	10,298	246,006	1,481	33,544	404,248
Argentina[2]	211,061[12]	99,858[12]	75,289[12]	449,196[12]	16,789[12]	352,726[12]	1,204,919[12]
Uruguay[4]	1,957	2,043	6,601	7,390	2,312	15,388	35,691
ASIA: Philippines	7,910	510	3,012	339	732	24,995	37,498
1921–1924							
AMERICA:							
United States[1]	169,881	338,457	152,937	635,755	66,867	980,702	2,344,599
Cuba	34,805	7,143	6,890	167,484	833	28,535	245,690
Argentina[2]	142,838	71,187	48,888	125,120	11,854	181,864	581,751
Uruguay[4]	770[3]	371[13]	1,527[13]	2,055[13]	448[13]	4,016[13]	9,187[13]
ASIA: Philippines	951	130	1,886	52	370	27,628	31,017

For reference notes see page 356.

TABLE 32.—DISTRIBUTION OF IMMIGRANTS

b. Per

Country of Immigration	Agriculture	Industry and mining	Transport and commerce	Domestic service and general labor	Liberal professions and public services	Other occupations, none or unknown	Total	Agriculture	Industry and mining	Transport and commerce
				1856–1860						1861–
AMERICA:										
United States[1]	12.1	10.4	6.5	16.6	0.3	54.1	100	7.2	10.2	6.5
Argentina[2]	47.1[3]	5.5[3]	4.1[3]	9.3[3]	0.6[3]	33.4[3]	100[3]	....	....	....
				1871–1875						1876–
AMERICA:										
United States[1]	8.7	10.4	2.8	25.1	0.7	52.2	100	10.3	10.7	3.9
Argentina[2]	....	....	....	....	....	....	...	38.6[5]	7.0[5]	3.3[5]
				1881–1885						1886–
AMERICA:										
United States[1]	7.9	8.9	2.3	26.9	0.4	53.6	100	6.3	9.3	2.9
Argentina[2]	....	....	....	....	....	....	....	54.1[7]	8.1[7]	3.1[7]
Uruguay[6]	11.5	3.6	5.0	11.5	2.2	66.3	100	18.3	2.8	3.0
				1896–1900						1901–
AMERICA:										
United States[1]	8.3	11.9	3.8	39.0	0.6	36.4	100	12.9	13.6	3.9
Argentina[2]	44.5[8]	7.8[8]	4.5[8]	19.7[8]	0.7[8]	22.9[8]	100[8]	....	....	....
Uruguay[6]	23.3	10.4	7.9	31.1	6.8	20.0	100	6.2[9]	17.1[9]	16.4[9]
				1911–1915						1916–
AMERICA:										
United States[1]	23.7	12.8	3.6	29.9	1.4	28.5	100	8.7	11.6	7.9
Cuba	17.7	4.7	9.2	43.3	1.3	23.8	100	23.8	4.1	2.5
Argentina[2]	..	..	....	....	....	....	...	17.5[12]	8.3[12]	6.2[12]
Uruguay[6]	5.6[11]	5.5[11]	14.5[11]	43.2[11]	2.0[11]	29.1[11]	100[11]	5.5	5.7	18.5
ASIA:										
Philippines	15.7	8.3	13.8	2.5	4.3	55.4	100	21.1	1.4	8.0

For reference notes see page 356.

(ALIENS), BY OCCUPATION, 1856-1924.

centages

Domestic service and general labor	Liberal professions and public services	Other occupations, none or unknown	Total	Agriculture	Industry and mining	Transport and commerce	Domestic service and general labor	Liberal professions and public services	Other occupations, none or unknown	Total	Country of Immigration
1865				1866–1870							
											AMERICA:
23.0	0.6	52.6	100	8.7	9.6	4.4	23.0	0.5	53.8	100	......United States[1]
....	....	....	...	48.7[4]	3.0[4]	2.5[4]	10.3[4]	0.3[4]	35.2[4]	100[4]	......Argentina[2]
1880											
											AMERICA:
25.5	0.8	48.7	100	....	....	....	....	....	....	...	......United States[1]
9.5[5]	0.8[5]	40.8[5]	100[5]	....	....	....	....	....	....	...	......Argentina[2]
1890				1891–1895							
											AMERICA:
34.6	0.6	46.3	100	5.5	8.3	3.1	33.1	0.5	49.5	100	......United States[1]
11.1[7]	0.6[7]	23.1[7]	100[7]	....	....	....	....	....	....	...	......Argentina[2]
9.8	1.2	64.8	100	13.6	3.1	5.1	15.4	3.3	59.6	100	......Uruguay[6]
1905				1906–1910							
											AMERICA:
43.3	1.0	25.3	100	24.8	12.7	3.1	31.1	1.1	27.2	100	......United States
....	....	....	....	31.9[10]	9.1[10]	6.1[10]	28.0[10]	0.8[10]	24.0[10]	100[10]	......Argentina[2]
35.9[9]	0.9[9]	23.5[9]	100[9]	....	....	....	....	....	....	...	......Uruguay[6]
1920				1921–1924							
											AMERICA:
26.2	3.3	42.4	100	7.2	14.4	6.5	27.1	2.9	41.8	100	......United States[11]
60.9	0.4	8.3	100	14.2	2.9	2.8	68.2	0.3	11.6	100	......Cuba
37.3[12]	1.4[12]	29.3[12]	100[12]	24.6	12.2	8.4	21.5	2.0	31.3	100	......Argentina[2]
20.7	6.5	43.1	100	8.4[13]	4.0[12]	16.6[13]	22.4[13]	4.9[13]	43.7[13]	100[13]	......Uruguay[6]
											ASIA:
0.9	2.0	66.7	100	3.1	0.4	6.1	0.2	1.1	89.1	100	......Philippines

TABLE 33.—DISTRIBUTION OF EMIGRANT ALIENS, BY OCCUPATION, 1906-1924

a. Absolute figures

1906-1910

Country of Emigration	Agriculture	Industry and mining	Transport and commerce	Domestic service and general labor	Liberal professions and public services	Other occupations, none or unknown	Total
AMERICA: United States...	23,451[1]	74,852[1]	21,111[1]	517,075	7,304[1]	179,518[1]	823,311[1]
ASIA: Philippines......	....	....	....	....	....	....	....

1911-1915

Country of Emigration	Agriculture	Industry and mining	Transport and commerce	Domestic service and general labor	Liberal professions and public services	Other occupations, none or unknown	Total
AMERICA: United States...	59,266	142,418	41,723	948,944	14,049	238,130	1,444,530
ASIA: Philippines......	142	575	1,742	933	322	1,581	5,295

1916-1920

Country of Emigration	Agriculture	Industry and mining	Transport and commerce	Domestic service and general labor	Liberal professions and public services	Other occupations, none or unknown	Total
AMERICA: United States...	32,167	59,746	30,770	419,213	12,624	147,944	702,464
ASIA: Philippines......	1,150	528	1,114	483	294	1,607	5,176

1921-1924

Country of Emigration	Agriculture	Industry and mining	Transport and commerce	Domestic service and general labor	Liberal professions and public services	Other occupations, none or unknown	Total
AMERICA: United States...	25,946	45,181	25,096	322,326	11,278	174,842	604,669
ASIA: Philippines......	1,677	246	937	133	241	1,610	4,844

For reference notes see page 356.

TABLE 34.—DISTRIBUTION OF EMIGRANT ALIENS, BY OCCUPATION, 1908-1924.

b. Percentages

Country of Emigration	Agriculture	Industry and mining	Transport and commerce	Domestic service and general labor	Liberal professions and public services	Other occupations, none or unknown	Total
1908–1910							
AMERICA: United States.............|	2.8[1]	9.1[1]	2.6[1]	62.8[1]	0.9[1]	21.8[1]	100[1]
1911–1915							
AMERICA: United States...........	4.1	9.9	2.9	65.7	1.0	16.5	100
ASIA: Philippines...........	2.7	10.9	32.9	17.6	6.1	29.9	100
1916–1920							
AMERICA: United States...........	4.6	8.5	4.4	59.7	1.8	21.1	100
ASIA: Philippines...........	22.2	10.2	21.5	9.3	5.7	31.0	100
1921–1924							
AMERICA: United States...........	4.3	7.5	4.2	53.3	1.9	28.9	100
ASIA: Philippines...........	34.6	5.1	19.3	2.7	5.0	33.2	100

For reference notes see page 356.

TABLE 35.—MIGRANTS IN TRANSIT (EUROPEAN COUNTRIES), OUTGOING, 1856-1924.

a. Absolute figures

Country of Transit	1856–1860	1861–1865	1866–1870	1871–1875	1876–1880	1881–1885	1886–1890	1891–1895	1896–1900	1901–1905	1906–1910	1911–1915	1916–1920	1921–1924
Belgium[1]		60,324	223,988	274,279	228,419	459,186	145,622	151,494	111,698	270,546	346,507	235,566[2]	24,646[3]	71,698
British Isles	35,636	59,443	119,980	157,881	133,296	207,540	494,153	464,599	414,240	842,960	998,022	769,940	136,548	438,129
France[4]	81,965	31,691	113,368	149,513	148,874	318,087	277,656	593,614	534,802	1,160,168	1,290,359	1,037,892	1,975[5]	128,416
Germany[4]	21,546						574,481							
Netherlands[6]			7,554 [7]	7,174	17,519	69,055	64,416	113,108	84,756	228,678	232,277	236,207	50,794	76,029
Total	139,147	151,458	464,890	588,847	528,108	1,053,868	1,556,328	1,322,815	1,145,496	2,502,352	2,867,165	2,279,605	213,963	714,272

TABLE 36.—MIGRANTS IN TRANSIT (EUROPEAN COUNTRIES), OUTGOING, 1856-1924 (cont.)

b. Percentages

Country of Transit	1856–1860	1861–1865	1866–1870	1871–1875	1876–1880	1881–1885	1886–1890	1891–1895	1896–1900	1901–1905	1906–1910	1911–1915	1916–1920	1921–1924
Belgium[1]		39.8	48.2	46.6	43.3	43.6	9.4	11.5	9.8	10.8	12.1	10.3[2]	11.5[3]	10.0
British Isles	25.6	39.2	25.8	26.8	25.2	19.7	31.8	35.1	36.2	33.7	34.8	33.8	63.8	61.3
France[4]	58.9	20.9	24.4	25.4	28.2	30.2	17.8	44.9	46.7	46.4	45.0	45.5	0.9[5]	18.0
Germany[4]	15.5						36.9							
Netherlands[6]			1.6[7]	1.2	3.3	6.6	4.1	8.6	7.4	9.1	8.1	10.4	23.7	10.6
Total	100.	100.	100.	100.	100.	100.	100.	100.	100.	100.	100.	100.	100.	100.

For reference notes see page 356.

NOTES (FOOTNOTES) TO INTERNATIONAL TABLES

TABLES 1 AND 2.—INTERCONTINENTAL EMIGRATION OF CITIZENS, 1846-1924.

[1] 1846-70 figures for Austria only, permit statistics according to national table I for Austria. 1871-1913 port statistics for Austria and Hungary combined.
Figures for Austria: 1871-75 according to table VI, 1876-1908 according to table VII, 1909-13 according to table VI (Oesterreichisches Statistisches Handbuch 1913) for Austria.
Figures for Hungary are taken from national table V for Hungary. Concerning the period 1916-24. f.
For the territory of Austria-Hungary are included: the number of emigrants from Austria, Hungary and Czechoslovakia, and 50% of the emigrants from Rumania, 75% of the emigrants of the Serb, Croat and Slovene State, and 33.3% of the emigrants from Poland.

[2] Exclusive of Hungary.

[3] No data for 1847 or 1848.

[4] 1911-13.

[5] 1920 only.

[6] Antwerp statistics.

[7] 1919 and 1920.

[8] 1853-55.

[9] 1,117,593 "passengers" from the United Kingdom, and 32,473 Irish "emigrants" embarked from April 1, 1923 to December 31, 1924. (See national table IV). For this period the "passenger" statistics of the United Kingdom do not comprise departures from the ports of the Irish Free State. The number of "passengers" (Citizens of Irish Free State and British Subjects) from ports of Irish Free State to Extra-European countries in 1924 was 13,829.

[10] From April 1, 1912 to December 31, 1915.

[11] 1869-70.

[12] 1857-60.

[13] Includes a certain number of aliens.

[14] These figures relate only to emigrants embarking at Hamburg and Bremen.

[15] Emigrants from Irish ports only.

[16] 1921 only.

[17] For 1880, emigrants via Rotterdam only.

[18] For 1851-70, includes continental emigration.

[19] 1868-70.

[20] Comprises alien emigrants residing in Switzerland down to 1881 inclusive.

[21] 1882-85.

[22] For 1891-1902, permanent emigrants only.

[23] 1901-04.

[24] 1908-10.

[25] Two-thirds of the total number of emigrants from the Polish Republic.

[26] Via German ports only; includes emigrants from Finland and Poland up to 1913.

[27] For 1899-1913, includes emigrants to the United Kingdom.

[28] The Union of the Soviet Republics only.

[29] 1921-23.

[30] 1909-10.

[31] From November 11, 1918 to March 31, 1921.

[32] This total does not include the emigrants proper from the British Isles (1911-24) and from Spain (1906-24), the emigrants from Ireland (1876-1924), the third class passengers from Portugal (1921-24) and the emigrants from Poland (1891-1915).

[33] 1921/22-1923/24.

[34] 1898-1900.

[35] Does not include figures for 1901.

[36] 1912-15.

[37] For 1920, excluding indentured laborers.

TABLE 3.—CONTINENTAL EMIGRATION OF CITIZENS, 1876-1924.

[1] 1911; for 1912 and 1913 emigration was at least as large as in 1911.

[2] 1911-13.

[3] 1919-20.

[4] 1899-1900.[6]

[5] 1921 only.

[6] 1898-1900.

TABLE 4.—INTERCONTINENTAL EMIGRATION OF ALIENS, 1846-1924.

[1] 1908-10.

[2] Second and third class passengers by sea.

[3] 1857-60.

[4] Passengers by foreign ocean commerce from Montevideo (all classes) according to Uruguay table VIII. Argentinians, Brazilians and Chilians are excluded.

[5] 1879-80.

[6] 1901-03.

[7] 1913-15.

[8] 1921 only.

[9] 1911-13.

[10] 1919-20.

[11] 1882-85.

[12]Departures according to Australia tables II and VI, but military forces and crews after 1917 deducted. Immigrants from New Zealand and Pacific Islands included.

[13]1904-05.

[14]Passengers.

[15]1921-23.

[16]Departures, except those going to British possessions in 1870 and those going to the Australian Commonwealth 1871-1919.

[17]Exclusive of the first three months of 1921.

[18]East Indian and Polynesian laborers.

[19]1883 missing.

[20]1916 and 1920.

[21]1921 and 1924.

[22]Indian immigrants departed according to Mauritius table II (1846-1900) and total emigration according to Mauritius table III (1901-24).

[23]1911-12.

[24]Permanent departures of passengers (according to South Africa table XI.)

[25]1918-20.

TABLE 5.—CONTINENTAL EMIGRATION OF ALIENS, 1886-1924.

[1]1908-10.

[2]1911-13.

[3]1919-20.

[4]Exclusive of 1920.

[5]Indian coolies from Penang.

[6]For 1923-24, emigrants from the Straits Settlements to Southern India. (See notes 4 and 6 in national tables.)

[7]Emigration to India.

[8]Indian coolies only (according to Ceylon table III).

TABLES 6 AND 7.—INTERCONTINENTAL IMMIGRATION OF ALIENS, 1821-1924.

[1]1817-26.

[2]1827-30.

[3]Including aliens in transit.

[4]1842-45.

[5]1821-67, alien passengers arrived; 1868-1903, immigrants arrived; 1904-06, aliens admitted, and 1907-24 immigrant aliens admitted. (According to United States tables I-III.)

[6]From October 1, 1830 to December 31, 1835.

[7]From January 1, 1841 to September 30, 1845.

[8]From October 1, 1845 to December 31, 1850.

[9]From January 1, 1866 to June 30, 1870.

[10]For 1834-75, the totals include all the British West Indian colonies; for 1876-1900, they include only British Guiana and Trinidad and Tobago; for 1901-05, British Guiana, Trinidad and Tobago, Bermuda and Jamaica; for 1906-24, Barbados has been added to the preceding colonies; for 1906-14 the figures include the Bahamas as well. The annual averages are the sums of the averages of the colonies in question. From 1902, and so far as data were available, the figures comprise not only coolies, but all immigrants (continental included). See also the notes attached to the tables for British West Indies, particularly with regard to the figures for coolies only and for all immigrants.

[11]Immigrants arriving from other parts of America, classed as continental immigrants, are not included in this table.

[12]East Indians introduced.

[13]1853-62.

[14]1863-72.

[15]Second and third class passengers by sea.

[16]1857-60.

[17]For 1821-1907, includes a certain number of Brazilians and citizens of other South American countries. For 1908-24, these have been excluded.

[18]Includes a certain number of citizens and continental immigrants up to 1878; since 1879 alien passengers by sea from abroad landing at the Port of Montevideo (all classes), excluding persons who are citizens of a South American State.

[19]1841 and 1842.

[20]Persons admitted according to Australia table V. Includes Pacific Islanders, Papuans and a small number of other immigrants from Oceania into Australia.

[21]Passengers.

[22]Arrivals, except those arriving from British possessions, 1853-70, and those arriving from the Australian Commonwealth, 1871-1919.

[23]Excluding extra-European British possessions.

[24]1853-55.

[25]East Indian and Polynesian laborers; 1901-08, indentured East Indians only.

[26]For 1834-75, immigration principally from East Indies (according to the Mauritius table I); for 1876-1900, East Indian immigrants (Mauritius table II); for 1901-24, immigrants from all countries (Mauritius table III).

[27]1834-39.

[28]1843-45.

[29]New arrivals (passengers).

[30]For 1900, the first six months.

[31]From July 1, 1905 to March 31, 1911.

[32]Intending settlers only.

[33]1911-13.

[34]1903-05.

[35]Bermuda, for 1904-05 only; Jamaica, except 1901.
[36]Barbados, for 1909-10 only; Jamaica, only for 1908-10.
[37]Bahamas, except 1915; British Guiana, immigrants from all countries from April 1, 1913 to December 31, 1915.
[38]For Bermuda, except 1917.
[39]For Barbados, except 1922; for Bermuda and British Guiana, except 1923; for Jamaica, 1921-22; for Trinidad and Tobago, 1921 only.
[40]1881-83.
[41]1873-82.
[42]1883-92.
[43]1893-95.
[44]These figures include a certain number of continental immigrants.
[45]Except 1924.
[46]1901-03.
[47]1921 only.
[48]Except 1901.
[49]1916 only.
[50]Except 1920.
[51]April 1, 1921 to December 31, 1924; only new arrivals of settlers.
[52]Except 1883.
[53]1902-05.
[54]Indentured East Indians only.
[55]1911-12.
[56]1913-15.

TABLE 8.—CONTINENTAL IMMIGRATION OF ALIENS, 1886-1924.

[1]1908-10. Figures for previous years incomplete and not comparable. (See explanatory notes to the U. S. tables.)
[2]For 1901-05, immigrants of American nationality; for 1906-24, immigrants whose last residence was in America.
[3]1908-10.
[4]1911-13.
[5]1919-20.
[6]1907-10.
[7]Chinese and East Indians.
[8]East Indians.
[9]Indian coolies only (according to Ceylon table III).
[10]1921-23.

TABLE 9.—INTERCONTINENTAL IMMIGRATION OF CITIZENS, 1876-1924.

[1]1911-13.
[2]1919-20.
[3]Irish Free State "immigrants" from April 1, 1923 to December 31, 1924 (5,579) have been added. (See national table IV for Irish Free State). The number of "passengers" (Citizens of Irish Free State and British Subjects) from extra-European countries to ports of Irish Free State in 1924 was 3,721. (See also note 9 to international table 1.)
[4]1912-15.
[5]Immigrants from America (according to Hungary table XXI).
[6]Entries in the population registers of persons arriving from a Dutch colony (according to Netherlands table VII).
[7]According to the returns of the shipping companies.
[8]1894-95.
[9]Exclusive of immigrants arriving from Mediterranean countries. Third class passengers; until 1901 aliens disembarked in Italian ports were included (see Italy table XXI).
[10]1887-90.
[11]1882-85.
[12]1896-99.
[13]1914-15.
[14]1921-23.
[15]1878/79-1880/81.
[16]1921/22-1923/24.
[17]1908-10.
[18]Including aliens and continentals.
[19]1902-05.

TABLE 10.—CONTINENTAL IMMIGRATION OF CITIZENS 1886-1924.

[1]1911-13.
[2]1919-20.

TABLE 11.—INTERCONTINENTAL EMIGRATION OF CITIZENS, BY COUNTRIES OF FUTURE RESIDENCE, 1866-1924.

[1]Passengers.
[2]1867-70.
[3]The data relating to the different quinquennial periods are frequently incomplete. Consult British India table IV for particulars as to dates.
[4]For 1871, by Hamburg only; for 1872-75, by Hamburg and Bremen.
[5]Emigrants by Hamburg only.

[6]Includes a small number of emigrants to other American countries.
[7]Includes aliens resident in Switzerland.
[8]Includes a small number of emigrants proceeding to Canada and Mexico.
[9]Until 1897, South America; from 1898 onwards, Central America and South America.
[10]The figures only relate to Central America.
[11]Includes Poland and Finland. Emigration by German ports only.
[12]1872-75.
[13]1879-80
[14]For 1876-78, the Italian emigration to the "United States" includes also the emigration to British North America.
[15]Includes Paraguay and Uruguay, for 1876-78.
[16]For Brazil the Italian emigration is given separately for 1878-80; for 1876-77, it is included in the column "Other American States".
[17]1878-80; for 1876-77, the Italian emigration to Oceania is included in the column "Other countries or countries of unknown destination".
[18]1881-84.
[19]1882-85.
[20]1885 only.
[21]Emigrants by Hamburg and Bremen.
[22]1892-95.
[23]Including Mexico.
[24]Except 1897.
[25]1900 only.
[26]1898-1900.
[27]Except 1903.
[28]1908-10.
[29]1911-13.
[30]From April 1, 1912 to December 31, 1915.
[31]1911-12.
[32]Barbary States and Egypt.
[33]1919-20.
[34]This figure includes all North American countries except Canada.
[35]From February 11, 1918 to March 31, 1920.
[36]After April 1, 1923 British subjects and citizens of the Irish Free State embarking directly from ports of the latter country, and after October 1, 1923 persons of the same description leaving also from ports of the United Kingdom, are not included.
[37]Includes Irish Free State emigrants for the period from October 1, 1923 to December 31, 1924. Until March 31, 1923 all Irish emigrants were included in the British statistics. There are no data regarding the destination of the Irish Free State emigrants for the 6 months from April 1 to September 30, 1923. (See also note 9 to international table 1).
[38]1921 only.
[39]Includes Mexico for the year 1924.
[40]This figure only relates to Turkey.
[41]1921-23.
[42]1921-22.

TABLE 12.—INTERCONTINENTAL EMIGRATION OF CITIZENS, BY COUNTRIES OF FUTURE RESIDENCE, 1866-1924.

[1]Passengers.
[2]1867-70.
[3]The data relating to the different quinquennial periods are frequently incomplete. Consult British India table IV for particulars as to dates.
[4]For 1871, by Hamburg only; for 1872-75, by Hamburg and Bremen.
[5]Emigrants by Hamburg only.
[6]Includes a small number of emigrants to other American countries.
[7]Includes aliens resident in Switzerland.
[8]Includes a small number of emigrants proceeding to Canada and Mexico.
[9]Until 1897, South America; from 1898 onwards, Central America and South America.
[10]The figures only relate to Central America.
[11]Includes Poland and Finland. Emigration by German ports only.
[12]1872-75.
[13]1879-80.
[14]For 1876-78, the Italian emigration to the "United States" includes also the emigration to British North America.
[15]Includes Paraguay and Uruguay, for 1876-78.
[16]For Brazil the Italian emigration is given separately for 1878-80; for 1876-77, it is included in the column "Other American States."
[17]1878-80; for 1876-77, the Italian emigration to Oceania is included in the column "Other countries or countries of unknown destination"
[18]1881-84.
[19]1882-85.
[20]1885 only.
[21]Emigrants by Hamburg and Bremen.
[22]1892-95.
[23]Including Mexico,
[24]Except 1897.
[25]1900 only.
[26]1898-1900.
[27]Except 1903.
[28]1908-10.
[29]1911-13.

[30]From April 1, 1912 to December 31, 1915.
[31]1911-12.
[32]Barbary States and Egypt.
[33]1919-20.
[34]This figure includes all North American countries except Canada.
[35]From February 11, 1918 to March 31, 1920.
[36]After April 1, 1923 British subjects and citizens of the Irish Free State embarking directly from ports of the latter country, and after October 1, 1923 persons of the same description leaving also from ports of the United Kingdom, are not included.
[37]Includes Irish Free State emigrants for the period from October 1, 1923 to December 31, 1924. Until March 31, 1923 all Irish emigrants were included in the British statistics. There are no data regarding the destination of the Irish Free State emigrants for the 6 months from April 1 to September 30, 1923. (See also note 9 to international table 1).
[38]1921 only.
[39]Includes Mexico for the year 1924.
[40]This figure only relates to Turkey.
[41]1921-23.
[42]1921-22.

TABLES 13 AND 14.—ALIEN IMMIGRATION, BY COUNTRIES OF LAST RESIDENCE, 1821-1924.

[1]Unless otherwise stated, the figures are for country of last residence.
[2]For 1821-68, alien   passengers arrived by nationalities, for 1869-98, immigrant aliens by countries of origin or nationality, for 1899-1924, immigrant aliens admitted by countries of last residence. —The national table shows when fiscal and when calendar years are involved (See general and explanatory notes).
[3]Immigrants classified by nationality.
[4]Immigrants into Canada from Norway included with the immigrants from Germany.
[5]Until 1870, Swedish immigrants are included in the figures for Norway.
[6]Finnish Immigrants included until 1870 and 1891-1919.
[7]Not including Poland up to 1898.
[8]Until 1895 immigrants from the Pacific Islands are included with those from Oceania.
[8 bis]The totals for Canada for the periods 1841-45 and 1846-50, do not agree with the number of immigrants by country of origin. (See national table I for Canada.)
[9]Passengers.
[10]1853-55.
[11]Other British Possessions included.
[12]Second and third class passengers by sea.
[13]1857-60.
[14]Immigrants from Hungary are included with those from Austria.
[15]From 1869 onwards immigrants from the Atlantic Islands which are Spanish Colonies (Canary and Balearic Islands) are included with those from Spain and immigrants from the Portuguese colonies (Cape Verde and Azores) are included with those from Portugal.
[16]Passengers from Hong Kong.
[16 bis]1871-72.
[17]Passengers from Australia, New Zealand, South Sea Islands and British New Guinea.
[18]Passengers from Australia.
[19]For more details, see Argentina Table V.
[20]Includes non-immigrants and aliens in transit bound for the United States.
[21]Passengers by sea landing at the port of Montevideo.
[22]Chilians.
[23]Immigrants from Singapore included.
[24]Immigrants from Java.
[25]Cubans.
[26]Immigrants from the United States for 1891 only.
[27]For 1900, 6 months ending June 30.
[28]Includes immigrants from Serbia and Montenegro for 1899-1919.
[29]1899-1900.
[30]1896-98. For 1899-1919, immigrants from Poland were included with those from Austria or Russia.
[31]Except 1896.
[32]1901-03.
[33]1902-05.
[34]Turkish n. e. s. and Armenian immigrants are classed under Turkey in Asia.
[35]Includes Hebrews.
[36]Syrians and Arabs.
[37]Syrians, Chaldeans and Arabs.
[38]Mauritians and St. Helena Negroes.
[39]Negroes (for 1919-20, also 20 immigrants of "other nationalities").
[40]American Indians, Creoles, Negroes, Maoris, Papuans, and unspecified.
[41]From July 1, 1905 to March 31, 1911.
[42]Immigrants from the Philippine Islands.
[43]1913-15.
[44]Includes immigrants from Macedonia.
[45]Other Caucasians.
[46]Includes Coreans.
[47]Porto-Ricans.
[48]Immigrants from "Other American countries."
[49]1916-19.
[50]1920 only.
[51]1921 only.
[52]1924 only.

TABLES 15 AND 16.—IMMIGRATION OF CITIZENS, BY COUNTRIES OF LAST RESIDENCE, 1876-1924.

[1]1882-85.
[2]1887-90.
[3]1896-99.
[4]1908-10.
[5]1911-13.
[6]April 1, 1912 to December 31, 1915.
[7]1914-15.
[8]North American countries, except Canada.
[9]1919-20.
[10]After April 1, 1923 British subjects and citizens of the Irish Free State disembarking at ports of the latter country, and after October 1, 1923 persons of the same description arriving also via ports of the United Kingdom, are not included.
[11]Exclusive of Irishmen disembarking at an Irish Free State port, between April 1, and September 30, 1923. For the period from October 1, 1923 to December 31, 1924, we have included Irish immigrants disembarked in the Irish Free State ports. (See also international table 1, Note 9.)
[12]1921-23.

TABLES 17 AND 18.—CONTINENTAL EMIGRATION OF CITIZENS, BY COUNTRY OF FUTURE RESIDENCE, 1876-1924.

[1]Includes Russia.
[2]Includes Luxemburg.
[3]Includes Norway and Denmark.
[4]Includes Baltic States and Poland.
[5]Includes Netherlands.
[6]1911-13.
[7]1919-20.
[8]Includes Czechoslovakia.
[9]Austria and Czechoslovakia.
[10]Belgium only.
[11]Includes Poland.

TABLES 19 AND 20.—DISTRIBUTION OF INTERCONTINENTAL EMIGRANT CITIZENS, BY SEX AND AGE, 1851-1924.

[1]If not otherwise stated, the age limit for the whole period is assumed to be under 15 years. However, for Portugal the limit is under 14 years, for the British Isles under 12 years, for Belgium and Finland under 16, and for Holland and France under 10. (See national tables.)
[2]Until 1884, permit statistics. The column "Children or young persons" includes emigrants under 17 years of age. After 1884 this column based on foreign port statistics includes emigrants under 15 years.
[3]Port statistics.
[4]Emigrants proper embarked at Irish ports.
[5]1857-60.
[6]1861-64.
[7]1865-69.
[8]1866-71.
[9]1872-75.
[10]1870-74.
[11]Before 1884 "children" include persons under 10 years; from 1884 onward they include persons under 14 years.
[12]Includes continental emigrants up to 1920, later port statistics. Until 1903 "children" signify persons under 14 years, from 1904 onward persons under 15 years.
[13]1871-80.
[14]1877-80.
[15]1875-81.
[16]1875-79.
[17]1878-79—1880-81.
[18]1881-84.
[19]According to the statistics of the port of Antwerp.
[20]1882-84.
[21]1882-85.
[22]1887-90.
[23]1894-95.
[24]Via Hamburg only.
[25]Passport statistics, emigrants for America.
[26]Emigrants proper (See Japan Table III last two columns.)
[27]1905-07.
[28]Heads of families and separate persons.
[29]1911-13.
[30]1911-12.
[31]From April 1, 1912 to December 31, 1913.
[32]1919-1920.
[33]Excludes Irishmen embarked at an Irish Free State port between April 1, and September 30, 1923, but includes those who embarked after October 1, 1923. (See also note 9, International Table 1.)
[34]1921 only.
[35]1921-22—1923-24.

TABLES 21 AND 22.—DISTRIBUTION OF EMIGRANT ALIENS, BY SEX AND AGE, 1924.

[1]All passengers departing. Up to 1919: "children," without indication of age; 1921-24: children, under 15 years.
[2]1853-55.
[3]Indian emigrants from Mauritius, "children," without indication of age.
[4]Oversea passengers from the port of Montevideo (all nationalities, including a small number of citizens). Children, 1881-1901, under 15 years; 1913-21, under 14 years.
[5]Excluding 1897.
[6]Emigrant aliens departed. Children, 1908-17, under 14 years, 1918-24, under 16 years.
[7]1901 only.
[8]"Departures" (According to Australia Table VII), children, under 12 years.
[9]1904-05.
[10]1908-10.
[11]1906-09.
[12]1913-15.
[13]Children, 1911-17, under 14 years; 1918-24, under 16 years.
[14]"Children," without indication of age.
[15]1912-15.
[16]1916-19.
[17]1921 only.

TABLES 23 AND 24.—DISTRIBUTION OF IMMIGRANT ALIENS, BY SEX AND AGE, 1924.

[1]The age limits for children during the whole period are under 13 years for Argentina, under 12 years for Australia, under 14 years for Cuba and under 15 years for Norway. Hawaii and Mauritius report children without indication of age.
[2]Up to 1867 figures for age groups relate to the "total number of passengers arrived" and those for sex to "alien passengers arrived." For 1868-72, all the figures concern "immigrants", for 1873-1905, "immigrants arrived", for 1906-24 "immigrant aliens admitted." Children, up to 1898, under 15 years, for 1899-1917, under 14 years, and for 1918-24, under 16 years.
[3]All passengers arrived, up to 1919, "children without indication of age"; for 1921-1924, under 15 years.
[4]Indian immigrants to Mauritius.
[5]1853-55.
[6]1857-60.
[7]Second and third class passengers by sea.
[8]1861-70.
[9]1871-80.
[10]Oversea passengers landing at the port of Montevideo (all nationalities, including a small number of citizens). Children: for 1881-1901, under 15 years, for 1913-21, under 14 years.
[11]No immigration in 1881.
[12]1881-90.
[13]No immigration in 1892.
[14]1891-1900.
[15]No immigration in 1898 and 1899.
[16]1901 only.
[17]"Arrivals" (according to Australia Table IV).
[18]1904-05.
[19]1901-10.
[20]1906-07.
[21]1913-15.
[22]1912-15.
[23]1911-20.
[24]Includes a small proportion of citizens.
[25]1918-20.
[26]1916-19.

TABLES 25 AND 26.—DISTRIBUTION OF IMMIGRANT CITIZENS, BY SEX AND AGE, 1876-1924.

[1]The age limit for children during the whole period is under 12 years for the British Isles, under 15 years for Sweden, and under 20 years for Hungary.
[2]Intercontinental migrants according to the statistics of communal registers.
[3]Intercontinental passengers, up to 1913 intercontinental migrants, as from 1912.
[4]1877-80.
[5]Entries in the population registers of persons arrived from Dutch colonies. (See Netherlands Table VII.)
[6]Includes a certain number of aliens.
[7]1878-79—1880-81.
[8]1884-85.
[9]Heads of families and separate persons.
[10]1907-08.
[11]1911-13.
[12]April 1, 1912 to December 31, 1915.
[13]1919-20.
[14]1916-17—1919-20.
[15]After April 1, 1923, British subjects and citizens of the Irish Free State disembarking directly at ports of the latter country, and after October 1, 1923, persons of the same description arriving also via ports of the United Kingdom, are not included in these figures.

TABLES 27 AND 28.—DISTRIBUTION OF INTERCONTINENTAL EMIGRANT CITIZENS, BY OCCUPATIONS, 1871-1924.

[1]In the absence of other indications, the figures relate to all emigrants regardless of age or sex, and where the members of a family carry on no trade, they are—except for Italy and Finland—comprised in the last group (other occupations, none. or unknown).

[2]Passenger statistics. The grouping by occupations does not correspond with that in the national table furnished by the Board of Trade. To suit the general requirements of the international table, the particulars as to occupations which were found in "Accounts and Papers" at the British Museum have been grouped into six classes.

[3]Male emigrants 15 years of age and over.

[4]1872-75.

[5]The figures for agriculture in 1872 and 1873 are included in the group "domestic service and general labor."

[6]1871-77, passport statistics (France Table IX), 1878-84, port statistics (France Table V). The passport statistics cover total emigration (except to Algeria), the port statistics intercontinental emigration only.

[7]Male emigrants over 15 years. The figures in this table for the period 1876-1915 will be found, in quinquennial form, in *Utwandringsstatistikk* (Norges offisielle statistikk. VII, 25, Kristiania, 1921, pp. 114-115). They do not altogether agree with those in Norway Table III which shows the annual figures.

[8]Includes a certain number of emigrants whose occupations are not specified.

[9]Continental emigration included. Up to 1903, persons over 14 years of age, from 1904, persons over 15 years. Members of families (adults) are classified under the occupation of their family heads.

[10]1877-80.

[11]1881-84.

[12]Includes a small proportion of aliens residing in Switzerland.

[13]1894-95.

[14]Emigrants 16 years of age and over through Antwerp.

[15]Includes continental emigration.

[16]Members of families are classified under the occupation of the family head.

[17]1893-95.

[18]Including a small proportion of continental emigrants.

[19]Passport statistics. Heads of families and single persons emigrating to America.

[20]1905-07.

[21]1911-13.

[22] 1919-20.

TABLES 29 AND 30.—DISTRIBUTION OF INTERCONTINENTAL IMMIGRANT CITIZENS, BY OCCUPATIONS, 1891-1924.

[1]Statistics of communal registers.

[2]Includes continental immigrants and aliens.

[3]Includes continental immigrants. Only heads of families and single persons are shown.

[4]1907-08.

[5]1911-13.

[6]1919-20.

TABLES 31 AND 32.—DISTRIBUTION OF IMMIGRANT ALIENS, BY OCCUPATIONS, 1856-1924.

[1]Up to 1867, "total number of passengers arrived"; 1868-72, "immigrants"; 1873-1905, "immigrants arrived"; 1906-24, "immigrant aliens admitted."

[2]Second and third class oversea passengers.

[3]1857-60.

[4]1861-70.

[5]1871-80.

[6]Oversea passengers landing at the port of Montevideo (all nationalities, including a small number of citizens).

[7]1881-90.

[8]1891-1900.

[9]1901-03.

[10]1901-10.

[11]1913-15.

[12]1911-20.

[13]1921 only.

TABLES 33 AND 34.—DISTRIBUTION OF EMIGRANT ALIENS, BY OCCUPATIONS, 1906-1924.

[1]1908-10.

TABLES 35 AND 36.—ALIEN MIGRANTS IN TRANSIT FROM OTHER EUROPEAN COUNTRIES OUTGOING, 1856-1924.

[1]Direct emigration through Antwerp.

[2]1911-13.

[3]1919-20.

[4]Up to 1870, through Hamburg and Bremen, afterwards through German ports.

[5]1920 only.

[6]Up to 1881, through Rotterdam only.

[7]1867-70.

INTERNATIONAL MIGRATION STATISTICS

PART II

NATIONAL TABLES

CANADA

I. Passenger Statistics (Tables I-IV)

Down to 1880 the figures in tables I, III, and IV relate as a rule to passengers of all classes arriving at the port of Quebec and, occasionally, in small numbers at Montreal. They also include passengers arriving from the American continent ("other countries").

According to the table furnished by the Canadian Government, these statistics are confined to the passenger traffic at the port of Quebec (Table I, years 1849-1880). The figures for the period 1829-1848, in table I, have been combined in the table supplied by the Government into quinquennial statements; but they roughly agree with our *annual* figures. However, our printed sources for table III suggest that passenger immigrants via Montreal also have been included. For the period 1842-1867 steerage passengers can be separated from cabin passengers. Table V gives total immigrants through all ports without migrants in transit.

II. Statistics of Intending Settlers (Tables V-IX)

From 1866 onwards (table V) the immigration returns do not relate to passengers generally, but, so far as could be ascertained, to immigrants proper. According to the official definition "immigrants are those who have never been in Canada before and who declare their intention to reside there permanently".

(a) With regard to the figures compiled at the ports, it appears that "returned Canadians, tourists, and saloon passengers are not included in our immigration figures". (*Immigration, Facts and Figures*, p. 10.) (Tables VI, IX.) And these three classes are defined as follows: "Returned Canadians are those who were born in Canada or who have been here before. Tourists are those who say they are in Canada on a visit. Saloon passengers are those travelling on first class tickets."

(b) However, as to overland statistics after 1908 (see below), only those Canadians who were domiciled abroad for less than two or three years were not included.

Table II connects the above tables with table VI. Inasmuch as in the different sources utilised in the tables, there are data common to certain years, it may be inferred that these tables rest in the main on the same definition of an immigrant.

Originally there were two bodies instructed to report the number of immigrants to the immigration authorities, the *Custom Houses* (immigrants reported with settlers' goods) and sundry *Agents* in close contact with the immigrants. The figures furnished by the agents commence in table V with the year 1866 and those supplied by the Custom Houses with 1875; but each is separately indicated only until 1891. In this connection it is stated that: "The number of immigrants reported to be distributed by the several agents will be found in excess of those

357

above given, and the fact arises from movements of immigrants between the stations, some of them being twice reported. The figures taken are those given by the agents at the points at which the immigrants enter the Dominions." (*Sessional Papers.* 1880-1881, vol. 7, p. XXI.)

Subsequently attempts were made to eliminate as far as possible figures reported more than once.

Recently the registration of immigrants at the ports has been in charge of immigration officers, while that of overland immigrants is entrusted to the Commissioners of Immigration at Ottawa, Winnipeg, and Vancouver, who are assisted by land agents, land guides, and immigration inspectors.[1]

Since Canada serves as a country of transit for many immigrants who later migrate to the United States, the two countries have arrived at an understanding according to which the movement of passengers between the two States is under joint control. The Commissioner of Immigration of the United States reported in 1907 that "the amicable relations existing between the Canadian immigration officials and those of this country made......it possible to build up a system of administration which could hardly be surpassed. There are located at the Canadian seaports and border ports exceptionally well qualified and efficiently organised employees, controlled and supervised by......the United States Commissioner of Immigration for Canada".

After the passing of the Act of February 20, 1907, "the agreement with the Canadian transportation companies", was "incorporated in the United States Regulations of July 1, 1907. (Rule 25)".[2]

In the Report of the Commissioner-General for 1908, speaking of emigration from Canada to the United States (there are no Canadian returns relating to emigration), an attempt is made to distinguish between real immigrants from Canada into the United States and the total number of "arrivals".

The immigrants to Canada are classified into those from the British Isles, those from the United States, and those from "other countries". This last group, in table II—as appears from the detailed figures of table VI—includes United States citizens entering Canada via ocean ports. The second group i. e., the immigrants from the United States into Canada include only immigrants over the land frontiers. This number "it is supposed, includes citizens and aliens who have resided for various periods in the latter country" i.e., the United States. (*Ibid.*, p. 143.)

Concerning the definition of real immigrants from the United States over the land frontiers, the Canadian Deputy Minister of Immigration and Colonisation in a letter dated April 23, 1923, states: "It is quite evident that these figures *fail to distinguish between immigrants and nonimmigrants, or in other words, between permanent settlers and transients.* Their collection was discontinued in 1892 and resumed again on an entirely different basis in 1897, but it was not until 1908 that our

[1]International Labour Office, *Emigration and Immigration* (Legislation and Treaties), Geneva, 1921, p. 225.

[2]*Annual Report of the Commissioner-General of Immigration* for the fiscal year ended June 30, 1907. Washington, 1907, p. 71.

inspectional service on the international boundary between Canada and the United States was organised for the collection of accurate data. The figures...showing the movement between 1897 and 1907 (inclusive) are the result of incomplete reports, but they are the most reliable figures obtainable."

We may suppose that by immigrants via the land frontiers since 1908-09 are signified only Canadians who are returning after two or three years' absence and aliens who have not resided formerly in the country. (*Globe*, May 3, 1924.)

Recently the returned Canadians have been classified as: Canadian-born citizens, British subjects with Canadian domicile, and Naturalized Canadians with domicile.

III. CHINESE IMMIGRATION (Table X)

Since 1885 the immigration of Chinese has been specially regulated by law. From that date the statistical returns distinguish between payers of the tax and persons exempt from the tax. For reasons unknown to us, the figures in table VI for Chinese immigration before 1912 (inclusive) are entirely different from those in table X.

TABLE I.—Immigration (cabin and other passengers) through the ports of Quebec and Montreal by country of origin, 1816-1880.

Year	Total	England	Ireland	Scotland	Germany and Norway	Other countries
1816	1,250	......	......	......	......	......
1817–26	over9,000[1]	......	......	......	......	......
1827	15,862	......	......	......	......	......
1828	12,697	......	......	......	......	......
1829	15,945	3,565	9,614	2,643	......	123[2]
1830	28,000	6,799	18,300	2,450	......	451[2]
1831	50,254	10,343	34,133	5,354	......	424[2]
1832	51,746	17,481	28,204	5,500	15	546[2]
1833	21,752	5,198	12,013	4,196	......	345[2]
1834	30,935	6,799	19,206	4,591	......	339[2]
1835	12,527	3,067	7,108	2,127	......	225[2]
1836	27,722	12,188	12,590	2,224	485	235[2]
1837	21,901	5,580	14,538	1,509	......	274[2]
1838	3,266	990	1,456	547	......	273[2]
1839	7,439	1,586	5,113	485	......	255[2]
1840	22,234	4,567	16,291	1,144	......	232[2]
1841	28,086	5,970	18,317	3,559	......	240[2]
1842	44,374	12,191	2,5532	6,095	......	556[2]
1843	21,727	6,499[3]	9,728[3]	5,006[3]	......	494[2]
1844	20,142	7,426[3,4]	9,498[3,4]	2,174[3,4]	......	217[2,4]
1845	25,375	8,511[3,5]	14,060[3,5]	2,011[3,5]	......	160[2,5]
1846	32,753	3,851	26,186	1,632	1,084	......
1847	74,408[6]	31,505[7]	54,310[7]	3,747[7]	......	......
1848	27,939	6,034[3]	16,582[3]	3,086[3]	1,395[3]	842[2]
1849	38,494	8,980	23,126	4,984	436	968
1850	32,292	9,887	17,976	2,879	849	701
1851	41,076	9,677	22,381	7,042	870	1,106
1852	39,176	9,276	15,983	5,477	7,256	1,184
1853	36,699	9,585	14,417	4,745	7,456	496
1854	53,180	18,175	16,165	6,446	11,537	857
1855	21,274	6,754	4,106	4,859	4,864	691
1856	22,439	10,353	1,688	2,794	7,343	261
1857	32,097	15,471	2,016	3,218	11,368	24
1858	12,810	6,441	1,153	1,424	3,578	214
1859	8,778	4,846	417	793	2,722	......
1860	10,150	6,481	376	979	2,314	......
1861	19,923	7,780	413	1,112	10,618	......
1862	22,176	6,877	4,545	2,979	7,728	47
1863	19,419	6,317	4,949	3,959	4,182	12
1864	19,147	5,013	3,767	2,914	7,453	......
1865	21,355	9,296	4,682	2,601	4,770	6
1866	28,648	7,235	2,230	2,222	16,958	3
1867	30,757	9,509	2,997	1,793	16,453	5
1868	34,300	16,173	2,585	1,924	13,607	11
1869	43,114	27,876	2,743	2,867	9,626	2
1870	44,475	27,183	2,534	5,356	9,396	6
1871	37,020	23,710	2,893	4,984	5,391	42
1872	34,743	21,712	3,274	5,022	4,414	321
1873	36,901	25,129	4,236	4,803	2,010	723
1874	23,894	17,631	2,503	2,491	857	412
1875	16,038	12,456	1,252	1,768	......	562
1876	10,901	7,720	688	2,131	......	362
1877	7,743	5,927	663	829	......	324
1878	10,295	7,500	913	1,425	......	457
1879	17,251	14,113	1,088	1,602	......	448
1880	24,997	18,647	2,485	2,845	......	1,020

For reference notes see page 370.

TABLE II.—Immigration to Canada by countries of last residence, 1881-1900

Years	Total	British Isles	United States	Other countries
1881	47,991	17,033	21,822	9,136
1882	112,458	41,283	58,372	12,803
1883	133,624	45,439	78,508	9,677
1884	103,824	31,787	65,886	6,151
1885	79,169	18,591	57,506	3,072
1886	69,152	23,507	40,650	4,995
1887	84,526	31,104	41,046	12,376
1888	88,766	30,852	44,952	12,962
1889	91,600	19,384	67,896	4,320
1890	75,067	21,793	50,336	2,938
1891	82,165	22,042	52,516	7,607
1892	30,996	22,636	. . . . . .	8,360
1893	29,633	20,071	. . . . . .	9,562
1894	20,829	16,004	. . . . . .	4,825
1895	18,790	14,956	. . . . . .	3,834
1896	16,835	12,384	. . . . . .	4,451
1897	21,716	11,383	2,412	7,921
1898	31,900	11,173	9,119	11,608
1899	44,543	10,660	11,945	21,938
6 months ended June 30, 1900	23,895	5,141	8,543	10,211

TABLE III.—Distribution of immigrants (steerage passengers) through Quebec and Montreal, by sex and age, 1832-1843.

Year	Total	Children				Adults[8]	
		Under 7 Years		7 to 14 Years		Males	Females
		Males	Females	Males	Females		
1832	51,746	14,864		. . . , .	. . . . .	19,830	17,052
1833	21,752	. . . . .		. . . . .	. . . . .	. . . . .	. . . . .
1834	30,935	7,681		. . . . .	. . . . .	13,565	9,685
1835	12,527	3,064		. . . . .	. . . . .	5,597	3,866
1836	27,728	5,448		. . . . .	. . . . .	14,447	7,833
1837	21,901	4,082		. . . . .	. . . . .	11,740	6,079
1838	3,266	672		. . . . .	. . . . .	1,646	948
1839	7,439	. . . . .		. . . . .	. . . . .	. . . . .	. . . . .
1840	22,234	. . . . .		. . . . .	. . . . .	. . . . .	. . . . .
1841	28,086	2,505	2,446	1,939	1,776	10,952	8,468
1842	43,760	4,528	4,187	2,902	2,582	17,173	12,388
1843	20,924	1,698	1,755	1,675	1,579	7,901	6,316

TABLE IV.—DISTRIBUTION OF CABIN AND STEERAGE PASSENGERS LANDED AND OF PASSENGERS IN TRANSIT (THROUGH QUEBEC AND MONTREAL) FOR THE UNITED STATES, BY SEX, AGE AND OCCUPATION, 1853-1867.

Year	Total	STEERAGE PASSENGERS										Cabin passengers	In transit for the United States[9]
		Total	Adults, by occupation						Adult women	Children (1 to 14 years)	Infants		
			Farmers & farm laborers	Artisans or tradesmen	Laborers unskilled	Domestic servants	Clerks, Accountants, etc.	Professional Men					
1853	35,968	12,421	3,974	1,560	6,667	146	74		11,548	10,392	1,607	731	11,504
1854	52,365											818	22,000
1855	20,243											1,067	5,500
1856												1,033[10]	9,352
1857		12,443	3,518	2,185	6,279	134	327					1,466[10]	
1858	7,058	4,442	1,651	932	1,593	266						1,720	
1859	8,599											1,551	
1860	18,259											1,664	
1861	20,037											2,139	
1862													
1863	18,112	7,679	2,198	2,098	3,147	23	203	10		10,433		1,307	
1864	17,937	7,836	2,908	1,878	2,962	4	78	6		10,101		1,210	
1865	19,795											1,560	
1866	27,084									16,481		1,564	
1867	28,715	12,234	4,687	2,777	4,508	6	160	96				2,042	

For reference notes see page 370.

TABLE V.—SETTLERS AND IMMIGRANTS IN TRANSIT, 1866-1891.

Year	Total settlers	Total Settlers		Immigrant passengers for United States
		Immigrants reported by agents as intending to settle.	Reported with settlers' goods by Custom houses.	
1866	. . . .	10,091	. . . .	41,704
1867	. . . .	14,666	. . . .	47,212
1868	. . . .	12,765	. . . .	58,683
1869	. . . .	18,630	. . . .	57,202
1870	. . . .	24,706	. . . .	44,313
1871	. . . .	27,773	. . . .	37,949
1872	. . . .	36,578	. . . .	52,608
1873	50,050	41,079	. . . .	49,059
1874	39,373	25,263	. . . .	40,649
1875	27,382	19,243	8,139	9,214
1876	25,633	14,499	11,134	10,916
1877	27,082	15,323	11,759	5,640
1878	29,807	18,372	11,435	11,226
1879	40,492	30,717	9,775	20,560
1880	38,505	27,544	10,961	47,112
1881	47,991	32,587	15,404	69,025
1882	112,458	81,904	30,554	80,692
1883	133,624	98,637	34,987	72,274
1884	103,824	68,633	35,191	62,772
1885	79,169	46,868	32,301	25,927
1886	69,152	43,875	25,277	53,429
1887	84,526	51,704	29,822	91,053
1888	88,766	57,106	31,660	85,708
1889	91,600	52,983	38,617	84,862
1890	75,067	41,549	33,518	103,854
1891	82,165	45,051	37,114	105,213

TABLE VI.—Distribution of immigrants to Canada

Fiscal

Nationality	1900–1901	1901–1902	1902–1903	1903–1904	1904–1905	1905–1906	Nine months ended March 31, 1907
British							
English	9,331	12,783	32,087	36,003	48,847	65,135	41,156
Irish	933	1,311	2,236	3,128	3,998	5,018	3,404
Scotch	1,476	2,853	7,046	10,552	11,744	15,846	10,729
Welsh	70	312	423	691	770	797	502
Total British	11,810	17,259	41,792	50,374	65,359	86,796	55,791
African, South	.....	.....	......	21	35	46	23
Albanian	.....	.....		.....	.....	.....	......
Argentinian	.....	.....					
Australian	3	11	46	58	204	322	185
Austro-Hungarian	5,692	8,557	13,095	11,137	10,089	10,170	4,045
Belgian	132	223	303	858	796	1,106	650
Brazilian	.....	.....		2	1	2	5
Bulgarian	.....	1	7	14	2	71	179
Chinese	7	2	.....	.....	.....	18	92
Cuban	.....	.....					
Dutch	25	35	223	169	281	389	394
French	360	431	937	1,534	1,743	1,648	1,314
German	984	1,048	1,887	2,985	2,759	1,796	1,903
Greek	81	161	193	191	98	254	545
Hawaiian	.....	.....					
Hebrew	2,765	1,015	2,066	3,727	7,715	7,127	6,584
Hindu	.....	.....		.....	45	387	2,124
Italian	4,710	3,828	3,371	4,445	3,473	7,959	5,114
Japanese	6	.....	.....	.....	354	1,922	2,042
Macedonian	.....	.....					
Malay	.....	5	.....				
Maltese	.....	.....	2	.....			
Mexican	.....	.....					
Montenegrin	.....	.....					
Negro	.....	.....		......	5	42	108
Newfoundland	.....	.....	335	519	190	340	1,029
New Zealand	.....	1	2	23	57	89	30
Persian	.....	.....	40	5	8	7	31
Polish	162	230	274	669	745	725	1,033
Portuguese	.....	.....	.....	......	1	6	2
Rumanian	152	551	438	619	270	396	431
Russian, not specified	1,044	2,467	5,505	1,955	1,887	3,152	1,927
Doukhobor	.....	12	.....	......	24	204	....
Finnish	682	1,292	1,734	845	1,323	1,103	1,049
Mennonite	.....	52	38	11	.....	.....	....
Scandinavian							
Danish	88	163	308	417	461	474	297
Icelandic	912	260	917	396	413	168	46
Norwegian	265	1,015	1,746	1,239	1,397	1,415	876
Swedish	485	1,013	2,477	2,151	1,847	1,802	1,077
Serbian	23	.....	2	10	7	19	4
Spanish	14	1	7	5	10	12	29
Swiss	30	17	73	128	150	172	112
Turkish							
Turkish, not specified	37	17	43	29	30	357	232
Arabian	98	70	46	58	48	19	31
Armenian	62	112	113	81	78	82	208
Egyptian	1	3	1	3	2	18	10
Syrian	464	1,066	847	369	630	336	277
United States citizens							
via ocean ports—	68	73	.....	58	109	123	89
West Indian	.....	.....	23	55	77	194	90
Other nationalities—	.....	.....					
Total continental, etc.	19,352	23,732	37,099	34,786	37,364	44,472	34,217
From the United States	17,987	26,388	49,473	45,171	43,543	57,796	34,659
Grand total	49,149	67,379	128,364	130,331	146,266	189,064	124,667

For reference notes see page 370.

BY NATIONALITY, JULY 1, 1900, TO MARCH 31, 1920.

years[11]

1907–1908	1908–1909	1909–1910	1910–1911	1911–1912	1912–1913	1913–1914	1914–1915	1915–1916	1916–1917	1917–1918	1918–1919	1919–1920
90,380	37,019	40,416	84,707	95,107	108,082	102,122	30,807	5,857	5,174	2,477	7,954	45,173
6,547	3,609	3,940	6,877	8,327	9,706	9,585	3,525	818	958	174	336	2,751
22,223	11,810	14,706	29,924	32,988	30,735	29,128	8,346	1,887	2,062	473	1,518	10,997
1032	463	728	1,505	1,699	2,019	1,787	598	102	88	54	106	682
120,182	52,901	59,790	123,013	138,121	150,542	142,622	43,276	8,664	8,282	3,178	9,914	59,603
76	53	97	86	1444	22	56	23	11	1	4	.....	23
.....	.....	.....	.....	.....	.....	3	4	.....	.....	.....	.....	.....
.....	.....	.....	.....	.....	.....	2	5	.....	.....	.....	.....	2
180	171	203	266	.184	106	106	51	32	18	34	35	88
21,376	10,798	9,757	16,285	21,651	21,875	28,323	7,150	15	1	.....	2	8
1,214	828	910	1,563	1,601	1,826	2,651	1,149	172	126	19	48	1,532
1	4	.....	13	.....	.....	5	.....	2	.....	.....	.....	.....
2,529	56	557	1,068	3,295	4,616	1,727	4,048	1	.....	.....	.....	1
1,884	1,887	2,156	5,278	6,247	7,445	5,512	1,258	88	393	769	4,333	544
.....	.....	.....	.....	.....	.....	10	1	1	3	1	.....	2
1,212	495	741	931	1,077	1,524	1,506	605	186	151	94	59	154
2,671	1,830	1,727	2,041	2,094	2,755	2,683	1,206	180	199	114	222	1,584
2,377	1,340	1,533	2,533	4,664	4,953	5,537	2,472	27	9	1	1	12
1,053	192	452	777	693	1,390	1,102	1,147	145	258	45	4	39
.....	.....	.....	.....	.....	.....	2	18	1	.....	.....	.....	.....
7,712	1,636	3,182	5,146	5,322	7,387	11,252	3,107	65	136	32	22	116
2,623	6	10	5	3	5	88	.....	1	.....	.....	.....	.....
11,212	4,228	7,118	8,359	7,590	16,601	24,722	6,228	388	758	189	49	1,165
7,601	495	271	437	765	724	856	592	401	648	883	1,178	711
.....	.....	.....	.....	.....	.....	17	132	.....	.....	.....	.....	.....
.....	.....	.....	.....	.....	128	402	19	4	109	144	2	405
.....	.....	.....	.....	3	9	9	.....	.....	.....	1	3	.....
.....	.....	.....	.....	.....	36	13	9	.....	1	.....	.....	.....
136	73	7	12	138	211	266	202	34	98	35	22	61
3,374	2,108	3,372	2,229	2,598	1,036	496	338	255	1,243	1,199	512	443
70	65	82	116	61	39	24	21	18	12	13	15	31
7	1	5	19	19	20	19	7	3	.....	2	2	.....
1,593	376	1,407	2,177	5,060	9,945	9,793	1,976	8	12	.....	4	76
2	2	2	13	6	9	58	8	.....	1	1	.....	3
949	278	293	511	793	1,116	1,504	361	4	4	.....	.....	21
6,281	3,547	4,564	6,621	9,805	18,623	24,485	5,201	40	25	42	42	51
.....	.....	.....	41	24	108	4	.....	.....	.....	.....	.....	.....
1,212	669	1,457	2,132	1,646	2,391	3,183	459	139	249	113	2	44
290	160	300	535	628	798	871	326	167	145	74	44	233
97	35	95	250	205	231	292	145	15	9	3	12	11
1,554	752	1,370	2,169	1,692	1,832	1,647	788	232	303	235	91	179
2,132	1,135	2,017	3,213	2,394	2,477	2,435	916	177	332	156	101	241
48	31	76	50	209	366	193	220	6	1	.....	1	12
61	32	42	197	191	296	1,138	755	11	76	28	12	15
195	129	211	270	230	246	269	209	42	30	12	11	100
489	236	517	469	632	770	187	33	.....	5	.....	.....	1
50	4	14	3	2	10	16	.....	.....	.....	.....	.....	.....
563	79	75	20	60	100	139	36	.....	3	2	.....	10
8	2	.....	3	.....	7	5	.....	.....	.....	.....	.....	.....
732	189	195	124	144	232	278	79	3	9	2	.....	18
133	94	186	203	143	121	121	41	15	20	28	21	55
278	159	203	455	393	495	719	389	47	315	307	223	66
.....	.....	.....	.....	.....	.....	.....	.....	.....	.....	.....	.....	20
83,975	34,175	45,206	66,620	82,406	112,881	134,726	41,734	2,936	5,703	4,582	7,073	8,077
58,312	59,832	103,798	121,451	133,710	139,009	107,530	59,779	36,937	61,389	71,314	40,715	49,656
262,469	146,908	208,794	311,084	354,237	402,432	384,878	144,789	48,537	75,374	79,074	57,702	117,336

TABLE VII.—Total immigration, calendar years 1903-1920.

1903[12]	129,193
1904[12]	125,183
1905[12]	141,897
1906	214,724
1907	277,373
1908	148,700
1909	184,281
1910	303,091
1911	350,374
1912	395,804
1913	418,838
1914	168,930
1915	48,466
1916	65,836
1917	86,451
1918	50,270
1919	117,633
1920	147,502

For reference notes see page 370.

TABLE VIII—Distribution of immigrants by nationality, 1920-1924.
(Calendar Years)

Nationality		1920	1921	1922	1923	1924
Albanian		2	6	1	6	2
African, South		73	35	31	57	97
Armenian		6	84	43	404	338
Australian		98	64	59	97	171
Argentinian		1	3	4	..	..
Austrian		51	53	59	61	97
Hungarian					162	1,107
Belgian		2,191	578	300	1,368	1,504
Bermuda		7	3	5	1	..
Brazilian		..	..	..	..	1
Bulgarian		4	26	15	163	170
Chilian		...	...	...	...	3
Chinese		1,329	2,732	810	811	7
Czechoslovak		273	155	123	1,934	2,872
Dutch		575	240	118	798	1,821
East Indian		...	...	..	..	10
Estonian		...	...	12	33	65
Finnish		1,198	333	654	6,019	6,123
French		984	364	289	324	351
German		112	195	177	1,263	2,560
Great Britain and Ireland	English	49,248	26,407	17,729	35,783	28,276
	Irish	6,122	4,108	3,217	8,231	10,760
	Scotch	19,486	12,551	9,531	25,107	17,305
	Welsh	951	744	528	989	1,271
Greek		297	195	187	294	215
Hebrew	N. E. S.	273	2,595	970	839	892
	Polish	291	6,136	2,415	1,207	828
	Russian	771			1,426	3,704
	German	...	...	...	3	2
	Austrian	..	..	..	..	2
Hindu		9	11	22	30	39
Italian		3,927	2,508	2,030	6,062	2,676
Jamaican		18	13	23	9	9
Japanese		525	481	395	404	510
Yugoslav		72	178	137	714	2,183
Latvian		..	..	..	18	20
Lithuanian		..	..	119	204	155
Luxemburger		16	1	7	40	69
Maltese		154	34	50	151	29
Mexican		..	..	..	1	..
Negro		142	41	47	40	34
New Zealand		21	35	34	23	121
Persian		1	9	1	13	10
Polish	(Polish N. E. S.)	3,476	...	...	4,157	...
	(Russian)	68	2,853	2,758		2,908
Portuguese		4	...	2	...	3
Rumanian		702	952	440	965	2,471
Russian		963	547	168	2,852	5,545
Scandinavian	Danish	478	603	297	1,025	2,066
	Icelandic	50	22	33	26	48
	Norwegian	412	489	448	1,670	3,216
	Swedish	645	509	666	3,295	2,550
Spanish		201	6	16	39	3
Swiss		211	205	115	1,527	758
Syrian		95	153	87	235	253
Turkish	N. E. S.	1	...	5	10	43
	Arabian	3	2	2	...	...
	Egyptian	364	11	2	3	3
	Armenian					
Ukrainian		478	93	38	816	49
Venezuelan		..	..	1	6	..
West Indian		106	30	52	57	40
Total oversea		97,485	67,393	45,272	111,772	106,366
CONTINENTAL						
Newfoundland		1,021	377	1,382	5,140	1,629
United States via ocean ports		120	70	36	101	127
United States		48,866	32,573	23,733	20,307	16,328
Total continental		50,007	33,020	25,151	25,548	18,084
Grand total		147,492	100,413	70,423	137,320	124,450

TABLE IX.—Distribution of immigrants, by sex and age, 1920-1924.

Calendar Year	Total	Children under 14 years	Adults	
			Males	Females
1920	147,492	28,240	69,482	49,770
1921	100,413	21,351	43,788	35,274
1922	70,423	14,551	31,509	24,363
1923	137,320	21,555	79,030	36,735
1924	124,450	21,999	65,752	36,699

TABLE X.—Chinese immigration, 1886-1924

Fiscal Year	Chinese.	
	Paying tax	Exempt from tax
1886-1891	1,590	222
1892	3,276	6
1893	2,244	14
1894	2,087	22
1895	1,440	22
1896	1,762	24
1897	2,447	24
1898	2,175	17
1899	4,385	17
1900	4,231	26
1901	2,518	26
1902	3,525	62
1903	5,245	84
1904	4,719	128
1905	8	69
1906	22	146
1907	91	200
1908	1,482	752
1909	1,411	695
1910	1,614	688
1911	4,515	805
1912	6,083	498
1913	7,078	367
1914	5,274	238
1915	1,155	103
1916	20	69
1917	272	121
1918	650	119
1919	4,066	267
1920	363	181
1921	885	1,550
1922	1,459	287
1923	652	59
1924	625	51
Total	82,369	7,959

TABLE XI.—IMMIGRANTS LANDED AT NEW BRUNSWICK, NOVA SCOTIA AND PRINCE EDWARD ISLAND, 1842-1866.

Year	New Brunswick		Nova Scotia	Prince Edward Island
	Total	In transit for the United States[9]		
1840	.....	....	....	....
1841	.....	....	....	....
1842	8,668[7]	....	2,333[7]	1,257[7]
1843	987[7]	....	1,203[7]	528[7]
1844	2,489[7]	....	747[7]	467
1845	6,412[7]	....	615[7]	193
1846	9,765	4,500	698[7]	286[7]
1847	14,959[6]	....	2,000[7]	536[7]
1848	4,020	4,020	140	59[7]
1849	2,671	....	298[7]	84
1850	1,507	....	174	88
1851	3,470	....	231	34
1852	2,165	....	165	32
1853	3,762	....	211	120
1854	3,618	....	161	143
1855	1,405	....	344[7]	91[7]
1856	712	200	457	86
1857	551	....	64[7]	36[7]
1858	309[7]	....	96[7]	316[7]
1859	229[7]	....	28[7]	9[7]
1860	294[7]	....	109[7]	16[7]
1861	545[7]	....	239[7]	136[7]
1862	548	....	363[7]	22[7]
1863	649	....	419[7]	21[7]
1864	396	....	433	....
1865	1,456	....	336	2
1866	197	....	1,139	....

SOURCES

Accounts and Papers, London, 1833 (vol. XXVI), 1835 (vol. XXXIX), 1836 (vol. XL), 1837 (vol. XLII), 1838 (vol. XL), 1839 (vol. XXXIX), 1842 (vol. XXXI), 1843 (vol. XXXIV, and 1844 (vol. XXXV).

The titles of the reports containing statistics of immigration into Canada change from year to year as follows: *Correspondence relating to Emigration, Annual Report on Emigration to Canada, Papers relating to Emigration, Copy of the Report from the Agent for Emigration in Canada*, etc.

Tables I (years 1816–42), III and XI.

For reference notes see page 370.

General Report of the Emigration Commissioners for the Years 1842 to 1873. (London, 1843 to 1874.)

Tables I (years 1842-48), IV and XII.

Canada Sessional Papers. 1880-81, 1889, 1892-1922. Ottawa.

Tables V and VIII.

Immigration Facts and Figures. Compiled under the direction of J. A. Calder, Minister of Immigration and Colonization, 1920, pp. 6-9.

Table VI.

Canada Year-Book, Ottawa, 1924, p. 1756.

Table X.

Labor Gazette (published monthly by the Department of Labor of Canada). Ottawa, 1920-25.

Tables VII and IX.

Information supplied by the Canadian Government.

Tables I (years 1849-80) and II.

NOTES

[1]Annual average.
[2]New Brunswick, Nova Scotia and ports on the St. Lawrence River, 1829-48.
[3]Arrived directly from the ports of the countries indicated.
[4]"Infants" not included in these figures.
[5]"Cabin passengers" not included in these figures. On the other hand, the 6th *Report* (1846) supplies the following classification, which includes "cabin passengers"; England, 8,449; Ireland, 13,668; Scotland, 2,113; Lower ports, 160; infants, 985.
[6]Excluding 15,330 emigrants for Canada and 2,113 for New Brunswick who died on the voyage or were placed in quarantine or hospital on their arrival.
[7]Statistical returns of emigration from the United Kingdom.
[8]For 1832 to 1838, over 7 years; for 1841 to 1843 over 14 years.
[9]Approximately estimated and already included in the columns for steerage and cabin passengers.
[10]Incomplete.
[11]For 1900-01 to 1905-06, the 12 months ending June 30; for the period 1907-08 to 1919-20, the 12 months ending March 31.
[12]To the monthly totals for the fiscal year 1902-03 5,245 persons from the United States were added. To the monthly totals for the fiscal year 1903-04 from

United States {7,479 persons (Customs entries)
               {1,930 persons (Repatriation societies)

were added.

To the monthly totals for the fiscal year 1904-05 from

United States {7,781 persons (Customs entries)
               {1,884 persons (Repatriation societies)

were added.
Note.—The above figures have not been included in the totals for the calendar years compiled from the *fiscal* returns.

TABLE I—Distribution of free immigrants by sex and age, 1884.

| | Sex | | | |
| Port of Embarkation | Males | | Females | |
	Under 14 years	Over 14 years	Under 14 years	Over 14 years
European: French ports.....	..	40	..	6
English ports.....	..	1	..	..
Spanish ports....	..	3	..	..
American: Newfoundland ports........	1	5	2	9
Nova Scotia ports	..	1	..	..
United States ports........	..	..	..	..
Total	1	50	2	15
Grand total	51		17	
	68			

SOURCE

Notices Coloniales. Paris, 1885, vol. III. p. 267.

NEWFOUNDLAND
TABLE I—IMMIGRANTS LANDED 1842-1865.

Year	Total	Year	Total	Year	Total	Year	Total
1842	490[1]	1848[1]	343[1]	1854	95[1]	1860	465[1]
1843	448[1]	1849[1]	321[1]	1855	94[1]	1861	239[1]
1844	684[1]	1850[1]	325[1]	1856	324	1862	34[1]
1845	618[1]	1851[1]	241[1]	1857	32[1]	1863	27[1]
1846	523[1]	1852[1]	299[1]	1858	138[1]	1864	33
1847	993[1]	1853[1]	173[1]	1859	281[1]	1865	32

TABLE II—IMMIGRATION AND EMIGRATION, 1903-1913.

Year[2]	Immigrants		Emigrants
	Aliens (intending settlers)	Citizens (returning residents)[3]	Chiefly citizens[3]
1903	643	8,535	9,554
1904	824	6,796	6,288
1905	884	6,220	6,885
1906	1,447	7,117	7,460
1907	851	6,160	7,029
1908	885	5,498	4,857
1909	536	4,810	7,540
1910	707	8,399	9,096
1911	653	7,612	7,711
1912	697	7,444	8,724
1913	785	7,967	8,445

TABLE III—IMMIGRATION AND EMIGRATION, 1903-1924[3].

Year	Immigrants		Emigrants	
	Total		To the United Kingdom	To all countries
	From the United Kingdom	From all countries		
1903[2]		13,647		12,731
1904[2]	Cannot	12,759	Cannot	9,766
1905[2]		12,478		10,618
1906[2]	be	10,839	be	12,107
1907[2]		10,973		12,196
1908[2]	stated.	9,993	stated.	10,247
1909[2]		793		5,457
1910[2]	701	11,370	688	12,539
1911[2]	818	12,034	690	12,390
1912[2]	654	11,912	683	9,179
1913[2]		13,788		14,255
1914[2]	Cannot	11,260	Cannot	10,825
1915[2]		8,169		9,247
1916[2]	be	12,080	be	13,419
1921		8,867		8,233
1922	stated.	—	stated.	—
1923		11,034		18,818
1924		14,214		11,801

SOURCES

General Reports of the Emigration Commissioners, 1843-72.

Table I (years 1842-65).

Royal Commission on the Natural Resources, Trade, and Legislation of certain Portions of His Majesty's Dominions. Minutes of Evidence taken in Newfoundland in 1914. London, 1915, pp. 1, 2.

Table II (years 1903-13).

Statistical Abstract for the several British Overseas Dominions and Protectorates. London, 1914, 1922, 1924.

Table III (years 1903-1921).

Statesman's Year-Book. London, 1924-26.

Table III, (years 1921, 1923, 1924).

NOTES

[1]Emigration figures of the United Kingdom.
[2]For the 12 months ended June 30 of the year stated.
[3]The differences between tables II and III are mainly due to the fact that the latter includes ordinary travellers, sportsmen and tourists.

UNITED STATES

The migration statistics are based on the provisions of the immigration acts. These require that the masters of arriving and departing vessels should deliver passenger lists to the collectors of customs. It is contended, however, that in the period before 1864 these lists were frequently prepared before the arrival of the vessel and did not allow for later events, such as deaths, which omissions are estimated at 50 percent.

The first immigration act is dated March 2, 1819, and relates to the supervision of passenger ships. Immigration statistics began to be reported to the Secretary of State quarterly and yearly from September 30 of that year. But to compare the migration statistics of the several years, one must be acquainted with the definition of the terms "passenger" and "immigrant" as settled in immigration acts or interpreted by administrative authorities.

I. Definition of "immigrant" and "emigrant"

From 1820 to 1867 the figures relate to *alien passengers* as such. Certain particulars (age and occupation for 1820-1867, and country of birth, for 1820-1855) are available only for passengers in general including citizens.

From 1868 to 1900 returns were prepared for *alien immigrants*, that is, passengers who arrive in the country and intend to reside there.

Until January 1, 1903, however, only third class passengers were counted as immigrants, and aliens who travelled first or second class were omitted.

On the other hand, down to the same date, passengers in transit were classed as immigrants.

Until 1907, aliens who had already on their first arrival been registered as immigrants were again reckoned among new immigrants, each time they returned.[1] After this date, only the first arrival counted.

From 1906 onward the figures relate to *immigrant aliens admitted*, and exclude "all aliens admitted who avowed an intention not to settle in the United States, and all returning to resume domiciles formerly acquired in this country". (*Annual Report*, 1906, p. 45.) That this definition still holds appears from the following recent communication:

"For statistical purposes immigrant aliens are those whose place of last permanent residence was in some foreign country, and who are coming to the United States with the intention of residing here permanently. Nonimmigrant aliens are of two classes: those whose place of last permanent residence was the United States, but who have been abroad for a short period of time, and those whose place of last permanent residence was in a foreign country, and who are coming to the United States without the intention of residing here permanently. The latter, or nonimmigrants, are merely travellers." (Letter of the Com-

[1] Willcox, Walter F. *Paper presented before the Committee on Basal Statistics of the Civic Federation's Immigration Department.*

missioner-General of Immigration to Professor Willcox, dated March 6, 1926.)

The immigration figures also omit aliens debarred and deported, and deserting seamen, even when a head tax has been paid for them.

Passengers departing from the seaports of the United States to foreign countries other than those of North America were reported from 1868 to 1907 (fiscal years ending June 30) through the courtesy of the owners or agents of vessels and not by statutory provisions. Such passengers were distinguished as cabin passengers and passengers other than cabin and classified both by sex and age (adults and children).

The Commissioner-General of Immigration states that "it is.probable that the departures given embrace nearly the entire passenger movement from the United States to foreign countries from our seaports". (Report 1907, p. 50.)

The statistics above referred to will be found in table XIV (1868-1902) and are quoted from a statistical summary in the above source; but we have not compared them with the corresponding figures contained in the reports of the Commissioner-General of Immigration. For recent years these passenger statistics which do not even distinguish aliens from citizens are of minor importance.

Emigrant aliens have been reported since 1908. According to the aforementioned letter, they stand in opposition to nonemigrant aliens or travellers: "The outgoing aliens," that letter says, "are similarly classified, *i. e.*, those who permanently change their country of residence are emigrants, and the travellers are nonemigrants. Residence for a year or more is regarded as permanent residence."

II. CONTINENTAL MIGRATIONS

Canadian, Cuban and Mexican citizens, arriving before 1908, directly from national ports, were not counted as immigrants, but if arriving via foreign ports were so counted.

Separate and complete figures showing migration *by land* from Canada and Mexico into the United States were first included in immigration statistics in the fiscal year ended June 30, 1908. From 1894 to 1902 the figures include European immigrants arriving in the Dominion of Canada destined to the United States, statistics which had never theretofore been furnished; from 1903 to 1907 they cover immigration into the United States via Canadian Atlantic seaports and all border stations; in 1908 for the first time the number of immigrant aliens admitted to the United States via land border stations was shown separately. (*Report of the Commissioner-General of Immigration* for 1908, p. 143.) The Commissioner-General of Immigration distinguishes immigrants and emigrants from and to Canada (and Mexico) according to nationality in the following way: (1) United States citizens; (2) Canadian (and Mexican) citizens; (3) citzens of other countries.

With regard to overland immigration, the immigrants are questioned at the frontier stations between the United States and Canada and Mexico respectively. Ordinary passengers and tourists are exempted from the more detailed examinations.

III. Citizens

The statistics of passengers inward and outward, which began to be published in 1820, did not distinguish citizens from aliens during the period 1868-1909. Prior to 1868 citizens are described as "passengers born in America" or "belonging to the United States," etc. The real migration statistics of the latter only date from 1910. As we are informed by the United States Commissioner-General of Immigration: "The figures for citizens, shown in Table I of the *Annual Report of the Commissioner-General of Immigration* for the fiscal year 1910 and the years following, cover all arrivals and departures, the latter including both the temporary and permanent class. Citizens leaving for permanent residence in some foreign country for a year or more are shown as such for the first time in the *Annual Report* for 1918. Table 47 (p. 137) of the Report for the fiscal year 1925 gives "the total number of citizens permanently departed during the eight years, as well as during each year, from 1918 to 1925, by principal countries of intended future permanent residence."

Citizens are further divided for statistical purposes into native-born and naturalised citizens.

IV. Fiscal and Calendar Years

The administrative year was frequently changed. Unless otherwise stated, it coincides with the fiscal year, *i. e.*

1820-31, the 12 months ending September 30.

1832, the 15 months ending December 31.

1833-42, calendar years.

1843, the 9 months ending September 30.

1844-49, the 12 months ending September 30.

1850, the 15 months ending December 31.

1851-67, calendar years.

1868, the 6 months ending June 30.

1869-1924, the 12 months ending June 30.

At our request the migration statistics relating to citizens were furnished for calendar years distinguishing intercontinental and continental directions (Canada and Mexico) during 1920-24.

V. Particulars

Sex and Age. Alien immigrants are distinguished since 1820 by sex (except for the year 1856, for which no figure is available). Before 1855 the sex of a certain number of persons was not recorded.

Three *age* groups are distinguished as a rule: (a) children; (b) up to 45 years, excluding children; (c) 45 years and over. Until 1898 the first group was designated, children under 15 years; from 1898 to 1917, less than 14 years; and from 1918, under 16 years.

Country of Origin and Nationality. Until 1898 the country of origin of the migrant aliens or their nationality or nativity was taken into consideration. After 1899, the country of last (or future) residence of the migrants and the "race or people" they belong to were both reported.

The table published after 1898, which shows nationality as well as country of last residence permits some comparison with earlier years,

TABLE I—Distribution of Alien Passengers Admitted, by Nationality 1820-1868.

Period	Total.	Europe						
		Austria-Hungary			Bel-gium	Den-mark	France	Ger-many
		Hun-gary	Other Austria (except Poland)	Total				
Year ending Sept. 30—								
1820	8,385	....	....	....	1	20	371	968
1821	9,127	....	....	....	2	12	370	383
1822	6,911	....	....	....	10	18	351	148
1823	6,354	....	....	....	2	6	460	183
1824	7,912	....	....	....	1	11	377	230
1825	10,199	....	....	....	1	14	515	450
1826	10,837	....	....	....	2	10	545	511
1827	18,875	....	....	....	7	15	1,280	432
1828	27,382	....	....	....	2	50	2,843	1,851
1829	22,520	....	....	....	....	17	582	597
1830	23,322	....	....	....	....	16	1,174	1,976
1831	22,633	....	....	....	1	23	2,038	2,413
15 mos. end. Dec.31,'32	60,482	....	....	....	....	21	5,361	10,194
Year ending Dec. 31—								
1833	58,640	....	....	....	....	173	4,682	6,988
1834	65,365	....	....	....	3	24	2,989	17,686
1835	45,374	....	....	....	1	37	2,696	8,311
1836	76,242	....	....	....	....	416	4,443	20,707
1837	79,340	....	....	....	....	109	5,074	23,740
1838	38,914	....	....	....	14	52	3,675	11,683
1839	68,069	....	....	....	1	56	7,198	21,028
1840	84,066	....	....	....	2	152	7,419	29,704
1841	80,289	....	....	....	106	31	5,006	15,291
1842	104,565	....	....	....	44	35	4,504	20,370
9 mos. end. Sept.30, '43	52,496	....	....	....	135	29	3,346	14,441
Year ending Sept. 30—								
1844	78,615	....	....	....	165	25	3,155	20,731
1845	114,371	....	....	....	541	54	7,663	34,355
1846	154,416	....	....	....	43	114	10,583	57,561
1847	234,968	....	....	....	1,473	13	20,040	74,281
1848	226,527	....	....	....	897	210	7,743	58,465
1849	297,024	....	....	....	590	8	5,841	60,235
1850	310,004	....	....	....	1,055	10	8,009	63,182
3 mos. end. Dec. 31, '50	59,976	....	....	....	25	10	1,372	15,714
Year ending Dec. 31—								
1851	379,466	....	....	....	....	14	20,126	72,482
1852	371,603	....	....	....	8	3	6,763	145,918
1853	368,645	....	....	....	87	32	10,770	141,946
1854	427,833	....	....	....	266	691	13,317	215,009
1855	200,877	....	....	....	1,506	528	6,044	71,918
1856	200,436	....	....	....	1,982	173	7,246	71,028
1857	251,306	....	....	....	627	1,035	2,397	91,781
1858	123,126	....	....	....	184	232	3,155	45,310
1859	121,282	....	....	....	25	499	2,579	41,784
1860	153,640	....	....	....	53	542	3,961	54,491
1861	91,918	2	49	51	153	234	2,326	31,651
1862	91,985	17	94	111	169	1,658	3,142	27,529
1863	176,282	28	57	85	301	1,492	1,838	33,162
1864	193,418	40	190	230	389	712	3,128	57,276
1865	248,120	322	100	422	741	1,149	3,583	83,424
1866	318,568	45	48	93	1,254	1,862	6,855	115,892
1867	315,722	25	667	692	789	1,436	5,237	133,426
6 mos. end. June 30, '68	138,840	....	....	192	14	819	1,989	55,831

TABLE I (continued).

| Period | Greece | Europe | | | | Malta | Nether-lands |
| | | Italy | | | | | |
		Italy (conti-nental)	Sardinia	Sicily	Total		
Year ending Sept. 30—							
1820............................	......	25	5	......	30	......	49
1821............................	......	62	......	......	62	......	56
1822............................	......	32	1	2	35	......	51
1823............................	......	32	1	......	33	1	19
1824............................	5	41	2	2	45	......	40
1825............................	......	58	17	......	75	1	37
1826............................	4	50	6	1	57	......	176
1827............................	......	35	......	......	35	1	245
1828............................	7	30	......	4	34	......	263
1829............................	1	16	......	7	23	......	169
1830............................	3	8	......	1	9	......	22
1831............................	......	28	......	......	28	......	175
15 months ending Dec.31,1832	1	2	......	1	3	2	205
Year ending Dec. 31—							
1833............................	1	1,693	......	6	1,699	5	39
1834............................	......	103	1	1	104	......	87
1835............................	7	56	......	4	61	......	124
1836............................	28	107	......	8	115	2	301
1837............................	5	36	......	......	36	......	312
1838............................	4	82	......	4	86	1	27
1839............................	......	76	6	2	84	30	85
1840............................	3	28	......	9	37	......	57
1841............................	......	166	......	13	179	66	214
1842............................	1	93	3	4	100	1	330
9 months ending Sept. 30, 1843	4	108	6	3	117	5	330
Year ending Sept. 30—							
1844............................	3	79	58	4	141	3	184
1845............................	2	63	69	5	137	......	791
1846............................	3	88	59	4	151	4	979
1847............................	......	160	......	4	164	......	2,631
1848............................	1	219	......	22	241	......	918
1849............................	......	208	......	1	209	......	1,190
1850............................	2	360	3	10	373	......	576
3 months ending Dec. 31, 1850	......	46	3	9	58	......	108
Year ending Dec. 31—							
1851............................	......	423	......	24	447	......	352
1852............................	10	297	10	44	351	......	1,719
1853............................	12	267	232	56	555	......	600
1854............................	1	984	219	60	1,263	2	1,534
1855............................	......	1,024	5	23	1,052	......	2,588
1856............................	2	962	380	23	1,365	......	1,395
1857............................	4	632	343	32	1,007	......	1,775
1858............................	......	889	257	94	1,240	2	185
1859............................	1	764	159	9	932	......	290
1860............................	1	770	185	64	1,019	1	351
1861............................	1	764	47	......	811	3	283
1862............................	5	541	25	......	566	......	432
1863............................	4	537	1	9	547	......	416
1864............................	5	597	......	3	600	......	708
1865............................	7	919	......	5	924	2	779
1866............................	10	1,287	......	95	1,382	3	1,716
1867............................	10	1,612	......	12	1,624	......	2,223
6 months ending June 30, 1868	......	......	......	......	891	......	345

TABLE I (continued).

Period	Europe						
	Nor-way and Sweden	Poland	Portu-gal	Russia (except Po-land)	Spain	Switzer-land	Turkey in Eu-rope
Year ending Sept. 30—							
1820	3	5	35	14	139	31	1
1821	12	1	18	7	191	93	......
1822	10	3	28	10	152	110	4
1823	1	3	24	7	220	47	2
1824	9	4	13	7	359	253	2
1825	4	1	13	10	273	166	......
1826	16	....	16	4	436	245	2
1827	13	1	7	19	414	297	1
1828	10	1	14	7	209	1,592	6
1829	13	....	9	1	202	314	1
1830	3	2	3	3	21	109	2
1831	13	....	....	1	37	63	......
15 months ending Dec. 31, 1832	313	34	5	52	106	129	......
Year ending Dec. 31—							
1833	16	1	633	159	516	634	1
1834	42	54	44	15	107	1,389	1
1835	31	54	29	9	183	548	......
1836	57	53	29	2	180	445	3
1837	290	81	34	19	230	383	......
1838	60	41	24	13	202	123	......
1839	324	46	19	7	428	607	1
1840	55	5	12	......	136	500	1
1841	195	15	7	174	215	751	6
1842	553	10	15	28	122	483	2
9 months ending Sept. 30, 1843	1,748	17	32	6	145	553	5
Year ending Sept. 30—							
1844	1,311	36	16	13	270	839	10
1845	928	6	14	1	304	471	3
1846	1,916	4	2	248	73	698	4
1847	1,307	8	5	5	158	192	2
1848	903	....	67	1	164	319	3
1849	3,473	4	26	44	329	13	9
1850	1,363	3	366	31	325	146	13
3 months ending Dec. 31, 1850	206	2	......	......	104	179	2
Year ending Dec. 31—							
1851	2,424	10	50	1	435	427	2
1852	4,103	110	68	2	391	2,788	3
1853	3,364	33	95	3	1,091	2,748	15
1854	3,531	208	72	2	1,433	7,953	7
1855	821	462	205	13	951	4,433	9
1856	1,157	20	128	9	786	1,780	5
1857	1,712	124	92	25	714	2,080	11
1858	2,430	9	177	246	1,282	1,056	17
1859	1,091	106	46	91	1,283	833	10
1860	298	82	122	65	932	913	4
1861	616	48	47	34	448	1,007	5
1862	892	63	72	79	348	643	11
1863	1,627	94	86	77	500	690	16
1864	2,249	165	240	256	917	1,396	11
1865	6,109	528	365	183	692	2,889	14
1866	12,633	412	344	287	718	3,823	18
1867	7,055	310	126	205	904	4,168	26
6 months ending June 30, 1868	11,166	....	174	141	384	1,945	4

TABLE I (continued).

Period	Europe						
	United Kingdom						Total Europe
	England	Scotland	Ireland	Wales	Not specified	Total	
Year ending Sept. 30—							
1820	1,782	268	3,614	......	360	6,024	7,691
1821	1,036	293	1,518	11	1,870	4,728	5,935
1822	856	198	2,267	13	154	3,488	4,418
1823	851	180	1,908	69	......	3,008	4,016
1824	713	257	2,345	33	261	3,609	4,965
1825	1,002	113	4,888	11	969	6,983	8,543
1826	1,459	230	5,408	6	624	7,727	9,751
1827	2,521	460	9,766	......	1,205	13,952	16,719
1828	2,735	1,041	12,488	17	1,559	17,840	24,729
1829	2,149	111	7,415	3	916	10,594	12,523
1830	733	29	2,721	7	384	3,874	7,217
1831	251	226	5,772	131	1,867	8,247	13,039
15 months ending Dec. 31,'1832	944	158	12,436	......	4,229	17,767	34,193
Year ending Dec. 31—							
1833	2,966	1,921	8,648	29	......	13,564	29,111
1834	1,129	110	24,474	1	9,250	34,964	57,510
1835	468	63	20,927	16	8,423	29,897	41,987
1836	420	106	30,578	2	12,578	43,684	70,465
1837	896	14	28,508	6	11,302	40,726	71,039
1838	157	48	12,645	......	5,215	18,065	34,070
1839	62	......	23,963	......	10,209	34,234	64,148
1840	318	21	39,430	......	2,274	42,043	80,126
1841	147	35	37,772	55	15,951	53,960	76,216
1842	1,743	24	51,342	38	20,200	73,347	99,946
9 months ending Sept. 30, 1843	3,517	41	19,670	......	4,872	28,100	49,013
Year ending Sept. 30—							
1844	1,357	23	33,490	3	12,970	47,843	74,745
1845	1,710	368	44,821	11	17,121	64,031	109,301
1846	2,854	305	51,752	187	18,874	73,932	146,315
1847	3,476	337	105,536	145	19,344	128,838	229,117
1848	4,455	659	112,934	348	29,697	148,093	218,025
1849	6,036	1,060	159,398	272	47,764	214,530	286,501
1850	5,276	627	133,806	49	35,727	175,485	250,939
3 months ending Dec. 31, 1850	1,521	233	30,198	193	7,459	39,604	57,384
Year ending Dec. 31—							
1851	5,306	966	221,253	211	45,004	272,740	369,510
1852	30,007	8,148	159,548	741	1,803	200,247	362,484
1853	28,867	6,006	162,649	222	2,481	200,225	361,576
1854	48,901	4,605	101,606	816	4,325	160,253	405,542
1855	38,871	5,275	49,627	1,176	2,250	97,199	187,729
1856	25,904	3,297	54,349	1,126	14,331	99,007	186,083
1857	27,804	4,182	54,361	769	25,724	112,840	216,224
1858	14,638	1,946	26,873	316	12,056	55,829	111,354
1859	13,826	2,293	35,216	332	9,712	61,379	110,949
1860	13,001	1,613	48,637	610	14,513	78,374	141,209
1861	8,970	767	23,797	461	9,477	43,472	81,200
1862	10,947	657	23,351	536	12,499	47,990	83,710
1863	24,065	1,940	55,916	705	40,172	122,798	163,733
1864	26,096	3,476	63,523	628	23,228	116,951	185,233
1865	15,038	3,037	29,772	146	64,244	112,237	214,048
1866	3,559	1,038	36,690	23	90,304	131,614	278,916
1867	36,972	7,582	72,879	143	7,944	125,520	283,751
6 months ending June 30, 1868	[2]	[2]	32,068	[2]	24,127	56,195	130,090

For reference notes see page 500.

TABLE I (continued).

Period	Central America	South America	West Indies	China	India	Japan
Year ending Sept. 30—						
1820	2	11	164	1	1	.....
1821	....	8	107	....	....	.....
1822	3	7	159	....	1	.....
1823	....	20	160	....	....	.....
1824	10	25	259	....	1	.....
1825	8	67	389	1	....	.....
1826	12	63	427	....	1	.....
1827	7	54	227	....	1	.....
1828	5	77	652	....	3	.....
1829	10	73	517	1	1	.....
1830	50	137	937	....	....	.....
1831	3	42	1,281	....	1	.....
15 months ending Dec. 31, 1832	6	174	1,256	....	4	.....
Year ending Dec. 31—						
1833	18	27	1,264	....	3	.....
1834	9	74	791	....	6	.....
1835	4	145	938	8	8	.....
1836	....	146	1,178	....	4	.....
1837	4	91	1,627	....	11	.....
1838	....	72	1,231	....	1	.....
1839	....	49	1,289	....	....	.....
1840	....	36	1,446	....	1	.....
1841	....	219	1,042	2	1	.....
1842	1	102	1,410	4	2	.....
9 months ending Sept. 30, 1843	12	62	880	3	2	.....
Year ending Sept. 30—						
1844	....	61	771	3	1	.....
1845	21	80	1,241	6	....	.....
1846	5	92	1,351	7	4	.....
1847	21	70	1,251	4	8	.....
1848	4	150	1,338	....	6	.....
1849	233	190	1,073	3	8	.....
1850	71	2,462	2,903	3	4	.....
3 months ending Dec. 31, 1850	....	91	268	....	....	.....
Year ending Dec. 31—						
1851	96	59	1,929	....	2	.....
1852	....	39	1,232	....	4	.....
1853	....	38	406	42	5	.....
1854	24	136	1,036	13,100	....	.....
1855	1	191	887	3,526	6	.....
1856	303	184	1,337	4,733	13	.....
1857	2	83	923	5,944	1	.....
1858	11	131	647	5,128	5	.....
1859	4	155	879	3,457	2	.....
1860	8	208	1,384	5,467	5	.....
1861	21	97	358	7,518	6	1
1862	27	146	585	3,633	5	.....
1863	2	94	491	7,214	1	.....
1864	2	152	718	2,975	6	.....
1865	....	148	851	2,942	5	.....
1866	4	294	895	2,385	17	7
1867	3	224	817	3,863	2	67
6 months ending June 30, 1868	....	82	419	5,157	....	.....

TABLE I (continued).

Period	Asia, not specified	Total Asia	Africa	Islands of the Atlantic[1]	Oceania
Year ending Sept. 30—					
1820	3	5	1	6	1
1821			2	1	
1822		1		6	2
1823				2	
1824		1		1	
1825		1	1	9	
1826		1		13	
1827		1	4	5	
1828		3	6	17	
1829		2	1	290	
1830			2	8	
1831		1	2	2	1
15 months ending Dec. 31, 1832		4	2	5	
Year ending Dec. 31—					
1833		3	1	8	
1834		6	1	32	
1835	1	17	14	18	3
1836		4	6	5	2
1837		11	2	5	
1838		1	10	8	
1839			8	7	1
1840		1	6	13	2
1841		3	14	3	3
1842	1	7	3	5	
9 months ending Sept. 30, 1843	6	11	6	8	5
Year ending Sept. 30—					
1844	2	6	14	24	
1845		6	4	7	
1846		11	1	18	
1847		12		24	1
1848	2	8	10	20	3
1849		11	3	48	
1850		7		180	17
3 months ending Dec. 31, 1850					
Year ending Dec. 31—					
1851		2	3	113	
1852		4		182	
1853		47	8	264	
1854		13,100		271	31
1855	8	3,540	14	177	12
1856	1	4,747	6	360	10
1857		5,945	25	679	12
1858		5,133	17	303	36
1859	2	3,461	11	418	48
1860	4	5,476	126	323	9
1861	3	7,528	47	287	21
1862	2	3,640	12	161	34
1863	1	7,216	3	227	29
1864	1	2,982	37	466	6
1865		2,947	49	553	73
1866	2	2,411	33	358	14
1867	29	3,961	25	391	1
6 months ending June 30, 1868	14	5,171	3		

For reference notes see page 500.

TABLE I (concluded).

Period	All other countries and countries not stated	Total inter-continental	British North America	Mexico	Total continental
Year ending Sept. 30—					
1820	294	8,174	209	1	210
1821	2,886	8,939	184	4	188
1822	2,106	6,702	204	5	209
1823	1,954	6,152	167	35	202
1824	2,386	7,647	155	110	265
1825	799	9,817	314	68	382
1826	241	10,508	223	106	329
1827	1,566	18,583	165	127	292
1828	537	26,026	267	1,089	1,356
1829	6,405	19,821	409	2,290	2,699
1830	13,799	22,150	189	983	1,172
1831	7,394	21,765	176	692	868
15 months ending Dec. 31, 1832	23,407	59,047	608	827	1,435
Year ending Dec. 31—					
1833	26,235	56,667	1,194	779	1,973
1834	5,037	63,460	1,020	885	1,905
1835	23	43,149	1,193	1,032	2,225
1836	824	72,630	2,814	798	3,612
1837	4,655	77,434	1,279	627	1,906
1838	1,835	37,227	1,476	211	1,687
1839	288	65,790	1,926	353	2,279
1840	103	81,733	1,938	395	2,333
1841	621	78,121	1,816	352	2,168
1842	610	102,084	2,078	403	2,481
9 months ending Sept. 30, 1843	599	50,596	1,502	398	1,900
Year ending Sept. 30—					
1844	86	75,707	2,711	197	2,908
1845	18	110,678	3,195	498	3,693
1846	2,546	150,339	3,855	222	4,077
1847	583	231,079	3,827	62	3,889
1848	472	220,030	6,473	24	6,497
1849	1,557	289,616	6,890	518	7,408
1850	45,131	301,710	7,796	498	8,294
3 months ending Dec. 31, 1850	554	58,297	1,580	99	1,679
Year ending Dec. 31—					
1851	135	371,847	7,438	181	7,619
1852	1,238	365,179	6,352	72	6,424
1853	720	363,059	5,424	162	5,586
1854	356	420,496	6,891	446	7,337
1855	145	192,692	7,761	420	8,181
1856	172	193,202	6,493	741	7,234
1857	21,610	245,503	5,670	133	5,803
1858	462	118,094	4,603	429	5,032
1859	929	116,854	4,163	265	4,428
1860	154	148,897	4,514	229	4,743
1861	72	89,631	2,069	218	2,287
1862	253	88,568	3,275	142	3,417
1863	927	172,722	3,464	96	3,560
1864	87	189,683	3,636	99	3,735
1865	7,672	226,341	21,586	193	21,779
1866	3,254	286,179	32,150	239	32,389
1867	2,878	292,051	23,379	292	23,671
6 months ending June 30, 1868	161	135,926	2,785	129	2,914

TABLE II—Distribution of immigrant aliens admitted, by country of origin
or nationality (fiscal year ended June 30) 1869-1898.

Country	1869	1870	1871	1872	1873	1874
Bohemia........................	......	......	......	......	......	......
Other Austria (except Poland)	1,495	4,424	4,884	4,182	5,765	7,888
Total...................	1,495	4,424	4,884	4,182	5,765	7,888
Hungary...................	4	1	3	228	1,347	962
Belgium..................	1,922	1,002	774	738	1,176	817
Denmark.................	3,649	4,083	2,015	3,690	4,931	3,082
France....................	3,879	4,009	3,138	9,317	14,798	9,644
Germany..................	131,042	118,225	82,554	141,109	119,671	87,291
Greece...................	8	22	11	12	23	36
Italy.....................	1,489	2,891	2,816	4,190	8,757	7,666
Netherlands..............	1,134	1,066	993	1,909	3,811	2,444
Norway...................	16,068	13,216	9,418	11,421	16,247	10,384
Portugal..................	87	255	290	416	24	60
Poland....................	184	223	535	1,647	3,338	1,795
Russia....................	343	907	673	994	1,560	3,960
Finland...................	......	......	......	24	74	113
Rumania..................	......	......	......	......	......	......
Spain.....................	1,123	663	558	595	541	485
Sweden...................	24,224	13,443	10,699	13,464	14,303	5,712
Switzerland...............	3,650	3,075	2,269	3,650	3,107	3,093
Turkey in Europe..........	18	6	23	20	53	62
United Kingdom.						
England..............	35,673	60,957	56,530	69,764	74,801	50,905
Scotland.............	7,751	12,521	11,984	13,916	13,841	10,429
Ireland..............	40,786	56,996	57,439	68,732	77,344	53,707
Wales................	660	1,011	899	1,214	840	665
U. K. not specified......	40,354	29,188	16,042	18	18	22
Total United Kingdom....	125,224	160,673	142,894	153,644	166,844	115,728
Other Europe.............	420	442	598	905	1,171	1,561
Total Europe............	315,963	328,626	265,145	352,155	397,541	262,783
China....................	12,874	15,740	7,135	7,788	20,292	13,776
India....................	3	24	14	12	15	17
Japan....................	63	48	78	17	9	21
Turkey in Asia............	2	......	4	......	3	6
Other Asia...............	7	13	9	8	6	18
Total Asia...............	12,949	15,825	7,240	7,825	20,325	13,838
Africa....................	72	31	24	41	28	58
Oceania..................	......	36	21	2,416	1,414	1,193
Central America...........	3	33	4	8	38	20
West Indies including						
Bermuda..............	2,236	1,682	1,251	1,350	1,654	1,829
South America............	91	69	96	102	166	144
Other countries...........	17	27	85	164	160	128
Total intercontinental.....	331,331	346,329	273,866	364,061	421,326	279,993
British North America.......	21,117	40,411	47,082	40,176	37,871	32,950
Mexico...................	320	463	402	569	606	386
Total continental.........	21,437	40,874	47,484	40,745	38,477	33,346
Grand total...............	352,768	387,203	321,350	404,806	459,803	313,339

TABLE II (continued).

Country	1875	1876	1877	1878	1879	1880
Bohemia..................	.....	.....	.....	.....	.....	.....
Other Austria (except Poland)	6,882	5,646	5,023	4,504	5,331	12,904
Total..................	6,882	5,646	5,023	4,504	5,331	12,904
Hungary..................	776	630	373	646	632	4,363
Belgium..................	615	515	488	354	512	1,232
Denmark..................	2,656	1,547	1,695	2,105	3,474	6,576
France..................	8,321	8,004	5,856	4,159	4,655	4,314
Germany..................	47,769	31,937	29,298	29,313	34,602	84,638
Greece..................	25	19	24	16	21	23
Italy..................	3,631	3,015	3,195	4,344	5,791	12,354
Netherlands..................	1,237	855	591	608	753	3,340
Norway..................	6,093	5,173	4,588	4,759	7,345	19,895
Portugal..................	763	471	1,291	660	392	260
Poland..................	984	925	533	547	489	2,177
Russia..................	7,982	4,765	6,579	3,037	4,434	4,854
Finland..................	15	10	20	11	19	160
Rumania..................	.....	.....	.....	.....	.....	11
Spain..................	601	518	665	457	457	389
Sweden..................	5,573	5,603	4,991	5,390	11,001	39,186
Switzerland..................	1,814	1,549	1,686	1,808	3,161	6,156
Turkey in Europe..........	27	38	32	29	29	24
United Kingdom:						
England..................	40,130	24,373	19,161	18,405	24,183	59,454
Scotland..................	7,310	4,582	4,135	3,502	5,225	12,640
Ireland..................	37,957	19,575	14,569	15,932	20,013	71,603
Wales..................	449	324	281	243	543	1,173
U. K. not specified.....	16	12	4	.....	4	6
Total United Kingdom....	85,862	48,866	38,150	38,082	49,968	144,876
Other Europe.............	1,335	834	1,117	783	1,193	959
Total Europe............	182,961	120,920	106,195	101,612	134,259	348,691
China..................	16,437	22,781	10,594	8,992	9,604	5,802
India..................	19	25	17	8	15	21
Japan..................	3	4	7	2	4	4
Turkey in Asia.............	1	8	3	7	31	4
Other Asia.................	39	125	19	5	6	8
Total Asia...............	16,499	22,943	10,640	9,014	9,660	5,839
Africa..................	54	89	16	18	12	18
Oceania..................	1,268	1,312	914	606	816	954
Central America...........	15	15	7	50	9	44
West Indies including Bermuda..................	1,832	1,413	1,410	1,033	1,141	1,362
South America.............	132	156	87	88	69	88
Other countries............	76	36	27	15	36	63
Total intercontinental.....	202,837	146,884	119,296	112,436	146,002	357,059
British North America.......	24,051	22,471	22,116	25,568	31,268	99,706
Mexico..................	610	631	445	465	556	492
Total continental........	24,661	23,102	22,561	26,033	31,824	100,198
Grand total..............	227,498	169,986	141,857	138,469	177,826	457,257

TABLE II (continued).

Country	1881	1882	1883	1884	1885	1886
Bohemia.............	....	6,602	5,462	8,239	6,352	4,314
Other Austria (except Poland)	21,109	13,619	10,923	13,534	11,574	11,946
Total.................	21,109	20,221	16,385	21,773	17,926	16,260
Hungary.................	6,826	8,929	11,240	14,798	9,383	12,420
Belgium.................	1,766	1,431	1,450	1,576	1,653	1,300
Denmark.................	9,117	11,618	10,319	9,202	6,100	6,225
France.................	5,227	6,004	4,821	3,608	3,495	3,318
Germany.................	210,485	250,630	194,786	179,676	124,443	84,403
Greece.................	19	126	73	37	172	104
Italy.................	15,401	32,159	31,792	16,510	13,642	21,315
Netherlands.................	8,597	9,517	5,249	4,198	2,689	2,314
Norway.................	22,705	29,101	23,398	16,974	12,356	12,759
Portugal.................	171	42	176	701	440	238
Poland.................	5,614	4,672	2,011	4,536	3,085	3,939
Russia.................	4,865	16,321	9,186	11,854	16,603	17,309
Finland.................	176	597	723	835	555	491
Rumania.................	30	65	77	238	803	494
Spain.................	484	378	262	300	350	344
Sweden.................	49,760	64,607	38,277	26,552	22,248	27,751
Switzerland.................	11,293	10,844	12,751	9,386	5,895	4,805
Turkey in Europe..........	72	69	86	150	138	176
United Kingdom:						
England.................	65,177	82,394	63,140	55,918	47,332	49,767
Scotland..............	15,168	18,937	11,859	9,060	9,226	12.126
Ireland.................	72,342	76,432	81,486	63,344	51,795	49,619
Wales.................	1,027	1,656	1,597	901	1,127	1,027
U. K. not specified......	4	4	10	71	28	9
Total United Kingdom....	153,718	179,423	158,092	129,294	109,508	112,548
Other Europe..............	1,110	1,432	1,433	1,488	1,599	1,016
Total Europe.............	528,545	648,186	522,587	453,686	353,083	329,529
China.................	11,890	39,579	8,031	279	22	40
India.................	33	10	9	12	34	17
Japan.................	11	5	27	20	49	194
Turkey in Asia.............	5	....	....	....	....	15
Other Asia.................	43	35	46	199	93	51
Total Asia..............	11,982	39,629	8,113	510	198	317
Africa.................	33	60	67	59	112	122
Oceania.................	1,191	889	747	900	679	1,136
Central America...........	29	20	9	23	24	32
West Indies including Bermuda.................	1,722	1,357	933	2,237	2,521	2,748
South America.............	110	91	77	65	44	246
Other countries............	103	99	79	98	71	73
Total intercontinental.....	543,715	690,331	532,612	457,578	356,732	334,203
British North America.......	125,391	98,295	70,241	60,584	38,291	....
Mexico.................	325	366	469	430	323	....
Total continental.........	125,716	98,661	70,710	61,014	38,614	....
Grand total..............	669,431	788,992	603,322	518,592	395,346	334,203

TABLE II (continued).

Country	1887	1888	1889	1890	1891	1892[3]
Bohemia....................	4,579	4,127	3,085	4,505	11,758	....
Other Austria(except Poland)	20,430	25,884	20,122	29,632	30,918	....
Total....................	25,009	30,011	23,207	34,137	42,676	} 76,937
Hungary...................	15,256	15,800	10,967	22,062	28,366	
Belgium...................	2,553	3,215	2,562	2,671	3,037	4,026
Denmark..................	8,524	8,962	8,699	9,366	10,659	10,125
France....................	5,034	6,454	5,918	6,585	6,770	4,678
Germany..................	106,865	109,717	99,538	92,427	113,554	119,168
Greece....................	313	782	158	524	1,105	660
Italy.....................	47,622	51,558	25,307	52,003	76,055	61,631
Netherlands...............	4,506	5,845	6,460	4,326	5,206	6,141
Norway...................	16,269	18,264	13,390	11,370	12,568	14,325
Portugal..................	110	23	57	158	918	3,400
Poland...................	6,128	5,826	4,922	11,073	27,497	40,536
Russia....................	28,944	31,256	31,889	33,147	42,145	} 81,511
Finland...................	1,822	2,231	2,027	2,451	5,281	
Rumania..................	2,045	1,186	893	517	957	....
Spain.....................	436	526	526	813	905	4,078
Sweden...................	42,836	54,698	35,415	29,632	36,880	41,845
Switzerland...............	5,214	7,737	7,070	6,993	6,811	6,886
Turkey in Europe..........	206	207	252	206	265	1,331
United Kingdom:						
England...............	72,855	82,574	68,503	57,020	53,600	34,309
Scotland..............	18,699	24,457	18,296	12,041	12,557	7,177
Ireland...............	68,370	73,513	65,557	53,024	55,706	51,383
Wales................	1,820	1,654	1,181	650	424	729
U. K. not specified......	4	7	12	19	24	....
Total United Kingdom....	161,748	182,205	153,549	122,754	122,311	93,598
Other Europe.............	1,389	1,628	1,984	2,465	2,119	....
Total Europe............	482,829	538,131	434,790	445,680	546,085	570,876
China....................	10	26	118	1,716	2,836	....
India.....................	32	20	59	43	42	....
Japan.....................	229	404	640	691	1,136	....
Turkey in Asia............	208	273	593	1,126	2,488	....
Other Asia................	136	120	315	872	1,176	....
Total Asia...............	615	843	1,725	4,448	7,678	....
Africa....................	40	65	187	112	103	....
Oceania..................	1,282	2,387	2,196	1,167	1,301	267
Central America...........	23	67	88	147	285	....
West Indies including Bermuda.................	4,881	4,895	4,944	3,248	4,133	....
South America............	366	440	427	438	664	....
Other countries...........	73	61	70	62	70	8,520
Total intercontinental.....	490,109	546,889	444,427	455,302	560,319	579,663
British North America.......	....	....	....	....	....	....
Mexico...................	....	....	....	....	....	....
Total continental........	....	....	....	....	....	....
Grand total...............	490,109	546,889	444,427	455,302	560,319	579,663

For reference notes see page 500.

TABLE II (concluded).

Country	1893[3]	1894[3]	1895[3]	1896	1897	1898
Europe						
Austria-Hungary............	57,420	38,638	33,401	65,103	33,031	39,797
Belgium..................	3,324	1,709	1,058	1,261	760	695
Bulgaria, Serbia and Monte-negro..................	....	....	....	....	....	....
Denmark.................	7,720	5,003	3,910	3,167	2,085	1,946
France, including Corsica....	3,621	3,080	2,628	2,463	2,107	1,990
Germany.................	78,756	53,989	32,173	31,885	22,533	17,111
Greece...................	1,072	1,356	597	2,175	571	2,339
Italy, including Sicily and Sardinia..............	72,145	42,977	35,427	68,060	59,131	58,613
Netherlands..............	6,199	1,820	1,388	1,583	890	767
Norway..................	15,515	9,111	7,581	8,855	5,842	4,938
Poland...................	16,374	1,941	790	691	4,165	4,726
Portugal, including Cape Verde, and Azores......	4,816	2,196	1,452	2,766	1,874	1,717
Rumania.................	....	729	523	785	791	900
Russian Empire...........	42,310	39,278	35,907	51,445	25,816	29,828
Spain, including Canary and Balearic Islands........	206	925	501	351	448	577
Sweden..................	35,710	18,286	15,361	21,177	13,162	12,398
Switzerland..............	4,744	2,905	2,239	2,304	1,566	1,246
Turkey in Europe..........	625	298	245	169	152	176
United Kingdom:						
England..............	27,931	17,747	23,443	19,492	9,974	9,877
Ireland...............	43,578	30,231	46,304	40,262	28,421	25,128
Scotland..............	6,215	3,772	3,788	3,483	1,883	1,797
Wales................	1,043	1,001	1,602	1,581	870	1,219
Not specified..........	....	....	....	9	25	1
Other Europe.............	....	60	24	....	....	....
Total Europe..........	429,324	277,052	250,342	329,067	216,397	217,786
Asia						
China...................	472	1,170	539	1,441	3,363	2,071
India...................	....	....	....	....	....	....
Japan...................	1,380	1,931	1,150	1,110	1,526	2,230
Turkey in Asia............	....	....	2,767	4,139	4,732	4,275
Other Asia...............	540	1,589	39	74	41	61
Total Asia.............	2,392	4,690	4,495	6,764	9,662	8,637
Africa...................	....	24	36	21	37	48
Oceania.................	248	244	155	112	199	201
Central America...........	....	32	16	12	5	5
West Indies incl. Jamaica....	2,593	3,177	3,096	6,828	4,101	2,124
South America............	....	39	36	35	49	39
Countries not specified......	5,173	70	....	....	....	....
Total intercontinental.....	439,730	285,328	258,176	342,839	230,450	228,840
British North America.......	....	194	244	278	291	352
Mexico..................	....	109	116	150	91	107
Total continental........	....	303	360	428	382	459
Grand total...............	439,730	285,631	258,536	343,267	230,832	229,299

For reference notes see page 500.

TABLE III—Admission of immigrant aliens, by country of last residence (fiscal year ended June 30) 1899-1924

Country	1899	1900	1901	1902	1903
Austria............................ Hungary...........................	} 62,491	114,847	113,390	171,989	206,011
Belgium...........................	1,101	1,196	1,579	2,577	3,450
Bulgaria[4].........................	52	108	657	851	1,761
Czechoslovakia....................					
Denmark..........................	2,690	2,926	3,655	5,660	7,158
Finland...........................					
France, including Corsica.......	1,694	1,739	3,150	3,117	5,578
Germany..........................	17,476	18,507	21,651	28,304	40,086
Greece............................	2,333	3,771	5,910	8,104	14,090
Italy, including Sicily and Sardinia...............................	77,419	100,135	135,996	178,375	230,622
Netherlands.......................	1,029	1,735	2,349	2,284	3,998
Norway...........................	6,705	9,575	12,248	17,484	24,461
Poland............................					
Portugal including Cape Verde and Azores......................	2,054	4,234	4,165	5,307	9,317
Rumania..........................	1,606	6,459	7,155	7,196	9,310
Russia[5]..........................	60,982	90,787	85,257	107,347	136,093
Spain, including Canary and Balearic Islands..............	385	355	592	975	2,080
Sweden...........................	12,797	18,650	23,331	30,894	46,028
Switzerland.......................	1,326	1,152	2,201	2,344	3,983
Turkey in Europe.................	80	285	387	187	1,529
United Kingdom:					
England.......................		9,951	12,214	13,575	26,219
Ireland........................	45,123	35,730	30,561	29,138	35,310
Scotland.......................		1,792	2,070	2,560	6,143
Wales.........................		764	701	763	1,275
Yugoslavia (Serb, Croat and Slovene Kingdom)................					
Other Europe.....................	6	2	18	37	5
Total Europe	297,349	424,700	469,237	619,068	814,507
China.............................	1,660	1,247	2,459	1,649	2,209
Japan............................	2,844	12,635	5,269	14,270	19,968
India.............................	17	9	22	93	94
Turkey in Asia...................	4,436	3,962	5,782	6,223	7,118
Other Asia.......................	15	93	61	36	577
Total Asia...................	8,972	17,946	13,593	22,271	29,966
Africa............................	51	30	173	37	176
Australia, Tasmania, and New Zealand.........................	456	214	325	384	1,150
Pacific Islands (not specified)....	354	214	173	182	199
Central America..................	159	42	150	305	678
South America...................	89	124	203	337	589
West Indies.......................	2,585	4,656	3,176	4,711	8,170
Other countries..................	217	13	1	103	25
Total intercontinental........	310,232	447,939	487,031	647,398	855,460
Canada...........................	1,322	396	540	636	1,058
Mexico...........................	161	237	347	709	528
Total continental............	1,483	633	887	1,345	1,586
Grand total..................	311,715	448,572	487,918	648,743	857,046

For reference notes see page 500.

TABLE III (continued).

Country	1904	1905	1906	1907	1908
Austria............................	} 177,156	111,990	111,598	144,992	82,983
Hungary..........................		163,703	153,540	193,460	85,526
Belgium..........................	3,976	5,302	5,099	6,396	4,162
Bulgaria[4]........................	1,325	2,043	4,666	11,359	10,827
Czechoslovakia...................	....	....	....	....	....
Denmark.........................	8,525	8,970	7,741	7,243	4,954
Finland...........................	....	....	....	....	....
France, including Corsica.......	9,406	10,168	9,386	9,731	8,788
Germany..........................	46,380	40,574	37,564	37,807	32,309
Greece...........................	11,343	10,515	19,489	36,580	21,489
Italy, including Sicily and Sardinia............................	193,296	221,479	273,120	285,731	128,503
Netherlands......................	4,916	4,954	4,946	6,637	5,946
Norway...........................	23,808	25,064	21,730	22,133	12,412
Poland............................	....	....	....	....	....
Portugal including Cape Verde and Azores......................	6,715	5,028	8,517	9,608	7,307
Rumania..........................	7,087	4,437	4,476	4,384	5,228
Russia[5].........................	145,141	184,897	215,665	258,943	156,711
Spain, including Canary and Balearic Islands...............	3,996	2,600	1,921	5,784	3,899
Sweden...........................	27,763	25,591	23,310	20,589	12,809
Switzerland.......................	5,023	4,269	3,846	3,748	3,281
Turkey in Europe................	4,344	4,542	9,510	20,767	11,290
United Kingdom:					
England.....................	38,626	64,709	49,491	56,637	47,031
Ireland......................	36,142	52,945	34,995	34,530	30,556
Scotland....................	11,092	16,977	15,866	19,740	13,506
Wales.......................	1,730	2,503	1,841	2,660	2,287
Yugoslavia (Serb, Croat and Slovene Kingdom).............	....	....	....	....	....
Other Europe....................	143	13	48	107	97
Total Europe................	767,933	974.273	1,018,365	1,199,566	691,901
China............................	4,309	2,166	1,544	961	1,397
Japan............................	14,264	10,331	13,835	30,226	15,803
India.............................	261	190	216	898	1,040
Turkey in Asia..................	5,235	6,157	6,354	8,053	9,753
Other Asia.......................	2,117	5,081	351	386	372
Total Asia..................	26,186	23,925	22,300	40,524	28,365
Africa............................	686	757	712	1,486	1,411
Australia, Tasmania, and New Zealand,....................	1,461	2,091	1,682	1,947	1,098
Pacific Islands (not specified)....	94	75	51	42	81
Central America.................	714	1,195	1,140	970	1,217
South America...................	1,667	2,576	2,757	2,779	2,315
West Indies......................	10,193	16,641	13,656	16,689	11,888
Other countries..................	90	161	33,012	22	17
Total intercontinental........	809.024	1,021,694	1,093,675	1,264,025	738,293
Canada..........................	2,837	2,168	5,063	19,918	38,510
Mexico...........................	1,009	2,637	1,997	1,406	6,067
Total continental. ·..........	3,846	4,805	7,060	21,324	44,577
Grand total....................	812,870	1.026,499	1,100,735	1,285,349	782,870

For reference notes see page 500.

TABLE III (continued).

Country	1909	1910	1911	1912	1913
Austria.....................	80,853	135,793	82,129	85,854	137,245
Hungary....................	89,338	122,944	76,928	93,028	117,580
Belgium	3,692	5,402	5,711	4,169	7,405
Bulgaria⁴	1,054	4,737	4,695	4,447	1,753
Czechoslovakia.............	....	....	....	....	....
Denmark...................	4,395	6,984	7,555	6,191	6,478
Finland....................	....	....	....	....	....
France, including Corsica.......	6,672	7,383	8,022	8,628	9,675
Germany....................	25,540	31,283	32,061	27,788	34,329
Greece.....................	14,111	25,888	26,226	21,449	22,817
Italy, including Sicily and Sardinia...................	183,218	215,537	182,882	157,134	265,542
Netherlands.................	4,698	7,534	8,358	6,619	6,902
Norway....................	13,627	17,538	13,950	8,675	8,587
Poland.....................	....	....	....	....	....
Portugal including Cape Verde and Azores...............	4,956	8,229	8,374	10,230	14,171
Rumania...................	1,590	2,145	2,522	1,997	2,155
Russia⁵	120,460	186,792	158,721	162,395	291,040
Spain, including Canary and Balearic Islands...........	2,616	3,472	5,074	6,327	6,167
Sweden.....................	14,474	23,745	20,780	12,688	17,202
Switzerland.................	2,694	3,533	3,458	3,505	4,104
Turkey in Europe.............	9,015	18,405	14,438	14,481	14,128
United Kingdom:					
England.................	32,809	46,706	52,426	40,408	43,363
Ireland.................	25,033	29,855	29,112	25,879	27,876
Scotland................	12,400	20,115	18,796	14,578	14,220
Wales..................	1,584	2,120	2,162	2,162	2,745
Yugoslavia (Serb, Croat and Slovene Kingdom)	....	....	....	....	....
Other Europe................	46	151	377	243	371
Total Europe...............	654,875	926,291	764,757	718,875	1,055,855
China......................	1,943	1,968	1,460	1,765	2,105
Japan.......................	3,111	2,720	4,520	6,114	8,281
India.......................	203	1,696	524	175	179
Turkey in Asia...............	7,506	15,212	10,229	12,788	23,955
Other Asia..................	141	1,937	695	607	838
Total Asia..................	12,904	23,533	17,428	21,449	35,358
Africa......................	858	1,072	956	1,009	1,409
Australia, Tasmania, and New Zealand...................	839	998	984	794	1,229
Pacific Islands (not specified)....	53	99	59	104	111
Central America..............	930	893	1,193	1,242	1,473
South America...............	1,906	2,151	3,049	2,989	4.248
West Indies.................	11,180	11,244	13,403	12,467	12,458
Other countries..............	49	43	39	15	23
Total intercontinental........	683,594	966,324	801,868	758,944	1,112,164
Canada.....................	51,941	56,555	56,830	55,990	73,802
Mexico.....................	16,251	18,691	19,889	23,238	11,926
Total continental...........	6,8192	75,246	76,719	79,228	85,728
Grand total.................	751,786	1,041,570	878,587	838,172	1,197,892

For reference notes see page 500.

TABLE III (continued).

Country	1914	1915	1916	1917	1918
Albania....................	....	....	....	....	....
Austria....................	134,831	9,215	3,171	857	53
Hungary...................	143,321	9,296	2,020	401	8
Belgium...................	5,763	2,399	986	398	73
Bulgaria[4].................	9,189	1,403	764	151	19
Czechoslovakia.............	....	....	....	....	....
Denmark..................	6,262	3,312	3,322	2,744	1,630
Estonia...................	....	....	....	....	....
Finland...................	....	....	....	....	....
France, including Corsica.......	9,296	4,811	4,156	3,187	1,798
Germany...................	35,734	7,799	2,877	1,857	447
Greece....................	35,832	12,592	27,034	23,974	1,910
Italy, incl. Sicily and Sardinia..	283,738	49,688	33,665	34,596	5,250
Latvia....................	....	....	....	....	....
Lithuania.................	....	....	....	....	....
Netherlands...............	6,321	3,144	2,910	2,235	944
Norway...................	8,329	7,986	5,191	4,659	2,578
Poland....................	....	....	....	....	....
Portugal, including Cape Verde and Azores...............	10,898	4,907	12,259	9,975	2,224
Rumania...................	4,032	481	90	66	59
Russia[5]..................	255,660	26,187	7,842	12,716	4,242
Spain, including Canary and Balearic Islands...........	7,591	2,762	5,769	10,232	4,295
Sweden...................	14,800	6,585	6,248	6,368	2,298
Switzerland...............	4,211	1,742	663	911	331
Turkey in Europe...........	8,199	1,008	313	152	15
United Kingdom:					
England..................	35,864	21,562	12,896	8,354	2,037
Ireland..................	24,688	14,185	8,639	5,406	331
Scotland.................	10,682	4,668	2,655	1,868	260
Wales....................	2,183	1,007	512	513	219
Yugoslavia (Serb, Croat and Slovene Kingdom)........	....	....	....	....	....
Other Europe..............	967	1,180	1,717	1,463	42
Total Europe..............	1,058,391	197,919	145,699	133,083	31,063
China....................	2,502	2,660	2,460	2,237	1,795
Japan....................	8,929	8,613	8,680	8,991	10,213
India....................	221	161	112	109	130
Syria, Mesopotamia and Pa'estine	....	....	....	....	....
Turkey in Asia..............	21,716	3,543	1,670	393	43
Other Asia................	905	234	282	1,026	520
Total Asia................	34,273	15,211	13,204	12,756	12,701
Africa....................	1,539	934	894	566	299
Australia, Tasmania and New Zealand...................	1,336	1,282	1,484	1,014	925
Pacific Islands (not specified) ...	110	117	90	128	165
Central America.............	1,622	1,252	1.135	2,073	2,220
South America.............	5,869	3,801	4,286	6,931	3,343
West Indies................	14,451	11,598	12,027	15,507	8,879
Other countries.............	136	31	31	77	47
Total intercontinental.......	1,117,727	232,145	178,850	172,135	59,642
Canada and Newfoundland.....	86,139	82,215	101,551	105,399	32,452
Mexico...................	14,614	12,340	18,425	17,869	18,524
Total continental...........	100,753	94,555	119,976	123,268	50,976
Grand total...............	1,218,480	326,700	298,826	295,403	110,618

For reference notes see page 500.

TABLE III (concluded).

Country	1919	1920	1921	1922	1923	1924
Albania....................	......	......	......	......	......	250
Austria....................	26	268	4,947	5,019	8,103	7,505
Hungary...................	27	84	7,702	5,756	5,914	5,806
Belgium...................	268	6,574	6,166	1,541	1,590	2,065
Bulgaria[4].................	22	90	585	297	392	550
Czechoslovakia.............	......	3,426	40,884	12,541	13,840	13,554
Denmark..................	1,352	3,137	6,260	2,709	4,523	5,281
Estonia...................	......	......	......	......	......	765
Finland...................	......	756	3,795	2,767	3,644	3,662
France,including Corsica.....	3,379	8,945	9,552	4,220	4,380	6,387
Germany..................	52	1,001	6,803	17,931	48,277	75,091
Greece....................	386	11,981	28,502	3,457	3,333	4,871
Italy, incl. Sicily and Sardinia	1,884	95,145	222,260	40,319	46,674	56,246
Latvia....................	......	......	......	......	......	1,473
Lithuania.................	......	......	......	......	......	2,369
Netherlands...............	1,098	5,187	6,493	1,990	3,150	3,783
Norway...................	1,995	4,445	7,423	5,292	11,745	11,986
Poland....................	......	4,813	95,089	28,635	26,538	28,806
Portugal, including Cape Verde and Azores........	1,222	15,472	19,195	1,950	2,384	2,769
Rumania..................	19	1,890	25,817	10,287	11,947	11,142
Russia[5]...................	1,403	995	6,398	17,143	17,507	12,649
Spain, including Canary and Balearic Islands........	1,573	18,821	23,818	665	841	932
Sweden...................	2,243	5,862	9,171	6,624	17,916	18,310
Switzerland...............	381	3,785	7,106	3,398	3,349	3,842
Turkey in Europe..........	10	1,933	6,391	1,660	3,743	1,481
United Kingdom: England...............	5,163	27,871	33,431	15,249	21,558	24,466
Ireland...............	474	9,591	28,435	10,579	15,740	17,111
Scotland..............	1,283	9,347	15,954	9,018	23,019	33,471
Wales................	351	1,253	1,757	886	1,182	1,553
Yugoslavia (Serb, Croat and Slovene Kingdom)......	......	1,888	23,536	6,047	6,181	5,835
Other Europe.............	16	1,735	4,894	405	450	328
Total Europe.............	24,627	246,295	652,364	216,385	307,920	364,339
China....................	1,964	2,330	4,009	4,406	4,986	6,992
Japan....................	10,064	9,432	7,878	6,716	5,809	8,801
India....................	171	300	511	360	257	183
Turkey in Asia............	19	5,033	11,735	1,998	2,183	2,820
Syria. Mesopotamia and Palestine..............	......	......	......	......	......	2,946
Other Asia................	456	410	901	783	470	323
Total Asia...............	12,674	17,505	25,034	14,263	13,705	22,065
Africa....................	189	648	1,301	520	548	900
Australia, Tasmania and New Zealand..........	1,234	2066	2,191	855	711	635
Pacific Islands (not specified)	76	119	90	60	48	44
Central America	2,589	2,360	2,254	970	1,275	2,000
South America.............	3,271	4,112	5,015	2,668	4,737	9,270
West Indies...............	8,826	13,808	13,774	7,449	13,181	17,559
Other countries............	46	702	130	25	15	58
Total intercontinental.....	53,532	287,615	702,153	243,195	342,140	416,870
Canada and Newfoundland..	57,782	90,025	72,317	46,810	117,011	200,690
Mexico...................	29,818	52,361	30,758	19,551	63,768	89,336
Total continental........	87,600	142,386	103,075	66,361	180,779	290,026
Grand total..............	141,132	430,001	805,228	309,556	522,919	706,896

For reference notes see page 500.

TABLE IV—Immigration of aliens (calendar years) 1833-1842 and 1851-1924.

Year	Total	Year	Total	Year	Total
1833	58,640	1869	385,394	1897	222,399
1834	65,365	1870	356,196	1898	255,407
1835	45,374	1871	346,938	1899	361,318
1836	76,242	1872	437,304	1900	472,126
1837	79,340	1873	422,991	1901	522,573
1838	38,914	1874	260,814	1902	739,289
1839	68,069	1875	191,231	1903	937,371
1840	84,066	1876	157,440	1904	808,257
1841	80,289	1877	130,507	1905	1,054,442
1842	104,565	1878	153,203	1906	1,214,836
1851	379,466	1879	250,565	1907	1,334,166
1852	371,603	1880	593,717	1908	410,319
1853	368,645	1881	720,047	1909	957,105
1854	427,833	1882	730,073	1910	1,071,885
1855	200,877	1883	569,904	1911	782,545
1856	195,857	1884	462,034	1912	1,026,360
1857	246,945	1885	350,284	1913	1,387,318
1858	119,501	1886	392,887	1914	688,495
1859	118,616	1887	516,933	1915	258,678
1860	150,237	1888	525,019	1916	355,767
1861	89,724	1889	431,935	1917	152,959
1862	89,007	1890	495,021	1918	115,916
1863	174,524	1891	595,251	1919	247,358
1864	193,195	1892	547,060	1920	708,562
1865	247,453	1893	492,408	1921	563,905
1866	314,917	1894	248,978	1922	381,167
1867	310,965	1895	324,329	1923	751,050
1868	289,145	1896	284,943	1924	354,770

TABLE V—Distribution of immigrant aliens admitted, by sex, 1820-1855.

Year	Total	Males	Females	Sex not stated
Year ending Sept. 30				
1820	8,385	4,871	2,393	1,121
1821	9,127	4,651	1,636	2,840
1822	6,911	3,816	1,013	2,082
1823	6,354	3,598	848	1,908
1824	7,912	4,706	1,393	1,813
1825	10,199	6,917	2,959	323
1826	10,837	7,702	3,078	57
1827	18,875	11,803	5,939	1,133
1828	27,382	17,261	10,060	61
1829	22,520	11,303	5,112	6,105
1830	23,322	6,439	3,135	13,748
1831	22,633	14,909	7,724	. . . . .
Oct. 1, 1831				
Dec. 31, 1832	60,482	39,287	21,095	100
Year ending Dec. 31				
1833	58,640	41,546	17,094	. . . . .
1834	65,365	38,796	22,540	4,029
1835	45,374	28,196	17,027	151
1836	76,242	47,865	27,553	824
1837	79,340	48,837	27,653	2,850
1838	38,914	23,474	13,685	1,755
1839	68,069	42,932	25,125	12
1840	84,066	52,883	31,132	51
1841	80,289	48,082	32,031	176
1842	104,565	62,277	41,907	381
January 1 to Sept. 30, 1843	52,496	30,069	22,424	3
Year ending Sept. 30				
1844	78,615	44,431	34,184	. . . . .
1845	114,371	65,015	48,115	1,241
1846	154,416	87,777	65,742	897
1847	234,968	136,086	97,917	965
1848	226,527	133,906	92,149	472
1849	297,024	177,232	119,280	512
1850	310,004	196,331	112,635	1,038
Oct. 1 to Dec. 31, 1850	59,976	32,990	26,805	181

TABLE VI—Distribution of immigrant aliens, by sex (calendar years)
1851-1924.

Year	Total	Males	Females	Sex not stated
1851	379,466	217,181	162,219	66
1852	370,603	210,314	157,717	2,572
1853	368,643	208,024	160,619	. . . .
1854	427,833	256,177	171,656	. . . .
1855	200,877	115,307	85,567	3

Year	Total	Males	Females	Year	Total	Males	Females
1856	200,436	115,846	84,590	1891	595,251	369,392	225,859
1857	251,306	146,215	105,091	1892	547,060	343,452	203,608
1858	123,126	73,033	50,093	1893	492,408	310,868	181,540
1859	121,282	69,498	51,784	1894	248,978	141,052	107,926
1860	153,640	88,537	65,103	1895	324,329	186,059	138,270
1861	91,921	54,904	37,017	1896	284,943	181,197	103,746
1862	91,986	52,815	39,171	1897	222,399	129,870	92,529
1863	176,272	105,858	70,414	1898	255,407	154,513	100,894
1864	193,418	114,364	79,054	1899	361,318	231,480	129,838
1865	248,083	149,441	98,642	1900	472,126	313,953	158,173
1866	318,571	197,775	120,796	1901	522,573	362,470	160,103
1867	295,642	178,169	117,473	1902	739,289	527,301	211,988
1868	289,145	177,302	111,843	1903	937,371	660,324	277,047
1869	385,394	235,196	150,198	1904	808,257	539,871	268,386
1870	356,196	214,822	141,374	1905	1,054,442	744,349	310,093
1871	346,938	204,728	142,210	1906	1,214,836	857,344	357,492
1872	437,304	258,287	179,017	1907	1,334,166	961,809	372,357
1873	422,991	256,682	166,309	1908	410,319	241,877	168,442
1874	260,814	159,936	100,878	1909	957,105	665,661	291,444
1875	191,231	121,928	69,303	1910	1,071,885	748,056	323,829
1876	157,440	102,960	54,480	1911	782,545	488,230	294,315
1877	130,507	84,265	46,242	1912	1,026,360	674,555	351,805
1878	153,203	94,647	58,556	1913	1,387,318	935,970	451,348
1879	250,565	159,007	91,558	1914	688,495	439,549	248,946
1880	593,717	365,788	227,929	1915	258,678	153,428	105,250
1881	720,047	442,245	277,802	1916	355,757	213,076	142,691
1882	730,073	458,215	271,858	1917	152,959	90,341	62,618
1883	569,904	341,744	228,160	1918	115,916	65,843	50,073
1884	462,034	272,444	189,590	1919	247,358	137,673	109,685
1885	350,284	199,598	150,686	1920	708,562	414,107	294,455
1886	392,887	240,139	152,748	1921	563,905	290,161	273,744
1887	515,933	322,026	194,907	1922	381,167	203,859	177,308
1888	525,019	326,556	198,463	1923	751,050	460,409	290,641
1889	431,935	258,268	173,667	1924	354,770	203,759	151,011
1890	495,021	308,602	186,419				

TABLE VII—Distribution of total number of passengers arrived in the United States from 1820 to 1867 and of immigrant aliens only from 1868 to 1924, by age.

Period	Total	Under 15 years	15 to 40 years	Over 40 years	Age not stated
Year ending Sept. 30, 1820	10,311	1,313	6,064	1,518	1,416
1821	11,644	170	7,047	1,396	3,031
1822	8,549	51	5,430	956	2,112
1823	8,265	17	5,314	984	1,950
1824	9,627	94	6,550	1,106	1,877
1825	12,858	1,825	9,392	1,151	490
1826	13,908	2,261	10,025	1,281	341
1827	21,777	3,905	14,089	2,148	1,635
1828	30,184	8,117	18,397	3,036	634
1829	24,513	3,686	11,603	1,764	7,460
1830	24,837	2,878	6,347	1,173	14,439
1831	23,880	7,040	13,598	1,863	1,379
1832	54,351	16,485	31,069	4,273	2,524
3 months ending Dec. 31, 1832	7,303	1,946	3,774	425	1,158
Year ending Dec. 31, 1833	59,925	17,425	35,002	4,855	2,643
1834	67,948	15,383	42,811	6,818	2,936
1835	48,716	10,635	32,412	5,431	238
1836	80,972	16,665	54,738	8,141	1,428
1837	84,959	16,014	54,312	8,421	6,212
1838	45,159	8,822	28,713	5,748	1,876
1839	74,666	15,167	51,063	7,201	1,235
1840	92,207	21,727	62,461	7,556	463
1841	87,805	19,732	58,864	8,590	619
1842	110,980	25,516	74,499	9,709	1,256
9 months ending Sept. 30, 1843	56,529	14,930	34,606	5,197	1,796
Year ending Sept. 30, 1844	84,764	19,913	54,745	8,655	1,451
1845	119,896	26,182	79,448	12,059	2,207
1846	158,649	36,878	103,263	17,160	1,348
1847	239,482	57,161	156,627	20,800	4,894
1848	229,483	53,213	151,148	23,066	2,056
1849	299,683	67,331	200,899	30,679	774
1850	315,334	62,543	181,468	26,085	45,238
3 months ending Dec. 31, 1850	65,570	13,825	43,609	7,621	425
Year ending Dec. 31, 1851	408,828	89,241	274,359	44,072	1,156
1852	397,343	90,274	246,076	43,394	17,599
1853	400,982	87,331	267,876	44,558	1,217
1854	460,474	100,013	312,301	47,377	783
1855	230,476	53,045	151,440	25,155	836
1856	224,496	42,732	141,986	19,905	19,873
1857	271,982	50,548	177,093	22,808	21,533
1858	144,906	25,914	102,921	15,545	526
1859	155,509	24,670	114,110	16,115	614
1860	179,691	28,620	133,919	16,795	357
1861	112,702	18,878	81,515	11,221	1,088
1862	114,463	20,641	80,725	12,888	209
1863	199,811	37,433	142,009	20,108	261
1864	221,535	41,912	151,711	27,778	134
1865	287,399	46,524	175,501	32,190	33,184
6 months ending June 30, 1866	185,892	27,011	112,692	18,034	28,155
Year ending June 30, 1867	342,162	65,335	236,017	40,810	....
1868	282,189	57,637	188,359	36,193	....
1869	352,768	79,803	232,397	40,568	....
1870	387,203	89,129	250,965	47,109	....
1871	321,350	71,148	210,366	39,836	....
1872	404,806	90,510	263,213	51,083	....

TABLE VII (continued)

Year	Total	Under 15 years	15 to 40 years	Over 40 years
1873	459,803	104,672	288,272	66,859
1874	313,339	63,578	199,840	49,921
1875	227,498	44,254	154,621	28,623
1876	169,986	27,875	121,734	20,377
1877	141,857	23,754	100,366	17,737
1878	138,469	24,285	95,938	18,246
1879	177,826	34,554	122,731	20,541
1880	457,257	87,154	327,662	42,441
1881	669,431	153,480	454,495	61,456
1882	788,992	171,021	540,677	77,294
1883	603,322	143,865	390,406	69,051
1884	518,592	123,562	335,572	59,458
1885	395,346	92,880	257,551	44,915
1886	334,203	66,188	232,118	35,897
1887	490,109	94,278	345,575	50,256
1888	546,889	97,287	396,990	52,612
1889	444,427	92,534	303,835	48,058
1890	455,302	86,404	315,054	53,844
1891	560,319	95,879	405,843	58,597
1892	623,084	89,167	491,839	42,078
1893	502,917	57,392	419,701	25,824
1894	314,467	41,755	258,162	14,550
1895	279,948	33,289	233,543	13,116
1896	343,267	52,741	254,519	36,007
1897	230,832	38,627	165,181	27,024
1898	229,299	38,267	164,905	26,127

Year	Total	Under 14 years	14–44 years	45 years and over
1899	311,715	43,983	248,187	19,545
1900	448,572	54,624	370,382	23,566
1901	487,918	62,562	396,516	28,840
1902	648,743	74,063	539,254	35,426
1903	857,046	102,431	714,053	40,562
1904	812,870	109,150	657,155	46,565
1905	1,026,499	114,668	855,419	56,412
1906	1,100,735	136,273	913,955	50,507
1907	1,285,349	138,344	1,100,771	46,234
1908	782,870	112,148	630,671	40,051
1909	751,786	88,393	624,876	38,517
1910	1,041,570	120,509	868,310	52,751
1911	878,587	117,837	714,709	46,041
1912	838,172	113,700	678,480	45,992
1913	1,197,892	147,158	986,355	64,379
1914	1,218,480	158,621	981,692	78,167
1915	326,700	52,982	244,472	29,246
1916	298,826	47,070	220,821	30,935
1917	295,403	47,467	214,616	33,320

		Under 16 years	16-44 years	
1918	110,618	21,349	76,098	13,171
1919	141,132	26,373	97,341	17,418
1920	430,001	81,890	307,589	40,522
1921	805,228	146,613	587,965	70,650
1922	309,556	63,710	210,164	35,682
1923	522,919	91,816	383,960	47,143
1924	706,896	132,264	513,788	60,844

TABLE VIII.—Distribution of total number of passengers arrived from 1820 to 1867 and of immigrant aliens only from 1868 to 1924, by occupation.

Year	Total	Agriculture	Industry and mining	Transport and commerce	Domestic service and general labor	Liberal professions and public services	Other occupations, none, or unknown
1820	10,311	874	691	1,332	473	105	6,836
1821	11,644	1,249	942	2,032	547	204	6,670
1822	8,549	834	787	2,041	434	151	4,302
1823	8,265	800	728	1,967	344	179	4,247
1824	9,627	918	713	2,450	394	187	4,965
1825	12,858	1,647	838	2,419	719	204	7,031
1826	13,908	1,382	1,499	2,573	786	190	7,478
1827	21,777	2,071	2,484	2,648	1,897	262	12,415
1828	30,184	2,542	3,294	2,902	3,049	331	18,066
1829	24,513	1,264	2,063	3,177	2,222	252	15,535
1830	24,837	1,424	1,402	1,770	742	136	19,363
1831	23,880	2,685	1,857	2,894	1,043	183	15,218
1832	61,654	8,502	9,413	6,344	3,379	176	33,840
1833	59,925	6,618	10,910	6,803	4,191	459	30,944
1834	67,948	7,160	6,524	3,687	4,110	561	45,906
1835	48,716	6,117	5,107	4,773	3,496	487	28,736
1836	80,972	8,770	8,084	4,174	8,788	472	50,684
1837	84,959	10,835	8,084	4,292	9,215	522	52,011
1838	45,159	6,667	4,768	4,912	3,726	459	24,627
1839	74,666	12,410	9,248	6,470	7,969	584	37,985
1840	92,207	18,476	9,943	6,179	9,823	481	47,305
1841	87,805	12,343	10,215	6,163	12,346	541	46,197
1842	110,980	12,966	13,686	5,843	17,215	744	60,526
1843	56,529	8,031	5,558	3,761	5,759	578	32,842
1844	84,764	9,831	8,660	4,776	10,899	755	49,843
1845	119,896	19,349	10,338	5,568	19,044	542	65,055
1846	158,649	27,944	12,655	4,784	21,542	592	91,132
1847	239,482	43,594	25,430	4,683	39,067	703	126,005
1848	229,483	31,670	24,311	3,801	50,656	517	118,528
1849	299,683	39,675	31,133	4,396	65,850	972	157,657
1850	315,334	42,873	25,077	7,692	49,843	918	188,931
1851	474,398	59,095	35,181	16,099	105,709	938	257,376
1852	397,343	58,023	26,008	12,670	76,209	572	223,861
1853	400,982	56,322	19,669	13,919	86,960	722	223,390
1854	460,474	87,188	35,050	16,591	85,730	699	235,216
1855	230,476	34,693	16,065	16,157	45,178	780	117,603
1856	224,496	24,722	17,756	12,142	38,767	462	130,647
1857	271,982	34,702	24,801	13,375	44,571	570	153,963
1858	144,906	20,506	17,374	11,585	23,459	662	71,320
1859	155,509	16,323	23,608	13,515	22,977	858	78,228
1860	179,691	21,742	18,135	12,414	32,683	792	93,925
1861	112,702	11,672	10,742	8,538	20,177	668	60,905
1862	114,463	9,274	9,696	10,056	21,451	788	63,198
1863	199,811	12,364	20,782	10,948	55,303	1,173	99,241
1864	221,535	13,848	22,851	13,153	63,669	1,120	106,894
1865	287,399	20,032	31,215	17,993	54,488	1,743	161,928
1866	359,957	30,335	35,617	21,275	67,531	2,242	202,957
1867	342,162	32,683	38,006	20,751	65,156	2,288	183,278
1868	282,189	23,070	28,431	12,304	65,720	1,398	151,266
1869	352,768	28,180	30,432	11,707	98,922	1,700	181,827
1870	387,203	35,730	32,615	10,171	98,911	1,831	207,945

TABLE VIII.—DISTRIBUTION OF TOTAL NUMBER OF PASSENGERS ARRIVED FROM 1820 TO 1867 AND OF IMMIGRANT ALIENS ONLY FROM 1868 TO 1924, BY OCCUPATION (continued).

Year	Total	Agri- culture	Industry and mining	Transport and commerce	Domestic service and gen- eral labor	Liberal professions and public services	Other oc- cupations, none or unknown
1871	321,350	27,293	30,595	8,312	79,798	2,247	173,105
1872	404,806	38,887	40,786	10,718	97,181	1,905	215,329
1873	459,803	37,752	44,022	11,825	120,975	2,980	242,249
1874	313,339	29,275	34,798	9,172	78,537	2,476	159,081
1875	227,498	16,915	29,870	8,653	57,740	2,426	111,984
1876	169,986	14,988	21,081	7,661	45,571	2,400	78,285
1877	141,857	13,557	17,984	7,358	30,797	1,885	70,276
1878	138,469	15,126	13,984	6,783	33,054	1,510	68,012
1879	177,826	20,201	18,368	7,936	43,927	1,639	85,755
1880	457,257	47,641	45,050	12,418	123,812	1,773	226,563
1881	669,431	59,471	60,466	14,405	167,608	2,812	364,669
1882	788,992	63,117	66,242	15,607	233,154	2,992	407,880
1883	603,322	40,243	56,137	13,667	164,493	2,450	326,332
1884	518,592	43,127	48,752	13,113	130,998	2,284	280,318
1885	395,346	28,265	34,215	11,710	103,593	2,097	215,466
1886	334,203	21,172	31,040	11,196	107,365	2,078	161,352
1887	490,109	31,589	45,605	14,217	168,914	2,882	226,902
1888	546,889	31,354	52,445	14,185	198,545	3,360	248,000
1889	444,427	29,909	43,495	13,420	142,534	2,815	212,254
1890	455,302	30,116	37,782	13,792	168,531	3,236	201,845
1891	560,319	37,282	47,918	17,564	200,414	3,431	253,710
1892	623,084	32,324	43,542	15,830	216,290	2,674	312,424
1893	502,917	27,597	41,408	14,615	162,836	2,600	253,861
1894	314,467	17,065	28,884	12,412	89,067	1,738	165,301
1895	279,948	11,652	26,480	10,693	85,493	1,935	143,695
1896	343,267	29,891	39,600	12,782	131,390	2,324	127,280
1897	230,832	23,039	28,070	11,789	70,880	1,732	95,322
1898	229,299	16,697	28,016	10,672	77,023	1,347	95,544
1899	311,715	21,749	37,571	11,685	126,139	1,972	112,599
1900	448,572	38,135	53,111	13,246	203,819	2,392	137,869
1901	487,918	58,413	56,075	14,645	203,965	2,665	152,155
1902	648,743	89,450	68,862	17,701	312,592	2,937	157,201
1903	857,046[6]	92,063	107,375[6]	29,167	413,328	6,999	208,114
1904	812,870	92,503	131,380	42,633	315,363	13,265	217,726
1905	1,026,499	163,220	156,832	45,380	412,923	13,643	234,501
1906	1,100,735	256,849	156,306	39,947	342,329	13,766	291,538
1907	1,285,349	340,057	169,698	35,971	412,728	12,600	314,295
1908	782,870	148,453	108,226	28,802	235,993	11,078	250,318
1909	751,786	181,914	75,088	21,870	239,368	8,086	225,460
1910	1,041,570	303,147	121,470	29,240	310,958	10,334	266,421
1911	878,587	188,234	129,568	31,560	263,149	12,035	254,041
1912	838,172	193,964	109,216	29,502	252,255	11,685	241,550
1913	1,197,892	335,975	140,042	35,612	361,210	13,469	311,584
1914	1,218,480	305,023	150,131	41,729	370,816	14,601	336,180
1915	326,700	32,510	43,696	22,360	88,125	12,279	127,730
1916	298,826	34,255	33,962	20,919	85,074	9,795	114,821
1917	295,403	31,159	34,225	23,231	83,000	8,403	115,385
1918	110,618	7,604	12,999	11,872	22,475	4,559	51,109
1919	141,132	9,016	17,494	14,212	24,528	6,272	69,610
1920	430,001	29,213	49,383	30,023	118,929	12,442	190,011
1921	805,228	56,977	100,288	48,329	263,042	14,592	322,000
1922	309,556	19,276	39,070	20,776	77,257	10,955	142,222
1923	522,919	41,473	82,875	34,323	135,775	16,542	211,931
1924	706,896	52,155	116,224	49,509	159,681	24,778	304,549

For reference notes see page 500.

TABLE IX.—Distribution of passengers arriving in the United States, by sex and country of birth, 1820-55.

Country	1820				1821			
	Total	Males	Females	Sex not stated	Total	Males	Females	Sex not stated
Belgium................	1	1	....	....	2	2	....	....
Denmark.............·...	20	11	7	2	12	10	2	....
France, including Corsica...	371	282	58	31	370	328	42	....
Germany...............	968	631	248	89	383	302	81	....
Great Britain and Ireland (not specified)........	2,249	1,179	640	430	1,870	1,276	594	....
England..............	1,782	967	561	254	1,036	749	287	....
Ireland..............	1,725	944	572	209	1,518	1,051	467	....
Scotland..............	268	173	75	20	293	220	73	....
Wales................	....	....	....	....	11	7	4	....
Greece...................	....	....	....	....	....	....	....	....
Italy, including Sardinia and Sicily.............	30	22	6	2	62	58	4	....
Netherlands.............	49	28	19	2	56	50	6	....
Norway and Sweden......	3	3	....	....	12	12	....	....
Poland................	5	5	....	....	1	1	....	....
Portugal, including Azores, Cape Verde Islands and Madeira..............	38	33	5	....	19	19	....	....
Russia.................	14	13	1	....	7	7	....	....
Spain,including Canary Is..	142	136	4	2	191	184	7	....
Switzerland.............	31	24	6	1	93	85	8	....
Turkey in Europe........	1	1	....	....	....	....	....	....
Other Europe...........	2	2	....	....	....	....	....	....
Total Europe..........	7,699	4,455	2,202	1,042	5,936	4,361	1,575	....
China..................	1	1	....	....	....	....	....	....
India..................	1	1	....	....	....	....	....	....
Turkey in Asia..........	....	....	....	....	....	....	....	....
Other Asia..............	3	....	2	1	....	....	....	....
Total Asia............	5	2	2	1	....	....	....	....
Africa..................	1	....	1	....	2	2	....	....
Australia................	....	....	....	....	....	....	....	....
Pacific Islands...........	1	1	....	....	....	....	....	....
Central America..........	2	2	....	....	....	....	....	....
South America..........	11	9	1	1	8	8	....	....
West Indies.............	164	102	46	16	107	91	16	....
Not stated..............	292	165	77	50	2,886	32	14	2,840
Total intercontinental...	8,175	4,736	2,329	1,110	8,939	4,494	1,605	2,840
British North America.....	209	134	64	11	184	153	31	....
Mexico................	1	1	....	....	4	4	....	....
Total continental......	210	135	64	11	188	157	31	....
Grand total...........	8,385	4,871	2,393	1,121	9,127	4,651	1,636	2,840
United States...........	1,926	1,576	287	63	2,517	2,215	302	....

TABLE IX.—DISTRIBUTION OF PASSENGERS ARRIVING IN THE UNITED STATES BY SEX AND COUNTRY OF BIRTH, 1820-55 (continued).

Country	1822				1823			
	Total	Males	Females	Sex not stated	Total	Males	Females	Sex not stated
Belgium	10	10	....	....	2	2	....	....
Denmark	18	18	....	....	6	4	2	....
France, including Corsica	351	323	28	....	461	408	53	....
Germany	148	125	23	....	183	159	24	....
Great Britain and Ireland (not specified)	1,075	838	237	....	857	663	194	....
England	856	650	206	....	851	663	188	....
Ireland	1,346	983	363	....	1,051	800	251	....
Scotland	198	156	42	....	180	140	40	....
Wales	13	8	5	....	69	53	16	....
Greece								
Italy, including Sardinia and Sicily	35	34	1	....	33	31	2	....
Netherlands	51	43	8	....	19	17	2	....
Norway and Sweden	10	10	....	....	1	1	....	....
Poland	3	3	....	....	3	3	....	....
Portugal, including Azores, Cape Verde Islands and Madeira	34	34	....	....	25	24	1	....
Russia	10	8	2	....	7	7	....	....
Spain, including Canary Is.	152	143	9	....	221	205	16	....
Switzerland	110	84	26	....	47	37	10	....
Turkey in Europe	4	2	2	....	2	2	....	....
Other Europe	....	....	....	....	....	....	....	....
Total Europe	4,424	3,472	952	....	4,018	3,219	799	....
China	....	....	....	....	....	....	....	....
India	1	1	....	....	....	....	....	....
Turkey in Asia	....	....	....	....	....	....	....	....
Other Asia	....	....	....	....	....	....	....	....
Total Asia	1	1	....	....	....	....	....	....
Africa	....	....	....	....	....	....	....	....
Australia	2	2	....	....	....	....	....	....
Pacific Islands	....	....	....	....	....	....	....	....
Central America	3	3	....	....	....	....	....	....
South America	7	7	....	....	20	18	2	....
West Indies	159	132	27	....	160	140	20	....
Not stated	2,106	23	1	2,082	1,954	43	3	1,908
Total intercontinental	6,702	3,640	980	2,082	6,152	3,420	824	1,908
British North America	204	171	33	....	167	143	24	....
Mexico	5	5	....	....	35	35	....	....
Total continental	209	176	33	....	202	178	24	....
Grand total	6,911	3,816	1,013	2,082	6,354	3,598	848	1,908
United States	1,638	1,502	136	....	1,911	1,715	196	....

TABLE IX.—Distribution of passengers arriving in the United States, by sex and country of birth, 1820-55 (continued).

Country	1824				1825			
	Total	Males	Females	Sex not stated	Total	Males	Females	Sex not stated
Belgium.................	1	1	....	....	1	1	....	....
Denmark................	11	11	....	....	14	14	....	....
France, including Corsica...	377	334	43	....	515	430	85	....
Germany................	230	199	31	....	450	344	106	....
Great Britain and Ireland (not specified).........	1,031	754	277	....	1,700	1,185	515	....
England...............	713	556	157	....	1,002	709	293	....
Ireland...............	1,575	1,133	442	....	4,157	2,729	1,428	....
Scotland..............	257	194	63	....	113	73	40	....
Wales.................	33	20	13	....	11	8	3	....
Greece..................	5	5	....	....	....	....	....	....
Italy, including Sardinia, and Sicily.............	45	45	....	....	75	63	12	....
Netherlands.............	40	31	9	....	37	31	6	....
Norway and Sweden......	9	9	....	....	4	3	1	....
Poland.................	4	4	....	....	1	....	1	....
Portugal, including Azores, Cape Verde Islands and Madeira..............	13	12	1	....	16	15	1	....
Russia.................	7	7	....	....	10	10	...	....
Spain, including Canary Is..	360	344	16	....	279	263	16	....
Switzerland.............	253	179	74	....	166	116	50	....
Turkey in Europe........	....	....	....	....	....	....	....	....
Other Europe...........	....	....	....	....	1	....	1	....
Total Europe..........	4,964	3,838	1,126	....	8,552	5,994	2,558	....
China..................	....	....	....	....	1	1	....	....
India..................	1	1	....	....	....	....	....	....
Turkey in Asia..........	2	2	....	....	....	....	....	....
Other Asia.............	....	....	....	....	....	....	....	....
Total Asia............	3	3	....	....	1	1	....	....
Africa..................	....	....	....	....	1	1	....	....
Australia...............	....	....	....	....	....	....	....	....
Pacific Islands...........	....	....	....	....	....	....	....	....
Central America.........	10	10	....	....	8	8	....	....
South America..........	25	25	....	....	67	66	1	....
West Indies.............	259	216	43	....	389	283	106	....
Not stated..............	2,386	393	180	1,813	799	311	165	323
Total intercontinental...	7,647	4,485	1,349	1,813	9,817	6,664	2,830	323
British North America.....	155	114	41	....	314	193	121	....
Mexico.................	110	107	3	....	68	60	8	....
Total continental.......	265	221	44	....	382	253	129	....
Grand total...........	7,912	4,706	1,393	1,813	10,199	6,917	2,959	323
United States...........	1,715	1,547	168	....	2,659	2,289	370	....

TABLE IX.—DISTRIBUTION OF PASSENGERS ARRIVING IN THE UNITED STATES, BY SEX AND COUNTRY OF BIRTH, 1820-55 (continued).

Country	1826				1827			
	Total	Males	Females	Sex not stated	Total	Males	Females	Sex not stated
Belgium................	2	2	....	....	7	7	....	....
Denmark...............	10	9	1	....	15	14	1	....
France, including Corsica...	545	465	80	....	1,281	879	402	....
Germany...............	511	400	111	....	432	345	87	....
Great Britain and Ireland (not specified).........	2,699	1,871	828	....	7,689	4,874	2,815	....
England...............	1,459	1,059	400	....	2,521	1,742	779	....
Ireland...............	3,333	2,184	1,149	....	3,282	2,137	1,145	....
Scotland..............	230	165	65	....	460	312	148	....
Wales................	6	6	....	....	....	....	....	....
Greece.................	4	4	....	....	....	....	....	....
Italy, including Sardinia and Sicily..............	57	52	5	....	35	33	2	....
Netherlands.............	176	100	76	....	245	149	96	....
Norway and Sweden......	16	14	2	....	13	11	2	....
Poland.................	....	....	....	....	1	1	....	....
Portugal, including Azores, Cape Verde Islands and Madeira...............	17	15	2	....	12	11	1	....
Russia.................	4	3	1	....	19	18	1	....
Spain,including Canary Is..	448	407	41	....	414	375	39	....
Switzerland.............	245	158	87	....	297	173	124	....
Turkey in Europe........	....	....	....	....	....	....	....	....
Other Europe...........	....	....	....	....	....	....	....	....
Total Europe...........	9,762	6,914	2,848	....	16,723	11,081	5,642	....
China..................	....	....	....	....	....	....	....	....
India..................	1	1	....	....	1	1	....	....
Turkey in Asia..........	2	2	....	....	1	1	....	....
Other Asia.............	....	....	....	....	....	....	....	....
Total Asia.............	3	3	....	....	2	2	....	....
Africa.................	....	....	....	....	4	2	2	....
Australia...............	....	....	....	....	....	....	....	....
Pacific Islands...........	....	....	....	....	79	44	35	....
Central America.........	12	10	2	....	7	7	....	....
South America...........	63	51	12	....	54	47	7	....
West Indies.............	427	341	86	....	227	197	30	....
Not stated..............	241	120	64	57	1,487	184	170	1,133
Total intercontinental...	10,508	7,439	3,012	57	18,583	11,564	5,886	1,133
British North America.....	223	166	57	....	165	124	41	....
Mexico.................	106	97	9	....	127	115	12	....
Total continental.......	329	263	66	....	292	239	53	....
Grand total...........	10,837	7,702	3,078	57	18,875	11,803	5,939	1,133
United States..............	3,071	2,516	555	....	2,902	2,362	540	....

TABLE IX.—DISTRIBUTION OF PASSENGERS ARRIVING IN THE UNITED STATES, BY SEX AND COUNTRY OF BIRTH, 1820-55 (continued).

Country	1828				1829			
	Total	Males	Females	Sex not stated	Total	Males	Females	Sex not stated
Belgium.................	2	2	....	....	....	....	....	....
Denmark................	50	25	25	....	17	11	6	....
France, including Corsica...	2,843	1,746	1,097	....	582	420	162	....
Germany................	1,851	1,155	696	....	597	404	193	....
Great Britain and Ireland (not specified)..........	8,781	5,330	3,451	....	5,225	3,254	1,971	....
England................	2,735	1,823	912	....	2,149	1,545	604	....
Ireland................	5,266	3,166	2,100	....	3,106	1,963	1,143	....
Scotland...............	1,041	646	395	....	111	89	22	....
Wales.................	17	8	9	....	3	3	....	....
Greece.................	7	5	2	....	1	1	....	....
Italy, including Sardinia and Sicily..............	34	32	2	....	23	21	2	....
Netherlands.............	263	152	111	....	169	113	56	....
Norway and Sweden......	10	7	3	....	13	10	3	....
Poland.................	1	1	....	....	....	....	....	....
Portugal, including Azores, Cape Verde Islands and Madeira..............	26	24	2	....	56	51	5	....
Russia..................	7	6	1	....	1	1	....	....
Spain, including Canary Is.	214	186	28	....	445	344	101	....
Switzerland.............	1,592	950	642	....	314	179	135	....
Turkey in Europe........	6	6	....	....	....	....	....	....
Other Europe...........	....	....	....	....	....	....	....	....
Total Europe..........	24,746	15,270	9,476	....	12,812	8,409	4,403	....
China..................	....	....	....	....	1	1	....	....
India..................	3	3	....	....	1	1	....	....
Turkey in Asia..........	....	....	....	....	1	1	....	....
Other Asia.............	....	....	....	....	....	....	....	....
Total Asia............	3	3	....	....	3	3	....	....
Africa..................	6	6	....	....	1	1	....	....
Australia...............	....	....	....	....	....	....	....	....
Pacific Islands..........	....	....	....	....	....	....	....	....
Central America........	5	5	....	....	10	8	2	....
South America..........	77	63	14	....	73	60	13	....
West Indies.............	652	539	113	....	517	430	87	....
Not stated.............	537	238	238	61	6,405	201	99	6,105
Total intercontinental..	26,026	16,124	9,841	61	19,821	9,112	4,604	6,105
British North America.....	267	164	103	....	409	258	151	....
Mexico.................	1,089	973	116	....	2,290	1,933	357	....
Total continental.......	1,356	1,137	219	....	2,699	2,191	508	....
Grand total...........	27,382	17,261	10,060	61	22,520	11,303	5,112	6,105
United States...........	2,802	2,185	617	....	1,993	1,635	358	....

TABLE IX.—Distribution of passengers arriving in the United States, by sex and country of birth, 1820-55 (continued).

Country	1830				1831			1832		
	Total	Males	Females	Sex not stated	Total	Males	Females	Total	Males	Females
Belgium.............	....	....	....	....	1	1	....	....	....	....
Denmark.............	16	11	5	....	23	20	3	21	19	2
France, including Corsica.....	1,174	712	462	....	2,038	1,332	706	5,363	3,703	1,660
Germany.............	1,976	1,158	818	....	2,413	1,524	889	10,194	6,133	4,061
Great Britain and Ireland (not specified)..................	2,358	1,591	767	....	5,992	3,678	2,314	11,545	7,129	4,416
England..................	733	448	285	....	251	169	82	944	598	346
Ireland..................	747	462	285	....	1,647	1,035	612	5,120	3,217	1,903
Scotland..................	29	25	4	....	226	157	69	158	113	45
Wales..................	7	7	....	....	131	81	50	....	....	....
Greece..................	3	3	....	....	....	....	....	1	1	....
Italy, including Sardinia and Sicily..................	9	9	....	....	28	25	3	3	3	....
Netherlands..................	22	16	6	....	175	147	28	205	130	75
Norway and Sweden..........	3	2	1	....	13	8	5	313	184	129
Poland..................	2	2	....	....	....	....	....	34	24	10
Portugal, including Azores, Cape Verde Islands and Madeira..................	11	8	3	....	2	2	....	10	9	1
Russia..................	3	3	....	....	1	.	1	52	32	20
Spain, including Canary Is....	21	18	3	....	37	32	5	106	74	32
Switzerland..................	109	62	47	....	63	63	....	129	77	52
Turkey in Europe...........	2	2	....	....	....	....	....	....	....	....
Other Europe.............	....	....	....	....	....	....	....	....	....	....
Total Europe..............	7,225	4,539	2,686	....	13,041	8,274	4,767	34,198	21,446	12,752
China..................	....	....	....	....	....	....	....	....	....	....
India..................	....	....	....	....	1	1	....	4	3	1
Turkey in Asia.............	....	....	....	....	....	....	....	....	....	....
Other Asia..................	....	....	....	....	....	....	....	....	....	....
Total Asia..............	....	....	....	....	1	1	....	4	3	1
Africa..................	2	2	....	....	2	2	....	2	1	1
Australia..................	....	....	....	....	....	....	....	....	....	....
Pacific Islands..............	....	....	....	....	1	1	....	....	....	....
Central America.............	50	43	7	....	3	3	....	6	5	1
South America..............	137	79	58	....	42	35	7	174	120	54
West Indies..............	937	771	166	....	1,281	1,066	215	1,256	943	313
Not stated..................	13,799	25	26	13,748	7,394	4,771	2,623	16,104	10,891	5,213
Total intercontinental......	22,150	5,459	2,943	13,748	21,765	14,153	7,612	51,744	33,409	18,335
British North America........	189	112	77	..	176	132	44	608	430	178
Mexico..................	983	868	115	....	692	624	68	827	757	70
Total continental..........	1,172	980	192	....	868	756	112	1,435	1,187	248
Grand total...............	23,322	6,439	3,135	13,748	22,633	14,909	7,724	53,179	34,596	18,583
United States..............	1,515	1,075	440	....	1,247	1,008	239	1,172	1,003	169

TABLE IX.—DISTRIBUTION OF PASSENGERS ARRIVING IN THE UNITED STATES, BY SEX AND COUNTRY OF BIRTH, 1820-55 (continued).

Country	1832 October, November, December				1833 1 January to 31 December			1834			
	Total	Males	Females	Sex not stated	Total	Males	Females	Total	Males	Females	Sex not stated
Belgium..................	....	....	....	....	....	....	....	3	3	....	....
Denmark.................	....	....	....	....	173	160	13	24	20	4	....
France, including Corsica..	....	....	....	....	4,682	3,392	1,290	2,989	1,892	1,097	....
Germany................	....	....	....	....	6,988	5,299	1,689	17,686	11,463	6,223	....
Great Britain and Ireland (not specified).........	....	....	....	....	4,137	2,410	1,727	26,952	16,362	10,590	....
England...............	....	....	....	....	2,966	2,522	444	1,129	648	430	51
Ireland...............	....	....	....	....	4,511	3,089	1,422	6,772	4,121	2,636	15
Scotland..............	....	....	....	....	1,921	1,898	23	110	57	53	....
Wales.................	....	....	....	....	29	16	13	1	1	....	....
Greece..................	....	....	....	....	1	1	....	....	....	....	....
Italy, including Sardinia and Sicily.............	....	....	....	....	1,699	1,697	2	105	85	20	....
Netherlands.............	....	....	....	....	39	33	6	87	45	42	....
Norway and Sweden.....	....	....	....	....	16	9	7	42	38	4	....
Poland..................	....	....	....	....	1	1	....	54	51	3	....
Portugal, including Azores, Cape Verde Islands and Madeira..............	....	....	....	....	638	636	2	73	67	6	....
Russia..................	....	....	....	....	159	156	3	15	12	3	....
Spain, including Canary Is..	....	....	....	....	519	490	29	110	102	8	....
Switzerland.............	....	....	....	....	634	630	4	1,389	849	540	....
Turkey in Europe........	....	....	....	....	1	1	....	1	1	....	....
Other Europe............	....	....	....	....	5	3	2	....	....	....	....
Total Europe..........	....	....	....	....	29,119	22,443	6,676	57,542	35,817	21,659	66
China...................	....	....	....	....	....	....	....	....	....	....	....
India...................	....	....	....	....	3	2	1	6	5	1	....
Turkey in Asia..........	....	....	....	....	....	....	....	....	....	....	....
Other Asia..............	....	....	....	....	....	....	....	....	....	....	....
Total Asia............	....	....	....	....	3	2	1	6	5	1	....
Africa..................	....	....	....	....	1	1	....	1	1	....	....
Australia...............	....	....	....	....	....	....	....	....	....	....	....
Pacific Islands..........	....	....	....	....	....	....	....	....	....	....	....
Central America.........	....	....	....	....	18	17	1	9	8	1	....
South America..........	....	....	....	....	27	18	9	74	60	13	1
West Indies.............	....	....	....	....	1,264	1,152	112	791	610	181	....
Not stated..............	....	....	....	....	26,235	16,422	9,813	5,037	901	186	3,950
Total intercontinental...	....	....	....	....	56,667	40,055	16,612	63,460	37,402	22,041	4,017
British North America.....	....	....	....	....	1,194	786	408	1,020	599	409	12
Mexico..................	....	....	....	....	779	705	74	885	795	90	....
Total continental.......	....	....	....	....	1,973	1,491	482	1,905	1,394	499	12
Grand total...........	7,303	4,691	2,512	100	58,640	41,546	17,094	65,365	38,796	22,540	4,029
United States...........	....	....	....	....	1,285	1,002	283	2,583	1,934	640	9

TABLE IX.—DISTRIBUTION OF PASSENGERS ARRIVING IN THE UNITED STATES, BY SEX AND COUNTRY OF BIRTH, 1820-55 (continued).

Country	1835				1836			
	Total	Males	Females	Sex not stated	Total	Males	Females	Sex not stated
Belgium.................	1	1	....	....	....	....	....	....
Denmark................	37	24	13	....	416	303	113	....
France, including Corsica...	2,696	2,030	666	....	4,443	2,972	1,471	....
Germany................	8,311	5,405	2,906	....	20,707	13,043	7,664	....
Great Britain and Ireland (not specified).........	24,202	14,322	9,743	137	41,004	25,197	15,807	....
England...............	468	340	128	....	420	276	144	....
Ireland...............	5,148	2,658	2,490	....	2,152	1,433	719	....
Scotland..............	63	32	31	....	106	74	32	....
Wales.................	16	10	6	....	2	2	....	....
Greece.................	7	7	....	....	28	27	1	....
Italy, including Sardinia and Sicily...........	60	47	13	....	115	95	20	....
Netherlands............	124	82	42	....	301	213	88	....
Norway and Sweden......	31	23	8	....	57	43	14	....
Poland.................	54	52	2	....	53	47	6	....
Portugal, including Azores, Cape Verde Islands and Madeira..............	46	40	6	....	34	27	7	....
Russia.................	9	7	2	....	2	2	....	....
Spain, including Canary Is..	183	154	29	....	180	154	26	....
Switzerland............	548	326	222	....	445	310	135	....
Turkey in Europe........	....	....	....	....	3	3	...	....
Other Europe...........	....	....	....	....	2	2	...	....
Total Europe..........	42,004	25,560	16,307	137	70,470	44,223	26,247	....
China..................	8	3	3	2	....	....	....	....
India..................	8	8	....	....	4	4	....	....
Turkey in Asia..........	....	....	....	....	....	....	....	....
Other Asia.............	1	1	....	....	....	....	....	....
Total Asia............	17	12	3	2	4	4	....	....
Africa.................	15	11	4	....	6	6	....	....
Australia..............	....	....	....	....	....	....	....	....
Pacific Islands.........	3	2	1	....	2	1	1	....
Central America........	4	4	....	....	....	....	....	....
South America.........	145	125	18	2	146	126	20	....
West Indies............	938	776	159	3	1,178	926	252	....
Not stated.............	23	11	5	7	824	....	....	824
Total intercontinental...	43,149	26,501	16,497	151	72,630	45,286	26,520	824
British North America.....	1,193	783	410	....	2,814	1,854	960	....
Mexico................	1,032	912	120	....	798	725	73	....
Total continental.......	2,225	1,695	530	....	3,612	2,579	1,033	....
Grand total...........	45,374	28,196	17,027	151	76,242	47,865	27,553	824
United States...........	3,342	2,556	764	22	4,730	3,594	1,136	....

TABLE IX.—Distribution of passengers arriving in the United States, by sex and country of birth, 1820-55 (continued)

Country	1837				1838			
	Total	Males	Females	Sex not stated	Total	Males	Females	Sex not stated
Belgium	....	....	....	....	14	9	5	....
Denmark	109	68	41	....	52	38	14	....
France, including Corsica	5,074	3,461	1,613	....	3,676	2.565	1,111	....
Germany	23,740	15,567	8,173	....	11,683	7,294	4,389	....
Great Britain and Ireland (not specified)	39,073	23,710	15,363	....	16,635	9,992	6,643	....
England	896	613	283	....	157	104	53	....
Ireland	737	428	309	....	1,225	700	525	....
Scotland	14	10	4	....	48	29	19	....
Wales	6	....	6	....	....	....	....	....
Greece	5	5	....	....	4	4	....	....
Italy, including Sardinia and Sicily	36	32	4	....	86	71	15	....
Netherlands	312	226	86	....	27	20	7	....
Norway and Sweden	290	179	111	....	60	44	16	....
Poland	81	72	9	....	41	36	5	....
Portugal, including Azores, Cape Verde Islands and Madeira	39	30	9	....	32	23	9	....
Russia	19	17	2	....	13	13	....	....
Spain, including Canary Is.	230	197	33	....	202	175	27	....
Switzerland	383	250	133	....	123	95	28	....
Turkey in Europe	....	....	....	....	....	....	....	....
Other Europe	....	....	....	....	....	....	....	....
Total Europe	71,044	44,865	26,179	....	34,078	21,212	12,886	....
China	....	....	....	....	....	....	....	....
India	11	6	5	....	1	1	....	....
Turkey in Asia	....	....	....	....	....	....	....	....
Other Asia	....	....	....	....	....	....	....	....
Total Asia	11	6	5	....	1	1	....	....
Africa	2	2	....	....	12	12	....	....
Australia	....	....	....	....	....	....	....	....
Pacific Islands,	....	....	....	....	....	....	....	....
Central America	4	2	2	....	....	....	....	....
South America	91	76	15	....	72	54	18	....
West Indies	1,627	1,277	350	....	1,231	967	264	....
Not stated	4,655	1,251	554	2,850	1,833	17	61	1,755
Total intercontinental	77,434	47,479	27,105	2,850	37,227	22,263	13,209	1,755
British North America	1,279	816	463	....	1,476	1,034	442	....
Mexico	627	542	85	....	211	177	34	....
Total continental	1,906	1,358	548	....	1,687	1,211	476	....
Grand total	79,340	48,837	27,653	2,850	38,914	23,474	13,685	1,755
United States	5,616	4,566	1,053	....	6,245	5,030	1,215	....

TABLE IX.—Distribution of passengers arriving in the United States, by sex and country of birth, 1820-55 (continued).

Country	1839				1840			
	Total	Males	Females	Sex not stated	Total	Males	Females	Sex not stated
Belgium.................	1	1	....	....	2	1	1	....
Denmark................	56	44	12	....	152	96	56	....
France, including Corsica...	7,200	4,837	2,363	....	7,419	4,843	2,576	....
Germany................	21,028	13,214	7,814	....	29,704	18,805	10,899	....
Great Britain and Ireland (not specified).........	32,973	19,999	12,974	....	41,027	25,045	15,982	....
England...............	62	46	16	....	318	219	99	....
Ireland................	1,199	796	403	....	677	386	291	....
Scotland.......	....	....	....	....	21	20	1	....
Wales................	....	....	....	....	.....	.....	....	....
Greece.....	....	....	....	....	3	3	....	....
Italy, including Sardinia and Sicily.............	84	72	12	....	37	36	1	....
Netherlands.............	85	53	32	....	57	36	21	....
Norway and Sweden......	324	188	136	....	55	40	15	....
Poland.................	46	34	12	....	5	5	....	....
Portugal, including Azores, Cape Verde Islands and Madeira..............	26	20	6	....	25	20	5	....
Russia.................	7	4	3	....	....	....	....	....
Spain,including Canary Is..	428	333	95	....	136	110	26	....
Switzerland.............	607	430	177	....	500	293	207	....
Turkey in Europe........	1	1	....	....	1	1	....	....
Other Europe...........	28	20	8	....	....	....	....	...
Total Europe..........	64,155	40,092	24,063	....	80,139	49,959	30,180	....
China..................	....	....	....	....	1	....	....	....
India..................	....	....	....	....	1	1	....	....
Turkey in Asia..........	....	....	....	....	....	....	....	....
Other Asia.............	....	....	....	....	....	....	....	....
Total Asia.......... ...	....	....	....	....	1	1	....	....
Africa..................	8	6	2	....	6	4	2	....
Australia...............	1	1	....	....	2	2	....	....
Pacific Islands...........	....	....	....	....	....	....	....	....
Central America.........	....	....	....	....	....	....	....	....
South America..........	49	38	11	....	36	31	5	....
West Indies.............	1,289	1,035	254	....	1,446	1,164	282	....
Not stated.............	288	111	165	12	103	35	17	51
Total intercontinental...	65,790	41,283	24,495	12	81,733	51,196	30,486	51
British North America.. ..	1,926	1,329	597	....	1,938	1,341	597	....
Mexico.................	353	320	33	....	395	346	49	....
Total continental.......	2,279	1,649	630	....	2,333	1,687	646	....
Grand total...........	68,069	42,932	25,125	12	84,066	52,883	31,132	51
United States...........	6,597	5,268	1,329	....	8,141	6,115	2,026	....

TABLE IX.—Distribution of passengers arriving in the United States, by sex and country of birth, 1820-55 (continued).

Country	1841				1842			
	Total	Males	Females	Sex not stated	Total	Males	Females	Sex not stated
Belgium	106	69	37	....	44	34	10	....
Denmark	31	19	12	....	35	28	7	....
France, including Corsica	5,006	3,431	1,575	....	4,505	2,982	1,523	....
Germany	15,291	9,330	5,961	....	20,370	12,290	8,080	....
Great Britain and Ireland (not specified)	50,432	29,434	20,998	....	66,698	39,136	27,562	....
England	147	119	28	....	1,743	982	761	....
Ireland	3,291	1,868	1,423	....	4,844	2,727	2,117	....
Scotland	35	28	7	....	24	12	12	....
Wales	55	43	12	....	38	24	14	....
Greece	....	....	....	....	1	1	....	....
Italy, including Sardinia and Sicily	179	152	27	....	100	81	19	....
Netherlands	214	124	90	....	330	188	142	....
Norway and Sweden	195	130	65	....	553	311	242	....
Poland	15	10	5	....	10	8	2	....
Portugal, including Azores, Cape Verde Islands and Madeira	10	10	....	....	19	17	2	....
Russia	174	101	73	....	28	22	6	....
Spain, including Canary Is.	215	170	45	....	123	106	17	....
Switzerland	751	471	280	....	483	318	165	....
Turkey in Europe	6	6	....	....	2	2	....	....
Other Europe	66	42	24	....	1	1	....	....
Total Europe	76,219	45,557	30,662	....	99,951	59,270	40,681	....
China	2	2	....	....	4	....	4	....
India	1	1	....	....	2	2	....	....
Turkey in Asia	....	....	....	....	....	....	....	....
Other Asia	....	....	....	....	1	1	....	....
Total Asia	3	3	....	....	7	3	4	....
Africa	14	8	6	....	3	2	1	....
Australia	....	....	....	....	....	....	....	....
Pacific Islands	3	....	3	....	....	....	....	....
Central America	....	....	....	....	1	1	....	....
South America	219	57	162	....	102	79	23	....
West Indies	1,042	848	194	....	1,410	1,155	255	....
Not stated	621	119	326	176	610	137	92	381
Total intercontinental	78,121	46,592	31,353	176	102,084	60,647	41,056	381
British North America	1,816	1,201	615	....	2,078	1,265	813	....
Mexico	352	289	63	....	403	365	38	....
Total continental	2,168	1,490	678	....	2,481	1,630	851	....
Grand total	80,289	48,082	32,031	176	104,565	62,277	41,907	381
United States	7,516	5,733	1,783	......	6,415	4,847	1,568	......

TABLE IX.—DISTRIBUTION OF PASSENGERS ARRIVING IN THE UNITED STATES, BY SEX AND COUNTRY OF BIRTH, 1820-55 (continued).

Country	1843 three first quarters 1843				1844 1 Oct. 1843 to 30 Sept. 1844			1845			
	Total	Males	Females	Sex not stated	Total	Males	Females	Total	Males	Females	Sex not stated
Belgium	135	81	54	....	165	112	53	541	345	196	....
Denmark	29	20	9	....	25	18	7	54	29	25	....
France, including Corsica	3,346	1,971	1,375	....	3,156	1,924	1,232	7,663	5,086	2,577	....
Germany	14,441	8,324	6,117	....	20,731	12,188	8,543	34,355	20,650	13,705	....
Great Britain and Ireland (not specified)	23,369	12,522	10,847	....	40,969	21,984	18,985	53,301	28,598	24,702	1
England	3,517	2,085	1,432	....	1,357	814	543	1,710	1,062	598	50
Ireland	1,173	678	495	....	5,491	2,811	2,680	8,641	3,855	3,964	822
Scotland	41	31	10	....	23	13	10	368	205	154	9
Wales	....	....	....	....	3	1	2	11	3	8	....
Greece	4	4	....	....	3	3	....	2	2	....	....
Italy, including Sardinia and Sicily	117	94	23	....	141	112	29	137	108	28	1
Netherlands	330	181	149	....	184	113	71	791	486	305	....
Norway and Sweden	1,748	1,019	729	....	1,311	879	432	928	557	371	....
Poland	17	15	2	....	36	27	9	6	6	....	....
Portugal, including Azores, Cape Verde Islands and Madeira	40	35	5	....	40	32	8	21	17	4	....
Russia	6	4	2	....	13	12	1	1	1	....	....
Spain, including Canary Is	145	112	33	....	270	214	56	304	249	55	....
Switzerland	553	318	235	....	839	513	326	471	293	178	....
Turkey in Europe	5	5	....	....	10	6	4	3	2	....	1
Other Europe	5	4	1	....	50	44	6	....	....	....	....
Total Europe	49,021	27,503	21,518	....	74,817	41,820	32,997	109,308	61,554	46,870	884
China	3	2	1	....	3	3	....	6	6	....	....
India	2	2	....	....	1	1	....	....	....	....	....
Turkey in Asia	....	....	....	....	....	....	....	....	....	....	....
Other Asia	6	3	3	....	2	2	....	....	....	....	....
Total Asia	11	7	4	....	6	6	....	6	6	....	....
Africa	6	4	2	....	14	9	5	4	4	....	....
Australia	....	....	....	....	....	....	....	....	....	....	....
Pacific Islands	5	3	2	....	....	....	....	....	....	....	....
Central America	12	11	1	....	....	....	....	21	14	7	....
South America	62	47	15	....	61	46	15	80	70	10	....
West Indies	880	695	185	....	771	589	182	1,241	1,036	204	1
Not stated	599	547	49	3	38	27	11	18	6	12	....
Total intercontinental	50,596	28,817	21,776	3	75,707	42,497	33,210	110,678	62,690	47,103	885
British North America	1,502	903	599	....	2,711	1,768	943	3,195	1,882	957	356
Mexico	398	349	49	....	197	166	31	498	443	55	....
Total continental	1,900	1,252	648	....	2,908	1,934	974	3,693	2,325	1,012	356
Grand total	52,496	30,069	22,424	3	78,615	44,431	34,184	114,371	65,015	48,115	1,241
United States	4,033	3,103	930	....	6,149	4,466	1,683	5,525	4,164	1,196	165

TABLE IX.—DISTRIBUTION OF PASSENGERS ARRIVING IN THE UNITED STATES, BY SEX AND COUNTRY OF BIRTH, 1820-55 (continued).

Country	1846				1847			
	Total	Males	Females	Sex not stated	Total	Males	Females	Sex not stated
Belgium..................	43	33	10	....	1,473	790	683	....
Denmark...............	114	68	46	....	13	10	2	1
France, including Corsica...	10,583	6,549	4,034	....	20,040	12,151	7,878	11
Germany...............	57,561	34,032	23,529	....	74,281	44,345	29,650	286
Great Britain and Ireland (not specified)..........	57,677	31,565	26,112	....	95,240	54,148	41,092	....
England...............	2,854	1,625	1,229	....	3,476	2,032	1,437	7
Ireland...............	12,949	6,388	6,561	....	29,640	16,066	13,359	215
Scotland..............	305	192	113	....	337	203	134	....
Wales................	147	82	65	....	145	77	68	....
Greece.................	3	3	....	....	....	....	....	....
Italy, including Sardinia and Sicily..............	151	123	28	....	164	109	55	....
Netherlands.............	979	575	404	....	2,631	1,576	1,055	....
Norway and Sweden......	1,916	1,123	793	....	1,307	738	442	127
Poland.................	4	4	....	....	8	3	5	....
Portugal, including Azores, Cape Verde Islands and Madeira..............	17	14	3	....	29	22	7	....
Russia.................	248	145	103	....	5	4	....	1
Spain, including Canary Is..	73	63	10	....	158	95	63	....
Switzerland.............	698	432	266	....	192	116	71	5
Turkey in Europe.........	4	4	....	....	2	2	....	....
Other Europe...........	4	4	....	....	....	....	....	....
Total Europe..........	146,330	83,024	63,306	....	229,141	132,487	96,001	653
China..................	7	3	4	....	4	1	3	....
India..................	4	1	3	....	8	3	5	....
Turkey in Asia...........	....	....	....	....	....	....	....	....
Other Asia..............	....	....	....	....	....	....	....	....
Total Asia.............	11	4	7	....	12	4	8	....
Africa..................	4	1	3	....	....	....	....	....
Australia...............	....	....	....	....	....	....	....	....
Pacific Islands...........	....	....	....	....	1	1	....	....
Central America..........	5	4	1	....	21	10	11	..
South America..........	92	78	14	....	70	49	21	....
West Indies.............	1,351	1,046	305	....	1,251	990	261	....
Not stated..............	2,546	920	729	897	583	71	200	312
Total intercontinental...	150,339	85,077	64,365	897	231,079	133,612	96,502	965
British North America.....	3,855	2,523	1,332	....	3,827	2,413	1,414	....
Mexico.................	222	177	45	....	62	61	1	...
Total continental.......	4,077	2,700	1,377	....	3,889	2,474	1,415	....
Grand total...........	154,416	87,777	65,742	897	234,968	136,086	97,917	965
United States...........	4,233	3,197	1,036	....	4,514	3,081	1,408	25

TABLE IX.—Distribution of passengers arriving in the United States, by sex and country of birth, 1820-55 (continued).

Country	1848				1849			
	Total	Males	Females	Sex not stated	Total	Males	Females	Sex not stated
Belgium.................	897	534	363	....	590	330	260	....
Denmark................	210	144	66	....	8	7	1	....
France, including Corsica..	7,743	4,850	2,893	....	5,841	3,878	1,963	....
Germany................	58,465	36,232	22,233	....	60,235	40,703	19,532	....
Great Britain and Ireland (not specified)..........	117,829	68,595	49,234	....	175,841	101,447	74,394	....
England..............	4,455	2,664	1,791	....	6,036	3,385	2,651	....
Ireland..............	24,802	13,444	11,358	....	31,321	16,605	14,716	....
Scotland.............	659	404	255	....	1,060	619	441	....
Wales................	348	214	134	....	272	154	118	....
Greece..................	1	1	....	....	....	....	....	....
Italy, including Sardinia and Sicily..............	241	175	66	....	209	158	51	....
Netherlands.............	918	534	384	....	1,190	711	479	....
Norway and Sweden......	903	580	323	....	3,473	2,168	1,305	....
Poland..................	....	....	....	....	4	4	....	....
Portugal, including Azores, Cape Verde Islands and Madeira...............	87	60	27	....	74	53	21	....
Russia..................	1	....	1	....	44	29	15	....
Spain, including Canary Is.	164	136	28	....	329	227	102	....
Switzerland.............	319	198	121	....	13	10	3	....
Turkey in Europe........	3	3	....	....	9	9	....	....
Other Europe...........	....	....	....	....	....	....	....	....
Total Europe..........	218,045	128,768	89,277	....	286,549	170,497	116,052	....
China..................	....	....	....	....	3	3	....	....
India...................	6	4	2	....	8	6	2	....
Turkey in Asia..........	....	....	....	....	....	....	....	....
Other Asia.............	2	2	....	....	....	....	....	....
Total Asia............	8	6	2	....	11	9	2	....
Africa..................	10	5	5	....	4	4	....	....
Australia...............	....	....	....	....	....	....	....	....
Pacific Islands...........	3	2	1	....	....	....	....	....
Central America.........	4	4	....	....	233	233	....	....
South America..........	150	106	44	....	190	150	40	....
West Indies.............	1,338	988	350	....	1,073	764	309	....
Not stated..............	472	....	....	472	1,556	804	310	442
Total intercontinental...	220,030	129,879	89,679	472	289,616	172,461	116,713	442
British North America.....	6,473	4,006	2,467	....	6,890	4,283	2,537	70
Mexico.................	24	21	3	....	518	488	30	....
Total continental.......	6,497	4,027	2,470	....	7,408	4,771	2,567	70
Grand total..........	226,527	133,906	92,149	472	297,024	177,232	119,280	512
United States...........	2,956	2,222	734	....	2,659	2,024	635	....

TABLE IX.—DISTRIBUTION OF PASSENGERS ARRIVING IN THE UNITED STATES, BY SEX AND COUNTRY OF BIRTH, 1820-55 (continued).

Country	1850				1850 Quarter ending December 31			
	Total	Males	Females	Sex not stated	Total	Males	Females	Sex not stated
Belgium.................	1,055	530	525	....	25	5	20	....
Denmark.................	10	9	1	....	10	7	3	....
France, including Corsica...	8,009	5,521	2,488	....	1,372	952	420	....
Germany.................	63,182	39,218	23,964	....	15,714	19,164	6,550	....
Great Britain and Ireland (not specified)..........	141,859	80,173	61,686	....	25,151	13,189	11,962	....
England...............	5,276	2,959	2,316	1	1,521	912	609	....
Ireland...............	27,674	13,463	14,211	....	12,506	6,411	6,095	....
Scotland..............	627	357	270	....	233	145	88	....
Wales.................	49	29	20	....	193	81	112	....
Greece.................	2	2	....	....	....	....	....	....
Italy, including Sardinia and Sicily..............	373	300	73	....	58	32	26	....
Netherlands.............	576	399	177	....	108	79	29	....
Norway and Sweden	1,363	819	544	....	206	146	60	....
Poland.................	3	2	1	....	2	2	....	....
Portugal, including Azores, Cape Verde Islands and Madeira...............	546	350	196	....	....	....	....	....
Russia.................	31	18	13	....	....	....	....	....
Spain, including Canary Is..	325	269	56	....	104	90	14	....
Switzerland.............	146	104	42	....	179	106	73	....
Turkey in Europe.........	13	13	....	....	2	2	....	....
Other Europe............	....	....	....	....	3	3	....	....
Total Europe..........	251,119	144,535	106,583	1	57,387	31,326	26,061	....
China..................	3	2	1	....	....	....	....	....
India..................	4	3	1	....	....	....	....	....
Turkey in Asia..........	....	....	....	....	....	....	....	....
Other Asia.............	....	....	....	....	....	....	....	....
Total Asia............	7	5	2	....	....	....	....	....
Africa.................	....	....	....	....	....	....	....	....
Australia..............	....	....	....	....	....	....	....	....
Pacific Islands..........	17	10	7	....	....	....	....	....
Central America.........	71	57	14	....	....	....	....	....
South America..........	2,462	1,726	736	....	91	81	10	....
West Indies.............	2,903	2,100	803	....	268	204	64	....
Not stated.............	45,131	42,659	1,669	803	551	325	45	181
Total intercontinental...	301,710	191,092	109,814	804	58,297	31,936	26,180	181
British North America.....	7,796	4,824	2,738	234	1,580	957	623	....
Mexico.................	498	415	83	....	99	97	2	....
Total continental........	8,294	5,239	2,821	234	1,679	1,054	625	....
Grand total...........	310,004	196,331	112,635	1,038	59,976	32,990	26,805	181
United States...........	5,330	4,573	757	....	5,594	5,292	302	....

TABLE IX.—DISTRIBUTION OF PASSENGERS ARRIVING IN THE UNITED STATES, BY SEX AND COUNTRY OF BIRTH, 1820-55 (continued).

Country	1851				1852			
	Total	Males	Females	Sex not stated	Total	Males	Females	Sex not stated
Belgium................	....	....	....	....	8	4	4	....
Denmark	14	13	1	....	3	3	....	....
France, including Corsica...	20,126	12,801	7,325	....	6,763	4,292	2,471	....
Germany...............	72,482	44,210	28,272	....	145,918	86,900	57,606	1,412
Great Britain and Ireland (not specified)..........	210,383	117,482	92,901	....	1,803	1,050	753	....
England..............	5,306	3,174	2,130	2	30,007	17,307	12,700	....
Ireland..............	55,874	29,287	26,587	....	159,548	85,715	73,808	25
Scotland.............	966	579	387	....	8,148	4,733	3,415	....
Wales................	211	149	62	....	741	432	309	....
Greece.................	....	....	....	....	10	7	3	....
Italy, including Sardinia and Sicily..............	447	347	100	....	351	304	47	....
Netherlands.............	352	276	76	....	1,719	983	736	....
Norway and Sweden......	2,424	1,448	976	....	4,103	2,440	1,663	....
Poland.................	10	9	1	....	110	101	9	....
Portugal, including Azores, Cape Verde Islands and Madeira..............	161	119	42	....	246	191	55	....
Russia.................	1	1	....	....	2	2	....	....
Spain, including Canary Is.	435	362	73	....	.391	310	81	....
Switzerland.............	427	284	143	....	2,788	1,786	1,002	....
Turkey in Europe........	2	2	....	....	3	3	....	....
Other Europe...........	....	....	....	....	473	290	183	....
Total Europe..........	369,621	210,543	159,076	2	363,135	206,853	154,845	1,437
China..................	....	....	....	....	....	....	....	....
India..................	2	1	1	....	4	2	2	....
Turkey in Asia..........	....	....	....	....	....	....	....	....
Other Asia.............	....	....	....	....	....	....	....	....
Total Asia..........	2	1	1	....	4	2	2	....
Africa.................	5	4	1	....	4	....	4	....
Australia...............	....	....	....	....	....	....	....	....
Pacific Islands..........	....	....	....	....	....	....	....	....
Central America.........	96	96	....	....	....	....	....	....
South America..........	59	41	18	....	39	26	13	....
West Indies............	1,929	1,491	438	....	1,232	850	382	....
Not stated.............	135	50	21	64	765	582	182	1
Total intercontinental...	371,847	212,226	159,555	66	365,179	208,313	155,428	1,438
British North America.....	7,438	4,780	2,658	....	6,352	4,091	2,261	....
Mexico.................	181	175	6	....	72	65	7	....
Total continental......	7,619	4,955	2,664	....	6,424	4,156	2,268	....
Grand total...........	379,466	217,181	162,219	66	371,603	212,469	157,696	1,438
United States...........	29,362	27,836	1,526	....	25,740	23,262	2,478	....

TABLE IX.—Distribution of passengers arriving in the United States, by sex and country of birth, 1820-55 (concluded).

Country	1853				1854				1855			
	Total	Males	Females	Sex not stated	Total	Males	Females	Sex not stated	Total	Males	Females	Sex not stated
Belgium..........	87	73	14	..	266	193	73		1,506	819	687	..
Denmark.........	32	29	3	..	691	407	284		528	287	241	..
France, including Corsica.........	10,770	6,729	4,041	..	13,317	8,812	4,505		6,044	3,869	2,175	..
Germany.........	141,946	84,217	57,729	..	215,009	127,116	87,893		71,918	40,543	31,375	..
Great Britain and Ireland (not specified).........	2,481	1,401	1,080	..	4,325	2,577	1,748		2,250	1,198	1,052	..
England........	28,867	16,075	12,792	..	48,901	28,989	19,912		38,871	21,986	16,885	..
Ireland.........	162,649	86,353	76,296	..	101,606	56,516	45,090		49,627	26,029	23,598	..
Scotland........	6,006	3,234	2,772	..	4,605	2,477	2,128		5,275	3,173	2,102	..
Wales..........	222	143	79	..	816	483	333		1,176	635	541	..
Greece..........	12	9	3	..	1	1	....		....	....	....	..
Italy, including Sardinia and Sicily............	555	400	155	..	1,263	861	402		1,052	863	189	..
Netherlands......	600	372	228	..	1,534	885	649		2,588	1,482	1,106	..
Norway and Sweden............	3,364	1,891	1,473	..	3,531	2,057	1,474		821	448	373	..
Poland...........	33	24	9	..	208	117	91		462	300	162	..
Portugal, including Azores,Cape Verde Islands and Madeira	359	242	117	..	340	287	53		381	307	74	..
Russia...........	3	3	....	..	2	2	....		13	12	1	..
Spain, including Canary Islands..	1,091	862	229	..	1,433	1,097	336		951	748	200	3
Switzerland......	2,748	1,638	1,110	..	7,953	4,802	3,151		4,433	2,488	1,945	..
Turkey in Europe..	15	15	....	..	7	7	....		9	7	2	..
Other Europe.....	....	....	....	..	2	2	....		....	....	....	..
Total Europe...	361,840	203,710	158,130	..	405,810	237,688	168,122		187,905	105,194	82,708	3
China............	42	42	....	..	13,100	12,427	673		3,526	3,524	2	..
India............	5	2	3	..	....	....	....		6	3	3	..
Turkey in Asia....	....	....	....	..	....	....	....		....	....	....	..
Other Asia........	....	....	....	..	....	....	....		8	7	1	..
Total Asia......	47	44	3	..	13,100	12,427	673		3,540	3,534	6	..
Africa............	8	6	2	..	6	2	4		16	14	2	..
Australia.........	....	....	....	..	11	11	....		4	2	2	..
Pacific Islands....	....	....	....	..	17	11	6		7	4	3	..
Central America...	....	....	....	..	24	21	3		1	1	....	..
South America....	38	23	15	..	136	79	57		191	151	40	..
West Indies.......	406	267	139	..	1,036	746	290		887	644	243	..
Not stated.......	720	408	240	72	356	297	59		145	87	58	..
Total intercontinental.......	363,059	204,458	158,529	72	420,496	251,282	169,214		192,696	109,631	83,062	3
British No.America	5,424	3,364	2,060	..	6,891	4,532	2,359		7,761	5,367	2,394	..
Mexico..........	162	136	26	..	446	363	83		420	309	111	..
Total continental...	5,586	3,500	2,086	..	7,337	4,895	2,442		8,181	5,676	2,505	..
Grand total.......	368,645	207,958	160,615	72	427,833	256,177	171,656		200,877	115,307	85,567	3
United States.....	32,337	28,774	3,563	..	32,641	28,710	3,931		29,599	24,874	4,716	9

TABLE IXa.—Distribution of immigrant aliens (fiscal years ending 30 June), by sex and country of origin (or nationality), 1869-98.

Country	1869			1870		
	Total	Males	Females	Total	Males	Females
Europe:						
Austria-Hungary..................	1,499	867	632	4,425	2,341	2,084
Belgium........................	1,922	1,122	800	1,002	718	284
Bulgaria, Serbia and Montenegro.....	....	....	....	....	....	....
Denmark........................	3,649	2,397	1,252	4,083	2,519	1,564
France, including Corsica..........	3,879	2,531	1,348	4,009	2,693	1,316
German Empire..................	131,042	77,438	53,604	118,225	70,688	47,537
Greece.........................	8	7	1	22	20	2
Italy, including Sicily and Sardinia....	1,489	1,076	413	2,891	2,132	759
Netherlands.....................	1,134	739	395	1,066	663	403
Norway........................	16,068	9,147	6,921	13,216	8,003	5,213
Poland.........................	184	138	46	223	140	83
Portugal, including Cape Verde and Azore Islands	507	302	205	697	450	247
Rumania........................	....	....	....	....	....	....
Russian Empire..................	343	228	115	907	550	357
Spain, including Canary and Balearic Islands........................	1,123	749	374	663	487	176
Sweden.........................	24,224	15,663	8,561	13,443	8,306	5,137
Switzerland.....................	3,650	2,373	1,277	3,075	2,002	1,073
Turkey in Europe.................	18	14	4	6	6	....
United Kingdom:						
England.......................	35,673	22,952	12,721	60,957	38,106	22,851
Ireland.......................	40,786	22,708	18,078	56,996	31,414	25,582
Scotland......................	7,751	4,915	2,836	12,521	7,605	4,916
Wales........................	660	460	200	1,011	574	437
Not specified..................	40,354	23,379	16,975	29,188	17,084	12,104
Other Europe....................	....	....	....	....	....	....
Total Europe..................	315,963	189,205	126,758	328,626	196,501	132,125
Asia:						
China..........................	12,874	11,900	974	15,740	14,624	1,116
India..........................	3	1	2	24	19	5
Japan..........................	63	53	10	48	46	2
Turkey in Asia...................	2	2	....	....	....	....
Other Asia......................	7	4	3	13	10	3
Total Asia....................	12,949	11,960	989	15,825	14,699	1,126
Africa..........................	72	47	25	31	26	5
Australia and New Zealand..........	....	....	....	36	17	19
Pacific Islands, not specified..........	....	....	....	....	....	....
British North American possessions....	21,120	11,888	9,232	40,414	22,726	17,688
Central America..................	3	3	....	33	31	2
Mexico.........................	320	225	95	463	358	105
South America...................	91	64	27	69	59	10
West Indies, including Jamaica.......	2,233	1,462	771	1,679	1,181	498
Countries not specified.............	17	11	6	27	14	13
Grand total...................	352,768	214,865	137,903	387,203	235,612	151,591

TABLE IXa.—Distribution of immigrant aliens (fiscal years ending 30 June), by sex and country of origin (or nationality), 1869-98 (continued).

Country	1871			1872		
	Total	Males	Females	Total	Males	Females
Europe:						
Austria-Hungary	4,887	2,557	2,330	4,410	2,465	1,945
Belgium	774	523	251	738	481	257
Bulgaria, Serbia and Montenegro	....	....	....	....	....	....
Denmark	2,015	1,347	668	3,690	2,534	1,156
France, including Corsica	3,138	1,993	1,145	9,317	6,061	3,256
German Empire	82,554	47,775	34,779	141,109	83,418	57,691
Greece	11	10	1	12	11	1
Italy, including Sicily and Sardinia	2,816	2,072	744	4,190	3,171	1,019
Netherlands	993	697	296	1,909	1,185	724
Norway	9,418	6,179	3,239	11,421	6,840	4,581
Poland	535	328	207	1,647	1,158	489
Portugal, including Cape Verde and Azore Islands	887	510	377	1,306	956	350
Rumania	....	....	....	....	....	....
Russian Empire	673	394	279	1,018	648	370
Spain, including Canary and Balearic Islands	558	423	135	595	435	160
Sweden	10,699	6,803	3,896	13,464	8,510	4,954
Switzerland	2,269	1,399	870	3,650	2,312	1,338
Turkey in Europe	23	19	4	20	16	4
United Kingdom:						
England	56,530	34,412	22,118	69,764	42,496	26,268
Ireland	57,439	30,939	26,500	68,732	36,548	32,184
Scotland	11,984	7,087	4,897	13,916	7,940	5,976
Wales	899	517	382	1,214	685	529
Not specified	16,042	9,128	6,914	18	12	6
Other Europe	1	....	1	15	11	4
Total Europe	265,145	155,112	110,033	352,155	207,893	144,262
Asia:						
China	7,135	6,786	349	7,788	7,605	183
India	14	8	6	12	7	5
Japan	78	77	1	17	17	....
Turkey in Asia	4	2	2	....	....	....
Other Asia	9	8	1	8	6	2
Total Asia	7,240	6,881	359	7,825	7,635	190
Africa	24	19	5	41	24	17
Australia and New Zealand	18	13	5	2,180	1,961	219
Pacific Islands, not specified	3	2	1	236	194	42
British North American possessions	47,164	27,195	19,969	40,204	20,965	19,239
Central America	4	2	2	8	7	1
Mexico	402	336	66	569	487	82
South America	96	71	25	102	75	27
West Indies, including Jamaica	1,169	749	420	1,322	837	485
Countries not specified	85	48	37	164	92	72
Grand total	321,350	190,428	130,922	404,806	240,170	164,636

TABLE IXa.—Distribution of immigrant aliens (fiscal years ending 30 June), by sex and country of origin (or nationality), 1869-98 (continued).

Country	1873			1874		
	Total	Males	Females	Total	Males	Females
Europe:						
Austria-Hungary..................	7,112	3,813	3,299	8,850	4,882	3,968
Belgium..........................	1,176	763	413	817	556	261
Bulgaria, Serbia and Montenegro....	....	....	....	....	....	....
Denmark.........................	4,931	3,326	1,605	3,082	1,824	1,258
France, including Corsica..........	14,798	9,500	5,298	9,644	5,856	3,788
German Empire.............⌢.....	149,671	86,411	63,260	87,291	49,554	37,737
Greece...........................	23	21	2	36	33	3
Italy, including Sicily and Sardinia....	8,757	6,878	1,879	7,666	6,140	1,526
Netherlands......................	3,811	2,282	1,529	2,444	1,409	1,035
Norway..........................	16,247	9,928	6,319	10,384	6,766	3,618
Poland...........................	3,338	2,224	1,114	1,795	1,078	717
Portugal, including Cape Verde and Azore Islands	1,185	807	378	1,611	1,132	479
Rumania.........................	....	....	....	....	....	....
Russian Empire...................	1,634	1,023	611	4,073	2,692	1,381
Spain, including Canary and Balearic Islands.........................	541	409	132	485	388	97
Sweden..........................	14,303	8,656	5,647	5,712	3,318	2,394
Switzerland......................	3,107	1,943	1,164	3,093	1,845	1,248
Turkey in Europe.................	53	39	14	62	47	15
United Kingdom:						
England.....................	74,801	45,024	29,777	50,905	29,921	20,984
Ireland......................	77,344	40,993	36,351	53,707	27,047	26,660
Scotland....................	13,841	8,254	5,587	10,429	6,301	4,128
Wales.......................	840	518	322	665	392	273
Not specified................	18	12	6	22	11	11
Other Europe...................	10	6	4	10	6	4
Total Europe........	397,541	232,830	164,711	262,783	151,198	111,585
Asia:						
China...........................	20,292	19,403	889	13,776	13,533	243
India............................	15	12	3	17	9	8
Japan...........................	9	9	....	21	18	3
Turkey in Asia...................	3	3	....	6	2	4
Other Asia......................	6	4	2	18	15	3
Total Asia....................	20,325	19,431	894	13,838	13,577	261
Africa...........................	28	22	6	58	39	19
Australia and New Zealand.........	1,135	992	143	960	782	178
Pacific Islands, not specified.........	279	238	41	233	206	27
British North American possessions....	37,891	20,461	17,430	33,020	21,792	11,228
Central America..................	38	31	7	12	10	2
Mexico..........................	606	483	123	386	311	75
South America...................	166	145	21	144	121	23
West Indies, including Jamaica.......	1,634	1,067	567	1,777	1,109	668
Countries not specified.............	160	92	68	128	80	48
Grand total..................	459,803	275,792	184,011	313,339	189,225	124,114

TABLE IXa.—Distribution of immigrant aliens (fiscal years ending 30 June), by sex and country of origin (or nationality), 1869-98 (continued).

Country	1875			1876		
	Total	Males	Females	Total	Males	Females
Europe:						
Austria-Hungary.................	7,658	4,129	3,529	6,276	3,484	2,792
Belgium........................	615	475	140	515	418	97
Bulgaria, Serbia and Montenegro....	....	....	....	....	....	....
Denmark........................	2,656	1,563	1,093	1,547	967	580
France, including Corsica..........	8,321	5,378	2,943	8,004	5,317	2,687
German Empire...................	47,769	27,576	20,193	31,937	18,673	13,264
Greece..........................	25	19	6	19	17	2
Italy, including Sicily and Sardinia....	3,631	2,812	819	3,015	2,312	703
Netherlands.....................	1,237	750	487	,855	560	295
Norway.........................	6,093	3,726	2,367	5,173	3,404	1,769
Poland..........................	984	586	398	925	568	357
Portugal, including Cape Verde and Azore Islands..................	1,939	1,261	678	1,277	745	532
Rumania........................	....	....	....	....	....	....
Russian Empire..................	7,997	4,384	3,613	4,775	2,776	1,999
Spain, including Canary and Balearic Islands........................	601	467	134	518	406	112
Sweden.........................	5,573	3,274	2,299	5,603	3,479	2,124
Switzerland......................	1,814	1,127	687	1,549	1,047	502
Turkey in Europe:................	27	25	2	38	29	9
United Kingdom:						
England.......................	40,130	24,497	15,633	24,373	14,949	9,424
Ireland.......................	37,957	18,029	19,928	19,575	8,938	10,637
Scotland......................	7,310	4,473	2,837	4,582	2,989	1,593
Wales........................	449	270	179	324	199	125
Not specified..................	16	15	1	12	6	6
Other Europe.....................	159	155	4	28	24	4
Total Europe..................	182,961	104,991	77,970	120,920	71,307	49,613
Asia:						
China...........................	16,437	16,055	382	22,781	22,521	260
India...........................	19	13	6	25	14	11
Japan...........................	3	3	....	4	4	....
Turkey in Asia...................	1	1	....	8	5	3
Other Asia......................	39	37	2	125	73	52
Total Asia.....................	16,499	16,109	390	22,943	22,617	326
Africa...........................	54	38	16	89	60	29
Australia and New Zealand..........	1,104	879	225	1,205	976	229
Pacific Islands, not specified..........	164	147	17	107	98	9
British North America possessions.....	24,097	16,189	7,908	22,505	15,299	7,206
Central America..................	11	10	1	12	6	6
Mexico..........................	610	481	129	631	466	165
South America...................	132	105	27	156	130	26
West Indies including Jamaica.......	1,790	958	832	1,382	809	573
Countries not specified.............	76	43	33	36	18	18
Grand total....................	227,498	139,950	87,548	169,986	111,786	58,200

TABLE IXa.—Distribution of immigrant aliens (fiscal years ending 30 June), by sex and country of origin (or nationality), 1869-98 (continued).

Country	1877			1878		
	Total	Males	Females	Total	Males	Females
Europe:						
Austria-Hungary	5,396	2,989	2,407	5,150	2,925	2,225
Belgium	488	379	109	354	231	123
Bulgaria, Serbia and Montenegro	....	....	....	....	....	....
Denmark	1,695	1,073	622	2,105	1,308	797
France, including Corsica	5,856	3,839	2,017	4,159	2,589	1,570
German Empire	29,298	17,732	11,566	29,313	18,019	11,294
Greece	24	19	5	16	16	....
Italy, including Sicily and Spain	3,195	2,321	874	4,344	3,126	1,218
Netherlands	591	391	200	608	392	216
Norway	4,588	2,950	1,638	4,759	3,034	1,725
Poland	533	382	151	547	362	185
Portugal, including Cape Verde and Azore Islands	2,363	1,725	638	1,332	885	447
Rumania	....	....	....	....	....	....
Russian Empire	6,599	3,838	2,761	3,048	1,757	1,291
Spain, including Canary and Balearic Islands	665	489	176	457	350	107
Sweden	4,991	2,919	2,072	5,390	3,272	2,118
Switzerland	1,686	1,193	493	1,808	1,236	572
Turkey in Europe	32	21	11	29	20	9
United Kingdom:						
England	19,161	12,045	7,116	18,405	11,448	6,957
Ireland	14,569	6,819	7,750	15,932	7,203	8,729
Scotland	4,135	2,843	1,292	3,502	2,145	1,357
Wales	281	169	112	243	145	98
Not specified	4	1	3	....	....	....
Other Europe	45	41	4	111	89	22
Total Europe	106,195	64,178	42,017	101,612	60,552	41,060
Asia:						
China	10,594	10,518	76	8,992	8,641	351
India	17	8	9	8	6	2
Japan	7	4	3	2	2	....
Turkey in Asia	3	3	....	7	4	3
Other Asia	19	16	3	5	4	1
Total Asia	10,640	10,549	91	9,014	8,657	357
Africa	16	10	6	18	12	6
Australia and New Zealand	912	767	145	606	508	98
Pacific Islands, not specified	2	2	....	....	....	....
British North America possessions	22,137	15,248	6,889	25,592	15,403	10 189
Central America	6	6	....	40	33	7
Mexico	445	349	96	465	376	89
South America	87	61	26	88	65	23
West Indies: including Jamaica	1,390	848	542	1,019	644	375
Countries not specified	27	15	12	15	9	6
Grand total	141,857	92,033	49,824	138,469	86,259	52,210

TABLE IXa.—Distribution of immigrant aliens (fiscal years ending 30 June), by sex and country of origin (or nationality), 1869-98 (continued).

Country	1879			1880		
	Total	Males	Females	Total	Males	Females
Europe:						
Austria-Hungary.....	5,963	3,391	2,572	17,267	10,247	7,020
Belgium.........................	512	320	192	1,232	784	448
Bulgaria, Serbia and Montenegro....	....	....	....	....	....	....
Denmark........................	3,474	2,244	1,230	6,576	4,466	2,110
France, including Corsica...........	4,655	2,954	1,701	4,314	2,802	1,512
German Empire..................	34,602	21,578	13,024	84,638	52,743	31,895
Greece........................	21	18	3	23	19	4
Italy, including Sicily and Sardinia....	5,791	4,252	1,539	12,354	8,695	3,659
Netherlands.....................	753	467	286	3,340	1,932	1,408
Norway........................	7,345	4,695	2,650	19,895	13,165	6,730
Poland.........................	489	335	154	2,177	1,442	735
Portugal, including Cape Verde and Azore Islands	1,374	916	458	808	495	313
Rumania.......................	....	....	....	11	8	3
Russian Empire..................	4,453	2,497	1,956	5,014	3,410	1,604
Spain, including Canary and Balearic Islands........................	457	352	105	389	305	84
Sweden........................	11,001	7,313	3,688	39,186	26,862	12,324
Switzerland.....................	3,161	2,167	994	6,156	4,212	1,944
Turkey in Europe.................	29	22	7	24	18	6
United Kingdom:						
England.......................	24,183	15,476	8,707	59,454	37,661	21,793
Ireland.......................	20,013	9,635	10,378	71,603	38,151	33,452
Scotland......................	5,225	3,443	1,782	12,640	8,072	4,568
Wales........................	543	351	192	1,173	730	443
Not specified..................	4	2	2	6	4	2
Other Europe....................	211	139	72	411	253	158
Total Europe..................	134,259	82,567	51,692	348,691	216,476	132,215
Asia:						
China.........................	9,604	9,264	340	5,802	5,732	70
India.........................	15	6	9	21	12	9
Japan.........................	4	3	1	4	4	....
Turkey in Asia...................	31	19	12	4	1	3
Other Asia.....................	6	4	2	8	8	....
Total Asia....................	9,660	9,296	364	5,839	5,757	82
Africa...........................	12	10	2	18	14	4
Australia and New Zealand..........	813	704	109	953	799	154
Pacific Islands, not specified..........	3	3	....	1	1	....
British North American possessions....	31,286	18,007	13,279	99,744	63,165	36,579
Central America...................	9	8	1	17	14	3
Mexico..........................	556	457	99	492	405	87
South America....................	69	50	19	88	64	24
West Indies, including Jamaica........	1,123	'753	370	1,351	892	459
Countries not specified..............	36	27	9	63	36	27
Grand total...................	177,826	111,882	65,944	457,257	287,623	169,634

TABLE IXa.—Distribution of immigrant aliens (fiscal years ending 30 June), by sex and country of origin (or nationality), 1869-98 (continued).

Country	1881			1882		
	Total	Males	Females	Total	Males	Females
Europe:						
Austria-Hungary	27,935	16,299	11,636	29,150	18,690	10,460
Belgium	1,766	1,186	580	1,431	892	539
Bulgaria, Serbia and Montenegro	....	....	....	....	....	....
Denmark	9,117	5,874	3,243	11,618	7,517	4,101
France, including Corsica	5,227	3,455	1,772	6,004	3,893	2,111
German Empire	210,485	128,399	82,086	250,630	148,466	102,164
Greece	19	17	2	126	125	1
Italy, including Sicily and Sardinia	15,401	11,579	3,822	32,159	27,488	4,671
Netherlands	8,597	5,086	3,511	9,517	5,620	3,897
Norway	22,705	14,511	8,194	29,101	17,929	11,172
Poland	5,614	3,595	2,019	4,672	3,419	1,253
Portugal, including Cape Verde and Azore Islands	1,215	803	412	1,436	916	520
Rumania	30	19	11	65	44	21
Russian Empire	5,041	3,247	1,794	16,918	11,639	5,279
Spain, including Canary and Balearic Islands	484	386	98	378	293	85
Sweden	49,760	31,317	18,443	64,607	41,335	23,272
Switzerland	11,293	7,499	3,794	10,844	7,047	3,797
Turkey in Europe	72	54	18	69	52	17
United Kingdom:						
England	65,177	40,401	24,776	82,394	51,575	30,819
Ireland	72,342	37,387	34,955	76,432	40,980	35,452
Scotland	15,168	9,503	5,665	18,937	12,108	6,829
Wales	1,027	650	377	1,656	1,097	559
Not specified	4	4	....	4	3	1
Other Europe	66	45	21	38	28	10
Total Europe	528,545	321,316	207,229	648,186	401,156	247,030
Asia:						
China	11,890	11,815	75	39,579	39,463	116
India	33	25	8	10	6	4
Japan	11	11	....	5	5	....
Turkey in Asia	5	5	....	....	....	....
Other Asia	43	30	13	35	30	5
Total Asia	11,982	11,886	96	39,629	39,504	125
Africa	33	21	12	60	39	21
Australia and New Zealand	1,188	986	202	878	740	138
Pacific Islands, not specified	3	3	....	11	7	4
British North American possessions	125,450	74,938	50,512	98,366	56,152	42,214
Central America	12	11	1	15	8	7
Mexico	325	247	78	366	292	74
South America	110	86	24	91	61	30
West Indies, including Jamaica	1,680	1,164	516	1,291	810	481
Countries not specified	103	71	32	99	45	54
Grand total	669,431	410,729	258,702	788,992	498,814	290,178

TABLE IXa.—Distribution of immigrant aliens (fiscal years ending 30 June), by sex and country of origin (or nationality), 1869-98 (continued).

Country	1883 Total	Males	Females	1884 Total	Males	Females	1885 Total	Males	Females
Europe:									
Austria-Hungary........	27,625	18,814	8,811	36,571	24,381	12,190	27,309	16,695	10,614
Belgium..............	1,450	957	493	1,576	1,059	517	1,653	1,007	646
Bulgaria, Serbia and Montenegro..........	....	....	....	....	....	....	....	....	....
Denmark..............	10,319	6,228	4,091	9,202	5,509	3,693	6,100	3,541	2,559
France,including Corsica.	4,821	3,247	1,574	3,608	2,293	1,315	3,495	2,271	1,224
German Empire.........	194,786	111,778	83,008	179,676	103,663	76,013	124,443	68,426	56,017
Greece...............	73	58	15	37	34	3	172	154	18
Italy, including Sicily and Sardinia........	31,792	28,222	3,570	16,510	12,657	3,853	13,642	9,864	3,778
Netherlands............	5,249	3,122	2,127	4,198	2,569	1,629	2,689	1,649	1,040
Norway..............	23,398	13,799	9,599	16,974	9,986	6,988	12,356	7,054	5,302
Poland...............	2,011	1,465	546	4,536	3,384	1,152	3,085	2,139	946
Portugal, including Cape Verde and Azore Islands.	1,573	1,048	525	1,927	1,225	702	2,024	1,323	701
Rumania.............	77	37	40	238	131	107	803	449	354
Russian Empire........	9,909	6,025	3,884	12,689	8,675	4,014	17,158	10,480	6,678
Spain, including Canary and Balearic Islands...	262	205	57	300	236	64	350	271	79
Sweden...............	38,277	22,916	15,361	26,552	15,459	11,093	22,248	12,491	9,757
Switzerland............	12,751	8,165	4,586	9,386	5,835	3,551	5,895	3,680	2,215
Turkey in Europe.......	86	52	34	150	138	12	138	110	28
United Kingdom:									
England..............	63,140	38,174	24,966	55,918	33,413	22,505	47,332	28,083	19,249
Ireland..............	81,486	41,495	39,991	63,344	31,280	32,064	51,795	25,187	26,608
Scotland.............	11,859	7,007	4,852	9,060	5,294	3,766	9,226	5,617	3,609
Wales...............	1,597	987	610	901	508	393	1,127	668	459
Not specified.........	10	7	3	71	51	20	28	11	17
Other Europe..........	36	27	9	262	148	114	15	8	7
Total Europe	522,587	313,835	208,752	453,686	267,928	185,758	353,083	201,178	151,905
Asia:									
China................	8,031	7,987	44	279	241	38	22	12	10
India................	9	4	5	12	9	3	34	27	7
Japan................	27	19	8	20	19	1	49	42	7
Turkey in Asia........	....	....	....	....	....	....	....	....	....
Other Asia............	46	37	9	199	168	31	93	81	12
Total Asia..........	8,113	8,047	66	510	437	73	198	162	36
Africa.................	67	36	31	59	43	16	112	85	27
Australia and New Zealand.................	554	428	126	502	339	163	449	305	144
Pacific Islands, not specified.................	193	113	80	398	295	103	230	163	67
British North American possessions.............	70,274	40,284	29,990	60,626	37,642	22,984	38,336	22,601	15,735
Central America.........	6	6	....	10	7	3	23	20	3
Mexico...............	469	377	92	430	290	140	323	238	85
South America.........	77	55	22	65	40	25	44	35	9
West Indies, including Jamaica...............	903	644	259	2,208	1,430	778	2,477	1,564	913
Countries not specified.....	79	38	41	98	58	40	71	31	40
Grand total.........	603,322	363,863	239,459	518,592	308,509	210,083	395,346	226,382	168,964

TABLE IXa.—Distribution of immigrant aliens (fiscal years ending 30 June), by sex and country of origin (or nationality), 1869-98 (continued).

Country	1886			1887		
	Total	Males	Females	Total	Males	Females
Europe:						
Austria-Hungary..................	28,680	19,554	9,126	40,265	26,898	13,367
Belgium........................	1,300	845	455	2,553	1,670	883
Bulgaria Serbia and Montenegro.....	....	....	....	....	....	....
Denmark.......................	6,225	3,875	2,350	8,524	5,448	3,076
France including Corsica..........	3,318	2,169	1,149	5,034	3,212	1,822
German Empire..................	84,403	46,738	37,665	106,865	61,097	45,768
Greece.........................	104	95	9	313	305	8
Italy, including Sicily and Sardinia....	21,315	15,340	5,975	47,622	37,442	10,180
Netherlands.....................	2,314	1,492	822	4,506	2,708	1,798
Norway........................	12,759	7,890	4,869	16,269	10,523	5,746
Poland.........................	3,939	2,852	1,087	6,128	4,150	1,978
Portugal, including Cape Verde and Azore Islands	1,194	821	373	1,360	869	491
Rumania........................	494	314	180	2,045	1,087	958
Russian Empire..................	17,800	11,555	6,245	30,766	20,070	10,696
Spain, including Canary and Balearic Islands........................	344	261	83	436	341	95
Sweden........................	27,751	17,019	10,732	42,836	27,359	15,477
Switzerland.....................	4,805	2,902	1,903	5,214	3,283	1,931
Turkey in Europe................	176	132	44	206	157	49
United Kingdom:						
England.......................	49,767	30,913	18,854	72,855	45,979	26,876
Ireland.......................	49,619	24,425	25,194	68,370	35,449	32,921
Scotland......................	12,126	7,584	4,542	18,699	12,133	6,566
Wales........................	1,027	614	413	1,820	1,211	609
Not specified..................	9	6	3	4	3	1
Other Europe...................	60	33	27	139	69	70
Total Europe..................	329,529	197,429	132,100	482,829	301,463	181,366
Asia:						
China..........................	40	25	15	10	8	2
India..........................	17	10	7	32	20	12
Japan..........................	194	160	34	229	218	11
Turkey in Asia..................	15	14	1	208	184	24
Other Asia.....................	51	51	....	136	133	3
Total Asia....................	317	260	57	615	563	52
Africa..........................	122	79	43	40	34	6
Australia and New Zealand..........	522	360	162	528	394	134
Pacific Islands, not specified..........	614	393	221	754	445	309
British North American possessions[7]...	17	15	2	9	9	....
Central America...................	29	23	6	19	13	6
Mexico[8]........................	....	....	....	....	....	....
South America....................	246	180	66	366	259	107
West Indies, including Jamaica........	2,734	1,927	807	4,876	3,447	1,429
Countries not specified..............	73	38	35	73	31	42
Grand total...................	334,203	200,704	133,499	490,109	306,658	183,451

TABLE IXa.—Distribution of immigrant aliens (fiscal years ending 30 June), by sex and country of origin (or nationality), 1869-98 (continued).

Country	1888			1889		
	Total	Males	Females	Total	Males	Females
Europe:						
Austria-Hungary..................	45,811	32,226	13,585	34,174	22,890	11,284
Belgium.......................	3,215	2,050	1,165	2,562	1,639	923
Bulgaria, Serbia and Montenegro....	....	....	....	....	....	....
Denmark.......................	8,962	5,649	3,313	8,699	5,301	3,398
France, including Corsica...........	6,454	4,354	2,100	5,918	3,789	2,129
German Empire..................	109,717	61,924	47,793	99,538	54,876	44,662
Greece........................	782	768	14	158	149	9
Italy, including Sicily and Sardinia...	51,558	42,206	9,352	25,307	18,273	7,034
Netherlands....................	5,845	3,487	2,358	6,460	3,794	2,666
Norway.......................	18,264	11,888	6,376	13,390	7,572	5,818
Poland........................	5,826	4,133	1,693	4,922	3,191	1,731
Portugal, including Cape Verde and Azore Islands	1,625	1,131	494	2,024	1,287	737
Rumania.......................	1,186	683	503	893	443	450
Russian Empire..................	33,487	22,425	11,062	33,916	21,661	12,255
Spain, including Canary and Balearic Islands.......................	526	411	115	526	411	115
Sweden.......................	54,698	34,762	19,936	35,415	19,919	15,496
Switzerland....................	7,737	5,040	2,697	7,070	4,525	2,545
Turkey in Europe................	207	161	46	252	202	50
United Kingdom:						
England......................	82,574	50,941	31,633	68,503	41,549	26,954
Ireland.......................	73,513	38,459	35,054	65,557	33,223	32,334
Scotland.....................	24,457	15,475	8,982	18,296	10,698	7,598
Wales........................	1,654	1,037	617	1,181	732	449
Not specified..................	7	5	2	12	8	4
Other Europe...................	26	18	8	17	7	10
Total Europe..................	**538,131**	**339,233**	**198,898**	**434,790**	**256,139**	**178,651**
Asia:						
China.........................	26	21	5	118	90	28
India.........................	20	15	5	59	50	9
Japan.........................	404	366	38	640	558	82
Turkey in Asia..................	272	230	43	593	499	94
Other Asia.....................	120	99	21	315	278	37
Total Asia.....................	**843**	**731**	**112**	**1,725**	**1,475**	**250**
Africa.........................	65	51	14	187	149	38
Australia and New Zealand..........	697	485	212	1,000	648	352
Pacific Islands, not specified..........	1,690	1,010	680	1,196	731	465
British North American possessions[7]...	15	12	3	28	22	6
Central America..................	67	54	13	81	62	19
Mexico[8]......................	....	....	....	....	....	....
South America...................	440	336	104	427	337	90
West Indies, including Jamaica........	4,880	3,428	1,452	4,923	3,422	1,501
Countries not specified..............	61	35	26	70	39	31
Grand total..................	**546,889**	**345,375**	**201,514**	**444,427**	**263,024**	**181,403**

TABLE IXa.—Distribution of immigrant aliens (fiscal years ending 30 June), by sex and country of origin (or nationality), 1869-98 (continued).

Country	1890			1891		
	Total	Males	Females	Total	Males	Females
Europe:						
Austria-Hungary..................	56,199	40,017	16,182	71,042	48,823	22,219
Belgium.......................	2,671	1,719	952	3,037	2,041	996
Bulgaria, Serbia and Montenegro....	....	....	....	....	....	....
Denmark.......................	9,366	5,713	3,653	10,659	6,455	4,204
France, including Corsica..........	6,585	3,863	2,722	6,770	4,087	2,683
German Empire..................	92,427	50,923	41,504	113,554	63,406	50,148
Greece........................	524	464	60	1,105	1,040	65
Italy, including Sicily and Sardinia....	52,003	40,852	11,151	76,055	60,775	15,280
Netherlands....................	4,326	2,655	1,671	5,206	3,184	2,022
Norway........................	11,370	6,601	4,769	12,568	7,644	4,924
Poland........................	11,073	7,613	3,460	27,497	18,064	9,433
Portugal, including Cape Verde and Azore Islands..................	2,600	1,669	931	2,999	1,843	1,156
Rumania.......................	517	260	257	957	472	485
Russian Empire.................	35,598	22,763	12,835	47,426	30,626	16,800
Spain, including Canary and Balearic Islands......................	813	619	194	905	690	215
Sweden.......................	29,632	16,532	13,100	36,880	21,746	15,134
Switzerland....................	6,993	4,406	2,587	6,811	4,275	2,536
Turkey in Europe................	206	171	35	265	224	41
United Kingdom:						
England......................	57,020	34,245	22,775	53,600	32,279	21,321
Ireland.......................	53,024	26,344	26,680	55,706	25,936	27,770
Scotland......................	12,041	6,833	5,208	12,557	7,318	5,239
Wales........................	650	384	266	424	278	146
Not specified..................	19	12	7	24	18	6
Other Europe...................	23	12	11	38	22	16
Total Europe..................	445,680	274,670	171,010	546,085	343,246	202,839
Asia:						
China.........................	1,716	1,401	315	2,836	2,608	228
India.........................	43	34	9	42	33	9
Japan.........................	691	601	90	1,136	1,023	113
Turkey in Asia..................	1,126	841	285	2,488	1,774	714
Other Asia.....................	872	770	102	1,176	1,024	152
Total Asia....................	4,448	3,647	801	7,678	6,462	1,216
Africa.........................	112	88	24	103	82	21
Australia and New Zealand..........	699	485	214	777	503	274
Pacific Islands, not specified.........	468	310	158	524	344	180
British North American possessions[7]....	183	111	72	234	138	96
Central America.................	142	110	32	278	185	93
Mexico[8]	....	....	....	....	....	....
South America..................	438	345	93	664	467	197
West Indies, including Jamaica........	3,070	2,052	1,018	3,906	2,592	1,314
Countries not specified.............	62	35	27	70	40	30
Grand total...................	455,302	281,853	173,449	560,319	354,059	206,260

TABLE IXa.—Distribution of immigrant aliens (fiscal years ending 30 june), by sex and country of origin (or nationality), 1869-98 (continued).

Country	1892			1893		
	Total	Males	Females	Total	Males	Females
Europe:						
Austria-Hungary	76,937	53,814	23,123	57,420	*	*
Belgium	4,026	2,656	1,370	3,324	*	*
Bulgaria, Serbia and Montenegro	*	*	*	*	*	*
Denmark	10,125	6,230	3,895	7,720	*	*
France, including Corsica	4,678	2,874	1,804	3,621	*	*
German Empire	119,168	66,897	52,271	78,756	*	*
Greece	660	604	56	1,072	*	*
Italy, including Sicily and Sardinia	61,631	47,399	14,232	72,145	*	*
Netherlands	6,141	3,634	2,507	6,199	*	*
Norway	14,325	8,910	5,415	15,515	*	*
Poland	40,536	26,514	14,022	16,374	*	*
Portugal, including Cape Verde and Azore Islands	3,400	2,094	1,306	4,816	*	*
Rumania	*	*	*	*	*	*
Russian Empire	81,511	48,807	32,704	42,310	*	*
Spain, including Canary and Balearic Islands	4,078	3,063	1,015	206	*	*
Sweden	41,845	24,684	17,161	35,710	*	*
Switzerland	6,886	4,359	2,527	4,744	*	*
Turkey in Europe	1,331	1,248	83	625	*	*
United Kingdom:						
England	34,309	21,213	13,096	27,931	*	*
Ireland	51,383	25,699	25,684	43,578	*	*
Scotland	7,177	4,266	2,911	6,215	*	*
Wales	729	466	263	1,043	*	*
Not specified	....	....	....	....	....	....
Other Europe	....	....	....	....	....	....
Total Europe	570,876	355,431	215,445	429,324	*	*
Asia:						
China	....	....	....	472	*	*
India	....	....	....	1,380	....	....
Japan	....	....	....	1,380	*	*
Turkey in Asia	....	....	....	....	....	....
Other Asia	....	....	....	540	....	....
Total Asia	....	....	....	2,392	*	*
Africa	....	....	....	....	....	....
Australia and New Zealand	267	171	96	248	*	*
Pacific Islands, not specified	....	....	....	....	....	....
British North American possessions	....	....	....	....	....	....
Central America	....	....	....	....	....	....
Mexico	....	....	....	....	....	....
South America	....	....	....	....	....	....
West Indies, including Jamaica	....	....	....	2,593	*	*
Countries not specified	8,520	6,262	2,258	5,173	*	*
Grand total	579,663	361,864	217,799	439,730	280,344	159,386

TABLE IXa.—Distribution of immigrant aliens (fiscal years ending 20 June), by sex and country of origin (or nationality), 1868-98 (continued).

Country	1894			1895		
	Total	Males	Females	Total	Males	Females
Europe:						
Austria-Hungary	38,638	*	*	33,401	*	*
Belgium	1,709	*	*	1,058	*	*
Bulgaria, Serbia and Montenegro	*	*	*	*	*	*
Denmark	5,003	*	*	3,910	*	*
France, including Corsica	3,080	*	*	2,628	*	*
German Empire	53,989	*	*	32,173	*	*
Greece	1,356	*	*	597	*	*
Italy, including Sicily and Sardinia	42,977	*	*	35,427	*	*
Netherlands	1,820	*	*	1,388	*	*
Norway	9,111	*	*	7,581	*	*
Poland	1,941	*	*	790	*	*
Portugal, including Cape Verde and Azore Islands	2,196	*	*	1,452	*	*
Rumania	729	*	*	523	*	*
Russian Empire	39,278	*	*	35,907	*	*
Spain, including Canary and Balearic Islands	925	*	*	501	*	*
Sweden	18,286	*	*	15,361	*	*
Switzerland	2,905	*	*	2,239	*	*
Turkey in Europe	298	*	*	245	*	*
United Kingdom:						
England	17,747	*	*	23,443	*	*
Ireland	30,231	*	*	46,304	*	*
Scotland	3,772	*	*	3,788	*	*
Wales	1,001	*	*	1,602	*	*
Not specified	....	....	....	....	....	....
Other Europe	60	*	*	24	*	*
Total Europe	277,052	*	*	250,342	*	*
Asia:						
China	1,170	*	*	539	*	*
India	....	....	....	....	....	....
Japan	1,931	*	*	1,150	*	*
Turkey in Asia	....	....	....	2,767	*	*
Other Asia	1,589	*	*	39	*	*
Total Asia	4,690	*	*	4,495	*	*
Africa	24	*	*	36	*	*
Australia and New Zealand	244	*	*	155	*	*
Pacific Islands, not specified	....	....	....	....	....	....
British North American possessions	194	*	*	244	*	*
Central America	32	*	*	16	*	*
Mexico	109	*	*	116	*	*
South America	39	*	*	36	*	*
West Indies, including Jamaica	2,177	*	*	3,096	*	*
Countries not specified	70	*	*	....	....	....
Grand total	285,631	169,274	116,357	258,536	149,016	109,520

TABLE IXa—Distribution of immigrant aliens (fiscal years ending 30 June), by sex and country of origin (or nationality), 1869-98 (concluded).

Country	1896			1897			1898		
	Total	Males	Females	Total	Males	Females	Total	Males	Females
Europe:									
Austria-Hungary........	65,103	43,125	21,978	33,031	18,773	14,258	39,797	23,086	16,711
Belgium..............	1,261	793	468	760	490	270	695	425	270
Bulgaria, Serbia and Montenegro.........	*	*	*	*	*	*	*	*	*
Denmark.............	3,167	1,749	1,418	2,085	1,212	873	1,946	1,204	742
France,including Corsica.	2,463	1,381	1,082	2,107	1,209	898	1,990	1,233	757
German Empire........	31,885	16,942	14,943	22,533	11,899	10,634	17,111	9,105	8,006
Greece..............	2,175	2,124	51	571	546	25	2,339	2,246	93
Italy, including Sicily and Sardinia.............	68,060	51,067	16,993	59,431	41,446	17,985	58,613	40,248	18,365
Netherlands...........	1,583	929	654	890	558	332	767	500	267
Norway..............	8,855	5,581	3,274	5,842	3,535	2,307	4,938	3,007	1,931
Poland..............	691	409	282	4,165	2,654	1,511	4,726	2,998	1,728
Portugal, including Cape Verde and Azore Islands.............	2,766	1,410	1,356	1,874	962	912	1,717	857	860
Rumania.............	785	453	332	791	413	378	900	519	381
Russian Empire........	51,445	32,163	19,282	25,816	13,894	11,922	29,828	17,104	12,724
Spain, including Canary and Balearic Islands...	351	293	58	448	407	41	577	511	66
Sweden..............	21,177	10,968	10,209	13,162	6,231	6,931	12,398	5,442	6,956
Switzerland...........	2,304	1,401	903	1,566	975	591	1,246	824	422
Turkey in Europe.	169	118	51	152	110	42	176	139	37
United Kingdom:									
England.............	19,492	11,178	8,314	9,974	5,998	3,976	9,877	5,943	3,934
Ireland.............	40,262	17,625	22,637	28,421	11,542	16,872	25,128	9,952	15,176
Scotland............	3,483	2,000	1,483	1,883	1,054	829	1,797	1,100	697
Wales..............	1,581	915	666	870	539	331	1,219	758	461
Not specified.........	9	4	5	25	18	7	1	1	....
Other Europe.........	....	....	....	....	....	....	....	....	....
Total Europe........	329,067	202,628	126,439	216,397	12 ,472	91,925	217,786	127,202	90,584
Asia:									
China...............	1,441	1,382	59	3,363	3,334	29	2,071	2,061	10
India...............	....	....	....	....	....	....	....	....	....
Japan...............	1,110	1,007	103	1,526	1,420	106	2,230	2,115	115
Turkey in Asia........	4,139	2,915	1,224	4,732	3,203	1,529	4,275	2,651	1,624
Other Asia...........	74	60	14	41	40	1	61	51	10
Total Asia..........	6,764	5,364	1,400	9,662	7,997	1,665	8,637	6,878	1,759
Africa.................	21	15	6	37	24	13	48	38	10
Australia and New Zealand.................	87	9 59	28	139	65	74	153	115	38
Pacific Islands, not specified...............	25	11	14	60	32	28	48	32	16
British North American possessions.	278	200	78	291	181	110	352	294	58
Central America.........	12	6	6	5	5	....	5	5	....
Mexico...............	150	64	86	91	42	49	107	39	68
South America..........	35	28	7	49	28	21	39	30	9
West Indies, including Jamaica..............	6,828	4,091	2,737	4,101	2,261	1,840	2,124	1,142	982
Countries not specified....	....	....	....	....	....	....	....	....	....
Grand total.........	343,267	212,466	130,801	230,832	135,107	95,725	229,299	135,775	93,524

For reference notes see page 500.

TABLE X.—DISTRIBUTION OF IMMIGRANT ALIENS ADMITTED, BY SEX AND RACE OR PEOPLE, 1899-1924.

Race or people	1899			1900		
	Total	Males	Females	Total	Males	Females
African (black)...................	412	220	192	714	414	300
Armenian.........................	674	471	203	982	748	234
Bohemian and Moravian............	2,526	1,262	1,264	3,060	1,562	1,498
Bulgarian, Serbian and Montenegrin..	94	85	9	204	200	4
Chinese..........................	1,638	1,627	11	1,250	1,241	9
Croatian and Slovenian.............	8,632	7,266	1,366	17,184	14,934	2,250
Cuban...........................	1,374	1,074	300	2,678	1,763	915
Dalmatian, Bosnian, Herzegovinian....	367	297	70	675	637	38
Dutch and Flemish................	1,860	1,226	634	2,702	1,765	937
East Indian.......................	15	12	3	9	8	1
English..........................	10,712	6,707	4,005	10.897	6,710	4,187
Finnish..........................	6,097	3,942	2,155	12,612	8,000	4,612
French...........................	2,278	1,428	850	2,095	1,311	784
German..........................	26,632	14,742	11,890	29,682	17,284	12,398
Greek............................	2,395	2,263	132	3,773	3,655	118
Hebrew..........................	37,415	21,153	16,262	60,764	36,330	24,434
Irish............................	32,345	13,720	18,625	35,607	16,674	18,933
Italian, North....................	13,091	9,746	3,345	17,316	13,540	3,776
Italian, South....................	65,639	45,587	20,052	84,346	63,684	20,662
Japanese.........................	3,395	3,171	224	12,628	12,260	368
Korean..........................	22	22	....	71	71	....
Lithuanian.......................	6,858	5,291	1,567	10,311	7,683	2,628
Magyar..........................	5,700	3,627	2,073	13,777	10,207	3,570
Mexican.........................	163	80	83	261	154	107
Pacific Islander...................	14	10	4	112	92	20
Polish...........................	28,466	18,191	10,275	46,938	32,152	14,786
Portuguese.......................	2,096	1,101	995	4,241	2,386	1,855
Rumanian........................	96	90	6	398	374	24
Russian..........................	1,774	1,261	513	1,200	886	314
Ruthenian (Russniak)..............	1,400	872	528	2,832	1,942	890
Scandinavian.....................	23,249	12,747	10,502	32,952	19,530	13,422
Scotch...........................	1,752	1,057	695	1,757	1,065	692
Slovak...........................	15,838	10,324	5,514	29,243	21,235	8,008
Spanish..........................	996	899	97	1,111	964	147
Spanish-American.................	....	....	....	97	83	14
Syrian...........................	3,708	2,446	1,262	2,920	1,813	1,107
Turkish..........................	28	26	2	184	174	10
Welsh...........................	1,359	853	506	762	455	307
West Indian (except Cuban).........	144	90	54	78	56	22
Other...........................	457	288	169	76	50	26
Not specified.....................	4	3	1	73	56	17
Total.....................	311,715	195,277	116,438	448,572	304,148	144,424

TABLE X.—DISTRIBUTION OF IMMIGRANT ALIENS ADMITTED, BY SEX AND RACE OR PEOPLE, 1899-1924 (continued).

Race or people	1901			1902		
	Total	Males	Females	Total	Males	Females
African (black)	594	299	295	832	492	340
Armenian	1,855	1,364	491	1,151	946	205
Bohemian and Moravian	3,766	1,943	1,823	5,590	3,278	2,312
Bulgarian, Serbian and Montenegrin	611	499	112	1,291	1,202	89
Chinese	2,452	2,413	39	1,631	1,587	44
Croatian and Slovenian	17,928	15,492	2,436	30,233	27,097	3,136
Cuban	1,622	1,019	603	2,423	1,693	730
Dalmatian, Bosnian, Herzegovinian	732	630	102	1,004	895	109
Dutch and Flemish	3,299	2,149	1,150	4,117	2,745	1,372
East Indian	20	18	2	84	82	2
English	13,488	8,041	5,447	14,942	8,967	5,975
Finnish	9,999	6,458	3,541	13,868	9,585	4,283
French	4,036	2,526	1,510	4,122	2,608	1,514
German	34,742	20,214	14,528	51,686	32,813	18,873
Greek	5,919	5,754	165	8,115	7,854	261
Hebrew	58,098	32,345	25,753	57,688	32,737	24,951
Irish	30,404	12,807	17,597	29,001	12,727	16,274
Italian, North	22,103	17,852	4,251	27,620	22,425	5,195
Italian, South	115,704	90,395	25,309	152,915	124,536	28,379
Japanese	5,249	4,887	362	14,455	10,589	3,866
Korean	47	46	1	28	26	2
Lithuanian	8,815	6,499	2,316	11,629	8,576	3,053
Magyar	13,311	9,627	3,684	23,610	18,348	5,262
Mexican	350	217	133	715	532	183
Pacific Islander	24	20	4	40	29	11
Polish	43,617	29,581	14,036	69,620	50,368	19,252
Portuguese	4,176	2,240	1,936	5,309	3,117	2,192
Rumanian	761	704	57	2,033	1,904	129
Russian	670	474	196	1,551	1,225	326
Ruthenian (Russniak)	5,288	3,903	1,385	7,533	5,836	1,627
Scandinavian	40,277	23,503	16,774	55,780	36,431	19,349
Scotch	2,004	1,202	802	2,432	1,497	935
Slovak	29,343	21,227	8,116	36,934	27,197	9,737
Spanish	1,202	1,072	130	1,954	1,758	196
Spanish-American	276	200	76	496	353	143
Syrian	4,064	2,729	1,335	4,982	3,337	1,645
Turkish	136	123	13	165	151	14
Welsh	674	391	283	760	468	292
West Indian (except Cuban)	82	62	20	137	92	45
Other	178	130	48	267	266	1
Not specified	....	....	....	....	....	....
Total	(a)487,918	331,055	(a)156,86	648,743	466,369	182,374

For reference notes see page 500.

TABLE X.—DISTRIBUTION OF IMMIGRANT ALIENS ADMITTED, BY SEX AND RACE OR PEOPLE, 1899-1924 (continued).

Country	1903			1904		
	Total	Males	Females	Total	Males	Females
African (black).....................	1,549	625	2,174	1,537	849	2,386
Armenian.........................	1,424	335	1,759	1,315	430	1,745
Bohemian and Moravian.............	5,820	3,771	9,591	6,657	5,254	11,911
Bulgarian, Serbian and Montenegrin....	6,315	164	6,479	4,385	192	4,577
Chinese..........................	2,152	40	2,192	4,209	118	4,327
Croatian and Slovenian..............	29,222	3,685	32,907	17,644	3,598	21,242
Cuban............................	1,945	999	2,944	3,346	1,465	4,811
Dalmatian, Bosnian, Herzegovinian....	1,544	192	1,736	1,904	132	2,036
Dutch and Flemish.................	4,312	2,184	6,496	5,191	2,641	7,832
East Indian.......................	70	13	83	241	17	258
English...........................	17,229	11,222	28,451	25,326	16,153	41,479
Finnish...........................	12 755	6,109	18,864	5,583	4,574	10,157
French...........................	4,450	2,716	7,166	6,696	4,861	11,557
German...........................	44,663	27,119	71,782	43,775	31,015	74,790
Greek............................	13,885	491	14,376	12,106	519	12,625
Hebrew...........................	43,985	32,218	76,203	65,040	41,196	106,236
Irish.............................	16,112	19,254	35,366	16,607	20,469	37,076
Italian, North.....................	30,477	6,952	37,429	28,784	7,915	36,699
Italian, South.....................	158,939	37,178	196,117	122,770	36,559	159,329
Japanese..........................	15,990	4,051	20,041	12,729	1,653	14,382
Korean...........................	496	68	564	1,723	184	1,907
Lithuanian........................	10,721	3,711	14,432	8,854	3,926	12,780
Magyar...........................	20,440	6,684	27,124	16,253	7,630	23,883
Mexican..........................	324	162	486	354	93	447
Pacific Islander....................	46	6	52	9	3	12
Polish............................	58,992	23,351	82,343	44,882	22,875	67,757
Portuguese........................	4,999	3,434	8,433	3,867	2,471	6,338
Rumanian.........................	4,472	268	4,740	3,994	370	4,364
Russian...........................	2,897	711	3,608	3,018	943	3,961
Ruthenian (Russniak)..............	7,695	2,148	9,843	6,904	2,688	9,592
Scandinavian......................	51,272	28,075	79,347	36,024	25,005	61,029
Scotch...........................	3,995	2,224	6,219	7,023	4,460	11,483
Slovak...........................	24,394	10,033	34,427	18,502	9,438	27,940
Spanish...........................	2,738	559	3,297	3,960	702	4,662
Spanish-American..................	691	287	978	1,141	525	1,666
Syrian............................	3,749	1,802	5,551	2,480	1,173	3,653
Turkish...........................	424	25	449	1,412	70	1,482
Welsh............................	836	442	1,278	1,173	647	1,820
West Indian (except Cuban)..........	943	554	1,497	1,123	819	1,942
Other............................	184	38	222	559	138	697
Not specified.....................	....	....	....	....	....	....
Total...............	613,146	243,900	857,046	549,100	263,770	812,870

TABLE X.—Distribution of immigrant aliens admitted, by sex and race or people, 1899-1924 (continued).

Race or people	1905			1906		
	Total	Males	Females	Total	Males	Females
African (black)...................	3,598	2,325	1,273	3,786	2,355	1,431
Armenian.......................	1,878	1,339	539	1,895	1,423	472
Bohemian and Moravian..........	11,757	6,662	5,095	12,958	7,418	5,540
Bulgarian, Serbian and Montenegrin..	5,823	5,562	261	11,548	11,104	444
Chinese.........................	1,971	1,883	88	1,485	1,397	88
Croatian and Slovenian...........	35,104	30,253	4,851	44,272	38,287	5,985
Cuban..........................	7,259	4,925	2,334	5,591	3,769	1,822
Dalmatian, Bosnian, Herzegovinian...	2,639	2,489	150	4,568	4,346	222
Dutch and Flemish...............	8,498	5,693	2,805	9,735	6,526	3,209
East Indian.....................	145	137	8	271	252	19
English.........................	50,865	31,965	18,900	45,079	28,010	17,069
Finnish.........................	17,012	11,907	5,105	14,136	9,525	4,611
French.........................	11,347	6,705	4,642	10,379	5,924	4,455
German.........................	82,360	49,647	32,713	86,813	51,427	35,386
Greek..........................	12,144	11,586	558	23,127	22,266	861
Hebrew.........................	129,910	82,076	47,834	153,748	80,086	73,662
Irish...........................	54,266	24,640	29,626	40,959	20,846	20,113
Italian, North..................	39,930	31,695	8,235	46,286	36,542	9,744
Italian, South..................	186,390	155,007	31,383	240,528	190,992	49,536
Japanese.......................	11,021	9,810	1,211	14,243	12,756	1,487
Korean.........................	4,929	4,506	423	127	103	24
Lithuanian......................	18,604	13,842	4,762	14,257	9,429	4,828
Magyar.........................	46,030	34,242	11,788	44,261	31,760	12,501
Mexican........................	227	152	75	141	93	48
Pacific Islander.................	17	13	4	13	10	3
Polish..........................	102,437	72,452	29,985	95,835	66,410	29,425
Portuguese......................	4,855	2,992	1,863	8,729	5,096	3,633
Rumanian.......................	7,818	7,244	574	11,425	10,561	864
Russian........................	3,746	2,700	1,046	5,814	4,750	1,064
Ruthenian (Russniak)............	14,473	10,820	3,653	16,257	12,310	3,947
Scandinavian....................	62,284	37,202	25,082	58,141	36,092	22,049
Scotch.........................	16,144	10,472	5,672	16,463	10,883	5,580
Slovak.........................	52,368	38,038	14,330	38,221	26,605	11,616
Spanish.........................	5,590	4,724	866	5,332	4,460	872
Spanish-American...............	1,658	1,146	512	1,585	1,105	480
Syrian..........................	4,822	3,248	1,574	5,824	4,100	1,724
Turkish........................	2,145	2,082	63	2,033	1,946	87
Welsh..........................	2,531	1,549	982	2,367	1,660	707
West Indian (except Cuban).......	1,548	892	656	1,476	869	607
Other..........................	356	292	64	1,027	970	57
Total....................	1,026,499	724,914	301,585	1,100,735	764,463	336,272

TABLE X.—DISTRIBUTION OF IMMIGRANT ALIENS ADMITTED, BY SEX AND RACE OR PEOPLE, 1899-1924
(continued).

Race or people	1907			1908		
	Total	Males	Females	Total	Males	Females
African (black).....................	5 235	3,332	1,903	4,626	2,839	1,787
Armenian..........................	2,644	1,874	770	3,299	2,097	1,202
Bohemian and Moravian............	13,554	8,142	5,412	10,164	5,495	4,669
Bulgarian, Serbian and Montenegrin..	27,174	26,423	751	18,246	17,416	830
Chinese............................	770	706	64	1,263	1,177	86
Croatian and Slovenian.............	47,826	40,538	7,288	20,472	15,476	4,996
Cuban.............................	5,475	3,747	1,728	3,323	2,339	984
Dalmatian, Bosnian, Herzegovinian ..	7,393	7,061	332	3,747	3,379	368
Dutch and Flemish.................	12,467	8,362	4,105	9,526	5,789	3,737
East Indian........................	1,072	1,056	16	1,710	1,702	8
English............................	51,126	33,100	18,026	49,056	29,727	19,329
Finnish............................	14,860	10,326	4,534	6,746	3,652	3,094
French............................	9,392	5,425	3,967	12,881	7,694	5,187
German............................	92,936	56,170	36,766	73,038	41,209	31,829
Greek.............................	46,283	44,647	1,636	28,808	26,972	1,836
Hebrew............................	149,182	80,530	68,652	103,387	56,277	47,110
Irish..............................	38,706	21,871	16,835	36,427	17,822	18,605
Italian, North.....................	51,564	40,949	10,615	24,700	17,269	7,431
Italian, South.....................	242,497	190,905	51,592	110,547	73,824	36,723
Japanese..........................	30,824	27,845	2,979	16,418	12,256	4,162
Korean............................	39	36	3	26	20	6
Lithuanian.........................	25,884	18,716	7,168	13,720	8,522	5,198
Magyar............................	60,071	44,804	15,267	24,378	15,504	8,874
Mexican...........................	91	74	17	5,682	3,968	1,714
Pacific Islander....................	3	2	1	2	1	1
Polish.............................	138,033	100,700	37,333	68,105	43,667	24,438
Portuguese........................	9,648	5,812	3,836	6,809	4,019	2,790
Rumanian.........................	19,200	17,779	1,421	9,629	8,478	1,151
Russian...........................	16,807	15,095	1,712	17,111	15,004	2,107
Ruthenian (Russniak)..............	24,081	18,451	5,630	12,361	8,820	3,541
Scandinavian......................	53,425	34,164	19,261	32,789	18,251	14,538
Scotch............................	20,516	13,666	6,850	17,014	10,209	6,805
Slovak............................	42,041	28,951	13,090	16,170	9,979	6,191
Spanish...........................	9,495	7,268	2,227	6,636	5,489	1,147
Spanish-American..................	1,060	734	326	1,063	752	311
Syrian............................	5,880	4,276	1,604	5,520	3,926	1,594
Turkish...........................	1,902	1,855	47	2,327	2,265	62
Welsh.............................	2,754	1,852	902	2,504	1,651	853
West Indian (except Cuban)........	1,381	778	603	1,110	560	550
Other.............................	2,058	1,954	104	1,530	1,416	114
Total......................	1,285,349	929,976	355,373	782,870	506,912	275,958

TABLE X.—Distribution of immigrant aliens admitted, by sex and race or people, 1899-1924 (continued).

Race or people	1909			1910		
	Total	Males	Females	Total	Males	Females
African (black)	4,307	2,601	1,706	4,966	2,961	2,005
Armenian	3,108	2,595	513	5,508	4,686	822
Bohemian and Moravian	6,850	3,998	2,852	8,462	4,874	3,588
Bulgarian Serbian and Montenegrin	6,214	5,756	458	15,130	14,253	877
Chinese	1,841	1,706	135	1,770	1,598	172
Croatian and Slovenian	20,181	15,710	4,471	39,562½	32,947	6,615
Cuban	3,380	2,322	1,058	3,331	2,342	989
Dalmatian, Bosnian and Herzegovinian	1,888	1,617	271	4,911	4,453	458
Dutch and Flemish	8,114	5,131	2,983	13,012½	8,742	4,270
East Indian	337	327	10	1,782	1,768	14
English	39,021	23,440	15,581	53,498,	32,199	21,299
Finnish	11,687	7,832	3,855	15,736	10,724	5,012
French	19,423	10,735	8,688	21,107₁	11,715	9,392
German	58,534	33,919	24,615	71,380	42,191	29,189
Greek	20,262	18,738	1,524	39,135½	36,580	2,555
Hebrew	57,551	31,057	26,494	84,260½	46,206	38,054
Irish	31,185	15,785	15,400	38,382½	21,075	17,307
Italian, North	25,150	18,844	6,306	30,780	23,754	7,026
Italian, South	165,248	135,080	30,168	192,673	151,249	41,424
Japanese	3,275	1,462	1,813	2,798	915	1,883
Korean	11	9	2	19	14	5
Lithuanian	15,254	10,284	4,970	22,714	15,360	7,354
Magyar	28,704	21,027	7,677	27,302	18,382	8,920
Mexican	15,591	10,111	5,480	17,760	11,617	6,143
Pacific Islander	7	3	4	61	45	16
Polish	77,565	50,597	26,968	128,348	91,275	37,073
Portuguese	4,606	2,886	1,720	7,657	4,887	2,770
Rumanian	8,041	7,036	1,005	14,199	12,602	1,597
Russian	10,038	8,794	1,244	17,294	14,918	2,376
Ruthenian (Russniak)	15,808	10,863	4,945	27,907	21,198	6,709
Scandinavian	34,996	22,232	12,764	52,037	35,019	17,018
Scotch	16,446	10,323	6,123	24,612	15,546	9,066
Slovak	22,586	16,168	6,418	32,416	23,642	8,774
Spanish	4,939	4,070	869	5,837	4,890	947
Spanish-American	890	604	286	900	645	255
Syrian	3,668	2,383	1,285	6,317	4,148	2,169
Turkish	820	781	39	1,283	1,237	46
Welsh	1,699	1,108	591	2,244	1,504	740
West Indian (except Cuban)	1,024	591	433	1,150	634	516
Other	1,537	1,444	93	3,330	3,243	87
Total	751,786	519,969	231,817	1,041,570	736,038	305,532

TABLE X.—Distribution of immigrant aliens admitted, by sex and race or people, 1899-1924
(continued).

Race or people	1911			1912		
	Total	Males	Females	Total	Males	Females
African (black)....................	6,721	4,086	2,635	6,759	3,828	2,931
Armenian..........................	3,092	2,643	449	5,222	4,476	746
Bohemian and Moravian (Czech)......	9,223	5,214	4,009	8,439	4,565	3,874
Bulgarian, Serbian and Montenegrin...	10,222	9,485	737	10,657	9,626	1,031
Chinese...........................	1,307	1,124	183	1,608	1,367	241
Croatian and Slovenian..............	18,982	13,466	5,516	24,366	17,383	6,983
Cuban.............................	3,914	2,762	1,152	3,155	2,098	1,057
Dalmatian, Bosnian and Herzegovinian.	4,400	3,809	591	3,672	3,152	520
Dutch and Flemish..................	13,862	8,778	5,084	10,935	6,808	4,127
East Indian........	517	511	6	165	153	12
English............................	57,258	32,980	24,278	49,689	27,133	22,556
Finnish...........................	9,779	5,645	4,134	6,641	3,354	3,287
French............................	18,132	10,254	7,878	18,382	10,327	8,055
German...........................	66,471	37,629	28,842	65,343	36,479	28,864
Greek.............................	37,021	34,105	2,916	31,566	28,521	3,045
Hebrew...........................	91,223	48,935	42,288	80,595	42,751	37,844
Irish..............................	40,246	21,283	18,963	33,922	17,012	16,910
Italian, North	30,312	22,522	7,790	26,443	18,507	7,936
Italian, South	159,638	116,244	43,394	135,830	94,460	41,370
Japanese..........................	4,575	1,409	3,166	6,172	1,930	4,242
Korean............................	8	....	8	33	14	19
Lithuanian.........................	17,027	10,473	6,554	14,078	8,098	5,980
Magyar...........................	19,996	11,640	8,356	23,599	13,792	9,807
Mexican...........................	18,784	12,423	6,361	22,001	15,367	6,634
Pacific Islander.....................	12	7	5	3	2	1
Polish.............................	71,446	42,339	29,107	85,163	50,028	35,135
Portuguese........................	7,469	4,843	2,626	9,403	5,938	3,465
Rumanian.........................	5,311	4,228	1,083	8,329	6,752	1,577
Russian...........................	18,721	16,280	2,441	22,558	19,464	3,094
Ruthenian (Russniak)	17,724	11,375	6,349	21,965	13,121	8,844
Scandinavian (Norwegians, Danes and Swedes)........................	45,859	28,757	17,102	31,601	19,073	12,528
Scotch............................	25,625	14,798	10,827	20,293	10,637	9,656
Slovak............................	21,415	13,173	8,242	25,281	15,639	9,642
Spanish...........................	8,068	6,405	1,663	9,070	6,900	2,170
Spanish-American...................	1,153	747	406	1,342	930	412
Syrian............................	5,444	3,609	1,835	5,525	3,646	1,879
Turkish...........................	918	830	88	1,336	1,256	80
Welsh.............................	2,248	1,471	777	2,239	1,419	820
West Indian (except Cuban).........	1,141	625	516	1,132	590	542
Other.............................	3,323	3,150	173	3,660	3,335	325
Total........................	878,587	570,057	308,530	838,172	529,931	308,241

TABLE X.—DISTRIBUTION OF IMMIGRANT ALIENS ADMITTED, BY SEX AND RACE OR PEOPLE, 1899-1924
(continued).

Race or people	1913			1914		
	Total	Males	Females	Total	Males	Females
African (black)	6,634	3,691	2,943	8,447	4,901	3,546
Armenian	9,353	7,893	1,460	7,785	6,533	1,252
Bohemian and Moravian (Czech)	11,091	6,328	4,763	9,928	5,367	4,561
Bulgarian, Serbian and Montenegrin	9,087	7,834	1,253	15,084	13,465	1,619
Chinese	2,022	1,692	330	2,354	2,052	302
Croatian and Slovenian	42,499	31,590	10,909	37,284	26,877	10,407
Cuban	3,099	2,126	973	3,539	2,452	1,087
Dalmatian, Bosnian and Herzegovinian	4,520	3,938	582	5,149	4,437	712
Dutch and Flemish	14,507	9,471	5,036	12,566	7,737	4,829
East Indian	188	184	4	172	163	9
English	55,522	31,320	24,202	51,746	28,920	22,826
Finnish	12,756	8,219	4,537	12,805	7,582	5,223
French	20,652	11,620	9,032	18,166	10,404	7,762
German	80,865	45,974	34,891	79,871	44,821	35,050
Greek	38,644	35 143	3,501	45,881	40,207	5,674
Hebrew	101,330	57,148	44,182	138,051	74,905	63,146
Irish	37,023	19,072	17,951	33,898	16,793	17,105
Italian, North	42,534	32,428	10,106	44,802	33,552	11,250
Italian, South	231,613	176,472	55,141	251,612	184,270	67,342
Japanese	8,302	3,157	5,145	8,941	3,292	5,649
Korean	64	15	49	152	58	94
Lithuanian	24,647	16,069	8,578	21,584	12,282	9,302
Magyar	30,610	16,637	13,973	44,538	27,517	17,021
Mexican	10,954	6,359	4,595	13,089	6,584	6,505
Pacific Islander	11	8	3	1	.....	1
Polish	174,365	115,772	58,593	122,657	72,837	49,820
Portuguese	13,566	8,696	4,870	9,647	6,260	3,387
Rumanian	13,451	10,373	3,078	24,070	19,748	4,322
Russian	51,472	45,633	5,839	44,957	38,010	6,947
Ruthenian (Russniak)	30,588	18,980	11,608	36,727	23,590	13,137
Scandinavian (Norwegians, Danes and Swedes)	38,737	25,243	13,494	36,053	22,996	13,057
Scotch	21,293	11,545	9,748	18,997	10,332	8,665
Slovak	27,234	16,242	10,992	25,819	15,009	10,810
Spanish	9,042	7,240	1,802	11,064	8,758	2,306
Spanish-American	1,363	978	385	1,544	1,032	512
Syrian	9,210	6,177	3,033	9,023	6,391	2,632
Turkish	2,015	1,866	149	2,693	2,591	102
Welsh	2,820	1,771	1,049	2,558	1,651	907
West Indian (except Cuban)	1,171	655	516	1,396	818	578
Other	3,038	2,585	453	3,830	3,553	277
Total	1,197,892	808,144	389,748	1,218,480	798,747	419,733

TABLE X.—Distribution of immigrant aliens admitted, by sex and race or people, 1899-1924 (continued).

Race or people	1915			1916			1917		
	Total	Males	Females	Total	Males	Females	Total	Males	Females
African (black)............	5,660	3,002	2,658	4,576	2,291	2,285	7,971	4,192	3,779
Armenian.................	932	685	247	964	775	189	1,221	1,017	204
Bohemian and Moravian (Czech).................	1,651	766	885	642	227	415	327	171	156
Bulgarian, Serbian and Montenegrin...............	3,506	3,215	291	3,146	2,968	178	1,134	1,050	84
Chinese..................	2,469	2,182	287	2,239	1,962	277	1,843	1,563	280
Croatian and Slovenian.....	1,942	1,254	688	791	425	366	305	220	85
Cuban...................	3,402	2,280	1,122	3,442	2,273	1,169	3,428	2,321	1,107
Dalmatian, Bosnian and Herzegovinian..........	305	230	75	114	88	26	94	88	6
Dutch and Flemish........	6,675	4,015	2,660	6,443	3,945	2,498	5,393	3,323	2,070
East Indian..............	82	70	12	80	70	10	69	64	5
English..................	38,662	20,069	18,593	36,168	18,727	17,441	32,246	15,981	16,265
Finnish..................	3,472	2,210	1,262	5,649	3,479	2,170	5,900	3,657	2,243
French..................	12,636	6,933	5,703	19,518	11,624	7,894	24,405	15,634	8,771
German..................	20,729	11,728	9,001	11,555	6,129	5,426	9,682	5,529	4,153
Greek...................	15,187	11,740	3,447	26,792	21,093	5,699	25,919	21,124	4,795
Hebrew..................	26,497	13,756	12,741	15,108	9,391	5,717	17,342	8,982	8,360
Irish....................	23,503	13,015	10,488	20,636	11,258	9,378	17,462	7,679	9,783
Italian, North.............	10,660	6,263	4,397	4,905	2,920	1,985	3,796	2,253	1,543
Italian, South.............	46,557	24,870	21,687	33,909	20,521	13,388	35,154	17,838	17,316
Japanese.................	8,609	3,762	4,847	8,711	4,033	4,678	8,925	4,162	4,763
Korean..................	146	91	55	154	70	84	194	75	119
Lithuanian...............	2,638	1,223	1,415	599	399	200	479	329	150
Magyar..................	3,604	1,905	1,699	981	351	630	434	209	225
Mexican.................	10,993	5,682	5,311	17,198	8,732	8,466	16,438	8,046	8,392
Pacific Islander...........	6	5	1	5	1	4	10	4	6
Polish...................	9,065	4,429	4,636	4,502	2,280	2,222	3,109	1,856	1,253
Portuguese...............	4,376	2,853	1,523	12,208	8,010	4,198	10,194	4,878	5,316
Rumanian................	1,200	852	348	953	530	423	522	398	124
Russian..................	4,459	3,355	1,104	4,858	4,057	801	3,711	2,758	953
Ruthenian (Russniak)......	2,933	1,907	1,026	1,365	1,135	230	1,211	925	286
Scandinavian (Norwegians, Danes and Swedes)......	24,263	14,375	9,888	19,172	11,527	7,645	19,596	12,121	7,475
Scotch..................	14,310	7,318	6,992	13,515	6,771	6,744	13,350	6,603	6,747
Slovak..................	2,069	970	1,099	577	210	367	244	134	110
Spanish.................	5,705	4,551	1,154	9,259	7,768	1,491	15,019	13,317	1,702
Spanish-American.........	1,667	1,111	556	1,881	1,336	545	2,587	1,906	681
Syrian..................	1,767	1,174	593	676	474	202	976	690	286
Turkish.................	273	241	32	216	207	9	454	434	20
Welsh...................	1,390	821	569	983	577	406	793	454	339
West Indian (except Cuban).	823	442	381	948	460	488	1,369	722	647
Other...................	1,877	1,671	206	3,388	3,135	253	2,097	1,772	325
Total...............	326,700	187,021	139,679	298,826	182,229	116,597	295,403	174,479	120,924

TABLE X.—Distribution of immigrant aliens admitted, by sex and race or people, 1909-1924 (continued).

Race or people	1918			1919		
	Total	Males	Females	Total	Males	Females
African (black)...................	5,706	2,774	2,932	5,823	3,008	2,815
Armenian.........................	221	147	74	282	196	86
Bohemian and Moravian (Czech).......	74	45	29	105	68	37
Bulgarian, Serbian and Montenegrin. ...	150	130	20	205	153	52
Chinese..........................	1,576	1,276	300	1,697	1,425	272
Croatian and Slovenian..............	33	26	7	23	21	2
Cuban...........................	1,179	816	363	1,169	803	366
Dalmatian, Bosnian and Herzegovinian.	15	15	....	4	3	1
Dutch and Flemish.................	2,200	1,492	708	2,735	1,723	1,012
East Indian.......................	61	57	4	68	52	*16
English..........................	12,980	5,832	7,148	26,889	14,866	12,023
Finnish..........................	1,867	1,242	625	968	788	180
French...........................	6,840	3,132	3,708	12,598	6,192	6,406
German..........................	1,992	1,174	818	1,837	1,008	829
Greek............................	2,602	2,149	453	813	696	117
Hebrew..........................	3,672	1,514	2,158	3,055	1,566	1,489
Irish............................	4,657	2,088	2,569	7,910	4,518	3,392
Italian, North....................	1,074	586	488	1,236	772	464
Italian, South....................	5,234	1,879	3,355	2,137	1,174	963
Japanese.........................	10,168	4,821	5,347	10,056	4,567	5,489
Korean..........................	149	59	90	77	6	71
Lithuanian.......................	135	96	39	160	119	41
Magyar..........................	32	14	18	52	24	28
Mexican..........................	17,602	10,642	6,960	28,844	18,834	10,010
Pacific Islander...................	17	12	5	6	4	2
Polish...........................	668	497	171	732	545	187
Portuguese.......................	2,319	1,349	970	1,574	1,089	485
Rumanian........................	155	124	31	89	66	23
Russian..........................	1,513	1,081	432	1,532	1,199	333
Ruthenian (Russniak)..............	49	36	13	103	79	24
Scandinavian (Norwegians, Danes and Swedes).........................	8,741	5,467	3,274	8,261	5,159	3,102
Scotch...........................	5,204	2,010	3,194	10,364	5,614	4,750
Slovak...........................	35	27	8	85	53	32
Spanish..........................	7,909	6,791	1,118	4,224	3,453	771
Spanish-American..................	2,231	1,580	651	3,092	2,175	917
Syrian...........................	210	143	67	231	157	74
Turkish..........................	24	23	1	18	11	7
Welsh............................	278	170	108	608	395	213
West Indian (except Cuban).........	732	361	371	1,223	529	694
Other............................	314	203	111	247	162	85
Total......................	110,618	61,880	48,738	141,132	83,272	57,860

TABLE X.—Distribution of immigrant aliens admitted, by sex and race or people, 1899-1924 (continued).

Race or people	1920			1921		
	Total	Males	Females	Total	Males	Females
African (black)	8,174	4,508	3,666	9,873	5,066	4,807
Armenian	3,762	1,466	1,296	10,212	4,986	5,226
Bohemian and Moravian (Czech)	415	173	242	1,743	733	1,010
Bulgarian, Serbian and Montenegrin	1,064	633	431	7,700	3,925	3,775
Chinese	2,148	1,719	429	4,017	3,304	713
Croatian and Slovenian	493	234	259	11,035	4,657	6,378
Cuban	1,510	1,012	498	1,523	1,013	510
Dalmatian, Bosnian and Herzegovinian	63	41	22	930	485	445
Dutch and Flemish	12,730	7,052	5,678	12,813	7,212	5,601
East Indian	160	138	22	353	339	14
English	58,366	29,923	28,443	54,627	27,654	26,973
Finnish	1,510	907	603	4,233	1,623	2,610
French	27,390	14,238	13,152	24,122	12,727	11,395
German	7,338	4,383	2,955	24,168	11,619	12,549
Greek	13,998	11,167	2,831	31,828	21,551	10,277
Hebrew	14,292	6,595	7,697	119,036	52,710	66,326
Irish	20,784	10,219	10,565	39,056	17,595	21,461
Italian, North,	12,918	6,599	6,319	27,459	18,786	8,673
Italian, South	84,882	44,112	40,770	195,037	126,528	68,509
Japanese	9,279	3,414	5,865	7,531	3,147	4,384
Korean	72	25	47	61	22	39
Lithuanian	422	274	148	829	337	492
Magyar	252	124	128	9,377	3,782	5,595
Mexican	51,042	34,042	17,000	29,603	17,546	12,057
Pacific Islander	17	11	6	13	8	5
Polish	2,519	1,436	1,083	21,146	7,482	13,664
Portuguese	15,174	11,056	4,118	18,856	13,479	5,377
Rumanian	898	530	368	5,925	3,032	2,893
Russian	2,378	1,657	721	2,887	1,625	1,262
Ruthenian (Russniak)	258	192	66	958	359	599
Scandinavian (Norwegians, Danes and Swedes)	16,621	9,790	6,831	25,812	15,690	10,122
Scotch	21,180	11,027	10,153	24,649	12,420	12,229
Slovak	3,824	1,325	2,499	35,047	15,026	20,021
Spanish	23,594	20,494	3,100	27,448	23,652	3,796
Spanish-American	3,934	2,564	1,370	3,325	2,190	1,135
Syrian	3,047	1,915	1,132	5,105	2,783	2,322
Turkish	140	118	22	353	276	77
Welsh	1,462	782	680	1,748	1,011	737
West Indian (except Cuban)	1,546	711	835	1,553	664	889
Other	1,345	1,019	326	3,237	2,378	859
Total	430,001	247,625	182,376	805,228	449,422	355,806

TABLE X.—Distribution of immigrant aliens admitted, by sex and race or people, 1899-1924 (concluded).

Race or people	1922			1923			1924		
	Total	Males	Females	Total	Males	Females	Total	Males	Females
African (black)............	5,248	1,964	3,284	7,554	3,436	4,118	12,243	5,558	6,685
Armenian................	2,249	909	1,340	2,396	1,018	1,378	2.940	1,226	1,714
Bohemian and Moravian (Czech)...............	3,086	1,426	1,660	5,537	2,880	2,657	6,869	3,713	3,156
Bulgarian, Serbian and Montenegrin...........	1,370	665	705	1,893	988	905	2,482	1,525	957
Chinese..................	4,465	3,622	843	4,074	3,239	835	4,670	3,732	938
Croatian and Slovenian.....	3,783	1,467	2,316	4,163	2,033	2,130	4,137	2,560	1,577
Cuban..................	698	456	242	1,347	885	462	1,412	972	440
Dalmatian, Bosnian and Herzegovinian..........	307	127	180	571	305	266	295	182	113
Dutch and Flemish........	3,749	1,905	1,844	5,804	3,441	2,363	7,840	4,561	3,279
East Indian..............	223	209	14	156	144	12	154	137	17
English..................	30,429	14,063	16,366	60,524	33,784	26,740	93,939	53,275	40,664
Finnish..................	2,506	951	1,555	3,087	1,395	1,692	3,975	2,157	1,818
French..................	13,617	6,793	6,824	34,371	18,972	15,399	48,632	28,967	19,665
German..................	31,218	14,441	16,777	65,543	34,249	31,294	95,627	53,717	41,910
Greek...................	3,821	1,679	2,142	4,177	1,474	2,703	5,252	2,256	2,996
Hebrew..................	53,524	22,216	31,308	49,719	23,826	25,893	49,989	25,258	24,731
Irish....................	17,191	6,851	10,340	30,386	16 451	13,953	42,364	24,273	18,091
Italian, North............	6,098	3,570	2,528	9,054	5,738	3,316	11,576	9,005	2,571
Italian, South............	35,056	19,726	15,330	39,226	26,646	12,580	47,633	34,018	13,615
Japanese................	6,361	2,683	3,678	5,652	2,489	3 163	8,481	3,784	4,697
Korean..................	88	31	57	104	53	51	122	68	54
Lithuanian...............	1,602	386	1,216	1,828	690	1,138	1,991	778	1,213
Magyar..................	6,037	2,708	3,329	6,922	3,316	3,606	7,446	3,746	3,700
Mexican.................	18,246	11,468	6,778	62,709	46,007	16,702	87,648	59,489	28,159
Pacific Islander...........	7	5	2	14	7	7	12	5	7
Polish..................	6,357	2,133	4,224	13,210	6,768	6,442	19,371	10,720	8,651
Portuguese..............	1,867	1 077	790	2,802	1,973	829	3,892	2,638	1,254
Rumanian...............	1,520	749	771	1,397	687	710	1,727	986	741
Russian.................	2,486	1,275	1,211	4,346	2,545	1,801	9,531	5,784	3,747
Ruthenian (Russniak)......	698	284	414	1,168	612	556	2,356	1,543	813
Scandinavian (Norwegians, Danes and Swedes)......	16,678	9,341	7,337	37,630	27,054	10,576	40,978	26,908	14,070
Scotch.	15,596	7,215	8,381	38,627	24,109	14,518	61,327	37,339	23,988
Slovak..................	6,001	3,160	2,841	6,230	3,499	2,731	5,523	3,398	2,125
Spanish.................	1,879	1,314	565	3,525	2,812	713	3,664	2,734	930
Spanish-American.........	1,446	906	540	1,990	1,225	765	3,065	1,865	1,200
Syrian..................	1,334	685	649	1,207	606	601	1,595	801	794
Turkish.................	40	35	5	237	108	129	355	179	176
Welsh...................	956	486	470	1,622	979	643	2,635	1,702	933
West Indian (except Cuban).	976	386	590	1,467	690	777	2,211	1,024	1,187
Other...................	743	374	369	650	389	261	937	603	334
Total...............	309,556	149,741	158,815	522,919	307,522	215,397	706,896	423,186	283,710

TABLE XI.—DISTRIBUTION OF IMMIGRANT ALIENS ADMITTED, BY AGE AND RACE OR PEOPLE, 1899-1924.

Race or people	1899			1900			1901			1902		
	Under 14 years	14 to 44 years	45 years and over	Under 14 years	14 to 44 years	45 years and over	Under 14 years	14 to 44 years	45 years and over	Under 14 years	14 to 44 years	45 years and over
African (black)	70	296	46	162	500	52	120	416	58	163	595	74
Armenian	119	513	42	110	837	35	242	1,534	79	115	978	58
Bohemian and Moravian	547	1,742	237	593	2,228	239	757	2,663	346	1,025	4,177	388
Bulgarian, Serbian and Montenegrin	5	86	3	1	197	6	54	540	17	30	1,218	43
Chinese	10	1,574	54	6	1,183	61	56	2,309	87	29	1,506	96
Croatian and Slovenian	398	7,869	365	667	15,819	698	745	16,576	607	989	27,870	1,374
Cuban	183	970	221	599	1,767	312	360	1,085	177	485	1,740	198
Dalmatian, Bosnian and Herzegovinian	17	340	10	37	613	25	40	664	28	45	895	64
Dutch and Flemish	425	1,284	151	704	1,768	230	769	2,232	298	956	2,856	305
East Indian		14	1		9	1	1	19		3	80	1
English	1,492	7,962	1,258	1,659	8,067	1,171	2,105	9,702	1,681	2,367	10,835	1,740
Finnish	586	5,299	212	1,393	10,799	420	1,099	8,557	343	1,289	12,209	370
French	261	1,813	204	234	1,672	189	432	3,253	351	573	3,227	322
German	5,290	19,227	2,114	5,638	21,868	2,176	6,490	25,706	2,546	9,582	38,703	3,401
Greek	314	2,018	64	388	3,296	89	506	5,238	175	687	7,227	201
Hebrew	8,987	26,019	2,409	13,092	44,239	3,433	14,731	39,830	3,537	15,312	38,937	3,439
Irish	1,189	29,913	1,243	1,382	32,993	1,232	1,347	27,821	1,236	1,183	26,651	1,167
Italian, North	1,466	10,810	815	1,574	14,822	920	1,830	19,156	1,117	2,215	24,029	1,376
Italian, South	12,373	47,148	6,118	12,532	65,213	6,601	15,794	90,317	9,593	16,954	123,745	12,216
Japanese	31	3,295	69	32	12,439	157	53	5,079	117	630	13,685	140
Korean		17	5		63	8	1	43	3	1	23	4
Lithuanian	448	6,276	134	790	9,347	174	712	7,986	117	949	10,479	201
Magyar	592	4,884	224	1,018	12,167	592	1,108	11,620	583	1,447	21,166	997
Mexican	27	117	19	55	175	31	42	278	31	84	597	34
Pacific Islander		14		7	101	4	1	21		7	33	
Polish	3,355	24,343	768	4,597	41,136	1,205	4,520	37,904	1,193	5,989	61,886	1,745
Portuguese	477	1,487	132	1,105	2,778	358	1,030	2,774	372	1,439	3,410	460
Rumanian	1	88	7	8	371	19	23	684	54	39	1,876	118
Russian	282	1,428	64	245	918	37	147	495	28	235	1,260	56
Ruthenian (Russniak)	119	1,246	35	216	2,540	76	252	4,850	186	300	6,996	237
Scandinavian	1,901	19,976	1,372	2,422	28,860	1,670	3,185	34,796	2,296	4,349	48,768	2,663
Scotch	257	1,283	212	284	1,289	184	311	1,482	211	379	1,765	288
Slovak	1,544	13,769	525	2,159	26,243	841	2,582	25,756	1,005	3,005	32,727	1,202
Spanish	26	877	93	61	917	133	105	1,020	77	105	1,697	152
Spanish-American				10	83	4	49	210	17	82	381	33
Syrian	731	2,799	178	599	2,200	121	798	3,080	186	842	3,974	166
Turkish	2	26		16	167	1	8	125	3	11	146	8
Welsh	350	925	84	196	510	56	113	485	76	142	553	65
West Indian (except Cuban)	15	117	12	4	72	2	9	72	1	17	103	17
Other	93	319	45	19	57		35	136	7	9	251	7
Not specified	4	4		10	59	4						
Total	43,983	248,187	19,545	54,624	370,382	23,566	62,562	396,516	28,840	74,063	539,254	35,426

TABLE XI.—DISTRIBUTION OF IMMIGRANT ALIENS ADMITTED, BY AGE AND RACE OR PEOPLE, 1899-1924 (continued).

Race or people	1903 Under 14 years	1903 14 to 44 years	1903 45 years or over	1904 Under 14 years	1904 14 to 44 years	1904 45 years or over	1905 Under 14 years	1905 14 to 44 years	1905 45 years or over	1906 Under 14 years	1906 14 to 44 years	1906 45 years or over
African (black)	242	1,811	121	306	1,907	173	433	2,974	191	346	3,286	154
Armenian	150	1,557	52	238	1,441	66	246	1,529	103	223	1,598	74
Bohemian and Moravian	1,856	7,224	511	2,694	8,511	706	2,620	8,442	695	2,678	9,578	702
Bulgarian, Serbian and Montenegrin	74	6,165	240	76	4,383	118	97	5,529	197	224	11,104	220
Chinese	32	2,055	105	90	3,804	433	28	1,666	277	67	1,210	208
Croatian and Slovenian	1,111	30,457	1,339	1,225	19,314	703	1,383	32,470	1,251	1,674	41,653	945
Cuban	610	1,987	347	913	3,401	497	1,346	15,225	688	963	4,090	538
Dalmatian, Bosnian and Herzegovinian	33	1,625	78	47	1,913	76	62	2,450	127	77	4,398	93
Dutch and Flemish	1,602	4,404	490	1,693	5,465	674	1,699	6,085	714	1,706	7,442	587
East Indian	5	75	3	18	221	19	3	122	20	15	245	11
English	4,270	20,649	3,532	5,812	29,793	5,874	6,956	36,726	7,183	6,081	33,935	5,063
Finnish	1,807	16,540	517	1,506	8,323	328	1,483	15,047	482	1,005	12,840	291
French	938	5,554	674	1,413	8,935	1,209	1,121	8,825	1,401	889	8,482	1,008
German	13,377	53,992	4,413	12,868	56,097	5,845	11,469	64,441	6,450	13,076	68,282	5,455
Greek	1,185	12,951	240	605	11,883	137	446	11,523	175	718	22,174	235
Hebrew	19,044	53,074	4,085	23,529	77,224	5,485	28,553	95,964	5,393	43,620	101,875	8,253
Irish	1,843	32,037	1,486	1,966	33,147	1,963	2,580	48,562	3,124	1,868	37,232	1,859
Italian, North	3,404	32,606	1,419	3,633	31,529	1,537	3,569	34,561	1,800	3,993	40,684	1,609
Italian, South	21,619	164,661	9,837	20,895	128,991	9,443	16,915	159,024	10,451	26,546	202,888	11,094
Japanese	515	19,344	182	190	13,832	360	124	10,588	309	146	13,821	276
Korean	43	520	1	133	1,756	18	325	4,557	47	21	103	3
Lithuanian	1,137	13,078	217	1,317	11,279	184	1,474	16,875	255	1,270	12,765	222
Magyar	2,141	23,721	1,262	2,441	20,358	1,084	3,864	39,926	2,240	3,974	38,746	1,541
Mexican	67	384	35	1	380	26	29	169	29	21	105	15
Pacific Islander	3	46	3	1	11		1	15	1	1	10	2
Polish	7,761	72,629	1,953	8,116	57,898	1,743	9,867	89,914	2,656	8,941	84,860	2,034
Portuguese	2,072	5,665	696	1,426	4,382	530	1,035	3,381	439	1,821	6,171	737
Rumanian	78	4,408	254	93	4,014	257	153	7,293	372	201	10,769	455
Russian	407	3,069	132	429	3,390	142	591	2,988	167	580	5,047	187
Ruthenian (Russniak)	467	9,084	292	549	8,781	262	661	13,321	491	592	15,262	403
Scandinavian	8,396	67,518	3,433	7,709	50,127	3,193	6,597	52,226	3,461	5,290	50,214	2,637
Scotch	960	4,600	659	1,923	8,217	1,343	2,270	12,109	1,765	2,117	12,978	1,368
Slovak	3,300	30,042	1,085	3,336	23,754	850	4,582	45,882	1,904	3,415	33,796	1,010
Spanish	282	2,722	293	331	3,878	453	403	4,612	575	378	4,509	445
Spanish-American	150	735	93	287	1,142	237	223	1,232	203	270	1,179	136
Syrian	952	4,379	220	621	2,902	130	742	3,843	237	886	4,712	226
Turkish	8	434	7	43	1,391	48	45	2,073	27	38	1,952	43
Welsh	253	895	130	340	1,306	174	464	1,726	341	297	1,851	219
West Indian (except Cuban)	202	1,175	120	232	1,513	197	187	1,209	152	218	1,123	135
Other	35	181	6	65	582	50	22	315	19	27	986	14
Total	102,431	714,053	40,562	109,150	657,155	46,565	114,668	855,419	56,412	136,273	913,955	50,507

TABLE XI.—DISTRIBUTION OF IMMIGRANT ALIENS ADMITTED, BY AGE AND RACE OR PEOPLE, 1899-1924 (continued).

Race or people	1907			1908			1909			1910		
	Under 14 years	14 to 44 years	45 years or over	Under 14 years	14 to 44 years	45 years or over	Under 14 years	14 to 44 years	45 years or over	Under 14 years	14 to 44 years	45 years or over
African (black)	500	4,510	225	421	4,021	184	341	3,803	163	449	4,315	202
Armenian	371	2,174	99	581	2,517	201	191	2,803	114	389	4,957	162
Bohemian and Moravian	2,539	10,446	569	2,216	7,425	523	1,440	5,051	359	1,503	6,493	446
Bulgarian, Serbian and Montenegrin	296	26,358	520	339	17,442	465	211	5,780	223	388	14,250	492
Chinese	85	662	23	150	1,064	49	232	1,514	95	221	1,397	152
Croatian and Slovenian	1,694	45,167	965	1,567	18,321	584	1,258	18,169	754	1,855	36,438	1,269
Cuban	790	4,305	380	445	2,582	296	536	2,554	290	550	2,516	265
Dalmatian, Bosnian, and Herzegovinian	109	7,075	209	115	3,568	64	80	1,737	71	173	4,594	144
Dutch and Flemish	2,560	9,249	658	2,250	6,602	674	1,757	5,760	597	2,630	9,611	771
East Indian	4	1,055	13	3	1,676	31	4	312	21	6	1,762	14
English	7,982	39,061	4,083	7,990	36,245	4,821	5,745	29,359	3,917	8,697	39,633	5,168
Finnish	967	13,559	334	670	5,946	130	818	10,652	217	1,235	14,182	319
French	1,002	7,844	546	1,920	9,919	1,042	4,444	13,177	1,802	4,918	14,114	2,075
German	14,845	73,379	4,712	13,899	54,402	4,737	9,882	44,359	4,293	12,165	54,142	5,073
Greek	819	45,169	295	868	27,617	323	778	19,155	329	1,041	37,589	505
Hebrew	37,696	103,779	7,707	26,013	71,388	5,986	15,210	38,465	3,876	21,869	57,191	5,200
Irish	2,243	35,316	1,147	2,656	32,188	1,583	1,990	27,937	1,258	2,837	33,916	1,629
Italian, North	4,008	46,089	1,467	2,775	21,115		2,178	22,041	931	2,722	27,014	1,044
Italian, South	24,890	207,339	10,268	18,465	83,956	8,126	14,509	142,793	7,946	20,065	160,859	11,749
Japanese	249	30,251	324	317	15,808	293	149	3,032	94	121	2,609	68
Korean	1	38		4	22			11			16	1
Lithuanian	1,563	23,928	393	1,256	12,173	291	1,088	13,694	472	1,813	20,381	520
Magyar	4,384	54,064	1,623	3,447	20,083	848	3,003	24,315	1,386	3,650	22,129	1,523
Mexican	7	78	6	1,002	4,195	465	3,721	10,498	1,372	4,078	11,951	1,731
Pacific Islander		3			1			6			53	8
Polish	9,602	125,904	2,527	7,818	58,682	1,605	7,397	68,070	2,098	9,798	115,112	3,438
Portuguese	2,431	6,581	636	1,697	4,655	457	908	3,404	294	1,526	5,691	440
Rumanian	248	18,314	638	304	8,904	421	328	7,276	437	389	12,778	1,032
Russian	740	15,774	293	960	15,787	364	377	9,469	192	1,102	15,849	343
Ruthenian (Russniak)	731	22,952	398	689	11,353	319	961	14,320	527	1,063	25,933	911
Scandinavian	4,840	46,606	1,979	3,727	27,517	1,545	2,804	30,698	1,494	4,452	45,588	1,997
Scotch	3,242	16,060	1,214	3,035	13,353	1,363	2,379	12,724	1,343	3,897	18,805	1,910
Slovak	3,766	37,319	956	2,323	5,697	494	2,145	19,758	683	2,787	28,537	1,092
Spanish	1,596	7,491	408	581	4,602	358	346	4,275	318	419	5,058	360
Spanish-American	159	803	98	167	811	85	141	669	80	123	687	90
Syrian	664	5,044	172	746	2,266	172	548	2,957	163	946	5,111	260
Turkish	18	1,863	41	41		20	33	771	16	21	1,245	17
Welsh	466	2,114	174	436	1,429	194	260	1,298	141	359	838	171
West Indian (except Cuban)	179	1,083	119	175		86	142	766	116	206		106
Other	58	1,965	35	60	1,874	41	59	1,444	34	44	3,252	34
Not specified												
Total	138,344	1,100,771	46,234	112,148	630,671	40,051	88,393	624,876	38,517	120,509	868,310	52,751

TABLE XI.—DISTRIBUTION OF IMMIGRANT ALIENS ADMITTED, BY AGE AND RACE OR PEOPLE, 1899-1924 (continued).

Race or people	1911			1912			1913			1914			1915		
	Under 14 years	14 to 44 years	45 years and over	Under 14 years	14 to 44 years	45 years and over	Under 14 years	14 to 44 years	45 years and over	Under 14 years	14 to 44 years	45 years and over	Under 14 years	14 to 44 years	45 years and over
African (black)	593	5,867	261	614	5,844	301	565	5,804	265	718	7,426	303	575	4,814	271
Armenian	205	2,783	104	290	4,779	153	718	8,309	326	538	6,960	287	107	762	63
Bohemian and Moravian (Czech)	1,748	7,003	472	1,610	6,339	490	2,006	8,539	546	1,972	7,482	474	409	1,133	109
Bulgarian, Serbian and Montenegrin	339	9,689	194	453	9,945	259	560	8,044	483	689	13,737	658	136	3,207	163
Chinese	112	1,049	146	207	1,327	74	189	1,530	303	144	1,736	474	118	1,860	491
Croatian and Slovenian	1,587	16,889	506	2,063	21,660	643	3,422	37,362	1,715	3,511	31,701	2,072	319	1,507	116
Cuban	585	2,950	379	455	2,389	311	396	2,368	335	488	2,685	366	562	2,472	368
Dalmatian, Bosnian and Herzegovinian	175	4,127	98	130	3,466	76	159	181	193	206	161	221	22	264	19
Dutch and Flemish	3,096	9,862	904	2,352	7,758	825	2,675	10,896	936	2,400	9,229	937	1,313	4,691	671
East Indian	9	504	4		157		1		6	2			3	75	4
English	9,920	41,835	5,503	8,395	35,774	5,520	8,915	40,296	6,311	8,060	37,393	6,293	5,992	27,173	5,497
Finnish	977	8,617	185	713	5,769	159	888	11,651	217	1,115	11,460	230	381	3,000	9
French	3,403	12,843	1,886	3,320	13,019	2,043	3,831	14,402	2,419	3,170	12,917	2,079	2,083	8,884	1,669
German	11,680	50,197	4,594	11,484	49,340	4,519	15,450	59,627	5,788	13,520	60,008	6,343	3,430	15,221	2,078
Greek	1,106	35,485	430	1,144	49,976	446	1,269	36,591	784	1,848	42,264	1,769	1,230	13,088	869
Hebrew	21,835	63,674	5,714	20,091	54,927	5,577	22,378	72,218	6,734	30,113	98,236	9,702	6,794	20,026	2,096
Irish	2,871	35,512	1,863	2,357	29,671	1,894	2,543	32,441	2,039	2,482	29,479	1,937	1,628	8,082	1,849
Italian, North	2,900	26,293	1,119	3,033	22,334	1,076	4,248	36,645	1,641	4,775	38,106	1,921	1,974		604
Italian, South	21,171	128,617	9,850	20,081	107,216	8,533	27,302	190,795	13,516	32,936	201,428	17,248	11,298	30,716	4,543
Japanese	300	4,184	91	328	5,546	29	437	7,290	575	438	8,135	466	487	7,724	3
Korean	1	7			30	1	13	51				9			
Lithuanian	1,382	15,331	314	1,186	12,635	257	1,760	22,438	449	2,040	19,059	485	398	2,177	398
Magyar	3,095	15,901	1,000	3,740	18,697	1,162	5,670	22,410	2,530	6,356	33,445	4,737	895	2,443	63
Mexican	4,111	12,946	1,727	4,188	15,910	1,903	3,048	6,931	975	4,409	7,358	1,322	3,134	6,542	266
Pacific Islander	2	1	1		1			8	3				6	6	
Polish	7,691	62,148	1,607	8,477	74,911	1,775	17,253	52,988	4,124	15,767	103,201	3,689	1,896	6,832	1,317
Portuguese	1,238	5,765	466	1,863	6,939	601	2,301	10,366	899	1,338	7,769	540	638	3,427	337
Rumanian	365	4,668	278	484	7,304	541	992	10,539	1,920	1,232	18,672	4,166	132	983	311
Russian	969	17,394	358	1,043	21,114	401	1,747	48,906	819	2,143	41,939	875	497	3,793	85
Ruthenian (Russniak)	855	16,542	327	1,255	20,314	396	2,365	47,250	973	2,680	32,579	1,468	334	2,440	169
Scandinavian (Norwegians, Danes, and Swedes)	4,127	39,923	1,809	2,867	27,270	1,464	3,038	34,056	1,643	3,068	31,345	1,640	2,139	20,757	1,367
Scotch	4,510	19,042	2,073	3,593	14,593	2,107	3,521	15,406	2,366	2,938	13,886	2,173	2,078	10,258	1,974
Slovak	2,534	18,224	657	2,997	21,519	765	4,205	22,048	981	4,232	19,998	1,589	616	4,828	137
Spanish	913	6,699	456	1,294	7,196	580	926	7,568	548	1,198	9,180	686	383	1,249	494
Spanish-American	169	885	99	193	1,029	120	203	1,065	95	245	1,187	112	258	1,402	160
Syrian	673	4,536	235	761	4,475	289	1,341	7,448	421	1,110	7,533	380	279	244	86
Turkish	34	858	26	25	1,283	28	70	1,903	42	47	2,602	44	17	998	12
Welsh	322	1,768	158	344	1,697	198	443	2,128	249	443	1,905	210	228	620	164
West Indian (except Cuban)	139	908	94	115	902	115	125	938	108	150	1,101	145	107	1,723	96
Other	95	3,175	53	151	3,243	86	185	2,751	102	92	3,630	108	77		77
Total	117,837	714,709	46,041	113,700	678,480	45,992	147,158	986,355	64,379	158,621	981,692	78,167	52,982	244,472	29,246

TABLE XI.—DISTRIBUTION OF IMMIGRANT ALIENS ADMITTED, BY AGE AND RACE OR PEOPLE, 1899-1924 (continued).

Race or people	1916			1917			1918			1919			1920		
	Under 14 years	14 to 44 years	45 years and over	Under 14 years	14 to 44 years	45 years and over	Under 16 years	16 to 44 years	45 years and over	Under 16 years	16 to 44 years	45 years and over	Under 16 years	16 to 44 years	45 years and over
African (black)	448	3,926	202	662	7,019	290	662	4,828	216	764	4,740	319	1,223	6,544	407
Armenian	95	817	52	85	1,074	62	45	152	24	48	706	28	481	2,066	215
Bohemian and Moravian (Czech)	209	380	53	86	200	41	6	48	17	18	72	15	79	296	40
Bulgarian, Serbian, Montenegrin	129	2,776	241	58	1,025	51	9	128	16	44	138	23	234	749	81
Chinese	149	1,737	353	135	1,481	227	129	1,178	269	172	1,278	247	242	1,712	194
Croatian and Slovenian	243	508	40	45	227	33	3	24	6	3	18	2	150	320	23
Cuban	547	2,540	355	548	2,521	359	365	755	59	310	783	76	429	1,003	78
Dalmatian, Bosnian, Herzegovinian	23	88	3	1	91	6					5		6	51	6
Dutch and Flemish	1,345	4,480	618	1,050	3,726	617	369	1,533	298	585	1,770	380	3,206	8,113	1,411
East Indian	4	71	5	2	64	1	13	56	1	6	57	5	11	146	3
English	5,683	24,833	5,652	5,185	21,127	5,934	2,274	7,879	2,827	4,328	17,917	4,644	10,645	39,718	8,003
Finnish	754	4,740	155	804	4,866	230	321	1,451	95	74	831	63	317	1,088	105
French	3,730	13,221	2,567	4,070	17,188	3,147	1,185	4,304	1,351	2,607	8,011	1,980	5,487	18,395	3,508
German	2,375	7,772	1,408	1,821	6,475	1,386	364	1,307	321	475	1,030	332	1,536	4,938	864
Greek	1,960	22,252	2,580	1,624	22,460	1,835	233	2,184	185	76	665	72	1,020	11,563	1,415
Hebrew	3,521	10,622	965	4,911	10,991	1,440	1,510	1,811	351	958	1,762	335	4,700	8,021	1,571
Irish	1,921	16,475	2,240	2,001	12,968	2,493	652	2,910	1,095	1,121	5,238	1,551	2,643	15,887	2,254
Italian, North	944	3,583	378	621	2,839	336	209	2,735	130	303	801	132	2,891	9,104	923
Italian, South	7,344	22,189	4,376	8,154	21,842	5,158	1,885	8,228	606	693	1,183	261	20,205	57,739	6,938
Japanese	504	7,696	511	716	7,663	546	1,417	2,743	523	1,397	8,018	641	1,342	7,462	475
Korean	14	136	4	14	364	23	13	130	6	5	70	9	3	67	2
Lithuanian	97	467	35	139	252	43	17	107	11	30	121	8	113	275	34
Magyar	363	540	78		1,777		9	20	3	23	21	8	101	125	26
Mexican	5,459	9,958	1,781	5,119	9,630	1,689	5,277	10,856	1,469	7,342	19,242	2,260	10,880	36,290	3,872
Pacific Islander	4	1		4	6		3	12	2	2	5		2	15	1
Polish	1,139	3,166	197	674	2,276	159	112	477	79	119	542	71	742	1,579	198
Portuguese	1,563	9,725	920	2,172	6,738	1,284	581	1,518	220	234	1,232	108	1,581	12,855	738
Rumanian	225	649	79	70	406	46	27	105	23	19	64	6	219	605	74
Russian	438	4,223	197	506	2,992	213	240	1,175	98	214	1,204	114	499	1,704	175
Ruthenian (Russniak)	164	1,115	86	247	878	86	6	35	8	30	63	10	55	194	9
Scandinavian (Norwegians, Danes, Swedes)	2,170	15,645	1,357	2,159	15,799	1,638	1,232	6,652	857	1,271	5,933	1,057	2,202	12,601	1,818
Scotch	1,906	9,487	2,122	1,957	8,968	2,425	777	3,263	1,164	1,560	6,965	1,839	3,637	14,752	2,791
Slovak	255	296	26	93	138	13	6	25	4	29	49	7	93	209	7
Spanish	575	8,069	615	716	13,470	833	701	6,701	507	473	3,375	376	1,593	20,791	1,210
Spanish-American	251	1,461	169	301	2,117	169	372	1,727	132	554	2,369	169	764	2,131	243
Syrian	123	492	61	220	683	73	33	160	17	57	152	22	739	2,927	177
Turkish	6	200	10	11	411	32	1	22	1	5	12		12	118	10
Welsh	145	705	133	109	542	142	64	132	82	94	406	108	248	1,015	199
West Indian (except Cuban)	113	723	112	174	1,059	136	171	493	68	297	809	117	262	1,156	128
Other	132	3,057	199	110	1,863	124	65	221	28	35	185	27	173	1,077	95
Total	47,070	220,821	30,935	47,467	214,616	33,320	21,349	76,098	13,171	26,373	97,341	17,418	81,890	307,589	40,522

TABLE XI.—DISTRIBUTION OF IMMIGRANT ALIENS ADMITTED, BY AGE AND RACE OR PEOPLE, 1899-1924 (concluded).

Race or people	1921			1922			1923			1924		
	Under 16 years	16 to 44 years	45 years and over	Under 16 years	16 to 44 years	45 years and over	Under 16 years	16 to 44 years	45 years and over	Under 16 years	16 to 44 years	45 years and over
African (black)	1,385	7,948	540	1,001	3,947	300	1,025	6,148	381	1,746	9,847	650
Armenian	2,084	7,352	776	481	1,571	197	572	1,572	252	770	1,796	374
Bohemian and Moravian (Czech)	293	1,290	160	463	2,431	192	784	4,417	336	1,226	5,176	467
Bulgarian, Serbian and Monte-negrin	1,443	5,762	495	298	959	113	407	1,340	146	361	1,947	174
Chinese	415	3,344	258	461	3,570	434	434	3,084	556	396	3,459	815
Croatian and Slovenian	2,308	8,226	501	786	2,819	178	742	3,180	241	492	3,349	296
Cuban	480	897	146	203	446	49	361	885	101	362	977	73
Dalmatian, Bosnian and Herze-govinian	153	722	55	46	242	19	62	478	31	36	234	25
Dutch and Flemish	2,957	8,608	1,248	811	2,386	552	1,326	3,874	604	1,803	5,243	794
East Indian	5	344	4	9	210			148			148	3
English	10,192	36,786	7,649	5,837	19,578	5,014	12,237	40,952	7,335	20,077	63,389	10,473
Finnish	704	3,216	313	283	2,081	142	363	2,546	178	546	3,207	222
French	4,085	16,849	3,188	2,630	9,121	1,866	9,155	21,604	3,612	10,686	33,191	4,755
German	4,845	16,292	3,031	4,602	22,999	3,617	8,056	52,405	5,082	13,022	75,818	6,787
Greek	3,881	24,791	3,156	620	2,741	460	609	3,128	440	893	3,733	626
Hebrew	34,675	71,269	13,092	18,113	27,190	8,221	13,900	29,216	6,603	13,803	29,501	6,685
Irish	3,550	32,765	2,741	2,117	13,388	1,686	3,642	24,166	2,578	5,740	33,006	3,618
Italian, North	3,164	22,853	1,442	946	4,741	411	1,247	7,294	513	1,115	9,871	590
Italian, South	29,765	150,130	15,142	6,419	24,909	3,728	5,223	30,689	3,314	7,927	37,300	2,406
Japanese	1,227	5,778	526	1,049	4,845	467	935	4,107	610	1,375	6,115	991
Korean	6	50	5	9	75	4	14	81	9	16	94	12
Lithuanian	223	512	94	376	1,090	136	435	1,233	160	562	1,231	198
Magyar	2,493	6,123	761	1,427	4,099	511	1,742	4,655	525	1,813	4,904	729
Mexican	7,153	20,039	2,411	3,968	12,685	1,593	11,054	47,255	4,400	19,131	62,606	5,911
Pacific Islander	4	9		7	7			9	1	1	11	
Polish	5,331	14,452	1,363	1,932	4,006	419	3,567	8,677	966	4,820	12,599	1,952
Portuguese	2,158	15,763	935	351	1,310	206	334	2,278	190	524	3,099	269
Rumanian	1,406	4,052	467	421	967	132	344	951	102	404	1,211	112
Russian	699	1,918	270	663	1,538	285	835	3,091	420	1,867	6,876	788
Ruthenian (Russniak)	269	647	42	208	454	36	443	670	55	724	1,522	110
Scandinavian (Norwegians, Danes and Swedes)	2,652	21,140	2,020	1,737	13,473	1,468	2,953	32,364	2,313	5,073	33,459	2,446
Scotch	4,493	26,047	3,187	3,005	10,402	2,189	6,118	28,609	3,900	11,472	43,806	6,049
Slovak	7,100	24,061	1,900	886	4,812	303	1,066	4,861	303	880	4,335	308
Spanish	1,853	2,506	1,534	284	1,377	218	366	2,927	232	475	2,967	222
Spanish-American	596	3,315	223	286	1,051	109	381	1,475	134	583	2,269	213
Syrian	1,427	2,559	363	391	822	121	352	718	137	478	966	151
Turkish	47	280	26	2	36	2	53	173	11	69	246	40
Welsh	317	1,194	237	206	593	157	304	1,130	188	502	1,841	292
West Indian (except Cuban)	334	1,107	112	201	713	62	230	1,121	116	341	1,719	151
Other	441		237	182	480	81	137	449	64	150	720	67
Total	146,613	587,965	70,650	63,710	210,164	35,682	91,816	383,960	47,143	132,264	513,788	60,844

TABLE XII.—Distribution of Immigrant Aliens Admitted, by Occupation and Race or People, 1899-1924.

Year	African (Black)						
	Agriculture	Industry	Commerce Finance	Laborers, Servants	Professional	Miscellaneous	Total
1899	31	36	51	126	12	156	412
1900	43	157	93	87	12	322	714
1901	21	108	76	131	10	248	594
1902	50	191	104	168	5	314	832
1903	426	313	290	612	15	518	2,174
1904	85	531	286	864	70	550	2,386
1905	102	1,062	399	1,133	80	822	3,598
1906	289	985	372	1,136	89	915	3,786
1907	614	1,358	374	1,607	151	1,131	5,235
1908	678	850	306	1,574	121	1,097	4,626
1909	897	749	205	1,253	72	1,131	4,307
1910	674	1,065	255	1,687	108	1,177	4,966
1911	1,091	1,414	283	2,349	113	1,471	6,721
1912	1,031	1,323	330	2,375	157	1,543	6,759
1913	1,297	1,324	314	1,939	146	1,614	6,634
1914	1,309	1 785	383	2,777	198	1 995	8,447
1915	698	1,151	308	1,852	129	1,522	5,660
1916	374	982	218	1,625	140	1,237	4,576
1917	685	2,073	641	2,630	199	1,743	7,971
1918	211	1,819	521	1,634	152	1,369	5,706
1919	632	1,459	529	1,472	188	1,543	5,823
1920	825	1,843	812	2,012	212	2,470	8,174
1921	930	2,194	929	2,643	234	2,943	9,873
1922	451	1,150	355	1,351	137	1,804	5,248
1923	560	1,808	544	2,273	256	2,113	7,554
1924	920	3,069	913	3,207	389	3,745	12,243
	Armenian						
1899	56	221	26	73	21	277	674
1900	134	298	30	170	21	329	982
1901	277	583	53	233	29	680	1,855
1902	248	365	44	169	17	308	1,151
1903	362	544	80	333	37	403	1,759
1904	134	575	105	403	36	492	1,745
1905	175	568	100	453	44	538	1,878
1906	350	516	74	388	47	520	1,895
1907	395	652	101	593	43	860	2,644
1908	571	674	100	667	47	1,240	3,299
1909	797	760	63	587	28	873	3,108
1910	1,425	1,246	167	1,016	65	1,589	5,508
1911	832	712	94	880	52	522	3,092
1912	1,461	1,411	120	1,449	64	717	5,222
1913	2,413	2,193	194	2,864	91	1,598	9,353
1914	2,093	1,559	147	2,534	75	1,377	7,785
1915	95	140	59	338	34	266	932
1916	25	182	51	481	17	208	964
1917	55	279	51	584	14	238	1,221
1918	7	54	15	25	13	107	221
1919	13	70	17	30	17	135	282
1920	53	338	137	674	96	1,464	2,762
1921	158	1,299	414	2,931	184	5,226	10,212
1922	46	465	103	348	103	1,184	2,249
1923	32	334	98	524	119	1,289	2,396
1924	16	410	123	370	197	1,824	2,940
	Bohemian and Moravian						
1899	273	371	40	446	21	1,375	2,526
1900	339	519	25	550	16	1,611	3,060
1901	332	642	33	764	35	1,910	3,766
1902	536	1,220	69	1,750	53	1,962	5,590
1903	712	2,518	121	2,861	83	3,296	9,591
1904	766	2,914	201	3,206	120	4,704	11,911
1905	914	2,706	229	3,443	110	4,355	11,757
1906	1,756	3,295	255	2,556	102	4,994	12,958
1907	2,268	3,509	219	2,461	70	5,027	13,554
1908	1,134	2,330	229	1,941	83	4,447	10,164
1909	931	1,448	131	1,058	55	3,227	6,850
1910	1,493	1,935	151	1,603	60	3,220	8,462
1911	1,392	2,259	230	2,017	93	3,232	9,223
1912	1,029	1,787	177	2,472	59	2,915	8,439
1913	1,165	2,653	247	3,163	100	3,763	11,091
1914	1,178	2,198	215	2,617	76	3,644	9,928
1915	103	295	56	402	34	761	1,651
1916	25	75	19	144	16	363	642
1917	30	58	14	43	11	171	327
1918	13	15	5	9	4	28	74
1919	9	19	6	11	7	53	105
1920	31	45	21	91	26	201	415
1921	129	249	70	621	35	639	1,743
1922	343	416	94	1,169	59	1,005	3,086
1923	504	908	172	1,701	119	1,733	5,537
1924	754	956	230	1,924	212	2,793	6,869

Year	Agriculture	Industry	Commerce Finance	Laborers, Servants	Professional	Miscellaneous	Total
			CROATIAN AND SLOVENIAN				
1899	1,480	484	223	5,119	4	1,322	8,632
1900	2,398	659	368	11,118	5	2,636	17,184
1901	3,185	722	403	11,419	9	2,190	17,928
1902	5,137	1,064	481	21,796	19	1,736	30,233
1903	4,217	1,066	649	24,534	35	2,406	32,907
1904	2,884	1,116	435	14,185	20	2,602	21,242
1905	5,622	1,232	554	24,546	31	3,119	35,104
1906	22,727	1,204	328	15,830	28	4,155	44,272
1907	22,863	1,434	210	17,797	35	5,487	47,826
1908	7,153	958	129	8,278	31	3,923	20,472
1909	6,887	445	84	9,214	11	3,540	20,181
1910	18,242	729	234	15,930	25	4,402	39,562
1911	5,551	913	162	8,620	25	3,711	18,982
1912	7,825	647	126	11,087	30	4,651	24,366
1913	13,163	1,084	191	20,584	43	7,434	42,499
1914	11,311	1,020	221	17,468	39	7,225	37,284
1915	170	197	47	912	13	603	1,942
1916	7	76	16	260	6	426	791
1917	3	79	26	97	5	95	305
1918	....	7	6	4	2	14	33
1919	1	5	2	8	2	5	23
1920	41	48	20	66	6	312	493
1921	1,358	454	178	4,184	27	4,834	11,035
1922	379	201	52	1,612	29	1,510	3,783
1923	804	275	121	1,402	21	1,540	4,163
1924	972	437	118	1,346	38	1,226	4,137
			BULGARIAN, SERBIAN AND MONTENEGRIN				
1899	13	4	2	54	1	20	94
1900	27	33	6	107	1	30	204
1901	128	58	12	254	....	159	611
1902	206	49	15	822	7	192	1,291
1903	515	140	55	5,566	4	199	6,479
1904	626	140	56	3,543	15	197	4,577
1905	1,521	181	33	3,798	14	276	5,823
1906	6,564	346	54	4,045	15	524	11,548
1907	16,018	618	124	9,528	13	873	27,174
1908	11,647	518	93	5,227	28	733	18,246
1909	2,456	95	16	2,494	9	1,144	6,214
1910	6,880	326	68	5,717	17	2,122	15,130
1911	4,249	424	75	4,606	13	855	10,222
1912	4,182	456	59	4,876	21	1,063	10,657
1913	3,082	348	56	4,251	19	1,331	9,087
1914	5,251	466	90	7,614	32	1,631	15,084
1915	282	144	30	2,688	23	339	3,506
1916	335	136	47	2,334	25	269	3,146
1917	117	169	22	672	21	133	1,134
1918	8	32	7	53	22	28	150
1919	10	41	9	50	15	80	205
1920	57	94	35	275	31	572	1,064
1921	944	523	162	2,993	39	3,039	7,700
1922	106	107	39	438	35	645	1,370
1923	269	135	52	509	40	888	1,893
1924	344	235	91	865	69	878	2,482
			DUTCH AND FLEMISH				
1899	397	224	81	303	20	835	1,860
1900	503	284	66	499	12	1,338	2,702
1901	514	415	85	732	28	1,525	3,299
1902	535	460	92	1,308	33	1,689	4,117
1903	1,078	827	288	1,727	121	2,455	6,496
1904	1,090	1,186	525	1,372	267	3,392	7,832
1905	1,594	1,348	566	1,268	249	3,473	8,498
1906	1,679	1,455	566	1,748	306	3,981	9,735
1907	1,725	2,076	514	2,490	261	5,401	12,467
1908	833	1,631	438	1,453	268	4,903	9,526
1909	1,077	1,055	311	1,237	203	4,231	8,114
1910	3,435	1,801	526	1,606	251	5,393	13,012
1911	2,909	1,909	553	1,873	317	6,301	13,862
1912	2,198	1,613	447	1,510	275	4,892	10,935
1913	3,289	2,307	528	2,159	309	5,915	14,507
1914	2,270	1,845	586	1,946	350	5,569	12,566
1915	830	843	482	1,092	311	3,117	6,675
1916	838	730	601	1,023	286	2,965	6,443
1917	774	683	566	713	227	2,430	5,393
1918	154	232	416	408	115	875	2,200
1919	231	376	478	195	146	1,309	2,735
1920	1,970	1,481	781	1,482	371	6,645	12,730
1921	1,782	1,565	928	1,732	331	6,475	12,813
1922	425	390	283	442	226	1,983	3,749
1923	853	771	419	533	277	2,951	5,804
1924	917	1,104	615	682	387	4,135	7,840

TABLE XII.—Distribution of immigrant aliens admitted, by occupation and race or people, 1899-1924 (continued).

Year	English and Welsh						
	Agriculture	Industry	Commerce Finance	Laborers, Servants	Professional	Miscellaneous	Total
1899	439	2,610	921	1,709	442	5,950	12,071
1900	417	2,764	791	1,896	368	5,423	11,659
1901	428	3.258	975	2,558	459	6,484	14,162
1902	529	3,672	1,085	2,903	576	6,937	15,702
1903	954	6,949	2,841	5,001	1,631	12,353	29,729
1904	1,259	9,819	4,943	5,792	2,987	18,499	43,299
1905	1,769	14,340	5,860	7,698	3,345	20,384	53,396
1906	1,514	13,222	4,664	5,967	3,131	18,948	47,446
1907	1,602	15,801	4,004	7,706	2,769	21,998	53,880
1908	1,977	12,178	4,178	7,982	2,725	22,520	51,560
1909	1,831	9,458	3,053	6,270	2,193	17,915	40,720
1910	2,936	14,528	3,982	8,694	2,605	22,997	55,742
1911	2,969	14,638	4,307	9,065	2,852	25,675	59,506
1912	2,780	10,937	3,930	8,263	2,755	23,263	51,928
1913	3,019	13,066	4,319	8,641	3,286	26,011	58,342
1914	2,836	11,244	4,420	7,951	3,375	24,478	54,304
1915	2,261	6,566	3,409	5,016	3,265	19,535	40,052
1916	2,260	5,755	3,720	4,115	2,535	18,766	37,151
1917	2,521	4,281	3,340	3,500	1,958	17,439	33,039
1918	738	1,598	1,357	1,131	908	7,526	13,258
1919	1,377	4,290	3,020	1,842	1,726	15,242	27,497
1920	3,132	9,715	6,091	5,803	3,409	31,678	59,828
1921	2,673	9,596	6,023	6,381	2,903	28,799	56,375
1922	1,557	4,437	2,810	3,657	1,969	16,955	31,385
1923	3,435	12,021	4,715	6,116	2,761	33,098	62,146
1924	5,984	18,797	7,822	9,389	3.872	50,710	96,574
	Finnish						
1899	807	55	78	3,759	....	1,398	6,097
1900	610	144	98	8,700	5	3,055	12,612
1901	284	137	66	7,280	5	2,227	9,999
1902	397	226	127	10,906	9	2,203	13,868
1903	522	512	282	13,477	34	4,037	18,864
1904	217	522	326	6,319	57	2,716	10,157
1905	1,833	689	467	11,165	63	2,795	17,012
1906	987	560	315	10,030	44	2,200	14,136
1907	881	559	216	11,025	47	2,132	14,860
1908	160	374	117	4,627	36	1,432	6,746
1909	508	465	151	8,536	14	2,013	11,687
1910	919	773	201	10,971	56	2,816	15,736
1911	430	722	193	6,399	56	1,979	9,779
1912	296	609	200	4,076	58	1,402	6,641
1913	664	912	228	8,986	60	1,906	12,756
1914	710	826	189	8,726	63	2,291	12,805
1915	93	465	117	1,948	36	813	3,472
1916	465	570	135	2,947	28	1,504	5,649
1917	615	658	230	2,808	19	1,570	5,900
1918	90	226	239	773	13	526	1,867
1919	24	188	189	356	17	194	968
1920	73	218	145	436	27	611	1,510
1921	231	276	277	1,926	53	1,470	4,233
1922	175	241	148	1,228	67	647	2,506
1923	302	375	141	1,328	52	889	3,087
1924	486	557	230	1,304	139	1,259	3,975
	German						
1899	2,516	3,625	1,114	5,041	205	14,131	26,632
1900	2,726	4,067	979	6,798	196	14,916	29,682
1901	2,977	4,899	1,268	7,834	273	17,491	34,742
1902	4,812	8,450	1,443	17,577	293	19,111	51,686
1903	6,394	12,956	3,096	21,890	1,075	26,291	71,782
1904	4,951	13,505	5,939	19,840	2,532	28,023	74,790
1905	8,126	14,262	5,894	24,671	2,448	26,959	82,360
1906	14,451	14,097	5,311	18,386	2,352	32,216	86,813
1907	17,756	14,983	4,599	17,681	1,996	35,921	92,936
1908	10,948	10,820	4,169	13,169	1,725	32,207	73,038
1909	11,194	7,479	3,405	10,367	1,455	24,634	58,534
1910	11,141	10,241	3,722	14,809	1,684	29,783	71,380
1911	8,972	11,207	4,019	14,460	1,893	25,920	66,471
1912	10,018	9,838	4,065	14,296	1,754	25,372	65,343
1913	13,481	11,459	4,381	16,887	2,017	32,640	80,865
1914	12,499	12,123	4,948	17,761	2,159	30,381	79,871
1915	1,727	2,785	2,704	3,825	1,235	8,453	20,729
1916	1,026	1,417	1,375	1,608	553	5,576	11,555
1917	1,200	1,220	1,160	1,182	442	4,478	9,682
1918	190	304	256	215	84	943	1,992
1919	273	173	144	125	59	1,063	1,837
1920	1,233	813	597	915	347	3,433	7,338
1921	2,536	2,720	1,350	5,679	749	11,134	24,168
1922	2,938	5,029	2,311	7,926	1,649	11,365	31,218
1923	6,460	14,156	5,885	15,378	3,128	20,536	65,543
1924	7,708	22,116	9,673	18,659	4,855	32,616	95,627

| Year | GREEK | | | | | | |
	Agriculture	Industry	Commerce Finance	Laborers, Servants	Professional	Miscellaneous	Total
1899	711	252	359	447	19	607	2,395
1900	1,105	355	369	1,187	14	743	3,773
1901	2,593	496	461	1,537	17	815	5,919
1902	3,934	634	511	1,724	16	1,296	8,115
1903	3,916	1,078	942	6,237	44	2,159	14,376
1904	3,319	1,170	992	5,988	89	1,067	12,625
1905	3,073	920	987	6,205	72	887	12,144
1906	5,434	1,071	1,417	13,521	98	1,586	23,127
1907	7,353	1,325	1,213	34,259	87	2,046	46,283
1908	2,992	637	755	21,752	92	2,580	28,808
1909	1,129	360	462	15,507	46	2,758	20,262
1910	5,127	1,079	961	28,457	84	3,427	39,135
1911	9,207	1,717	1,205	21,522	121	3,249	37,021
1912	8,546	2,241	1,283	16,506	122	2,868	31,566
1913	9,514	1,670	1,033	23,197	98	3,132	38,644
1914	4,658	2,052	2,033	31,848	149	5,141	45,881
1915	716	1,036	1,071	9,173	101	3,090	15,187
1916	4,076	970	750	16,438	110	4,448	26,792
1917	4,860	1,316	1,204	14,840	99	3,600	25,919
1918	72	314	410	1,294	42	470	2,602
1919	7	156	262	132	43	213	813
1920	458	778	1,004	8,967	106	2,685	13,998
1921	871	1,370	1,699	19,260	153	8,475	31,828
1922	159	250	348	1,563	85	1,416	3,821
1923	65	233	335	1,902	135	1,507	4,177
1924	110	309	430	1,795	182	2,426	5,252

| Year | HEBREW | | | | | | |
	Agriculture	Industry	Commerce Finance	Laborers, Servants	Professional	Miscellaneous	Total
1899	319	11,862	1,736	3,291	197	20,010	37,415
1900	679	20,517	2,464	6,319	253	30,532	60,764
1901	396	17,684	2,676	4,795	294	32,253	58,098
1902	392	17,261	2,824	10,438	279	26,494	57,688
1903	399	25,979	3,463	13,703	499	23,160	76,203
1904	396	43,248	5,457	17,663	843	38,629	106,236
1905	683	57,618	7,281	16,159	1,163	47,006	129,910
1906	1,928	48,787	6,023	18,217	1,094	77,699	153,748
1907	2,416	53,100	6,101	16,582	1,045	69,938	149,182
1908	1,995	34,330	4,563	14,287	713	47,499	103,387
1909	1,281	17,121	2,743	6,468	456	29,482	57,551
1910	1,962	30,985	4,603	7,057	619	39,034	84,260
1911	1,402	36,899	5,035	8,337	736	38,814	91,223
1912	1,245	32,176	4,620	7,856	781	33,917	80,595
1913	2,324	41,610	7,087	10,125	972	39,212	101,330
1914	3,394	55,213	10,080	15,295	1,226	52,843	138,051
1915	345	8,698	2,231	2,423	485	12,315	26,497
1916	177	4,308	1,799	1,069	436	7,319	15,108
1917	170	3,729	1,729	1,429	318	9,967	17,342
1918	14	435	262	110	79	2,772	3,672
1919	23	467	374	89	76	2,026	3,055
1920	101	1,997	1,411	1,315	291	9,177	14 292
1921	1,667	18,042	8,688	22,812	1,557	66,270	119,036
1922	542	7,133	3,214	9,239	1,121	32,275	53,524
1923	726	9,331	4,156	7,389	1,593	26,524	49,719
1924	675	8,791	4,355	6,028	2,220	27,920	49,989

| Year | IRISH | | | | | | |
	Agriculture	Industry	Commerce Finance	Laborers, Servants	Professional	Miscellaneous	Total
1899	1,361	1,234	673	24,842	123	4,112	32,345
1900	1,781	1,442	600	27,107	105	4,572	35,607
1901	990	1,401	626	20,816	116	6,455	30,404
1902	1,330	1,600	695	21,704	118	3,554	29,001
1903	1,304	2,378	1,577	25,064	280	4,763	35,366
1904	1,945	3,056	1,582	24,715	570	5,208	37,076
1905	3,064	4,759	2,199	36,421	611	7,212	54,266
1906	3,293	3,939	1,827	25,152	605	6,143	40,959
1907	2,969	3,873	1,860	23,369	521	6,114	38,706
1908	2,373	3,508	2,006	20,996	711	6,833	36,427
1909	1,862	2,772	1,496	18,155	504	6,396	31,185
1910	4,232	4,190	1,973	20,519	604	6,864	38,382
1911	3,896	4,394	2,304	21,618	712	7,322	40,246
1912	3,199	3,322	1,827	18,399	703	6,472	33,922
1913	4,312	3,640	1,958	18,954	794	7,365	37,023
1914	3,595	3,090	1,799	17,328	922	7,164	33,898
1915	2,647	2,454	1,509	10,147	863	5,883	23,503
1916	2,246	2,365	1,749	6,979	815	6,482	20,636
1917	1,353	2,161	1,523	5,035	693	6,697	17,462
1918	304	659	479	568	254	2,393	4,657
1919	518	1,191	829	811	429	4,132	7,910
1920	1,769	2,606	1,761	6,081	906	7,661	20,784
1921	3,517	4,089	2,583	18,170	1,053	9,644	39,056
1922	1,262	1,764	1,182	6,770	702	5,511	17,191
1923	2,938	4,198	2,119	9,577	1,018	10,536	30,386
1924	4,432	6,338	3,043	12,169	1,269	15,113	42,364

Year	FRENCH						
	Agriculture	Industry	Commerce Finance	Laborers, Servants	Professional	Miscellaneous	Total
1899	364	521	147	367	61	818	2,278
1900	298	471	85	435	45	761	2,095
1901	613	892	156	872	79	1,424	4,036
1902	627	885	163	873	96	1,478	4,122
1903	603	1,720	540	1,495	389	2,419	7,166
1904	611	2,382	1,120	2,029	1,023	4,392	11,557
1905	699	2,280	1,278	1,924	1,133	4,033	11,347
1906	740	1,826	1,052	1,947	1,129	3,685	10,379
1907	779	1,885	632	1,810	802	3,484	9,392
1908	980	2,412	744	2,967	611	5,167	12,881
1909	1,117	3,057	640	4,554	535	9,520	19,423
1910	1,615	3,029	701	4,703	629	10,430	21,107
1911	1,349	3,016	863	4,486	817	7,601	18,132
1912	1,384	3,014	790	4,485	763	7,946	18,382
1913	1,524	3,218	861	4,642	923	9,484	20,652
1914	1,182	2,858	907	4,396	906	7,917	18,166
1915	777	1,879	620	2,955	818	5,587	12,636
1916	1,701	2,450	814	5,024	750	8,779	19,518
1917	2,137	2,395	1,015	8,151	763	9,944	24,405
1918	374	931	388	879	569	3,699	6,840
1919	749	1,641	734	1,699	898	6,877	12,598
1920	2,358	3,376	1,467	4,738	1,354	14,097	27,390
1821	1,875	3,272	1,342	4,950	1,163	11,520	24,122
1922	1,041	1,555	696	2,881	652	6,792	13,617
1923	3,507	3,465	1,172	6,799	760	18,668	34,371
1924	4,683	5,582	1,985	12,012	1,047	23,323	48,632
ITALIAN (North)							
1899	1,342	2,425	378	4,827	74	4,045	13,091
1900	2,234	3,150	333	7,689	97	3,813	17,316
1901	3,360	4,245	365	9,663	126	4,344	22,103
1902	6,488	5,147	442	11,424	116	4,003	27,620
1903	6,724	6,270	876	17,578	253	5,728	37,429
1904	5,472	5,975	1,095	16,257	492	7,408	36,699
1905	7,621	6,050	1,090	17,043	455	7,671	39,930
1906	7,688	6,762	1,146	20,722	523	9,445	46,286
1907	8,611	7,428	857	23,984	405	10,279	51,564
1908	3,771	3,219	502	9,758	276	7,174	24,700
1909	4,141	2,793	342	11,099	189	6,586	25,150
1910	4,731	3,396	444	14,901	318	6,990	30,780
1911	3,365	3,937	468	15,080	438	7,024	30,312
1912	2,345	3,596	551	12,699	374	6,878	26,443
1913	4,454	5,728	680	21,855	447	9,370	42,534
1914	4,421	5,847	678	22,827	508	10,521	44,802
1915	454	1,437	293	4,014	231	4,231	10,660
1916	119	772	176	1,748	203	1,887	4,905
1917	98	757	184	1,450	126	1,181	3,796
1918	16	218	73	299	85	383	1,074
1919	15	214	87	257	88	575	1,236
1920	684	1,749	442	4,266	245	5,532	12,918
1921	2,919	4,606	880	11,591	258	7,205	27,459
1922	678	945	289	1,931	112	2,143	6,098
1923	1,125	1,457	379	2,996	160	2,937	9,054
1924	1,795	2,384	625	3,447	286	3,039	11,576
ITALIAN (South)							
1899	3,888	7,613	1,543	25,277	238	27,080	65,639
1900	4,788	8,818	1,829	45,623	263	23,025	84,346
1901	26,718	11,499	1,535	48,858	410	26,684	115,704
1902	39,486	13,715	1,810	63,325	406	34,173	152,915
1903	33,331	22,551	2,982	92,288	532	44,433	196,117
1904	43,204	21,486	4,198	52,582	716	37,143	159,329
1905	65,840	19,151	3,803	64,709	676	32,211	186,390
1906	74,906	28,140	4,640	81,184	800	50,858	240,528
1907	67,379	24,467	4,054	91,927	701	53,969	242,497
1908	21,704	12,156	2,077	36,660	550	37,400	110,547
1909	54,396	9,413	2,137	61,547	294	37,461	165,248
1910	88,793	15,250	2,490	45,737	426	39,977	192,673
1911	55,081	15,731	2,484	42,527	495	43,320	159,638
1912	43,933	14,317	2,593	35,276	564	39,147	135,830
1913	87,157	18,936	1,495	67,280	521	53,524	231,613
1914	89,053	20,521	4,892	72,076	608	64,462	251,612
1915	6,430	4,439	1,082	12,701	309	21,596	46,557
1916	7,441	3,261	675	9,658	212	12,662	33,909
1917	5,139	3,607	553	11,954	122	13,779	35,154
1918	42	812	160	1,382	59	2,779	5,234
1919	14	281	152	421	82	1,187	2,137
1920	2,776	10,327	2,560	29,693	616	38,910	84,882
1921	16,706	28,208	4,635	84,259	824	60,405	195,037
1922	2,192	5,647	1,336	12,418	445	13,018	35,056
1923	4,351	5,772	1,488	15,782	450	11,383	39,226
1924	3,998	8,978	1,622	15,011	838	17,186	47,633

TABLE XII.—DISTRIBUTION OF IMMIGRANT ALIENS ADMITTED, BY OCCUPATION AND RACE OR PEOPLE, 1899-1924 (continued).

Year	Agriculture	Industry	Commerce Finance	Laborers, Servants	Professional	Miscellaneous	Total
\multicolumn{8}{c}{JAPANESE}							
1899	1,684	80	661	256	92	622	3,395
1900	6,705	1,053	1,223	2,200	563	884	12,628
1901	2,059	367	901	1,011	167	744	5,249
1902	5,665	536	1,747	1,731	222	4,554	14,455
1903	10,843	502	1,903	704	274	5,815	20,041
1904	6,948	489	1,447	1,791	373	3,334	14,382
1905	6,292	236	1,001	950	280	2,262	11,021
1906	8,973	239	789	1,030	256	2,956	14,243
1907	21,479	369	995	1,500	610	5,871	30,824
1908	7,164	314	968	1,428	378	6,166	16,418
1909	659	37	173	267	139	2,000	3,275
1910	339	24	140	129	104	2,062	2,798
1911	1,054	29	172	94	180	3,046	4,575
1912	2,371	100	233	209	296	2,963	6,172
1913	3,763	134	290	283	315	3,517	8,302
1914	3,462	97	327	227	289	4,539	8,941
1915	2,839	171	474	434	480	4,211	8,609
1916	3,626	206	454	456	509	3,460	8,711
1917	3,540	174	446	487	379	3,899	8,925
1918	2,844	186	879	429	495	5,335	10,168
1919	2,406	173	778	272	427	6,000	10,056
1920	2,273	175	517	176	273	5,865	9,279
1921	1,515	135	507	213	434	4,727	7,531
1922	1,339	121	425	152	354	3,970	6,361
1923	1,040	92	351	207	257	3,705	5,652
1924	1,310	198	540	299	282	5,852	8,481
\multicolumn{8}{c}{LITHUANIAN}							
1899	145	190	9	4,798	2	1,714	6,858
1900	783	302	21	6,527	6	2,672	10,311
1901	267	437	41	5,552	11	2,507	8,815
1902	133	425	18	8,718	11	2,324	11,629
1903	262	580	12	11,123	6	2,449	14,432
1904	412	811	30	9,048	16	2,463	12,780
1905	1,427	1,192	48	13,056	13	2,868	18,604
1906	4,029	1,025	45	6,435	25	2,698	14,257
1907	10,756	1,753	74	9,612	27	3,662	25,884
1908	4,894	715	37	5,183	25	2,866	13,720
1909	7,211	527	49	3,941	6	3,520	15,254
1910	11,873	1,143	36	5,512	17	4,133	22,714
1911	8,028	1,086	46	4,834	18	3,015	17,027
1912	6,480	610	30	4,581	13	2,364	14,078
1913	13,291	954	48	6,817	24	3,513	24,647
1914	9,726	963	59	6,855	36	3,945	21,584
1915	722	187	31	977	8	713	2,638
1916	21	143	17	197	11	210	599
1917	29	92	23	129	11	195	479
1918	2	29	21	36	7	40	135
1919	2	30	15	42	4	67	160
1920	4	91	15	95	8	209	422
1921	29	114	33	172	9	472	829
1922	63	123	28	696	18	674	1,602
1923	106	176	41	516	22	967	1,828
1924	146	196	57	418	58	1,116	1,991
\multicolumn{8}{c}{MAGYAR}							
1899	495	345	33	2,795	12	2,020	5,700
1900	1,723	666	42	7,413	16	3,917	13,777
1901	2,065	582	64	6,311	21	4,268	13,311
1902	5,439	1,292	80	13,025	23	3,751	23,610
1903	4,091	1,988	136	15,828	87	4,994	27,124
1904	3,430	2,058	278	12,485	214	5,418	23,883
1905	14,556	2,670	251	19,853	234	8,466	46,030
1906	19,636	3,025	317	11,356	198	9,729	44,261
1907	30,123	4,212	390	13,140	249	11,957	60,071
1908	8,585	2,195	249	5,272	172	7,905	24,378
1909	14,148	863	121	5,000	55	8,517	28,704
1910	4,528	1,238	142	12,952	86	8,356	27,302
1911	2,385	1,527	172	9,027	129	6,756	19,996
1912	5,378	1,347	189	8,602	126	7,957	23,599
1913	6,671	1,618	217	10,438	129	11,537	30,610
1914	13,732	2,337	293	14,879	159	13,138	44,538
1915	549	268	62	1,009	85	1,631	3,604
1916	29	61	14	119	14	744	981
1917	33	47	18	58	11	267	434
1918	5	1	2	2	....	22	32
1919	8	6	1	2	....	35	52
1920	16	20	12	29	8	167	252
1921	536	754	253	2,653	161	5,020	9,377
1922	316	640	156	1,990	156	2,779	6,037
1923	620	724	187	1,804	217	3,370	6,922
1924	885	795	190	1,355	350	3,871	7,446

| Year | MEXICAN | | | | | | |
	Agriculture	Industry	Commerce Finance	Laborers, Servants	Professional	Miscellaneous	Total
1899	5	18	24	3	4	109	163
1900	4	26	61	19	2	149	261
1901	6	36	109	30	4	165	350
1902	5	51	344	26	11	278	715
1903	9	22	158	49	17	231	486
1904	3	25	201	58	33	127	447
1905	4	16	68	22	18	99	227
1906	2	9	30	9	15	76	141
1907	....	12	22	5	15	37	91
1908	155	510	152	2,462	73	2,329	5,682
1909	307	818	198	6,508	113	7,647	15,591
1910	248	1,205	376	7,410	135	8,386	17,760
1911	444	1,315	454	7,852	251	8,468	18,784
1912	271	962	458	11,190	186	8,934	22,001
1913	234	599	387	3,280	188	6,266	10,954
1914	247	649	552	2,601	294	8,746	13,089
1915	288	716	831	1,542	707	6,909	10,993
1916	290	620	546	4,195	324	11,223	17,198
1917	337	924	727	3,143	288	11,019	16,438
1918	439	1,140	675	5,496	220	9,632	17,602
1919	574	1,728	819	11,715	272	13,736	28,844
1920	934	2,971	1,742	22,213	588	22,594	51,042
1921	618	2,020	1,417	9,006	655	15,887	29,603
1922	243	920	587	7,328	291	8,877	18,246
1923	598	1,863	784	36,861	331	22,272	62,709
1924	1,281	4,190	1,792	42,548	565	37,272	87,648
	POLISH						
1899	809	1,294	48	15,608	22	10,685	28,466
1900	4,245	1,824	79	24,243	29	16,518	46,938
1901	3,424	1,746	88	22,776	39	15,544	43,617
1902	2,668	2,890	118	49,401	41	14,502	69,620
1903	2,386	3,623	162	60,079	50	16,043	82,343
1904	2,129	3,679	212	46,762	136	14,839	67,757
1905	8,363	4,900	243	70,428	160	18,343	102,437
1906	33,082	5,715	272	38,107	191	18,468	95,835
1907	55,235	7,788	338	52,440	273	21,959	138,033
1908	21,568	4,335	237	25,049	186	16,730	68,105
1909	31,503	2,354	148	26,268	66	17,226	77,565
1910	67,246	5,727	240	34,443	139	20,553	128,348
1911	27,696	5,223	218	22,324	170	15,815	71,446
1912	34,418	4,495	229	29,166	200	16,655	85,163
1913	82,637	8,915	392	49,540	244	32,637	174,365
1914	49,528	6,623	358	36,890	213	29,045	122,657
1915	1,919	632	74	3,045	82	3,313	9,065
1916	120	437	61	1,550	38	2,296	4,502
1917	109	353	62	1,227	40	1,318	3,109
1918	32	67	22	298	20	229	668
1919	24	136	36	224	43	269	732
1920	90	339	108	446	122	1,414	2,519
1921	651	2,021	640	7,082	263	10,489	21,146
1922	244	469	129	1,874	142	3,499	6,357
1923	1,163	1,492	258	3,406	169	6,722	13,210
1924	2,753	2,094	318	4,458	293	9,455	19,371
	PORTUGUESE						
1899	94	35	36	1,336	3	592	2,096
1900	61	50	199	3,080	4	847	4,241
1901	285	80	269	2,565	9	968	4,176
1902	218	114	228	2,746	....	2,003	5,309
1903	3,467	187	135	1,825	7	2,812	8,433
1904	633	203	317	2,970	31	2,184	6,338
1905	372	180	126	2,498	31	1,648	4,855
1906	581	188	151	4,853	29	2,927	8,729
1907	448	241	127	4,934	31	3,867	9,648
1908	499	223	166	3,106	23	2,792	6,809
1909	345	119	59	2,526	24	1,533	4,606
1910	762	175	73	4,081	20	2,546	7,657
1911	1,057	278	123	3,642	31	2,328	7,469
1912	1,715	239	180	3,987	42	3,240	9,403
1913	3,154	326	215	5,588	51	4,232	13,566
1914	2,584	273	219	3,766	28	2,777	9,647
1915	812	172	133	1,876	36	1,347	4,376
1916	2,964	298	270	5,443	43	3,190	12,208
1917	705	313	310	4,978	59	3,829	10,194
1918	170	176	225	820	42	886	2,319
1919	108	168	256	465	49	528	1,574
1920	1,865	1,006	817	8,224	74	3,188	15,174
1921	2,192	879	896	9,889	68	4,932	18,856
1922	38	50	138	638	45	958	1,867
1923	197	169	302	1,083	57	994	2,802
1924	186	367	481	1,396	69	1,393	3,892

Year	RUMANIAN						
	Agriculture	Industry	Commerce Finance	Laborers, Servants	Professional	Miscellaneous	Total
1899	17	6	4	57	. . . .	12	96
1900	11	38	8	304	. . . .	37	398
1901	33	30	7	613	1	77	761
1902	122	77	19	1,663	6	146	2,033
1903	353	190	20	3 927	11	239	4,740
1904	402	221	50	3,366	23	302	4,364
1905	2,223	204	46	4,876	14	455	7,818
1906	8,592	248	38	1,849	25	673	11,425
1907	14,991	398	53	2,638	18	1,102	19,200
1908	6,984	232	57	1,305	28	1,023	9,629
1909	4,784	90	18	1,430	13	1,706	8,041
1910	6,628	207	24	5,864	21	1,455	14,199
1911	1,908	192	35	2,142	17	1,017	5,311
1912	3,940	223	35	2,736	18	1,377	8,329
1913	6,513	281	38	3,917	23	2,679	13,451
1914	13,780	340	59	6,207	31	3,653	24,070
1915	360	66	30	391	13	340	1,200
1916	29	52	22	351	6	493	953
1917	48	52	19	241	18	144	522
1918	8	19	17	32	25	54	155
1919	4	13	9	21	4	38	89
1920	53	77	63	215	30	460	898
1921	411	655	386	1,446	74	2,953	5,925
1922	123	142	59	343	38	815	1,520
1923	127	133	41	318	40	738	1,397
1924	224	205	74	281	62	881	1,727

Year	RUSSIAN						
	Agriculture	Industry	Commerce Finance	Laborers, Servants	Professional	Miscellaneous	Total
1899	84	153	33	829	7	668	1,774
1900	138	75	79	379	11	518	1,200
1901	29	69	21	267	20	264	670
1902	179	119	36	778	12	427	1,551
1903	149	446	110	2 121	66	716	3,608
1904	88	475	200	2,179	119	900	3,961
1905	251	507	243	1,467	133	1,145	3,746
1906	1,716	443	149	2,122	146	1,238	5,814
1907	5,976	1,058	128	7,713	115	1,818	16 807[10]
1908	7,560	1,073	122	6,195	158	2,003	17,111
1909	5,039	370	69	3,026	56	1,478	10,038
1910	7,379	960	102	6,076	126	2,651	17,294
1911	10,405	1,138	140	4,832	153	2,053	18,721
1912	12,607	1,241	155	6,126	126	2,303	22,558
1913	26,749	1,593	181	18,882	129	3,938	51,472
1914	20,495	1,824	256	17,550	163	4,669	44,957
1915	553	359	142	2,176	160	1,069	4,459
1916	136	418	178	2,734	349	1,043	4,858
1917	156	350	204	1,621	214	1,166	3,711
1918	30	157	227	409	151	539	1,513
1919	51	244	169	481	95	492	1,532
1920	157	255	168	668	114	1,016	2,378
1921	174	313	295	477	150	1,478	2,887
1922	105	179	215	308	236	1,443	2,486
1923	207	588	374	547	433	2,197	4,346
1924	581	1,481	723	1,197	995	4,554	9,531

Year	RUTHENIAN						
	Agriculture	Industry	Commerce Finance	Laborers, Servants	Professional	Miscellaneous	Total
1899	80	14	. . . .	768	. . . .	538	1,400
1900	174	32	4	1,572	2	1,048	2,832
1901	568	58	4	3,080	1	1,577	5,288
1902	783	95	3	5,531	4	1,117	7,533
1903	604	159	7	8,162	6	905	9,843
1904	656	177	16	7,623	9	1,111	9,592
1905	2,336	200	8	10,514	7	1,408	14,473
1906	6,572	387	17	7,904	18	1,359	16,257
1907	12,779	418	20	8,949	11	1,904	24,081
1908	6,295	305	21	4,040	25	1,675	12,361
1909	8,119	170	17	4,239	14	3,249	15,808
1910	17,273	488	16	7,054	12	3,064	27,907
1911	8,883	413	20	6,037	23	2,348	17,724
1912	10,389	359	17	8,273	23	2,904	21,965
1913	15,270	546	37	9,596	23	5,116	30,588
1914	18,324	715	43	11,861	30	5,754	36,727
1915	861	105	4	1,345	4	614	2,933
1916	209	79	15	744	2	316	1,365
1917	216	59	8	498	5	425	1,211
1918	3	7	2	18	. . . .	19	49
1919	6	13	1	37	. . . .	46	103
1920	20	21	8	111	4	94	258
1921	64	42	7	353	7	485	958
1922	74	25	5	216	9	369	698
1923	197	48	9	199	11	704	1,168
1924	500	182	36	438	25	1,175	2,356

Year	SCANDINAVIAN						
	Agriculture	Industry	Commerce Finance	Laborers, Servants	Professional	Miscellaneous	Total
1899	2,262	1,524	1,358	13,355	135	4,615	23,249
1900	2,583	1,939	1,764	21,123	126	5,417	32,952
1901	2,619	2,764	1,875	25,187	164	7,668	40,277
1902	2,976	3,976	2,780	36,646	232	9,170	55,780
1903	4,880	7,911	4,455	46,008	629	15,464	79,347
1904	4,560	7,191	4,848	29,756	784	13,890	61,029
1905	5,805	7,079	5,807	30,187	707	12,699	62,284
1906	5,653	6,866	4,545	29,062	844	11,171	58,141
1907	5,803	6,230	3,935	25,419	647	11,391	53,425
1908	2,964	3,549	2,072	16,038	442	7,724	32,789
1909	3,758	4,020	2,271	17,946	366	6,635	34,996
1910	7,939	7,372	3,109	24,362	602	8,653	52,037
1911	6,902	6,668	2,626	20,646	702	8,315	45,859
1912	5,465	4,228	1,923	13,718	527	5,740	31,601
1913	6,643	5,462	2,165	17,228	599	6,640	38,737
1914	6,416	5,032	2,107	15,033	687	6,778	36,053
1915	3,720	3,583	1,624	9,515	652	5,169	24,263
1916	3,154	2,814	1,540	6,060	680	4,924	19,172
1917	3,229	2,778	2,336	5,448	702	5,103	19,596
1918	597	1,201	1,953	2,129	308	2,553	8,741
1919	967	1,038	1,678	1,427	374	2,777	8,261
1920	2,586	1,966	2,542	3,540	828	5,159	16,621
1921	3,765	3,686	4,477	6,378	898	6,608	25,812
1922	2,719	2,724	1,775	4,338	713	4,409	16,678
1923	7,961	8,394	4,198	7,840	1,587	7,650	37,630
1924	6,664	7,597	4,508	8,415	2,014	11,780	40,978
	SCOTCH						
1899	79	434	116	330	66	727	1,752
1900	70	482	97	288	42	778	1,757
1901	46	559	108	330	46	915	2,004
1902	68	751	100	452	60	1,001	2,432
1903	268	1,948	373	1,204	295	2,131	6,219
1904	380	3,634	955	1,396	536	4,582	11,483
1905	596	6,021	1,333	2,232	541	5,421	16,144
1906	584	6,279	1,251	1,846	631	5,872	16,463
1907	737	7,617	1,370	2,286	784	7,722	20,516
1908	829	4,447	1,278	2,581	652	7,227	17,014
1909	867	5,196	1,119	2,533	566	6,165	16,446
1910	1,326	7,844	1,644	3,580	869	9,349	24,612
1911	1,277	7,453	1,908	4,177	778	10,032	25,625
1912	1,096	4,645	1,569	3,732	707	8,544	20,293
1913	1,128	4,960	1,590	3,623	997	8,995	21,293
1914	1,048	4,214	1,557	3,352	956	7,870	18,997
1915	832	2,823	1,152	2,245	926	6,332	14,310
1916	907	2,263	1,424	1,869	751	6,301	13,515
1917	1,021	2,076	1,342	1,716	656	6,539	13,350
1918	247	715	496	686	303	2,784	5,204
1919	490	1,957	1,016	874	567	5,460	10,364
1920	1,033	3,985	2,182	2,438	1,182	10,360	21,180
1921	983	5,278	2,344	3,116	1,088	11,840	24,649
1922	631	2,801	1,419	2,087	887	7,771	15,596
1923	1,331	12,373	2,922	3,846	1,786	16,369	38,627
1924	2,484	16,912	4,914	5,914	3,015	28,088	61,327
	SLOVAK						
1899	1,023	579	16	8,994	11	5,215	15,838
1900	2,789	973	22	16,826	6	8,627	29,243
1901	2,906	721	42	16,486	16	9,172	29,343
1902	4,684	1,268	32	22,350	18	8,582	36,934
1903	3,375	1,340	48	22,604	16	7,044	34,427
1904	2,444	1,157	51	17,788	20	6,480	27,940
1905	10,563	1,710	40	30,500	19	9,536	52,368
1906	18,203	1,403	63	10,214	25	8,313	38,221
1907	21,888	1,571	58	10,376	31	8,117	42,041
1908	6,762	586	26	4,000	18	4,778	16,170
1909	12,779	475	19	3,480	4	5,829	22,586
1910	17,055	693	26	8,804	10	5,828	32,416
1911	8,827	658	21	6,767	7	5,135	21,415
1912	11,597	608	26	6,936	10	6,104	25,281
1913	10,908	762	45	7,443	8	8,068	27,234
1914	10,468	648	30	6,766	8	7,899	25,819
1915	516	35	13	504	3	998	2,069
1916	4	19	5	82	2	465	577
1917	8	23	9	40	5	159	244
1918	....	3	9	3	9	11	35
1919	4	9	1	3	17	51	85
1920	214	168	91	723	76	2,552	3,824
1921	3,310	1,989	554	14,977	279	13,938	35,047
1922	857	414	121	2,770	38	1,801	6,001
1923	1,330	478	78	2,180	46	2,118	6,230
1924	1,063	454	89	2,074	53	1,790	5,523

TABLE XII.—Distribution of immigrant aliens admitted, by occupation and race or people, 1899-1924 (concluded).

Year	SPANISH						
	Agriculture	Industry	Commerce Finance	Laborers, Servants	Professional	Miscellaneous	Total
1899	56	244	294	178	36	188	996
1900	50	393	300	143	16	207	1,111[11]
1901	137	346	287	193	19	220	1,202
1902	161	588	500	365	41	299	1,954
1903	251	458	971	811	119	687	3,297
1904	306	1,028	1,413	671	252	992	4,662
1905	480	1,435	1,550	817	234	1,074	5,590
1906	395	1,365	1,275	884	243	1,170	5,332
1907	700	1,894	1,308	1,938	189	3,466	9,495
1908	541	1,422	1,033	1,522	206	1,912	6,636
1909	319	853	765	981	147	1,874	4,939
1910	629	1,141	1,075	1,383	172	1,437	5,837
1911	1,146	1,290	1,473	1,787	191	2,181	8,068
1912	1,890	1,053	1,437	1,879	250	2,561	9,070
1913	1,604	1,208	1,515	2,441	234	2,040	9,042
1914	1,895	1,309	1,706	3,306	272	2,576	11,064
1915	323	941	1,369	1,161	442	1,469	5,705
1916	929	1,576	1,972	2,704	261	1,817	9,259
1917	1,279	2,257	2,897	6,215	288	2,083	15,019
1918	893	1,109	1,324	2,851	173	1,559	7,909
1919	310	687	882	1,035	158	1,152	4,224
1920	3,983	1,726	2 174	11 630	301	3,780	23,594
1921	3,777	2,213	2,809	13,713	299	4,637	27,448
1922	50	153	355	359	135	827	1,879
1923	49	293	691	1,345	120	1,027	3,525
1924	65	317	688	1,183	146	1,265	3,664

Year	SYRIAN						
	Agriculture	Industry	Commerce Finance	Laborers, Servants	Professional	Miscellaneous	Total
1899	790	717	231	313	29	1,628	3,708
1900	545	447	141	406	30	1,351	2,920
1901	859	536	246	680	33	1,710	3,064
1902	1,286	555	239	1,024	26	1,852	4,982
1903	1,035	772	417	1,451	43	1,833	5,551
1904	525	630	401	895	28	1,174	3,653
1905	973	578	534	1,236	47	1,454	4,822
1906	1,536	737	498	1,191	47	1,815	5,824
1907	1,837	737	330	1,275	44	1,657	5,880
1908	1,531	680	332	1,235	47	1,695	5,520
1909	622	397	206	639	22	1,782	3,668
1910	1,246	920	350	1,270	45	2,486	6,317
1911	1,234	729	341	1,298	49	1,793	5,444
1912	1,021	763	350	1,610	25	1,756	5,525
1913	1,876	1,232	405	2,792	62	2,843	9,210
1914	1,758	968	415	3,401	48	2,433	9,023
1915	134	199	240	503	32	659	1,767
1916	18	72	169	93	14	310	676
1917	19	83	265	180	7	422	976
1918	7	20	50	38	2	93	210
1919	2	20	53	22	3	131	231
1920	166	316	467	546	45	1,507	3,047
1921	243	465	594	980	71	2,752	5,105
1922	40	139	207	111	32	805	1,334
1923	17	108	162	131	27	762	1,207
1924	37	124	227	130	42	1,035	1,595

For reference notes see page 500.

TABLE XIII.—DISTRIBUTION, BY RACE OR PEOPLE AND COUNTRY OF LAST RESIDENCE, OF IMMIGRANT ALIENS ADMITTED, 1899-1924[45].

Year	African						Armenian						Bulgarian and Montenegrin					
	Total	Portugal	British North America	Central America	South America	West Indies	Total	Greece	Russian Empire	Turkey in Europe	Turkey in Asia	British North America	Total	Austria	Hungary	Bulgaria, Serbia and Montenegro	Turkey in Europe	British North America
1899	412	...	1	...	...	388	674	...	...	...	670	...	94	41	...	48	...	...
1900	714	...	...	...	...	703	982	...	1	71	910	...	204	34	...	97	69	...
1901	594	...	...	...	...	520	1,855	...	...	163	1,692	...	611	41	...	560	9	...
1902	832	...	...	...	...	805	1,151	...	...	108	1,041	...	1,291	461	...	820	3	...
1903	2,174	934	...	1	2	1,134	1,759	...	17	95	1,660	...	6,479	4,227	...	1,705	540	...
1904	2,386	439	5	3	25	1,762	1,745	...	10	96	1,578	...	4,577	2,088	...	1,211	1,228	...
1905	3,598	347	9	37	66	3,034	1,878	2	130	101	1,483	...	5,823	2,579	...	1,830	1,327	1
1906	3,786	301	9	91	43	3,018	1,895	21	341	102	1,420	35	11,548	3,224	...	4,473	3,647	23
1907	5,235	349	105	99	48	4,561	2,644	3	62	74	1,666	111	27,174	6,223	...	11,053	9,412	179
1908	4,626	705	102	116	77	3,563	3,299	17	50	182	2,681	89	18,246	3,759	...	10,369	3,319	594
1909	4,307	615	172	107	30	3,340	3,108	15	52	67	2,839	52	6,214	1,823	...	990	2,393	868
1910	4,966	778	212	120	38	3,769	5,508	4	152	208	4,921	73	15,130	493	4,147	4,588	4,969	670
1911	6,721	1,101	304	154	111	4,973	3,092	47	250	288	2,422	71	10,222	308	1,753	4,516	3,050	335
1912	6,759	1,103	329	245	94	4,885	5,222	3	909	349	4,242	74	10,657	352	2,403	4,079	3,146	467
1913	6,634	972	338	277	91	4,891	9,353	13	872	442	7,369	114	9,087	1,036	3,213	1,528	1,589	1,443
1914	8,447	1,711	342	348	111	5,724	7,785	96	41	353	6,097	122	15,084	743	3,677	8,312	782	835
1915	5,660	838	286	252	98	4,104	932	9	44	67	526	117	3,506	18	202	988	39	1,717
1916	4,576	653	364	160	100	3,257	964	5	103	28	112	258	1,134	3	17	489	...	866
1917	7,971	940	409	622	135	5,769	1,221	26	26	12	83	228	150	...	...	131	...	404
1918	5,706	407	142	906	158	3,993	221	14	115	5	13	35	205	...	...	5	3	93
1919	5,823	329	274	799	268	4,027	282	9	...	4	9	76	...	...	...	21	...	112
1920	8,174	845	415	417	193	6,059	2,762	82	66	762	1,493	103	1,064	5	...	Bulgaria 37 / Serb, Croat & Slovene State 492	2	245
1921	9,873	1,364	414	543	197	7,046	10,212	715	32	3,193	5,371	53	7,700	30	12	Bulgaria 451 / Serb, Croat & Slovene State 5,681	11	147
1922	5,248	201	172	188	154	4,424	2,249	119	16	875	836	71	1,370	4	11	Bulgaria 216 / Serb, Croat & Slovene State 916	11	59
1923	7,554	164	292	171	171	6,580	2,396	109	28	1,337	658	44	1,893	16	1	Bulgaria 297 / Serb, Croat & Slovene State 1,266	3	90
1924	12,243	128	494	511	375	10,630	2,940	465	26	307	728	113	2,482	20	5	Bulgaria 374 / Serb, Croat & Slovene State 1,440	6	136

For reference notes see page 500.

TABLE XIII.—DISTRIBUTION, BY RACE OR PEOPLE AND COUNTRY OF LAST RESIDENCE, OF IMMIGRANT ALIENS ADMITTED 1899-1924[2]
(continued).

Year	Dutch and Flemish				Croatian and Slovenian							English and Welsh						
	Total	Belgium	Netherlands	British North America	Total	Austria	Hungary	Czecho-slovakia	Italy	Kingdom of S.C.S.	British North America	Total	France	United Kingdom	British North America	Austra-lia	Mexico	West Indies
1899	1,860	846	1,003		8,632	8,612						12,071		10,802	659	309	5	144
1900	2,702	968	1,715		17,184	17,163						11,659		10,742	388	184		322
1901	3,299	946	2,335	2	17,928	17,905						14,162		13,032	491	265		316
1902	4,117	1,835	2,270		30,233	30,223						15,702		14,550	454	363		293
1903	6,496	2,452	3,975		32,907	32,892						29,729		26,926	900	896	12	763
1904	7,832	2,588	4,822	1	21,242	21,105						43,299	16	38,294	2,358	1,128	124	933
1905	8,498	3,382	4,767	8	35,104	34,932					16	47,446	185	40,279	749	1,413	431	1,543
1906	9,735	3,958	5,704	34	44,272	43,157					96	53,396	217	48,168	1,214	1,093	262	1,340
1907	12,467	5,216	6,456	228	47,826	47,125					428	53,880	160	45,638	4,674	1,222	88	1,398
1908	9,526	2,929	5,704	473	20,181	19,782					452	51,560	147	38,342	10,614	588	45	1,115
1909	8,114	2,740	4,574	383	20,472	19,473					489	40,720	128	27,613	10,977	525	56	787
1910	13,012	4,621	7,383	499	39,562	16,455	22,330				499	55,742	196	40,129	13,487	509	71	718
1911	13,862	4,589	8,192	621	18,982	7,615	10,537				491	59,506	196	42,307	15,017	530	151	643
1912	10,935	3,386	6,420	699	24,366	8,849	14,958				325	51,928	215	34,339	15,195	428	196	664
1913	14,507	6,340	6,681	935	42,499	17,797	22,970				1,239	58,342	242	38,383	17,312	755	158	590
1914	12,566	4,731	6,002	1,250	37,284	15,558	19,657				1,254	54,304	236	31,151	20,373	709	232	616
1915	6,675	1,566	2,923	1,587	1,942	564	606				680	40,052	199	16,591	21,200	690	107	471
1916	6,443	836	2,675	2,280	791	343	80				336	37,151	151	9,208	25,568	774	176	586
1917	5,393	334	2,087	2,231	305	63	11				165	33,039	113	5,580	25,437	552	132	446
1918	2,200	51	911	723	33	6	3				15	13,258	34	1,189	10,545	531	114	178
1919	2,735	203	1,037	922	23	4			5		12	27,497	175	4,397	20,948	838	121	265
1920	12,730	5,774	4,978	1,293	493		2	66	101	230	71	59,828	278	25,312	30,922	1,478	146	476
1921	12,813	5,095	5,933	1,130	11,035	153	48	1,820	1,299	6,821	83	56,375	193	29,306	23,575	1,447	157	489
1922	3,749	978	1,764	726	3,783	140	20	442	553	2,548	32	31,385	145	13,602	16,044	524	131	310
1923	5,804	1,024	2,836	1,599	4,163	329	32	181	478	3,057	25	62,146	92	20,316	39,983	461	127	361
1924	7,840	1,360	3,287	2,811	4,137	190	27	287	1,008	2,425	62	96,574	144	23,314	71,426	358	130	402

For reference notes see page 500.

TABLE XIII.—DISTRIBUTION, BY RACE OR PEOPLE AND COUNTRY OF LAST RESIDENCE, OF IMMIGRANT ALIENS ADMITTED, 1899-1924² (continued).

Year	Finnish			French				
	Total	Russian Empire and Finland	British North America	Total	Belgium	France	Switzerland	British North America
1899	6,097	6,048	2	2,278	206	1,666	221	38
1900	12,612	12,515	....	2,095	218	1,714	108	4
1901	9,999	9,966	....	4,036	612	3,090	266	13
1902	13,868	13,854	....	4,122	712	3,089	236	3
1903	18,864	18,776	....	7,166	949	5,488	423	4
1904	10,157	10,077	6	11,557	1,284	9,193	699	48
1905	17,012	16,671	59	11,347	1,378	8,188	621	61
1906	14,136	13,461	97	10,379	851	6,957	467	80
1907	14,860	14,311	355	9,392	860	7,084	410	308
1908	6,746	6,303	330	12,881	964	6,659	362	4,205
1909	11,687	11,202	398	19,423	701	4,941	351	12,850
1910	15,736	14,999	600	21,107	472	5,279	504	14,214
1911	9,779	8,942	710	18,132	714	5,681	517	10,472
1912	6,641	5,708	816	18,382	434	5,813	392	11,044
1913	12,756	11,156	1,453	20,652	636	6,423	510	12,362
1914	12,805	10,968	1,602	18,166	574	5,930	492	10,338
1915	3,472	1,650	1,749	12,636	209	2,390	255	9,026
1916	5,649	3,834	1,733	19,518	60	1,793	131	16,690
1917	5,900	3,745	1,978	24,405	18	1,785	211	21,723
1918	1,867	1,086	637	6,840	7	1,076	109	5,277
1919	968	243	651	12,598	51	2,618	125	9,444
1920	1,510	640¹³	743	27,390	589	6,445	564	19,087
1921	4,233	3,424¹³	480	24,122	495	5,859	947	15,906
1922	2,506	2,190¹³	222	13,617	239	2,900	463	9,625
1923	3,087	2,692¹³	330	34,371	176	2,937	411	30,438
1924	3,975	2,853¹³	512	48,632	177	3,551	333	43,959

For reference notes see page 500.

TABLE XIII.—DISTRIBUTION, BY RACE OR PEOPLE AND COUNTRY OF LAST RESIDENCE, OF IMMIGRANT ALIENS ADMITTED, 1899-1924 (continued).

Year	Total	German											Greek				
		Austria	Hungary	Czechoslovakia	Germany	Poland	Russian Empire	Rumania	Serb-Croat-Slovene State	Switzerland	United Kingdom	British North America	Total	Greece	Turkey in Europe	Turkey in Asia	British North America
1899	26,632	4,313		*	15,609	*	5,383	183	*	936	66	5	2,395	2,330	25	13	5
1900	29,682	6,901		*	16,484	*	5,349	58	*	807	1	2	3,773	3,771			
1901	34,742	7,816		*	19,468	*	5,643	120	*	1,625	3	1	5,919	5,910	5	1	
1902	51,686	16,249		*	24,785	*	8,542	313	*	1,716			8,115	8,101	1		
1903	71,782	23,597		*	34,213	*	10,485	210	*	2,930	5		14,376	14,082	260	8	
1904	74,790	22,507		*	40,526	*	7,128	159	*	3,662	29	3	12,625	11,259	1,246	60	16
1905	82,360	33,642		*	35,325	*	6,722	96	*	3,094	110	18	12,144	10,390	1,198	135	56
1906	86,813	34,848		*	31,855	*	10,279	225	*	2,991	1,171	91	23,127	19,398	2,766	106	354
1907	92,936	40,497		*	32,276	*	13,480	266	*	2,996	802	290	46,283	36,404	7,060	1,353	433
1908	73,038	27,576		*	28,162	*	10,009	256	*	2,522	841	1,121	28,808	21,415	5,114	1,295	457
1909	58,534	21,096		*	22,694	*	7,781	47	*	2,016	740	2,468	20,262	14,059	4,462	996	361
1910	71,380	6,841	19,483	*	27,177	*	10,016	71	*	2,612	602	3,031	39,135	25,675	8,959	3,693	411
1911	66,471	6,323	15,027	*	27,787	*	8,779	100	*	2,379	680	3,898	37,021	26,086	7,569	2,309	400
1912	65,343	6,265	14,859	*	24,402	*	11,031	57	*	2,510	661	4,041	31,566	21,288	7,134	2,147	946
1913	80,865	8,113	16,002	*	28,037	*	17,857	51	*	2,910	650	5,406	38,644	22,437	9,374	5,192	937
1914	79,871	8,378	20,530	*	29,027	*	9,889	68	*	3,039	639	6,287	45,881	34,832	3,631	4,946	892
1915	20,729	1,102	1,652	*	6,787	*	905	22	*	1,207	585	5,679	15,187	11,223	647	1,460	906
1916	11,555	251	401	*	2,559	*	63		*	429	1,459	6,180	26,792	22,589	229	1,279	663
1917	9,682	141	101	*	1,698	*	39	1	*	597	444	5,917	25,919	22,006	111	205	156
1918	1,992	8		*	418	*	10		*	137	227	1,209	2,602	1,784	9	7	263
1919	1,837	3	1	*	35	*			*	204	33	1,456	813	368	2	1	396
1920	7,338	39	5	85	762	26	9	52	106	2,744	24	2,985	13,998	10,893	565	259	289
1921	24,168	1,842	520	1,674	5,131	810	75	1,097	4,023	5,094	81	2,857	31,828	26,232	1,649	553	396
1922	31,218	3,868	531	832	16,940	367	180	1,227	1,615	2,469	97	2,056	3,821	3,115	279	51	109
1923	65,543	6,344	274	951	46,663	519	318	2,418	930	2,454	63	3,313	4,177	3,057	460	179	134
1924	95,627	6,075	244	905	71,406	243	300	3,040	726	2,999	83	7,077	5,252	4,001	108	195	273

For reference notes see page 500.

TABLE XIII.—DISTRIBUTION, BY RACE OR PEOPLE AND COUNTRY OF LAST RESIDENCE, OF IMMIGRANT ALIENS ADMITTED, 1899-1924[12] (continued).

Hebrew

Year	Total	Austria	Hungary	Czecho-slovakia	France	Germany	Ru-mania	Russia	Poland	United King-dom	Turkey in Europe	Turkey in Asia	Syria, Palestine and Irak (Mesopotamia)	Africa	British North America	Mexico	South America	West Indies
1899	37,415	11,071		*	9	405	1,343	24,275	....	174	24	57	*	7	5	..	11	..
1900	60,764	16,920		*	17	337	6,183	37,011	....	133	64	50	*	3	....	1	1	3
1901	58,098	13,006		*	20	272	6,827	37,660	....	110	82	72	†	8	....	..	9	..
1902	57,668	12,848		*	9	182	6,589	37,846	....	55	20	118	*		....	..	7	2
1903	76,203	18,759		*	11	477	8,562	47,689	....	420	161	144	*	6	....	..	8	1
1904	106,236	20,211		*	32	669	6,446	77,544	....	817	169	50	*	19	8	2	9	9
1905	129,910	17,352		*	327	734	3,854	92,388	....	14,299	83	90	*	192	11	4	65	11
1906	153,748	14,884		*	479	979	3,872	125,234	....	6,113	252	209	*	278	429	6	86	34
1907	149,182	18,885		*	306	734	3,605	114,932	....	7,032	588	330	*	317	1,818	6	243	12
1908	103,387	15,293		*	425	869	4,455	71,978	....	6,260	379	256	*	457	2,393	..	150	6
1909	57,551	8,431		*	325	652	1,390	39,150	....	3,385	346	344	*	295	2,780	..	120	18
1910	84,260	10,704	2,438	*	339	705	1,701	59,824	....	4,098	953	435	*	234	2,262	2	167	20
1911	91,223	10,101	2,684	*	425	799	2,188	65,472	....	4,895	723	454	*	167	2,420	13	285	14
1912	80,595	8,535	2,222	*	587	629	1,512	58,389	....	4,308	760	621	*	218	1,896	12	318	28
1913	101,330	11,831	3,371	*	693	806	1,640	74,033	....	4,001	1,007	1,046	*	330	1,467	10	409	39
1914	138,051	15,355	5,099	*	803	1,127	2,646	102,638	....	3,614	1,408	844	†	299	2,559	27	721	33
1915	26,497	1,806	718	*	913	282	321	14,496	....	2,129	156	324	*	319	3,404	18	476	69
1916	15,108	479	147	*	1,472	98	55	2,138	....	1,909	23	235	*	370	6,450	31	316	82
1917	17,342	99	22	*	275	91	21	6,801	....	1,483	12	82	*	113	6,347	41	271	71
1918	3,672	7	2	*	59	4	1	2,036	....	156		2	*	38	1,099	7	79	30
1919	3,055		1	*	70		3	503	....	157	3		*	7	2,114	15	52	19
1920	14,292	155	31	232	458	67	1,304	460	3,793	1,304	490	829	*	101	3,326	46	148	15
1921	119,036	2,091	1,930	4,160	795	838	18,238	4,661	74,755	2,405	1,139	1,296	*	233	3,269	24	301	25
1922	53,524	572	1,093	1,665	420	600	7,107	14,415	22,373	1,125	241	287	*	140	1,958	41	322	56
1923	49,719	732	965	908	433	864	7,150	14,264	14,125	1,112	1,201	417	*	67	4,486	68	1,074	991
1924	49,989	538	903	886	432	1,986	5,535	10,268	12,185	1,478	269	882	1,298	109	7,421	316	2,002	638

For reference notes see page 500.

TABLE XIII.—DISTRIBUTION, BY RACE OR PEOPLE AND COUNTRY OF LAST RESIDENCE, OF IMMIGRANT ALIENS ADMITTED, 1899-1924[12]
(continued).

Year	Italian								Irish			
	Total	Austria	France	Italy	Switzer-land	United Kingdom	British North America	South America	Total	United Kingdom		British North America
										Total	Ireland	
1899	78,730	1,050	18	77,408	165	19	23	12	32,345	32,302	*	23
1900	101,662	1,287	1	100,128	218	6		10	35,607	35,595	*	1
1901	137,807	1,463	8	135,983	302			38	30,404	30,374	*	4
1902	180,535	1,714		178,368	382			26	29,001	28,994	*	
1903	233,546	2,170	35	230,564	574	15	3	34	35,366	35,308	*	12
1904	196,028	1,985	23	193,183	605	22	10	101	37,076	36,747	*	156
1905	226,320	2,355	448	221,247	441	493	110	548	54,266	53,809	*	132
1906	286,814	1,962	399	272,861	265	493	943	592	40,959	36,953	*	191
1907	294,061	1,506	857	285,494	201	627	3,887	660	38,706	37,660	*	705
1908	135,247	1,121	565	128,318	283	456	3,348	419	36,427	33,119	*	3,038
1909	190,398	1,151	449	183,020	239	276	4,332	380	31,185	27,011	*	3,950
1910	223,453	1,858	579	215,315	318	308	3,900	456	38,382	32,808	*	5,310
1911	189,950	1,250	657	182,620	388	326	3,242	555	40,246	33,842	*	6,147
1912	162,273	1,048	768	156,832	438	358	1,687	446	33,922	27,960	*	5,618
1913	274,147	1,962	915	265,155	484	424	3,509	649	37,023	29,930	*	6,763
1914	296,414	1,784	876	283,258	460	352	7,504	1,043	33,898	26,284	*	7,215
1915	57,217	245	261	49,379	127	184	5,950	576	23,503	15,100	*	8,056
1916	38,814	17	110	32,946	57	91	4,786	443	20,636	9,445	*	10,754
1917	38,950	39	94	33,468	50	58	4,298	531	17,462	5,751	*	11,504
1918	6,308	6	28	5,076	59	21	763	150	4,657	409	*	4,080
1919	3,373	1	55	1,809	19	18	1,094	145	7,910	753	*	6,947
1920	97,800	1	213	93,069	277	175	1,555	323	20,784	10,900	*	9,614
1921	222,496	29	475	217,661	676	158	1,261	607	39,056	30,968	27,773	7,748
1922	41,154	5	113	39,429	322	76	615	311	17,191	11,826	10,357	5,160
1923	48,280	18	139	45,822	284	70	1,099	544	30,386	18,109	15,367	12,000
1924	59,209	19	692	54,729	280	149	1,543	1,080	42,364	20,454	16,778	21,727

For reference notes see page 500.

TABLE XIII.—DISTRIBUTION, BY RACE OR PEOPLE AND COUNTRY OF LAST RESIDENCE, OF IMMIGRANT ALIENS ADMITTED, 1899-1924[12]
(continued).

Year	Lithuanian					Magyar					
	Total	Russia	Lithuania	United Kingdom	British North America	Total	Austria	Hungary	Czecho-slovakia	Rumania	British North America
1899	6,858	6,838	*			5,700		5,657	*		1
1900	10,311	10,927	*			13,777		13,776	*		
1901	8,815	8,805	*			13,311		13,310	*		
1902	11,629	9,975	*	2		23,610		23,609	*		
1903	14,432	14,420	*	6		27,124		27,113	*	2	
1904	12,780	12,707	*	868		23,883		23,851	*	12	
1905	18,604	17,649	*	382		46,030		45,871	*	11	3
1906	14,257	13,697	*	879	15	44,261		42,848	*	5	180
1907	25,884	24,811	*	272	106	60,071		59,593	*	3	368
1908	13,720	13,270	*	373	101	24,378		23,826	*	4	426
1909	15,254	14,595	*	691	207	28,704		27,941	*	3	653
1910	22,714	21,676	*	512	192	27,302	424	26,394	*	2	348
1911	17,027	16,210	*	268	172	19,996	308	19,308	*	7	244
1912	14,078	13,576	*	340	142	23,599	356	22,818	*	1	281
1913	24,647	23,873	*	256	251	30,610	399	29,422	*	10	558
1914	21,584	20,808	*	112	338	44,538	340	43,390	*	6	501
1915	2,638	2,218	*	41	202	3,604	46	3,061	*	1	338
1916	599	136	*	41	393	981	6	578	*	3	346
1917	479	73	*	3	344	434	5	123	*		275
1918	135	50	*	6	72	32		2	*		26
1919	160	20	*	20	130	52			*		48
1920	422	29	*	102	362	252	3	22	39	13	137
1921	829	472	*	41	133	9,377	146	4,956	2,402	766	122
1922	1,602	1,394	*	77	32	6,037	104	4,017	918	519	85
1923	1,828	1,537	*	113	77	6,922	115	4,535	731	980	271
1924	1,991	38	1,287		119	7,446	163	4,498	620	1,150	471

For reference notes see page 500.

TABLE XIII.—DISTRIBUTION, BY RACE OR PEOPLE AND COUNTRY OF LAST RESIDENCE, OF IMMIGRANT ALIENS ADMITTED, 1899-1924[a] (continued).

Year	Polish								Portuguese			Rumanian				
	Total	Austria	Hungary	Germany	Poland	Russia	British North America	South America	Total	Portugal	South America	Total	Austria	Hungary	Rumania	British North America
1899	28,466	11,660		1,271		15,517		1	2,096	2,054	2	96		29	60	
1900	46,938	22,802		1,633		22,500			4,241	4,234	3	398		175	214	
1901	43,617	20,288		1,844		21,475	1		4,176	4,164	10	761		557	204	
1902	69,620	32,429		3,313		33,859		3	5,309	5,307		2,033		1,735	267	
1903	82,343	37,499		5,252		39,548		18	8,433	8,381	14	4,740		4,173	514	
1904	67,757	30,243		4,901		32,577		15	6,338	6,242	49	4,364		3,851	426	
1905	102,437	50,785		3,858		47,224	8	25	4,855	4,630	97	7,818		7,261	423	
1906	95,835	43,803		4,108		46,204	249	37	8,729	8,198	101	11,425		10,811	297	33
1907	138,033	59,719		3,888		73,122	820	43	9,648	9,212	125	19,200		18,429	339	111
1908	68,105	26,423		2,320		37,947	1,057	39	6,809	6,571	103	9,629		8,791	333	229
1909	77,565	36,483		1,320		37,770	1,709	55	4,606	4,287	102	8,041		7,484	113	333
1910	128,348	60,565	110	2,176		63,635	1,388	47	7,657	7,418	105	14,199	387	13,072	267	291
1911	71,446	27,430	85	2,160		40,193	1,109	80	7,469	7,218	145	5,311	190	4,582	145	155
1912	85,163	30,459	190	1,689		51,244	1,139	98	9,403	9,096	179	8,329	256	7,199	346	126
1913	174,365	54,997	336	3,658		112,345	2,226	239	13,566	13,164	239	13,451	484	11,955	375	253
1914	122,657	48,970	285	3,217		66,278	3,143	218	9,647	9,134	302	24,070	501	21,622	1,182	344
1915	9,065	2,479	27	250		4,486	1,547	52	4,376	4,028	217	1,200	25	675	101	257
1916	4,502	1,498	4	80		277	2,279	89	12,208	11,554	356	953		306	15	388
1917	3,109	356	2	14		360	2,056	76	10,194	8,952	1,008	522	1	8	24	265
1918	668	4				125	481	30	2,319	1,777	434	155	1		50	72
1919	732		3	1		54	585	4	1,574	875	487	89			12	67
1920	2,519	13	1	12	849	31	1,310	14	15,174	14,477	436	898	3	4	487	296
1921	21,146	184	38	157	18,253	209	983	128	18,856	17,633	563	5,925	18	8	5,207	233
1922	6,357	41	11	68	5,242	121	492	51	1,867	1,666	115	1,520	4	9	1,213	114
1923	13,210	97	32	135	11,290	195	964	104	2,802	2,173	486	1,397	9	4	1,032	196
1924	19,371	92	15	274	15,687	149	2,039	196	3,892	2,576	1,021	1,727	6	8	960	426

For reference notes see page 500.

TABLE XIII.—DISTRIBUTION, BY RACE OR PEOPLE AND COUNTRY OF LAST RESIDENCE, OF IMMIGRANT ALIENS ADMITTED, 1899-1924[a] (continued).

Year	Russian							Ruthenian				
	Total	Austria	Russian Empire	Latvia, Lithuania and Poland	Turkey	China	British North America	Total	Austria	Hungary	Russia	British North America
1899	1,774	65[14]	1,657	*	....	....	2	1,400	....	1,371	29	....
1900	1,200	28[14]	1,165	*	....	....	....	2,832	....	2,832	....	....
1901	672	....	655	*	....	3	....	5,288	....	5,276	12	....
1902	1,551	7[14]	1,536	*	....	4	....	7,533	....	7,533	....	....
1903	3,608	22[14]	3,565	*	2	....	....	9,843	....	9,819	24	....
1904	3,961	25[14]	3,907	*	4	....	1	9,592	....	9,415	173	....
1905	3,746	82[14]	3,278	*	4	....	5	14,473	....	14,250	178	....
1906	5,814	67[14]	5,282	*	10	11	29	16,257	....	15,689	259	18
1907	16,807	195[14]	16,085	*	6	11	149	24,081	....	23,751	150	166
1908	17,111	198[14]	16,324	*	11	7	262	12,361	....	12,100	37	201
1909	10,038	232[14]	9,099	*	1	6	393	15,808	....	15,236	70	454
1910	17,294	306	14,768	*	9	23	345	27,907	24,005	3,433	102	297
1911	18,721	133	17,581	*	3	13	413	17,724	15,160	1,908	196	309
1912	22,558	358	21,101	*	10	10	487	21,965	17,284	3,591	384	528
1913	51,472	366	48,472	*	7	8	1,981	30,588	24,700	3,879	1,074	656
1914	44,957	319	40,241	*	....	12	3,483	36,727	27,936	4,110	2,543	1,597
1915	4,459	16	2,030	*	....	11	1,880	2,933	1,329	409	158	976
1916	4,858	2	1,026	*	....	22	3,289	1,365	43	2	2	1,301
1917	3,711	....	1,006	*	....	12	2,370	1,211	29	8	7	1,158
1918	1,513	....	686	*	....	17	549	49	2	....	4	43
1919	1,532	....	370	*	....	10	933	103	....	....	1	101
1920	2,378	....	269	22	15	33	1,624	258	....	....	....	240
1921	2,887	6	793	202	71	123	747	958	2	....	13	246
1922	2,486	3	884	214	105	230	390	698	....	....	9	149
1923	4,346	16	1,060	198	635	859	656	1,168	1	....	14	605
1924	9,531	11	1,715	575	1,367	2,037	1,584	2,356	21	....	14	1,838

For reference notes see page 500.

TABLE XIII.—DISTRIBUTION, BY RACE OR PEOPLE AND COUNTRY OF LAST RESIDENCE, OF IMMIGRANT ALIENS ADMITTED 1899-1924[12] (continued).

Year	Scandinavian								Scotch			Slovak			Czecho-slovakia	Serb-Croat-Slovene State
	Total	Denmark	Norway	Sweden	Finland	Russia	United Kingdom	British North America	Total	United Kingdom	British North America	Total	Austria	Hungary		
1899	23,249	2,685	6,704	12,771		1,012	1	8	1,752	1,709	18	15,838		15,757	*	*
1900	32,952	2,922	9,572	18,567		1,859	1	···	1,757	1,742	···	29,243		29,183	*	*
1901	40,277	3,654	12,245	23,306		1,025	1	···	2,004	1,994	3	29,343		29,243	*	*
1902	55,780	5,660	17,484	30,878		1,727	1	···	2,432	2,419	···	36,934		36,931	*	*
1903	79,347	7,154	24,460	45,947		1,571	6	5	6,219	6,139	12	34,427		34,412	*	*
1904	61,029	8,450	23,768	27,660		871	41	11	11,483	11,226	74	27,940		27,895	*	*
1905	62,284	8,787	25,008	26,642		690	533	129	16,144	15,641	149	52,368		52,282	*	*
1906	58,141	7,643	21,693	23,203		937	359	325	16,463	15,048	380	38,221		36,550	*	*
1907	53,425	7,163	22,043	20,534		1,416	494	1,278	20,516	18,347	1,734	42,041		41,815	*	*
1908	32,789	4,811	12,354	12,684		527	249	1,759	17,014	12,602	4,122	16,170		15,979	*	*
1909	34,996	4,280	13,607	14,347		591	208	1,634	16,446	11,431	4,819	22,586		22,374	*	*
1910	52,037	6,761	17,508	23,590		1,398	334	2,024	24,612	18,625	5,745	32,416	904	31,299	*	*
1911	45,859	7,274	13,903	20,593		730	268	2,646	25,625	18,575	6,640	21,415	472	20,673	*	*
1912	31,601	5,956	8,579	12,469		414	200	3,545	20,293	13,585	6,401	25,281	659	24,358	*	*
1913	38,737	6,083	8,511	17,007		892	189	5,595	21,293	13,226	7,712	27,234	911	25,923	*	*
1914	36,053	5,820	8,278	14,565		743	155	5,988	18,997	10,002	8,604	25,819	1,059	24,306	*	*
1915	24,263	3,109	7,908	6,448		121	179	6,137	14,310	4,488	9,521	2,069	80	1,880	*	*
1916	19,172	2,926	5,088	5,578		267	165	4,777	13,515	2,427	10,763	577	64	425	*	*
1917	19,596	2,329	4,567	6,222		455	186	5,188	13,350	1,693	11,371	244	7	103	*	*
1918	8,741	1,578	2,518	2,267		134	200	1,392	5,204	279	4,706	35	3		*	*
1919	8,261	1,320	1,972	2,216		15	104	2,329	10,364	1,406	8,684	85	15		*	*
1920	16,621	3,021	4,385	5,790	74	8	181	2,682	21,180	9,050	11,756	3,824	26	13	2,680	825
1921	25,812	5,963	7,277	9,027	261	24	311	2,197	24,649	14,534	9,737	35,047	137	130	28,056	5,010
1922	16,678	2,544	5,217	6,520	547	13	127	1,460	15,596	8,477	6,805	6,001	50	22	5,426	336
1923	37,630	4,361	11,663	17,799	897	6	108	2,419	38,627	21,279	17,045	6,230	56	23	5,703	251
1924	40,978	4,993	11,862	18,125	733	9	110	4,516	61,327	30,400	30,630	5,523	62	40	4,428	457

For reference notes see page 500.

TABLE XIII.—DISTRIBUTION, BY RACE OR PEOPLE AND COUNTRY OF LAST RESIDENCE, OF IMMIGRANT ALIENS ADMITTED, 1899-1924[12] (concluded).

Year	Spanish						Syrian			
	Total	France	Spain	Central America	South America	West Indies	Total	Turkey in Europe and Turkey in Asia	Syria	British North America
1899	996	….	385	2	8	538	3,708	3,678	….	….
1900	1,111	….	354	3	11	734	2,920	2,891	….	….
1901	1,202	….	591	….	11	579	4,064	3,984	….	….
1902	1,954	9	947	4	36	954	4,982	4,938	….	….
1903	3,297	2	1,974	45	112	1,083	5,551	5,407	….	….
1904	4,662	24	3,850	76	148	389	3,653	3,232	….	….
1905	5,590	98	2,405	77	129	2,118	4,822	4,161	….	7
1906	5,332	73	1,701	122	290	2,080	5,880	4,807	….	46
1907	9,495	92	5,452	105	283	2,800	5,824	5,105	….	133
1908	6,636	80	3,722	117	229	2,020	3,520	4,709	….	178
1909	4,939	52	2,520	48	95	1,890	3,668	3,023	….	197
1910	5,837	69	3,353	1,113	218	1,694	6,317	5,579	….	172
1911	8,068	73	4,861	148	228	2,199	5,444	4,499	….	229
1912	9,070	143	6,125	120	223	1,932	5,525	4,718	….	141
1913	9,042	157	6,026	118	325	1,957	9,210	8,272	….	134
1914	11,064	145	7,324	139	369	2,335	9,023	7,822	….	220
1915	5,705	90	2,414	119	347	1,860	1,767	1,044	….	255
1916	9,259	81	5,439	80	394	2,735	676	30	….	234
1917	15,019	226	9,774	165	680	3,424	976	5	….	290
1918	7,909	243	4,210	124	309	2,404	210	8	….	61
1919	4,224	48	1,501	106	329	1,675	231	2	….	103
1920	23,594	324	18,522	112	320	3,585	504	2,332	….	174
1921	27,448	360	23,167	129	573	2,469	5,105	4,157	….	145
1922	1,879	29	546	45	183	716	1,334	754	….	90
1923	3,525	42	729	46	275	2,109	1,207	670	….	154
1924	3,664	57	791	65	467	1,769	1,595	122	690	332

For reference notes see page 500.

TABLE XIV.—Total passengers departed for foreign countries and distribution, by sex and age, of passengers other than cabin, 1868-1902.

Year	Total passengers departed	Total	Passengers other than cabin					
			Adults			Children		
			Total	Males	Females	Total	Males	Females
1868	66,422	33,905	30,723	22,197	8,526	3,182	1,777	1,405
1869	70,569	36,971	*	*	*	*	*	*
1870	78,040	44,480	40,640	31,905	8,735	3,840	2,452	1,388
1871	82,895	45,748	41,000	29,896	11,104	4,748	2,755	1,993
1872	83,320	43,372	36,904	27,227	9,677	6,468	4,013	2,455
1873	113,813	61,672	57,206	42,060	15,146	4,466	2,349	2,117
1874	131,657	82,524	72,800	53,160	19,640	9,724	5,473	4,251
1875	156,073	106,376	93,537	67,581	25,956	12,839	7,303	5,536
1876	129,159	82,709	73,387	53,297	20,090	9,322	5,235	4,087
1877	128,456	75,863	67,195	49,659	17,536	8,668	4,985	3,683
1878	116,177	61,000	54,360	40,813	13,547	6,640	3,835	2,805
1879	102,088	50,648	44,475	33,947	10,528	6,173	3,597	2,576
1880	96,063	41,229	37,142	28,805	8,337	4,087	2,334	1,753
1881	104,102	48,074	43,923	33,860	10,063	4,151	2,390	1,761
1882	131,799	62,943	57,266	45,458	11,808	5,677	3,684	1,993
1883	156,204	77,958	69,660	53,662	15,998	8,298	5,126	3,172
1884	185,765	101,042	89,945	68,882	21,063	11,097	6,988	4,109
1885	241,314	153,466	137,536	103,962	33,574	15,930	9,188	6,742
1886	201,293	112,615	102,150	78,468	23,682	16,465	6,735	3,730
1887	193,897	102,446	92,060	67,146	24,914	10,386	5,677	4,709
1888	211,212	114.234	104,543	77,755	26,788	9,691	6,221	3,470
1889	239,557	139,655	126,739	95,723	31,016	12,916	7,479	5,437
1890	238,139	132,254	116,024	83,110	32,914	16,230	8,698	7,532
1891	246,506	139,398	124,126	89,034	35,092	15,272	9,268	6,004
1892	256,556	151,404	135,436	96,834	38,602	15,968	9,999	5,969
1893	230,664	135,495	121,699	88,315	33,384	13,796	8,352	5,444
1894	,312,771	190,840	165,735	112,941	52,794	25,105	15,798	9,307
1895	329,558	216,665	188,796	123,845	64,951	27,869	17,257	10,612
1898	225,411	130,857	115,067	78,621	36,446	15,790	10,001	5,789
1899	256,008	127,761	112,478	78,061	34,417	15,283	8,836	6,447
1900	293,404	137,499	114,498	78,230	36,268	23,001	13,906	9,095
1901	306,710	158,155	139,145	96,795	42,350	19,010	10,968	8,042
1902	326,760	168,648	148,325	99,966	48,359	20,323	12,067	8,256

TABLE XV.—EMIGRATION OF ALIENS, BY COUNTRY OF FUTURE RESIDENCE, 1908-24.

Country	1908	1909	1910	1911	1912	1913	1914	1915
Albania	*	*	*	*	*	*	*	*
Austria	64,607	27,782	26,424	45,160	46,137	28,760	35,013	6,776
Belgium	853	431	655	1,017	1,103	803	1,149	333
Bulgaria[4]	3,280	1,594	1,566	3,154	3,577	9,664	2,553	964
Czechoslovakia	*	*	*	*	*	*	*	*
Denmark	689	460	433	469	665	608	629	412
Estonia	*	*	*	*	*	*	*	*
Finland	*	*	*	*	*	*	*	*
France (including Corsica)	3,107	2,817	4,025	3,148	3,473	3,430	2,927	5,751
Germany	6,770	4,905	6,216	6,042	5,785	4,759	5,136	1,419
Great Britain:								
England	5,019	3,076	4,554	5,441	6,700	5,969	7,275	7,715
Ireland	2,023	1,380	1,754	1,984	3,082	2,894	3,632	2,218
Scotland	1,499	743	1,099	1,528	2,195	2,179	2,464	1,847
Wales	87	51	84	145	185	157	234	169
Greece	6,131	5,606	8,144	9,376	11,461	30,603	11,124	9,775
Hungary	65,590	21,631	20,866	41,182	42,423	29,904	39,987	5,059
Italy (including Sicily and Sardinia)	166,733	83,300	52,323	72,640	108,388	88,021	84,351	96,903
Latvia	*	*	*	*	*	*	*	*
Lithuania	*	*	*	*	*	*	*	*
Netherlands	330	308	463	461	564	599	690	612
Norway	2,275	1,328	1,028	1,400	2,310	1,710	2,797	1,211
Poland	*	*	*	*	*	*	*	*
Portugal (including Cape Verde and Azores Islands)	1,056	1,025	1,082	1,459	1,916	1,965	2,055	2,661
Rumania	1.267	434	445	669	550	319	348	244
Russia[5]	37,777	19,707	17,362	27,053	34,681	26,923	47,451	18,297
Spain (including Canary and Balearic Islands)	1,116	1,079	1,463	1,396	1,581	2,029	2,254	3,042
Sweden	2,574	1,159	1,006	1,615	2,490	1,989	2,240	953
Switzerland	684	658	759	667	510	449	432	349
Turkey in Europe	3,084	1,267	1,988	4,688	5,926	4,809	2,528	164
Yugoslavia (Serb, Croat and Slovene State)	*	*	*	*	*	*	*	*
Other European countries	5	6	16	10	22	16	26	80
Total Europe:	376,556	180,747	153,755	230,704	285,724	248,559	257,295	167,954
China	3,923	3,411	2,371	2,762	2,609	2,303	2,112	2,011
Japan	3,431	3,819	4,366	3,354	1,485	731	756	840
India	128	48	69	92	182	240	164	179
Syria, Palestine, Iraq (Mesopotamia)	*	*	*	*	*	*	*	*
Turkey in Asia	1,847	1,650	1,548	1,905	1,551	1,313	2,243	593
Other Asiatic countries	221	205	160	59	104	103	167	214
Total Asia:	9,550	9,133	8,514	8,172	5,931	4,690	5,442	3,837
Africa	133	140	215	275	266	209	196	85
Australia, Tasmania and New Zealand	241	442	345	474	645	645	745	608
Pacific Islands (not specified)	33	38	31	30	43	29	30	17
Central America	505	302	390	347	328	482	437	436
South America	880	925	1,073	1,183	1,319	1,367	1,376	988
West Indies	4,247	3,306	3,519	4,584	4,864	4,223	4,237	6,243
Other countries	4	2	37	61	31	14	38	30
Total intercontinental	392,149	195,035	167,879	245,830	299,151	260,218	269,796	180,198
Canada	2,629	30,478	34,194	49,373	33,506	46,981	31,818	23,225
Mexico	295	289	363	463	605	991	1,724	651
Total continental:	2,924	30,767	34,557	49,836	34,111	47,972	33,542	23,876
Grand total:	395,073	225,802	202,436	295,666	333,262	308,190	303,338	204,074

For reference notes see page 500.

TABLE XV.—Emigration of aliens, by country of future residence, 1908-24 (concluded).

Country	1916	1917	1918	1919	1920	1921	1922	1923	1924
Albania	*	*	*	*	*	*	*	*	284
Austria	230	126	5	201	2,274	1,399	579	247	217
Belgium	24	15	41	634	1,846	1,430	1,203	672	517
Bulgaria[4]	250	191	700	2,891	3,587	2,923	660	156	233
Czechoslovakia	*	*	*	*	11,147	15,452	7,846	2,074	1,568
Denmark	513	489	304	599	1,477	922	690	511	510
Estonia	*	*	*	*	*	*	*	*	11
Finland	*	*	*	*	1,473	2,386	1,179	396	360
France (including Corsica)	2,231	2,064	3,176	3,792	4,477	3,026	2,557	1,507	1,249
Germany	439	315	28	26	3,069	5,263	4,362	1,529	1,178
Great Britain:									
England	5,130	2,798	1,239	4,482	8,099	7,839	6,434	5,505	4,361
Ireland	1,304	1,027	280	988	3,735	1,905	2,182	1,368	1,282
Scotland	1,332	678	141	569	1,488	1,187	915	705	827
Wales	118	69	24	54	141	180	60	34	60
Greece	4,829	2,034	2,986	15,482	20,314	13,423	7,506	2,988	7,250
Hungary	592	112	1	100	14,233	12,153	4,307	895	522
Italy (including Sicily and Sardinia)	72,507	12,542	8,645	38,245	88,909	48,192	53,651	23,329	22,904
Latvia	*	*	*	*	*	*	*	*	67
Lithuania	*	*	*	*	*	*	*	*	335
Netherlands	351	227	139	596	1,017	849	860	482	345
Norway	1,359	1,633	1,730	1,952	3,022	2,406	1,427	946	955
Poland	*	*	*	*	18,190	42,572	33,581	5,439	2,594
Portugal (including Cape Verde and Azores Islands)	2,396	1,353	1,976	3,447	4,728	5,167	5,877	2,620	3,357
Rumania	49	16	7	39	21,506	9,297	3,795	1,169	1,096
Russia[5]	5,259	5,947	4,983	1,868	1,933	15,229	6,407	2,434	572
Spain (including Canary and Balearic Islands)	1,816	2,491	3,250	6,280	3,841	3,966	6,793	2,557	2,967
Sweden	1,412	969	1,169	1,738	3,109	2,913	1,903	1,179	830
Switzerland	201	159	172	403	1,103	900	886	546	390
Turkey in Europe	18	24	24	47	1,812	405	201	125	128
Yugoslavia (Serb, Croat and Slovene State	*	*	*	*	28,474	13,034	9,733	2,064	1,991
Other European countries	49	88	480	98	1,429	827	703	179	28
Total Europe:	102,409	35,367	31,500	84,531	256,433	215,245	166,297	61,656	58,988
China	2,203	1,871	2,352	2,199	3,102	5,451	6,362	3,715	3,847
Japan	770	750	1,583	2,195	4,249	4,375	4,368	2,869	2,155
India	123	176	229	161	189	281	267	146	161
Syria, Palestine, Iraq (Mesopotamia)	*	*	*	*	*	*	*	*	492
Turkey in Asia	14	8	5	26	1,731	2,534	1,731	773	211
Other Asiatic countries	867	356	212	79	170	246	86	90	77
Tota Asia:	3,977	3,161	4,381	4,660	9,441	12,887	12,814	7,593	6,943
Africa	93	108	100	74	121	197	133	113	108
Australia, Tasmania and New Zealand	445	35	36	362	490	742	645	442	485
Pacific Islands (not specified)	10	382	418	19	29	50	34	22	34
Central America	495	530	489	413	602	703	955	550	567
South America	997	993	1,071	914	1,398	1,647	1,787	1,447	1,052
West Indies	5,059	5,891	3,891	3,806	5,502	5,050	5,252	4,183	4,081
Other countries	36	4	14	17	25	36	30	9	4
Total intercontinental	113,521	46,471	41,900	94,796	274,041	236,557	187,947	76,015	72,262
Canada	15,712	18,994	27,170	10,726	7,668	5,456	4,480	2,775	2,601
Mexico	532	812	25,515	18,000	6,606	5,705	6,285	2,660	1,926
Total continental:	16,244	19,806	52,685	28,726	14,274	11,161	10,765	5,435	4,527
Grand total:	129,765	66,277	94,585	123,522	288,315	247,718	198,712	81,450	76,789

For reference notes see page 500.

TABLE XVI.—DISTRIBUTION, BY SEX AND AGE, OF EMIGRANT ALIENS DEPARTED, 1908-24.

Year	Sex			Age		
	Total	Males	Females	Under 14 years	14–44 years	45 years and over
1908	395,073	342,883	52,190	14,011	345,920	35,142
1909	225,802[15]	159,009	37,085	9,804	165,778	20,512
1910	202,436	154,842	47,594	13,741	167,440	21,255
1911	295,666	238,922	56,744	15,889	248,021	31,756
1912	333,262	275,970	57,292	13,026	282,111	38,125
1913	308,190	251,808	56,382	13,245	264,137	30,808
1914	303,338	242,208	61,130	13,117	256,044	34,177
1915	204,074	168,072	36,002	10,453	170,088	23,533
1916	129,765	106,625	23,140	6,131	111,331	12,303
1917	66,277	48,427	17,850	5,085	50,964	10,228
				Under 16 years	16–44 years	45 years and over
1918	94,585	71,352	23,233	9,862	69,893	14,830
1919	123,522	101,167	22,355	7,352	86,006	30,164
1920	288,315	237,748	50,567	10,705	203,374	74,236
1921	247,718	189,134	58,584	10,820	177,798	59,100
1922	198,712	143,223	55,489	9,499	143,081	46,132
1923	81,450	54,752	26,698	4,539	57,183	19,728
1924	76,789	57,313	19,476	3,717	54,544	18,528

TABLE XVII.—DISTRIBUTION, BY SEX (CALENDAR YEARS), OF EMIGRANT ALIENS DEPARTED, 1908-24.

Year	Total	Males	Females	Year	Total	Males	Females
1908	341,426[16]	278,027	53,063	1917	67,652	53,592	14,060
1909	187,831[17]	131,431	37,028	1918	80,612	59,012	21,600
1910	260,439	206,279	54,160	1919	261,718	216,819	44,899
1911	352,423	290,875	61,548	1920	261,721	205,216	56,505
1912	299,385	244,000	55,385	1921	245,978	184,923	61,055
1913	274,209	219,064	55,145	1922	115,973	79,815	36,158
1914	293,635	239,110	54,525	1923	70,610	49,969	20,641
1915	160,641	134,605	26,036	1924	90,121	70,341	19,780
1916	69,725	49,180	20,545				

For reference notes see page 500.

TABLE XVIII.—Distribution of emigrant aliens departed, by occupation, 1908-24.

Year	Total	Agriculture	Industry	Commerce	Laborers and servants	Professional	Other and unknown
1908	395,073	10,770	35,786	7,299	290,269	2,218	48,731
1909	225,802	6,207	19,798	6,583	129,095	1,806	62,313
1910	202,436	6,474	19,268	7,229	97,711	3,280	68,474
1911	295,666	18,387	30,489	8,859	183,187	2,883	51,861
1912	333,262	12,243	33,265	8,793	222,728	3,056	53,177
1913	308,190	10,525	28,933	8,933	207,824	2,925	49,950
1914	303,338	11,830	32,350	8,823	194,850	2,873	52,612
1915	204,074	6,281	17,381	6,315	140,355	2,312	31,430
1916	129,765	4,505	11,650	5,466	86,600	2,097	19,447
1917	66,277	4,859	8,351	4,929	28,806	1,930	17,402
1918	94,585	4,851	13,087	5,847	37,246	2,589	30,965
1919	123,522	3,335	8,823	5,894	76,939	2,629	25,902
1920	288,315	14,617	17,835	8,634	189,622	3,379	54,228
1921	247,718	12,989	18,446	8,014	140.719	3,422	64,128
1922	198,712	8,101	14,638	8,103	105,270	3,313	59,287
1923	81,450	2,842	6,341	4,750	36,419	2,537	28,561
1924	76,789	2,014	5,756	4,229	39,918	2,006	22,866

TABLE XIX.—DISTRIBUTION OF EMIGRANT ALIENS DEPARTED, BY SEX AND RACE OR PEOPLE, 1908-24.

Year	African (black)			Armenian			Bohemian and Moravian			Bulgarian, Serbian and Montenegrin			Chinese			Croatian and Slovenian		
	Total	Males	Females	Total	Males	Females	Total	Males	Females	Total	Males	Females	Total	Males	Females	Total	Males	Females
1908	889	645	244	234	221	13	1,051	755	296	5,965	5,843	122	3,898	3,760	138	28,589	26,753	1,836
1909	1,027	743	284	541	490	51	699	449	250	2,312	2,235	77	3,397	3,325	72	8,981	7,861	1,120
1910	926	626	300	521	492	29	943	601	342	2,720	2,606	114	2,383	2,334	49	7,133	6,110	1,023
1911	913	598	315	999	901	98	1,208	806	402	6,472	6,250	222	2,716	2,660	56	13,735	12,245	1,490
1912	1,288	893	395	718	682	36	1,149	780	369	7,349	7,142	207	2,549	2,483	66	13,963	12,529	1,434
1913	1,671	1,127	544	676	640	36	871	545	326	13,525	13,222	303	2,250	2,204	46	10,209	9,098	1,111
1914	1,805	1,195	610	1,250	1,199	51	1,011	638	373	5,780	5,461	319	2,059	2,005	54	14,440	12,790	1,650
1915	1,644	1,022	622	444	434	10	219	127	92	2,354	2,271	83	1,959	1,918	41	2,381	2,020	361
1916	1,684	1,044	640	659	654	5	42	10	32	290	268	22	2,148	2,093	55	76	30	46
1917	1,497	915	582	133	126	7	59	52	7	325	312	13	1,799	1,735	64	24	18	6
1918	1,291	774	517	1,238	1,236	2	455	441	14	918	900	18	2,062	1,979	83	31	28	3
1919	976	607	369	11	11	...	412	404	8	3,241	3,177	64	2,961	2,844	117	154	152	2
1920	1,275	759	516	584	573	11	259	175	84	23,844	21,584	2,260	5,253	5,112	141	7,481	6,928	553
1921	1,807	1,129	678	605	595	10	564	375	189	9,940	8,674	1,266	6,146	5,943	203	3,306	2,927	379
1922	2,183	1,147	1,036	253	228	25	4,246	2,697	1,549	5,877	4,879	998	3,788	3,625	163	3,997	3,338	659
1923	1,525	721	804	69	62	7	1,716	943	773	1,864	1,400	464	3,736	3,553	183	233	179	54
1924	1,419	731	718	60	54	6	1,287	841	446	1,544	1,266	278				381	302	79

Year	Cuban			Dalmatian, Bosnian, Herzegovinian			Dutch and Flemish			East Indian			English			Finnish		
	Total	Males	Females	Total	Males	Females	Total	Males	Females	Total	Males	Females	Total	Males	Females	Total	Males	Females
1908	2,089	1,340	749	1,046	999	47	1,198	931	267	124	122	2	5,320	3,473	1,847	3,463	2,770	693
1909	1,243	852	391	515	477	38	727	527	200	41	39	2	3,800	2,326	1,474	1,057	787	270
1910	1,556	1,086	471	432	410	22	1,192	828	364	80	70	10	6,508	4,192	2,316	1,276	993	283
1911	2,234	1,531	703	935	873	62	1,689	1,254	435	75	70	5	9,432	6,293	3,139	4,219	3,615	604
1912	1,963	1,377	586	927	893	34	1,816	1,301	515	164	161	3	10,341	6,566	3,775	4,148	3,306	842
1913	1,264	835	429	849	824	25	2,148	1,600	548	213	212	1	10,794	6,797	3,997	3,053	2,221	832
1914	947	659	288	878	847	31	2,252	1,605	647	143	134	9	11,187	7,005	4,182	2,941	2,028	913
1915	2,536	1,632	904	105	100	5	1,340	1,068	272	162	158	4	10,372	6,944	3,428	845	596	249
1916	1,454	997	457	4	4		742	525	217	91	87	4	7,826	4,366	3,460	543	358	185
1917	2,395	1,625	770	3	3		742	541	201	136	135	1	6,316	3,494	2,822	1,256	1,057	199
1918	1,141	757	384	13	11	2	698	540	158	154	154	...	12,810	9,907	2,903	1,596	1,305	291
1919	898	595	303	2	1	1	1,356	889	467	106	105	1	9,406	5,382	4,024	497	384	113
1920	1,598	1,053	545	1,533	1,401	132	3,016	1,867	1,149	162	153	9	11,659	5,677	5,982	1,447	1,002	445
1921	1,059	720	339	909	704	205	2,405	1,474	931	137	136	1	11,622	5,755	5,867	2,480	1,634	846
1922	909	613	296	549	373	176	2,157	1,340	817	218	205	13	9,663	4,792	4,876	1,254	764	490
1923	751	475	276	201	113	88	1,252	703	549	113	105	8	7,979	3,562	4,417	445	255	190
1924	961	616	345	183	108	75	990	560	430	149	138	11	6,505	3,124	3,381	411	231	180

TABLE XIX.—DISTRIBUTION OF EMIGRANT ALIENS DEPARTED, BY SEX AND RACE OR PEOPLE, 1908-24 (continued).

Year	French			German			Greek			Hebrew			Irish			Italian (North)			Italian (South)			Polish		
	Total	Males	Females	Total	Males	Females	Total	Males	Females	Total	Males	Females	Total	Males	Females	Total	Males	Females	Total	Males	Females	Total	Males	Females
1908	3,063	1,838	1,225	14,418	10,070	4,348	6,763	6,597	166	7,702	6,004	1,698	2,441	1,193	1,248	19,507	17,467	2,040	147,828	134,783	13,045	46,727	39,148	7,579
1909	2,637	1,543	1,094	10,116	6,299	3,817	5,923	5,744	179	5,859	4,122	1,737	1,578	732	846	16,122	14,083	2,039	67,683	59,035	8,648	18,919	14,514	4,405
1910	4,029	2,427	1,602	13,303	8,053	5,250	8,814	8,464	350	5,689	4,222	1,467	2,472	1,270	1,202	13,431	11,389	2,042	41,772	36,259	5,513	16,884	12,133	4,751
1911	3,400	2,094	1,306	15,243	10,070	5,173	11,134	10,787	347	6,401	4,951	1,450	3,300	1,958	1,342	14,209	12,152	2,057	62,009	55,542	6,467	31,952	25,808	6,144
1912	4,189	2,654	1,535	15,026	10,147	4,879	13,323	12,976	347	7,418	5,648	1,770	4,086	2,125	1,961	13,006	11,285	1,721	96,881	88,987	7,894	37,764	30,628	7,136
1913	4,019	2,550	1,469	11,871	7,613	4,258	31,556	31,115	441	6,697	5,215	1,482	4,458	2,439	2,019	10,995	9,378	1,617	79,057	70,619	8,438	24,107	18,886	5,221
1914	2,930	1,819	1,111	11,977	7,485	4,492	11,266	10,776	490	6,826	5,161	1,665	4,689	2,274	2,415	12,663	10,707	1,956	72,767	64,949	7,818	35,028	27,834	7,194
1915	5,799	4,726	1,073	2,749	1,680	1,069	9,767	9,344	423	1,524	1,103	421	2,948	1,579	1,369	7,539	6,373	1,166	89,969	81,566	8,403	7,912	6,251	1,661
1916	2,297	1,339	958	873	277	596	4,855	4,572	283	199	140	59	1,851	868	983	4,020	3,385	635	68,981	64,802	4,179	358	240	118
1917	2,829	1,587	1,242	767	440	327	2,082	1,982	100	329	228	101	1,736	815	921	3,478	3,057	421	10,016	8,819	1,197	119	87	32
1918	5,427	3,258	2,169	563	341	222	2,952	2,894	58	687	523	164	3,071	2,523	548	1,041	854	187	8,135	7,549	586	1,035	995	40
1919	5,472	3,102	2,370	343	215	128	15,562	15,274	288	373	294	79	1,934	987	947	1,195	975	220	36,980	34,975	2,005	153	110	43
1920	7,026	3,826	3,200	4,178	2,737	1,441	20,319	19,051	1,268	358	261	97	4,635	1,961	2,674	8,159	6,872	1,287	80,955	72,046	8,909	18,392	16,781	1,611
1921	3,836	2,052	1,784	6,770	4,028	2,742	13,470	12,406	1,064	483	343	140	2,535	1,001	1,534	11,447	9,354	2,093	37,032	30,548	6,484	42,207	32,941	9,266
1922	3,464	1,828	1,636	5,715	3,260	2,455	7,649	6,943	706	830	640	190	2,485	1,202	1,283	7,448	5,738	1,710	46,562	37,525	9,037	31,004	20,349	10,655
1923	1,896	990	906	2,217	1,189	1,028	3,060	2,701	359	413	281	132	1,511	584	927	2,538	1,899	639	21,029	16,197	4,832	5,278	3,361	1,917
1924	1,305	670	635	1,832	993	830	7,335	6,864	471	260	175	85	1,581	700	881	2,704	2,168	536	20,363	17,468	2,895	2,590	1,857	733

Year	Japanese			Korean			Lithuanian			Magyar			Mexican			Pacific Islander		
	Total	Males	Females	Total	Males	Females	Total	Males	Females	Total	Males	Females	Total	Males	Females	Total	Males	Females
1908	5,323	4,586	737	188	174	14	3,388	2,828	560	29,276	24,941	4,335	173	120	53	7	3	4
1909	3,894	3,196	698	114	95	19	1,990	1,547	443	11,109	8,162	2,947	158	108	50	4	4	…
1910	4,377	3,476	901	137	120	17	1,812	1,361	451	10,533	7,367	3,166	210	153	57	1	1	…
1911	3,351	2,721	630	41	35	6	2,430	1,865	565	18,975	14,827	4,148	319	256	63	1	1	…
1912	1,501	1,167	334	55	48	7	4,141	3,190	951	17,575	13,348	4,227	325	248	77	4	3	1
1913	733	561	172	44	38	6	3,276	2,412	864	11,496	8,235	3,271	910	773	137	5	5	…
1914	794	615	179	47	40	7	5,522	4,162	1,360	14,254	10,339	3,915	1,670	1,482	188	4	2	2
1915	825	676	149	29	27	2	988	722	266	2,262	1,548	714	573	446	127	6	5	1
1916	780	635	145	45	41	4	28	26	2	394	33	361	559	401	158	2	2	…
1917	722	581	141	77	63	14	38	32	6	123	46	77	759	511	248	3	2	1
1918	1,558	1,215	343	23	21	2	45	35	10	41	37	4	25,084	14,281	10,803	1	1	…
1919	2,127	1,715	412	21	…	…	7	6	1	10	10	…	17,793	11,643	6,150	…	…	…
1920	4,238	3,181	1,057	33	29	4	719	635	84	14,619	12,502	2,117	6,412	3,975	2,437	5	2	2
1921	4,352	3,249	1,103	50	42	8	4,507	3,510	997	12,457	8,752	3,705	5,519	3,421	2,098	…	2	…
1922	4,353	3,086	1,267	55	45	10	4,606	3,185	1,421	4,758	2,890	1,868	5,770	3,616	2,154	5	1	1
1923	2,844	2,043	801	27	20	7	1,109	715	394	1,039	541	498	2,479	1,477	1,002	6	6	5
1924	2,120	1,537	583	…	…	…	381	266	115	587	360	227	1,878	1,261	617	1	1	1

TABLE XIX.—DISTRIBUTION OF EMIGRANT ALIENS DEPARTED, BY SEX AND RACE OR PEOPLE, 1908-24 (concluded).

Year	Portuguese			Rumanian			Russian			Ruthenian (Russniak)			Norwegians, Danes and Swedes (Scandinavian)			Scotch			Slovak		
	Total	Males	Females	Total	Males	Females	Total	Males	Females	Total	Males	Females	Total	Males	Females	Total	Males	Females	Total	Males	Females
1908	898	633	265	5,264	5,008	256	7,507	6,500	1,007	3,310	2,906	404	5,801	3,933	1,868	1,596	1,085	511	23,573	19,992	3,581
1909	815	563	252	1,247	1,106	141	4,112	3,380	732	1,656	1,379	277	3,106	1,905	1,201	903	515	388	8,861	6,749	2,112
1910	906	591	315	1,834	1,625	209	5,682	4,675	1,007	1,719	1,375	344	5,032	3,514	1,518	1,992	1,322	670	9,259	6,872	2,387
1911	1,388	927	461	5,230	4,790	440	8,439	7,258	1,181	3,838	3,301	537	8,036	6,259	1,777	3,083	2,202	881	15,561	12,645	2,916
1912	1,747	1,275	472	5,824	5,363	461	9,744	8,588	1,156	5,521	4,721	800	10,380	8,009	2,371	3,456	2,300	1,156	12,526	10,139	2,387
1913	1,583	1,128	455	3,156	2,811	345	10,548	9,040	1,508	5,327	4,643	684	9,291	6,989	2,302	4,118	2,706	1,412	9,851	7,678	2,173
1914	1,848	1,397	451	3,837	3,359	478	17,491	15,615	1,876	5,049	4,164	885	8,073	5,511	2,562	3,923	2,484	1,439	11,786	9,406	2,380
1915	2,526	1,962	564	899	786	113	11,256	10,464	792	860	672	188	3,473	2,283	1,190	2,714	1,768	946	1,398	1,023	375
1916	2,185	1,552	633	138	89	49	4,716	4,297	419	17		17	3,954	2,436	1,518	2,096	1,184	912	74	5	69
1917	1,313	946	367	61	44	17	6,393	5,716	677	21	10	11	4,550	3,182	1,368	1,618	879	739	34	17	17
1918	2,016	1,689	327	61	50	11	4,926	4,386	540	25	20	5	4,665	3,533	1,132	3,307	2,672	635	453	451	2
1919	3,525	3,008	517	60	51	9	1,717	1,527	190	2		2	4,865	3,187	1,678	1,687	919	768	1,150	1,124	26
1920	4,859	3,413	1,446	21,490	19,221	2,269	1,151	939	212	693	614	79	8,246	4,531	3,715	2,577	1,095	1,482	11,568	10,191	1,377
1921	5,144	3,683	1,461	8,603	6,532	2,071	11,085	9,928	1,157	465	421	44	6,944	3,827	3,117	2,027	950	1,077	17,625	14,120	3,505
1922	6,052	4,553	1,499	4,219	2,880	1,339	2,891	2,308	583	448	318	130	4,417	2,569	1,848	1,659	834	825	3,451	2,277	1,174
1923	2,721	1,933	788	1,098	708	390	1,611	1,259	352	29	21	8	2,936	1,476	1,460	1,129	514	615	387	241	146
1924	3,465	2,690	775	1,085	777	308	734	557	177	52	39	13	2,662	1,426	1,236	1,281	649	632	475	362	113

Year	Spanish			Spanish-American			Syrian			Turkish			Welsh			West Indian (except Cuban)			Other			Not specified		
	Total	Males	Females	Total	Males	Females	Total	Males	Females	Total	Males	Females	Total	Males	Females	Total	Males	Females	Total	Males	Females	Total	Males	Females
1908	1,977	1,696	281	333	228	105	1,700	1,355	345	1,276	1,232	44	163	108	55	375	220	155	630	623	7			
1909	1,794	1,538	256	305	220	85	1,141	907	234	698	673	25	102	65	37	375	199	176	533	515	18			
1910	2,323	1,958	365	387	271	116	1,077	851	226	1,058	1,006	52	195	142	53	388	222	166	806	749	57			
1911	2,518	2,234	284	374	278	96	1,173	951	222	1,633	1,579	54	255	202	53	344	184	160	1,113	1,088	25			
1912	2,569	2,252	317	343	248	95	972	780	192	1,366	1,332	34	301	215	86	530	277	253	1,470	1,423	47			
1913	3,181	2,692	489	457	310	147	797	616	181	1,297	1,266	31	298	231	67	584	299	285	1,511	1,468	43			
1914	3,214	2,810	404	542	379	163	1,200	950	250	890	861	29	395	284	111	677	361	316	769	750	19			
1915	4,347	3,931	416	560	386	174	433	355	78	208	191	17	253	180	73	480	252	228	504	482	22			
1916	2,792	2,439	353	612	367	245	120	100	20	41	33	8	214	154	60	603	300	303	262	165	97			
1917	3,524	3,090	434	736	494	242	110	85	25	54	47	7	130	78	52	520	258	262	209	133	76	20,644	12,628	8,016
1918	4,182	3,763	419	799	554	245	160	129	31	58	53	5	263	232	31	426	217	209	1,001	884	117	25,540	15,133	10,407
1919	7,489	6,952	537	1,126	768	358	132	116	16	275	273	2	195	112	83	336	170	166	235	165	70	15,201	8,818	6,383
1920	5,144	4,328	816	1,536	1,023	513	1,652	1,451	201	1,340	1,314	26	167	83	84	626	285	341	1,457	1,079	378	19,838	11,197	8,641
1921	4,961	4,211	750	1,791	1,200	591	1,599	1,302	297	713	690	23	201	95	106	656	286	370	1,802	1,629	173	17,819	9,995	7,824
1922	7,838	7,088	750	1,200	675	525	1,396	1,061	335	272	253	19	195	93	102	820	384	436	1,518	1,148	370	16,888	9,001	7,887
1923	3,193	2,629	564	1,071	675	396	651	482	169	124	104	20	101	35	66	716	284	432	308	220	88	10,744	5,741	5,003
1924	3,674	3,071	603	906	597	309	439	334	105	297	276	21	77	47	30	600	274	326	422	351	71	9,098	4,987	4,111

TABLE XX.—DISTRIBUTION OF EMIGRANT ALIENS DEPARTED, BY RACE OR PEOPLE AND COUNTRY OF FUTURE RESIDENCE, 1908-24[18]

Year	African Total	African Portugal	African West Indies	African British North America	Armenian Total	Armenian Turkey in Europe	Armenian Turkey in Asia	Bulgarian, Serbian and Montenegrin Total	Austria	Hungary	Bulgaria and Serbia and Montenegro	Turkey in Europe	British North America	Crotian and Slovenian Total	Austria	Hungary	Czecho-slovakia	Serb-Croat-Slovene State	British North America
1908	889	243	609		234	6	159	5,965		1,475	3,125	1,140	2	28,589	28,364				
1909	1,104	279	705		561	39	425	2,422		591	1,414	180	144	9,014	8,686				
1910	926	246	523		521	40	407	2,720	322	440	1,456	272	190	7,133	4,760	1,990			98
1911	913	155	700		999	226	676	6,472	702	1,192	3,006	1,100	304	13,735	8,974	3,753			288
1912	1,288	268	1,153		718	109	561	7,349	793	1,034	3,462	1,843	114	13,963	9,594	3,651			846
1913	1,671	464	1,433		676	26	599	13,525	749	822	9,593	2,004	277	10,209	6,473	2,773			634
1914	1,805	290	1,366		1,250	27	1,090	5,780	766	1,733	2,479	603	62	14,440	8,500	5,672			905
1915	1,644	224	1,328		444		181	2,354	173	125	1,923	16	26	2,381	1,884	384			200
1916	1,684	308	1,263		659	2	8	290		7	247		14	76	28	26			62
1917	1,497	168	978		1,263	20		325		3	190		89	24	4	1			11
1918	1,291	148	890		1,238	21	1	918			566		345	31	2				19
1919	976	11			11			3,241	12	8	2,858	47	355	154	59	61			4
1920	1,275	80	1,072		584	110	435	23,844	32	16	23,327	1	9	7,481	29	96	307	6,853	13
1921	1,807	5	1,537		605	48	470	9,940	3	13	9,736	4	6		42	38	308	2,812	3
1922	2,183	5	2,067		253	9	207	5,877		2	5,684		52	3,997	12		3	3,850	7
1923	1,525		1,445		69	10	36	1,864		1	1,834	1	3	233	1	5	1	219	
1924	1,449	9	1,351		60	2	24	1,544		3	1,500		3	381				360	1

Year	Dutch and Flemish Total	Belgium	Nether-lands	British North America	English and Welsh Total	United Kingdom	British North America	Australia	Finnish Total	Russia and Finland	British North America	French Total	France	British North America
1908	1,198	698	314	176	5,483	4,432	427	145	3,463	3,360	7	3,063	2,593	18
1909	903	386	283	191	5,232	2,692	1,816	328	1,427	1,035	371	2,862	2,316	237
1910	1,192	467	437	334	6,703	4,046	1,886	208	1,276	692	550	4,029	3,316	207
1911	1,689	813	442	298	9,687	4,924	3,882	276	4,219	1,603	2,555	3,400	2,580	385
1912	1,816	884	521	777	10,642	6,294	3,088	398	3,053	2,430	1,660	4,189	2,906	869
1913	2,148	684	582	390	11,092	5,622	4,495	375	2,941	1,906	1,131	4,019	2,363	668
1914	2,252	1,038	672	259	11,582	6,932	3,590	462	845	2,252	668	2,930	3,018	272
1915	1,340	284	596	233	10,625	7,455	2,170	354	543	727	104	5,799	5,458	119
1916	742	19	337	382	8,046	4,927	2,006	317	1,256	379	146	2,297	1,931	122
1917	742	14	225	399	13,236	2,695	2,529	308	1,596	471	773	2,829	1,695	912
1918	698	29	128	332	9,562	1,146	10,888	327	497	357	658	5,427	2,303	4,074
1919	1,356	301	591	166	11,854	4,283	4,055	290	1,447	931	84	7,026	4,070	2,575
1920	3,016	1,490	986	199	11,789	7,867	2,528	347	2,480	1,354[13]	34	2,836	2,450	2,110
1921	2,405	1,189	807	183	9,822	7,595	2,289	511	1,254	2,284[13]	60	3,464	2,220	650
1922	2,157	838	802	84	8,045	6,433	1,826	429	445	1,129[13]	23	1,896	1,281	515
1923	1,252	520	466	74	6,582	5,572	1,140	314	411	379[13]	23	1,305	1,033	198
1924	990	476	325			4,252	1,145	318		355[13]	21			83

For reference notes see page 500.

TABLE XX.—DISTRIBUTION OF EMIGRANT ALIENS DEPARTED, BY RACE OR PEOPLE AND COUNTRY OF FUTURE RESIDENCE, 1908-24[18]
(continued)

Year	German Total	German Austria	German Hungary	German Russia	German Germany	German Switzerland	German British North America	German South America	Greek Total	Greek Greece	Greek Turkey in Europe	Greek Turkey in Asia	Hebrew Total	Hebrew Austria	Hebrew Hungary	Hebrew Russia	Hebrew Rumania	Hebrew United Kingdom
1908	14,418	7,058		6,014	408	463	32	68	6,763	6,027	418	19	7,702	1,758		5,439	158	174
1909	13,541	4,278		4,602	338	455	3,445	78	6,275	5,478	191	50	6,105	1,398		3,898	87	132
1910	13,303	2,543	2,120	5,850	503	497	1,296	96	8,814	8,013	340	36	5,689	1,161	248	3,295	101	186
1911	15,243	2,736	3,496	5,543	517	428	1,999	103	11,134	9,272	1,264	55	6,401	1,445	382	3,375	78	188
1912	15,026	1,575	4,205	5,314	519	363	2,556	117	13,323	11,418	1,714	28	7,418	1,664	457	4,448	122	279
1913	11,871	969	2,915	4,445	396	332	2,374	111	31,556	30,531	746	4	6,697	955	256	3,505	94	206
1914	11,977	1,039	3,407	4,735	811	341	1,208	98	11,266	10,947	117	7	6,826	1,324	257	4,174	94	247
1915	2,749	175	407	1,313	167	190	301	30		9,596	27	24	1,524	189	36	873	32	151
1916	873	58	78	432	20	80	32	36	4,855	4,757	7		199	1	2	45	6	27
1917	767	49	15	313	7	90	66	52	2,082	1,899	1		329	2	3	183		11
1918	563	1		17	21	101	304	21	2,952	2,786		1	687			284		2
1919	343		1			109	137	2	15,562	15,426	2		373		9	98	12	71
1920	4,178	87	71	3,002	2	384	118	63	20,319	20,186	18	11	358	8	6	12	18	66
1921	6,770	219	202	5,063	12	487	98	74	13,470	13,327	17	2	483	8	8	77	58	53
1922	5,715	37	93	4,199	16	494	137	74		7,443	28	15	830	1	10	28	23	44
1923	2,217	127	5	1,410	1	334	127	45	3,060	2,970	9		413		10	22	17	26
1924	1,832	48	3	1,130	3	272	168	30	7,335	7,209		4	260	3	12	14		12

Year	Irish Total	Irish Great Britain	Irish Ireland	Irish British North America	Italian Total	Italian Italy	Italian British North America	Italian South America	Magyar Total	Magyar Austria	Magyar Hungary	Magyar British North America	Polish Total	Polish Austria	Polish Hungary	Polish Germany	Polish Russia	Polish Poland	Polish British North America
1908	2,441	2,304		81	167,335	166,179	46	320	29,276		29,118	4	46,727	28,048		367	18,187		2
1909	2,059	1,478		551	86,439	82,896	2,639	275	11,507		11,026	399	19,290	10,292		154	8,421		371
1910	2,472	1,890		498	55,203	52,137	1,993	322	10,533	2,159	8,030	284	16,884	9,406	203	154	6,705		370
1911	3,306	3,184		1,005	76,218	72,416	2,445	364	18,975	2,411	16,207	269	31,952	18,157	342	274	12,276		796
1912	4,086	2,971		770	109,887	108,253	451	359	17,575	1,386	16,001	124	37,764	22,266	280	242	14,701		169
1913	4,458	3,705		1,339	90,052	87,914	1,387	345	11,496	575	10,647	237	24,107	13,325	103	146	9,701		779
1914	4,689	2,359		895	85,430	84,253	417	275	14,254	325	13,734	147	35,028	15,657	91	214	18,779		230
1915	2,948	1,425		504	97,508	96,813	157	175	2,262	62	2,107	79	7,912	2,992	68	62	4,694		64
1916	1,851	1,072		353	73,001	72,485	175	148	394	6	374	5	358	88		1	229		27
1917	1,736	306		610	13,494	12,521	652	89	123	28	85	10	119	17			53		40
1918	3,071	1,019		862	38,175	37,945	367	42	41			3	153				26		1,006
1919	1,934	3,768		794	89,114	88,691	103	28	10				1,035	117	6	6	48		72
1920	4,635			2,674	48,479	47,886	80	84	14,614	398	13,933	16	18,392	21	3	29	67	17,769	28
1921	2,535	121	1,729	537	54,010	53,340	95	110	12,457	259	11,648	29	42,207	14	23	13	203	41,572	76
1922	2,485	160	1,712	423	23,567	23,234	45	94	4,758	33	4,131	23	31,004	11	10	8	88	30,618	53
1923	1,511	119	1,070	227	23,067	22,808	31	95	1,039	14	856	17	5,278	2		4	7	5,125	52
1924	1,581	129	1,189	189			40	65	587	6	478		2,590				4	2,474	62

For reference notes see page 500.

TABLE XX —DISTRIBUTION OF EMIGRANT ALIENS DEPARTED, BY RACE OR PEOPLE AND COUNTRY OF FUTURE RESIDENCE, 1908-24[18] (concluded).

Year	Portuguese Total	Portugal	South America	Rumanian Total	Austria	Hungary	Rumania	Russian Total	Austria	Hungary	Russia	British North America	Ruthenian Total	Austria	Hungary	Russia	British North America
1908	898	794	25	5,264		4,294	882	7,507		710	6,636	8	3,310	3,256		50	
1909	816	735	45	1,352		928	282	5,125		137	3,819	1,017	1,672	1,625		30	16
1910	906	830	53	1,834	388	1,023	318	5,682	107	37	4,223	1,157	1,719	1,266	409	38	4
1911	1,388	1,284	46	5,230	1,060	3,455	390	8,439	343	52	6,508	1,422	3,838	2,939	780	103	7
1912	1,747	1,641	71	5,824	444	4,857	186	9,744	537	124	8,139	591	5,521	3,766	912	133	686
1913	1,583	1,488	59	3,156	134	2,677	220	10,548	392	55	7,980	1,947	5,327	2,379	1,054	41	2,141
1914	1,848	1,755	64	3,837	141	3,356	198	17,491	447	65	15,703	1,073	5,049	3,540	103	67	371
1915	2,526	2,434	62	138	56	588	47	11,256	90	12	10,501	517	860	613		40	104
1916	2,185	2,082	86	61	2	41	9	4,716			4,106	432	17	16	1		
1917	1,313	1,183	100	61			5	6,393			5,106	1,142	21	2	1		17
1918	2,016	1,826	146	60			36	4,926			3,634	1,177	25			1	25
1919	3,525	3,434	62		3			1,717			1,297	251					2
1920	4,859	4,633	191	21,490		19	21,343	1,151	47	2	768	77	693	165	6	314	1
1921	5,144	5,027	76	8,603	15	15	8,474	11,085	10	2	10,025	75	465	9	3	207	4
1922	6,052	5,829	94	4,219		6	3,200	2,891	12		1,593	42	448		1	17	8
1923	2,721	2,606	100	1,098		1	1,046	1,611			1,247	26	29				2
1924	3,465	3,320	117	1,085	3	4	1,017	734	5		489	61	52				6

Year	Scandinavian Total	Denmark	Norway	Sweden	British North America	Scotch Total	United Kingdom	British North America	Slovak Total	Austria	Hungary	Czecho-slovakia	Serb-Croat-Slovene State	Spanish Total	Spain	Central America	Mexico	South America	West Indies
1908	5,801	673	2,244	2,539	40	1,596	1,460	47	23,573		23,426			1,977	1,035	53	29	73	698
1909	7,257	450	1,323	1,146	4,179	1,618	809	740	8,894		8,790			1,834	1,016	39	36	55	589
1910	5,032	425	1,016	985	2,403	1,992	1,127	782	9,259	2,583	6,221			2,323	1,396	32	30	90	616
1911	8,036	455	1,374	1,568	4,338	3,083	1,568	1,389	15,561	3,807	11,209			2,518	1,338	35	24	95	807
1912	10,380	635	2,210	2,391	4,853	3,456	2,173	1,155	12,526	1,747	10,734			2,569	1,558	53	69	172	622
1913	9,291	595	1,698	1,973	4,820	4,118	2,181	1,816	9,851	1,004	8,831			3,181	1,983	56	27	204	751
1914	8,073	617	1,191	2,209	2,276	3,923	2,485	1,312	11,786	1,179	10,565			3,214	2,209	54	28	176	668
1915	3,473	406	1,346	942	799	2,714	1,856	768	1,398	184	1,198			4,347	2,985	65	40	139	1,078
1916	3,954	501	1,631	1,400	557	2,096	1,363	635	34					2,792	2,405	60	33	70	809
1917	4,550	480	1,724	966	1,340	1,618	711	855	453	6	60			3,524	3,185	52	90	101	798
1918	4,665	297	1,935	1,163	1,325	3,307	187	3,010	1,150	1	2			4,182				61	759
1919	4,865	590		1,729	468	1,687	596	1,051		118				7,489	6,241	47	117	80	967
1920	8,246	1,435	2,996	3,093	496	2,577	1,524	945	11,568	39	29	10,218	1,163	5,144	3,756	29	60	105	1,162
1921	6,944	879	2,377	2,885	429	2,027	1,216	639	17,625	46	46	14,106	2,769	4,961	3,834	103	97	127	722
1922	4,417	659	1,368	1,831	315	1,659	879	610	3,451	2	140	3,028	314	7,838	6,696	122	177	217	552
1923	2,936	490		1,164	163	1,129	660	387	387	1	13	312	38	3,193	2,491	48	52	212	358
1924	2,662	480	946	821	237	1,281	840	348	475	3	5	198	235	3,674	2,937	88	26	130	436

For reference notes see page 500.

TABLE XXI.—United States citizens permanently departed, by principal
countries of intended future permanent residence (fiscal years ended
30 June), 1918-24.

Year	Number departed	Intended future permanent residence						
		Europe	Asia	Canada and Newfoundland	Mexico	West Indies	Central and South America	Other countries
1918	56,998	1,786	2,333	34,697	9,015	3,818	4,957	392
1919	39,543	3,976	2,094	21,716	2,934	2,564	5,944	315
1920	64,564	20,776	5,715	25,094	1,915	4,564	6,165	335
1921	71,391	33,284	5,461	23,059	1,766	3,547	4,010	264
1922	79,198	50,197	5,297	15,036	1,877	2,871	3,639	281
1923	36,260	16,739	4,566	9,023	1,203	2,479	1,875	375
1924	29,661	10,397	3,400	10,537	594	2,925	1,561	247

TABLE XXII.—United States citizens permanently departed (calendar years),
1920-24.

Year	Number departed	Year	Number departed
1920	40,893	1923	19,052
1921	65,645	1924	17,354
1922	38,219		

TABLE XXIII.—DISTRIBUTION, BY PRINCIPAL RACES OR PEOPLES, OF IMMIGRANT ALIENS ADMITTED FROM AUSTRIA-HUNGARY, 1899-1910.

Year	Total	Bohemian and Moravian	Bulgarian, Serbian and Montenegrin	Croatian and Slovenian	Dalmatian, Bosnian and Herzegovinian	German	Hebrew	Italian	Magyar	Polish	Rumanian	Russian	Ruthenian (Russniak)	Slovak	Not specified
1899	62,491	2,382	41	8,612	367	4,313	11,071	1,050	5,657	11,660	29	65	1,371	15,757	2
1900	114,847	3,056	34	17,163	672	6,901	16,920	1,287	13,776	22,802	175	28	2,832	29,183	7
1901	113,390	3,766	41	17,905	717	7,816	13,006	1,463	13,310	20,288	557	..	5,276	29,243	..
1902	171,989	5,589	461	30,223	1,004	16,249	12,848	1,714	23,609	32,429	1,735	7	7,533	36,931	..
1903	206,011	9,577	4,227	32,892	1,723	23,597	18,759	2,170	27,113	37,499	4,173	22	9,819	34,412	..
1904	177,156	11,838	2,088	21,105	2,023	22,507	20,211	1,985	23,851	30,243	3,851	25	9,415	27,895	..
1905	275,693	11,593	2,579	34,932	2,552	33,642	17,352	2,355	45,871	50,785	7,261	82	14,250	52,282	..
1906	265,138	12,635	3,224	43,157	4,424	34,848	14,884	1,962	42,848	43,803	10,811	67	15,689	36,550	..
1907	338,452	13,363	6,223	47,125	7,263	40,497	18,885	1,506	59,593	59,719	18,429	195	23,751	41,815	..
1908	168,509	9,899	3,759	19,782	3,685	27,576	15,293	1,121	23,826	26,423	8,791	198	12,100	15,979	..
1909	170,191	6,609	1,823	19,473	1,805	21,096	8,431	1,151	27,941	36,483	7,484	232	15,236	22,374	..
1910	258,737	8,162	4,640	38,785	4,812	26,324	13,142	1,858	26,818	60,675	13,459	331	27,438	32,203	..

TABLE XXIIIa.—DISTRIBUTION, BY PRINCIPAL RACES OR PEOPLES, OF IMMIGRANT ALIENS ADMITTED FROM AUSTRIA, 1910-24.

Year	Total	Bohemian and Moravian	Bulgarian, Serbian and Montenegrin	Croatian and Slovenian	Dalmatian, Bosnian and Herzegovinian	German	Hebrew	Italian	Magyar	Polish	Rumanian	Russian	Ruthenian (Russniak)	Slovak	Not specified
1910	135,793	8,035	493	16,455	4,790	6,841	10,704	1,827	424	60,565	387	306	24,005	904	..
1911	82,129	8,488	308	7,615	4,249	6,323	10,101	1,250	308	27,430	190	133	15,160	472	..
1912	85,854	7,840	352	8,849	3,506	6,265	8,535	1,048	356	30,459	256	358	17,284	659	..
1913	137,245	10,362	1,036	17,797	4,120	6,113	11,831	1,962	399	54,997	484	366	24,700	911	..
1914	134,831	9,127	743	15,558	4,606	8,378	15,335	1,784	340	48,970	501	319	27,936	1,059	..
1915	9,215	1,254	18	564	203	1,102	1,806	245	46	2,479	25	16	1,329	80	..
1916	3,171	428	3	343	13	251	479	17	6	1,498	..	2	43	64	..
1917	857	98	..	63	15	141	99	39	5	356	1	..	29	7	..
1918	53	5	..	1	7	8	7	6	..	..	1	..	2	3	..
1919	26	5	..	..	..	3	..	1	..	..	..	..	..	15	..
1920	268	14	5	4	5	39	155	1	3	13	3	..	..	26	..
1921	4,947	87	30	153	202	1,842	2,091	29	146	184	18	6	2	137	..
1922	5,019	70	4	140	136	3,868	572	5	104	41	4	3	..	50	..
1923	8,103	76	16	329	261	6,344	732	18	115	97	9	16	1	56	..
1924	7,505	134	20	190	141	6,075	538	19	163	92	6	11	21	62	..

TABLE XXIIIb.—DISTRIBUTION, BY PRINCIPAL RACES OR PEOPLES, OF IMMIGRANT ALIENS ADMITTED FROM HUNGARY, 1910-24.

Year	Total	Bohemian and Moravian	Bulgarian, Serbian and Montenegrin	Croatian and Slovenian	Dalmatian, Bosnian and Herzegovinian	German	Hebrew	Italian	Magyar	Polish	Rumanian	Russian	Ruthenian (Russniak)	Slovak	Not specified
1910	122,944	127	4,147	22,330	22	19,483	2,438	31	26,394	110	13,072	25	3,433	31,299	...
1911	76,928	185	1,753	10,537	24	15,027	2,684	36	19,308	85	4,582	9	1,908	20,673	...
1912	93,028	191	2,403	14,958	50	14,859	2,222	51	22,818	190	7,199	67	3,591	24,358	...
1913	117,580	179	3,213	22,970	144	16,002	3,371	70	29,422	336	11,955	37	3,879	25,923	...
1914	143,321	225	3,677	19,657	171	20,530	5,099	61	43,390	285	21,622	56	4,110	24,306	...
1915	9,296	27	202	606	5	1,652	718	11	3,061	27	675	11	409	1,880	...
1916	2,020	8	67	80	...	401	147	...	578	4	306	...	2	425	...
1917	401	2	17	11	...	101	22	...	123	2	8	1	8	103	...
1918	8	...	...	3	...	1	2	...	2	...	...	...	...	...	...
1919	27	6	...	...	...	...	1	...	...	3	...	...	...	...	...
1920	84	3	...	2	...	5	31	1	22	1	4	...	...	13	...
1921	7,702	17	12	48	5	520	1,930	15	4,956	38	8	13	2	130	...
1922	5,756	22	11	20	6	531	1,093	2	4,017	11	9	3	1	22	...
1923	5,914	14	1	32	8	274	965	1	4,535	32	4	5	...	23	...
1924	5,806	26	5	27	1	244	903	18	4,498	15	8	3	...	40	...

TABLE XXIV.—DISTRIBUTION, BY PRINCIPAL RACES OR PEOPLES, OF IMMIGRANT ALIENS ADMITTED FROM BELGIUM, 1899-1924.

Year	Total	Dutch and Flemish	French	German	Year	Total	Dutch and Flemish	French	German
1899	1,101	846	206	18	1912	4,169	3,386	434	111
1900	1,196	968	218	4	1913	7,405	6,340	636	147
1901	1,579	946	612	18	1914	5,763	4,731	574	141
1902	2,577	1,835	712	22	1915	2,399	1,566	209	180
1903	3,450	2,452	949	41	1916	986	836	60	10
1904	3,976	2,588	1,284	69	1917	398	334	18	10
1905	5,302	3,382	1,378	211	1918	73	51	7	4
1906	5,099	3,958	851	103	1919	268	203	51	7
1907	6,396	5,216	860	126	1920	6,574	5,774	589	21
1908	4,162	2,929	964	122	1921	6,166	5,095	495	29
1909	3,692	2,740	701	135	1922	1,541	978	239	51
1910	5,402	4,621	472	150	1923	1,590	1,024	176	31
1911	5,711	4,589	714	131	1924	2,065	1,360	177	55

TABLE XXV.—DISTRIBUTION, BY PRINCIPAL RACES OR PEOPLES, OF IMMIGRANT ALIENS ADMITTED FROM FRANCE (INCLUDING CORSICA), 1899-1924.

Year	Total	Dutch and Flemish	English	French	German	Hebrew	Italian, south and north
1899	1,694	1	. . .	1,666	. . .	9	18
1900	1,739	. . .	. . .	1,714	7	17	1
1901	3,150	. . .	. . .	3,090	11	20	8
1902	3,117	. . .	. . .	3,089	6	9	4
1903	5,578	. . .	. . .	5,488	41	11	35
1904	9,406	15	16	9,193	38	32	23
1905	10,168	83	184	8,188	402	327	448
1906	9,386	127	216	6,957	504	479	399
1907	9,731	142	160	7,084	337	306	857
1908	8,788	125	147	6,659	396	425	565
1909	6,672	118	128	4,941	312	325	449
1910	7,383	143	193	5,279	381	339	579
1911	8,022	87	195	5,681	363	425	657
1912	8,628	119	213	5,813	416	587	768
1913	9,675	148	240	6,423	452	693	915
1914	9,296	170	230	5,930	469	803	876
1915	4,811	136	197	2,390	241	913	261
1916	4,156	131	149	1,793	54	1,472	110
1917	3,187	87	112	1,785	35	275	94
1918	1,798	48	33	1,076	12	59	28
1919	3,379	67	175	2,618	17	70	55
1920	8,945	195	275	6,445	108	458	213
1921	9,552	153	192	5,859	196	795	475
1922	4,220	21	144	2,900	143	420	113
1923	4,380	20	92	2,937	154	433	139
1924	6,387	23	144	3,551	223	432	692

TABLE XXVI.—Distribution, by principal races or peoples, of immigrant aliens admitted, from Czechoslovakia, 1920-24.

	1920	1921	1922	1923	1924
Total	3,426	40,884	12,541	13,840	13,554
Bohemian and Moravian	225	1,325	2,798	5,029	5,943
Croatian and Slovenian	66	1,820	442	181	287
German	85	1,674	832	951	905
Hebrew	232	4,160	1,665	908	886
Magyar	39	2,402	918	731	620
Russian	3	89	79	39	112
Ruthenian (Russniak)	....	199	137	174	123
Slovak	2,680	28,056	5,426	5,703	4,428

TABLE XXVII.—Distribution, by principal races or peoples, of immigrant aliens, from Germany, 1899-1924.

Year	Total	German	Hebrew	Polish	Year	Total	German	Hebrew	Polish
1899	17,476	15,609	405	1,271	1912	27,788	24,402	629	1,689
1900	18,507	16,484	337	1,633	1913	34,329	28,037	806	3,658
1901	21,651	19,468	272	1,844	1914	35,734	29,027	1,127	3,217
1902	28,304	24,785	182	3,343	1915	7,799	6,787	282	250
1903	40,086	34,213	477	5,252	1916	2,877	2,559	98	80
1904	46,380	40,526	669	4,901	1917	1,857	1,698	91	14
1905	40,574	35,325	734	3,858	1918	447	418	4	4
1906	37,564	31,855	979	4,108	1919	52	35	...	1
1907	37,807	32,276	734	3,888	1920	1,001	762	67	12
1908	32,309	28,162	869	2,320	1921	6,803	5,131	838	157
1909	25,540	22,694	652	1,320	1922	17,931	16,940	600	68
1910	31,283	27,177	705	2,176	1923	48,277	46,663	864	135
1911	32,061	27,787	799	2,160	1924	75,091	71,406	1,986	274

TABLE XXVIII.—Distribution, by principal races or peoples, of immigrant aliens admitted from Italy, 1899-1924.

Year	Total	Italian (North)	Italian (South)	Year	Total	Italian (North)	Italian (South)
1899	77,419	11,821	65,587	1912	157,134	23,314	133,518
1900	100,135	15,799	84,329	1913	265,542	37,531	227,624
1901	135,996	20,324	115,659	1914	283,738	39,424	243,834
1902	178,375	25,485	152,883	1915	49,688	8,079	41,300
1903	230,622	34,571	195,993	1916	33,665	2,885	30,091
1904	193,296	34,056	159,127	1917	34,596	1,853	31,615
1905	221,479	35,802	185,445	1918	5,250	520	4,556
1906	273,120	40,940	231,921	1919	1,884	542	1,267
1907	285,731	47,814	237,680	1920	95,145	11,442	81,627
1908	128,503	21,494	106,824	1921	222,260	25,952	191,709
1909	183,218	22,220	160,800	1922	40,319	5,422	34,007
1910	215,537	26,699	188,616	1923	46,674	7,996	37,826
1911	182,882	26,694	155,926	1924	56,246	9,098	45,631

TABLE XXIX.—Distribution, by principal races or peoples, of immigrant aliens admitted from Poland, 1920-24.

Year	Total	German	Hebrew	Polish	Russian	Ruthenian (Russniak)
1920	4,813	26	3,793	849	22	8
1921	95,089	810	74,755	18,253	202	388
1922	28,635	367	22,373	5,242	214	362
1923	26,538	519	14,125	11,290	198	296
1924	28,806	243	12,185	15,687	293	288

TABLE XXX.—Distribution, by principal races or peoples, of immigrant aliens admitted from Portugal, 1899-1924.

Year	Total	African (black)	Portuguese	Year	Total	African (black)	Portuguese
1899	2,054	....	2,054	1912	10,230	1,103	9,096
1900	4,234	....	4,234	1913	14,171	972	13,164
1901	4,165	....	4,164	1914	10,898	1,711	9,134
1902	5,307	....	5,307	1915	4,907	838	4,028
1903	9,317	934	8,381	1916	12,259	653	11,554
1904	6,715	439	6,242	1917	9,975	940	8,952
1905	5,028	347	4,630	1918	2,224	407	1,777
1906	8,517	301	8,198	1919	1,222	329	875
1907	9,608	349	9,212	1920	15,472	845	14,477
1908	7,307	705	6,571	1921	19,195	1,364	17,633
1909	4,956	615	4,287	1922	1,950	201	1,666
1910	8,229	778	7,418	1923	2,384	164	2,173
1911	8,374	1,101	7,218	1924	2,769	128	2,576

TABLE XXXI.—Distribution, by principal races or peoples, of immigrant aliens admitted from Rumania, 1899-1924.

Year	Total	German	Hebrew	Rumanian	Magyar
1899	1,606	183	1,343	60	....
1900	6,459	58	6,183	214	....
1901	7,155	120	6,827	204	....
1902	7,196	313	6,589	267	....
1903	9,310	210	8,562	514	2
1904	7,087	159	6,446	426	12
1905	4,437	96	3,854	423	11
1906	4,476	225	3,872	297	5
1907	4,384	266	3,605	339	3
1908	5,228	256	4,455	333	4
1909	1,590	47	1,390	113	3
1910	2,145	71	1,701	267	2
1911	2,522	100	2,188	145	7
1912	1,997	57	1,512	346	1
1913	2,155	51	1,640	375	10
1914	4,032	68	2,646	1,182	6
1915	481	22	321	101	1
1916	90	....	55	15	3
1917	66	1	21	24	....
1918	59	....	1	50	....
1919	19	....	3	12	....
1920	1,890	52	1,304	487	13
1921	25,817	1,097	18,238	5,207	766
1922	10,287	1,227	7,107	1,213	519
1923	11,947	2,418	7,150	1,032	980
1924	11,142	3,040	5,535	960	1,150

TABLE XXXII.—Distribution, by Principal Races or Peoples, of Immigrant Aliens Admitted from Russia and Finland, 1899-1924.

Year	Total	Armenian	Finnish	German	Hebrew	Lithuanian	Polish	Russian	Ruthenian	Scandinavian
1899	60,982	...	6,048	5,383	24,275	6,838	15,517	1,657	29	1,012
1900	90,787	1	12,515	5,349	37,011	10,297	22,500	1,165	...	1,859
1901	85,257	...	9,966	5,643	37,660	8,805	21,475	655	12	1,025
1902	107,347	...	13,854	8,542	37,846	9,975	33,859	1,536	...	1,727
1903	136,093	...	18,776	10,485	47,689	14,420	39,548	3,565	24	1,571
1904	145,141	17	10,077	7,128	77,544	12,707	32,577	3,907	173	871
1905	184,897	10	16,671	6,722	92,388	17,649	47,224	3,278	178	690
1906	215,665	130	13,461	10,279	125,234	13,697	46,204	5,282	259	937
1907	258,943	341	14,311	13,480	114,932	24,811	73,122	16,085	150	1,416
1908	156,711	62	6,303	10,009	71,978	13,270	37,947	16,324	37	527
1909	120,460	50	11,202	7,781	39,150	14,595	37,770	9,099	70	591
1910	186,792	52	14,999	10,016	59,824	21,676	63,635	14,768	102	1,398
1911	158,721	152	8,942	8,779	65,472	16,210	40,193	17,581	196	730
1912	162,395	250	5,708	11,031	58,389	13,576	51,244	21,101	384	414
1913	291,040	909	11,156	17,857	74,033	23,873	112,345	48,472	1,074	892
1914	255,660	872	10,968	9,889	102,638	20,808	66,278	40,241	2,543	743
1915	26,187	41	1,650	905	14,496	2,218	4,486	2,030	158	121
1916	7,842	44	3,834	63	2,138	136	277	1,026	2	267
1917	12,716	103	3,745	39	6,801	73	360	1,006	7	455
1918	4,242	26	1,086	10	2,036	50	125	686	4	134
1919	1,403	115	243	...	503	20	54	370	1	15
1920[19]	1,751	66	640	9	460	29	31	269	...	74
1921[19]	10,193	32	3,424	75	4,661	472	209	793	13	261
1922[19]	19,910	16	2,190	180	14,415	1,394	121	884	9	547
1923[19]	21,151	28	2,692	318	14,264	1,537	195	1,060	14	897
1924[19]	16,311	26	2,853	300	10,268	38	149	1,715	14	733

TABLE XXXIII.—Distribution, by principal races or peoples, of immigrant aliens admitted from the Serb, Croat and Slovene State, 1920-24.

Year	Total	Bohemian	Bulgarian and Moravian	Croatian and Slovenian	German	Magyar	Slovak
1920	1,888	13	492	230	106	12	825
1921	23,536	35	5,681	6,821	4,023	775	5,010
1922	6,047	43	916	2,548	1,615	303	336
1923	6,181	115	1,266	3,057	930	123	251
1924	5,835	230	1,440	2,425	726	173	457

TABLE XXXIV.—Distribution, by principal races or peoples, of immigrant aliens admitted from Switzerland, 1899-1924.

Year	Total	French	German	Italian	Year	Total	French	German	Italian
1899	1,326	221	936	165	1912	3,505	392	2,519	438
1900	1,152	108	807	218	1913	4,104	510	2,910	484
1901	2,201	266	1,625	302	1914	4,211	492	3,039	460
1902	2,344	236	1,716	382	1915	1,742	255	1,207	127
1903	3,983	423	2,930	574	1916	663	131	429	57
1904	5,023	699	3,662	605	1917	911	211	597	50
1905	4,269	621	3,094	441	1918	331	109	137	59
1906	3,846	467	2,991	265	1919	381	125	204	19
1907	3,748	410	2,996	201	1920	3,785	564	2,744	277
1908	3,281	362	2,522	283	1921	7,106	947	5,094	676
1909	2,694	351	2,016	239	1922	3,398	463	2,469	322
1910	3,533	504	2,612	318	1923	3,349	411	2,454	284
1911	3,458	517	2,379	388	1924	3,842	333	2,999	280

TABLE XXXV.—Distribution, by principal races or peoples, of immigrant aliens, admitted from Turkey in Europe, 1899-1924.

Year	Total	Armenian	Bulgarian, Serbian and Montenegrin	Greek	Hebrew	Russian	Syrian	Turkish
1899	80	....	...	25	24	....	....	18
1900	285	71	69	....	64	....	6	66
1901	387	163	9	5	82	....	....	92
1902	187	108	3	1	20	....	1	54
1903	1,529	95	540	260	161	....	41	362
1904	4,344	96	1,228	1,246	169	2	116	1,216
1905	4,542	101	1,327	1,198	83	4	75	1,664
1906	9,510	102	3,647	2,766	252	1	454	1,543
1907	20,767	74	9,412	7,060	588	3	952	1,124
1908	11,290	182	3,319	5,114	379	9	48	1,177
1909	9,015	67	2,393	4,462	346	2	22	528
1910	18,405	208	4,969	8,959	953	....	43	724
1911	14,438	288	3,050	7,569	723	....	60	432
1912	14,481	349	3,146	7,134	760	1	64	368
1913	14,128	442	1,589	9,374	1,007	1	48	303
1914	8,199	353	782	3,631	1,408	5	50	504
1915	1,008	67	39	647	156	....	8	25
1916	313	28	....	229	23	....	....	8
1917	152	12	3	111	12	....	....	12
1918	15	5	....	9	....	....	....	....
1919	10	4	....	2	3	....	....	....
1920	1,933	762	2	565	490	13	30	28
1921	6,391	3,199	11	1,649	1,139	44	137	90
1922	1,660	875	11	279	241	76	24	15
1923	3,743	1,337	3	460	1,201	579	39	32
1924	1,481	307	6	108	269	704	26	24

TABLE XXXVI.—DISTRIBUTION, BY PRINCIPAL RACES OR PEOPLES, OF IMMIGRANT ALIENS ADMITTED FROM THE UNITED KINGDOM, 1899-1924.

Year	Total	English	Welsh	Scotch	Irish	French	German	Hebrew	Italian	Lithuanian	Polish	Scandinavian	Spanish
1899	45,123	9,445	1,357	1,709	32,302	...	66	174	19	...	2	1	9
1900	48,237	9,981	761	1,742	35,595	4	1	133	6	...	...	1	3
1901	45,546	12,358	674	1,994	30,374	2	3	110	...	...	7	1	13
1902	46,036	13,790	760	2,419	28,994	1	5	55	...	...	1	1	2
1903	68,947	25,652	1,274	6,139	35,308	25	29	420	15	2	13	6	6
1904	87,590	36,486	1,808	11,226	36,747	29	110	817	22	6	8	41	18
1905	137,134	45,702	2,466	15,641	53,809	297	1,171	14,299	493	868	444	533	339
1906	102,193	38,111	2,168	15,048	36,953	270	802	6,113	493	382	259	359	233
1907	113,567	43,098	2,540	18,347	37,660	271	841	7,032	627	879	337	494	333
1908	93,380	36,171	2,171	12,602	33,119	229	740	6,260	456	272	173	249	240
1909	71,826	26,203	1,410	11,431	27,011	196	602	3,385	276	373	147	208	66
1910	98,796	38,164	1,965	18,625	32,808	241	680	4,098	308	691	213	334	53
1911	102,496	40,543	1,764	18,575	33,842	252	661	4,895	326	512	171	268	52
1912	83,027	32,681	1,858	13,585	27,960	253	650	4,308	358	268	145	200	66
1913	88,204	36,016	2,367	13,226	29,930	239	639	4,001	424	340	156	189	55
1914	73,417	29,274	1,877	10,002	26,284	210	585	3,614	352	256	137	155	39
1915	41,422	15,756	835	4,488	15,100	237	1,459	2,129	184	112	68	179	51
1916	24,702	8,835	373	2,427	9,445	187	444	1,909	91	41	26	165	33
1917	16,141	5,393	187	1,693	5,751	130	227	1,483	58	41	18	186	50
1918	2,847	1,154	35	279	409	51	33	156	21	3	6	200	50
1919	7,271	4,293	104	1,406	753	48	24	157	18	6	21	104	20
1920	48,062	24,440	872	9,050	10,900	116	81	1,304	175	20	41	181	58
1921	79,577	27,995	1,311	14,534	30,968	131	97	2,405	158	102	147	311	123
1922	35,732	12,917	685	8,477	11,826	53	63	1,125	76	41	15	127	20
1923	61,499	19,409	907	21,279	18,109	59	83	1,112	70	77	36	108	13
1924	76,601	22,085	1,229	30,400	20,454	69	87	1,478	149	113	61	110	16

TABLE XXXVII.—Distribution, by principal races or peoples, of immigrant aliens, admitted from Turkey in Asia, 1899-1924.

Year	Total	Armenian	Greek	Hebrew	Syrian	Turkish
1899	4,436	670	13	57	3,678	5
1900	3,962	910	....	50	2,885	115
1901	5,782	1,692	1	72	3,984	33
1902	6,223	1,041	....	118	4,937	105
1903	7,118	1,660	8	50	5,366	33
1904	5,235	1,578	60	144	3,116	174
1905	6,157	1,483	135	90	4,086	266
1906	6,354	1,420	106	209	4,353	186
1907	8,053	1,666	1,353	330	4,153	383
1908	9,753	2,681	1,295	256	4,661	731
1909	7,506	2,839	996	344	3,001	190
1910	15,212	4,921	3,693	435	5,536	450
1911	10,229	2,422	2,309	454	4,439	359
1912	12,788	4,242	2,147	621	4,654	796
1913	23,955	7,369	5,192	1,046	8,224	1,385
1914	21,716	6,097	4,946	844	7,772	1,683
1915	3,543	526	1,460	324	1,036	84
1916	1,670	112	1,279	235	30	7
1917	393	83	205	82	5	10
1918	43	13	7	2	8	3
1919	19	9	1	....	2	...
1920	5,033	1,493	259	829	2,302	48
1921	11,735	5,371	553	1,296	4,020	90
1922	1,998	836	51	287	730	8
1923	2,183	658	179	417	631	158
1824	2,820	728	195	882	96	83

TABLE XXXVIII.—DISTRIBUTION, BY PRINCIPAL RACES OR PEOPLES, OF IMMIGRANT ALIENS ADMITTED FROM BRITISH NORTH AMERICA, 1899-1924.

Year	Total	English	Welsh	Scotch	Irish	Bulgarian, Serbian, Montenegrin	Croatian and Slovenian	Dutch and Flemish	Finnish	French	German	Greek	Hebrew	Italian	Japanese	Magyar	Polish	Russian	Ruthenian (Russniak)	Scandinavian
1899	1,322	659		18	23				2	38	5	5	5	23	522	1		2		8
1900	396	388			1					4	2									
1901	540	491		3	4					13	1				1					
1902	636	454								3					179					
1903	1,058	900		12	12			2		4	3				97					5
1904	2,837	2,357	1	74	156			1	6	48	18			3	113		1			11
1905	2,168	740	9	149	132	1	16	8	59	61	91	16	8	10	523	3	8	5		129
1906	5,063	1,191	23	380	191	23	96	34	97	80	290	56	11	110	145	180	249	29	18	325
1907	19,918	4,515	159	1,734	705	179	428	228	355	308	1,121	354	429	943	304	368	820	149	166	1,278
1908	38,510	10,296	318	4,122	3,038	594	452	473	330	4,205	2,468	433	1,818	3,887	645	426	1,057	262	201	1,759
1909	51,941	10,708	269	4,819	3,950	868	489	383	398	12,850	3,031	457	2,393	3,348	195	653	1,709	393	454	1,634
1910	56,555	13,236	251	5,745	5,310	670	499	499	600	14,214	3,082	361	2,780	3,900	74	348	1,388	345	297	2,024
1911	56,830	14,574	443	6,640	6,147	335	491	621	710	10,472	3,898	411	2,262	3,242	33	244	1,109	413	309	2,646
1912	55,990	14,837	358	6,401	5,618	467	325	699	816	11,044	4,041	400	2,420	1,687	32	281	1,139	487	528	3,545
1913	73,802	16,898	414	7,712	6,763	1,443	1,239	935	1,453	12,362	5,406	946	1,896	3,509	41	558	2,226	1,981	656	5,595
1914	86,139	19,730	643	8,604	7,215	835	1,254	1,250	1,602	10,338	6,287	937	1,467	7,504	28	501	3,143	3,483	1,597	5,988
1915	82,215	20,677	523	9,521	8,056	1,717	680	1,587	1,749	9,026	5,679	892	2,559	5,950	41	338	1,517	1,880	976	6,137
1916	101,551	24,994	574	10,763	10,754	866	336	2,208	1,733	16,690	6,180	906	3,404	4,786	70	346	2,279	3,289	1,301	4,777
1917	105,399	24,857	580	11,371	11,504	404	165	2,231	1,978	21,723	5,917	663	6,450	4,298	46	275	2,056	2,370	1,158	5,188
1918	32,452	10,326	219	4,706	4,080	93	15	723	637	5,277	1,209	156	6,347	763	28	26	481	549	43	1,392
1919	57,782	20,462	486	8,684	6,947	112	12	922	651	9,444	1,456	263	1,099	1,094	67	48	585	933	101	2,329
1920	90,025	30,398	524	11,756	9,614	245	71	1,293	743	19,087	2,985	396	2,114	1,555	42	137	1,310	1,624	240	2,682
1921	72,317	23,177	398	9,737	7,748	147	83	1,130	480	15,906	2,857	289	3,326	1,261	22	122	983	747	246	2,197
1922	46,810	15,784	260	6,805	5,160	59	32	726	222	9,625	2,056	109	1,958	615	24	85	492	390	149	1,460
1923	117,011	39,295	688	17,045	12,000	90	25	1,599	330	30,438	3,313	134	4,486	1,099	12	271	964	656	605	2,419
1924	200,690	70,064	1,362	30,630	21,727	136	62	2,811	512	43,959	7,077	273	7,421	1,543	38	471	2,039	1,584	1,838	4,516

TABLE XXXIX.—Distribution, by principal races or peoples, of immigrant aliens admitted from Mexico, 1899-1924.

Year	Total	English	German	Mexican	Spanish
1899	161	5	3	144	2
1900	237	. . . .	. . . .	237	. . . .
1901	347	. . . .	. . . .	345	. . . .
1902	709	. . . .	. . . .	709	. . . .
1903	528	12	2	468	20
1904	1,009	123	94	440	116
1905	2,637	430	431	147	355
1906	1,997	261	287	82	315
1907	1,406	74	139	31	322
1908	6,067	44	45	5,641	109
1909	16,251	55	126	15,534	181
1910	18,691	69	198	17,690	258
1911	19,889	151	175	18,704	289
1912	23,238	195	164	21,937	327
1913	11,926	157	114	10,908	203
1914	14,614	229	232	12,998	395
1915	12,340	103	180	10,908	572
1916	18,425	174	152	17,017	348
1917	17,869	132	204	16,246	433
1918	18,524	113	35	17,433	432
1919	29,818	121	18	28,740	413
1920	52,361	143	66	50,893	422
1921	30,758	157	62	29,489	355
1922	19,551	130	117	18,208	260
1923	63,768	123	166	62,672	221
1924	89,336	129	251	87,575	291

TABLE XL.—Distribution, by races or peoples, of immigrant aliens admitted from the West Indies, 1899-1924.

Year	Total	Africa	Cuba	English	French	Spanish	Spanish American	Syrian	West Indian
1899	89	388	1,285	144	7	538	. . .	. . .	137
1900	124	703	2,677	322	14	734	. . .	. . .	76
1901	203	520	1,622	316	4	579	1	4	82
1902	337	805	2,389	293	31	954	12	14	130
1903	589	1,134	2,894	762	124	1,083	277	101	1,441
1904	1,667	1,762	4,783	933	48	389	137	194	1,697
1905	2,576	3,034	7,178	1,539	229	2,118	176	148	1,373
1906	2,757	3,018	4,448	1,334	164	2,080	248	175	1,300
1907	2,779	4,561	5,433	1,396	128	2,800	151	111	1,276
1908	2,315	3,563	3,289	1,113	131	2,020	152	110	1,039
1909	1,906	3,340	3,331	785	76	1,890	83	141	930
1910	2,151	3,769	3,281	716	65	1,694	100	165	1,061
1911	13,403	4,973	3,832	637	92	2,199	95	150	1,041
1912	12,467	4,885	3,098	662	90	1,932	144	142	1,041
1913	12,458	4,891	3,029	582	98	1,957	140	111	1,074
1914	14,451	5,724	3,440	610	106	2,335	120	87	1,267
1915	11,598	4,104	3,319	467	105	1,860	145	122	729
1916	12,027	3,257	3,381	579	118	2,735	185	117	814
1917	15,507	5,769	3,364	439	118	3,424	155	91	1,249
1918	8,879	3,993	1,145	178	32	2,404	101	16	642
1919	8,826	4,027	1,136	265	51	1,675	147	19	1,075
1920	13,808	6,059	1,462	475	75	3,585	220	32	1,375
1921	13,774	7,046	1,472	489	82	2,469	178	59	1,367
1922	7,449	4,424	667	306	30	716	80	25	801
1923	13,181	6,580	1,299	357	47	2,109	77	45	1,308
1924	17,559	10,630	1,348	389	56	1,769	158	20	1,878

TABLE XLI.—Distribution, by races or peoples, of emigrant aliens departed for Austria-Hungary, 1908-09.

Year	Total	Bohemian and Moravian	Bulgarian, Serbian and Montenegrin	Croatian and Slovenian	Dalmatian, Bosnian and Herzegovinian	German	Hebrew	Italian	Magyar	Polish	Rumanian	Russian	Ruthenian	Slovak
1908	130,197	1,016	1,475	28,364	1,009	7,058	1,758	302	29,118	28,048	4,294	710	3,256	23,426
1909	49,413	675	591	8,686	490	4,278	1,398	259	11,026	10,292	928	137	1,625	8,790

TABLE XLIa.—Distribution, by races or peoples, of emigrant aliens departed for Austria, 1910-24.

Year	Total	Bohemian and Moravian	Bulgarian, Serbian and Montenegrin	Croatian and Slovenian	Dalmatian, Bosnian and Herzegovinian	German	Hebrew	Italian	Magyar	Polish	Rumanian	Russian	Ruthenian	Slovak
1910	26,424	887	322	4,760	388	2,543	1,161	294	2,159	9,406	388	107	1,266	2,583
1911	45,160	1,088	702	8,974	820	2,736	1,445	492	2,411	18,157	1,060	343	2,939	3,807
1912	46,137	1,009	793	9,594	879	1,575	1,664	378	1,386	22,266	444	537	3,766	1,747
1913	28,760	787	749	6,473	838	969	955	120	575	13,325	134	392	2,379	1,004
1914	35,013	961	766	8,500	870	1,039	1,324	147	325	15,657	141	447	3,540	1,179
1915	6,776	174	173	1,884	93	175	189	60	62	2,992	56	90	613	184
1916	230	23		28	1	58	1	1	6	88	2		16	6
1917	126	15		4		49	2	1	28	17			2	6
1918	5	1		2		1								1
1919	201	2	12	59						6				118
1920	2,274	21	32	29	1,311	87	8	1	398	117	3	47	165	39
1921	1,399	14	6	42	707	219	8	8	259	21	15	10	9	46
1922	579	11	3	12	327	127	1	2	33	14		12		2
1923	244	5		1	147	37	3	1	14	11	3	1		1
1924	217	1			141	48		1	6	2		5		3

TABLE XLIb.—DISTRIBUTION, BY RACES OR PEOPLES, OF EMIGRANT ALIENS DEPARTED FOR HUNGARY, 1910-24.

Year	Total	Bohemian and Moravian	Bulgarian, Serbian and Montenegrin	Croatian and Slovenian	Dalmatian, Bosnian and Herzegovinian	German	Hebrew	Italian	Magyar	Polish	Rumanian	Russian	Ruthenian	Slovak
1910	20,866	....	440	1,990	....	2,120	248	....	8,030	203	1,023	....	409	6,221
1911	41,182	....	1,192	3,753	....	3,496	382	....	16,207	342	3,455	....	780	11,209
1912	42,423	....	1,034	3,651	....	4,205	457	....	16,001	280	4,857	....	912	10,734
1913	29,904	....	822	2,773	....	2,915	256	....	10,647	103	2,677	....	763	8,831
1914	39,987	....	1,733	5,672	....	3,407	257	....	13,734	91	3,356	....	1,054	10,565
1915	5,059	....	125	384	....	407	36	....	2,107	68	588	....	103	1,198
1916	592	....	7	26	....	78	2	....	374	....	41	....	1	60
1917	112	....	3	1	....	15	3	....	85	....	....	....	1	2
1918	1	....	....	....	....	1	....	....	....	....	....	....	....	....
1919	100	....	8	....	....	....	....	....	....	....	....	....	....	....
1920	14,233	....	16	61	....	71	9	....	13,933	3	19	....	6	29
1921	12,153	....	13	96	....	202	6	....	11,648	23	15	....	3	46
1922	4,307	....	2	38	....	93	8	....	4,131	10	6	....	1	140
1923	895	....	1	3	....	5	10	....	856	3	1	....	....	13
1924	522	....	3	5	....	3	12	....	478	....	4	....	....	5

TABLE XLII.—Distribution, by principal races or peoples, of emigrant aliens departed for Czechoslovakia, 1920-24.

Year	Total	Bohemian and Moravian	Slovak	Year	Total	Bohemian and Moravian	Slovak
1920	11,147	180	10,218	1923	2,074	1,639	312
1921	15,452	412	14,106	1924	1,568	1,236	198
1922	7,846	4,100	3,028				

TABLE XLIII.—Distribution, by principal races or peoples, of emigrant aliens departed for Germany, 1908-24.

Year	Total	German	Polish	Year	Total	German	Polish
1908	6,770	6,014	367	1917	315	313	1
1909	4,905	4,602	154	1918	28	25	..
1910	6,216	5,850	154	1919	26	17	..
1911	6,042	5,543	274	1920	3,069	3,002	6
1912	5,785	5,314	242	1921	5,263	5,063	29
1913	4,759	4,445	146	1922	4,362	4,199	13
1914	5,136	4,735	214	1923	1,529	1,410	8
1915	1,419	1,313	62	1924	1,178	1,130	4
1916	439	432	1				

TABLE XLIV.—Distribution, by principal races or peoples, of emigrant aliens departed for Italy, 1908-24.

Year	Total	Italian (north)	Italian (south)	Year	Total	Italian (north)	Italian (south)
1908	166,733	18,967	147,212	1916	72,507	3,799	68,686
1909	83,300	15,555	67,341	1917	12,542	3,046	9,475
1910	52,323	11,891	40,246	1918	8,645	801	7,780
				1919	38,245	1,132	36,813
1911	72,640	12,475	59,941	1920	88,909	7,986	80,705
1912	108,388	12,097	96,156				
1913	88,021	10,197	77,717	1921	48,192	11,125	36,761
1914	84,351	12,103	72,150	1922	53,651	7,156	46,184
1915	96,903	7,245	89,568	1923	23,329	2,381	20,853
				1924	22,904	2,652	20,156

TABLE XLV.—Distribution, by principal races or peoples, of emigrant aliens departed for Portugal, 1908-24.

Year	Total	African	Portuguese	Year	Total	African	Portuguese
1908	1,056	243	794	1917	1,353	168	1,183
1909	1,025	279	735	1918	1,976	148	1,826
1910	1,082	246	830	1919	3,447	11	3,434
1911	1,459	155	1,284	1920	4,728	80	4,633
1912	1,916	268	1,641	1921	5,167	95	5,027
1913	1,965	464	1,488	1922	5,877	5	5,829
1914	2,055	290	1,755	1923	2,620	1	2,606
1915	2,661	224	2,434	1924	3,357	9	3,320
1916	2,396	308	2,082				

TABLE XLVI.—Distribution, by principal races or peoples, of emigrant aliens departed for Rumania, 1908-24.

Year	Total	Hebrew	Rumanian	Year	Total	Hebrew	Rumanian
1908	1,267	158	882	1916	49	2	47
1909	434	87	282	1917	16	6	9
1910	445	101	318	1918	7	. .	5
1911	669	78	542	1919	39	. .	36
1912	550	122	390	1920	21,506	12	21,343
1913	319	94	186	1921	9,297	18	8,474
1914	348	94	220	1922	3,795	58	3,200
1915	244	32	198	1923	1,169	23	1,046
				1924	1,096	17	1,017

TABLE XLVII.—Distribution, by principal races or peoples, of emigrant aliens departed for Russia and Finland, 1908-24.

Year	Total	Finnish	German	Hebrew	Lithuanian	Polish	Russian
1908	37,777	3,360	408	5,439	3,282	18,187	6,636
1909	19,707	1,035	338	3,989	1,944	8,421	3,819
1910	17,362	692	503	3,295	1,765	6,705	4,223
1911	27,053	1,603	517	3,375	2,364	12,276	6,508
1912	34,681	2,430	519	4,448	4,112	14,701	8,139
1913	26,923	1,906	396	3,505	3,263	9,701	7,980
1914	47,451	2,252	811	4,174	5,480	18,779	15,703
1915	18,297	727	167	873	965	4,694	10,501
1916	5,259	379	20	45	26	229	4,106
1917	5,947	471	7	183	33	53	5,106
1918	4,983	931	21	284	21	26	3,634
1919	1,868	357	1	98	4	48	1,297
1920[19]	3,406	1,354	2	12	702	67	768
1921[19]	17,615	2,284	12	77	4,333	203	10,025
1922[19]	7,586	1,129	16	28	4,429	88	1,593
1923[19]	2,830	379	1	22	1,078	7	1,247
1924[19]	932	355	3	14	29	4	489

TABLE XLVIII.—Distribution, by principal races' or peoples, of emigrant aliens departed for the Serb-Croat-Slovene State, 1920-24.

Year	Total	Bul-garian	Croatian and Slov-enian	Slovak	Year	Total	Bul-garian	Croatian and Slov-enian	Slovak
1920	28,474	19,769	6,853	1,163	1923	2,064	1,685	219	38
1921	13,034	6,888	2,812	2,769	1924	1,991	1,276	360	235
1922	9,733	5,051	3,850	314					

TABLE XLIX.—Distribution, by principal races or peoples, of emigrant aliens departed for Switzerland, 1908-24.

Year	Total	French	German	Italian	Year	Total	French	German	Italian
1908	684	115	463	68	1917	159	48	90	18
1909	658	88	455	78	1918	172	55	101	12
1910	759	133	497	78	1919	403	232	109	10
1911	667	113	428	89	1920	1,103	372	384	44
1912	510	74	363	39	1921	900	114	487	100
1913	449	59	332	40	1922	886	172	494	76
1914	432	39	341	22	1923	546	75	334	40
1915	349	51	190	18	1924	390	57	272	10
1916	201	79	80	13					

TABLE L.—Distribution, by principal races or peoples, of emigrant aliens departed for Turkey, 1908-24.

Year	Total	Armenian	Bulgarian, Serbian and Montenegrin	Greek	Syrian	Turkish
1908	4,931	165	1,150	437	1,555	1,057
1909	2,917	464	192	241	1,045	535
1910	3,536	447	275	376	872	856
1911	6,593	902	1,143	1,319	1,001	1,446
1912	7,477	670	1,887	1,742	819	1,253
1913	6,122	625	2,023	750	628	1,193
1914	4,771	1,117	612	124	949	769
1915	757	183	24	51	269	129
1916	32	10	..	7	1	1
1917	32	21	...	2	4	5
1918	29	22	...	...	2	3
1919	73	1	...	2	53	3
1920	3,543	545	49	29	1,466	1,303
1921	2,939	518	11	19	1,337	691
1922	1,932	216	5	43	1,192	223
1923	898	46	...	9	542	102
1924	339	26	1	4	8	274

TABLE LI.—Distribution, by principal races or peoples, of emigrant aliens departed for British North America, 1908-24.

Year	Total	English	Welsh	Scotch	Irish	Bulgarian, Serbian and Montenegrin	Croatian, Slovenian	Dutch and Flemish	Finnish	French	German	Italian	Magyar	Polish	Russian	Ruthenian	Scandinavian
1908	2,629	423	4	47	81	2	....	....	7	18	32	46	4	2	8	....	40
1909	30,478	1,747	69	740	511	144	97	176	371	237	3,445	2,639	399	371	1,017	16	4,179
1910	34,194	1,828	58	782	498	190	288	191	550	207	1,296	1,993	284	370	1,157	4	2,403
1911	49,373	3,803	79	1,389	1,005	304	846	334	2,555	385	1,999	2,445	269	796	1,422	7	4,338
1912	33,506	2,997	91	1,155	770	114	634	298	1,660	869	2,556	451	124	169	591	686	4,853
1913	46,981	4,377	118	1,816	1,339	277	905	777	1,131	668	2,374	1,387	237	779	1,947	2,141	4,820
1914	31,818	3,479	111	1,312	895	62	200	390	668	272	1,208	417	147	230	1,073	371	2,276
1915	23,225	2,133	37	768	504	26	62	259	104	119	301	157	79	64	517	104	799
1916	15,712	1,954	52	635	353	14	11	233	146	122	32	175	6	27	432	....	557
1917	18,994	2,483	46	855	610	89	19	382	773	912	66	652	5	40	1,142	17	1,340
1918	27,170	10,662	226	3,010	2,674	345	4	399	658	4,074	304	367	10	1,006	1,177	25	1,325
1919	10,726	3,964	91	1,051	862	355	13	332	84	2,575	137	103	7	72	251	2	468
1920	7,668	2,479	49	945	794	9	3	166	34	2,110	118	80	3	28	75	1	496
1921	5,456	2,240	49	639	537	6	7	199	60	650	98	95	16	76	77	4	429
1922	4,480	1,768	58	610	423	52	....	183	23	515	137	45	29	53	42	8	315
1923	2,775	1,112	28	387	227	3	1	84	23	198	127	31	23	52	26	2	163
1924	2,601	1,130	15	348	189	3	1	74	21	83	168	40	17	62	61	6	237

500 INTERNATIONAL MIGRATION STATISTICS

SOURCES

a. W. J. Bromwell, *History of Immigration to the United States*, exhibiting the number, sex, age, occupation and country of birth of passengers arriving in the United States by sea from foreign countries, from September 30, 1819, to December 31, 1855, compiled entirely from official data. Redfield, N. Y., 1856.

Tables I, V, VII, VIII, IX (years 1820-55).

b. ————*Arrivals of Alien Passengers and Immigrants in the United States from 1820 to 1892.* Treasury Department, Washington, 1893.

Tables I, II, IV, VIII, IX, except for the years 1892-95; V, from 1857; VI, from 1868; VII, from 1869; for all tables up to 1892 inclusive.

c. *Immigration into the United States showing number, nationality, sex, age, occupation, destination, etc., from 1820 to 1903,* Monthly Summary of Commerce and Finance of the United States, June 1903. Treasury Department, Washington, 1903, pp. 4333-4444.

Tables I-III, V-XII, XIV (from the start); IV (from 1857); for all tables up to 1902 inclusive.

d. *Statistical Review of Immigration, 1820-1910.* (*Reports of the Immigration Commission.* Senate, Washington, 1911.)

Tables I-III, VII, X-XIII, XXI-XXXVIII (from the start); V (from 1869); VIII and IX (from 1899); for all tables up to 1910 inclusive.

e. *Annual Reports of the Commissioner-General of Immigration for the fiscal years ended June 30* (1896-1924).

All tables containing statistics for the years 1896-1924; all years in this period.

f. *Information supplied by the Commissioner-General of Immigration.*

Tables XXI and XXII.

For 1892-95, the totals as well as the figures of sex, age, occupation and country of origin furnished from the sources *b* and *c* do not correspond with those furnished by the sources *d* and *e*. Unless otherwise indicated, the figures have been taken from the sources *b* and *c*, as they supply more details.

NOTES

[1]Azores, Bermuda, Canary Islands, Cape Verde, Madeira and St. Helena.
[2]Included in "United Kingdom not specified".
[3]Figures given in the *Statistical Review of Immigration* (above-mentioned source under *d*, the totals in which agree with the Summaries in the *Annual Reports*, but not with those from source *c*).
[4]Including Serbia and Montenegro for 1899-1919.
[5]Including Finland for 1899-1919.
[6]Detail 54 more than total.
[7]Including only Bermuda and British Honduras, 1886-91. No records for other British North American possessions.
[8]No records.
[9]Including Pacific Islands.
[10]The figures given for the different occupations total 16,808.
[11]The figures given for the different occupations, 1,109.
[12]Where the immigrants to the United States come almost exclusively from one country, their "race or people" is not indicated. •
[13]Finland only.
[14]1899-1909 including Hungary.
[15]29,708 emigrants, sex and age unknown, left the United States via the Canadian border.
[16]Sex of 10,336 persons unknown.
[17]Sex of 19,372 persons unknown.
[18]Where emigrants leave the United States almost exclusively for one country, their "race or people' is not indicated.
[19]For 1920-24, the figures of Finns and Scandinavians refer to Finland, those of other nationalities refer to Russia.

MEXICO

These statistics were first collected in 1909. In that year they were published in a separate volume which contained particulars not collected or not published later. For instance, aliens were classified not only according to their nationality, but also according to the country of their last permanent residence.

The statistics relate to both the continental and intercontinental migrations of citizens and aliens. However, after 1910 the distinction between these two forms of migration cannot be exactly drawn. The majority of aliens arrive from or proceed to overseas countries, while the contrary is the case for citizens.

TABLE I.—DISTRIBUTION OF IMMIGRANTS (CITIZENS AND ALIENS DISTINGUISHED) BY SEX AND AGE, 1909-10.

Age	1909			1910		
	Total	Males	Females	Total	Males	Females
Up to 5 years..........	2,403	1,202	1,201	3,297	1,719	1,578
6 to 12 "	2,486	1,340	1,146	2,896	1,531	1,365
13 to 18 "	3,420	2,203	1,217	4,705	3,213	1,492
19 to 40 "	35,974	27,027	8,947	56,612	44,880	11,732
41 years and over.......	14,165	11,311	2,854	19,399	15,704	3,695
Total..............	58,448	43,083	15,365	86,909	67,047	19,862
Of which: repatriated citizens.............	16,069	11,792	4,277	37,227	29,436	7,791
alien immigrants.......	42,379	31,291	11,088	49,682	37,611	12,071

TABLE II.—DISTRIBUTION OF IMMIGRANTS, BY OCCUPATION AND SEX, 1909.

Occupation	Total	Males	Females
Total...........................	58,448	43,083	15,365
Doctors........................	538	531	7
Engineers......................	2,059	2,056	3
Other liberal professions.........	775	772	3
Farmers.......................	5,484	5,479	5
Masons........................	241	241	..
Merchants.....................	5,313	5,283	30
Carpenters.....................	641	641	..
Domestic servants..............	196	81	115
Smiths........................	252	252	...
Industrials....................	536	536	...
Miners........................	2,335	2,335	...
Mechanics.....................	1,208	1,207	1
Industrial workers..............	117	117	...
Shoemakers....................	220	220	...
Independent....................	779	756	23
Debarred from occupation through age or sex..................	16,912	2,272	14,640
Other occupations...............	20,842	20,304	538
Total.....................	58,448	43,083	15,365

TABLE III.—DISTRIBUTION OF IMMIGRANTS, BY COUNTRY OF LAST RESIDENCE, 1909.

EUROPE	Germany	571
	Spain	4,165
	France	1,081
	Great Britain	1,767
	Italy	158
	Other countries	733
ASIA	China	2,962
	Japan	31
	Other countries	62
AMERICA	Canada	139
	South America	220
	United States	42,374
	Central America	581
	Cuba	3,604
	Total continental	46,559
	Total intercontinental	11,889
	General total	58,448

TABLE IV.—DISTRIBUTION OF IMMIGRANT ALIENS BY NATIONALITY, 1909-24[1]

Nationality	1909	1910	1911	1912	1913	1914	1915	1916	1917	1918	1919	1920	1921	1922	1923	1924
German	1,271	1,255	1,224	1,154	937	275	258	465	388	80	206	924	1,200	1,165	1,524	1,845
Spanish	5,635	5,927	5,269	5,321	4,487	1,393	1,856	2,872	4,395	2,347	3,282	4,184	8,364	5,979	5,904	3,869
French	923	1,058	1,044	1,102	1,145	294	179	300	482	273	910	881	969	952	819	713
English	2,424	3,176	3,302	3,268	3,288	1,856	832	1,221	1,078	644	1,114	1,242	1,723	3,284	2,983	3,377
Italian	499	517	628	705	472	119	177	125	350	136	216	374	1,177	714	1,689	1,592
Other European	1,514	1,543	1,527	2,433	1,314	314	289	555	1,174	397	489	1,595	2,509	1,459	3,141	3,837
Chinese	3,487	4,681	3,370	4,973	4,910	1,491	474	228	377	774	1,151	2,669	1,320	721	1,125	880
Japanese	135	175	198	278	306	225	116	493	610	456	515	181	1,070	311	283	320
Arab			53	54	88	17	26	75	144	5	37					
Other Asiatic	55	66	104	129	738	162	56	23	241	57	275	38	612	957	1,962	715
North American	25,169	29,564	19,733	19,864	8,628	2,603	2,377	5,525	8,264	3,804	5,885	7,817	15,429	18,532	20,198	20,978
Guatemalan			26	22	18	16	11	8	19	31	567	661	1,358	1,158	1,125	976
Cuban	931	937	737	841	634	275	486	367	658	491	551					
Central American	217	665	175	101	106	101	67	144	102	161	156	518	521	368	288	346
South American	119	118	220	422	120	41	34	115	186	62	242	311	819	414	397	186
Other nationalities																1,087
Total	42,379	49,682	37,610	40,667	27,191	9,182	7,238	12,516	18,468	9,718	15,596	21,395	37,071	36,014	41,438	40,721
Continental[2]	26,317	31,166	20,671	20,828	9,386	2,995	2,941	6,044	9,043	4,487	7,159	8,996	17,308	20,058	21,611	22,300
Intercontinental	16,062	18,516	16,939	19,839	17,805	6,187	4,297	6,472	9,425	5,231	8,437	12,399	19,763	15,956	19,827	18,421

For reference notes see page 505.

TABLE V.—DISTRIBUTION OF EMIGRANT ALIENS BY NATIONALITY, 1911-24.

Nationality	1911	1912	1913	1914	1915	1916	1917	1918	1919	1920	1921	1922	1923	1924	
German	1,118	1,169	1,072	369	139	413	121	11	101	294	724	1,006	986	1,079	
Spanish	5,065	5,073	4,460	1,609	3,175	3,414	3,365	2,445	4,183	2,925	4,296	4,032	3,981	3,676	
French	1,139	1,009	1,129	344	196	445	336	303	639	547	724	739	747	764	
English	3,287	2,842	2,983	1,647	444	640	419	516	571	707	796	963	2,148	1,738	
Italian	561	564	585	146	110	145	205	152	312	380	389	409	750	579	
Other European	1,299	1,471	1,261	241	149	485	471	325	434	761	1,111	694	1,428	965	
Chinese	810	550	866	460	186	373	636	519	745	1,066	1,023	960	870	972	
Japanese	92	124	128	72	210	232	186	100	142	126	125	196	194	198	
Arab	108	86	148	32	30	153	58	9	33						
Other Asiatic	108	86	258	60	30	59	63	33	365	6	48	381	748	363	
North American	20,501	23,986	11,796	1,713	1,715	3,604	2,977	3,172	4,271	4,716	10,200	13,358	16,795	16,962	
Guatemalan	68	69	64	15	46	7	1		339						
Cuban	890	928	869	303	322	559	621	573	578	1,076	1,709	1,299	2,122	1,066	
Other Nor h American	164	189	103	8	6	9	44	21	27	323	346	201	287	363	
Central American	184	188	169	66	60	37	49	153	65	262	333	259	239	238	
South American	202	145	87	42	10	139	101	103	159						
African			2	5	2	6	2								
Other nationalities			10					2	2	61	422	841	1,186	880	
Total	35,596	38,479	25,990	7,132	6,830	10,720	9,655	8,456	12,968	13,250	22,246	25,338	32,481	29,843	
Continental²	21,643	25,171	12,898	2,097	2,143	4,207	3,648	3,919	5,253	6,115	12,255	14,858	19,204	18,391	
Intercontinental	13,953	13,308	13,092	5,035	4,687	6,513	6,007	4,537	7,715	7,135	9,991	10,480	13,277	11,452	

TABLE VI.—DISTRIBUTION OF IMMIGRANTS, BY OCCUPATION, 1922-24.

Occupation	1922	1923	1924
Agriculture................................	17,235	29,604	35,001
Industry and mining........................	7,726	10,262	10,593
Transport and commerce.................. ...	11,701	13,541	12,903
Domestic service and general labor.	20,202	18,960	22,887
Liberal professions and public services..........	4,671	5,994	7,179
Other occupations, none or unknown...........	29,324	54,445	61,944
Total................................	90,859	132,806	150,507

SOURCES

Estadistica de Immigración formada por la Dirección General de Estadistica a cargo del Dr. Antonio Peñafiel. No. 1. Año de 1909. Mexico, 1910, pp. 308-319.

Tables I-III (year 1909).

Boletin del Departemento de la Estadistica Nacional. September and November 1924. Mexico, 1924.

Tables IV and V (years 1911-23); VI (years 1922 and 1923).

Estadistica Nacional. Organ of the Department of National Statistics. Año II, Numero 27, Febrero 15, 1926. Mexico, 1926.

Tables IV-VI (year 1924).

Information supplied by the Department of National Statistics.

Tables I and IV (year 1910).

NOTES

[1]In addition, 13 Africans and 2,854 persons, the nationality of whom is not distinguished and the year of immigration of whom is not indicated, immigrated during the period 1911-23.
[2]North Americans, Guatemalans, Cubans and Central Americans.

WEST INDIES

TABLE I.—IMMIGRATION TO THE WEST INDIAN COLONIES, BY COUNTRY OF ORIGIN AND COLONY OF IMMIGRATION, 1834-72.

Immigrants introduced into:	from:	1834	1835	1836	1837	1838	1839	1840	1841	1842	1843
JAMAICA	Great Britain	2	358	613	360	....	.....	......	1,333	19	.....
	Madeira	....	24	67	....	....	.....	......	....	....	....
	Sierra Leone	....	....	....	....	....	.....	......	592	292	301
	St. Helena	....	....	....	....	....	.....	......	....	400	....
	East Indies	....	....	....	....	....	.....	......	....	....	....
	China	....	....	....	....	....	.....	......	....	....	....
	Canada	....	....	....	....	....	.....	......	25	....	110
	United States	....	....	....	....	....	.....	71	161	3	23
	West Indies	....	....	....	....	....	.....	......	94	314	....
	Havana	....	....	....	....	....	.....	......	....	....	....
	Direct from captured slavers	....	....	....	....	....	.....	......	....	....	....
	Germany	....	506	532	....	....	.....	......	....	....	....
	Total	2	888	1,212	360	....	.....	71	2,205	1,028	434
TRINIDAD	United States						314	909	63	.....	3
	West Indies						692	1,106	1,719	1,956	2,075
	Rio de Janeiro						.....	......	....	....	....
	Sierra Leone		No record of any migration				.....	......	170	514	476
	Madeira						.....	......	....	....	....
	St. Helena						.....	......	....	402	289
	East Indies						.....	......	....	....	....
	Cape Verde						.....	......	....	....	....
	China						.....	......	....	....	....
	Total						1,006	2,015	1,952	2,872	2,843
BRITISH GUIANA	Africa	....	....	....	....	....	.....	......	....	....	....
	British West Indies	....	157	807	698	653	.....	869	2,740	471	37
	East Indies	....	....	....	....	406	.....	......	....	....	....
	St. Helena	....	....	....	....	....	.....	......	....	1,112	86
	Sierra Leone	....	....	....	....	....	.....	......	415	148	239
	Kroo Coast	....	....	....	....	....	.....	......	....	....	....
	Foreign West Indies	....	....	174	713	314	37	2	51	13	....
	Madeira	....	429	....	....	....	.....	......	4,312	348	45
	Azores	....	....	....	....	....	.....	......	....	....	....
	Rio de Janeiro	....	....	....	....	91	.....	......	578	563	....
	Surinam	....	....	....	252	58	.....	4	....	....	31
	China	....	....	....	....	....	.....	......	....	....	....
	Great Britain	....	....	....	....	....	.....	......	....	....	....
	Cape Verde	....	....	....	....	....	.....	......	....	....	....
	Not stated	....	....	143	132	388	155	1	....	....	112
	Total[2]	....	586	1,124	1,795	1,910	192	876	8,096	2,655	550
ST. LUCIA	Great Britain	....	.....	18	18	....	1	17	....	....	....
	France	....	.....	1	....	1	....	6	....	23	....
	Germany	....	.....	....	....	....	....	29	....	....	....
	British West Indies	....	.....	....	....	....	....	78	....	....	....
	Sierra Leone	....	.....	....	....	....	....	....	....	....	....
	St. Helena	....	.....	....	....	....	....	....	....	....	....
	East Indies	....	.....	....	....	....	....	....	....	....	....
	Total	....	.....	19	18	1	1	130	.....	23	....
ST. VINCENT	Madeira	....	....	....	....	....					
	St. Helena	....	....	....	....	136					
	Sierra Leone	....	....	....	....	....					
	East Indies	....	....	....	....	....					
	Total				136[4]						
GRENADA	Madeira	....	....	....	....	....	....	....	....	....	....
	St. Helena	....	....	....	....	....	....	....	....	....	....
	Sierra Leone	....	....	....	....	....	....	....	....	....	....
	Saba	....	....	....	....	....	....	....	....	....	....
	East Indies	....	....	....	....	....	....	....	....	....	....
	Total	....	....	....	....	....	....	....	....	....	....

For reference notes see page 521.

TABLE I.—IMMIGRATION TO THE WEST INDIAN COLONIES, BY COUNTRY OF ORIGIN AND COLONY OF IMMIGRATION, 1834-72 (continued).

Immigrants introduced into:	from:	1844	1845	1846	1847	1848	1849	1850	1851	1852	1853
JAMAICA	Great Britain		13								
	Madeira										167
	Sierra Leone	339	42			1,148	228	177	317		
	St. Helena	201		463		743	773		452		
	East Indies		261	1,851	2,438						
	China										
	Canada		35								
	United States										
	West Indies		255	127							
	Havana				71	49	79	61	39	16	32
	Direct from captured slavers							230			
	Germany										
	Total	540	606	2,441	2,509	1,940	1,080	468	808	16	199
TRINIDAD	United States	12				32					
	West Indies	1,708	990								
	Rio de Janeiro	504			52		323				
	Sierra Leone	246	420		399	207	255	471			
	Madeira			379	346						
	St. Helena	60		100	231		1,290	304		14	4
	East Indies		225	2,456	2,077	634			173	1,309	2,089
	Cape Verde										
	China										988
	Total	2,530	1,635	2,935	3,105	873	1,868	775	173	1,323	3,081
BRITISH GUIANA	Africa										
	British West Indies		722	428							
	East Indies		816	4,019	3,477	3,545			517	2,805	2,022
	St. Helena			819	10	876		719		15	
	Sierra Leone	378	1,425	278	457	821		428	453	140	
	Kroo Coast				108						273
	Foreign West Indies										
	Madeira	140	668	5,975	3,755	300	86	1,040	1,101	1,009	2,567
	Azores								164		
	Rio de Janeiro	145					111	72		113	
	Surinam										
	China										647
	Great Britain								21		
	Cape Verde										
	Not stated	255									
	Total[3]	918	3,631	11,519	7,807	5,542	197	2,259	2,256	4,082	5,509
ST. LUCIA	Great Britain										
	France										
	Germany										
	British West Indies										
	Sierra Leone							365	186		
	St. Helena								568		
	East Indies										
	Total							365	754		
ST. VINCENT	Madeira				460	86					
	St. Helena							575			
	Sierra Leone						234				
	East Indies										
	Total				460	86	234	575			
GRENADA	Madeira				421				10		
	St. Helena						85				
	Sierra Leone						711	261			
	Saba									23	
	East Indies										
	Total				421		796	261	10	23	

For reference notes see page 521.

TABLE I.—IMMIGRATION TO THE WEST INDIAN COLONIES, BY COUNTRY OF ORIGIN AND COLONY OF IMMIGRATION, 1834-72 (continued).

Immigrants introduced into:	from:	1854	1855	1856	1857	1858	1859	1860	1861	1862	1863
JAMAICA	Great Britain										
	Madeira										
	Sierra Leone		212								
	St. Helena								390		
	East Indies							47	259	608	533
	China							598	1,523	1,982	542
	Canada	472[1]									
	United States										
	West Indies										
	Havana										
	Direct from captured slavers				362						
	Germany										
	Total	472	212		362			645	2,172	2,590	1,075
TRINIDAD	United States										
	West Indies										
	Rio de Janeiro										
	Sierra Leone							226			
	Madeira										
	St. Helena					30	4	470			
	East Indies	687	291	628	1,414	2,083	3,363	2,169	2,544	1,603	1,801
	Cape Verde				172						
	China									467	
	Total	687	291	628	1,586	2,113	3,367	2,865	2,544	2,070	1,801
BRITISH GUIANA	Africa					281		625	40	558	373
	British West Indies										69
	East Indies	1,928	2,342	1,259	2,596	1,404	3,426	5,450	3,737	5,625	2,354
	St. Helena			65							
	Sierra Leone										
	Kroo Coast										
	Foreign West Indies										
	Madeira	648	1,055	180	342	1,484	684	135	35	29	
	Azores										
	Rio de Janeiro										
	Surinam										
	China						699	1,942	3,368	2,590	296
	Great Britain										
	Cape Verde			766		53					
	Not stated										
	Total	2,576	3,397	2,270	2,938	3,222	4,809	8,152	7,180	8,802	3,092
ST. LUCIA	Great Britain										
	France										
	Germany										
	British West Indies										
	Sierra Leone										
	St. Helena									179	
	East Indies						555	660		320	
	Total						555	660		499	
ST. VINCENT	Madeira										
	St. Helena							94	119	14	
	Sierra Leone										
	East Indies								260	307	
	Total							94	379	321	
GRENADA	Madeira										
	St. Helena							92	122	57	114
	Sierra Leone										
	Saba										
	East Indies				283	362	299			1,097	
	Total				283	362	299		122	1,154	114

For reference notes see page 521.

TABLE I.—IMMIGRATION TO THE WEST INDIAN COLONIES, BY COUNTRY OF ORIGIN AND COLONY OF IMMIGRATION, 1834-72 (continued).

Immigrants introduced into:	from:	1864	1865	1866	1867	1868	1869	1870	1871	1872
JAMAICA	Great Britain									
	Madeira									
	Sierra Leone									
	St. Helena				11					
	East Indies					1,625	1,393	906	1,355	1,525
	China									
	Canada									
	United States									
	West Indies									
	Havana									
	Direct from captured slavers									
	Germany									
	Total					1,636	1,393	906	1,355	1,525
TRINIDAD	United States									
	West Indies			1,322						
	Rio de Janeiro									
	Sierra Leone									
	Madeira									
	St. Helena									
	East Indies	949	2,759	473	3,267	1,367	3,329	1,892	1,508	3,607
	Cape Verde									
	China		593	597						
	Total	949	3,352	2,402	3,267	1,367	3,329	1,892	1,508	3,607
BRITISH GUIANA	Africa	390	42							
	British West Indies	4,297	2,482	757	355	559	980	631	591	
	East Indies	2,709	3,216	2,526	3,909	2,528	7,168	4,943	2,706	3,550
	St. Helena									
	Sierra Leone									
	Kroo Coast									
	Foreign West Indies									
	Madeira		118	134	304	219	240	454²	260	
	Azores									
	Rio de Janeiro									
	Surinam									
	China	509	1,691	789						
	Great Britain									
	Cape Verde									
	Not stated									
	Total	7,905	7,549	4,206	4,568	3,306	8,388	6,028	3,557	3,550
ST LUCIA	Great Britain									
	France									
	Germany									
	British West Indies									
	Sierra Leone									
	St. Helena									
	East Indies									
	Total									
ST. VINCENT	Madeira									
	St. Helena									
	Sierra Leone									
	East Indies			214	477		343		325	
	Total			214	477		343		325	
GRENADA	Madeira									
	St. Helena									
	Sierra Leone									
	Saba									
	East Indies			260					269	
	Total			260					269	

For reference notes see page 521.

TABLE Ia.—RETURN OF IMMIGRANTS INTRODUCED INTO THE WEST INDIAN COLONIES, BY COUNTRY OF ORIGIN AND ISLES OF IMMIGRATION, SINCE THE ABOLITION OF SLAVERY 1834-72 (continued).

Immigrants introduced into:	from:	1834	1835	1836	1837	1838	1839	1840	1841	1842	1843
ANTIGUA	Madeira										
	Great Britain										
	British West Indies										
	Cape Verde										
	China										
	Total										
ST. KITTS	Trinidad										
	Sierra Leone										
	Great Britain										
	St. Helena										
	Madeira										
	East Indies										
	Total										
NEVIS	Madeira										
TOBAGO	Sierra Leone										
	St. Helena										
	Total										
DOMINICA	Liberated Africans from the Don Francisco					401					
	Refugees from French Islands					327					
	British West Indies					76					
	Great Britain					4					
	Total					808					
BAHAMAS	Wrecked Slavers										
HONDURAS	China										
	United States										
	British West Indies										
	Total										
TOTAL TO WEST INDIES[7]	Great Britain	2	358	631	378		1	17	1,333	19	
	Madeira		453	67					4,312	348	45
	Cape Verde										
	Azores										
	Sierra Leone								1,177	954	1,016
	St. Helena									1,914	375
	East Indies					406					
	China										
	Canada							25			110
	United States						314	980	224	3	26
	British West Indies		157	807	698	653	692	2,053	4,553	2,741	2,112
	Havannah & F. Indies			174	713	314	37	2	51	13	
	Saba										
	Rio de Janeiro						91		578	563	
	Direct from captured and wrecked slavers										
	Malta										
	Kroo Coast										
	Germany		506	532				29			
	France		1		1			6		23	
	Not stated			143	132	388	155	1			112
	Surinam				252	58		4			31
	Trinidad										
	Total	2	1,474	2,355	2,173	1,911	1,199	3,092	12,253	6,578	3,827

TABLE Ia.—RETURN OF IMMIGRANTS INTRODUCED INTO THE WEST INDIAN COLONIES, BY COUNTRY OF ORIGIN AND ISLES OF IMMIGRATION, SINCE THE ABOLITION OF SLAVERY, 1834-72 (continued).

Immigrants introduced into:	from:	1844	1845	1846	1847	1848	1849	1850	1851	1852	1853
ANTIGUA	Madeira				1,068	7	132	63	180	21	335
	Great Britain										
	British West Indies										19
	Cape Verde										
	China										
	Total				1,068	7	132	63	180	21	354
ST. KITTS	Trinidad				5						
	Sierra Leone							95			
	Great Britain										
	St. Helena								137		
	Madeira										
	East Indies										
	Total				5			95	137		
NEVIS	Madeira			59	368						
TOBAGO	Sierra Leone								46		
	St. Helena								246		
	Total								292		
DOMINICA	Liberated Africans from the Don Francisco										
	Refugees from French Islands										
	British West Indies										
	Great Britain										
	Total										
BAHAMAS	Wrecked Slavers										
HONDURAS	China										
	United States										
	British West Indies										
	Total										
TOTAL TO WEST INDIES	Great Britain		13						21		
	Madeira	140	668	6,413	6,418	393	218	1,103	1,290	1,030	3,069
	Cape Verde										
	Azores								164		
	Sierra Leone	963	1,887	278	856	2,176	1,888	1,523	816	140	273[6]
	St. Helena	261		1,382	241	1,619	2,148	2,303	698	29	4
	East Indies		1,302	8,326	7,992	4,179			690	4,114	4,111
	China										1,635
	Canada		35								
	United States	12				32					
	British West Indies	1,708	1,967	555							19
	Havannah & F. Indies				71	49	79	61	39	16	32
	Saba									23	
	Rio de Janeiro	649			52		434	72		113	
	Direct from captured and wrecked slavers							230			
	Malta										
	Kroo Coast				108						
	Germany										
	France										
	Not stated	255									
	Surinam										
	Trinidad				5						
	Total	3,938	5,872	16,954	15,743	8,448	4,767	5,292	3,719	5,465	9,143

For reference notes see page 521.

TABLE Ia.—RETURN OF IMMIGRANTS INTRODUCED INTO THE WEST INDIAN COLO-
NIES, BY COUNTRY OF ORIGIN AND ISLES OF IMMIGRATION, SINCE THE
ABOLITION OF SLAVERY, 1834-72 (continued).

Immigrants introduced into:	from:	1854	1855	1856	1857	1858	1859	1860	1861	1862	1863
ANTIGUA	Madeira..............	167	....	....	....	44	....	....	11	....	191
	Great Britain.........	....	....	....	....	....	....	....	....	....	....
	British West Indies...	....	....	....	....	12	26	....	....	....	1,005
	Cape Verde...........	....	....	195	12	....	....	....	....	....	....
	China...............	....	....	....	....	....	....	....	....	....	100⁵
	Total.............	167	....	195	12	56	26	....	11	....	1,296
ST. KITTS	Trinidad............	....	....	....	....	....	....	....	....	....	223
	Sierra Leone.........	....	....	....	....	....	....	....	....	....	....
	Great Britain........	....	....	....	....	....	1	....	....	....	....
	St. Helena..........	....	....	....	....	....	....	....	....	....	....
	Madeira............	....	....	106	157	253	103	77	43	50	219
	East Indies.........	....	....	....	....	....	....	....	337	...:	....
	Total............	....	....	106	157	254	103	77	380	50	442
NEVIS	Madeira............	....	....	....	....	....	....	....	....	....	....
TOBAGO	Sierra Leone.........	....	....	....	....	....	....	....	....	....	....
	St. Helena..........	....	....	....	....	....	....	....	....	225	....
	Total...	....	....	....	....	....	....	....	....	225	....
DOMINICA	Liberated Africans from the Don Franci.co...	....	....	....	....	....	....	....	....	....	....
	Refugees from French Islands	....	....	....	....	....	....	....	....	....	....
	British West Indies ...	....	....	....	....	....	....	....	....	....	....
	Great Britain........	....	....	....	....	....	....	....	....	....	....
	Total.	....	....	....	....	....	....	....	....	....	....
BAHAMAS	Wrecked Slavers.	....	....	....	....	....	....	389	....	....	....
HONDURAS	China....	....	....	....	....	....	....	....	....	....	....
	United States	....	....	....	....	....	....	....	....	....	....
	British West Indies ...	....	....	....	....	....	....	....	....	....	....
	Total.	....	....	....	....	....	....	....	....	....	....
TOTAL TO WEST INDIES	Great Britain...... ..	....	....	....	....	1	....	....	....	....	....
	Madeira....	815	1,267	286	499	1,781	787	212	89	79	410
	Cape Verde..........	....	....	961	184	53	....	....	....	....	....
	Azores.....	....	....	....	....	....	....	....	....	....	....
	Sierra Leone.........	....	....	....	65	....	281	....	851	430	558	596
	St. Helena	....	....	....	....	30	4	703	500	1,083	647
	East Indies.........	2,615	2,633	1,887	4,293	3,849	7,643	8,877	8,401	10,934	4,697
	China.....	472	....	....	....	....	699	1,942	3,368	3,057	396
	Canada.............	....	....	....	....	....	....	....	....	....	....
	United States........	....	....	....	....	....	....	....	....	....	....
	British West Indies...	....	....	....	....	12	26	....	....	....	1,074
	Havannah & F. Indies.	....	....	....	....	....	....	....	....	....	....
	Saba................	....	....	....	....	....	....	....	....	....	....
	Rio de Janeiro.	.. ..	....	....	....	....	....	....	....	....	....
	Direct from captured and wrecked slavers.	....	....	....	362	....	....	389	....	....	....
	Malta.....	....	....	....	....	....	....	....	....	....	....
	Kroo Coast..........	....	..	....	....	....	....	....	....	....	....
	Germany............	....	....	....	....	....	....	....	....	....	....
	France..	....	....	....	....	....	....	....	....	....	....
	Not stated...........	....	....	....	....	....	....	....	....	....	....
	Surinam.	....	....	....	....	....	....	....	....	....	....
	Trinidad.....	....	....	....	....	....	....	....	....	....	....
	Total...........	3,902	3,900	3,199	5,338	6,007	9,159	12,974	12,788	15,711	7,820

For reference notes see page 521.

TABLE Ia.—RETURN OF IMMIGRANTS INTRODUCED INTO THE WEST INDIAN COLO-
NIES, BY COUNTRY OF ORIGIN AND ISLES OF IMMIGRATION, SINCE THE
ABOLITION OF SLAVERY, 1834-72 (concluded).

Immigrants introduced into:	from:	1864	1865	1866	1867	1868	1869	1870	1871	1872
ANTIGUA	Madeira............									
	Great Britain........									
	British West Indies....						4			
	Cape Verde									
	China...............									
	Total...........						4			
ST. KITTS	Trinidad...........									
	Sierra Leone........									
	Great Britain......									
	St. Helena..........									
	Madeira............			15	51					
	East Indies.........									
	Total............			15	51					
NEVIS	Madeira............									
TOBAGO	Sierra Leone........									
	St. Helena...........									
	Total............									
DOMINICA	(Liberated Africans from the Don Francisco)................									
	Refugees from French Islands.............									
	British West Indies....									
	Great Britain........									
	Total									
BAHAMAS	Wrecked Slavers......									
HONDURAS...	China...............		474							
	United States........					178	319			
	British West Indies...		129							
	Total...........		603			178	319			
TOTAL TO WEST INDIES	Great Britain........									
	Madeira............		118	149	355	219	240	454	260	
	Cape Verde.........									
	Azores......									
	Sierra Leone........	390	42							
	St. Helena..........					11				
	East Indies.........	3,658	5,975	3,473	9,278	3,895	12,233	7,741	6,163	8,682
	China...............	509	2,758	1,386						
	Canada.............									
	United States........					178	319			
	British W. Indies.....	4,297	2,611	2,089	355	563	980	631	591	
	Havannah & F.Indies..									
	Saba...............									
	Rio de Janeiro.									
	Direct from captured and wrecked slavers...									
	Malta..............									
	Kroo Coast.........									
	Germany...........									
	France.............									
	Not stated......									
	Surinam............									
	Trinidad...........									
	Total...........	8,854	11,504	7,097	10,177	4,996	13,453	8,826	7,014	8,682

TABLE II.—IMMIGRANTS AND LIBERATED AFRICANS INTRODUCED INTO THE WEST INDIA COLONIES, BY COLONY OF IMMIGRATION, 1873-75.

	1873	1874	1875
Jamaica	1,562	1,356	1,250
British Guiana	11,592	7,610	4,907
Trinidad	2,901	1,717	3,275
St. Vincent	.....	333	.....
Nevis	.....	315	.....

TABLE III.—IMMIGRANTS INTO THE WEST INDIES, BY COUNTRY OF ORIGIN, 1873-75.

	1873	1874	1875
Total	11,592	11,331	9,432
Madeira	187	189	114
East Indies	7,512	9,740	8,871
China	.....	388	.....
British West Indies	3,893	1,014	447

TABLE IV.—IMMIGRANTS, LIBERATED AFRICANS AND KROOMEN RETURNED TO THEIR OWN COUNTRIES FROM THE BRITISH WEST INDIA COLONIES, 1843-72.

Years	Jamaica	Br. Guiana	Trinidad	St. Vincent	St. Lucia	Grenada
1843–49	48	868[8]	...	..	...	...
1850	.....	247	...	..	...	...
1851	.....	927	376	..	...	...
1852	.....	519	241	..	...	...
1853	1,167	211	601	..	...	...
1854	429	251	...	..	...	...
1855	.....	...	177	..	...	...
1856	...	260	280	..	...	...
1857	.....	595	343	..	...	...
1858	126	323	359	..	...	...
1859	.....	798	...	..	...	...
1860	.....	...	...	..	...	...
1861	74	...	303	..	...	...
1862	.....	399	...	..	...	...
1863	.....	...	...	..	...	...
1864	.....	447	...	..	...	...
1865	.....	462	521	..	...	...
1866	.....	...	...	..	...	...
1867	4	451	...	..	...	...
1868	.....	...	...	..	298	76
1869	.....	407	372	..	...	...
1870	.....	407[9]	408	..	...	...
1871	925	423[10]	163	34	165	...
1872	421	987[11]	398	..	...	110

For reference notes see page 521.

BAHAMAS

TABLE V.—IMMIGRATION AND EMIGRATION OF ALIENS (CONTRACT LABORERS), 1906-14.

Year	Arrived	Sent home
1906	5,815	5,603
1907	6,497	6,303
1908	3,670	4,064
1909	3,764	3,680
1910	4,185	3,685
1911	4,469	4,094
1912	4,026	4,280
1913	5,095	5,046
1914	2,715	2,792

TABLE VI.—DISTRIBUTION OF EMIGRANT AND IMMIGRANT CITIZENS FROM AND INTO FLORIDA, BY SEX, 1911-15.

	Emigrants			Immigrants		
Year	Total	Males	Females	Total	Males	Females
1911	3,230	2,832	848	1,964	1,521	443
1912	2,628	1,909	719	2,548	1,922	626
1913	3,422	2,547	875	2,396	1,779	617
1914	3,758	2,806	952	3,059	2,302	757
1915	1,511	1,008	503	2,702	1,959	743
1916	2,734	1,945	789	1,895	1,296	599
1917	1,750	1,147	603	2,090	1,524	566
1918	3,521	2,977	544	1,396	1,069	327

BARBADOS

TABLE VII.—IMMIGRATION AND EMIGRATION, 1909-24.

Year	Immigrants	Emigrant
1909	11,764	. . . . .
1910	17,932	. . . . .
1911	17,525	. . . . .
1912	15,218	. . . . .
1913	14,435	15,116
1914	11,898	9,029
1915	8,838	6,614
1916	8,677	6,655
1917	8,262	6,595
1918	8,209	5,013
1919	12,783	3,404
1920	13,168	15,846
1921	13,156	12,949
1922	. . . . .	. . . . .
1923	11,611	11,676[12]
1924	12,427	11,609

For reference notes see page 521.

BERMUDA

TABLE VIII.—IMMIGRATION AND EMIGRATION, 1904-24.

Year	Immigrants[13]		Emigrants to all countries
	From all countries	From the United Kingdom	
1904	936	. .	667
1905	599	. .	937
1906	625	. .	1,485
1907	637	. .	1,255
1908	105	3	238
1909	104	7	179
1910	153	20	102
1911	73	7	157
1912	157	1	94
1913	205	. .	160
1914	338	. .	132
1915	177	. .	103
1916	291	. .	171
1917	. . .	. .	. . .
1918	183	. .	147
1919	58	. .	137
1920	79	. .	125
1921	197	. .	92
1922	467	. .	497
1923	676[14]	. .	507
1924	696[14]	. .	466

BRITISH GUIANA

TABLE IX.—IMMIGRATION, BY COUNTRY OF LAST RESIDENCE, 1868-81.

Year	Total	East Indies	Barbados	Madeira	China
1868	3,306	2,528	559	219	. . .
1869	8,388	4,168	980	240	. . .
1870	6,028	4,943	631	454	. . .
1871	3,557	2,706	591	260	. . .
1872	6,620	3,556	2,697	367	. . .
1873	11,592	7,512	3,893	187	. . .
1874	7,615	6,011	1,024	192	388
1875	4,907	4,346	447	114	. . .
1876	3,525	2,931	542	52	. . .
1877	5,538	4,403	934	201	. . .
1878	10,778	9,101	1,385	290	. . .
1879	7,493	6,055	680	243	515
1880	5,207	4,377	600	230	. . .
1881	4,423	3,956	246	221	. . .

For reference notes see page 521.

BRITISH GUIANA

TABLE X.—EMIGRATION, BY COUNTRY OF FUTURE RESIDENCE, 1869-81..

Year	Total	East Indies	China
1869	526	526	..
1870	421	407	14
1871	438	423	15
1872	1,126	988	138
1873	937	905	32
1874	467	467	..
1875	839	837	2
1876	492	492	..
1877	1,052	1,052	..
1878	1,071	1,071	..
1879	1,122	1,122	..
1880	1,583	1,582	1
1881	1,566	1,566	..

TABLE XI.—IMMIGRATION FROM INDIA OF INDENTURED IMMIGRANTS (COOLIES), BY SEX, AND OTHER IMMIGRANTS, 1882-1900.

Year	Total	Males	Females	Immigrants from India at their own expense	Grand total
1882	3,165	2,211	954	..	3,165
1883	2,497	1,720	777	..	2,497
1884	4,707	3,187	1,520	..	4,707
1885	7,258	5,061	2,197	46	7,304
1886	3,511	2,350	1,161	56	3,567
1887	4,356	3,002	1,354	35	4,391
1888	2,892	1,968	924	16	2,908
1889	3,510	2,452	1,058	37	3,547
1890	4,574	3,102	1,472	43	4,617
1891	4,978	3,323	1,655	29	5,007
1892	4,658	3,175	1,483	35	4,693
1893	5,236	3,621	1,615	..	5,236
1894	7,160	4,971	2,189	29	7,189
1895	2,412	1,642	770	13	2,425
1896	2,380	1,556	824	28	2,408
1897	1,194	806	388	11	1,205
1898	2,387	1,607	780	12	2,399
1899	4,274	2,971	1,303	27	4,301
1900	4,464	2,942	1,522	6	4,470

TABLE XII.—EMIGRATION TO THE EAST INDIES (COOLIES), BY SEX, 1882-1900.

Year	Total	Males	Females
1882	1,109[15]	700	388
1883	1,482[16]	1,003	464
1884	1,554	1,020	534
1885	1,761	1,166	595
1886	1,889	1,237	652
1887	1,420	949	471
1888	1,938	1,305	633
1889	2,042	1,309	733
1890	2,125	1,373	752
1891	2,151	1,431	720
1892	2,014	1,342	672
1893	1,848	1,221	627
1894	1,998	1,350	648
1895	2,071	1,289	782
1896	2,059	1,365	694
1897	1,529	1,098	431
1898	1,238	850	388
1899	1,145	817	328
1900	1,017	726	291

TABLE XIII.—IMMIGRANTS AND EMIGRANTS FROM ALL COUNTRIES AND INDENTURED EAST INDIANS, 1900-24.

Year[17]	Immigrants		Emigrants	
	From all countries	East Indian indentured	To all countries	Returned East Indian
1900	. . . . .	4,464	. . . . .	1,017
1901	. . . . .	4,228	. . . . .	1,150
1902	. . . . .	1,947	. . . . .	1,684
1903	. . . . .	2,967	. . . . .	1,802
1904	. . . . .	1,314	. . . . .	1,625
1905	. . . . .	2,704	. . . . .	2,762
1906	. . . . .	2,257	. . . . .	1,982
1907	. . . . .	1,855	. . . . .	1,837
1908	. . . . .	1,799	. . . . .	1,366
1909	. . . . .	2,512	. . . . .	1,392
1910	. . . . .	2,174	. . . . .	1,720
1911	. . . . .	1,768	. . . . .	1,069
1912	. . . . .	2,206	. . . . .	759
1913	14,338	1,346	12,378	681
1914	13,149	819	10,436	742
1915	9,985	1,165	8,661	. . . . .
1916	10,679	1,220	9,032	. . . . .
1917	10,464	825	9,708	. . . . .
1918	10,809	. . . . .	9,013	. . . . .
1919	10,416	. . . . .	10,958	. . . . .
1920	13,155	. . . . .	13,765	. . . . .
1921	10,409	. . . . .	10,783	473
1922	9,009	. . . . .	8,991	211
1923	9,460	. . . . .	8,719	846
1924	9,358	1,047	9,391	1,391

For reference notes see page 521.

TABLE XIV.—DISTRIBUTION OF IMMIGRANTS AND EMIGRANTS, BY SEX AND NATIONALITY OR RACE, 1924.

Nationality or race	Immigrants			Emigrants		
	Males	Females	Total	Males	Females	Total
Total..........	6,895	2,463	9,358	6,714	2,677	9,391
Europeans other than Portuguese..........	1,035	473	1,508	1,031	473	1,504
Portuguese.........	267	172	439	308	233	541
East Indians[18].......	877	170	1,047	793	219	1,012
East Indian immigrants.............	....	....	....	270	109	379
Chinese.............	288	71	359	317	90	407
Blacks..............	2,964	914	3,878	2,550	874	3,424
Mixed..............	1.464	663	2,127	1,445	679	2,124

JAMAICA

TABLE XV.—IMMIGRATION AND EMIGRATION, 1900-22.

Year[17]	Immigrants		Emigrants
	From all countries	East Indians indentured	To all countries
1900	.....	661	......
1901	......	...	......
1902	3,905	...	3,124
1903	3,212	659	3,257
1904	2,846	.	5,922
1905	11,310	812	15,233
1906	.....	814	......
1907	......	609	......
1908	17,496	417	18,329
1909	16,680	...	19,672
1910	9,121	1,118	13,977
1911	18,495	813	18,320
1912	27,163	1,985	28,957
1913	23,925	293	26,529
1914	15,218	...	12,330
1915	10,539	...	12,868
1916	7,616	617	10,163
1917	10,194	...	18,869
1918	6,586[19]	...	10,720[19]
1919	13,690	...	28,070
1920	32,496	...	30,259
1921[20]	25,445	...	22,887
1922[20]	14,197	...	13,002
1923[20]	12,116	...	17,031
1924[20]	5,247	...	7,284

For reference notes see page 521.

TRINIDAD AND TOBAGO

TABLE XVI.—TOTAL NUMBER OF COOLIES INTRODUCED INTO AND SENT AWAY FROM TRINIDAD AT THE PUBLIC EXPENSE, 1868-1900.[21]

Year	Arrivals	Departures	Year	Arrivals	Departures
1868	3,267	. . .	1885	1,706	614
1869	2,202	. . .	1886	2,185	544
1870[22]	1,889	. . .	1887	2,179	680
1871	1,508	157	1888	1,860	435
1872	3,604	398	1889	3,252	668
1873	2,897	. . .	1890	2,915	603
1874	2,061	. . .	1891	2,908	. . .
1875	3,274	2	1892	3,254	696
1876	1,517	480	1893	1,927	706
1877	1,636	466	1894	2,519	707
1878	3,057	477	1895	2,766	949
1879	2,134	. . .	1896	3,087	712
1880	3,123	457	1897	1,834	747
1881	2,655	473	1898	1,292	746
1882	2,629	5	1899	1,171	720
1883	2,053	511	1900	646	653
1884	3,147	677			

TABLE XVII.—IMMIGRATION AND EMIGRATION OF INDENTURED EAST INDIANS, 1900–24.

Year[17]	Immigrants	Emigrants	Year	Immigrants	Emigrants
1900	627	710	1911	3,181	526
1901	2,553	735	1912	2,419	640
1902	2,348	750	1913	1,189	816
1903	2,458	721	1914	443	. . .
1904	1,265	728	1915	624	580
1905	3,796	904	1916	1,286	744
1906	2,502	783	1917	707	. . .
1907	1,860	752	1922	*	1,075
1908	2,445	726	1923	*.	994
1909	2,511	588	1924	*	886
1910	3,228	622	. . . .	. . . .	. . .

TABLE XVIII.—IMMIGRATION AND EMIGRATION, (TOTAL AND UNITED KINGDOM), 1918-21.

Year	Immigrants		Emigrants	
	From the United Kingdom	From all countries	To the United Kingdom	To all countries
1918	88	11,933	70	11,177
1919	892	19,703	352	16,474
1920	867	20,157	403	18,054
1921	895	20,948	707	17,882
1922	800	18,957	853	16,725
1923	866	17,645	841	19,309

For reference notes see page 521.

General Reports of the Emigration Commissioners for the years 1850 (p. 130), 1858 (p. 100), 1861 (p. 81), and 1873 (pp. 64 and 76-77). London.

Tables I and IV.

Colonisation Circular, issued by Her Majesty's Colonial Land and Emigration Commissioners, No. 34. London, 1877, pp. 399-400.

Tables II and III.

Statistical Tables relating to the Colonial and other Possessions of the United Kingdom. London. Parts XIV-XVII.

Tables IX-XII and XVI.

Statistical Abstract for the several British Overseas Dominions and Protectorates. Statistical Department, Board of Trade. London, 1914, 1922, 1924, 1926.

Tables VII, VIII, XIII, XV, XVII and XVIII (years 1900-23).

Colonial Reports (Annual), London:

Bahamas, for the years 1910-24.

Tables V and VI.

Barbados, for the years 1910-24.

Table VII (years 1909-12 and 1923).

Bermuda, for 1923 and 1924.

Table VIII (years 1923 and 1924).

British Guiana, for 1921 and 1922.

Table XIII (years 1921 and 1922).

Jamaica, years 1923-24.

Report of the Immigration Agent-General for British Guiana for the year 1923, Georgetown, 1925, p. 2.

Table XIII (year 1923).

Information supplied by the British Government (Ministry of Labor).
Tables VII (years 1923 and 1924); VIII (years 1922 and 1924); XIII (year 1924) and XVII (years 1922-24).

Information supplied by the British Government (Foreign Office).
Tables XIII (year 1922); XV (year 1922).

(There is frequently a discrepancy between the figures given by the different sources.)
[1] Includes 205 Chinese brought from Panama.
[2] Of this number, 1 man, 3 women, 2 boys and 3 infants were from Teneriffe.
[3] During the period 1835 to 1842, 208 immigrants came from Malta and 70 from the United States. During the period 1843 to 1856, 21 immigrants came from Great Britain. These figures are not included in the annual totals.
[4] During the period 1834 to 1842, there arrived at St. Vincent, 136 immigrants, the country of origin of whom is not stated.
[5] Received from a French vessel stranded at Barbuda.
[6] Previously indicated as coming from the Kroo Coast.
[7] The annual totals to the West Indies do not include the totals for the period 1834 to 1842 for St. Vincent and Dominica.
[8] This figure includes 550 Negroes and liberated Africans.
[9] Plus 14 Chinese not included in this figure.
[10] Plus 1 family of 15 Chinese.
[11] Plus 138 Chinese.

[11b]After 1918 no full statistics of the above were given; only the following statement was made concerning immigration and emigration (Colonial Report for the years 1916 to 1924.

1919 Emigrants exceeded immigrants by............3,243
1920   do   do   do 2,170
1921   do   do   do   192
1922 Immigrants exceeded emigrants by............ 443

The 1923-24 Report does not contain the section "Vital Statistic" from which the 1919 to 1922 figures were taken.

[12]Of which number 2,535 emigrated to United States; about 307 of the remainder departed for Cuba to work on the sugar crop.

[13]Declared settlers.

[14]Including 97 immigrants subject to Immigration Law, in 1923 and 103 in 1924.

[15]Including 21 infants, sex not stated.

[16]Including 15 infants, sex not stated.

[17]For 1900-14 the figures refer to the 12 months ended March 31 of the years following those stated. For 1915 the figures refer to the nine months ended December 31 of the year stated. The other years are calendar years.

[18]Persons of East Indian origin, but born or residing in British Guiana.

[19]Excluding troops.

[20]The *Colonial Report for Jamaica* for the years 1923 and 1924 gives the following figures:

Years	Emigrants	Immigrants
1921	15,199	17,463
1922	6,733	6,931
1923	7,778	5,029
1924	7,284	5,247

[21]These figures differ from those given in tables I and II.

[22]Total number of immigrants from all parts.

*The notes are not arranged according to pages but follow the sequence of the countries of immigration running through several pages.

CUBA

Statistics are compiled in Cuba not only of the movement of travellers, but also of immigration. These have been published since 1902 showing nationality, country of departure, and other particulars. The definition of the term, 'Immigrant' is the same as in the United States.

Cuban statistics are published annually by the Finance Department. (*Immigración y Movimiento de Pasajeros en el Año 1919*. Havana.)

TABLE I.—DISTRIBUTION OF IMMIGRANT ALIENS ADMITTED, BY SEX, 1901-24.

Year	Total	Males	Females
1901	22,894	19,201	3,693
1902	11,986	9,496	2,490
1903	18,054	14,929	3,125
1904	29,116	24,372	4,744
1905	54,219	45,807	8,412
1906	34,556	28,141	6,415
1907	32,436	26,670	5,766
1908	27,999	22,369	5,630
1909	31,286	25,425	5,861
1910	37,764	31,105	6,659
1911	38,053	31,055	6,998
1912	38,296	30,863	7,433
1913	43,507	34,904	8,603
1914	25,911	20,527	5,384
1915	32,795	26,476	6,319
1916	55,121	47,354	7,767
1917	57,097	49,587	7,510
1918	37,321	30,369	6,952
1919	80,488	71,100	9,388
1920	174,221	163,949	10,272
1921	58,948	49,819	9,129
1922	25,993	19,468	6,525
1923	75,461	63,348	12,113
1924	85,288	75,442	9,846

TABLE II.—DISTRIBUTION OF IMMIGRANT ALIENS ADMITTED, BY AGE, 1911-24.

Year	Under 14 years	14 to 45 years	45 and over
1911	3,622	31,813	2,618
1912	3,550	31,973	2,773
1913	4,136	36,893	2,478
1914	1,962	23,115	834
1915	2,275	28,930	1,590
1916	3,706	48,990	2,425
1917	2,818	52,018	2,261
1918	1,638	34,583	1,100
1919	2,143	74,959	3,386
1920	2,061	170,618	1,542
1921	2,782	55,470	696
1922	1,762	23,757	474
1923	2,425	71,144	1,892
1924	1,883	82,530	875

TABLE III.—Distribution of immigrant aliens admitted, by occupation, 1911-24.

Year	Total	Agri-culture	Industry and mining	Transport and commerce	Domestic service and general labor	Liberal professions and public services	Other occupations, none, or unknown
1911	38,053	6,236	2,064	3,558	16,659	353	9,183
1912	38,296	5,750	2,075	3,572	16,913	455	9,531
1913	43,507	7,997	2,094	3,842	18,796	484	10,294
1914	25,911	4,124	1,148	3,009	10,650	590	6,390
1915	32,795	7,467	1,078	2,373	14,340	382	7,155
1916	55,121	18,046	2,130	3,337	23,499	502	7,607
1917	57,097	20,191	1,472	1,748	26,692	302	6,692
1918	37,321	14,898	3,022	1,505	12,611	263	5,022
1919	80,488	11,812	5,724	1,763	52,173	174	8,842
1920	174,221	31,398	4,226	1,945	131,031	240	5,381
1921	58,948	12,563	2,188	2,437	34,160	291	7,309
1922	25,993	296	1,408	1,740	17,344	227	4,978
1923	75,461	17,080	2,149	1,437	45,746	228	8,821
1924	85,288	4,866	1,398	1,276	70,234	87	7,427

TABLE IV.—DISTRIBUTION OF IMMIGRANT ALIENS ADMITTED, BY NATIONALITY, 1901-24.

Nationality	1901	1902	1903	1904	1905	1906	1907	1908	1909	1910	1911	1912
Albanian												
African												
German	145	69	82	138	181	108	72	134	103	113	128	119
North American	650	1,063	1,281	1,549	1,861	2,097	1,769	2,074	2,146	1,767	1,369	1,642
South American	165	121	150	188	230	193	113	121	184	155	134	153
West Indian	166	73	219	359	811	1,559	1,735	1,229	1,155	2,022	1,484	78
Armenian											29	38
Arab	31	29	31	48	168	178	23	17	19	18	18	2
Australian												
Austrian											12	25
Hungarian											21	12
Belgian												1
Bulgarian												44
Canadian											12	26
Central American												20
Corean												
Chinese	756	145	18	132	152	7					46	118
Czechoslovak												
Dominican												5
Egyptian												
Spanish	17,330	8,877	14,691	23,759	47,902	26,923	25,330	21,305	24,662	30,913	32,104	32,531
English	698	403	332	413	460	1,017	1,870	1,656	1,560	993	932	545
Irish							4	11	20			8
Scotch											2	3
Filipino												
Finnish												1
French	264	171	172	255	350	320	291	272	240	259	263	257
Greek							64	79	40	14	13	14
Haitian												111
Hawaiian												
Hebrew											16	13
Netherlander											15	91
East Indian												
Italian	380	222	267	262	317	221	223	233	194	200	146	195
Yugoslav											2	831
Jamaican												5
Japanese												
Lithuanian												
Mexican	256	127	149	221	279	145					220	235
Palestinian											1	1
Persian											4	4
Polish	781	84	92	363	572	816					464	411
Porto-Rican											24	65
Portuguese												
Rumanian											1	1
Russian											12	28

TABLE IV.—DISTRIBUTION OF IMMIGRANT ALIENS ADMITTED, BY NATIONALITY, 1901-24 (continued).

Nationality	1901	1902	1903	1904	1905	1906	1907	1908	1909	1910	1911	1912
Syrian	295	232	115	313	405	236	......	......	......	......	217	209
Danish	45	32	48	107	112	98	101	85	77	103	65	34
Norwegian											33	32
Swedish											20	46
Swiss	......	......	......	......	......	......	......	......	......	......	12	18
Ukrainian	......	......	......	......	......	......	......	......	......	......	......	......
Turkish	105	31	38	100	152	289	248	190	277	210	223	320
Latvian	......	......	......	......	......	......	......	......	......	......	......	......
European (not specified)	......	......	......	......	......	......	75	103	82	92	11	......
Other	218	219	159	260	267	349	518	490	527	905	......	1
Total	22,285[1]	11,898[1]	17,844[1]	28,467[1]	54,219	34,556	32,436	27,999	31,286	37,764	38,053	38,296

For reference notes see page 533.

TABLE IV.—DISTRIBUTION OF IMMIGRANT ALIENS ADMITTED, BY NATIONALITY, 1901-24 (continued).

Nationality	1913	1914	1915	1916	1917	1918	1919	1920	1921	1922	1923	1924
Albanian										6	21	11
African	141	92	65	55	26	4	5	115	142	82	158	432
German	1,371	958	910	1,209	1,013	771	1,227	1,065	1,003	776	689	599
North American	222	170	187	336	233	313	709	765	238	124	314	390
South American	22	38	115	27	195	37		131	591		103	1,185
West Indian										35		
Armenian	1	2	10	20	9		3	45	26	35	103	237
Arab	71	17	16	15	17			15	33	15	14	15
Australian	1											
Hungarian	30	22	16	15		5	12	11		15		2
Belgian	3	8	11	10	15	5	12	11	4	20	5	2
Bulgarian	7	1		5	3		2			4	13	552
Canadian	28	29	16	19	18	14	22	11	2	9	13	13
Central American	33		72	109	197	249	460	159	36	44	9	321
Corean		2		7								2
Chinese	9	1		6	3	237	1,236	9,203	1,858	3	188	263
Czechoslovak											7	
Dominican	91	88	80	129	78	208	142	153	86	20	150	443
Egyptian	8	11	1	7		2	7	2	16	75	11	6
Spanish	34,278	20,140	24,501	37,615	34,795	14,293	39,573	94,294	26,340	16,397	46,439	41,070
English	997	350	329	326	567	255	745	1,320	561	537	464	779
Irish	6	5	3	5	4	1	1	3			3	
Scotch	10	5	4	3			1	3			3	
Filipino	2	1		3	3							
Finnish	4	1	4	2	4	7	1	4	5	1	3	5
French	273	225	130	169	173	118	188	504	366	210	215	232
Greek	22	17	12	34	30	14	36	57	35	142	473	913
Haitian	1,200	98	2,453	4,922	10,136	10,640	10,044	35,971	12,483	639	11,088	21,013
Hawaiian									8	1		
Hebrew												
Netherlander	12	11	8	30	26	100	57	318	39	19	21	66
East Indian	90	48	24	40	2	1	7		1		1	200
Italian	239	242	113	164	77	51	100	316	316	356	2,053	1,437
Yugoslav									1		182	365
Jamaican	2,258	1,791	1,834	7,133	7,889	9,184	24,187	27,088	12,469	4,455	5,844	5,086
Japanese	2	2	3	262	34	12	31	14	87	23	19	187
Lithuanian	2											369
Mexican	279	452	714	662	526	244	263	378	199	142	218	304
Palestinian					4				2	269	10	566
Persian			2									14
Polish							2	5	1	349	1,581	2,554
Porto-Rican	635	527	840	1,277	805	395	1,005	629	388	259	420	444
Portuguese	99	45	38	227	52	9	132	240	403	108	444	442
Rumanian	6		8				5	4	46	294	169	951
Russian	97	19	33	29	15	8	3	19	371	294	1,139	1,005

TABLE IV.—DISTRIBUTION OF IMMIGRANT ALIENS ADMITTED, BY NATIONALITY, 1901-24 (concluded).

Nationality	1913	1914	1915	1916	1917	1918	1919	1920	1921	1922	1923	1924
Syrian	495	197	62	59	23	31	91	637	230	230	1,059	1,373
Danish	65	24	35	99	18	30	63	40	11	12	13	16
Norwegian	13	13	7	10	33	19	12	9	4	12	19	17
Swedish	21	9	12	9	18	19	6	20	20	10	55	31
Swiss	17	21	11	11	12	14	13	71	17	15	68	38
Ukrainian									78	44	158	34
Turkish	336	205	71	68	33	13	79	572	159	137	803	1,148
Latvian												25
European (not specified)	13	27	1	2		18	6	21	16	8		
Other												
Total	43,507	25,911	32,795	55,121	57,097	37,321	80,488	174,221	58,948	25,993	75,461	85,288

TABLE V.—IMMIGRANT ALIENS ADMITTED, BY COUNTRY OF DEPARTURE, 1904-24.

Country	1904	1905	1906	1907	1908	1909	1910	1911	1912	1913	1914
Germany	75	52	41	36	43	42	32	34	54	40	29
Austria										4	4
Belgium									7	2	3
Denmark								8	16	9	2
Spain and Canary Islands	22,308	45,294	24,612	20,007	21,320	22,075	28,380	[2]30,080	[2]30,660	[2]32,140	[2]17,764
France	265	209	208	257	385	370	411	312	233	120	241
Greece									1		32
Netherlands								4	1	1	1
England	27	63	134	95	66	58	64	99	99	59	1
Italy	85	134	76	81	52	7	1	9	17	58	54
Norway								4	4	1	16
Poland										7	6
Portugal								4	12	7	8
Rumania											
Russia											
Serb-Croat-Slovene State											
Sweden										1	
Switzerland								6	8		
Turkey								90	203	244	5
Ukraine											
Other	58	62	236	179	246	130	48				
Total Europe	22,818	45,814	25,307	20,665	22,112	22,682	28,936	30,650	31,315	32,687	18,168
China	42	51							2		
India											
Japan											
Syria	52	174				5			128	439	34
Turkey											
Total Asia	94	225				5			130	439	34
Morocco										2	
Total Africa										2	

For reference notes see page 533.

TABLE V.—IMMIGRANT ALIENS ADMITTED, BY COUNTRY OF DEPARTURE, 1904-24 (continued).

Country	1904	1905	1906	1907	1908	1909	1910	1911	1912	1913	1914
North America									16	8	6
South America	225	252	138	73	447	27	13	198	89	83	57
Dutch West Indies											
British West Indies									21	27	7
French West Indies											
West Indies (not specified)	1,164	1,506	3,700	4,192	3,242	3,359	3,862	2,736	201	25	15
Danish West Indies	63	33	27	20	3	1	45	42	397	35	
Central America (not specified)											468
Barbados											5
Costa Rica										1,010	
Canada								7	12		
United States	2,497	3,274	2,556	1,996	2,649	3,181	3,217	2,469	2,884	2,763	2,901
Haiti								221	172	1,422	120
Honduras, British									3		
Jamaica									1,269	2,716	1,792
Martinique											
Mexico	1,740	2,333	1,859	1,720	1,828	1,144	969	965	873	992	1,217
Panama								141	213	147	100
Porto Rico	515	782	969	916	946	887	722	591	523	943	738
San Domingo								33	174	205	283
Venezuela											
Other countries, not specified									4	2	
Total America	6,204	8,180	9,249	8,917	9,115	8,599	8,828	7,403	6,851	10,378	7,709
Australia											
Hawaii											
Pacific Isles (not specified)											
Philippine Islands										1	
Total Oceania										1	
Grand total	29,116	54,219	34,556	29,572	31,227	31,286	37,764	38,053	38,296	43,507	25,911
Continental immigration	6,204	8,180	9,249	8,917	9,115	8,599	8,828	7,403	6,851	10,378	7,709
Intercontinental immigration	22,912	46,039	25,307	20,655	22,112	22,687	28,936	30,650	31,445	33,129	18,202

TABLE V.—IMMIGRANT ALIENS ADMITTED, BY COUNTRY OF DEPARTURE, 1904-24 (continued).

Country	1915	1916	1917	1918	1919	1920	1921	1922	1923	1924
Germany	16	10	7		1	95	82	77	61	688
Austria	5				1	12	5	9		2
Belgium	2	2				8	1	9	10	
Denmark						13			12	
Spain and Canary Islands	[b]23,183	36,286	33,757	13,378	32,157	94,226	27,027	16,141	46,466	40,191
France	46	37	13		6,311	436	249	327	4,475	10,996
Greece					108	55	5	131	99	2
Netherlands			3	2	25	17	71	6	866	316
England	21	34	3	3	8	344	192	261	502	554
Italy	7	1		2	154	275	111	272	1,226	762
Norway	10				71	13	51	10	7	
Poland				1	4		148	7		289
Portugal					58	243	24	77	151	3
Rumania		1	1	3	3	1	74	253	25	191
Russia					5	14	186	279	305	
Serb-Croat-Slovene State					3	7	5	34	5	
Sweden					2				1	2
Switzerland		3	2		16		4	21	34	
Turkey					77	67	57	109	42	
Ukraine						566	49			
Other					444	70		91	2	
Total Europe	23,290	36,374	33,786	13,389	39,448	96,462	28,341	18,114	54,289	54,026
China	1		7	7	1,100	9,203	1,857			
India				4	1			1	1	105
Japan					13	14		12	6	94
Syria						43	36	16		
Turkey								3	20	
Total Asia	1		7	11	1,114	9,260	1,893	32	27	199
Morocco										
Total Africa										

TABLE V.—IMMIGRANT ALIENS ADMITTED, BY COUNTRY OF DEPARTURE, 1904-24 (continued).

Country	1915	1916	1917	1918	1919	1920	1921	1922	1923	1924
North America	7									
South America	38				151	928	454	134	321	436
Dutch West Indies			93	160	66	444	5		8	8
British West Indies		26		69	98	3,110	171	6	7	15
French West Indies							52		22	
West Indies (not specified)	87	862	656	12	261		5,955			
Danish West Indies			593	659	449	288	62	36	401	203
Central America (not specified)	743	520	629	251						
Barbados										
Costa Rica										
Canada	1,988	2,468	2,237	1,705	2,652	1,387	1,161	993	1,145	1,194
United States	2,416	4,829	9,730	10,870	10,136	36,115	12,043	848	10,966	20,415
Haiti	47		11			133				
Honduras, British										
Jamaica	1,649	6,005	5,866	7,317	23,859	24,461	7,868	5,016	6,127	5,372
Martinique	1	1,324	735	414	453	178	191	228	927	313
Mexico	1,297	666	1,609	1,100	136					
Panama	1,091	1,576	975	629	931	987	452	304	549	581
Porto Rico	134	469	170	379	726	460	290	265	668	297
San Domingo										
Venezuela										
Other countries, not specified				4	2		10	16	2	2,219
Total America	9,498	18,745	23,304	23,569	39,926	68,491	28,714	7,846	21,143	31,045
Australia	2	2						1		
Hawaii				110						18
Pacific Islands (not specified)	4									
Philippine Islands				242		4			2	
Total Oceania	6	2		352		4		1	2	18
Grand total	32,795	55,121	57,097	37,321	80,488	174,221	58,948	25,993	75,461	85,288
Continental immigration	9,498	18,745	23,304	23,569	39,926	68,491	28,714	7,846	21,143	31,045
Intercontinental immigration	23,297	36,376	33,793	13,752	40,562	105,730	30,234	18,147	54,318	54,243

SOURCES

Immigración y Movimiento de Passajeros. Cuban Republic. Secretaria de Hacienda, Statistical Section. Havana, 1916, 1920, 1921, 1925.

Tables I (years 1902-1924); all other tables (years 1911-24).

Statistica della Emigrazione italiana per l'Estero negli anni 1906, 1907, 1908 e 1909, 1910 e 1911. (Roma, 1908, 1910, 1913.)

Tables I (year 1901); IV (years 1901-06); V (years 1904-10).

Conférence internationale de l'Emigration et de l'Immigration. Rome, May 15-31, 1924. Published by the Italian Commissariat-General of Emigration. Rome, 1924, Vol. I, p. 446.

Table IV (years 1907-10).

NOTES

[1]Our source indicates the following number of Cuban arrivals who are not included in our tables: 1901 609; 1902, 88; 1903, 210; 1904, 649.
[2]Refer to Spain only.

GUADELOUPE

TABLE I.— MIGRATION MOVEMENTS OF THE EAST INDIAN POPULATION, 1854-83

Year	Total introduced	Repatriated	Year	Total introduced	Repatriated
1854	314	...	1869	915	...
1855	437	...	1870	884	...
1856	1,071	...	1871	935	344
1857	1,358	...	1872	462	...
1858	1,411	...	1873	1,414	...
1859	1,733	...	1874	1,263	...
1860	808	...	1875	778	...
1861	1,939	65	1876	1,321	...
1862	906	...	1877	1,231	305
1863	1,729	243	1878	2,213	...
1864	636	...	1879	2,141	...
1865	462	297	1880	2,672	...
1866	1,235	...	1881	2,770	...
1867	3,144	...	1882	978	508
1868	1,370	386	1883	1,275	

TABLE II.—PASSENGERS ARRIVED AT GUADELOUPE FROM EUROPE AND DEPARTED FROM GUADELOUPE TO EUROPE, 1923-24.[1]

Year	Passengers from Europe disembarked	Passengers embarked for Europe
1923	772	793
1924	749	910

SOURCES

Notices Coloniales. Paris, 1885. Vol. III, p. 501.

Table I.

Information supplied by the French Government.

Table II.

NOTE

[1]The figures refer to the towns of Pointe à Pitre and Basse-Terre.

MARTINIQUE

TABLE I.—DISTRIBUTION OF EXTRA-EUROPEAN IMMIGRANTS IN 1883

		Came by	
		the *Neva*	the *Cecile*
EAST INDIANS	Males	312	309
	Females	124	116
	Children { Males	13	19
	Females	11	21
	Total..................	460	465

TABLE II.—DISTRIBUTION OF IMMIGRANTS[1], BY SEX AND NATIONALITY, 1923-24.

Nationality	1923		1924	
	Males	Females	Males	Females
English.............	2	2	2	3
Netherlander.......	1	.	1	.
Italian	9	.	9	.
Venezuelan.........	3	.	3	.
Total.........	15	2	15	3

For reference notes see page 536.

TABLE III.—DISTRIBUTION OF EMIGRANTS², BY SEX, AGE AND COUNTRY OF DESTINATION, 1923-24.

Year	Total	Age and sex of emigrants								Country of destination							
		Up to 15 years		16-20 years		21-40 years		over 40 years		Belgium	Brazil	Colombia	Colon	United States	Panama	Venezuela	International passengers
		Males	Females	Males	Females	Males	Females	Males	Females								
1923	238	·	6	12	18	74	100	12	22	·	·	42	8	4	4	92	88
1924	272	·	9	13	23	72	86	28	35	3	2	15	18	35	3	115	81

SOURCE

Notices Coloniales.   Paris, 1885. p. 312.

Table I.

Information supplied by the French Government (General Secretariat, Colony of Martinique).

Tables II-III.

NOTES

¹Mostly for commercial purposes.
²Natives emigrating for work.

TABLE I.—IMMIGRATION OF ALIENS,[1] BY COUNTRY OF LAST RESIDENCE, AND EMIGRATION OF ALIENS, 1853-1924.

YEAR	IMMIGRANTS							EMI-GRANTS
	Total	Dutch East Indies	Madeira	China	West Indies	Nether-lands	British India	
1853–1862	770	8	275	487	....	..	....	....
1863–1872	4,625	21	205	2,015	2,382	2	....	....
1873–1882	6,964	94	....	....	214	87	6,569	....
1883–1892	8,806	94	....	....	79	..	8,633	3,401
1893	1,092	....	....	....	....	..	1,092 ⎫	
1894	1,788	582	....	....	....	..	1,206 ⎬ 836	
1895	1,615	....	....	....	....	..	1,615 ⎪	
1896	1,169	....	....	....	....	..	1,169 ⎭	
1897	898	898	....	....	....	..	....	....
1898	1,176	560	....	....	....	..	616	743
1899	669	55	....	....	....	..	614	214
1900	1,375	1,375	....	....	....	..	....	265
1901	1,325	1,325	....	....	....	..	....	....
1902	1,562	231	....	....	....	..	1,331	....
1903	1,263	609	....	....	....	..	654	717
1904	422	170	....	....	....	..	252	402
1905	699	526	....	....	....	..	173	883
1906	1,016	384	....	....	....	..	632	339
1907	2,924	1,250	....	....	....	..	1,674	431
1908	2,811	944	....	....	....	..	1,867	217
1909	2,072	648	....	....	....	..	1,424	501
1910	949	471	....	....	....	..	478	223
1911	....	....	....	....	....	..	....	....
1912	1,691	487	....	....	....	..	1,204	413
1913	1,329	378	....	....	....	..	951	668
1914	1,740	173	....	....	....	..	1,567	395
915	....	....	....	....	....	..	....	....
1916	303	....	....	....	....	..	303	....
917	1, 87	1,187	....	....	....	..	....	....
1918	1,175	1,175	....	....	....	..	....	....
1919	2,126	2,126	....	....	....	..	....	1,302
1920	3,559	3,559	....	....	....	..	....	1,312
1921	....	....	....	....	....	..	....	886
1922	1,975	1,975	....	....	....	..	....	....
1923	657	657	....	....	....	..	....	....
1924	1,135	1,135	....	....	....	..	....	....

TABLE II.—DISTRIBUTION OF JAVANESE IMMIGRANTS AND EMIGRANTS, BY SEX, AGE AND OCCUPATION, 1923.

Total	Sex		Age			Occupation					
	Males	Females	Up to 15 years	16–45 years	46 years and over	Agri-culture	Indus-try and mining	Trans-port and com-merce	Domes-tic ser-vice and general labor	Public services and liberal profes-sions	Other occupa-tions, none or unknown
Immigrants											
657	479	178[2]	26	631	..	450	41	11	27	..	128
Emigrants											
205	142	63	7	185	13	145	..	..	..	..	60[3]

SOURCES

Jaarcijfers voor het Koninkrijk der Nederlanden Kolonien. 1899 and 1919. The Hague. Table I (years 1853-99, 1913-19).

Information received from the Central Statistical Bureau of the Netherlands. The Hague. Tables I (years 1897-1912, 1920-24); II (year 1923).

NOTES

[1] Immigration includes only persons intending to work on the plantations.
[2] Including 47 women not engaged, who accompany their husbands.
[3] Including unemployables.

VENEZUELA

TABLE I.—IMMIGRATION AND EMIGRATION, 1919-21, 1924.

Year	Immigrants	Emigrants
1919	12,433	12,879
1920	11,178	11,883
1921	10,086	9,152
1924	13,070	11,170

SOURCE

Statesman's Year-Book, 1923. London, 1923, pp. 1403 and 1926, London, 1926, p 1403.

Table I (years 1919-21, 1924).

ARGENTINA

Migration statistics were compiled until May 30, 1872, by the Port Prefect of Buenos Aires, after that date by the Immigration Commissariat. The movement of alien passengers who arrived in or left the country directly by sea has been recorded since 1857. As a result, in certain tables first class passenger could be separated from the commencement, and this permitted second and third class passengers to be distinguished as "immigrants." In the reports which relate to those immigrants who did not arrive at Buenos Aires by a direct route, but reached Argentina by river navigation (via Montevideo), the passenger classes began to be recorded April 15, 1880. Hence for the period prior to that date it has been impossible to indicate separately second and third class river passengers ("immigrants"). Tourists and passengers travelling from one river station to another were also included in the statistics. As a result, the figures in table VI have only a slight relation to overseas immigrants. The latter were not separately recorded until after July 1, 1923 (12,044 for 1923, and 15,027 for 1924). (Information supplied on May 13, 1926, by Mr. J. Ramos, formerly Commissioner-General for Immigration.) In determining the aggregate overseas migration before 1924, it is advisable, therefore, to exclude those arriving and departing by the river route.

TABLE I.—DISTRIBUTION, BY SEX, OF IMMIGRANT ALIENS (SECOND AND THIRD CLASS PASSENGERS), BY SEA, 1857-1924.

Year	Total	Males	Females	Year	Total	Males	Females
1857	4,951	3,929	1,022	1891	28,266	18,228	10,038
1858	4,658	3,668	990	1892	39,973	26,369	13,604
1859	4,735	3,985	750	1893	52,067	34,952	17,115
1860	5,656	4,520	1,136	1894	54,720	37,196	17,524
1861	6,301	5,041	1,260	1895	61,226	42,410	18,816
1862	6,716	5,465	1,251	1896	102,673	75,079	27,594
1863	10,408	8,204	2,204	1897	72,978	51,547	21,431
1864	11,682	8,916	2,766	1898	67,130	47,635	19,495
1865	11,767	9,009	2,758	1899	84,442	62,235	22,207
1866	13,696	10,293	3,403	1900	84,851	61,900	22,951
1867	13,225	10,031	3,194	1901	90,127	65,061	25,066
1868	25,919	19,950	5,969	1902	57,992	40,479	17,513
1869	28,958	22,488	6,470	1903	75,227	53,833	21,394
1870	30,898	22,592	8,306	1904	125,567	90,080	35,487
1871	15,088	11,926	3,162	1905	177,117	130,563	46,554
1872	26,218	20,800	5,418	1906	252,536	186,514	66,022
1873	48,382	31,572	16,810	1907	209,103	151,918	57,185
1874	40,674	28,659	12,015	1908	255,710	185,134	70,576
1875	18,332	12,994	5,338	1909	231,084	164,493	66,591
1876	14,532	10,549	3,983	1910	289,640	213,169	76,471
1877	14,675	10,546	4,129	1911	225,772	162,007	63,765
1878	23,624	16,599	7,025	1912	323,403	237,989	85,414

(continued on next page)

TABLE I.—Distribution, by sex, of immigrant aliens (second and third class passengers), by sea, 1857-1924 (continued).

Year	Total	Males	Females	Year	Total	Males	Females
1879	32,717	22,778	9,939	1913	302,047	215,871	86,176
1880	26,643	17,124	9,519	1914	115,321	76,217	39,104
1881	31,431	19,867	11,564	1915	45,290	27,957	17,333
1882	41,041	27,253	13,788	1916	32,990	19,680	13,310
1883	52,472	35,174	17,298	1917	18,064	10,909	7,155
1884	49,623	33,294	16,329	1918	13,701	8,358	5,343
1885	80,618	59,329	21,289	1919	41,299	26,756	14,543
1886	65,655	46,683	18,972	1920	87,032	56,110	30,922
1887	94,608	67,745	26,863	1921	98,086	65,382	32,704
1888	129,115	92,540	36,575	1922	129,263	91,364	37,899
1889	218,744	150,275	68,469	1923[1]	195,063	141,680	53,383
1890	77,815	53,027	24,788	1924	159,939	110,446	49,493

TABLE II.—Distribution, by age, of immigrant aliens (second and third class passengers), by sea (in decades), 1857-1924.

Year	Total	Up to 1 year	1 to 7 years	8 to 12 years	13 to 20 years	21 to 30 years	31 to 40 years	41 to 50 years	51 to 60 years	Over 60 years
1857–1860	20,000	961	1,468	1,047	4,496	6,153	2,966	1,984	684	241
1861–1870	159,570	1,472	2,124	8,589	30,217	67,080	28,112	15,677	4,555	1,744
1871–1880	260,885	3,756	23,419	15,120	44,555	101,919	42,014	22,175	5,388	2,539
1881–1890	841,122	12,111	70,225	47,324	151,847	311,315	141,808	75,477	23,514	7,501
1891–1900	648,326	9,547	57,758	35,128	118,703	223,434	113,041	66,240	18,058	6,417
1901–1910	1,764,103	25,828	158,806	95,375	320,821	603,898	308,489	181,364	51,502	18,018
1911–1920	1,204,919	12,014	100,617	64,102	270,867	369,797	211,798	119,653	41,281	14,792
1921–1924	582,531	6,637	32,319	20,607	113,331	232,095	100,861	47,381	21,320	7,800
1857–1924	5,481,276	72,326	446,736	287,292	1,054,837	1,916,691	949,089	529,951	166,302	59,052

For reference notes see page 547.

TABLE IIa.—DISTRIBUTION, BY SEX AND AGE, OF IMMIGRANT ALIENS (SECOND AND THIRD CLASS PASSENGERS), BY SEA, 1921-24.

Age	1921			1922			1923			1924		
	Total	Males	Females	Total	Males	Females	Total	Males	Females	Total	Males	Females
Up to 4 years	4,737	2,683	2,054	6,371	3,366	3,005	9,460	4,977	4,483	10,224	5,318	4,906
5 to 13 "	5,492	2,812	2,680	7,237	3,901	3,336	10,871	5,815	5,056	9,168	4,948	4,220
14 to 21 "	21,188	15,334	5,854	27,890	19,990	7,900	42,300	30,676	11,624	36,178	25,966	10,212
22 to 30 "	38,354	25,958	12,396	48,898	38,193	10,705	73,299	56,627	16,672	53,322	37,901	15,421
31 to 40 "	15,783	9,952	5,831	22,460	14,445	8,015	34,571	26,395	8,176	28,047	20,207	7,840
41 to 50 "	7,751	5,723	2,028	10,213	7,536	2,677	15,403	11,430	3,973	14,014	10,382	3,632
51 to 60 "	3,432	2,220	1,212	4,523	2,959	1,564	6,828	4,537	2,291	6,537	4,360	2,177
61 to 70 "	1,088	565	523	1,348	803	545	1,888	990	898	1,943	1,067	876
71 years and over	261	135	126	323	171	152	443	233	210	506	297	209
Total	98,086	65,382	32,704	129,263	91,364	37,899	195,063	141,680	53,383	159,939	110,446	49,493

TABLE III.—DISTRIBUTION, BY OCCUPATION, OF IMMIGRANT ALIENS (SECOND AND THIRD CLASS PASSENGERS), BY SEA (IN DECADES), 1857-1924.

Year	Total	Agriculture	Industry and mining	Transport and commerce	Domestic service and general labor	Liberal professions and public services	Other occupations, none, or unknown
1857 to 1860	20,000	9,421	1,105	823	1,850	124	6,677
1861 to 1870	159,570	77,671	4,699	4,053	16,373	554	56,220
1871 to 1880	260,885	100,701	18,319	8,653	24,780	2,064	106,368
1881 to 1890	841,122	454,919	67,686	26,217	93,115	5,288	193,897
1891 to 1900	648,326	288,429	50,613	29,068	127,415	4,364	148,437
1901 to 1910	1,764,103	562,884	161,092	107,983	493,685	14,248	424,211
1911 to 1920	1,204,919	211,061	99,858	75,289	449,196	16,789	352,726
1921 to 1924	582,351[2]	142,838	71,187	48,888	125,120	11,854	181,864

TABLE IIIa.—Distribution, by occupation, of immigrant aliens (second and third class passengers), by sea, 1921-24.

Year	Total	Agri-culture	Industry and mining	Transport and commerce	Domestic service and general labor	Liberal and public services	Other occupations, none, or unknown
1921	98,086	11,146	7,311	11,551	34,003	2,900	31,175
1922	129,263	16,030	10,867	12,506	46,299	3,967	39,594
1923	195,063	59,375	31,574	13,795	27,865	2,967	59,487
1924	159,939	56,287	23,237	11,112	16,953	2,659	49,691

TABLE IV.—Emigration of aliens (second and third class passengers) by sea, 1871-1924.

Year	Total	Year	Total	Year	Total
1871	10,686	1889	40,649	1907	90,190
1872	9,153	1890	48,794	1908	85,412
1873	18,236	1891	72,380	1909	94,644
1874	21,340	1892	29,893	1910	97,854
1875	25,578	1893	26,055	1911	120,709
1876	13,487	1894	20,586	1912	120,260
1877	18,350	1895	20,390	1913	156,829
1878	14,860	1896	20,415	1914	178,684
1879	23,696	1897	31,192	1915	111,459
1880	20,377	1898	30,802	1916	73,348
1881	22,374	1899	38,397	1917	50,995
1882	8,720	1900	38,334	1918	24,075
1883	9,510	1901	48,697	1919	42,279
1884	14,444	1902	44,558	1920	57,187
1885	14,585	1903	40,610	1921	44,638
1886	13,907	1904	38,923	1922	45,993
1887	13,630	1905	42,869	1923	46,810
1888	16,842	1906	60,124	1924	46,105

TABLE V.—Distribution, by nationality, of immigrant and emigrant aliens (second and third class passengers), by sea, 1857-1924.

Year	ITALIAN		SPANISH		FRENCH		BRITISH	
	Immi-grants	Emi-grants	Immi-grants	Emi-grants	Immi-grants	Emi-grants	Immi-grants	Emi-grants
1857	3,021	1,216	854	356	276	138	98	16
1858	2,976	1,151	784	531	193	109	112	37
1859	3,009	1,612	802	288	251	125	149	130
1860	3,349	1,633	930	376	385	155	159	138
1861	4,807	2,646	786	369	148	53	127	66
1862	4,902	2,514	934	480	203	106	141	72
1863	7,836	3,979	1,092	503	397	195	164	85
1864	8,422	5,507	1,608	818	426	213	219	116
1865	7,697	3,853	1,981	1,010	513	218	213	110
1866	9,212	4,861	2,074	274	609	341	418	217
1867	7,221	4,133	3,186	789	991	484	526	361
1868	18,937	9,667	3,834	950	1,223	722	744	289
1869	21,419	12,902	3,744	1,055	1,465	729	892	455
1870	23,101	13,854	3,388	812	2,396	1,018	453	235
1871	8,170	5,518	2,554	1,113	1,988	1,281	694	475
1872	14,769	9,977	4,411	1,822	4,602	3,164	968	671
1873	26,878	18,845	9,185	4,018	7,431	5,001	1,612	980
1874	23,904	16,910	8,272	3,570	5,654	4,008	1,336	801
1875	9,130	6,422	4,036	1,788	2,633	1,825	1,288	964
1876	6,950	5,876	3,463	1,530	2,064	1,303	834	583
1877	7,556	5,389	2,700	1,205	1,996	1,310	808	558
1878	13,514	10,474	3,371	1,517	2,025	1,120	789	616
1879	22,774	17,729	3,422	1,872	2,149	1,477	784	667
1880	18,416	17,696	3,112	1,395	2,175	1,522	588	313
1881	20,506	3,330	3,444	1,413	3,612	1,651	1,149	382
1882	29,587	2,691	3,520	1,118	3,382	979	826	269
1883	37,043	4,631	5,023	1,753	4,286	1,092	891	302
1884	31,983	1,315	6,832	1,516	4,731	1,169	1,021	337
1885	63,501	15,514	4,314	939	4,752	1,013	1,104	308
1886	43,328	13,265	9,895	1,974	4,662	1,244	1,682	552
1887	65,139	16,936	15,618	2,009	7,036	1,827	1,038	280
1888	75,029	10,179	25,407	4,938	17,105	3,636	1,426	479
1889	88,647	13,048	71,151	4,798	27,173	7,064	5,967	1,489
1890	39,122	47,408	13,560	3,814	17,104	4,805	1,108	746
1891	15,511	57,920	4,290	10,159	2,915	2,595	272	286
1892	27,850	14,678	5,650	2,938	2,115	1,160	224	98
1893	37,977	13,024	7,100	4,161	1,612	1,007	273	112
1894	37,699	19,905	8,122	5,127	2,107	1,108	385	209
1895	41,203	11,341	11,288	7,824	2,448	1,591	329	106
1896	75,202	14,705	18,051	9,666	3,486	1,082	429	208
1897	45,678	23,516	18,316	1,229	2,835	1,629	562	409
1898	39,135	20,644	18,716	1,663	2,449	1,546	632	329
1899	53,295	25,604	19,798	7,520	2,473	1,606	477	235
1900	52,143	23,138	20,383	7,876	3,160	881	421	146
1901	58,314	22,089	18,066	5,634	2,788	1,918	439	363
1902	32,314	12,315	13,911	4,353	2,378	1,609	405	361
1903	42,358	16,280	21,917	10,018	2,491	888	560	573
1904	67,598	23,970	39,851	19,020	2,902	2,043	734	694
1905	88,950	26,122	53,029	19,533	3,475	2,199	1,368	1,337
1906	127,348	37,534	79,517	12,556	3,698	2,296	1,690	966
1907	90,282	57,686	82,606	18,486	4,125	2,888	1,659	872
1908	93,479	48,065	125,497	23,701	3,823	2,903	1,879	864
1909	93,528	51,642	86,798	27,464	4,120	2,833	2,026	912
1910	102,019	48,398	131,466	23,719	4,380	2,741	1,825	1,227
1911	58,185	60,329	118,723	39,801	4,916	3,159	1,730	1,385
1912	80,583	48,063	165,662	41,118	5,180	3,249	3,134	1,475
1913	114,252	59,920	122,271	59,133	4,696	4,083	2,132	2,127
1914	36,122	60,602	52,186	77,646	2,590	6,636	1,263	4,860
1915	11,309	55,775	25,250	45,205	1,253	2,285	744	1,554
1916	5,205	21,364	21,768	42,558	775	1,329	573	1,084
1917	1,698	11,422	12,499	33,838	659	1,000	214	681
1918	855	3,608	9,188	17,545	761	680	163	429
1919	8,966	8,380	20,824	21,599	2,128	1,398	1,749	850
1920	30,213	20,915	40,722	29,172	2,300	2,791	1,858	2,464
1921	39,965	16,329	40,119	18,182	1,244	1,681	1,172	1,095
1922	57,827	14,472	43,305	19,289	1,794	1,704	1,053	899
1923	91,992	14,153	48,428	19,063	1,545	1,317	860	1,035
1924	73,119	16,200	45,691	16,763	1,237	1,326	864	1,026
Total	2,604,029	1,292,789	1,780,295	756,262	226,894	120,258	64,426	45,370

TABLE V.—DISTRIBUTION, BY NATIONALITY, OF IMMIGRANT AND EMIGRANT ALIENS (SECOND AND THIRD CLASS PASSENGERS), BY SEA, 1857-1924 (continued).

Year	AUSTRO-HUNGARIAN		GERMAN		SWISS		BELGIAN		RUSSIAN	
	Immi-grants	Emi-grants	Immi-grants	Emi-grants	Immi-grants	Emi-grants	Immi-grants	Emi-grants	Immi-grants	Emi-grants
1857	82	21	74	40	68	38	17	2	8	1
1858	75	38	61	22	74	50	21	5	17	10
1859	69	30	43	17	77	49	30	9	55	13
1860	71	34	62	39	67	44	27	6	40	18
1861	54	25	57	35	85	47	44	3	10	..
1862	73	29	72	68	92	34	39	11	28	3
1863	87	33	83	27	109	52	51	18	47	19
1864	67	26	97	41	124	40	61	27	64	28
1865	89	48	117	59	138	69	56	30	36	9
1866	94	39	122	84	164	102	68	35	78	39
1867	71	50	185	106	187	90	44	31	41	27
1868	92	44	215	48	210	115	86	46	29	10
1869	121	78	202	66	386	129	43	30	34	47
1870	67	22	148	79	499	232	27	7	52	11
1871	50	24	155	112	436	227	22	4	20	8
1872	62	17	269	129	623	289	38	18	18	2
1873	187	65	793	555	1,628	934	145	89	37	18
1874	156	61	392	174	679	219	48	19	59	11
1875	93	48	354	118	376	208	38	11	88	34
1876	136	60	231	151	373	111	74	63	37	14
1877	37	29	303	122	340	163	83	47	27	24
1878	901	407	387	96	533	238	75	16	49	5
1879	1,760	1,605	490	188	717	406	78	25	77	46
1880	879	515	445	114	581	199	57	19	..	5
1881	490	101	591	167	635	156	140	28	22	1
1882	672	277	1,128	319	913	234	183	96	26	3
1883	1,056	389	1,388	313	1,293	463	383	101	28	14
1884	1,329	514	1,261	387	1,359	208	175	44	13	..
1885	1,982	528	1,546	814	1,094	180	973	215	31	6
1886	1,015	310	1,131	303	1,284	446	479	350	918	60
1887	1,498	241	1,333	334	1,420	615	839	74	955	37
1888	2,333	791	1,536	450	1,479	288	3,201	414	512	28
1889	4,225	1,028	2,999	213	1,571	244	8,666	897	1,332	55
1890	1,918	734	1,271	626	959	173	762	584	318	112
1891	263	296	832	410	352	241	241	217	2,953	2,608
1892	552	470	785	206	364	183	146	55	1,623	410
1893	685	557	748	344	546	262	233	114	966	321
1894	440	339	971	156	516	218	248	101	3,132	894
1895	549	384	1,067	288	465	232	211	77	2,336	1,042
1896	963	697	1,032	278	679	612	318	121	575	201
1897	1,768	828	987	391	390	208	207	126	617	10
1898	593	211	779	417	261	88	149	40	1,459	229
1899	950	207	732	666	343	65	139	70	1,686	1,124
1900	2,024	188	760	673	355	122	117	50	2,119	153
1901	2,742	1,827	836	603	363	298	117	96	2,086	1,826
1902	2,135	1,710	1,029	295	267	600	148	81	1,753	1,351
1903	1,378	830	1,000	216	275	469	174	123	1,429	1,363
1904	2,237	1,145	1,151	767	339	86	206	145	4,393	2,205
1905	5,346	2,262	1,836	508	573	96	263	88	10,078	8,343
1906	6,120	2,302	2,178	479	503	117	230	136	17,424	1,153
1907	4,659	1,160	2,322	1,371	486	141	209	81	9,530	1,932
1908	3,485	1,359	2,469	1,710	665	94	239	56	8,560	2,252
1909	4,452	3,928	3,201	2,296	760	108	339	58	16,475	3,004
1910	5,236	1,084	3,282	2,760	710	151	349	70	12,765	2,964
1911	4,703	993	3,593	2,830	805	112	425	91	9,713	3,288
1912	6,545	1,495	4,337	3,528	1,005	163	405	101	20,832	5,526
1913	4,317	1,821	4,620	4,331	880	164	477	39	18,626	9,417
1914	2,055	1,946	2,318	4,473	553	277	297	205	5,387	12,237
1915	187	142	323	204	269	319	131	128	750	1,005
1916	69	66	149	109	123	187	48	73	404	1,126
1917	32	8	18	15	50	56	34	36	280	578
1918	7	5	10	1	51	36	24	28	235	267
1919	155	66	1,992	999	325	167	169	174	131	325
1920	728	139	4,798	1,855	517	378	183	233	439	337
1921	571	174	4,113	1,784	644	309	94	97	306	531
1922	783	306	6,514	2,496	681	251	189	111	672	403
1923	2,177	308	10,138	1,989	751	337	146	80	2,990	1,283
1924	1,072	288	10,238	3,388	578	470	164	137	1,427	473
Total	91,869	37,802	100,699	49,252	37,017	14,709	24,142	6,812	169,257	70,899

ARGENTINA 545

TABLE V.—Oversea immigration and emigration (second and third class passengers), by nationality (1857-1924) (continued).

Year	NETHERLANDER Immigrants	Emigrants	PORTUGUESE Immigrants	Emigrants	DANISH Immigrants	Emigrants	AMERICAN U. S. A. Immigrants	Emigrants	SWEDISH Immigrants	Emigrants
1857	4	1	2	....						
1858	11	8	37	5	....	....	....	....	....	
1859	22	13	49	4						
1860	5	6	68	30						
1861	7	....	33	18						
1862	1	....	7	1						
1863	....	2	18	4						
1864	4	....	14	....						
1865	27	16	19	3						
1866	8	....	72	22	....	....	....	....	....	....
1867	41	29	87	31						
1868	16	....	113	41						
1869	2	3	1	1						
1870	5	....	54	3						
1871	....	2	90	40						
1872	4	....	62	13						
1873	1	....	21	6						
1874	9	10	77	54						
1875	4	4	94	39	304	....	819	....	187	....
1876	3	1	38	7						
1877	40	13	80	41						
1878	21	4	59	13						
1879	12	....	81	28						
1880	....	2	101	60						
1881	25	16	119	56						
1882	5	1	98	18						
1883	9	....	108	27						
1884	40	8	136	26						
1885	34	37	182	78	1,472	....	1,200	....	741	....
1886	48	39	374	166						
1887	67	30	153	46						
1888	68	23	331	110						
1889	4,007	710	209	73						
1890	395	164	160	119						
1891	4	10	44	114						
1892	26	3	93	31						
1893	27	14	192	140						
1894	18	5	200	119						
1895	36	17	178	114	976	464	777	422	325	151
1896	61	10	219	165						
1897	31	8	195	54						
1898	51	33	175	101						
1899	26	24	197	43						
1900	43	23	205	145						
1901	35	19	156	574						
1902	37	14	141	435						
1903	72	20	202	279						
1904	139	104	518	433						
1905	149	30	674	567	3,316	1,028	2,640	1,772	462	274
1906	147	17	885	682						
1907	178	76	1,118	251						
1908	214	57	2,083	258						
1909	327	223	1,651	300						
1910	281	313	2,848	355						
1911	246	284	2,575	608						
1912	274	266	4,959	912						
1913	292	329	3,619	1,359						
1914	10	234	1,397	1,530						
1915	19	86	859	988	4,576	2,081	2,631	2,971	508	703
1916	70	43	466	829						
1917	41	13	197	432						
1918	26	19	320	509						
1919	130	95	330	426						
1920	156	209	886	689						
1921	103	103	1,160	566						
1922	220	181	1,692	688	2,252	296	961	362	441	43
1923	138	136	2,873	669						
1924	179	106	1,742	917						
Total	8,751	4,266	38,196	17,465	12,896	3,869	9,028	5,527	2,664	1,171

TABLE V.—Oversea immigration and emigration (second and third class passengers), by nationality (1857-1924) (concluded).

Year	TURKISH		POLISH		YUGOSLAV		NOT SPECIFIED		TOTAL	
	Immi-grants	Emi-grants	Immi-grants	Emi-grants	Immi-grants	Emi-grants	Immi-grants	Emi-grants	Immi-grants	Emi-grants
1857									4,951	.....
1858	....	....	....	....	....	....	1,416	336	4,658	8,900
1859									4,735	
1860									5,656	.....
1861									6,301	.....
1862									6,716	.....
1863									10,408	.....
1864									11,682	.....
1865	....	....	....	....	....	....	5,547	3,393	11,767	82,976
1866									13,696	
1867									13,225	.....
1868									25,919	.....
1869									28,958	.....
1870									30,898	.....
1871									15,088	.....
1872									26,218	
1873									48,382	.....
1874									40,674	.....
1875	672	....	....	....	....	....	3,665	4,069	18,332	175,763
1876									14,532	
1877									14,675	.....
1878									23,624	.....
1879									32,717	.....
1880									26,643	.....
1881									31,431	22,374
1882									41,041	8,720
1883									52,472	9,510
1884									49,623	11,444
1885	3,537	....	....	....	....	....	2,235	4,530	80,618	14,585
1886									65,655	13,907
1887									94,608	13,630
1888									129,115	16,842
1889									218,744	40,649
1890									77,815	48,794
1891									28,266	72,380
1892									39,973	29,893
1893									52,067	26,055
1894									54,720	20,586
1895	11,583	1,011	....	....	....	....	4,407	8,042	61,226	20,390
1896									102,673	20,415
1897									72,978	31,192
1898									67,130	30,802
1899									84,442	38,397
1900									84,851	38,334
1901									90,127	48,697
1902									57,992	44,558
1903									75,227	40,610
1904									125,567	38,923
1905	66,558	31,160	....	....	....	....	34,857	17,469	177,117	42,869
1906									252,536	60,124
1907									209,103	90,190
1908									255,710	85,412
1909									231,084	94,644
1910									289,640	97,854
1911									225,772	120,709
1912									323,403	120,260
1913									302,047	156,829
1914									115,321	178,684
1915	59,272	20,220	685	601	1,753	627	38,799	25,151	45,290	111,459
1916									32,990	73,348
1917									18,064	50,995
1918									13,701	24,075
1919									41,299	42,279
1920									87,032	57,187
1921									98,086	44,638
1922	15,563	1,122	24,029	578	7,497	388	29,038	17,642	129,263	45,993
1923									195,063	46,810
1924									159,939	46,105
Total	157,185	53,513	24,714	1,179	9,250	1,015	119,968	80,632	5,481,276	2,562,790

TABLE VI.—Arrivals and departures of second and third class passengers by river shipping, 1867-1924.

Year	Arrivals[2]	Departures	Year	Arrivals[2]	Departures
1867	3,821	. . . . .	1896	32,532	25,506
1868	3,315	. . . . .	1897	32,165	26,265
1869	8,976	. . . . .	1898	28,060	22,734
1870	9,069	. . . . .	1899	26,641	23,844
1871	5,845	. . . . .	1900	21,051	17,083
1872	10,819	. . . . .	1901	35,824	31,554
1873	27,950	. . . . .	1902	38,088	38,774
1874	27,603	. . . . .	1903	37,444	35,853
1875	23,704	. . . . .	1904	35,511	27,674
1876	16,433	. . . . .	1905	44,505	39,903
1877	21,650	. . . . .	1906	49,713	38,728
1878	19,334	. . . . .	1907	48,821	47,873
1879	22,438	. . . . :	1908	47,402	41,620
1880	15,008	21,201	1909	47,064	42,864
1881	16,053	15,944	1910	49,188	38,551
1882	10,462	10,139	1911	55,850	51,332
1883	10,771	20,220	1912	55,714	52,736
1884	28,182	28,555	1913	62,224	34,814
1885	28,104	27,909	1914	67,338	42,324
1886	29,532	29,611	1915	37,374	22,263
1887	21,944	20,442	1916	49,465	42,203
1888	26,537	26,762	1917	33,601	33,001
1889	42,165	40,013	1918	36,961	35,833
1890	54,486	53,898	1919	28,580	25,431
1891	28,266	9,552	1920	17,085	10,503
1892	35,321	13,960	1921	14,064	9,379
1893	32,253	22,739	1922	17,785	13,750
1894	25,951	20,813	1923	14,797	13,451
1895	19,762	16,422	1924	17,338	16,626

SOURCES

Resumen Estadistico del Movimiento Migratorio en la Republica Argentina. Años 1857-1924. Ministry of Agriculture. Buenos Aires, 1925.

Tables I, II, III, V (years 1857-1924); IIa, IIIa (years 1921-24); IV (years, 1881-1924); VI (years 1867-79).

Annuario de la Dirección General de Estadistica correspondiente al año 1896. Tomo II. Buenos Aires; 1897, p. 190.

Tables IV, V (years 1871-80); VI (years 1867-79).

Information supplied by the Department of Immigration, Ministry of Agriculture.

Table VI (years 1880-1924).

NOTES

[1]As from July 1923, the intercontinental immigrants who arrived in Argentina by river are included n the number of intercontinental immigrants.

[2]Details total 581,751.

[3]The figures for the years 1867-79 have been obtained by deducting the figures for overseas immigrants given in the *Resumen Estadistico* from those for all immigrants given in the *Annuario.*

BRAZIL

(a) Before 1898 the immigration statistics collected in the ports were elaborated by the Inspectorate General of Lands and Colonisation. When this authority ceased to function, the work was transferred to the Statistical Department of Rio de Janeiro. After 1908 these statistics were published by the Ministry of Agriculture, Industry and Commerce.

Table I is an official compilation based on immigration figures taken from diverse and dissimilar sources. (See Explanatory Notes 1-10.) European emigration data are utilised.

In general, the figures are for third class passengers arriving by sailing vessels or steamships in Brazilian ports.[1] Shipping and railway companies are required to supply the proper authorities regularly with lists of their passengers.

More complete statistics are available after 1908. These are arranged according to a more detailed list of nationalities. The immigration data since 1921, so far as known, relate to second class and third class passengers arriving at the ports of Belém, Recife, São Salvador, Rio de Janeiro, Santos, Paranagua, Florianopolis and Rio Grande. (Table IV.) The corresponding annual emigration figures are available only for the years 1920 and 1921. (Table VIII.)[2]

(b) Concerning these tables, which more or less refer to Brazil as a whole, we possess immigration and emigration statistics based on the passenger lists of vessels arriving and departing at the ports of Rio de Janeiro and Santos. These tables show certain details about the migrants.

The source whence we derived the emigrant figures for 1899-1904 (*Statistica della Emigrazione italiana per l'Estero* negli anni 1904 e 1905, pp. 140-141) in table VI (for Rio de Janeiro and Santos) notes, on the basis of Brazilian information, that passengers of all classes are included but that 80 per cent of these may be regarded as emigrants.

---

[1] See also Oliveira Martins, *L'Emigration Portugaise*, extract from the *Bulletin de l'Institut international de statistique*, Vol. VI, part 2, Rome. p. 12.

[2] According to Oliveira Martins, the number of departures during the period 1855 to 1863 was 35,037, as against 71,499 arrivals. He does not specify particular years. For 1863-73, he had at his disposal, apart from Brazilian sources, only the departures for the Port of Rio de Janeiro—32,132 departures as against 66,258 arrivals. (*Ibid.*, p. 13.)

TABLE I.—DISTRIBUTION OF IMMIGRANTS ADMITTED BY NATIONALITY, 1820-1907.

Year	Total	German	Austrian	Belgian	French	Spanish	English	Italian	Portuguese	Russian	Swedish	Swiss	Turco-Arab	Other, including Brazilian
1820	1,682											1,682[1]		
1821														
1822														
1823	126													126[2]
1824	909													909[2]
1825	828													828[2]
1826	1,088													1,088[2]
1827	2,060	1,261												799
1828	2,412	723												1,689
1829														
1830														
1831														
1832														
1833														
1834														
1835	1,180							180						1,000[3]
1836	604	207							120					277[3]
1837	396													396
1838	389								141					248
1839	269	63							206					
1840	555	191				10			159					195
1841	568	332			100				48					88
1842	694				59									635
1843														
1844	53	53												
1845	435				64							17		354
1846	2,350	1,500		2			292	5	78			8		465[4]
1847	28											28		
1848	40											40		
1849	2,072	643			50	122			178			245		834
1850	4,425	400			20	5			53			321		3,626
1851	2,731	1,221			52	17		2	231			468		740
1852	10,935	2,214		13				22	8,329[5]		21	180		156
1853	9,189	846							7,384[5]		74	604		281
1854	11,798	532							9,839		28	173		1,226
1855	14,008	1,822				37			9,159		79	92		2,819
1856	14,244	2,639							9,340		42	8		2,215
1857	18,529	2,333		5	51				9,327		60	161		6,592
1858	20,114	3,165							9,342		143	276		7,188
1859	15,774	3,748		8	18				5,914			112		5,974
1860	13,003	2,211		44	15		4		6,460			193		4,076
1861	14,295	4,037		376	233		164	431	5,625		185	240		3,004
1862	7,642	367							4,420		119	89		2,647
1863														

For reference notes see page 557.

TABLE I.—DISTRIBUTION OF IMMIGRANTS ADMITTED BY NATIONALITY, 1820-1907 (continued).

Year	Total	German	Austrian	Belgian	French	Spanish	English	Italian	Portuguese	Russian	Swedish	Swiss	Turco-Arab	Other, including Brazilian
1864	9,578	234	....	....	1,166	83	68	2,092	5,097	....	....	....	....	838
1865	6,452	275	....	....	....	....	....	500	3,784	....	....	....	....	1,893
1866	7,699	360[6]	....	....	....	....	418	....	4,724	....	....	....	....	2,197
1867	10,902	1,128[6]	104	33	598	218	867	....	4,822	....	....	2	....	4,082
1868	11,315	3,779[a]	....	20	538	332	375	841	4,425	....	1	64	....	151
1869	11,527	375	....	....	16	38	1,026	1,052	4,458	....	76	58	....	2,430
1870	5,158	6	....	....	....	....	375	7	5,347	4	....	187	2	379
1871	12,431	296	....	32	777	510	3	1,626	8,124	7	64	62	....	467
1872	19,219	1,103	14	33	1,048	727	515	1,808	12,918	41	2	141	....	357
1873	14,742	1,082	17	....	....	....	1,051	5	1,310	7	9	287	8	12,000[7]
1874	20,332	1,435	....	73	328	39	147	1,171	6,644	30	14	134	21	11,863
1875	14,590	1,308	290	132	1,214	763	363	6,820	3,692	956	53	302	....	6,001
1876	30,747	3,530	4,028	....	383	23	635	13,582	7,421	3,011	67	409	15	2,747
1877	29,468	2,310	1,728	....	183	929	....	11,836	7,965	2,158[8]	125	316	....	906
1878	24,456	1,535	1,185	....	264	911	52	10,245	6,236	1,904[8]	....	....	....	596
1879	22,788	2,022	318	....	240	1,275	51	2,705	8,841	7	....	....	6	129
1880	30,355	2,385	292	5	194	2,677	229	12,428	12,101	426	14	88	38	363
1881	11,548	1,851	83	24	249	3,961	239	15,724	13,144	305	51	70	....	400
1882	29,589	1,804	94	19	152	2,660	158	10,102	10,621	10	....	30	....	139
1883	34,015	2,348	251	16	243	710	100	21,765	12,509	19	2	94	6	77
1884	24,890	251	651	101	233	952	90	20,430	8,683	457[8]	....	70	16	2,120
1885	35,440	1,719	524	212	218	1,317	93	104,353	7,611	275[8]	16	43	43	1,024
1886	33,486	2,414	728	1,082	241	1,766	72	36,124	6,287	146[8]	....	396	....	1,356
1887	55,965	1,147	274	387	478	4,736	129	104,353	10,205	....	....	....	....	1,891
1888	133,253	782	1,156	308	608	9,012	76	104,353	18,289	....	....	51	....	2,248
1889	65,246	1,903	550	471	2,844	12,008	193	36,124	15,240	27,125[8]	354	254	....	1,295
1890	107,474	4,812	2,246	24	1,921	22,146	1,959	31,275	25,174	11,817	2,008[9]	198	3	881
1891	216,760	5,285	4,244	37	575	10,471	100	132,326	32,349	158	37	58	....	2,033
1892	86,203	800	574	9	616	38,998	91	55,049	17,797	155	....	40	....	593
1893	134,805	1,368	2,737	28	309	5,986	28	58,552	28,986	57	8	21	....	3,216
1894	60,984	790	798	22	286	17,641	63	34,872	17,041	275	....	93	....	1,002
1895	167,618	973	10,108	28	327	24,154	106	97,344	36,055	592	7	153	....	4,787
1896	158,132	1,070	11,365	18	225	19,466	103	96,505	22,299	569	14	90	648	1,575
1897	146,362	930	3,665	6	255	8,024	101	104,510	13,558	258	4	119	978	2,553
1898	78,109	535	924	13	217	5,399	166	49,086	15,105	412	6	30	1,823	2,700
1899	54,629	521	1,826	25	233	4,834	47	30,846	10,989	147	8	23	874	2,453
1900	40,300	217	2,089	5	212	8,584	35	19,671	8,250	99	14	17	781	3,775
1901	85,306	166	511	17	151	3,588	85	59,869	11,261	108	27	15	772	3,535
1902	52,204	265	696	29	302	4,466	362	32,111	11,606	371	2	46	481	3,010
1903	34,062	1,231	474	18	228	10,046	123	12,970	11,378	287	....	98	1,097	2,239
1904	46,164	797	387	15	224	25,329	119	12,857	17,318	996	....	68	1,446	2,658
1905	70,295	650	427	26	109	24,441	....	17,360	20,181	751	1	10	1,193	3,473
1906	73,672	1,333	1,012	....	202	9,235	....	20,777	21,706	703	8	12	1,480	2,251
1907	67,787	845	522	....	....	....	....	18,238	25,681	....	....	....	....	10,716[10]

For reference notes see page 557.

TABLE II.—Distribution of immigrants admitted by nationality, 1908-24.

Nationality	1908	1909	1910	1911	1912	1913	1914	1915
Albanian								
Argentinian	329	176	477	624	500	353	362	178
Armenian								
Australian								
Austrian	5,317	4,008	2,636	3,352	3,045	2,255	971	104
Belgian	87	99	83	293	255	223	160	79
Bolivian	20	29	25	163	12	9	25	2
Bulgarian								
Chilian	13	18	23	19	43	42	43	22
Chinese	13	6	12	16	57	176	95	21
Colombian								
Costa Rican								
Cuban								
Czechoslovak								
Danziger								
Dane	22	25	14	65	56	74	37	27
Egyptian								
English	1,109	778	1,087	1,157	1,077	825	462	311
Equatorian								
Estonian								
Finnish								
French	992	1,241	1,134	1,397	1,513	1,532	696	410
German	2,931	5,413	3,902	4,251	5,733	8,004	2,811	169
Greek	99	94	113	250	453	375	232	143
Guatemalan								
Haitian								
Hindu								
Hungarian	55	57	284	780	300	223	23	1
Italian	13,873	13,668	14,163	22,914	31,785	30,886	15,542	5,779
Japanese	830	31	948	28	2,909	7,122	3,675	65
Latvian								
Lithuanian								
Luxemburger								
Mexican								
Montenegrin								
Moroccan								
Netherlander	1,037	1,036	197	247	243	256	123	41
North American	338	272	344	275	370	265	173	113
Norwegian								
Panamanian								
Paraguayan								
Persian								
Peruvian	41	43	86	65	6	13	16	5
Polish								
Portuguese	37,628	30,577	30,857	47,493	76,530	76,701	27,935	15,118
Rumanian	13	13	46	57	63	56	36	32
Russian	5,781	5,663	2,462	14,013	9,193	8,251	2,958	640
Serbian	7	53	90	8	37	72	6	2
Spanish	14.862	16,219	20,843	27,141	35,492	41,064	18,945	5,895
Swedish	19	35	424	1,110	59	25	20	2
Swiss	442	262	156	229	281	304	182	75
Transvaalian								
Turco-Arab	3,170	4,027	5,257	6,319	7,302	10,886	3,456	514
Ukrainian								
Uruguayan	64	82	144	229	133	123	124	60
Venezuelan	3	2	173	19	1	3	3	
Yugoslav								
Other	1,441	163	771	1,061	439	215	121	525
Total aliens	90,536	84,090	86,751	133,575	177,887	190,333	79,232	30,333
Brazilian: Total citizens	4,159	1,320	1,813	2,392	2,295	2,350	3,340	1,873
Continental alien immigrants[11]	470	350	928	1,119	695	543	573	267
Intercontinental alien immigrants	90,066	83,740	85,823	132,456	177,192	189,790	78,659	30,066

For reference marks see page 557.

TABLE II.—Distribution of immigrants admitted by nationality, 1908-24 (continued).

Nationality	1916	1917	1918	1919	1920	1921	1922	1923	1924
Albanian					4				
Argentinian	388	680	141	177	191	196	404	419	393
Armenian								1	45
Australian							8		
Austrian	155	18	1	548	757	760	808	2,163	919
Belgian	35	30	9	220	132	117	124	75	98
Bolivian	6	3		23	2	3	15	17	10
Bulgarian					10	12	40	24	7
Chilian	9	14	6	14	20	28	65	43	47
Chinese	29	12	2	53	6	49	12	37	77
Colombian			1	1	1	3	6	4	14
Costa Rican							8	4	1
Cuban				6	3	5	1	4	4
Czechoslovak					92	221	307	539	610
Danziger								2	2
Dane	41	3	2	31	46	100	140	58	63
Egyptian			2	3	80	29	21	55	69
English	244	243	69	369	658	492	532	584	537
Equatorian				1		5	19	2	
Estonian								73	107
Finnish	4			1	1	15	13	26	21
French	292	273	226	690	838	633	725	609	634
German	364	201	1	466	4,120	7,915	5,038	8,254	22,168
Greek	160	47	18	40	94	61	98	101	85
Guatemalan				1	2				2
Haitian									
Hindu				2		45	11		4	29
Hungarian	19				5	87	97	163	826	996
Italian	5,340	5,478	1,050	5,231	10,005	10,779	11,277	15,839	13,844
Japanese	165	3,899	5,599	3,022	1,013	840	1,225	895	2,673
Latvian									21
Lithuanian					6	10	992	923	80
Luxemburger				2	3	21	12	9	22
Mexican				11	14	28	9	17	13
Montenegrin				1		1			
Moroccan				1	13	2	16	3	9
Netherlander	48	11	5	96	145	118	125	130	117
North American	164	126	48	138	295	338	270	233	191
Norwegian			2	33	5	23	13	68	22
Panamanians								8	
Paraguayans				1		3	7	14	6
Persians							8	4	23
Peruvians	4	6	8	11	11	16	31	40	53
Polish					576	653	739	1,105	2,025
Portuguese	11,981	6,817	7,981	17,068	33,883	19,981	28,622	31,866	23,267
Rumanian	20	16	6	11	845	1,107	340	1,983	6,340
Russian	516	644	181	330	245	1,526	279	777	559
Serbian	4		1	7					
Spanish	10,306	11,113	4,225	6,627	9,136	9,523	8,869	10,140	7,238
Swedish	9	3	3	13	38	32	51	40	30
Swiss	119	45	17	178	404	445	552	564	374
Transvaalian				1	3	2			
Turco-Arab	603	259	93	504	4,854	1,865	2,278	4,829	4,078
Ukrainian					14	161	471	176	35
Uruguayans	105	274	94	81	100	117	215	166	203
Venezuelan	1	1		1	1	8	3	6	2
Yugoslav					37	22	56	790	7,889
Other	118	61		10	207	103			
Total aliens	31,245	30,277	19,793	36,027	69,042	58,476	65,007	84,549	96,052
Brazilian: Total citizens	2,758	915	708	1,871	1,985	2,308	1,960	2,130	2,073
Continental alien immigrants[11]	513	978	249	309	325	376	759	707	714
Intercontinental alien immigrants	30,732	29,299	19,544	35,718	68,717	58,100	64,248	83,842	95,338

For reference notes see page 557.

TABLE III.—DISTRIBUTION OF IMMIGRANT ALIENS ADMITTED AT RIO DE JANEIRO AND SANTOS, BY SEX, AGE AND OCCUPATION, 1890-1913.

Year	Total	Sex		Age				Occupation			
		Males	Females	Under 3 years	3 to 7 years	7 to 12 years	12 years and over	Agriculture	Artisans	Laborers	Other occupations
1890	85,172	58,395	26,777		18,712		66,460	67,338	15,254	2,580	
1891	191,151	134,248	56,903		44,070		147,081	164,194	20,039	6,918	
1892											
1893	127,279	83,117	41,283		29,353		95,047	85,555	.....	9,283	29,562
1894[12]	33,733	24,387	9,346		6,518		27,215	31,835	.....	1,734	164
1895[12]	91,773	60,146	31,627		25,111		66,662	87,712	1,833	.....	2,228
1896	157,948	94,330	63,618		53,942		104,006	128,318	.....	3,204	26,426
1908	85,549[13]	63,569	20,522	3,823	4,557	5,298	70,413	41,570		43,979	
1909	78,777	54,491	24,286	4,274	5,151	6,284	63,068	43,720		35,057	
1910	78,584	54,852	23,732	3,987	4,748	6,799	63,050	57,451		21,133	
1911	126,037	83,472	42,565	8,127	9,899	12,729	95,282	99,124		26,913	
1912	175,936	117,445	58,491	9,582	13,224	16,626	136,504	134,141		41,795	
1913	189,184	.....	.....	.....	.....	.....	.....	142,316		46,868	

For reference notes see page 557.

TABLE IV.—Distribution of immigrants admitted, by sex, 1920-22.

Year	Total	Males	Females
1920	71,027	49,080	21,947
1921	60,784	40,278	20,506
1922	66,967	46,103	20,864

TABLE V.—Distribution of immigrants, by age and occupation, 1922.

Total......	66,967
Age	
over 12 years....	56,652
up to 12 years....	10,315
Occupation	
Agriculture....	18,511
Artisans....	1,782
General labor....	29,173
Other occupations....	17,501

TABLE VI.—DISTRIBUTION OF EMIGRANTS DEPARTED VIA RIO DE JANEIRO AND SANTOS, BY NATIONALITY, 1899–1907.

Year	Total	Austro-Hungarian	French	German	English, Irish, Scotch	Italian	Portuguese	Spanish	Syrian, Armenian and other Ottoman subjects	North American	Other foreign nationalities	Brazilian
1899	31,319[4]	122	....	....	....	20,406	4,317	1,194	....	....	1,825	2,652
1900	38,143[4]	221	....	....	....	26,046	5,084	2,556	....	....	2,028	2,208
1901	40,707[14]	146	....	....	....	29,181	4,640	1,687	....	....	2,748	2,305
1902	35,570[14]	....	....	....	....	21,687	....	....	....	....	....	....
1903	45,130[15]	207	477	527	703	32,757	4,330	2,842	772	208	2,491	2,503
1904	54,235[16]	235	648	616	632	27,676	10,742	5,304	572	267	4,483	3,108
1905	54,509	357	792	1,217	948	30,459	11,039	5,037	2,001	447	2,586	2,296
1906	65,453	302	486	1,174	372	31,763	13,063	10,862	2,339	79	950	3,108
1907	58,169	560				27,368	14,272	8,520			705	2,294

For reference notes see page 557.

TABLE VII.—Emigration via Rio de Janeiro and Santos, by country of
destination, 1904-12.

Year	Total	Europe	La Plata Republic	Other countries
1904	49,610	35,647	8,789	5,174
1905	54,509	37,982	11,749	4,778
1906	65,453	42,010	17,337	6,106
1907	58,169	41,049	11,374	5,746
1908	58,558	41,201	13,007	4,350
1909	55,095	41,863	12,557	675
1910	55,769	40,845	14,315	609
1911	56,136	42,781	12,810	545
1912	68,461	.....	......	......

TABLE VIII.—Distribution of second and third class emigrants departed,
by nationality, 1920 and 1921.

Nationality	1920	1921	Nationality	1920	1921
Argentinian	386	393	Yugoslav	13	12
Armenian	3	2	Luxemburger	1	1
Austrian	97	130	Mexican	28	14
Belgian	110	104	Moroccan	3	16
Bolivian	2	7	Netherlander	100	81
Brazilian	1,715	1,380	North American	322	409
Bulgarian	1	12	Norwegian	7	17
Chilian	35	17	Paraguayan	4	6
Chinese	13	16	Peruvian	19	29
Colombian	1	5	Polish	303	442
Cuban	7	3	Portuguese	16,086	16,625
Czechoslovak	12	47	Rumanian	54	335
Dane	19	58	Russian	239	641
Dominican	1	0	Senegalese	9	0
Egyptian	4	5	Serbian	16	27
English	578	619	Spanish	5,206	4,064
Equatorian	157	4	Swedish	26	12
French	631	608	Swiss	111	135
German	981	1,236	Tripolitan	6	0
Greek	172	104	Turco-Arab	1,537	842
Guatemalan	1	0	Ukrainian	2	16
Hindu	87	17	Uruguayan	142	118
Hungarian	20	18	Venezuelan	2	3
Italian	6,143	5,913	Others	131	147[17]
Japanese	216	195			
Total				35,759	34,885

For reference notes see page 557.

SOURCES

Boletino Commemorativo da Exposiçao nacional de 1908. Rio de Janeiro, 1908. pp. 82-85.

Table I.

Information supplied by the Ministry of Agriculture, Industry and Commerce.

Table II (years 1908-24); IV (year 1921); VIII (years 1920, 1921).

Statistica della Emigrazione italiana all'Estero, 1891-1915. Rome, 1892 to 1916 (Publication of the Statistical Department).

Tables III, VI, VII.

Relatorio apresentado ao Sr. Presidente da Republica pelo Ministro de Estado dos Negocios da Agricultura, Industria e Commercio, par Ildefonso Simoes Lopes. Rio de Janeiro, 1921, p. 20.

Table IV, (year 1920).

Relatorio apresentado ao Presidente da Republica dos Estados Unidos do Brasil pelo Ministro de Estado da Agricultura, Industria e Commercio, par Miguel Calmon du Pin e Almeida. 1922. Rio de Janeiro, 1925.

Tables IV and V (year 1922).

NOTES*

[1]The first inhabitants of the Colony of Nova Friburgo, founded in 1819, arrived at the commencement of 1820 (Relatorio do Imperio de 1855).

[2]Memorandum by J. Candido Gomes on the Memorial of the Minister of Prussia respecting the Colony of S. Leopoldo, Rio de Janeiro, July 15, 1863.

[3]Statistics of the Depot of the Society for Promoting the Colonisation of Rio de Janeiro. (Reports of the Division of Affairs of the Empire, 1836-38.)

[4]Statistical and Descriptive Statement specially prepared in homage of the Hon. Elihu Root, Secretary of State of the United States of North America, S. Paulo, 1906.

[5]Table furnished by the Portuguese consulate (Relatorio do Imperio de 1856).

[6]Table showing German emigration from the Port of Hamburg to Brazil in 1868, by Dr. Hermann Blumenau. (Appendices to the Report of the Ministry of Agriculture, Commerce and Public Works for 1869.)

[7]Statistics of immigration from 1855 to 1890. (Report of the General Inspectorate of Lands and Colonisation, May 31, 1891.)

[8]Including Poles.

[9]Report of the General Inspectorate of Lands and Colonisation, by Candido Ferreira de Arbreu, Engineer. (Appendices to the Report of the Ministry of Industry, Railways and Public Works, 1892.)

[10]Report of the Population Service for 1907 by the Chief Engineer J. F. Goncalves Junior, 1908. Relatorios do Imperio de 1837, 1838, 1839, 1840, 1844, 1847, 1848, 1852, 1853, 1854, 1856, 1857, 1858. Reports of the Ministry of Agriculture, Commerce and Public Works, 1867, 1871, 1874, 1876, 1882, 1 84, 1885, 1888. Reports of the Ministry of Agriculture, Commerce and Public Works for 1891 and 1892. Reports of the Ministry of Industry, Railways and Public Works from 1893 to 1907.

[11]Continental alien immigrants: Argentinians, Bolivians, Chilians, Equadorians, Paraguayans, Peruvians, Uruguyans, Venezuelans.

[12]The figures for 1894 and 1895 are for the Port of Rio de Janeiro only.

[13]Classification by sex and age is lacking in respect of 1,458 immigrants through the Port of Santos in 1908.

[14]There is no indication of the number of passengers who left via Rio de Janeiro; classification by nationality of 13,883 passengers of other than Italian nationality who departed from Sao Paulo in 1902 is lacking.

[15]Does not include passengers of other than Italian nationality who departed via Rio de Janeiro.

[16]This figure does not include 4,625 first and second class passengers whose nationalities are not indicated.

[17]Including 12 Latvians, 3 from Barbados, 3 from Haiti, 1 from Costa Rica, 1 from Finland, 1 from Persia and 1 from the Transvaal.

*1-10 are original footnotes to table 1.

PARAGUAY

The Department of Land and Colonisation (*Dirección de Tierras y Colonias*) publishes figures relating to immigrants who arrive and are registered by the Immigration Office at Asunción. It also indicates the country of origin and the occupation of the immigrants.[1]

[1]Its latest publication, *Memoria correspondiente al año 1927*, presentada al Ministerio de Hacienda por Genaro Romero, President del Departemento di Tierras y Colonias, Asuncion, 1928, contains the figures of Table Ia and brings them up to the end of 1927.

TABLE I.—DISTRIBUTION OF IMMIGRANTS, BY NATIONALITY, 1881-1906 and 1922-23.[1]

Nationality	1881	1882	1883	1884	1885	1886	1887	1888	1889	1890	1891	1892	1893	1894
German	96	197	141	152	21	67	141	193	200	90	64	92	46	44
Austrian		7				7	60	77	60	45	15		5	6
Hungarian		12												
Argentinian			22	10	7		18	15	44	31	4	28	27	20
Australian													6	2
Arabian														
Belgian		1	6	10	1		8	17	47	26	2	1	4	1
Boer														
Bolivian							17	2			2			1
Brazilian						2	11	1	1		4	6	20	5
Colombian														
Cuban													2	
Chilian				1		1	4	4	3		1	4	5	
Danish		1					12		6	1			2	
Spanish		3				3	54	264	280	120	64	38	49	7
French			23	53	4	2	92	184	351	165	85	239	177	41
Greek							12	1	2	2				
Dutch	1								7					
Italian		1	2		2	3	261	277	710	292	104	43	53	19
English			1			3	17	26	33	13	8	34	9	3
Irish									1	1				
North American						1	29	4	27	6		2	4	4
Portuguese							3			1				
Peruvian										2				
Rumanian	1	4				1	1		1	1			2	
Russian	2	5		3		1	30	40	74	2	1	9	2	8
Swiss		1	22	48	12	25	5	1	6	15	10	10	42	36
Swedish				1			20	11	27	5	1	4	1	2
Uruguayan				6		2				2	2			4
Other alien														
Total alien	100	233	217	284	47	114	804	1,117	1,881	821	367	510	457	203
Paraguayan		3	1			1	3	2	5	2	1	2	1	2
Grand total	100	236	218	284	47	115	807	1,119	1,886	823	368	512	458	205

For reference notes see page 563.

TABLE I.—DISTRIBUTION OF IMMIGRANTS, BY NATIONALITY, 1881-1906 and 1922-23[1] (continued).

Nationality	1895	1896	1897	1898	1899	1900	1901	1902	1903	1904	1905	1906	1922	1923
German	92	25	19	17	15	18	26	45	35	33	83	131	100	54
Austrian	1	8	1	1	2	3	11	11	1	15	8	20	4	11
Hungarian													11	3
Argentinian	36	17	36	2	15	18	75	127	69	73	86	98	7	10
Australian							4	15	1	1				
Arabian														
Belgian		1	2	1		1		4			4	13		
Boer									5			7		
Bolivian					5				11	7	91	2		
Brazilian							3			1			1	
Colombian												22		
Cuban							1				1			
Chilian							1	2		1	4			
Danish	3						2	1	5			3		
Spanish	24	12	16	6	63	25	91	72	4	51	70	206	22	26
French		35	15	17	34	23	33	17	51	32	18	64	6	2
Greek									7			4		
Dutch	18	55	4	326	104	25	1	4	1		3			1
Italian	32	20	25	21	50	12	158	215	63	88	138	377	5	8
English	1		52	6			17	15	8	16	8	15		
Irish	4		1				17	2	19	5	3		3	
North American								2			4	68		
Portuguese						1		1			1	7		
Peruvian											11			
Rumanian														
Russian	2	13	10		1	8	8	5	2	1	2	79	3	
Swiss	38	10	1	3	13	2	7	7	1	7	2	5	26	4
Swedish							2	1				2		
Uruguayan	11				10		4	23	26	8	20	33	2	1
Other alien													11[2]	4[3]
Total alien	262	196	182	400	312	136	461	569	309	339	557	1,156	201	124
Paraguayan	8	4	5		8	4	10	15	7	11	42	70		
Grand total	270	200	187	400	320	140	471	584	316	350	599	1,226	201	124

TABLE Ia.—IMMIGRANTS (CHIEFLY ALIENS), 1907-23.

Year	Total	Year	Total
1907	1,774	1916	298
1908	870	1917	326
1909	634	1918	270
1910	418	1919	349
1911	446	1920	330
1912	704	1921	557
1913	1,512	1922[1]	201
1914	1,616	1923[1]	124
1915	366		

TABLE II.—DISTRIBUTION OF IMMIGRANTS BY SEX AND AGE, 1881-1906.

Year[1]	Total	Males	Females	Up to 12 years	12 to 50 years	over 50 years
1881	100	73	27	19	81	..
1882	236	137	99	73	163	..
1883	218	138	80	57	155	6
1884	284	179	105	96	170	18
1885	47	24	23	15	26	6
1886	115	84	31	25	83	7
1887	807	744	63	40	749	18
1888	1,119	858	261	169	911	39
1889	1,886	1,590	296	238	1,594	54
1890	823	643	180	198	605	20
1891	368	268	100	77	280	11
1892	512	321	191	162	325	25
1893	458	294	164	136	303	19
1894	205	136	69	51	145	9
1895	270	155	115	82	175	13
1896	200	131	69	53	136	11
1897	187	126	61	50	127	10
1898	400	263	137	159	229	12
1899	320	225	95	75	239	6
1900	140	95	45	31	102	7
1901	471	318	153	151	306	14
1902	584	411	173	153	409	22
1903	316	227	89	84	226	6
1904	350	226	124	93	243	14
1905	599	399	200	172	418	9
1906	1,226	988	238	232	994	..

For reference notes see page 563.

TABLE IIa.—DISTRIBUTION OF IMMIGRANT ALIENS, BY SEX AND AGE, 1922 AND 1923.

Sex and age	1922[1]	1923[1]
Total	201	124
Males	129	79
Females	72	45
Adults:		
Total	163	101
Males	113	68
Females	50	33
Minors:		
Total	38	23
Males	16	11
Females	22	12

TABLE III.— DISTRIBUTION OF IMMIGRANTS (CHIEFLY ALIENS), BY OCCUPATION, 1881-1906 AND 1922-23.

Year[1]	Total	Agri-culture	Industry and mining	Transport and commerce	Domestic service and general labor	Liberal pro-fessions and public services	Other occu-pations, none or unknown
1881	100	28	25	11	...	4	32
1882	236	88	35	3	...	2	108
1883	218	98	13	9	...	3	95
1884	284	108	1	..	...	.	175
1885	47	14	..	..	...	.	33
1886	115	33	12	4	...	4	62
1887	807	93	237	26	285	3	163
1888	1,119	197	339	35	106	4	438
1889	1,886	261	504	45	515	3	558
1890	823	212	184	16	95	2	314
1891	368	168	61	4	13	1	121
1892	512	156	21	6	7	.	322
1893	458	153	40	2	3	3	257
1894	205	88	16	7	3	.	91
1895	270	95	17	2	3	5	148
1896	200	51	7	..	31	7	104
1897	187	76	17	..	4	1	89
1898	400	136	40	3	...	9	212
1899	320	136	35	1	1	1	146
1900	140	68	14	2	2	1	53
1901	471	152	64	10	5	2	238
1902	584	117	95	23	119	4	226
1903	316	115	56	21	12	2	110
1904	350	116	81	14	3	6	130
1905	599	155	113	18	13	2	298
1906	1,226	420	387	36	62	7	314
1922	201	87	31	18	14	6	45
1923	124	52	14	7	9	10	32

SOURCES

Datos estadisticos sobre el movimiento de Immigración en el Paraguay desde 1882 hasta 1907. Department of Immigration and Colonisation. Asuncion, 1908.

Tables I, II, III (years 1881-1906).

Information supplied by the Office for Land and Land Settlement, Asunción.

Tables I, Ia, IIa (years 1922 and 1923).

Nuestra emigración. Bulletin of the Spanish Association of San Rafael for the protection of emigrants. Año VIII, No. 92, Madrid, October 1924, p. 159.

Table Ia (years 1907-21).

NOTES

[1]For 1881, from August 1, 1881 to March 31 following, for the years 1882-1906, fiscal years ending April 1 to March 31 of the following year. 1922 and 1923 are calendar years.
[2]Including 2 Polish, 3 Latvian and 6 Finnish.
[3]Czechoslovak.

URUGUAY

According to the method employed in preparing the returns, three types of statistics may be distinguished. I. Passenger statistics; II. Statistics of wage earners in search of work; III. Statistics of immigrants housed at the Immigrants' Hostel at Montevideo.

I. Passenger Statistics

The passenger movement tables relate (a) to the total movement of passengers by foreign commerce in all ports of the Republic; (b) to the movement of passengers by foreign commerce (ocean and river combined) through the Port of Montevideo; and (c) to the movement of passengers by foreign commerce through the Port of Montevideo.

(1) *Movement of passengers by foreign ocean and river commerce through all ports.* (Table Ia, years 1893-1924.)—This table comprises passengers of every class who arrived in Uruguay as passengers by ocean or river. We quote also figures indicating the difference between arrivals and departures, as this difference is of some importance for our enquiry.

The corresponding table relating to passengers classified according to their last or future residence, shows that this movement is confined almost entirely to travel to and from Argentina. For example, in 1921, of a total of 118,451 passengers entered by all ports, 104,211 had arrived from Argentina. However, the statistics of nationalities show that the citizens of the continental countries are far more feebly represented among the passengers than their countries as countries of last residence. Of passengers arrived in 1921, only 33,847 were Argentinians. The same proportions hold approximately of departures. On the other hand, immigration from European countries is decidedly feebler than European immigration. For instance, in 1921, 2,902 passengers arrived from Spain, whilst 10,044 Spaniards arrived.

(2) *Movement of passengers by foreign ocean and river commerce through the Port of Montevideo.*—This table refers to the Port of Montevideo. Totals have been published since 1877 in the *Anuario Estadistico*, and data concerning sex, age, occupation, and nationality since 1904-1905. We refrain from reproducing these figures as a large number of the migrants are practically transients travelling by river and as our tables relate on the whole only to the Port of Montevideo.

(3) *Movement of passengers by foreign ocean commerce through the port of Montevideo.* (Tables I, IIa, III, IV, IVb, VI, VII, VIII.)—These tables only include persons who, regardless of passenger class, arrived by sea at the Port of Montevideo or departed from this port in order to go abroad. Continental migrations and migrations of transients are included only so far as they are by sea.

The earliest data relate to the period 1835-42 (tables I and IV). We may assume that migrants at that date were almost exclusively European

immigrants who intended to take up their abode permanently in Uruguay. The publication of the statistics was resumed, after a protracted interruption, in 1866. (Table I.)

From 1879 onwards particulars were furnished in regard to sex, age, occupation, and nationality (Tables I, IIa, III, IVb); but these were again interrupted between 1902 or 1904 and 1912.

Beginning with 1877, emigration returns are also available. (Tables I, VI and VIII.) In Table I as it is here throughout a question of passenger statistics—we have indicated for 1879-1903 and 1913-21 the excess of arriving over departing aliens.

The Act of June 10, 1890 adopted a definition of immigrants which is correct in principle; "foreigners of good repute and capable of work who arrive in the Republic by second or third class with the intention of settling there." (Act of June 10, 1890.)

Unfortunately this definition was not applied in the collection of the port statistics.

II. STATISTICS OF MIGRATION OF WORKERS (WAGE EARNERS IN SEARCH OF WORK) (1867-90.) (Tables II, IVa.)

(1) The table entitled *Immigrants who applied for work at the Commissariat-General of Immigration*, 1867-90, approximates to a correct conception of the signification of the term immigrant.

These immigrants represent 5 to 12 per cent of the passenger arrivals by sea at Montevideo. (Table I.) These figures, too, do not present an exact account of the actual volume of real immigration, since the immigrants were not bound to announce their arrival at the Commissariat. As a measure of economy the Commissariat was abolished in 1891.

(2) *Migrant Workers, 1920-21.* (Tables IX-IXd.) These tables, which were communicated to the International Labour Office without accompanying particulars as to method, comprise probably the whole volume of the migration of workers, that is, the continental and overseas migrations of citizens and aliens.

When a comparison is made between the nationality and the country of origin of the migrants, the same phenomenon is revealed as that already noticed in the passenger statistics. For instance, in 1920, of a total of 14,901 immigrants, 11,739 arrived from Argentina, whilst the number of immigrant workers of Argentine nationality did not exceed 4,896.

In the same year direct overseas immigration accounted for 1,409 persons, while the number of immigrants of European nationality was 7,842. The number of direct immigrants arriving from Europe is relatively modest, and many entered via other countries, especially through Argentina or after having found temporary employment in the latter country. It is quite possible that a certain number of the immigrants had been for a time domiciled in Argentina and came to Uruguay in search of temporary employment.

The available data make it difficult to ascertain the correct number

of real overseas immigrants (direct and indirect) who have reached the country with the intention of residing therein for at least a year. For this reason we have contrasted the statistics of the immigration and the emigration of workers, in order to emphasise this phenomenon year by year.

III.   Statistics of Immigrants housed at the Immigrants' Hostel
       at Montevideo   (Table V, years 1908-24)

(1) By a Decree of October 11, 1912, the Director of the Immigrants' Hostel at Montevideo is charged with the duty of supervising immigration. The persons dealt with in his account coincide no doubt with immigrants proper. Continental immigrants are included in this place.

Of course, we are here far from comprehending all immigrants, as no one is bound to reside at the Immigrants' Hostel.

TABLE I.—Passengers inward and outward (citizens and aliens) by Foreign Ocean Commerce
at the Port of Montevideo (all classes), 1835-42 and
1866-1923.

Year	Immigrants			Emigrants			Excess of alien arrivals over alien departures
	Total	Citizens	Aliens	Total	Citizens	Aliens	
1835	613		613[1]				
1836	3,146		3,146[1]				
1837	2,583		2,583[1]				
1838	5,424		5,424[1]				
1839	1,163		1,163[1]				
1840	2,475		2,475[1]				
1841	7,860		7,860[1]				
1842	9,874		9,874[1]				
1866	9,326						
1867	17,356						
1868	16,892						
1869	20,435						
1870	21,148						
1871	17,912						
1872	11,516						
1873	24,339						
1874	13,759						
1875	5,298						
1876	5,570						
1877	6,168			6,376			
1878	9,464			6,259			
1879	10,710[2]		10,829	7,009	...	6,965	3,864
1880	9,281[2]	152	9,051	6,829	282	6,558	2,493
1881	8,309[2]	201	8,135	6,286	386	5,953	2,182
1882	10,116	162	9,954	6,179	464	5,715	4,239
1883	11,086	143	10,943	6,089	332	5,757	5,186
1884	11,954	162	11,792	6,040	331	5,709	6,083
1885	15,679	234	15,445	6,729	319	6,410	9,035
1886	12,291	191	12,100	6,542	189	6,353	5,747
1887	12,867	200	12,667	6,252	203	6,049	6,618
1888	16,581	216	16,365	7,601	269	7,332	9,033
1889	27,349	304	27,045	10,658	182	10,476	16,569
1890	24,117	187	23,930	19,852	108	19,744	4,186

For reference notes see page 581.

TABLE I.—Passengers inward and outward (citizens and aliens) by foreign ocean commerce at the Port of Montevideo (all classes), 1835-42 and 1866-1923 (concluded).

Year	Immigrants			Emigrants			Excess of alien arrivals over alien departures
	Total	Citizens	Aliens	Total	Citizens	Aliens	
1891	11,916	339	11,577	19,809	181	19,628	—8,051
1892	11,871	187	11,684	8,827	286	8,541	3,143
1893	9,543	187	9,356	6,339	133	6,206	3,150
1894	11,875	195	11,680	6,016	113	5,903	5,777
1895	9,158	142	9,016	6,387	65	6,322	2,694
1896	10,505	107	10,398	5,918	192	5,726	4,672
1897	9,140	309	8,831	6,779	338	6,441	2,390
1898	9,467	230	9,237	6,411	251	6,160	3,077
1899	9,006	207	8,799	5,830	212	5,618	3,181
1900	8,892	396	8,496	6,705	570	6,135	2,361
1901	9,620	334	9,286	6,664	276	6,388	2,898
1902	6,883	204	6,679	6,941	319	6,622	57
1903	7,268	278	6,990	6,247	272	5,975	1,015
1904	7,008			5,901			
1905	7,878			6,078			
1906	8,664			5,793			
1907	8,580			6,458			
1908	8,904			5,863			
1909	9,340			7,775			
1910	11,231			8,388			
1911	13,883			8,781			
1912	17,984			9,507			
1913	16,639	494	16,145	12,380	660	11,720	4,425
1914	10,454	637	9,817	11,571	611	10,960	—1,143
1915	5,595	511	5,084	6,876	470	6,406	—1,322
1916	4,694	465	4,229	4,962	566	4,396	—167
1917	4,394	443	3,951	3,975	324	3,651	300
1918	5,212	546	4,666	4,258	449	3,809	857
1919	11,301	804	10,497	5,955	659	5,296	5,201
1920	10,090	845	9,245	7,058	1,044	6,014	3,231
1921	9,187	936	8,251	5,297	953	4,344	3,907
1922	10,817			6,183			
1923	17,418			6,611			

TABLE Ia.—MOVEMENT OF PASSENGERS BY FOREIGN OCEAN AND RIVER COM-
MERCE THROUGH ALL PORTS, 1893-1924.

Year	Arrivals	Departures	Excess of arrivals over departures
1893	71,462	67,911	3,551
1894	71,304	61,338	9,966
1895	55,418	50,180	5,238
1896	80,184	74,190	5,994
1897	74,329	69,065	5,264
1898	71,475	66,799	4,676
1899	77,990	67,920	10,070
1900	62,588	54,643	7,945
1901	97,447	88,223	9,224
1902	96,249	88,289	7,960
1903	98,240	88,360	9,880
1904	83,249	79,597	3,652
1905	126,624	113,525	13,099
1906	135,962	121,699	14,263
1907	149,418	129,755	19,663
1908	153,785	133,016	20,769
1909	165,638	145,554	20,084
1910	173,741	155,726	18,015
1911	195,389	170,922	24,467
1912	248,085	222,157	25,928
1913	261,148	232,644	28,504
1914	264,232	251,098	13,134
1915	212,236	203,233	9,003
1916	220,527	204,525	16,002
1917	173,421	164,386	9,035
1918	180,687	177,254	3,433
1919	158,186	145,287	12,899
1920	137,639	125,867	11,772
1921	118,451	106,888	11,563
1922	165,435	152,339	13,096
1923	172,503	157,078	15,425
1924	173,833	158,533	15,300

TABLE II.—Distribution of immigrants who applied for work at the Commissariat-General of Immigration, by sex, age and occupation, 1867-90

Year	Total	Sex and age			Occupation			
		Children	Adults		Artisans	Workers and shepherds	Employees	Not specified
			Males	Females				
1867	1,913	77	1,744	92	462	484	237	730
1868	2,479	200	2,061	218	672	349	221	1,237
1869	1,861	102	1,613	146	433	236	199	993
1870	1,305	123	1,036	146	171	336	138	660
1871	743	45	626	72	114	154	105	370
1872	916	66	756	94	161	212	136	407
1873	1,480	133	1,183	164	237	301	218	724
1874	2,708	279	2,129	300	535	736	309	1,128
1875	1,493	215	1,097	181	257	449	115	622
1876	1,469	180	1,158	131	292	440	145	592
1877	1,913	316	1,306	291	321	710	150	732
1878	1,594	237	1,167	190	397	612	131	454
1879	1,587	200	1,206	181	555	277	134	521
1880	1,933	340	1,328	265	361	931	114	527
1881	1,416	267	993	156	220	618	82	496
1882	1,124	176	824	124	311	584	7	311
1883	1,067	124	832	111	139	449	72	407
1884	1,272	115	1,039	118	127	481	113	551
1885	1,857	83	1,663	111	255	649	109	844
1886	1,383	127	1,131	125	157	388	72	766
1887	1,406	91	1,192	123	125	482	61	738
1888	1,622	115	1,393	114	211	468	111	832
1889	10,446	2,804	5,950	1,692	1,523	5,565	65	3,293
1890	881	3,091	3,881	1,844	598	7,421	18	779

TABLE IIa.—Distribution of passengers inward by foreign ocean commerce at the Port of Montevideo (all classes), by sex and age, 1879-1901 and 1913-21.

Year	Total	Males under 15 years	Adults	Females under 15 years	Adults
1879	10,829	1,104	7,215	546	1,964
1880	9,203	751	6,285	510	1,657
1881	8,336	589	6,102	362	1,283
1882	10,116	972	6,642	493	2,009
1883	11,086	1,037	7,536	459	2,054
1884	11,954	671	8,869	405	2,009
1885	15,679	1,053	11,543	506	2,577
1886	12,291	682	9,220	433	1,956
1887	12,867	807	9,652	390	2,018
1888	16,581	918	12,468	363	2,832
1889	27,349	1,846	20,010	716	4,777
1890	24,117	1,188	17,826	672	4,431
1891	11,916	627	9,178	168	1,943
1892	11,871	572	9,121	275	1,903
1893	9,543	839	6,716	422	1,566
1894	11,875	696	8,819	448	1,912
1895	9,158	292	7,836	146	884
1896	10,505	392	8,761	259	1,093
1897	9,140	423	7,464	203	1,050
1898	9,467	562	7,503	341	1,061
1899	9,006	739	6,369	441	1,457
1900	8,892	813	5,836	615	1,628
1901	9,620	767	6,711	518	1,624
1913	16,639	585[3]	13,459[4]	418[3]	2,177[4]
1914	10,454	376[3]	8,038[4]	287[3]	1,753[4]
1915	5,595	453[3]	3,468[4]	363[3]	1,312[4]
1916	4,694	349[3]	2,747[4]	306[3]	1,292[4]
1917	4,394	344[3]	2,654[4]	334[3]	1,062[4]
1918	5,212	492[3]	2,826[4]	451[3]	1,443[4]
1919	11,301	1,039[3]	6,035[4]	1,044[3]	3,183[4]
1920	10,090	819[3]	5,543[4]	739[3]	2,989[4]
1921	9,187	659[3]	5,345[4]	635[3]	2,548[4]

For reference notes see page 581.

TABLE III.—DISTRIBUTION OF PASSENGERS INWARD BY FOREIGN OCEAN COMMERCE AT THE PORT OF MONTEVIDEO (ALL CLASSES), BY OCCUPATION, 1879-1921.

Year	Farmers and shepherds	Merchants	Industrial	General labor	Intellectual or liberal professions	Religious callings	Independent	Domestic service	Other occupations	No occupation
1879	3,278	706	783	1,220	659	15	29	99	649	3,391
1880	1,757	590	641	797	137	34	31	218	374	4,624
1881	950	516	374	624	178	6	17	140	169	5,362
1882	1,195	430	244	867	230	11	45	108	344	6,642
1883	1,120	413	277	895	233	26	28	161	465	7,468
1884	1,307	576	410	1,486	169	34	32	278	389	7,273
1885	1,993	906	765	1,686	358	19	23	306	409	9,214
1886	1,488	536	338	1,245	195	19	7	184	639	7,640
1887	1,515	476	410	1,435	168	14	9	147	615	8,078
1888	2,306	517	670	1,873	260	29	23	181	509	10,213
1889	7,379	655	796	2,417	178	40	.	183	630	15,071
1890	4,415	625	422	1,370	162	27	5	129	548	16,414
1891	1,334	639	226	934	323	22	9	106	429	7,894
1892	742	404	262	803	88	20	18	113	385	9,035
1893	1,414	665	269	1,311	182	42	21	107	266	5,266
1894	1,836	614	257	3,071	203	32	38	71	1,397	4,356
1895	2,059	427	671	1,684	879	5	89	152	358	2,834
1896	2,537	391	586	4,020	953	39	88	94	378	1,419
1897	2,382	694	948	2,720	536	57	73	113	711	906
1898	2,535	691	1,029	2,862	872	25	39	148	669	597
1899	2,186	751	1,127	2,371	538	55	32	173	633	1,140
1900	1,540	1,185	1,180	1,920	82	53	77	214	688	1,953
1901	718	1,276	817	3,326	69	31	52	186	579	2,566
1902	307	1,275	1,698	2,167	32	5	43	134	514	708
1903	455	1,348	1,540	2,658	40	29	29	68	387	714
1913	1,049	2,007⁵	852⁶	8,299	58	57	86	154	1,572	2,505
1914	533	1,640⁵	658⁶	4,133	132	44	76	151	1,076	2,011
1915	258	1,101⁵	297⁶	1,249	342	25	74	148	388	1,713
1916	190	990⁵	512⁶	747	236	53	95	169	196	1,506
1917	339	918⁵	420⁶	620	205	43	49	61	187	1,552
1918	195	945⁵	493⁶	982	216	30	39	50	216	2,046
1919	488	1,750⁵	997⁶	1,808	801	106	134	246	432	4,539
1920	745	1,998⁵	761⁶	1,441	551	71	93	126	423	3,881
1921	770	1,527⁵	643⁶	1,673	370	78	116	110	493	3,407

TABLE IV.—DISTRIBUTION OF PASSENGERS INWARD AT THE PORT OF MONTEVIDEO, BY NATIONALITY, 1835-42.

Year	Total	French	Spanish	Italian	Brazilian	English	German	Others
1835	613	43	481	34	37	10	...	8
1836	3,146	998	1,209	512	246	88	38	55
1837	2,583	442	1,227	522	178	180	2	32
1838	5,424	2,071	2,359	468	161	156	77	132
1839	1,163	342	280	382	59	63	4	33
1840	2,475	835	370	771	45	59	298	97
1841	7,860	3,816	948	2,737	112	170	7	70
1842	9,874	5,218	1,607	2,519	82	124	227	97
Total:	33,138	13,765	8,481	7,945	920	850	653	524
Proportion (percent)	100	41.54	25.59	23.98	2.78	2.56	1.97	1.58

For reference notes see page 581.

TABLE IVa.—PASSENGERS INWARD BY FOREIGN OCEAN COMMERCE AT THE PORT OF MONTEVIDEO (ALL CLASSES) AND DISTRIBUTION OF IMMIGRANTS WHO APPLIED FOR WORK AT THE COMMISSARIAT-GENERAL OF IMMIGRATION, BY NATIONALITY, 1867-90.

| Year | Passengers inward | Nationality of immigrants who applied for work | | | | | | | | | |
		Total	Spanish	Italians	French	English	Germans	Swiss	Argentinians	Portuguese	Others
1867	17,356	1,913	360	743	256	161	104	33	31	54	171
1868	16,892	2,479	508	1,093	358	241	100	38	24	49	68
1869	20,435	1,861	620	592	244	146	119	30	22	44	44
1870	21,148	1,305	514	376	205	61	37	17	15	18	62
1871	17,912	743	308	214	106	16	32	9	12	13	33
1872	11,516	916	423	202	181	44	26	10	1	12	17
1873	24,339	1,480	606	346	359	26	27	35	20	22	39
1874	13,759	2,708	1,086	961	437	16	54	74	21	22	37
1875	5,298	1,493	609	402	279	8	55	53	51	12	24
1876	5,570	1,469	453	500	271	11	37	47	43	4	103
1877	6,160	1,913	571	569	358	35	54	121	85	34	86
1878	9,464	1,594	529	492	208	10	72	48	46	19	170
1879	10,829	1,587	387	721	230	31	43	52	63	14	46
1880	9,203	1,933	405	939	258	42	74	74	73	9	59
1881	8,336	1,416	435	646	128	12	38	25	62	11	59
1882	10,116	1,124	370	518	76	25	41	14	22	14	44
1883	11,086	1,067	428	380	...	7	75	18	31	15	113
1884	11,954	1,272	428	537	103	12	62	13	41	8	68
1885	15,679	1,857	607	916	98	19	41	11	40	14	111
1886	12,291	1,383	653	553	61	8	29	7	24	16	32
1887	12,867	1,406	618	423	104	26	46	14	18	34	123
1888	16,581	1,622	738	513	176	27	45	14	12	43	54
1889	27,349	10,446	1,399	6,932	670	78	126	22	14	41	1,164
1890	24,117	8,816	1,073	7,341	170	14	16	13	3	19	167

TABLE IVb.—DISTRIBUTION OF PASSENGER ALIENS INWARD BY FOREIGN OCEAN COMMERCE AT THE PORT OF MONTEVIDEO (ALL CLASSES), BY NATIONALITY, 1879-1921.

Year	Total	Germans	Argentinians	Austrians and Hungarians	Belgians	Brazilians	Chilians	Spanish	French	English	Italians	North Americans	Portuguese	Swiss	Russians	Other nationalities
1879	10,829	211	75	40	…	542	46	2,935	800	277	4,648	18	137	53	…	1,047
1880	9,051	295	67	25	11	682	41	1,846	825	261	4,176	22	111	…	…	689
1881	8,135	400	55	62	13	685	40	1,589	844	531	3,686	22	154	…	…	54
1882	9,954	453	48	59	61	919	47	2,487	978	531	4,045	12	122	38	…	154
1883	10,943	392	72	85	11	781	55	2,951	872	472	4,573	36	84	43	…	516
1884	11,792	437	70	96	14	619	14	2,886	991	330	5,364	34	144	89	…	704
1885	15,445	413	72	75	12	726	25	3,175	978	624	8,865	29	139	67	…	305
1886	12,100	464	75	76	21	675	10	2,667	1,001	825	5,510	17	202	51	…	506
1887	12,667	303	62	62	30	415	22	3,416	835	429	5,422	21	76	78	…	1,496
1888	16,365	474	90	76	29	706	28	4,147	876	326	6,671	39	155	55	…	2,693
1889	27,045	319	68	378	34	631	17	4,747	1,091	314	15,047	44	89	122	…	4,144
1890	23,930	213	73	182	32	901	26	4,606	976	369	12,873	39	86	43	…	3,511
1891	11,577	262	103	116	35	973	24	1,945	736	189	4,559	37	118	53	…	2,427
1892	11,684	271	77	155	23	923	23	2,097	555	201	4,966	17	76	27	…	2,273
1893	9,356	222	74	85	23	671	14	1,585	348	494	2,894	29	64	40	…	2,813
1894	11,680	244	89	323	2	2,305	16	2,031	460	216	4,255	43	63	32	…	1,601
1895	9,016	153	98	66	33	382	15	2,116	542	256	3,557	20	41	62	…	1,675
1896	10,398	228	58	168	44	588	10	2,501	388	199	5,046	10	56	61	…	1,041
1897	8,831	287	48	102	69	672	26	2,552	483	225	3,651	20	41	73	…	582
1898	9,237	338	40	87	89	673	27	3,339	814	342	2,894	25	35	78	…	456
1899	8,799	290	62	71	20	426	29	3,110	697	283	3,219	26	57	95	…	414
1900	8,496	290	65	126	31	685	50	2,815	451	252	3,211	58	119	32	…	311
1901	9,286	336	63	177	43	715	33	2,708	512	209	3,777	46	76	17	…	574
1902	6,679	277	27	110	42	333	23	1,884	479	243	2,823	31	91	64	…	252
1903	6,990	189	47	113	20	339	25	2,209	356	291	2,961	11	142	95	…	192
1913	16,145	430	26	…	…	627	…	5,751	478	490	4,097	45	…	…	…	4,201
1914	9,817	261	34	…	…	301	…	3,340	328	415	2,723	120	…	…	…	2,295
1915	5,084	154	163	…	…	621	…	2,260	176	333	335	154	…	…	…	888
1916	4,229	71	114	…	21	598	…	1,973	149	226	405	205	130	…	99	238
1917	3,951	43	213	…	20	642	…	1,717	169	135	329	144	147	…	143	249
1918	4,666	31	174	…	15	643	…	2,411	186	194	405	148	130	…	100	229
1919	10,497	289	328	…	94	1,244	…	4,883	587	852	676	315	364	…	219	646
1920	9,245	233	263	…	125	688	…	4,081	491	683	1,161	318	318	…	60	824
1921	8,251	237	172	…	71	510	…	3,443	400	513	1,409	267	183	…	90	956

TABLE V.—DISTRIBUTION OF IMMIGRANTS HOUSED AT THE IMMIGRANTS' HOSTELRY AT MONTEVIDEO, BY NATIONALITY, 1908-24.

Nationality	1908	1909	1910	1911	1912	1913	1914	1915	1916	1917	1918	1919	1920	1921	1922	1923	1924
Albanian																11	7
Arab		10													12	2	
Argentinian		9	4	11	23	32	16	23	18	150	289	135	566	325	183	223	107
Armenian	2															90	29
Australian																	
Austrian		40	252	295	242	144	176	46	48	15	5	2	2	11	18	71	59
Belgian		1	5	6	8	28						15	3	6	16		
Bolivian					1									2		2	
Brazilian	1	3	16	22	63	52	136	65	18	84	132	343	423	255	322	367	106
Bulgarian		24	30	30	7	9	1		15	5				10	10	37	91
Chilian		14	4	13	23	6	7	12	7	4	2	5	3	3	36	4	4
Colombian			6		3		1								3		
Cuban		2			4			2		2							
Czechoslovak														3	3	55	60
Danish		3	6	6	2	45	12	2			1	2	5			5	1
English		39	29	47	32						1	3	14	51		9	5
Estonian																	2
French	2	24	79	73	83	135	15	2			1	5	20	6	13	6	3
German		38	96	66	134	108	48	41	5	14		7	15	37	66	421	1,067
Greek		16	13	8	17	5	2		22	14				7	11	59	2
Hungarian					3		5		2					1	11	282	108
Italian	22	185	416	307	300	431	171	89	30	31	34	101	228	253	226	871	852
Japanese		5				3	3				3		3		1	1	
Latvian																12	32
Lithuanian											1	1		2	2	1	146
Mexican		1	1	5	2								1				2
Montenegrin		1	19			7											
Netherlander		1	5	2	3	2		1	1				13	4	2	2	1
Nicaraguan																	
North American		5	1	8	5	6	11			1	4	2	6	13		2	5
Norwegian		1	2		1			2			1	1			2		
Paraguayan											1					2	2
Persian										1	4					5	
Peruvian				3			3					2			5	2	2
Polish															2	126	214
Porto-Rican	23															2	
Portuguese		120	107	117	265	318	160	121	61	35	16	92	144	80	52	99	93
Rumanian							1							40	17	145	168
Russian		41	9	16	140	1,943	1,093	375	345	147	94	106	246	202	85	340	522
Serbian				3	1								6		9	21	31
Serb, Croat and Slovene																133	298
Spanish	207	681	1,330	1,293	1,866	1,987	1,083	615	235	287	338	994	1,422	1,053	669	1,229	823
Swedish		3	3		13	3	1	1	1		3						
Swiss		6	7	9	2	3	6	3	15	3	3	6	2	5	14	9	14
Syrian															1	11	1
Turkish		41			43	67	5		11	2	1			2	3	151	235
Ukrainian						1		1	1					1		127	34
Venezuelan		1	4														
Total	257	1,315	2,446	2,340	3,286	5,343	2,959	1,408	835	795	934	1,822	3,122	2,372	1,792	4,932	5,126

TABLE VI.—Distribution of passengers outward by foreign ocean commerce at the Port of Montevideo (all classes), by sex and age, 1879-1921.

Year	Total	Males		Females	
		Under 15 years	Adults	Under 15 years	Adults
1879	6,965	472	5,368	260	865
1880	6,840	456	5,186	161	1,037
1881	6,339	443	4,960	115	821
1882	6,179	757	4,334	194	894
1883	6,089	606	4,493	85	905
1884	6,040	318	4,545	127	1,050
1885	6,729	378	5,138	192	1,021
1886	6,542	327	5,064	194	957
1887	6,252	490	4,756	118	888
1888	7,601	378	6,195	129	899
1889	10,658	507	8,149	366	1,636
1890	19,852	764	15,354	477	3,257
1891	19,809	729	15,901	221	2,958
1892	8,827	591	6,704	243	1,289
1893	6,339	394	4,641	215	1,089
1894	6,016	391	4,346	233	1,046
1895	6,387	138	5,675	73	501
1896	5,918	243	4,934	79	662
1897	6,779[7]	338	5,425	161	865
1898	6,411	321	5,406	176	508
1899	5,830	296	4,653	186	695
1900	6,705	385	4,769	284	1,267
1901	6,664	355	5,287	203	819
1913	12,380	495[3]	9,950[4]	356[3]	1,579[4]
1914	11,571	357[3]	9,283[4]	243[3]	1,688[4]
1915	6,876	301[3]	5,188[4]	238[3]	1,149[4]
1916	4,962	238[3]	3,385[4]	248[3]	1,091[4]
1917	3,975	266[3]	2,699[4]	216[3]	794[4]
1918	4,258	279[3]	2,876[4]	260[3]	843[4]
1919	5,955	398[3]	3,479[4]	368[3]	1,440[4]
1920	7,058	401[3]	4,527[4]	414[3]	1,716[4]
1921	5,297	324[3]	3,280[4]	285[3]	1,408[4]

For reference notes see page 581.

TABLE VII.—DISTRIBUTION OF PASSENGERS OUTWARD BY FOREIGN OCEAN COMMERCE AT THE PORT OF MONTEVIDEO (ALL CLASSES), BY OCCUPATION, 1879-1921.

Year	Farmers and shepherds	Merchants	Industrials	General labor	Intellectual or liberal professions	Religious callings	Independent	Domestic service	Other occupations	No occupation
1879	172	822	212	2,686	113	12	14	61	305	2,568
1880	105	764	106	1,916	116	11	16	100	378	3,328
1881	121	729	97	1,256	141	32	7	155	377	3,424
1882	65	678	84	1,264	126	25	28	40	243	3,626
1883	113	729	79	875	178	37	23	56	278	3,721
1884	162	906	98	1,063	431	28	20	47	245	3,040
1885	570	791	130	1,088	213	11	10	48	288	3,580
1886	345	475	87	873	150	8		54	310	4,240
1887	112	576	16	370	237	20		8	261	4,652
1888	414	602	51	334	151	26		13	97	5,913
1889	432	637	43	361	147	21	2	19	151	8,845
1890	1,281	410	128	392	110	2	3	22	182	17,322
1891	2,507	479	93	330	116	6		8	230	16,040
1892	491	624	465	815	191	33	24	41	392	5,751
1893	851	674	798	832	183	17	7	34	227	2,716
1894	538	685	862	848	85	24	70	17	263	2,624
1895	652	360	591	804	904	20	41	112	786	2,117
1896	1,456	532	711	1,524	434	31	76	46	541	567
1897	1,245	765	832	1,903	510	40	38	67	346	1,033
1898	2,003	425	559	2,118	522	20	85	45	393	241
1899	1,335	621	622	1,985	310	54	22	89	350	442
1900	892	1,177	1,097	1,859	228	34	30	105	460	823
1901	428	1,126	1,081	2,154	43	37	38	54	661	1,042
1902	200	1,660	1,471	2,319	49	24	37	80	521	580
1903	118	1,368	1,429	2,150	37	35	44	39	391	636
1913	435	1,431[5]	738[5]	6,419	104	34	113	79	1,238	1,789
1914	538	1,247[5]	685[5]	6,105	81	37	133	123	791	1,831
1915	90	1,037[5]	951[5]	1,782	155	25	83	66	1,529	1,158
1916	100	998[5]	843[5]	1,260	185	30	42	143	161	1,200
1917	35	1,259[5]	505[5]	994	68	6	29	5	67	1,007
1918	112	1,121[5]	636[5]	890	108	14	22	25	177	1,153
1919	109	1,654[5]	787[5]	854	260	61	61	72	163	1,934
1920	125	2,086[5]	1,134[5]	1,022	276	48	91	46	179	2,051
1921	121	1,216[5]	1,025[5]	606	259	55	52	51	188	1,724

For reference notes see page 581.

TABLE VIII.—DISTRIBUTION OF PASSENGER ALIENS OUTWARD BY FOREIGN OCEAN COMMERCE AT THE PORT OF MONTEVIDEO (ALL CLASSES), BY NATIONALITY, 1879-1921.

Year	Total	German	Argentinian	Austrian and Hungarian	Belgian	Brazilian	Chilian	Spanish	French	English	Italian	North American	Portuguese	Swiss	Russian	Other nationalities
1879	6,965	122	26	4	5	542	19	1,329	643	298	3,234	29	121	10		588
1880	6,558	205	27	9	17	564	12	1,501	656	196	2,975	13	112			283
1881	5,953	196	25	4	23	638	12	1,030	671	388	2,805	43	82			42
1882	5,715	245	29	12	4	768	31	1,206	571	320	2,369	27	67	11		36
1883	5,757	259	74	13	7	546	23	1,216	610	264	2,427	15	56	15		235
1884	5,709	253	41	25	9	388	20	1,069	505	300	2,740	21	94	19		227
1885	6,410	217	13	8		474	5	1,255	895	417	2,835	5	38	13		226
1886	6,353	140	17	13	4	414	8	1,040	913	315	3,219	4	90	6		174
1887	6,049	208	34	12	2	271	2	966	396	253	1,706	4	29	41		2,123
1888	7,332	227	29	32	37	503	11	1,202	274	345	2,536	23	39	53		2,056
1889	10,476	196	24	66	22	584	11	1,158	268	185	3,556	9	80	71		4,231
1890	19,744	172	23	98	85	625	11	1,940	612	271	8,780	20	55	51		7,064
1891	19,628	150	13	31	11	586	19	2,332	688	216	9,073	17	40	91		6,287
1892	8,541	115	23	132	92	666	9	1,697	247	211	3,925	34	14	16		1,441
1893	6,206	99	22	14	6	374	15	1,207	181	261	2,373	42	26	7		1,590
1894	5,903	106	11	28	11	387	140	952	177	219	2,540	8	48	1		1,192
1895	6,322	93	30	19	32	1,062	17	1,230	314	150	1,867	23	78	15		1,549
1896	5,726	112	22	107	30	727	21	1,866	362	156	2,526	24	27	30		349
1897	6,441	144	34	40	5	550	13	2,045	388	230	2,785	19	27	31		299
1898	6,160	210	17	49	15	660	16	1,822	485	241	2,044	11	14	53		213
1899	5,618	235	21	81	21	394		1,821	525	214	2,257	20	31	82		286
1900	6,135	179	25	77	14	703	20	1,879	313	208	2,319	35	33	50		155
1901	6,388	240	19	41	2	536	22	2,036	306	206	2,391	6	37	51		376
1902	7,072	173	14	35		340	16	1,809	363	201	2,953	13	94	38		371
1903	5,975	161	9			367	7		248	345	2,765	28	58	18		209
1913	11,720	271	59			318		4,032	253	314	3,533	49				2,750
1914	10,960	213	32			207		4,226	179	241	3,546	76				2,098
1915	6,406	68	26			595		2,835	148	193	1,760	108	106			520
1916	4,396	59	54		15	471		2,602	149	103	662	102	30		43	184
1917	3,651	24	20		7	426		2,084	282	124	652	21	46		68	58
1918	3,809	4	56		15	665		1,867	381	328	734	102	127		27	102
1919	5,296	173	99		29	994		1,967	243	497	894	161	126		116	286
1920	6,014	144	95		44	992		2,037		311	942	194	101		51	559
1921	4,344	158	96		30	446		1,327				276			26	388

TABLE IX.—INTERCONTINENTAL AND CONTINENTAL IMMIGRATION AND EMIGRATION OF WORKERS, 1920-21.

Year	IMMIGRANTS			EMIGRANTS			EXCESS OF IMMIGRATION OVER EMIGRATION		
	Total	Intercontinental	Continental	Total	Intercontinental	Continental	Total	Intercontinental	Continental
1920	14,901	1,409	12,078	13,820	449	12,163	1,081	960	85
1921[8]	11,045	4,403	6,642	11,002	2,822	8,180	43	1,581	1,538

TABLE IXa.—DISTRIBUTION OF IMMIGRANT AND EMIGRANT WORKERS, BY COUNTRY OF ORIGIN AND DESTINATION, 1920-21.

Country	Immigrants		Emigrants	
	1920	1921[8]	1920	1921[8]
Argentina	11,739	} 6,642	11,946	} 8,180
Brazil	339		217	
Spain	1,130		316	
Italy	108		82	
France	74	} 4,403	48	} 2,822
England	13		3	
Portugal	84		405	
Other countries	31		803	
Unspecified	1,383			
Total	14,901	11,045	13,820	11,002

TABLE IXb.—DISTRIBUTION OF IMMIGRANT AND EMIGRANT WORKERS BY SEX AND AGE, 1920-21.

Year	Immigrants								Emigrants							
	Total	Men	Women	Under 15 years	From 16 to 21	From 22 to 50	51 and over	Unspecified	Total	Men	Women	Under 15 years	From 16 to 21	From 22 to 50	51 and over	Unspecified
1920	14,901	14,814	87	399	1,823	11,614	694	371	13,820	13,790	30	313	2,003	9,980	1,212	312
1921[8]	11,045	10,335	710	35	586	5,690	694	4,042	11,002	10,749	253	89	871	6,466	650	2,926

For reference notes see page 581.

TABLE IXc.—DISTRIBUTION OF IMMIGRANT AND EMIGRANT WORKERS, BY OCCUPATION, 1920-21.

	Immigrants		Emigrants	
	1920	1921[g]	1920	1921[g]
Masons	21	6	25	17
Coopers	7	...	...	...
Butchers	1	...	...	...
Carpenters	36	26	17	425
Cooks	10	8	9	204
Drivers	2	...	...	...
Dressmakers	9	...	...	...
Chauffeurs	8	4	...	204
Cabinet makers	7	...	...	...
Clerks	294	212	169	181
Farmers	5	...	...	...
Sculptors	...	7	1	27
Electricians	15	4	4	7
Engine stokers	18	...	...	...
Photographers	1	...	...	...
Blacksmiths	10	...	5	...
Oven men	1	...	...	...
Gardeners	2	547	...	47
Workers	421	10	2	3
Machinists	14	...	...	...
Sailors	219	159	291	216
Mechanicians	64	37	31	11
Milliners	35	6	...	2
Waiters	5	...	...	...
Laborers	16	13	10	4
Bakers	4	4	1	3
Hairdressers	10	...	...	...
Unskilled workers	285	928	399	327
Stonecutters	4	...	...	...
Painters	11	10	8	4
Day laborers	13,031	7,033	12,743	8,195
Hewers	9	6	6	6
Domestic servants	231	977	29	123
Sadlers	1	...	...	...
Slaters	3	...	...	...
Lightermen	2	...	...	...
Bootmakers	22	16	60	3
Other occupations	66	1,032	9	993
Unspecified	...	...	...	...
Total	14,901	11,045	13,820	11,002

For reference notes see page 581.

TABLE IXd.—DISTRIBUTION OF IMMIGRANT AND EMIGRANT WORKERS, BY NATIONALITY, 1920-21.

Nationality	IMMIGRANTS		EMIGRANTS	
	1920	1921[8]	1920	1921[8]
Uruguayans	1,395	3,186	1,038	2,267
Argentinians	4,896	1,669	3,825	1,749
Brazilians	186	267	204	172
North Americans	....	72	....	57
Spaniards	4,174	1,744	4,006	2,255
Italians	2,090	947	2,107	1,265
Frenchmen	202	79	264	131
Englishmen	324	178	339	96
Germans	119	87	127	105
Portuguese	239	146	134	54
Austrians	49	19	79	52
Russians	305	152	414	217
Greeks	55	28	140	29
Turks	285	81	216	121
Other nationalities	582	2,390	927[*]	2,432
Total	14,901	11,045	13,820	11,002

For reference notes see page 581.

URUGUAY

SOURCES

Apuntos estadisticos para la Exposición universal de Paris, 1878, p. 28, cited in *Statistica della Emigrazione italiana all' Estero*, nel 1878, Rome, 1880, p. CCIX. The figures of the French edition of the same publication (Résumé statistique pour *l'Exposition Universelle de Paris*, par la Direction Statistique de la Republique, Montevideo, 1878, p. 33.), which were consulted in the Library of the Royal Statistical Society in London, are in some cases slightly different.

Tables I and IV (years 1835-42).

Sintesis estadistica de la Republica oriental del Uruguay, Agosto de 1925, Montevideo, 1925, p. 5.

Table Ia (years 1921-24).

Anuario estadistico de la Republica Oriental del Uruguay, año 1884 to 1921. Montevideo, 1885 to 1923.

All other figures.

NOTES

We may assume all these passengers to be aliens. Table IV indicates the different nationalities; it is not probable that there the nationals are included in the figures given for "other"; even if so, their number would be very small. In the source there is no indication as to the class in which the passengers travelled.

[2]These figures do not agree with the totals given in table IIa.
[3]Under 14 years.
[4]14 years and over.
[5]1913-21 includes merchants and mariners.
[6]1913-21 includes industrials, artisans and laborers.
[7]The sum of the figures given for sex and age is 6,789.
[8]The figures for 1921 include data for the first ten months of the year only, as the documents for the last two months were destroyed by a fire.
[9]Including 68 the nationality of whom is not specified.

CHILE

A Chilian Emigration Agency was established in Europe in 1845, its object being to recruit immigrants in Germany. European immigration, as a result of this recruiting effort, commenced in 1850.[1] However, the available statistical data are deficient. In 1884 the recruiting was taken over by an authorised company.

According to the Immigration Regulations of October 15, 1895, the General Agency of Colonisation and Immigration and another company were authorised to recruit immigrants. The former Agency prepared lists of immigrants and transmitted them to the competent Government authority at the landing port. These authorities forwarded quarterly reports to the Ministry of Colonisation which compiles immigration statistics. (Tables I and II.)

After 1910 we are without immigration statistics. These are replaced by the statistics of passenger movements, where only the excess of arrivals over departures interests us. (Tables III and IV.)

TABLE I.—IMMIGRATION OF ALIENS, 1850-1910.

Year	Immigrants
1850–1859	1,688
1869	7
1890	11,001
1894	395
1898	564
1900	936
1907	8,810
1909	2,561
Total 1850-1910	60,970

[1]*Boletin de la Oficina del Trabajo*, año 1922, núm. 19. Santiago de Chile, 1922, pp. 4-5.

TABLE II.—DISTRIBUTION BY SEX, AGE, NATIONALITY AND OCCUPATION OF IMMIGRANTS ADMITTED IN 1909.

Total	2,561
Adults:	
Men	972
Women	706
Children	883
Nationality:[1]	
Spanish	1,738
Portuguese	447
French	176
Italian	107
Other	91
Occupation:[1]	
Without occupation	1,648
Farmers or farm laborers	432
Unskilled workers	105
Mechanicians	36
Carpenters	46
Masons and building operatives	28
Glaziers	20
Clerks	20
Traders	17
Bakers	15
Tailors	13
Painters	5
Miners	4
Students	3
Teachers	4
Garment workers	8

TABLE III.—PASSENGERS ARRIVED AND DEPARTED BY SEA, 1908-23.

Year	Arrivals	Departures	Year	Arrivals	Departures
1908	25,775	12,759	1916	19,896	18,966
1909	19,014	15,867	1917	22,004	12,370
1910	25,788	16,798	1918	9,039	9,292
1911	24,845	23,841	1919	8,586	8,172
1912	27,645	15,482	1920	12,184	9,071
1913	23,579	19,179	1921	13,772	7,419
1914	40,822	15,110	1922	11,731	7,375
1915	13,086	7,126	1923	12,137	8,091

For reference notes see page 581.

TABLE IV.—PASSENGERS ARRIVED AND DEPARTED BY THE TRANS-ANDES RAILWAY, 1913-23.

Year	Arrivals	Departures	Year	Arrivals	Departures
1913	11,814	9,069	1919	7,072	6,952
1914	6,325	5,944	1920	9,938	9,320
1915	4,240	3,282	1921	8,154	7,653
1916	5,982	5,953	1922	7,797	8,114
1917	8,072	6,639	1923	9,861	9,192
1918	8,914	8,146	....	....	....

SOURCES

Boletin de la Oficina del Trabajo. Santiago de Chile, 1922. No. 19, year XII (1922), p. 4, etc.

Table I, (years 1850-1910); II (year 1909).

Annuario Estatistico de la Republica de Chile. Vol. I. "Demografia". Año 1925, Santiago de Chile, 1924, p. XI.

Tables III (years 1908-23); IV (years 1913-23).

NOTE

1The figures given for the different nationalities total 2,559 and those given for the occupations 2,404.

AUSTRIA

I.—PERMIT STATISTICS

The Emigration Patent of Joseph II, dated August 10, 1784, stipulated that emigrants must apply for a special authorisation and that the frontiers were not to be crossed without a passport. On this basis annual returns ("emigration tables") were to be prepared. The forms of the tables to be forwarded to the Court Office were also prescribed (Sec.47). The Court Chancery Decree of September 19, 1816, entrusted to the provincial authorities with the concurrence of the local authorities the granting of authorisation to female emigrants, but male emigrants had to obtain authorisation direct from the Court Office. The provincial authority was required, "in addition to presenting its half-yearly returns of authorisations granted by it to female emigrants, to present also half-yearly returns of emigration authorisations granted by the Court Chancery". (*State Archives*, Index, Vienna.) As these half-yearly returns were not drawn up on a uniform basis, a Court Chancery Decree of October 9, 1817, prescribed new forms for male and female emigrants.

By virtue of the Exchequer Decree of March 17, 1820, and the Decree of February 8, 1823, the political authorities were required—up to the year 1884—to send in yearly "emigration tables" showing all persons who left the Monarchy and who "proceeded to a foreign country with the object of not returning, whether the said persons had obtained the permission of the authorities or whether they had crossed the frontier without it". These tables contain special headings for the sex and the age of the emigrants, as well as for the wealth which they intend to take abroad. The "emigration tables" thus related both to authorised and unauthorised emigration and were framed with a view to providing a general survey of the extent of permanent emigration, not merely to other parts of Europe, but also to overseas countries.

Emigration from Hungary, Transylvania, and the "military frontier" was from the beginning excluded from these tables.

We were able to trace these migration statistics to their initial stages, that is, to a date even preceding the Decree of 1820, for the year 1819, in the lithographed Statistical Tables of the Austrian Monarchy (*Tafeln zur Statistik der oesterreichischen Monarchie*), second year, 1829.[1] With respect to subsequent years, these data are to be found in the same annual publication up to the year 1854; but for the years 1841 and 1842, t,ie particulars are not available, and for the year 1843 we were only able to find them in the same form in Bächer's study *Bevölkerungsverhältnisse der österreichisch-ungarischen Monarchie*, Vienna, 1846. Finally, for the years 1855-84, the particulars are contained in the *Statistische Monatsschrift*, Vienna, 1876 to 1884.

So long as in pursuance of the Emigration Patent of 1832, formal authorisation was required from the competent provincial authority by

[1] In the library of the "Bundesamt für Statistik."

any intending emigrant, no serious objection could be made to the statistics based thereon. But throughout the time before the principle of freedom of emigration was established under Article 4 of the Constitutional Law of December 21,1867 (*Reichsgesetzblatt*, No. 142), these particulars were not wholly complete or reliable.[1] After 1867 an increasing number of cases of emigration occurred without the knowledge of the authorities, and the data of the "emigration tables" when compared with the figures of the port statistics in transit countries were proved to be so incomplete that the Central Statistical Commission found itself compelled, in 1884, to abandon entirely the preparation of these statistics.[2]

II. PORT STATISTICS

Permit statistics were replaced by particulars taken from the reports of the consular authorities in the most important emigration ports. These were instructed by a Decree of the Ministry for Foreign Affairs, dated May 26, 1889, to keep records compiled on a uniform basis. Furthermore, the diplomatic and consular officers in the leading American immigration ports of New York, Rio de Janeiro, Buenos Aires and Valparaiso were instructed to furnish quarterly reports on the statistics and the legal aspect of immigration, Austrian and Hungarian subjects being dealt with separately. To supplement these reports, reference was also included to the reports of the police authorities in Trieste.

From 1884 onwards, therefore, the *Statistische Monatshefte* merely published the data respecting *overseas emigration*. Brief surveys were also published yearly in the *Statistisches Handbuch*. The material annually published by the Central Commission—which is very incomplete and not uniformly presented—was officially reproduced in abridged form, for the period 1876-1910, by Dr. von Englisch in the *Statistische Monatshefte* for 1913. This study contains not only the particulars collected in all European ports with respect to Austrian intercontinental migrants in transit, classified according to countries of destination, but a particularly complete classification according to sex, age and occupation, and in addition—though in this case not year by year—a classification according to ports, including Hamburg, Bremen, Gerstemünde, Stettin, Antwerp, Amsterdam, Rotterdam, Havre, Cherbourg, Boulogne, Bordeaux, Marseilles, Genoa, Naples, Trieste, Fiume, and some smaller ports. The indirect statistics relating to countries of immigration were also carefully worked out.

---

[1]Cf. the following remark in vols. I and II of the new series of the *Tafeln zur Statistik der Oesterreichischen Monarchie*: "The official data upon immigration and emigration from and to countries indicated cannot be regarded as complete since, in the majority of cases, emigration takes place without authorisation, and cannot be recorded until some time after the proceedings against unauthorised emigrants have been completed and most of immigrants prefer to be regarded for as long as possible as resident strangers. For these reasons, the official records give very low figures and are highly inadequate."

[2] *Statistische Monatshefte*, 10th year, p. 441.

III. Frontier Statistics (seasonal workers)

Finally, Dr. von Englisch's study contains the first particulars about seasonal workers emigrating via Oswicin, Czczakowa, Oderberg, Bodenbach and Tetschen to Germany, France, Denmark and Sweden, the data being taken from the records of the eastern frontier authorities. These statistics indicate, in certain years, a larger number of seasonal migrants than the German Central Office for Workers reported. Similarly it contains particulars regarding the return of intercontinental or continental emigrants.

The different issues of the *Statistisches Handbuch* complete these statistics up to the year 1913 inclusive.

IV. Passport Statistics

The emigration statistics of the Austrian Republic are compiled by the Migration Office of the Bundeskanzleramt, and are based on the passports granted to emigrants. It is also one of the duties of this Office to advise intending emigrants.

Statistics about migration into and out from Austria supplementing the figures in the Austrian national tables will be found in other parts of the present volume. Statistics about the number of migrants from Austria to Argentina (1857-1924), Brazil (1868-1924), Cuba (1901-24), United States (1861-1924), Uruguay (1879-1903), Palestine (1922-24), Australia (1902-24) and Canada (1900-24) will be found in the national tables for those countries. Statistics about the number of migrants returning to Austria from Argentina (1857-1924) United States (1908-24) and Uruguay (1879-1903) will be found in the national tables for those countries.

TABLE I.—EMIGRATION, BY PROVINCE, 1819-84.

Year	Total	Lower Austria	Upper Austria	Salzburg	Styria	Carinthia	Carniola	Austrian littoral[1]	Tyrol	Vorarlberg	Bohemia	Moravia	Silesia	Galicia	Bukovina	Dalmatia	Lombardy	Venice
1819	1,323	171	135		22	2		2	97		263	116		248			139	128
1820	1,603	55	115		9	3			108		121	37		763		740	273	119
1821	2,656	59	111		1	1			114		96	74		1,035		376	368	57
1822	2,474	67	101		1	2			117		124	53		1,182		463	338	103
1823	2,337	62	62		3	1			115		165	500		797		346	23	107
1824	1,349	62	74		7	5		4	88		197	258		234		44	32	58
1825	912	77	103		4	1		8	124		122	141		195		85	29	97
1826	794	55	51			3			117		128	92		63		179	24	116
1827	833	67	94		2			5	116		139	63		65		148	62	87
1828	1,084	60	108		1	2			138		215	237		26		1,517	47	111
1829	2,449	57	57			3		1	118		290	127		51		498	55	123
1830	1,319	70	162		1	2			97		274	89		10		112	38	77
1831	966	61	115						91		349	61		7		27	54	96
1832	754	52	135		9	1		1	119		200	120		27		78	31	62
1833	843	78	148		4	2			98		172	131		21		5	24	81
1834	915	63	126		3	5			89		235	223		31		8	60	74
1835	785	55	119			4		1	116		237	129		23			37	54
1836	761	44	127			1			113		248	140		25		12	29	33
1837	1,205	36	110		1	4		1	527		251	139		27		8	22	77
1838	915	75	103		1	2		2	124		320	120		15			31	115
1839	782	50	136			1			93		228	123		19		1	49	46
1840	662	50	115		2		1	6	128		144	128		111	2	3	38	39
1846	745	64	70		4	5	1		71		165	139		11		4	50	49
1849	469	26	56	10	3				32		103	20	102	2			22	62
1850	635	58	70	30	44	2	1		70		166	13	108	5			70	57
1851	2,842	188	117	28	18				75		341	11	49	5		8	1,919	59
1852	1,288	50	362	37	20	5	2	7	149		427	37	85	30		1	54	55
1853	4,779	147	169	32	9	9	7		180		3,419	272	224	1		3	60	35
1854	7,223	54	214	13	38	23	4		221		6,128	298	147	14		9	62	20
1855	4,005	68	173	18	32		1	8	79		3,021	502	32	53		15		
1856	2,779	87	125	20	20	15	5	19	123		2,088	185		34		15		
1857	2,836	31	62	19	15		3	13	225		2,167	51	73	70	5	12		
1858	2,126	44	49	27	9	6	4	11	416		1,341	75	53	97	4	10		
1859	1,431	42	40	22		1	13	21	200		842	65	43	140	24	7		
1860	2,032	55	50	20			15	17	134		1,302	258	50	159	15	1		
1861	2,513	45		28			5	25	85		1,927	88	64	60	9	3		
1862	1,582	30	31	7	2	3	37	29	85		1,246	55	25	51	13	3		
1863	1,515	48	37	22	1	1	55	63	87		1,124	52	29	61	9	13		
1864	2,322	65	91	22	7	7	27	17	69		1,950	38	57	66	10	11		
1865	2,954	101	86	30	2	2	28	3	101		2,417	158	59	68	7	2		
1866	3,807	97	90	28	13	2	15	34	124		3,089	371	66	134	8	13		
1867	9,299		104	23	15	5		812	169		7,430	71	126	298				
1868	4,149	46		14		4		50	235		3,220		64		4			

TABLE I.—Emigration, by Province, 1819-84 (continued).

Year	Total	Lower Austria	Upper Austria	Salzburg	Styria	Carinthia	Carniola	Austrian littoral[1]	Tyrol	Vorarlberg	Bohemia	Moravia	Silesia	Galicia	Bukovina	Dalmatia	Lombardy	Venice
1869	5,559	68	79	36	5	1	14	34	...	178	4,507	297	61	259	7	13	...	...
1870	5,920	170	73	18	3	...	4	47	...	162	4,519	656	101	144	...	23	...	...
1876[a]	9,246	47	36	15	3	...	4	21	3,409	...	4,098	901	80	627	5	...	...	...
1877	5,877	66	19	13	2	5	4	56	1,902	...	3,066	377	52	308	3	4	...	...
1878	5,554	42	27	15	5	3	7	1,004	1,103	32	2,383	625	149	145	8	9	...	...
1879	5,929	60	31	15	2	6	6	1,289	600	57	2,991	604	186	78	1	2	...	...
1880	10,145	70	29	25	4	1	2	174	348	36	6,411	2,230	110	691	6	4	...	...
1881	13,341	328	75	35	12	...	8	65	943	...	8,517	1,934	200	1,198	2	29	...	...
1882	7,759	111	36	12	17	...	20	244	732	...	5,566	497	89	436	6	5	...	...
1883	7,366	86	107	22	22	5	20	426	...	705	3,557	765	164	1,474	6	7	...	...
1884	7,215	43	57	10	13	7	27	272	...	1,336	3,391	946	67	1,038	8	...	...	...

TABLE II.—DISTRIBUTION OF AUTHORIZED AND UNAUTHORIZED EMIGRANTS, BY SEX AND AGE, 1830-54.

Year	Total	Authorized					Unauthorized				
		Total	Sex		Age		Sex		Age		Total
			Males	Females	Up to 17 years	Over 17 years	Males	Females	Up to 17 years	Over 17 years	
1830	1,319	704	385	319	128	576	366	249	216	399	615
1831	966	729	392	337	150	579	127	110	71	166	237
1832	754	659	354	305	115	544	59	36	17	78	95
1833	843	689	374	315	87	602	114	40	37	117	154
1834	915	850	551	299	139	711	45	20	21	44	65
1835	785	735	433	302	93	642	34	16	...	43	50
1836	761	745	412	333	127	618	11	5	1	15	16
1837	1,205	1,145	601	544	309	836	36	24	24	36	60
1838	915	847	475	372	208	639	37	31	22	46	68
1839	782	760	413	347	147	613	11	11	4	18	22
1840	662	643	367	276	94	549	10	9	...	19	19
1843	756	712	376	336	135	577	24	20	19	25	44
1846	745	725	468	257	86	639	11	9	8	12	20
1849	469	464	275	189	105	359	5	...	...	5	5
1850	635	620	363	257	130	490	10	5	...	14	15
1851	2,842	977	554	423	289	688	1,800	65	40	1,825	1,865
1852	1,288	1,253	685	568	483	770	25	10	3	32	35
1853	4,779	4,754	2,442	2,312	2,087	2,667	21	4	1	24	25
1854	7,223	7,111	3,669	3,442	3,237	3,874	75	37	9	103	112

For reference notes see page 600.

TABLE III.—DISTRIBUTION OF EMIGRANTS, BY SEX AND AGE, 1850-84.

Year	Total	Sex		Age				
		Males	Females	Up to 7 years	From 7 to 17 years	From 17 to 40 years	From 40 to 50 years	50 years and over
1850	508	278	230	38	60	328	69	13
1851	864	474	390	107	148	446	124	39
1852	1,179	627	552	241	217	559	110	52
1853	4,684	2,403	2,281	554	1,501	1,786	681	162
1854	7,141	3,691	3,450	1,631	1,586	2,726	865	333
1855	4,005	2,027	1,978	889	913	1,489	467	247
1856	2,779	1,459	1,320	591	634	1,065	319	170
1857	2,836	1,500	1,336	589	626	1,045	455	121
1858	2,126	1,139	987	352	477	880	303	114
1859	1,431	804	627	233	278	666	177	77
1860	2,032	1,124	908	399	446	894	205	88
1861	2,513	1,370	1,143	593	495	1,059	270	96
1862	1,582	890	692	338	300	692	180	72
1863	1,515	863	652	266	280	694	185	90
1864	2,322	1,288	1,034	488	472	992	285	85
1865	2,954	1,572	1,382	659	620	1,249	316	110
1866	3,807	1,996	1,811	901	771	1,577	422	136
1867	9,299	4,829	4,470	2,057	1,956	3,822	978	486
1868	4,149	2,216	1,933	797	903	1,829	448	172
1869	5,559	2,882	2,677	1,132	1,102	2,577	486	262
1870	5,920	3,134	2,786	1,106	1,134	2,691	627	362
1871	6,169	3,218	2,881	1,040	1,303	2,684	603	469
1872	6,927	3,703	3,224	1,423	1,431	2,891	748	434
1873	5,873	3,197	2,676	1,113	1,198	2,450	756	356
1874	10,012	5,524	4,488	2,010	2,157	3,818	1,263	764
1875	9,259	5,030	4,229	1,992	1,865	3,626	992	784
1876	5,877	3,264	2,613	1,175	1,207	2,523	563	409
1871 to 80	71,685	38,772	32,913	14,595	14,954	29,338	8,041	4,757
1881	13,341	7,201	6,140	2,565	2,947	5,715	1,404	710
1882	7,759	4,313	3,446	1,292	1,620	3,495	902	450
1883	7,366	4,022	3,344	1,337	1,437	3,345	827	420
1884	7,215	4,231	2,984	1,147	1,245	3,686	792	345

TABLE IV.—IMMIGRATION, BY PROVINCE, 1819-54.

Year	Total	Lower Austria	Upper Austria	Salzburg	Styria	Carinthia	Carniola	Austrian littoral[1]	Tyrol and Vorarlberg	Bohemia	Moravia	Silesia	Galicia	Bukovina	Dalmatia	Lombardy	Venice
1819	4,860	117	106	…	37	1	…	…	51	223	672		2,859		…	586	208
1820	5,807	22	123	…	…	…	…	…	53	79	149		4,655		…	387	339
1821	5,982	29	107	…	7	6	…	…	37	117	130		4,788		88	557	116
1922	5,406	10	132	…	…	…	…	…	22	123	82		4,526		8	384	119
1823	2,961	22	142	…	3	5	…	6	44	91	79		2,388		29	114	38
1824	1,345	10	60	…	2	…	…	…	42	129	80		778		66	124	54
1825	841	9	75	…	…	4	…	13	48	132	58		233		71	62	136
1826	862	9	86	…	…	2	…	20	57	106	90		267		50	44	131
1827	987	12	43	…	…	1	…	13	44	141	78		446		54	68	87
1828	998	13	77	…	3	…	…	8	53	135	52		393		152	26	86
1829	1,007	6	89	…	5	…	…	9	71	76	59		223		375	14	80
1830	759	9	84	…	1	1	…	10	62	81	36		89		168	55	163
1831	491	11	70	…	…	…	…	16	45	77	44		101		45[a]	20	62
1832	1,099	24	91	…	1	1	…	15	72	78	45		569		77	42	84
1833	1,358	67	118	…	8	…	…	…	56	79	42		860		11	42	75
1834	665	118	129	…	…	…	…	8	44	98	43		117		26	28	54
1835	928	140	119	…	1	2	…	51	60	114	49		268		13	44	67
1836	883	131	165	…	13	2	…	11	54	104	61		259		7	36	40
1837	898	280	171	…	…	3	…	12	62	79	80		77		8	76	51
1838	935	260	181	…	2	7	…	18	74	118	46		23		114	31	65
1839	974	284	185	…	1	4	…	19	93	73	68		136		70	16	22
1840	924	332	199	…	…	6	…	31	97	94	51		35		18	11	52
1846	1,143	439	256	…	17	1	1	23	122	68	76		57		2	50	27
1849	675	194	88	37	2	…	1	39	70	55	5	5	4	111	1	62	…
1850	904	268	103	28	9	3	…	53	58	83	16	14	51	35	…	195	23
1851	962	278	56	22	25	14	1	77	46	126	14	23	16		…	208	21
1852	1,108	302	86	45	21	7	…	58	52	118	10	34	67		…	274	34
1853	3,338	536	63	35	13	1	1	393	32	95	11	26	58		5	2,062	12
1854	1,917	313	49	43	23	3	5	187	32	98	22	32	9	26		1,061	9

For reference notes see page 600.

TABLE V.—Distribution of immigrants, by sex and age, 1830-54.

Year	IMMIGRATION				
	Total	Children	Adults		Professionals included in total
			Males	Females	
1830	759	103	395	261	163
1831	491	75	253	163	91
1832	1,099	277	503	319	108
1833	1,358	356	586	416	104
1834	665	70	372	223	157
1835	928	186	469	273	151
1836	883	147	465	271	171
1837	898	115	495	288	223
1838	935	120	534	281	230
1839	974	154	546	274	248
1840	924	101	550	273	247
1841	....	....	....	....	....
1842	....	....	....	....	....
1843	1,055	164	614	277	272
1844	....	....	....	....	....
1845	....	....	....	....	....
1846	1,143	175	700	268	313
1847	....	....	....	....	....
1848	....	....	....	....	....
1849	675	99	403	173	148
1850	904	122	614	168	240
1851	962	172	612	178	238
1852	1,108	185	713	210	284
1853	3,338	1,392	1,443	503	492
1854	1,917	718	871	328	273

TABLE VI.—INTERCONTINENTAL EMIGRATION OF CITIZENS, BY PORTS OF EMBARKATION, 1871-1913.

Year	Total	Hamburg	Bremen	Marseilles	Le Havre	Bordeaux	Trieste	Genoa	Antwerp	Amsterdam	Rotterdam	Other German ports	Boulogne	Cherbourg	Fiume
1871	9,205	935	8,270		111										
1872	9,014	1,734	7,169												
1873	10,266	2,642	7,624												
1874	8,974	2,018	6,956												
1875	11,055	2,033	4,561	72	4,273	116									
1876	10,832	3,730	4,079	1,038	1,978	7									
1877	6,723	3,093	3,271	11	259	9									
1878	5,130	1,730	3,087	54	103										
1879	7,366	1,887	4,508	868	193										
1880	20,993	6,807	13,786	207	278										
1881	24,712	11,518	12,741	175	559										
1882	18,119	7,634	9,737	189	494	18									
1883	19,581	8,883	9,968	218	387	35									
1884	21,039	11,206	9,352	59	118[4]	94[4]									
1885	16,372	8,837	7,260	634	217[4]	36[4]									
1886	19,403	12,271	6,654	225[4]	528[4]	24[4]									
1887	20,156	8,680	10,808	116[4]	499[4]	28[4]									
1888	24,819	13,784	10,495	13[4]	705[4]	23[4]									
1889	30,114	10,849	10,419	161[4]	1,317[4]	37[4]		5,219	1,692[4]	394	566	37			
1890	38,706	15,005	13,035	221[4]	1,363[4]	48[4]		4,183	2,581[4]	1,553	578	196			
1891	53,778	16,669	17,081	85[4]	1,378[4]	28[4]		4,802	10,508[4]	1,576	1,619	27			
1892	50,274	13,858	17,454	114[4]	2,068[4]	78[4]		2,738	11,811[4]	1,246	1,600	47			
1893	48,840	8,456	18,769	19[4]	1,428[4]	34[4]		3,060	12,934[4]	1,382	2,045	29			
1894	18,783	4,536	5,339	844	3,275[4]	70[4]		1,776	3,985[4]	416	1,185				
1895	46,016	7,274	11,969	35[4]	2,627[4]	24		11,951	8,412[4]	483	2,541	6			
1896	51,492	9,096	15,555	321	843[4]	94		9,513	11,031[4]	372	2,421	554			
1897	25,104	7,669	7,492	363	1,586[4]	27[4]		3,970	1,923	528	1,653	647			
1898	32,341	8,962	12,213	684	6,341[4]			2,166	2,612	371	4,089	262			
1899	55,905	15,065[5]	21,276	629[4]				1,812	5,252	235	5,135			7	
1900	62,605	18,887[5]	27,763					3,728	7,396		4,831			10[4]	
1901	65,083	14,782[5]	37,783[5]					2,151	7,302		3,065			153[4]	
1902	93,687	24,331[5]	51,321[5]				19	1,574	8,053		8,408[5]				
1903	102,316	37,231[5]	44,795[5]					1,831[6]	9,849	1	8,592[5]				
1904	78,996	28,172[5]	30,698[5]				1,981	2,013[6]	9,551		5,403[5]		14	33	1,145
1905	123,729	28,621[5]	49,466[5]		7,167		8,750	2,622[6]	20,336		5,074[5]		116	61	1,632
1906	136,354	36,647[5]	52,549[5]		5,595		8,265	3,779[6]	22,005		4,797[5]			60	2,643
1907	177,354	51,890[5]	61,389[5]		5,752		8,893	2,471[6]	36,721		8,083[5]			64	1,975
1908	58,932	18,261[5]	17,469[5]		2,272		4,098	1,609[6]	12,404	18	2,635		2	53	131
1909	129,808	40,497[5]	45,788[5]		3,203		7,773	2,036[6]	23,012		6,445			639	328
1910	138,915	42,637[5]	45,258[5]		5,302		7,531	2,396[6]	25,115		9,994		43	222	417
1911	91,868	25,382[5]	22,381[5]		4,187		8,415	1,113[6]	20,013	65	9,230		5	791	286
1912	131,227	32,983[5]	40,955[5]		5,880		9,062	916[6]	28,653	338	11,331			615	494
1913	194,462	51,319[5]	70,622[5]		7,174		13,394	765[6]	32,354	106	17,250			891	587

For reference notes see page 600.

TABLE VII.—INTERCONTINENTAL EMIGRATION (FROM ALL PORTS OF EMBARKATION), BY COUNTRY OF DESTINATION, 1871-1910.

Year	Total available	United States	Canada	Argentina	Brazil	Other American States	Africa	Australia	Asia	Not known
1871[7]	935	902	..	..	6	27	..	..	..	..
1872[8]	8,903	8,614	8	2	195	77	..	7	..	..
1873[8]	10,265	9,224	..	1	804	207	..	29	..	..
1874[8]	8,974	8,564	11	2	143	136	..	118	..	..
1875[8]	6,594	6,419	..	3	44	40	5	88	1	183
1876	7,809	6,173	6	4	1,433	4	..	..	..	..
1877	6,365	4,717	..	..	1,506	142	..	..	..	..
1878	4,817	4,605	..	..	66	34	112	..	..	..
1879	7,395	7,387	..	8	..	..	..	..	..	..
1880	19,873	19,302	..	400	..	171	..	..	..	..
1881	24,259	21,462	..	2,615	..	182	..	16	..	..
1882	17,071	17,071	..	..	325	..	..	19	..	..
1883	18,851	18,460	31	..	333	19	3	8	..	..
1884	21,558	20,115	56	4,243	291	1,032	5	12	..	..
1885	22,325	17,523	17	73	273	238	3	14	..	..
1886	19,803	19,330	61	1,273	144	50	2	10	1	..
1887	26,358	24,830	33	1,347	1,705	62	11	17	..	..
1888	30,969	27,751	78	5,424	395	57	54	11	10	..
1889	29,635	23,399	246	1,801	2,889	95	197	94	5	..
1890	38,069	32,848	261	1,315	2,856	62	1	51	..	..
1891	48,470	41,643	2,490	707	1,754	68	2	52	3	..
1892	50,273	46,203	824	1,056	1,975	732	6	16	..	..
1893	48,839	44,115	967	512	1,380	663	27	89	5	..
1894	18,805	16,252	379	948	11,459	239	..	457	..	..
1895	46,344	33,661	39	1,368	11,549	148	36	324	..	..
1896	47,655	32,697	1,124	1,478	2,097	424	48	729	..	..
1897	26,722	18,047	4,220	441	856	508	18	30	3	..
1898	33,945	27,653	4,126	583	1,942	119	31	338	4	..
1899	55,598	47,277	5,708	1,734	1,361	23	12	41	..	..
1900	62,605	53,930	5,122	2,312	445	108	72	51	11	..
1901	65,083	59,581	2,561	1,753	262	60	18	6	..	..
1902	93,687	80,908	10,629	1,113	320	66	71	464	..	..
1903	102,634	85,572	15,035	4,622	265	14	7	285	7	503
1904	79,017	60,983	12,649	12,772	293	110	68	330	22	..
1905	123,756	98,670	11,489	15,013	297	157	87	241	10	..
1906	136,414	110,599	9,924	13,601	408	154	42	178	8	..
1907	177,653	139,756	23,494	3,423	3,919	103	62	13	9	..
1908	58,323	42,943	7,704	5,835	2,020	85	34	23	2	..
1909	132,537	112,791	11,801	6,273	1,042	41	151	..	..	..
1910	141,865	113,218	20,839	..	..	315	..	..	4	..

TABLE VIII.—DISTRIBUTION OF EMIGRANTS VIA HAMBURG AND BREMEN, BY SEX, 1890-1910.

Year	Hamburg			Bremen		
	Total	Males	Females	Total	Males	Females
1890	15,005	9,338	5,667	13,035	7,957	5,078
1891	16,669	. . . .	. . . .	17,081	. . . .	. . . .
1892	13,858	. . . .	. . . .	17,454	. . . .	. . . .
1893	8,456	. . . .	. . . .	18,769	. . . .	. . . .
1894	4,536	2,322	2,214	5,339	2,828	2,511
1895	7,274	3,843	3,431	11,969	6,683	5,286
1896	9,096	4,992	4,104	15,555	8,660	6,895
1897	7,669	4,008	3,661	7,492	3,912	3,580
1898	8,962	4,673	4,289	12,213	7,067	5,146
1899	15,065	8,500	6,565	21,945	. . . .	. . . .
1900	18,887	11,778	7,109	27,763	. . . .	. . . .
1901	14,782	9,860	4,922	37,783	. . . .	. . . .
1902	24,331	16,801	7,530	51,321	. . . .	. . . .
1903	39,266[9]	25,241	11,990	44,793	. . . .	. . . .
1904	28,172	18,493	9,679	30,698	. . . .	. . . .
1905	28,621	19,710	8,911	49,466	. . . .	. . . .
1906	36,647	25,100	11,547	52,549	. . . .	. . . .
1907	51,890	34,779	17,111	61,389	. . . .	. . . .
1908	18,261	10,575	7,686	17,469	. . . .	. . . .
1909	40,497	26,375	14,122	45,788	. . . .	. . . .
1910	42,637	28,688	13,949	45,258	. . . .	. . . .

TABLE IX.—DISTRIBUTION OF EMIGRANTS THROUGH THE PORTS OF HAMBURG AND BREMEN, BY AGE, 1890-1910.

Year	Total	Under 15 years	15 to 40 years	41 years and over
1890	28,040	5,743	18,613	3,684
1894	9,875	2,663	5,981	1,231
1895	19,243	4,058	13,154	2,031
1896	24,651	6,350	15,577	2,724
1897	15,161	4,521	8,812	1,828
1898	21,175	4,996	13,894	2,285
1899	36,341	6,682	26,337	3,322
1900	46,650	7,253	34,930	4,467
1901	52,565	5,983	41,975	4,607
1902	75,652	8,445	58,894	8,313
1903	84,059[9]	11,153	62,827	8,044
1904	58,870	9,249	43,918	5,703
1905	78,087	9,725	61,559	6,803
1906	89,196	10,150	72,156	6,890
1907	113,279	13,102	91,787	8,390
1908	35,730	7,760	24,510	3,460
1909	86,285	11,037	67,522	7,726
1910	87,895	9,458	70,529	7,908

For reference notes see page 600.

TABLE X.—Distribution of emigrants through the Ports of Hamburg
and Bremen, by occupation, 1890-1910.

Year	Total	Agri-culture	In-dustry	Com-merce	Liberal pro-fessions	General workers[10]	Other oc-cupa-tions	Occu-pations unknown
1890	28,040	1,149	1,896	1,887	144	8,226	5,907	8,831
1894	9,875	833	1,679	542	55	3,049	854	2,863
1895	19,243	1,458	1,576	653	79	8,586	2,042	4,849
1896	24,651	6,246	1,315	743	80	8,039	2,630	5,598
1897	15,161	5,669	933	596	64	3,035	804	4,060
1898	21,175	7,536	1,772	745	92	3,799	1,064	6,167
1899	36,341	20,524	3,527	1,314	186	32	783	9,975
1900	46,650	29,864	4,816	1,927	222	62	1,323	8,436
1901	52,565	41,539	4,110	1,369	180	98	416	4,853
1902	75,652	56,870	7,275	1,816	206	1,494	1,815	6,176
1903	84,059[9]	58,437	9,351	1,882	215	103	2,447	9,589
1904	58,870	34,842	7,503	1,909	305	207	5,574	8,530
1905	78,087	50,577	9,374	1,837	319	242	5,898	9,840
1906	89,196	53,783	15,065	2,544	1,187	134	9,918	6,565
1907	113,279	70,345	15,950	3,599	569	249	10,785	11,782
1908	35,730	20,680	4,820	1,563	421	122	3,335	4,789
1909	86,285	58,444	9,288	2,438	465	135	6,530	8,985
1910	87,895	55,553	10,783	2,758	502	94	9,649	8,556

TABLE XI.—Continental emigration (seasonal) totals, according to the
records of the frontier police, 1906-11.

Years	Totals	Years	Totals
1906	110,639	1909	317,902
1907	151,876	1910	313,229
1908	157,669	1911	343,224

TABLE XII.—Emigrants and immigrants from Bosnia and Herzegovina
(emigrants, fugitives and returned emigrants), 1883-1905.

Year	Departed	Returned	Year	Departed	Returned
1883	1,472	....	1895	504	42
1884	1,876	....	1896	334	40
1885	2,561	....	1897	328	36
1886	838	103	1898	477	25
1887	790	104	1899	1,173	29
1888	1,382	89	1900	8,312	228
1889	680	105	1901	4,916	132
1890	776	114	1902	998	1,245
1891	1,927	55	1903	309	698
1892	1,187	262	1904	285	309
1893	727	174	1905	497	171
1894	276	81	....	....	....

For reference notes see page 600.

TABLE XIII.—NUMBER OF EMIGRANTS FROM BOSNIA AND HERZEGOVINA TO AMERICA, ACCORDING TO PASSPORTS ISSUED, 1904-13.

Year	Number	Year	Number
1904	199	1909	26
1905	1,418	1910	23
1906	3,533	1911	1,600
1907	6,118	1912	1,865
1908	654	1913	543

TABLE XIV.—DISTRIBUTION OF EMIGRANT CITIZENS TO EXTRA-EUROPEAN COUNTRIES, BY SEX AND AGE, 1921-24.

Year	Total	Sex		Age	
		Males	Females	Children	Adults
1921	5,176	2,779	2,397	1,856	3,320
1922	10,579	6,021	4,558	3,735	6,844
1923	15,497	9,927	5,570	4,847	10,650
1924	2,650	1,629	1,021	789	1,861

TABLE XV.—DISTRIBUTION OF EMIGRANT CITIZENS TO EXTRA-EUROPEAN COUNTRIES, BY OCCUPATION, 1921-24.

Year	Total	Agri-culture	Industry and mining	Transport and commerce	Domestic service and general labor	Liberal professions and civil servants	Other occupations, none or unknown
1921	5,176	915	1,142	385	675	213	1,846
1922	10,579	2,471	2,039	581	1,102	325	4,061
1923	15,497	2,791	4,197	872	1,230	417	5,990
1924	2,650	382	626	225	149	145	1,123

TABLE XVI.—INTERCONTINENTAL EMIGRATION OF CITIZENS, BY COUNTRY OF DESTINATION, 1921-24.

Year	Total	United States	Canada	Mexico	Central America	Brazil	Argentina	Other South American States	All America	Palestine	Persia	Turkey	Dutch Indies	China and Japan	Other Asiatic countries	All Asia	Africa	Australia	French and British colonies	Other countries
1921	5,176	4,157	14	15	1	649	198	31	5,065	17	3	..	73	7	1	101	10	..	..	..
1922	10,579	8,256	25	22	2	1,472	585	38	10,400	38	1	..	30	6	27	102	75	2	..	..
1923	15,497	9,385	72	57	.	3,452	2,267	80	15,313	23	5	17	14	12	..	71	56	5	19	33
1924	2,650	810	68	35	.	780	631	72	2,396	31	.	27	8	12	..	78	86	13	21	56

TABLE XVII.—DISTRIBUTION OF EMIGRANTS TO EXTRA-EUROPEAN COUNTRIES, BY OCCUPATION AND COUNTRY OF DESTINATION, 1921-24.

Country	Year	Total	Agriculture	Industry and mining	Transport and commerce	Liberal professions and civil servants	Domestic service	Occupations not specified	Dependents
TOTAL.........	1921	5,176	915	1,142	385	213	675	948	898
	1922	10,579	2,471	2,039	581	325	1,102	1,484	2,577
	1923	15,497	2,791	4,197	872	417	1,230	2,032	3,958
	1924	2,650	382	626	225	145	149	252	871
UNITED STATES...	1921	4,157	737	813	324	150	651	854	628
	1922	8,256	1,976	1,610	440	213	1,024	1,292	1,701
	1923	9,385	1,708	2,399	481	182	1,003	1,534	2,078
	1924	810	72	170	45	30	60	109	324
CANADA...	1921	14	2	1	1	1	3	3	3
	1922	25	4	3		1	4	4	8
	1923	72	16	13	6	..	4	12	15
	1924	68	30	7	2	6	6	9	14
BRAZIL...	1921	649	138	219	17	13	6	32	224
	1922	1,472	410	191	46	45	23	57	700
	1923	3,452	680	809	132	113	85	249	1,384
	1924	780	166	155	35	44	14	53	313
ARGENTINA...	1921	198	27	58	24	11	11	34	33
	1922	585	75	174	67	45	24	74	126
	1923	2,267	349	881	215	76	122	187	437
	1924	631	92	187	70	27	46	43	166
OTHER SOUTH AMERICAN STATES...	1921	47	6	15	5	3	2	12	4
	1922	62	..	19	11	3	6	15	8
	1923	137	21	42	20	16	2	15	21
	1924	107	13	37	17	20	3	6	11
ASIA...	1921	101	4	31	13	34	2	11	6
	1922	102	6	24	3	12	2	26	29
	1923	71	5	27	6	9	2	10	12
	1924	78	4	31	15	6	2	7	13
AFRICA...	1921	10	1	5	1	1	..	2	..
	1922	75	..	18	13	6	19	14	5
	1923	56	1	11	6	8	11	14	5
	1924	86	..	20	23	8	14	13	8
AUSTRALIA...	1921	..	..	..	..	..	..	..	..
	1922	2	..	..	..	..	..	2	..
	1923	5	..	5	..	..	..	..	..
	1924	13	..	2	4	..	..	1	6
NOT SPECIFIED...	1921	..	..	..	..	..	..	..	..
	1922	..	..	..	..	..	..	..	..
	1923	52	11	10	6	7	1	11	6
	1924	77	5	17	14	10	4	11	16

SOURCES

Tafeln zur Statistik der Oesterreichischen Monarchie, 1829, 1830-40, 1846, 1849, 1851, 1852-54.

Tables I (years 1819-54), II, IV, V.

Becker: Vienna, 1846.

Tables II (1843); V (1843).

Mitteilungen aus dem Gebiete der Statistik (Annual), Nos. XVII and XIX, Vienna, 1870 and 1872.

Tables I (years 1855-70); III (years 1850-70).

Statistische Monatschrift. Issued by the K. K. Statistische Zentral-Kommission. Nos. II, V, VIII, X and XII. Vienna, 1876, 1879, 1882, 1884, 1886.

Oesterreichisches Statistisches Handbuch, Nos. XIV, XV, XX, XXII, XXIX, XXXII, Vienna.

Tables VI, VII.

ENGLISH, Dr. K. von, "Die Oesterreichische Auswanderungsstatistik", in *Statistische Monatschrift*, new series, No. XVIII, Brünn, 1913.

Tables VII, X, XIX.

Statistica della Emigrazione italiana per l'Estero, negli anni 1897, 1898, 1899, 1900-01, 1902-03, 1904-05, 1906-07, 1908-09, 1910-11, 1912-13. Rome. (Taken from the annual reports of the consulates communicated to the General Statistical Bureau of Italy.)

Tables VIII, IX.

Bericht des K. K. Reichsfinanzministeriums über die Verwaltung von Bosnien und der Herzegovina, 1906 and 1914-16.

Tables XI and XII.

Statistisches Handbuch für die Republik Oesterreich. Nos. III, VI. Vienna.

Tables XIII-XVI.

NOTES

[1] As from 1849 entitled: Görz, Gradiska, Istria, Trieste and district.
[2] For the years 1871 to 1875 the totals are 6 169, 6 099, 6 927, 5 873 and 10 012 respectively.
[3] Incomplete.
[4] Including Hungarian emigrants.
[5] Including the Austrian emigrants who embarked for England (*e.g.* 1,286 in 1899).
[6] As from 1903, the figures also include the emigrants who departed through the Port of Naples.
[7] Through the Port of Hamburg only.
[8] Through the Ports of Hamburg and Bremen.
[9] Includes 2,035 persons the sex, age and occupation of whom are unknown.
[10] These figures refer to the Port of Bremen only.

BELGIUM

I. Statistics of Local Population Registers (Tables I-X)

Since 1841 the Minister of the Interior has published emigration and immigration figures drawn from local population registers. The returns include citizens and domiciled aliens who leave the country in order to settle abroad and also persons who arrive and intend to take up their abode in Belgium. These population movements comprise intercontinental as well as continental migrations. So far as the continental emigration and immigration of citizens or aliens are concerned, the publications furnish no separate figures for individual years before 1884.

The figures relating to the intercontinental emigration of citizens (available separately since 1884) fall far below the corresponding figures of our second source, the port statistics of Antwerp (available separately for citizens since 1885) and are not as accurate.

II. Statistics of the Port of Antwerp (Tables XI-XIII)

The port statistics of Antwerp were collected after 1843 by the Emigration Commission and, more recently, by the Government Emigration Commissioner. Citizens, and aliens classified according to nationality, have been distinguished since 1886.

In addition to direct emigration, figures are given concerning departures by an indirect route (*e. g.*, via England); but they only distinguish between citizens and aliens (mainly in transit.)

Only combined data, if any at all, are available for the earlier years. This characterises particularly the first period when the paramount significance of Antwerp lay in its transit traffic and when a large proportion of the Germans who migrated to the United States went through this port.

For the period 1844-1846 we have found exact returns of intercontinental "steerage passengers sailing from this port," in the reports of the German consul at Antwerp to the Ministry for Foreign Affairs in Berlin. The Emigration Commission of this port placed these data at the disposal of the German consul.

For the year 1844 these figures not only agree with those of Höfken and Hübner, but also with those of the United States *Senate Report*.[1] But while the two authors, just mentioned, speak only of German emigration (Hübner includes Swiss), the *Report* of the Senate Committee identifies the figures with the number of emigrants embarked for the United States. For 1845 and 1846 this *Report* quotes lower figures (4,549 and 11,402) than the other sources mentioned above. In fact, according to Duval the transport of emigrants via Antwerp to Brazil and Buenos Aires started in 1857.[2] The discrepancy is probably to be

---

[1] *Report* of the Select Committee of the U. S. Senate on the Sickness and Mortality on Board Emigrant Ships. Washington, 1854.

[2] Duval, Jules, *Histoire de l'Emigration européenne, asiatique et africaine.* (Paris, 1862), p. 124.

explained on the assumption that the United States *Report* did not include indirect emigrants (via England). On the other hand, Hübner appears to be mistaken in confining the figures to German and other alien migrants (in contrast to the report of the German consul). As a matter of fact, the emigration of non-Germans through Antwerp was of comparatively little significance before 1850.

According to the United States statistics for the period 1840-60, the Belgians, other than transients, arriving in the States were in 1847, 1,473; again in 1850, 1,080, 1855, 1,506, and in 1856, 1,982. For other years their number did not exceed a few hundred, sometimes falling even much below that figure. Since Hübner's figures for Antwerp agree with the official statements of the consul (1844-46), we have, in the absence of original figures, availed ourselves of his data until 1854. Probably they relate also to the aggregate amount of emigration, includi g therefore Belgians, Dutch and Swiss, who, to a limited extent, emigrated through this port.[1]

Statistics about migration into and out from Belgium supplementing the figures in the Belgian national tables will be found in other sections of the present volume. Statistics about the number of migrants from Belgium to South Africa (1913-24), Brazil (1847-1924), United States (1820-1924), Argentina (1857-1924), Australia (1902-24) and Canada (1900-24) will be found in the national tables for those countries. Statistics about the number of migrants returning to Belgium from Argentina (1857-1924) and the United States (1908-24) will be found in the national tables for those countries.

Immigrants landing at Antwerp are also included in the statistics of this port.

[1]In the *Documents statistiques de la Belgique* quoted above, figures for Antwerp for the period 1851-60 are given. They are, however, considerably below those of Hübner and agree exactly with those of the communal registers, which—as already mentioned— fall generally considerably below the Antwerp figures comprising always the transit figures as well. Accordingly, we have not utilised these figures until 1860 when they again deviate from those of the communal registers.

TABLE I.—EMIGRATION AND IMMIGRATION (TAKEN FROM THE COMMUNAL REGISTERS), 1841-91.

Year	Emigrants	Immigrants	Year	Emigrants	Immigrants
1841	3,792	2,919	1867	9,729	11,829
1842	4,240	2,825	1868	9,867	11,171
1843	3,947	4,083	1869	11,619	10,741
1844	4,239	2,703	1870	7,326	16,571
1845	6,477	2,992	1871	13,171	16,708
1847	6,292	4,417	1872	11,040	15,789
1848	5,046	5,428	1873	7,981	15,792
1849	5,052	3,862	1874	8,217	16,762
1850	6,385	4,237	1875	10,157	15,372
1851	6,081	4,144	1876	13,124	14,446
1852	7,781	5,006	1877	11,847	15,075
1853	9,530	4,912	1878	11,646	14,325
1854	7,995	5,035	1879	12,474	14,234
1855	9,546	5,156	1880	15,064	16,490
1856	13,261	5,592	1881	15,822	17,692
1857	8,587	6,652	1882	16,257	18,104
1858	8,081	7,750	1883	15,208	17,499
1859	8,406	7,664	1884	13,993	16,558
1860	9,339	8,295	1885	13,236	18,310
1861	10,218	8,856	1886	17,029	19,804
1862	9,465	9,201	1887	17,528	19,286
1863	9,131	8,848	1888	23,041	21,213
1864	10,650	9,169	1889	23,190	22,150
1865	12,015	9,600	1890	21,675	21,458
1866	14,349	10,626	1891	18,994	20,741

TABLE II.—DISTRIBUTION OF EMIGRANT CITIZENS TO EXTRA-EUROPEAN COUNTRIES, BY SEX AND OCCUPATION. 1884-1924

Year	Total	Males	Females	Agriculture			Industry and commerce			Liberal professions and brain-workers			Other occupations		
				Total	Males	Females	Total	Males	Females	Total	Males	Females	Total	Males	Females
1884	525	331	194	...	...	...	...	...	...	...	...	...	...	...	...
1885	354	270	134	...	...	...	...	...	...	...	...	...	...	...	...
1886	1,001	650	351	237	159	78	365	289	76	37	33	4	362	169	193
1887	1,641	985	656	397	268	129	692	452	240	30	23	7	522	242	280
1888	5,059	3,298	1,761	1,674	1,157	517	1,341	1,031	310	224	159	65	1,820	951	869
1889	4,677	2,862	1,815	1,810	1,131	679	1,456	993	463	104	82	22	1,307	656	651
1890	1,822	1,146	676	443	295	148	651	467	184	179	117	62	549	267	282
1891	1,752	1,112	640	445	294	151	807	583	224	87	66	21	413	169	244
1892	2,586	1,606	980	794	531	263	914	682	232	58	48	10	820	345	475
1893	2,122	1,292	830	556	368	188	805	591	214	62	49	13	699	284	415
1894	620	385	235	126	88	38	221	153	68	39	31	8	234	113	121
1895	876	572	304	194	127	67	333	270	63	19	18	1	330	157	173
1896	578	363	215	130	81	49	223	164	59	65	48	17	160	70	90
1897	551	337	214	81	55	26	196	129	67	28	27	1	246	126	120
1898	565	345	220	73	56	17	241	162	79	53	49	4	198	78	120
1899	600	396	204	130	95	35	204	159	45	67	57	10	199	85	114
1900	876	585	291	385	256	129	249	185	64	34	28	6	208	116	92
1901	1,019	662	357	293	212	81	335	270	65	26	22	4	365	158	207
1902	1,695	1,110	585	507	383	124	573	458	115	72	63	9	543	206	337
1903	2,101	1,418	683	576	453	123	766	638	128	81	70	11	678	257	421
1904	2,269	1,464	805	487	367	120	908	674	234	83	70	13	791	353	438
1905	2,540	1,660	880	749	566	183	831	649	182	112	95	17	848	350	498
1906	3,637	2,517	1,120	1,135	843	292	1,167	932	235	136	121	15	1,199	621	578
1907	4,374	2,854	1,520	1,393	1,024	369	1,481	1,152	329	130	103	27	1,370	575	795
1908	2,054	1,270	784	310	212	98	789	612	177	123	102	21	832	344	488
1909	2,391	1,520	871	611	438	173	859	665	194	104	74	30	817	343	474
1910	3,918	2,536	1,382	984	689	295	1,390	1,071	319	239	198	41	1,305	578	727
1911	2,481	1,513	968	530	378	152	910	665	245	138	99	39	903	371	532
1912	3,417	2,187	1,230	756	520	236	1,361	1,030	331	261	217	44	1,039	420	619
1913	5,037	3,202	1,835	1,538	1,036	502	1,730	1,366	364	390	284	106	1,379	516	863
1919	1,841	882	959	306	172	134	610	384	226	166	106	60	759	220	539
1920	4,751	2,514	2,237	1,317	739	578	1,523	1,058	465	283	184	99	1,628	533	1,095
1921	2,018	1,106	912	250	152	98	606	472	134	181	129	52	981	353	628
1922	2,041	1,095	946	126	75	51	659	514	145	199	153	46	1,057	353	704
1923	1,885	1,057	828	202	115	87	636	486	150	187	140	47	860	316	544
1924	1,928	1,118	810	188	128	60	619	529	90	231	157	74	890	304	586

TABLE III.—INTERCONTINENTAL EMIGRATION OF CITIZENS, BY COUNTRY OF DESTINATION, 1884-1924.

Year	Total	Belgian Congo	Other African countries	Canada	Other North American countries	Argentina	Other South American countries	Asia and Dutch East Indies	New Zealand Australia and Pacific Islands	Other countries
1884	525				356	143				26
1885	354				279	44				31
1886	1,001	21			694	208		14	7	57
1887	1,641	17			1,059	533		4	5	13
1888	5,059	15			1,278	3,631		48	2	85
1889	4,677	37			1,569	2,924		36	13	98
1890	1,822	38			1,316	367		16	3	82
1891	1,752	42			1,430	222		19	3	37
1892	2,586	40			2,196	297		30	3	20
1893	2,122	42			1,859	157		32	4	28
1894	620	53			363	144		22	6	32
1895	876	50			657	108		25	9	27
1896	578	55			358	122		24	6	13
1897	551	38			330	114		15	4	50
1898	565	71			289	92		15	2	96
1899	600	74			375	79		43	10	19
1900	876	80			701	56		12	2	25
1901	1,019	35			876	59		11	1	37
1902	1,695	58			1,376	159		31	8	63
1903	2,101	95			1,745	180		35	4	42
1904	2,269	85			1,893	220		24	1	46
1905	2,540	101			2,162	174		37	2	64
1906	3,637	152			3,015	357		47	2	64
1907	4,374	129			3,808	283		71	19	64
1908	2,054	122			1,628	205		32	9	58
1909	2,391	138			1,840	288		57	4	64
1910	3,918	213			3,270	330		61	14	30
1911	2,481	188			1,948	266		23	6	50
1912	3,417	338	156	721	1,789	81	175	36	25	96
1913	5,037	434	88	1,034	2,917	130	291	69	6	68
1919	1,841	238	57	368	799	38	109	32	17	183
1920	4,751	509	119	743	2,941	34	163	80	23	139
1921	2,018	420	96	202	870	22	165	49	21	173
1922	2,041	452	74	185	987	39	68	63	19	154
1923	1,885	561	61	291	733	22	66	73	25	53
1924	1,928	806	86	343	435	27	71	89	44	27

TABLE IV.—DISTRIBUTION OF EMIGRANT CITIZENS TO EUROPEAN COUNTRIES, BY SEX AND OCCUPATION, 1884-1924.

Year	Total	Males	Females	Agriculture Total	Agriculture Males	Agriculture Females	Industry and commerce Total	Industry and commerce Males	Industry and commerce Females	Liberal professions and brain-workers Total	Liberal professions and brain-workers Males	Liberal professions and brain-workers Females	Other occupations Total	Other occupations Males	Other occupations Females
1884	7,572	3,916	3,656	....	....	....	....	....	....	....	....	....	....	....	....
1885	6,491	3,364	3,127	....	....	....	....	....	....	....	....	....	....	....	....
1886	8,210	4,327	3,883	1,343	748	595	2,423	1,656	767	415	289	126	4,029	1,634	2,395
1887	7,980	4,089	3,891	1,140	632	508	3,095	1,836	1,259	322	212	110	3,423	1,409	2,014
1888	10,361	5,514	4,847	1,477	835	642	3,790	2,456	1,334	317	238	79	4,777	1,985	2,792
1889	9,272	4,999	4,273	1,499	816	683	2,991	2,050	941	375	258	117	4,407	1,875	2,532
1890	10,668	5,635	5,033	1,766	926	840	3,560	2,301	1,259	528	325	203	4,814	2,083	2,731
1891	9,991	5,268	4,723	1,265	692	573	3,395	2,309	1,086	440	278	162	4,891	1,989	2,902
1892	12,289	6,545	5,744	1,307	727	580	4,486	3,000	1,486	622	387	235	5,874	2,431	3,443
1893	12,818	6,880	5,938	1,516	825	691	4,544	3,127	1,417	475	309	166	6,283	2,619	3,664
1894	10,417	5,479	4,938	1,228	728	500	3,179	2,202	977	435	271	164	5,575	2,278	3,297
1895	9,842	5,242	4,600	1,126	639	487	3,728	2,496	1,232	282	186	96	4,706	1,921	2,785
1896	10,612	5,709	4,903	1,206	704	502	3,448	2,409	1,039	519	358	161	5,439	2,238	3,201
1897	11,317	6,089	5,228	1,136	656	480	3,785	2,685	1,100	446	343	103	5,950	2,405	3,545
1898	11,631	6,475	5,156	1,432	855	577	3,871	2,862	1,009	444	317	127	5,884	2,441	3,443
1899	12,340	6,632	5,708	1,260	681	579	4,206	3,022	1,184	568	380	188	6,306	2,549	3,757
1900	12,616	6,925	5,691	1,472	871	601	4,091	2,911	1,180	409	302	107	6,644	2,841	3,803
1901	9,343	5,066	4,277	921	573	348	3,311	2,370	941	423	300	123	4,688	1,823	2,865
1902	10,927	5,749	5,178	1,155	676	479	3,793	2,691	1,102	425	296	129	5,554	2,086	3,468
1903	11,502	6,088	5,414	1,051	613	438	4,227	2,974	1,253	530	375	155	5,694	2,126	3,568
1904	12,483	6,499	5,984	1,241	700	541	4,586	3,142	1,444	520	338	182	6,136	2,319	3,817
1905	12,102	6,365	5,737	1,208	678	530	4,281	3,039	1,242	517	365	152	6,096	2,283	3,813
1906	13,913	7,500	6,413	1,411	837	574	4,785	3,392	1,393	562	404	158	7,155	2,867	4,288
1907	13,729	7,395	6,334	1,285	760	525	5,159	3,665	1,494	585	408	177	6,700	2,562	4,138
1908	15,226	8,270	6,956	1,384	810	574	5,680	4,117	1,563	593	422	171	7,569	2,921	4,648
1909	17,033	8,965	8,068	1,708	967	741	6,498	4,564	1,934	721	473	248	8,106	2,961	5,145
1910	17,475	9,419	8,056	1,820	1,097	723	6,949	4,927	2,022	743	524	219	7,963	2,871	5,092
1911	15,649	8,338	7,321	1,479	859	620	6,370	4,553	1,817	726	488	238	7,074	2,428	4,646
1912	16,341	8,488	7,853	1,828	1,026	802	6,544	4,616	1,928	635	396	239	7,334	2,450	4,884
1913	17,271	9,083	8,188	1,993	1,106	887	6,634	4,745	1,889	925	578	347	7,719	2,654	5,065
1919	36,530	17,919	18,611	5,690	3,189	2,501	11,946	8,178	3,768	1,556	994	562	17,338	5,558	11,780
1920	32,155	16,159	15,996	5,261	3,023	2,238	10,142	7,317	2,825	1,597	1,000	597	15,155	4,819	10,336
1921	18,086	9,011	9,075	3,412	1,922	1,490	5,811	4,081	1,730	804	547	257	8,059	2,461	5,598
1922	21,991	11,136	10,855	3,786	2,122	1,664	7,193	5,247	1,946	774	525	249	10,238	3,242	6,996
1923	18,969	9,673	9,296	2,907	1,696	1,211	6,819	4,765	2,054	797	526	271	8,446	2,686	5,760
1924	17,142	8,875	8,267	2,800	1,602	1,198	6,017	4,383	1,634	656	458	198	7,669	2,432	5,237

TABLE V.—CONTINENTAL EMIGRATION OF CITIZENS, BY COUNTRY OF DESTINATION, 1884-1924.

Year	Total	Germany	Austria-Hungary	Spain and Portugal	France	Great Britain and Ireland	Italy	Luxemburg	Netherlands	Russia	Switzerland	Other countries
1884	7,572	318	7	20[1]	6,209	103	19	89	753	18	21	15
1885	6,491	348	2	9[1]	5,206	64	20	118	697	11	11	5
1886	8,210	336	23	37	6,646	92	26	121	797	18	37	77
1887	7,980	307	5	65	6,582	54	15	103	790	18	9	32
1888	10,361	606	11	26	8,055	436	74	68	999	9	10	67
1889	9,272	471	5	40	7,303	86	70	49	1,145	19	16	68
1890	10,668	579	10	49	8,525	298	35	115	964	12	24	57
1891	9,991	508	12	63	7,876	85	42	105	1,211	19	54	16
1892	12,289	550	13	180	9,887	176	49	147	1,181	28	35	43
1893	12,818	638	16	42	10,455	136	36	129	1,257	36	26	47
1894	10,417	486	32	29	7,593	116	48	137	1,057	34	19	53
1895	9,842	570	46	32	8,145	110	25	104	1,167	98	51	46
1896	10,612	650	41	104	8,155	133	32	80	1,072	284	31	40
1897	11,317	816	26	48	7,985	191	60	83	1,153	723	31	35
1898	11,631	943	94	50	8,454	169	57	121	1,339	781	27	50
1899	12,340	1,008	67	50	8,824	269	77	157	1,282	830	42	115
1900	12,616	1,125	40	48	6,517	246	58	233	1,408	514	31	84
1901	9,343	908	23	32	7,821	196	43	180	1,104	213	36	95
1902	10,927	907	33	73	8,091	210	88	175	1,310	241	32	43
1903	11,502	949	10	86	8,720	304	64	223	1,476	176	26	53
1904	12,483	1,127	46	127	8,751	224	116	124	1,562	308	70	75
1905	12,102	976	13	110	9,824	225	87	217	1,400	213	54	57
1906	13,913	1,217	17	66	9,856	284	140	192	1,717	222	53	170
1907	13,729	1,111	17	117	11,291	315	156	232	1,496	256	64	95
1908	15,226	1,198	45	71	13,334	306	157	216	1,561	167	78	130
1909	17,033	1,059	35	66	13,531	292	122	187	1,588	205	84	92
1910	17,475	947	43	58	11,817	301	151	282	1,594	408	53	96
1911	15,649	1,013	51	48	12,422	272	96	203	1,727	235	64	94
1912	16,341	967	31	124		258	80	253	1,690	255	93	129
1913	17,271	977	58	63	13,367	307	92	163	1,680	300	132	142
1919	36,530	1,759	31	91	29,464	1,147	117	439	3,289	34	106	53
1920	32,155	1,190	....	92	25,921	1,279	129	425	2,774	32	133	180
1921	18,086	729	....	51	15,110	297	75	175	1,523	4	47	75
1922	21,991	664	....	47	18,897	407	55	211	1,449	16	58	187
1923	18,969	355	....	108	16,899	248	59	253	877	9	52	109
1924	17,142	310	....	77	15,034	182	124	215	1,064	8	54	74

For reference notes see page 618.

TABLE VI.—DISTRIBUTION OF IMMIGRANT CITIZENS FROM EXTRA-EUROPEAN COUNTRIES, BY SEX AND OCCUPATION, 1884–1924.

Year	Total	Males	Females	Agriculture			Industry and commerce			Liberal professions and brain-workers			Other occupations		
				Total	Males	Females	Total	Males	Females	Total	Males	Females	Total	Males	Females
1884	78	57	21	..	..	..	..	..	..	..	..	..	..	..	..
1885	53	38	15	..	..	..	..	..	..	..	..	..	..	..	..
1886	157	102	55	64	36	28	36	24	12	8	5	3	49	37	12
1887	81	53	28	27	17	10	34	25	9	..	..	..	20	11	9
1888	203	117	86	65	43	22	59	42	17	3	3	..	76	29	47
1889	476	306	170	190	115	75	141	112	29	7	7	..	138	72	66
1890	364	240	124	72	55	17	127	94	33	14	14	..	151	77	74
1891	244	156	88	72	50	22	63	43	20	14	8	6	95	55	40
1892	272	194	78	63	50	13	99	75	24	9	7	2	101	62	39
1893	426	297	129	122	95	27	142	109	33	8	5	3	154	88	66
1894	601	425	176	138	113	25	258	208	50	13	13	..	192	91	101
1895	330	218	112	70	55	15	151	112	39	7	6	1	102	45	57
1896	446	271	175	72	48	24	209	145	64	15	12	3	150	66	84
1897	437	284	153	72	52	20	158	118	40	13	11	2	194	103	91
1898	436	276	160	102	64	38	199	136	63	31	28	3	104	48	56
1899	325	195	130	65	44	21	136	101	35	18	13	5	106	37	69
1900	336	212	124	82	43	39	160	117	43	12	11	1	82	41	41
1901	327	191	136	73	51	22	123	90	33	15	13	2	116	37	79
1902	468	300	168	82	58	24	238	162	76	14	13	1	134	67	67
1903	391	273	118	71	54	17	180	144	36	31	27	4	109	48	61
1904	601	407	194	117	90	27	272	209	63	32	27	5	180	81	99
1905	515	362	153	124	96	28	208	163	45	23	22	1	160	81	79
1906	569	394	175	109	84	25	247	205	42	19	16	3	194	89	105
1907	787	548	239	130	116	14	360	284	76	30	26	4	267	122	145
1908	1,113	759	354	212	170	42	481	374	107	44	41	3	376	174	202
1909	777	500	277	168	115	53	314	240	74	41	36	5	254	109	145
1910	898	618	280	158	128	30	394	333	61	44	39	5	302	118	184
1911	869	601	268	136	115	21	391	307	84	41	36	5	301	143	158
1912	969	666	303	178	128	50	411	340	71	76	69	7	304	129	175
1913	1,181	829	352	285	225	60	491	413	78	65	54	11	340	137	203
1919	936	612	324	120	87	33	400	329	71	60	55	5	356	141	215
1920	1,333	809	524	256	177	79	496	405	91	82	68	14	499	159	340
1921	1,233	766	467	223	141	82	496	395	101	81	72	9	433	158	275
1922	1,499	916	583	212	145	67	642	521	121	74	66	8	571	184	387
1923	1,121	641	480	168	99	69	414	320	94	74	60	14	465	162	303
1924	1,190	743	447	123	83	40	516	427	89	75	66	9	476	167	309

TABLE VII.—INTERCONTINENTAL IMMIGRATION OF CITIZENS, BY COUNTRY OF ORIGIN, 1884-1924.

Year	Total	Belgian Congo	Other African countries	Canada	Other North American countries	Argentina	Other South American countries	Asia and Dutch East Indies	Australia and Pacific Islands	Other countries
1884	78				32					46
1885	53				46					7
1886	157				81	20		20		36
1887	81	1			42	22		5		11
1888	203	1			87	83		12	2	18
1889	476	7			146	277		16		30
1890	364	11			119	198		16	1	19
1891	244	13			81	132		16		2
1892	272	9			115	125		16	2	5
1893	426	9			298	105		7	2	5
1894	601	15			382	181		19	1	3
1895	330	9			246	62		10		3
1896	446	24			338	69		7	1	7
1897	437	14			282	108		14		19
1898	436	15			293	113		7	1	7
1899	325	17			221	68		14	2	3
1900	336	16			233	66		14	2	5
1901	327	20			225	65		8	1	8
1902	468	35			258	132		23	4	16
1903	391	50			245	62		15		19
1904	601	41			472	51		25	4	8
1905	515	18			405	52		24	4	12
1906	569	16			415	90		24	1	23
1907	787	26			658	70		29	3	1
1908	1,113	60			858	143		33	3	16
1909	777	58			596	76		36	3	8
1910	898	70			669	109		35	8	7
1911	869	121			590	106		37	3	12
1912	969	66	57	130	568	43	57	35	3	10
1913	1,181	142	42	173	662	41	62	25	5	29
1919	936	153	46	180	382	37	65	24	4	45
1920	1,333	157	74	182	745	36	83	34	4	18
1921	1,233	196	38	261	625	28	47	19	10	9
1922	1,499	252	77	225	789	28	70	51	7	
1923	1,121	337	29	196	449	25	37	36	8	4
1924	1,190	314	115	145	397	18	138	54	8	1

TABLE VIII.—DISTRIBUTION OF IMMIGRANT CITIZENS FROM EUROPEAN COUNTRIES, BY SEX AND OCCUPATION, 1884–1924.

Year	Total	Sex		Agriculture			Industry and commerce			Liberal professions and brain-workers			Other occupations		
		Males	Females	Total	Males	Females	Total	Males	Females	Total	Males	Females	Total	Males	Females
1884	3,874	2,951	1,823	...	...	...	...	...	...	...	...	...	...	...	...
1885	3,984	2,123	1,861	...	...	...	...	...	...	...	...	...	...	...	...
1886	4,024	2,046	1,978	619	355	264	1,169	754	415	143	103	40	2,093	834	1,259
1887	3,895	2,010	1,885	741	426	315	1,391	811	580	125	82	43	1,638	691	947
1888	5,269	2,773	2,496	946	521	425	1,510	992	518	181	120	61	2,632	1,140	1,492
1889	5,313	2,822	2,491	1,005	525	480	1,515	1,018	497	207	119	88	2,586	1,160	1,426
1890	5,208	2,761	2,447	1,011	539	472	1,878	1,214	664	201	116	85	2,118	892	1,226
1891	4,624	2,489	2,135	766	434	332	1,425	978	447	236	136	100	2,197	941	1,256
1892	5,977	3,191	2,786	954	523	431	2,048	1,362	686	227	141	86	2,748	1,165	1,583
1893	6,247	3,321	2,926	880	481	399	1,884	1,321	563	244	157	87	3,239	1,362	1,877
1894	6,631	3,503	3,128	816	465	351	2,120	1,484	636	331	211	120	3,364	1,343	2,021
1895	6,091	3,266	2,825	865	518	347	2,165	1,463	702	222	135	87	2,839	1,150	1,689
1896	6,186	3,295	2,891	841	474	367	2,137	1,461	676	202	125	77	3,006	1,235	1,771
1897	6,769	3,641	3,128	709	403	306	2,260	1,590	670	267	181	86	3,533	1,467	2,066
1898	9,775	5,343	4,432	966	591	375	2,380	1,709	671	295	186	109	6,134	2,857	3,277
1899	6,672	3,769	2,903	805	493	312	2,471	1,763	708	367	229	138	3,029	1,284	1,745
1900	7,914	4,367	3,547	928	575	353	3,089	2,201	888	347	218	129	3,550	1,373	2,177
1901	8,287	4,548	3,739	996	617	379	3,141	2,249	892	271	178	93	3,879	1,504	2,375
1902	7,371	3,943	3,428	845	509	336	2,673	1,860	813	274	159	115	3,579	1,415	2,164
1903	8,380	4,429	3,951	907	531	376	3,173	2,203	970	393	204	189	3,907	1,491	2,416
1904	8,306	4,423	3,883	1,005	566	439	3,445	2,325	1,120	400	211	189	3,456	1,321	2,135
1905	7,374	3,964	3,410	785	482	303	2,865	2,004	861	283	185	98	3,441	1,293	2,148
1906	8,139	4,441	3,698	814	489	325	3,118	2,199	919	285	203	82	3,922	1,550	2,372
1907	8,088	4,295	3,793	834	491	343	3,257	2,271	986	413	227	186	3,584	1,306	2,278
1908	8,324	4,516	3,808	827	493	334	3,372	2,334	1,038	376	240	136	3,749	1,449	2,300
1909	8,142	4,476	3,666	814	488	326	3,336	2,327	1,009	335	226	109	3,657	1,435	2,222
1910	8,972	4,888	4,084	974	576	398	3,623	2,637	986	424	291	133	3,951	1,384	2,567
1911	8,674	4,771	3,903	797	477	320	3,836	2,757	1,079	325	214	111	3,716	1,323	2,393
1912	10,355	5,707	4,648	974	623	351	4,284	3,195	1,089	437	303	134	4,660	1,586	3,074
1913	8,191	4,446	3,745	770	464	306	3,366	2,466	900	443	294	149	3,612	1,222	2,390
1919	18,954	8,789	10,165	1,810	1,053	757	5,068	3,342	1,726	877	599	278	11,199	3,795	7,404
1920	12,786	6,139	6,647	1,465	845	620	4,168	3,038	1,130	665	358	307	6,488	1,898	4,590
1921	9,198	4,667	4,531	987	603	384	3,291	2,357	934	466	305	161	4,454	1,402	3,052
1922	9,517	4,837	4,680	1,078	664	414	3,510	2,505	1,005	430	250	180	4,499	1,418	3,081
1923	10,748	5,434	5,314	1,077	640	437	3,743	2,676	1,067	365	254	111	5,563	1,864	3,699
1924	10,165	5,461	4,704	1,054	660	394	4,300	3,269	1,031	318	206	112	4,493	1,326	3,167

TABLE IX.—CONTINENTAL IMMIGRATION OF CITIZENS, BY COUNTRY OF ORIGIN, 1884-1924.

Year	Total	Germany	Austria-Hungary	Spain and Portugal	France	Great Britain and Ireland	Italy	Luxemburg	Netherlands	Russia	Switzerland	Other countries
1884	3,874	303	5	6	2,773	95	31	62	569	5	19	6
1885	3,984	176	6	16	3,027	35	16	85	596	...	3	24
1886	4,024	245	2	25	3,017	46	8	103	507	6	12	53
1887	3,895	197	10	10	3,063	41	5	39	497	8	7	28
1888	5,269	746	7	32	3,568	51	9	127	676	1	5	44
1889	5,313	358	17	30	3,955	53	33	79	659	19	21	99
1890	5,208	396		23	3,814	52	38	77	697	22	16	56
1891	4,624	244	8	4	3,596	33	4	66	646	2	1	20
1892	5,977	289	8	30	4,687	79	14	76	759	3	16	16
1893	6,247	396	10	98	4,685	71	27	100	823	5	16	16
1894	6,631	471	9	53	5,040	69	11	115	824	11	7	21
1895	6,091	314	10	14	4,797	79	8	82	742	19	10	16
1896	6,186	416	8	46	4,601	100	24	109	799	53	9	21
1897	6,769	402	20	40	5,088	103	18	103	906	44	8	37
1898	9,775	638	191	34	5,719	234	37	171	2,376	146	24	205
1899	6,672	468	20	29	4,682	123	23	115	923	257	23	9
1900	7,914	610	25	26	5,582	89	38	92	1,028	397	10	17
1901	8,287	760	46	40	5,895	121	34	179	888	283	14	27
1902	7,371	602	13	17	5,173	112	14	115	861	395	32	37
1903	8,380	601	19	21	6,147	103	40	171	977	217	36	40
1904	8,306	710	37	67	5,879	127	62	129	962	277	30	26
1905	7,374	621	5	86	5,113	94	50	161	960	228	35	21
1906	8,139	683	7	49	5,637	176	79	162	1,059	223	40	24
1907	8,088	664	12	76	5,547	152	125	152	1,080	214	32	34
1908	8,324	711	26	66	5,708	156	86	198	1,090	171	52	60
1909	8,142	719	6	44	5,857	118	84	145	919	173	33	44
1910	8,972	779	21	31	6,370	174	76	190	1,092	165	23	51
1911	8,674	611	15	33	6,317	135	137	166	1,041	130	43	46
1912	10,355	910	55	32	7,222	159	84	246	1,340	145	73	89
1913	8,191	659	14	59	5,927	117	50	129	967	136	71	62
1919	18,954	573	12	63	9,753	3,380	100	310	4,383	229	90	61
1920	12,786	532	:	86	8,689	693	116	252	2,176	86	76	80
1921	9,198	274	:	35	6,861	511	75	123	1,143	76	37	63
1922	9,517	266	:	25	7,186	385	100	161	1,213	48	44	89
1923	10,748	354	:	88	7,981	695	70	122	1,298	50	31	59
1924	10,165	433	:	68	7,018	210	865	135	1,217	26	41	152

For reference notes see page 618.

TABLE X.—CONTINENTAL AND INTERCONTINENTAL IMMIGRATION AND EMIGRATION OF
ALIENS, 1884-1924.

Year	IMMIGRATION			EMIGRATION		
	Total	Continental	Inter-continental	Total	Continental	Inter-continental
1884	12,606	12,341	265	5,896	5,718	178
1885	14,273	13,926	347	6,391	6,155	236
1886	15,623	15,397	226	7,818	7,651	167
1887	15,310	15,028	282	7,907	7,667	240
1888	15,741	15,480	261	7,621	7,085	536
1889	16,361	15,970	391	9,241	8,655	586
1890	15,886	15,657	229	9,185	8,796	389
1891	15,873	15,574	299	7,251	7,013	238
1892	15,525	15,233	292	7,657	7,370	287
1893	15,013	14,645	368	7,177	6,929	248
1894	17,403	16,804	599	7,265	7,048	217
1895	17,055	16,712	343	7,899	7,696	203
1896	17,869	17,582	287	8,572	8,331	241
1897	19,666	19,269	397	9,962	9,742	220
1898	17,182	16,837	345	10,664	9,901	763
1899	19,367	19,011	356	10,017	9,597	420
1900	20,981	20,655	326	11,572	11,384	188
1901	20,525	20,191	334	9,348	9,144	204
1902	21,565	21,203	362	10,506	10,216	290
1903	25,510	25,144	366	11,368	11,013	355
1904	26,708	26,207	501	12,550	12,163	387
1905	29,031	28,451	580	13,321	12,899	422
1906	28,674	28,211	463	15,308	14,656	652
1907	30,046	29,441	605	14,247	13,707	540
1908	28,718	28,095	623	15,014	14,541	473
1909	30,569	29,948	621	15,766	15,249	517
1910	35,080	34,018	1,062	17,461	16,745	716
1911	31,519	30,720	799	14,877	14,297	580
1912	31,656	30,788	868	16,017	15,476	541
1913	36,134	35,055	1,079	19,016	18,029	987
1919	30,153	29,203	950	19,387	19,005	382
1920	30,185	28,782	1,403	16,401	15,702	699
1921	13,958	13,317	641	7,339	6,875	464
1922	19,594	18,602	992	8,572	8,053	519
1923	22,875	22,168	707	10,236	9,847	389
1924	39,921	38,104	1,817	12,817	12,286	531

TABLE XI.—EMIGRATION, LIKEWISE IMMIGRATION, THROUGH THE PORT OF ANTWERP, 1843-1924.

Year	Citizens and Aliens		Year	Citizens and Aliens	
	Emigrants	Immigrants (returned emigrants)		Emigrants	Immigrants (returned emigrants)
1843	3,179	....	1884	28,576	8,254
1844	2,961	....	1885	25,659	9,785
1845	5,221	....	1886	24,650	5,780
1846	13,178	....	1887	36,413	7,432
1847	14,613	....	1888	39,527	7,923
1848	11,073	....	1889	40,896	8,400
1849	10,260	....	1890	38,671	9,757
1850	7,016	....	1891	51,487	11,313
1851	9,243	....	1892	46,600	11,635
1852	14,428	....	1893	43,124	13,167
1853	15,262	....	1894	15,915	12,808
1854	25,843	....	1895	20,690	7,665
			1896	24,384	9,664
1860	2,442	....	1897	15,793	7,690
1861	2,123	....	1898	16,711	7,083
1862	3,072	....	1899	26,835	6,766
1863	2,881	....	1900	40,763	9,033
1864	5,827	....	1901	46,336	9,339
1865	3,507	....	1902	62,799	9,308
1866	3,277	....	1903	72,486	13,261
1867	8,198	....	1904	65,453	16,520
1868	1,790	....	1905	83,815	12,601
1869	8,873	....	1906	106,775	19,890
1870	126	....	1907	121,247	31,071
1871	.....	....	1908	40,471	30,848
1872	1,408	....	1909	73,320	14,918
1873	6,294	....	1910	81,497	19,271
1874	5,316	....	1911	63,922	23,460
1875	4,735	2,202	1912	87,971	19,394
1876	7,374	1,842	1913	114,472	20,499
1877	5,082	1,657			
1878	7,541	1,627	1919	2,067	1,764
1879	9,828	1,813	1920	38,032	10,416
1880	19,990	1,300	1921	56,727	11,834
1881	47,523	2,385	1922	15,568	2,783
1882	35,120	4,212	1923	17,200	....
1883	32,644	6,357	1924	12,922	....

TABLE XII.—DIRECT AND INDIRECT EMIGRATION, VIA ANTWERP, 1890-1924.

Year	Total	Direct emigration	Indirect emigration[4]	Year	Total	Direct emigration	Indirect emigration[4]
1890	38,671	36,660	2,011	1906	106,775	87,797	18,978
1891	51,487	48,856	2,631[5]	1907	121,247	100,318	20,929
1892	46,600	43,580	3,020	1908	40,471	35,559	4,912
1893	43,124	38,010	5,114	1909	73,320	67,509	5,811
1894	15,915	13,737	2,178	1910	81,497	71,692	9,805
1895	20,690	18,982	1,708	1911	63,922	59,599	4,323
1896	24,384	23,407	977	1912	87,971	83,201	4,770
1897	15,793	14,960	833	1913	114,472	100,624	13,348
1898	16,711	15,983	728				
1899	26,835	25,886	949	1919	2,067	326	1,741
1900	40,763	37,491	3,272	1920	38,032	31,984	6,048
1901	46,336	38,663	7,673	1921	56,727	39,626	17,101
1902	62,709	54,574	8,225	1922	15,568	12,860	2,708
1903	72,486	64,254	8,232	1923	17,200	14,742	2,458
1904	65,453	51,260	14,193	1924	12,922	9,686	3,236
1905	83,815	76,735	7,080				

For reference notes see page 618.

TABLE XIII.—DISTRIBUTION OF EMIGRANT CITIZENS TO EXTRA-EUROPEAN COUNTRIES THROUGH THE PORT OF ANTWERP, BY SEX, AGE AND COUNTRY OF DESTINATION, 1885-1924.

Year	Total			Under 16 years			16 years and over			Country of destination[5]					
										America		South America	Asia	Australia and New Zealand	Africa
	Males	Females	Total	Males	Females	Total	Males	Females	Total	Canada	North America (excluding Canada)				
1885	852	434	1,286	181	179	360	671	255	926	....	....				
1886	1,316	732	2,048	322	315	637	994	417	1,411	....	....				
1887	2,555	1,279	3,834	569	566	1,135	1,986	713	2,699		2,917	286	1		
1888	5,296	2,498	7,794	1,390	1,079	2,469	3,906	1,419	5,325		2,130	4,724			
1889	5,363	3,043	8,406	1,765	1,397	3,162	3,598	1,646	5,244		2,061	5,878			
1890	1,972	1,004	2,976	442	346	788	1,530	658	2,188		1,987	561		7	10
1891	2,351	1,105	3,456	479	389	868	1,872	716	2,588		2,718	340		15	5
1892	3,456	1,718	5,174	745	685	1,430	2,711	1,033	3,744	745	4,297	117		8	
1893	2,719	1,162	3,881	498	412	910	2,221	750	2,971	3,757		113		13	2
1894	821	446	1,267	188	149	337	633	297	930	236	903	115		10	1
1895	830	488	1,318	155	169	324	675	319	994	218	942	148		1	12
1896	927	502	1,429	175	146	321	752	356	1,108	139	1,010	232		5	5
1897	584	339	923	110	109	219	474	230	704	90	650	149		6	42
1898	608	320	928	89	93	182	519	227	746		759	147		6	28
1899	953	503	1,456	152	168	320	801	335	1,136	77	1,269	98		5	17
1900	1,471	744	2,215	273	220	493	1,198	524	1,722		2,106	104	3		12
1901	1,867	902	2,769	310	294	604	1,557	608	2,165	159	2,508	77		7	5
1902	2,354	1,110	3,464	401	377	778	1,953	733	2,686	397	2,955	94	1	7	15
1903	2,847	1,270	4,117	537	442	979	2,310	828	3,138	486	3,520	94		6	12
1904	2,786	1,405	4,191	544	456	1,000	2,242	949	3,191	849	3,177	151		1	15
1905	3,076	1,416	4,492	466	482	948	2,610	934	3,544	1,092	3,229	167	3	1	13
1906	4,090	1,528	5,618	530	449	979	3,560	1,079	4,639	976	4,501	136	1		4
1907	4,505	1,918	6,423	717	618	1,335	3,788	1,300	5,088	1,159	5,179	76		2	
1908	1,841	1,066	2,907	362	349	711	1,479	717	2,196	690	2,103	113		1	4
1909	2,583	1,067	3,650	484	356	840	2,099	711	2,810	817	2,701	128		1	
1910	3,964	1,616	5,580	572	527	1,099	3,392	1,089	4,481	1,196	4,247	117		4	
1911	3,144	1,442	4,586	490	449	939	2,654	993	3,647	1,515	2,826	200		5	15
1912	3,115	1,287	4,402	441	392	833	2,674	895	3,569	1,405	2,844	143		18	17
1913	5,352	2,238	7,590	643	603	1,246	4,709	1,635	6,344	2,072	5,314	202		9	
1919	975	992	1,967	315	292	607	660	700	1,360	1,923		44			
1920	5,213	4,171	9,384	1,171	1,088	2,259	4,042	3,083	7,125	9,235		149	10		
1921	1,206	994	2,200	286	252	538	920	742	1,662	2,148		52		1	
1922	519	408	927	92	105	197	427	303	730	368	523	36			
1923	1,376	886	2,262	271	241	512	1,105	645	1,750	1,495	728	39			
1924	1,611	1,312	2,923	270	281	551	1,341	1,031	2,372[6]	1,816	1,000	104			3

For reference notes see page 618.

TABLE XIV.—DISTRIBUTION OF EMIGRANT CITIZENS TO EXTRA-EUROPEAN COUNTRIES, BY OCCUPATION, THROUGH THE PORT OF ANTWERP, 1886–1924.

Year	16 years and over	Agriculture	Industry and commerce	General labor	Other occupations	No occupation or occupation not specified	
						Males	Females
1886	1,411	238	103	359	156	168	387
1887	2,699	410	87	1,179	380	313	327
1888	5,325	1,737	83	310	2,219	685	291
1889	5,244	1,772	9	536	1,750	823	354
1890	2,188	549	16	110	764	458	291
1891	2,588	731	29	353	517	549	409
1892	3,744	1,884	15	1,090	326	53	376
1893	2,971	1,480	24	762	327	16	362
1894	930	277	23	247	122	44	217
1895	994	146	55	11	113	399	270
1896	1,108	185	37	52	236	326	272
1897	704	136	20	42	318	13	175
1898	746	191	18	65	313	4	155
1899	1,136	368	23	91	422	10	222
1900	1,722	497	30	128	684	25	358
1901	2,165	746	24	148	826	13	408
1902	2,686	1,152	43	135	827	14	515
1903	3,138	1,098	32	259	1,147	13	589
1904	3,191	901	46	196	1,304	19	725
1905	3,544	1,361	27	308	1,137	14	697
1906	4,639	2,093	43	411	1,316	16	760
1907	5,088	2,050	24	517	1,516	25	956
1908	2,196	539	24	167	862	23	581
1909	2,810	1,154	18	365	742	7	524
1910	4,481	1,976	25	635	997	10	834
1911	3,647	1,739	8	639	574	10	677
1912	3,569	1,133	9	1,158	728	14	527
1913	6,344	2,464	93	2,232	870	7	678
1914	....	....	....	....	....	....	....
1915	....	....	....	....	....	....	....
1916	....	....	....	....	....	....	....
1917	....	....	....	....	....	....	....
1918	1,360	163	9	426	122	....	631
1919	7,125[7]	1,954	91	1,753	1,266	9	1,990
1920	1,662	606	22	217	346	73	468
1921	730	235	8	77	184	3	225
1922	1,750	645	29	237	252	1	584
1923							
1924	2,372[8]	637	127[9]	....	649[10]	11	948

For reference notes see page 618.

TABLE XV.—DISTRIBUTION OF EMIGRANT ALIENS DIRECT TO EXTRA-EUROPEAN COUNTRIES THROUGH THE PORT OF ANTWERP, BY NATIONALITY, AND THEIR TOTAL INDIRECT INTERCONTINENTAL EMIGRATION THROUGH THIS PORT, 1886-1924.

Direct emigration.

Year	Total	Austrian	Hungarian	French	German	British	Italian	Luxemburger	Dutch	Poles	Rumanian	Russian	Swiss	Czecho-slovakian	Americans (without further distinction)	Other nationalities	Total	Aliens who departed indirectly
1886	22,602		805	487	10,031	4,665	693	686	297				1,454		649	84	20,302	2,300
1887	32,579		3,338	763	16,348	4,682	624	1,118	454			451	1,139		819	85	30,546	2,033
1888	31,733		1,147	930	17,646	3,995	600	1,217	493			1,176	960		820	292	29,232	2,501
1889	32,490		1,571	1,644	14,762	6,017	611	1,947	996			1,132	990		1,074	471	31,455	1,035
1890	35,695		6,428	609	16,036	2,438	794	1,097	497			1,372	1,100		863	389	34,087	1,608
1891	48,031		9,808	719	22,801	2,282	1,683	1,382	664			3,076	940		780	257	45,785	2,246
1892	41,426		11,811	489	17,720	1,204	1,533	1,335	981			4,313	1,263		1,098	199	39,528	1,898
1893	39,243		12,934	542	11,476	1,105	1,085	765	793			817	1,005		711	873	35,321	3,922
1894	14,648		3,985	155	4,182	640	342	319	174			3,933	359		1,318	89	12,823	1,825
1895	19,372		8,412	184	4,930	427	423	257	232			795	544		1,424	86	18,037	1,335
1896	22,955		11,031	212	5,267	651	899	303	514			905	360		1,194	119	22,189	766
1897	14,870		5,064	160	3,578	536	452	165	232			2,360	300		1,052	186	14,200	670
1898	15,783		5,880	113	2,888	604	413	111	180			3,664	269		887	262	15,203	580
1899	25,379		12,705	148	2,904	741	996	153	231			5,358	229		833	435	24,590	783
1900	38,548		17,087	210	3,381	982	1,936	301	247			7,478	297		1,373	2,459	35,510	3,038
1901	43,567		18,585	234	3,391	1,189	2,405	387	296			7,203	376		1,178	1,187	36,224	7,343
1902	59,335	8,060	14,367	308	5,810	1,029	2,533	373	351			15,726	559		862	1,570	51,708	7,627
1903	68,369	9,859	18,115	366	5,646	978	2,720	302	375			19,448	621		678	1,752	60,911	7,458
1904	61,262	9,562	10,864	314	4,449	738	2,619	289	360			16,065	531		928	1,670	48,629	12,633
1905	79,323	20,337	14,246	341	4,728	622	4,565	304	400			24,479	411		794	1,731	73,074	6,249
1906	101,157	22,005	13,831	342	4,406	803	4,035	219	346			35,724	320		571	1,384	83,805	17,352
1907	114,824	36,720	17,293	290	3,826	1,733	4,231	292	346			28,533	314		437	2,389	95,474	19,350
1908	37,564	12,408	4,440	273	2,036	1,505	418	78	149			10,720	234		731	473	33,693	3,871
1909	69,670	23,012	11,388	117	2,285	3,331	526	80	254			24,401	165		512	942	65,187	4,483
1910	75,917	25,127	8,667	143	2,404	5,470	359	85	293			25,879	125		594	1,341	68,348	7,569
1911	59,336	20,026	6,534	205	1,988	6,466	422	70	443			20,356	148		544	908	57,114	2,222
1912	83,569	28,655	9,469	151	2,082	1,204	633	82	466			30,614	92		756	1,668	81,134	2,435
1913	106,882	32,354	7,938	180	2,293	1	3,485	59	406			48,029	186		339	845	97,318	9,564
1919	100								59						4		64	36
1920	28,648	115	116	143	157	31	2,924	111	1,259	9,521		814	224		870	3,117	24,582	4,066
1921	54,527	273	1,331	51	197	17	465	15	102	23,817	3,565	3,116	77	5,180	633	1,315	38,311	16,216
1922	14,641	120	293	21	107	9	4	7	76	5,180	802	3,987	48	3,337	624	423	12,351	2,290
1923	14,938	81	186	36	180	15	390	68	360	7,167	501	1,751	90	650	726	676	13,317	1,621
1924	9,999	77	138	122	448	152	92	132	499	1,035	608	1,483	188	559	1,470	716	7,719	2,280

SOURCES

Statistique générale de la Belgique. Exposé de la situation du Royaume. Ministry of the Interior. Decennial period 1841-50; Vol. II, p. 44, Brussels, 1852. Decennial period 1851-60: Vol. II, p. 161, Brussels, 1865. 1861-75: Brussels, 1885, pp. 594-595.

Table I (years 1841-75).

Documents statistiques de la Belgique. Vols. IX-XIII. "Navigation".

Table XI (years 1843, 1850-67).

Annuaire Statistique de la Belgique, 1876-1922. Brussels, 1877-1924.
All tables not said to be taken from other sources.
Information supplied by the Belgian Government (Ministry of the Interior).

Tables II-X (years 1923-24).

Information supplied by the Emigration Commission of the Belgian Government at Antwerp.

Tables XI-XV (years 1923-24).

Letter dated July 15, 1847, of the German consul at Antwerp to the Prussian Ministry of Foreign Affairs. Preussisches Geheimes Staatsarchiv Rep. 1, Auswanderung ausser Europa 11, vol. IV.
Hübner, *Jahrbuch für Volkswirtschaft und Statistik,* vols. I-IV, Leipzig, 1853.

NOTES

[1]Spain only.
[2]Emigrants to ports in the United States.
[3]*Idem* for the first six months only.
[4]This heading includes emigrants who went from Antwerp by sea to other European ports to embark for non-European countries.
[5]For 1887-91, the countries of destination are indicated only in report of direct emigration.
[6]Exclusive of 131 passengers who departed for the Congo.
[7]Our source gives 7,125, but the details total 7,127.
[8]15 years and over.
[9]Of whom 49 persons in "industry" and 78 in "commerce and transport".
[10]Includes 71 persons in "liberal professions".

)

BRITISH ISLES

I. Historical Tables

1. The shipping lists which form the basis of table I (Emigration from the Port of London in 1635) indicate the name and the age of the emigrant as well as the destination of each ship (Virginia, New England, St. Christopher and Barbados, Island of Providence, Summer Islands "Bermudas"). Our table has been compiled by adding the names in the shipping lists. The name Francis has been treated as that of a man, except where it was expressly stated that a woman was referred to.

2. Table II (England) is a summary of the weekly lists of emigrants established at the command of the Treasury by the Custom-House officers in the following ports of emigration: London, Liverpool, Dover, Southwood, Bristol, those going to Europe, to Ireland and to the Isle of Man not being included.

The weekly figures concerning these ports for the year 1774 begin with December 11, 1773, and go on to December 26, 1774, but the following weeks are missing: April 12 to 19, April 26 to May 3, May 3 to 10. 51 weeks are given.

The figures for the year 1775 begin with December 26, 1774, and go on to December 31, 1775. The only week missing is November 6 to 13. 52 weeks are given.

The figures for the year 1776 begin on December 31, 1775, and go on to April 7, 1776.

As regards *sex*, all convicts have been classed as males. Practically all persons under "sex not stated" are children whose names are not given.

The large number whose ages are not stated usually includes those sailing to other ports of Europe. In the latter case information does not seem to have been exacted. The entry is sometimes found "These all refused further information" or "were obstinate and refused any information." There are also occasionally large numbers of convicts whose ages are not given.

3. Table III concerns emigration from Scotland to North America and Virginia during 1774-1775. The lists are established on the same principle as those underlying table II. They were drawn up on the basis of a letter of the Lords Commissioners of His Majesty's Treasury of December 8, 1773, which was addressed to the Commissioners of Customs for account of Persons Emigrating from Scotland to America, etc. (U. S. at Public Record Office, London, T 17, 20, p. 478). However these lists do not include passengers to the continent of Europe.

The lists of emigrants are written on loose sheets of paper, following no time order. Below are the dates for which lists are to be found in the Record Office:

1774: February 3 to 10, May 2, May 7, May 13 to 20, May 16, May 18, August 12 to 18, August 19 to 25, September 8 to 15, Sep-

tember 30 to October 7, October 7 to 14, October 17 to 23, November 14, December 2.

1775: March 30, April 7 to 14, April 28, May 1, May 9, May 26, May 31, June 9 to 16, July 7 to 14, July 13, July 14 to 21, July 28, September 3, September 4.

2 lists are undated.

Where the sex is "not stated," we are dealing mainly with children whose names are not furnished in the lists. Where the age of the children was not shown, we have placed them in the column headed "under 14."

There is not the same variety of *trades* as amongst the English emigrants. Most of the Scotch are farmers or weavers. The number of merchants is extremely small. The lists render it probable that the passengers were genuine emigrants in search of employment who took with them their wives and children. Usually the reasons given for their emigrating are the high rents and the general poverty of their country. It is sometimes stated that they are without means of subsistence in their own country. Where no occupation or employment is indicated, the statement is sometimes found that the passengers were generally of the labouring class or that "only five were people of any consequence".

II. STATISTICS OF INTERCONTINENTAL PASSENGERS

1. *Methods Employed and Competent Authorities*

The statistical reports to the Treasury regarding emigration appear to have been suspended during the period of the American Revolution. Whether these reports were resumed after that War, we have been unable to ascertain. In the Archives which we searched we could find neither passenger lists nor other statistical material dating before 1815. The regular emigration or passenger statistics start with that year. Like the earlier statistics, they are based on returns compiled by Custom-House officers and their staffs in the several ports. The data for these returns have been obtained from the masters of British vessels in pursuance of the Act of June 24, 1803, "for regulating the vessels carrying passengers from the United Kingdom to His Majesty's plantations and settlements abroad, or to foreign parts, with respect to the number of such passengers"

This first "Emigration Act" provided that British ships sailing overseas may, on pain of certain penalties, only carry one person for every two tons and foreign ships only one person for every five tons. Moreover, the Custom-House officers were instructed to ascertain, on the basis of the passenger lists delivered by the masters of vessels, whether the number of persons shipped was within the prescribed limit. These lists were preserved by the Customs authorities who issued the clearance papers.

From that period onward the materials for the tables relating to the movement of passengers between the United Kingdom and extra-European countries have been drawn from the returns furnished by masters of vessels leaving the ports of the United Kingdom for, or ar-

riving at such ports from, places out of Europe and not within the Mediterranean Sea.

The Act of July 5, 1825, extended the protection accorded to emigrants on foreign vessels, although notable exceptions were made for British vessels, as in the case of those proceeding from Ireland to British North America. In the course of the following years this legal protection was steadily extended to diverse other types of vessels. The improvement dates most especially from the amended Passenger Act of 1842 (5 and 6 Victoria, ch. 63), and was carried further in the Acts of 1849, 1852, 1853, 1855, 1863, 1870, 1889, 1894.

The Customs authorities were charged at first with the administration of the Passenger Acts. Special inspectors were not appointed, perhaps because, prior to the age of steamboats, emigration went through a multitude of ports. On the basis of the material furnished by the Customs authorities, the Colonial Department published the first statistical reports on the movement of passengers.[1] The financial assistance of emigrants and all questions relating to their settlement in the Colonies were entrusted in 1837 to an Agent General for Emigration and to a Board of Colonisation (South Australian) Commissioners, and three years later the Office of the Colonial Land and Emigration Commissioners was established. These Commissioners, from the time of their second annual report in 1841, for thirty years published passenger (emigration) statistics, adding frequently new particulars and making further improvements, but always in accordance with the actual state of the legislation dealing with the protection of emigrants.

All powers and duties conferred and imposed on them by the Passenger Acts of 1855 and 1863 were transferred to the Board of Trade by the Merchant Shipping Act of 1872, and the information available in respect of the passenger movement from 1815 onward was incorporated in their report entitled *Emigration from the United Kingdom, 1873*. From that date, annual reports were published by the Board of Trade up to 1913. For the later publications of the Board, see our references.

Mr. A. W. Flux, head of the Statistical Department of the Board of Trade, responding to our request for additional information, kindly forwarded us on February 4, 1927, a full memorandum on British migration statistics. This has enabled us to check our study regarding the bases of the migration figures at various periods, from 1841 onward. The same authority had previously favoured us with ten statistical tables covering the period 1815-1924. For that reason the Board of Trade is quoted as authority even in cases where the same figures had previously been found in printed publications.

2. *Definitions.*

The primary object of the Passenger Act was, not to find a suitable basis for emigration statistics, but rather to afford protection to a certain category of passengers.

[1]See *General Index to Accounts and Papers etc.*, printed by the order of the House of Commons or presented by command: 1801-1852, p. 343. Ordered by the House of Commons to be printed August 16, 1853.

The statistics relate to all intercontinental passengers, and not exclusively to persons intending to reside overseas. These passengers are officially divided into cabin and steerage passengers; but neither the two combined nor the steerage passengers alone cover the groups of emigrants proper. Nevertheless, until 1860 one would not be far wrong in treating all passengers, even the few cabin passengers, as persons who sailed for overseas countries with a view to changing their abode.

To identify the number of passengers, minus those paying for cabins, or the number of steerage passengers with the number of emigrants would be a doubtful procedure. Originally, these distinctions were made not for statistical purposes but for administrative ends and were adapted to the regulations then in force. Their object was to discriminate between emigrants for whose benefit a supervision of the ship's accommodation was maintained, and other passengers. A comparison of third class passengers, a new category since 1908 on British vessels, with steerage passengers is not practicable, because the two classes are not coextensive.

Before 1863 the masters only of such vessels as carried steerage passengers were required to furnish passenger lists to the Customs authorities. By reason of the voluntary nature of information from masters of ships carrying only cabin passengers more of them were recorded in some years than in others. During the period 1842 to 1852 travellers in vessels not governed by the Passenger Acts were generally entered in the column "cabin passengers". From 1853 to 1863, travellers whose age and sex were not distinguished, as in the case of infants, were entered in a separate column, the remark being made in some years (1853 and 1854) that they consisted mainly of cabin passengers. The figures for cabin passengers fluctuate remarkably from year to year, and one cannot tell for which years they are complete.

After 1863 the statistics comprised all classes of outward passengers, but the Emigration Commissioners do not seem to have published the number of cabin passengers separately in their annual reports until after 1876, nor is the information available in any official source.

After 1860 a new and graver source of error crept into the passenger statistics. With traffic improvements, and lower fares, especially through the introduction of steamships, the ratio of general travellers to emigrants rose. This was particularly true of cabin passengers as compared to other classes.

That disadvantage, however, was balanced in part by clearer definitions beginning with 1853, which permitted a division of passengers into aliens and citizens. German authorities estimated at 2,000 the number of aliens who sailed from British ports in 1844, and the number of these rapidly increased from 1847 onward. Thus in 1853, when aliens were distinguished from citizens for the first time, the British statistics record 31,459 alien passengers, and 20,349 whose nationality was not ascertained, but most of whom were aliens. For decades this class of passenger of unknown nationality was considerable: at the commencement of the sixties, over 20,000; later, under 10,000; and only since 1908 has it disappeared. Even to-day the particular nationality of alien passengers is not recorded.

3. *Immigration.*

The arrival of extra-European passengers has been recorded since 1854, although masters of vessels were not required by law to supply lists of such passengers. These statistics, however, for the years before 1870 are incomplete and otherwise defective. (See explanatory notes Nos. 11-14). After that date the master of every vessel who brought steerage passengers to the United Kingdom from places out of Europe was required to deliver a list at the port of arrival, and from these lists tables of immigration were compiled. Moreover, masters of vessels arriving from places out of Europe and carrying passengers other than steerage often furnished information about such passengers although it was not required.

In these circumstances, a comparison between the number of citizens departing and the number arriving furnishes the most reliable statistical measure of emigration. Although for the period 1870 to 1876 the number of immigrant citizens cannot be separately indicated, we may compare the inward and outward movement of migrants by supposing that the proportion of aliens among the immigrants was not large.

4. *Demographical Particulars.*

The regulations concerning the registration of *age* and *sex* were as follows. Prior to 1856 those aged 14 and over were regarded for the purposes of the Passenger Act as adults. From 1853 to 1876, infants under 12 months (males and females from 1861 onward) were distinguished from children 1 to 12 years old. After 1856 and until 1908, all persons of 12 years of age and upwards were considered as adults.

After April 1, 1912, the ages of "emigrants" and "immigrants" were grouped as follows: under 12, 12 to 17, 18 to 30, 31 to 45, 46 years and over, 'age not stated'. Males and females were distinguished.

During the period 1854-1902 the adult outward British and Irish passengers were classified—according to the information supplied by the Board of Trade—by occupation into a number of groups varying from 39 to 53 for males and from 6 to 8 for females.[1] Similar particulars were shown for the years 1877 to 1902 about passengers classified as "foreigners" and "nationality not distinguished".

The *countries* of arrival or departure have been grouped usually as follows: British North America, Australia and New Zealand, United States, and "all other places". However, in the above-quoted official printed reports we found annual figures for the West Indies and South Africa (table IVa); detailed particulars referring to emigration to the Australian Colonies (table IVc); as well as statistics concerning emigration to British North America during the period 1842-75 (table IVc). Detailed tables of the outward movement will be found in the annual reports (1841-1902) relating to the East Indies, British West Indies,

---

[1] However, for the years before 1877 we could only find in the Parliamentary Papers figures indicating the occupations of the British overseas emigrants for the two years 1857 and 1867. The source of the figures for 1857 was the Government Emigration Board, Downing Street, and for 1867 the Statistical and Commercial Department of the Board of Trade.

Cape of Good Hope and Natal (including from 1841 all passengers, the British being distinguished after 1877), Central and South America, and "all other places". "Cape of Good Hope and Natal" was given separately for inward passengers, and British were distinguished after 1882. After 1894 "all other places" was divided into India (including Ceylon), other British Colonies, and other foreign countries (for both outward and inward passengers). After 1904 Natal was distinguished from the Cape of Good Hope and after 1906 New Zealand from Australia.

III. STATISTICS OF INTERCONTINENTAL MIGRANTS

As passenger statistics had ceased to represent the movement of migrants, particulars about the past and future residence of passengers were published from April 1, 1912. By this means it became possible to separate migrants from other passengers. Passengers stating that they were changing their residence from or to the United Kingdom were classed as emigrants or immigrants respectively.

IV. PASSENGERS TO AND FROM THE CONTINENT OF EUROPE

Statistics of passengers travelling between the United Kingdom and the Continent were based on returns voluntarily furnished to the Board of Trade by the shipping companies, etc. Accordingly, the statistics for the years up to and including 1907 are less complete than those which have been furnished since 1908. (Tables XXVII and XXIX.) These figures do not include travellers by air.

Besides the voluntary returns mentioned above, lists of alien passengers were required to be furnished to the Customs authorities (under Act 6 Will. IV, ch. II) by the masters of certain vessels arriving with aliens on board. These lists, which contained the names and descriptions of aliens, were summarised for the years 1890-1905. (Table XXVIII) The Aliens Act, 1905, transferred the duties relating to alien passengers to the Home Office and statistics of the alien passenger movement since 1906 have been published in the Annual Reports of the Inspector under the Aliens Act. This Act was superseded by the Aliens Restriction Acts, 1914 and 1919. These statistics (Table XXX) date from 1921, classify aliens by nationality and include persons travelling by air between the United Kingdom and the continent of Europe.

Alien wage earners, equipped with a permit from the Ministry of Labour, may be counted among immigrants proper and can be also classified separately.

V. TRANSIT

We have included in tables IV and XII all alien passengers who embark in the British Isles for an overseas destination or who arrive from overseas. The overwhelming majority of these should be regarded as transmigrants. However, it is only since 1921 that "transmigrants" and "persons in transit," in the strict sense of the word, have been recorded

in the statistics compiled by the Home Office in connection with the Aliens Act.

Table XXXI refers to alien transmigrants as defined in Article 4 (1) of the Aliens Order, *i. e.*, migrants in transit for whom shipping companies give a guarantee that they will leave British territory as quickly as possible. Figures relating to arrivals (table V of the source) and departures (table VI of the source) of transmigrants show that the guarantee is honoured. To these transmigrants it has been necessary to add the aliens who are given in table II of the source under the heading "in transit". This heading refers to aliens admitted to the country as aliens in transit on their own responsibility. The figures given under this heading have here been divided between outgoing and returning migrants in transit in the same proportion as the outgoing and returning transmigrants. "Transmigrants" and "aliens in transit" are classified in our source according to nationality.

Statistics about migration into and out from the British Isles supplementing the figures in the British national tables will be found in other sections of the present volume. Statistics about the number of migrants from the British Isles or their divisions to Canada (1829-80 and 1900-24), Australia or colonies later combined into that Commonwealth (1851-1924), New Zealand (1853-1919), Argentina (1857-1924), Brazil (1861-1924), Cuba (1902-24), United States (1820-1924), Mexico (1909-24), and Hungary (1879-1924), will be found in the national tables for those countries. Statistics about the number of migrants returning to the British Isles from the Cape of Good Hope (1900-12), Natal (1911-12), Australia or colonies later combined into that Commonwealth (1851-1919), New Zealand (1853-1919), Argentina (1857-1924), United States (1908-24), Mexico (1911-24) and Uruguay (1879-1921) will be found in the national tables for those countries.

TABLE I.—INTERCONTINENTAL EMIGRATION FROM THE PORT OF LONDON, BY SEX, AGE AND COUNTRY OF DESTINATION, 1635.

Total	Sex		Age				
	Males	Females	Under 14 years	15-24 years	25-54 years	55 years and over	Age not stated
4,890	4,029	861	517	2,897	1,454	21	1

Total	Country of destination				
	Barbados and St. Christopher	Bermuda	New England	Virginia	Providence Island
4,890	1,407	220	1,178	2,013	72

TABLE II.—EMIGRATION FROM ENGLAND BY SEX, AGE AND COUNTRY OF DESTINATION, 1774-76.

Year	Sex				Age					Country of destination			
	Total	Males	Females	Unknown	Up to 14 years	15-24 years	25-54 years	55 years and over	Not stated	North America	West Indies	Europe	Other countries or country unknown
1774	7,756	6,430	977	349	400	2,277	2,823	51	2,205	3,746	370	3,515	125
1775	5,113	4,304	712	97	174	1,127	2,156	34	1,622	1,856	115	3,123	19
1776 (up to April 7)	455	394	57	4	2	32	156	2	265	...	44	408	3

TABLE III.—INTERCONTINENTAL EMIGRATION FROM SCOTLAND, BY SEX, AGE AND COUNTRY OF FUTURE RESIDENCE, 1774-75.

Year	Total	Sex			Age					Country of future residence	
		Males	Females	Not stated	Under 14 years	15-24 years	25-54 years	55 years and over	Not stated	North America	West Indies
1774	1,253	789	422	42	349	378	501	15	10	1,185	68
1775 (up to July 13)	1,180	653	402	125	386	360	410	12	12	1,140	40

TABLE IV.—PASSENGERS TO EXTRA-EUROPEAN COUNTRIES, BY COUNTRY OF DESTINATION, 1815-1924.

Year	Total	Citizens	Aliens	Nationality unknown	British North America	Australia	New Zealand	East Indies[1]	South Africa[2]	Other British Colonies and possessions[3]	United States	Other countries
1815	2,081	....	....	....	680	....	....	....	....	....	1,209	192
1816	12,510	....	....	....	3,370	....[4]	....[4]	....	....	....	9,022	118
1817	20,634	....	....	....	9,797	....[4]	....[4]	....	....	....	10,280	557
1818	27,787	....	....	....	15,136	....[4]	....[4]	....	....	....	12,429	222
1819	34,787	....	....	....	23,534	....[4]	....[4]	....	....	....	10,674	579
1820	25,729	....	....	....	17,921	....[4]	....[4]	....	....	....	6,745	1,063
1821	18,297	....	....	....	12,955	....[4]	....[4]	....	....	....	4,958	384
1822	20,429	....	....	....	16,013	....[4]	....[4]	....	....	....	4,137	279
1823	16,550	....	....	....	11,355	....[4]	....[4]	....	....	....	5,032	163
1824	14,025	....	....	....	8,774	....[4]	....[4]	....	....	....	5,152	99
1825	14,891	....	....	....	8,741	485[4]	....[4]	....	....	....	5,551	114
1826	20,900	....	....	....	12,818	903	....	....	....	....	7,063	116
1827	28,003	....	....	....	12,648	715	....	....	....	....	14,526	114
1828	26,092	....	....	....	12,084	1,056	....	....	....	....	12,817	135
1829	31,198	....	....	....	13,307	2,016	....	....	....	....	15,678	197
1830	56,907	....	....	....	30,574	1,242	....	....	....	....	24,887	204
1831	83,160	....	....	....	58,067	1,561	....	....	....	....	23,418	114
1832	103,140	....	....	....	66,339	3,733	....	....	....	....	32,872	196
1833	62,527	....	....	....	28,808	4,093	....	....	....	....	29,109	517
1834	76,222	....	....	....	40,060	2,800	....	....	....	....	33,074	288
1835	44,478	....	....	....	15,573	1,860	....	....	....	....	26,720	325
1836	75,417	....	....	....	34,226	3,124	....	....	....	....	37,774	293
1837	72,034	....	....	....	29,884	5,054	....	....	....	....	36,770	326
1838	33,222	....	....	....	4,577	14,021	....	....	....	....	14,332	292
1839	62,207	....	....	....	12,658	15,786	....	....	....	....	33,536	227
1840	90,743	....	....	....	32,293	15,850	....	....	....	....	40,642	1,958
1841	118,592	....	....	....	38,164	32,625	....	....	368	2,130	45,017	288
1842	128,344	....	....	....	54,123	8,534	....	....	587	813	63,852	435
1843	57,212	....	....	....	23,518	3,478	....	182	203	816	28,335	680
1844	70,686	....	....	....	22,924	2,229	....	176	161	496	43,660	1,040
1845	93,501	....	....	....	31,803	830	....	166	496	854	58,538	814
1846	129,851	....	....	....	43,439	2,347	....	109	545	488	82,239	684
1847	258,270	....	....	....	109,680	4,949	....	86	445	364	142,154	592
1848	248,089	....	....	....	31,065	23,904	....	1,180	1,445	855	188,233	1,407
1849	299,498	....	....	....	41,367	32,191	....	1,212	3,211	801	219,450	1,266
1850	280,849	....	....	....	32,961	16,037	....	1,172	4,624	986	223,078	1,991

For reference notes see page 658.

TABLE IV.—PASSENGERS TO EXTRA-EUROPEAN COUNTRIES, BY COUNTRY OF DESTINATION, 1815-1924 (continued).

Year	Total	Citizens	Aliens	Nationality unknown	British North America	Australia	New Zealand	East Indies[1]	South Africa[2]	Other British Colonies and possessions[3]	United States	Other countries
1851	335,966	.....	.....	.....	42,605	21,532		1,180	718	893	267,357	1,681
1852	368,764	.....	.....	.....	32,873	87,881		1,442	834	780	244,261	693
1853	329,937	278,129	31,459	20,349	34,522	61,401		928	369	600	230,885	1,232
1854	323,429	267,047	37,704	18,678	43,761	83,237		1,321	375	601	193,065	1,069
1855	176,807	150,023	10,554	16,230	17,966	52,309		1,285	487	584	103,414	762
1856	176,554	148,284	9,474	18,796	16,378	44,584		1,402	466	661	111,837	1,226
1857	212,875	181,051	12,624	19,200	21,001	61,248		966	1,003	681	126,905	1,071
1858	113,972	95,067	4,560	14,345	9,704	39,295		1,065	2,916	484	59,716	792
1859	120,432	97,093	4,442	18,897	6,689	31,013		6,241	4,842	464	70,303	880
1860	128,469	95,989	4,536	27,944	9,786	24,302		2,435	2,516	577	87,500	1,353
1861	91,770	65,197	3,619	22,954	12,707	23,738		1,249	2,350	633	49,764	1,329
1862	121,214	97,763	3,311	20,140	15,522	41,843		1,268	1,852	626	58,706	1,397
1863	223,758	192,864	7,833	23,061	18,083	53,054		1,159	1,208	1,046	146,813	2,395
1864	208,900	187,081	16,942	4,877	12,721	40,942		1,267	1,400	1,906	147,042	3,622
1865	209,801	174,891	28,619	6,291	17,211	37,283		1,091	1,037	1,930	147,258	3,991
1866	204,882	170,053	26,691	8,138	13,255	24,097		911	724	1,556	161,000	3,339
1867	195,953	156,982	31,193	7,778	15,503	14,466		810	696	1,710	159,275	3,493
1868	196,325	138,187	51,956	6,182	21,062	12,809		624	1,105	1,530	155,532	3,655
1869	258,027	186,300	65,752	5,975	33,891	14,901		750	717	1,386	203,001	3,381
1870	256,940	202,511	48,396	6,033	35,295	17,065		1,420	1,005	1,872	196,075	4,208
1871	252,435	192,751	53,246	6,438	32,671	12,227		1,644	1,070	1,879	198,843	4,101
1872	295,213	210,494	79,023	5,696	32,205	15,876		1,841	1,841	2,188	233,747	7,514
1873	310,612	228,345	72,198	10,069	37,208	26,428		2,912	2,838	2,175	233,073	5,978
1874	241,014	197,272	38,465	5,277	25,450	53,958		3,015	4,023	1,821	148,161	4,586
1875	173,809	140,675	31,347	1,787	17,378	35,525		4,094	5,628	1,828	105,046	4,310
1876	138,222	109,469	25,584	3,169	12,327	33,191		4,428	6,634	1,823	75,533	4,286
1877	119,971	95,195	21,289	3,487	9,289	31,071		4,507	5,321	1,468	64,027	4,288
1878	147,663	112,902	31,697	3,064	13,836	37,214		4,310	4,930	1,423	81,557	4,393
1879	217,163	164,274	49,480	3,409	22,509	42,178		4,384	7,665	1,430	134,590	4,407
1880	332,294	227,542	100,369	4,383	29,340	25,438		4,527	9,803	1,543	257,274	4,369
1881	392,514	243,002	144,381	5,131	34,561	24,093		1,499	14,229	1,522	307,973	5,637
1882	413,288	279,366	130,029	3,893	53,475	38,604		4,458	13,614	1,794	295,539	5,804
1883	397,157	320,118	73,260	3,779	53,566	73,017		4,219	6,713	1,834	252,226	5,582
1884	303,901	242,179	57,733	3,989	37,043	45,944		4,549	4,699	1,614	203,519	6,553
1885	264,385	207,644	53,783	2,958	22,928	40,689		4,211	3,960	1,479	184,470	6,648
1886	330,801	232,900	94,370	3,531	30,121	44,055		4,645	4,659	1,776	238,386	7,159
1887	396,494	281,487	108,572	6,435	44,406	35,198		4,858	5,658	1,565	296,901	7,908

For reference notes see page 658.

TABLE IV.—PASSENGERS TO EXTRA-EUROPEAN COUNTRIES, BY COUNTRY OF DESTINATION, 1815-1924 (concluded)

Year	Total	Citizens	Aliens	Nationality unknown	British North America	Australia	New Zealand	East Indies[1]	South Africa[2]	Other British Colonies and possessions[3]	United States	Other countries
1888	398,494	279,928	113,230	5,336	49,107	31,725		5,164	7,705	1,787	293,087	9,919
1889	342,641	253,795	83,466	5,380	38,056	28,834		5,247	15,671	1,860	240,395	12,578
1890	315,980	218,116	94,515	3,349	31,897	21,570		5,494	12,083	1,953	233,522	9,461
1891	334,543	218,507	112,275	3,761	33,752	19,957		5,605	10,686	2,091	252,016	10,436
1892	321,397	210,042	107,351	4,004	41,866	16,183		6,088	11,641	1,928	235,221	8,470
1893	307,633	208,814	95,123	3,696	50,381	11,412		5,718	16,158	1,992	213,212	8,760
1894	226,827	156,030	67,032	3,765	23,633	11,151		5,310	16,760	3,728	159,431	6,814
1895	271,772	185,181	82,818	3,773	22,357	10,809		5,528	25,988	3,777	195,632	7,681
1896	241,952	161,925	76,015	4,012	22,590	10,710		6,085	35,840	4,184	154,496	8,047
1897	213,280	146,460	62,932	3,888	22,669	12,396		6,076	28,801	4,411	132,048	6,879
1898	205,171	140,644	60,551	3,976	27,487	11,020		5,899	25,635	4,415	123,703	7,012
1899	240,696	146,362	90,020	4,314	33,669	12,268		5,198	18,863	4,511	159,143	7,044
1900	298,561	168,825	124,722	5,014	50,007	15,723		5,418	25,518	4,985	189,391	7,519
1901	302,575	171,715	124,354	6,506	42,898	15,754		5,294	28,553	6,927	194,941	8,208
1902	386,779	205,662	174,291	6,826	67,600	14,675		5,859	51,886	6,705	232,099	7,955
1903	449,006	259,950	181,539	7,517	99,582	12,573		6,532	62,824	7,050	251,941	8,504
1904	453,877	271,435	174,354	8,088	91,684	14,210		7,054	32,278	6,943	291,945	9,763
1905	459,662	262,077	188,422	9,163	108,118	15,488		7,274	31,166	7,159	276,636	13,821
1906	557,737	325,137	229,142	3,458	141,786	11,039	8,550	8,031	26,323	7,628	338,612	15,768
1907	634,949	395,680	239,040	229	185,831	16,445	8,622	8,601	23,264	7,924	366,396	17,866
1908	386,411	263,199	123,212	....	95,428	22,161	11,739	8,867	21,944	9,014	198,321	18,937
1909	474,378	288,761	185,617	....	113,318	27,727	10,623	9,420	24,649	9,160	259,933	19,548
1910	618,859	397,848	221,011	....	196,305	36,289	9,957	9,598	30,838	10,709	303,364	21,799
1911	623,425	454,527	168,898	....	213,361	69,055	12,239	10,041	34,528	10,095	250,969	23,137
1912	656,835	467,666	189,169	....	219,136	83,742	13,722	9,896	31,888	10,850	262,066	25,535
1913	701,691	469,640	232,051	....	231,718	65,101	13,787	10,267	29,706	11,868	313,848	25,396
1914	451,438	293,204	158,234	....	120,791	41,178	7,845	12,402	23,799	11,013	213,048	21,362
1915	126,507	104,919	21,588	....	20,596	12,192	3,160	8,242	13,071	8,405	52,835	8,006
1916	93,889	76,479	17,410	....	19,631	5,151	2,231	4,197	8,943	6,833	41,332	5,571
1917	27,871	20,578	7,293	....	6,898	1,351	872	992	3,316	3,555	9,099	1,788
1918	22,824	17,319	5,505	....	3,450	1,860	637	2,309	2,655	2,920	7,204	1,789
1919	201,504	180,232	21,272	....	91,383	13,534	4,290	10,986	8,021	11,930	47,732	13,628
1920	437,879	352,811	85,068	....	147,640	36,469	13,291	19,763	32,574	15,831	152,748	19,563
1921	377,507	268,259	109,248	....	100,428	35,209	11,367	16,928	32,739	14,581	149,943	16,312
1922	343,624	248,287	95,337	....	86,326	44,625	12,764	12,311	23,948	13,691	132,236	17,723
1923[5]	463,285	337,567	125,718	....	158,359	45,265	10,451	11,798	21,160	13,238	182,758	20,256
1924	371,306	263,480	107,826	....	129,507	47,357	12,512	12,832	25,237	15,009	108,301	20,551

For reference notes see page 658.

TABLE IVa.—EMIGRANTS TO BRITISH WEST INDIES AND THE CAPE OF GOOD HOPE, 1821-40.

Year	West Indies	Cape of Good Hope	Year	West Indies	Cape of Good Hope
1821	1,772	404	1831	....	114
1822	1,423	192	1832	....	196
1823	1,911	184	1833	....	517
1824	1,353	119	1834	....	288
1825	1,082	114	1835	....	325
1826	1,913	116	1836	....	293
1827	1,156	114	1837	....	326
1828	1,211	135	1838	....	292
1829	1,251	197	1839	....	227
1830	....	204	1840	1,938	513

TABLE IVb.—EMIGRATION TO THE SEVERAL AUSTRALIAN COLONIES, 1838-75.

Year	Total	New South Wales	Queensland	Victoria	Tasmania	South Australia	Western Australia	New Zealand
1838	14,021	10,189	....	3	571	3,143	115	....
1839	15,786[7]	8,455	....	1,161	328	4,856	268	....
1840	15,850	7,648	....	3,473	299	2,748	224	1,458
1841	32,625	17,492	....	9,894	806	175	357	3,901
1842	8,534	1,450	....	864	2,448	145	563	3,064
1843	3,478	2,439	....	627	24	45	....	343
1844	2,229	1,179	....	934	1	47	....	68
1845	830	73	....	423	20	300	....	14
1846	2,347	36	....	81	....	2,224	....	6
1847	4,949	726	....	387	8	3,512	....	316
1848	23,904	7,622	....	7,399	218	7,852	62	751
1849	32,191	8,403	....	10,562	535	10,855	11	1,825
Total 10 years	126,937	47,068	....	34,644	4,359	27,903	1,217	11,746
1850	16,037	3,661	....	4,682	270	5,103	316	2,005
1851	31,532	4,508	....	6,212	800	7,048	287	2,677
1852	87,881	12,736	....	63,719	1,417	7,552	739	1,718
1853	61,401	10,673	....	40,469	991	6,883	965	1,420
1854	83,237	14,647	....	51,291	4,312	11,457	480	1,050
1855	52,309	14,050	....	21,072	3,457	11,333	96	2,301
1856	44,584	9,810	....	24,314	1,815	4,512	129	4,004
1857	61,248	10,379	....	40,921	2,113	3,646	382	3,807
1858	39,295	7,214	....	21,666	306	3,982	255	5,872
1859	31,013	5,439	....	14,030	931	1,556	499	8,558
Total 10 years	498,537	93,117	....	288,376	16,412	63,072	4,148	33,412
1860	24,302	3,671	303	12,979	483	1,245	379	5,242
1861	23,738	1,626	2,480	14,256	258	422	141	4,555
1862	41,843	4,100	8,575	15,353	387	1,365	623	11,440
1863	53,054	6,379	10,339	20,261	38	1,898	220	13,919
1864	40,942	4,689	7,183	13,909	50	2,842	299	11,970
1865	37,283	2,623	12,551	9,713	40	5,145	174	7,037
1866	24,097	1,648	6,054	8,531	7	3,392	167	4,298
1867	14,466	1,318	454	7,898	25	624	163	3,984
1868	12,809	1,318	685	6,566	18	351	168	3,703
1869	14,901	796	2,318	8,649	315	161	26	2,636
Total 10 years	287,435	28,168	50,942	118,115	1,621	17,445	2,360	68,784
1870	17,065	1,043	2,593	9,103	27	311	56	3,932
1871	12,227	966	1,315	6,570	11	381	36	2,948
1872	15,876	1,102	2,380	5,269	196	281	32	6,616
1873	26,428	941	5,689	5,680	713	1,544	30	11,651
1874	53,958	1,579	8,382	5,223	13	1,958	99	36,704
1875	35,525	2,157	5,482	5,673	2	2,819	629	18,763
Total 38 years	1,102,897	194,785	76,783	479,817	24,253	123,713	8,990	194,556

For reference notes see page 658.

TABLE IVc.—EMIGRATION TO BRITISH NORTH AMERICA, BY COUNTRY OF DESTINATION, 1842-75.

Year	Total	Canada	New Brunswick	Nova Scotia and Cape Breton	Newfoundland	Prince Edward Island	Vancouvers Island	Other Places in British North America
1842	54,123	41,375	8,668	2,333	490	1,257	...	...
1843	23,518	20,350	987	1,203	448	528	...	2
1844	22,924	18,747	2,489	747	684	257	...	...
1845	31,803	23,884	6,412	615	618	242	...	32
1846	43,439	32,242	9,690	698	523	286	...	...
1847	109,680	89,562	16,589	2,000	993	536	...	...
1848	31,065	25,582	4,346	702	343	59	33	...
1849	41,367	37,520	3,016	298	321	148	64	...
1850	32,961	30,439	1,774	174	325	122	127	...
1851	42,605	38,451	3,533	231	241	128	21	...
Total 10 years	433,485	358,152	57,504	9,001	4,986	3,563	245	34
1852	32,873	30,011	2,201	165	299	144	5	48
1853	34,522	30,163	3,812	211	173	120	...	43
1854	43,761	39,792	3,570	161	95	143	...	...
1855	17,966	15,953	1,591	237	94	91	...	...
1856	16,378	14,769	742	457	215	86	9	100
1857	21,001	20,148	612	64	32	36	25	84
1858	9,704	8,764	309	96	138	316	21	60
1859	6,689	6,095	229	28	281	9	47	...
1860	9,786	8,848	294	109	465	16	54	...
1861	12,707	11,688	545	239	136	7	36	56
Total 10 years	205,387	186,231	13,905	1,767	1,928	968	197	391
1862	15,522	13,277	632	363	34	22	1,119	75
1863	18,083	16,984	434	419	27	21	118	80
1864	12,721	11,759	396	433	33	8	92	...
1865	17,211	16,544	249	336	32	2	41	7
1866	13,255	11,891	197	1,139	14	1	6	7
1867	15,503	14,877	203	305	86	24	3	5
1868	21,062	20,810	191	23	28	10	...	...
1869	33,891	33,688	157	6	19	...	...	21
1870	35,295	35,109	145	28	13	...	...	...
1871	32,671	32,003	605	17	44	...	...	2
Total 10 years	215,214	206,942	3,209	3,069	330	88	1,379	197
1872	32,205	29,984	113	2,043	62	...	...	3
1873	37,208	33,751	866	2,454	124	2	...	11
1874	25,450	22,432	321	2,654	33	10	...	...
1875	17,378	15,478	134	1,733	18	8	...	7
Total 34 years	966,327	852,970	76,052	22,721	7,481	4,639	1,821	643

TABLE V.—PASSENGERS OUTWARD, BY SEX AND AGE, 1843-76.

Year	Total			Cabin or other passengers, as described in Note 8		Total			Steerage Adults		Steerage Children[9]		Steerage Infants	
	Males	Females	Total	Males	Females	Males	Females	Total	Males	Females	Males	Females	Males	Females
1843			57,212			28,526	23,694	52,220	20,782	16,347	7,744	7,347		
1844			70,686			35,037	30,760	65,797	26,319	22,155	8,718	8,605		
1845			93,501			46,331	41,807	88,138	35,273	30,447	11,058	11,360		
1846			129,851			65,491	58,441	123,932	49,864	43,394	15,627	15,047		
1847			258,270			138,622	112,838	251,460	100,119	76,652	38,503	36,186		
1848			248,089			132,218	103,513	235,731						
1849			299,498			156,108	128,662	284,770						
1850			280,849			142,044	123,300	265,344						
1851			335,966			172,301	147,049	319,350						
1852			368,764			193,633	154,770	348,403						
1853			329,937			163,296	142,270	305,566	128,787	109,145	34,509	33,125	10,192	
1854			323,429			166,988	131,088	298,076	134,789	108,918	32,199	30,170	10,573	
1855			176,807			83,063	75,869	158,932	65,363	58,950	17,700	16,919	5,557	
1856			176,554			86,494	69,477	155,971	72,670	56,395	13,824	13,082	5,074	
1857			212,875			110,289	81,605	191,894	94,806	66,879	15,483	14,726	7,029	
1858			113,972			55,492	43,731	99,223	47,345	35,921	8,147	7,810	3,332	
1859			120,432			54,666	48,203	102,869	46,236	40,073	8,430	8,130	3,046	
1860			128,469			55,210	46,442	101,652	48,529	39,945	6,681	6,497	3,085	
1861	50,832	40,938	91,770			38,914	31,384	70,298	33,973	26,612	4,941	4,772	2,224	
1862	70,533	50,681	121,214	10,908	4,686	59,625	45,995	105,620	50,288	37,094	7,538	7,190	1,799	1,711
1863	129,480	94,278	223,758	13,026	6,225	116,454	88,053	204,507	96,461	69,202	15,795	14,852	4,198	3,999
1864	121,474	87,426	208,900	3,179	1,520	118,295	85,906	204,201	98,158	67,087	15,805	14,780	4,332	4,039
1865	126,938	82,863	209,801	3,664	2,056	123,274	80,807	204,081	103,519	62,664	15,719	14,307	4,036	3,836
1866	125,596	79,286	204,882	5,077	2,732	120,519	76,554	197,073	102,225	59,962	14,610	13,023	3,684	3,569
1867	118,088	77,865	195,953	4,972	2,729	113,116	75,136	188,252	94,937	58,845	14,306	13,064	3,873	3,227
1868	119,254	77,071	196,325	3,950	2,178	115,304	74,893	190,197	94,766	57,014	16,185	14,136	4,353	3,743
1869	160,244	97,783	258,027	3,836	2,100	156,408	95,683	252,091	128,499	70,881	21,597	19,265	6,312	5,537
1870	154,465	102,475	256,940	3,967	2,063	150,498	100,412	250,910	121,760	74,949	22,445	20,153	6,293	5,310
1871	153,148	99,287	252,435	4,130	1,866	149,018	97,421	246,439	122,401	74,040	21,157	18,552	5,460	4,829
1872	179,048	116,165	295,213	3,632	1,946	175,416	114,219	289,635	145,445	87,123	23,927	21,592	6,044	5,504
1873	183,804	245,068	428,872	2,439	1,739	181,365	273,306	454,671	148,237	243,329	26,318	23,835	6,810	6,142
1874	139,825	214,479	354,304			139,825	214,479	354,304	113,397	189,580	21,625	20,489	4,803	4,410
1875	103,885	69,924	173,809	362	188	103,523	69,736	173,259	86,980	54,799	13,554	12,257	2,989	2,680
1876	84,200	54,022	138,222	1,154	801	83,046	53,221	136,267	70,663	42,119	10,104	9,125	2,279	1,977

For reference notes see page 658.

TABLE VI.—PASSENGER CITIZENS OUTWARD, BY SEX AND AGE, 1877-1912.

Year	Children up to 12 years		Adults	
	Males	Females	Males	Females
1877	7,730	7,218	49,090	31,157
1878	8,866	8,583	58,852	36,601
1879	14,530	13,511	87,801	48,432
1880	20,171	18,421	112,513	76,437
1881	23,007	21,167	122,668	76,160
1882	27,019	24,946	139,243	88,158
1883	33,851	31,565	150,994	103,708
1884	23,211	21,191	117,778	79,999
1885	17,525	16,386	104,221	69,512
1886	19,790	18,323	118,988	75,799
1887	24,848	22,988	143,798	89,853
1888	24,713	22,167	143,129	89,919
1889	19,883	17,946	131,147	84,819
1890	15,181	14,081	111,861	76,993
1891	15,169	13,582	112,156	77,600
1892	14,093	12,853	108,063	75,033
1893	13,892	12,489	109,367	73,066
1894	9,494	8,832	78,631	59,073
1895	10,938	9,967	93,287	70,989
1896	9,285	7,915	85,385	59,340
1897	7,949	7,415	75,573	55,523
1898	7,739	7,442	73,154	52,309
1899	7,949	7,416	73,749	57,248
1900	9,353	8,814	86,749	63,909
1901	10,533	9,394	86,575	65,213
1902	13,083	11,993	106,923	73,663
1903	16,993	15,603	140,667	86,687
1904	18,772	17,207	139,232	96,224
1905	18,587	16,064	139,147	88,279
1906	24,439	21,628	173,931	105,139
1907	30,918	27,995	207,847	128,920
1908	19,359	17,810	128,856	97,174
1909	20,421	18,518	146,684	103,138
1910	29,493	27,338	204,318	136,699
1911	36,686	34,921	226,314	156,606
1912	40,103	38,555	220,656	168,352

TABLE VII.—ADULT PASSENGER CITIZENS TO EXTRA-EUROPEAN COUNTRIES, BY OCCUPATION AND SEX, 1857, 1867 and 1877-1911.

Year	Total male and female adults	Adult Males						Adult Females				
		Total	Agricultural	Commercial and professional	Skilled trades	Laborers	Miscellaneous or not stated	Total	Domestic and other service	Dressmakers and other trades	Teachers, clerks and professions	Miscellaneous or not stated
1857	95,628	67,565	13,587	3,974	12,289	33,769	3,946	28,063	10,003	306	18	17,736
1867	88,554	62,662	5,612	7,549	8,598	38,388	2,515	25,892	8,443	468	64	16,917
1877	80,247	49,090	6,555	10,997	9,654	9,816	12,068	31,157	6,917	205	394	23,641
1878	95,453	58,852	9,393	13,351	9,157	13,701	13,250	36,601	8,771	208	104	27,518
1879	136,233	87,801	9,481	14,535	18,403	28,504	16,878	48,432	10,152	348	96	37,836
1880	188,950	112,513	11,133	15,438	15,959	50,064	19,919	76,437	18,757	277	110	57,293
1881	198,828	122,668	6,847	14,984	16,438	59,823	24,576	76,160	18,512	235	150	57,263
1882	227,401	139,243	10,004	16,711	16,654	69,732	26,142	88,158	21,460	459	157	66,082
1883	254,702	150,994	14,352	17,853	22,205	70,834	25,750	103,708	29,574	777	125	73,232
1884	197,777	117,778	14,338	16,734	16,200	48,114	22,392	79,999	19,532	542	132	59,793
1885	173,733	104,221	14,310	13,882	14,572	32,807	28,650	69,512	19,593	629	190	49,100
1886	194,787	118,988	21,911	17,071	23,111	34,238	22,657	75,799	20,396	964	164	54,275
1887	233,651	143,798	30,180	17,176	27,312	44,785	24,345	89,853	23,985	2,005	234	63,629
1888	233,048	143,129	30,116	17,281	26,062	42,340	27,330	89,919	22,661	1,866	167	65,225
1889	215,066	131,147	21,625	17,572	23,724	37,166	31,060	84,819	22,621	1,543	216	60,430
1890	188,854	111,861	14,918	17,080	16,162	34,848	28,853	76,993	20,066	1,607	279	55,041
1891	189,756	112,156	18,501	16,829	14,068	33,647	29,111	77,600	18,392	1,936	280	56,992
1892	183,096	108,063	15,467	16,018	12,813	32,583	31,182	75,033	19,626	1,850	395	53,162
1893	182,433	109,367	13,975	18,414	21,359	27,265	28,354	73,066	20,070	2,532	320	50,144
1894	137,704	78,631	8,694	15,937	14,567	17,227	22,206	59,073	17,265	1,544	299	39,965
1895	164,276	93,287	9,144	18,033	18,538	24,683	22,889	70,989	22,774	2,119	307	45,789
1896	144,725	85,385	8,131	19,262	17,376	18,798	21,818	59,340	18,371	1,467	262	39,240
1897	131,096	75,573	7,651	18,630	13,717	14,421	21,154	55,523	16,138	1,480	233	37,672
1898	125,463	73,154	7,575	18,425	14,591	13,521	19,042	52,309	15,730	1,318	259	35,002
1899	130,997	73,749	8,120	17,273	11,590	17,011	19,755	57,248	19,210	1,416	274	36,348
1900	150,658	86,749	9,209	16,822	16,887	20,057	23,774	63,909	20,663	1,435	256	41,555
1901	151,788	86,575	9,054	16,924	16,713	16,237	27,647	65,213	17,334	1,560	666	45,653
1902	180,586	106,923	13,146	15,903	25,445	19,935	32,494	73,663	14,259	1,854	686	56,864
1903	227,354	140,667	15,508	14,865	36,146	36,671	37,477	86,687	15,817	2,357	1,698	66,815
1904	235,456	139,232	21,028	13,577	28,279	41,433	34,915	96,224	21,345	2,867	1,737	70,275
1905	227,426	139,147	21,778	13,380	28,858	41,568	33,563	88,279	18,337	2,609	1,351	65,982
1906	279,070	173,931	25,473	17,612	39,285	50,844	40,717	105,139	22,617	3,392	1,656	77,474
1907	336,767	207,847	26,446	18,572	46,642	64,450	51,737	128,920	26,345	3,895	1,812	96,868
1908	226,030	128,856	15,184	15,229	28,010	26,994	43,379	97,174	20,850	2,848	2,165	71,311
1909	249,822	146,684	21,128	17,181	32,971	32,502	42,902	103,138	24,357	3,454	2,225	73,102
1910	341,017	204,318	24,174	20,856	48,361	54,765	56,162	136,699	31,526	5,002	2,769	97,402
1911	382,920	226,314	33,232	25,070	48,585	54,409	65,018	156,606	36,397	5,816	3,751	110,642

TABLE VIII.—PASSENGER CITIZENS OUTWARD TO EXTRA-EUROPEAN COUNTRIES, BY COUNTRY OF DESTINATION, 1853-1924.

Year	Total	United States	British North America	Australia and New Zealand	Cape of Good Hope and Natal	All other places
1853	278.129	190,952	31,779	54,818	580	
1854	267,047	153,627	35,679	77,526	215	
1855	150,023	86,239	16,110	47,284	390	
1856	148,284	94,931	11,299	41,329	725	
1857	181,051	105,516	16,803	57,858	874	
1858	95,067	49,356	6,504	36,454	2,753	
1859	97,093	57,096	2,469	28,604	8,924	
1860	95,989	67,879	2,765	21,434	3,911	
1861	65,197	38,160	3,953	20,597	2,487	
1862	97,763	48,726	8,328	38,828	1,881	
1863	192,864	130,528	9,665	50,157	2,514	
1864	187,081	130,165	11,371	40,073	5,472	
1865	174,891	118,463	14,424	36,683	5,321	
1866	170,053	131,840	9,988	23,682	4,543	
1867	156,982	126,051	12,160	14,023	4,748	
1868	138,187	108,490	12,332	12,332	5,033	
1869	186,300	146,737	20,921	14,457	4,185	
1870	202,511	153,466	27,168	16,526	5,351	
1871	192,751	150,788	24,954	11,695	5,314	
1872	210,494	161,782	24,382	15,248	9,082	
1873	228,345	166,730	29,045	25,137	7,433	
1874	197,272	113,774	20,728	52,581	10,189	
1875	140,675	81,193	12,306	34,750	12,426	
1876	109,469	54,554	9,335	32,196	13,384	
1877	95,195	45,481	7,720	30,138	4,834	7,022
1878	112,902	54,694	10,652	36,479	4,337	6,740
1879	164,274	91,806	17,952	40,959	6,895	6,662
1880	227,542	166,570	20,902	24,184	9,059	6,827
1881	243,002	176,104	23,912	22,682	12,905	7,399
1882	279,366	181,903	40,441	37,289	12,063	7,670
1883	320,118	191,573	44,185	71,264	5,742	7,354
1884	242,179	155,280	31,134	44,255	3,954	7,556
1885	207,644	137,687	19,838	39,395	3,268	7,456
1886	232,900	152,710	24,745	43,076	3,897	8,472
1887	281,487	201,526	32,025	34,183	4,909	8,844
1888	279,928	195,986	34,853	31,127	6,466	11,496
1889	253,795	168,771	28,269	28,294	13,884	14,577
1890	218,116	152,413	22,520	21,179	10,321	11,683
1891	218,507	156,395	21,578	19,547	9,090	11,897
1892	210,042	150,039	23,254	15,950	9,891	10,908
1893	208,814	148,949	24,732	11,203	13,097	10,833
1894	156,030	104,001	17,459	10,917	13,177	10,476
1895	185,181	126,502	16,622	10,567	20,234	11,256

TABLE VIII.—PASSENGER CITIZENS OUTWARD TO EXTRA-EUROPEAN COUNTRIES, BY COUNTRY OF DESTINATION, 1853-1924 (concluded).

Year	Total	United States	British North America	Australia and New Zealand	Cape of Good Hope and Natal	All other places
1896	161,925	98,921	15,267	10,354	24,594	12,789
1897	146,460	85,324	15,571	12,061	21,109	12,395
1898	140,644	80,494	17,640	10,693	19,756	12,061
1899	146,362	92,482	16,410	11,467	14,432	11,571
1900	168,825	102,797	18,443	14,922	20,815	11,848
1901	171,715	104,195	15,757	15,350	23,143	13,270
1902	205,662	108,498	26,293	14,345	43,206	13,320
1903	259,950	123,663	59,652	12,375	50,206	14,054
1904	271,435	146,445	69,681	13,910	26,818	14,581
1905	262,077	122,370	82,437	15,139	26,307	15,824
1906	325,137	144,817	114,859	19,331	22,804	23,326
1907	395,680	170,264	151,216	24,767	20,925	28,508
1908	263,199	96,869	81,321	33,569	19,568	31,872
1909	288,761	109,700	85,887	37,620	22,017	33,537
1910	397,848	132,192	156,990	45,701	27,297	35,668
1911	454,527	121,814	184,860	80,770	30,767	36,316
1912	467,666	117,310	186,147	96,800	28,216	39,193
1913	469,640	129,169	196,278	77,934	25,855	40,404
1914	293,204	92,808	94,482	48,013	21,124	36,777
1915	104,919	37,763	19,434	14,907	11,699	21,116
1916	76,479	28,884	18,953	7,191	7,905	13,546
1917	20,578	3,981	6,415	2,203	2,794	5,185
1918	17,319	3,445	3,218	2,487	2,374	5,795
1919	180,232	32,765	89,102	17,757	7,761	32,847
1920	352,811	90,811	134,079	49,357	29,019	49,545
1921	268,259	67,499	84,145	46,073	28,138	42,404
1922	248,287	61,826	69,690	56,851	21,414	38,506
1923[5]	337,567	101,063	121,941	55,156	18,938	40,469
1924	263,480	39,057	99,717	58,500	22,452	43,754

TABLE IX.—INWARD MOVEMENT OF PASSENGERS (INCLUDING TRANSMIGRANTS) FROM EXTRA-EUROPEAN COUNTRIES[10] 1854-74.

Year	Total	Year	Total
1854	12,578[11]	1865	33,543
1855	22,821	1866	31,122
1856	20,619[12]	1867	36,646
1857	18,839[13]	1868	33,626[14]
1858	23,704	1869	36,047
1859	19,913	1870	41,528
1860	24,434	1871	45,016
1861	32,003	1872	41,689
1862	16,024[11]	1873	74,946
1863	17,565	1874	118,129
1864	25,835		

For reference notes see page 658.

TABLE X.—INWARD MOVEMENT OF PASSENGER CITIZENS FROM EXTRA-EUROPEAN
COUNTRIES, 1876-1924.

Year	Total	Year	Total
1876	71,404	1901	99,699
1877	63,890	1902	104,115
1878	54,944	1903	112,914
1879	37,936	1904	144,581
1880	47,007	1905	122,712
1881	52,707	1906	130,466
1882	54,711	1907	160,588
1883	73,804	1908	172,043
1884	91,356	1909	149,068
1885	85,468	1910	164,139
1886	80,018	1911	192,718
1887	85,475	1912	199,181
1888	94,133	1913	227,643
1889	103,070	1914	229,870
1890	109,470	1915	129,652
1891	103,037	1916	84,654
1892	97,780	1917	21,026
1893	102,119	1918	15,414
1894	118,309	1919	153,230
1895	109,418	1920	180,064
1896	101,742	1921	149,321
1897	95,221	1922	148,405
1898	91,248	1923[5]	147,184
1899	100,246	1924[5]	175,069
1900	97,637		

TABLE XI.—Passengers inward (citizens) from extra-european countries, by sex and age, 1877-1913.

Year	Total	Children	Adults	
			Males	Females
1877	63,890	9,876	35,405	18,609
1878	54,944	7,913	31,343	15,688
1879	37,936	5,559	21,035	11,342
1880	47,007	6,287	26,007	14,713
1881	52,707	7,258	28,780	16,669
1882	54,711	8,117	30,277	16,317
1883	73,804	8,698	45,928	19,178
1884	91,356	11,394	55,959	24,003
1885	85,468	11,134	49,969	24,365
1886	80,018	9,362	46,842	23,814
1887	85,475	10,080	50,170	25,225
1888	94,133	11,265	56,131	26,737
1889	103,070	13,207	59,154	30,709
1890	109,470	15,460	60,640	33,370
1891	103,037	14,257	55,912	32,868
1892	97,780	12,741	53,022	32,017
1893	102,119	12,224	58,244	31,651
1894	118,309	17,126	62,478	38,705
1895	109,418	15,289	55,676	38,453
1896	101,742	14,169	52,771	34,802
1897	95,221	13,540	49,480	32,201
1898	91,248	13,097	47,115	31,036
1899	100,246	13,738	51,945	34,563
1900	97,637	12,897	49,332	35,408
1901	99,699	13,036	50,218	36,445
1902	104,115	12,341	53,151	38,623
1903	112,914	12,730	60,810	39,374
1904	144,581	16,848	78,687	49,046
1905	122,712	14,445	65,250	43,017
1906	130,466	15,683	70,929	43,854
1907	160,588	19,352	87,413	53,823
1908	172,043	21,755	93,960	56,328
1909	149,068	18,554	78,324	52,190
1910	164,139	19,928	86,547	57,664
1911	192,718	23,807	101,883	67,028
1912	199,181	25,688	104,714	68,779
1913	227,643	29,593	120,651	77,399

TABLE XII.—PASSENGERS INWARD FROM EXTRA-EUROPEAN COUNTRIES, CITIZENS BY COUNTRY OF DEPARTURE AND ALIENS (TOTALS ONLY), 1870-1924.

Year	Grand total	Citizens						Aliens
		Total	United States	British North America	Australia and New Zealand	Cape of Good Hope and Natal	All other countries	
1870	49,157	49,157[15]	46,505			2,652		
1871	53,827	53,827[15]	47,726	3,997	1,994	110		
1872	70,181	70,181[15]	.....	.....	.....	.....		.....
1873	86,416	86,416[15]	68,536	5,862	2,574	9,444		.....
1874	118,129	118,129[15]	100,527	7,791	1,892	7,919		.....
1875	94,228	94,228[15]	80,045	6,577	2,108	5,498		.....
1876	93,557	71,404	54,697	6,629	2,579		7,499	22,153
1877	81,848	63,890	44,878	5,687	4,637		8,688	17,958
1878	77,951	54,944	34,040	6,204	4,207		10,493	23,007
1879	53,973	37,936	20,048	3,497	4,967		9,424	16,037
1880	68,316	47,007	26,518	4,688	5,910		9,891	21,309
1881	77,105	52,707	29,781	5,761	5,877	11,288		24,398
1882	82,804	54,711	28,468	6,097	6,871	6,499	6,776	28,093
1883	100,503	73,804	46,703	7,021	6,844	5,913	7,323	26,699
1884	123,466	91,356	61,466	8,861	8,312	5,460	7,257	32,110
1885	113,549	85,468	57,604	9,321	7,946	4,574	6,023	28,081
1886	108,879	80,018	52,909	7,167	8,980	3,842	7,120	28,861
1887	119,013	85,475	58,343	6,848	10,258	3,086	6,940	33,538
1888	128,879	94,133	64,031	8,817	10,387	3,481	7,417	34,746
1889	147,398	103,070	71,392	8,642	10,438	4,869	7,729	44,328
1890	155,910	109,470	74,740	9,525	10,223	6,507	8,475	46,440
1891	151,369	103,037	68,808	9,000	9,712	5,753	9,764	48,332
1892	143,747	97,780	62,698	9,310	10,606	6,147	9,019	45,967
1893	141,054	102,119	67,428	9,159	10,198	6,491	8,843	38,935
1894	185,799	118,309	83,523	10,256	9,106	6,866	8,558	67,490
1895	175,674	109,418	71,059	10,671	9,608	8,304	9,776	66,256
1896	159,913	101,742	59,212	9,539	9,348	14,161	9,482	58,171
1897	155,114	95,221	53,635	9,940	7,505	14,951	9,190	59,893
1898	139,346	91,248	50,728	9,794	7,060	14,092	9,574	48,098
1899	162,111	100,246	53,643	8,395	7,578	20,621	10,009	61,865
1900	175,747	97,637	54,819	10,640	8,663	13,398	10,117	78,110
1901	165,018	99,699	58,312	8,636	8,780	14,206	9,765	65,319
1902	170,874	104,115	56,881	11,563	9,979	15,162	10,530	66,759
1903	199,685	112,914	58,271	13,786	8,682	22,189	9,986	86,771
1904	241,896	144,581	79,655	18,397	8,670	27,651	10,208	97,315
1905	205,193	122,712	61,373	19,934	7,888	23,086	10,431	82,481
1906	230,165	130,466	58,876	23,596	9,411	25,964	12,619	99,699
1907	293,633	160,588	70,320	33,691	10,871	25,712	19,994	133,045
1908	342,922	172,043	65,418	39,866	13,146	24,348	29,265	170,879
1909	261,325	149,068	53,323	33,509	12,418	19,539	30,279	112,257
1910	298,779	164,139	58,623	41,309	12,976	18,983	32,248	134,640
1911	350,429	192,718	72,082	50,095	15,001	23,240	32,300	157,711
1912	340,696	199,181	71,493	52,586	17,074	23,983	34,045	141,515
1913	372,618	227,643	77,014	68,622	20,671	25,478	35,858	144,975
1914	359,892	229,870	77,171	64,689	22,286	24,653	41,071	130,022
1915	147,189	129,652	47,296	31,483	11,228	15,006	24,639	17,537
1916	98,583	84,654	30,813	21,857	7,221	10,535	14,228	13,929
1917	34,042	21,026	6,138	2,416	2,701	3,402	6,369	13,016
1918	25,970	15,414	5,492	2,346	459	1,256	5,861	10,556
1919	193,601	153,230	39,736	59,423	9,441	11,645	32,985	40,371
1920	283,705	180,064	41,028	58,644	20,373	20,632	39,387	103,641
1921	227,583	149,321	33,743	45,096	14,611	19,427	36,444	78,262
1922	224,462	148,405	34,137	39,024	16,555	19,867	38,822	76,057
1923[5]	210,509	147,184	30,215	40,024	17,297	18,702	40,946	63,325
1924[5]	253,432	175,069	35,806	53,248	21,508	21,144	43,363	78,363

For reference notes see page 658.

TABLE XIII.—EXCESS OF OUTWARD OVER INWARD PASSENGERS 1870-1924—PASSENGERS OF BRITISH NATIONALITY.

Year	Total	To British North America	To Australia and New Zealand	To Cape of Good Hope and Natal	To other British Possns.	To all British Possns.	To United States	To other foreign countries	To all foreign countries
1870[16]	153,354	.....	.....	.....	.....	.....	.....	.....	.....
1871	138,924	20,957	9,701	†	‡5,204	.....	103,062	†	.....
1872	140,313	φ	φ	φ	φ	.....	φ	φ	.....
1873	141,929	23,183	22,563	†	‡††2,011	.....	98,194	†	φ
1874	79,143	12,937	50,689	†	‡2,270	.....	13,247	†	.....
1875	46,447	5,729	32,642	†	‡6,928	.....	1,148	†	.....
1876	38,065	2,706	29,617	†	‡5,885	.....	††143	†	.....
1877	31,305	2,033	25,501	†	‡3,168	.....	603	†	.....
1878	57,958	4,448	32,272	†	‡584	.....	20,654	†	.....
1879	126,338	14,455	35,992	†	‡4,133	.....	71,758	†	.....
1880	180,535	16,214	18,274	†	‡5,995	.....	140,052	†	.....
1881	190,295	18,151	16,805	†	‡9,016	.....	146,323	†	.....
1882	224,655	34,344	30,418	5,564	‡894	.....	153,435	†	.....
1883	246,314	37,164	64,420	††171	‡31	.....	144,870	†	.....
1884	150,823	22,273	35,943	††1,506	‡299	.....	93,814	†	.....
1885	122,176	10,517	31,449	††1,306	‡1,433	.....	80,083	†	.....
1886	152,882	17,578	34,096	55	‡1,352	.....	99,801	†	.....
1887	196,012	25,177	23,925	1,823	‡1,904	.....	143,183	†	.....
1888	185,795	26,036	20,740	2,985	‡4,079	.....	131,955	†	.....
1889	150,725	19,627	17,856	9,015	‡6,848	.....	97,379	†	.....
1890	108,646	12,995	10,956	3,814	‡3,208	.....	77,673	†	.....
1891	115,470	12,578	9,835	3,337	‡2,133	.....	87,587	†	.....
1892	112,262	13,944	5,344	3,744	‡1,899	.....	87,341	†	.....
1893	106,695	15,573	1,005	6,606	‡1,990	.....	81,521	†	.....
1894	37,721	7,203	1,811	6,311	2,704	17,399	20,478	††156	20,322
1895	75,763	5,951	959	11,930	1,028	19,868	55,443	452	55,895
1896	60,183	5,728	1,006	10,433	2,323	19,490	39,709	984	40,693
1897	51,239	5,631	4,556	6,158	2,627	18,972	31,689	578	32,267
1898	49,396	7,846	3,633	5,664	2,541	19,684	29,766	††54	29,712
1899	46,116	8,015	3,889	††6,189	1,602	7,317	38,839	††40	38,799
1900	71,188	7,803	6,259	7,417	1,959	23,438	47,978	††228	47,750
1901	72,016	7,121	6,570	8,937	2,611	25,239	45,883	894	46,777
1902	101,547	14,730	4,366	28,044	2,552	49,692	51,617	238	51,855
1903	147,036	45,866	3,693	28,017	3,460	81,036	65,392	608	66,000
1904	126,854	51,284	5,240	††833	3,848	59,539	66,790	525	67,315
1905	139,365	62,503	7,251	3,221	4,084	77,059	60,997	1,309	62,306
1906	194,671	91,263	9,920	††3,160	7,155	105,178	85,941	3,552	89,493
1907	235,092	117,525	13,896	††4,787	4,799	131,433	99,944	3,715	103,659
1908	91,156	41,455	20,423	††4,780	1,494	58,592	31,451	1,113	32,564
1909	139,693	52,378	25,202	2,478	1,664	81,722	56,377	1,594	57,971
1910	233,709	115,681	32,725	8,314	2,158	158,878	73,569	1,262	74,831
1911	261,809	134,765	65,769	7,527	2,231	210,382	49,732	1,695	51,427
1912	268,485	133,561	79,726	4,233	2,468	219,988	45,817	2,680	48,497
1913	241,997	127,656	57,263	377	3,339	188,635	52,155	1,207	53,362
1914	63,334	29,793	25,727	††3,529	943	52,934	15,637	††5,237	10,400
1915	††24,733	††12,049	3,679	††3,307	17	††11,660	††9,533	††3,540	††13,073
1916	††8,175	††2,904	††30	††2,630	969	††4,595	††1,929	††1,651	††3,580
1917	††448	3,999	††498	††608	††165	2,728	††2,157	††1,019	††3,176
1918	1,905	872	2,028	1,118	599	4,617	††2,047	††665	††2,712
1919	27,002	29,679	8,316	††3,884	††3,065	31,046	††6,971	2,927	††4,044
1920	172,747	75,435	28,994	8,387	5,630	118,436	49,783	4,528	54,311
1921	118,938	39,049	31,462	8,711	4,856	84,078	33,756	1,104	34,860
1922	99,882	30,666	40,296	1,547	††802	71,707	27,689	486	28,175
1923[17]	190,383	81,917	37,859	236	††782	119,230	70,848	305	71,153
1924	88,411	46,469	36,992	1,308	518	85,287	3,251	††127	3,124

†Included with "Other British Possessions", further details not being available.
‡These figures include the balance of the British Passenger movement with countries not specified as British or Foreign.
φNot available.
††Excess inward.

TABLE XIV.—EMIGRANT CITIZENS TO EXTRA-EUROPEAN COUNTRIES, 1912-24.

Year	Total	Year	Total
1912[18]	326,959	1919	146,935
1913	389,394	1920	285,102
1914	214,893	1921	199,477
1915	76,911	1922	174,096
1916	52,926	1923[19]	256,284
1917	10,004	1924[19]	155,374
1918	10,621		

For reference notes see page 658.

TABLE XV.—EMIGRANT CITIZENS TO EXTRA-EUROPEAN COUNTRIES, BY SEX AND AGE, 1912-24.

Year	Total	Sex		Under 12 years		12 to 17 years		18 to 30 years		31 to 45 years		46 years and over		Age (12 and over) not stated		Adults		Children
		Males	Females	Males	Females	Males	Females	Males	Females	Males	Females	Males	Females	Males	Females	Males	Females	
1912[8]	326,959	175,076	151,883	30,922	30,053	8,939	8,206	73,902	57,340	31,503	28,159	9,152	9,491	20,658	18,634	144,154	121,830	60,975
1913	389,394	214,021	175,373	35,483	34,267	11,690	9,767	100,102	71,547	43,864	36,883	11,676	12,063	11,206	10,846	178,538	141,106	69,750
1914	222,012[20]	......	......	......												96,054	88,153	36,983
1915	82,649[20]	......	......	......												34,563	34,451	13,635
1921	199,477[21]	95,818[21]	103,659[21]	16,356	16,105	6,257	6,032	38,565	40,578	24,246	27,662	9,929	12,606	......	......	78,997	86,878	32,461
1922	174,096[21]	90,338[21]	83,758[21]	13,265	12,942	6,801	5,063	39,417	32,793	21,742	21,904	9,011	10,894	......	......	77,073	70,816	26,207
1923	267,554[21]	159,445[21]	108,109[21]	18,418	18,225	10,839	7,163	81,122	44,273	36,561	26,039	12,361	12,294	......	......	135,870[19]	84,178[19]	36,236[19]
1924[9]	155,374[21]	81,190[21]	74,184[21]	13,929	13,821	8,358	4,870	33,932	26,727	17,328	19,327	7,527	9,338	......	......	67,261	60,363	27,750

For reference notes see page 658.

TABLE XVI.—EMIGRANT CITIZENS, 18 YEARS OF AGE AND OVER, TO EXTRA-EUROPEAN COUNTRIES, BY OCCUPATION AND SEX, 1912, 1913 AND 1921-24.

OCCUPATION	1912[18]	1913	1921	1922	1923[19]	1924[19]
MALES						
Agricultural.................	23,289	33,815	13,454	12,937	26,223	18,984
Commercial, finance and insurance.................	19,779	31,248	12,404	9,706	12,960	9,438
Professional.................			5,583	4,404	4,387	3,761
Skilled trades:						
Mining and quarrying.......			3,577	4,836	7,300	2,774
Metal and engineering.......	38,816	51,413	8,016	10,536	24,724	7,742
Building....................			1,345	1,525	3,642	1,507
Other......................			8,151	7,835	16,867	6,906
Transport and communications..................			3,096	3,009	4,573	2,745
Laborers not in agriculture or transport............	30,942	29,484	9,661	7,022	19,017	6,834
Other and ill-defined occupations.................	11,330	17,890	7,918	8,462	10,495	8,240
Total[21]...............	124,156	163,850	73,205	70,272	130,188	68,931
FEMALES						
Domestic, hotel, etc., service	31,983	40,772	21,986	18,025	23,580	18,797
Commercial, finance and insurance.................	3,379	5,830	4,471	3,099	4,289	3,079
Professional.................			4,999	4,180	3,674	2,720
Clothing trades.............	5,765	7,245	2,148	1,809	2,365	1,502
Wife or housewife (not otherwise described)...........	58,325	69,942	38,904	30,824	39,106	29,537
Other and ill-defined occupations.................			9,014	7,816	9,707	7,298
Total[21]...............	99,452	123,789	81,522	65,753	82,721	62,933

For reference notes see page 658.

TABLE XVII.—EMIGRANT CITIZENS TO EXTRA-EUROPEAN COUNTRIES BY COUNTRY OF FUTURE PERMANENT RESIDENCE, 1912-24.

Year	Total	British Empire							Foreign Countries		
		British North America	Australia	New Zealand	South Africa	India including Ceylon	Other British possessions	Total	United States	Other foreign countries	Total
1912[18]	326,959	148,422	59,997	10,746	10,543	5,378	4,710	239,796	79,683	7,480	87,163
1913	389,394	190,854	56,779	14,255	10,916	6,810	5,432	285,046	94,691	9,657	104,348
1914	214,893	78,570	32,425	7,873	7,785	6,962	5,141	138,756	69,655	6,482	76,137
1915	76,911	16,772	9,394	2,985	5,700	5,053	4,359	44,263	29,400	3,248	32,648
1916	52,926	13,544	4,075	1,632	3,528	2,561	2,696	28,036	22,782	2,108	24,890
1917	10,004	2,486	1,147	567	1,072	599	1,084	6,955	2,379	670	3,049
1918	10,621	1,709	2,010	581	1,324	1,658	983	8,265	1,714	642	2,356
1919	146,935	79,109	12,545	4,455	4,756	7,771	6,733	115,369	23,867	7,699	31,566
1920	285,102	118,837	28,974	14,853	15,157	12,188	8,585	198,594	77,151	9,357	86,508
1921	199,477	67,907	27,751	11,513	12,903	9,830	6,873	136,777	56,393	6,307	62,700
1922	174,096	45,818	39,099	12,259	8,772	7,054	5,408	118,410	49,902	5,784	55,686
1923	256,284	88,290	39,967	9,392	7,629	6,344	5,440	157,062	93,076	6,146	99,222
1924	155,374	63,016	38,599	11,061	7,568	6,630	5,343	132,217	17,315	5,842	23,157

For reference notes see page 658.

OCCUPATION, SEX AND COUNTRY OF FUTURE PERMANENT RESIDENCE, 1921-24.

Occupation	Year	Country of Future Residence British Empire								Foreign Countries		
		Total	British North America	Australia	New Zealand	South Africa	India including Ceylon	Other British possessions	Total	United States	Other foreign countries	Total
MALES												
Agricultural	1921	13,454	6,906	2,312	945	379	203	211	10,956	2,346	152	2,498
	1922	12,937	5,087	4,602	851	287	181	116	11,124	1,689	124	1,813
	1923	26,223	16,898	4,096	721	269	224	225	22,433	3,668	122	3,790
	1924	18,984	10,098	3,490	969	278	257	249	15,341	3,516	127	3,643
Commercial, finance and insurance	1921	12,404	3,397	1,477	577	1,127	770	926	8,274	3,214	916	4,130
	1922	9,706	2,042	1,900	506	690	562	702	6,402	2,508	796	3,304
	1923	12,960	3,791	1,932	387	567	625	723	8,025	3,974	961	4,935
	1924	9,438	3,121	2,026	438	610	571	732	7,498	1,007	933	1,940
Professional	1921	5,583	1,095	448	156	586	826	874	3,985	1,012	586	1,598
	1922	4,404	660	519	112	486	606	752	3,135	750	519	1,269
	1923	4,387	774	478	117	433	479	690	2,971	832	584	1,416
	1924	3,761	716	483	89	420	448	649	2,805	462	494	956
Skilled Trades — Mining and quarrying	1921	3,577	899	525	284	233	39	56	2,036	1,503	38	1,541
	1922	4,836	1,044	1,169	535	97	41	51	2,937	1,847	52	1,899
	1923	7,300	2,119	719	321	64	45	62	3,330	3,950	20	3,970
	1924	2,774	1,284	763	286	75	35	48	2,491	254	29	283
Skilled Trades — Metal and engineering	1921	8,016	1,909	1,253	578	919	531	429	5,619	2,047	350	2,397
	1922	10,536	2,065	2,216	633	418	509	378	6,219	3,956	361	4,317
	1923	24,724	6,068	2,185	387	396	498	417	9,951	14,274	499	14,773
	1924	7,742	2,884	1,700	406	380	528	405	6,303	900	539	1,439
Skilled Trades — Building	1921	1,345	441	197	136	122	9	16	921	400	24	424
	1922	1,525	403	376	87	43	11	11	931	585	9	594
	1923	3,642	1,226	440	151	66	7	23	1,913	1,717	12	1,729
	1924	1,507	581	483	167	51	6	24	1,312	171	24	195
Skilled Trades — Other	1921	8,151	2,497	1,378	586	721	208	153	5,543	2,447	161	2,608
	1922	7,835	1,856	2,001	652	320	167	174	5,170	2,544	121	2,665
	1923	16,867	4,643	2,180	473	224	176	133	7,829	8,886	152	9,038
	1924	6,906	2,844	2,055	527	291	178	135	6,030	731	145	876
Transport and communications	1921	3,096	952	567	172	151	193	173	2,208	731	157	888
	1922	3,009	603	972	234	71	140	139	2,159	668	182	850
	1923	4,573	1,310	1,027	129	64	162	139	2,831	1,582	160	1,742
	1924	2,745	1,020	854	181	69	98	129	2,351	239	155	394
Laborers not in agriculture or transport	1921	9,661	4,466	864	371	49	5	14	5,769	3,865	27	3,892
	1922	7,022	1,560	1,972	290	28	9	21	3,880	3,133	9	3,142
	1923	19,017	6,291	2,302	216	23	6	9	8,847	10,159	11	10,170
	1924	6,834	3,537	1,563	275	25	20	11	5,431	1,387	16	1,403
Other and ill-defined occupations	1921	7,918	2,081	1,321	502	690	577	501	5,672	1,827	419	2,246
	1922	8,462	1,809	2,109	488	680	543	483	6,112	1,957	393	2,350
	1923	10,495	2,684	2,532	368	630	446	666	7,326	2,779	390	3,169
	1924	8,240	2,359	2,422	495	702	518	526	7,022	763	455	1,218
Grand total[22]	1921	73,205	24,643	10,342	4,307	4,977	3,361	3,353	50,983	19,392	2,830	22,222
	1922	70,272	17,129	17,836	4,388	3,120	2,769	2,827	48,069	19,637	2,566	22,203
	1923	130,188	45,804	17,891	3,270	2,736	2,668	3,087	75,456	51,821	2,911	54,732
	1924	68,931	28,444	15,839	3,833	2,901	2,659	2,908	56,584	9,430	2,917	12,347

For reference notes see page 658.

TABLE XVIII.—EMIGRANTS (BRITISH SUBJECTS), 18 YEARS OF AGE AND OVER, TO EXTRA-EUROPEAN COUNTRIES, BY OCCUPATION, SEX AND COUNTRY OF FUTURE PERMANENT RESIDENCE, 1921-24 (continued).

Occupation	Year	Total	Country of Future Residence — British Empire							Foreign Countries		
			British North America	Australia	New Zealand	South Africa	India including Ceylon	Other British possessions	Total	United States	Other foreign countries	Total
FEMALES												
Domestic, hotel, etc., service	1921	21,986	7,094	1,526	1,042	294	82	128	10,166	11,736	84	11,820
	1922	18,025	5,523	1,896	1,045	181	117	91	8,853	9,065	107	9,172
	1923	23,580	7,699	2,047	1,066	168	117	69	11,166	12,240	174	12,414
	1924	18,797	7,520	2,825	1,099	229	287	126	12,086	6,544	167	6,711
Commercial, finance and insurance	1921	4,471	1,358	592	241	361	83	57	2,692	1,683	96	1,779
	1922	3,099	737	541	152	237	49	24	1,740	1,285	74	1,359
	1923	4,289	1,143	508	147	209	47	35	2,089	2,122	78	2,200
	1924	3,079	1,155	563	161	218	69	60	2,226	761	92	853
Professional	1921	4,999	1,046	404	193	664	700	347	3,354	1,205	440	1,645
	1922	4,180	742	479	191	500	474	253	2,639	1,130	411	1,541
	1923	3,674	713	471	126	386	383	207	2,286	971	417	1,388
	1924	2,720	585	427	96	322	322	186	1,938	506	276	782
Clothing trades	1921	2,148	557	280	112	123	29	14	1,115	1,021	12	1,033
	1922	1,809	406	349	127	75	15	6	978	818	13	831
	1923	2,365	601	326	71	66	11	3	1,078	1,276	11	1,287
	1924	1,502	600	329	90	44	12	5	1,080	414	8	422
Wife or housewife (not otherwise described)	1921	38,904	14,636	5,828	2,235	2,589	2,508	1,360	29,156	8,711	1,037	9,748
	1922	30,824	9,115	6,654	2,455	1,812	1,651	990	22,677	7,182	965	8,147
	1923	39,106	12,814	6,389	1,759	1,521	1,357	964	24,804	13,297	1,005	14,302
	1924	29,537	11,411	6,843	2,106	1,511	1,369	953	24,193	4,407	937	5,344
Other and ill-defined occupations	1921	9,014	1,444	1,361	591	1,011	1,143	625	6,175	2,143	696	2,839
	1922	7,816	1,088	1,390	540	898	780	541	5,237	2,023	556	2,579
	1923	9,707	2,202	1,598	315	940	745	458	6,258	2,922	527	3,449
	1924	7,298	1,351	1,690	359	924	875	597	5,796	930	572	1,502
Grand total[25]	1921	81,522	26,135	9,991	4,414	5,042	4,545	2,531	52,658	26,499	2,365	28,864
	1922	65,753	17,611	11,309	4,510	3,703	3,086	1,905	42,124	21,503	2,126	23,629
	1923	82,721	25,172	11,339	3,484	2,660	2,660	1,736	47,681	32,828	2,212	35,040
	1924	62,933	22,622	12,677	3,911	3,248	2,934	1,927	47,319	13,562	2,052	15,614

For reference notes see page 658.

TABLE XIX.—IMMIGRANT CITIZENS FROM EXTRA-EUROPEAN COUNTRIES, 1912-24.

Year	Total	Year	Total
1912[18]	59,681	1919	93,023
1913	85,709	1920	86,055
1914	104,462	1921	71,367
1915	92,388	1922	68,026
1916	57,931	1923[19]	57,606
1917	12,254	1924[19]	64,112
1918	8,772		

For reference notes see page 658.

TABLE XX.—IMMIGRANT CITIZENS FROM EXTRA-EUROPEAN COUNTRIES, BY SEX AND AGE, 1912-24.

Year	Total	Males	Females	Under 12 years		12-17 years		18-30 years		31-45 years		46 years and over		Age (12 and over) not stated		Adults		Children
				Males	Females	Males	Females	Males	Females	Males	Females	Males	Females	Males	Females	Males	Females	
1912[18]	59,681	34,833	24,848	4,893	4,766	472	517	10,479	6,610	8,765	5,085	3,755	2,420	6,469	5,450	29,940	20,082	9,659
1913	85,709	50,582	35,127	6,961	7,149	770	994	18,199	10,899	15,232	8,465	5,549	3,591	3,871	4,029	43,621	27,978	14,110
1914	108,417	....	....	....	....	....	....	....	....	....	....	....	....	....	....	56,385[20]	34,735[20]	17,810[20]
1915	95,268[20]	....	....	....	....	....	....	....	....	....	....	....	....	....	....	46,622[20]	30,421[20]	18,225[20]
1921	71,367[21]	36,382[21]	34,985[21]	6,437	6,379	1,153	1,283	9,430	9,191	11,895	10,967	7,125	6,796	....	....	29,603	28,237	12,816
1922	68,026[21]	32,081[21]	35,945[21]	6,230	6,427	1,109	1,357	7,796	9,521	10,071	11,178	6,664	7,245	....	....	25,851	29,518	12,657
1923[19]	58,859[21]	28,457[21]	30,402[21]	5,391	5,377	940	1,218	7,707	7,905	8,509	9,447	5,848	6,355	....	....	22,617	24,321	10,668
1924[19]	64,112[21]	33,102[21]	31,010[21]	5,636	5,538	1,124	1,190	9,593	8,040	10,145	9,751	6,552	6,414	....	....	27,466	25,472	11,174

For reference notes see page 658.

TABLE XXI.—IMMIGRANT CITIZENS, 18 YEARS OF AGE AND OVER, FROM EXTRA-EUROPEAN COUNTRIES, BY OCCUPATION AND SEX, 1912, 1913 AND 1921-24.

OCCUPATION	1912[18]	1913	1921	1922	1923[19]	1924[19]
MALES						
Agricultural........................	2,631	3,745	2,884	2,373	2,243	2,649
Commercial, finance and insurance.....	5,828	10,292	5,810	5,151	4,348	4,693
Professional.......................			3,467	3,622	2,807	2,814
Skilled trades:						
Mining and quarrying...............			1,249	737	779	1,355
Metal and engineering..............	8,770	14,948	2,881	2,557	2,893	4,118
Building...........................			614	408	482	687
Other..............................			3,495	2,546	2,130	3,317
Transport and communications........			1,257	1,190	1,026	1,147
Laborers not in agriculture or transport.	3,345	5,895	2,287	1,545	1,262	1,945
Other and ill-defined occupations.......	3,935	5,334	4,848	4,613	4,156	4,697
Total[21].......................	24,509	40,214	28,792	24,742	22,126	27,422
FEMALES						
Domestic, hotel, etc., service..........	3,028	3,943	2,932	3,531	2,797	3,590
Commercial, finance and insurance	1,010	1,698	959	952	880	1,130
Professional.......................			1,989	2,296	1,967	1,686
Clothing trades.....................	464	711	499	493	344	380
Wife or housewife (not otherwise described).......................	9,946	16,836	15,676	15,066	12,399	13,286
Other and ill-defined occupations......			5,268	5,823	5,420	5,349
Total[21].......................	14,448	23,188	27,323	28,161	23,807	25,421

For reference notes see page 658.

TABLE XXII.—IMMIGRANT CITIZENS FROM EXTRA-EUROPEAN COUNTRIES, BY COUNTRY OF LAST PERMANENT RESIDENCE, 1912-1924

| Year | Total | British Empire | | | | | | | Foreign Countries | | |
		British North America	Australia	New Zealand	South Africa	India including Ceylon	Other British possessions	Total	United States	Other foreign countries	Total
1912[18]	59,681	16,383	6,451	1,829	8,022	4,229	3,192	40,106	14,726	4,849	19,575
1913	85,709	26,288	12,351	2,446	10,541	5,928	3,971	61,525	16,619	7,565	24,184
1914	104,462	33,684	13,515	2,880	11,289	8,138	4,991	74,497	20,444	9,521	29,965
1915	92,388	39,088	8,345	1,704	9,112	5,624	5,175	69,048	16,138	7,202	23,340
1916	57,931	23,354	5,817	1,288	6,272	3,018	3,140	42,889	11,044	3,998	15,042
1917	12,254	1,965	1,946	339	1,818	874	1,437	8,379	2,163	1,712	3,875
1918	8,772	2,152	590	133	670	1,302	1,225	6,072	1,302	1,398	2,700
1919	93,023	34,435	6,171	2,304	6,215	12,233	5,660	67,018	20,571	5,434	26,005
1920	86,055	24,341	12,854	2,568	7,313	11,999	4,802	63,877	17,084	5,094	22,178
1921	71,367	21,055	8,861	1,568	5,894	9,393	5,776	52,547	13,925	4,895	18,820
1922	68,026	16,197	8,310	2,223	7,509	9,809	5,639	49,687	12,611	5,728	18,339
1923[19]	57,606	12,424	8,384	2,204	7,103	8,750	5,573	44,438	7,042	6,126	13,168
1924[19]	64,112	15,822	8,295	2,321	6,919	8,734	5,265	47,356	10,880	5,876	16,756

For reference notes see page 658.

TABLE XXIII.—IMMIGRANT CITIZENS, 18 YEARS OF AGE AND OVER, FROM EXTRA-EUROPEAN COUNTRIES, BY OCCUPATION, SEX AND COUNTRY OF LAST PERMANENT RESIDENCE, 1924.

Occupation	Total	British Empire							Foreign Countries		
		British North America	Australia	New Zealand	South Africa	India including Ceylon	Other British possessions	Total	United States	Other foreign countries	Total
MALES											
Agricultural	2,649	1,150	427	179	152	210	208	2,326	221	102	323
Commercial, finance and insurance	4,693	875	566	146	491	580	498	3,156	803	734	1,537
Professional	2,814	292	251	67	270	629	613	2,122	291	401	692
Trades { Mining and quarrying	1,355	490	81	28	121	37	47	804	528	23	551
Metal and engineering	4,118	1,053	255	59	223	546	279	2,415	1,301	402	1,703
Building	687	280	78	11	49	4	20	442	239	6	245
Other	3,317	1,237	285	81	176	153	91	2,023	1,215	79	1,294
Transport and communications	1,147	268	116	32	86	150	95	747	221	179	400
Laborers not in agriculture or transport	1,945	823	321	60	13	5	8	1,230	708	7	715
Other and ill-defined occupations	4,697	963	615	179	632	636	478	3,503	828	366	1,194
Grand total[24]	27,422	7,431	2,995	842	2,213	2,950	2,337	18,768	6,355	2,299	8,654
FEMALES											
Domestic, hotel, etc., service	3,590	888	793	249	265	151	68	2,414	1,057	119	1,176
Commercial, finance and insurance	1,130	338	176	43	183	32	17	789	291	50	341
Professional	1,686	242	245	58	246	265	136	1,192	257	237	494
Clothing trades	380	131	86	14	40	5	2	278	97	5	102
Wife or housewife (not otherwise described)	13,286	3,080	1,816	520	1,543	2,004	1,100	10,063	2,062	1,161	3,223
Other and ill-defined occupations	5,349	905	745	229	780	923	440	4,022	742	585	1,327
Grand total[25]	25,421	5,584	3,861	1,113	3,057	3,380	1,763	18,758	4,506	2,157	6,663

For reference notes see page 658.

TABLE XXIV.—IMMIGRATION AND EMIGRATION OF ALIENS FROM AND TO EXTRA-EUROPEAN COUNTRIES, BY SEX AND AGE, 1912-15.

Year	Immigration					Emigration				
	Total	Adults		Children		Total	Adults		Children	
		Males	Females	Males	Females		Males	Females	Males	Females
1912[18]	2,944	1,656	904	198	186	7,879	3,996	2,217	823	843
1913	3,759	2,203	1,103	250	203	9,732	5,261	2,470	1,030	971
1914[20]	3,955	2,282	1,164	489		7,119	3,840	2,090	1,122	
1915[20]	3,308	2,089	874	345		5,735	2,741	2,049	945	

TABLE XXV.—IMMIGRATION AND EMIGRATION OF ALIENS, FROM AND TO EXTRA-EUROPEAN COUNTRIES, BY COUNTRY OF LAST AND FUTURE PERMANENT RESIDENCE, 1912-13.

Country of last permanent residence

Year	Total	British Empire							Foreign Countries		
		British North America	Australia	New Zealand	South Africa	India including Ceylon	Other British possessions	Total	United States	Other foreign countries	Total
1912[18]	2,944	61	44	5	120	20	56	306	1,469	1,169	2,638
1913	3,759	139	78	4	206	26	52	505	1,388	1,866	3,254

Country of future permanent residence

Year	Total	British Empire							Foreign Countries		
		British North America	Australia	New Zealand	South Africa	India including Ceylon	Other British possessions	Total	United States	Other foreign countries	Total
1912[18]	7,879	1,891	170	17	245	27	43	2,393	4,186	1,300	5,486
1913	9,732	2,108	257	59	285	21	45	2,775	5,357	1,600	6,957

For reference notes see page 658.

TABLE XXVI.—IMMIGRATION AND EMIGRATION OF ALIENS FROM AND TO EXTRA-EUROPEAN COUNTRIES, BY OCCUPATION AND SEX, 1912-13.

	Year	Males						Females				
		Total	Agricultural	Commercial and professional	Skilled trades	Laborers	Miscellaneous or not stated	Total	Domestic and other service	Dress-makers and other trades	Teachers, clerks and professions	No stated occupation
I. Immigrants.....	1912[18]	1,123	51	403	257	98	314	176	63	40	73	...
	1913	1,996	67	845	427	136	521	256	113	58	85	...
II. Emigrants......	1912[18]	3,448	202	685	1,452	501	608	599	310	200	89	...
	1913	4,954	278	1,142	1,996	738	800	727	368	252	107	...

For reference notes see page 658.

TABLE XXVII.—PASSENGER MOVEMENT BETWEEN THE UNITED KINGDOM AND
EUROPEAN COUNTRIES, 1890-1924.

Year	Outward	Inward	Balance inward. (—Balance outward)
1890	392,925	450,514	57,589
1891	418,003	504,445	86,442
1892	405,998	490,165	84,167
1893	395,362	468,642	73,280
1894	477,318	490,330	13,012
1895	493,946	522,449	28,503
1896	479,913	518,869	38,956
1897	569,150	587,000	17,850
1898	590,226	620,123	29,897
1899	609,570	666,230	56,660
1900	669,292	748,725	79,433
1901	613,843	702,555	88,712
1902	636,311	773,624	137,313
1903	699,901	814,441	114,540
1904	718,560	802,949	84,389
1905	742,830	850,563	107,733
1906	798,141	932,340	134,199
1907	835,994	949,379	113,385
1908	1,026,377	1,002,110	— *24,267*
1909	951,238	1,045,501	94,263
1910	1,040,942	1,153,606	112,664
1911	1,083,241	1,115,086	31,845
1912	1,075,312	1,149,717	74,405
1913	1,184,412	1,309,874	125,462
1914	853,636	1,053,870	200,234
1915	431,573	447,038	15,465
1916	219,017	212,491	— *6,526*
1917	201,953	182,484	— *19,469*
1918	189,225	171,229	— *17,996*
1919	569,922	425,183	—*144,739*
1920†	738,860	725,253	— *13,607*
1921†	830,558	855,343	24,785
1922†	898,182	916,398	18,216
1923†	1,038,154	1,103,016	64,862
1924†	1,131,363	1,172,951	41,588

TABLE XXVIII.—ALIENS ARRIVED FROM EUROPE (EXCLUDING TRANSMIGRANTS)[26], BY SEX AND AGE, 1891-1905.

Year	Total	Men	Women	Children
1891	28,270	17,225	7,550	3,495
1892	22,137	13,765	6,250	2,122
1893	31,056	19,349	8,833	2,874
1894	28,682	17,023	8,419	3,240
1895	30,528	19,132	8,381	3,015
1896	35,448	22,539	9,948	3,411
1897	38,851	24,075	10,701	4,075
1898	40,785	25,420	11,053	4,312
1899	50,884	32,053	13,581	5,250
1900	62,505	39,487	16,024	6,994
1901	55,464	34,050	14,518	6,856
1902	66,471	42,841	16,109	7,521
1903	69,168	45,219	16,714	7,235
1904	82,845	55,967	18,469	8,409
1905	74,386	43,965	19,804	10,617

TABLE XXIX.—PASSENGER MOVEMENT BETWEEN THE UNITED KINGDOM AND EUROPEAN COUNTRIES, DISTINGUISHING BRITISH AND ALIENS: 1906-13 and 1921-24.

Year	Outward to Europe			Inward from Europe			Balance inward (—Balance outward)		
	British	Aliens	Total	British	Aliens	Total	British	Aliens	Total
1906	....	....	798,141	466,840	465,500	932,340	....	....	134,199
1907	500,062	335,932	835,994	468,636	480,743	949,379	—31,426	144,811	113,385
1908	606,610	419,767	1,026,377	602,821	399,289	1,002,110	—3,789	—20,478	—24,267
1909	612,278	338,960	951,238	622,953	422,548	1,045,501	10,675	83,588	94,263
1910	665,174	375,768	1,040,942	677,523	476,083	1,153,606	12,349	100,315	112,664
1911	663,119	420,122	1,083,241	671,555	443,531	1,115,086	8,436	23,409	31,845
1912	670,638	404,674	1,075,312	677,183	472,534	1,149,717	6,545	67,860	74,405
1913	761,019	423,393	1,184,412	763,420	546,454	1,309,874	2,401	123,061	125,462
1921	553,098	282,832	835,930	561,903	298,798	860,701	8,805	15,966	24,771
1922	639,050	264,879	903,929	640,392	282,622	923,014	1,342	17,743	19,085
1923	777,191	267,684	1,044,875	783,644	327,823	1,111,467	6,453	60,139	66,592
1924	811,880	327,778	1,139,658	826,684	355,830	1,182,514	14,804	28,052	42,856

For reference notes see page 658.

TABLE XXX.—ALIENS LANDED HOLDING PERMITS ISSUED BY THE MINISTRY OF LABOR, CLASSIFIED BY NATIONALITY, SEX AND AGE, 1921-1924.

Nationality	1921				1922				1923				1924			
	Total	Children under 16 years	Adults Males	Adults Females	Total	Children under 16 years	Adults Males	Adults Females	Total	Children under 16 years	Adults Males	Adults Females	Total	Children under 16 years	Adults Males	Adults Females
Belgian	170	5	74	91	106	2	68	36	142	5	88	49	142	10	78	54
Bulgarian	1			1	2		1	1	2			2	2		1	1
Chinese	15	2	11	2	2		1	1	5		2	3	2		2	
Czechoslovakian	46		14	32	31		12	19	38	4	17	17	34	1	15	18
Dutch	149	9	71	69	115	5	64	46	169	2	125	42	203	5	155	43
Finnish	10		3	7	5		1	4	11		6	5	18		12	6
French	528	13	177	338	291	4	159	128	416	6	224	186	658	10	307	341
Greek	5		5		6		5	1	9		7	2	10		5	5
Italian	577	21	388	168	215	14	124	77	194	11	123	60	208	4	138	66
Yugoslav	3		2	1	1			1	1		1		7		4	3
Polish	48	6	25	17	39		23	16	53	2	28	23	58	2	41	15
Russian	48	1	24	23	31	2	16	13	48		28	20	187	4	114	69
Scandinavian including Danish	489	1	179	309	403		140	263	377	7	168	202	521	8	247	266
Spanish and Portuguese	69	3	26	40	51	5	30	16	43	2	29	12	78	8	45	25
Swiss	631	3	108	520	523	3	88	432	499		133	366	652	3	166	483
United States	128	4	80	44	143	7	92	44	374	32	208	134	290	14	174	102
German									78	2	44	32	259	5	170	84
Austrian									21		13	8	35		22	13
Hungarian	5		3	2					8	1	5	2	31	1	26	4
Ottoman					51	1	35	15	3		1	2	2		2	
Other nationalities	85	16	48	21					114	14	60	40	136	3	91	42
Total	3,007	84	1,238	1,685	2,015	43	859	1,113	2,605	88	1,310	1,207	3,533	78	1,815	1,640

TABLE XXXI.—INTERCONTINENTAL TRANSMIGRANTS AND MIGRANTS IN TRANSIT, 1921-24.

Year	Outgoing	Returning
1921	72,531	41,887
1922	48,868	28,934
1923	89,435	13,121
1924	57,922	19,145

SOURCES

HOTTEN, John Camden (Editor). *Original Lists of Emigrants to America,* 1600-1700. London, 1874, pp. 35-145.

Table I.

"An account of the passengers who have taken their passage on board any Ship or Vessel to go out of this Kingdom from any port in England with a description of their Quality, Occupation or Employment, former residence, to what port or place they propose to go and on what account and for what purpose they leave this country from . . . . to . . . . distinguishing each port."

MS at Public Record Office, London, ref: Treasury $\frac{47}{9}$, $\frac{47}{10}$ and $\frac{47}{11}$.

Tables II and III.

Accounts and Papers, 1830, vol. XXIX, p. 435. (Paper 65.)

Table IVa (years 1821-29).

Accounts and Papers, 1833, vol. XXVI, p. 282.

Table IVa (years 1830-32).

General Report of the Emigration Commissioners. London, 1843-73.

Tables IV and V (years 1843-1872).

Colonisation Circular, No. 34, issued by Her Majesty's Colonial Land and Emigration Commissioners, London, 1877, pp. 27-36.

Tables IV (years 1815-75), IVb, IVc, and IX; V (year 1875).

Copy of Tables (formerly Statistical Tables) *relating to Emigration and Immigration from and to the United Kingdom* for the years 1877-1913. London.

Accounts and Papers.

Tables VI, XI and XXVIII; VII, X (years 1877-1913); VIII, XII and XIII (years 1880-1913); XV, XVI, XX, XXI, XXIV, XXV and XXVI (years 1912-13); XXVII (years 1890-1913).

Accounts and Papers, 1868-69, vol. L (Returns of the Number of Emigrants, Natives of Great Britain or Ireland, who left the United Kingdom, etc.), p. 487.

Table VII (years 1857 and 1867).

Idem, 1877, vol. LXXXV, p. 634.

Table V (year 1876).

Returns relating to Post Office and Savings Bank. Accounts and Papers, 1875, XLII, p. 579.

Table V (years 1873 and 1874).

Board of Trade Journal and Commercial Gazette, March 27, 1924; August 28, 1924; September 18, 1924; January 8, 1925; March 26, 1925; August 27, 1925;

Tables XIV, XVII, XVIII, XIX, XXII (years 1921-24) and XXIII; XV, XVI, XX and XXI.

Passenger Movement from and to the United Kingdom, December 1914. London, December 1915.

Tables XXIV, XV and XX (years 1914-15).

Alien Restriction Acts, 1914 and 1919, Alien Order, 1920, Statistics in regard to Alien Passengers, London, 1922-25.

Tables XXX and XXXI (years 1921-24).

Information supplied by the British Government, Board of Trade.

Tables IV. VIII, X, XII, XIII, XXVII and XXIX; VII (years 1877-1911).

Montgomery, Martin Robert: *Statistics of the Colonies of the British Empire,* London, 1839.

Table IVa (years 1833-40).

NOTES

[1]Since 1903 entitled "India, including Ceylon".
[2]Prior to 1903 entitled "Cape of Good Hope".
[3]Up to 1893 the heading of this column is "British West Indies".
[4]In the *Colonisation Circular,* 1877, p. 327, is the following note:
"The Customs returns do not record any emigration to Australia during these 10 years but it appears from other sources that there went out in 1821, 320; in 1822, 875; in 1823, 543; in 1824, 780; and in 1825, 458 persons. These numbers have not been included in the totals of this table."
N. B. 1825 is already the eleventh year, for which in the text the figure 485 is given, whereas the note gives 458.
[5]From April I, 1923, the figures are exclusive of passengers who departed from ports in the Irish Free State.
[6]Prior to December 10, 1859, this colony formed part of New South Wales; the numbers for Queensland are therefore included in those under the head of New South Wales up to the end of 1859.
[7]For 718 of this number the colony is not distinguished.
[8]The figures given in this column are classed under different headings in the source.
1843-52: "Cabin passengers", with a note: The emigration officer being unable to specify the description or sex of the passengers proceeding in ships not under the Passenger Act (forming but a small proportion of the whole), they have been tabulated as cabin passengers. 1853-60: Age and sex "not distinguished". To which is added in 1853, "this includes Infants and Cabin passengers, etc.;" and in 1854: "chiefly Cabin passengers". 1862-76: "not distinguished as to age".
[9]For 1843-47, under 14 years; for 1853-55, from 1 to 14 years; for 1856-76, from 1 to 12 years.
[10]Approximate number of passengers from places out of Europe landed at the chief ports of arrival in the United Kingdom.
[11]Number landed at Liverpool; returns from the other ports wanting.
[12]Returns for 1856 wanting. Numbers estimated by the *Colonisation Circular* on the average of the preceding and subsequent years.
[13]Return from London wanting.
[14]Return from Glasgow wanting,
[15]For the years 1870-75 the figures refer to all passengers.
[16]The excess outward to the North American continent in 1870 was 134,129; to all other places 19,225. The inward figures for this year are not further classified.
[17]From April 1, 1923, the figures are exclusive of passengers who departed from, or arrived at, ports in the Irish Free State.
[18]Nine months ending December 31, 1912.
[19]The figures for the fourth quarter of 1923 and the whole of 1924 are exclusive of emigrants from the Irish Free State, and of emigrants from Great Britain or Northern Ireland who may have embarked at Irish Free State ports.
[20]Provisional figures.
[21]Includes emigrants of 12 years of age and over, whose ages were not specified.
[22]Includes 465 males of 12 years of age and over in 1921, 102 in 1922, 144 in 1923, and 57 in 1924, whose ages were not specified.
[23]Includes 676 females of 12 years of age and over in 1921, 162 in 1922, 115 in 1923 and 84 in 1924, whose ages were not specified.
[24]Includes 57 males of 12 years of age and over, whose ages were not specified.
[25]Includes 84 females of 12 years of age and over, whose ages were not specified.
[26]Aliens other than seamen not stated in the Alien Lists to be en route to America or other places. It was however ascertained from information supplied to officers of His Majesty's Customs or obtained from other sources that a certain number of passengers included in this table were en route to other countries though the fact was not stated in the Alien Lists, viz.:

1897	2,676	1903	9,739
1898	2,336	1904	7,697
1899	2,889	1905	8,440

CZECHOSLOVAKIA

I. Port Statistics

(Tables I-III)

These tables give the number of emigrants departed by sea, 1922-24, as ascertained from the returns of the shipping companies. Data for sex and occupation are not available for the years prior to 1924.

II. Passport Statistics

(a) Emigration Statistics

(Tables IV-X)

The statistics based on the returns of the passport offices begin in 1920. In the first two years, however, the data do not enable us to distinguish intercontinental from continental emigration (table IV). From 1922 onward we are able to record occupations separately for both principal destinations (tables VI and IX) for 1924, as also with sex and age combined (tables V and VIII). For 1922-24 we also present a table (XI) with sex and age combined for all emigrants.

Apart from passport statistics there are data concerning those seasonal emigrant workers who are equipped with collective identity papers furnished by the district employment exchanges. These figures will be found separately, together with the countries of destination, in table X. (See also note 3.)

(b) Immigration Statistics

(Table XII)

The statistics of immigration cover alien immigrants as well as returning Czechoslovakians. They are based on the consular registration of individuals who have obtained a residence permit, either to earn a livelihood in the country or to take up their abode there for any other reason.

These statistics are incomplete and provisional. They are incomplete because it is not necessary to inform Czechoslovakian agents abroad if one is to enter the country. On the other hand, the number of returning citizens does not agree with the number registered, because Czechoslovakians settled in certain European countries usually hold passports valid for two years, during which period the holders may return without notification and in such cases they are not included in the statistics.

Statistics about the number of migrants from Czechoslovakia to Brazil (1920-24) Canada (1920-24) Cuba (1919-24) United States (1882-1920) and Argentina (1882-1924) will be found in the national tables for those countries. Statistics about the number of migrants returning to Czechoslovakia from the United States (1908-24) will be found in the national tables for the latter country.

TABLE I.—Intercontinental emigration of citizens, by country of future residence (port statistics), 1922-24.

Year	Total	United States	Canada	Argentina	Brazil	Other American States	Other countries
1922	14,343	13,561	110	457	205	3	7
1923	18,343	11,037	2,029	4,932	248	90	7
1924	6,626	2,541	2,832	1,065	111	71	6

TABLE II.—Distribution of emigrant citizens to extra-European countries, by sex and age (port statistics), 1924.

Age	Total	Males	Females
Total.................	6,626	4,574	2,052
Up to 14 years	1,015	540	475
15 to 21 years	537	257	280
Over 21 years	5,074	3,777	1,297

TABLE III.—Distribution of emigrant citizens to extra-European countries, by occupation (port statistics), 1924.

Occupation	No. of emigrants
Agriculture, forestry, fishery.................................	3,462
Industry, mining, handicrafts..............................	1,208
Trade, finance, transport...........................	195
Public services and liberal professions.........................	106
Wage-earners, general labor, domestic servants	436
No occupation, other or unknown occupations.................	1,219
Total......................	6,626

TABLE IV.—Emigration of citizens to all parts, by country of future residence (passport statistics), 1920-21.[1]

Year	Total	Austria	Germany	Hungary	Serb, Croat and Slovene State	France	United States	Other countries
1920	34,942	4,492	5,197	2,445	1,114	1,308	16,893	3,493
1921	35,212	6,119	3,783	2,259	1,603	533	17,150	3,765

For reference notes see page 665.

TABLE V.—Distribution of Emigrants to extra-European countries, by sex AND AGE (PASSPORT STATISTICS), 1924.

Age	Total	Males	Females
Up to 4 years	1,866	941	925
5– 9 years	984	512	472
10–14 "	1,218	606	612
15–19 "	3,746	1,299	2,447
20–29 "	16,199	10,338	5,861
30–39 "	7,096	5,299	1,797
40–49 "	2,835	2,194	641
50–59 "	707	400	307
60–69 "	264	91	173
70 and over	50	18	32
Unknown	215	113	102
Total,	35,180	21,811	13,369

TABLE VI.—Distribution of emigrants to extra-European countries, by OCCUPATION (PASSPORT STATISTICS), 1922-24.

Year	Total	Agri-culture, forestry, fishery	Industry, mining, handicrafts	Trade, finance, transport	Public ser-vices and liberal pro-fessions	Wage-earn-ers, general labor, domestic servants	No occupa-tion, other or unknown occupa-tions
1922	20,761	5,546	4,019	575	185	5,367	5,069
1923	15,889	4,625	4,871	440	191	3,772	1,990
1924	35,180	10,752	7,053	965	314	8,589	7,507

TABLE VII.—Intercontinental emigration of citizens, by country of FUTURE RESIDENCE (PASSPORT STATISTICS), 1922-24.

Year	Total	United States	Canada	Argentina	Brazil	Other American countries	Other countries
1922	20,761	18,291	36	520	219	1,651	44
1923	15,889	6,700	2,531	5,974	384	265	35
1924[2]	35,180	30,846	3,059	1,026	126	68	55

For reference notes see page 665.

TABLE VIII.—DISTRIBUTION OF EMIGRANT CITIZENS TO EUROPEAN COUNTRIES, BY SEX AND AGE, 1924.

Age	Total	Males	Females
Up to 4 years	757	368	389
5– 9 years	280	141	139
10–14 "	398	200	198
15–19 "	2,789	2,062	727
20–29 "	9,528	7,686	1,842
30–39 "	3,170	2,559	611
40–49 "	1,388	1,218	170
50–59 "	491	423	68
60–69 "	131	83	48
70 years and over	49	21	28
Not specified	76	64	12
	19,057	14,825	4,232

TABLE IX.—DISTRIBUTION OF EMIGRANTS TO EUROPEAN COUNTRIES, BY OCCUPATION, 1922–24.

Year	Total	Agriculture, forestry, fishery	Industry mining, handicrafts	Trade, finance, transport	Liberal professions, public services	Wage earners, general labor, domestic servants	No occupations, other or unknown occupations
1922	17,935	1,416	10,488	914	487	2,691	1,939
1923	16,369	1,536	9,494	520	331	2,999	1,489
1924	19,057	4,381	7,864	480	315	4,346	1,671

TABLE X.—CONTINENTAL EMIGRATION OF CITIZENS, BY COUNTRY OF FUTURE RESIDENCE, DISTINGUISHING SEASONAL EMIGRANTS WITHOUT PASSPORTS FROM EMIGRANTS WITH INDIVIDUAL PASSPORTS, 1922-24.

Year	Total	Seasonal emigrants without passports[3]				Emigrants with individual passports									
		Total	Austria	Germany	Serb, Croat and Slovene State	Total	France	Austria	Germany	Hungary	Serb, Croat and Slovene State	Rumania	Poland	Russia	Other European countries
1922	31,558	13,623	7,723	4,045	1,855	17,935	3,457	4,214	5,208	894	1,555	1,042	694	212	659
1923	24,334	7,965	7,965	....	....	16,369	5,957	1,852	750	4,144	1,058	1,054	292	519	743
1924	29,371	10,314[4]	10,137	177	....	19,057	12,525	1,656	1,085	1,785	429	318	225	451	583

For reference notes see page 665.

TABLE XI.—Distribution of emigrants, by sex and age (passport statistics)[5], 1922–24.

Age	1922			1923			1924		
	Total	Males	Females	Total	Males	Females	Total	Males	Females
Up to 4 years	1,835	885	950	1,431	747	684	2,625	1,310	1,315
5– 9 years	1,274	641	633	721	355	366	1,267	655	612
10–14 "	1,571	798	773	1,034	542	492	1,617	807	810
15–19 "	6,154	3,169	2,985	3,537	2,443	1,094	6,541	3,366	3,175
20–29 "	17,091	11,469	5,622	15,047	12,016	3,031	25,793	18,077	7,716
30–39 "	6,866	4,877	1,989	6,666	5,383	1,283	10,301	7,892	2,409
40–49 "	2,843	2,144	699	2,724	2,306	418	4,239	3,426	813
50–59 "	1,095	723	372	843	645	198	1,201	826	375
60–69 "	524	226	298	235	123	112	396	175	221
70 years and over	176	82	94	90	38	52	100	40	60
Not specified	...	..	..	13	13	..	293	178	115
Total	39,429	25,014	14,415	32,341	24,611	7,730	54,373	36,752	17,621

TABLE XII.—Immigration, by country of origin, 1922-24.

Country of origin	1922	1923	1924[6]
Austria...................................	3,972	3,408	2,303
Germany..................................	197	544	264
Hungary..................................	2,687	1,419	857
Poland...................................	956	379	343
Rumania.................................	18	17	88
Serb, Croat and Slovene State..............	488	252	378
Italy.....................................	172	165	93
Switzerland...............................	79	40	41
Union of Socialist Soviet Republics...........	71	177	578
Bulgaria..................................	342	127	573
Turkey in Europe..........................	360	85	25
Other European countries...................	75	73	57
United States.............................	5,786	1,567	2,695
Canada..................................	57	7	36
Argentina................................	88	378	372[7]
Other American countries...................	20	11	14
Other countries...........................	75	25	14
Total	15,443	8,674	8,731

For reference notes see page 665.

SOURCES

Information supplied by the Ministry of Social Affairs, Prague.

Tables I-XI (years 1920-24).

Information supplied by the Office of Statistics of Czechoslovakia, Prague.

Table XII (year 1924).

Rapports de l'Office de Statistique de la République Tchécoslovaque, VI⁰ année (1925), No. 18, p. 141; No. 24, p. 197.

Tables XII (years 1922-23); VIII (year 1924) (seasonal emigration).

Mitteilungen des Statistischen Staatsamtes der Czechoslowakischen Republik. V. Jahrg. (1924), Nos. 25-26, p. 222.

Table VIII (years 1922-23) (seasonal emigration).

NOTES

[1] These figures are incomplete: 21 reports of administrative districts are missing in 1920 and 10 in 1921.

[2] The high figure for 1924 is explained by the fact that on learning of the new restrictions upon alien immigration into the United States many people who intended to emigrate there asked for their passports early in 1924 in order to be included as soon as possible within the quota for Czechoslovakia.

[3] Mass emigration for seasonal agricultural work has been arranged by a special international convention. No passports are required. The data are taken from the annual reports of these exchanges. These figures, however, do not represent the total number of seasonal workers who emigrated. In 1922, 2,998 and in 1923, 2,676 persons emigrated with *individual passports* for seasonal work.

[4] Including 4,982 women.

[5] The figures for emigration to all parts include 733 emigrants in 1922, 83 in 1923 and 136 in 1924 without indication of country of future residence and therefore exceed by these numbers respectively the totals of the intercontinental and continental emigration (tables VII and IX).

[6] Provisional figures.

DENMARK

Statistics of emigration to overseas countries are compiled in conformity with the Act of May 1, 1868, concerning the supervision of the transport of emigrants.   On June 30, 1873, the Minister of Justice instructed the police authorities to notify emigration agents that every contract with emigrants must contain information on points mentioned in the Circular (number of persons to be transported, their surnames, ages, etc.).   The Circular of the Ministry of Justice dated July 2, 1873, notified emigration agents that the accuracy of this information must be certified by the agent or his clerk either by an endorsement on the contract, or a statement attached to it, and that he must not give this certificate unless he had an intimate knowledge of the emigrants, or they had supplied him with certificates issued by the proper police authority, bailiff, parish minister, or, failing them, by two persons of good standing known to the agent; these certificates must accompany the contract when the latter is submitted to the Chief of Police for examination.   According to a Circular of the Minister of Justice, dated July 21, 1899, the contract must also contain information as to the port of destination.

The declarations made in accordance with this Circular are tabulated by the Statistical Department in conformity with a Circular of April 28, 1869.

Statistics about the number of migrants from Denmark to Argentina (1871-1924), Canada (1900-24), United States (1820-1924), and Australia (1902-24) will be found in the national tables for those countries.   Statistics about the number of migrants returning to Denmark from Argentina (1891-1924) and the United States (1908-24) will be found in the national tables for those countries

TABLE I.—DISTRIBUTION OF EMIGRANTS TO NON-EUROPEAN COUNTRIES, BY SEX AND AGE, 1869-1924.

Year	Total	Males	Females	Under 15 years		15 to 19 years		20 to 24 years		25 to 29 years		30 to 39 years		40 to 59 years		60 years and over	
				Males	Females	Males	Females	Males	Females	Males	Females	Males	Females	Males	Females	Males	Females
1869	4,359	2,796	1,563	....						....							....
1870	3,525	2,275	1,250	....						....							....
1871	3,906	2,489	1,417	....						....							....
1872	6,893	4,415	2,478	1,452						5,395							46
1873	7,200	4,422	2,778	1,553						5,596							51
1874	3,322	1,920	1,402	830						2,450							42
1875	2,088	1,143	945	541						1,520							27
1876	1,581	907	674	388						1,157							36
1877	1,877	1,130	747	463						1,378							36
1878	2,972	1,914	1,058	666						2,277							29
1879	3,103	1,948	1,155	682						2,368							53
1880	5,658	3,554	2,104	1,348						4,247							63
1881	7,985	4,855	3,130	2,064						5,813							108
1882	11,614	7,112	4,502	2,750						8,679							185
1883	8,375	4,936	3,439	2,075						6,180							120
1884	6,307	3,761	2,546	1,452						4,751							104
1885	4,346	2,414	1,932	929						3,334							83
1886	6,263	3,827	2,436	1,241						4,924							98
1887	8,801	5,457	3,344	1,650						7,041							110
1888	8,659	5,342	3,317	1,492						7,070							97
1889	8,967	5,455	3,512	1,683						7,180							104
1890	10,298	6,078	4,220	2,068						8,061							169
1891	10,382	6,118	4,264	2,091						8,154							137
1892	10,422	6,020	4,402	2,113						8,211							98
1893	9,150	5,301	3,849	1,737						7,299							114
1894	4,105	2,203	1,902	744						3,297							64
1895	3,607	1,986	1,621	595						2,945							67
1896	2,876	1,602	1,274	397						2,410							69
1897	2,260	1,285	975	323						1,875							62
1898	2,340	1,338	1,002	294						1,991							55
1899	2,799	1,627	1,172	380						2,369							50
1900	3,570	2,119	1,451	478						2,999							93
1901	4,657	2,857	1,800	676						3,886							95
1902	6,823	4,296	2,527	1,045						5,660							118
1903	8,214	5,305	2,909	597	557	1,111	540	1,811	693	898	443	568	378	272	232	48	66
1904	9,034	5,622	3,412	659	662	1,060	670	1,929	838	934	481	661	416	312	279	67	66
1905	8,051	5,161	2,890	525	531	1,055	528	1,850	772	870	493	574	338	237	181	50	47
1906	8,516	5,366	3,150	596	571	1,119	561	1,889	834	875	489	564	405	265	239	58	51
1907	7,890	4,996	2,894	535	448	1,085	517	1,691	787	815	473	552	341	259	262	59	66

TABLE I.—DISTRIBUTION OF EMIGRANTS TO NON-EUROPEAN COUNTRIES, BY SEX AND AGE, 1869-1924 (continued).

Year	Total		Under 15 years		15 to 19 years		20 to 24 years		25 to 29 years		30 to 39 years		40 to 59 years		60 years and over	
	Total	Males	Females	Males	Females	Males	Females	Males	Females	Males	Females	Males	Females	Males	Females	Males	Females
1908	4,558	2,691	1,867	287	236	512	343	873	485	477	333	330	249	173	165	39	56
1909	6,782	4,313	2,469	445	388	826	416	1,495	622	748	416	510	364	239	220	50	43
1910	8,890	5,657	3,233	575	580	1,193	535	1,938	818	972	532	631	446	299	262	49	60
1911	8,303	5,312	2,991	504	497	1,151	513	1,874	823	903	497	561	395	273	227	46	39
1912	8,636	5,675	2,961	445	494	1,220	477	2,095	819	986	523	620	388	274	211	35	49
1913	8,846	5,634	3,212	472	476	1,243	551	2,026	911	984	547	588	429	273	257	48	41
1914	6,203	3,762	2,441	364	377	850	399	1,231	601	639	473	448	351	193	203	37	37
1915	3,302	1,811	1,483	241	207	429	273	494	381	242	254	257	218	132	125	24	25
1916	4,265	2,311	1,954	279	268	568	297	546	518	371	338	349	312	166	174	32	47
1917	1,614	900	714	93	120	144	76	172	161	177	126	189	136	108	82	17	13
1918	793	416	377	84	67	65	28	62	55	57	75	87	88	55	46	6	18
1919	3,341	2,069	1,272	166	153	265	128	554	237	341	234	367	260	304	199	72	61
1920	6,300	4,034	2,266	299	327	611	245	1,383	502	812	424	554	399	273	252	102	117
1921	5,309	3,345	1,964	260	269	502	261	1,166	423	656	334	475	386	217	208	69	83
1922	4,094	2,475	1,619	232	259	354	148	813	338	434	280	379	328	215	201	48	65
1923	7,601	5,143	2,458	415	390	682	237	1,915	534	1,042	495	660	449	364	256	65	97
1924	6,319	4,422	1,897	334	348	585	150	1,646	368	864	359	643	369	287	236	63	67

TABLE II.—DISTRIBUTION OF MALE EMIGRANTS, 15 YEARS OF AGE AND OVER, BY OCCUPATION, 1872-1924.

Year	Total	Agriculture	Domestic service and general labor	In-dustry	Commerce	Shipping	Other occupations
1872	3,645	2,921		516	22	41	145
1873	3,610	2,843		523	34	36	174
1874	1,493	178	884	316	11	18	86
1875	873	108	514	174	7	9	61
1876	674	88	355	140	9	15	67
1877	881	99	425	245	16	16	80
1878	1,566	164	998	291	13	8	92
1879	1,578	183	840	383	31	17	124
1880	2,816	427	1,372	677	45	52	243
1881	3,791	674	1,803	921	56	60	277
1882	5,688	967	2,704	1,454	89	72	402
1883	3,858	643	1,893	914	64	61	283
1884	3,049	446	1,489	749	169	52	144
1885	1,959	246	886	544	126	40	117
1886	3,192	411	1,464	931	200	55	131
1887	4,625	546	2,265	1,290	229	63	232
1888	4,560	485	2,410	1,153	245	67	200
1889	4,613	556	2,116	1,285	101	75	480
1890	4,973	374	2,496	1,379	335	81	308
1891	5,061	507	2,392	1,363	340	86	373
1892	5,018	491	2,323	1,436	317	96	355
1893	4,434	417	2,029	1,256	81	72	579
1894	1,835	129	862	504	40	42	258
1895	1,675	115	696	478	31	48	307
1896	1,415	113	596	377	135	27	167
1897	1,120	79	454	282	128	14	163
1898	1,190	147	504	277	113	44	105
1899	1,434	205	609	362	143	23	92
1900	1,857	236	809	512	146	47	107
1901	2,552	320	1,058	789	196	43	146
1902	3,781	771	1,315	1,190	281	42	182
1903	4,708	538	1,895	1,547	348	107	273
1904	4,963	453	2,064	1,613	447	126	260
1905	4,636	333	2,298	1,316	390	81	218
1906	4,770	332	2,367	1,340	376	90	265
1907	4,461	720	1,721	1,222	375	93	330
1908	2,404	470	884	557	208	46	239
1909	3,868	633	1,365	1,095	347	70	358
1910	5,082	962	1,776	1,450	418	94	382
1911	4,808	1,017	1,721	1,253	419	91	307
1912	5,230	1,342	1,892	1,154	412	101	329
1913	5,162	1,211	1,915	1,199	438	82	317
1914	3,398	701	1,275	814	290	52	266
1915	1,578	230	548	374	215	35	176
1916	2,032	226	694	468	333	59	252
1917	807	74	149	177	208	75	124
1918	332	64	61	52	59	28	68
1919	1,903	245	310	277	613	75	383
1920	3,735	917	917	877	572	110	342
1921	3,085	877	813	671	400	75	249
1922	2,243	595	511	525	382	42	188
1923	4,728	1,216	1,236	1,190	612	116	358
1924	4,088	1,106	1,218	829	506	123	306

TABLE III.—EMIGRATION BY COUNTRY OF DESTINATION, 1869-1924.

Year	Total	United States	Canada	Other American States	Australia	Africa	Asia
1869	4,359	4,340	12	..	7	...	.
1870	3,525	3,264	54	2	205	...	.
1871	3,906	3,249	22	49	579	4	3
1872	6,893	5,941	43	45	862	1	1
1873	7,200	5,926	246	23	1,003	1	1
1874	3,319	2,258	98	13	950	...	.
1875	2,073	1,663	47	34	329	...	.
1876	1,581	1,336	23	11	198	12	1
1877	1,877	1,374	27	32	107	337	.
1878	2,972	2,300	95	18	530	29	.
1879	3,103	2,845	164	50	44	...	.
1880	5,649	5,475	145	...	29	...	.
1881	7,985	7,823	105	18	29	10	.
1882	11,614	11,385	193	7	15	14	.
1883	8,375	8,280	72	6	15	2	.
1884	6,307	6,149	123	12	15	7	1
1885	4,346	4,211	45	21	66	1	2
1886	6,263	5,558	68	565	65	1	6
1887	8,802	8,185	190	371	56	...	.
1888	8,658	8,268	214	119	48	1	8
1889	8,967	8,271	157	423	107	2	7
1890	10,298	9,524	365	315	87	3	4
1891	10,382	9,789	327	179	73	9	5
1892	10,422	9,763	501	77	62	14	5
1893	9,150	8,551	434	99	35	26	5
1894	4,105	3,719	224	63	31	60	8
1895	3,607	3,287	111	121	34	47	7
1896	2,876	2,479	81	157	47	108	4
1897	2,260	1,963	47	104	48	82	16
1898	2,340	2,073	101	54	49	50	13
1899	2,799	2,611	78	55	18	21	16
1900	3,570	3,253	150	89	17	33	28
1901	4,657	4,288	143	124	31	60	11
1902	6,823	6,383	189	128	45	54	24
1903	8,214	7,474	393	146	51	128	22
1904	9,034	8,405	384	144	43	38	20
1905	8,051	7,158	453	347	55	19	19
1906	8,516	7,596	484	309	64	18	45
1907	7,890	6,945	408	373	83	29	52
1908	4,558	3,704	245	435	110	16	48
1909	6,782	5,682	468	476	79	22	55
1910	·8,890	7,574	658	512	81	28	37

TABLE III.—EMIGRATION BY COUNTRY OF DESTINATION, 1869-1924 (concluded).

Year	Total	United States	Canada	Other American States	Australia	Africa	Asia
1911	8,303	6,809	744	549	116	35	50
1912	8,636	5,972	961	1,447	187	29	40
1913	8,846	6,774	975	869	148	31	49
1914	6,203	5,123	560	326	120	35	39
1915	3,302	3,059	104	84	53	2	..
1916	4,265	4,031	152	...	...	...	..
1917	1,614	1,589	25	66	9	4	3
1918	793	775	18	...	...	...	..
1919	3,341	2,922	165	250	2	...	2
1920	6,300	5,236	580	444	27	13	..
1921	5,309	3,986	689	536	75	13	10
1922	4,094	2,956	351	723	52	11	1
1923	7,601	5,813	1,081	651	44	10	2
1924	6,319	3,567	2,286	397	24	10	35

SOURCE

Return furnished by the Department of Statistics of Denmark at Copenhagen.

FRANCE

A continuous series of port and passport statistics began to be published after the Imperial Decree of January 15, 1855. Partial and occasional data had been collected earlier but they had not been utilised in statistical publications.

I. PORT STATISTICS

(Tables I-IV)

Following a suggestion of the Ministry for Foreign Affairs, the Ministry of the Interior undertook in 1837-39 a statistical enquiry into the number of citizens and aliens emigrating through the French ports of Dunkirk, Havre, St. Malo, Brest, Nantes, La Rochelle, Bordeaux, Bayonne, Cette et Agde, and Marseilles. These data were discovered in the National Archives of Paris under the following heading: "Etat numérique des Passagers tant Français qu'Etrangers qui pendant les trois dernières années se sont embarqués pour les Deux Amériques, dans les ports de France, d'après les rapports qu'ont addressés M. M. les Préfets des Départements maritimes." (F⁷ 12237.) (Numerical statement concerning passengers whether French or aliens, who during the last three years have embarked for the two Americas in French ports, compiled on the basis of reports furnished by the Prefects of the maritime Departments.)[1]

The port statistics of Havre, collected from 1837 to 1839, concern seagoing passengers as a whole. The information supplied by the Prussian consul at Havre for the year 1840 has reference to steerage passengers. The report furnished to the American Senate Commission, whence we derive our figures for 1843-46, speaks in general terms of "emigrants to the United States". It is probable, however, that in this case also it is a matter of totals. At that period the number of French emigrants was insignificant. This is well illustrated by the American source, which distinguishes for the first six months of 1847, 150 French, 600 Swiss, and 12,250 German emigrants. Hübner, speaking of the figures for 1855 and 1856, states that, in addition to Germans, they comprise Frenchmen, Swiss, and others. In view of the foregoing considerations, we decided to enter the emigration figures for Havre in the "total" column.

These port statistics were placed upon a systematic basis by the above-mentioned Imperial Decree of 1855 (which was incorporated in the Emigration Act of 1860), in virtue of which the Emigration Commissioners appointed in the ports by the Ministry of the Interior are entrusted with the supervision of emigration. These officers received orders to ensure the observance of Article 22 of the Decree, which con-

---

[1]The data thus supplied were coordinated and compiled by us, but the result cannot be accepted without certain reservations. For instance, only in some ports were citizens distinguished from aliens.

stituted the groundwork of the port statistics (compulsory lists of emigrants).[1] However, the *Rapports* make it clear that the Emigration Commissioners at the ports did not confine themselves to the collection of data relating to emigration vessels under legal control, for, on the one hand, they included emigrants embarked on vessels not subject to the emigration regulations, and, on the other—for certain years—passengers not under contract to authorised agents, whose embarkation could only be ascertained after sailing. (See explanatory notes 2 to 5.)

In the ports to which no Emigration Commissioners were appointed, the control and the collection of the figures was assigned to the police authorities. As a matter of fact, however, statistical data were only collected in the course of years in few ports, and consecutively scarcely in any, nor were the forms used throughout identical. These data were subsequently digested and published by the Emigration Section of the Ministry of the Interior in special Reports addressed to the Minister.

The statistics for

> 1857-58 relate to Havre, Bordeaux, Bayonne, St. Nazaire;
> 1859-64 relate to Havre, Bordeaux, Bayonne;
> 1865-81 relate to Havre, Bordeaux, Bayonne, Marseilles.

According to the previously mentioned Decree of 1855 and the corresponding text of the Emigration Act of July 11, 1860, only steerage passengers, *i. e.*, those travelling third or lowest class were deemed emigrants.

A Decree of March 9, 1861, defined an emigrant as a passenger who paid for his passage on a sailing ship or steamer, including food, a weekly amount of less than 40 francs. This did not apply to passengers who took their meals at the captain's or officers' table. In case of doubt, the Emigration Commissioner's decision was final.

The above definitions relate as much to citizens as to aliens. In regard to the returns concerning emigrant aliens, see p. 105ff.

II. Passport Statistics

(Tables V-VIII)

According to the Act of 10 Vendémiaire in the year IV of the Revolution, every person, whether of French or foreign nationality, who travelled in France or sought to enter or leave French territory, was required to

---

[1]*Article* 22.—The master or shipowner shall, "twenty-four hours before the departure of the ship, hand to the Emigration Commissioner an exact list of the passengers embarked, with particulars of the age, sex, nationality and destination of each person. Where fresh emigrant passengers report for embarkation after this list has been handed in, the master or shipowner shall furnish the Emigration Commissioner with as many supplementary lists as may be necessary, prepared in the above-mentioned manner.

The original list, with any supplementary lists, a duplicate of which is to be attached to the ship's papers, shall be finally endorsed and signed at the time of the departure by the Emigration Commissioner and by the master or shipowner. Once these final lists have been closed, no further emigrant shall be admitted on board."

carry a passport. More detailed instructions were embodied in the passport regulations of August 23, 1816.

Applications of *French* citizens for passports had to be addressed, through the local authorities, to the Ministry of the Interior. Portions of such lists of applications (not relating solely to emigration and covering certain periods of mass emigration) have been found in the National Archives in Paris for the first half of 1816 and in the Archives of the Bas-Rhin Department for the period 1808 to 1828. (See Introduction). Later the passports applied for by individuals intending to settle abroad were of a special character. J. Duval secured passport statistics for the years preceding 1857, the year in which the regular publication of these statistical reports commenced. He derived his data for his *Histoire de l'émigration au XIXe siècle* (Paris, 1862) from the files of the Emigration Section of the Ministry for Foreign Affairs. His figures ("number of persons to whom passports were delivered permitting them to settle abroad, and who may therefore be classed as emigrants"), together with those subsequently published in the official reports, form a comparable series.

1. For the first year common to both reports (1856) the figures are identical.[1] For the year following (1857) Duval's figures deviate in a few units (9), whilst the figures for Algiers coincide.

2. The definition of the term "emigrant" is also identical in both sources.

3. The statistical data refer in each instance to intercontinental and continental emigration, but of the countries of destination only Algiers is singled out for special treatment.

With regard to a continuous record by Prefects of the emigration of French citizens, a special Order was issued on June 26, 1855. It was laid down that each Prefecture should send in a monthly statement on emigration to foreign countries, indicating the name, age, sex, commune of domicile, and occupation of each emigrant. In addition, a second statement was to be sent, dealing with emigration to Algiers (professional men, workmen, or others).

In an Order of the Minister of the Interior, issued to the Prefects on November 26, 1855, the following definition of the term "emigrant" is given which agrees with that of Duval. "Generally speaking, emigrants are persons proceeding abroad or to Algiers with the object of taking up permanent residence there, and with intent to live in that country on the proceeds of their labour or professional activities."

Duval's emigration figures relating to Algiers before 1855 are the result of earlier Decrees issued by the Ministry of the Interior. In this connection we may note that after an Order dated January 21, 1843, had been promulgated, it was necessary to resort to a further Order (March 29, 1843), calling upon the Prefects to forward special quarterly reports on the subject of subsidised emigration to Algiers. This Order, however, was only partly complied with. (Circular letter of January 15, 1855). A regular record of emigrants to Algiers was published from 1856 to

---

[1]The first official Report and all the following decrees exist only in one manuscript **copy at the** "Prefecture de Police" (Paris).

1864; for the following years there is only one return for 1877 in the passport statistics table.[1]

The first report submitted by the Emigration Section to the Minister of the Interior, which is available only in manuscript in the archives of the Police Prefect, relates to the period from July 1, 1855, to the end of 1856. For later periods, until 1877, the port statistics, and also the passport statistics (tables V-VIII), both of which appeared in printed reports, have been used. (Tables entitled "French Emigration by Departments" in contradistinction to "French Emigration through Ports".)

In addition to these statistical data, diverging official totals for emigrant citizens classified by Departments have been found for the years 1854-60, these figures being "based on the passports delivered to travellers intending to settle abroad." (Gustave Lagneau, *L'Emigration de France*. Compte rendu de l'Académie des sciences morales et politiques, 44e année, 1884, t. 22, II semestre, p. 520.) Lagneau cites the *Statistique de la France*, 2e série, t. X, p. LXVIII, and t. XI, p. XCII. Here are his figures:

	1854	18,415
	1855	19,957
French emigrants who left their De-	1856	15,858
partments, registered by the	1857	17,958
passport and emigration services	1858	14,010
	1859	12,911
	1860	12,297

The totals of the passport statistics before 1877 as given in the *Rapports* and in the source just quoted do not agree with the port statistics. For 1878 to 1881, on the contrary, the *Rapport* does not contain separate passport statistics relating to intercontinental and continental emigrants, but only the intercontinental returns of the Emigration Commissioners from the ports previously mentioned. The first table of the report for 1878-81 is entitled "French Emigration by Sea" and specifies the Department in which the emigrants had resided and the totals are identical with the sum of the returns from the several ports. Presumably the Commissioners ascertained the Department of previous residence from the passports or from the transport contracts concluded with the shipping companies.

In 1884, the functions of the Emigration Commissioners of Paris, Havre and Marseilles were merged in those of the Railway Police Commissioners. These latter have retained the significant title "Acting Emigration Commissioners". They have continued to register the number of emigrants who had signed a transport contract with an emigration agent and departed through a French port (Bayonne, St. Nazaire, Bordeaux, Havre and Marseilles). Bodio, too, obtained his statistical data from the Police Commissioner (Directeur de la Sûreté générale) (see *Statistica della Emigrazione italiana per l'Estero* for 1891, p. 37), clas-

---

[1]However, the port statistics contain figures which do not appear in the tables: 1878, 870; 1879, 649; 1880, 252; and 1881, 231 emigrants to Algiers. (*Mouvement de l'Emigration en France*, 1878-1891, p. 15.)

sified, on the one hand, by the above ports and, on the other hand, by sex, age, nationality and occupation, except for the period 1885 to 1889. Citizens and aliens, without subdivision for nationality, are distinguished for these years. After 1892, to judge by a statement of the Deputy Police Commissioner on March 29, 1926, the Minister of the Interior received from the special Commissioners only the annual totals for the emigration movements "of Frenchmen embarked in French ports and travelling to America". The *Annuaire Statistique de la France* published these data until 1913.

A table dealing with the years 1910 to 1924 was placed at our disposal. Its statistics comprise all individuals proceeding for a long residence abroad, including those having no intention to return—whose number is insignificant. (Letter of May 8, 1926.)

In France, after 1891, not even the total number of emigrant aliens in transit were published.

III. STATISTICAL DATA RELATING TO LABOUR IMMIGRATION
(Tables VII and VIII)

Data on this subject are collected at the frontier stations by the inspectors. The table relating to immigration states the number of alien workers entering the country (omitting the dependents), who have been examined according to the regulations in force. Serious exception may be taken to the completeness and the accuracy of the data furnished.

These immigration figures depend on a compulsory system of control, while the departing emigrants are not required to announce at the frontier their intention to leave the country. The table relating to such departures is therefore incomplete.

Statistics about the number of migrants from France to South Africa (1913-24), Argentina (1857-1924), Brazil (1842-1924), Canada (1900-24), Cuba (1902-24), Mexico (1909-24), Paraguay (1883-1906), United States (1820-1924), Uruguay (1867-1921), and Australia (1902-24), will be found in the national tables for those countries. Statistics about the number of migrants returning to France from Argentina (1857-1924), Mexico (1911-24), United States (1908-24), and Uruguay (1879-1903), will be found in the national tables for those countries.

TABLE I.—DISTRIBUTION OF EMIGRANTS FROM FRENCH PORTS, BY NATIONALITY, 1837-39 and 1856-91.

Year	Grand total	Total citizens	Total aliens	German	English	American	Austrian	Belgian	Spanish and Portuguese	Dutch	Italian	Luxemburger	Swiss	Other nationalities	Nationality not distinguished	Alsace-Lorraine
1837	10,843															
1838	7,773															
1839	12,041															
1856	32,406		17,997[1]	13,133						859	396		2,748	861		
1857	15,467	5,721	26,685	19,821		497		41	657	276	519	801	3,845	226		
1858	11,732	3,735	11,732	8,266	2	425	13	17	578	54	150	179	1,803	247		
1859	12,798	2,586	10,212	6,850		489		22	403	20	382	29	1,656	214		
1860	18,869	3,530	15,339	11,011		579			797		203	63	1,943	220		
1861	14,108	2,687	11,421	5,272					686		380		1,828	820		
1862	10,474	2,334	8,140	3,633					585		456		1,763	734		
1863	12,666	2,384	10,282	3,230					541		278		1,772	670		
1864	18,245	3,103	15,142	7,423	1	498	2	84	680	6	502		2,236	1,526		
1865	19,173	4,715	14,458	8,626	6	1,135	47	20	781		913		2,764	783		
1866	29,090	5,752	23,338	13,328	1	1,093	1	20	1,493		1,531		3,953	1,825		
1867	31,025	6,047	24,978	11,109		707		6	2,517		3,886		4,207	2,744		
1868	27,855	6,406	21,449	6,382		982		13	1,972		5,352		4,120	2,910		
1869	36,600	7,898	28,702	5,643		736		8	2,910	4	9,636		4,886	4,628		
1870	26,113	4,600	21,513	3,171	1	488	8	9	2,647		8,622		3,512	2,816		
1871	14,556	5,947	8,609	312	6	1,450	7	11	580		4,388		1,245	1,573		
1872	49,679	15,829	33,850	2,502	1	677	5	14	1,163	2	18,265		5,724	4,725		
1873	48,024	8,404	39,620	6,800	4	833	89	12	1,169		21,727		6,397	2,827		
1874	60,356	7,163	53,193	1,556	5	809	4,461	154	785	1	17,610		3,420	27,879		
1875	26,893	4,284	22,609	1,276	79	927	3,023	128	1,083		12,084		2,264	119		
1876	23,424	2,190	21,234	934	40	866	359	114	721		12,760		2,278	81		
1877	20,074	2,116	17,958	1,410	79	1,910	313	64	662	3	12,997		1,826	121		
1878	24,543	2,316	22,227	2,561	75	1,066	971	63	1,515		13,988		2,864	85		
1879	35,174	3,634	31,540	10,907	142	862	400	122	1,846		19,190		5,516	185	4,540[2]	
1880	44,949	4,612	40,337	10,355	958	870	453	76	2,150		16,283		8,355	300	5,035[2]	
1881	50,663	4,456	46,207	9,716	358	765	748		1,123		20,387		11,390	1,195	4,673[3]	
1882	56,076	4,858	51,218	7,497	109	692	730		1,169		26,217		11,872	622	5,699[3]	
1883	52,353	4,011	48,342	5,479	114	761	481		1,633		23,544		13,484	648	2,435[2]	
1884	37,449	6,100	31,349		113				3,020		11,823		9,018	654	969[2]	
1885	36,487	6,063	30,424												3,791[4]	
1886	42,932	7,314	35,618												2,775[5]	
1887	72,119	11,170	60,949													
1888	94,675	23,339	71,336													
1889	89,155	31,354	57,801													
1890	72,512	20,560	51,952	5,239	148	847	1,547		4,724		26,919		7,941	4,587		
1891	57,815	6,217	51,598	4,705	53	829	1,464		1,396		28,639		7,692	6,820		

For reference notes see page 685.

TABLE II.—EMIGRATION THROUGH THE PORT OF HAVRE, 1837-40, 1843-91.

Year	Total	Citizens	Aliens	Year	Total	Citizens	Aliens
1837	8,331	1,376	6,955	1866	24,172	3,535	20,637
1838	4,122	744	3,378	1867	22,753	3,305	19,448
1839	10,110	1,216	8,894	1868	18,327	3,230	15,097
1840	19,348	.....	.....	1869	22,650	3,617	19,033
1843	8,553	.....	.....	1870	13,960	2,107	11,853
1844	16,660	.....	.....	1871	7,907	3,930	3,977
1845	23,500	.....	.....	1872	35,664	12,752	22,912
1846	32,381	.....	.....	1873	30,757	5,913	24,844
1847	39,417[6]	.....	.....	1874	45,767	4,798	40,969
1848	25,506	.....	.....	1875	17,538	2,837	14,701
1849	33,848	.....	.....	1876	13,470	1,281	12,189
1850	32,687	.....	.....	1877	10,703	979	9,724
1851	44,243	.....	.....	1878	16,205	1,265	14,940
1852	24,289	.....	.....	1879	17,725	1,781	15,944
1853	38,566	.....	.....	1880	30,867	2,645	28,222
1854	95,894	.....	.....	1881	31,942	2,530	29,412
1855	21,500	.....	.....	1882	32,510	2,973	29,537
1856	23,307	.....	17,997	1883	28,502	2,406	26,096
1857	34,240[7]	3,754	30,486	1884	21,634	2,231	19,403
1858	18,270[7]	2,116	16,154	1885	17,143	2,018	15,125
1859	15,392[7]	1,532	13,860	1886	18,947	2,892	16,055
1860	21,186[7]	1,689	19,497	1887	30,220	4,554	25,666
1861	11,416[7]	1,019	10,397	1888	38,525	10,628	27,897
1862	8,393[7]	877	7,516	1889	38,065	10,745	27,320
1863	9,293[7]	627	8,666	1890	39,922	9,076	30,846
1864	14,707[7]	1,408	13,299	1891	34,930	3,172	31,758
1865	15,715	3,008	12,707	....	.....	.....	.....

TABLE III.—DISTRIBUTION OF EMIGRANT CITIZENS, BY SEX AND AGE (PORT STATISTICS), 1865-91.

Year	Total	Adults		Children
		Males	Females	
1865	4,715	3,150	1,159	406
1866	5,752	3,819	1,447	486
1867	6,047	4,030	1,568	449
1868	6,406	4,270	1,715	421
1869	7,898	5,390	2,105	403
1870	4,600	3,091	1,306	203
1871	5,947	4,024	1,536	387
1872	15,829	10,914	3,571	1,344
1873	8,404	5,596	2,135	673
1874	7,163	4,412	2,009	742
1875	4,284	2,730	1,019	535
1876	2,190	1,383	535	272
1877	2,116[8]	1,330	628	158

For reference notes see page 685.

TABLE III.—DISTRIBUTION OF EMIGRANT CITIZENS BY SEX AND AGE (PORT STATISTICS), 1865-91 (continued).

	Total	Males	Females
1878	2,316	1,549	767
1879	3,634	2,425	1,209
1880	4,612	3,132	1,480
1881	4,456	3,022	1,434
1882	4,858	3,297	1,561
1883	4,011	2,790	1,221
1884	6,100	4,294	1,806
1890	20,560	13,270	7,290
1891	6,217	4,044	2,173

TABLE IV.—DISTRIBUTION OF EMIGRANT CITIZENS, BY AGE (PORT STATISTICS), 1878-91.

Year	Total	Under 10 years	10 to 20 years	21 to 50 years	51 years and over
1878–81	12,827[9]	1,477	2,397	8,195	758
1882	3,538[10]	687	786	1,769	296
1883	4,011	563	569	2,667	212
1884	6,100	620	801	4,303	376
1890	20,560	3,450	4,437	12,122	551
1891	6,217	678	1,479	3,805	255

TABLE V.—DISTRIBUTION OF EMIGRANT CITIZENS, BY OCCUPATION (PORT STATISTICS), 1878-91.

Year	Total	Agricultural population	Industrial population	Other occupations
1878	2,316	476	1,112	728
1879	3,634	1,514	959	1,161
1880	4,612	1,365	1,333	1,914
1881	4,456	2,052	486	1,918
1882	4,858	2,146	747	1,965
1883	4,011	983	1,170	1,858
1884	6,100	2,891	1,064	2,145
1890	20,560	8,695	6,397	5,468
1891	6,217	2,319	2,388	1,510

For reference notes see page 685.

TABLE VI.—INTERCONTINENTAL EMIGRATION OF CITIZENS, 1892-1924.

Year	Emi-grants	Year	Emi-grants	Year	Emi-grants	Year	Emi-grants	Year	Emi-grants
1892	6,000	1899	5,000	1906	6,000	1913	5,701	1920	4,012
1893	6,000	1900	5,000	1907	8,000	1914	3,057	1921	1,762
1894	4,000	1901	4,000	1908	5,000	1915	743[11]	1922	1,223
1895	5,000	1902	4,000	1909	5,000	1916	693[11]	1923	1,630
1896	5,000	1903	6,000	1910	5,114	1917	359[11]	1924	1,568
1897	5,000	1904	5,000	1911	6,166	1918	149[11]	....	.....
1898	4,000	1905	5,000	1912	5,834	1919	5,439[11]	....	.....

TABLE VII.—EMIGRATION OF CITIZENS TO FOREIGN COUNTRIES AND TO ALGERIA (PASS-PORT STATISTICS), 1853-64.

Year	Total	To foreign countries	To Algeria
1853	9,694	5,257	4,437
1854	18,079	10,395	7,684
1855	19,957	10,155	9,802
1856	17,997	9,433	8,564
1857	18,809	10,817	7,992
1858	13,813	9,004	4,809
1859	9,164	6,786	2,378
1860	10,087	7,443	2,644
1861	8,752	6,334	2,418
1862	6,800	5,036	1,764
1863	5,771	4,285	1,486
1864	5,431	4,057	1,374

For reference notes see page 685.

TABLE VIII.—DISTRIBUTION OF EMIGRANT CITIZENS, BY SEX AND AGE (PASSPORT STATISTICS), 1857-77.

Year	Total	Males	Females	Children and young persons	Under 1 year		1-10 years		11-20 years		21-30 years		31-40 years		41-50 years		Over 50	
					Males	Females	Males	Females	Males	Females	Males	Females	Males	Females	Males	Females	Males	Females
1857	10,817	7,190	3,627	......	39	35	488	428	1,529	720	2,552	1,315	1,562	647	669	257	351	225
1858	9,004	6,135	2,869	......	34	45	385	367	1,248	519	2,152	990	1,389	549	628	244	299	155
1859	6,786	4,680	2,106	......	27	24	237	233	1,156	398	1,516	796	1,027	398	470	160	247	97
1860	7,443	5,175	2,268	......	25	31	292	262	1,379	519	1,761	794	1,036	373	434	171	248	118
1861	6,334	4,476	1,858	......	22	20	216	180	1,137	387	1,594	705	869	315	385	132	253	119
1862	5,036	3,499	1,537	......	25	18	163	190	894	343	1,176	520	710	262	332	107	199	97
1863	4,285	2,967	1,318	......	13	9	135	124	763	339	1,112	464	542	185	237	114	165	83
1864	4,057	2,826	1,231	......	11	10	110	112	707	295	1,047	434	547	211	198	68	206	101
1865[12]	4,489	2,430	707	1,352	56		214		1,084				2,649				340	
1866[12]	4,531	2,223	788	1,520	58		218		1,273				2,474				319	
1867[12]	4,938	2,518	740	1,680	50		198		1,423				2,753				360	
1868[12]	5,274	2,570	830	1,874	49		256		1,552				2,882				341	
1869[12]	4,837	2,362	770	1,705	49		252		1,355				2,650				350	
1870[12]	4,845	2,752	816	1,277	79		274		966				2,841				559	
1871[12]	7,109	4,038	1,186	1,885	66		315		1,578				4,283				739	
1872[12]	9,581	5,119	1,420	3,042	65		502		2,459				5,443				745	
1873[12]	7,561	3,918	1,224	2,419	63		394		1,907				4,305				472	
1874[12]	7,080	3,679	1,230	2,171	87		563		1,513				3,968				624	
1875[12]	4,464	3,269	1,195	......	39		214		1,015				2,676				293	
1876[12]	2,867	2,135	732	......	26		171		681				1,661				227	
1877[13]	3,666	2,457	1,209	......	46		351		725				2,146				303	

For reference notes see page 685.

TABLE IX.—DISTRIBUTION OF EMIGRANT CITIZENS, BY OCCUPATION, SEX AND AGE (PASSPORT STATISTICS), 1857-77.

Year	Grand total	Agricultural population				Industrial population				Other occupations			
		Total	Males	Females	Children	Total	Males	Females	Children	Total	Males	Females	Children
1857	10,817	2,477	1,762	580	135	4,346	2,956	1,149	241	3,994	2,169	1,621	204
1858	9,004	1,912	1,359	445	101	3,966	2,818	920	228	3,126	1,693	1,249	184
1859	6,786	1,436	1,095	282	59	2,802	2,007	640	155	2,548	1,398	1,018	132
1860	7,443	1,691	1,323	297	71	2,204	1,609	445	150	3,548	2,066	1,340	142
1861	6,334	1,882	1,351	438	93	2,384	1,866	633	85	1,868	1,112	656	100
1862	5,036	1,393	966	360	67	2,047	1,447	486	114	1,596	944	571	81
1863	4,285	1,293	980	268	45	1,581	1,041	461	79	1,411	839	514	58
1864	4,057	987	751	207	29	1,457	1,037	367	53	1,613	974	578	61
1865	4,343	1,512	....	....	....	1,316	....	....	....	1,515	....	....	....
1866	4,342	1,864	....	....	....	1,208	....	....	....	1,270	....	....	....
1867	4,784	2,007	....	....	....	1,238	....	....	....	1,539	....	....	....
1868	5,080	2,311	....	....	....	1,230	....	....	....	1,539	....	....	....
1869	4,656	1,988	....	....	....	1,239	....	....	....	1,429	....	....	....
1870	4,719	1,477	....	....	....	1,386	....	....	....	1,856	....	....	....
1871	6,981	2,113	....	....	....	2,000	....	....	....	2,868	....	....	....
1872	9,214	3,431	....	....	....	2,584	....	....	....	3,199	....	....	....
1873	7,141	2,547	....	....	....	2,120	....	....	....	2,474	....	....	....
1874	6,755	2,342	....	....	....	1,804	....	....	....	2,609	....	....	....
1875	4,237	1,120	....	....	....	1,524	....	....	....	1,593	....	....	....
1876	2,766	997	....	....	....	918	....	....	....	851	....	....	....
1877	3,571	1,592	....	....	....	742	....	....	....	1,237	....	....	....

TABLE X.—DISTRIBUTION OF EMIGRANT CITIZENS TO ALGERIA, BY SEX AND AGE (PASSPORT STATISTICS), 1857-64.

Year	Total	Males	Females	Under 1 year		1-10 years		10-20 years		20-30 years		30-40 years		40-50 years		Over 50 years	
				Males	Females	Males	Females	Males	Females	Males	Females	Males	Females	Males	Females	Males	Females
1857	7,992	4,691	3,301	55	28	658	627	836	603	1,113	821	953	614	653	372	423	236
1858	4,809	2,819	1,990	36	25	408	346	442	317	688	552	623	383	380	194	242	173
1859	2,378	1,343	1,035	8	13	194	147	214	172	280	299	311	210	202	105	134	89
1860	2,644	1,522	1,122	16	22	216	179	248	180	373	345	334	203	180	124	155	69
1861	2,418	1,347	1,071	12	10	196	146	186	174	311	325	303	204	206	110	133	102
1862	1,764	1,019	745	13	14	140	119	171	128	209	174	237	156	141	95	108	59
1863	1,486	878	608	15	7	119	93	142	101	188	150	200	111	120	76	94	70
1864	1,374	803	571	7	9	118	98	125	83	192	141	183	97	109	84	69	59

TABLE XI.—DISTRIBUTION OF EMIGRANT CITIZENS TO ALGERIA, BY OCCUPATION, SEX AND AGE (PASSPORT STATISTICS) 1857-64.

Year	Total	Agricultural population				Industrial population				Other occupations			
		Total	Males	Females	Children	Total	Males	Females	Children	Total	Males	Females	Children
1857	7,992	3,595	2,045	1,113	437	2,899	1,607	1,041	251	1,498	620	742	136
1858	4,809	1,855	1,131	547	177	1,654	923	569	162	1,300	492	656	152
1859	2,378	789	498	232	59	837	427	338	72	752	299	366	87
1860	2,644	868	594	207	67	644	375	209	60	1,132	421	570	141
1861	2,418	762	451	232	79	1,005	520	393	92	651	242	358	61
1862	1,764	623	366	184	73	670	365	233	72	471	187	237	47
1863	1,486	503	316	152	35	574	313	196	65	409	162	201	46
1864	1,374	481	294	135	52	501	264	189	48	392	173	185	34

TABLE XII.—DISTRIBUTION OF ALIEN LABORERS WHO ENTERED FRANCE, BY NATIONALITY AND OCCUPATION, 1920-24.

Nationality	1920			1921			1922			1923			1924		
	Total	Agri-culture	In-dustry	Total	Agri-culture	In-dustry	Total	Agri-culture	In-dustry	Total	Agri-culture	In-dustry	Total	Agri-culture	In-dustry
Belgian	28,422	15,021	13,401	26,260	20,313	5,947	24,677	13,144	11,533	33,912	8,805	25,107	40,256	16,477	23,779
Spanish	53,306	35,943	17,363	28,310	26,773	1,537	45,392	38,740	6,652	36,497	28,980	7,517	38,960	32,265	6,695
Portuguese	6,741	.....	6,741	45	.....	45	6,771	.....	6,771	11,767	3,791	7,976	6,715	.....	6,715
Greek	131	.....	131	36	.....	36	12	.....	12	412	.....	412	903	.....	903
Italian	85,314	9,788	75,526	11,542	4,382	7,160	56,730	7,235	49,495	112,475	9,462	103,013	99,155	15,274	83,881
Polish	16,363	1,712	14,651	11,313	1,968	9,345	36,832	8,462	28,370	54,673	23,226	31,447	41,014	17,749	23,265
Russian	25	.....	25	256	.....	256	2,780	.....	2,780	3,346	2	3,344	4,359	767	3,592
Czechoslovakian	907	.....	907	.....	.....	.....	886	.....	886	4,330	3,065	1,265	10,340	5,939	4,401
Other nationalities	2,733	465	2,268	2,293	621	1,672	19,036	3,028	16,008	16,115	1,291	14,824	23,653	1,714	21,939
Total	193,942	62,929	131,013	80,055	54,057	25,998	193,113	70,606	122,507	273,527	78,622	194,905	265,355	90,185	175,170

TABLE XIII.—DISTRIBUTION OF ALIEN LABORERS WHO LEFT FRANCE, BY NATIONALITY, 1920-24.

Nationality	1920	1921	1922	1923	1924
Belgian..............	894	6,580	1,236	3,832	2,740
Spanish.............	708	23,097	11,727	11,203	13,805
Portuguese..........	6,330	3,934	1,432	4,052	7,093
Greek..............	278	702	138	61	....
Italian..............	777	23,197	33,484	39,383	23,920
Polish..............	2,866	4,113	1,850	77	89
Russian.............	....	....	8	....	....
Czechoslovakian.....	44	124	13	1,343	105
Other nationalities...	254	789	421	...	...
Total..........	12,151	62,536	50,309	59,951	47,752

SOURCES

Return supplied by the Ministry of the Interior to the Ministry of Foreign Affairs. MS. in the Archives Nationales in Paris. (F. 712337.)

Tables I and II (years 1837-39).

Rapport à S. E. le Ministre de l'Intérieur sur l'Emigration, 1856. MS. in the archives of the Public Security Section, Ministry of the Interior, Paris.

Tables I, II and VII (year 1856).

Idem (printed) 1857 and 1858; 1859 and 1860; 1861 and 1862; 1863 and 1864; 1865 to 1874; 1875 to 1877; 1878 to 1881. Paris, 1859, 1861, 1863, 1866, 1876, 1879 and 1883.

Tables I-XI (years 1857-81).

Annuaire Statistique. Ministry of Labour and Social Welfare, 33rd vol., 1913. Paris' 1914, p. 164.

Table VI (years 1892-1909).

Bulletin du Ministère du Travail et de l'Hygiène, 33rd year, July-August-September 1926. Paris, pp. 265d-266.

Tables XII and XIII.

Information supplied by the Ministry of the Interior.

Table VI (years 1910-24).

Duval, Jules. *Histoire de l'Emigration européenne, asiatique et africaine au XIXe siècle*. Paris, 1862, p. 105.

Table VII (years 1853-55).

Report of the German consul at Havre to the Prussian Ministry of Foreign Affairs dated February 16, 1841. Preuss. Geh. Staatsarchiv H. H. Rep. 1, Ger. 2, Vol. IX.

Statistica della Emigrazione italiana per gli anni 1884 e 1885, pp. LXXX-LXXXII, and 1891, pp. 38-40. Rome.

Tables I and II (years 1882-91); III-V (years 1882-84, 1890 and 1891).

Report of the Select Committee of the Senate of the United States on the Sickness and
Mortality on Board Emigrant Ships. Washington, 1854, p. 40.

Table II, (years 1843-46).

Hübner, *Jahrbuch für Voll swirtschaft und Statistik*, vols. I-V. Leipzig, 1853-57

Table II (years 1847-56).

NOTES

[1]Only includes alien emigrants embarked at Havre.
[2]Refers to emigrants embarked on vessels not subject to the emigration regulations.
[3]These figures include 4,526 emigrants in 1859 and 5,176 in 1860 embarked on vessels not subject to
the emigration regulations.
[4]In this figure are included 1,894 emigrants embarked on vessels not subject to the emigration regulations, 1,146 passengers not under contract to authorized agents and the embarkation of whom could only
be ascertained after sailing, and 751 emigrants through the Port of Marseilles without distinction of nationality.
[5]Includes 1,959 emigrants embarked on vessels not subject to the emigration regulations and 816
emigrants through the Port of Marseilles without distinction of nationality.
[6]The American source gives, for the first six months of 1847, a total of 16,000, comprising 15,250
Germans, 600 Swiss and 150 French.
[7]Includes a certain number of emigrants regarded as aliens who departed from Havre on vessels not
subject to the emigration regulations as follows:

1857	4,540	1861	2,435
1858	5,035	1862	969
1859	4,526	1863	3,040
1860	5,176	1864	1,959

[8]In this year 63 children under 10 years of age who emigrated through the Port of Bordeaux are included in the figures for adults.
[9]For 2,191 emigrants age not stated.
[10]For 1,320 emigrants age not stated.
[11]Figures for Havre, Bordeaux and Marseilles in 1915 and 1916; for Bordeaux, 1917 and 1918; *in
1919, except St. Nazaire, and in the first six months Cherbourg.
[12]As from 1865 the totals of emigrants distinguished by sex are greater than those of the emigrants
distinguished by age, probably because the former totals also include emigrants whose ages were not determined. Nevertheless, the figures of "children and minors" do not correspond exactly with the sum of
persons up to 20 years.
[13]In 1877 emigrants to Algeria are included.

GERMANY

I. EMIGRATION STATISTICS
Permit Statistics.

Previous to 1871 the local authorities in various German States received instructions at different dates about keeping a continuous record of emigrants. Intending emigrants were obliged to have permits. Exact data concerning emigrants could be thus obtained when an application for a permit was made. The granting of this permit was regulated in the laws and decrees of the German States. These regulations varied in stringency and the temptation to emigrate without a permit varied accordingly. Moreover, instances of clandestine emigration came to the knowledge of the authorities in a haphazard way. For example, cases of emigration without permit were not statistically noted in Prussia until after 1855.[1]

Permits were required for intercontinental and continental emigration, as well as for migrating from one German State to another. But in a large number of German States migration to other German States, not to mention migration to non-Germanic countries, was not allowed.

The Commission entrusted in 1870 with the reorganisation of the statistics of the German Customs Union, proposed to the Council of the North German States Federation, that the arrival and departure of migrants should cease to be locally recorded. This form of statistical registration was then discontinued and in its place the central authorities prescribed the collection at all ports of embarkation of certain data bearing on intercontinental migration.[2]

II. PORT STATISTICS
German Ports.

Before 1873 port statistics of migration were collected and compiled by the port authorities; after that date the Federal Statistical Office regularly published comprehensive migration reports in the *Vierteljahrshefte zur Statistik des deutschen Reichs.*

At Bremen and Hamburg, port statistics of migration go back to 1832 and 1836 respectively.[3] They were collected under various police orders relating to the regulation of emigration. The shipping agents are bound to supply the authorities with lists of intercontinental emigrants. From 1846 onwards Hamburg, and from 1866 onwards Bremen, distinguished between citizens and aliens. But the countries of future residence of emigrant citizens were not noted in Bremen until 1866 and in Hamburg until 1871. In Bremen emigrants were defined:

[1]Compare *Zeitschrift des Königl. Preussischen Statistischen Bureaus,* 13th year, 1873, Berlin, 1873, p. 7.
[2]*Statistik des deutschen Reichs,* Bd. II.; *Vierteljahrshefte zur Statistik des deutschen Reichs* für das Jahr 1873, 1. Jahrg., II. Heft, p. 129.
[3]In the other ports, such as Stettin, data were not continuously collected and the figures are accordingly of limited value.

(a) Europeans who leave their country with the intention of settling overseas;

(b) Europeans who, mostly at an early age, leave their country with the intention of taking advantage of the more favorable labor market overseas, but contemplate returning after the lapse of a number of years;

(c) Former Europeans who, as naturalised Americans, etc., have returned, perhaps with their families, to Europe, and are about to return to their adopted country;

(d) Tourists from extra-European countries, on the way home.

In Hamburg:

(a) All passengers on emigrant vessels,[1] that is, such vessels as depart for a transatlantic destination with more than 25 passengers on board;

(b) A few persons carried by other vessels, but whom the shipping agents in their reports to the police authorities expressly describe as emigrants.[2]

Bremen, accordingly, recorded only the real emigrants among the European passengers, whilst Hamburg identified as emigrants not only a portion of the non-European passengers (as Bremen did), but also a certain percentage of ordinary European passengers.

Even for subsequent periods no uniform definition of the term "migrant" existed. In the report *"Die überseeische Auswanderung in den Jahren 1922 und 1923* (Overseas Emigration in 1922 and 1923) (vol. 307 of *Statistik des deutschen Reichs*), the following remark occurs: "The recorded number of emigrants will not coincide with the actual number, in that cabin passengers are generally excluded from the list of emigrants. An unequivocal definition of the term 'emigrant' is still a desideratum".

Aliens, like citizens, were entered in the passenger lists and included in the emigration statistics.

Under the Order of May 18, 1851, "relating to the conveyance of emigrants who proceed from Hamburg to other continents by way of intermediate ports in Europe", Hamburg has taken statistical note of *indirect emigration*, more especially via English ports. Indirect emigration via Bremen was far less important and was not recorded.[3] Tables II and III allow consequently for indirect emigration since 1852.[4]

The expert commission of 1870 deliberately excluded emigration by sea to other European countries, contending that there were extreme difficulties in distinguishing between ordinary and emigrant passengers. Notwithstanding this decision, a certain number of such passengers were

[1]The following definition of an emigrant will be found in the *Statistik des Hamburgischen Staates* (Heft 17, Hamburg, 1895): "Emigrants from Hamburg are persons who travel by a vessel authorised to carry emigrant passengers." Hence nonemigrants in the statistical sense, mainly citizen tourists and Americans returning home, were included.

[2]Prior to 1870, those who travelled on vessels not confined to carrying passengers were also registered as emigrants in Hamburg. (*Ibid.*, p. 133, note 1.)

[3]Compare Lindemann, M., "Legislation and Arrangements in favor of Emigrants at Bremen," in *Auswanderung und Auswanderungspolitik in Deutschland*, Schriften des Vereins für Sozialpolitik, Leipzig, 1892, p. 430.

[4]*Statistik des Deutschen Reichs*, 1873, pp. 132 and 123, note 1.

statistically noted during the period 1899 to 1923, in table VI (totals). We have taken no account of these figures but they could not be eliminated from tables VII and VIII.

From 1871 onwards the tables include emigration via German and foreign ports, save for table VII which is confined to data relating to German ports.

Foreign Ports (Table IV.)

For the years 1837 to 1839 data are available for Havre. In the document quoted already, and found in the *Archives Nationales* in Paris special reference is made to the fact that the alien emigrants, apart from a number of Swiss, were of German nationality. The German consul at Havre reported in 1840 that the emigrants embarking at that port (19,348) were almost exclusively of German nationality and that their number exceeded those departing through Bremen or Hamburg. Early in the '40's, German emigration through foreign ports assumed such proportions that the Prussian Ministry for Foreign Affairs on May 9, 1845, addressed a circular letter, not only to its ambassadors at Hamburg and Bremen, but also to its consuls at Havre, Rotterdam and Antwerp, instructing them to pay particular attention to German emigration and to communicate to the Ministry the most reliable statistical and other data on the subject.[1] Unfortunately only a few of the reports could be traced in the Prussian General State Archives (Preussisches Geheimes Staatsarchiv); but those that were found tend to confirm the reliability of other and more complete semi-official sources.

No data were obtained for the years 1841 and 1842. Beginning with 1843, official figures are available for the Port of Antwerp, and these relate chiefly to emigration from Germany. For the years 1844 and 1845 comprehensive statistics relating to "emigration of Germans" from the most important ports (Havre, Dunkirk, Antwerp, Dutch and English ports) will be found in Höfken. (See Historical Introduction.) For the years 1846 to 1854 Table IV, following Hübner, gives the total number of "German emigrants" leaving through foreign ports. Hübner's figures refer to Antwerp, Rotterdam, and Havre, and for certain years (1844 and 1852) to Amsterdam, but include, for 1846, Dunkirk with 1,475 and, for 1850, Genoa with 132 German emigrants. Hübner's detailed figures for the ports of France and the Netherlands, as well as for Antwerp, are reproduced but the emigrants who were not German citizens could not be deducted. However, the reports of the Prussian consular offices in these ports confirm on the whole the reliability of Hübner's figures.

In respect of English ports, Hübner presents an estimate of the number of those passengers who proceeded overseas from Hamburg via England. These are included in the emigrant totals for Hamburg, *viz.*: 500, for 1846; 1,000, for 1847; 1,000, for 1848; 2,000, for 1849; 4,000, for 1850; 5,000, for 1851; and 8,625, for 1852. But the last year

[1] The Ministry for Foreign Affairs to Ambassador Hänlein at Hamburg, Consul Carp at Rotterdam, Consul Saportes at Antwerp, and Consul Werner at Havre. (*Preussisches Geheimes Staatsarchiv*, Rep. 1, "Emigration to Overseas Countries," (II, vol. 1.)

Hübner quotes another figure (31,068), which is inserted under the heading "other ports," both German and foreign. As emigration through German ports other than Hamburg and Bremen[1] and through foreign ports other than those mentioned in the table was insignificant, the excess must be due to migration through English ports. For the year 1853 the number of emigrants who proceeded overseas indirectly from Hamburg via England was 10,511. In that year the British statistics showed 31,459 alien passengers and 20,349 whose nationality was not ascertained, the majority of both these classes being probably of German nationality. For the same year (1853) the German consul at Liverpool reports that 20,000 Germans emigrated through that port,[2] which was the most important for emigrants from Germany. So far as it is a matter of indirect travel through other continental ports to England for overseas migration, the figures are very likely in great part duplicate data.

For the following years also the emigration totals for alien passengers embarking in British ports are given in table IV, British Isles. These passengers, until the seventies, were for the most part German citizens. For the periods 1857-84 and 1890-91 detailed figures of German emigrants are available for Havre and for certain other French ports—the latter, however, being practically negligible for German emigration—in the printed *Rapports* submitted to the French Minister of the Interior. These emigrants are even classified according to the German State whence they came, such as Hesse, Bavaria, Württemberg, Prussia.

After 1871 the *Statistisches Reichsamt* published detailed figures regarding German emigrants embarking at Antwerp, also totals for Havre, Rotterdam and Amsterdam (1885 onward).

III. Statistics of Alien Seasonal Workers

With regard to the seasonal movement of workers from continental countries, official statistics were based on the reports of the Central Office for Workers (Deutsche Arbeiterzentrale). In conformity with the Decree of the Prussian Minister of the Interior, December 20, 1907, this organisation had to keep the register of alien immigrant workers. In order to obtain authorisation to remain and to find employment in the country, these workers had to be in possession of an identification card issued at the frontier by the Central Office and renewed annually.

These seasonal workers were supposed to have left Germany by December 1, but in fact a not unimportant proportion remained through the winter. Efforts were made to trace them; different identification cards were supplied to new immigrants and to those others who had not spent the winter abroad.

However, the number of certificates issued cannot be considered as conclusive, since registration did not exist in all the Federated States. In Bavaria, Hesse and in the Hanseatic towns, it was not obligatory. In

[1]Höfken quotes the following figures for Stettin: 114, for 1845; 329, for 1846; and 74, for 1847.

[2]Consul Burckhardt at Liverpool to the Minister for Foreign Affairs in Berlin on February 8, 1854.

Baden it became obligatory in 1917, while in Saxony and Württemberg it was not completely enforced until 1920. Furthermore, even in the States where it was obligatory, experience had shown that a fairly large number of foreign workers succeeded in evading it at the frontiers.

Foreign workers who crossed the frontier without being [registered had to obtain an identification card issued by the local authority of the place in which the worker was employed, but this check was always incomplete and inaccurate, owing to the lack of collaboration between employers and the local authorities, and to the subterfuges of the workers.[1]

Moreover, it is not the number of persons but the number of identity cards issued to individuals which is recorded, and workers frequently had to obtain such cards several times in the same year.

For these reasons the number of foreign workers employed in Germany was probably larger than that indicated by the figures of the Central Office. A memorandum drawn up by the Federal Statistical Office gives the statistical information supplied by the Central Office for Workers for the years 1910 to 1920. As the frontier records were incomplete, one of the tables (Appendix 9, p. 30) shows the yearly immigration and emigration of alien workers on the following basis. By deducting from the total of the identification cards issued the number of those alien workers who were in the country at the commencement of the year, the number of alien workers who immigrated during the year was obtained and by taking the difference at the close of the year between the total number of identification cards issued and the number of those holding cards who remained for the winter, the number of seasonal workers departed during the year was obtained. (*Ibid.*, p. 12.)

In 1920 the obligatory return of seasonal immigrants to their country of origin was abolished in virtually all German States. This diminished the interest of the authorities in the control of the entry of new immigrants at the frontiers.

Strictly speaking, the German continental migration statistics represent since 1921 the number of alien workers placed by the frontier offices of the German Central Office for Workers, as these statistics are directly connected with the actual migration movements, and in view of the fact that industrial immigration has almost ceased since the War and that the much reduced number of agricultural workers is recruited almost exclusively by the frontier offices of the German Central Office for Workers, the new immigration figures may be said to correspond closely to the facts.

On the other hand, the statistics based on the number of identification cards issued include also the contingents of alien workers who have been for successive years employed in the territory of the Reich and whose cards require to be renewed annually, exemption from this provision being granted in exceptional circumstances. At all events, the latter form of statistics reflects the development of the conditions created by these migrations and may be regarded as indirect migration statistics of minor accuracy.

Statistics about the number of migrants from Germany to Palestine

[1]"Continental Immigration in Germany, Control and Statistics," *International Labour Review*, 1924, No. 1; Ferenczi, *Continental Migrations of Workers in Europe.*

(1922-24), South Africa (1913-24), Argentina (1857-1924), Brazil (1828-1924), Canada (1848-74 and 1900-24), Cuba (1902-24), Mexico (1909-24), Paraguay (1881-1906), United States (1820-1924), Uruguay (1879-1921) and Australia (1902-24) will be found in the national tables for those countries. Statistics about the number of migrants returning to Germany from Argentina (1857-1924), Mexico (1911-24), United States (1908-24) and Uruguay (1879-1921) will be found in the national tables for those countries.

TABLE I.—Emigration from Germany (statistics of authorized and clandestine emigration supplied by the various States), 1836-70.

Year[1]	Volume of emigration from various German States (cf. col. 6)				Remarks
	Total	To other German States	Intercontinental, to Europe (Germany excepted) or destination unknown	Emigrated clandestinely (without a permit). Included in foregoing columns	States to which the figures in col. 2 apply.
1. 1836 1837 1838 1839 1840	2. 6,944 6,922 3,601 7,040· 7,590	3. 1,049 1,114 1,160 1,379 1,342	4. 5,895 5,808 2,441 5,661 6,248	5. 1,240 1,396 704 1,188 1,146	6. Bavaria.
1841 1842 1843 1844 1845	4,459 4,155 6,553 8,826 23,316	1,302 1,420 1,369 1,480 1,191	3,157 2,735 5,184 7,346 22,125	745 885 826 975 3,103	Bavaria, Wurttemberg, electorate of Hesse. } Baden, 1843-47 as above, including } 20,519 emigrants in Prussia[2] ∫ all[3]
1846 1847 2848 1849 1850	38,933 41,866 23,928 23,214 22,602	1,332 1,218 1,012 922 934	37,601 40,648 22,916 22,292 21,668	4,605 5,572 3,835 4,258 4,530	as above, including Baden
1851[5]	37,707	1,025	36,282	5,689	as above, including Oldenburg[4]
1852	82,179	690	81,489	7,283	as above, including } (Kingdom of) Saxony Hesse-Nassau and Sax- } 1853-55, 4,209 in all[3] ony-Weimar-Eisenach ∫
1853 1854 1855	84,754 126,282 46,244	989 1,067 1,041	83,765 125,215 45,203	8,278 9,291 8,649	as above, including Mecklenburg-Schwerin } ibid. 1856-58, 2,094[3] Mecklenburg-Strelitz ∫
1856 1857 1858 1859 1860	50,699 68,536 34,804 32,002 40,429	1,213 1,365 1,367 1,753 1,997	49,486 67,171 33,437 30,249 38,432	10,129 15,166 6,331 5,539 8,158	and Brunswick as above, including } ibid. 1859-61, 2,771[3] Hanover ∫
1861	31,700	1,842	29,458	5,394	
1862	31,734	4,794	26,940	4,948	as above, but exclusive } ibid. 1862-64, 1876 of the electorate of { emigrants[2] Hesse and Oldenburg
1863 1864 1865	33,960 39,896 54,253	5,327 5,306 4,916	28,633 34,590 49,337	5,407 7,256 10,098	as above, but exclusive of Hesse-Nassau
1866 1867 1868 1869 1870	48,450 78,064 77,120 75,915 57,629	3,948 4,957 3,832 4,618 8,024	44,502 73,107 73,288 71,297 49,605	10,739 18,351 19,834 19,870 15,278	as above, but exclusive of Weimar-Eisenach and including (Kingdom of) Saxony and (since 1867) Hesse-Nassau (in Prussia)

For reference notes see page 708.

TABLE II.—EMIGRATION OF CITIZENS AND ALIENS THROUGH GERMAN PORTS (HAMBURG AND BREMEN), 1832-70.

Year	Total	Citizens	Aliens	Year	Total	Citizens	Aliens
1832[6]	10,344	. . . . .	. . . . .	1852	87,586	82,461	5,125
1833[6]	8,891	. . . . .	. . . . .	1853	87,760	81,523	6,237
1834[6]	13,086	. . . . .	. . . . .	1854	127,694	116,190	11,504
1835[6]	6,185	. . . . .	. . . . .	1855	50,202	45,241	4,961
1836	17,007	. . . . .	. . . . .	1856	62,720	58,713	4,007
1837	17,514	. . . . .	. . . . .	1857	81,014	75,927	5,087
1838	10,267	. . . . .	. . . . .	1858	42,976	38,438	4,538
1839	13,981	. . . . .	. . . . .	1859	35,253	31,714	3,539
1840	14,526	. . . . .	. . . .	1860	46,511	42,136	4,375
1841	11,001	. . . . .	. . . .	1861	30,939	27,362	3,577
1842	14,234	. . . . .	. . . . .	1862	35,264	28,778	6,486
1843	11,683	. . . . .	. . . . .	1863	42,856	36,083	6,773
1844	21,631	. . . . .	. . . . .	1864	52,756	47,802	4,954
1845	34,210	. . . . .	. . . . .	1865	87,549	77,648	9,901
1846	37,229	. . . . .	. . . . .	1866	106,657	84,403	22,254
1847	41,310	. . . . .	. . . . .	1867	116,860	88,725	28,135
1848	36,532	. . . . .	. . . . .	1868	116,483	96,025	20,458
1849	34,249	. . . . .	. . . . .	1869	110,813	88,529	22,284
1850	33,206	. . . . .	. . . . .	1870	79,337	59,100	20,237
1851	49,772	49,214	558	. . . .	. . . . . .	. . . . .	. . . . .

For reference notes see page 708.

TABLE IIa.—EMIGRATION THROUGH BREMEN (DIRECT) AND THROUGH HAMBURG (DIRECT AND INDIRECT), 1832-1870.

Year	Through Bremen	Through Hamburg			Direct emigration through Bremen and and Hamburg
		Total	Direct	Indirect	
1832	10,344	. . . . .	. . . . .	. . . . .	10,344
1833	8,891	. . . . .	. . . . .	. . . . .	8,891
1834	13,086	. . . . .	. . . . .	. . . . .	13,086
1835	6,185	. . . . .	. . . . .	. . . . .	6,185
1836	14,137	2,870	2,870	. . . . .	17,007
1837	15,087	2,427	2,427	. . . . .	17,514
1838	9,312	955	955	. . . . .	10,267
1839	12,412	1,569	1,569	. . . . .	13,981
1840	12,806	1,720	1,407	313	14,213
1841	9,594	1,407	1,377	30	10,971
1842	13,619	615	615	. . . . .	14,234
1843	9,927	1,756	1,756	. . . . .	11,683
1844	19,857	1,774	1,774	. . . . .	21,631
1845	31,822	2,388	2,388	. . . . .	34,210
1846	32,372	4,857	4,857	. . . . .	37,229
1847	33,682	7,628	7,628	. . . . .	41,310
1848	29,947	6,585	6,585	. . . . .	36,532
1849	28,629	5,620	5,620	. . . . .	34,249
1850	25,776	7,430	7,430	. . . . .	33,206
1851	37,493	12,279	12,279	. . . . .	49,772
1852	58,551	29,035	21,916	7,119	80,467
1853	58,111	29,457	18,946	10,511	77,057
1854	76,875	50,819	32,310	18,509	109,185
1855	31,550	18,652	15,663	2,989	47,213
1856	36,517	26,203	24,286	1,917	60,803
1857	49,448	31,566	28,894	2,672	78,342
1858	23,177	19,799	18,822	977	41,999
1859	22,011	13,242	12,753	489	34,764
1860	30,296	16,215	14,913	1,302	45,209
1861	16,540	14,399	13,724	675	30,264
1862	15,187	20,077	18,560	1,517	33,747
1863	18,175	24,681	22,060	2,621	40,235
1864	27,701	25,055	19,957	5,098	47,658
1865	44,665	42,884	37,212	5,672	81,877
1866	61,877	44,780	39,040	5,740	100,917
1867	73,971	42,889	38,214	4,675	112,185
1868	66,433	50,050	43,628	6,422	110,061
1869	63,519	47,294	41,424	5,870	104,943
1870	46,781	32,556	27,442	5,114	74,223

TABLE III.—EMIGRATION VIA HAMBURG AND BREMEN, BY COUNTRY OF DESTINATION, 1832-70.

Year	Total	Country		Australia	Other countries
		America			
		Via Bremen	Via Hamburg		
1832	10,344[6]	.....	......	.....	...
1833	8,891[6]	.....	.....	.....	...
1834	13,086[6]	.....	.....	.....	...
1835	6,185[6]	.....	.....	.....	...
1836	17,007	11,600	2,870	.....[7]	...[7]
1837	17,514	14,372	2,427	.....[7]	...[7]
1838	10,267	9,312	539	345[7]	71[7]
1839	13,981	12,421	1,569	.....[7]	...[7]
1840	14,526	12,650	1,720	.....[7]	...[7]
1841	11,001	9,501	1,134	258[7]	15[7]
1842	14,234	13,563	495	120[7]	...[7]
1843	11,683	9,844	1,756	.....[7]	...[7]
1844	21,631	19,145	1,774	.....[7]	...[7]
1845	34,210	31,358	2,388	.....[7]	...[7]
1846	37,229	31,607	4,857	.....[7]	...[7]
1847	41,310	40,422		888	...
1848	36,532	34,881		1,651	...
1849	34,249	32,472		1,754	23
1850	33,206[8]	32,545		518	8
1851	49,772[8]	48,796		788	4
1852	87,586[8]	78,684		1,195	17
1853	87,568[9]	85,700		1,865	26
1854	127,694	122,760		4,907	27
1855	50,202	47,034		3,119	49
1856	62,720	60,739		1,891	90
1857	81,014	78,745		2,179	90
1858	42,976	38,688		1,650	2,638
1859	35,253	33,987		1,060	206
1860	46,511	45,507		440	564
1861	30,939	29,539		766	634
1862	35,264	34,163		938	163
1863	42,856	40,247		2,516	93
1864	52,756	52,032		650	74
1865	87,549	84,687		2,834	28
1866	106,657	106,031		573	53
1867	116,860[9]	116,607		144	65
1868	116,483	49,851[7]		151[7]	48[7]
1869	110,813	47,188[7]		73[7]	33[7]
1870	79,337	31,285[7]		1,259[7]	12[7]

For reference notes see page 708.

TABLE IIIa.—DIRECT EMIGRATION THROUGH HAMBURG*, BY COUNTRY OF DESTINATION, 1836-70.

Year	Total	United States	Rest of North America	Mexico, Central America, West Indies	Argentina	Brazil	Chile	Rest of South America	Africa	Asia	Australia
1836	2,870	2,870									
1837	2,427	2,177				250					
1838	955	484				55			71		
1839	1,569	1,415				154					345
1840	1,407	1,407		20							
1841	1,377	1,071									
1842	615	495				13			15		258
1843	1,756	1,756									120
1844	1,774	1,774									
1845	2,388	2,388									
1846	4,857	3,960	399			498					
1847	7,628	4,857	1,431			758					
1848	6,585	5,439	775								1,069
1849	5,620	4,741	315			37					1,468
1850	7,430	3,800	593	190		240	215				368
1851	12,279	5,879	647	128		1,950	245				530
1852	21,916	8,533	3,508	49	23	2,047	581	43	20		1,195
1853	18,969	13,886	2,104	81	76	546	326	57	17	6	1,825
1854	32,310	14,027	4,530	42	66	1,395	263	67	16	10	4,880
1855	15,663	21,001	1,586	84	80	1,978	192	102	29	12	2,996
1856	24,293	8,708	3,195	158	81	1,529	703	101	52	42	1,747
1857	28,894	16,782	4,208	21	41	1,772	332	40	2,580	8	1,233
1858	18,822	20,949	749	17	23	3,431	160	37	163	8	969
1859	12,753	10,823	906	27	64	1,757	151	35	533	8	1,041
1860	14,913	8,650	536	17	45	897	167	11	586	13	436
1861	13,724	9,370	1,791	20	52	1,017	107	13	102	18	762
1862	18,560	12,205	2,019	14	47	1,025	74	12	33	21	934
1863	22,060	14,300	2,678	14	28	847	199	14	32	15	2,494
1864	19,957	15,721	1,633	248	168	447	83	47		15	641
1865	37,212	17,050	1,396	224	199	414	96	48	33	11	2,832
1866	39,040	32,000	2,447	17	96	417	41	40	41	8	549
1867	38,170	35,074	2,638		18	1,155	41	7	47	3	143
1868	43,628	33,996	2,669	6	71	3,425	30	73	23	1	151
1869	41,424	37,274	369	7	8	3,475	62	5	3	10	73
1870	27,442	24,874	97			1,169	18			9	1,259

*The indirect emigrants through Hamburg, included in table IIa, proceeded mainly to the United States; also 109 in 1853 and 1,621 in 1854 to British North America, 4 in 1854 to Argentina, 1 in 1858 and 9 in 1864 to Africa, and 25 in 1853, 27 in 1854, 14 in 1855, 49 in 1856, 6 in 1858, 13 in 1859, and 4 in 1860 to Australia. The countries of destination of the indirect emigrants for the year 1852 are unknown

TABLE IV.—EMIGRATION OF CITIZENS THROUGH GERMAN AND FOREIGN PORTS, 1844-54.

Year	Total	German ports* Hamburg and Bremen	Foreign ports
1844	45,655	21,631	24,024
1845	73,259	34,210	39,049
1846	93,752	37,229	56,523
1847	108,457	41,310	67,147
1848	80,900	36,532	44,368
1849	87,102	34,249	52,853
1850	78,549	33,206	45,343
1851	105,691	49,214	56,477
1852	154,962	82,461	72,501
1853	137,272	81,523	55,749
1854	240,427	116,190	124,237

*See table II.

TABLE V.—DISTRIBUTION OF EMIGRANTS VIA HAMBURG, BY SEX AND AGE, 1855-70.

Year	Total	Details of sex and age available.				
		Total	Males	Females	Up to 10 years	Over 10 years
1855	18,652	18,215	10,981	7,234	3,749	14,466
1856	26,203	25,739	14,973	10,766	5,431	20,308
1857	31,566	31,240	17,730	13,510	6,465	24,775
1858	19,799	19,450	11,089	8,361	4,357	15,093
1859	13,242	13,023	7,947	5,076	2,248	10,775
1860	16,215	15,992	9,693	6,299	2,568	13,424
1861	14,399	14,215	8,414	5,801	2,994	11,221
1862	20,077	19,890	11,559	8,331	4,305	15,585
1863	24,681	24,487	14,824	9,663	5,331	19,156
1864	25,055	24,842	15,140	9,702	5,009	19,833
1865	42,884	42,550	26,318	16,232	8,491	34,059
1866	44,780	44,367	26,919	17,448	8,669	35,698
1867	42,889	42,547	25,131	17,416	8,783	33,764
1868	50,050	49,927	29,488	20,439	11,148	38,779
1869	47,294	47,087	28,137	18,950	9,915	37,172
1870	32,556	32,506	19,230	13,276	7,027	25,479

TABLE VI.—VOLUME OF INTERCONTINENTAL EMIGRATION OF CITIZENS, 1871-1924.

Year	Total	Through German ports	Through foreign ports		
			Antwerp	Rotterdam and Amsterdam	French ports
1871	76,224	75,912	. . . . .	. . . . .	312
1872	128,152	124,534	1,116	. . . . .	2,502
1873	110,438	100,040	3,598	. . . . .	6,800
1874	47,671	43,536	1,576	. . . . .	2,559
1875	32,329	28,707	2,066	. . . . .	1,556
1876	29,644	23,880	4,488	. . . . .	1,276
1877	22,898	20,128	1,836	. . . .	934
1878	25,627	23,241	976	. . . . .	1,410
1879	35,888	29,238	4,089	. . . . .	2,561
1880	117,097	94,966	11,224	. . . . .	10,907
1881	220,902	184,369	26,178	. . . . .	10,355
1882	203,585	169,216	24,653	. . . . .	9,716
1883	173,616	143,951	22,168	. . . . .	7,497
1884	149,065	126,511	17,075	. . . . .	5,479
1885	110,119	88,900	14,742	3,596	2,881
1886	83,225	66,647	10,040	3,188	3,350
1887	104,787	79,473	16,132	4,107	5,075
1888	103,951	80,671	14,057	3,787	5,436
1889	96,070	74,101	12,657	3,501	5,811
1890	97,103	74,820	13,765	3,340	5,178
1891	120,089	93,145	19,069	3,178	4,697
1892	116,339	90,183	17,554	4,471	4,131
1893	87,677	71,008	11,532	1,918	3,219
1894	40,964	33,566	4,158	1,454	1,786
1895	37,498	29,226	4,924	1,407	1,941
1896	33,824	25,771	5,199	1,144	1,710
1897	24,631	18,801	3,769	650	1,411
1898	22,221	17,173	3,064	600	1,384
1899	24,323[10]	19,786	2,870	1,008	654
1900	22,309[10]	16,690	3,305	1,949	286
1901	22,073[10]	16,467	3,307	1,903	286
1902	32,098	23,530	5,792	2,278	498
1903	36,310	27,614	5,457	2,579	660
1904	27,984	22,018	4,215	1,454	297
1905	28,075	21,966	4,337	1,519	253
1906	31,074	25,474	3,972	1,379	249
1907	31,696	26,380	3,313	1,770	233
1908	19,883	16,722	1,774	1,300	87
1909	24,921	18,315	1,952	4,536	118
1910	25,531	21,409	1,863	2,108	151
1911	22,690	18,706	1,345	2,452	187
1912	18,545	13,734	1,433	3,261	117
1913	25,843	18,440	1,662	5,601	140
1914	11,803	9,224	654	1,840	85
1915	528	. . . . .	. . . . .	528	. . . . .
1916	326	. . . . .	. . . . .	326	. . . . .
1917	9	. . . . .	. . . . .	9	. . . . .
1918	. . . . .	. . . . .	. . . . .	. . . . .	. . . . .
1919	3,144	. . . . .	. . . . .	3,144	. . . . .
1920	8,458	869	. . . . .	7,589	. . . . .
1921	23,451	18,184	197	5,070	. . . . .
1922	36,527	35,887	. . . . .	640	. . . . .
1923	115,416	113,812	. . . . .	1,604	. . . . .
1924	58,328[11]	56,058	448	1,800	. . . . .

For reference notes see page 708.

TABLE VII.—DISTRIBUTION OF EMIGRANT CITIZENS, BY SEX AND AGE, 1871-1924.

Year	Total	Males	Females	Sex not distinguished	Under 14 years[12]		14-21 years[12]		21-50 years[12]		50 years and over		Age not stated		Sex unknown
					M.	F.	M.	F.	M.	F.	M.	F.	M.	F.	
1871	76,224	41,685	34,227	312											312
1872	128,152	70,787[13]	54,863[13]	2,502	3,525	3,670	10,984	9,856	56,334	41,385					2,502
1873	110,438	56,679[13]	46,959[13]	6,800	3,234	3,149	9,717	9,350	43,883	34,565					6,800
1874	47,671	24,194[13]	20,918[13]	2,559	1,258	1,217	4,246	4,104	18,857	15,702					2,559
1875	32,329	16,946[13]	13,827[13]	1,556	690	714	2,735	2,486	13,653	10,698			1	1	1,556
1876	29,644	16,044[13]	12,035[13]	1,565	689	691	2,443	2,357	13,054	9,063			22	25	1,565
1877	22,898	12,895[13]	9,069[13]	934	482	470	1,864	1,777	10,619	6,830			3	2	934
1878	25,627	14,409[13]	9,808[13]	1,410	555	526	1,994	1,890	11,984	7,446			41	19	1,410
1879	35,888	20,106	13,221	2,561	895	873	2,590	2,406	16,580	9,923			53	25	2,561
1880	117,097	63,778	42,412	10,907	3,575	3,421	9,077	8,693	51,073	30,273			53	25	10,907
1881	220,902	123,235	87,312	10,355	7,863	7,145	22,159	19,943	93,094	60,152			119	72	10,355
1882	203,585	110,652	83,035	9,898	6,310	6,301	18,925	17,673	85,309	59,003			108	58	9,898
1883	173,616	93,800	72,319	7,497	5,060	4,722	15,841	15,062	72,780	52,495			119	40	7,497
1884	149,065	81,089	62,497	5,479	20,821	19,052	15,150	12,727	41,089	26,694	3,905	3,978	124	46	5,479
1885	110,119	55,827	47,815	6,477	14,223	13,678	10,733	10,322	27,272	20,265	3,517	3,500	82	50	6,477
1886	83,225	41,898	34,789	6,538	9,464	9,223	8,199	7,631	21,776	15,378	2,453	2,557	6		6,538
1887	104,787	55,192	43,875	5,720	11,600	11,216	12,493[14]	10,767[14]	28,225	18,823	2,868	3,069	292		5,720
1888	103,951	54,243	44,264	5,444	12,181	11,661	10,499	10,036	28,428	19,260		2,934	154	373	5,444
1889	96,070	49,497	40,686	5,887	11,247	10,463	10,013	9,300	25,353	17,975	2,730	2,810	45	138	5,887
1890	97,103	50,019	40,906	5,178	11,173	10,788	9,758	9,633	26,258	18,389	2,785		23	27	5,178
1891	120,089	62,958	52,434	4,697	15,055	14,387	11,325	11,511	33,234	22,848	3,301	3,069	23	17	4,697
1892	116,339	61,882	49,512	4,945	14,343	13,441	11,485	10,953	32,975	21,844	3,056	3,268	3	6	4,945
1893	87,677	47,272	36,706	3,699	9,317	8,748	9,319	8,899	26,117	16,563	2,516	2,496	11		3,699
1894	40,964	20,482	18,346	2,136	3,755	3,754	4,271	4,856	11,138	8,236	1,307	1,499	12	1	2,136
1895	37,498	17,498	16,298	2,245	3,088	2,966	3,853	4,453	10,939	7,683	1,066	1,191	4	5	2,245
1896	33,824	17,549	14,513	1,762	2,719	2,746	3,470	4,042	10,482	6,668	874	1,055	3	2	1,762
1897	24,631	12,972	10,248	1,411	1,831	1,741	2,494	2,770	7,931	4,921	713	816	2		1,411
1898	22,221	11,667	9,170	1,384	1,568	1,568	2,044	2,352	7,417	4,483	636	767	9		1,384
1899	24,323	12,899	10,215	1,209	1,846	1,777	2,380	2,439	7,962	5,026	711	821	18	2	1,209
1900	22,309	11,114	9,257	1,938	1,816	1,887	2,249	2,134	6,465	4,204		725	15	4	1,938
1901	22,073	11,557	8,635	1,881	2,004	1,930	2,142	2,930	6,869	3,919	575	648	11	3	1,881
1902	32,098	17,608	12,230	2,260	3,215	3,122	2,899	2,936	10,854	5,412	625	763	13		2,260
1903	36,310	19,543	14,199	2,568	3,884	3,781	3,205	2,547	11,745	6,605	698	877	10		2,568
1904	27,984	15,244	11,302	1,438	2,755	2,629	2,795	2,493	9,063	5,362	618	760	24	4	1,438
1905	28,075	15,439	11,127	1,509	2,627	2,582	2,569	2,676	9,651	5,302	582	750	22	3	1,509
1906	31,074	17,179	12,541	1,354	3,133	3,028	2,866	2,804	10,523	6,044	633	790			1,354
1907	31,696	17,288	12,661	1,747	3,134	2,935	2,781	1,739	10,736	6,205	615	716			1,747
1908	19,883	10,707	8,205	971	1,653	1,607	1,679	1,760	6,617	4,155	567	566	191	138	971
1909	24,921	13,561	9,093	2,267	1,761	1,684	1,852	1,760	8,056	4,168	565	539	1,327	942	2,267

For reference notes see page 708.

TABLE VII.—DISTRIBUTION OF EMIGRANT CITIZENS, BY SEX AND AGE, 1871-1924 (continued).

Year	Total	Males	Females	Sex not distinguished	Under 14 years[2]		14-21 years[2]		21-50 years[2]		50 years and over		Age not stated		Sex unknown
					M.	F.	M.	F.	M.	F.	M.	F.	M.	F.	
1910	25,531	14,581	9,522	1,428	2,130	1,950	2,201	2,075	9,197	4,703	623	542	428	252	1,428
1911	22,690	12,876	8,519	1,295	1,643	1,660	1,902	1,784	8,016	4,175	578	480	737	420	1,295
1912	18,545	10,387	6,289	1,869	1,510	1,494	1,517	1,131	6,185	2,883	281	283	894	498	1,869
1913	25,843	13,578	9,175	3,090	2,083	1,977	1,683	1,672	7,968	4,083	402	374	1,442	1,069	3,090
1914	11,803	6,505	4,132	1,166	920	894	953	736	4,038	1,998	206	218	388	286	1,166
1915	528			528											528
1916	326			326											326
1917	9			9											9
1918															
1919	3,144			3,144											3,144
1920	8,458	4,434	2,527	1,497	97	92	74	44	297	194	41	30	3,925	2,167	1,497
1921	23,451	12,750	9,399	1,302	1,672	1,664	1,870	1,303	5,661	4,382	848	784	2,699	1,266	1,302
1922	36,527	19,389	16,766	372	2,076	2,082	3,261	3,150	12,536	10,033	1,323	1,426	193	75	372
1923	115,416	66,032	48,227	1,157	5,904	5,880	13,499	10,511	44,174	29,154	2,157	2,533	298	149	157
1924	58,328	35,114	22,354	860	5,045	4,839	6,160	2,861	21,805	13,025	1,324	1,172	780	457	860

For reference notes see page 708.

TABLE VIII.—EMIGRATION OF CITIZENS, BY COUNTRY OF DESTINATION, 1871-1924.

Year	Grand total	Europe	North America			South America						America Total	Africa	Asia	Australia	Destination unknown (emigrants through French ports)
			British North America	United States	Mexico, Central America and the West Indies	Brazil	Uruguay	Argentina	Chile	Peru	Other South American States	Total				
1871	76,224	....	9	73,816	58	920	....	62	100	35	66	75,066	18	11	817	312
1872	128,152	....	690	119,780	99	3,232	....	160	61	45	397	124,464	2	12	1,172	2,502
1873	110,438	....	49	96,641	60	5,048	7	232	92	78	87	102,294	4	9	1,331	6,800
1874	47,671	....	138	42,492	107	1,019	....	165	115	60	78	44,174	5	33	900	2,559
1875	32,329	....	38	27,834	73	1,387	....	126	113	75	63	29,709	1	37	1,026	1,556
1876	29,644	....	11	22,767	43	3,432	....	104	100	34	566	27,057	54	31	1,226	1,276
1877	22,898	....	11	18,240	268	1,069	....	87	79	53	70	19,877	750	31	1,306	934
1878	25,627	....	89	20,373	96	1,048	....	201	94	82	72	22,055	394	50	1,718	1,410
1879	35,888	....	44	30,808	76	1,630	....	216	113	48	64	32,999	23	31	274	2,561
1880	117,097	....	222	103,115	119	2,119	....	189	122	12	97	105,995	27	36	132	10,907
1881	220,902	....	286	206,189	114	2,102	....	362	210	38	152	209,453	314	35	745	10,355
1882	203,585	....	383	189,373	104	1,286	....	599	311	39	152	192,247	335	40	1,247	9,716
1883	173,616	....	591	159,894	84	1,583	....	668	186	42	145	163,193	772	50	2,104	7,497
1884	149,065	....	728	139,339	59	1,253	1	692	306	59	219	142,655	230	35	666	5,479
1885	110,119	....	692	102,224	63	1,713	10	726	682	56	111	106,268	294	72	604	2,881
1886	83,225	....	330	75,591	68	2,045	....	637	206	25	122	79,034	191	116	534	3,350
1887	104,787	....	270	95,976	98	1,152	....	908	135	17	127	98,683	302	227	500	5,075
1888	103,951	....	199	94,364	93	1,129	....	1,225	157	29	219	97,415	331	230	539	5,436
1889	96,070	....	88	84,424	137	2,412	....	1,519	218	41	240	89,079	422	262	496	5,811
1890	97,103	....	307	89,762	116	4,117	26	1,033	260	16	356	95,993	471	165	474	....
1891	120,089	....	976	113,046	170	3,779	16	665	126	10	167	118,955	599	97	438	....
1892	116,339	....	1,577	111,806	129	796	11	699	234	11	104	115,367	476	120	376	....
1893	87,677	....	6,136	78,249	93	1,173	14	684	210	29	96	86,684	586	146	261	....
1894	40,964	....	1,490	35,902	117	1,288	9	751	131	14	126	39,828	760	151	225	....
1895	37,498	....	1,100	32,503	124	1,405	3	795	232	8	97	36,267	886	134	211	....
1896	33,824	....	634	29,007	148	1,001	17	745	498	6	104	32,160	1,346	144	174	....
1897	24,631	....	539	20,346	155	936	2	642	314	25	88	23,047	1,115	145	324	....
1898	22,221	....	208	18,563	162	821	....	629	180	33	90	20,731[15]	1,104	223	163	....
1899	24,323	1,626	126	19,805	162	896	35	521	166	22	36	21,824[15]	554	178	141	....
1900	22,309	1,388	144	19,703	33	364	15	275	1	....	6	20,541	183	1	196	....

For reference notes see page 708.

TABLE VIII.—EMIGRATION OF CITIZENS, BY COUNTRY OF DESTINATION, 1871-1924 (continued).

Year	Grand total	Europe	North America: British North America	North America: United States	Mexico, Central America and the West Indies	America — South America: Brazil	Uruguay	Argentina	Chile	Peru	Other South American States	Total	Africa	Asia	Australia	Destination unknown (emigrants through French ports)
1901	22,073	1,199	11	19,912	26	402	9	231	1	…	4	20,596	55	6	217	…
1902	32,098	1,183	183	29,211	2	807	20	316	19	…	6	30,564	114	2	235	…
1903	36,310	857	480	33,649	2	693	17	232	1	…	…	35,074	226	…	153	…
1904	27,984	719	332	26,085	…	355	4	312	…	…	…	27,088	78	2	97	…
1905	28,075	672	243	26,005	1	333	7	674	…	…	…	27,262	57	…	84	…
1906	31,074	310	540	29,226	2	182	10	686	…	…	1	30,645	33	…	86	…
1907	31,696	153	333	30,431	…	167	5	404	…	…	…	31,343	37	1	163	…
1908	19,883	157	260	17,951	…	326	3	515	…	…	462	19,517	33	…	175	…
1909	24,921	164	367	19,930	…	367	10	448	…	…	3,431	24,553	26	…	178	…
1910	25,531	77	460	22,773	…	353	5	793	…	…	926	25,310	16	…	128	…
1911	22,690	98	511	18,900	…	363	6	990	…	…	1,558	22,328	18	…	246	…
1912	18,545	90	891	13,706	…	225	59	1,278	…	…	1,970	18,129	4	…	322	…
1913	25,843	68	1,306	19,124	…	140	24	1,085	…	…	3,705	25,384	32	…	359	…
1914	11,803	51	580	9,614	…	77	2	281	…	…	958[16]	11,512	8	…	232	…
1915	528	…	…	467	…	…	…	…	…	…	61[16]	528	…	…	…	…
1916	326	…	…	291	…	…	…	…	…	…	35[16]	326	…	…	…	…
1917	9	…	…	6	…	…	…	…	…	…	3[16]	9	…	…	…	…
1918	…	…	…	…	…	…	…	…	…	…	…	…	…	…	…	…
1919	3,144	…	…	213	…	…	…	…	…	…	2,931[16]	3,144	…	…	…	…
1920	8,458	1	…	1,429	231	131	…	588	…	…	6,078	8,457	…	…	…	…
1921	23,451	770	…	9,080	992	6,872	1	2,056	…	…	3,289	22,290	391	…	…	…
1922	36,527	57	3	24,605	253	5,261	7	4,996	35	15	673	35,848	607	15	…	…
1923	115,416	328	768	92,808	408	8,920	82	9,640	109	18	1,524	114,277	635	125	51	…
1924	58,328	…	2,221	22,475	716	21,016	420	8,125	133	21	2,138	57,265	1,000	60	3	…

For reference notes see page 708.

TABLE IX.—DISTRIBUTION OF EMIGRANT CITIZENS, BY OCCUPATION AND SEX, 1899-1924.

Year	Total	Agriculture and forestry		Mining, etc., industry, building trade		Transport, commerce, etc.		Domestic service		Wage-earners, various		Liberal professions, etc.		No occupation or not specified		No particulars available		Sex unknown
		Males	Females	Males	Females	Males	Females	Males	Females	Males	Females	Males	Females	Males	Females	Males	Females	
1899	24,323	3,022	1,238	3,455	816	3,936	498	63	290	177	45	521	163	1,594	7,093	131	72	1,209
1900	22,309	3,796	3,457	3,789	1,864	2,333	808	60	1,313	166	186	444	169	526	1,460			1,938
1901	22,073	4,219	3,319	4,451	1,904	2,049	625	77	2,139	259	189	312	110	190	349			1,881
1902	32,098	6,542	5,307	7,615	3,107	2,424	705	136	2,281	340	260	326	146	225	424			2,260
1903	36,310	7,489	6,055	8,162	3,679	2,962	1,080	198	2,552	185	142	339	216	208	475			2,568
1904	27,984	5,633	4,970	5,759	2,451	3,075	969	116	2,262	150	100	331	139	180	411			1,438
1905	28,075	5,430	4,380	6,006	2,676	3,066	1,205	136	2,156	163	124	470	316	168	270			1,509
1906	31,074	5,981	5,105	7,198	2,923	2,968	1,010	121	2,666	92	82	540	279	279	476			1,354
1907	31,696	5,654	5,266	7,332	2,903	3,071	975	165	2,560	132	84	560	263	374	610			1,747
1908	19,883	2,899	2,905	4,100	1,756	2,536	788	92	1,936	69	55	585	263	235	364	191	138	971
1909	24,921	3,196	2,574	5,445	2,183	2,496	633	109	1,879	109	58	609	318	270	506	1,327	942	2,267
1910	25,531	4,159	2,913	6,029	2,300	2,748	847	130	1,958	95	60	606	366	386	826	428	252	1,428
1911	22,690	3,506	2,188	4,915	1,969	2,644	813	79	1,975	80	49	613	391	302	714	737	420	1,295
1912	18,545	3,209	1,901	4,138	1,763	1,442	486	101	1,229	219	113	283	162	101	137	894	498	1,869
1913	25,843	4,171	2,469	5,489	2,468	1,868	683	90	1,867	142	58	182	219	194	342	1,442	1,069	3,090
1914	11,803	1,913	1,225	2,763	1,042	1,076	333	62	920	95	55	125	135	83	136	388	286	1,166
1915	528																	528
1916	326																	326
1917	9																	9
1918																		
1919	3,144																	3,144
1920	8,458	217	137	135	77	90	48	85	49	12	10	40	22	15	17	3,925	2,167	1,497
1921	23,451	4,483	3,102	2,233	1,044	1,953	973	332	708	312	149	444	338	541	1,819	2,699	1,266	1,302
1922	36,527	4,612	3,486	7,400	4,894	3,854	2,912	249	1,956	824	694	1,062	1,103	1,112	1,646	193	75	372
1923	115,416	11,805	5,098	34,869	12,392	11,397	4,801	710	11,315	2,186	853	2,400	2,054	2,828	11,565	298	149	1,157
1924	58,328	13,525	5,058	12,719	5,458	4,755	2,049		2,691			904	928	1,721	5,713	780	457	860

TABLE X.—Volume of alien intercontinental transit migration (outgoing movement), 1871-1924.

Year	Total	Through Bremen	Through Hamburg	Through other German ports
1871	26,828	14,858	11,970	...
1872	30,290	13,499	16,791	...
1873	32,377	14,633	17,744	...
1874	32,144	12,726	19,350	68
1875	27,874	11,890	15,984	...
1876	26,720	10,693	16,027	...
1877	21,696	9,851	11,845	...
1878	23,130	10,154	12,976	...
1879	22,525	10,826	11,699	...
1880	54,803	28,703	26,100	...
1881	62,967	24,257	38,706	4
1882	62,524	20,081	42,057	386
1883	57,363	23,556	33,799	8
1884	68,986	27,345	41,618	23
1885	66,247	31,645	34,068	534
1886	99,827	36,585	62,919	323
1887	92,989	44,186	48,359	444
1888	106,386	42,526	63,081	779
1889	106,808	55,093	51,285	430
1890	168,471	93,345	74,421	705
1891	196,080	80,148	112,658	3,274
1892	151,412	69,521	80,676	1,215
1893	98,288	69,548	28,362	378
1894	52,760	30,230	22,530	...
1895	95,074	53,832	41,100	142
1896	95,803	54,492	40,424	887
1897	64,419	37,239	26,247	933
1898	83,805	51,660	31,712	433
1899	130,646	77,092	53,554	...
1900	160,129	86,888	73,241	...
1901	166,626	101,463	65,163	...
1902	221,432	129,369	92,063	...
1903	268,227	158,681	109,546	...
1904	219,096	119,352	99,744	...
1905	284,787	172,011	112,776	...
1906	325,990	191,690	134,300	...
1907	363,615	216,883	146,732	...
1908	106,499	64,504	41,995	...
1909	239,637	132,455	107,182	...
1910	254,618	143,983	110,635	...
1911	183,233	102,845	80,388	...
1912	290,386	161,977	128,409	...
1913	413,857	229,854	184,003	...
1914	150,416	82,334	68,030	52
1915	......	.....	.....	...
1916	......	.....	.....	...
1917	......	.....	.....	...
1918	......	.....	.....	...
1919	......	.....	.....	...
1920	1,975	1,966	9	...
1921	19,422	6,003	13,414	5
1922	38,393	12,495	25,896	2
1923	51,934	18,868	33,066	...
1924	18,667	5,709	12,958	...

TABLE XI.—ALIEN EMIGRATION THROUGH GERMAN PORTS, BY COUNTRY OF ORIGIN, 1871-1924.

Year	Total	Russia	Norway, Sweden and Denmark	Great Britain	Netherlands	Belgium, Luxemburg and France	Spain and Portugal	Italy	Switzerland	Austria	Hungary	Rumania	Turkey in Europe	Other Balkan States	America — United States[17]	America — Other countries	Africa	Asia	Australia	Countries not distinguished and other non-European countries[17]
1871	26,828	2,480	2,569	104	75	81	1	63	3,050	9,500	9,500	2	…	2	8,467	…	…	…	…	434
1872	30,290	5,892	3,332	57	47	54	8	69	1,414	9,498	…	…	35	…	9,420	…	…	…	…	464
1873	32,377	6,038	3,100	29	29	31	6	78	716	11,228	…	…	62	…	10,609	…	…	…	…	451
1874	32,144	9,264	2,391	38	27	48	6	110	345	9,919	…	…	19	…	9,408	…	…	…	…	569
1875	27,874	6,752	1,691	36	31	28	1	327	184	7,659	…	…	30	…	10,666	…	…	…	…	469
1876	26,720	7,636	1,221	40	18	25	9	170	141	8,434	…	…	26	…	8,533	…	…	…	…	467
1877	21,696	5,005	1,219	29	16	6	2	42	192	7,016	…	…	36	…	7,637	…	…	…	…	496
1878	23,130	6,584	2,050	37	26	11	1	30	196	5,620	…	…	17	…	8,050	…	…	…	…	508
1879	22,525	3,138	3,681	36	24	12	3	23	90	8,154	…	15	14	2	6,829	…	…	…	…	506
1880	54,803	5,162	12,709	66	21	23	2	32	148	28,639	…	16	2	…	7,432	…	…	…	…	549
1881	62,967	9,409	9,725	68	49	39	4	110	269	35,517	…	64	3	2	7,187	…	…	…	…	521
1882	62,524	11,601	7,144	82	34	40	10	52	206	34,932	…	171	2	3	7,675	…	…	…	…	572
1883	57,363	7,619	6,729	61	40	64	1	44	253	33,746	…	157	17	…	8,114	…	…	…	…	523
1884	68,986	17,423	4,945	45	69	54	7	101	213	33,767	…	1,071	25	10	10,536	…	…	…	…	719
1885	66,247	18,763	3,155	41	71	40	327	70	379	28,585	…	570	44	19	13,581	…	…	…	…	628
1886	99,827	33,783	5,284	63	67	56	18	69	213	44,303	…	3,144	…	12	11,936	…	…	…	…	828
1887	92,989	29,554	10,019	54	111	50	14	134	244	19,647	18,335	1,066	129	14	12,704	…	…	…	…	914
1888	106,386	39,307	7,559	45	111	37	7	95	203	24,516	17,712	2,492	96	22	13,068	…	…	…	…	1,116
1889	106,808	36,629	7,915	54	231	37	7	156	176	21,305	22,228	728	65	20	15,967	…	…	…	…	1,290
1890	168,471	85,548	7,055	105	77	43	4	107	210	28,236	27,422	1,380	37	21	17,026	…	…	…	…	1,200
1891	196,080	109,515	9,730	68	41	41	7	110	191	33,777	21,419	1,671	28	80	17,990	…	…	…	…	1,412
1892	151,412	74,681	7,956	58	50	31	3	54	168	31,359	20,313	724	38	23	14,699	…	…	…	…	1,255
1893	98,288	40,545	2,225	64	62	50	6	70	211	27,254	13,932	723	33	122	11,453	…	…	…	…	1,541
1894	52,760	17,792	1,224	187	62	33	4	28	131	9,875	5,427	430	18	6	16,283	…	…	…	…	1,258
1895	95,074	36,725	1,264	120	43	37	19	22	86	19,249	17,536	634	27	12	18,074	…	…	…	…	1,241
1896	95,803	32,127	590	102	46	31	8	39	123	25,205	15,005	689	57	15	20,263	…	…	…	…	1,492
1897	64,419	18,107	474	70	61	27	11	46	103	15,808	9,880	552	20	20	17,886	…	…	…	…	1,349
1898	83,805	27,853	397	43	62	25	5	31	93	21,437	17,056	855	38	14	14,600	…	…	…	24	1,274
1899	130,646	57,394	386	78	83	38	5	70	147	37,010	32,800	2,043	38	88	73	231	77	61	16	…
1900	160,129	66,263	222	37	27	10	…	67	85	46,075	41,320	5,699	35	103	35	42	76	12	…	…
1901	166,626	57,164	260	27	41	43	13	140	100	51,911	55,153	1,530	56	81	29	21	25	24	8	…
1902	221,432	73,124	271	11	29	24	6	995	387	74,775	69,335	1,982	187	124	22	10	8	132	10	…

For reference notes see page 708.

TABLE XI.—ALIEN EMIGRATION THROUGH GERMAN PORTS, BY COUNTRY OF ORIGIN, 1871-1924 (continued).

Year	Total	Russia	Norway, Sweden and Denmark	Great Britain	Netherlands	Belgium, Luxemburg and France	Spain and Portugal	Italy	Switzerland	Austria	Hungary	Rumania	Turkey in Europe	Other Balkan States	America United States	America Other countries	Africa	Asia	Australia	Countries not distinguished and other non-European countries[17]
1903	268,227	87,495	252	29	24	26	191	2,597	576	80,713	93,029	1,388	1,266	541	13	13	10	63	1	
1904	219,096	105,554	1,250	206	29	27	39	773	397	57,354	50,695	1,318	445	854	17	31	6	76	25	
1905	284,787	97,080	612	32	70	62	14	457	616	76,829	104,521	1,660	940	1,675	16	26	21	138	18	
1906	325,990	129,184	510	50	61	222	39	391	697	87,494	100,464	1,298	3,219	2,060	7	11	27	237	19	
1907	363,615	119,352	445	45	42	73	83	383	787	110,444	112,788	3,424	7,054	8,537	7	31	23	77	7	
1908	106,499	46,376	548	27	92	50	29	96	805	34,273	22,682	1,029	231	243	7	31	7	18	5	
1909	239,637	89,718	624	39	72	50	30	245	587	83,220	61,641	985	941	1,330	5	8	13	97	12	
1910	254,618	105,662	902	29		42	27	186	642	84,427	56,861	1,547	1,562	2,579	1	2	7	65	5	
1911	183,233	84,180	1,273	35	91	53	8	91	611	53,767	39,008	1,140	1,029	1,837	4	4	5	95	2	
1912	290,386	127,747	730	9	61	21	56	1,152	440	79,561	74,333	1,026	1,602	3,514	4	1	34	93	2	
1913	413,857	208,719	333	31	157	21	47	615	607	126,167	73,574	1,979	179	1,283	17	16	2	108	2	
1914	150,416	60,585	136	13	43	16	79	514	478	37,403	47,266	1,097	120	2,562	16	51	2	35		
1915																				
1916																				
1917																				
1918																				
1919																				
1920	1,975[18]	2			2			2		14		4								
1921	19,422[18]	473	95	18	32	11	8	14	85	2,771	1,391	1,423	1	18						
1922	38,393[18]	2,479	425	21	38	74	41	124	1,261	6,759	2,775	4,912	8	824	3	2		1		
1923	51,934[18]	4,233	479	15	76	60	49	130	1,398	9,253	3,290	8,497	2	513		1		5	13	
1924	18,667[18]	1,482	343	64	43	60	12	83	686	1,877	762	2,808	98	129				2		53

For reference notes see page 708.

TABLE XII.—ALIEN EMIGRATION THROUGH GERMAN PORTS, BY COUNTRY OF DESTINATION, 1871-1924.

Year	Grand total	Europe (Great Britain)	AMERICA								Africa	Asia	Australia
			United States	British North America	Mexico and other Central American States	Brazil	South America			Total			
							Argentina	Uruguay	Not specified and other S. American States				
1871	26,828	....	25,241	9	55	249	35	....	141	25,730	4	2	1,092
1872	30,290	....	28,136	8	90	387	66	....	280	28,967	5	5	1,313
1873	32,377	....	29,635	....	71	996	93	....	332	31,127	6	3	1,241
1874	32,144	....	28,557	1,581	186	294	90	....	221	30,929	1	11	1,203
1875	27,874	....	23,564	2,821	105	167	121	....	129	26,907	3	1	963
1876	26,720	....	22,254	1,362	137	2,046	101	....	98	25,998			681
1877	21,696	....	16,310	197	113	3,261	865	....	112	20,858	26	15	235
1878	23,130	....	18,820	374	118	2,307	293	....	83	21,995	561	42	891
1879	22,525	....	21,448	275	141	359	190	....	63	22,476	230	14	34
1880	54,803	....	54,022	79	48	352	189	....	75	54,765	10	11	17
1881	62,967[19]	....	61,971	76	39	443	176	....	114	62,819	63	10	71
1882	62,524[19]	....	61,080	190	26	233	197	....	125	61,851	133	17	137
1883	57,363[19]	....	56,096	65	36	561	224	....	95	57,077	76	15	187
1884	68,986	....	67,294	207	31	645	304	....	150	68,631	139	72	144
1885	66,247	....	64,203	324	67	541	636	....	178	65,949	131	20	147
1886	99,827	....	95,611	510	73	1,487	1,548	....	175	99,404	95	45	283
1887	92,989	....	89,479	335	71	893	1,451	....	174	92,403	114	136	336
1888	106,386	....	102,385	693	67	1,045	1,391	....	162	105,743	159	201	283
1889	106,808	....	101,217	632	65	884	2,975	....	267	106,040	270	122	376
1890	168,471	....	134,582	1,016	76	30,520	1,187	....	209	167,590	458	70	353
1891	196,080	....	174,664	3,344	91	13,913	2,833	....	190	195,035	553	118	374
1892	151,412	....	144,448	3,474	58	760	1,749	....	108	150,597	445	63	307
1893	98,288	....	93,438	2,362	46	1,118	823	....	101	97,888	150	59	191
1894	52,760	....	49,321	859	74	918	820	....	83	52,075	499	75	111
1895	95,074	....	87,918	1,283	65	2,497	1,701	....	66	93,530	1,361	63	120
1896	95,803	....	84,149	1,679	69	6,606	1,267	....	101	93,871	1,678	94	160
1897	64,419	....	55,698	4,868	81	878	1,607	....	108	63,240	785	102	292
1898	83,805	....	74,679	4,563	129	980	1,955	4	47	82,353	844	87	521
1899	130,646	16,056	105,151	6,033	44	982	1,635	....	25	113,874	649	23	44
1900	160,129	19,067	133,124	5,403	7	444	1,566	....	2	140,546	481	....	35

For reference notes see page 708.

TABLE XII.—ALIEN EMIGRATION THROUGH GERMAN PORTS, BY COUNTRY OF DESTINATION, 1871-1924 (continued).

Year	Grand total	Europe (Great Britain)	United States	British North America	Mexico and other Central American States	Brazil	Argentina	Uruguay	Not specified and other S. American States	Total	Africa	Asia	Australia
1901	166,626	12,348	147,972	3,202	7	298	2,129	8		153,616	593	1	68
1902	221,432	17,163	194,266	6,626	2	383	1,688	6		202,971	1,217		81
1903	268,227	17,039	235,118	11,883	2	460	1,610	9		249,082	2,012		94
1904	219,096	22,859	185,454	6,688	10	508	3,219	4		195,883	292		62
1905	284,787	19,792	249,868	2,997	11	262	11,671	13		264,822	139		34
1906	325,990	7,385	303,668	640	5	179	13,886	3	2	318,383	162		60
1907	363,615	4,255	346,871	3,025	22	319	8,877	22		359,136	102		122
1908	106,499	2,333	86,314	1,840	10	8,550	7,252			103,966	111		89
1909	239,637	2,953	215,625	3,874	1	4,915	12,035	16		236,466	139		79
1910	254,618	2,752	233,056	8,538	20	1,948	8,129	17		251,708	70		88
1911	183,233	3,008	152,262	9,493	132	12,021	5,944	24		179,876	159		190
1912	290,386	3,725	242,541	17,210	116	6,314	19,818	26		286,025	431		205
1913	413,857	4,814	352,251	34,980	21	7,185	13,582	441		408,460	437		146
1914	150,416	2,075	131,938	10,993	3	1,830	3,030	221		148,015	223		103
1915													
1916													
1917													
1918													
1919													
1920	1,975		1,975										
1921	19,422	60	18,012	748	87	702	540	16	263	19,254	108		
1922	38,393	23	29,953	933	272	2,651	4,451	63	732	38,169	199	2	
1923	51,934	72	34,234	1,874	654	3,946	11,478	222	820	51,658	136	68	
1924	18,667		4,980			4,721	5,132			18,403	233	31	

TABLE XIII.—Continental migration of alien workers, 1910-24.

Year	Number of newly immigrated alien workers (identified)	Number of workers who departed again	Year	Number of newly immigrated alien workers (identified)	Number of workers who departed again
1910	444,798	444,321	1918	175,461	617,321
1911	497,797	475,369	1919	167,580	172,044
1912	515,737	512,740	1920	206,714	......
1913	549,990	512,277	1921	21,687	......
1914	500,327	278,933	1922	29,917	......
1915	108,593	121,957	1923	29,642	......
1916	142,060	111,144	1924	29,118	......
1917	179,381	142,133	....	......	......

SOURCES

Information supplied by the *Statistisches Reichsamt.*
Tables I, II, V-XII, III (except the figures concerning Bremen, from 1836 to 1846); XIII (years 1921-24).

Die überseeische Auswanderung in den Jahren 1922-23, in *Statistik des deutschen Reiches,* vol. 307, Berlin.

Tables VI-XII (years 1901-23).

Denkschrift des deutschen Reichstages, 1922. No. 8, p. 30.

Table XIII (years 1910-20).

Report of the Select Committee of the Senate of the United States on the Sickness and Mortality on Board Emigrant Ships. Washington, 1854, pp. 43, 44 and 46.

Table III (years 1836-41, Bremen).

Höfken, Dr. Gust. *Deutsche Auswanderung und Kolonisation mit Hinblick auf Ungarn.* Wien, 1850, p. 37.

Table IV (years 1844-45).

Hübner, *Jahrbuch für Volkswirtschaft und Statistik.* vols. I-V, Leipzig, 1853-57.

Table IV (years 1846-54).

NOTES

[1] For Prussia (1845-53) and Bavaria the figures refer to the period October 1 to September 30; the year 1854 for Prussia comprises the period October 1, 1853 to December 31, 1854.
[2] Prussia up to 1866 excludes Hanover, Hesse, Nassau and Schleswig-Holstein.
[3] These figures have not been included in the yearly columns.
[4] Oldenburg up to 1854 excludes the principalities of Lübeck and Birkenfeld.
[5] As from 1851 only emigrants from the German Empire.
[6] Bremen only.
[7] Hamburg only.
[8] Including in 1850, 135; in 1851, 184 and in 1852, 7,690, whose country of destination is not stated.

[9]Note in the Hamburg publication: "In the years 1853 and 1867 the figures show inexplicable differences (of 23 and 44 respectively)".
[10]Including emigrants via Liverpool: 5 in 1899, 79 in 1900 and 110 in 1901.
[11]Including 22 emigrants via Danzig.
[12]For the years 1872-83 the age groups are: "under one year","1 to 10 years," "over 10 years".
[13]The total of German emigrants disagrees with the total of emigrants by age groups, as the latter include persons of Luxemburg nationality, who cannot be distinguished and the number of whom by sex was:

Year	Males	Females
1872	56	48
1873	155	105
1874	167	105
1875	132	71
1876	143	77
1877	92	33
1878	127	56

[14]Includes 2,177 males and 1,234 females over 14 years of age.
[15]Includes 45 in 1898 and 55 in 1899 to "other parts of America".
[16]"Other parts of America" and "America without further specification".
[17]Up to 1898, inclusive of passengers carried on emigrant ships but who did not belong to the emigrant class.
[18]Includes emigrants from the following countries: Danzig, Memel, Finland, Estonia, Latvia, Lithuania, Poland, Ukraine, Czechoslovakia, Serb-Croat-Slovene State.

Year	Danzig	Memel	Finland	Estonia	Latvia	Lithua-nia	Poland	Ukraine	Czecho-slovakia	Serb-Croat-Slovene
1920	..	..	..	.	1	69	1127	3	715	36
1921	58	..	18	2	60	1,023	3,190	24	6,883	1,824
1922	89	19	65	29	707	2,005	2,993	1,265	9,466	2,008
1923	363	27	76	147	1,204	2,159	2,726	878	12,984	3,356
1924	133	13	30	105	222	1,305	1,022	131	2,858	4,346

[19]Includes 4 in 1881, 386 in 1882 and 8 in 1883, whose country of destination is not stated.

HUNGARY

I. Permit Statistics of Immigrants

(Tables I-IV)

Tables I,[1] II,[2] and IV deal with the transit statistics, and table III[3] with the annual returns concerning settlers during one or the other of the two main periods (1768-71 and 1784-86) of State-assisted colonising activity.

The Imperial and Royal Department of Official Statistics (Vienna), of which von Czoernig was Director, compiled, on the basis of the monthly returns preserved in the Archives, immigration statistics which relate to aliens migrating into Hungary via Vienna and coming from Germany or France.

Only those immigrants were to be accepted as settlers who had presented themselves to the Hungarian-Transylvanian Court Chancery at Vienna and were provided with passports. Furthermore, emigrants recruited abroad and going via Vienna had a personal interest in calling at the Chancery, as they might receive not only their travelling expenses (including free transport, maintenance and equipment), but a plot of land tax-free. (See in this connection the Immigration Patent of Joseph II, September 21, 1782, to be found in Czoernig, vol. 3, p. 371.) These settlers included manufacturers, traders and professional as well as agricultural workers, and special lists of them were kept (Table IV).

The data are only available to the close of 1786. With regard to the continuation of these colonisation statistics Czoernig observes: "As colonisation at the cost of the State had stopped, 1,788 families may have been provided for in the subsequent years. Reckoning 5 persons to a family, the total number of immigrants settled at State expense under the rule of Emperor Joseph II, 1780-1790, may be estimated at 38,000."

II. Statistics of Foreign Ports

(Tables V-VII)

As the national statistics commenced in 1899, for earlier years—in addition to the records of the countries of immigration—the statistics of the ports of embarkation have been used. Of these, the German ports before 1871 were almost the only important ones. From 1884 onwards the consuls had to prepare special reports on Hungarian emigration. The figures for Antwerp and Genoa were of notable dimensions, those for Amsterdam and Rotterdam of less account. With the year 1904, as a consequence of Governmental initiative, Fiume came to play

---

[1]Statement concerning settlers who, in the years 1768-71, proceeded from Vienna to the Banat.
[2]Settlers from Germany who either applied for or were provided with passports at the Hungarian Transylvanian Court Chancery, permitting them to emigrate to Hungary.
[3]Summary statement of the progress of colonisation in Hungary.

a leading rôle as the national port. Returns for the less important numbers emigrating via Havre, Cherbourg and Liverpool began to appear in the years immediately preceding the war. Detailed information about Hungarian emigrants via foreign ports is available only for Hamburg (from 1871) and Bremen (from 1890).

III. NATIONAL PASSPORT STATISTICS

(Tables VIII-XVIII)

From 1899 to 1904 the statistics of emigration were based on the very incomplete returns of village burgomasters and notaries. Owing to the increase in emigration, it was decided to combine these figures with the figures supplied by the passport offices in accordance with the provisions of Act VI of 1903, in virtue of which:—

1. The authorities which issued passports were to forward every month a copy of their passport register to the Central Statistical Office of the Kingdom of Hungary.

2. Communal and district notaries or, in towns which had a town council, the prefects of police were to keep a register of the names of persons to whom passports for emigration had been issued, and to prepare an emigration report concerning such persons. The prefects of police of municipalities who had the right to issue passports did not keep a register; they merely prepared a statistical report concerning the persons to whom a passport had been issued with a view to emigration. The reports concerning persons who actually emigrated were to be forwarded monthly to the Central Statistical Office.

3. The same authorities were to keep a record of any persons known to have emigrated without passports, and to compile a statistical report concerning such persons.

4. They also were to keep a register and compile a statistical report in regard to returned emigrants. This report was to be forwarded to the local police authorities and to mayors of villages.

Hungarian statistics, which were suspended in consequence of the war, did not appear for the years 1916 to 1920, inclusive.

The institution of a compulsory passport system during the war made the compilation of statistics more difficult, for it is not easy to distinguish intercontinental emigrants from other travellers. The Hungarian Minister of the Interior, by Decree No. 12000-XI-1921, ordered that, in the case of all persons travelling to America (except minors for whom "affidavits" suffice), the police authorities should endeavour by all means in their power to ascertain whether travellers are emigrants within the meaning of paragraph 1 of the aforesaid Act, that is to say, whether they are going abroad with the intention of earning a living there permanently. It was presumed that the person is an emigrant unless he can prove the contrary.

IV. Statistics of Contracts

(Table XIX)

The passport statistics are actually very incomplete. We are therefore making use of the more accurate ones furnished by the shipping companies to the Commissioner of Emigration, and drawn up in accordance with the transport contracts.

V. Permit Statistics of Immigration

(Table XX)

In regard to immigration, Hungarian statistics deal also with aliens to whom the authorities have issued permits to reside in the country. Under Act V of 1903 all aliens who intend to live in Hungary must apply to the proper authorities for a certificate of residence. The publication of these statistics was suspended in 1915.

Statistics about the number of migrants from Hungary to Argentina (1921-24), Brazil (1908-24), Canada (1923-24), Cuba (1923-24), and the United States (1861-1924), will be found in the national tables for those countries. Statistics about the number of migrants returning to Hungary from the United States (1908-24) will be found in the national tables for that the latter country.

TABLE I.—IMMIGRATION (TRANSIT BY VIENNA), 1768-71.

Year	Month	Families	Persons
1768	January	3	12
	February	2	8
	March	34	136
	April	30	120
	May	202	812
	June	96	412
	July	27	112
	August	13	50
	September	17	68
	October	12	50
	November	16	64
	December	10	44
	Total	462	1,888
1769	January	10	45
	February	3	15
	March	50	212
	April	138	556
	May	348	1,297
	June	103	424
	July	20	64
	August	23	70
	September	21	67
	October	40	161
	November	39	131
	December	20	82
	Total	815	3,124
1770	January	13	28
	February	23	50
	March	125	357
	April	930	2,402
	May	500	1,968
	June	335	1,235
	July	140	545
	August	152	536
	September	175	546
	October	268	980
	November	244	600
	December	309	1,145
	Total	3,214	10,392
1771	January	5	19
	February	10	32
	March	129	445
	April	10	35
	May	57	287
	June	116	526
	July	13	48
	August	3	12
	September	13	82
	October	12	54
	November	19	65
	Total	387	1,605
	Grand total	4,878	17,009

TABLE II.—Immigration (transit by Vienna), 1784-86.[1]

Year	Month	Families	Persons
1784	April	524	2,190
	May	480	1,964
	June	204	988
	July	312	1,502
	August	269	1,287
	September	241	1,229
	October	195	973
		2,225	10,133
1785	February	5	18
	March	10	24
	April	130	598
	May	1,841	8,699
	June	1,154	5,522
	July	412	2,075
	August	334	1,594
	September	209	958
	October	338	1,524
	November	197	818
	December	13	24
		4,643	21,854
1786	January	7	24
	February	5	20
	March	50	183
	April	219	1,081
	May	886	3,864
	June	372	1,609
	July	234	950
	August	156	665
	September	121	465
	October	91	392
		2,143	9,253

TABLE III.—Immigration. (Newly arrived families settlers[3]) in the years 1784-87.

1784[2]	1785	1786	1787[3]
548	1,726	2,794	1,887

For reference notes see page 728.

TABLE IV.—IMMIGRANTS. SPECIAL RETURN OF SKILLED TRADES[4], NOVEMBER 1, 1785, to OCTOBER 31, 1786.

Trade	Total	Trade	Total
Bakers	24	Plasterers	2
Miners	14	Serge makers	2
Tinsmiths	1	Strap maker	1
Distillers	1	Tanners	7
Brewers	8	Saddlers	3
Brush makers	5	Silk weavers	2
Book binders	2	Soap boilers	3
Box lacquerers	2	Rope maker	1
Turners	5	Grinders	2
Coopers	21	Locksmiths	8
Dyers	2	Smiths	18
Butchers	16	Tailors	66
Gardeners	9	Shoe makers	72
Glass blower	1	Plate-glass polisher	1
Glazier	1	Steel worker	1
Braziers	5	Stone breaker	1
Flax comber	1	Masons	2
Hammer smiths	2	Stucco workers	2
Glove makers	3	Thatchers	3
Blacksmiths	23	Stocking makers	12
Hat makers	2	Stocking knitter	1
Chimney sweeper	1	Joiners	23
Cheese maker	1	Snuffbox maker	1
Skin dresser	1	Pipe makers	2
Basket makers	2	Potters	7
Cotton printers	2	Cloth makers	9
Art linen weavers	2	Wheelwrights	25
Copper smiths	1	Tarvers	2
Linen printers	3	Woolen cloth makers	6
Linen weavers	124	Wool comber	1
Painter	1	Textile weavers	9
Bricklayers	84	Brick makers	11
Cutler	1	Tiler	1
Flour millers	47	Carpenters	59
Nailsmiths	14	Compass maker	1
Oil millers	2	Tinder maker	1
Paper maker	1	Ticking maker	1
Potash maker	1		
		Total	805

For reference notes see page 728.

TABLE V.—INTERCONTINENTAL EMIGRATION OF CITIZENS, 1871-1913.

Year	Total	Hamburg	Bremen	Other German ports	Amsterdam	Rotterdam	Genoa	Antwerp	Trieste	Fiume	Le Havre	Cherbourg	Liverpool	Naples
1871	294	236	58											
1872	595	457	138											
1873	962	764	198											
1874	927	701	226											
1875	1,065	787	278											
1876	625	501	124											
1877	652	495	157											
1878	803	661	142											
1879	1,759	1,292	467											
1880	8,766	8,146	620											
1881	11,257	10,453	804											
1882	17,520	16,060	1,460											
1883	14,839	11,478	3,361											
1884	13,195	7,885	5,310											
1885	12,348	4,179	8,169											
1886	25,149	12,176	12,973											
1887	18,271	9,598	8,673											
1888	17,630	8,179	9,451											
1889	25,144	4,873	17,177	56	166		1,567	940						
1890	31,470	5,418	21,850	14	374	421	1,448	1,434						
1891	33,000	4,124	17,289	15	784	946	1,046	5,443						
1892	35,125	2,645	17,667	6	1,808	4,314	721	6,555						
1893	22,996	1,867	12,059	1	135	5,729	1,078	7,178						
1894	8,044	1,366	4,061	6	20	679	108	2,212						
1895	25,858	3,679	13,857		445	277	190	4,675						
1896	24,649	3,082	11,726	197	404	3,012	1,210	6,122						
1897	14,106	1,584	8,092	204	175	2,105	673	2,820						
1898	22,802	2,135	14,758	163	74	1,751	816	3,268						
1899	43,394	4,855	27,945		58	2,301	782	7,453						
1900	54,767	9,691	31,629			3,072	678	9,697						
1901	71,474	12,806	42,347			4,506	533	11,282						
1902	91,762	21,485	47,850			8,026	34	14,367						
1903	119,944	23,008	70,021		1	8,439	338	18,115						
1904	97,340	13,508	37,187		5	4,391	255	10,864	525	22,016			9,068	23
1905	170,430	27,664	76,857		6	8,809	197	14,246	867	35,961	5,101		716	50
1906	178,170	27,246	73,218		10	6,587	358	13,831	3,621	49,332	3,412		542	7
1907	209,169	33,636	79,152		10	13,794	149	17,293	6,028	47,620	9,523		1,963	17
1908	49,365	6,436	16,246			1,874	187	4,440	1,805	15,411	2,952			6
1909	129,337	19,199	42,442			6,559	285	11,387	4,729	36,824	6,732	1,160		4
1910	119,901	21,261	35,600			5,873	184	8,667	4,299	36,834	6,608	575		
1911	73,654	14,885	24,123		5	4,182	148	6,534	2,379	18,532	2,401	465		
1912	120,516	29,557	39,659			6,949	97	9,469	3,959	21,922	8,845	59		
1913	119,159	29,944	39,264			9,312	49	7,939	4,345	20,847	6,279	22	1,158	

TABLE VI.—INTERCONTINENTAL EMIGRATION OF CITIZENS, BY COUNTRY OF DESTINATION (FROM 1871 to 1884 HAMBURG STATISTICS; FROM 1892-1913, HAMBURG AND BREMEN STATISTICS).

Year	United States	Canada	Argentina	Brazil	West Indies	Other American countries	Asia	Africa	Australia	Great Britain
1871	234			1	1					
1872	452			5						
1873	762			2	1				13	
1874	681		4	6		1			21	
1875	758			3				1		
1876	486			14				1		
1877	471			23						
1878	661		1							
1879	1,261		1						3	
1880	8,135	2	1	6						
1881	10,443	1	1	8						
1882	16,014	38	2	1		2		3	3	
1883	11,443	7	8	21		2		3		
1884	7,828	26		18				3		
1892	20,113	63	59	75	1	1				
1893	13,667	241	4	16						
1894	5,353	57	1	11	4	1		7	2	
1895	17,081	138	1	306		1				
1896	14,660	85	19	53	1	2		184		
1897	9,701	122	14	5		9	2	23	3	
1898	16,966	48	3	4		1		27	6	137
1899	32,545	92	2	6			1	15		186
1900	40,963	161	6	1		2		1		172
1901	54,678	275	9	10		7		2		206
1902	68,421	655	26	17				10		108
1903	90,979	1,566	61	64				251	3	75
1904	50,056	420	114	4		4		19		104
1905	101,195	343	2,839	28				12		25
1906	98,537	227	1,660	2		12		1		11
1907	111,634	302	836	3				1		13
1908	22,079	87	481	22					1	18
1909	60,894	276	428	24						3
1910	56,232	261	362	3					1	18
1911	38,360	427	190	6						20
1912	67,978	768	400	42				1	4	18
1913	68,027	899	225	44				4	6	13

TABLE VII.—Distribution of emigrant citizens to extra-European countries through the Port of Hamburg, by sex, 1871-84.

Year	Total	Males	Females	Males percent
1871	236	176	60	74.58
1872	457	333	124	72.87
1873	764	509	255	66.62
1874	701	435	266	62.05
1875	787	511	276	64.93
1876	501	341˙	160	68.06
1877	495	316	179	63.84
1878	661	406	255	61.42
1879	1,262	805	457	63.79
1880	8,146	5,210	2,936	63.96
1881	10,453	7,797	2,656	74.59
1882	16,060	......	......	.....
1883	11,478	......	......	.....
1884	7,885	......	......	.....

TABLE VIII.—Emigration, by country of destination, 1899-1913.

Year	Number of emigrants			
	America	Germany	Rumania	Other countries
1899	26,515	490	7,436	2,752
1900	31,092	1,024	4,653	2,119
1901	45,196	967	6,710	2,504
1902	56,346	836	4,580	2,293
1903	61,466	734	3,567	2,690
1904	57,695	2,115	7,534	3,144
1905	142,169	5,972	11,021	6,699
1906	149,932	5,275	8,795	5,200
1907	172,200	7,354	7,790	5,638
1908	38,214	4,229	6,457	4,042
1909	100,424	2,627	6,639	3,625
1910	85,248	2,465	5,451	3,160
1911	53,502	2,720	5,586	2,249
1912	92,664	2,607	7,291	2,101
1913	84,084	2,170	8.868	1,599

TABLE IX.—Distribution of emigrants (heads of families and separate persons) to America, by occupation; 1905-07 and 1911-13.

Occupation	Number of emigrants								Percent of total	
	1905	1906	1907	1911	1912	1913	1905–07	1911–13	1905–07	1911–13
Farmers..............	13,419	11,836	12,345	4,864	8,621	8,701	37,600	22,186	11.1	15.3
Farm servants and workers............	55,566	60,492	71,789	16,796	32,483	26,154	187,847	75,433	55.4	51.8
Miners..............	1,735	751	805	330	602	262	3,291	1,194	0.9	0.8
Employers...........	2,193	2,607	2,989	1,178	1,631	1,896	7,789	4,705	2.3	3.2
Traders..............	137	215	283	100	202	299	635	601	0.2	0.4
Skilled and unskilled workers and general labor in trade and industry.............	10,737	13,079	14,964	3,104	4,515	3,924	38,780	11,543	11.4	7.9
Liberal professions.....	251	421	369	206	164	216	1,041	586	0.3	0.4
General labor, not otherwise distinguished ...	12,058	11,577	14,952	4,426	7,262	6,558	38,587	18,246	11.4	12.5
Domestic servants.....	6,188	7,123	6,284	2,115	2,732	3,133	19,595	7,980	5.8	5.5
Other occupations or occupation unknown.	1,238	1,402	1,617	770	1,104	1,377	4,257	3,251	1.2	2.2
Total............	103,522	109,503	126,397	33,889	59,316	52,520	339,422	145,725	100.00	100.00

TABLE X.—Distribution of emigrants from Hungary Proper to
America, by sex, 1901-13.

Year	Total	Males		Females	
		Number	Percent	Number	Percent
1901	38,391	28,586	74.5	9,805	25.5
1902	46,563	35,021	75.2	11,542	24.8
1903	49,936	36,363	72.8	13,573	27.2
1904	54,150	37,513	69.3	16,637	30.7
1905	119,965	86,300	71.9	33,665	28.1
1906	128,109	89,531	69.9	38,578	30.1
1907	149,372	107,722	72.1	41,650	27.9
1908	35,384	22,579	63.8	12,805	36.2
1909	89,035	62,209	69.9	26,826	30.1
1910	71,323	45,927	64.4	25,396	35.6
1911	47,046	24,111	51.2	22,935	48.8
1912	78,425	45,663	58.2	32,762	41.8
1913	71,409	33,131	46.4	38,278	53.6
1901–1913	979,108	654,656	66.9	324,452	33.1

TABLE XI.—Distribution of emigrants (heads of families and separate persons)
from Hungary Proper to America, by age, (triennial totals only)
1905-07; 1911-13.

	Age	1905–07	1911–13
Number of emigrants	Under 20 years	82,675	25,195
	20 to 29 years	123,324	50,722
	30 to 39 years	87,832	34,583
	40 to 49 years	40,673	27,469
	50 years and over	4,918	7,756
Per cent of total	Under 20 years	24.4	17.3
	20 to 29 years	36.3	34.8
	30 to 39 years	25.9	23.7
	40 to 49 years	12.0	18.9
	50 years and over	1.4	5.3

TABLE XII.—Distribution of emigrants from Hungary Proper to Europe, by
sex, 1901-13.

Year	Males	Females	Year	Males	Females
1901	5,628	3,479	1908	7,833	4,680
1902	4,089	2,433	1909	6,464	4,375
1903	3,423	2,021	1910	4,974	3,923
1904	7,042	4,448	1911	4,996	3,800
1905	11,666	7,088	1912	5,477	4,782
1906	10,583	5,784	1913	5.105	6,208
1907	11,990	6,127			
			1901–1913	89,270	59,148

TABLE XIII.—Distribution of emigrants (heads of families and separate persons) to Germany, Rumania, and other countries (excluding America), by age, 1905-13.

Year	Up to 19 years	20 to 49 years	50 years and over	Year	Up to 19 years	20 to 49 years	50 years and over
1905	3,082	12,871	2,042	1911	716	5,790	1,249
1906	2,485	10,967	1,681	1912	693	6,498	1,507
1907	2,518	12,065	1,872	1913	609	5,860	2,386

TABLE XIV.—Distribution of emigrants (heads of families and separate persons) from Hungary Proper to Europe, by occupation, 1905-07 and 1911-13.

Occupation	Number of emigrants								Percent of total	
	1905	1906	1907	1911	1912	1913	1905–07	1911–13	1905–07	1911–13
Independent farmers..........	848	778	773	454	493	628	2,399	1,575	6.18	7.57
Farm servants and workers...	7,118	6,225	6,677	3,175	3,856	4,550	20,020	11,581	51.62	55.72
Miners.....................	505	392	1,116	261	233	164	2,013	658	5.19	3.16
Employers..................	320	333	284	134	243	173	937	550	2.41	2.64
Traders....................	99	94	100	40	45	51	293	136	0.75	0.65
Skilled and unskilled workers and general labor in trade and industry...............	1,854	1,858	1,660	797	828	540	5,372	2,165	13.85	10.41
Liberal professions...........	208	242	273	140	121	130	723	391	1.86	1.88
General labor, not otherwise distinguished..............	1,045	1,047	1,225	475	516	659	3,317	1,650	8.55	7.93
Domestic servants...........	1,189	1,016	781	463	581	620	2,986	1,664	7.70	8.00
Other occupations, or occupation unknown.............	291	196	241	116	171	125	728	412	1.87	1.98
Total..................	13,477	12,181	13,130	6,055	7,087	7,640	38,788	20,782	99.98	99.94

TABLE XV.—Emigration and immigration of citizens, by constituent parts of the Kingdom, 1899-1913.

Year	EMIGRATION			IMMIGRATION		
	Total	Hungary Proper	Croatia and Slavonia	Total	Hungary Proper	Croatia and Slavonia
1899	37,193	32,998	4,195	4,739	4,739	....
1900	38,888	34,712	4,176	6,169	6,169	....
1901	55,377	47,498	7,879	8,493	7,465	1,028
1902	64,055	53,085	10,970	11,463	9,834	1,629
1903	68,457	55,380	13,077	20,212	17,030	3,182
1904	70,488	65,640	4,848	16,870	14,022	2,848
1905	165,861	138,719	27,142	17,566	14,850	2,716
1906	169,202	144,476	24,726	27,612	23,622	3,990
1907	192,982	167,489	25,493	51,236	43,528	7,708
1908	52,942	47,897	5,045	53,770	46,106	7,664
1909	113,315	99,874	13,441	16,985	14,913	2,072
1910	96,324	80,220	16,104	24,722	21,403	3,319
1911	64,057	55,842	8,215	32,787	28,071	4,716
1912	104,663	88,684	15,979	23,635	20,245	3,390
1913	96,721	82,722	13,999	21,780	18,148	3,632

TABLE XVI.—DISTRIBUTION OF EMIGRANT CITIZENS, BY CONSTITUENT PARTS OF THE KINGDOM AND BY SEX, 1899-1913.

Year	Number of emigrants						Percentage					
	Total		Hungary proper		Croatia Slavonia		Total		Hungary proper		Croatia Slavonia	
	Males	Females	Males	Females	Males	Females	Males	Females	Males	Females	Males	Females
1899	25,294	11,899	21,632	11,366	3,662	533	68.0	32.0	*65.6	34.4	87.3	12.7
1900	27,762	11,126	24,268	10,444	3,494	682	71.4	28.6	69.9	30.1	83.7	16.3
1901	41,235	14,142	34,214	13,284	7,021	858	74.5	25.5	72.0	28.0	89.1	10.9
1902	48,933	15,122	39,110	13,975	9,823	1,147	76.4	23.6	73.7	26.3	89.5	10.5
1903	51,402	17,055	39,786	15,594	11,616	1,461	75.1	24.9	71.8	28.2	88.8	11.2
1904	48,476	22,012	44,555	21,085	3,921	927	68.8	31.2	67.9	32.1	80.9	19.1
1905	122,059	43,802	97,966	40,753	24,093	3,049	73.6	26.4	70.6	29.4	88.8	11.2
1906	121,282	47,920	100,114	44,362	21,168	3,558	71.7	28.3	69.3	30.7	85.6	14.4
1907	140,977	52,005	119,712	47,777	21,265	4,228	73.1	26.9	71.5	28.5	83.4	16.6
1908	34,151	18,791	30,412	17,485	3,739	1,306	64.5	35.5	63.5	36.5	74.1	25.9
1909	79,434	33,881	68,673	31,201	10,761	2,680	70.1	29.9	68.8	31.2	80.1	19.9
1910	63,700	32,624	50,901	29,319	12,799	3,305	66.1	33.9	63.5	36.5	79.5	20.5
1911	34,668	29,389	29,107	26,735	5,561	2,654	54.1	45.9	52.1	47.9	67.7	32.3
1912	62,307	42,356	51,140	37,544	11,167	4,812	59.5	40.5	57.7	42.3	69.9	30.1
1913	46,308	50,413	38,236	44,486	8,072	5,927	47.9	52.1	46.2	53.8	57.7	42.3
Total 1899–1913	947,988	442,537	789,826	405,410	158,162	37,127	68.2	31.8	66.1	33.9	81.0	19.0

TABLE XVII.—DISTRIBUTION OF EMIGRANT CITIZENS (HEADS OF FAMILIES AND SEPARATE PERSONS), BY CONSTITUENT PARTS OF THE KINGDOM AND BY AGE, 1905-13.

	Year	under 20 years			20-29 years			30-39 years			40-49 years			50 years and over		
		Total	Hungary proper	Croatia and Slavonia	Total	Hungary proper	Croatia and Slavonia	Total	Hungary proper	Croatia and Slavonia	Total	Hungary proper	Croatia and Slavonia	Total	Hungary proper	Croatia and Slavonia
Number of emigrants	1905	33,384	26,160	7,224	49,364	40,956	8,408	37,655	31,568	6,087	18,679	15,290	3,389	3,849	3,276	573
	1906	37,882	31,073	6,809	50,355	42,743	7,612	36,175	30,643	5,532	17,497	14,743	2,754	3,538	2,912	626
	1907	37,839	31,316	6,523	60,667	52,652	8,015	40,801	35,284	5,517	20,813	17,718	3,095	4,190	3,539	651
	1911	8,129	6,338	1,791	17,552	15,010	2,542	12,129	10,586	1,543	6,694	5,887	807	2,506	2,199	307
	1912	12,861	9,361	3,500	29,221	24,360	4,861	22,751	19,345	3,406	11,876	10,284	1,592	3,491	3,131	360
	1913	13,387	10,515	2,872	20,652	16,793	3,859	11,511	9,519	1,992	18,653	16,267	2,386	7,896	7,116	780
Percent of total	1905	23.3	22.3	28.1	34.5	34.9	32.8	26.4	26.9	23.7	13.1	13.1	13.2	2.7	2.8	2.2
	1906	26.1	25.4	29.2	34.6	35.0	32.6	24.9	25.1	23.7	12.0	12.1	11.8	2.4	2.4	2.7
	1907	23.0	22.3	27.4	36.9	37.5	33.7	24.8	25.1	23.2	12.7	12.6	13.0	2.6	2.5	2.7
	1911	17.3	15.8	25.6	37.4	37.6	36.4	25.8	26.4	22.1	14.2	14.7	11.5	5.3	5.5	4.4
	1912	16.0	14.1	25.5	36.4	36.6	35.5	28.4	29.1	24.8	14.8	15.5	11.6	4.4	4.7	2.6
	1913	18.6	17.5	24.2	28.6	27.9	32.4	16.0	15.8	16.8	25.9	27.0	20.0	10.9	11.8	6.6

TABLE XVIII.—DISTRIBUTION OF EMIGRANT CITIZENS (HEADS OF FAMILIES AND SEPARATE PERSONS), BY OCCUPATION, 1905-13.

Occupation	Number of emigrants								Percent of total	
	1905	1906	1907	1911	1912	1913	1905–07	1911–13	1905–07	1911–13
Independent farmers...	26,438	23,999	26,397	8,320	16,773	16,724	76,834	41,817	17.0	21.0
Farm servants and workers..........	72,280	75,437	86,165	21,827	39,727	32,893	233,882	94,447	51.6	47.4
Miners and general mine labor........	2,342	1,156	1,931	608	848	432	5,429	1,888	1.2	0 9
Independent industrial workers..........	2,822	3,404	3,720	1,460	2,113	2,352	9,946	5,925	2.2	3.0
Merchants...........	308	369	460	174	278	390	1,137	842	0.3	0.4
Skilled and unskilled workers and general labor in trade and industry	15,282	17,120	18,619	5,127	6,552	5,080	51,021	16,759	11.3	8.4
Liberal professions....	586	815	802	465	439	470	2,203	1,374	0.5	0.7
General labor not otherwise distinguished....	13,373	12,944	16,693	5,016	7,963	7,344	43,010	20,323	9.5	10.2
Domestic servants.....	7,650	8,419	7,394	2,754	3,647	4,148	23,463	10,549	5.2	5.3
Other occupations or occupation unknown...	1,850	1,784	2,129	1,259	1,860	2,266	5,763	5,385	1.2	2.7
Total............	142,931	145,447	164,310	7,010	80,200	72,099	452,688	199,309	100.0	100.0

TABLE XIX.—DISTRIBUTION OF EMIGRANT CITIZENS, BY LANGUAGE, 1905-13.

Year	Magyar	German	Slovak	Rumanian	Ruthenian	Croatian	Serbian	Other languages
1905	43,754	28,303	38,770	17,747	7,287	17,523	10,376	2,101
1906	52,121	30,551	32,904	20,859	4,920	16,016	9,950	1,881
1907	58,739	37,611	32,737	26,491	5,088	16,589	13,514	2,213
1911	20,143	13,221	11,595	8,227	2,269	5,338	2,512	752
1912	31,478	16,803	17,029	18,620	3,761	9,961	5,908	1,103
1913	29,301	14,124	14,827	20,656	3,002	8,805	4,892	1,114

TABLE XX.—DISTRIBUTION OF EMIGRANT CITIZENS, BY LANGUAGE AND COUNTRY OF DESTINATION, (QUADRENNIAL TOTALS) 1910-13.

Language (race)	Number of emigrants						Percent of total					
	Germany	Rumania	Other Balkan countries	Other European countries	America	Other parts of the world	Germany	Rumania	Other Balkan countries	Other European countries	America	Other parts of the world
Magyar	1,736	4,196	388	628	99,258	278	17.4	15.4	15.0	10.9	31.5	37.6
German	4,364	2,211	419	856	52,903	153	43.8	8.1	16.2	14.8	16.8	20.7
Slovak	574	40	105	620	60,118	4	5.8	0.1	4.1	10.7	19.0	0.5
Rumanian	2,110	20,251	107	344	39,644	15	21.2	74.5	4.1	5.9	12.6	2.0
Ruthenian	3	309	13	44	12,466	2	0.0	1.1	0.5	0.8	3.9	0.3
Croatian	737	76	775	2,240	29,821	272	7.4	0.3	29.9	38.8	9.5	36.7
Serbian	219	74	676	412	18,348	13	2.2	0.3	26.1	7.1	5.8	1.8
Other languages	219	39	106	636	2,940	3	2.2	0.2	4.1	11.0	0.9	0.4
Total	9,962	27,196	2,589	5,780	315,498	740	100.0	100.0	100.0	100.0	100.0	100.0

TABLE XXI.—Immigration of citizens, by country of last residence, 1901-13.

Year	America	Germany	Rumania	Other countries
1901	6,801	195	1,135	362
1902	9,803	131	1,146	383
1903	18,816	151	1,062	183
1904	15,822	143	648	257
1905	13,926	1,015	1,772	853
1906	23,976	985	1,747	904
1907	47,175	1,731	1,606	724
1908	50,801	1,276	1,073	620
1909	14,867	770	842	506
1910	22,890	576	678	578
1911	30,993	586	817	391
1912	22,263	474	559	339
1913	20,302	436	731	311

TABLE XXII.—Immigration of citizens from America, by constituent parts of the Kingdom, 1899-1913.

Year	Hungary Proper	Croatia and Slavonia	Total	Year	Hungary Proper	Croatia and Slavonia	Total
1899	3,582	....	....	1907	40,483	6,692	47,175
1900	4,937	....	....	1908	43,937	6,864	50,801
1901	5,960	841	6,801	1909	13,288	1,579	14,867
1902	8,400	1,403	9,803	1910	20,071	2,819	22,890
1903	15,730	3,086	18,816	1911	26,688	4,305	30,993
1904	13,187	2,635	15,822	1912	19,201	3,062	22,263
1905	11,968	1,958	13,926	1913	16,996	3,306	20,302
1906	20,910	3,066	23,976	....	....	....	....

TABLE XXIII.—Distribution of immigrant citizens returned, by sex, 1905-13.

Year	Total		Percent of total		Percent of emigrants	
	Males	Females	Males	Females	Males	Females
1905	14,489	3,077	82.5	17.5	11.9	7.0
1906	23,289	4,323	84.3	15.7	19.2	9.0
1907	45,017	6,219	87.9	12.1	31.9	12.0
1908	45,805	7,965	85.2	14.8	134.1	42.4
1909	12,984	4,001	76.4	23.6	16.3	11.8
1910	19,529	5,193	79.0	21.0	30.7	15.9
1911	26,651	6,136	81.3	18.7	76.9	20.9
1912	18,836	4,799	79.7	20.3	30.2	11.3
1913	17,339	4,441	79.6	20.4	37.4	8.8

TABLE XXIV.—DISTRIBUTION OF IMMIGRANT CITIZENS (HEADS OF FAMILIES AND SEPARATE PERSONS), BY AGE, 1907-13.

Year	Total	Under 20 years	20 to 29 years	30 to 39 years	40 to 49 years	50 years and over
1907	46,262	2,149	16,967	16,873	8,563	1,710
1908	46,550	2,422	19,301	15,504	7,676	1,647
1911	27,115	560	9,725	10,023	5,477	1,330
1912	19,116	356	6,508	7,243	3,917	1,092
1913	17,758	323	5,703	6,618	3,875	1,239

TABLE XXV.—DISTRIBUTION OF IMMIGRANT CITIZENS (HEADS OF FAMILIES AND SEPARATE PERSONS), BY OCCUPATION, 1907-13.

Year	Independent farmers	Farm servants and workers	Miners and general mine labor	Independent industrial workers	Merchants	Skilled and unskilled workers and general labor in trade and industry	Liberal professions	General labor not otherwise distinguished	Domestic servants	Other occupations and occupation unknown
					Number					
1907	1,952	9,135	4,452	499	44	24,263	71	3,792	1,123	571
1908	1,568	7,526	5,511	651	67	25,745	75	3,656	1,206	545
1911	950	4,242	3,071	356	30	14,648	55	2,581	680	502
1912	656	2,810	2,596	315	29	10,430	51	1,444	475	310
1913	686	2,596	2,258	238	28	9,761	31	1,363	469	328
					Percentages					
1907	4.2	19.8	9.6	1.1	0.1	53.2	0.2	8.2	2.4	1.2
1908	3.4	16.2	11.8	1.4	0.1	55.3	0.2	7.9	2.6	1.1
1911	3.5	15.7	11.3	1.3	0.1	54.0	0.2	9.5	2.5	1.9
1912	3.4	14.7	13.6	1.7	0.1	54.6	0.3	7.5	2.5	1.6
1913	3.9	14.6	12.7	1.3	0.2	55.0	0.2	7.7	2.6	1.8

TABLE XXVI.—DISTRIBUTION OF IMMIGRANT CITIZENS, BY LANGUAGE, 1905-13.

Year	Total	Magyar	German	Slovak	Rumanian	Ruthenian	Croatian	Serbian	Other languages
1905	17,566	4,575	2,453	4,038	2,506	1,012	1,885	930	167
1906	27,612	7,797	3,987	6,562	3,102	1,560	2,711	1,670	223
1907	51,236	14,866	6,541	11,331	6,843	2,371	5,445	3,270	569
1908	53,770	15,057	7,595	13,538	5,548	2,408	5,697	3,358	569
1909	16,985	4,637	3,472	3,582	1,902	810	1,596	845	141
1910	24,722	7,674	4,065	4,952	2,881	1,078	2,217	1,632	223
1911	32,787	9,729	4,912	6,321	4,613	1,505	3,290	2,125	292
1912	23,635	6,445	3,985	4,929	2,925	1,400	2,279	1,373	279
1913	21,780	5,825	3,268	4,717	2,565	1,121	2,248	1,832	204
1905-07	96,414	27,238	12,981	21,931	12,451	4,943	10,041	5,870	959
1908-13	173,679	49,387	27,297	38,039	20,434	8,322	17,327	11,165	1,708

TABLE XXVII.—IMMIGRATION OF ALIENS, BY COUNTRY OF ORIGIN, 1907-15.

Year	Total	Austria	Germany	Italy	Rumania	Serbia	Bulgaria	Bosnia and Herzegovina	Other countries
1907	14,447	11,303	352	1,069	403	334	308	...	678
1908	15,433	12,312	422	1,189	183	193	356	...	778
1909	15,599	11,833	683	1,240	233	336	437	...	837
1910	10,256	7,801	591	286	206	331	405	...	636
1911	11,895	8,960	792	328	232	420	463	...	700
1912	9,660	7,104	637	221	197	403	437	...	661
1913	9,300	6,751	713	558	124	286	257	...	611
1914	9,234	6,761	523	400	156	353	489	105	447
1915	4,157	3,306	331	64	91	44	140	42	139

TABLE XXVIII.—IMMIGRATION OF ALIENS, BY LANGUAGE (RACE), 1907-15.

Year	Total	Magyar	German	Slovak	Rumanian	Ruthenian	Croatian	Serbian	Polish	Czecho-Moravian	Italian	Other languages
1907	14,447	87	4,018	1,068	353	807	148	466	3,583	1,769	1,260	888
1908	15,433	55	4,071	1,236	133	1,772	101	285	3,385	1,988	1,378	1,029
1909	15,599	79	4,684	811	133	901	25	470	3,827	2,275	1,346	1,048
1910	10,256	62	3,863	539	104	191	46	412	2,226	1,472	337	1,004
1911	11,895	49	4,656	292	173	225	99	529	2,830	1,524	367	1,151
1912	9,660	38	3,733	342	131	142	142	486	1,760	1,591	262	1,033
1913	9,300	22	4,031	221	82	236	63	413	1,319	1,621	614	678
1914	9,234	51	3,543	412	106	163	165	304	1,171	1,222	988	1,109
1915	4,157	29	2,215	277	41	45	32	18	359	698	123	320

TABLE XXIX.—DISTRIBUTION OF EMIGRANTS TO EXTRA-EUROPEAN COUNTRIES, BY AGE, 1921-24.

Year	Total	Number of emigrants							Country of destination			
		over ten years				under 10 years						
		Males		Females		Boys	Girls	Infants	United States	Canada	South America	Other countries
		Married	Single	Married	Single							
1921	6,004[3]	902	1,355	1,319	1,637	364	349	78	Almost exclusively to the United States.			
1922	5,544[5]	791	1,216	1,269	1,337	443	410	78	Immigration into Canada prohibited.			
1923	5,087[5]	618	1,141	1,415	965	467	415	66	Only a few persons to South America.			
1924	1,710	648	331	322	201	92	95	21	457	1,094	158	1

SOURCES

Kivándorlás és Visszavándorlás, 1899-1913 (Emigration et retour des émigrés des pays de la Ste. Couronne Hongroise de 1899 à 1913) (Published by the Central Statistical Office for Hungary, with titles and preface translated into French). Budapest, 1918.

Tables V (p. 47); VI (years 1892-1912) (p. 48); VIII (p. 16); IX (p. 37); X(p. 37); XI (p. 49); XII (p. 65); XIII (p. 9); XIV (p. 8); XV (pp. 4-5); XVI (p. 9); XVII (p.8); XVIII (p. 33); XIX (p. 17); XX (p. 33); XXI (p. 40); XXII (p. 73); XXIII (p. 39); XXIV (p. 42); XXV (p. 40); XXVI (p. 43).

Annuaire Statistique Hongrois, for the years 1908 to 1915 (published by the Central Statistical Office for Hungary). The issue for 1915 appeared in Budapest in 1921.

Tables XXVII and XXVIII.

Information supplied by the Emigration Commissariat of Hungary.

Table XXIX.

Statistik des Hamburgischen Staats.

Tables VI (years 1871-84), and VII.

Czoernig, K. von, *Ethnographie der oesterreichischen Monarchie,* vol. III. Vienna, 1857.

Tables I (p. 23); II (p. 67); III (p. 71); IV (p. 68).

NOTES

[1]The immigration occurred between April 18, 1784 and the end of October 1786.
[2]From the third quarter only.
[3]To the fourth quarter only.
[4]Contains a special list of origins included in the table II for the period August 1, 1785 to October 31, 1785, and November 1, 1785 to October 31, 1786 respectively.
[5]Almost exclusively to the United States. Immigration into Canada still prohibited. Only a few persons to South America.

IRISH FREE STATE (IRELAND)

I. IRELAND

(Tables I-III)

Irish emigration statistics cover the period from May 1, 1851, to December 31, 1921. They indicate the number of emigrants proper who left the ports of Ireland for Great Britain, the colonies or foreign countries. (Table II.) These figures differ, of course, from the number of Irish passengers recorded in the British statistics. The Irish statistics contain two sets of figures, one for the "Natives of Ireland" and one for"Natives and those belonging to other countries combined". Particulars as to age are published for the latter group only (table III). The number of alien emigrants who left Irish ports (difference between totals of tables I and III) was very small. This is the reason why no tables are given for total or alien emigration.

It is possible to distinguish only in totals between emigrants bound for Great Britain and intercontinental emigrants (table II).

II. IRISH FREE STATE

(Tables IV-VIII)

The Irish Free State Department of Statistics has compiled statistical data from April 1, 1923. The emigration statistics include British subjects and citizens of the Free State who leave the Free State, after residing there for at least one year, with the intention of settling in a country outside Europe and the Mediterranean Sea. The immigration statistics include persons of the said nationalities who enter the Free State with the intention of settling there for at least a year after residence in a country outside Europe and the Mediterranean Sea.

The emigration figures cover emigrants from the Free State leaving directly through ports of the Free State (from April 1923), and also indirectly from ports of Great Britain and Northern Ireland (from October 1923). The statistics of immigration include immigrants arriving at ports of the Free State (from April 1923) and also indirectly through ports of Great Britain and Northern Ireland (from October 1923).

All Irish emigrants and immigrants for the period January to March 1923 are included in the statistics of the British Board of Trade. Emigrants from the Free State who left through ports of Great Britain and Northern Ireland during the period April to September and immigrants who returned during the same period through ports of Great Britain and Northern Ireland are included in the statistics for the United Kingdom for 1923.

For the period April 1 to September 30, 1923, a careful estimate made by the Dublin Statistical Department gave the number of indirect emigrants as 6,813, and that of indirect immigrants as 687. (See also *Industrial and Labor Information*, vol. 13, No. 5, pp. 190-193.)

These migrants have had to be taken into account in the national table giving the total emigration from Ireland in the second and third quarters of 1923.

Statistics about the number of migrants from Ireland to Canada (1829-80) and the United States (1820-1924) will be found in the national tables for those countries. Statistics about the number of migrants returning to Ireland from the United States (1908-24) will be found in the national tables for the latter country.

TABLE I.—DISTRIBUTION OF EMIGRANTS (NATIVES) TO GREAT BRITAIN, BRITISH COLONIES AND FOREIGN COUNTRIES, BY SEX, 1851-1921.

Year	Total	Males	Females	Year	Total	Males	Females
1851[1]	152,060	. . . . .	. . . . .	1886	63,135	31,950	31,185
1852	190,322	. . . . .	. . . . .	1887	82,923	43,176	39,747
1853	173,148	. . . . .	. . . . .	1888	78,684	41,310	37,374
1854	140,555	. . . . .	. . . . .	1889	70,477	36,226	34,251
1855	91,914	. . . . .	. . . . .	1890	61,313	31,361	29,952
1856	90,781	47,570	43,211	1891	59,623	30,046	29,577
1857	95,081	52,242	42,839	1892	50,867	25,495	25,372
1858	64,337	35,101	29,236	1893	48,147	23,044	25,103
1859	80,599	43,752	36,847	1894	35,895	15,318	20,577
1860	84,621	42,658	41,963	1895	48,703	21,398	27,305
1861	64,292	32,373	31,919	1896	38,995	17,751	21,244
1862	70,117	36,546	33,571	1897	32,535	13,966	18,569
1863	117,229	61,306	55,923	1898	32,241	14,030	18,211
1864	114,169	60,692	53,477	1899	41,232	18,621	22,611
1865	101,497	55,214	46,283	1900	45,288	21,901	23,387
1866	99,467	59,561	39,906	1901	39,613	18,127	21,486
1867	80,624	45,215	35,409	1902	40,190	18,765	21,425
1868	61,018	35,412	25,606	1903	39,789	18,671	21,118
1869	66,568	39,614	26,954	1904	36,902	17,165	19,737
1870	74,855	43,884	30,971	1905	30,676	16,082	14,594
1871	71,240	41,358	29,882	1906	35,344	19,230	16,114
1872	78,102	46,212	31,890	1907	39,082	21,124	17,958
1873	90,149	51,930	38,219	1908	23,295	10,480	12,815
1874	73,184	39,096	34,088	1909	28,676	14,916	13,760
1875	51,462	26,097	25,365	1910	32,457	17,737	14,720
1876	37,587	20,077	17,510	1911	30,573	16,671	13,902
1877	38,503	20,847	17,656	1912	29,344	15,325	14,019
1878	41,124	20,916	20,208	1913	30,967	16,452	14,515
1879	47,065	25,807	21,258	1914	20,314	10,660	9,654
1880	95,517	49,937	45,580	1915	10,659	6,567	4,092
1881	78,417	40,106	38,311	1916	7,302	1,743	5,559
1882	89,136	46,978	42,158	1917	2,111	838	1,273
1883	108,724	55,264	53,460	1918	980	442	538
1884	75,863	38,054	37,809	1919	2,975	1,137	1,838
1885	62,034	30,873	31,161	1920	15,531	6,044	9,487
				1921	13,635	5,308	8,327

For reference notes see page 736.

TABLE II. EMIGRATION OF NATIVES BY COUNTRY OF DESTINATION, 1876-1921.

Year	Colonies and Foreign Countries							Great Britain
	Total	United States	Canada	South Africa	Australia	New Zealand	Other countries	
1876	20,800	14,887	677	...	3,635	1,558	43	16,787
1877	18,232	12,018	490	...	3,527	2,070	127	20,271
1878	22,476	14,720	660	...	4,251	2,524	321	18,648
1879	31,567	23,361	1,622	...	3,052	3,166	366	15,498
1880	81,968	74,636	3,052	...	2,576	1,477	227	13,549
1881	67,794	61,459	2,916	...	2,795	492	132	10,623
1882	78,480	65,962	7,268	...	4,614	380	256	10,656
1883	98,623	79,798	11,070	...	6,009	1,656	90	10,101
1884	66,873	56,808	4,060	...	5,051	809	145	8,990
1885	56,205	49,655	2,170	...	3,867	429	84	5,829
1886	57,817	50,723	2,588	...	4,212	208	86	5,318
1887	77,861	69,789	3,769	...	3,896	322	85	5,062
1888	72,988	66,906	2,686	...	3,110	87	199	5,696
1889	66,438	59,723	1,742	...	3,038	90	1,845	4,039
1890	56,841	52,685	1,517	...	2,338	126	175	4,472
1891	55,481	52,273	1,078	...	1,824	145	161	4,142
1892	48,937	46,550	989	...	1,216	101	81	1,930
1893	46,795	45,243	872	...	511	94	75	1,352
1894	34,308	33,096	540	...	457	114	101	1,587
1895	46,948	45,298	732	...	629	93	196	1,755
1896	37,081	35,216	654	...	545	77	589	1,914
1897	30,254	28,760	397	...	676	61	360	2,281
1898	29,432	27,855	456		837	36	248	2,809
1899	37,091	35,433	397	...	1,005	56	200	4,141
1900	39,238	37,765	472	...	834	64	103	6,050
1901	33,349	31,942	569	178	595	56	9	6,264
1902	35,472	33,683	732	476	496	74	11	4,718
1903	36,142	33,501	1,493	678	380	67	23	3,647
1904	33,434	30,580	2,083	298	336	123	14	3,468
1905	27,189	24,134	2,360	324	285	69	17	3,487
1906	31,279	27,079	3,404	295	343	105	53	4,065
1907	35,120	30,006	4,296	226	365	143	84	3,962
1908	20,389	16,861	2,531	148	607	126	116	2,906
1909	26,145	21,774	3,043	148	782	272	126	2,531
1910	30,361	24,905	4,416	165	613	179	83	2,096
1911	28,558	22,010	5,478	113	765	166	26	2,015
1912	27,477	20,466	5,788	147	842	189	45	1,867
1913	29,818	21,758	6,673	214	915	220	38	1,149
1914	19,267	15,272	2,909	118	768	172	28	1,047
1915	7,761	6,681	597	68	347	53	15	2,898
1916	4,856	4,207	485	19	100	27	18	2,446
1917	203	88	79	13	13	9	1	1,908
1918	101	12	54	1	32	....	2	879
1919	1,902	848	947	8	60	....	2	1,073
1920	14,949	12,288	2,109	60	212	203	31	582
1921	13,248	11,417	1,422	37	170	170	77	387

TABLE III.—DISTRIBUTION OF EMIGRANTS (NATIVES AND OTHERS NOT DISTINGUISHED), BY AGE, 1856-1920.

Year	Total[2]	under 1 year	1-4 years	5-14 years	15-24 years	25-34 years	35-44 years	45-54 years	55-64 years[3]	65 years and over[3]	Age not specified
1856[4]	90,781	952	4,284	10,824	44,009	18,322	6,995	3,877	1,280	238	...
1857[4]	95,081	991	3,751	9,336	46,647	21,326	7,331	4,083	1,305	272	39
1858	68,093	596	3,426	5,750	28,477	17,268	5,050	2,516	748	129	377
1859	84,599	682	4,549	6,542	36,111	22,763	6,372	2,609	718	141	112
1860	87,626	833	4,517	7,487	40,758	20,764	6,313	2,800	719	94	3,341
1861	66,396	936	4,122	6,393	26,878	15,777	5,932	2,325	525	73	3,435
1862	72,730	663	4,689	6,883	30,125	15,904	5,366	2,705	626	75	5,694
1863	117,820	918	7,208	11,840	51,012	25,511	7,897	4,618	1,083	197	7,536
1864	114,903	936	7,934	10,934	44,134	28,073	7,470	5,390	1,145	147	8,740
1865	103,046	691	5,865	9,393	42,542	24,218	6,801	3,781	907	196	8,702
1866	101,251	367	4,942	8,503	48,758	27,135	7,125	2,746	862	144	669
1867	81,724	369	3,365	7,425	40,129	19,958	5,515	2,986	927	158	892
1868	62,190	279	2,395	4,750	29,672	18,182	3,850	1,803	584	61	614
1869	67,555	272	2,298	4,723	32,339	20,095	4,681	1,843	571	79	636
1870	75,480	360	2,694	5,697	34,409	22,951	5,849	1,975	724	77	744
1871	72,004	309	2,611	5,594	33,962	20,450	5,259	1,846	574	71	564
1872	78,781	293	2,661	6,361	36,895	24,289	5,332	2,098	733	87	32
1873	90,992	401	3,794	7,703	44,163	25,620	5,862	2,571	790	78	10
1874	74,779	516	4,064	7,831	31,707	20,012	6,568	2,931	1,026	118	6
1875	52,397	485	3,219	5,400	20,915	14,249	4,871	2,323	748	158	29

For reference notes see page 736.

TABLE III.—DISTRIBUTION OF EMIGRANTS (NATIVES AND OTHERS NOT DISTINGUISHED), BY AGE, 1856-1920 (continued).

Year	Total	Under 1 year	1-4 years	5-14 years	15-24 years	25-34 years	35-44 years	45-54 years	55-59 years	60 years and over	Age not specified
1876	38,315	383	2,023	3,592	14,596	10,774	4,611	1,698	542	87	9
1877	41,225	503	2,232	3,818	16,128	11,602	4,126	1,832	365	600	19
1878	41,626	447	2,593	4,034	17,935	10,595	3,524	1,656	317	525	...
1879	47,364	402	2,256	3,945	22,472	12,170	3,840	1,621	248	410	...
1880	95,859	748	4,469	8,486	52,178	20,370	5,797	2,675	548	559	29
1881	78,719	636	3,694	7,221	44,837	15,045	4,173	2,134	447	434	98
1882	89,566	818	4,347	8,560	50,096	16,888	5,328	2,474	456	546	53
1883	108,916	1,017	6,451	14,264	56,321	17,582	7,413	4,239	683	791	155
1884	76,043	594	4,039	8,225	39,386	14,196	5,307	3,103	627	566	...
1885	62,420	469	2,677	5,020	34,835	12,087	4,099	2,353	430	442	8
1886	63,416	479	2,331	4,299	36,682	12,871	3,778	2,101	364	435	76
1887	83,202	591	2,847	5,453	50,572	15,692	4,347	2,526	512	467	195
1888	79,211	566	2,742	4,981	48,631	14,863	4,171	2,178	393	448	238
1889	70,800	599	2,565	4,617	43,160	13,261	3,697	1,877	390	461	173
1890	61,435	422	2,064	3,780	38,209	11,550	3,045	1,598	369	357	41
1891	59,868	393	1,839	3,421	38,653	10,762	2,721	1,502	276	299	2
1892	51,000	380	1,497	2,779	32,456	9,966	2,226	1,219	261	201	15
1893	48,246	292	1,157	2,406	31,199	9,814	1,913	1,045	213	191	16
1894	35,959	329	855	1,669	20,736	9,152	1,726	994	240	251	7
1895	48,934	240	1,093	1,894	28,547	12,954	1,986	1,400	321	305	2
1896	39,226	237	874	1,659	21,785	11,063	1,779	1,107	293	252	10
1897	32,906	227	716	1,392	18,627	8,676	1,922	927	284	273	5
1898	33,865	221	874	1,434	18,664	9,199	1,922	1,008	281	259	3
1899	43,760	305	1,184	1,898	24,308	11,963	2,434	1,086	311	270	1
1900	47,107	357	1,464	2,227	26,871	11,875	2,566	1,126	341	319	...
1901	39,870	308	1,391	2,073	22,473	9,590	2,473	933	290	246	21
1902	40,101	279	1,196	1,985	22,506	10,407	2,349	899	350	285	9
1903	40,659	312	1,302	2,277	21,983	10,913	2,333	886	348	280	25
1904	37,415	280	1,067	2,042	23,520	7,805	1,463	773	251	189	15
1905	31,172	220	957	1,601	19,470	6,739	1,252	585	176	157	...
1906	35,918	238	1,294	2,028	21,649	8,186	1,630	569	197	127	2
1907	39,562	259	1,294	2,172	23,914	9,294	1,685	644	158	140	2
1908	23,952	136	968	1,557	13,626	5,812	1,184	433	126	108	3
1909	29,230	121	745	1,306	17,716	7,505	1,220	421	90	103	...
1910	32,923	122	817	1,310	19,923	8,693	1,429	425	95	109	2
1911	31,058	131	809	1,431	18,618	7,981	1,405	475	105	103	2
1912	29,799	136	724	1,424	18,625	6,963	1,301	437	92	95	...
1913	31,339	139	817	1,553	19,672	7,096	1,387	457	107	109	2
1914	20,583	80	482	967	13,288	4,527	813	284	73	69	...
1915	10,792	31	229	479	5,847	3,173	761	198	36	36	...
1916	7,366	42	300	671	4,242	1,162	537	291	61	60	...
1917	2,129	28	222	585	422	377	369	100	8	18	...
1918	983	10	125	322	108	186	171	49	7	5	...
1919	3,114	36	280	543	809	782	392	161	46	65	...
1920	15,585	90	333	910	9,646	3,370	701	323	96	116	...

TABLE IV.—Distribution of emigrants and immigrants of Saorstat nationality, by sex and age[5], 1923-24.

Year	Total	Emigration					
		Children under 12 years			Adults of 12 years and over		
		Total	Males	Females	Total	Males	Females
1923 April-Sept.	9,977	....	....	....	....	....	....
Oct.-Dec.	3,419	180	....	....	3,239	1,502	1,737
1924	19,077	817	412	405	18,260	10,282	7,978

Year	Total	Immigration					
		Children under 12 years			Adults of 12 years and over		
		Total	Males	Females	Total	Males	Females
1923 April-Sept.	2,543	....	....	....	....	....	....
Oct.-Dec.	537	48	....	....	489	213	276
1924	2,499	280	131	149	2,219	2,081	1,138

TABLE V.—Distribution of adult emigrants and immigrants (over 18 years of age) of Saorstat nationality, by occupation and sex[5], 1924.

Occupation	Emigration			Immigration		
	Total	Males	Females	Total	Males	Females
Agriculture and laborers not in transport or communications....................	8,083	8,083	....	440	440	...
Domestic, hotel, etc., service..	5,670	....	5,670	552	...	552
Commercial, finance and insurance.................	692	515	177	160	109	51
Professional and independent.	511	278	233	158	109	49
Skilled trades..............	669	669	...	157	157	...
Transport and communications....................	141	141	...	43	43	...
Clothing trades............	95	...	95	19	...	19
Wife or housewife not otherwise described.......	967	...	967	325	...	325
Other and ill-defined occupations...................	617	331	286	324	200	124
Total.............	17,445	10,017	7,428	2,178	1,058	1,120

For reference notes see page 736.

TABLE VI.—Emigration and immigration (Saorstat nationality), by country of future or last residence[5] [6], 1923-24.

Year	Emigration				
	Total	United States	British North America	Australia	Other countries
1923 (Oct.-Dec.)	3,419	2,610	389	190	230
1924	19,077	12,016	5,237	1,138	686

Year	Immigration				
	Total	United States	British North America	Australia	Other countries
1923 (Oct.-Dec.)	537	349	68	41	79
1924	2,499	1,460	333	203	503

TABLE VII.—Distribution of emigrant and immigrant aliens, by sex and age during the nine months ended 31 December 1924.[5]

Immigration				Emigration			
Total	Males	Females	Children under 12 years	Total	Males	Females	Children under 12 years
891	425	301	165	213	96	68	49

TABLE VIII.—Immigration and emigration of aliens, by country of last or future residence[5], during nine months ended 31 December 1924.

Immigration			Emigration			
Total	United States	Other countries	Total	United States	British North America	Other countries
891	880	11	213	197	4	12

For reference notes see page 736.

SOURCES

Emigration Statistics of Ireland, 1876-1920.   Accounts and Papers.

Tables I (years 1851-1920); II, III, IV (years 1876-1920).

Agricultural Statistics for Ireland, 1858-75, London.

Tables II, III (years 1856-75).

Emigration Statistics, Ireland.   Return of the Number of Emigrants (Natives of Ireland) who left Irish Ports during the month of December 1921.   By Authority of the Registrar-General.   Dublin, 1922.

Tables I, II, III (year 1921).

Information supplied by the Government of the Irish Free State, Dublin.

Tables V, VII (years 1923, 1924); VI, VIII, IX (year 1924).

NOTES

[1]From May 1, the date at which the collection of these returns commenced.
[2]This total does not correspond in every year with the total indicated in the source for total emigrants (natives and those belonging to other countries).
[3]From 1877 to 1920 these age groups are 55-59 and 60 years and over.
[4]The figures for 1856 and 1857 correspond with those given in table I as referring to Natives of Ireland.
[5]The figures include emigrants from Great Britain embarked at Irish Free State ports (see Introduction).
[6]Residence for a year or more is treated as permanent residence.

NETHERLANDS

I. Statistics compiled by the Municipalities and relating to the Emigration of Citizens by Sea

(Tables I-II)

Returns relating to the overseas emigration of citizens were first prepared by the municipalities (1831-81) and published in the Official Gazette. This was undertaken "in pursuance of a Circular Letter of the Minister for Home Affairs of December 21, 1847. The Letter required the municipalities to forward to him annually the figures concerning emigration to America and other overseas countries. These figures were for the first time furnished for the year 1848, and thereto were joined, as far as possible, data for previous years".

The Central Statistical Office has furnished a table giving the aggregate figures of emigrants passing through Dutch ports. This table can be supplemented by another which was found in a report addressed to the King, and which gives the same aggregate figures, but classifies them according to sex and age (see sources).

Data for the year 1880 are lacking; but for 1881 the recorded number of emigrants is to all appearance excessive (10,100). As the port statistics of Rotterdam—by far the most important emigration port— only recorded for this year 3,360 Dutch emigrants (table III) and the United States immigration statistics reported a total of 3,340 Dutch immigrants, it is likely that in the number of 10,100 alien emigrants are included or, possibly, the table refers not only to Dutch but to other ports.

Generally speaking, the figures for the period 1867-74 (table I) do not agree with the Rotterdam statistics, although for the succeeding period, 1874-79—if we disregard some insignificant deviations—they accord well enough with the Rotterdam figures for emigrant citizens. (Table IV.)

II. Port Statistics

(Tables III-V)

In conformity with the Act of June 1, 1861, amended by the Act of July 15, 1869, the commission charged with the function of supervising the transport of emigrants at Amsterdam, Rotterdam (Flushing and Harlingen) publishes a quarterly list of emigrants. This list includes only those who are travelling to overseas countries and who embark in Dutch ports.

No distinction is drawn between ordinary passengers and emigrants, but the passengers are classified according to sex, age, occupation and class in which they are travelling. Voyages during which transshipment takes place in British ports are referred to as "interrupted voyages" and are included in the total.

For the Port of Rotterdam original documents are only available since 1867 (no distinction was made until 1881 between aliens and citizens). For the Port of Amsterdam, these documents only date back to 1882.

III. STATISTICS OF POPULATION REGISTERS

(Tables VI-VIII)

The emigration statistics developed from the population registers are based on the departures from communes there recorded. These departures are brought to the attention of the local authority by the declarations required of those who intend to depart by the Royal Decree of 1861 (*Rec. des Lois 94*). The Article runs as follows: "Each person leaving a commune with the intention of taking up his residence in a Dutch colony or abroad is struck off from the population register after he has made a declaration to this effect and so soon as his departure has been confirmed." Conformably to a Ministerial instruction the records thus made are, for statistical purposes, cast into tabular form by the local authorities.

The names of the persons who left the country without notifying the Population Office of their intention to depart are crossed off the list a year after their absence has been noted.

The statistics mention the total number of emigrants and their sex.

With regard to immigration, the names of the persons who come from abroad and settle in the country are entered on the population register. The statistical returns give merely the number of such persons, classified by sex. If persons entering the country do not have their names immediately entered on the population register, they are entered on a visitors' register; if, later, they declare their intention to settle in the country, their names are officially entered on the population register and are included with the other names in the statistics.

In addition to the tables relating to emigration and immigration (tables VI-VII), a special table (VIII) is published referring to the persons officially struck off or entered in the population registers. Only after adding the numbers in this table to those of emigrants and immigrants in the previously mentioned two tables do we reach the actual grand totals.

Table VI relates mainly to aliens, but it also comprises a certain number of citizens who departed from their communes without giving due notice and remained away for over a year. This is subject, however, to the provision that the persons involved were not entered on some other communal register. Such incorporations of citizens took place in a wholesale manner, notably in years where certain communes, or portions of them, were incorporated in other communes. This explains the high figures for the years 1921 and 1923, the individuals concerned being struck off one register and entered on another.

Emigration figures for the years 1843 to 1853 are to be found for Dutch ports in the above-cited United States *Report* and in Hübner's *Jahrbuch*.

For the period 1843-45 the United States source only has been utilised, because (a) for 1843 we have only the figures furnished by this source, because (b) it gives separate figures for Rotterdam and Amsterdam; and because (c) its data reflect a more general phenomenon, as they include the number of emigrants of all nationalities departing for the United States. This latter was the principal country of destination for the emigrants leaving from Dutch ports, whilst, on the contrary, Hübner includes only German emigrants without distinguishing their countries of destination. The difference between our two sources in regard to the year 1844 is negligible. For 1845 Hübner does not supply any figures at all, and another source (Höfken) gives the same figure for Rotterdam as the American source. For 1846 the latter source quotes an improbable figure (5,010), one far inferior to that of Hübner (13,120), which, it should be noted, does not include Amsterdam. From 1847 onwards we reproduce Hübner's figures, which are derived, as shown by his figures for other countries, from the most reliable official documents. In some years the number of Dutch immigrants arriving in the United States was so high (2,631, for 1847; 1,190, for 1849; and 1,719, for 1852) that presumably Hübner's figures refer exclusively to German and other transmigrants.

•Statistics about the number of migrants from the Netherlands to South Africa (1913-24), Argentina (1857-1924), Brazil (1908-24). Canada (1900-24), Cuba (1911-24), United States (1820-1924) and Australia (1902-24) will be found in the national tables for those countries. Statistics about the number of migrants returning to the Netherlands from Argentina (1857-1924) and the United States (1908-24) will be found in the national tables for those countries.

TABLE I.—EMIGRATION OF CITIZENS THROUGH DUTCH PORTS, 1831-81.

Year	Total	Year	Total	Year	Total
1831	1	1848	2,160	1865	1,567
1832	1	1849	2,078	1866	3,295
1833	..	1850	774	1867	4,187
1834	..	1851	1,196	1868	2,972
1835	6	1852	1,184	1869	3,436
1836	13	1853	1,646	1870	1,644
1837	1	1854	3,611	1871	2,069
1838	..	1855	2,077	1872	3,486
1839	9	1856	1,924	1873	3,867
1840	2	1857	1,663	1874	1,042
1841	..	1858	1,177	1875	786
1842	24	1859	497	1876	620
1843	67	1860	862	1877	594
1844	171	1861	757	1878	563
1845	680	1862	819	1879	1,105
1846	1,755	1863	1,054	1880	....
1847	5,322	1864	740	1881	10,100

TABLE II.—INTERCONTINENTAL EMIGRATION OF CITIZENS, BY SEX AND AGE, 1831-56.

Year	Total	Heads of families and unmarried	Females	Children	Servants
1831–47	8,053	2,334	1,357	4,281	81
1848	2,160	678	322	1,131	29
1849	2,078	623	320	1,108	27
1850	774	282	112	373	7
1851	1,196	401	178	599	18
1852	1,184	422	179	578	5
1853	1,646	647	256	735	8
1854	3,611	1,256	582	1,759	14
1855	2,077	677	327	1,060	13
1856	1,924	623	283	997	21

TABLE III.—EMIGRATION FROM DUTCH PORTS TO UNITED STATES PORTS, 1843-53.

Year	Total	From Rotterdam	From Amsterdam	Year	Total	From Rotterdam	From Amsterdam
1843	1,648	1,387	261	1849	....	8,695	...
1844	2,363	2,143	220	1850	....	5,640	...
1845	5,131	4,549	582	1851	....	3,000	...
1846	....	9,547	....	1852	2,698	....	...
1847	....	13,060	....	1853	....	1,789	...
1848	....	7,784	....	....	....	....	...

TABLE IV.—EMIGRATION THROUGH DUTCH PORTS DISTINGUISHING CITIZENS AND ALIENS, 1867-1924.[1]

Year	Total	Citizens	Aliens	Year	Total	Citizens	Aliens
1867	4,161	1,776	2,385	1896	12,787	1,387	11,400
1868	2,546	969	1,577	1897	9,036	792	8,244
1869	2,726	1,452	1,274	1898	14,119	851	13,268
1870	3,441	1,123	2,318	1899	20,296	1,347	18,949
				1900	34,794	1,899	32,895
1871	2,844	1,592	1,252				
1872	3,662	2,176	1,486	1901	34,343	1,874	32,469
1873	5,091	3,172	1,919	1902	45,886	2,301	43,585
1874	2,241	1,066	1,175	1903	53,590	2,963	50,627
1875	2,099	757	1,342	1904	49,854	2,440	47,414
				1905	56,880	2,297	54,583
1876	2,356	598	1,758				
1877	2,373	574	1,799	1906	50,954	2,548	48,406
1878	2,781	563	2,218	1907	62,402	4,393	58,009
1879	4,603	1,048	3,555	1908	20,545	3,030	17,515
1880	11,549	3,360	8,189	1909	50,318	2,939	47,379
				1910	64,188	3,220	60,968
1881	18,171	4,414	13,757				
1882	34,321	7,304	27,017	1911	43,838	2,638	41,200
1883	19,643	4,855	14,788	1912	72,509	2,155	70,354
1884	11,278	3,729	7,549	1913	87,813	2,330	85,483
1885	8,090	2,146	5,944	1914	35,815	2,174	33,641
				1915	6,603	1,074	5,529
1886	11,924	2,024	9,900				
1887	19,192	5,018	14,174	1916	7,458	911	6,547
1888	18,137	4,628	13,509	1917	2,944	867	2,077
1889	22,334	9,111	13,223	1918	1,197	1,160	37
1890	17,136	3,526	13,610	1919	8,213	2,439	5,774
				1920	42,337	5,978	36,359
1891	32,109	4,075	28,034				
1892	28,327	6,290	22,037	1921	35,799	3,286	32,513
1893	39,260	4,820	34,440	1922	12,685	2,158	10,527
1894	15,138	1,146	13,992	1923	22,529	5,648	16,881
1895	15,919	1,314	14,603	1924	19,245	3,137	16,108

For reference notes see page 746.

TABLE V.—Distribution of citizens emigrated through Dutch ports, by sex, age and country of destination, 1882-1924.

Year	Total[2]	Males	Females	Children under 10 years	North America	South America[3]	Australia	Africa
1882	7,304[4]	3,111	1,941	2,273	7,230	16	12	46
1883	4,855	2,118	1,372	1,365	4,798	3	18	36
1884	3,729	1,672	1,131	926	3,654	4	7	64
1885	2,146	1,010	597	539	2,121	. . .	7	18
1886	2,024	930	509	585	2,002	5	8	9
1887	5,018	2,861	1,030	1,127	5,018	. . .	. .	. .
1888	4,628	2,333	1,105	1,190	4,298	330	. .	. .
1889	9,111	3,377	2,543	3,191	5,050	4,020	. .	41
1890	3,526	1,454	1,133	939	3,282	167	. .	77
1891	4,075	1,784	1,247	1,044	3,923	. . .	. .	152
1892	6,290	2,773	1,821	1,696	6,211	. . .	. .	79
1893	4,820	2,262	1,248	1,310	4,820	. . .	. . .	. .
1894	1,146	583	322	241	1,146	. . .	. .	. .
1895	1,314	667	366	281	1,277	. . .	. .	37
1896	1,387	680	400	307	1,241	51	. .	95
1897	792	433	197	162	. . . .	. . .	. .	. .
1898	851	439	226	186	781	. . .	. .	70
1899	1,347	674	332	341	1,260	. . .	. . .	87
1900	1,899	907	477	515	1,893	. . .	. .	6
1901	1,874	950	525	399	1,874	. . .	. .	. .
1902	2,301	1,136	595	570	2,298	. . .	. .	3
1903	2,963	1,385	748	830	. . . .	. . .	. .	. .
1904	2,440	1,178	597	665	2,424	. . .	. .	16
1905	2,297	1,127	544	626	2,282	. . .	. .	15
1906	2,548	1,224	624	700	2,509	29	. .	10
1907	4,393	2,296	1,012	1,085	4,331	59	. .	3
1908	3,030	1,344	814	872	1,848	1,176	. .	6
1909	2,939	1,358	706	875	1,703	1,223	. .	13
1910	3,220	1,736	762	722	2,984	227	. .	9
1911	2,638	1,426	604	608	2,364	257	. .	7
1912	2,155	1,150	504	501	1,803	352	. .	. .
1913	2,330	1,271	527	532	2,100	226	. .	4
1914	2,174	1,150	533	491	1,954	70	. .	. .
1915	1,074	567	278	229	1,009	48	. .	. .
1916	911	454	264	193	869	33	. .	. .
1917	867	462	277	128	821	43	. .	. .
1918	1,160	495	451	214	1,072	48	. .	9
1919	2,439	1,264	808	367	2,159	237	. .	. .
1920	5,978	2,977	1,940	1,061	5,781	182	. .	. .
1921	3,286	1,556	1,155	575	3,099	165	. .	20
1922	2,158	1,115	745	298	1,912	195	. .	47
1923	5,648	3,134	1,548	966	5,373	207	. .	59
1994	3,137	1,860	786	491	2,605	394	. .	37

For reference notes see page 746.

TABLE VI.—Distribution of emigrant citizens, by sex and destination, 1865-1924.

Year	To Dutch colonies			To foreign countries		
	Total	Males	Females	Total	Males	Females
1865	537	351	186	7,816	4,367	3,449
1866	892	657	235	9,536	5,379	4,157
1867	584	397	187	10,459	5,771	4,688
1868	572	369	203	9,258	4,902	4,356
1869	1,615	1,330	285	13,157	7,451	5,706
1870	615	394	221	7,913	4,299	3,614
1871	1,110	873	237	10,637	5,774	4,863
1872	832	564	268	11,916	6,389	5,527
1873	1,897	1,629	268	12,762	6,734	6,028
1874	1,029	787	242	8,761	4,529	4,232
1875	858	519	339	8,177	4,269	3,908
1876	806	523	283	7,759	3,881	3,878
1877	788	465	323	6,778	3,331	3,447
1878	770	458	312	7,290	3,547	3,743
1879	870	535	335	9,551	4,927	4,624
1880	822	532	290	11,836	6,048	5,788
1881	2,766	2,380	386	16,025	8,628	7,397
1882	4,245	3,940	305	15,582	8,441	7,141
1883	3,168	2,719	449	13,625	7,257	6,368
1884	3,223	2,853	370	12,977	6,846	6,131
1885	3,268	2,895	373	11,740	6,160	5,580
1886	3,348	3,073	275	12,127	6,279	5,848
1887	2,947	2,570	377	14,597	7,800	6,797
1888	3,406	3,020	386	15,608	8,425	7,183
1889	2,890	2,481	409	20,146	10,728	9,418
1890	3,045	2,683	362	15,987	8,390	7,597
1891	3,032	2,627	405	16,839	8,919	7,920
1892	3,852	3,416	436	17,553	9,151	8,402
1893	4,308	3,859	449	18,562	10,077	8,485
1894	5,939	5,386	553	15,159	8,120	7,039
1895	3,565	3,006	559	14,857	8,033	6,824
1896	4,166	3,662	504	18,992	10,594	8,398
1897	4,108	3,641	467	19,446	10,526	8,920
1898	4,077	3,482	595	21,293	11,555	9,738
1899	3,782	3,277	505	25,117	13,733	11,384
1900	3,090	2,564	526	22,042	11,804	10,238
1901	3,583	2,989	594	19,181	9,911	9,270
1902	4,641	4,023	618	19,789	10,154	9,635
1903	4,546	3,791	755	23,748	12,605	11,143
1904	3,580	2,878	702	24,110	12,850	11,260
1905	3,808	3,096	712	23,658	12,421	11,237
1906	3,304	2,488	816	27,574	14,801	12,773
1907	4,229	3,394	835	34,149	18,581	15,568
1908	4,707	3,729	978	29,931	15,530	14,401
1909	4,815	3,677	1,138	32,252	17,474	14,778
1910	5,147	4,080	1,067	29,932	15,954	13,978
1911	5,382	4,008	1,374	33,478	17,840	15,638
1912	5,732	3,983	1,749	33,284	17,594	15,690
1913	6,499	4,527	1,972	33,568	18,156	15,412
1914	4,897	3,062	1,835	24,916	13,068	11,848
1915	4,215	2,505	1,710	12,864	6,852	6,012
1916	3,605	2,275	1,330	7,493	3,862	3,631
1917	2,330	1,603	727	6,489	3,091	3,398
1918	2,904	2,015	889	17,729	7,846	9,883
1919	5,239	3,057	2,182	40,183	19,755	20,428
1920	7,970	4,679	3,291	27,964	14,467	13,497
1921	8,280	4,830	3,450	22,655	11,547	11,108
1922	7,224	4,064	3,160	26,252	13,200	13,052
1923	5,490	3,205	2,285	31,275	15,780	15,495
1924	6,053	3,637	2,416	38,437	15,148	23,289

TABLE VII. —Distribution of immigrants, by sex and country of origin, 1865-1924

Year	From Dutch colonies			From foreign countries		
	Total	Males	Females	Total	Males	Females
1865	1,875	1,525	350	5,072	2,878	2,194
1866	1,154	822	332	5,150	2,863	2,287
1867	1,732	1,338	394	5,084	2,754	2,330
1868	1,978	1,531	447	5,388	2,945	2,443
1869	1,466	961	505	6,056	3,280	2,776
1870	2,063	1,645	418	5,692	3,244	2,448
1871	1,628	1,229	399	5,327	2,873	2,454
1872	1,711	1,213	498	6,424	3,535	2,889
1873	1,724	1,162	562	6,549	3,522	3,027
1874	1,679	1,109	570	6,673	3,699	2,974
1875	1,739	1,199	540	7,457	3,828	3,629
1876	1,699	1,195	504	8,185	4,181	4,004
1877	2,021	1,450	571	9,934	5,470	4,464
1878	2,895	2,147	748	10,751	6,085	4,666
1879	3,255	2,591	664	10,755	5,869	4,886
1880	2,615	2,007	608	9,308	5,275	4,033
1881	3,050	2,410	640	10,806	5,938	4,868
1882	4,236	3,485	751	11,058	6,045	5,013
1883	3,298	2,580	718	11,151	5,926	5,225
1884	2,791	2,175	616	11,296	5,961	5,335
1885	3,083	2,439	644	10,569	5,449	5,120
1886	3,240	2,633	607	10,622	5,463	5,159
1887	3,154	2,550	604	10,381	5,294	5,087
1888	2,590	1,964	626	10,836	5,867	4,969
1889	3,231	2,409	822	12,109	6,202	5,907
1890	2,627	2,020	607	10,521	5,343	5,178
1891	2,568	1,948	620	12,642	6,648	5,994
1892	2,787	2,061	726	13,129	6,921	6,208
1893	3,166	2,451	715	12,797	7,030	5,767
1894	2,833	2,058	775	12,847	6,976	5,871
1895	2,873	2,153	720	11,885	6,409	5,476
1896	3,379	2,732	647	13,231	6,990	6,241
1897	3,947	3,146	801	15,217	8,369	6,848
1898	3,526	2,758	768	15,726	8,410	7,316
1899	4,363	3,484	879	17,677	9,527	8,150
1900	4,262	3,477	785	19,802	10,682	9,120
1901	3,970	3,061	909	20,421	10,815	9,606
1902	4,721	3,654	1,067	19,818	10,292	9,526
1903	4,834	3,802	1,032	20,723	11,139	9,584
1904	4,326	3,342	984	19,366	10,099	9,267
1905	4,817	3,609	1,208	20,353	10,763	9,590
1906	4,546	3,280	1,266	21,677	11,400	10,277
1907	4,639	3,407	1,232	22,630	12,053	10,577
1908	4,826	3,631	1,195	25,128	13,362	11,766
1909	4,301	2,964	1,337	27,885	14,636	13,249
1910	4,436	3,084	1,352	26,711	14,391	12,320

TABLE VII.—DISTRIBUTION OF IMMIGRANTS, BY SEX AND COUNTRY OF ORIGIN, 1865-1924—continued

Year	From Dutch colonies			From foreign countries		
	Total	Males	Females	Total	Males	Females
1911	5,011	3,205	1,806	28,544	15,292	13,252
1912	5,201	3,349	1,852	31,000	16,616	14,384
1913	5,999	4,046	1,953	33,966	18,631	15,335
1914	5,363	3,359	2,004	46,372	24,893	21,479
1915	3,697	2,324	1,373	28,819	14,325	14,494
1916	4,731	3,119	1,612	46,172	22,951	23,221
1917	2,555	1,703	852	47,994	24,527	23,467
1918	1,073	853	220	21,582	9,949	11,633
1919	7,245	4,526	2,719	25,041	12,895	12,146
1920	8,663	5,068	3,595	32,961	17,265	15,696
1921	7,316	4,111	3,205	23,001	9,893	13,108
1922	9,027	5,471	3,556	33,796	10,867	22,929
1923	7,421	4,300	3,121	43,737	13,487	30,250
1924	7,199	4,113	3,086	34,085	14,447	19,638

TABLE VIII.—OFFICIAL REGISTRATION AND CANCELLATION IN THE POPULATION REGISTERS, BY SEX, 1879-1905.

Year	Registered		Cancelled		Year	Registered		Cancelled	
	Males	Females	Males	Females		Males	Females	Males	Females
1879	2,541	1,475	12,273	3,468	1893	1,438	1,140	2,343	1,839
1880	3,581	2,228	10,526	1,785	1894	1,260	1,029	2,219	1,755
1881	2,641	4,818	4,596	1,687	1895	1,547	1,064	3,258	2,153
1882	1,840	4,083	2,574	1,844	1896	1,469	1,067	6,677	6,317
1883	1,183	973	1,074	1,551	1897	1,825	1,344	2,779	2,225
1884	5,249	4,979	6,048	5,356	1898	1,996	1,486	2,480	1,975
1885	1,156	904	1,885	1,335	1899	2,533	2,291	5,550	2,839
1886	993	852	1,857	1,444	1900	3,449	3,048	1,131	791
1887	1,042	859	2,283	1,595	1901	3,049	2,529	2,148	1,752
1888	996	832	2,591	1,975	1902	2,633	1,982	2,644	2,293
1889	1,557	1,381	5,354	4,369	1903	2,808	2,084	4,766	4,002
1890	2,526	2,195	1,949	1,434	1904	2,548	2,108	4,032	3,326
1891	1,934	1,749	1,697	1,304	1905	1,928	1,477	3,466	2,837
1892	1,663	1,413	2,247	1,790	....	....	....	....	....

TABLE IX.—CONTINENTAL EMIGRATION AND IMMIGRATION OF LABORERS, 1811.

Department	Emigrants	Immigrants
Mouth of the Meuse	41	4,019
Mouth of the Ysel	550	800
Ems, West	640	2,277
Ems, East	....	885
Friesland	....	3,665
Overijssel	625	44
Zuider Zee	....	8,928
Total	1,856	20,618

SOURCES

Jaarcijfers voor Nederland, 1915, 1920, 1924.   The Hague.

Tables IV, VII (years 1906-24).

Information supplied by the Central Statistical Bureau of the Netherlands.

Tables I, V-VIII; IV (years 1867-1905).

Proposals Addressed by the State Commission constituted by the Royal Decree of June 16, 1857, No. 90, to F. H. von Vlissingen and nine others, concerning the European colonisation of the Dutch Indies, with seven appendices.   The Hague, 1858.

Table II.

Report of the Select Committee of the Senate of the United States on the Sickness and Mortality on board Emigrant Ships.   Washington, 1854, p. 42.

Table III (years 1843-45).

M. D'Alphonse, (Intendant of the Interior in Holland).   *Aperçu sur la Hollande.* Published under the regime and by order of the French Government.

Table IX.

Statistica della Emigrazione italiana avvenuta nell'anno 1891.   Roma, 1892, p. 36. *Statistica della Emigrazione italiana per l'Estero* negli anni 1898 e 1899 ad 1906 e 1907. Rome, 1900-08.

Table IV (years 1882-1905, totals and aliens).

Hübner, *Jahrbuch für Volkswirtschaft und Statistik*. vols. I-IV, Leipzig, 1852-56.

Table III (years 1846-53).

NOTES

[1]For 1867-81, the figures refer to the Port of Rotterdam only.
[2]Including emigrants the country of destination of whom is not indicated.
[3]Includes Central America as from 1898.
[4]The total of emigrants by sex and age gives the figure 7,325.

NORWAY

I. Statistics of Transport Contracts
(Tables I-IV)

Statistics of Norwegian emigration date from 1821. They are now compiled in conformity with the Act of May 22, 1869, concerning the supervision of emigrant transportation. According to Section 6 of this Act, emigration agents must make a written contract with every emigrant and have it approved by the chief of police who reports on emigration at the end of each year.

On these reports the statistics of emigration are based. They apply only to emigration of Norwegian subjects intending to settle in countries outside Europe but include also a certain number of aliens domiciled in Norway.

II. Statistics of Police Registers
(Tables V-VII)

Statistics of immigration are compiled in conformity with the Act of June 24, 1915, amending and completing the Act of May 4, 1901, upon the registration of travellers and aliens. It applies to all aliens domiciled in the country for more than four months. According to Section 3, persons who are not domiciled in Norway (both aliens and Norwegians) must register when they come from overseas or continental countries in case they desire to settle or seek employment in Norway. An Act of May 4, 1917, provides that no one may stay within the country more than three days without notifying the authorities. The increase in the figures for 1917 probably shows the effect of the new Act, but the data for the preceding year are markedly incomplete.

The immigration statistics are not yet entirely reliable It is difficult to obtain exact information regarding Norwegians of American nationality who have returned to Norway, as they frequently fail to report their arrival.

The tables for the period 1918-24 include persons in search of employment or intending to settle in Norway.

Since 1916, the police authorities have submitted reports in regard to immigrants registered under this Act.

Statistics about the number of migrants from Norway to South Africa (1913-24), Canada (1900-24) and the United States (1820-1924) will be found in the national tables for those countries. Statistics about the number of migrants returning to Norway from the United States (1908-24) will be found in the national tables for the latter country.

TABLE I.—Intercontinental emigration of citizens, 1821-65.

Year	Emigrants	Year	Emigrants	Year	Emigrants	Year	Emigrants
1821	1	1842	700	1850	3,700	1858	2,500
1825	53	1843	1,600	1851	2,640	1859	1,800
1836	200	1844	1,200	1852	4,030	1860	1,900
1837	200	1845	1,100	1853	6,050	1861	8,900
1838	100	1846	1,300	1854	5,950	1862	5,250
1839	400	1847	1,600	1855	1,600	1863	1,100
1840	300	1848	1,400	1856	3,200	1864	4,300
1841	400	1849	4,000	1857	6,400	1865	4,000

TABLE II.—Distribution of emigrant citizens to extra-European countries, by sex and age, 1866-1924.

Year	Total	Sex		under 5 years		5-9 years	
		Males	Females	Males	Females	Males	Females
1866[1]	15,455	9,149	6,306	1,051	1,012	842	750
1867[1]	12,830	7,081	5,749	974	930	803	737
1868[1]	13,219	7,415	5,804	814	800	692	699
1869[1]	18,056	10,155	7,901	1,148	1,014	950	896
1870[1]	14,788	8,169	6,619	1,101	989	805	731
1871[1]	11,361	6,364	4,997	786	720	530	451
1872[1]	13,322	7,193	6,129	769	804	605	535
1873[1]	9,917	5,379	4,538	621	603	372	355
1874[1]	4,357	2,214	2,143	246	264	159	167
1875[1]	4,032	2,157	1,875	224	236	149	152
1876[1]	4,355	2,403	1,952	263	247	154	148
1877	3,206	1,701	1,505	174	160	102	101
1878	4,863	2,713	2,150	276	259	162	164
1879	7,609	4,708	2,900	441	401	164	182
1880	20,212	12,260	7,952	1,308	1,244	502	500
1881	25,976	14,910	11,066	1,855	1,769	819	812
1882	28,804	16,538	12,266	2,029	1,928	894	798
1883	22,167	12,358	9,809	1,589	1,532	777	671
1884	14,776	8,044	6,732	986	882	445	418
1885	13,981	7,272	6,709	884	795	493	433
1886	15,158	8,611	6,547	817	741	398	371
1887	20,741	12,714	8,027	957	896	459	392
1888	21,452	13,138	8,314	935	916	493	429
1889	12,642	7,076	5,566	546	566	287	261
1890	10,991	5,878	5,113	525	469	277	256
1891	13,341	7,784	5,557	398	373	340	321
1892	17,049	10,119	6,930	533	534	425	362
1893	18,778	11,236	7,542	635	571	439	418
1894	5,642	2,926	2,716	189	204	139	135
1895	6,207	3,305	2,902	172	173	130	141
1896	6,679	4,064	2,615	150	164	101	90
1897	4,669	2,712	1,957	127	114	59	65
1898	4,859	2,845	2,014	119	103	79	83
1899	6,699	4,149	2,550	159	161	123	85
1900	10,931	6,873	4,058	266	270	157	146
1901	12,745	8,131	4,614	355	334	193	172
1902	20,343	13,633	6,710	607	555	327	283
1903	26,784	17,394	9,390	886	920	474	445
1904	22,264	13,506	8,758	902	805	552	520
1905	21,059	12,935	8,124	689	669	458	410
1906	21,967	13,871	8,096	536	510	367	219
1907	22,135	13,872	8,263	496	515	416	440
1908	8,497	4,275	4,222	203	236	244	225
1909	16,152	10,094	6,058	261	267	234	250
1910	18,912	12,291	6,621	323	309	308	271
1911	12,477	7,556	4,921	198	188	161	153
1912	9,105	5,056	4,049	176	170	157	151
1913	9,876	6,185	3,691	178	152	160	156
1914	8,522	4,797	3,725	133	123	110	115
1915	4,572	2,122	2,450	118	87	100	95
1916	5,212	2,306	2,906	119	128	123	126
1917	2,518	1,329	1,189	77	53	78	99
1918	1,226	538	688	41	50	42	43
1919	2,432	1,105	1,327	62	63	59	75
1920	5,581	3,115	2,466	125	123	108	91
1921	4,627	2,436	2,191	94	104	78	90
1922	6,456	3,955	2,501	138	125	125	107
1923	18,287	13,184	5,103	353	324	211	244
1924	8,492	6,013	2,479	195	188	156	141

For reference notes see page 754.

TABLE II.—Distribution of emigrant citizens to extra-European countries, by sex and age, 1866-1924 (continued).

Year	10-14 years		15-19 years		20-29 years		30-39 years		40-49 years	
	Males	Females	Males	Females	Males	Females	Males	Females	Males	Females
1866[1]	579	456	1,036	548	2,890	1,677	1,616	904	681	557
1867[1]	595	533	616	482	1,829	1,183	1,160	913	660	543
1868[1]	602	495	812	535	2,023	1,357	1,261	891	700	556
1869[1]	783	666	1,129	776	2,971	2,134	1,823	1,189	801	684
1870[1]	658	489	1,086	760	2,208	1,714	1,279	916	552	553
1871[1]	493	380	827	544	1,910	1,465	1,003	715	470	394
1872[1]	513	474	955	708	2,278	1,857	1,101	831	561	490
1873[1]	378	302	818	563	1,749	1,446	749	612	372	320
1874[1]	198	168	344	261	659	659	281	252	144	159
1875[1]	161	131	335	226	701	580	246	241	167	124
1876[1]	155	113	369	261	865	637	276	234	146	133
1877	108	101	270	212	598	488	200	179	111	92
1878	158	157	452	295	1,002	702	339	253	143	128
1879	190	165	646	354	2,138	1,039	652	391	240	167
1880	485	459	1,599	826	5,339	2,839	1,796	1,077	695	476
1881	756	626	2,038	1,170	5,694	3,814	2,103	1,524	951	646
1882	796	737	2,522	1,412	6,184	4,223	2,306	1,634	987	745
1883	635	594	2,033	1,200	4,429	3,357	1,613	1,207	678	587
1884	469	418	1,526	920	2,883	2,407	923	787	394	394
1855	457	415	1,486	1,047	2,403	2,360	791	756	350	411
1886	377	403	1,692	1,011	3,368	2,391	1,038	792	483	314
1887	509	420	2,272	1,204	5,555	3,289	1,725	949	731	394
1888	464	454	2,475	1,273	5,803	3,304	1,818	1,019	685	391
1889	300	278	1,474	917	2,935	2,301	865	642	355	294
1890	283	276	1,341	888	2,329	2,026	631	633	258	251
1891	341	293	1,413	924	3,559	2,322	982	702	419	259
1892	432	356	1,984	1,164	4,681	2,899	1,146	867	523	320
1893	415	356	2,224	1,250	5,193	3,273	1,312	854	574	341
1894	131	128	596	457	1,152	1,107	399	375	186	130
1895	119	113	624	514	1,309	1,239	523	403	270	144
1896	132	131	1,125	565	1,762	1,082	428	320	242	126
1897	86	91	756	421	1,109	833	315	247	163	94
1898	97	80	736	440	1,299	856	273	250	152	93
1899	104	109	986	515	1,950	1,071	437	339	210	121
1900	162	163	1,664	862	3,381	1,707	728	453	299	188
1901	207	183	1,926	957	3,998	1,999	798	521	399	201
1902	294	270	3,319	1,397	6,699	2,794	1,496	783	577	305
1903	429	392	3,986	1,857	8,417	3,831	1,985	1,101	799	441
1904	424	376	3,216	1,770	5,865	3,472	1,544	1,060	634	411
1905	356	334	3,322	1,707	5,765	3,368	1,484	961	570	365
1906	366	354	3,440	1,668	6,585	3,455	1,574	983	691	588
1907	318	291	3,448	1,720	6,768	3,740	1,542	980	580	329
1908	164	175	1,131	923	1,809	1,785	424	556	176	153
1909	189	181	2,643	1,404	5,068	2,801	1,127	714	366	235
1910	237	208	3,282	1,455	6,189	3,099	1,302	814	441	222
1911	137	138	2,117	1,159	3,905	2,389	657	572	236	168
1912	140	152	1,452	955	2,389	1,808	450	504	170	156
1913	138	114	1,705	844	3,100	1,660	570	472	215	150
1914	120	107	1,516	874	2,296	1,726	363	473	151	146
1915	86	95	684	500	772	1,094	202	351	84	107
1916	106	99	817	587	616	1,223	286	444	141	156
1917	69	57	270	152	426	430	208	229	129	93
1918	35	28	73	69	130	229	102	162	55	54
1919	63	52	196	150	395	454	204	273	61	108
1920	70	65	612	401	1,421	1,032	471	440	188	147
1921	54	52	380	316	1,171	916	408	431	150	144
1922	57	78	572	378	1,808	1,042	747	494	350	166
1923	129	130	1,764	729	6,982	2,368	2,281	854	1,066	259
1924	87	90	652	257	3,162	1,071	1,109	488	472	121

For reference notes see page 754.

TABLE II.—Distribution of emigrant citizens to extra-European countries, by sex AND AGE, 1866-1924 (concluded).

Year	50-59 years		60-69 years		70-79 years		80 years and over		age unknown	
	Males	Females	Males	Females	Males	Females	Males	Females	Males	Females
1866[1]	294	254	104	104	51	44	5	..	..	..
1867[1]	281	275	109	107	52	42	2	4	..	..
1868[1]	347	292	120	138	44	41	..	..	..	..
1869[1]	405	342	113	140	32	59	..	1	..	..
1870[1]	324	311	122	122	32	32	2	2	..	..
1871[1]	239	221	82	87	20	20	4	..	..	..
1872[1]	280	283	105	122	21	22	5	2	..	1
1873[1]	210	225	90	97	19	15	1	..	..	..
1874[1]	124	152	52	47	6	14	1	..	..	..
1875[1]	102	113	57	53	14	16	1	3	..	..
1876[1]	116	130	47	39	10	7	..	1	2	2
1877	90	126	35	37	9	7	1	1	3	1
1878	116	106	49	63	15	14	..	3	1	6
1879	149	122	68	65	17	12	1	..	2	2
1880	350	338	142	152	38	32	2	5	4	4
1881	477	436	172	219	34	42	5	4	6	4
1882	563	523	200	220	45	42	6	1	6	3
1883	387	420	175	197	33	40	5	3	4	1
1884	268	316	120	163	28	19	..	3	2	5
1885	266	337	112	127	27	26	1	2	2	..
1886	264	315	139	176	29	27	2	1	4	5
1887	326	301	138	143	32	30	6	4	4	5
1888	308	330	132	163	19	20	2	3	4	12
1889	190	189	96	103	20	11	2	1	6	3
1890	141	200	75	97	16	15	..	..	2	2
1891	196	215	101	115	27	27	2	2	6	4
1892	241	259	122	146	29	23	2	..	1	..
1893	277	272	112	162	43	28	1	2	11	15
1894	73	106	47	60	11	11	..	..	3	3
1895	101	103	39	54	9	14	1	..	8	4
1896	63	83	45	44	11	8	2	1	3	1
1897	56	52	33	31	5	7	1	..	2	2
1898	42	60	35	34	10	10	1	..	2	5
1899	112	82	46	46	19	14	2	2	1	5
1900	132	149	54	86	26	29	2	2	2	3
1901	153	149	70	69	25	22	4	6	3	1
1902	210	203	74	97	22	18	6	1	2	4
1903	265	242	85	114	39	45	5	2	24	..
1901	247	212	69	99	21	21	6	2	26	10
1905	204	209	59	74	24	24	3	1	1	2
1906	244	211	40	81	18	20	4	2	6	5
1907	226	179	52	57	23	11	3	1	..	..
1908	90	101	22	54	10	12	1	1	1	1
1909	161	136	30	58	12	12	2	..	1	..
1910	145	158	50	71	11	10	..	1	3	3
1911	88	91	43	47	12	13	..	..	2	3
1912	75	92	35	49	9	10	1	..	2	2
1913	83	93	28	40	8	9	..	..	..	1
1914	67	96	25	45	14	17	1	2	1	1
1915	44	74	22	38	9	9	..	..	1	..
1916	69	85	23	48	6	10	..	..	..	..
1917	55	44	11	26	5	5	1	1	..	..
1918	22	29	13	15	5	2	..	1	20	6
1919	34	67	18	68	12	17	1	..	..	..
1920	69	82	35	63	15	17	..	5	1	..
1921	59	53	29	67	11	17	2	1	..	..
1922	117	44	27	43	12	22	2	2	..	..
1923	327	94	51	68	15	30	3	2	2	1
1924	143	81	27	33	8	9	2	..	..	..

For reference notes see page 754.

TABLE III.—DISTRIBUTION OF MALE EMIGRANT CITIZENS, OVER 15 YEARS OF AGE, TO EXTRA-EUROPEAN COUNTRIES, BY OCCUPATION,[2] 1871-1924.

Year	Total	Agriculture and breeding	Fishery	Mining	Industry	Transport and commerce	Domestic service	Liberal professions and public services	General labor	Other occupations	No occupation
1871	4,555	1,114	56	26	631	236	78	56	2,347		11
1872	5,276	1,272	25	33	853	412	27	67	2,573		14
1873	4,030	922	57	13	561	316	69	68	2,012		12
1874	1,611	643	8		157	100	11	25	663		4
1875	1,623	693	4	.	168	94	33	36	590		3
1876	1,832	335	18	2	181	115	87	31	1,057		1
1877	1,317	372	15	7	139	82	25	12	652		9
1878	2,117	426	31	1	136	79	27	13	1,394		11
1879	3,914	443	44		507	201	47	41	2,618		11
1880	9,965	969	31	4	2,019	721	111	103	5,995		9
1881	11,480	1,091	142	5	1,999	915	111	105	7,094		11
1882	12,819	1,417	167	3	1,746	1,180	280	140	7,852		20
1883	9,357	1,067	92	12	1,301	1,115	198	101	5,451		25
1884	6,144	935	27	13	745	826	101	71	3,410		19
1890	4,793	943	22	7	593	894	55	101	2,071		107
1891											
1892											
1893	9,697	1,960	87	.	1,110	1,734	473	70	4,145	...	108
1894	2,467	503	27	10	308	789	107	29	658	...	43
1895	2,924	488	17	3	431	1,150	71	26	657	...	80
1896	3,681	814	61	4	448	1,046	138	23	1,094	...	55
1897	2,440	570	50	2	339	668	100	21	651	...	39
1898	2,550	666	42	2	311	539	64	18	821	...	87
1899	3,763	913	68	1	451	837	91	15	1,294	...	93
1900	5,288	193	48	1	883	1,269	150	36	2,606	...	102
1901	7,376	1,234	87	7	1,381	1,396	162	38	2,855	...	216
1902	12,405	1,975	163	12	2,533	2,275	198	41	4,906	...	302
1903	15,605	2,230	295	3,302		2,766	24	79	6,378	...	531
1904[3]	11,628	2,418	607	2,916		3,020	54	89	2,060	...	464
1905	11,432	4,438	658	2,881		2,675	44	88	260	...	388
1906	12,602	4,324	731	3,621		2,849	18	88	359	...	612
1907	12,642	2,965	1,112	3,473		2,644	32	94	1,804	...	518
1908	3,664	923	254	764		786	18	31	692	...	196
1909	9,410	2,668	882	2,837		2,047	49	71	1,346	...	64
1910	11,423	4,074	1,158	2,283		2,234	30	63	933	...	94
1911	7,060	2,728	584	1,708		1,527	45	59	333	...	76
1912	4,583	1,787	267	1,089		1,114	5	26	225	...	70
1913	5,709	2,091	430	1,526		1,284	10	47	268	...	53
1914	4,434	1,762	392	1,035		911	7	30	232	...	65
1915	1,818	673	86	454		503	13	34	19	...	36
1916	1,958	577	55	526		693	8	27	31	...	41
1917	1,105	140	17	228		667	4	16	22	...	11
1918	420	40	3	96		216	2	25	18	...	20
1919	922	146	24	195		412		26	11	81	27
1920	2,812	662	188	843		776		38	114	162	29
1921	2,210	636	174	686		496		24	25	131	38
1922	3,635	989	186	1,400		766		31	28	184	51
1923	12,491	3,330	924	4,662		2,417		85	185	749	139
1924	5,575	1,949	376	1,638		993		53	40	439	87

For reference notes see page 754.

TABLE IV.—Intercontinental emigration, by country of future residence, 1867-1924.

Year	Total	United States	British North America	Other American countries	Oceania	Africa	Asia
1867	12,829	12,828	....	..	1	...	..
1868	13,211	13,209	....	..	2	...	..
1869	18,070	18,055	....	..	15	...	..
1870	14,838	14,788	....	..	50	...	..
1871	12,276	12,055	....	..	221	...	..
1872	13,865	13,081	....	..	784	...	..
1873	10,352	9,998	....	..	354	...	..
1874	4,601	4,565	....	..	36	...	..
1875	4,048	3,972	....	..	76	...	..
1876	4,355	4,313	....	..	42	...	..
1877	3,206	3,195	....	..	11	...	..
1878	4,863	4,833	....	..	30	...	..
1879	7,608	7,607	....	..	1	...	..
1880	20,212	19,615	....	..	595[4]	2	..
1881	25,976	25,956	....	..	19[5]	1	..
1882	28,804	28,788	....	..	10	6	..
1883	22,167	22,164	3	..	...	...	..
1884	14,776	14,755	5	2	14	...	..
1885	13,981	13,970	2	..	9	...	..
1886	15,158	15,116	7	..	35	...	..
1887	20,741	20,706	21	2	12	...	..
1888	21,452	21,348	79	4	13	8	..
1889	12,642	12,597	19	8	17	...	1
1890	10,991	10,898	51	20	21	1	..
1891	13,341	13,249	79	7	5	...	1
1892	17,049	16,814	223	3	6	3	..
1893	18,778	18,690	75	1	6	6	..
1894	5,642	5,591	22	3	2	24	..
1895	6,207	6,153	6	2	3	43	..
1896	6,679	6,584	22	1	10	59	3
1897	4,669	4,580	3	..	2	82	2
1898	4,859	4,805	13	1	6	34	..
1899	6,699	6,466	51	..	148	34	..
1900	10,931	10,655	112	19	99	46	..
1901	12,745	12,488	143	77	7	30	..
1902	20,343	19,225	1,028	3	4	83	..
1903	26,784	24,998	1,477	1	5	303	..
1904	22,264	20,836	1,373	8	3	44	..
1905	21,059	19,638	1,390	1	4	25	1
1906	21,967	20,449	1,476	14	1	26	1
1907	22,135	20,615	1,490	16	3	11	..
1908	8,497	7,850	610	18	9	10	..
1909	16,152	15,237	880	12	12	9	2
1910	18,912	17,361	1,513	13	8	17	..
1911	12,477	11,122	1,304	23	2	24	2
1912	9,105	7,776	1,287	15	12	11	4
1913	9,876	8,568	1,281	12	5	10	..
1914	8,522	7,723	775	1	10	9	4
1915	4,572	4,388	169	..	3	5	7
1916	5,212	4,865	320	3	...	3	21
1917	2,518	2,344	168	4	...	...	2
1918	1,226	1,179	30	..	...	...	17
1919	2,432	2,287	130	9	...	...	6
1920	5,581	5,216	325	24	...	10	6
1921	4,627	4,131	448	24	4	..	20
1922	6,456	5,867	517	26	19	20	7
1923	18,287	16,152	2,064	39	6	9	17
1924	8,492	5,065	3,365	23	7	8	24

For reference notes see page 754.

TABLE V.—Distribution of alien immigrants (including a small percentage of citizens), by sex and age, 1918-24.

Age	Sex	1918	1919	1920	1921	1922	1923	1924
Under 5 years.........	Males	47	86	89	26	26	18	10
	Females	47	86	88	34	32	18	10
5- 9 years...........	Males	43	82	100	32	24	25	10
	Females	56	73	85	32	24	20	13
10-14 years...........	Males	77	58	83	31	21	21	10
	Females	41	71	81	41	16	21	17
15-19 years...........	Males	867	1,107	762	214	161	139	123
	Females	440	668	700	286	283	294	144
20-29 years...........	Males	3,563	4,898	3,341	1,145	904	943	653
	Females	1,102	1,740	1,986	918	810	850	451
30-39 years...........	Males	1,915	2,014	1,568	635	492	457	310
	Females	365	518	626	328	272	245	163
40-49 years...........	Males	820	724	589	283	160	181	112
	Females	118	159	182	94	84	72	47
50-59 years...........	Males	293	241	239	110	105	69	53
	Females	73	92	76	43	41	38	21
60-69 years...........	Males	84	93	83	56	31	25	27
	Females	22	26	29	16	10	13	11
70 years and over.....	Males	9	18	22	6	27	37	30
	Females	9	10	16	2	27	29	43
Unknown............	Males	194	124	87	38	...	...	...
	Females	75	50	76	36	...	...	...
Total............	Males	7,912	9,445	6,963	2,576	1,951	1,915	1,338
	Females	2,348	3,493	3,945	1,830	1,599	1,600	920
Grand total..........		10,260	12,938	10,908	4,406	3,550	3,515	2,258

TABLE VI.—Distribution of immigrants, by occupation and sex, 1918-24.[6]

Occupation	1918		1919-20		1922		1923		1924	
	Males	Fe-males	Males	Fe-males	Males	Fe-males	Males	Fe-males	Males	Fe-males
Agriculture, forestry.........	1,208	12	2,954	252	474	10	452	2	378	9
Fishery.....................	23	..	117	19	13	..	8	..	5	..
Industry....................	3,207	141	6,868	936	666	58	696	53	509	25
Commerce...................	230	61	464	233	107	49	97	40	48	13
Shipping...................	691	...	776	48	78	...	39	...	74	...
Other transport	38	...	212	25	28	...	14	1	7	...
Liberal professions...........	183	120	362	336	116	83	131	74	54	70
Domestic service or occupation not specified.............	1,984	1,645	11	4,233	...	954	...	1,046	1	564
Independent or in receipt of a pension..................	3	2	...	...	...	...	...	...	...	...
No occupation...............	210	158	...	...	...	...	...	...	...	...
Occupation unknown.........	135	209	...	...	...	...	...	...	...	...
Other occupations, including:	...[7]	...[7]	599	184	84	14	106	16	74	8
Higher civil servants.....	...	...	...	...	21	2	30	...	22	...
Office employees..........	...	...	...	...	20	12	26	16	23	8
Engineers................	...	...	...	...	27	...	43	...	26	...
Other or no occupation.......	...	...	4,045	1,172	385	431	372	368	188	231
Total.................	7,912	2,348	16,408	7,438	1,951	1,599	1,915	1,600	1,338	920

For reference notes see page 754.

TABLE VII.—IMMIGRATION, BY COUNTRY OF LAST RESIDENCE, 1916-24.

Country of last residence	1916	1917	1918	1919	1920	1921	1922	1923	1924
Sweden..........	3,647	14,891	7,037	8,796	6,307	2,168	1,920	1,777	1,044
Denmark.........	906	2,404	1,370	1,243	1,201	675	501	667	459
Germany.........	196	492	197	727	1,428	483	441	580	226
England..........	181	238	120	248	169	98	66	67	85
France...........	10	32	16	30	38	22	25	10	18
Russia...........	440	795	901	131	64	48	52	16	10
Austria..........	18	24	2	9	58	32	18	19	14
Other European countries.........	85	160	55	278	213	124	151	142	112
America..........	541	911	471	1,437	1,375	698	356	215	269
Other countries.....	21	33	25	25	20	32	16	20	19
Unknown.........	60	748	66	14	35	26	4	2	2
Total..........	6,105	20,728	10,260	12,938	10,908	4,406	3,550	3,515	2,258

SOURCES

Utvanderingsstatistikk (Emigration Statistics), Norges offisielle Statistikk, VII, 25' Christiania, 1921.

Tables I, IV (years 1876-1918).

Tabeller vedkommente Folkemaengdens Bevaegelse, 1850-70, 1871, etc., Christiania, 1873, etc.

Tables II (years 1866-76); III (years 1871-1913).

Information supplied by the Central Statistical Bureau of Norway.

Tables II (years 1877-1924); III (years 1914-24); IV, V, VI, VII.

NOTES

[1]For the years 1866 to 1876 the figures refer only to emigrants departed to the United States.
[2]The figures for the years 1871 to 1913 taken from the *Tabeller vedkommende Folkemaengdens Bevaegelse* differ slightly from the quinquennial figures published in the *Utvandringsstatistikk*, Christiania, 1921.
[3]As from 1904, a large number of agricultural laborers, previously classed as "laborers", are, by reason of a more exact classification of emigrants, grouped under "agriculture".
[4]Includes 593 for the Sandwich Islands.
[5]Includes 2 for the Sandwich Islands.
[6]After 1918, occupations were grouped by a new method employed for the census of December 1, 1920. The main difference was assembling occupations such as directors, office managers, accountants and clerks, under the head, "other occupations".
[7]For 1918, distributed over the various occupations.
[8]Including immigrants from Sweden.

SWEDEN

Since 1882, Swedish emigration and immigration statistics have been derived from the annual ecclesiastical lists (prepared for Stockholm by the registrars of births, marriages, and deaths), lists of emigrants since 1856, and lists of immigrants since 1875.

For the period 1885-93, Swedish emigration tables are almost complete, because the Order of June 4, 1884, concerning emigration required that an emigration certificate, issued by the clergyman of the parish of origin, should be submitted before the emigration contract received the visa of the police authorities.

After 1893, statistics again became somewhat incomplete because no permission to emigrate was given to persons who had not performed their military service. This gave rise to secret emigration, not appearing on the parish registers.

The statistics of these registers concern only an inconsiderable number of aliens.

It should also be noted that statistics of immigration include only immigrants registered as intending permanent residence and exclude the considerable number of aliens who found a temporary refuge in Sweden.

Statistics about the number of migrants from Sweden to South Africa (1913-24), Argentina (1871-1924), Brazil (1853-1924), Canada (1900-24), United States (1820-1924), and Australia (1902-24), will be found in the national tables for those countries. Statistics about the number of migrants returning to Sweden from Argentina (1891-1900) and the United States (1908-24) will be found in the national tables for those countries.

TABLE I.—EMIGRATION, BY COUNTRY OF FUTURE RESIDENCE, 1871-1924.

Year	Extra-European countries				European countries					
	Total	United States	Other American countries	Asia, Africa, Oceania	Total	Norway	Denmark	Finland	Russia	Other countries
1871	13,188	13,053[1]		135	4,262	1,350	1,383	355		1,174
1872	11,968	11,891[1]		77	3,947	1,356	1,329	381		881
1873	9,642	9,562[1]		80	3,938	1,501	1,329	295		813
1874	3,569	3,433[1]		136	4,222	1,560	1,610	357		695
1875	3,688	3,641[1]		47	6,039	1,918	2,836	468		817
1876	3,786	3,747[1]		39	5,632	1,880	2,421	460		871
1877	2,997	2,959[1]		38	4,613	1,807	1,701	420		685
1878	4,400	4,265[1]		135	4,632	1,696	1,626	500		810
1879	12,866	12,806[1]		60	4,771	1,557	2,020	374		820
1880	36,398	36,322[1]		76	5,711	1,714	2,657	463		877
1881	40,762	40,658[1]	22	82	5,230	1,460	2,601	313	85	771
1882	44,585	44,410[1]	16	159	5,593	1,551	2,743	339	67	893
1883	25,911	25,733[1]	17	161	5,694	1,577	2,831	355	87	844
1884	17,895	17,700[1]	17	178	5,665	1,604	2,980	238	52	791
1885	18,466	18,243[1]	27	196	5,027	1,261	2,579	215	54	918
1886	28,271	27,943[1]	174	154	4,618	1,194	2,177	273	76	898
1887	46,556	46,265[1]	100	191	4,230	1,166	2,000	306	44	714
1888	45,864	45,583[1]	105	176	4,459	1,077	2,173	379	53	777
1889	29,067	28,546[1]	357	164	4,296	1,225	1,864	428	78	701
1890	30,128	29,498[1]	482	148	4,084	1,358	1,545	423	37	721
1891	38,318	36,150[1]	2,028	140	4,458	1,615	1,622	464	53	704
1892	41,275	40,996[1]	130	149	4,229	1,507	1,671	349	28	674
1893	37,504	37,327[1]	87	90	3,365	1,270	1,275	228	26	566
1894	9,678	9,533[1]	61	84	3,680	1,300	1,516	270	43	551
1895	15,104	14,989[1]	45	70	3,851	1,273	1,568	243	54	713
1896	15,175	14,874	105	196	4,376	1,458	1,769	404	70	675
1897	10,314	10,109	89	116	4,245	1,597	1,538	402	40	668
1898	8,683	8,534	64	85	4,980	2,057	1,774	395	60	694
1899	12,028	11,842	54	132	4,848	2,188	1,588	295	65	712
1900	16,434	16,209	110	115	4,227	1,482	1,687	279	20	759
1901	20,464	20,306	74	84	4,152	1,495	1,514	330	50	763
1902	33,477	33,151	201	125	3,630	1,164	1,374	260	40	792
1903	35,975	35,439	345	191	3,550	1,066	1,389	238	69	788
1904	18,968	18,533	355	80	3,416	1,059	1,278	284	31	764
1905	20,862	20,520	279	63	3,184	874	1,101	365	29	815
1906	21,692	21,242	391	59	3,012	876	1,155	292	43	646
1907	19,818	19,325	427	66	3,160	764	1,140	345	43	868
1908	9,246	8,873	287	86	3,253	906	1,109	360	51	827
1909	18,894	18,331	461	102	3,098	849	929	356	81	880
1910	24,647	23,529	1,001	117	3,169	891	921	360	104	893
1911	16,770	15,571	1,091	108	3,227	993	946	396	82	810
1912	14,689	13,896	660	133	3,428	1,087	1,017	373	102	849
1913	17,224	16,329	741	154	3,122	958	968	297	75	824
1914	10,006	9,589	341	76	2,954	926	797	237	77	917
1915	4,672	4,538	55	79	2,840	968	1,013	206	42	611
1916	7,488	7,268	168	52	3,083	1,220	1,295	133	59	376
1917	2,571	2,462	85	24	3,869	1,694	1,686	107	65	317
1918	1,498	1,416	60	22	3,355	1,190	1,598	237	41	289
1919	4,008	3,777	141	90	3,329	1,612	1,036	242	14	425
1920	7,093	6,691	293	109	3,149	1,353	915	227	5	649
1921	5,881	5,430	315	136	3,069	956	823	284	19	987
1922	8,985	8,455	363	167	2,812	875	768	285	15	869
1923	26,559	24,948	1,483	128	2,679	858	772	422	14	613
1924	8,401	7,036	1,240	125	2,270	692	630	269	15	664

For reference notes see page 762.

TABLE II.—DISTRIBUTION OF EMIGRANTS, BY SEX AND AGE, 1851-1924.

Year	Total	Sex		Age			
		Males	Females	Under 15 years	15-25 years	25-50 years	50 years and over
1851	1,102	617	485	336	.....	.....	....
1852	3,314	1,905	1,409	1,218	.....	.....	....
1853	2,998	1,773	1,225	962	.....	.....	....
1854	4,243	2,434	1,809	1,331	.....	.....	....
1855	1,087	651	436	207	.....	.....	....
1856	1,130	638	492	392	.....	.....	....
1857	1,831	989	842	649	...	.....	....
1858	571	344	227	172	.....	.....	....
1859	276	174	102	47	.....	.....	....
1860	348	194	154	112	.....	.....	....
1861	2,286	1,282	1,004	435	780	1,001[2]	70
1862	2,535	1,350	1,185	532	855	1,049	99
1863	3,127	1,778	1,349	682	1,038	1,310[2]	97
1864	5,177	3,131	2,046	1,071	1,782	2,158[2]	166
1865	6,691	3,944	2,747	1,662	1,946	2,875[2]	208
1866	7,206	4,274	2,932	1,688	2,236	3,014	268
1867	9,334	5,582	3,752	1,973	3,243	3,766	352
1868	27,024	15,716	11,308	6,549	8,254	11,189	1,032
1869	39,064	22,569	16,495	9,301	12,186	15,931	1,646
1870	20,003	10,913	9,090	4,976	6,303	7,832	892
1871	17,450	9,944	7,506	3,713	6,081	6,956[2]	700
1872	15,915	8,796	7,119	3,054	6,071	6,164[2]	626
1873	13,580	7,193	6,387	2,719	5,213	5,082[2]	566
1874	7,791	3,946	3,845	1,532	3,007	2,900[2]	352
1875	9,727	5,049	4,678	1,607	4,188	3,513[2]	419
1876	9,418	4,927	4,491	1,619	3,968	3,432	399
1877	7,610	3,874	3,736	1,356	3,051	2,823[2]	380
1878	9,032	4,710	4,322	1,507	3,762	3,364[2]	399
1879	17,637	10,345	7,292	3,015	7,328	6,666[2]	628
1880	42,109	24,704	17,405	7,860	16,683	16,087[2]	1,479
1881	45,992	25,695	20,297	9,701	17,860	16,681[2]	1,750
1882	50,178	28,007	22,171	10,453	19,862	17,639[2]	2,224
1883	31,605	17,131	14,474	6,497	13,100	10,480[2]	1,528
1884	23,560	12,117	11,443	4,405	10,249	7,785[2]	1,121
1885	23,493	11,937	11,556	4,103	10,498	7,751[2]	1,141
1886	32,889	18,828	14,061	4,856	15,660	11,094[2]	1,279
1887	50,786	29,235	21,551	7,388	23,942	17,522[2]	1,934
1888	50,323	28,875	21,448	7,304	23,609	17,616[2]	1,794
1889	33,363	17,321	16,042	5,517	15,281	11,196[2]	1,369
1890	34,212	17,842	16,370	5,668	16,133	11,066[2]	1,345
1891	42,776	23,301	19,475	7,203	19,546	14,421[2]	1,606
1892	45,504	25,167	20,337	7,539	20,791	15,324[2]	1,850
1893	40,869	22,298	18,571	6,532	19,818	12,849[2]	1,670
1894	13,358	5,520	7,838	2,404	6,160	4,197[2]	597
1895	18,955	8,575	10,380	2,640	9,959	5,556[2]	800

For reference notes see page 762.

TABLE II.—DISTRIBUTION OF EMIGRANTS, BY SEX AND AGE, 1851–1924 (cont.).

Year	Total	Sex		Age			
		Males	Females	Under 15 years	15–25 years	25–50 years	50 years and over
1896	19,551	9,606	9,945	2,221	10,741	5,833	756
1897	14,559	6,426	8,133	1,759	7,830	4,347[2]	623
1898	13,663	6,179	7,484	1,781	7,102	4,194	586
1899	16,876	7,764	9,112	2,155	9,044	4,905[2]	772
1900	20,661	10,445	10,216	2,319	11,498	5,944	900
1901	24,616	13,591	11,025	2,548	14,132	6,991	945
1902	37,107	22,093	15,014	4,024	20,519	11,364	1,200
1903	39,525	22,893	16,632	5,486	20,027	12,644	1,368
1904	22,384	10,833	11,551	3,714	11,117	6,574	979
1905	24,046	13,423	10,623	3,083	12,559	7,479	925
1906	24,704	13,752	10,952	3,211	13,255	7,322	916
1907	22,978	12,815	10,163	3,097	12,023	7,010	848
1908	12,499	6,014	6,485	1,923	5,959	4,016	601
1909	21,992	13,413	8,579	2,645	11,140	7,466	741
1910	27,816	16,796	11,020	3,999	13,394	9,573	850
1911	19,997	11,065	8,932	2,969	9,726	6,583	719
1912	18,117	9,548	8,569	2,649	9,144	5,643	681
1913	20,346	11,569	8,777	2,503	10,578	6,566	699
1914	12,960	7,033	5,927	1,844	6,529	4,138	449
1915	7,512	3,576	3,936	1,265	3,293	2,540	414
1916	10,571	5,317	5,254	1,672	5,279	3,011	609
1917	6,440	2,636	3,804	1,252	2,436	2,333	419
1918	4,853	1,867	2,986	1,058	1,433	1,898	464
1919	7,337	2,821	4,516	1,334	2,645	2,741	617
1920	10,242	4,795	5,447	1,328	4,297	3,931	686
1921	8,950	4,073	4,877	1,217	3,276	3,823	634
1922	11,797	6,653	5,144	1,311	5,007	4,844	635
1923	29,238	20,325	8,913	2,837	12,697	12,788	916
1924	10,671	6,226	4,445	1,548	3,925	4,659	539

TABLE III.—DISTRIBUTION OF EMIGRANTS, BY OCCUPATION, 1891-1924.

Year	Total	Agri-culture	Indus-try	Trade	Ship-ping	Dom-mestic service	General labor	Other oc-cupation	Occupa-tion unknown
1891	42,776	7,128	6,849	588	643	9,812	12,895	1,018	3,843
1892	45,504	8,723	6,857	831	550	9,573	14,836	1,023	3,111
1893	40,869	8,001	5,670	740	589	8,329	11,269	793	2,478
1894	13,358	2,147	1,734	271	224	3,295	4,002	282	1,403
1895	18,955	4,880	2,713	460	323	4,341	4,776	476	986
1896	19,551	5,632	2,898	422	307	4,589	4,452	441	810
1897	14,559	3,797	2,274	354	277	3,563	3,113	391	790
1898	13,663	3,379	2,430	333	211	3,126	3,030	592	562
1899	16,876	4,528	2,967	346	250	3,512	3,881	665	727
1900	20,661	6,318	3,588	397	299	3,872	4,678	590	919
1901	24,616	7,140	4,826	572	299	4,347	5,904	612	916
1902	37,107	10,847	7,335	739	449	5,273	10,413	795	1,256
1903	39,525	11,196	9,695	976	583	5,139	9,243	2,626	67
1904	22,384	6,218	5,113	617	348	3,333	5,053	1,650	52
1905	24,046	8,323	5,730	729	406	2,266	4,889	1,659	44
1906	24,704	8,073	5,891	776	445	2,526	5,266	1,687	40
1907	22,978	7,121	5,801	808	389	2,248	5,054	1,524	33
1908	12,499	3,531	3,342	577	222	1,376	2,558	870	23
1909	21,992	6,543	6,146	812	350	1,664	5,167	1,259	51
1910	27,816	8,887	9,634	886	483	2,088	4,297	1,518	23
1911	19,997	6,357	6,784	819	337	1,832	1,921	1,770	177
1912	18,117	5,932	5,524	821	351	1,724	1,946	1,674	145
1913	20,346	7,070	6,149	878	365	1,878	2,119	1,748	139
1914	12,960	4,415	3,978	583	229	1,255	1,145	1,243	112
1915	7,512	1,877	2,588	444	117	895	645	848	98
1916	10,571	2.944	3,642	532	144	1,188	951	1,043	127
1917	6,440	1,345	2,573	383	75	1,133	169	607	155
1918	4,853	633	1,751	366	71	903	393	600	136
1919	7,337	1,564	2,224	534	138	1,360	293	1,001	223
1920	10,242	2,706	3,039	587	170	1,544	827	1,150	219
1921	8,950	2,075	2,618	813	144	1,278	757	782	483
1922	11,797	3,520	3,585	805	191	1,261	1,032	952	451
1923	29,238	9,204	11,129	1,739	430	1,719	2,130	2,017	870
1924	10,671	3,122	3,165	962	160	857	949	949	507

TABLE IV.—IMMIGRATION, BY COUNTRY OF LAST RESIDENCE, 1876-1924.

Year	Extra-European countries				European countries					
	Total	United States	Other American countries	Asia, Africa, Oceania	Total	Norway	Denmark	Finland	Russia	Other countries
1876	842	837[1]		5	2,370	451	1,177	285		457
1877	737	733[1]		4	2,551	432	1,230	365		524
1878	510	493[1]		17	2,331	498	1,015	334		484
1879	392	361[1]		31	2,200	465	944	399		392
1880	410	404[1]		6	2,599	634	957	521		487
1881	574	563[1]	3	8	2,383	498	953	365	98	469
1882	830	805[1]	15	10	2,737	540	1,227	351	127	492
1883	1,377	1,346[1]	13	18	2,776	597	1,148	406	100	525
1884	1,961	1,940[1]	1	20	2,950	647	1,286	413	100	504
1885	2,430	2,397[1]	5	28	3,362	772	1,486	420	70	614
1886	1,908	1,882[1]	5	21	3,316	667	1,600	368	76	605
1887	1,818	1,774[1]	18	26	2,824	622	1,283	266	122	531
1888	2,270	2,229[1]	14	27	2,551	667	1,090	242	54	498
1889	2,800	2,743[1]	16	41	2,704	637	1,203	281	57	526
1890	3,235	3,174[1]	36	25	2,795	668	1,167	258	63	639
1891	3,632	3,552[1]	42	38	2,482	619	940	341	72	510
1892	3,827	3,718[1]	75	34	2,684	727	1,012	276	85	584
1893	4,938	4,827	75	36	2,439	548	970	325	52	544
1894	7,455	7,343	59	53	2,970	746	1,159	337	39	689
1895	5,464	5,394[1]	22	48	3,064	717	1,255	465	49	578
1896	4,504	4,441	25	38	3,303	758	1,189	589	55	712
1897	4,956	4,849	45	62	2,905	604	1,036	368	71	826
1898	4,727	4,648	30	49	3,247	712	1,175	425	70	865
1899	4,469	4,359	31	79	3,727	836	1,282	557	102	950
1900	4,149	4,024	33	92	3,868	1,115	1,238	653	89	773
1901	3,719	3,621	32	66	3,902	1,120	1,190	609	143	840
1902	3,387	3,297	57	33	3,397	909	1,073	588	90	737
1903	3,612	3,537	15	60	4,011	1,255	1,025	775	144	812
1904	4,573	4,505	27	41	4,689	1,509	1,137	905	259	879
1905	4,165	4,110	11	44	4,444	1,609	1,097	642	328	768
1906	4,614	4,511	50	53	4,967	1,588	984	787	529	1,079
1907	4,778	4,677	55	46	4,135	1,320	881	660	342	932
1908	6,421	6,308	41	72	3,397	888	815	514	254	926
1909	4,988	4,854	88	46	3,083	728	667	550	251	887
1910	4,735	4,609	58	68	3,407	894	714	642	213	944
1911	4,558	4,411	98	49	3,194	713	700	747	143	891
1912	5,181	4,681	416	84	3,115	713	651	623	158	970
1913	4,917	4,684	162	71	3,490	724	807	672	257	1,030
1914	4,864	4,647	128	89	3,772	697	741	741	386	1,207
1915	3,223	3,055	96	72	3,134	640	751	586	373	785
1916	3,159	2,989	101	69	3,554	819	745	635	445	910
1917	2,478	2,344	74	60	3,333	920	869	358	405	781
1918	1,630	1,565	43	22	3,302	957	725	748	281	591
1919	3,573	3,436	78	59	4,236	915	838	724	287	1,472
1920	5,601	5,341	153	107	5,240	1,149	1,033	757	318	1,983
1921	4,605	4,387	121	97	3,946	1,099	797	541	227	1,282
1922	3,237	3,079	86	72	3,066	895	652	441	133	945
1923	2,433	2,258	93	82	3,394	869	564	380	89	1,492
1924	2,539	2,320	142	77	3,403	1,056	573	436	82	1,256

For reference notes see page 762.

TABLE V.—DISTRIBUTION OF IMMIGRANTS, BY SEX AND AGE, 1875-1924.

Year	Sex			Age			
	Total	Males	Females	Under 15 years	15–25 years	25–50 years	50 years and over
1875	2,805	.....	.....	.....	.....	.....	...
1876	3,212	1,922	1,290	507	909	1,666[2]	130
1877	3,288	1,972	1,316	532	984	1,661[2]	111
1878	2,841	1,631	1,210	496	807	1,421[2]	117
1879	2,592	1,461	1,131	503	741	1,260[2]	88
1880	3,009	1,619	1,390	652	837	1,385[2]	135
1881	2,957	1,635	1,322	558	884	1,411[2]	104
1882	3,567	2,035	1,532	694	1,058	1,666[2]	149
1883	4,153	2,464	1,689	757	1,210	2,008[2]	178
1884	4,911	3,016	1,895	820	1,375	2,499[7]	217
1885	5,792	3,423	2,369	1,024	1,564	2,961[2]	243
1886	5,224	2,990	2,234	946	1,430	2,594[2]	254
1887	4,642	2,636	2,006	800	1,210	2,359[2]	273
1888	4,821	2,862	1,959	860	1,242	2,485[2]	234
1889	5,504	3,234	2,270	1,025	1,273	2,898[2]	308
1890	6,030	3,584	2,446	1,080	1,337	3,229[2]	384
1891	6,114	3,700	2,414	1,055	1,275	3,407[2]	377
1892	6,511	3,877	2,634	1,184	1,343	3,587[2]	397
1893	7,377	4,648	2,729	1,204	1,519	4,156[2]	498
1894	10,425	6,409	4,016	1,756	2,338	5,640[2]	691
1895	8,528	4,908	3,620	1,523	1,917	4,581[2]	507
1896	7,807	4,293	3,514	1,434	1,808	4,095[2]	470
1897	7,861	4,400	3,461	1,332	1,764	4,273[2]	492
1898	7,974	4,333	3,641	1,472	1,786	4,279[2]	437
1899	8,196	4,291	3,905	1,655	1,916	4,143[2]	482
1900	8,017	4,267	3,750	1,575	1,937	4,020[2]	485
1901	7,621	3,994	3,627	1,578	1,794	3,781[2]	468
1902	6,784	3,608	3,176	1,239	1,772	3,321[2]	452
1903	7,623	4,046	3,577	1,552	1,954	3,610[2]	507
1904	9,262	5,093	4,169	1,782	2,243	4,599[2]	638
1905	8,609	4,662	3,947	1,769	1,980	4,303	557
1906	9,581	5,080	4,501	1,857	2,351	4,741	632
1907	8,913	4,809	4,104	1,638	2,079	4,616	580
1908	9,818	5,534	4,284	1,703	2,065	5,373	677
1909	8,071	4,446	3,625	1,459	1,653	4,349	610
1910	8,142	4,385	3,757	1,514	1,703	4,316	609
1911	7,752	4,238	3,514	1,465	1,504	4,093	690
1912	8,296	4,579	3,717	1,577	1,599	4,378	742
1913	8,407	4,644	3,763	1,565	1,706	4,406	730
1914	8,636	4,801	3,835	1,431	1,789	4,630	786
1915	6,357	3,421	2,936	974	1,352	3,367	664
1916	6,713	3,506	3,207	1,243	1,316	3,511	643
1917	5,811	3,018	2,793	950	1,264	3,094	503
1918	4,932	2,514	2,418	814	1,214	2,505	399
1919	7,809	3,934	3,875	1,310	1,532	4,314	653
1920	10,841	5,414	5,427	1,831	1,911	6,119	980
1921	8,551	4,252	4,299	1,382	1,488	4,805	876
1922	6,303	3,039	3,264	1,099	1,070	3,354	780
1923	5,827	2,722	3,105	986	1,185	2,996	660
1924	5,942	2,867	3,075	1,064	1,279	2,942	657

For reference notes see page 762.

TABLE VI.—DISTRIBUTION OF IMMIGRANTS, BY OCCUPATION, 1891-1924.

Year	Total	Agri-culture	Indus-try	Trade	Ship-ping	Do-mestic service	General labor	Other oc-cupations	Occupa-tion unknown
1891	6,114	1,220	1,229	152	116	978	1,529	166	724
1892	6,511	1,288	1,474	163	118	977	1,699	203	589
1893	7,377	1,523	1,526	189	167	1,066	2,177	198	531
1894	10,425	2,182	2,082	277	189	1,462	3,102	252	879
1895	8,528	2,164	1,922	270	173	1,134	1,998	286	581
1896	7,807	1,846	1,556	289	141	1,203	1,957	273	542
1897	7,861	1,752	1,885	287	149	1,149	1,876	208	555
1898	7,974	1,748	2,071	321	165	1,109	1,798	325	437
1899	8,196	1,623	2,394	351	125	963	1,812	375	553
1900	8,017	1,730	2,221	367	124	899	1,614	416	646
1901	7,621	1,632	2,123	360	126	877	1,776	306	421
1902	6,784	1,568	1,709	335	98	864	1,408	278	524
1903	7,623	1,651	2,281	388	122	847	1,626	661	47
1904	9,262	1,851	3,016	476	152	903	2,108	718	38
1905	8,609	1,856	2,889	488	133	734	1,836	646	27
1906	9,581	1,839	3,344	525	205	751	1,986	883	48
1907	8,913	1,892	2,942	474	168	792	1,921	696	28
1908	9,818	2,623	2,877	482	188	671	2,229	701	47
1909	8,071	2,197	2,190	429	174	631	1,765	656	29
1910	8,142	2,307	2,749	424	156	720	1,115	634	37
1911	7,752	2,197	2,385	465	129	646	883	852	195
1912	8,296	2,207	2,559	482	157	656	1,069	1,004	162
1913	8,407	2,273	2,788	452	144	679	956	998	117
1914	8,636	2,210	3,000	477	139	679	917	1,079	135
1915	6,357	1,574	1,986	603	82	562	551	862	137
1916	6,713	1,516	1,940	746	157	680	654	825	195
1917	5,811	1,626	1,780	704	105	579	131	686	200
1918	4,932	1,083	1,533	466	74	553	419	624	180
1919	7,809	1,801	2,480	776	135	865	398	1,044	310
1920	10,841	2,137	3,709	840	133	1,310	1,063	1,325	324
1921	8,551	1,922	2,373	721	140	1,144	842	837	572
1922	6,303	1,367	1,587	536	91	797	692	737	496
1923	5,827	1,111	1,677	635	81	763	426	624	510
1924	5,942	1,065	1,786	658	66	699	510	630	528

SOURCES

Annuaire statistique de la Suède. Central Statistical Bureau of Sweden. Stockholm, 1914-24.

Ut- och Inwandering. (Annual) Central Statistical, Bureau of Sweden. Stockholm, 1911-23.

Information supplied by the Government.

NOTES

[1]Includes a small number of migrants whose destination or country of origin is unknown.
[2]Includes a small number of migrants whose age is unknown.

SWITZERLAND

Under the first Federal Emigration Act of December 24, 1880, the statistics compiled by the Federal Emigration Office relate only to emigration to countries outside Europe for which emigrants have concluded a contract with a Swiss transportation agency. There is no record of emigration to countries within Europe.

At first (1867-80) these Federal statistics included only Swiss citizens or aliens settled in Switzerland who were transported overseas by agencies having headquarters in Switzerland. They are exceedingly incomplete because the information supplied by the cantons is inadequate. After 1882 the statistics included persons thus sent abroad who had stayed only temporarily in Switzerland or had come to Switzerland merely for the purpose of concluding an emigration contract. In 1888 the revised Emigration Act was put in force and from that date the statistics have been based on the returns of the agencies. Since the same year emigrants have been classified according to the purpose of their journey. From 1903 onwards the agencies have been required to report the number of emigrants in transit who have passed through their hands. Every emigrant travelling to an extra-European country, with the intention of settling there or of staying for more than a year, must furnish certain information on a form supplied to him.

The figures prior to 1890—at which period the agencies had already made the necessary preparations for providing a statistical return— require critical examination.

Statistics about the number of migrants from Switzerland to South Africa (1913-24), Argentina (1857-1924), Brazil (1846-1924), Canada (1900-24), United States (1820-1924), Paraguay (1881-1906), Uruguay (1867-1903), and Australia (1902-24), will be found in the national tables for those countries. Statistics about the number of migrants returning to Switzerland from Argentina (1857-1924), United States (1908-24), and Uruguay (1879-1903), will be found in the national tables for those countries.

TABLE I.—INTERCONTINENTAL EMIGRATION (CITIZENS AND ALIENS DISTINGUISHED), 1868-1924.

Year	Total	Citizens	Aliens	Year	Total	Citizens	Aliens
1868	5,007	....	....	1897	2,508	1,778	730
1869	5,206	....	....	1898	2,288	1,694	594
1870	3,494	....	....	1899	2,493	1,701	792
1871	3,852	....	....	1900	3,816	2,650	1,166
1872	4,899	....	....	1901	3,921	2,968	953
1873	4,957	....	....	1902	4,707	3,617	1,090
1874	2,672	....	....	1903	5,817	4,669	1,148
1875	1,772	....	....	1904	4,818	3,727	1,091
1876	1,741	....	....	1905	5,049	3,780	1,269
1877	1,691	....	....	1906	5,296	3,835	1,461
1878	2,608	....	....	1907	5,710	4,384	1,326
1879	4,288	....	....	1908	3,656	2,801	855
1880	7,255	....	....	1909	4,915	3,716	1,199
1881	10,935	....	....	1910	5,178	4,084	1,094
1882	11,962	10,896	1,066	1911	5,512	4,285	1,227
1883	13,502	12,758	744	1912	5,871	4,399	1,472
1884	9,608	8,975	633	1913	6,191	4,705	1,486
1885	7,583	6,928	655	1914	3,869	3,119	750
1886	6,342	5,803	539	1915	1,976	1,693	283
1887	7,558	6,801	757	1916	1,464	1,249	215
1888	8,346	7,432	914	1917	656	536	120
1889	8,430	7,445	985	1918	304	204	100
1890	7,712	6,693	1,019	1919	3,063	2,554	509
1891	7,516	6,521	995	1920	9,276	7,988	1,288
1892	7,835	6,629	1,206	1921	'7,129	6,102	1,027
1893	6,177	5,229	948	1922	5,787	4,924	863
1894	3,849	2,863	986	1923	8,006	7,121	885
1895	4,268	3,107	1,161	1924	4,140	3,454	686
1896	3,330	2,441	889	....	....	....	....

TABLE II.—DISTRIBUTION OF EMIGRANTS TO EXTRA-EUROPEAN COUNTRIES, BY SEX, 1887-1924.

Year	Males	Females	Year	Males	Females
1887	4,713	2,845	1906	3,363	1,933
1888	5,257	3,089	1907	3,694	2,016
1889	5,385	3,045	1908	2,248	1,408
1890	4,802	2,910	1909	3,207	1,708
1891	4,564	2,952	1910	3,431	1,747
1892	4,804	3,031	1911	3,653	1,859
1893	3,808	2,369	1912	3,875	1,996
1894	2,297	1,552	1913	4,092	2,099
1895	2,525	1,743	1914	2,515	1,354
1896	2,007	1,323	1915	1,023	953
1897	1,476	1,032	1916	782	682
1898	1,403	885	1917	344	312
1899	1,540	953	1918	188	116
1900	2,438	1,378	1919	1,807	1,256
1901	2,509	1,412	1920	6,169	3,107
1902	3,121	1,586	1921	4,340	2,789
1903	3,849	1,968	1922	3,485	2,302
1904	3,084	1,734	1923	5,274	2,732
1905	3,261	1,788	1924	2,555	1,585

TABLE III.—DISTRIBUTION OF EMIGRANTS TO EXTRA-EUROPEAN COUNTRIES, BY SEX AND AGE, 1887-1924.

Year	Under 5 years			5-9 years			10-14 years			15-19 years			20-29 years		
	Total	Males	Females	Total	Males	Females	Total	Males	Females	Total	Males	Females	Total	Males	Females
1887	676	345	331	448	220	228	360	210	150	1,304	871	433	2,942	1,916	1,026
1888	702	338	364	435	243	192	372	204	168	1,529	1,050	479	3,247	2,144	1,103
1889	714	358	356	473	247	226	413	239	174	1,581	1,103	478	3,298	2,177	1,121
1890	614	306	308	405	222	183	372	220	152	1,521	993	528	2,981	1,956	1,025
1891	614	299	315	400	193	207	363	204	159	1,384	929	455	2,945	1,861	1,084
1892	603	297	306	373	204	169	380	203	177	1,589	1,061	528	3,018	1,938	1,080
1893	442	232	210	319	178	141	290	159	131	1,163	764	399	2,480	1,592	888
1894	230	115	115	133	50	83	171	92	79	684	438	246	1,444	875	569
1895	274	138	136	218	107	111	175	106	69	758	439	319	1,539	945	594
1896	200	92	108	151	78	73	124	69	55	554	363	191	1,259	761	498
1897	170	77	93	120	67	53	106	61	45	397	254	143	889	534	355
1898	153	77	76	101	55	46	67	31	36	357	231	126	853	532	321
1899	141	61	80	87	41	46	98	59	39	402	258	144	932	584	348
1900	227	111	109	182	94	88	129	70	59	543	370	173	1,454	976	478
1901	242	121	121	159	77	82	128	71	57	574	400	174	1,612	1,099	513
1902	259	123	136	176	83	93	183	115	68	771	551	220	1,948	1,387	561
1903	390	185	205	233	114	119	199	113	86	992	699	293	2,503	1,781	722
1904	316	146	170	205	112	93	175	99	76	778	536	242	1,981	1,354	627
1905	304	177	127	205	105	100	172	92	80	800	569	231	2,066	1,392	674
1906	336	163	173	244	122	122	219	108	111	739	492	247	2,234	1,534	700
1907	364	179	185	240	118	122	166	86	80	931	652	279	2,485	1,721	764
1908	193	84	109	155	75	80	135	79	56	583	376	207	1,421	912	509
1909	272	134	138	200	97	103	143	71	72	748	543	205	2,116	1,440	676
1910	293	149	144	229	127	102	175	90	85	839	596	243	2,219	1,556	663
1911	307	167	140	215	101	114	138	76	62	835	604	231	2,435	1,696	739
1912	319	154	165	191	101	90	175	91	84	950	681	269	2,595	1,794	801
1913	338	170	168	236	112	124	182	93	89	1,020	727	293	2,729	1,921	808
1914	211	114	97	175	94	81	134	75	59	552	395	157	1,671	1,129	542
1915	117	66	51	86	44	42	63	30	33	272	149	123	811	393	418
1916	71	37	34	56	24	32	57	34	23	225	137	88	599	309	290
1917	40	20	20	29	14	15	31	15	16	96	58	38	239	123	116
1918	18	10	8	20	10	10	27	18	9	65	56	9	65	39	26
1919	118	70	48	131	63	68	119	62	57	398	264	134	1,308	830	478
1920	359	173	186	304	162	142	252	116	136	1,313	979	334	4,477	3,228	1,249
1921	327	171	156	227	111	116	202	107	95	879	602	277	3,189	2,032	1,157
1922	241	125	116	217	111	106	205	112	93	828	541	287	2,566	1,637	929
1923	357	187	170	244	140	104	188	98	90	1,061	807	254	4,099	2,905	1,194
1924	230	118	112	160	91	69	132	65	67	456	335	121	1,808	1,183	625

TABLE III.—DISTRIBUTION OF EMIGRANTS TO EXTRA-EUROPEAN COUNTRIES, BY SEX AND AGE, 1887-1924 (continued).

Year	30-39 years			40-49 years			50-59 years			60-69 years			70 years and over		
	Total	Males	Females	Total	Males	Females	Total	Males	Females	Total	Males	Females	Total	Males	Females
1887	983	646	337	460	296	164	293	157	136	80	43	37	12	9	3
1888	1,116	709	407	536	351	185	279	152	127	108	53	55	22	13	9
1889	1,069	731	338	524	336	188	256	139	117	89	47	42	13	8	5
1890	950	594	356	453	295	158	286	144	142	112	59	53	18	13	5
1891	995	614	381	456	270	186	257	139	118	90	49	41	12	6	6
1892	1,047	610	437	456	281	175	262	147	115	91	53	38	16	10	6
1893	800	494	306	347	207	140	230	129	101	92	46	46	14	7	7
1894	584	368	216	299	174	125	197	117	80	88	53	35	19	15	4
1895	718	441	277	288	180	108	196	107	89	88	55	33	14	7	7
1896	568	357	211	231	145	86	150	85	65	73	45	28	20	12	8
1897	462	276	186	187	106	81	119	71	48	49	27	22	9	3	6
1898	418	258	160	167	111	56	116	72	44	53	33	20	3	3	.
1899	463	302	161	201	122	79	111	72	39	46	34	12	12	7	5
1900	712	438	274	293	201	92	180	110	70	76	45	31	20	16	4
1901	695	436	259	287	180	107	137	79	58	76	39	37	11	7	4
1902	847	546	301	301	188	113	143	80	63	61	36	25	18	12	6
1903	925	602	323	355	224	131	143	79	64	63	43	20	14	9	5
1904	770	493	277	339	195	144	175	105	70	66	36	30	13	8	5
1905	850	535	315	380	231	149	190	112	78	67	37	30	15	11	4
1906	853	547	306	394	237	157	183	103	80	76	45	31	18	12	6
1907	917	571	346	380	227	153	147	88	59	64	39	25	16	13	3
1908	660	420	240	295	175	120	139	79	60	60	39	21	15	9	6
1909	814	527	287	370	236	134	166	102	64	64	40	24	22	17	5
1910	824	535	289	345	222	123	180	107	73	57	34	23	17	15	2
1911	919	603	316	428	260	168	141	90	51	79	45	34	15	11	4
1912	926	614	312	411	260	151	208	124	84	83	47	36	13	9	4
1913	1,031	652	379	377	251	126	190	112	78	68	41	27	20	13	7
1914	635	405	230	323	199	124	128	75	53	28	22	6	12	7	5
1915	351	194	157	160	86	74	74	37	37	34	17	17	8	7	1
1916	244	129	115	136	69	67	52	30	22	17	9	8	7	4	3
1917	125	63	62	50	31	19	29	13	16	11	5	6	6	2	4
1918	44	21	23	35	17	18	20	10	10	5	2	3	5	4	1
1919	471	255	216	270	139	131	152	69	83	77	44	33	19	11	8
1920	1,466	880	586	603	361	242	325	181	144	140	70	70	37	19	18
1921	1,330	774	556	535	316	219	293	149	144	127	68	59	20	10	10
1922	948	537	411	416	235	181	246	132	114	97	46	51	23	9	14
1923	1,308	730	578	430	256	174	209	98	111	89	42	47	21	11	10
1924	770	441	329	343	192	151	144	82	62	83	40	43	14	8	6

TABLE IV.—DISTRIBUTION OF EMIGRANTS TO EXTRA-EUROPEAN COUNTRIES, BY OCCUPATION AND SEX, 1882-1924.

Year	Extraction and production of raw material			Working up of raw material			Trade			Transport and communications		
	Total	Males	Females	Total	Males	Females	Total	Males	Females	Total	Males	Females
1882	4,256	3,394	862	2,212	1,745	467	336	293	43	79	71	8
1883[1]	4,901	3,800	1,101	2,181	1,702	479	275	239	36	51	46	5
1884[1]	3,295	2,487	808	1,945	1,411	534	352	284	68	111	99	12
1885	2,511	2,135	376	1,195	1,033	162	364	243	121	44	44	
1886	2,213	1,834	379	1,013	835	178	289	255	34	22	21	1
1887	2,485	2,084	401	1,470	1,185	285	303	281	22	64	63	1
1888	2,689	2,150	539	1,819	1,487	332	378	336	42	57	57	
1889	2,894	2,412	482	1,620	1,319	301	470	336	134	60	59	1
1890	2,484	2,114	370	1,461	1,160	301	489	332	157	44	44	
1891	2,642	2,066	576	1,297	1,025	272	410	319	91	40	38	2
1892	2,145	1,941	204	1,742	1,339	403	627	426	201	44	44	
1893	1,692	1,557	135	1,342	981	361	619	368	251	25	25	
1894	998	927	71	793	566	227	479	307	172	32	31	1
1895	992	915	77	895	652	243	544	372	172	39	39	
1896	769	727	42	689	516	173	363	281	82	39	38	1
1897	589	554	35	373	297	76	277	224	53	29	28	1
1898	559	515	44	456	340	116	252	214	38	22	22	
1899	582	546	36	482	379	103	278	231	47	41	40	1
1900	1,063	985	78	686	567	119	365	321	44	49	49	
1901	1,135	1,045	90	748	610	138	326	270	56	53	52	1
1902	1,427	1,268	159	987	852	135	392	310	82	58	58	
1903	1,554	1,455	99	1,378	1,137	241	428	404	24	74	73	1
1904	1,222	1,137	85	1,084	879	205	506	396	110	66	66	
1905	1,317	1,223	94	1,051	873	178	479	386	93	54	54	
1906	1,176	1,110	66	1,112	921	191	533	445	88	82	82	
1907	1,320	1,261	59	1,244	1,047	197	596	484	112	80	80	
1908	834	770	64	698	585	113	476	374	102	50	47	3
1909	1,173	1,119	54	1,084	953	131	662	518	144	50	47	
1910	1,334	1,281	53	1,209	1,041	168	536	444	92	35	35	
1911	1,322	1,268	54	1,363	1,184	179	621	515	106	40	40	
1912	1,277	1,223	54	1,540	1,326	214	713	589	124	60	59	1
1913	1,536	1,470	66	1,582	1,352	230	657	522	135	71	71	
1914	977	956	21	840	734	106	451	345	106	65	65	
1915	228	210	18	300	236	64	352	276	76	30	30	
1916	153	144	9	277	199	78	263	212	51	21	20	1
1917	63	57	6	93	73	20	122	97	25	12	12	
1918	32	22	10	24	22	2	69	64	5	6	4	2
1919	363	343	20	467	397	70	619	535	84	1	1	
1920	2,196	2,106	90	1,850	1,645	205	1,585	1,337	248	22	21	1
1921	1,609	1,546	63	1,373	1,172	201	980	747	233	110	104	6
1922	1,137	1,083	54	1,217	1,049	168	847	673	174	64	62	2
1923	1,883	1,844	39	1,771	1,583	188	1,176	971	205	56	52	4
1924	776	761	15	622	540	82	724	627	97	95	84	11
										31	29	2

For reference notes see page 771.

TABLE IV.—DISTRIBUTION OF EMIGRANTS TO EXTRA-EUROPEAN COUNTRIES, BY OCCUPATION AND SEX, 1882-1924 (continued).

Year	Public administration, justice, science and the arts			Domestic service, other occupations			Students, persons of independent means, no occupation or occupation unknown.		
	Total	Males	Females	Total	Males	Females	Total	Males[2]	Females[2]
1882	124	91	33	437	87	350	4,518	2,040	2,478
1883[1]	120	79	41	375	75	300	5,599	2,457	3,142
1884[1]	110	63	47	370	6	364	3,425	1,724	1,701
1885	79	54	25	301	8	293	3,089	153	671
1886	73	28	45	460	94	366	2,272	116	393
1887	90	32	58	559	72	487	2,587	996	1,591
1888	119	49	70	696	116	580	2,588	1,062	1,526
1889	119	65	54	602	61	541	2,665	1,133	1,532
1890	127	48	79	593	56	537	2,514	1,048	1,466
1891	102	68	34	941	76	865	2,084	972	1,112
1892	110	40	70	676	80	596	2,491	934	1,557
1893	127	53	74	415	43	372	1,957	781	1,176
1894	111	40	71	258	22	236	1,178	404	774
1895	107	39	68	313	21	292	1,378	487	891
1896	110	34	76	285	27	258	1,075	384	691
1897	64	22	42	259	13	246	917	338	579
1898	99	38	61	179	19	160	721	255	466
1899	88	40	48	194	28	166	828	276	552
1900	97	38	59	255	36	219	1,301	442	859
1901	101	58	43	260	29	231	1,298	445	853
1902	79	21	58	225	37	188	1,539	575	964
1903	74	30	44	491	88	403	1,818	662	1,156
1904	86	31	55	338	40	298	1,516	535	981
1905	132	43	89	343	40	303	1,673	642	1,031
1906	111	35	76	384	62	322	1,898	708	1,190
1907	124	39	85	458	116	342	1,888	667	1,221
1908	117	23	94	274	40	234	1,207	409	798
1909	244	110	134	302	24	278	1,415	448	967
1910	201	93	108	346	54	292	1,512	478	1,034
1911	224	113	111	397	40	357	1,525	474	1,051
1912	298	126	172	341	49	292	1,631	491	1,140
1913	285	131	154	316	29	287	1,750	523	1,227
1914	176	71	105	193	11	182	1,202	368	834
1915	224	79	145	196	9	187	655	193	462
1916	186	73	113	121	2	119	452	140	312
1917	61	33	28	52	1	51	259	79	180
1918	28	17	11	11	1	10	139	61	78
1919	326	169	157	157	9	148	1,109	333	776
1920	591	326	265	483	21	462	2,461	630	1,831
1921	529	238	291	500	27	473	2,074	548	1,526
1922	400	155	245	504	19	485	1,626	454	1,172
1923	480	272	208	706	13	693	1,895	507	1,388
1924	398	240	158	341	17	324	1,248	341	907

For reference notes see page 771.

TABLE V.—INTERCONTINENTAL EMIGRATION, BY COUNTRY OF FUTURE RESIDENCE, 1871-1924.

Year	Total	United States	Canada	Mexico	America	Brazil	Uruguay	Argentina	Chile	Other South American States	Australia	Africa	Asia	Unknown
1871	3,852	2,729		...	146			731			109	92	16	29
1872	4,899	3,288		...	158			1,150			60	177	14	52
1873	4,957	3,462		...	183			997			121	139	6	49
1874	2,672	1,631		...	82			796			49	58	7	49
1875	1,772	866		...	76			642			74	77	9	28
1876	1,741	1,011			70			393			146	72	13	36
1877	1,691	1,027			91			244			117	167	11	34
1878	2,608	1,602			38			570			144	183	24	47
1879	4,288	2,964			143			811			75	157	27	111
1880	7,255	5,792			153			952			53	192	19	94
1881	10,935	9,996			134			624			28	100	8	45
1882	11,962	11,069			96			778			14	4	...	1
1883	13,502	11,619			8			1,852			20	2	1	...
1884	9,608	8,359			5			1,193			50	1	...	...
1885	7,583	5,934			7			1,608			24	9	1	...
1886	6,342	4,863			6			1,442			16	14	1	...
1887	7,558	6,445	3		...	241	51	732	40	12	29	5	...	...
1888	8,346	6,759	5		2	83	17	1,334	107	17	16	5	1	
1889	8,430	6,963	3		...	39	33	1,294	30	23	23	15	7	
1890	7,712	6,909	8		...	79	29	629	9	6	23	15	5	
1891	7,516	6,920	16		8	184	19	282	4	11	47	17	8	
1892	7,835	7,340	2		16	49	11	358	14	6	20	10	9	
1893	6,177	5,637	52		2	50	16	317	34	30	21	15	3	
1894	3,849	3,285	21		7	48	8	401	13	26	17	20	3	
1895	4,268	3,697	11		3	108	19	354	31	...	13	29	3	
1896	3,330	2,787	2		2	56	8	410	21	4	9	28	3	
1897	2,508	2,149	3		6	55	12	233	5	2	7	33	3	
1898	2,288	1,988	5		2	48	7	168	16	4	16	33	1	
1899	2,493	2,159	9		3	10	3	245	2	6	9	37	10	
1900	3,816	3,341	47		2	16	21	266	35	1	16	50	21	
1901	3,921	3,520	3		...	42	6	236	12	6	39	18	40	
1902	4,707	4,227	6		5	45	12	230	32	5	77	48	20	
1903	5,817	5,286	17		8	39	14	238	30	14	79	65	27	
1904	4,818	4,279	40	4	12	46	8	308	7	7	71	23	13	...
1905	5,049	4,349	73	7	12	53	12	471	...	8	26	16	22	...

TABLE V.—INTERCONTINENTAL EMIGRATION, BY COUNTRY OF FUTURE RESIDENCE, 1871-1924 (continued).

Year	Total	United States	Canada	Mexico	America	Brazil	Uruguay	Argentina	Chile	Other South American States	Australia	Africa	Asia	Unknown
1906	5,296	4,609	109	11	10	29	9	442	2	1	21	15	38	....
1907	5,710	4,945	133	14	11	45	20	432	21	4	32	25	28	....
1908	3,656	2,855	55	5	6	61	11	553	3	14	38	24	31	....
1909	4,915	3,798	103	7	6	72	28	720	7	23	94	27	30	....
1910	5,178	4,072	184	11	14	72	40	683	9	24	28	16	25	....
1911	5,512	3,969	227	14	1	118	14	997	8	8	80	36	40	....
1912	5,871	4,195	209	13	16	228	21	969	17	21	113	32	37	....
1913	6,191	4,367	391	5	9	257	49	874	26	12	114	41	46	....
1914	3,869	2,890	251	1	36	145	17	367	6	15	86	36	19	....
1915	1,976	1,547	12	..	40	64	6	156	4	5	11	73	58	....
1916	1,464	1,180	1	3	11	67	3	105	....	10	3	44	37	....
1917	656	489	..	..	2	37	..	57	....	5	3	31	32	....
1918	304	186	..	6	1	26	..	31	....	9	1	32	12	....
1919	3,063	1,913	18	6	25	253	..	390	....	44	..	262	152	....
1920	9,276	7,049	205	14	43	533	..	559	....	106	39	409	319	....
1921	7,129	4,911	261	39	36	496	..	637	....	127	85	328	209	....
1922	5,787	3,708	141	27	46	629	..	687	....	77	84	232	156	....
1923	8,006	4,585	1,503	35	29	514	..	618	....	87	99	391	145	....
1924	4,140	1,427	{695}		49	317	..	463	...	154	187	616	232	....

SOURCES

Annuaire statistique de la Suisse, 1915 and 1924. Berne, 1916 and 1925.

Table I (years 1868-1915); all tables (year 1924).

Emigration de la Suisse pour les pays d'outre-mer, 1887-1923. Report published by the Federal Bureau of Statistics from 1887 to 1891, and by the Federal Office of Emigration from 1892 to 1923. Berne.

All tables (years 1887-1923).

Information supplied by the Federal Office of Emigration.

Tables IV, V (year 1886).

L. Karrer, *Die Auswanderung aus der Schweiz.* Berne, 1887. Appendix III, pp. 228, 236.

Tables IV (years 1882-85), V (years 1871-85).

NOTES

[1]In 1883 and 1884 the adult dependants are distributed over the various occupational groups. In the other years, all dependants are included under the head "no occupation".

[2]In the years 1885-1908 the statistics only distinguish the adults by sex among the emigrants without occupation, whereas the total in this category includes the children. Classification by sex has now been established for the purpose of this work by deducting the total of emigrants of each sex in active occupations from the general total of emigrants of each sex (table III).

DANZIG

The Senate of the Free City of Danzig has issued detailed statistics of emigration since January 1, 1921. These statistics relate to persons using the port of Danzig as their point of departure to an overseas country. The figures concerning transit are in this instance far more important than those relating to citizens.

TABLE I.—INTERCONTINENTAL EMIGRATION OF CITIZENS, 1921-23.

Year	Emigrants
1921	24
1922	13
1923	20[1]

TABLE II.—ALIEN MIGRANTS IN TRANSIT TO EXTRA-EUROPEAN COUNTRIES, 1920-24.

Year	Migrants
1920	30,578
1921	32,727
1922	24,871
1923	21,219
1924	8,196[2]

SOURCE

Information supplied by the Senate of the Free City of Danzig.

Tables I and II.

NOTES

[1]First seven months of the year only. From August 1923 to January 1926 no distinction was made between citizens of Danzig and aliens; the totals have been added to those of migrants in transit.
[2]Exclusive of July.

ESTONIA.

Table I refers to ordinary passengers and its figures are derived from reports prepared at the frontier stations.

Tables II to V, which relate to the year 1924, are based on passports issued. The statistics draw no distinction between emigrants and non-emigrants. Accordingly, attempts have been made to ascertain the number of those whose passports have been extended by the diplomatic representatives of Estonia in foreign countries. Moreover, separate note has been taken of persons holding passports for European countries or proceeding overseas. The first group covers persons of all occupations, while from the second group have been excluded traders, sailors and students, because these classes, although possessing passports, retain domicile in Estonia. It is, of course, probable that some belonging to other occupational groups retain their Estonian domicile although they have received passports. The actual number of emigrants, accordingly, should be regarded as falling somewhat below the figures in the tables.

Statistics about the number of migrants from Estonia to Brazil (1923-24) and the United States (1924) will be found in the national tables for those countries.

TABLE I.—NUMBER OF PERSONS WHO CROSSED THE FRONTIERS, 1920-24.

	1920	1921	1922	1923	1924
Arrivals	19,476	46,554	35,879	39,719	35,330
Departures	195	30,288	30,336	38,068	35,734
Excess of arrivals (+) and departures (—)	+19,281	+16,266	+5,543	+1,651	—404

TABLE II.—DISTRIBUTION OF INTERCONTINENTAL AND CONTINENTAL EMIGRANT CITIZENS, BY SEX AND AGE, 1924.

	Total	Intercontinental	Continental		Total	Intercontinental	Continental
Grand total	1,222[1]	726	471	30-39 years	301[1]	195	100
Males	628[1]	441	173	40-49 years	139[1]	89	46
Females	594[1]	285	298	50-59 years	63[1]	28	35
Under 14 years	130[1]	58	72	60 years and over	56[1]	4	51
15-19 years	98[1]	58	39	Not stated	52[1]	26	20
20-29 years	383[1]	268	108				

For reference notes see page 774.

TABLE III.—Distribution of intercontinental and continental emigrant citizens, by occupation, 1924.

Occupation	Total[1]		Intercontinental		Continental	
	Head of the family	Dependents	Head of the family	Dependents	Head of the family	Dependents
Farmers..................	30	15	25	15	4	..
Agricultural workers........	76	24	59	17	17	7
Manufacturers and traders...	16	12	14	6	2	6
Workers:						
Skilled workers...........	311	104	215	57	87	41
Unskilled workers........	57	16	26	10	31	6
Shop assistants...........	15	2	10	1	5	1
Domestic servants........	37	3	15	1	21	1
Seamen...................	25	3	25	3	..	..
Officials..................	70	5	50	2	18	2
Liberal professions..........	48	16	25	6	22	10
Students..................	39	1	34	1	5	..
Occupation unknown........	170	50	68	12	100	38
Housewives...............	53	24	19	10	33	14
Total..............	947	275	585	141	345	126

TABLE IV.—Emigration of citizens, by country of destination, 1924.

Latvia............................	155	Spain......................	1
Lithuania........................	6	Italy......................	3
Finland..........................	60	Yugoslavia.................	3
Union of Socialist Soviet Republics....	116	Palestine..................	2
Poland..........................	8	Egypt.....................	1
Sweden..........................	12	China.....................	5
Norway..........................	1	United States..............	170
Denmark.........................	4	Canada....................	39
Germany.........................	44	North America.............	50
Netherlands......................	10	Argentina.................	42
France...........................	23	Brazil.....................	86
England..........................	5	South America.............	14
Belgium..........................	13	America (no detailed indication)........	281
Switzerland......................	2	Australia..................	36
Austria...........................	5	Not specified..............	25
		Total.....................	1,222

TABLE V.—Distribution of intercontinental and continental emigrant citizens, by race or people, 1924.

Nationality	Total	Intercontinental	Continental	Nationality	Total	Intercontinental	Continental
Estonian.....	957[1]	661	273	Finnish..............	9	2	7
German.....	79[1]	18	60	Jewish..............	28	19	9
Russian.....	72[1]	14	57	Polish...............	6	..	6
Swedish.....	30	10	20	Other nationalities.....	4	1	3
Latvian.....	22	1	21	Nationality not stated..	15	..	15

SOURCE

Information supplied by the Government.

NOTE

[1]Including countries not specified.

FINLAND

Finland possesses two types of migration statistics: those established by administrative methods and passenger returns from transportation companies.

1. Emigration statistics are prepared in the following way: the Governors of the different districts send yearly lists of persons who have received passports. Forms are used on which passports for countries situated outside Europe are distinguished and detailed information about holders of them is given.

State officials obtain the necessary information about returning emigrants at the annual meetings at which tax lists are revised and forward it to the Governors.

2. Passenger statistics of transportation companies about returning emigrants give higher figures than those found in the above-mentioned sources. They exceed the true number because (a) they include a small number of alien immigrants, and (b) they relate as a rule to the aggregate movement of passengers regardless of the period of intended residence. On the other hand, the particulars in the tax lists relate to emigrants who have returned with the object of resuming their domicile.

Statistics about the number of migrants from Finland to Brazil (1919-24), Canada (1900-24) and the United States (1899-1924) will be found in the national tables for those countries. Statistics about the number of migrants returning to Finland from the United States (1908-24) will be found in the national tables for the latter country.

TABLE I.—DISTRIBUTION OF EMIGRANTS TO EXTRA-EUROPEAN COUNTRIES, BY SEX AND AGE, 1882-1924.

Year	Total (according to passports taken out)	Sex		Age and Sex													
		Males	Females	Under 16 years		16 to 20 years		21 to 30 years		31 to 40 years		41 to 50 years		Over 50 years		Age unknown	
				Males	Females	Males	Females	Males	Females	Males	Females	Males	Females	Males	Females	Males	Females
1882[1]	1,559	1,296	263	32	33	1,095				120		148			14	21	96
1883[1]	1,616	1,352	264	30	32	1,179				154		123			12	20	66
1884[2]	889	689	200	46	53	538				114		80			8	25	25
1885[2]	439	274	165	35	31	199				39		15			3	25	92
1886[2]	1,324	1,042	282	52	44	137	10	696			52	129			4	28	172
1887[2]	6,117[3]	5,067	1,050	158	128	507	33	2,330			138	522			24	36	393
1888[3]	4,205[3]	3,231	974	108	104	307	39	1,521			176	303			25	26	315
1889[3]	4,340[3]	3,262	1,078	132	98	475	76	1,366			152	298			22	1	423
1890[2]	5,982[3]	4,170	1,812	226	218	790	199	1,560			449	328			47	130	451
1891[2]	4,869[3]	3,414	1,455	229	192	669	280	1,312			436	256			47	40	144
1892[2]	6,620	4,496	2,124	542	492	1,381	582	2,095			911	442			93	36	46
1893[4]	9,117	6,277	2,840	845	657	1,612	792	3,116			1,202	649			150	55	39
1894[5]	1,380	637	743	149	152	153	141	249			360	60			56	26	34
1895[5]	4,020	2,063	1,957	287	298	575	506	989			1,011	178			89	34	53
1896[5]	5,185	3,078	2,107	250	284	906	536	1,600			1,159	268			112	25	45
1897[5]	1,916	866	1,050	95	100	265	309	430			562	47			52	29	27
1898[5]	3,467	2,001	1,466	198	217	658	431	934			722	130			103	36	38
1899[5]	12,075	7,599	4,476	743	726	2,282	1,233	3,937			2,108	519			335	81	107
1900	10,397	6,265	4,132	730	703	1,529	1,053	2,704	1,653	847	413	317	171	112	96	26	43
1901	12,561	8,237	4,324	678	706	1,944	1,033	3,734	1,831	1,267	429	448	162	124	94	42	69
1902	23,152	16,075	7,077	1,233	1,267	4,294	1,705	7,314	2,853	2,225	742	746	287	192	157	71	66
1903	16,964	10,449	6,515	1,018	1,050	2,857	1,716	4,307	2,693	1,577	632	516	252	127	120	47	52
1904	10,952	6,158	4,794	814	888	1,610	1,236	2,539	1,811	851	510	247	149	71	103	26	97
1905	17,427	12,001	5,426	820	813	3,067	1,533	5,559	2,209	1,801	539	548	142	158	101	48	89
1906	17,517	11,921	5,596	710	691	3,331	1,700	5,726	2,350	1,524	523	452	130	112	97	66	105
1907	16,296	10,470	5,826	632	666	2,691	1,780	5,176	2,500	1,380	545	396	136	108	96	87	103
1908	5,812	3,313	2,499	397	406	644	601	1,592	974	478	326	118	70	41	56	43	66
1909	19,144	12,509	6,635	967	952	2,498	1,716	6,385	2,915	2,014	736	428	149	130	84	87	83
1910	19,007	12,444	6,563	970	967	2,910	1,704	6,059	2,795	1,885	752	439	163	129	109	52	73
1911	9,372	4,821	4,551	611	622	1,058	1,237	2,140	1,876	716	570	191	103	62	97	43	46
1912	10,724	5,652	5,072	695	676	1,251	1,474	2,642	2,082	748	585	216	132	73	106	27	17
1913	20,057	12,919	7,138	827	869	2,858	2,092	6,817	3,059	1,816	795	464	189	106	96	31	38
1914	6,474	3,651	2,823	403	368	710	711	1,719	1,169	595	396	156	101	47	58	21	20
1915	4,041	2,583	1,458	295	280	548	263	1,192	552	427	273	89	50	24	31	8	9
1916	5,325	2,249	3,076	564	620	486	754	517	1,050	409	452	207	126	64	65	2	9
1917	2,773	1,258	1,515	380	369	300	291	215	442	191	274	126	70	42	41	4	28
1918	1,900	1,331	569	128	137	224	89	708	193	192	87	59	29	16	17	4	17
1919	1,085	538	547	162	147	71	79	130	127	117	113	37	37	21	21		23
1920	5,595	2,516	3,079	434	476	399	751	1,080	1,086	410	417	126	175	67	157		17
1921	3,557	1,280	2,277														
1922	5,715	2,766	2,949														
1923	13,835	9,125	4,710														
1924	5,429	3,745	1,684														

TABLE II.—DISTRIBUTION OF EMIGRANTS, BY OCCUPATION, 1893-1924.

Year	Total	Agriculture						Artisans		Factory workers	
		Farmer landowners		Tenants		Tenants and farm laborers					
		Males	Females	Males	Females	Males	Females	Males	Females	Males	Females
1893	9,117	2,302	824	993	297	1,747	895	340	150	43	15
1894	1,380	189	164	67	65	201	288	35	44	5	5
1895	4,020	867	598	236	229	608	621	64	50	6	3
1896	5,185	1,245	695	430	253	925	634	76	51	6	6
1897	1,916	358	284	93	90	276	344	21	21	.	5
1898	3,467	804	439	281	193	608	489	51	28	3	1
1899	12,075	3,033	1,360	1,203	577	2,276	1,516	193	92	11	23
1900	10,397	2,112	1,046	1,057	507	1,950	1,491	216	113	18	11
1901	12,561	2,773	1,125	1,302	501	2,240	1,409	346	141	50	33
1902	23,152	4,879	1,690	2,353	791	4,027	1,888	1,098	466	299	129
1903	16,964	2,963	1,350	1,406	754	2,467	1,529	799	452	233	168
1904	10,952	1,887	972	749	508	1,507	1,261	334	262	58	88
1905	17,427	4,039	1,323	1,850	603	3,311	1,573	415	226	94	89
1906	17,517	3,922	1,358	1,679	641	3,276	1,616	480	218	142	93
1907	16,296	3,337	1,377	1,369	602	2,832	1,630	575	252	146	87
1908	5,812	929	587	371	230	978	779	168	110	44	30
1909	19,144	4,068	1,524	1,566	768	3,380	1,857	545	316	165	112
1910	19,007	4,044	1,533	1,535	692	3,113	1,738	618	322	236	160
1911	9,372	1,530	1,002	468	428	1,088	1,189	340	237	89	87
1912	10,724	1,860	1,168	556	478	1,296	1,257	361	297	81	95
1913	20,057	4,073	1,622	1,455	712	3,096	1,669	698	443	183	190
1914	6,474	1,038	562	293	260	866	728	232	164	90	73
1915	4,041	1,208	354	164	102	475	362	152	76	43	32
1916	5,325	964	792	160	190	507	844	112	140	28	65
1917	2,773	367	388	77	110	267	352	85	86	30	36
1918	1,900	431	151	115	47	225	125	80	30	47	19
1919	1,085	152	138	15	14	109	113	44	36	10	13
1920	5,595	985	582	119	218	422	610	147	166	74	120
1921	3,557	323	508	52	108	184	298	111	114	51	51
1922	5,715	1,120	705	113	142	342	333	250	190	77	68
1923	13,835	3,899	1,207	404	178	944	542	830	356	359	170
1924	5,429	1,549	389	113	36	386	128	332	190	155	96

TABLE II.—DISTRIBUTION OF EMIGRANTS, BY OCCUPATION, 1893-1924 (continued).

Year	Traders and seamen		Domestic servants		General labor and persons without definite occupation		Civil servants		Other occupations		Occupation not stated	
	Males	Females	Males	Females	Males	Females	Males	Females	Males	Females	Males	Females
1893	219	88	147	338	352	152	35	20	89	65	10	6
1894	50	21	18	93	46	37	5	6	21	20	..	..
1895	74	39	68	284	94	79	6	12	37	27	3	15
1896	76	35	156	293	104	75	15	10	42	34	3	21
1897	27	19	32	215	31	28	3	7	19	26	6	11
1898	57	32	100	188	69	51	9	9	10	23	9	13
1899	117	74	278	531	389	196	32	21	39	53	28	33
1900	112	46	164	553	470	240	28	26	105	69	33	30
1901	243	95	179	499	922	360	43	27	115	79	24	55
1902	501	187	378	917	2,097	758	158	63	180	68	105	120
1903	365	197	254	875	1,622	910	108	101	152	62	80	117
1904	261	133	133	644	1,068	690	58	71	63	36	40	129
1905	339	140	307	628	1,401	619	89	61	117	64	39	100
1906	372	128	413	763	1,303	443	120	7	134	61	80	198
1907	286	113	292	881	1,346	519	76	78	138	60	73	227
1908	94	49	41	294	558	235	26	18	38	20	66	147
1909	290	118	213	763	1,946	728	117	94	136	45	83	310
1910	331	135	172	811	2,002	810	135	79	146	54	112	229
1911	210	110	46	608	821	546	69	54	95	55	65	235
1912	204	125	80	766	985	538	68	71	84	47	77	230
1913	343	195	197	1,002	2,438	795	124	82	178	89	134	339
1914	138	82	31	359	804	350	27	29	64	43	68	173
1915	104	53	19	122	296	207	29	25	53	19	40	106
1916	68	69	11	289	274	346	20	35	26	37	79	269
1917	66	46	4	136	262	201	14	26	53	25	33	109
1918	48	9	2	23	287	87	23	5	45	8	28	65
1919	37	28	2	31	88	74	13	12	43	13	25	75
1920	114	103	10	309	375	354	84	64	80	52	106	501
1921	71	90	7	262	288	251	29	36	69	72	95	487
1922	119	95	13	376	496	259	22	36	122	118	92	627
1923	302	172	28	438	1,747	509	118	60	266	174	228	904
1924	161	65	9	214	806	258	39	26	134	88	61	194

TABLE III.—INTERCONTINENTAL EMIGRATION, BY COUNTRY OF DESTINATION AND SEX, 1882-1917.

Year	America		Other non-European countries		Year	America		Other non-European countries	
	Males	Females	Males	Females		Males	Females	Males	Females
1882	1,296	263	...	..	1901	8,219	4,317	18	7
1883	1,352	264	...	..	1902	15,991	7,066	84	11
1884	689	200	...	..	1903	10,330	6,491	119	24
1885	274	165	...	..	1904	6,102	4,787	56	7
					1905	11,966	5,424	35	2
1886	1,042	282	...	..					
1887	5,067	1,050	...	..	1906	11,906	5,593	15	3
1888	3,231	974	...	..	1907	10,465	5,825	5	1
1889	3,262	1,078	...	..	1908	3,311	2,497	2	2
1890	4,170	1,812	...	..	1909	12,490	6,627	19	8
					1910	12,435	6,559	9	4
1891	3,414	1,455	...	..					
1892	4,496	2,124	...	..	1911	4,796	4,550	25	1
1893	6,277	2,840	...	..	1912	5,642	5,066	10	6
1894	637	743	...	..	1913	12,901	7,136	18	2
1895	2,063	1,957	...	..	1914	3,637	2,819	14	4
					1915	2,568	1,455	15	3
1896	3,049	2,136	...	..					
1897	866	1,050	...	..	1916	2,244	3,074	5	2
1898	1,956	1,511	...	..	1917	1,250	1,508	8	7
1899	7,562	4,509	...	..	....	....	....	....	..
1900	6,260	4,128	5	4	....	....	....	...	..

TABLE IV.—DISTRIBUTION OF IMMIGRANT CITIZENS, BY SEX AND AGE, 1894-1916, AND TOTAL, 1894-1924.[6]

Year	Total	Sex		Age									
		Males	Females	Under 16 years		16 to 20 years		21 to 39 years[7]		40 years and over[7]		Age unknown	
				Males	Females	Males	Females	Males	Females	Males	Females	Males	Females
1894	630	550	80	7	4	14	1	361	64	124	6	44	5
1895	646	561	85	6	7	12	4	407	58	131	7	5	9
1896	894	744	150	22	15	10	1	529	102	172	13	11	19
1897	693	579	114	12	17	7	8	381	80	137	8	42	1
1898	572	464	108	12	12	1	1	296	83	113	7	42	5
1899	291	248	43	4	2	5		156	31	61	6	22	3
1900	1,043	819	224	38	33	15	2	554	118	173	6	39	43
1901	1,148	871	277	82	79	13	4	575	167	199	28	2	7
1902	901	727	174	58	42	11	5	502	108	153	20	3	4
1903	1,740	1,450	290	53	59	41	12	1,089	183	266	15	1	3
1904	1,764	1,421	343	63	87	38	18	1,059	204	256	33	5	5
1905	1,259	926	333	78	84	19	7	674	192	146	29	9	23
1906	1,602	1,210	392	86	62	26	13	881	267	208	27	9	17
1907	3,783	2,997	786	134	141	101	26	2,358	528	390	33	14	28
1908	3,183	2,482	701	138	168	64	13	1,963	442	297	63	20	36
1909	1,601	1,123	478	122	120	15	14	825	285	150	42	11	17
1910	1,641	1,223	418	67	79	11	7	962	285	169	42	14	10
1911	2,423	1,864	559	103	133	36	16	1,484	356	216	37	25	25
1912	2,159	1,618	541	97	96	29	18	1,249	361	184	29	59	33
1913	2,068	1,506	562	114	127	17	14	1,154	343	207	33	14	43
1914	1,840	1,370	470	70	81	17	18	1,074	312	200	35	9	16
1915	478	369	109	16	19	2	5	286	74	59	43	6	7
1916	221	159	62	5	7	2	4	106	37	34	4	12	9
1917	673												
1918	140												
1919	731												
1920	1,553												
1921	1,322												
1922	588												
1923	379												
1924	604												

For reference notes see page 782.

TABLE V.—Distribution of immigrant citizens, by country of last residence and sex, 1894-1916.

Year	Total	America		Other non-European countries	
		Males	Females	Males	Females
1894	630	499	79	51	1
1895	646	539	79	22	6
1896	894	688	147	56	3
1897	693	537	111	42	3
1898	572	430	107	34	1
1899	291	224	42	24	1
1900	1,043	813	221	6	3
1901	1,148	869	277	2	..
1902	901	718	173	9	1
1903	1,740	1,442	289	8	1
1904	1,764	1,416	343	5	..
1905	1,259	918	333	8	..
1906	1,602	1,206	392	4	..
1907	3,783	2,997	786	..	..
1908	3,183	2,481	701	1	..
1909	1,601	1,120	477	3	1
1910	1,641	1,221	418	2	..
1911	2,423	1,860	558	4	1
1912	2,159	1,608	539	10	2
1913	2,068	1,501	562	5	..
1914	1,840	1,359	468	11	2
1915	478	366	109	3	..
1916	221	153	62	6	..

TABLE VI.—Departures and arrivals, according to the returns of the shipping companies, 1894-1924.

Year	Departures	Arrivals	Year	Departures	Arrivals	Year	Departures	Arrivals
1894	1,075	2,074	1904	10,351	5,406	1914	5,786	4,457
1895	2,981	1,757	1905	18,341	3,930	1915	2,566	....
1896	4,942	1,880	1906	16,466	6,790	1916	4,558	....
1897	2,557	1,825	1907	16,056	10,809	1917	1,694	....
1898	3,667	2,689	1908	6,248	12,440	1918	....	....
1899	12,357	1,619	1909	20,283	4,880	1919	107	....
1900	10,642	2,579	1910	19,571	5,348	1920	3,250	....
1901	12,659	3,176	1911	9,945	7,688	1921	....	3,026
1902	21,753	2,857	1912	11,447	6,892	1922	....	1,413
1903	16,087	5,268	1913	21,370	6,533	1923	....	1,227
	....	....		....	....	1924	....	2,283

TABLE VII.—INDIRECT STATISTICS.   IMMIGRATION INTO THE UNITED STATES, BY SEX, 1872-98.

Year	Total	Males	Females	Year	Total	Males	Females
1872	24	16	8	1886	491	348	143
1873	74	68	6	1887	1,822	1,529	293
1874	113	91	22	1888	2,231	1,850	381
1875	15	13	2	1889	2,027	1,573	454
1876	10	7	3	1890	2,451	1,666	785
1877	20	13	7	1891	5,281	3,747	1,534
1878	11	5	6	1892	5,099	3,527	1,572
1879	19	17	2	1893	6,651	4,563	2,088
1880	160	144	16	1894	2,400	1,416	984
1881	176	133	43	1895	2,437	1,309	1,128
1882	597	485	112	1896	6,308	3,725	2,583
1883	723	549	174	1897	3,066	1,458	1,608
1884	835	538	297	1898	2,607	1,374	1,233
1885	555	377	178				

SOURCE

Statistik Arsbok för Finland.   Helsingfors, 1894 to 1925.

NOTES

[1]The figures refer to passports to America taken out by persons of the province of Wasa.
[2]The figures refer to passports to America taken out by persons of the provinces of Wasa and Uleaborg.
[3]Includes persons specified by sex and age combined:

1887........4,269
1888........2,924
1889........3,043
1890........4,398
1891........3,605

[4]The figures refer to passports to America.
[5]The age figures refer to persons who took passports to America. They aggregate in 1899 slightly less than the total number of passports.
[6]Including children born outside Europe as follows:

	Males	Females		Males	Females
1900		82	1908	99	115
1901	56	57	1909	84	79
1902	42	27	1910	35	57
1903	37	40	1911	44	63
1904	39	55	1912	55	57
1905	33	44	1913	56	60
1906	55	36	1914	44	46
1907	79	83	1915	3	9
			1916	1	1

[7]After 1911 the corresponding age groups are "21 to 40 years" and "41 years and over".

LATVIA

For the period 1919-24, the Latvian statistics cover in a general way the movements of migrants, refugees, prisoners of war, and others, who have changed their domicile because of the contingencies of war or on account of the post-war situation.

We may distinguish between arrivals from and departures to Russia and arrivals from and departures to other countries. (Table I.) The former have been classed in certain groups, such as refugees and Soviet soldiers. (Tables II and III.) Transmigrants coming from or proceeding to Russia (tables IV and V) are classed according to their country of destination or origin. They form a group distinct from those persons who intend to reside in the country for a certain time or permanently.

TABLE I.—ARRIVALS AND DEPARTURES,[1][2] BY COUNTRY OF ORIGIN AND DESTINATION, 1919-24.

Year	Arrivals			Departures		
	Total	from Russia	from other countries	Total	to Russia	to other countries
1919	8,700	5,087	3,613	372	308	64
1920	93,533	87,967	5,566	7,336	4,312	3,024
1921	94,881	91,788	3,093	6,922	3,886	3,036
1922	23,046	22,804	242	1,019	985	34
1923	8,019	8,019	....	565	565	....
1924	4,792	4,792	....	....	....	....

TABLE II.—ARRIVALS FROM RUSSIA,[2] BY GROUPS OF MIGRANTS 1919-24.

Year	Total	Refugees	Soldiers of the Red Army	Prisoners of war	Deserters	Subjects by choice	Hostages	Sent by institutions	Children repatriated by the Latvian Red Cross	Through various countries
1919	5,087	4,638	.....	153	296	....	..	...	..	...
1920	87,967	85,841	.....	...	1,610	....	..	250	..	266
1921	91,788	74,680	10,930	561	5,398	.....	52	147	20	...
1922	22,804	15,712	465	...	4,595	1,801	75	102	54	...
1923	8,019	3,567	.....	...	2,464	1,933	42	...	13	...
1924	4,792	1,458	....	...	858	2,476	..	...	..	...

TABLE III.—DEPARTURES TO RUSSIA[2], BY GROUPS OF MIGRANTS, 1919-23.

Year	Total	Emigrants and refugees	Prisoners of war	Expelled Communists	Hostages
1919	308	308	....	...	...
1920	4,312	2,553	1,759	...	...
1921	3,886	1,370	2,267	249	...
1922	985	846	8	31	100
1923	565	401	....	63	101

For reference notes see page 784.

TABLE IV.—ARRIVALS FROM RUSSIA EN ROUTE TO OTHER COUNTRIES, 1919-24.

Arrivals en route to	1919	1920	1921	1922	1923	1924
Lithuania						
Refugees	8	9,938	69,778	13,176	720	721
Prisoners		1,192		16		
Subjects by choice					215	52
Prisoners of war exchanged by the Red Cross and repatriated in Germany		3,641	15,426	4,536	7	
Refugees from Poland repatriated by the Lithuanian echelons		136	2,309	45		
Hostages and prisoners of war repatriated in Hungary			860	1,217		
Lithuania				332	1,549	611
Austria			279	32	7	
Germany				1,091	141	5
Switzerland					5	
Estonia		18		6	3	
America		7	11	4,633	11,259	934
British Isles					30	6
France					18	5
Belgium					13	1
Palestine					21	47
Denmark		25				
Canada					1,086	1,250
Brazil					29	192
Argentina					582	713
Cuba						357
Mexico						494
Uruguay						47
Mennonites for:						
Canada					2,056	3,958
Germany					536	
Returned to Russia (raftsmen)					2,809	165
Entered into Latvia with transit visa (without other indication)					200	
Various countries			9		597	227	398
Total	8	14,966	88,663	25,681	21,513	9,956

TABLE V.—ARRIVALS FROM VARIOUS COUNTRIES EN ROUTE TO RUSSIA, 1919-24.

Year	Total	Refugees	With transit visas	Prisoners	Prisoners of war from Germany exchanged by the Red Cross	America	Exchanged Communists from Hungary	England	Palestine	Prisoners of war from Germany
1919	....	...	.	...	....	....	...	..	..	...
1920	2,888	...	.	...	745	2,143	...	..	..	...
1921	43,984	812	.	535	33,038	9,453	90	1	55	...
1922	5,094	24	7	21	4,108	485	449	..	..	...
1923	981	...	.	41	....	707	...	40	..	193
1924	....	...	.	...	....	....	...	..	..	...

SOURCE

Information supplied by the Government.

NOTES

[1] Consisting mainly of aliens.
[2] Exclusive of transmigrants.

LITHUANIA

No statistics about migration have been obtained from the government of Lithuania.

Statistics about the number of migrants from Lithuania to South Africa (1922-24), Brazil (1920-24), Cuba (1921-24), United States (1924), Palestine (1922-24), Argentina (1922-24), and Canada (1921-24) will be found in the national tables for those countries.

Statistics about the number of migrants returning to Lithuania from the United States (1924) will be found in the national tables for that country.

POLAND

I. Statistics of Congress Poland
(Tables I-V)

The Statistical Committee of Warsaw (pre-war Russia) collected from time to time statistics relating to ten governments formerly constituting Congress Poland, but this was not done either continuously or systematically. Nor are the results contained in any publications. Some of them were inserted in various issues of the "Proceedings" of the above Committee; others were not published at all. The Director of the Statistical Office of the Republic of Poland has kindly supplied returns for all the years for which information was collected and, in transmitting them, has added the following statement:

1. These statistics relate to the territory of the former Kingdom of Poland or of the Congress, as delimited by the Treaty of Vienna of 1815. This territory approximately corresponds at present to five of the central provinces (voiévodies) of the Polish Republic, namely, Warsaw, Lodz, Kielce, Lublin and Bialystok, with these exceptions that the northern portion of the ancient government of Suwalki is now incorporated in Lithuania, and the eastern portion of the province of Bialystok comprises those departments which during Russian rule did not belong to Congress Poland.

2. The emigration figures were collected by the former Statistical Committee of Warsaw with the aid of the communal administrations. They are somewhat inexact and incomplete, more particularly with regard to the earlier period, but are not without value. In fact, these figures faithfully reflect the general tendencies of the migrations, both in regard to the fluctuations of the grand total and the direction taken by the stream of emigrants. However, the classification of emigrants to America into temporary and permanent is not quite correct.

3. The figures supplied do not comprise emigration to Russia. Data on this subject exist for certain years, but are very incomplete.

4. No data are available relating to (a) temporary emigration for countries other than Germany in 1890 and 1900-03, and (b) the division of permanent emigrants according to country of destination (or immigration) for the period 1890-1903.

5. For the last years before the war (1909-13 and partly 1904-08) detailed information is available concerning (a) the division more of emigrants into peasant proprietors, landless peasants (rural proletariat), and skilled and unskilled workers, and (b) their classification according to religion. Similarly, territorial division is indicated in these statistics.

II. Statistics of the Republic of Poland
(Tables VI-X)

During the period 1920-23 emigration officials reported on the intercontinental emigration of citizens, and in subsequent years these statis-

tics have been prepared by the National Emigration Office on the basis of data furnished by the authorised shipping companies.

On the other hand, the number of emigrants to continental countries has been ascertained from the visas granted. The figures relating to emigration and immigration from France have been furnished to the Emigration Office by the French Mission at Poznan.

Statistics about the number of migrants from Poland to the United States by sex (1869-98), and both sexes combined (1899-1924), to South Africa (1922-24), Argentina (1921-24), Australia (1902-24), Brazil (1920-24), Canada (1900-24), Cuba (1911-24) and Palestine (1922-24) will be found in the national tables for those countries. Statistics about the number of migrants returning to Poland from Argentina (1911-24) and the United States (1908-24) will be found in the national tables for those countries.

TABLE I.—PERMANENT EMIGRATION FROM CONGRESS POLAND, 1890-1903.

Year	Emigrants	Year	Emigrants	Year	Emigrants
1890	19,323	1895	7,124	1900	9,838
1891	17,499	1896	6,180	1901	11,439
1892	13,127	1897	5,733	1902	9,121
1893	8,784	1898	7,766	1903	10,896[1]
1894	5,623	1899	8,670	....	.....

TABLE II.—PERMANENT EMIGRATION FROM CONGRESS POLAND, BY COUNTRY OF DESTINATION, 1904 AND 1908-13.

Year	Total	North America	South America	Other countries	Year	Total	North America	South America	Other countries
1904	17,239	14,573	471	2,195	1911	21,686	12,375	8,152	1,159
1908	35,646	26,963	3,854	4,829	1912	20,302	15,416	3,306	1,580
1909	17,252	14,137	1,453	1,662	1913	17,163	14,349	1,528	1,286
1910	15,117	12,844	1,174	1,099	....	....	....	....	....

For reference notes see page 791.

TABLE III.—Distribution of permanent emigrants from Congress Poland, by sex, occupation and country of destination, 1909-13.

Year	Country of destination	Total	Males	Females	Occupation			
					Farmers	Farm laborers	Industrial workers	Other occupations or occupation unknown
1909	North America....	14,137	9,004	5,133	4,120	6,207	663	3,147
	South America....	1,453	1,064	389	255	567	113	518
	Other countries....	1,662	1,094	568	441	467	125	629
	Total............	17,252	11,162	6,090	4,816	7,241	901	4,294
1910	North America....	12,844	8,388	4,456	3,754	6,076	253	2,761
	South America....	1,174	827	347	204	534	69	367
	Other countries....	1,099	690	409	121	415	78	485
	Total............	15,117	9,905	5,212	4,079	7,025	400	3,613
1911	North America....	12,375	7,874	4,501	3,253	6,238	287	2,597
	South America....	8,152	4,412	3,740	2,082	5,555	87	428
	Other countries....	1,159	745	414	98	558	59	444
	Total............	21,686	13,031	8,655	5,433	12,351	433	3,469
1912	North America....	15,416	9,820	5,596	3,991	7,329	411	3,685
	South America....	3,306	1,893	1,413	610	2,056	144	496
	Other countries....	1,580	1,066	514	114	541	75	850
	Total............	20,302	12,779	7,523	4,715	9,926	630	5,031
1913	North America....	14,349	8,881	5,468	4,310	7,244	342	2,453
	South America....	1,528	986	542	336	622	73	497
	Other countries....	1,286	826	460	133	632	68	453
	Total............	17,163	10,693	6,470	4,779	8,498	483	3,403

TABLE IV.—Distribution of permanent emigrants from Congress Poland, by religion, 1909-13.

Year	Catholic	Greek Orthodox	Protestant	Jewish	Other faiths or faith unknown
1909	11,838	52	1,145	3,696	521
1910	10,884	66	871	2,960	336
1911	17,500	167	810	2,921	288
1912	14,393	139	1,125	4,255	390
1913	12,612	61	1,014	2,953	523

TABLE V.—Temporary emigration from Congress Poland, by country of destination, 1890-1913.

Year	Total	Germany	Denmark	France	America	Other countries[2]
1890	. . . . . .	17,275	. . . . .	. . .	. . . . .	. . . . .
1900	. . . . . .	119,184	. . . . .	. .	. . . . .	. . . . .
1901	. . . . . .	139,664	. . . . .	. . .	. . . . .	. . . . .
1902	. . . . . .	135,657	. . . . .	. . .	. . . . .	. . . . .
1903	150,265	141,731	247	. . .	8,267	20
1904	149,081	137,701	814	1	10,453	112
1908	254,895	235,074	4,196	[3]	12,399	3,226[3]
1909	288,977	260,702	4,117	342	20,760	3,056
1910	302,681	275,441	3,645	508	20,119	2,968
1911	326,375	296,561	4,395	802	20,822	3,795
1912	360,291	322,838	3,721	621	28,110	5,001
1913	377,674	343,415	5,507	601	25,074	3,077

TABLE VI.—Distribution of emigrants from the Polish Republic to extra-European countries, by occupation, 1922 and 1923.

Year	Total	Agri-culture	Artisans	Mer-chants	Laborers	Liberal pro-fessions	No definite oc-cupations
1922[4]	46,773	6,250	7,262	1,690	3,319	2,549	25,703
1923	5,613	1,106	1,093	119	75	349	2,871

TABLE VII.—Intercontinental emigration from the Polish Republic, by country of future residence, 1920-24.

Year	Total	Argen-tina	Brazil	Canada	United States	Other American coun-tries	Pales-tine	Other countries
1920	74,121	. . . .	. . . .	. . . .	90,101	. . . .	6,115	. . . .
1921	107,046	2,257	253	7,571	27,723	. . . .	2,232	749
1922	38,716	3,311	776	3,717	23,709	6,809	1,973	957
1923	55,401	4,977	98	2,851	4,290	1,973	5,724	14,984
1924	22,511	5,590	2,513	2,271				150

For reference notes see page 791.

TABLE VIII.—Distribution of Emigrants from the Polish Republic to European
Countries, by Sex, Age and Occupation, 1924.

```
Farmers...................................................................4,942
Miners....................................................................2,775
Industrial workers.........................................................983
Unskilled workers........................................................7,156
Merchants..................................................................70
Liberal professions.......................................................138
Domestic service..........................................................734
Other occupations.........................................................103
No occupation:
    Females..............................................................2,345
    Children.............................................................6,890

                            Total..............................26,136

                              ⎧ Males   .........................11,343
               Comprising ⎨ Females...........................7,900
                              ⎩ Children..........................6,893
```

TABLE IX.—Continental emigration from the Polish Republic, by country
of future residence, 1920-24.

Year	Total	England	Belgium	France	Germany	Austria-Hungary, Czecho-slovakia	Switzer-land	Other coun-tries
1920	26,846	...	...	....	..	...	..	...
1921	12,129	388	189	988	180	...	..	210
1922	31,373	199	...	29,840	34	503	61	736
1923	72,020	92	32	70,895	17	150	55	21
1924	52,082	...	...	....	..	..	..	...

TABLE X.—Intercontinental immigration of citizens into the Polish Republic,
1920-23.

Year	Immigrants	Year	Immigrants
1920	70,000	1922	11,116
1921	78,817	1923	6,693

SOURCES

Troudy Warszawskawo Statisticzeskawo Komiteta. (Publication of the Warsaw Statistical Committee.) Parts XIX and XXII for 1890 and Part XXXIX for 1908; also an unpublished return of the Central Statistical Bureau of the Polish Republic based on the archives of the former (Russian) Statistical Committee of Warsaw (for 1909-13) and furnished by the Central Statistical Bureau.

Tables I, II, III, IV and V.

Revue Mensuelle de Statistique. Published by the Central Statistical Bureau of the Polish Republic. Warsaw, April 1922 and April 1923.

Biuletyn Urzedu Emigracyjnego (Bulletin of the Emigration Office). Warsaw, April 1925.

Information supplied by the Central Statistical Bureau of the Polish Republic.

Tables VI, VII, VIII, IX (years 1920-23); X.

Przeglad Emigracyiny, Warsaw, first quarter 1926.

Table IX (year 1924).

NOTES

[1]For 1903, emigration from the towns is not included; it amounted in 1902 to 2,060 and in 1904 to 13,031 persons.
[2]Emigrants to Russia are not included.
[3]France is included under "other countries".
[4]These figures refer to the total of emigrants and include aliens.

RUSSIA

I. Frontier Statistics of Travellers

(Tables I-VI)

Records have been kept since 1828 of persons, whether emigrants or ordinary travellers, whether citizens or aliens who entered or left European Russia. The data were elaborated by the Russian Customs authorities on the basis of the passport registers or, in the case of Austrian subjects, of identification cards. Until 1850 travellers who arrived from or departed to Russian Poland were recorded but in 1851 the customs barriers between Russian Poland and the rest of Russia were removed. Passenger traffic between the two districts thereafter was regarded as internal, and statistical facts concerning these currents of migration ceased to be recorded.[1]

Emigration to overseas countries is not distinguished in these statistics. They are concerned only with arrivals in and departures from European Russia, from and to Asia and continental Europe, without distinguishing emigrants proper from the mass of ordinary travellers.

From the beginning the statistics paid close attention to the nationalities of alien travellers. In table III will be found such a statement for the period 1828 to 1915, with an estimate of the resulting net balance. But no final conclusions can be drawn from the figures. These statistics are characterised as follows in Vessélovsky's *Annuaire des finances russes* (8th year, St. Petersburg, 1879): "The figures for the period 1857-76 enable us to estimate the results realised in two decades relative to the migration of individuals between the Empire and foreign countries, the traffic facilities, the increase in comfort, the development of commerce and industry, and the character of the current and counter-current of arrivals and departures." The same authority showed the excess of citizens departing over those arriving and the excess of aliens arriving over those departing, concluding that there had been a net increase in population.

The statistics about individuals presenting "short-dated cards" at the frontiers (tables II and VI) are even less complete, because checking these papers without seriously disturbing the traffic was very difficult.

II Port Statistics

(Tables VII-IX)

The statistics of German seaports furnish another method of ascertaining the volume of Russian emigration. They relate to emigration overseas and, after 1899, to the British Isles. For the post-war period

[1]See *Statistica dell'Emigrazione italiana, per l'Estero*, 1891, 1898-1913, Rome, 1892-1915.

German statistics also are serviceable, since they furnish totals for Russians, but full particulars are not available. Tables IV and V for Latvia, showing transit of Russians according to their origins and destinations, are also useful in this connection.

Statistics about the number of migrants from pre-war or post-war Russia to Palestine (1922-24), South Africa (1913-24), Argentina (1857-1924), Brazil (1871-1924), Canada (1900-24), Cuba (1911-24), United States (1820-1924) and Australia (1902-24) will be found in the national tables for those countries. Statistics about the number of migrants returning to Russia from Argentina (1857-1924) and the United States (1908-24) will be found in the national tables for those countries.

TABLE I.—CITIZEN AND ALIEN PASSENGERS WITH PASSPORTS OUTWARD AND INWARD ACROSS THE FRONTIER OF RUSSIA DURING THE IMPERIAL PERIOD (1828-1915)

Year	Total Arrivals	Total Departures	Citizens Arrivals	Citizens Departures	Aliens Arrivals	Aliens Departures	Across the European frontier of Russia — Total Arrivals	Total Departures	Citizens Arrivals	Citizens Departures	Aliens Arrivals	Aliens Departures
1828	32,856	31,718	24,771	24,572	8,085	7,146	30,811	29,972	24,552	24,102	6,259	5,870
1829	31,982	31,097	22,928	22,472	9,054	8,625	30,657	27,782	22,087	20,466	8,570	7,316
1830	59,674	57,630	38,822	39,141	20,852	18,489	57,356	54,645	38,517	37,961	18,839	16,684
1831	98,574	66,358	71,469	48,603	27,105	17,755	94,850	63,452	70,736	47,046	24,114	16,406
1832	52,842	50,040	35,647	33,338	17,195	16,702	50,059	46,343	34,708	31,591	15,351	14,752
1833	50,181	49,762	30,428	31,212	19,753	18,550	46,412	44,084	29,217	28,580	17,195	15,504
1834	64,413	66,654	41,806	44,024	22,607	22,630	58,760	58,023	40,860	40,989	17,900	17,034
1835	57,634	53,227	40,146	35,488	17,488	17,739	54,642	49,907	39,223	36,835	15,419	13,072
1836	64,655	59,528	43,103	41,416	21,552	18,112	59,422	56,364	41,738	40,535	17,684	15,829
1837	69,434	67,521	43,980	45,284	25,454	22,237	66,279	62,585	42,657	42,911	23,622	19,674
1838	74,553	70,716	45,778	45,703	28,775	25,013	70,624	65,334	44,426	43,320	26,198	22,014
1839	79,397	72,087	52,089	45,740	27,308	26,347	73,885	67,482	49,835	43,339	24,050	24,143
1840	45,470	43,581	27,600	26,500	17,870	17,081	40,755	36,773	25,595	22,148	15,160	14,625
1841	45,100	41,527	23,521	22,314	21,579	19,213	39,864	35,390	21,335	18,862	18,529	16,528
1842	45,944	45,081	24,051	26,985	21,893	18,096	40,103	39,258	20,839	22,378	19,264	16,880
1843	49,058	45,291	24,726	24,963	24,332	20,328	42,549	38,182	21,238	19,870	21,311	18,312
1844	52,122	46,133	25,658	25,528	26,464	20,605	45,493	39,293	22,098	20,551	23,395	18,742
1845	53,683	48,191	25,971	25,866	27,712	22,325	46,733	41,135	22,306	20,813	24,427	20,322
1846	53,623	48,490	23,212	25,819	30,411	22,671	46,692	40,173	20,560	20,936	26,132	19,237
1847	64,965	63,594	40,744	42,927	24,221	20,667	59,969	59,020	38,574	39,198	21,395	19,822
1848	45,194	46,580	34,814	35,995	10,380	10,585	41,423	42,130	32,886	32,792	8,537	9,338
1849	62,872	50,439	52,867	41,641	10,005	8,798	53,318	41,874	49,136	36,021	4,182	5,853
1850	29,207	27,156	12,186	14,723	17,021	12,433	17,426	17,618	8,100	8,523	9,326	9,095
1851	35,014	32,246	12,338	17,567	22,676	14,679	21,246	20,860	6,879	8,601	14,367	12,259
1852	50,668	51,490	15,474	19,717	35,194	31,773	35,531	40,758	10,170	11,618	25,361	29,140
1853	114,860	89,442	27,238	31,856	87,622	57,586	102,193	80,287	23,399	25,133	78,794	55,154
1854	87,924	74,929	21,756	21,430	66,168	53,499	82,704	69,775	19,188	16,866	63,516	52,909
1855	69,753	87,484	16,085	19,509	53,668	67,975	63,289	82,557	12,895	15,883	50,394	66,674
1856	94,520	60,466	23,958	23,375	70,562	37,091	83,871	52,925	18,558	17,542	65,313	35,383
1857	126,589	129,640	39,043	41,205	87,546	88,435	113,815	116,952	34,098	32,043	79,717	84,909
1858	272,895	244,003	70,912	78,117	201,983	165,886	254,448	231,393	66,576	69,485	187,872	161,908
1859	315,860	315,212	78,558	120,143	237,302	195,069	288,897	295,512	72,675	110,582	216,222	184,930
1860	368,607	519,436	91,412	286,678	277,195	232,758	339,804	498,047	84,857	275,582	254,947	222,465
1861	359,358	333,367	74,226	101,434	285,132	231,933	334,115	308,025	68,400	89,125	265,715	218,900
1862	344,748	302,125	66,796	73,335	277,952	228,790	312,072	273,437	59,216	63,771	252,856	209,666
1863	279,675	238,190	51,317	56,102	228,358	182,088	250,198	212,820	45,321	46,832	204,877	165,988
1864	328,219	396,762	54,964	174,730	273,255	222,032	304,480	258,995	49,138	49,939	255,342	209,056
1865	385,602	317,452	59,719	69,994	325,883	247,458	359,335	290,069	53,294	56,676	306,041	233,393
1866	426,038	373,011	64,711	74,169	361,327	298,842	394,571	344,672	57,249	62,761	337,322	281,911
1867	490,978	431,901	117,542	126,102	373,436	305,799	455,033	400,794	110,409	114,869	344,624	285,925
1868	485,773	418,051	103,888	109,640	381,885	308,411	448,636	389,178	98,333	102,162	350,303	287,016
1869	483,802	455,451	162,734	145,032	321,068	310,419	443,740	422,912	156,349	136,865	287,391	286,047
1870	572,328	553,517	152,900	174,530	419,428	378,987	543,855	529,666	146,866	167,569	396,989	362,097
1871	532,154	503,068	122,824	150,538	409,330	352,530	500,774	480,087	118,519	143,787	382,255	336,300

TABLE I.—CITIZEN AND ALIEN PASSENGERS WITH PASSPORTS OUTWARD AND INWARD ACROSS THE FRONTIER OF RUSSIA DURING THE IMPERIAL PERIOD 1828-1915 (continued).

Year	Total		Citizens		Aliens		Across the European frontier of Russia: Total		Citizens		Aliens	
	Arrivals	Departures	Arrivals	Departures	Arrivals	Departures	Arrivals	Departures	Arrivals	Departures	Arrivals	Departures
1872	739,752	676,900	192,904	211,657	546,848	465,243	702,358	645,786	188,652	198,997	513,706	446,789
1873	821,200	802,372	209,033	245,667	612,167	556,705	790,064	777,268	204,322	236,357	585,742	540,911
1874	855,944	801,544	256,978	293,443	598,966	508,101	820,661	781,427	252,477	286,025	568,184	495,402
1875	355,705	323,115	63,345	73,443	292,360	249,672	328,476	309,687	60,599	704,56	267,877	239,231
1876	324,090	282,813	63,240	63,809	260,850	219,004	306,113	272,157	60,981	62.294	245,132	209,863
1877	302,624	276,033	52,225	60,911	250,399	215,122	288,120	269,490	51,238	60,660	236,882	208,830
1878	339,617	255,531	73,740	73,494	265,877	182,037	324,999	248,269	72,315	72,485	252,684	175,784
1879	286,836	241,000	54,969	69,413	231,867	171,587	257,881	218,465	53,625	62,040	204,256	156,425
1880	281,487	212,531	50,441	49,191	231,046	163,340	262,055	198,185	46,711	45,511	215,344	152,674
1881	316,303	295,295	42,446	68,138	273,857	227,157	262,925	240,886	37,590	62,418	225,335	178,468
1882	353,253	299,673	46,599	60,616	306,654	239,057	315,202	270,330	43,133	57,279	272,069	213,051
1883	304,397	271,707	39,395	62,156	265,002	209,551	268,193	244,150	36,445	60,076	231,748	184,074
1884	281,322	254,443	38,121	56,326	243,201	198,117	245,424	225,053	36,148	53,439	209,276	171,614
1885	320,994	272,087	61,378	71,279	259,616	200,808	281,225	239,948	58,928	68,637	222,297	171,311
1886	294,246	258,113	56,469	79,872	237,777	178,241	251.433	223,599	53,944	68,905	197,489	154,694
1887	297,778	298,602	47,262	69,632	250,516	228,970	250,919	258,465	44,465	63,332	206,454	195,133
1888	326,238	321,165	53,760	70,586	272,478	250,579	278,098	280,924	50,565	63,381	227,533	217,543
1889	406,625	424,022	82,694	118,100	323,931	305,922	353,722	382,661	79,144	115,630	274,578	267,031
1890	372,150	393,951	66,050	107,395	306,090	286,556	318,077	354,245	64,598	105,469	253,479	248,776
1891	364,126	401,468	95,625	137,590	268,501	263,878	309,740	357,628	94,098	135,289	215,642	222,339
1892	326,653	345,843	98,029	134,954	228,624	210,889	260,551	296,070	87,329	123,306	173,222	172,764
1893	341,451	368,031	93,314	141,091	248,137	226,940	266,209	312,750	81,216	129,746	184,993	183,004
1894	343,999	348,902	87,224	114,748	256,775	234,154	275,323	293,020	82,936	108,554	192,387	184,466
1895	391,127	383,111	117,803	147,753	273,324	235,358	307,543	318,075	109,320	136,914	198,223	181,161
1896	396,933	412,597	128,206	156,044	268,727	256,553	336,021	356,199	117,900	144,984	218,121	211,215
1897	419,596	399,576	133,306	159,384	286,290	240,192	348,099	354,281	125,889	150,143	222,210	204,138
1898	416,725	402,215	136,593	175,983	280,132	226,232	347,201	351,520	131,589	163,238	215,612	188,282
1899	407,730	406,988	142,132	187,351	265,598	219,637	320,175	346,027	136,320	177,038	185,855	168,989
1900	443,220	451,135	194,981	229,931	248,239	221,204	370,611	391,457	187,310	219,710	183,301	171,747
1901	484,608	470,578	192,964	232,810	291,644	237,768	321,790	342,978	157,356	192,490	164,434	150,488
1902	489,391	456,755	189,625	220,034	299,766	236,721	316,194	336,329	165,755	196,561	150,439	139,768
1903	493,836	513,163	178,615	246,662	315,221	266,501	340,098	392,206	168,310	230,296	171,788	161,910
1904	421,812	466,570	144,802	214,847	277,010	251,723	296,664	358,849	136,092	202,643	160,572	156,206
1905	394,324	483,348	146,904	243,939	247,420	239,409	296,297	386,951	136,943	229,855	159,354	157,096
1906	536,700	596,283	202,798	329,853	333,902	266,430	372,127	483,234	189,813	306,474	182,314	176,760
1907	565,767	581,407	207,836	304,019	357,931	277,388	373,025	449,670	192,665	282,515	180,360	167,155
1908	547,707	530,599	206,847	245,559	340,860	285,040	376,351	396,287	189,761	227,113	186,590	169,174
1909	585,697	569,736	214,687	272,711	371,010	297,025	407,263	444,419	200,739	255,227	206,524	189,192
1910	719,380	720,367	292,060	366,688	427,320	353,679	503,818	553,078	273,422	344,748	230,396	208,330
1911	778,612	787,775	336,297	403,915	442,315	383,860	561,067	608,526	307,891	374,098	253,176	234,428
1912	859,416	884,644	366,964	462,484	492,452	422,160	596,309	675,568	317,172	411,811	279,137	263,757
1913	919,981	950,391	403,967	529,210	516,014	421,181	610,203	706,736	239,581	463,338	370,622	243,398
1914	615,666	603,520	244,679	303,370	370,987	300,150	319,373	365,788	181,469	235,432	137,904	130,356
1915	202,429	172,576	49,565	46,347	152,864	126,229	25,281	23,160	13,652	5,416	11,629	17,744

Included in the figures for 1856-1874 are passengers with short-dated cards.

TABLE Ia.—CITIZEN AND ALIEN PASSENGERS MOVEMENT.
BALANCE INWARD AND OUTWARD 1828-1915.

Year	Citizens balance inward (+) or outward (—)	Aliens balance inward (+) or outward (—)	Year	Citizens balance inward (+) or outward (—)	Aliens balance inward (+) or outward (—)
1828	+ 450	+ 389	1872	— 10,345	+ 66,917
1829	+ 1,621	+ 1,254	1873	— 32,035	+ 44,831
1830	+ 556	+ 2,155	1874	— 33,548	+ 72,782
1831	+ 23,690	+ 7,708	1875	— 9,857	+ 28,646
1832	+ 3,117	+ 599	1876	— 1,313	+ 35,269
1833	+ 637	+ 1,691	1877	— 9,422	+ 28,052
1834	— 129	+ 866	1878	— 170	+ 76,900
1835	+ 2,388	+ 2,347	1879	— 8,415	+ 47,831
1836	+ 1,203	+ 1,855	1880	+ 1,200	+ 62,670
1837	— 254	+ 3,948	1881	— 24,828	+ 46,867
1838	+ 1,106	+ 4,184	1882	— 14,146	+ 59,018
1839	+ 6,496	— 93	1883	— 23,631	+ 47,674
1840	+ 3,447	+ 535	1884	— 17,291	+ 37,662
1841	+ 2,473	+ 2,001	1885	— 9,709	+ 50,986
1842	— 1,539	+ 2,384	1886	— 14,961	+ 42,795
1843	+ 1,368	+ 2,999	1887	— 18,867	+ 11,321
1844	+ 1,547	+ 4,653	1888	— 12,816	+ 9,990
1845	+ 1,493	+ 4,105	1889	— 36,486	+ 7,547
1846	— 376	+ 6,895	1890	— 40,871	+ 4,703
1847	— 624	+ 1,573	1891	— 41,191	— 6,697
1848	+ 94	— 801	1892	— 35,977	+ 458
1849	+ 13,115	— 1,671	1893	— 48,530	+ 1,989
1850	— 423	+ 231	1894	— 25,618	+ 7,921
1851	— 1,722	+ 2,108	1895	— 27,594	+ 17,062
1852	— 1,448	— 3,779	1896	— 27,084	+ 6,906
1853	— 1,734	+ 23,640	1897	— 24,254	+ 18,072
1854	+ 2,322	+ 10,607	1898	— 31,649	+ 27,330
1855	— 2,988	— 16,280	1899	— 40,718	+ 14,866
1856	+ 1,016	+ 29,930	1900	— 32,400	+ 11,554
1857	+ 2,055	— 5,192	1901	— 35,134	+ 13,946
1858	— 2,907	+ 25,964	1902	— 30,806	+ 10,671
1859	— 37,907	+ 31,292	1903	— 61,986	+ 9,878
1860	— 190,725	+ 32,482	1904	— 66,551	+ 4,366
1861	— 20,725	+ 46,815	1905	— 92,912	+ 2,258
1862	— 4,555	+ 43,190	1906	— 11,6661	+ 5,554
1863	— 1,511	+ 38,889	1907	— 89,850	+ 13,205
1864	— 801	+ 46,286	1908	— 37,352	+ 17,416
1865	— 3,382	+ 72,648	1909	— 54,488	+ 17,332
1866	— 5,512	+ 55,411	1910	— 71,326	+ 22,066
1867	— 4,460	+ 58,699	1911	— 66,207	+ 18,748
1868	— 3,829	+ 63,287	1912	— 94,639	+ 15,380
1869	+ 19,484	+ 1,344	1913	— 223,757	+ 127,224
1870	— 20,703	+ 34,892	1914	— 53,963	+ 7,548
1871	— 25,268	+ 45,955	1915	+ 8,236	— 6,115

TABLE II.—CITIZEN AND ALIEN PASSENGERS OUTWARD AND INWARD ACROSS THE FRONTIER OF RUSSIA DURING THE IMPERIAL PERIOD, WITH SHORT-DATED CARDS (1875-1915).

| Year | Total | | Citizens | | Aliens | | Across the European frontier of Russia | | | | | |
| | | | | | | | Total | | Citizens | | Aliens | |
	Arrivals	Departures	Arrivals	Departures	Arrivals	Departures	Arrivals	Departures	Arrivals	Departures	Arrivals	Departures
1875	558,709	533,523	237,356	262,010	321,353	271,513	553,098	528,622	236,288	258,400	316,810	270,232
1876	568,389	559,256	242,844	288,435	325,545	270,821	554,035	547,642	241,672	285,003	312,363	262,639
1877	563,843	568,069	233,252	270,161	330,591	297,908	556,508	561,219	233,124	269,929	323,384	291,290
1878	563,070	582,385	233,376	269,536	329,694	312,849	538,207	564,424	233,201	269,207	305,006	295,217
1879	537,517	575,374	192,998	236,474	344,519	338,900	524,638	559,098	191,892	236,171	332,746	322,927
1880	582,688	620,948	212,263	250,434	370,425	370,514	568,293	607,097	212,046	249,856	356,247	357,241
1881	461,014	448,449	197,202	216,933	263,812	231,516	456,095	445,621	197,123	216,846	258,972	228,775
1882	592,354	585,707	258,920	288,864	333,434	296,843	592,352	585,707	258,920	288,864	333,434	296,843
1883	604,808	592,914	263,291	273,387	341,577	319,527	604,868	592,914	263,291	273,387	341,577	319,527
1884	649,628	635,875	299,777	323,975	349,851	311,900	649,628	635,875	299,777	323,975	349,851	311,900
1885	696,550	649,476	287,789	304,432	408,761	345,044	696,550	649,476	287,789	304,432	408,761	345,044
1886	822,384	779,387	319,448	332,647	502,936	446,740	822,384	779,387	319,448	332,647	502,936	446,740
1887	923,702	888,765	376,834	386,666	546,868	502,099	923,702	888,765	376,834	386,666	546,868	502,099
1888	1,090,971	1,066,469	423,116	473,615	667,855	592,854	1,090,971	1,066,469	423,116	473,615	667,855	592,854
1889	1,542,995	1,509,588	533,323	530,798	1,009,672	978,790	1,542,995	1,509,588	533,325	530,798	1,009,672	978,790
1890	1,957,321	1,919,839	572,114	584,646	1,385,207	1,335,193	1,957,321	1,919,839	572,114	584,646	1,385,207	1,335,193
1891	2,228,491	2,249,768	629,716	666,910	1,598,775	1,582,858	2,228,491	2,249,768	629,716	666,910	1,598,775	1,582,858
1892	1,549,371	1,555,284	610,000	627,982	939,371	927,302	1,549,371	1,555,284	610,000	627,982	939,371	927,302
1893	1,757,154	1,749,362	668,415	692,179	1,088,739	1,057,183	1,757,154	1,749,362	668,415	692,179	1,088,739	1,057,183
1894	1,699,923	1,702,412	693,886	708,622	1,006,037	993,790	1,699,923	1,702,412	693,886	708,622	1,006,037	993,790
1895	2,585,199	2,579,921	1,177,716	1,094,019	1,407,483	1,485,902	2,585,199	2,579,921	1,177,716	1,094,019	1,407,483	1,485,902
1896	2,769,654	2,781,407	1,238,315	1,285,595	1,531,339	1,495,812	2,725,645	2,743,418	1,231,549	1,276,930	1,494,096	1,466,488
1897	3,452,143	3,479,695	1,385,675	1,446,472	2,066,468	2,033,223	3,409,850	3,441,733	1,379,417	1,440,365	2,030,433	2,001,368
1898	3,634,959	3,664,542	1,672,422	1,731,747	1,962,537	1,932,795	3,588,024	3,629,481	1,660,012	1,721,116	1,928,012	1,908,365
1899	3,520,576	3,564,082	1,876,091	1,968,790	1,644,485	1,595,292	3,477,387	3,531,808	1,862,512	1,957,209	1,614,875	1,574,599
1900	3,448,773	3,507,566	1,885,728	1,980,038	1,563,045	1,527,528	3,404,399	3,467,691	1,871,632	1,967,299	1,532,767	1,500,392
1901	4,464,235	4,497,882	2,191,485	2,268,854	2,272,750	2,229,028	4,426,177	4,462,957	2,176,683	2,253,397	2,249,494	2,209,560
1902	5,358,381	5,404,694	2,468,657	2,546,962	2,889,724	2,857,732	5,323,869	5,374,084	2,454,176	2,531,206	2,869,693	2,842,878
1903	5,580,122	5,648,067	2,928,888	3,030,213	2,651,234	2,617,854	5,335,884	5,607,341	2,907,167	3,008,409	2,628,717	2,598,932
1904	5,869,203	5,897,215	3,344,202	3,401,596	2,525,001	2,495,619	5,830,740	5,860,325	3,326,642	3,383,776	2,504,098	2,476,549
1905	7,358,421	7,497,986	4,253,004	4,393,624	3,105,417	3,104,362	7,319,472	7,462,390	4,235,622	4,375,203	3,083,850	3,087,187
1906	8,604,353	8,692,190	6,012,539	6,053,311	2,591,814	2,638,879	8,551,043	8,642,239	5,996,659	6,035,913	2,554,384	2,606,326
1907	8,934,439	9,057,873	6,354,304	6,005,517	2,580,135	2,557,356	8,874,177	9,000,770	6,337,792	6,482,773	2,536,385	2,517,997
1908	8,186,226	8,233,200	5,712,734	5,786,197	2,473,492	2,447,003	8,126,291	8,178,231	5,702,093	5,775,234	2,424,198	2,402,997
1909	10,313,360	10,339,016	7,161,379	7,223,149	3,151,981	3,115,867	10,239,906	10,269,653	7,145,596	7,207,074	3,094,310	3,062,579
1910	10,115,088	10,217,130	7,174,402	7,256,332	2,940,686	2,960,798	9,988,579	10,101,429	7,152,508	7,233,597	2,836,071	2,867,832
1911	10,504,059	10,549,227	7,410,424	7,490,793	3,093,635	3,058,434	10,342,355	10,401,903	7,379,238	7,458,449	2,963,117	2,943,454
1912	11,357,970	11,397,735	7,958,553	8,042,681	3,399,417	3,355,054	11,017,651	11,079,195	7,866,988	7,948,266	3,150,663	3,130,929
1913	12,130,115	12,072,652	8,561,122	8,595,030	3,568,993	3,477,622	11,730,893	11,743,335	8,461,642	8,491,506	3,269,251	3,251,829
1914	6,083,560	6,522,070	4,474,780	4,942,076	1,608,780	1,579,994	5,858,922	6,314,801	4,410,310	4,672,723	1,448,612	1,442,678
1915	218,397	201,201	91,130	96,557	127,267	104,644	3,154	3,238	2,154	2,390	1,000	848

TABLE III.—DISTRIBUTION OF ALIEN PASSENGERS WITH PASSPORTS OUTWARD AND INWARD ACROSS THE FRONTIER OF RUSSIA DURING THE IMPERIAL PERIOD, (by nationality) 1828-1915.

YEAR	GERMANY Arrivals	GERMANY Departures	AUSTRIA Arrivals	AUSTRIA Departures	FRANCE Arrivals	FRANCE Departures	ENGLAND Arrivals	ENGLAND Departures	UNITED STATES Arrivals	UNITED STATES Departures	SWITZERLAND Arrivals	SWITZERLAND Departures	BELGIUM Arrivals	BELGIUM Departures	HOLLAND Arrivals	HOLLAND Departures
1828	2,285	1,942	2,625	2,806	234	190	325	255	3	15	110	117	..	..	8	6
1829	3,112	2,451	4,000	3,615	251	174	382	377	4	22	65	42	..	..	58	33
1830	8,317	7,157	4,568	4,259	210	234	402	474	6	33	105	67	..	..	16	22
1831	11,263	9,107	5,126	3,044	247	198	555	514	3	11	202	108	..	..	25	26
1832	3,613	2,157	7,432	7,301	1,233	1,147	497	534	24	59	114	82	..	..	45	28
1833	3,581	3,378	10,095	7,192	299	209	375	456	12	29	155	126	9	1	24	20
1834	4,166	3,505	9,494	8,957	317	277	454	532	14	28	95	84	4	4	31	33
1835	2,648	2,275	10,043	7,899	398	467	382	357	28	21	43	42	..	..	87	71
1836	2,894	2,729	10,940	9,993	469	364	645	698	18	24	44	40	15	1	33	14
1837	4,417	3,579	15,645	13,081	586	554	711	713	15	17	88	59	6	..	48	57
1838	4,955	4,397	15,691	13,106	795	750	738	781	19	13	169	87	23	33	66	85
1839	5,620	4,559	13,575	15,571	666	428	551	723	33	15	128	88	46	21	61	43
1840	3,974	3,253	7,579	8,355	513	349	418	410	30	27	152	98	28	16	53	38
1841	4,632	3,036	10,367	10,102	710	553	376	456	42	84	158	138	31	12	58	32
1842	4,865	3,184	10,661	10,527	733	556	494	507	20	38	143	137	25	25	35	57
1843	6,040	4,002	10,827	10,820	633	490	530	568	24	44	180	169	24	26	83	68
1844	6,654	4,367	11,600	11,061	991	731	654	626	80	63	221	174	37	44	105	88
1845	7,185	4,639	11,758	11,165	1,055	809	685	702	112	68	244	201	..	48	152	111
1846	8,295	6,009	11,678	9,297	1,079	755	517	505	61	44	230	163	74	45	142	57
1847	5,146	3,927	12,067	12,630	708	538	647	555	56	45	164	138	42	37	85	43
1848	2,560	2,386	3,252	4,526	291	318	418	478	14	80	86	69	34	41	40	59
1849	2,063	2,331	735	1,651	288	325	486	602	33	42	50	65	30	39	19	53
1850	4,308	4,313	2,337	2,046	675	565	721	789	36	64	147	134	46	46	15	89
1851	6,252	5,204	4,986	4,171	765	668	674	714	30	52	181	165	79	54	47	50
1852	15,209	20,221	6,969	5,779	783	747	660	794	40	31	163	160	138	75	56	77
1853	54,522	45,735	21,364	6,375	732	748	727	937	14	63	187	140	67	77	38	78
1854	45,161	45,549	17,339	5,592	91	350	44	474	53	47	77	93	28	28	25	42
1855	39,230	56,779	10,244	8,511	111	180	114	139	121	48	106	85	59	33	53	42
1856	35,842	21,954	23,440	9,153	1,125	894	1,041	1,008	135	138	336	227	146	117	49	74
1857	58,654	63,840	11,489	15,762	2,048	1,209	1,119	601	145	62	334	231	174	81	66	35
1858	123,279	106,800	50,375	45,597	2,302	1,492	2,039	1,582	150	117	523	504	317	163	64	68
1859	147,284	127,903	54,387	48,270	2,494	1,547	1,577	1,096	320	189	504	441	278	250	68	64
1860	180,051	147,075	57,582	66,062	4,998	2,321	2,395	2,188	126	151	887	414	613	234	58	52
1861	173,074	140,494	68,105	70,189	2,091	1,631	1,254	1,073	150	111	570	292	221	132	72	98
1862 [1]	166,125	131,198	74,797	63,674	1,228	624	1,022	900	74	114	369	300	164	163	75	68
1863 [2]	122,453	104,543	69,331	53,750	839	1,038	1,146	811	161	81	314	299	184	141	72	80
1864	171,079	162,958	73,164	37,824	965	718	1,149	876	124	108	179	272	169	146	106	80
1865	201,411	164,917	92,907	59,886	742	646	1,156	727	254	84	306	283	147	145	267	79
1866	218,643	186,591	105,220	84,222	903	858	1,110	1,033	571	295	476	368	208	254	517	180
1867	213,443	193,140	109,838	75,737	764	851	1,170	878	387	374	486	354	338	332	794	366
1868	196,103	184,282	138,565	89,644	1,124	1,034	1,114	863	314	479	483	383	160	185	464	571
1869	243,545	172,081	18,842	94,285	1,946	1,820	1,665	1,193	474	325	590	552	170	155	553	435
1870	240,084	234,688	132,641	108,475	2,596	2,154	1,925	1,206	300	529	793	655	328	223	684	450
1871	229,746	223,355	130,292	96,994	2,014	1,373	1,460	1,493		232	739	428	129	105	135	204

For reference notes see page 810.

TABLE III.—DISTRIBUTION OF ALIEN PASSENGERS WITH PASSPORTS OUTWARD AND INWARD ACROSS THE FRONTIER OF RUSSIA DURING THE IMPERIAL PERIOD (by nationality) 1828-1915 (continued).

YEAR	GERMANY		AUSTRIA		FRANCE		ENGLAND		UNITED STATES		SWITZERLAND		BELGIUM		HOLLAND	
	Arrivals	Departures	Arrivals	Departures	Arrivals	Departures	Arrivals	Departures	Arrivals	Departures	Arrivals	Departures	Arrivals	Departures	Arrivals	Departures
1872[1]	312,856	290,573	170,181	132,753	2,973	2,401	2,305	1,771	428	310	1,997	1,562	366	257	38	45
1873	384,988	361,243	162,895	150,265	3,070	2,749	3,414	1,906	596	557	2,402	2,118	614	566	318	275
1874[2]	398,328	340,590	138,161	128,211	3,230	2,960	2,102	1,536	599	517	1,172	1,121	415	383	269	255
1875	131,235	121,192	108,871	99,106	4,241	2,862	4,192	1,619	946	687	1,180	913	775	606	324	381
1876	121,846	107,250	96,966	83,627	4,663	2,963	4,141	2,539	945	657	1,185	958	716	652	304	331
1877	119,404	108,808	94,375	77,510	6,476	5,123	3,289	2,690	936	786	983	929	561	491	460	435
1878	126,930	91,361	99,044	62,821	6,118	4,956	3,307	2,860	971	887	654	553	552	436	164	253
1879	97,474	80,534	78,104	50,996	4,684	5,335	2,693	3,132	652	997	973	980	639	643	222	118
1880	89,284	65,178	99,246	66,149	4,141	3,976	2,750	2,339	576	812	907	579	751	533	120	126
1881	112,831	81,565	94,439	78,912	2,918	3,284	1,498	1,792	330	323	639	798	321	291	101	156
1882	99,693	80,509	141,179	103,716	4,897	5,390	2,546	3,025	397	408	2,860	3,641	370	109	162	218
1883	72,639	57,074	135,851	107,056	3,128	1,905	2,546	2,392	590	502	674	581	108	157	53	59
1884	61,712	52,665	126,409	100,293	1,692	1,411	1,761	2,132	653	594	699	670	202	318	78	66
1885	68,337	52,808	129,010	97,644	4,717	2,536	2,919	2,382	511	366	1,169	951	381	510	217	260
1886	58,598	47,779	116,083	86,622	3,380	3,095	2,803	2,574	827	413	1,142	919	417	461	163	152
1887	65,234	62,759	119,769	109,143	2,625	3,523	2,182	2,611	453	529	825	1,119	340	694	88	115
1888	94,503	89,953	109,278	105,007	3,018	3,130	3,099	2,856	706	781	1,182	1,177	768	1,271	103	95
1889	923,112	905,717	324,485	307,842	4,554	4,154	4,781	3,706	2,503	1,583	1,836	1,584	1,219	2,763	310	280
1890	1,265,126	1,232,326	329,920	314,087	7,043	5,462	5,555	4,687	3,131	2,841	2,462	2,016	2,876	1,900	404	392
1891	1,484,237	1,495,576	292,278	272,396	5,983	6,509	4,909	4,058	3,011	2,430	2,027	1,988	1,802	1,892	318	320
1892[2]	875,237	871,621	210,869	200,977	5,420	6,419	4,185	3,769	2,714	2,490	1,699	2,090	1,883	2,006	308	291
1893	1,018,183	991,372	222,653	218,904	5,300	5,427	5,301	3,490	2,209	1,925	1,714	1,638	2,705	2,314	285	216
1894	922,021	916,146	231,955	226,877	6,794	7,886	4,533	3,662	3,067	2,637	2,332	2,342	2,000	2,302	437	397
1895	1,298,867	1,383,597	262,943	247,097	6,847	6,991	5,411	4,378	2,399	1,319	3,273	2,926	2,327	1,972	434	491
1896	78,666	80,508	97,395	96,377	7,368	8,346	4,367	4,707	1,624	1,373	2,275	1,849	3,387	3,038	583	693
1897	65,362	64,466	109,819	103,760	9,130	7,112	4,367	3,354	2,311	1,796	2,823	2,299	4,456	4,660	827	737
1898	49,905	43,794	110,120	101,292	10,967	8,906	5,727	5,079	2,555	2,140	3,200	2,817	5,747	5,470	514	501
1899	43,993	40,106	93,136	88,838	7,251	6,745	5,900	5,394	3,227	2,773	3,184	2,982	6,498	5,817	742	611
1900	62,161	58,351	77,141	72,958	6,679	6,519	4,306	4,203	3,961	3,711	2,515	2,783	6,415	4,561	576	693
1901	43,688	40,312	78,649	71,385	6,588	5,410	4,990	4,505	3,447	3,074	2,446	2,357	4,797	4,205	454	441
1902	36,870	34,470	65,342	60,911	8,740	8,301	6,136	5,485	3,702	3,511	2,654	2,592	4,418	3,866	798	600
1903	45,969	43,130	72,674	69,159	9,770	9,778	5,425	4,501	4,573	4,218	2,818	2,700	3,950	2,504	928	734
1904	45,354	41,922	67,034	67,903	9,158	8,968	4,934	4,648	4,192	4,082	2,097	2,261	2,567	2,833	721	553
1905	45,667	45,398	71,467	70,602	7,302	6,934	5,758	4,909	3,326	2,917	1,690	1,794	2,335	2,114	633	711
1906	47,715	46,315	68,749	84,867	8,424	8,240	7,375	5,875	2,978	2,784	1,786	1,913	2,171	1,779	1,021	929
1907	52,589	46,681	75,648	70,228	8,840	8,877	9,828	7,421	3,111	2,558	2,018	2,085	2,393	1,841	1,224	994
1908	53,113	45,160	73,298	68,449	10,692	10,426	10,024	8,814	3,857	3,586	2,666	2,343	2,328	2,476	1,579	1,366
1909	60,922	56,259	75,816	70,888	11,256	10,397	12,676	9,557	4,737	4,293	2,915	3,027	3,054	3,278	1,849	1,419
1910	67,531	59,655	85,151	79,598	13,789	12,298	11,599	10,211	5,660	4,989	3,806	3,401	3,665	4,262	2,009	1,487
1911	80,756	74,551	93,263	85,955	14,297	13,412	13,287	11,633	5,239	4,938	3,407	3,014	4,894	5,654	2,383	1,539
1912	92,198	85,630	94,935	87,642	17,418	15,990			5,963	5,682	5,998	5,734	5,909	5,056	2,884	2,209
1913	91,446	84,914	76,710	69,675	20,010	17,242	14,678	12,434	7,702	6,766	7,720	6,779	6,314	2,730	5,177	3,478
1914	42,608	42,931	35,218	29,169	9,471	10,569	7,612	7,640	3,976	3,087	3,417	3,690	3,153	124	2,294	1,600
1915	12	7,339	197	1,291	1,046	1,184	1,110	1,198	471	428	268	220	220		91	95

For reference notes see page 810.

TABLE III.—DISTRIBUTION OF ALIEN PASSENGERS WITH PASSPORTS OUTWARD AND INWARD ACROSS THE FRONTIER OF RUSSIA DURING THE IMPERIAL PERIOD (by nationality) 1828-1915 (continued).

YEAR	ITALY Arrivals	ITALY Departures	BULGARIA Arrivals	BULGARIA Departures	ROUMANIA Arrivals	ROUMANIA Departures	GREECE Arrivals	GREECE Departures	DENMARK Arrivals	DENMARK Departures	SWEDEN AND NORWAY Arrivals	SWEDEN AND NORWAY Departures	SERBIA Arrivals	SERBIA Departures	SPAIN Arrivals	SPAIN Departures	PORTUGAL Arrivals	PORTUGAL Departures
1828	110	109	....	....	74	42	49	27	81	81	58	69	....	....	3	2	1	5
1829	80	66	....	....	263	149	74	51	118	116	86	65	....	....	3	....	2	2
1830	666	649	....	....	182	120	2,295	1,156	105	70	49	66	....	....	5	....	4	1
1831	1,013	416	....	....	246	78	3,025	721	122	76	35	17	....	....	2	8	....	....
1832	61	45	....	....	650	897	287	997	148	70	86	52	2	38	11	6	1	5
1833	338	321	....	....	1,048	492	425	591	124	80	50	41	1	2	11	9	2	2
1834	54	39	....	....	2,314	1,581	321	439	60	103	27	128	13	....	12	....	7	4
1835	9	5	....	....	826	954	172	188	66	60	55	47	....	....	....	....	....	....
1836	67	42	....	....	770	599	480	240	129	108	39	63	13	152	8	15	2	3
1837	118	75	....	....	308	270	327	228	148	153	61	97	....	....	1	13	....	....
1838	136	160	....	....	510	376	605	445	344	312	80	51	....	....	2	6	....	....
1839	76	69	....	....	685	653	470	288	427	273	97	60	....	....	5	1	1	7
1840	124	40	....	....	699	578	290	162	143	106	112	115	....	....	24	4	2	2
1841	90	129	....	....	930	678	220	203	132	148	78	76	....	....	11	21	4	7
1842	85	71	....	....	986	704	109	160	107	95	79	66	....	....	15	10	6	13
1843	97	94	....	....	1,084	847	294	217	115	94	79	66	....	....	17	10	8	15
1844	117	125	....	....	1,133	96	366	270	141	120	98	74	....	....	18	36	15	4
1845	128	167	....	....	1,134	927	394	311	166	139	111	85	....	....	17	54	10	9
1846	213	75	....	....	1,849	875	620	339	159	104	119	121	....	....	....	67	....	4
1847	74	98	....	....	952	919	533	278	130	122	127	104	....	....	4	7	2	1
1848	38	106	....	....	793	588	250	203	54	78	50	54	....	....	10	2	8	3
1849	33	48	....	....	51	96	251	148	37	55	57	87	....	....	6	....	5	6
1850	121	99	....	....	284	251	343	133	56	90	50	57	....	....	1	11	4	11
1851	190	166	....	....	405	321	359	253	71	93	70	70	....	....	12	2	2	2
1852	136	161	....	....	526	312	262	312	90	120	62	84	....	....	15	15	2	11
1853	163	146	....	....	277	265	216	129	96	176	59	106	....	....	13	10	2	2
1854	58	133	....	....	299	148	227	246	43	34	33	61	....	....	18	8	....	....
1855	25	118	....	....	91	128	722	493	49	46	39	136	....	....	7	9	....	....
1856	635	150	....	....	1,058	569	967	503	170	172	115	133	....	....	4	4	....	....
1857	451	205	....	....	2,451	1,271	876	597	217	154	75	80	....	....	....	14	....	....
1858	438	324	....	....	5,189	3,629	738	461	144	171	141	117	....	....	....	....	....	....
1859	542	342	....	....	6,003	3,211	922	351	169	123	123	58	....	....	....	....	....	....
1860	941	424	....	....	3,195	2,361	709	436	330	161	85	63	....	....	....	....	....	....
1861	566	456	....	....	9,496	2,663	510	496	235	142	97	74	....	....	....	....	....	....
1862	342	306	....	....	5,174	3,381	1,018	258	305	162	116	104	....	....	....	....	....	....
1863 [1]	382	356	....	....	3,075	2,840	1,147	718	161	122	62	70	....	....	....	....	....	....
1864 [1]	456	361	....	....	3,831	3,288	1,044	817	189	133	168	65	....	....	....	....	....	....
1865 [2]	440	316	....	....	4,488	3,666	1,140	828	92	74	80	41	....	....	....	....	....	....
1866	436	480	....	....	5,291	4,508	1,615	895	81	106	122	108	....	....	....	....	....	....
1867	670	510	....	....	10,815	9,211	1,444	1,132	123	154	148	532	....	....	....	....	....	....
1868	526	449	....	....	5,485	5,198	1,617	1,363	79	189	53	33	....	....	....	....	....	....
1869	585	384	....	....	12,286	10,104	1,657	1,080	134	228	185	168	....	....	....	....	....	....
1870	887	663	....	....	8,935	8,089	1,942	1,017	160	404	622	491	....	....	....	....	....	....
1871	687	515	....	....	7,557	6,881	....	762	446	....	535	445	....	....	....	....	....	....

For reference notes see page 810.

TABLE III.—DISTRIBUTION OF ALIEN PASSENGERS WITH PASSPORTS OUTWARD AND INWARD ACROSS THE FRONTIER OF RUSSIA DURING THE IMPERIAL PERIOD (by nationality) 1828-1915 (continued).

YEAR	ITALY Arrivals	ITALY Departures	BULGARIA Arrivals	BULGARIA Departures	ROUMANIA Arrivals	ROUMANIA Departures	GREECE Arrivals	GREECE Departures	DENMARK Arrivals	DENMARK Departures	SWEDEN AND NORWAY Arrivals	SWEDEN AND NORWAY Departures	SERBIA Arrivals	SERBIA Departures	SPAIN Arrivals	SPAIN Departures	PORTUGAL Arrivals	PORTUGAL Departures
1872[1]	1,641	1,253	....	....	8,941	9,207	2,991	1,612	512	463	259	247	....	....	....	....	....	....
1873[1 & 2]	1,572	1,162	....	....	14,875	10,892						353	....	....	....	....	....	....
1874[2]	1,907	1,724	....	....	11,226	9,868	3,107	2,440	451	618	369	309	....	....	....	....	....	....
1875	1,918	1,342	....	....	3,416	3,997	2,245	1,596	426	391	327	321	147	160	....	43	42	34
1876	1,875	1,459	....	....	3,869	3,227	2,389	1,539	488	434	353	331	345	669	44	71	26	37
1877	1,762	1,805	857	442	3,447	2,625	1,237	1,563	518	490	373	344	930	215	47	69	9	3
1878	1,846	1,587	491	735	2,687	1,930	3,385	4,151	589	524	400	92	544	408	68	33	4	6
1879	1,745	2,336	560	636	2,674	2,104	3,973	2,489	409	305	274	114	92	99	58	35	32	1
1880	1,727	1,799	1,013	1,015	2,294	2,175	3,546	2,792	466	426	363	338	78	55	33	39	5	3
1881	1,373	1,315	1,122	1,032	4,848	4,322	3,059	2,461	528	360	379	269	40	67	33	27	2	4
1882	1,594	1,207	958	875	3,805	3,864	3,642	4,274	339	357	391	342	87	82	29	25	5	7
1883	1,197	1,163	983	1,073	4,101	3,363	4,693	3,363	296	317	359	294	194	109	27	25		
1884	974	872	800	808	3,222	3,720	4,018	3,720	232	186	372	410	113	96	18	42	12	3
1885	1,063	1,184	949	955	2,771	3,189	3,987	3,948	265	198	327	312	83	70	103	122	8	11
1886	1,183	866	875	796	3,841	2,841	4,324	3,445	265	248	670	541	126	82	92	75	7	13
1887	1,174	1,081	948	944	4,800	3,855	4,062	3,750	278	235	691	650	160	147	63	68	8	25
1888	1,129	955	813	804	7,620	4,827	3,619	2,958	213	233	675	645	158	147	65	71	10	22
1889	1,849	1,874	885	785	5,609	7,285	3,620	3,324	274	230	1,292	1,130	228	239	115	79	41	29
1890	3,505	2,127	949	848		5,775	4,038	3,612	607	616	1,413	1,122	297	331	147	122	268	292
1891	2,937	2,058	1,039	861		5,884	4,052	3,851	659	638	1,454	1,214	232	201	160	162	17	17
1892	2,723	1,824	1,219	1,116	6,048	3,581	2,934	2,720	695	610	1,449	1,250	218	208	160	146	47	13
1893	2,210	1,859	1,282	1,274	5,761	3,090	3,210	3,206	495	377	1,199	924	245	216	144	176	33	36
1894	3,309	2,156	1,705	1,531		5,663	3,319	2,921	514	545	1,708	1,318	168	172	225	173	54	29
1895	2,201	1,604	1,799	1,803	3,571	5,405	3,259	3,152	498	399	1,365	1,161	519	504	150	128	50	54
1896	2,177	1,823	2,057	1,896		3,405	3,459	3,128	416	380	1,486	960	367	238	360	298	114	158
1897	2,839	2,355	2,537	2,354	3,505	3,315	3,577	3,269	633	582	1,923	1,509	492	417	425	308	146	106
1898	3,157	2,521	3,409	2,805	3,349	3,029	3,857	3,433	1,212	922	2,368	1,786	537	314	501	312	41	79
1899	2,288	2,014		3,795	3,522	3,363	3,387	3,369	1,950	2,121	1,888	1,193	343	281	158	181	32	21
1900	1,641	1,480	5,396	4,454	2,885	2,656	3,138	2,870	1,143	984	1,330	1,097	340	340	206	186	36	9
1901	1,928	1,658	5,676	4,773	3,364	3,125	3,343	3,059	1,041	837	1,310	988	457	468	163	170	10	5
1902	2,788	2,455	5,773	4,863	3,333	3,335	3,526	3,159	884	701	1,344	1,146	541	560	231	146	26	60
1903	2,640	2,265	6,679	5,371	3,890	3,705	4,255	3,941	1,018	852	1,590	1,213	697	667	268	244	71	75
1904	2,374	2,566	7,856	6,008	3,928	3,868	4,012	3,679	1,237	988	1,241	1,158	418	503	201	256	64	108
1905	1,893	2,054	7,005	6,622	3,114	3,142	2,756	2,760	979	926	1,079	871	660	612	184	254	46	74
1906	1,758	1,725	7,503	7,018	3,205	3,154	3,846	3,345	980	1,269	947	839	522	464	372	353	153	149
1907	1,906	1,692	8,996	7,070	3,637	3,548	3,971	3,257	1,525	1,379	1,354	909	591	508	636	487	192	204
1908	2,432	2,448	9,213	8,878	4,418	3,650	3,632	3,458	1,779	1,639	1,408	1,065	490	560	465	363	397	127
1909	2,917	2,520	8,972	7,868	5,419	3,739	4,174	3,657	1,802	1,343	1,929	1,455	594	561	523	442	393	371
1910	3,152	2,711	8,785	8,785	3,993	3,239	3,463	3,185	2,431	1,851	2,327	1,602	727	606	540	477	358	365
1911	2,822	2,510			4,610	4,803	4,514	3,958	2,681	2,226	2,299	1,647	847	848	474	401	341	323
1912	3,997	3,872			5,754	4,908	3,801	4,248	2,623	2,038	2,567	1,722	893	1,064	621	610	393	350
1913	5,601	5,218			5,122	4,293	3,853	3,590	3,902	2,572	2,524	2,046	791	774	623	507	358	348
1914	3,304	3,635	7,764	6,187	4,290	4,293	3,849	2,984	1,994	1,437	1,442	1,430	744	758	295	252	141	134
1915	509	533	1,679	820	1,063	1,245	1,897	2,339	401	378	718	651	161	127	17	7	2	3

For reference notes see page 810.

TABLE III.—DISTRIBUTION OF ALIEN PASSENGERS WITH PASSPORTS OUTWARD AND INWARD ACROSS THE FRONTIER OF RUSSIA DURING THE IMPERIAL PERIOD (by nationality) 1828-1915 (continued).

YEAR	MONTENEGRO Arrivals	MONTENEGRO Departures	PERSIA Arrivals	PERSIA Departures	CHINA Arrivals	CHINA Departures	TURKEY Arrivals	TURKEY Departures	JAPAN Arrivals	JAPAN Departure	KHIVA AND BOKHARI Arrivals	KHIVA AND BOKHARI Departures	OTHER Arrivals	OTHER Departures	TOTAL Arrivals	TOTAL Departures
1828			882	786		1	329	293			658	230	250	170	8,085	7,146
1829			89	787	2	2	65	167			269	391	131	115	9,054	8,625
1830			194	915	1	1	1,818	2,070			398	295	1,511	892	20,852	18,489
1831			311	207			2,105	1,666			481	127	2,342	1,433	27,105	17,755
1832			330	545		1	1,701	1,374			360	270	600	1,091	17,195	16,702
1833			1,168	671		5	591	2,602			202	328	1,243	1,983	19,753	18,550
1834			3,077	1,127			1,059	4,363			193	120	895	1,291	22,607	22,630
1835			806	437			1,179	1,243			230	116	516	557	17,488	14,739
1836			1,110	522			1,729	1,160			288	206	1,225	1,148	21,552	18,112
1837			639	472			930	914			181	151	1,732	1,815	25,454	22,237
1838			1,087	780			1,576	1,259			247	246	1,633	1,691	28,775	25,013
1839			1,368	757			1,527	830			340	274	1,046	2,043	27,308	26,347
1840			811	336			1,414	789			459	338	1,166	1,725	17,870	17,081
1841			881	445			1,098	974			597	410	325	190	21,579	19,213
1842			1,332	687			1,475	1,019			600	56	379	840	21,893	18,096
1843			1,495	800			1,699	1,051			565	83	487	584	24,332	20,328
1844			1,585	862			1,691	1,165			586	86	920	655	26,464	20,605
1845			1,582	887			1,843	1,233			644	107	383	985	27,712	22,325
1846			1,827	1,000			1,982	1,559			632	722	192	195	30,411	22,671
1847			1,631	548			1,154	432			298	233	147	146	24,221	20,667
1848			960	1,040			1,047	783			253	111	189	67	10,380	10,585
1849			3,268	1,379			2,457	2,011			134	135	51	168	10,005	8,798
1850			5,004	762			2,651	2,122			113	70	167	67	17,021	12,433
1851			5,098	670			3,100	1,629			308	254	72	37	22,676	14,679
1852			5,561	511			4,007	2,003			261	146	46	62	35,194	31,773
1853			5,628	330			2,842	1,847			566	217	27	25	87,662	57,586
1854			2,196	1,091			97	104			392	224		29	66,168	53,499
1855			3,069	967			18	88			147	25		17	53,668	67,975
1856			2,156	900			2,303	765					1,303	316	70,562	37,091
1857			2,593	5,677			5,542	2,904					1,231	436	87,546	88,435
1858			6,987	4,822			8,233	3,376					931	585	201,983	165,886
1859			12,059	8,309			10,012	5,024					914	523	237,302	195,069
1860			11,943	13,462			11,816	5,446					1,059	548	277,195	232,758
1861			9,241	9,004			18,333	5,308					942	465	285,132	231,933
1862			14,880	8,269			11,715	3,634					980	442	277,952	228,790
1863			11,657	9,206			16,974	7,869					616	366	228,358	182,088
1864 [1]			10,210	13,988			9,581	5,760					701	358	273,255	222,032
1865 [2]			12,409	17,551			9,585	6,160					685	310	325,883	247,458
1866 [2]			17,055	16,508			9,075	4,467					796	335	361,327	298,842
1867			18,642	20,327			13,117	5,186					902	377	373,436	305,799
1868			22,014	13,682			13,644	6,268					190	150	381,885	310,471
1869			24,815	13,279			13,694	7,215					177	144	321,068	378,987
1870			15,316	13,892			12,095	6,229					231	120	419,428	352,530
1871			20,088	12,165			13,062	5,940					198		409,330	465,243
1872			21,699				19,266	8,628					395	268	546,848	556,705
1873			18,453				14,543	9,004					500	392	612,167	

For reference notes see page 810.

TABLE III.—DISTRIBUTION OF ALIEN PASSENGERS WITH PASSPORTS OUTWARD AND INWARD ACROSS THE FRONTIER OF RUSSIA DURING THE IMPERIAL PERIOD (by nationality) 1828-1915 (concluded).

Year	Montenegro		Persia		China		Turkey		Japan		Khiva and Bokhara		Other		Total	
	Arrivals	Departures	Arrivals	Departures	Arrivals	Departures	Arrivals	Departures	Arrivals	Departures	Arrivals	Departures	Arrivals	Departures	Arrivals	Departures
1874[1][2]			22,544	9,976			15,527	8,112					488	552	598,966	508,101
1875	21	17	20,157	8,337	3	1	10,688	5,985	25	18	17	29	125	49	292,360	249,672
1876	19	33	11,448	7,275			9,581	4,978	24	19	14	9	68	32	260,850	219,004
1877	22	19	12,787	6,027			2,205	1,942	21	15	2	9	14		250,399	215,122
1878	48	16	10,470	5,088			7,623	5,243			3	18	26	1	265,877	182,037
1879	46	32	21,141	11,468		2	14,875	8,635	6	1	38	1	22		231,867	171,587
1880	46	26	10,070	6,215	50	40	13,571	9,093	12	2	30				231,046	163,340
1881	115	89	39,899	40,841	51	35	12,567	11,677	13	15	55	47			273,857	227,157
1882	36	39	25,384	18,316	40	30	14,869	11,788	61	26	11	35	147	70	306,654	239,057
1883	49	39	24,741	20,195	40	3	13,859	9,033	9	15	30	9	134	85	265,002	209,551
1884	57	31	26,724	20,367	1	9	11,890	9,117	11	8	10	37	526	422	243,201	198,117
1885	51	20	27,152	22,550	2	22	14,274	10,340	16	7	18	95	459	395	259,616	200,808
1886	31	43	29,994	15,959	23	47	13,692	10,598	33	24	32	52	304	601	237,777	178,241
1887	65	43	32,523	24,400	43	142	14,427	12,244	21	38	68	15	758	973	250,516	228,970
1888	45	54	30,553	24,424	98	132	17,239	11,312	49	24	69	106	191	149	272,478	250,579
1889	149	151	36,401	27,875	127	227	17,528	14,533	20	44	129	140	100	119	1,333,603	1,284,712
1890	106	65	37,566	24,986	65	154	19,200	15,828	13	22	49	106	247	953	1,691,297	1,621,749
1891	51	65	37,656	29,994	35	157	18,637	15,478	16	10	80	344	198	668	1,867,276	1,847,736
1892[2]	33	31	42,513	26,153	17	218	10,566	10,730	26	11	167	423	99	115	1,167,995	1,138,191
1893	65	50	45,906	33,242	2,409	2,024	18,159	12,346	31	13	106	417	102	58	1,336,876	1,284,123
1894	36	20	50,073	35,883	2,553	2,016	15,435	13,384	43	25	171	499	4,646	94	1,262,812	1,227,944
1895	43	21	60,000	43,904	2,726	2,667	15,899	10,993	95	31	163	314	4,429	109	1,680,807	1,721,260
1896	68	43	25,843	20,340	3,607	2,975	22,161	17,390	53	82	3,071	391	4,907	805	268,727	256,553
1897	73	113	44,054	21,628	4,256	2,326	18,880	14,140	111	37	191	5,152	3,770	548	286,290	240,192
1898	154	124	39,928	24,077	3,005	3,166	24,079	14,123	531	79	111	131	4,055	730	280,132	219,637
1899	99	53	57,268	34,607	5,442	4,908	22,972	14,773	2,947	738	315	125	2,340	606	265,598	226,232
1900	130	96	39,565	32,175	50,266	27,049	22,683	14,235	3,248	1,325	247	463	267	84	248,239	221,204
1901	111	79	51,742	38,536	50,129	23,615	23,209	19,625	3,109	984	619	462	2,143	3,431	291,644	237,768
1902	102	138	67,724	49,872	29,465	25,240	21,424	21,424	12	1,030	733	1,011	2,776	4,446	299,766	236,721
1903	165	145	74,698	53,272	18,206	18,575	33,234	23,132	210	471	576	980	6,832	5,628	315,221	266,501
1904	162	158	66,751	51,643	19,303	21,855	24,459	24,459	6,299	55	889	1,023	1,144	4,142	277,010	251,723
1905	118	110	52,014	46,597	55,575	40,585	20,013	16,736	4,265	2,088	784	1,146	233	330	247,420	239,409
1906	156	136	63,495	32,658	78,149	52,555	22,225	14,551	4,148	2,985	589	845	8,777	5,278	333,962	266,430
1907	200	225	57,184	43,323	57,987	46,577	28,049	13,477	4,353	3,437	952	1,033	14,864	5,117	357,931	277,388
1908	209	226	58,424	47,183	41,434	51,543	31,355	18,077	4,614	3,978	1,061	1,367	7,973	7,035	340,860	285,040
1909	397	370	64,505	47,073	67,349	51,543	30,234	30,234	5,288	5,368	1,216	1,288	4,089	6,910	371,010	297,025
1910	466	449	80,507	63,911	47,797	50,690	48,174	29,911	4,839	3,995	1,345	1,085	3,396	7,843	427,320	353,679
1911	352	386	84,184	64,490	64,168	48,934	44,563	33,054	4,069	3,140	1,403	1,820	4,748	4,135	442,315	383,860
1912	653	783	103,297	74,332	63,842	56,331	44,983	36,877	3,455	3,255	1,616	1,922	4,207	2,747	492,452	422,160
1913	641	391	127,994	91,642	75,746	56,694	47,141	38,667	4,069	3,155	1,585	1,606	4,033	4,207	516,014	421,181
1914	254	209	108,121	75,227	60,464	34,127	47,141	36,386	3,455	3,255	667	1,448	4,694	4,694	370,987	300,150
1915	83	50	71,229	62,380	60,464	34,127	2,020	1,556	4,288	2,779	542	633	4,376	6,872	152,864	126,229

[1] The figures for 1856-1874 inclusive, do not mention respectively nationals of Serbia, Spain, Portugal, Montenegro, China, Japan, Khiva and Bokhara but those passengers are included in the column "Others".

[2] For the same period and for the years 1889-1895, this table does not include only passengers across the frontier, with passports, but also passengers with short-dated cards and passports valid for 8 months.

TABLE IV.—DISTRIBUTION OF ALIEN PASSENGERS OUTWARD AND INWARD ACROSS THE FRONTIER OF RUSSIA DURING THE IMPERIAL PERIOD, WITH SHORT-DATED CARDS, BY NATIONALITY (1875-1915).

Year	Germany Arrivals	Germany Departures	Austria Arrivals	Austria Departures	Roumania Arrivals	Roumania Departures	Persia Arrivals	Persia Departures	China Arrivals	China Departures	Other Countries Arrivals	Other Countries Departures	Total Arrivals	Total Departures
1875	291,269	248,442	16,432	13,945	9,109	7,845	285	159			4,258	1,122	321,353	271,513
1876	281,055	235,435	22,814	19,032	8,494	8,173	7,051	7,141			6,131	1,040	325,545	270,821
1877	286,346	260,289	22,258	15,555	14,780	15,446	6,214	6,364			993	254	330,591	297,908
1878	277,582	275,182	20,308	13,012	7,116	7,016	24,678	17,491			10	148	329,694	312,849
1879	293,950	298,661	30,717	17,949	7,827	6,169	11,156	7,841			869	8,280	344,519	338,900
1880	317,075	323,155	29,662	24,759	9,498	9,322	13,856	8,673			334	4,605	370,425	370,514
1881	229,749	206,169	20,939	15,214	8,284	7,392	4,783	2,721			57	20	263,812	231,516
1882	294,606	263,286	29,364	24,985	9,440	8,538					24	34	333,434	296,843
1883	298,326	283,309	35,374	29,003	7,877	7,215							341,577	319,527
1884	293,758	269,887	46,497	34,624	9,594	7,388					2	1	349,851	311,900
1885	337,005	287,101	61,533	48,140	10,223	9,803							408,761	345,044
1886	399,987	355,641	93,388	82,242	9,530	8,814					31	43	502,936	446,740
1887	401,791	364,189	142,924	135,896	2,153	2,014							546,868	502,099
1888	494,846	431,236	172,753	161,405	256	213							667,855	592,854
1889													1,009,672	978,790
1890													1,385,207	1,335,193
1891													1,598,775	1,582,858
1892													939,371	927,302
1893													1,088,739	1,057,183
1894													1,006,037	933,790
1895													1,407,483	1,485,902
1896	1,286,269	1,260,967	204,763	202,602	2,921	2,798	30,678	24,086	5,291	2,674	1,417	2,685	1,531,339	1,495,812
1897	1,797,163	1,771,492	230,014	226,920	3,049	2,784	34,375	30,177	1,398	1,640	469	210	2,066,468	2,033,223
1898	1,713,564	1,699,995	209,032	203,381	5,343	4,917	32,838	22,077	1,574	1,203	186	1,222	1,962,537	1,932,795
1899	1,424,841	1,389,202	185,091	180,700	4,855	4,604	27,515	19,118	2,008	1,492	175	176	1,644,485	1,595,292
1900	1,303,148	1,278,534	226,442	218,835	3,068	2,919	28,308	25,677	1,702	999	377	564	1,563,045	1,527,528
1901	2,016,551	1,983,252	228,858	222,423	3,825	3,569	20,751	17,419	2,496	1,952	269	413	2,272,750	2,229,028
1902	2,633,032	2,617,310	231,462	220,517	4,772	3,542	17,026	12,890	2,974	1,922	458	551	2,889,724	2,857,732
1903	2,362,867	2,341,271	261,007	253,057	4,477	4,214	19,199	16,642	3,292	2,265	392	405	2,651,234	2,617,854
1904	1,970,336	1,960,057	530,876	513,743	2,769	2,582	12,623	13,004	8,276	6,058	121	175	2,525,001	2,495,619
1905	2,448,986	2,431,941	632,490	653,145	2,261	2,023	16,416	14,245	5,093	2,920	171	88	3,105,417	3,104,362
1906	1,907,864	1,875,553	642,637	727,190	3,796	3,438	32,302	29,016	5,087	3,505	128	177	2,591,814	2,638,879
1907	1,800,036	1,788,346	732,632	726,147	3,689	3,403	38,352	36,031	5,380	3,271	46	158	2,580,135	2,557,356
1908	1,748,790	1,733,205	671,922	666,572	3,464	3,131	44,531	41,155	4,721	2,794	64	146	2,473,492	2,447,003
1909	2,446,625	2,416,822	641,500	640,099	6,153	5,643	52,357	49,990	5,162	3,268	184	45	3,151,981	3,115,867
1910	2,216,286	2,255,871	609,375	608,770	3,369	3,156	82,698	74,888	21,368	17,467	7,590	646	2,940,686	2,960,798
1911	2,244,089	2,232,061	711,888	704,729	7,103	6,632	108,582	95,721	19,517	16,707	2,456	2,584	3,093,635	3,058,434
1912	2,463,970	2,443,797	677,356	678,320	9,319	8,797	165,374	144,405	72,603	68,048	10,795	11,687	3,399,417	3,355,054
1913	2,617,317	2,603,400	644,542	641,348	7,387	7,081	149,589	125,135	116,513	72,940	33,645	27,718	3,568,993	3,477,622
1914	1,070,272	1,069,499	370,805	366,072	7,530	7,103	134,063	116,299	18,354	14,222	7,756	6,799	1,608,780	1,579,994
1915					984	832	79,919	68,271	41,034	31,085	5,330	4,456	127,267	104,644

[1]For the years 1889-1895, the number of persons who crossed the frontier, with short-dated cards, is included in table III (with passports).

TABLE V.—DISTRIBUTION OF CITIZEN AND ALIEN PASSENGERS WITH PASSPORTS, INWARD AND OUTWARD ACROSS THE FRONTIER OF RUSSIA DURING THE IMPERIAL PERIOD, BY SEX (1884-1915).

YEAR	TOTALS				CITIZENS				ALIENS			
	Arrivals		Departures		Arrivals		Departures		Arrivals		Departures	
	Men	Women	Men	Women	Men	Women	Men	Women	Men	Women	Men	Women
1884	223,704	57,618	201,829	52,614	28,106	10,015	43,817	12,509	195,598	47,603	158,012	40,105
1885	251,016	69,978	214,743	57,344	39,733	21,645	49,703	21,576	211,283	48,333	165,040	35,768
1886	231,258	62,988	202,861	55,251	38,503	17,966	59,618	20,254	192,755	45,022	143,243	34,998
1887	231,081	66,697	228,248	70,354	33,135	14,127	51,449	18,183	197,946	52,570	176,799	52,171
1888	244,281	81,957	236,301	84,864	36,392	17,368	47,861	22,725	207,889	64,589	188,440	62,139
1890	301,407	95,526	305,360	107,237	94,297	33,909	114,256	41,788	207,110	61,617	191,104	65,449
1897	324,196	95,400	291,420	108,156	103,467	29,839	117,115	42,269	220,729	65,561	174,305	65,887
1898	320,342	96,383	298,783	103,432	100,603	35,990	123,786	52,197	219,739	60,393	174,997	51,235
1899	310,403	97,327	297,495	109,493	99,388	42,744	125,590	61,761	211,015	54,583	171,905	47,732
1900	326,828	116,392	324,843	126,292	137,819	57,162	157,787	72,144	189,009	59,230	167,056	54,148
1901	387,650	96,958	361,273	109,305	145,777	47,187	167,615	65,195	241,873	49,771	193,658	44,110
1902	390,931	98,460	347,630	109,125	141,323	48,302	155,913	64,121	249,608	50,158	191,717	45,004
1903	388,547	105,289	386,807	126,356	129,904	48,711	171,558	75,104	258,643	56,578	215,249	51,252
1904	323,376	98,436	344,418	122,152	97,365	47,437	140,659	74,188	226,011	50,999	203,759	47,964
1905	298,841	95,483	337,839	145,509	97,485	49,419	144,016	99,923	201,356	46,064	193,823	45,586
1906	403,868	132,832	415,690	180,593	128,576	74,222	201,824	128,029	275,292	58,610	213,866	52,564
1907	434,182	131,585	422,777	158,630	137,586	70,250	196,338	107,681	296,596	61,335	226,439	50,949
1908	409,822	137,885	385,367	145,232	135,578	71,269	156,337	89,222	274,222	66,616	229,030	56,010
1909	436,974	148,723	405,021	164,715	144,252	70,435	175,627	97,084	292,744	78,288	229,394	67,631
1910	543,758	175,622	526,898	193,469	202,472	89,588	246,677	120,011	341,286	86,034	280,221	73,458
1911	583,946	194,666	571,424	216,351	235,262	101,035	268,795	135,120	348,684	93,631	302,629	81,231
1912	636,480	222,936	635,631	249,013	251,333	115,631	310,136	152,348	385,147	107,305	325,495	96,665
1913	693,306	226,675	690,214	260,177	286,211	117,756	363,512	165,698	407,095	108,919	326,702	94,479
1914	495,046	120,620	458,968	144,552	179,534	65,145	207,549	95,821	315,512	55,475	251,419	48,731
1915	190,128	12,301	150,206	22,370	43,575	5,990	41,643	4,704	146,553	6,311	108,563	17,666

Note: The department for foreign trade did not publish for the years 1889-1895 in its table of the register of persons who crossed the frontier, figures showing the distribution by sex.

TABLE VI.—DISTRIBUTION OF CITIZEN AND ALIEN PASSENGERS WITH SHORT DATED CARDS, INWARD AND OUTWARD ACROSS THE FRONTIER OF RUSSIA, DURING THE IMPERIAL PERIOD, BY SEX (1884-1915).

YEAR	TOTAL				CITIZENS				ALIENS			
	Arrivals		Departures		Arrivals		Departures		Arrivals		Departures	
	Men	Women	Men	Women	Men	Women	Men	Women	Men	Women	Men	Women
1884	457,962	191,666	444,987	190,888	207,618	92,159	227,746	96,229	250,344	99,507	217,241	94,659
1885	482,465	214,085	455,220	194,256	198,576	89,213	214,440	89,992	283,889	124,872	240,780	104,264
1886	562,759	259,625	541,211	238,176	226,670	92,778	236,293	96,354	336,089	166,847	304,918	141,822
1887	614,052	309,650	595,824	292,941	267,142	109,692	275,802	110,864	346,910	199,958	320,022	182,077
1888	708,381	382,590	695,582	370,887	297,776	125,340	329,819	143,796	410,605	257,250	365,763	227,091
1896	1,624,863	1,144,791	1,629,191	1,152,216	811,270	427,045	837,067	448,528	813,593	717,746	792,124	703,688
1897	1,789,102	1,663,041	1,806,318	1,673,377	927,139	458,536	960,728	485,744	861,963	1,204,505	845,590	1,187,633
1898	1,880,248	1,754,711	1,894,934	1,769,608	1,110,742	561,680	1,150,557	581,190	769,506	1,193,031	744,377	1,188,418
1899	1,897,481	1,623,095	1,933,725	1,630,357	1,194,122	681,969	1,255,525	713,265	703,359	941,126	678,200	917,092
1900	1,921,133	1,527,640	1,961,946	1,545,620	1,241,125	644,603	1,303,456	676,582	680,008	883,037	658,490	869,038
1901	2,321,160	2,143,075	2,346,799	2,151,083	1,431,583	759,902	1,486,900	781,954	889,577	1,383,173	859,899	1,369,129
1902	2,693,349	2,665,032	2,730,059	2,674,635	1,605,014	863,643	1,661,447	885,515	1,088,335	1,801,389	1,068,612	1,789,120
1903	2,937,841	2,642,281	2,988,136	2,659,931	1,876,866	1,052,022	1,943,818	1,086,395	1,060,975	1,590,259	1,044,318	1,573,536
1904	3,232,274	2,636,929	3,264,316	2,632,899	2,137,693	1,206,509	2,185,913	1,215,683	1,094,581	1,430,420	1,078,403	1,417,216
1905	3,980,560	3,177,861	4,070,365	3,427,621	2,716,237	1,336,767	2,805,935	1,587,689	1,264,323	1,841,094	1,264,430	1,839,932
1906	4,888,011	3,716,342	4,967,057	3,725,133	3,605,818	2,406,721	3,617,998	2,435,313	1,282,193	1,309,621	1,349,059	1,289,820
1907	4,861,475	4,072,964	4,939,445	4,118,428	3,598,291	2,756,013	3,687,254	2,813,263	1,263,184	1,316,951	1,252,191	1,305,165
1908	4,376,352	3,809,874	4,397,663	3,835,537	3,155,537	2,557,197	3,191,208	2,594,989	1,220,815	1,252,677	1,206,455	1,240,548
1909	5,703,983	4,609,377	5,714,404	4,624,612	4,126,703	3,034,676	4,155,271	3,067,878	1,577,280	1,574,701	1,559,133	1,556,734
1910	5,694,386	4,420,702	5,697,046	4,520,084	4,191,255	2,983,147	4,215,638	3,040,694	1,503,131	1,437,555	1,481,408	1,479,390
1911	6,042,685	4,461,374	6,073,998	4,475,229	4,418,083	2,992,341	4,475,102	3,015,691	1,624,602	1,469,033	1,598,896	1,459,538
1912	6,508,917	4,849,053	6,529,026	4,868,709	4,743,318	3,215,235	4,801,716	3,240,965	1,765,599	1,633,818	1,727,310	1,627,744
1913	6,983,857	5,146,258	6,938,568	5,134,084	5,129,521	3,431,601	5,169,551	3,425,479	1,854,336	1,714,657	1,769,017	1,708,605
1914	3,584,065	2,499,495	3,811,465	2,710,605	2,676,607	1,798,173	2,929,201	2,012,875	907,458	701,322	882,264	697,730
1915	206,231	12,166	189,293	11,908	81,221	9,909	86,298	10,259	125,010	2,257	102,995	1,649

Note: The department for foreign trade did not publish for the years 1889-1895 in its table of the register of persons who crossed the frontier, figures showing the distribution by sex.

TABLE VII.—Intercontinental emigration of citizens, according to statistics of German ports of embarkation, 1871-1924.[1]

Year	Total	via Ham-burg	via Bre-men	Through other German ports	Year	Total	via Ham-burg	via Bre-men	Through other German ports
1871	2,480	2,393	87	....	1895	36,725	19,461	17,133	131
1872	5,892	5,772	120	....	1896	32,127	18,270	13,805	52
1873	6,038	5,856	182	....	1897	18,107	8,841	9,266	...
1874	9,236	8,881	355	....	1898	27,853	13,663	14,220	...
1875	6,752	5,982	770	....	1899[2]	57,394	30,941	26,453	...
1876	7,636	5,970	1,666	....	1900	66,263	40,452	25,811	...
1877	5,005	3,253	1,752	....	1901	57,164	36,395	20,769	...
1878	6,584	4,564	2,020	....	1902	73,124	43,994	29,130	...
1879	3,138	2,398	740	....	1903	87,495	47,558	39,937	...
1880	5,162	4,857	305	....	1904	105,554	55,835	49,719	...
1881	9,409	9,068	341	....	1905	97,080	55,702	41,378	...
1882	11,400	11,052	348	....	1906	129,184	68,808	60,376	...
1883	7,619	6,994	625	....	1907	119,352	58,424	60,928	...
1884	17,415	14,423	2,992	....	1908	46,376	17,090	29,286	...
1885	18,550	13,783	4,767	....	1909	89,718	48,774	40,944	...
1886	33,724	29,216	4,508	....	1910	105,662	47,943	57,719	...
1887	29,355	22,482	6,873	....	1911	84,180	37,962	46,218	...
1888	38,747	31,501	7,246	....	1912	127,747	62,436	65,311	...
1889	35,874	24,875	10,999	....	1913	208,719	99,602	109,117	...
1890	85,548	42,429	42,661	458	1920	2	....	....	...
1891	109,515	76,791	29,503	3,221	1921	473	....	....	...
1892	74,681	54,149	19,416	1,116	1922	2,479	1,904	575	...
1893	40,545	11,732	28,811	2	1923	4,233	2,774	1,459	...
1894	17,792	7,495	10,297	....	1924	1,482	....	....	...

TABLE VIII.—INTERCONTINENTAL EMIGRATION OF CITIZENS, ACCORDING TO STATISTICS OF THE PORTS OF HAMBURG AND BREMEN, BY COUNTRY OF DESTINATION, 1871-1913, 1920-24.[3]

Year	Total	AMERICA								Africa	Asia	Australia
		United States	British North America	Central America and Mexico	West Indies	Brazil	La Plata	Chile and Peru	Other South American States			
1871	2,480	2,477				1	1	1				
1872	5,892	5,857		1	1	9			1	1		21
1873	6,038	6,021				2		1				10
1874	9,236	7,703	1,518		1	9	4	1			1	4
1875	6,752	3,927	2,821		1	1		1				1
1876	7,636	5,765	1,356			512					1	2
1877	5,005	2,357	184		2	1,583	757			121		1
1878	6,584	3,961	326			2,091	166		1	38		1
1879	3,138	2,923	212			1			2			
1880	5,162	5,050	72			7	30		1		1	1
1881	9,409	9,368	2		3	5	1		2	26		2
1882	11,400	11,304	19			1	5	2		65		4
1883	17,619	17,527	13			16	16	3	12	19		13
1884	17,415	17,261	41			5	23		5	61	2	17
1885	18,550	18,355	109	1	2	25	15	2	1	38		2
1886	33,724	32,143	232			169	1,155	6	6	5		8
1887	29,355	28,219	234	4		42	762	3	12	25	7	47
1888	38,747	37,560	522	1	1	79	516	1	2	41		25
1889	35,874	34,022	297	1	1	12	1,356	1	3	133		48
1890	85,548	55,145	666		1	29,226	144		8	307	3	48
1891	109,515	93,848	2,716			10,051	2,394		3	394	34	75
1892	74,681	70,343	2,520			142	1,330	4	1	303	1	37
1893	40,545	39,054	957			149	311			35	1	38
1894	17,792	16,678	340			54	407			311	1	1
1895	36,725	33,180	694		1	373	1,278			1,195		4
1896	32,127	29,415	439			425	599	1	1	1,235		11
1897	18,107	16,507	460	2	2	178	425			510	2	23
1898	27,853	25,230	364	2	3	111	1,463		2	611	1	43
1899	44,201	42,082	227	1	1	115	1,251		3	504	4	16
1900	51,626	49,580	104			241	1,253			444	1	
1901	46,888	44,714	200			159	1,255			551		9
1902	58,474	55,368	878			228	800			1,179		21
1903	72,223	68,105	1,262			146	1,048			1,641		21
1904	84,120	80,892	325	5		348	2,280			255		15
1905	78,469	72,425	122	2		82	5,724			114		

For reference notes see page 810.

TABLE VIII.—INTERCONTINENTAL EMIGRATION OF CITIZENS, ACCORDING TO STATISTICS OF THE PORTS OF HAMBURG AND BREMEN, BY COUNTRY OF DESTINATION, 1871-1913, 1920-24.[3] (continued).

Year	Total	United States	British North America	Central America and Mexico	West Indies	Brazil	La Plata	Chile and Peru	Other South American States	Africa	Asia	Australia
				AMERICA								
1906	122,191	112,764	167	2	...	50	9,026	...	...	157	...	25
1907	115,387	109,272	273	22	...	88	5,621	...	...	92	...	19
1908	44,233	33,958	148	7	...	4,421	5,594	...	...	94	...	11
1909	87,022	73,541	836	7	...	2,953	9,545	...	...	137	...	10
1910	103,138	94,593	1,868	7	...	720	5,858	...	...	70	...	22
1911	81,384	63,478	3,001	94	...	10,109	4,503	...	...	154	...	45
1912	124,290	98,838	4,259	108	...	5,357	15,274	...	...	424	...	30
1913	204,237	168,061	17,433	15	...	6,093	12,162	...	...	431	...	42
1920	2	...	...	...	...	....	....	...	...	...	...	...
1921	473	...	...	...	...	...	...	...	...	...	...	...
1922	2,479	2,054	...	...	...	...	...	...	...	...	...	...
1923	4,233	3,280	...	...	...	...	...	...	...	...	...	...
1924	1,482	...	...	...	...	...	...	...	...	...	...	...

For reference notes see page 810.

TABLE IX.—Distribution of citizens, seasonal emigrants to Germany (agricultural workers bearing 8-month passports), by sex, 1898-1913.

Year	Total	Males	Females	Year	Total	Males	Females
1898	71,428	......	......	1906	493,260	267,793	225,467
1899	103,338	......	......	1907	542,095	289,856	252,239
1900	86,571[3]	......	......	1908	569,527	312,518	257,009
1901	228,014	143,040	84,974	1909	513,059	293,012	220,047
1902	283,536	168,104	115,432	1910	636,826	360,502	276,324
1903	274,124	160,495	113,629	1911	739,969	433,827	306,142
1904	293,270	167,430	125,840	1912	793,716	467,965	325,751
1905	397,024	212,754	184,270	1913	849,792	478,392	371,400

TABLE X.—Immigration of agricultural laborers (citizens) from Germany only (according to their 8-month passports), by sex, 1901-13.

Year	Total	Males	Females	Year	Total	Males	Females
1901	212,782	129,432	83,350	1908	552,972	302,275	250,697
1902	286,145	167,454	118,691	1909	498,122	280,104	218,018
1903	262,431	154,625	107,806	1910	633,885	352,217	281,668
1904	294,014	167,543	126,471	1911	736,697	422,391	314,306
1905	378,711	198,971	179,740	1912	766,505	441,801	324,704
1906	464,970	251,595	213,375	1913	836,875	478,190	358,685
1907	511,476	273,202	238,274	....	....	......	......

SOURCES

Communication of the Central Statistical Administration of the U. R. S. S.

Tables I-IV
(Table Ia has been compiled by the author)

Information supplied by the *Statistisches Reichsamt.*

Table VII, (totals); VIII (years 1920-24, totals).

"Die überseeische Auswanderung in den Jahren 1922 und 1923." Sonderabdruck aus Band 307 der Statistik des Deutschen Reichs.

Tables VI and VII, years 1922-1923.

NOTES

[1]For 1871-1913 the table refers to Russia in Europe, including former Finland and Russian Poland.
[2]For 1899-1913 including emigrants to the United Kingdom.
[3]Only a part of the total migration in the year.

ITALY

Prior to 1876, the intercontinental emigration movement from Italy which had been in existence for at least half a century and had increased in importance from 1860 onwards, had not been covered by detailed statistics prepared by a central body.

From time immemorial there had been migration from Italy to the Balkans, the Levant, North Africa, Egypt, Corsica, and also to the neighbouring European States, France, Switzerland, Austria, etc.[1] In the nineteenth century, this short distance emigration underwent an enormous development, and up to 1885 to 1890, greatly exceeded the overseas emigration. At the Italian census of 1861,[2] the first attempt was made to determine the amount of temporary emigration to other parts of Europe.

I. Statistics of the Port of Genoa

(Table I)

Overseas emigration began after the Napoleonic wars, and up to the sixties was limited to northern Italy. The earliest particulars regarding Italian emigration, authorised and unauthorised, are for 1819 and later years in the provinces of Lombardy and Venice—then under Austrian rule. They are found in the *Tafeln zur Statistik der Oesterreichischen Monarchie*. It is impossible, however, to distinguish the overseas from the continental emigration, especially to other parts of Italy. According to the immigration statistics of the South American countries and the United States, the emigration movement from the northern part of Italy (Liguria, Piedmont, Lombardy and Venice) assumed greater proportions during the period 1840-60.[3] It was not until the sixties that the movement spread to southern and central Italy. But as late as the eighties Italy lagged far behind the northern and western European States in the matter of overseas emigration. The emigrants, destined almost exclusively for South America, even when they went from southern Italy, passed through Genoa. As this fact had long been clearly established,[4] it seemed important to secure accurate statistics for that port.

[1]Correnti, Cesare, *Annuario statistico italiano.* Anno 1, 1857-58. Turin and Milan, 1858, p. 441.

[2]*Censimento generale della poplazione* (31 dicembre 1861). Published by the Ministry of Agriculture, Industry and Commerce, Florence, 1864-66, 3 vols. Table V, periodical emigration, by month, sex, and occupation.

[3]Argentina remained, for a long time, the principal goal of emigrants. Continuous official statistics are available from 1857 onwards (3,021 Italian immigrants): also 4,902 Italians in 1862 and 18,937 in 1868. To Brazil in 1836, 1,807 and in 1864, 2,092; to Uruguay, in 1835, 34, and in 1842, 2,519; to United States, in 1920, 34, representing a negligible quantity until the seventies (in 1867, 1,624). In Mexico, the first Italian settlers are reported for the year 1858.

[4]Carpi reproduces the statistics of the Port of Genoa with the following remark: "These tables only include persons embarking in Genoa. The development of emigration

The first overseas shipping line was started at Genoa in 1840.[1] In 1846 there was a regular traffic via Marseilles and Spain to La Plata and Brazil. In the sixties, the traffic to La Plata underwent a considerable development. Thenceforward, up to 1869, Genoa statistics represented those of all Italy.[2] In the Port of Genoa particulars regarding emigration were collected at a very early date.[3] Thus detailed estimates were found for the year 1845 (20,000)[4] and for 1859 (5,000).[5] A legal basis for the compilation of regular passenger lists, and hence for the preparation of emigration statistics, was provided by Ordinance No. 3251, February 11, 1859, of the kingdom of Sardinia "concerning the regulation of passenger traffic on overseas routes". Article 43 of this Ordinance reads as follows:

"Before the second inspection, the Captain shall be required to furnish to the Director-General of the Health Administration the list of persons intending to embark. This must be accompanied by particulars of the quality and quantity of the ship's provisions loaded on board, and similarly of drugs prepared according to the formulas given under Section C of the Ordinance and accompanied by corresponding samples."

In the works of Carpi[6] and of Florenzano the figures of table I are given with very slight variations respecting overseas emigration (in all probability almost exclusively to South America) for the years 1861-70.

In Genoa, I endeavoured in vain to find the original lists upon which these statistics were based, searching for them in the Marine Office of the port and at Police Headquarters. In the former office, the passenger

via foreign ports underwent a particularly rapid development from 1869 to 1873, with this peculiarity, that during the last years of the period indicated, thousands of emigrants embarked in the remaining Italian ports, more particularly in Naples, whilst during the years preceding 1869, the number of such emigrants was small." (*Delle colonie e dell'emigrazione d'italiani all'estero*. Milano, 1874, Part 3, pp. 243-254).

Florenzano, on the other hand, in his study, *Della emigrazione italiana in America*, Napoli, 1874, states that "the Italian ports in which emigrants embark are: Palermo, Naples, Livorno, Savona and Genoa. All, or nearly all of the ships sailing from these ports call at Genoa which has become the centre of this great movement of our compatriots, whether as the main starting point for emigrants from Southern and Central Italy, or as the point of departure for the Northern migratory movement from Piedmont, Lombardy and Venice."

[1]*Della storia del porto di Genova dall'origine all'anno* 1892. Genova, 1892.

[2]Prof. Benini, the Chairman of the Consiglio Superiore di Statistica made personal investigations at my request into legislative measures concerning migration statistics in the former States of Italy. He also enlisted the assistance of his colleagues at various universities. But the result was absolutely negative. (Letter of April 6, 1926.)

[3]"Emigration statistics were prepared throughout by the port authorities of Genoa, the consequence being that useful comparisons can be made with earlier years. The statistics of returned emigrants recently engaged our attention and caused us considerable trouble, since the transshipping via Marseilles had to be taken into account." (H. Malnate.)

[4]Dassore, Carlo, *L'emigrazione per l'America meridionale dal Porto di Genova durante l'anno* 1883, Genova, 1884, p. 1. *Il porto di Genova*, Note statistiche, Genova, 1869, p. 16, refers, in quoting this number, to Banthero, *Genova e le due Riviera*, Genova, 1846 (Pelles). In spite of arduous research, we were unable to trace this figure in that publication. Perhaps it is a misprint (20,000 instead of 2,000).

[5]*Delle Emigrazione transoceaniche dei Italiani ed in espezie dei quelli di Liguria*, Genova, 1868, p. 27.

[6]*Ibid*, vol. 1, p. 53, for the year 1870.

lists had been destroyed by fire, and in the latter, the archives had been disposed of. The closeness with which these Genoa figures must have approximated the number of overseas emigrants from all Italy can be seen from particulars which Carpi gives for other Italian ports for 1870, namely, 2,933 foreign-bound passengers embarked at Naples and 268 at Messina[1] while 772 passengers travelled to Alexandria via Venice and Trieste. Florenzano obtained from the Prefect of Genoa for 1872 and 1873 statistical tables of emigrants classified according to their provinces of origin; these statistics show that even at that time approximately 50 per cent. of the emigrants passing through Genoa came from the provinces of southern and central Italy.[2]

For these two years (1872-73) particulars are available showing the classification of emigrants passing through Genoa, according to sex, age and occupation, and the number of alien emigrants in transit.

Florenzano, besides, rightly points out that Genoa emigration statistics do not include clandestine emigrants who embarked on foreign ships outside Italian harbours. Many overseas emigrants passed the continental frontiers as temporary emigrants or without obtaining a passport. Finally, a growing number of Italians travelled openly by railway[3] to foreign emigration ports.

Particulars are available after 1856 for Italian emigrants travelling via French ports to North or South America. These enable us to supplement the Genoa statistics. The figures for emigrants via French ports show how the overseas emigration of Italians, including that to North America, underwent considerable development during the sixties and seventies. But Genoa was preponderant even when the official statistics of the Italian Statistical Department (South America) began to appear,[4] and retained this preponderance up to the War as a starting point for emigrants to South America, notwithstanding the fact that Naples (along with Havre and Marseilles) became the center for emigration to North America).[5]

[1] *Ibid.*, vol. 1, p. 53.

[2] *Ibid.*, 124-126. According to Florenzano these figures appear also in the Genoa papers *Commercio* and *Il Corrente Mercantile.*

[3] According to a report by the Prefect of Turin, 12,000 emigrants left via Modena in the year 1872.

[4] In the year 1876 Italian emigrants were distributed over various ports in the following manner:

Genoa	19,483
Naples	4,495
Palermo	7,957
Marseilles	6,305
Bordeaux	740
Havre	5,715
Boulogne-sur-Mer	. . . .
Antwerp	. . . .
Hamburg and Bremen	170

[5] Lucca, A. Paolo Emilio, *Della Emigrazione Europea e in particolare di quella Italiana.* Milano, Torino, Roma, 1909. Part I, p. 133.

II. Carpi's Statistics

(Tables II-VII)

One of Carpi's claims to recognition, is that in 1869 he made the first attempt to examine the growing Italian emigration, continental and intercontinental, and obtained the co-operation of all the Italian Prefects.[1] He did not distinguish between continental and overseas movements but as he gave the countries of destination, it became possible, in the statistical work of Luigi Bodio, to apply to these statistics the distinction between temporary and permanent emigrants and after making some few alterations[2] to stamp them with an official character. The tables offer a general survey of emigration properly so called (propria), temporary (temporanea) and clandestine, during the years 1869-75.

Carpi's passport statistics for the year 1869 (23,325 emigrants) giving the authorised emigration properly so called (preponderantly to non-European countries) differ but little from those of the Port of Genoa (22,201 emigrants). Of Carpi's 14,040 clandestine emigrants as officially recorded—and hence not complete—some small portion must have passed through Italian ports, but the greater part should be ascribed to emigration through foreign ports or to other parts of Europe. For various reasons, particularly the increase in emigration from other ports, his figures for the period 1871 to 1873 differ more from those of Genoa. The number of emigrants via Genoa alone during these years was 10,651,[3] 20,364 and 26,183, and that of emigrants to non-European countries (authorised and clandestine), as reported by Carpi, was 18,607, 35,398 and 42,715.

III. Statistics of the National Statistical Department

(Tables VII-XII and XX-XXI)

From 1876 to 1920 the Statistical Department (Direzione Generale della Statistica) published official reports annually. Up to 1904 the statistics were based upon municipal certificates approving applications for emigration.

Persons to whom passports were issued were not necessarily recorded as emigrants. An "emigrant" is a person to whom the following definition of emigrant in the Emigration Act of November 13, 1919, applies.

Except as specially provided to the contrary, any citizen shall be deemed to be an emigrant for the purposes of the laws and regulations respecting emigration, if he or she leaves the country

---

[1]The works of Carpi, which provide reliable and comparable data for the years 1869-75, are the following: *Dell'emigrazione italiana all'estero*, Firenze, 1871; *Delle colonie e dell'emigrazione d'italiani all'estero*, 4 volumes (the first three containing the statistical tables), Milano, 1874; *Statistica illustrata dell'emigrazione all'estero* (1874-76), Roma, 1878.

[2]*Statistica della emigrazione italiana all'estero nell* 1878, Roma, 1878, p. 3 ff., also *Archivio di Statistica*, anno I, fasc. 1, Roma, 1876, p. 15 ff.; *idem*, anno II, fasc. 1, p. 124.

[3]Florenzano, *op. cit.*, p. 123.

exclusively for purposes of manual work or in order to carry on business in a small way,or goes to rejoin wife or husband, parents or other ascendants, childern or other descendants, brother or sister, aunt or uncle, nephew or niece, or connections by marriage of the or connections by marriage by the same degrees who have previously emigrated for purposes of work, or who is returning to a foreign destination whither he had formerly gone as an emigrant under the conditions specified in this section.

Up to 1903, Italian statistics distinguished periodical and seasona' from permanent emigration, but it was not always possible to rely on these distinctions, which were based on the emigrant's declarations. Accordingly, from January 1, 1904, onwards, it was considered preferable to abandon the attempt to distinguish between seasonal emigrants and permanent emigrants and thenceforth to classify emigrants according to their place of destination (intercontinental and continental emigration).

In 1915 the method by which this statistical material was obtained was altered, substituting for the quarterly examination of passports a system of forms prepared by the local police for every emigrant. This reform made it possible to give more exact information. It facilitated the task of compiling statistics, reproducing the information given on the passports, and made it possible to adopt a uniform method in the preparation and classification of statistical data.

The publication of these data in the *Statistica della emigrazione italiana per l'estero* gave only figures in regard to the territorial distribution of emigration (by communes) of citizens to places in Europe, on the one hand, and to trans-oceanic countries, on the other.

The statistics of returned citizen emigrants were based on the passenger lists transmitted to the Italian authorities by the masters of ships arriving in ports and on lists of passengers landing at Havre.

IV. STATISTICS OF THE DEPARTMENT OF EMIGRATION
(Tables XIII-XIX and XXII-XXV)

The statistics of the Department of Emigration (Commissariato Generale dell' Emigrazione) with regard to emigration to overseas countries were at first drawn from passenger lists. They concern Italian overseas emigrants embarking and disembarking at ports of the Kingdom or leaving the country to embark at foreign ports. All emigrants going to countries on the Mediterranean coast, including Morocco, are considered as continental. The emigration statistics for 1920 do not contain the figures relating to Italians who embarked at foreign ports during the first six months of that year.

Until 1920, the Department of Emigration collected statistical information relating to trans-oceanic emigration only; but after that date continental emigration was included. The introduction of a new regulation made it possible to extend the scope of the statistics of the Department, which, unlike the statistics of the National Statistical Department,

aim at establishing actual emigration figures. In order to facilitate the compilation of statistics, special passports with two counterfoils are issued to emigrants; one marked "expatriated", the other marked "repatriated". These counterfoils contain the information required to ascertain the extent of the emigration movement, especially according to place of destination. They are detached from the emigrant's passport by the frontier police authorities and sent to the statistical branch of the Department of Emigration.

The statistics of Italian emigrants and immigrants proceeding to and returning from continental countries, are based on the entry and exit slips detached from emigrants' passports. As many emigrants travel with ordinary passports or use the same passport twice or oftener, these statistics do not fully cover continental migration. The figure for 1924, however, is corrected by an estimate based on other sources, to allow for this supplementary movement.

In respect of the statistics of occupations we may note that until 1903 only persons *over 14 years* of age were shown, while for the subsequent period of 1904-15 the occupations of persons *over 15 years* of age are given. Later, the definition of adults was again modified: for 1916-20, to *15 years and over* and for 1921-24, to *over fifteen years*.

Statistics about the number of migrants from Italy to France (1921-24), Tunis (1904-24), Argentina (1857-1924), Brazil (1836-1924), Canada (1900-24), Cuba (1902-24), Mexico (1909-24), Paraguay (1882-1906), United States (1820-1924), Uruguay (1867-1924) and Australia (1902-24) will be found in the national tables for those countries. Statistics about the number of migrants returning to Italy from Argentina (1857-1924), Mexico (1911-24), United States (1908-24), and Uruguay (1879-1903 and 1913-21), will be found in the national tables for those countries.

TABLE I.—Emigration to America, 1856-73.

Year	Through French ports	Via Genoa	Year	Through French ports	Via Genoa
1856	396	....	1865	913	5,742[1]
1857	519	....	1866	1,531	8,790
1858	150	....	1867	3,286	18,447
1859	382	....	1868	5,352	.18,129[1]
1860	203	....	1869	9,636	23,325
1861	380	5,525	1870	8,622	15,473
1862	456	4,287	1871	4,388	10,651
1863	278	5,071[1]	1872	18,265	20,364
1864	502	4,879	1873	21,727	26,183

TABLE II.—Emigration of citizens (statistics of Carpi), 1869-76.

Year	Total	Authorized	Clandestine	Year	Total	Authorized	Clandestine
1869	143,109	127,757	15,352	1873	151,781	139,860	11,921
1870	110,458	101,815	8,643	1874	108,639	91,239	17,400
1871	122,478	111,410	11,068	1875	104,016	76,602	27,414
1872	146,265	140,680	5,585	1876	45,170	19,783	25,387

TABLE III.—Distribution of citizen emigrants, by sex (statistics of Carpi), 1871-76.

Year	Total			Authorized			Clandestine		
	Total	Males	Females	Total	Males	Females	Total	Males	Females
1871	122,383	110,742	11,641	111,315	100,419	10,896	11,068	10,323	745
1872	146,265	132,056	14,209	140,680	126,831	13,849	5,585	5,225	360
1873	152,309	135,031	17,278	139,754	124,050	15,704	12,555	10,981	1,574
1874	108,601	99,251	9,350	91,239	83,464	7,775	17,362	15,787	1,575
1875	103,338	95,016	8,322	76,085	70,396	5,689	27,253	24,620	2,633
1876	44,971	35,142	9,829	19,783	13,296	6,487	25,188	21,846	3,342

For reference notes see page 842.

TABLE IV.—DISTRIBUTION OF CITIZEN EMIGRANTS, BY AGE (STATISTICS OF CARPI), 1872-76.

Age	Total					Authorized					Clandestine			
	1872²	1873	1874	1875	1876	1872	1873	1874	1875	1876	1873	1874	1875	1876
Up to 10 years.	4,172	4,742	2,550	1,794	6,419³	4,172	4,599	2,283	1,472	4,426³	143	267	322	659
10-15 years.	5,070	5,365	6,508	5,231		5,070	4,991	5,733	4,423		374	775	808	1,334
15-20 years.	9,937	11,547	12,665	13,720		9,937	9,242	9,883	10,237		2,305	2,782	3,483	4,142
20-30 years.	43,300	53,322	38,007	33,034	37,792⁴	43,300	49,220	30,929	24,090	15,357⁴	4,102	7,078	8,944	5,786
30-40 years.	40,732	42,483	28,350	29,006		40,732	39,363	24,526	19,628		3,120	3,824	9,378	7,941
40-50 years.	25,790	23,584	13,531	15,023		25,790	22,197	11,629	11,598		1,387	1,902	3,425	3,606
50 years and over.	11,679	10,738	6,646	6,127		11,679	10,248	5,874	5,154		490	772	973	960
Total.	140,680	151,781	108,257	103,935	44,211	140,680	139,860	90,857	76,602	19,783	11,921	17,400	27,333	24,428

TABLE V.—DISTRIBUTION OF CITIZEN EMIGRANTS, BY OCCUPATION (STATISTICS OF CARPI), 1869-76.

Occupation	Total							Authorized							Clandestine					
	1869	1870	1872²	1873	1874	1875	1876²	1869	1870	1872	1873	1874	1875	1876²	1869	1870	1873	1874	1875	1876
Traders.	3,449	3,112	4,217	5,484	2,819	2,524	333	3,339	2,929	4,217	5,275	2,542	2,027	333	110	183	209	277	497	333
Liberal professions.	660	7,868	3,811	3,752	7,232	6,482	1,106	247	7,579	3,811	3,693	6,432	5,258	1,106	413	289	59	800	1,224	1,106
Industry.	24,382	3,870	7,942	10,486	5,278	6,148	1,748	24,176	3,743	7,942	9,636	4,698	4,716	1,748	206	127	850	580	1,432	1,748
General labor.	1,067	28,455	60,023	62,004	50,566	51,326	10,649	24	26,414	60,023	56,718	41,723	37,230	10,649	1,043	2,041	5,286	8,843	14,096	10,649
Agriculture.	93,389	56,617	55,141	59,311	32,110	28,821	9,617	81,195	51,509	55,141	55,430	26,580	20,961	9,617	12,194	5,108	3,881	5,530	7,860	9,617
Domestic service.	444	390	2,369	2,922	1,874	1,424	510	439	390	2,369	2,764	1,574	1,052	510	5	.....	158	300	372	510
Other occupations.	19,718	5,531	7,177	7,495	7,754	6,452	1,424	18,337	4,963	7,177	6,017	6,822	4,752	1,424	1,381	568	1,478	932	1,700	1,424
Total.	143,109	105,843	140,680	151,454	107,633	103,177	25,387	127,757	97,527	140,680	139,533	90,371	75,996	25,387	15,352	8,316	11,921	17,262	27,181	25,387

For reference notes see page 842.

TABLE VI.—EMIGRATION OF CITIZENS, BY COUNTRY OF DESTINATION (STATISTICS OF CARPI). 1869-76.

Country	Total							Authorized							Clandestine				
	1869[2]	1870	1872[2]	1873	1874	1875	1876	1869[2]	1870	1872	1873	1874	1875	1876	1870	1873	1874	1875	1876
America (no further distinction)	22,660	16,392	33,352	39,267	18,574	10,006	3,471	22,660	15,759	33,352	37,499	16,732	8,671		633	1,768	1,842	1,335	3,471
United States and Canada							824							824					
Mexico, Central and South America							13,476							13,476					
Brazil	3	40						3	40										
India	14	118						14	118										
Japan	1	1					6	1	1										6
Asia	111	145		520	437	195		111	145		518	417	185			2	20	10	
Persia	5	1,000						5	990						10				
Egypt	1,533		1,909				308	1,533		1,909				308					
Tunis	78	213					67	78	213					67					
Algeria	848	696		2,725	1,562	1,435	337	848	696		2,680	1,437	1,115	337		45	125	320	
Africa	16						174	16											174
Ionian Islands																			
Oceania			137	203	97	177	28			137	191	83	31			12	14	146	28
Total intercontinental	25,269	18,605	35,398	42,715	20,670	11,813	18,691	25,269	17,962	35,398	40,888	18,669	10,002	15,012	643	1,827	2,001	1,811	3,679
France and Corsica	32,197	22,693	33,368	33,901	24,222	35,588	14,956	32,197	21,874	33,368	31,352	18,000	20,539	2,559	819	2,549	6,222	15,049	12,397
Spain	377	1,679					299	377	1,679					299[7]					
Switzerland	3,633	3,856					634	3,633	3,739					634	117				
Turkey	337	736					265	337	736					265					
Greece	141	181						141	181										
Russia	360	360		1,000	977	767	314	360	360		956	857	675	77		44	120	92	237
Austria-Hungary	33,325	39,361	44,726	44,525	30,730	22,859	3,600	33,325	35,639	44,726	38,982	27,417	19,338	447	3,722	5,543	3,313	3,521	3,153
Istria	4		14					4		14									
England	458	676					88	458	571[6]					88	105				
Germany	1,416	4,043		15,204	15,787	17,184	2,014	1,416	3,636		13,932	13,814	15,046	228	407	1,272	1,973	2,138	1,786
Saxony		1							1										
Prussia	200	1,233	12,433					200	1,233	12,433									
Danube States	165	715						165	715										
Bavaria	791	617						791	617										
Belgium	52	108					41	52	108					41					
Netherlands	3	15						3	15										
Malta	161	160						161	160										
Valona	30							30											
Serbia	1							1											
Scandinavia							43							43					
Other European countries	4,910	3,725		14,436	15,831	15,207	3,878	4,910	3,725		13,750	12,196	10,404			686	3,635	4,803	3,878
Total continental	78,561	80,158	90,541	109,066	87,547	91,605	26,132	78,561	74,988	90,541	98,972	72,284	66,002	4,681	5,170	10,094	15,263	25,603	21,451

For reference notes see page 842.

TABLE VII.—EMIGRATION OF CITIZENS TO EXTRA-EUROPEAN AND MEDITERRANEAN COUNTRIES, 1876-1920.

Year	Total	Extra-European countries	Mediterranean countries	Year	Total	Extra-European countries	Mediterranean countries
1876	108,771	19,848	88,923	1899	308,339	140,767	167,572
1877	99,213	21,385	77,828	1900	352,782	166,503	186,279
1878	96,268	21,203	75,065	1901	533,245	279,674	253,571
1879	119,831	37,286	82,545	1902	531,509	284,654	246,855
1880	119,901	33,258	86,643	1903	507,976	282,435	225,541
1881	135,832	41,064	94,768	1904	471,191	252,366	218,825
1882	161,562	59,826	101,736	1905	726,331	447,083	279,248
1883	169,101	64,283	104,818	1906	787,977	511,935	276,042
1884	147,017	56,319	90,698	1907	704,675	415,901	288,774
1885	157,193	73,481	83,712	1908	486,674	238,573	248,101
1886	167,829	82,877	84,952	1909	625,637	399,282	226,355
1887	215,665	130,302	85,363	1910	651,475	402,779	248,696
1888	290,736	204,700	86,036	1911	533,844	262,779	271,065
1889	218,412	123,589	94,823	1912	711,446	403,306	308,140
1890	217,244	114,949	102,295	1913	872,598	559,566	313,032
1891	293,631	187,575	106,056	1914	479,152	233,214	245,938
1892	223,667	114,246	109,421	1915	146,019	66,517	79,502
1893	246,751	138,982	107,769	1916	142,364	74,140	68,224
1894	225,323	111,898	113,425	1917	46,496	13,013	33,483
1895	293,181	184,518	108,663	1918	28,311	4,010	24,301
1896	307,482	194,247	113,235	1919	253,224	105,833	147,391
1897	299,855	172,078	127,777	1920	614,611	409,239	205,372
1898	283,715	135,912	147,803	....	......	.....	.....

TABLE VIII.—DISTRIBUTION OF CITIZEN EMIGRANTS, BY SEX AND AGE, 1876-1914.

Year	Total	Males	Females	Children up to 14 years included in foregoing columns	Year	Total	Males	Females	Children up to 14 years included in foregoing columns
1876	108,771	95,187	13,584	7,778	1896	307,482	238,519	68,963	50,388
1877	99,213	85,199	14,014	10,489	1897	299,855	227,790	72,065	50,704
1878	96,268	82,510	13,758	9,761	1898	283,715	226,993	56,722	38,622
1879	119,831	100,172	19,659	13,329	1899	308,339	255,223	53,116	35,172
1880	119,901	100,726	19,175	11,989	1900	352,782	291,568	61,214	34,911
1881	135,832	117,042	18,790	12,176	1901	533,245	432,926	100,319	56,260
1882	161,562	136,750	24,812	15,612	1902	531,509	439,809	91,700	48,161
1883	169,101	146,245	22,856	13,039	1903	507,976	422,735	85,241	46,569
1884	147,017	125,911	21,106	12,829	1904	471,191	387,826	83,365	50,399[9]
1885	157,193	128,243	28,950	18,023	1905	726,331	603,552	122,779	76,371[9]
1886	167,829	135,890	31,939	20,045	1906	787,977	642,716	145,261	83,585[9]
1887	215,665	171,579	44,086	28,295	1907	704,675	574,432	130,243	72,237[9]
1888	290,736	210,611	80,125	56,181	1908	486,674	402,517	84,157	48,467[9]
1889	218,412	175,657	42,755	27,063	1909	625,637	507,765	117,872	64,351[9]
1890	217,244[8]	175,971	39,883	26,249	1910	651,475	531,197	120,278	69,498[9]
1891	293,631	219,823	73,808	52,144	1911	533,844	430,961	102,883	55,400[9]
1892	223,667	175,949	47,718	30,732	1912	711,446	579,585	131,861	72,491[9]
1893	246,751	194,365	52,386	33,598	1913	872,598	710,358	162,240	89,385[9]
1894	225,323	178,739	46,584	31,987	1914	479,152	385,147	94,005	57,781[9]
1895	293,181	220,179	73,002	51,285	....	.....	......	......	......

For reference notes see page 842.

TABLE VIIIa.—DISTRIBUTION OF CITIZEN EMIGRANTS, BY SEX AND AGE, 1915-20.

Age	1915			1916			1917			1918			1919			1920		
	Total	Males	Fe-males	Total	Males	Fe-males	Total	Males	Fe-males	Total	Males	Fe-males	Total	Males	Fe-males	Total	Males	Fe-males
Up to 10 years	19,374	10,088	9,286	17,520	9,086	8,434	5,429	2,782	2,647	2,309	1,192	1,117	21,096	11,161	9,935	32,978	17,333	15,645
10 to 14 years	8,582	4,962	3,620	10,690	6,219	4,471	2,819	1,499	1,320	1,250	649	601	11,752	6,320	5,432	20,916	11,506	9,410
15 to 20 years	15,034	8,389	6,645	13,414	3,751	9,663	4,968	1,264	3,704	2,104	746	1,358	27,699	15,437	12,262	100,647	68,212	32,435
21 to 35 years	50,246	28,714	21,532	42,228	18,355	23,873	14,768	4,872	9,896	8,350	3,220	5,130	111,812	72,085	39,727	318,773	237,385	81,388
36 to 55 years	43,206	32,846	10,360	48,273	35,389	12,884	13,757	7,814	5,943	11,328	7,932	3,396	67,685	50,983	16,702	117,025	90,302	26,723
56 to 65 years	7,254	5,074	2,180	7,781	5,310	2,471	3,480	2,259	1,221	2,117	1,386	731	9,136	5,336	3,800	17,108	9,812	7,296
65 years and over	2,323	1,502	821	2,458	1,493	965	1,275	711	564	853	524	329	4,044	2,179	1,865	7,164	3,700	3,464
Total	146,019	91,575	54,444	142,364	79,603	62,761	46,496	21,201	25,295	28,311	15,649	12,662	253,224	163,501	89,723	614,611	438,250	176,361

TABLE IX.—Distribution of citizen emigrants (permanent and temporary distinguished), by sex and age, 1876-1903.

Year	Permanent emigrants				Temporary emigrants			
	Total	Males	Females	Children up to 14 years included in foregoing columns	Total	Males	Females	Children up to 14 years included in foregoing columns
1876	19,756	13,268	6,488	4,426	89,015	81,919	7,096	3,352
1877	21,087	13,409	7,678	5,922	78,126	71,790	6,336	4,567
1878	18,535	12,398	6,137	4,281	77,733	70,112	7,621	5,480
1879	40,824	28,632	12,192	7,896	79,007	71,540	7,467	5,433
1880	37,934	26,285	11,649	7,286	81,967	74,441	7,526	4,703
1881	41,607	30,201	11,406	7,295	94,225	86,841	7,384	4,881
1882	65,748	49,789	15,959	10,381	95,814	86,961	8,853	5,231
1883	68,416	53,782	14,634	8,795	100,685	92,463	8,222	4,244
1884	58,049	44,368	13,681	8,010	88,968	81,543	7,425	4,819
1885	77,029	56,161	20,868	13,207	80,164	72,082	8,082	4,816
1886	85,355	61,512	23,843	15,262	82,474	74,378	8,096	4,783
1887	127,748	91,935	35,813	23,252	87,917	79,644	8,273	5,043
1888	195,993	127,902	68,091	48,704	94,743	82,709	12,034	7,477
1889	113,093	81,267	31,826	19,905	105,319	94,390	10,929	7,158
1890	104,733[8]	74,396	28,947	18,006	112,511	101,575	10,936	8,243
1891	175,520	116,019	59,501	42,061	118,111	103,804	14,307	10,083
1892	107,369	71,853	35,516	23,964	116,298	104,096	12,202	6,768
1893	124,312	86,839	37,473	24,095	122,439	107,526	14,913	9,503
1894	105,455	71,354	34,101	22,307	119,868	107,385	12,483	9,680
1895	169,513	111,688	57,825	40,598	123,668	108,491	15,177	10,687
1896	183,620	126,806	56,814	39,624	123,862	111,713	12,149	10,764
1897	165,429	106,957	58,472	39,829	134,426	120,833	13,593	10,875
1898	126,787	85,809	40,978	26,848	156,928	141,184	15,744	11,774
1899	131,308	94,807	36,501	24,462	177,031	160,416	16,615	10,710
1900	153,209	113,800	39,409	22,685	199,573	177,768	21,805	12,226
1901	251,577	183,877	67,700	40,546	281,668	249,049	32,619	15,714
1902	245,217	190,540	54,677	31,765	286,292	249,269	37,023	16,396
1903	230,841	181,825	49,016	26,522	277,135	240,910	36,225	20,047

For reference notes see page 842.

TABLE X.—DISTRIBUTION OF CITIZEN EMIGRANTS OVER 14 YEARS OF AGE (PERMANENT AND TEMPORARY DISTINGUISHED), BY OCCUPATION, 1876-1903.

Occupation	1876[10]	1877[10]	1878[10]			1879			1880		
	Total	Total	Per-manent	Tem-porary	Total	Per-manent	Tem-porary	Total	Per-manent	Tem-porary	Total
Persons in agriculture	20,970	47,496[11]	8,175	27,098	35,273	21,153	27,415	48,568	18,082	30,332	48,414
Clay and earth workers, etc.	38,250		1,235	14,138	15,373	3,216	18,287	21,503	3,979	19,926	23,905
Masons and stoneworkers			505	12,367	12,872	1,283	13,466	14,749	964	13,984	14,948
Artisans and workers	31,973	30,300	2,131	9,421	11,552	4,081	7,963	12,044	4,141	7,553	11,694
Traders, persons in industry	1,985	2,143	649	1,780	2,429	879	1,332	2,211	783	1,294	2,077
Liberal professions	721	758	203	764	967	331	767	1,098	415	495	910
Domestic servants	1,847	1,649	327	1,358	1,685	379	913	1,292	388	631	1,019
Itinerants	1,729	2,189	286	1,878	2,164	211	1,283	1,494	391	1,131	1,522
Theatrical artists	760	322	46	436	482	38	169	207	76	209	285
Indigents	320	318	65	291	356	77	209	286	5	272	277
Other occupations and conditions	2,095	2,802	428	1,941	2,369	966	1,369	2,335	936	1,234	2,170
Occupation unknown	343	747	204	781	985	314	401	715	488	203	691
Total	100,993	88,724	14,254	72,253	86,507	32,928	73,574	106,502	30,648	77,264	107,912

Occupation	1881			1882			1883			1884			1885		
	Per-manent	Tem-porary	Total	Per-manent	Tem-porary	Total	Per-manent	Tem-porary	Total	Per-manent	Tem-porary	Total	Per-manent	Tem-porary	Total
Persons in agriculture	19,375	35,215	54,590	32,755	36,645	69,400	37,864	40,449	78,313	29,309	31,678	60,987	38,059	31,980	70,039
Clay and earth workers, etc.	5,936	23,515	29,451	8,441	28,747	37,188	8,301	31,173	39,474	7,320	28,175	35,495	7,932	21,496	29,428
Masons and stoneworkers	1,207	18,212	19,419	2,784	12,847	15,631	2,711	14,633	17,344	2,826	14,505	17,331	3,505	12,318	15,823
Artisans and workers	4,668	6,513	11,181	6,035	5,931	11,966	6,099	4,958	11,057	6,029	4,381	10,410	8,491	4,015	12,506
Traders, persons in industry	865	1,332	2,197	1,300	1,471	2,771	1,361	1,123	2,484	1,287	1,156	2,443	1,547	986	2,533
Liberal professions	254	509	763	708	626	1,334	463	499	962	401	525	926	598	485	1,083
Domestic servants	467	983	1,450	819	989	1,808	646	865	1,511	788	838	1,626	1,196	870	2,066
Itinerants	211	1,055	1,266	455	835	1,290	307	701	1,008	192	753	945	201	831	1,032
Theatrical artists	86	215	301	115	320	435	80	414	494	66	438	504	104	466	570
Indigents	20	388	408	63	409	472	9	12	21	69	222	291	11	198	209
Other occupations and conditions	955	1,263	2,218	1,550	1,467	3,017	1,528	1,348	2,876	1,443	1,203	2,646	1,749	1,095	2,844
Occupation unknown	268	144	412	342	296	638	252	266	518	309	275	584	429	608	1,037
Total	34,312	89,344	123,656	55,367	90,583	145,950	59,621	96,441	156,062	50,039	84,149	134,188	63,822	75,348	139,170

For reference notes see page 842.

TABLE X.—DISTRIBUTION OF CITIZEN EMIGRANTS OVER 14 YEARS OF AGE (PERMANENT AND TEMPORARY DISTINGUISHED), BY OCCUPATION, 1876–1903 (cont.).

Occupation	1886 Per-manent	1886 Tem-porary	1886 Total	1887 Per-manent	1887 Tem-porary	1887 Total	1888 Per-manent	1888 Tem-porary	1888 Total	1889 Per-manent	1889 Tem-porary	1889 Total	1890 Per-manent	1890 Tem-porary	1890 Total
Persons in agriculture	44,013	36,464	80,477	68,548	46,599	115,147	103,010	44,183	147,193	58,439	48,679	107,118	53,027	37,693	90,720
Clay and earth workers, etc.	8,354	17,442	25,796	13,629	17,997	31,626	17,371	22,894	40,265	11,620	25,646	37,266	11,349	32,688	44,037
Masons and stoneworkers	3,291	14,805	18,096	5,923	9,453	15,376	7,665	10,303	17,968	5,398	11,377	16,775	5,213	19,079	24,292
Artisans and workers	8,247	3,376	11,623	8,426	3,933	12,359	9,731	4,153	13,884	8,272	5,019	13,291	7,257	6,998	14,255
Traders, persons in industry	1,547	1,292	2,839	2,495	1,201	3,696	2,342	1,203	3,545	2,175	1,263	3,438	1,839	1,366	3,205
Liberal professions	631	438	1,069	751	548	1,299	631	457	1,088	928	733	1,661	839	706	1,545
Domestic servants	1,269	1,046	2,315	1,318	771	2,089	1,731	862	2,593	1,515	801	2,316	1,382	1,152	2,534
Itinerants	275	720	995	248	754	1,002	468	655	1,123	340	871	1,211	408	1,353	1,761
Theatrical artists	119	508	627	135	511	646	211	489	700	269	624	893	86	461	547
Indigents	62	83	145	14	145	159	9	479	488	173	546	719	34	30	64
Other occupations and conditions	1,741	1,128	2,869	2,273	777	3,050	3,045	1,182	4,227	3,148	1,950	5,098	2,853	2,422	5,275
Occupation unknown	544	389	933	736	185	921	1,075	406	1,481	911	652	1,563	1,050	320	1,370
Total	70,093	77,691	147,784	104,496	82,874	187,370	117,289	87,266	234,555	93,188	98,161	191,349	85,337	104,268	189,605

Occupation	1891 Per-manent	1891 Tem-porary	1891 Total	1892 Per-manent	1892 Tem-porary	1892 Total	1893 Per-manent	1893 Tem-porary	1893 Total	1894 Per-manent	1894 Tem-porary	1894 Total	1895 Per-manent	1895 Tem-porary	1895 Total
Persons in agriculture	85,598	36,558	122,156	49,901	38,913	88,814	54,595	41,302	95,897	55,485	27,816	83,301	90,369	32,045	122,414
Clay and earth workers, etc.	19,457	33,337	52,794	11,264	33,650	44,914	17,286	36,914	54,200	11,855	40,627	52,482	16,476	38,721	55,197
Masons and stone workers	8,209	22,142	30,351	5,476	24,385	29,861	6,486	19,473	25,959	4,077	28,110	32,187	4,598	28,483	33,081
Artisans and workers	10,128	8,553	18,681	7,251	5,420	12,671	8,374	7,318	15,692	4,827	6,622	11,449	7,175	6,731	13,906
Traders, persons in industry	2,092	1,126	3,218	1,724	1,352	3,076	2,856	1,417	4,273	1,718	2,030	3,748	1,947	1,363	3,310
Liberal professions	1,381	718	2,099	663	583	1,246	1,185	785	1,970	691	837	1,528	947	901	1,848
Domestic servants	1,945	1,197	3,142	1,894	1,394	3,288	2,225	1,436	3,661	983	1,236	2,219	1,163	1,241	2,404
Itinerants	550	1,246	1,796	660	1,353	2,013	978	1,170	2,148	267	609	876	489	669	1,158
Theatrical artists	145	681	826	181	458	639	424	589	1,013	245	442	687	264	470	734
Indigents	130	232	362	248	272	520	342	280	622	227	60	287	544	445	989
Other occupations and conditions	2,511	1,814	4,325	2,826	1,036	3,862	3,575	1,337	4,912	1,959	1,085	3,044	3,203	1,186	4,389
Occupation unknown	1,313	424	1,737	1,317	714	2,031	1,891	915	2,806	814	714	1,528	1,740	726	2,466
Total	133,459	108,028	241,487	83,405	109,530	192,935	100,217	112,936	213,153	83,148	110,188	193,336	128,915	112,981	241,896

TABLE X.—DISTRIBUTION OF CITIZEN EMIGRANTS OVER 14 YEARS OF AGE (PERMANENT AND TEMPORARY DISTINGUISHED), BY OCCUPATION, 1876-1903 (concluded).

Occupation	1896			1897			1898			1899			1900		
	Permanent	Temporary	Total	Permanent	Temporary	Total	Permanent	Temporary	Total	Permanent	Temporary	Total	Permanent	Temporary	Total
Persons in agriculture	94,391	34,864	129,255	81,147	31,300	112,447	62,560	40,175	102,735	65,206	39,258	104,464	76,075	64,585	140,660
Clay and earth workers, etc.	19,886	35,136	55,022	16,727	44,627	61,354	13,586	50,207	63,793	15,183	67,272	82,455	23,855	61,845	85,700
Masons and stoneworkers	6,388	26,244	32,632	6,520	30,667	37,187	4,731	33,761	38,492	4,435	35,890	40,325	7,659	36,636	44,295
Artisans and workers	9,086	8,505	17,591	7,451	7,763	15,214	7,205	11,758	18,963	8,488	12,303	20,791	9,369	9,920	19,289
Traders, persons in industry	2,280	1,467	3,747	2,687	1,869	4,556	1,706	1,857	3,563	2,160	1,968	4,128	2,286	2,057	4,343
Liberal professions	1,222	954	2,176	1,587	969	2,556	1,068	983	2,051	1,356	1,444	2,800	1,015	1,825	2,840
Domestic servants	1,618	875	2,493	1,590	1,178	2,768	1,603	1,508	3,111	1,574	1,433	3,007	1,167	2,226	3,393
Itinerants	892	1,608	2,500	827	2,103	2,930	455	2,265	2,720	640	2,116	2,756	307	1,747	2,054
Indigents	330	508	838	429	665	1,094	172	576	748	243	531	774	151	855	1,006
Theatrical artists	972	515	1,487	164	542	706									
Other occupations and conditions	5,214	1,673	6,887	5,284	1,599	6,883	5,545	1,774	7,319	6,574	2,866	9,440	7,612	3,191	10,803
Occupation unknown	1,717	749	2,466	1,187	269	1,456	1,308	290	1,598	987	1,240	2,227	1,028	2,460	3,488
Total	143,996	113,098	257,094	125,600	123,551	249,151	99,939	145,154	245,093	106,846	166,321	273,167	130,524	187,347	317,871

Occupation	1901			1902			1903		
	Permanent	Temporary	Total	Permanent	Temporary	Total	Permanent	Temporary	Total
Persons in agriculture	129,758	82,340	212,098	121,142	85,204	206,346	113,824	83,246	197,070
Clay and earth workers, etc.	39,048	84,947	123,995	43,106	90,080	133,186	43,346	93,744	137,090
Masons and stoneworkers	13,306	60,960	74,266	14,423	55,306	69,729	11,169	38,766	49,935
Artisans and workers	14,107	15,444	29,551	18,143	19,565	37,708	18,841	20,414	39,255
Traders, persons in industry	2,761	2,190	4,951	3,310	3,147	6,457	2,644	3,611	6,255
Liberal professions	1,727	2,582	4,309	1,702	2,080	3,782	2,067	2,202	4,269
Domestic servants	1,813	3,239	5,052	2,201	4,816	7,017	1,947	4,236	6,183
Itinerants	605	1,423	2,028	605	1,868	2,473	705	1,764	2,469
Theatrical artists	150	681	831	278	874	1,152	180	1,037	1,217
Other occupations or conditions	5,530	5,995	11,525	6,216	5,121	11,337	7,343	5,395	12,738
Occupation unknown	2,226	6,153	8,379	2,326	1,835	4,161	2,253	2,673	4,926
Total	211,031	265,954	476,985	213,452	269,896	483,348	204,319	257,088	461,407

TABLE Xa.—DISTRIBUTION OF CITIZEN EMIGRANTS OVER 14 YEARS OF AGE IN 1903 AND OVER 15 YEARS OF AGE, 1904-15, BY OCCUPATION, 1903-1915.

Occupation	1903	1904	1905	1906	1907	1908	1909	1910	1911	1912	1913	1914	1915
Persons in agriculture, shepherds, and woodcutters, etc	197,070	136,998	232,108	256,720	212,759	138,969	194,084	192,953	137,673	194,211	257,293	119,137	22,152
Masons, laborers, stoneworkers, brickmakers (fornaciori), etc	49,935	49,799	74,960	75,500	73,173	57,133	55,628	70,010	64,920	86,267	95,489	61,140	8,952
Auxiliary workers in other earth-working industries, and the building trade	137,090	132,320	195,361	194,490	183,129	139,488	177,005	170,247	148,849	189,364	221,858	124,155	18,098
Workers in other industries	39,255	53,188	71,875	89,481	81,977	50,215	61,532	66,010	56,588	76,437	102,902	58,489	31,587
Hotel, restaurant and innkeepers, druggists, pork-butchers (salumai), bakers, greengrocers, etc	3,050	3,321	4,814	5,235	4,869	3,007	3,853	6,012	4,782	6,964	7,970	4,783	1,091
Persons in other trades and in transport { heads and clerks	3,205	1,909	2,663	2,746	2,540	2,036	2,098	2,527	2,547	3,623	3,307	8,119	8,380
office boys, commission-aires, waiters		3,739	5,519	7,980	7,188	4,400	6,071	6,905	6,051	8,071	10,451		
Itinerants	2,469	2,960	4,232	4,419	3,693	1,967	2,803	3,468	2,697	3,701	4,070		
Doctors, chemists, midwives, lawyers, engineers, teachers	3,325	1,339	2,021	2,391	2,454	1,832	2,049	2,474	2,139	2,901	2,484	2,301	1,567
Painters, sculptors, designers, engravers, photographers	944	995	1,156	1,576	1,984	1,008	1,072	1,298	1,085	1,413	1,918	1,073	558
Theatrical and musical artists	1,217	1,607	2,316	2,180	2,187	1,657	1,872	2,189	1,821	2,087	2,260	1,607	949
Persons in domestic service (addetti ai servizi domestici)	6,183	8,364	13,283	14,941	14,142	10,237	13,459	14,601	13,868	17,571	19,044	11,856	1,776
Persons attending to domestic duties (attendenti alle cure domestiche)	12,738	13,925	23,507	29,209	28,508	18,478	27,902	28,718	21,683	28,353	37,076	19,403	19,322
Other occupations or conditions		8,145	12,126	13,099	9,793	5,861	8,700	10,625	10,208	12,947	13,442	6,662	1,946
Occupation or condition unknown	4,926	2,183	4,019	4,425	4,042	1,919	3,158	3,940	3,533	5,045	3,649	2,646	1,685
Total	461,407	420,792	649,960	704,392	632,438	438,207	561,286	581,977	478,444	638,955	783,213	421,371	118,063

TABLE Xb.—Distribution of citizen emigrants, 15 years of age and over, by occupation, 1916-20.

Occupation	1916	1917	1918	1919	1920
Persons in agriculture	26,442	3,920	2,452	34,258	148,407
Persons in extracting industries	1,238	817	237	3,500	11,071
Clay and earth workers	18,429	4,645	2,439	29,198	109,915
Masons, bricklayers, stoneworkers, brickmakers (fornaciaris)	6,642	2,070	1,803	18,813	54,756
Persons in siderurgical, metallurgical and engineering industries	2,007	819	786	8,879	15,565
Joiners, cabinetmakers, calkers, carpenters, carriage makers, etc	2,009	573	533	4,844	13,022
Spinners, weavers, dyers and other persons in the textile industry	800	310	128	1,361	2,493
Shoemakers, saddlers and other workers in leather and hides	1,953	621	555	4,634	15,059
Persons in the clothing and furnishing industries	6,546	2,674	1,160	9,974	26,219
Persons in food industries	984	372	425	3,014	5,756
Persons in industries not before indicated	608	368	231	1,720	1,853
Workers and other persons in industries without other specification	8,130	3,142	2,077	18,570	43,270
Persons in public services	1,968	1,271	869	5,854	8,114
Persons in the transport trade	1,886	601	812	7,111	12,682
Persons in the wholesale and retail trade	2,504	831	642	3,941	3,342
Persons in commerce	1,342	770	581	5,257	2,616
Public and private employees	946	437	370	2,270	1,991
Persons in religious professions	340	179	189	726	709
Liberal professions, lawyers, doctors, engineers, etc	942	388	270	1,700	936
Painters, sculptors, architects, designers, photographers, engravers	317	190	224	1,181	1,251
Theatrical artists and musicians	715	267	179	930	1,628
Persons in domestic service	3,663	1,718	925	3,979	5,361
Persons not in occupations	2,585	1,011	687	4,690	2,508
Persons attending to domestic duties	20,099	9,660	5,889	37,695	69,770
Occupations and conditions unknown or not specified	1,059	594	289	6,277	2,423
Total	114,154	38,248	24,752	220,376	560,717

TABLE XI.—EMIGRATION OF CITIZENS, BY COUNTRY OF DESTINATION, 1876-1920.

Country of destination	1876	1877	1878	1879	1880	1881	1882	1883	1884	1885	1886	1887
EUROPE:												
Northern and Eastern — Russia in Europe, Baltic States, Poland	566	166	373	264	278	437	218	328	214	255	281	366
Norway, Sweden, Denmark	75	15	7	17	4	39	12	77	29	30	10	14
Great Britain and Ireland	257	560	700	686	469	1,094	512	379	336	486	349	675
Western — Netherlands, Belgium, Luxemburg	236	134	197	179	203	157	271	543	218	1,386	134	470
France (including the Principality of Monaco)	34,509	33,333	33,552	39,713	43,172	50,735	53,037	46,768	38,523	33,438	35,706	31,185
Switzerland	18,655	13,498	10,782	10,401	13,074	10,245	8,476	6,348	5,509	4,583	4,346	5,561
Central — Germany	9,623	9,058	6,916	6,700	4,277	5,793	7,662	12,376	4,271	4,532	3,811	4,676
Austria, Czechoslovakia	20,534	17,944	18,391	18,617	20,493	20,503	12,101	17,252	22,226	16,962	19,166	28,591
Hungary							8,329	9,535	10,470	10,744	13,181	7,130
Southern — Portugal, Spain	886	436	500	587	753	793	1,252	931	580	829	900	900
Gibraltar, Malta												
Greece, Turkey in Europe, Serb-Croat-Slovene State	1,038[12]	1,371[12]	949	2,156	1,189	1,436	1,512	3,839	4,707	3,877	1,789	2,019
Other European countries (Bulgaria, Rumania, Albania) (not specified)	?*			744	312	875	548	289	475	1,110	733	887
Total (Europe)	86,379[12]	76,515[12]	72,367	80,004	84,224	92,107	93,930	98,665	87,558	78,232	80,406	82,474
AFRICA: — Tripoli	1,472	385	1,493	1,419	1,390	1,552	3,325	2,882	1,636	3,423	2,243	1,375
Algeria	304	282	585	467	260	265	2,235	1,867	637	818	1,557	633
Tunis												
Morocco	768	646	620	637	758	837	2,213	1,374	850	1,194	740	867
Egypt			246	156	147	138	82	712	631	782	424	576
Other African countries (not specified)	?*											
Total (Africa)	2,544	1,313	2,944	2,679	2,555	2,792	7,855	6,835	3,754	6,217	4,964	3,451
ASIA: — Turkey in Asia		?	20	42	27	52	53	49	65	96	62	61
Other Asiatic countries (not specified)	?	?										
Total (Asia)	?	?										
OCEANIA	?	?	80	31	15	10	29	164	173	158	231	216
AMERICA:												
Northern — Canada	1,441	976	1,993	94	45	26	76	81	265	611	1,720	1,632
United States	...[13]	211[15]	1,637[15]	3,114	5,711	11,842	18,593	21,256	10,582	12,485	26,920	37,221
Mexico	...[13]											
Central — Guatemala, Salvador, Honduras, Nicaragua				4,757	4,641	1,601	3,310	3,755	1,065	1,150	706	773
Costa Rica, Panama, Antilles												
Colombia, Venezuela, Guiana	...[13]											
South — Ecuador	...[13]	...[13]	304	233	209	178	431	423	224	433	473	472
Peru, Bolivia, Chile	...[13]	222[13]	440	270	188	285	531	317	350	366	321	313
Brazil	...[13]	...[13]	4,533	7,999	6,080	6,766	9,074	7,590	6,116	12,311	11,334	31,445
Argentina	3,461	5,733	8,645	13,197	12,003	15,899	22,997	24,127	31,927	37,710	36,534	52,383
Paraguay				439	463	721	725	923	923	847	647	821
Uruguay					879		804	1,025	947	1,497	1,202	1,295
Other American countries (not specified)	14,708	14,027	3,191	6,442	2,861	3,226	3,154	3,891	2,849	5,080	2,309	3,108
Total (America)	19,610	21,169	20,743	37,075	33,080	40,871	59,695	63,388	55,467	72,490	82,166	129,463
Total (Europe and Mediterranean countries)												
Total (non-European countries)												
Grand total	108,711[14]	99,213[16]	96,268[17]	119,831	119,901	135,832	161,562	169,101	147,017	157,195	167,829	215,665

*The interrogation marks given here are found in our source.

For reference notes see page 842.

TABLE XI.—EMIGRATION OF CITIZENS, BY COUNTRY OF DESTINATION, 1876-1920 (continued).

Country of destination	1888	1889	1890	1891	1892	1893	1894	1895	1896	1897	1898	1899
EUROPE:												
Northern and Eastern — Russia in Europe, Baltic States, Poland	315	283	251	257	213	336	355	546	906	1,292	1,217	1,795
Norway, Sweden, Denmark	29	4	138	173	49	152	199	58	29	75	20	50
Great Britain and Ireland	553	523	842	773	488	635	619	434	489	616	890	1,269
Western — Netherlands, Belgium, Luxemburg	188	243	150	206	110	262	93	197	282	509	208	431
France (including the Principality of Monaco)	27,882	27,487	29,310	31,248	32,391	28,719	23,380	18,746	17,967	19,566	22,927	25,047
Switzerland	6,237	9,163	10,707	13,195	13,676	9,645	10,435	13,878	18,311	25,266	27,613	29,282
Central — Germany	10,105	17,951	15,215	13,880	15,580	15,245	16,584	14,939	17,245	21,080	26,852	40,283
Austria, Czechoslovakia	23,916	25,670	31,241	25,629	21,610	20,315	23,166	25,791	29,240	30,440	33,399	31,872
Hungary	8,032	6,716	6,946	11,866	12,625	13,510	14,866	12,346	11,907	13,081	14,266	14,820
Portugal, Spain	583	837	380	457	294	236	1,284	576	555	560	521	652
Gibraltar, Malta	......	......	......	......	......	......	......	......	......	......	......	......
Southern — Greece, Turkey in Europe, Serb-Croat-Slovene, Bulgaria, Rumania, Albania	3,217	2,280	3,630	4,733	9,398	13,595	17,398	15,607	8,970	10,852	14,779	14,673
Other European countries (not specified)	1,884	1,474	1,449	1,468	591	1,832	2,378	2,155	4,027	1,973	1,836	2,725
Total (Europe)	82,941	92,631	100,259	103,885	107,025	104,482	110,757	105,273	109,928	125,310	144,528	162,899
AFRICA: Tripoli	1,436	765	744	718	805	1,054	810	956	1,304	936	1,074	1,150
Algeria	751	639	522	583	618	765	828	1,121	898	593	1,003	1,246
Tunis	......	......	......	......	......	......	......	......	......	......	......	......
Morocco	902	773	754	830	894	1,300	752	986	1,025	928	1,174	2,170
Egypt	......	......	......	......	......	......	......	......	......	......	......	......
Other African countries (not specified)	245	236	208	270	230	530	273	369	707	269	300	282
Total (Africa)	3,334	2,413	2,228	2,401	2,547	3,649	2,663	3,432	3,934	2,726	3,551	4,848
ASIA: Turkey in Asia	34	31	49	89	144	267	376	403	155	89	72	231
Other Asiatic countries (not specified)	......	......	......	......	......	......	......	......	......	......	......	......
Total (Asia)	34	31	49	89	144	267	376	403	155	89	72	231
OCEANIA	163	156	291	784	144	54	68	154	467	436	371	427
AMERICA: *Northern* — Canada	1,347	447	67	163	211	382	805	783	397	139	328	1,021
United States	32,945	25,434	47,952	44,359	42,953	49,765	31,668	37,851	53,486	47,000	56,375	63,156
Central — Mexico	388	593	391	1,160	730	582	936	1,350	904	952	654	752
Guatemala, Salvador, Honduras, Nicaragua, Costa Rica, Panama, Antilles, Guiana, Ecuador	......	......	......	......	......	......	......	......	......	......	......	......
South — Colombia, Venezuela, Guiana, Ecuador	252	444	535	876	612	506	268	338	912	831	371	515
Peru, Bolivia, Chile	359	375	3,334	896	734	657	192	461	669	770	260	408
Brazil	97,730	16,953	16,233	108,414	36,448	45,324	41,628	98,090	76,665	80,984	38,659	26,574
Argentina	64,223	69,008	36,695	24,125	25,331	32,541	32,557	41,029	56,026	36,712	33,938	44,168
Paraguay	971	1,335	941	1,559	2,006	2,414	843	1,593	1,011	1,468	2,339	1,505
Uruguay	764	4,515	3,716	1,818	1,205	1,257	983	862	967	1,358	516	975
Other American countries (not specified)	5,285	3,877	4,553	3,062	3,577	4,871	1,579	1,562	1,961	1,080	1,753	860
Total (America)	204,264	123,181	114,417	186,472	113,807	138,299	111,459	183,919	192,998	171,294	135,193	139,934
Total (Europe and Mediterranean countries)												
Total (non-European countries)												
Grand total	290,736	218,412	217,244	293,631	223,667	246,751	225,323	293,181	307,482	299,855	283,715	308,339

TABLE XI.—EMIGRATION OF CITIZENS, BY COUNTRY OF DESTINATION, 1876-1920 (continued),

Country of destination	1900	1901	1902	1903	1904	1905	1906	1907	1908	1909
EUROPE:										
Northern and Eastern										
Russia in Europe, Baltic States, Poland	1,320	977	2,060	1,049	1,572	1,508	1,512	1,565	931	900
Norway, Sweden, Denmark	23	115	105	97	256	210	151	111	115	250
Great Britain and Ireland	1,453	3,328	3,763	3,963[18]	3,994[18]	3,762[18]	5,576[18]	4,344[18]	3,346[18]	3,974[18]
Western										
Netherlands, Belgium, Luxemburg	331	881	859	631[19]	1,776	2,313	2,497	2,961	2,107	1,953
France (including the Principality of Monaco)	39,292	59,162	59,777	48,993	45,559	58,002	62,497	63,105	57,702	56,863
Switzerland	27,761	45,785	50,233	45,780	52,263	75,080	80,019	83,026	76,708	66,931
Central										
Germany	49,243	46,934	52,885	53,553	55,049	71,624	68,295	75,885	59,780	53,391
Austria, Czechoslovakia	45,338	69,328	44,138	45,819	35,853	44,412	32,650	37,072	31,276	26,247
Hungary	6,972	7,119	10,181	5,733	3,584	6,101	6,871	4,881	5,722	4,742
Southern										
Portugal, Spain	894	560	968	670	629	757	819	550	424	584
Gibraltar, Malta										
Greece, Turkey in Europe, Serb-Croat-Slovene, Bulgaria, Rumania, Albania	5,018	2,138	3,432	3,001	2,742	2,894	3,754	2,862	2,842	3,788
Other European countries (not specified)	3,402	7,971	7,665	6,654	665	319	242	58		
Total (Europe)	181,047	244,298	236,066	215,943	203,942	266,982	264,883	276,420	240,953	219,623
AFRICA:										
Tripoli							277	189	265	232
Algeria	1,586	1,899	2,620	2,260	568[20]	350[20]	5,223	7,031	1,576	1,512
Tunis	2,245	5,447	6,123	5,405	9,645	7,051	2,740	2,361	3,152	2,705
Morocco										
Egypt	1,373	1,757	1,916	1,787	4,496	4,509	2,516	2,467	2,007	2,126
Other African countries (not specified)	213	396	1,112	1,239	1,889	1,162	813	637	351	523
Total (Africa)	5,417	9,499	11,771	10,691	16,598	13,072	11,569	12,685	7,351	7,098
ASIA:										
Turkey in Asia	156			146	174	356	403	306	148	157
Other Asiatic countries (not specified)		382	319	394	202	432	959	297	179	263
Total (Asia)	156	382	319	540	376	788	1,362	603	327	420
OCEANIA	535	890	767	389	701	765	815	664	638	830
AMERICA:										
Northern										
Canada	1,686	3,497	2,951	2,528	4,748	5,930	10,032	10,436	5,988	8,786
United States	87,714	121,139	193,772	197,855	168,789	316,797	358,569	298,124	131,501	280,351
Mexico					981	1,026	1,190	504	306	660
Central										
Guatemala, Salvador, Honduras, Nicaragua, etc.	2,069	997	766	1,012	227	418	369	293	179	334
Colombia, Venezuela, Guiana, Ecuador	454	421	445	319	620[21]	600[21]	787[21]	1,829[21]	544[22]	724[21]
Peru, Bolivia, Chile	409	739	679	539	1,383	1,034	1,055	1,676	754	838
Southern										
Brazil	27,438	82,159	40,434	27,707	19,724	30,079	27,808	21,298	15,558	19,263
Argentina	40,393	59,881	36,778	43,915	51,779	86,158	107,227	78,493	80,699	84,949
Paraguay	1,257	2,926	588	458						
Uruguay	1,070	1,283	613	787	1,325	2,682	2,311	1,650	1,876	1,761
Other American countries (not specified)	3,137	5,134	5,560	5,293						
Total (America)	165,627	278,176	282,586	280,413	249,574	444,724	509,348	414,303	237,405	397,666
Total (European and Mediterranean countries)				225,541	218,825	279,248	276,042	288,744	248,101	226,355
Total (non-European countries)				282,435	252,366	447,083	511,935	415,931	238,573	399,282
Grand total	352,782	533,245	531,509	507,976	471,191	726,331	787,977	704,675	486,674	625,637

For reference notes see page 842.

TABLE XI.—EMIGRATION OF CITIZENS, BY COUNTRY OF DESTINATION, 1876-1920 (concluded).

Country of destination	1910	1911	1912	1913	1914	1915	1916	1917	1918	1919	1920
EUROPE:											
Northern and Eastern Russia in Europe, Baltic States, Poland.	1,134	1,283	1,372	1,334	1,341	119	59	18	7	81	90
Norway, Sweden, Denmark	145	117	205	98	652	39	20	5	3	77	60
Great Britain and Ireland	3,607	3,510	3,563	3,884	3,620	2,338	2,306	554	584	6,129	5,126
Western Netherlands, Belgium, Luxemburg	2,554	2,472	3,570	3,369	1,961	247	10	6	4	2,152	2,497
France (including Principality of Monaco)	60,956	63,370	74,089	83,435	68,126	36,297	44,350	22,566	16,948	98,281	157,025
Switzerland	79,843	88,777	89,258	90,019	62,404	27,519	17,565	7,783	5,062	20,838	24,277
Central Germany	53,648	64,950	75,507	81,947	55,159	3,343	12			1,334	2,821
Austria, Czechoslovakia	28,670	30,151	34,157	33,706	32,161	2,443				2,068	2,859
Hungary	7,563	4,948	7,853	5,327	8,561	109				33	111
Southern Portugal, Spain	758	625	709	1,003	646	693	395	230	128	529	554
Gibraltar, Malta	373	528	417	327	190	113	89	32	39	172	124
Greece, Turkey in Europe, Serb-Croat-Slovene, Bulgaria, Rumania, Albania	3,130	3,235	3,671	3,178	6,657	908	392	243	210	2,631	2,525
Other European countries (not specified)				[23]		221	11	2	1	17	102
Total (Europe)	242,381	263,966	294,371	307,627	241,478	74,389	65,209	31,439	22,986	134,342	198,171
AFRICA: Tripoli	229	1,032	7,428		737			245	183	1,986	1,229
Algeria	1,711	1,295	1,445	1,460	1,651	657	395	1,589	838	7,941	3,923
Tunis	2,375	2,585	2,898	2,257	148	3,149	2,056	76	140	566	427
Morocco					1,615	235	136	134	133	2,379	1,473
Egypt	1,730	1,910	1,826	1,403	800	1,058	428	42	15	220	251
Other African countries (not specified)	625	571	2,128	1,421		207	102				
Total (Africa)	6,670	7,393	15,725	6,541	4,951	5,306	3,117	2,086	1,309	13,092	7,303
ASIA: Turkey in Asia	270	277	172	285	309	14			21	177	149
Other Asiatic countries (not specified)	223	228	251	138	252	86	39	17	6	135	107
Total (Asia)	493	505	423	423	561	100	39	17	27	312	256
OCEANIA	1,079	1,608	1,214	1,682	1,397	347	167	14	4	347	697
AMERICA: *Northern* Canada	10,209	9,094	18,901	30,699	11,589	761	1,532	233	69	2,185	8,475
United States	262,554	191,087	267,637	376,776	167,481	51,720	66,295	11,459	2,793	82,492	349,042
Mexico	459	1,020	758	707	311	39	29	16	31	104	130
Central Guatemala, Salvador, Honduras, Nicaragua, etc.	206	346	545	811	197	89	47	9	15	219	574
Colombia, Venezuela, Guiana, Ecuador	602[22]	770[22]	893[22]	468	307	97	36	10	3	182	397
Peru, Bolivia, Chile	661	1,061	1,530	1,162	667	204	85	31	22	492	556
Southern Brazil	19,331	22,287	35,562	31,952	14,017	3,604	1,524	426	361	5,588	10,563
Argentina	104,718	32,719	72,154	111,500	34,822	8,762	3,981	672	640	12,834	37,431
Paraguay and Uruguay	2,072	1,988	1,643	2,250	1,374	299	131	55	21	372	693
Other American countries (not specified)						302	172	29	30	663	323
Total (America)	400,852	260,372	399,713	556,325	230,765	65,877	73,832	12,940	3,985	105,131	408,184
Total (European and Mediterranean countries)	248,696	271,065	308,140	313,032	245,938	79,502	68,224	33,483	24,301	147,391	205,372
Total (non-European countries)	402,779	262,779	403,306	559,566	233,214	66,517	74,140	13,013	4,010	105,833	409,239
Grand total	651,475	533,844	711,446	872,598	479,152	146,019	142,364	46,496	28,311	253,224	614,611

For reference notes see page 842.

TABLE XII.—DISTRIBUTION OF CITIZEN EMIGRANTS, BY OCCUPATION AND COUNTRY OF DESTINATION, 1915-20.

Country of destination and year		Total	Persons in agriculture	Clay and earth workers	Masons, bricklayers, stone-workers (brick-makers), (paviers)	Siderurgical, metallurgical and engineering industry	Spinning and weaving	Tailors, seamstresses, clothing industry	Other industries and workers not specified	Persons in commerce and transport	Liberal professions, artists and employees	Domestic servants and persons attending to domestic service	Persons not in occupations	Occupations and conditions unknown or not specified
British Isles	1915	1,910	162	299	47	23	4	42	252	630	91	237	101	22
	1916	1,807	193	304	34	26	7	68	245	417	86	336	73	18
	1917	468	34	51	11	8	.....	15	43	117	40	116	29	4
	1918	485	12	16	2	7	.....	20	83	141	40	127	34	3
	1919	5,392	350	380	79	73	1	99	985	1,916	203	974	182	150
	1920	4,609	514	1,071	109	66	5	121	772	956	125	812	46	12
France	1915	30,408	3,050	5,590	2,782	929	200	1,165	5,219	3,692	1,352	5,154	920	355
	1916	37,932	4,433	7,838	3,082	933	208	1,458	4,990	3,141	1,234	9,310	923	382
	1917	19,508	1,773	3,136	1,126	444	117	912	2,532	2,018	708	6,100	467	175
	1918	15,296	1,661	1,789	1,051	501	53	636	2,448	1,817	605	4,192	350	193
	1919	88,265	10,173	15,019	11,429	4,308	416	2,352	16,743	7,364	2,308	14,562	1,148	2,443
	1920	146,202	17,727	36,275	31,766	5,073	670	2,498	28,943	4,664	1,634	15,762	526	664
Switzerland	1915	24,596	2,253	2,813	3,660	480	305	602	5,536	2,947	1,347	3,100	1,219	334
	1916	14,795	1,000	1,134	1,763	369	149	506	2,766	1,517	949	3,654	839	149
	1917	6,615	449	510	626	163	48	315	1,297	553	327	1,968	250	109
	1918	4,443	264	340	530	146	33	153	897	399	268	1,256	114	43
	1919	19,034	1,352	1,226	2,594	1,037	239	678	4,007	2,215	1,055	3,458	732	441
	1920	22,934	1,606	2,776	6,073	902	266	736	5,350	960	665	3,343	143	114
Other European countries (not specified)	1915	7,784	303	907	832	201	34	140	1,935	1,220	855	818	333	206
	1916	900	21	26	59	22	3	23	117	226	194	117	72	20
	1917	501	10	9	52	8	2	12	76	104	93	86	42	7
	1918	359	32	6	18	12	.....	9	72	65	53	68	20	4
	1919	8,134	335	779	804	371	14	106	1,421	1,653	713	1,310	460	168
	1920	11,023	520	1,768	1,735	502	32	140	2,458	1,108	713	1,721	194	132
Mediterranean countries	1915	4,506	155	389	413	231	11	109	1,112	770	428	640	135	113
	1916	2,524	115	279	270	136	5	104	431	290	180	581	90	43
	1917	1,792	62	147	100	89	.....	38	744	173	78	280	55	26
	1918	1,178	102	116	144	71	1	30	234	149	93	189	35	14
	1919	11,703	1,125	769	1,384	979	13	217	1,750	1,722	857	1,763	386	738
	1920	6,516	662	469	824	418	3	256	1,103	543	518	1,547	115	58

TABLE XII.—DISTRIBUTION OF CITIZEN EMIGRANTS, BY OCCUPATION AND COUNTRY OF DESTINATION, 1915-20 (cont.).

Country of destination and year	Total	Persons in agriculture	Clay and earth workers	Masons, bricklayers, stone-workers (brickmakers), (paviers)	Siderurgical, metallurgical and engineering industry	Spinning and weaving	Tailors, seamstresses, clothing industry	Other industries and workers not specified	Persons in commerce and transport	Liberal professions, artists and employees	Domestic servants and persons attending to domestic service	Persons not in occupations	Occupations and conditions unknown or not specified
Canada													
1915	588	164	164	27	3	6	9	79	21	3	86	11	15
1916	1,270	716	236	21	6	6	35	98	19	4	117	4	8
1917	170	72	24	2	1	1	13	21	7	1	26	..	2
1918	44	15	5	..	..	1	3	..	1	..	17	1	1
1919	1,944	541	436	63	43	8	58	296	90	11	344	24	30
1920	8,077	2,626	2,811	382	123	3	176	1,143	165	17	613	11	7
United States													
1915	37,555	13,201	6,799	802	368	307	2,466	4,853	1,609	375	5,960	293	522
1916	50,126	18,907	8,168	1,233	421	351	4,067	5,682	1,555	315	8,668	378	381
1917	8,097	1,403	708	112	72	126	1,289	1,033	157	113	2,561	90	246
1918	1,944	270	110	29	18	30	269	193	157	62	755	29	22
1919	67,889	16,261	9,181	1,719	1,449	497	5,650	8,823	5,173	808	16,321	1,021	986
1920	315,083	105,300	59,716	11,656	7,003	1,186	19,946	45,190	14,991	2,161	46,187	952	595
Brazil													
1915	2,629	529	339	83	74	30	113	417	280	140	492	93	39
1916	1,159	197	128	38	36	7	75	164	137	71	221	70	15
1917	364	36	29	13	16	4	28	54	43	38	71	25	8
1918	328	34	27	6	10	5	13	54	47	36	68	26	2
1919	4,806	930	385	172	152	43	232	720	593	242	734	246	357
1920	9,225	3,359	997	332	329	64	474	1,331	527	170	1,357	92	193
Argentina													
1915	6,723	2,144	660	241	156	63	294	859	713	306	1,038	187	62
1916	2,978	789	261	96	42	57	192	342	299	139	625	97	39
1917	537	69	25	9	14	9	65	62	72	40	142	38	12
1918	542	56	28	18	15	5	24	62	99	55	110	65	5
1919	10,767	2,822	849	461	383	101	504	1,139	1,091	436	1,796	367	818
1920	33,561	14,997	3,465	1,659	976	248	1,734	3,253	2,418	376	3,665	175	595

TABLE XII.—DISTRIBUTION OF CITIZEN EMIGRANTS, BY OCCUPATION AND COUNTRY OF DESTINATION, 1915-20 (concluded).

Country of destination and year		Total	Persons in agriculture	Clay and earth workers	Masons, bricklayers, stoneworkers (brickmakers), (paviers)	Siderurgical, metallurgical and engineering industry	Spinning and weaving	Tailors, seamstresses, clothing industry	Other industries and workers not specified	Persons in commerce and transport	Liberal professions, artists and employees	Domestic servants and persons attending to domestic service	Persons not in occupations	Occupations and conditions unknown or not specified
Other non-European countries	1915	1,364	191	138	65	35	12	49	218	235	123	215	66	17
	1916	663	71	55	46	16	7	18	87	99	88	133	39	4
	1917	196	13	6	9	4	3	7	31	52	23	28	15	5
	1918	133		2	5	6	....	3	15	29	20	32	13	2
	1919	2,442	369	174	108	84	29	78	398	346	174	412	124	146
	1920	3,487	896	567	220	173	16	138	488	422	136	344	34	53
Total	1915	118,063	22,152	18,098	8,952	2,500	972	4,989	20,480	12,117	5,020	17,740	3,358	1,685
	1916	114,154	26,442	18,429	6,642	2,007	800	6,546	14,922	7,700	3,260	23,762	2,585	1,059
	1917	38,248	3,920	4,645	2,070	819	310	2,674	5,893	3,473	1,461	11,378	1,011	594
	1918	24,752	2,452	2,439	1,803	786	128	1,160	4,058	2,904	1,232	6,814	687	289
	1919	220,376	34,258	29,198	18,813	8,879	1,361	9,974	36,282	22,163	6,807	41,674	4,690	6,277
	1920	560,717	148,407	109,915	54,756	15,565	2,493	26,219	90,031	26,754	6,515	75,351	2,288	2,423

TABLE XIII.—Intercontinental emigration of citizens, by country of destination, 1902-24.

Year	Total	Canada	United States	Brazil	La Plata	Australia	Other non-European countries
1902	246,374	. . . . .	191,710	23,479	30,375	62	748
1903	265,566	. . . . .	214,157	10,515	39,763	53	1,078
1904	211,726	. . . . .	142,327	9,809	57,674	54	1,862
1905	350,951	. . . . .	252,521	14,297	82,534	4	1,595
1906	414,719	. . . . .	292,059	12,413	109,107	. . . .	1,140
1907	372,579	. . . . .	283,671	11,836	75,836	. . . .	1,236
1908	167,511	. . . . .	70,668	9,596	86,356	. . . .	891
1909	337,019	. . . . .	246,121	9,295	80,762	182	659
1910	327,247	627	222,235	8,434	95,249	126	576
1911	212,500	13	155,835	18,011	37,666	114	861
1912	292,811	303	208,434	23,488	59,309	318	959
1913	428,484	1,584	305,240	21,303	99,214	390	753
1914	162,492	842	125,812	9,162	25,371	844	461
1915	38,226	81	28,907	2,575	6,400	132	131
1916	50,541	703	44,994	1,312	3,490	. . . .	42
1917	8,966	181	8,197	151	435	. . . .	2
1918	1,978	43	1,545	118	268	. . . .	4
1919	56,885	560	41,606	4,135	10,175	. . . .	409
1920	211,227	3,325	169,379	8,593	28,575	. . . .	1,355
1921	198,891	2,635	142,514	10,391	40,936	1,064	1,351
1922	128,529	2,496	52,182	9,860	59,758	3,432	801
1923	186,192	7,236	65,299	15,436	95,616	1,043	1,562
1924	137,517	2,802	44,568	11,792	71,718	4,502	2,135

TABLE XIV.—Distribution of citizen emigrants to extra-European countries, by sex and age, 1921-24.

Year	Total	Males	Females	Children under 15 years			Adults		
				Total	Males	Females	Total	Males	Female
1921	198,891	130,359	68,532	34,580	18,575	16,005	164,311	111,784	52,527
1922	128,529	94,482	34,047	19,295	10,626	8,669	109,234	83,856	25,378
1923	186,192	148,163	38,029	24,659	13,734	10,925	161,533	134,429	27,104
1924	137,517	99,478	38,039	25,342	13,930	11,412	112,175	85,548	26,627

TABLE XV.—Distribution of citizen emigrants over 15 years of age to extra-European countries, by occupation, 1921-24.

Year	Total	Agriculture	Industry and mining	Transport and commerce	Domestic service and general labor	Liberal professions and public services	Other or no occupations
1921	160,804	61,102	43,011	3,477	35,283	2,786	15,145
1922	108,518	55,665	26,366	3,316	18,694	2,012	2,465
1923	160,469	70,989	53,348	4,714	22,849	3,473	5,096
1924	110,784	47,633	32,716	3,506	21,957	2,957	2,015

TABLE XVI.—DISTRIBUTION OF CITIZEN EMIGRANTS TO EUROPEAN COUNTRIES, BY SEX AND AGE (UNDER AND OVER 15 YEARS), 1921-24.

| Year | Total | Children | Adults | | |
			Total	Males	Females
1921	60,846	5,670	55,176	36,610	18,566
1922	123,030	8,746	114,284	87,691	26,593
1923	170,226	16,510	153,716	114,067	39,649
1924	201,591	18,274	183,317	136,444	46,873

TABLE XVII.—DISTRIBUTION OF CITIZEN EMIGRANTS OVER 15 YEARS OF AGE TO EUROPEAN COUNTRIES, BY OCCUPATION, 1921-24

Year	Total	Agri-culture	Industry and mining	Transport and commerce	Domestic service and general labor	Liberal professions and public services	Other or no occupations
1921	55,176	7,928	26,279	1,776	15,670	2,337	1,186
1922	114,284	11,408	70,862	2,025	26,644	2,327	1,018
1923	153,716	19,500	86,756	2,888	40,399	2,951	1,222
1924	183,317	27,036	99,310	2,457	49,166	3,630	1,718

TABLE XVIII.—CONTINENTAL EMIGRATION OF CITIZENS, BY COUNTRY OF DESTINATION (ACCORDING TO THE SCHEDULES DETACHED FROM THE EMIGRANTS' PASSPORTS) 1921-24.

Year	Total	France	Switzerland	Austria, Czechoslovakia	Germany	Belgium	Luxemburg	Great Britain and Ireland	Scandinavia	Russia, Poland	Spain and Portugal	Balkans Serb-Croat-Slovene State	Greece	Turkey	Egypt	Tunis	Algeria	Morocco	Other countries
1921	60,846	36,179	6,543	4,091	1,085	2,130	335	1,786	23	35	363	4,896	75	44	629	1,797	499	313	23
1922	123,030	85,815	5,241	2,719	1,261	15,385	5,547	867	32	26	277	2,865	7	39	201	1,920	512	279	37
1923	170,226	142,990	6,906	1,303	350	11,214	841	724	62	20	315	2,158	59	69	364	1,965	643	193	50
1924	201,591	173,664	10,119	1,673	643	7,907	1,923	573	67	27	363	1,160	129	48	332	1,911	778	95	179

TABLE XIX.—CONTINENTAL EMIGRATION OF CITIZENS BY COUNTRY OF DESTINATION (CORRECTED TABLE, IN ACCORDANCE WITH ADDITIONAL INFORMATION), 1921-24.

Year	Total	France	Switzerland	Austria, Czechoslovakia	Germany	Belgium	Luxemburg	Great Britain and Ireland	Scandinavia	Russia, Poland	Spain Portugal	Serb-Croat-Slovene State	Greece	Turkey	Egypt	Tunis	Algeria	Morocco	Other countries
1921	88,295	49,499	9,318	6,814	1,747	3,608	460	2,462	38	59	576	8,585	239	104	1,042	2,544	598	450	152
1922	170,155	113,625	7,718	5,031	2,026	21,751	8,200	1,296	113	55	429	4,498	222	138	689	2,595	663	376	730
1923	229,854	190,589	9,573	2,026	561	15,199	1,099	1,129	107	42	526	3,211	199	177	941	3,034	874	258	309
1924	271,089	231,090	13,887	2,374	1,032	10,219	2,489	898	106	49	532	1,884	236	93	825	3,703	1,139	176	357

TABLE XX.—Intercontinental immigration distinguishing citizens and aliens
AND FIRST AND SECOND CLASS PASSENGERS, 1884-1920.

Year	Total	Citizens	Aliens	1st and 2nd class	Year	Total	Citizens	Aliens	1st and 2nd class
1884	12,908	......	.....	2,785	1904	172,661	168,379	4,282	16,293
1887	18,039	......	.....	1,969	1905	126,008	119,858	6,150	6,240
1888	27,281	......	.....	1,268	1906	165,691	157,987	7,704	8,970
1889	33,576	......	.....	2,879	1907	256,904	248,428	8,476	11,714
1890	45,880	......	.....	2,195	1908	331,331	300,834	30,497	15,922
1891	60,710	......	.....	2,407	1909	140,626	134,210	6,416	13,977
1892	51,699	......	.....	5,130	1910	168,689	161,148	7,541	15,065
1893	53,634	......	.....	3,722	1911	226,900	218,998	7,902	18,800
1894	55,221	......	.....	2,774	1912	189,395	182,990	6,405	18,266
1895	53,962	......	.....	5,632	1913	196,976	188,978	7,998	21,151
1896	58,607	......	.....	7,535	1914	229,049	219,178	9,871	21,088
1897	63,893	......	.....	7,176	1915	170,615	167,925	2,690	9,237
1898	71,687	......	.....	5,484	1916	39,943	39,039	904	3,901
1899	69,441	......	.....	5,891	1917	17,227	16,885	342	2,144
1900	80,570	......	.....	12,479	1918	9,180	9,025	125	1,420
1901	77,567	......	.....	26,136	1919	100,393	89,833	10,560	13,200
1902	95,336	92,707	2,629	12,154	1920	121,075	78,498	42,577	15,355
1903	124,590	120,645	3,945	12,437	....	......	......	.....	.....

TABLE XXI.—INTERCONTINENTAL IMMIGRATION (THIRD CLASS PASSENGERS), BY COUNTRY OF LAST RESIDENCE, 1884-1920.[24]

Year	Total	United States	Canada	Brazil	La Plata Republics	Central America	Other American countries	Other countries
1884[25]	12,908	2,667	.....	72	10,169	..	.....	.....
1887[25]	18,039	3,000	.....	317	14,517	..	129	76
1888[25]	27,281	6,072	.....	1,136	19,998	..	75	.....
1889[25]	33,576	4,734	.....	3,603	25,125	..	101	13
1890[25]	45,880	2,881	.....	1,510	41,476	..	13	.....
1891[25]	60,710	10,170	.....	2,583	47,957	..	.....	.....
1892[25]	51,699	12,695	.....	7,566	31,438	..	.....	.....
1893[25]	53,634	22,912	.....	10,906	19,816	..	.....	.....
1894[25]	55,221	26,845	.....	5,300	22,209	..	867	.....
1895[25]	53,962	17,039	.....	16,654	19,319	..	950	.....
1896[25]	58,607	20,885	.....	16,794	19,997	..	931	.....
1897[25]	63,893	22,292	.....	20,192	20,540	..	869	.....
1898[25]	71,687	24,735	.....	17,489	28,110	..	1,353	.....
1889[25]	69,441	31,289	.....	8,972	28,033	..	1,147	.....
1900[25]	80,570	31,966	.....	17,733	29,419	..	689	763
1901[25]	77,567	24,678	.....	21,224	29,204	..	604	1,857
1902[26]	92,707	52,216	.....	29,701	23,813	..	1,018	742
1903[26]	120,645	78,233	.....	29,740	26,813	..	1,050	1,191
1904[27]	168,379	129,231	.....	16,667	21,472	..	1,009	
1905[28]	119,858	77,636	.....	18,985	22,184	..	756	297
1906[28]	157,987	109,258	.....	17,236	30,393	..	859	241
1907[28]	248,428	176,727	.....	20,721	49,867	..	928	185
1908[28]	300,834	240,877[29]	.....	14,675	44,196	..	1,060	26
1909[28]	134,210	73,806[29]	326	14,071	45,232	..	732	43
1910[28]	161,148	106,705[29]	.....	10,808	42,888	..	720	27
1911[28]	218,998	156,205[29]	.....	10,568	51,483	..	688	54
1912[28]	182,990	129,649[29]	.....	9,031	43,593	..	717	.....
1913[28]	188,978	122,589[29]	1,647	12,742	51,151	..	833	16
1914[28]	219,178	156,274[29]	26	12,865	48,413	..	810	790
1915[28]	167,925	104,265[29]	.....	11,489	51,322	..	621	228
1916[27]	39,039	17,248[29]	463	2,305	18,324	63	636	
1917[27]	16,885	8,763[29]	369	897	6,697	71	88	
1918[27]	9,025	4,057[29]	532	1,069	3,227	58	82	
1919[27]	89,833	76,910[29]	2,786	2,130	7,677	63	267	
1920[27]	78,498	53,407[29]	1,167	4,664	18,783	87	390	

For reference notes see page 842.

TABLE XXII.—Immigration of citizens, by country of last residence, 1921-24

	Country of last residence	1921[30]	1922[30]	1923[30]	1924[31]
	Grand total...................	123,999	110,786	119,738	172,811
Intercontinental	Total......................	93,916	55,145	40,240	65,390
	Canada.....................	2,477	535	272	495
	United States.................	73,116	36,886	24,359	42,746
	Central America..............	57	57	54	107
	Brazil.......................	3,928	3,940	3,338	4,652
	Argentina...................	13,553	13,165	11,152	16,040
	Uruguay.....................	520	388	460	604
	Africa.......................	16	10	95	171
	Australia....................			353	328
	Other countries..............	249	164	157	247
Continental	Total......................	30,083	55,641	79,498	107,421
	France......................	20,069	36,096	63,396	88,243
	Switzerland..................	4,727	3,738	5,374	8,671
	Austria, Czechoslovakia........	1,838	2,228	1,401	1,663
	Germany....................	230	538	365	439
	Holland and Belgium...........	219	7,101	4,773	4,057
	Luxemburg..................	84	2,652	1,434	872
	Great Britain and Ireland.......	209	350	540	540
	Scandinavia..................	5	18	20	35
	Russia and Poland.............	9	7	8	25
	Spain and Portugal............	150	102	199	253
	Balkans, Serb, Croat and Slovene State........................	1,583	1,435	1,073	1,034
	Greece......................	32	9	20	118
	Turkey......................	5	3	8	27
	Egypt.......................	114	434	149	299
	Tunis.......................	491	669	409	671
	Algeria......................	284	183	241	384
	Morocco.....................	29	65	58	49
	Other countries..............	5	13	30	41

TABLE XXIII.—Distribution of citizen immigrants from extra-European countries, by sex and age, 1921-24.

Year	Total			Children			Adults		
	Total	Males	Females	Total	Males	Females	Total	Males	Females
1921	93.916	73,333	20,583	18,762	9,793	8,969	75,154	63,540	11,614
1922	55,145	41,555	13.590	11,539	6,089	5,450	43,606	35,466	8,140
1923	40,240	32,179	8,061	6,261	3,296	2,965	33,979	28,883	5,096
1924[31]	65,390	54,219	11,171	7,853	4,097	3,756	57,537	50,122	7,415

For reference notes see page 842.

TABLE XXIV.—Distribution of citizen immigrants from European countries, by sex and age, 1921-24.

Year	Total			Children			Adults		
	Total	Males	Females	Total	Males	Females	Total	Males	Females
1921[30]	30,083	21,755	8,328	....	....	....	30,083	21,755	8,328
1922[30]	55,641	44,556	11,085	....	....	....	55,641	44,556	11,085
1923[30]	79,498	63,983	15,515	....	....	....	79,498	63,983	15,515
1924	107,421	81,783	25,638	5,932	3,173	2,759	101,489	78,610	22,879

TABLE XXV.—Alien migrants in transit to and from extra-European countries, 1920-24.

Year	Outgoing	Returning
1920	18,140	42,577
1921	12,660	20,037
1922	7,232	7,455
1923	13,824	4,778
1924	10,914	6,465

SOURCES

Carpi, L.: Delle Colonie e della Emigrazione italiana all' Estero. Milan, 1874 (4 vols.); vol. I, p. 53 and vol. III, p. 243.

Tables I (figures for Genoa); II-VI.

Florenzano, G.: Della Emigrazione italiana in America. Naples, 1874; pp. 122-141.

Table I (figures for Genoa).

Rapport à S. E. le Ministre de l'Intérieur sur l'Emigration. Reports for 1857 and 1858, 1859 and 1860, 1861 and 1862, 1863 and 1864, 1865 and 1874. Paris.

Table I (figures for French ports).

Statistica della Emigrazione italiana all'Estero, 1878-1920. 'Rome, 1880 to 1925 (publication of the Direzione Generale della Statistica).

Tables VII-XII, XIX, XX.

Conférence internationale de l'émigration et de l'immigration, Rome, 1924. Documents préparatoires et considérations générales sur les problèmes de l'émigration et de l'immigration. I (Published by the Generale Commissariato della Emigrazione), Rome, 1924.

Table XIII, years 1902-20.

Information supplied by the General Emigration Department.

Tables XIII, (years 1921-24); XIV-XVIII, XXI-XXIV.

For reference notes see page 842.

NOTES

[1]In Florenzano the corresponding figures are 5,070 for 1863, 9,742 for 1865 and 18,120 for 1868; the disparities are probably due to printing errors.

[2]Authorized emigration only.

[3]Under 14 years of age for authorized and under 15 years for clandestine emigration.

[4]Over 14 years of age for authorized and over 15 years for clandestine emigration.

[5]Clandestine emigration only.

[6]England and Australia.

[7]Spain and Portugal.

[8]Including 1,390 emigrants embarked for America whose sex and age were not stated.

[9]Children up to 15 years since 1904.

[10]No comparison can be instituted between the figures for 1876 to 1878 owing to a change in their classification during these three years.

[11]Agricultural workers, and general labor attached to agriculture.

[12]Including a certain number of emigrants to the Levant.

[13]Included in "American States not distinguished".

[14]Including 238 emigrants shown under the general head "other countries".

[15]Not including the Antilles Islands placed under "American States not distinguished".

[16]Including 216 emigrants for "other places in Africa, Asia and Oceania".

[17]Including 114 emigrants for "other places in Asia and Oceania".

[18]Including British possessions in the Mediterranean.

[19]Not including the emigrants to Luxemburg classed with those en route to Germany.

[20]Tripoli and Morocco.

[21]For 1904 and 1905 the Antilles Islands are included under the head "Colombia, Venezuela, Guiana, Ecuador".

[22]For 1906-12 Panama is included under the head "Colombia, Venezuela, Guiana, Ecuador".

[23]After January 1, 1913, Italians en route to Tripoli were not reckoned as emigrants.

[24]Not including immigrants from the North of Africa classified in the Italian statistics as continental migrants.

[25]For 1884-1901, Italians and foreigners travelling third class and disembarking at Italian ports.

[26]For 1902 and 1903, Italians and foreigners of all classes landed at Italian ports. The totals, however, show the number of Italian third class passengers only.

[27]For 1904 and 1916-20, only third class Italian passengers landed at Italian ports.

[28]For 1905-15, third class Italian passengers landed at Italian ports and at Havre.

[29]Including migrants sent back to Italy immediately on their arrival in the United States as follows:

Year	No.	Year	No.
1908	654	1914	3,613
1909	1,762	1915	901
1910	3,438	1916	1,071
1911	2,778	1917	134
1912	3,150	1918	39
1913	3,883	1919	203
		1920	553

[30]For 1921-23, the figures of continental immigrants are of adults only.

[31]Including Italians immigrated through foreign ports.

PORTUGAL

I. PASSENGER STATISTICS

(Tables I-III)

The Statistical Department in the Ministry of Finance basing itself on the reports of the local authorities has published information concerning emigration since 1855. The statistics are compiled from the passport registers and include only authorised emigration. No investigation of clandestine emigration is made. Emigration from Madeira and the Azores is included, but citizens proceeding to Portuguese colonies not being obliged to procure passports (Act of April 27, 1907) are not included.[1] Passport statistics are compiled also for all the Portuguese overseas colonies.

II. PORT STATISTICS

(Table IV)

Statistics of embarkations and disembarkations at Lisbon and Oporto have been available since 1919. All third class passengers are regarded as emigrants. No separate particulars are available for the different passenger classes, and passengers to and from Madeira and the Azores are excluded.

Statistics about the number of migrants from Portugal to Argentina (1857-1924), Brazil (1837-1924), Cuba (1911-24), United States (1820-1924), Uruguay (1867-1924) and Hawaii (1911-24) will be found in the national tables for those countries. Statistics about the number of migrants returning to Portugal from Argentina (1858-1924), United States (1908-24), Uruguay (1879-1903 and 1916-21) and Hawaii (1911-24) will be found in the national tables for those countries.

[1]*Statistica della Emigrazione Italiana per l'Estero negli anni* 1912 e 1913, Roma, p. 141.

TABLE I.—DISTRIBUTION OF CITIZEN EMIGRANTS, BY SEX, AGE AND COUNTRY OF FUTURE RESIDENCE, 1855-1924.

Year	Total	Sex		Age		Country of future residence				
		Males	Females	Under 14 years	14 years and over	Europe	America	Asia	Oceania	Africa
1855–65	80,821									
1866[1]	6,046									
1867[1]	7,200									
1868[1]	6,742	45,196	6,313							
1869[1]	8,415									
1870[1]	10,409									
1871[1]	12,697									
1872	17,284	15,371	1,913	2,665	14,619	....	16,935	12	....	337
1873	12,989	11,077	1,912	2,233	10,756	....	12,614	5	....	370
1874	14,835	12,683	2,152	2,540	12,295	....	14,547	9	....	279
1875	15,440	13,684	1,756	2,733	12,707	....	15,084	4	....	352
1876	11,035	9,667	1,368	1,987[2]	9,018[10]	....	10,725	9	....	301
1877	11,057	9,074	1,983	1,939	9,118	....	10,725	13	....	319
1878	9,926	8,214	1,712	1,165	8,761	....	9,558[3]	7[3]	....	362[8]
1879	13,208	10,431	2,777	2,228	10,980	....	12,893	10	....	305
1880	12,597	10,388	2,209	1,757	10,840	....	12,218	16	....	363
1881	14,637	12,046	2,591	2,134	12,503	....	14,267	10	....	360
1882	18,272	14,625	3,647	2,573	15,699	....	17,722	71	....	479
1883	19,251	15,066	4,185	3,315	15,936	....	18,706	7	....	588
1884	17,518	13,740	3,778	2,492	15,026	....	16,924	7	....	587
1885	15,004	11,471	3,533	2,615	12,389	1,851	11,853	18	424	858
1886	13,998	10,644	3,354	2,522	11,476	260	13,039	3	426	270
1887	16,932	13,600	3,332	2,462	14,470	411	15,803	4	292	422
1888	23,981	18,414	5,567	5,188	18,793	349	22,952	19	5	656
1889	20,614	15,818	4,796	3,928	16,686	967	18,305	....	2	1,340
1890	29,421	21,944	7,477	6,307	23,114	476	27,038	12	16	1,879
1891	33,585	25,090	8,495	6,919	26,666	351	31,654	1	5	1,574
1892	21,074	15,195	5,879	4,451	16,623	302	19,573	10	....	1,189
1893	30,383	23,482	6,901	5,771	24,612	290	28,829	6	6	1,252
1894	26,911	21,011	5,900	4,791	22,120	255	25,237	....	15	1,404
1895	44,746	32,365	12,381	11,367	33,379	327[4]	42,562[4]	2[4]	617[4]	1,239[4]
1896	27,980	19,343	8,637	7,653	20,327	355	26,461	3	16	1,145
1897	21,612	15,734	5,878	5,183	16,429	243	19,809	3	16	1,541
1898	23,510	17,691	5,819	5,171	18,339	230	21,422	4	....	1,854
1899	17,776	13,142	4,634	3,566	14,210	235	15,874	1	133	1,533
1900	21,306	15,578	5,728	4,506	16,800	445	18,908	5	20	1,928
1901	20,646	15,051	5,595	4,259	16,387	207	18,426	1	56	1,956
1902	24,170	17,032	7,138	5,341	18,829	290	21,916	8	16	1,940
1903	21,611	15,931	5,680	4,369	17,242	320	19,339	10	22	1,920
1904	28,311	20,917	7,394	5,714	22,597	384	25,967	8	....	1,952
1905	33,622	25,425	8,197	6,531	27,091	304	31,236	8	....	2,074
1906	38,094	28,741	9,353	7,026	31,068	369	34,098	7	1,335	2,285
1907	41,944	32,139	9,805	7,746	34,198	107	40,145	13	1,043	636
1908	40,056	31,539	8,517	7,221	32,835	83	39,957	....	1	15
1909	38,213	29,646	8,567	6,607	31,606	67	37,285	1	851	9
1910	39,502	30,762	8,740	6,205	33,297	45	39,349	....	79	29
1911	59,652	43,062	16,590	12,134	47,518	253	59,141	....	239	19
1912	88,920	62,154	26,766	18,674	70,246	328	88,375	....	127	90
1913	77,633	52,911	24,722	16,928	60,705	406	77,004	3	32	188
1914	25,722	15,570	10,152	6,051	19,671	112	25,570	1	....	39
1915	19,298	11,917	7,381	4,050	15,248	384	18,820	2	21	71
1916	24,721	12,607	12,114	5,818	18,903	2,262	21,639	13	4	803
1917	15,689	8,340	7,349	3,505	12,184	3,330	11,583	14	....	762
1918	11,672	7,185	4,487	2,349	9,323	3,138	7,655	1	4	874
1919	36,901	25,748	11,153	4,638	32,263	7,924	26,849	3	....	2,125
1920	64,651	48,066	16,585	6,020	58,631	4,945	58,587	3	1	1,115
1921	24,523	17,937	6,586	2,013	22,510	5,141	18,375	22	3	982
1922	39,709	31,669	8,040	1,985	37,724	8,432	30,521	4	1	752
1923	40,072	32,086	7,986	2,056	38,016	11,155	28,383	8	2	524
1924	29,644	22,849	6,795	1,683	28,961	11,963	17,283	15	....	383

For reference notes see page 847.

TABLE II.—DISTRIBUTION OF CITIZEN EMIGRANTS, BY SEX AND AGE, 1913-21.

Year	Children			Over 14 years		
	Total	Males	Females	Total	Males	Females
1913	16,928	9,684	7,244	60,705	43,227	17,478
1914	6,051	3,509	2,542	19,671	12,061	7,610
1915	4,050	2,274	1,776	15,248	9,643	5,605
1916	5,818	3,280	2,538	18,903	9,327	9,576
1917	3,505	2,026	1,479	12,184	6,314	5,870
1918	2,349	1,357	992	9,323	5,828	3,495
1919	4,638	2,749	1,889	32,263	22,999	9,264
1920	6,020	3,545	2,475	58,631	44,521	14,110
1921	2,013	1,166	847	22,510	16,771	5,739

TABLE III.—EMIGRATION OF CITIZENS TO AMERICA, BY COUNTRY OF FUTURE RESIDENCE, 1913-21, AND 1923-24.

Year	North America	South America		
		Argentina	Brazil	Other countries
1913	11,440	. . .	64,402	1,162
1914	5,927	254	19,341	48
1915	7,070	252	11,435	63
1916	11,513	128	9,988	10
1917	4,551	89	6,934	9
1918	1,438	113	6,100	4
1919	5,222	339	21,218	70
1920	24,136	746	33,641	64
1921	3,589	856	13,829	101
1923	3,700	1,847	22,270	566
1924	1,052	979	14,960	292

TABLE IV.—EMIGRATION AND IMMIGRATION OF CITIZENS (THIRD CLASS PASSENGERS EMBARKED AND DISEMBARKED AT PORTUGUESE PORTS), 1919-24.

Year	Passengers embarked			Passengers disembarked		
	Total	Males	Females	Total	Males	Females
1919	21,614	14,663	6,951	*	*	*
1920	46,410	36,106	10,304	16,307	11,962	4,345
1921	17,915	12,797	5,118	20,232	15,646	4,586
1922	29,037	22,227	6,810	20,480	15,720	4,760
1923	30,792	22,314	8,478	15,512	12,111	3,401
1924	22,279	16,008	6,271	9,973	8,022	1,951

TABLE V.—DISTRIBUTION OF CITIZEN EMIGRANTS OF ALL CLASSES, EMBARKED AT LISBON OR OPORTO, BY SEX, OCCUPATION AND DESTINATION, 1919-24.[5]

Year	Total	Sex		Destination[6]						Unknown[7]	Total[8]	Occupations			
		Males	Females	Brazil		Montevideo and Buenos Aires		United States				Artisans		General laborers	
				Males	Females	Males	Females	Males	Females			Males	Females	Males	Females
1919	24,278	16,265	8,013	13,135	6,868	196	141	1,946	657	1,335	8,268	1,955	52	6,143	118
1920	50,223	38,551	11,672	26,333	9,549	387	129	10,436	1,741	1,648	27,707	4,100	37	23,397	173
1921	20,595	14,477	6,118	12,375	5,510	358	47	951	198	1,156	8,001	649	4	7,344	4
1922	31,601	24,005	7,596	21,293	6,821	644	199	1,239	366	1,039	16,680	2,501	..	14,161	18
1923	36,311	25,974	10,337	22,164	9,065	1,592	336	1,624	589	941	17,837	1,986	6	15,699	146
1924	25,742	18,230	7,512	15,314	6,651	1,354	497	955	150	821	12,104	1,405	4	10,675	20

TABLE VI.—DISTRIBUTION OF CITIZEN IMMIGRANTS OF ALL CLASSES, DISEMBARKED AT LISBON OR OPORTO, BY SEX, COUNTRY OF EMBARKATION AND OCCUPATION, 1920-24

Year	Total	Sex		Country of Embarkation						Unknown[7]	Total[8]	Occupations			
		Males	Females	Brazil		Montevideo and Buenos Aires		United States				Artisans		General laborers	
				Males	Females	Males	Females	Males	Females			Males	Females	Males	Females
1920	20,896	14,840	6,056	11,781	5,076	514	119	1,689	553	1,164	6,527	1,353	81	4,857	236
1921	23,329	17,803	5,526	12,728	4,643	211	46	3,920	659	1,122	8,463	783	..	7,680	..
1922	24,420	18,450	5,970	15,509	5,220	87	30	1,435	457	1,682	9,570	961	..	8,609	..
1923	21,047	15,943	5,104	13,864	4,605	328	132	1,275	250	593	6,549	696	12	5,837	4
1924	13,547	10,503	3,044	7,194	2,204	721	199	1,988	431	810	6,362	474	..	5,888	..

For reference notes see page 847.

SOURCES

Table I (years 1855-65) (calculated).

First Parliamentary Enquiry relating to Portuguese Emigration by the Commission of the Chamber of Deputies. Lisbon, 1873, pp. 495, 502, 503.

Table I (years 1866-71).

Statistica della Emigrazione italiana all' Estero. Rome, 1886 to 1915. Figures for 1872-81 taken from *Emigraçao relatorio e Projeto de regulamento pelo primeiro official da Direcçao geral de administraçao politica e civil,* by Comm. Luciano Cordeiro. Lisbon, 1883, p. 80. Figures for 1882-84 supplied to the Italian Directorate-General of Statistics by Comm. Luciano Cordeiro, and for 1885-1912 by the Portuguese administration or statistical authorities.

Table I (years 1872-1912).

Portuguese Republic, Ministry of Finance, Statistical Section. *Estatistica Demographia.* Movements of Population. Lisbon, 1919 to 1926.

Tables I, II, III (years 1913-2)4.

Ministry of the Interior. Commissioner-General of Emigration Services. *Boletim de Emigração,* 1920 to 1921. Lisbon, 1920 to 1926.

Tables IV, V, VI (years 1920-24).

Information supplied by M. Francisco de Melo e Noronha, Commissioner-General of Emigration. Lisbon.

J. Fayn, Mining engineer, Consul of H. M. The King of the Netherlands at Liège. *Le Portugal et ses Richesses naturelles à l'Exposition Universelle de Vienne de 1873.* Liége, 1874, pp. 5, 6.

Tables III-IV (year 1919).

NOTES

[1]Madeira and the Azores are included. The figures in the other tables (II-IV) refer to passengers embarked and disembarked at Portuguese ports. Madeira and the Azores are not included.
[2]Age specified for only 11,005 emigrants.
[3]Country of destination indicated for only 9,927 emigrants.
[4]Country of destination indicated for only 44,747 emigrants.
[5]Passengers mostly between 20 and 40 years of age.
[6]528 passengers (364 males, 164 females) embarked for Africa (other than Portuguese colonies) and 7 to Asia during the years 1919 to 1925. (Note. It was not possible to distinguish and eliminate the figures for 1925.)
[7]This column represents the difference between the total and the sum of the figures given for the various countries.
[8]These totals have been obtained by adding the figures for the two occupational groups.

SPAIN

I.—Passenger Statistics compiled by the Geographical and Statistical Institute

(Tables I-III)

By a Decree of April 21, 1861, the General Commission of Statistics (Comisión General de Estadística), called into being by a Royal Order of 1856, was reorganised and renamed *Junta general de estadística*. It consisted of two sections, one geographical, the other statistical. The Order of July 15,1865, created a Department for geography and another for statistics and the *Junta* was retained as a consultative body. In 1870 the Geographical Institute was founded and, three years later, it was entrusted with the compilation of statistics. Since 1882 it has published the *Estadística del movimento de buques y pasajeros por mar*. The statistics are based on the manifests required by the Royal Order of August 13, 1883, from the masters of vessels. No vessel carrying passengers to places abroad may leave the port without delivering the manifest to the sanitary authority. For arriving passengers other forms are prescribed. The officials of the *Sanidad marítima* transmit these forms monthly to the Institute which digests and publishes them. These statistics cover all arrivals and departures, including persons proceeding abroad from the Balearic Isles, the Canaries and Ceuta.

Emigration data began to be collected from the year 1865, but unfortunately they are to be found only in private sources.

II. Emigration and Immigration Statistics

(Tables IV-IX)

Since 1909 the Superior Council of Emigration has compiled and published monthly statistics of intercontinental emigration, and since 1915 corresponding statistics have appeared for immigration.

The statistics of emigrant and immigrant citizens are based on information supplied by the emigration officers in the form of lists of names which are transmitted to the Superior Council after the emigrants have embarked. These lists are copied from the slips detached from the special identification papers held by the emigrants.

For the purpose of these statistics the term "emigrant" is defined as "a Spanish subject who wishes to leave Spain, and to be conveyed on payment of a fare or free of charge, in the third or in any other class recognised by the Superior Emigration Council as being equivalent thereto, to any place in America, Asia, or Oceania". The term "immigrant" is defined likewise as "anyone who returns to Spain from America, Asia, or Oceania, with a third class ticket or a ticket of an equivalent class".

Consequently, Spanish migration statistics do not include (a) persons

who emigrate to European countries or to Africa, or (b) persons who travel first or second class or even in a "superior" third class.

Statistics about the number of migrants from Spain to Argentina (1857-1924), Brazil (1850-1924), Canada (1900-24), Cuba (1902-24), Mexico (1909-24), Paraguay (1887-1906) United States (1820-1924), Uruguay (1867-1903), Australia (1902-24) and Hawaii (1911-24) will be found in the national tables for those countries. Statistics about the number of migrants returning to Spain from Argentina (1857-1924), Mexico (1911-24), United States (1908-24), Uruguay (1879-1903) and Hawaii (1912-24) will be found in the national tables for those countries.

TABLE I.—Passengers outward and inward by sea, 1882-1923.

Year	Outward	Inward	Balance outward (—) or inward (+)	Year	Outward	Inward	Balance outward (—) or inward (+)
1882	71,806	58,520	—13,286	1903	57,261	54,689	— 2,572
1883	59,261	55,360	— 3,901	1904	87,291	57,147	— 30,144
1884	42,843	38,004	— 4,839	1905	126,067	62,037	— 64,030
1885	40,316	39,720	— 596				
				1906	126,771	73,908	— 52,863
1886	62,025	57,436	— 4,589	1907	130,640	79,352	— 51,288
1887	66,979	52,827	—14,152	1908	159,137	87,775	— 71,362
1888	76,398	52,844	—23,554	1909	142,717	92,042	— 50,675
1889	125,807	53,403	—72,404	1910	191,761	99,839	— 91,922
1890	65,860	54,796	—11,064				
				1911	175,567	105,055	— 70,512
1891	68,037	62,857	— 5,180	1912	257,264	123,270	—133,994
1892	66,406	58,148	— 8,258	1913	220,399	147,746	— 72,653
1893	76,526	56,693	—19,833	1914	129,576	192,057	+ 62,481
1894	81,189	66,498	—14,691	1915	96,424	115,508	+ 19,084
1895	121,166	56,694	—64,472				
				1916	100,336	96,530	— 3,806
1896	166,269	67,405	—98,864	1917	66,028	71,192	+ 5,164
1897	73,535	82,691	+ 9,156	1918	36,254	51,131	+ 14,877
1898	59,543	137,238	+77,695	1919	107,083	87,150	— 19,933
1899	53,862	116,584	+62,722	1920	189,517	102,303	— 87,214
1900	63,020	57,382	— 5,638				
				1921	95,759	127,552	+ 31,793
1901	56,906	53,063	— 3,843	1922	93,591	86,275	— 7,316
1902	51,593	58,223	+ 6,630	1923	123,804	69,399	— 54,405

TABLE II.—PASSENGERS OUTWARD BY SEA, BY COUNTRY OF DESTINATION, 1882-1923.

Country	1882	1883	1884	1885	1886	1887	1888	1889	1890	1891	1892	1893	1894	1895	1896	1897
EUROPE:																
Austria-Hungary		1														
Belgium	3	1	3			4	13	5	9	10	2	10	22	12	5	24
Denmark	1		9													
France	1,729	1,611	669			1,000	1,012	691	327	374	300	376	390	362	491	562
Gibraltar	1,454	1,409	1,548			983	973	511	424	689	608	783	749	294	559	705
Great Britain and Ireland	854	825	536			873	951	964	1,160	1,073	1,324	1,408	1,226	1,242	1,558	1,343
Greece	4	107				34	54	38	81	29	26	23	37	47	62	22
Germany		18	28			208	707	281	303	296	295	503		271	322	134
Italy	342	236	240			6	18	3	3		7		10,523			
Netherlands	146	129	7							32	45	55	1	41	37	25
Portugal	6,358	585	237			159	178	144	757				121			
Rumania	3															
Russia	5	1				3	17	10								
Norway and Sweden			2						64	10	14	9	30	14	5	11
Turkey										1	1					
Other European countries			6			4	6	68	24	24	7	7	63	33	10	20
Total	10,899	4,923	3,285	3,446	3,195	3,274	3,929	2,715	3,152	2,523	2,628	3,175	13,161	2,316	3,049	2,846
ASIA[1]:																
Aden			2													
China																6
British India	2		2	1		2	2	9	1	2	15	0				
Turkey in Asia					5											
Total	2		4	1	5	2	2	9	1	2	15	0				6
AFRICA:																
Algeria	17,437	16,887	10,535	15,947	23,885	19,590	19,043	20,537	15,438	19,287	17,433	16,508	18,630	14,591	17,584	16,611
Fernando Po	24	23	15	39	211	81	86	49	54	38	36	15	15	21	10	10
Rio de Oro	17			144	40	165	128	128	94	66	32				98	100
Egypt	64	3	11	10	6	173	269	212	168	148	112	124	127	174	212	218
Madeira	43	53	46	54	79	318	1,111	1,137	915	1,393	1,386	1,207	1,229	845	1,133	1,215
Morocco	36	125	136	173	310	88	90	79	65	71	74	77	138	96	168	42
Other African countries		54	17	68	53											
Total	17,621	17,145	10,760	16,435	24,584	20,415	20,727	22,142	16,734	21,003	19,073	17,931	20,139	15,727	19,205	18,196

TABLE II.—PASSENGERS OUTWARD BY SEA, BY COUNTRY OF DESTINATION, 1882-1923 (continued).

Country	1882	1883	1884	1885	1886	1887	1888	1889	1890	1891	1892	1893	1894	1895	1896	1897
AMERICA:																
Brazil	2,247	1,134	533	387	332	560	2,604	7,527	5,186	10,023	3,606	11,172	4,526	10,355	11,993	8,156
Colombia	104	33	12	17	31	73	87	25	53	38	38	37	17	32	70	49
Chile	10	4	56	55	197	66	208	3,835	961	22	53	66	82	70	174	129
Ecuador	3		1	4	4											
Guatemala	10		7	3	11											
Mexico	414	1,075	1,012	493	624	696	891	1,558	1,240	1,209	1,215	1,001	953	939	1,126	1,570
Peru	240	217	22	17	7	13	51	24			5	22				
Argentina[2]	3,245	4,265	6,949	5,864	7,211	13,685	22,595	58,135	9,561	3,821	4,593	6,799	7,069	7,732	11,603	10,376
St. Thomas	241	136														
United States	57	135	259	42	9	1	37	21	19	20	40	119	43	13	11	16
Newfoundland	3		1	3	1											
Uruguay	992	1,886	1,045	1,000	1,123	1,691	1,998	3,802	1,869	788	648	672	822	982	869	673
Venezuela	516	658	110	129	139	155	198	776	1,471	765	817	362	359	330	320	257
Cuba	30,730	24,959	14,097	8,319	21,650	22,754	19,445	21,421	21,194	22,886	30,306	28,234	29,193	76,780	90,527	24,328
Porto Rico	1,897	943	1,564	2,803	980	1,839	1,776	1,716	2,662	2,876	1,531	3,734	2,733	4,251	2,587	2,694
Other American countries	12	3	13	44	11	80	99	42	69	131	158	541	105	57	54	49
Total	40,721	35,448	25,681	19,180	32,330	41,624	49,989	98,882	44,285	42,579	43,010	52,759	45,902	101,541	119,334	48,297
OCEANIA:																
Philippine Islands	2,460	1,743	3,112	1,254	1,911	1,663	1,751	2,059	1,679	1,927	1,680	2,661	1,985	1,578	24,681	4,185
Australia and New Zealand													2	4		5
Other countries	1	1							9	3						
Total	2,461	1,744	3,112	1,254	1,911	1,663	1,751	2,059	1,688	1,930	1,680	2,661	1,987	1,582	24,681	4,190
Grand total	71,806[3]	59,260	42,843[3]	40,316	62,025	66,979[3]	76,398	125,807	65,860	68,037	66,406	76,526	81,189	121,166	166,269	73,535

For reference notes see page 862.

TABLE II.—PASSENGERS OUTWARD BY SEA, BY COUNTRY OF DESTINATION, 1882-1923 (continued).

Country	1898	1899	1900	1901	1902	1903	1904	1905	1906	1907	1908	1909	1910	1911	1912	1913
EUROPE:																
Austria-Hungary	17	....	....	....	....	....	....	....	....	....	....	....	....	....	....	....
Belgium	....	15	....	....	....	....	....	....	....	....	....	....	....	....	....	3
Denmark	....	....	....	....	....	....	....	....	....	....	....	....	....	....	....	....
France	434	642	332	294	341	529	769	1,144	948	776	612	1,518	1,589	1,690	4,811	5,160
Gibraltar	543	606	578	882	824	746	870	796	836	694	572	559	1,297	79	3,426	872
Great Britain and Ireland	1,085	1,066	1,735	2,042	1,567	2,015	1,682	1,708	1,355	2,183	1,858	1,603	2,109	2,177	2,610	3,459
Greece	54	26	50	54	94	115	113	214	241	202	294	403	351	339	478	281
Germany	144	204	875	152	117	154	286	90	116	198	168	156	116	59	175	430
Italy	....	....	....	....	....	....	....	....	....	....	....	....	....	....	....	....
Netherlands	30	63	....	....	....	....	....	....	....	....	....	....	....	....	....	....
Portugal	....	....	....	....	....	....	....	....	....	....	....	....	....	....	....	....
Rumania	....	....	....	....	....	....	....	....	....	....	....	....	....	....	....	....
Russia	....	....	....	....	....	....	....	....	....	....	....	....	....	....	....	....
Turkey	....	....	....	....	....	....	....	....	....	....	....	....	....	....	....	....
Norway and Sweden	4	4	....	....	....	....	....	....	....	....	....	....	....	....	....	....
Other European countries	8	93	190	178	121	42	62	74	62	72	63	95	191	97	95	489
Total	2,319	2,719	3,760	3,602	3,064	3,601	3,782	4,026	3,558	4,125	3,567	4,334	5,653	4,441	11,595	10,694
ASIA:[1]																
Aden	2	....	....	....	....	....	....	....	....	....	....	....	....	....	....	....
China	....	....	....	....	....	....	....	....	....	....	....	....	....	....	....	....
British India	....	....	....	....	....	....	....	....	....	....	....	....	....	....	....	....
Turkey in Asia	....	....	....	....	....	....	....	....	....	....	....	....	....	....	....	....
Total	2	....	4	8	235	22	230	25	18	214	20	254	18	169	213	45
AFRICA:																
Algeria	12,851	15,448	17,020	14,668	20,171	16,482	21,301	26,453	21,723	17,726	23,596	17,468	24,560	22,825	29,928	28,269
Fernando Po	2	2	....	....	....	....	....	....	....	....	....	....	....	....	....	....
Rio de Oro	66	33	....	....	....	....	....	....	....	....	....	....	....	....	....	....
Egypt	207	78	....	....	....	....	....	....	....	....	....	....	....	....	....	....
Madeira	1,046	1,144	1,036	1,471	1,788	1,845	1,881	2,097	2,530	4,068	2,927	2,409	3,510	4,312	4,574	8,476
Morocco	42	49	623	755	638	478	280	323	383	371	443	277	328	205	224	366
Other African countries	....	....	....	....	....	....	....	....	....	....	....	....	....	....	....	....
Total	14,214	16,754	18,679	16,894	22,597	18,805	23,462	28,873	24,636	22,165	26,966	20,154	28,398	27,342	34,726	37,111

TABLE II.—PASSENGERS OUTWARD BY SEA, BY COUNTRY OF DESTINATION, 1882-1923 (continued.)

Country	1898	1899	1900	1901	1902	1903	1904	1905	1906	1907	1908	1909	1910	1911	1912	1913
AMERICA:																
Brazil	3,869	2,301	3,385	2,919	1,161	1,641	5,404	17,924	19,748	4,830	4,974	12,075	13,669	6,082	10,067	10,857
Colombia	37	251	....	....	....	....	....	....	....	....	....	....	....	....	....	....
Chile	99	75	....	....	....	....	....	....	....	....	....	....	....	....	....	....
Ecuador	....	....	....	....	....	....	....	....	....	....	....	....	....	....	....	....
Guatemala	....	....	....	....	....	....	....	....	....	....	....	....	....	....	....	....
Mexico	1,386	2,400	2,924	2,972	2,457	2,650	3,236	3,758	4,447	4,766	3,958	3,758	3,565	3,722	3,553	3,136
Peru	....	....	....	....	....	....	....	....	....	....	....	....	....	....	....	....
Argentina	12,832	10,743	13,161	11,558	9,137	14,656	29,216	33,293	48,749	58,453	91,632	71,024	103,128	94,478	154,726	110,912
St. Thomas	....	....	....	....	....	....	....	....	....	....	....	....	....	....	....	....
United States	2	278	....	....	....	....	....	....	....	....	....	....	....	....	....	....
Newfoundland	....	....	....	....	....	....	....	....	....	....	....	....	....	....	....	....
Uruguay	705	557	863	709	576	566	516	628	686	1,042	1,254	2,088	2,382	2,915	2,888	3,442
Venezuela	135	98	192	164	130	191	110	65	61	84	32	92	129	217	169	287
Cuba	21,632	16,203	18,267	16,059	10,323	12,804	19,450	35,807	21,301	22,819	19,870	23,741	28,748	31,762	34,485	37,544
Porto Rico	1,424	970	718	466	556	543	517	475	644	566	718	830	689	799	840	843
Other American countries	46	32	427	635	523	966	792	698	2,370	8,904	5,734	3,805	4,887	3,005	3,058	5,010
Total	42,167	33,908	39,937	35,482	24,863	34,017	59,241	92,648	98,006	101,464	128,172	117,413	157,197	143,080	209,786	172,031
OCEANIA:																
Philippine Islands	831	297	640	907	830	813	575	487	550	456	398	547	471	535	541	566
Australia and New Zealand	10	184	....	....	....	....	....	....	....	....	....	....	24	....	9	....
Other countries	....	....	....	13	....	3	1	8	3	2,216	14	15	....	....	....	1
Total	841	481	640	920	834	816	576	495	553	2,672	412	562	495	535	550	567
Grand total	59,543	53,862	63,020	56,906	51,593	57,261	87,291	126,067	126,771	130,640	159,137	142,717	191,761	175,567	257,264[3]	220,399[3]

For reference notes see page 862.

TABLE II.—PASSENGERS OUTWARD BY SEA, BY COUNTRY OF DESTINATION, 1882-1923 (continued).

Country	1914	1915	1916	1917	1918	1919	1920	1921	1922	1923
EUROPE:										
Germany	355	3	....	....	....	810	137	155	430	894
Belgium	11	....	....	....	....	16	24	7	11	....
France	4,520	6,155	6,100	148	3	46	69	794	679	797
Gibraltar	108	23	2	....	3	17	2	6	6	7
Great Britain	3,290	963	1,123	73	9	1,279	708	557	559	773
Italy	2,916	1,462	154	261	457	5,499	5,174	1,837	511	617
Portugal	229	23	15	....	....	93	108	50	89	268
Other European countries	442	260	466	128	89	1,493	209	162	105	65
Total	11,871	8,889	7,860	610	561	9,253	6,431	3,568	2,430	3,421
ASIA:	24	46	96	18	17	85	103	99	8	28
AFRICA:										
Algeria	19,381	13,052	7,564	198	4	5,812	8,624	5,901	6,944	5,913
Egypt	74	60	99	3	10	41	23	33	17	9
Morocco	8,242	7,230	5,625	5,428	5,025	3,860	5,206	6,135	6,411	6,397
Spanish colonies	127	143	154	184	90	162	117	108	224	256
Other African countries	186	2	3	55	4	94	96	58	114	54
Total	28,010	20,487	13,445	5,868	5,133	9,969	14,066	12,235	13,710	12,629
AMERICA:										
Argentina	48,343	25,313	22,894	14,437	11,278	24,942	39,760	40,247	42,137	41,720
Brazil	5,764	2,574	2,409	1,442	909	2,504	3,127	2,524	2,004	1,533
Colombia	441	133	110	157	67	139	179	172	138	95
Costa Rica	125	33	2	1	....	1	....	6	....	....
Cuba	24,572	32,137	42,599	32,874	15,460	49,770	99,487	26,163	24,111	47,689
Chile	311	45	48	....	....	118	187	127	169	258
United States	3,017	2,061	5,579	5,883	979	2,655	18,575	1,411	510	185
Mexico	2,030	1,170	2,052	2,699	413	2,184	2,144	4,617	3,614	3,279
Panama	382	408	369	287	77	213	297	347	280	152
Porto Rico	988	811	723	422	241	527	898	866	500	314
Uruguay	2,475	1,537	1,392	927	832	4,078	3,387	2,407	3,329	3,081
Venezuela	305	234	144	141	113	298	335	278	183	137
Other American countries	440	54	53	25	14	41	48	118	114	210
Total	89,193	66,510	78,374	59,295	30,383	87,469	168,425	79,283	77,089	98,653

TABLE II.—PASSENGERS OUTWARD BY SEA, BY COUNTRY OF DESTINATION, 1882-1923 (concluded).

Country	1914	1915	1916	1917	1918	1919	1920	1921	1922	1923
OCEANIA:										
Philippine Islands........	478	492	561	237	160	307	492	574	354	213
Other Pacific islands	.....	.....	.....	.....	.....	.....	.....	.....	.....	.....
Total.........	478	492	561	237	160	307	492	574	354	213
Grand total.........	129,576	96,424	100,336	66,028	36,254	107,083	189,517	95,759	93,591	114,944

TABLE III.—PASSENGERS INWARD BY SEA, BY COUNTRY OF ORIGIN, 1882-99 AND 1914-23.

Country	1882	1883	1884	1885	1886	1887	1888	1889	1890	1891	1892	1893	1894	1895	1896	1897	1898	1899
EUROPE:																		
Austria-Hungary	13	2	1															
Belgium	50	18	183			78	120	72	39	37	23	30	28	64	102	118	109	85
Denmark	3																	
France	10,569	5,933	3,232			5,247	5,825	4,346	3,541	4,221	2,634	1,610	1,399	2,044	2,755	3,204	2,637	2,083
Gibraltar	4,151	3,172	2,327			2,124	1,502	1,668	1,222	1,899	1,911	1,963	1,594	1,013	1,046	790	404	551
Great Britain and Ireland	1,525	833	1,022			1,622	2,386	2,388	2,514	2,623	2,464	2,085	2,105	2,430	2,496	2,171	2,228	2,074
Greece	49	108	81			69	177	131	88	140	67	52	67	133	84	63	73	75
Germany	558	46	474			382	1,451	1,212	717	1,055	981	819	8,753	1,786	1,965	1,815	1,400	1,423
Italy	142	468	35															
Netherlands	239	4	87															
Portugal		197	1			90	107	112	96	109	95	98	101	68	96	22	21	158
Rumania																		
Russia	7																	
Norway and Sweden	35	44	7			33	37	11	27	15	23	42	35	32	17	19	24	12
Turkey	1	2	6			14	166	105	8	13								
Other European countries									38	29	62	9	55	38	21	41	37	94
Total	17,342	10,827	7,456	7,946	9,740	9,690	11,791	10,062	8,318	10,171	8,334	6,717	14,137	7,608	8,582	8,243	6,933	6,555
ASIA:																		
China	6												4	4	2	2		
British India	8	1	1						1	2	2						78	
Turkey in Asia																		
Total	14	1	1						1	2	2		4	4	2	2	78	
AFRICA:																		
Algeria	20,191	19,568	11,867	13,660	23,937	18,572	19,245	19,232	15,661	18,107	18,289	20,765	20,736	15,686	16,451	15,523	14,932	15,139
Cape Verde	65	41	38	72	235	61	68	54	85	45	111	8	16	126	135	301	314	224
Fernando Po	96				103	159	128	96	94	96			29		98	98	67	35
Rio de Oro					14													
Egypt	15	1	8															
Madeira	68	109	71	110	126	205	153	175	163	166	162	180	124	100	202	250	138	173
Morocco	143	364	367	102	811	1,201	1,281	1,691	1,635	1,755	1,887	1,478	1,542	1,171	1,490	1,510	1,152	1,301
Other African countries	14	93	28	469	100	230	96	98	141	135	234	254	309	273	239	241	203	256
Total	20,592	20,176	12,379	14,413	25,326	20,428	20,971	21,346	17,779	20,304	20,683	22,685	22,756	17,356	18,615	17,925	16,806	17,128

TABLE III.—PASSENGERS INWARD BY SEA, BY COUNTRY OF ORIGIN, 1882-99 AND 1914-23 (continued).

Country	1882	1883	1884	1885	1886	1887	1888	1889	1890	1891	1892	1893	1894	1895	1896	1897	1898	1899
AMERICA:																		
Brazil	2	48	76	176	219	220	593	628	675	1,078	1,404	1,017	1,195	1,057	1,356	1,510	1,177	1,718
Colombia	78	25	33	44	33	53	72	68	37	97	38	20	24	33	31	16	18	25
Chile		11		3	5	12	18	22	14	34	41	26	16	29	42	48	61	38
Ecuador				5														
Guatemala				2														
Mexico	384	264	876	351	338	320	579	658	717	689	703	613	529	591	571	689	949	891
Peru		6		1	3		6	8			2	18						
La Plata (Argentina)[2]	1,260	1,307	1,080	1,168	1,484	2,430	3,007	5,034	7,199	7,860	5,682	4,673	4,023	3,187	4,141	6,240	5,204	8,429
St. Thomas			6	8		3	1											
United States	69	25	97	23	46	16	77	90	28	38	47	144	31	20	4	21	1,762	6
Newfoundland	2	1	3	2	4													
Uruguay	181	297	232	346	739	980	1,003	1,495	2,595	2,748	1,848	1,444	1,266	834	1,372	1,582	1,124	1,332
Venezuela	24	128	108	229	86	143	201	196	206	397	610	182	500	537	358	341	236	427
Cuba	16,481	19,710	12,870	11,984	14,177	15,626	11,213	10,200	13,552	15,980	14,952	15,168	18,180	21,894	28,367	37,273	85,846	63,712
Porto Rico	881	1,263	1,206	1,576	2,574	1,203	1,304	1,985	1,780	1,419	1,713	2,081	1,791	1,523	1,685	1,536	9,818	2,066
Other American countries	10				2	20	31	37	50	43	27	15	41	56	29	39	92	124
Total	19,372	23,085	16,587	15,918	19,710	21,026	18,105	20,421	26,853	30,383	27,067	25,401	27,596	29,761	37,956	49,295	106,287	78,768
OCEANIA:																		
Philippine Islands	1,198	1,232	1,581	1,442	2,660	1,680	1,970	1,570	1,837	1,995	2,029	1,883	1,999	1,967	2,248	7,205	7,134	14,110
Australia and New Zealand				1									6	2	2			
Other countries	2	3							8	2						20		23
Total	1,200	1,235	1,581	1,443	2,660	1,680	1,970	1,570	1,845	1,997	2,029	1,883	2,005	1,969	2,250	7,225	7,134	14,133
Grand total	58,520	55,360	38,004	39,720	57,436	52,827[3]	52,844[3]	53,403[3]	54,796	62,857	58,148[3]	56,693[3]	66,498	56,694	67,405	82,691	137,238	116,584

For reference notes see page 862.

TABLE III.—PASSENGERS INWARD BY SEA, BY COUNTRY OF ORIGIN, 1882-99 AND 1914-23 (concluded).

Country	1914	1915	1916	1917	1918	1919	1920	1921	1922	1923
EUROPE:										
Germany	544	10	23	4	.....	371	389	413	1,011	2,109
Belgium	160	76	4	2	1	6	24	25	36	48
France	11,584	3,392	2,813	1,787	653	776	387	2,182	1,370	1,471
Gibraltar	357	433	140	38	24	90	73	211	241	499
Great Britain	4,057	1,019	1,168	228	26	1,099	1,469	1,263	1,244	1,311
Italy	4,893	2,086	557	141	755	2,969	4,505	2,183	808	1,004
Portugal	363	131	102	175	19	377	105	111	116	234
Other European countries	536	389	291	47	35	416	318	291	120	177
Total	22,494	7,536	5,098	2,422	1,513	6,104	7,270	6,679	4,946	6,853
ASIA:	54	27	118	34	.....	65	54	17	27	10
AFRICA:										
Algeria	34,386	12,328	7,891	339	96	4,931	8,742	6,917	6,528	5,727
Egypt	56	130	262	15	16	2	41	41	33	7
Morocco	15,380	14,850	11,334	9,285	6,697	5,964	6,911	8,297	9,197	8,155
Spanish colonies	70	242	1,147	420	296	345	280	292	295	208
Other African countries	1,029	396	201	112	4	242	523	438	434	316
Total	50,921	27,946	20,835	10,171	7,109	11,484	16,497	15,985	16,487	14,413
AMERICA:										
Argentina	67,635	43,539	36,083	27,538	19,285	22,368	29,840	17,612	19,523	17,046
Brazil	9,916	5,412	4,400	3,002	1,573	2,983	2,972	2,100	2,618	2,459
Colombia	185	153	194	165	98	276	323	222	156	152
Costa Rica	86	26	16						13	9
Cuba	23,460	20,051	20,463	18,726	15,957	32,360	34,962	60,627	31,953	14,901
Chile	188	72	103	14	14	11	81	127	188	294
United States	3,249	2,327	2,231	4,051	2,490	5,870	3,358	17,938	4,124	1,981
Mexico	4,337	3,174	2,410	2,188	976	2,120	1,932	3,013	3,152	2,199
Panama	1,133	569	477	289	155	538	513	285	188	164
Porto Rico	767	697	684	518	355	974	1,421	669	569	389
Uruguay	6,641	3,186	2,495	1,617	1,400	1,504	1,566	1,217	1,369	1,169
Venezuela	362	275	320	279	166	315	433	270	277	286
Other American countries	120	60	62	44	8	56	241	248	313	254
Total	118,079	79,541	69,938	58,417	42,477	69,375	77,642	104,328	64,443	41,303
OCEANIA:										
Philippine Islands	537	457	516	148	32	122	840	543	372	277
Other Pacific islands	3	1	25	.....	.....	.....	.....	.....	.....	7
Total	540	458	541	148	32	122	840	543	372	284
Grand total	192,088	115,508	96,530	71,192	51,131	87,150	102,303	127,552	86,275	62,863

TABLE IV.—DISTRIBUTION OF EMIGRANTS TO EXTRA-EUROPEAN COUNTRIES, BY SEX AND AGE, 1909-24.

Year	Total	Males	Females	Up to 15 years		15 to 23 years		over 23 years	
				Males	Females	Males	Females	Males	Females
1909	111,058	......	......	....	....	....	....	....	....
1910	160,936	113,879	47,057	....	....	....	....	....	....
1911	139,683			....	....	....	.!..	....	....
1912	194,443	139,999	54,444	....	....	....	....	....	....
1913	151,000	105,864	45,136	....	....	....	....	....	....
1914	66,596	45,279	21,317	....	....	....	....	....	...
1915	50,359	36,420	13,939	....	....	....	....	....	....
1916	62,247			....	....	....	....	....	....
1917	43,051	33,860	9,191	....	....	....	....	....	....
1918	20,168	14,562	5,606	2,010	1,231	6,037	1,539	6,515	2,836
1919	69,472	52,452	17,020	5,876	3,362	20,855	4,534	25,721	9,124
1920	150,566	121,031	29,535	7,939	5,127	46,857	8,556	66,235	15,852
1921	62,527	42,543	19,984	....	....	....	....	....	....
1922	64,119	42,356	21,763	4,313	3,283	15,774	6,438	22,269	12,042
1923	93,246	66,002	27,244	....	....	....	....	....	....
1924	86,920	60,198	26,722	....	....	....	....	....	....

TABLE V.—DISTRIBUTION OF EMIGRANTS TO EXTRA-EUROPEAN COUNTRIES, BY OCCUPATION, 1920-22.

Occupation	1920	1921	1922
Agriculture.................................	20,859	6,133	9,976
Industry and mining........................	3,464	1,711	2,028
Transport and commerce....................	3,905	2,660	2,538
Domestic service and general labor.........	85,407	28,438	24,412
Liberal professions and public services......	106	122	91
Other occupations, none, or unknown.........	36,835	23,415	25,074
Total............................	150,576[4]	62,479	64,119

For reference notes see page 862.

TABLE VI.—INTERCONTINENTAL EMIGRATION, BY COUNTRY OF DESTINATION, 1909-24.

Country	1909	1910	1911	1912	1913	1914	1915	1916	1917	1918	1919	1920	1921	1922	1923	1924
Argentina	69,110	109,415	96,009	147,640	101,636	38,515	19,283	17,722	8,677	6,373	20,351	35,227	35,688	39,193	41,716	40,784
Dutch West Indies		1														
Brazil	13,409	14,514	6,831	9,641	9,075	4,070	1,899	1,809	868	622	2,110	2,657	2,119	1,903	1,709	1,622
Canada			6	72										26		
Colombia	11	38	71	8	48	34	14									
Costa Rica	622	1,416	803	304	307	46	9	19	24	5	6	20				
Cuba	20,960	27,542	28,938	29,386	31,989	19,048	26,476	36,730	28,251	11,869	40,427	90,417	19,328	18,062	44,275	39,500
Chile	1,255	1,755	726	770	602	275	25	38			84	148		140		
Ecuador	3	1	4	6	4	1		1			7	6				
United States	660	1,064	714	1,013	2,185	1,727	842	3,675	3,772	613	1,604	17,623	611	60		
Guatemala	4	5	2	2		1										
Haiti		1				1										
British India		2														
Jamaica	2,457	2,264	2,155	2,051	1,541	818	434	966	954	162	703	910		1,538	1,671	958
Mexico		1	1	1		1										
Nicaragua			4	4	110	114	110	88	28	4	17	35		110		
Panama	40	34	8	19	43	18	2	8	2		2	3		10		
Peru	39	41	118	23	10	119	128	138	78	34	56	98		6		
Philippines	217	226	287	185	146	14										
Porto Rico	16	3	23	15	61											
Dominican Republic		2	3	2	1	1										
Salvador	2,198	2,501	2,859	3,186	3,139	1,685	1,044	1,010	350	469	3,937	3,131	2,329	3,030	3,515	3,587
Uruguay	56	110	91	115	103	108	93	43	47	17	168	291	2,452	39		
Venezuela														2	360	469
Other countries																
	111,058	160,936	139,683	194,443	151,000	66,596	50,359	62,247	43,051	20,168	69,472	150,566	62,527	64,119	93,246	86,920

TABLE VII.—Distribution of immigrants from extra-European countries, by sex and age, 1916-24.

Year	Total	Males	Females	Up to 15 years	15 to 40 years	over 40 years
1916	46,423	35,553	10,870	6,256	29,895	10,272
1917	37,701	.....	.....	.....	.....	.....
1918	28,406	22,813	5,593	3,248	17,969	7,189
1919	47,175	37,207	9,968	6,249	29,231	11,695
1920	46,534	35,599	10,935	6,914	27,550	12,070
1921	71,966	62,551	9,415	.....	.....	.....
1922	50,144	39,107	11,037	.....	.....	.....
1923	32,081	23,610	8,471	.....	.....	.....
1924	36,499	28,095	8,404	.....	.....	.....

TABLE VIII.—Distribution of immigrants from extra-European countries, by occupation, 1920-22.

Occupation	1920	1921	1922
Agriculture	1,482	669	2,936
Industry and mining	1,011	1,120	1,192
Transport and commerce	3,370	3,625	2,783
Domestic service and general labor	28,607	57,865	30,072
Liberal professions and public services	79	77	70
Other occupations, none, or unknown	11,985	13,083	14,044
Total	46,534	76,439	51,097

TABLE IX.—Intercontinental immigration, by country of origin, 1916-24.

Country of origin	1916	1917	1918	1919	1920	1921	1922	1923	1924
Argentina	27,026	19,320	13,085	15,346	19,194	10,540	15,581	14,639	14,501
Dutch West Indies	9	1	.....	2	.....	.....	.....	.....	.....
Brazil	2,838	1,667	222	1,756	2,297	1,605	2,359	2,052	1,958
Colombia	26	12	15	8	15	.....	.....	.....	.....
Costa Rica	7	.....	.....	.....	.....	.....	.....	.....	.....
Cuba	12,731	13,410	12,315	25,192	21,164	49,993	26,590	12,079	15,070
Chile	8	.....	.....	.....	3	.....	.....	.....	.....
Ecuador	.....	.....	.....	.....	8	.....	.....	.....	.....
United States	1,015	1,497	1,524	2,979	1,966	8,304	2,818	.....	.....
Mexico	569	579	292	534	433	.....	.....	.....	.....
Panama	126	82	63	119	95	.....	.....	.....	.....
Peru	.....	.....	.....	.....	2	.....	.....	.....	.....
Philippines	.....	.....	.....	.....	3	.....	.....	.....	.....
Porto Rico	116	84	48	141	104	.....	.....	.....	.....
Uruguay	1,828	957	797	1,024	1,172	788	1,087	1,022	1,010
Venezuela	124	92	45	74	78	.....	.....	.....	.....
Other countries	.....	.....	.....	.....	.....	736	1,709	2,289	3,960
Total	46,423	37,701	28,406	47,175	46,534	71,966	50,144	32,081	36,499

SOURCES

Estadistica de Pasageros por Mar, 1919. Madrid, 1923 (p. 9). (Published by the Statistical Department.)

Tables I (years 1882-1919); II and III (totals).

Annuario Estadistico de España, 6th year (1919) and 10th year (1923-24). Madrid, 1921 (p. 42) and 1925 (pp. 56-59).

Tables I, II and III (years 1914-23).

Boletin de la Dirección General de Emigración, First year, No. 1. Madrid, 1925, pp. 200-1.

Tables IV-VI (years 1923-24).

Information supplied by the Emigration Department.

Tables IV-VII, also II and III (years 1882-1913).

Statistica della Emigrazione italiana all' Estero, published by the Italian Statistical Department for the years: 1884-85 (p. LXV), 1891 (p. 46), 1895 (p. 117), 1897 (p. 115) 1898-99 (p. 126), 1900-01 (p. 78), 1902-03 (p. 122), 1904-05 (p. 128), 1906-07 (p. 139), 1908-09 (p-135), 1910-11 (p. 141), 1912-13 (pp. 143, 147).

Tables II and III (years 1882-1913).

Resumen de la Migración espannola in 1920, 1921 and 1922. Madrid, 1923 and 1924 (Published by the Consejo superior de Emigración.)

Tables V and VIII (years 1920-22).

NOTES

[1] The Philippine Islands are included in Oceania.
[2] For 1882-84, called La Plata; later, Argentina.
[3] Does not agree with the totals by country.
[4] In the source the total is given as 150,566.

BULGARIA

Statistics about the number of migrants from Bulgaria to Argentina (1921-24), Canada (1901-24), Cuba (1912-24) and the United States (1899-1924) will be found in the national tables for those countries. Statistics about the number of migrants returning to Bulgaria from the United States (1908-24) will be found in the national tables for the latter country.

TABLE I.—Permanent emigration by families and by persons, classified by sex and age, 1893-1902.

Age	Sex	1893	1894	1895	1896	1897	1898	1899	1900	1901	1902
Number of families		2,509	1,926	1,195	492	658	2,031	1,949	1,813	2,029	1,997
Number of persons		11,619	8,932	5,244	2,044	2,908	6,955	7,672	7,790	9,495	9,865
	Males	5,861	4,487	2,586	1,019	1,438	3,790	4,031	3,936	4,655	4,817
	Females	5,758	4,445	2,658	1,025	1,470	3,165	3,641	3,854	4,840	5,048
Up to 15 years	Males	2,861	2,205	1,285	480	651	1,515	1,709	1,715	2,136	2,252
	Females	2,502	1,886	1,199	421	629	1,829	1,560	1,570	2,028	2,058
15 to 20 years	Males	405	273	149	68	103	314	369	374	421	444
	Females	435	318	180	69	91	230	296	332	433	493
20 to 25 years	Males	213	185	82	38	47	224	210	162	205	164
	Females	381	267	149	66	75	187	196	225	311	334
25 to 30 years	Males	357	207	131	59	90	310	279	232	240	247
	Females	417	312	182	78	115	242	260	264	297	316
30 to 40 years	Males	647	483	292	107	186	486	494	422	490	485
	Females	727	605	335	150	216	416	434	446	560	525
40 to 50 years	Males	582	497	285	126	166	430	401	372	453	409
	Females	563	472	295	105	148	325	380	343	466	486
50 to 60 years	Males	454	390	205	86	101	274	302	303	346	395
	Females	399	303	174	75	101	219	275	332	360	434
60 to 70 years	Males	223	162	91	38	63	159	196	223	246	294
	Females	199	136	78	38	51	138	151	187	236	256
70 to 80 years	Males	64	42	23	11	21	42	50	47	76	85
	Females	85	72	28	19	29	50	47	75	107	104
80 years and over	Males	28	17	13	6	8	29	12	20	24	24
	Females	21	26	17	4	15	21	32	35	35	29
Age unknown	Males	27	26	30	……	2	7	9	66	18	18
	Females	29	48	21	……	……	8	10	45	7	13

TABLE II.—DISTRIBUTION OF PERMANENT EMIGRANTS, BY SEX AND OCCUPATION, 1893-1902.

Year	Agriculture, etc.		Mining and quarrying		Industry		Transport and communications		Commerce		Other occupations	
	Males	Females	Males	Females	Males	Females	Males	Females	Males	Females	Males	Females
1893	5,345	5,173	1	.	162	155	67	60	67	53	219	317
1894	3,863	3,806	.	.	215	194	64	53	22	24	323	365
1895	2,130	2,190	2	.	145	123	32	30	68	73	209	242
1896	771	780	.	1	98	96	20	18	36	35	94	95
1897	1,202	1,244	.	.	93	90	26	26	37	38	80	72
1898	2,723	2,715	11	.	431	192	62	41	80	79	483	142
1899	3,216	3,282	13	.	321	168	38	17	68	45	375	129
1900	3,360	3,499	8	.	220	144	21	15	34	25	293	171
1901	4,240	4,554	1	.	137	91	55	37	27	27	196	131
1902	4,349	4,644	.	2	191	144	37	32	43	24	196	202

TABLE III.—DISTRIBUTION OF PERMANENT EMIGRANTS, BY SEX, RELIGION AND COUNTRY OF DESTINATION, 1893-1902.

Year	Religion	Turkey Males	Turkey Females	Serbia Males	Serbia Females	Rumania Males	Rumania Females	Austria-Hungary Males	Austria-Hungary Females	Other countries Males	Other countries Females
1893	Orthodox Greek	30	23	59	47	15	7	4	2	2	2
	Jewish	1									
	Mohammedan	5,739	5,665			2	6				
	Catholic	1	1					2	2		
	Protestant					6	3				
	Total	5,771	5,689	59	47	23	16	6	4	2	2
1894	Orthodox Greek	39	39	14	13	10	8	5		17	
	Mohammedan	4,375	4,360	1	1	7	3				
	Jewish	7	15			6	2				
	Armenian Gregorian	1	1								
	Catholic			3	3			1		1	
	Total	4,422	4,415	18	17	23	13	6		18	
1895	Orthodox Greek	44	34	36	21	18	13	2	1	11	5
	Mohammedan	2,437	2,558	5		3	3				
	Jewish	8	10	1	4		1				
	Catholic	3	1	4	1	2	4	11	2	1	
	Total	2,492	2,603	46	26	23	21	13	3	12	5
1896	Orthodox Greek	14	4	11	12	16	5	3	2	6	
	Mohammedan	932	968			6	4				
	Jewish	12	15			1	1	2	2		
	Catholic		1					12	10	4	1
	Total	958	988	11	12	23	10	17	14	10	1

TABLE III.—DISTRIBUTION OF PERMANENT EMIGRANTS, BY SEX, RELIGION AND COUNTRY OF DESTINATION, 1893-1902 (continued).

Year	Religion	Turkey		Serbia		Rumania		Austria-Hungary		Other countries	
		Males	Females	Males	Females	Males	Females	Males	Females	Males	Females
1897	Orthodox Greek	21	17	20	22	12	19	1	2	3	1
	Mohammedan	1,362	1,392	1	..	1	3	..	..	..	..
	Jewish	1	2	..	..	3	2	..	..	..	..
	Armenian Gregorian	3	1	1	1	1	2	..	..	1	1
	Catholic	1	1	..	..	1	1	..	..	3	2
	Protestant	..	..	..	..	..	..	..	..	2	1
	Total	1,388	1,413	22	23	18	27	1	2	9	5
1898	Orthodox Greek	565	40	81	28	58	19	17	11	21	3
	Mohammedan	2,972	3,006	..	..	5	8	..	..	..	..
	Jewish	26	17	2	1	..	1	2	1	..	..
	Armenian Gregorian	9	5	7	7	2	1	15	11	6	4
	Catholic	..	..	..	..	..	..	1	..	1	2
	Protestant	..	..	..	..	..	..	..	..	..	..
	Total	3,572	3,068	90	36	65	29	35	23	28	9
1899	Orthodox Greek	346	20	65	24	31	12	10	2	25	9
	Mohammedan	3,412	3,477	1	5	3	5	..	..	..	..
	Jewish	51	33	2	1	..	..	6	3	11	..
	Armenian Gregorian	1	3	..	..	1	..	..	..	..	4
	Catholic	7	3	9	8	3	3	28	23	14	5
	Protestant	1	..	..	..	..	..	1	..	3	1
	Total	3,818	3,536	77	38	38	20	45	28	53	19

TABLE III.—DISTRIBUTION OF PERMANENT EMIGRANTS, BY SEX, RELIGION AND COUNTRY OF DESTINATION, 1893-1902 (concluded).

Year	Religion	Turkey		Serbia		Rumania		Austria-Hungary		Other countries	
		Males	Females	Males	Females	Males	Females	Males	Females	Males	Females
1900	Orthodox Greek	162	18	102	69	34	12	3	1	27	13
	Mohammedan	3,514	3,673			5	10				
	Jewish	18	13	2	2	1	2	4	1		
	Armenian Gregorian	5	2				1			3	
	Catholic	4	7	7	7	6	3	28	15	7	4
	Protestant	1				1				2	1
	Total	3,704	3,713	111	78	47	28	35	17	39	18
1901	Orthodox Greek	110	9	28	21	8	4	2	2	14	3
	Mohammedan	4,452	4,763			12	7				
	Jewish			2	2		3	5	6		
	Armenian Gregorian		1			4	1				
	Catholic	1		3	4	3		5	10	2	1
	Protestant	1	2	1	1	1				1	
	Total	4,564	4,775	34	28	28	15	12	18	17	4
1902	Orthodox Greek	56	1	31	21	20	2	1		7	8
	Mohammedan	4,662	4,968				1				
	Jewish	6	6			1	3	1	2	3	5
	Armenian Gregorian	3	7			2	2			6	1
	Catholic	2	3	3	3	3	2	4	9	6	3
	Protestant						1				
	Total	4,729	4,985	34	24	26	11	6	11	22	17

SOURCE

Statistique de l'émigration de la Principauté, dans des pays étrangers, 1893-1902.

Sofia, 1905.

Tables I-III

GREECE

Statistics about the number of migrants from Greece to Palestine (1924), Argentina (1921-24), Brazil (1908-24), Canada (1900-24), Cuba (1902-24), United States (1824-1924) and Australia (1902-24) will be found in the national tables for those countries. Statistics about the number of migrants returning to Greece from the United States (1908-24) will be found in the national tables for the latter country.

TABLE I.—INTERCONTINENTAL EMIGRATION OF CITIZENS, 1913, 1920-21.

Year	Total
1913	38,077
1920	12,243
1921	4,142

TABLE II.—DISTRIBUTION OF EMIGRANTS, BY SEX, NATIONALITY AND COUNTRY OF DESTINATION, 1923.

Destination	Greek subjects			Aliens		
	Total	Males	Females	Total	Males	Females
North America.............	6,422	2,759	3,663	1,439	1,102	337
South America.............	464	392	72	132	94	38
Canada...................	277	206	71	77	50	27
Australia.................	722	539	183	62	40	22
India....................	37	21	16	47	29	18
Europe and North African littoral...............	7,355	4,535	2,820	2,372	1,520	852
Total..............	15,277[1]	8,452	6,825	4,129	2,835	1,294

SOURCES

Conférence internationale de l'Emigration et de l'Immigration. Rome, May 15-31, 1924. Italian Commissariat-General for Emigration, Rome, 1924, p. 453.

Table I (years 1913, 1920-21).

Information supplied by the Government.

Table II (year 1923).

NOTE

[1]The information gives 15,077 as total; the sum of the different countries, however, is 15,277.

MALTA

There are annual figures of emigration for the fiscal years 1911 to 1915. A summary for 1910-18 is given in note 2.

The Malta Emigration Department, which now compiles the statistics on the basis of the applications for passports was established in October 1919. Accurate emigration data are available from November 11, 1918.

The figures are for British subjects born in Malta and Gozo, except tourists and travellers.

TABLE I.—DISTRIBUTION OF MALTESE EMIGRANTS, BY SEX, AGE, OCCUPATION AND COUNTRY OF DESTINATION, 1911-12—1924-25

Year[1]		Total	Australia	Barbary States	Canada	Egypt	France	British Isles	United States	Other countries
1911-12		658	223	391	44	....	....	....	....	....
1912-13		1,755	365	876	514	....	....	....	....	....
1913-14		1,568	433	493	642	....	....	....	....	....
1914-15		550	215	315	20	....	....	....	....	....
1915-16		775	216	541	18	....	....	....	....	....
1918-20[2]	Men: Skilled	....	6	319	310	380	397	155	1,310	9
	Men: Unskilled	....	14	303	206	9	642	28	375	1
	Total	4,464	20	622	516	389	1,039	183	1,685	10
	Women	576	8	221	48	72	28	23	176	....
	Children	561	16	205	47	72	25	19	177	....
	Total	5,601	44	1,048	611	533	1,092	225	2 038	10
1920-21	Men: Skilled	3,450	71	567	24	551	286	153	1,540	258
	Men: Unskilled	1,646	140	571	25	6	139	32	719	14
	Total	5,096	211	1,138	49	557	425	185	2,259	272
	Women	545	23	179	32	23	16	10	258	4
	Children	545	44	141	44	41	20	3	251	1
	Total	6,186	278	1,458	125	621	461	198	2,768	277
1921-22	Men: Skilled	1,583	108	443	13	191	260	187	29	352
	Men: Unskilled	544	277	190	7	7	53	7	1	2
	Total	2,127	385	633	20	198	313	194	30	354
	Women	242	30	96	8	35	10	19	20	24
	Children	216	44	75	11	22	4	15	24	21
	Total	2,585	459	804	39	255	327	228	74	399
1922-23	Men: Skilled	1,737	65	419	49	238	255	166	41	504
	Men: Unskilled	896	303	243	38	7	288	6	7	4
	Total	2,633	368	662	87	245	543	172	48	508
	Women	247	17	130	21	24	20	13	13	9
	Children	254	21	119	19	33	24	13	16	9
	Total	3,134	406	911	127	302	587	198	77	526

For reference notes see page 874.

TABLE I.—DISTRIBUTION OF MALTESE EMIGRANTS, BY SEX, AGE, OCCUPATION AND COUNTRY OF DESTINATION, 1911-12—1924-25 (concluded).

Year [1] [2]		Total	Australia	Barbary States	Canada	Egypt	France	British Isles	United States	Other countries
1923-24	Men: Skilled.........	1,822	87	286	16	121	271	209	49	783
	Unskilled.........	996	319	179	133	25	214	55	13	58
	Total.........	2,818	406	465	149	146	485	264	62	841
	Women.........	283	30	127	22	25	39	21	10	9
	Children.........	306	34	122	20	27	65	8	19	11
	Total.........	3,407	470	714	191	198	589	293	91	861
1924-25	Men: Skilled.........	1,780	129	296	15	128	242	283	63	624
	Unskilled.........	956	482	186	7	2	213	31	18	17
	Total.........	2,736	611	482	22	130	455	314	81	641
	Women.........	286	38	108	15	32	15	17	49	12
	Children.........	255	43	67	2	44	24	9	58	8
	Total.........	3,277	692	657	39	206	494	340	188	661

For reference notes see page 874.

TABLE II.—DISTRIBUTION OF MALTESE IMMIGRANTS, BY SEX AGE, OCCUPATION AND COUNTRY OF LAST RESIDENCE, 1920-21—1924-25

Year[1]		Total	Australia	Barbary States	Canada	Egypt	France	British Isles	United States	Other countries
1920-21	Men: Skilled...	2,409	...	...	...	...	...	...	...	...
	Unskilled...	1,118	...	...	...	...	...	...	...	...
	Total...	3,527	...	...	...	...	...	...	...	...
	Women...	149	...	...	...	...	...	...	...	...
	Children...	162	...	...	...	...	...	...	...	...
	Total...	3,838	...	...	...	...	...	...	...	...
1921-22	Men: Skilled...	2,242	13	441	33	315	139	371	538	392
	Unskilled...	759	75	259	47	12	72	17	255	22
	Total...	3,001	88	700	80	327	211	388	793	414
	Women...	231	1	93	3	90	4	2	19	19
	Children...	290	1	111	1	142	4	6	13	12
	Total...	3,522	90	904	84	559	219	396	825	445
1922-23	Men: Skilled...	1,594	17	480	17	156	77	220	105	522
	Unskilled...	599	92	323	6	17	71	11	45	34
	Total...	2,193	109	803	23	173	148	231	150	556
	Women...	157	2	105	...	17	5	8	8	12
	Children...	184	4	118	...	32	5	7	12	6
	Total...	2,534	115	1,026	23	222	158	246	170	574
1923-24	Men: Skilled...	1,893	15	460	31	173	75	215	91	833
	Unskilled...	635	37	350	11	12	123	19	43	40
	Total...	2,528	52	810	42	185	198	234	134	873
	Women...	127	1	80	...	14	3	7	8	14
	Children...	170	...	97	...	33	2	10	11	17
	Total...	2,825	53	987	42	232	203	251	153	904
1924-25	Men: Skilled...	1,713	27	426	41	150	80	177	166	646
	Unskilled...	603	94	210	54	13	117	5	84	26
	Total...	2,316	121	636	95	163	197	182	250	672
	Women...	115	...	68	4	3	13	1	9	17
	Children...	169	...	99	3	7	21	2	13	24
	Total...	2,600	121	803	102	173	231	185	272	713

For reference notes see page 874.

SOURCES

Colonial Reports (Annual).   Malta.   London, 1914-16.

Table I (years 1911/12-1915/16).

Information supplied by the British Government (Ministry of Labor).

Table I (years 1918-20).

Reports on Emigration.   Malta, 1921-25.

Tables I, II (years 1920/21-1924/25).

NOTES

[1]Fiscal years ending March 31.
[2]Return showing the number of persons who left Malta in the years 1910-18 for countries to which it may be assumed that they went in order to acquire domicile, and who may therefore be classed as emigrants

Australia	1,862	France	1,533
Barbary States	1,949	South America	59
Canada	1,807	United States	1,109
Egypt	1,124		
		Total	9,443

Information supplied by the British Government.
[3]From November 11, 1918 to March 31, 1920.

RUMANIA

In a letter of January 15,1926, the Director-General of the National Statistical Department gave information about Rumanian pre-war migration statistics. He wrote: "Aside from the stream of emigration to America, which took place among the Jewish population in 1903 and 1904, the migration question did not exist in Rumania before the war, and, so far as we know, migration statistics were not published concerning this event."

In pursuance of an Order of the Minister of Labour, issued in agreement with the Minister of the Interior, frontier stations have been instructed since 1920 to compile migration statistics. These statistics cover continental and intercontinental emigration and immigration of citizen and alien wage earners, but exclude persons visiting or leaving the country for business purposes.

Statistics about the number of migrants from Rumania to Palestine (1922-24), Argentina (1921-24), Brazil (1908-24), Canada (1900-24), Cuba (1911-24) and the United States (1880-1924) will be found in the national tables for those countries. Statistics about the number of migrants returning to Rumania from the United States (1908-24) will be found in the national tables for the latter country.

TABLE I.—Intercontinental Emigration and Immigration of Citizens, 1920-24.[1]

Year	Emigrants	Immigrants	Year	Emigrants	Immigrants
1920	10,000	2,500	1923	12,723	679
1921	2,058	2,546	1924	3,105	973
1922	16,812	1,662	....	......	....

TABLE II.—Intercontinental Emigration and Immigration of Citizens,[1] by Country of Future or Last Residence, 1922-24.

Year	Emigrants			Immigrants		
	1922	1923	1924	1922	1923	1924
America.......	16,239	7,394	2,788	1,662	628	929
Argentina......	7	2	4	....	....	....
Armenia.......	....	1	....	....	1	....
Australia......	....	3	....	....	14	....
Brazil.........	....	4,656	54	....	0	....
Canada........	....	....	41	....	....	....
Egypt.........	....	5	22	....	10	36
Palestine......	566	662	196	....	25	7
Persia.........	....	....	....	....	1	1
Total......	16,812	12,723	3,105	1,662	679	973

For reference notes see page 877.

TABLE III.—Continental immigration and emigration of alien workers, 1920-24.[2]

Year	Immigrants	Emigrants	Year	Immigrants	Emigrants
1920	13,000	10,000	1923	12,203	7,937
1921	15,274	9,199	1924	9,888	7,248
1922	13,603	12,169	....	....	..

TABLE IV.—Continental immigration and emigration of alien workers, by country of last or future residence, 1922-24.[2]

Country	Immigrants			Emigrants		
	1922	1923	1924	1922	1923	1924
Albania........	114	82	53	62	41	39
Germany......	845	1,156	1,138	481	396	546
Austria........	877	783	538	623	374	421
Belgium.......	9	....	....	....	....	....
Bulgaria.......	3,109	3,609	4,521	3,191	2,748	2,294
Spain..........	....	1	5	1	....	....
France........	42	40	40	64	147	426
British Isles....	10	5	6	22	8	3
Greece.........	224	294	240	212	216	347
Hungary.......	1,431	1,227	692	3,509	595	514
Italy..........	1,301	106	126	398	82	140
Netherlands...,.	....	1	....	....	....	....
Poland........	846	1,228	655	428	875	828
Portugal......	....	....	....	....	1	....
Russia........	27	3	....	20	....	....
Switzerland....	11	19	....	....	....	....
Czechoslovakia.	1,732	1,639	884	1,421	889	489
Turkey........	529	213	115	407	276	325
Serb-Croat-Slovene State	2,452	1,797	875	1,330	1,289	876
Total......	13,559[3]	12,203	9,888	12,169	7,937	7,248

For reference notes see page 877.

TABLE V.—Distribution of emigrants, by occupation, 1923-24.

Occupation	1923	1924
Agricultural workers:		
Superintending staff	194	107
General laborers	3,864	2,033
Industrial workers:		
Superintending staff	310	449
Skilled workers:		
Iron workers	832	900
Wood workers	680	463
Food-industry workers	626	2,097
Clothing-industry workers	569	530
Building-trade workers	625	738
Miners	129	125
Employees:		
In industry and trade (office and shop employees, salesmen, etc.)	467	424
Domestic service and general labor:		
Servants, governesses, nurses, etc.	259	254
Unskilled workers	12,105[4]	2,233
Total	20,660	10,353

TABLE VI.—Distribution of immigrants, by occupation, 1923-24.

Occupation	1923	1924
Agricultural workers:		
Superintending staff	53	822
General labor	3,727	4,247
Industrial workers:		
Superintending staff	466	347
Skilled workers		
Iron workers	990	924
Wood workers	939	579
Food-industry workers	1,136	622
Clothing-industry workers	842	509
Building-trade workers	836	836
Miners	227	126
Employees:		
In industry and trade (office and shop employees, salesmen, etc.)	290	532
Domestic service and general labor:		
Servants, governesses, nurses, etc.	269	234
Unskilled workers	3,107[4]	1,083
Total	12,882	10,861

SOURCE

Information supplied by the Government.

NOTES

[1] Including aliens.
[2] Including citizens.
[3] This total does not correspond with that given in table III.
[4] For 1923 the figures represent industrial unskilled labor.

SERB, CROAT AND SLOVENE STATE

I. PRE-WAR SERBIA

The following explanation is made about the figures in tables I to III. "The Serbian police authorities keep registers of persons who cross the frontiers. These registers are utilised by the statistical department for the purpose of preparing comparative tables to discover whether there is an excess of emigrants over immigrants or the reverse."

Moreover, no precise data are available about migration on the side of Austria-Hungary during the years 1860 to 1862 and so the data about migration on the side of Turkey and Rumania have been ignored. Only the principal data concerning the three frontiers have been retained.

II. SERB, CROAT AND SLOVENE STATE

The emigration statistics are based on the contracts of emigrants with transport companies.

Statistics about the number of pre-war migrants from the area now included in the Serb, Croat and Slovene State to the United States and also about the number of pre-war migrants returning from that country can be approximated by combining certain racial statistics of migration into and out from the the latter country. They are shown in tables XIII and XIV.

PRE-WAR SERBIA

TABLE I.—PASSENGERS INWARD AND OUTWARD, BY COUNTRY OF ORIGIN OR DESTINATION, 1860-75.

Year	Total			Austria-Hungary			Turkey			Rumania		
	Inward	Outward	Balance inward (+) or outward (—)	Inward	Outward	Balance inward (+) or outward (—)	Inward	Outward	Balance inward (+) or outward (—)	Inward	Outward	Balance inward (+) or outward (—)
1860	99,034	97,332	+1,702	56,216	56,112	+104	37,408	35,920	+1,488	5,410	5,300	+110
1861	115,785	109,860	+5,925	65,541	64,859	+682	43,694	38,671	+5,023	6,550	6,330	+220
1862	73,258	75,020	-1,762	41,354	46,553	-5,199	27,569	23,802	+3,767	4,335	4,665	-330
1863	80,109	73,011	+7,098	45,142	36,610	+8,532	30,988	32,255	-1,267	3,979	4,146	-167
1864	79,687	68,103	+11,584	44,907	36,387	+8,520	30,090	27,142	+2,948	4,690	4,574	+116
1865	84,385	80,281	+4,104	48,558	46,729	+1,827	31,023	28,769	+2,254	4,804	4,783	+21
1866	99,816	100,483	-667	63,925	65,993	-2,068	28,751	27,159	+1,592	7,140	7,331	-191
1867	95,035	99,264	-4,229	55,886	61,477	-5,591	32,878	31,165	+1,713	6,271	6,622	-351
1868	104,922	95,362	+9,560	57,756	50,775	+6,981	41,005	37,918	+3,087	6,161	6,669	-508
1869	97,638	89,114	+8,524	50,657	48,017	+2,460	41,117	35,384	+5,733	5,864	5,713	+151
1870	98,121	95,369	+2,752	49,497	47,441	+2,056	43,149	42,711	+438	5,475	5,217	+258
1871	100,521	101,805	-1,284	49,542	50,926	-1,384	44,019	43,678	+341	6,960	7,201	-241
1872	104,594	107,369	-2,775	50,969	54,578	-3,609	44,921	44,004	+917	8,704	8,787	-83
1873	120,362	120,000	+362	58,643	60,383	-1,740	51,951	50,496	+1,455	9,768	9,121	+647
1874	111,847	106,087	+5,760	54,279	54,735	-456	45,242	39,858	+5,384	12,326	11,494	+832
1875	83,255	78,772	+4,483	36,680	37,664	-984	35,056	29,061	+5,995	11,519	12,047	-528
Total...	1,548,369	1,497,232	+51,137	829,552	819,239	+10,313	608,861	567,993	+40,868	109,956	110,000	-44
Annual average..	96,773	93,577	+3,196	51,847	51,202	+645	38,054	35,500	+2,554	6,872	6,875	-3

TABLE II.—Citizen passengers outward and inward across the frontier, 1889-1908.

Year	Outward	Inward	Balance outward (—) or inward (+)	Year	Outward	Inward	Balance outward (—) or inward (+)
1889	62,664	57,738	—4,926	1899	103,721	96,137	—7,584
1890	94,074	91,134	—2,940	1900	115,661	117,309	+1,648
1891	51,615	47,102	—4,513	1901	91,086	82,195	—8,891
1892	49,665	48,634	—1,031	1902	84,675	75,369	—9,306
1893	61,429	59,245	—2,184	1903	75,535	68,186	—7,349
1894	150,067	142,891	—7,176	1904	87,476	78,875	—8,601
1895	38,205	34,958	—3,247	1905	71,622	61,078	—10,544
1896	151,336	150,911	— 425	1906	66,400	49,426	—16,974
1897	117,096	115,411	—1,685	1907	69,334	55,142	—14,192
1898	121,936	113,980	—7,956	1908	62,025	53,587	—8,438

TABLE III.—Alien passengers inward and outward across the frontier, by nationality, 1889-1908.

Year	Total			Austro-Hungarian			Bulgarian		
	Inward	Outward	Balance inward (+) or outward (—)	Inward	Outward	Balance inward (+) or outward (—)	Inward	Outward	Balance inward (+) or outward (—)
1889	150,664	127,743	+22,921	105,833	98,758	+ 7,075	8,407	6,437	+ 1,970
1890	151,248	135,835	+15,413	113,844	105,958	+ 7,886	6,171	5,053	+ 1,118
1891	61,898	54,604	+ 7,294	24,756	23,180	+ 1,576	8,487	7,294	+ 1,193
1892	82,607	77,594	+ 5,013	26,762	25,693	+ 1,069	7,700	6,792	+ 908
1893	95,161	94,673	+ 488	56,280	57,573	— 1,293	7,639	6,408	+ 1,231
1894	196,571	188,555	+ 8,016	147,993	141,518	+ 6,475	7,581	6,781	+ 800
1895	78,730	73,985	+ 4,745	29,006	25,676	+ 3,330	7,881	7,632	+ 249
1896	216,176	207,684	+ 8,492	157,814	155,224	+ 2,590	10,440	9,057	+ 1,383
1897	222,829	208,983	+13,846	163,188	156,666	+ 6,522	10,936	9,778	+ 1,158
1898	178,476	160,318	+18,158	110,610	102,034	+ 8,576	11,223	9,729	+ 1,494
1899	162,521	146,805	+15,716	96,451	89,821	+ 6,630	13,829	11,672	+ 2,157
1900	210,669	203,760	+ 6,909	141,724	141,819	— 95	13,730	12,559	+ 1,171
1901	146,727	140,319	+ 6,408	78,277	75,942	+ 2,335	20,329	18,921	+ 1,408
1902	146,124	128,912	+17,212	77,115	66,462	+10,653	17,840	15,806	+ 2,034
1903	141,605	130,679	+10,926	73,408	69,729	+ 3,679	17,679	16,838	+ 841
1904	170,658	142,139	+28,519	69,330	63,144	+ 6,186	16,687	14,444	+ 2,243
1905	111,364	97,874	+13,490	11,091	8,989	+ 2,102	21,485	19,581	+ 1,904
1906	107,395	99,142	+ 8,253	7,629	6,323	+ 1,306	24,345	24,131	+ 214
1907	120,840	105,258	+15,582	17,940	19,323	— 1,383	21,838	19,638	+ 2,200
1908	91,022	96,151	— 5,129	25,707	26,050	— 343	12,316	10,390	+ 1,926

TABLE III.—ALIEN PASSENGERS INWARD AND OUTWARD ACROSS THE FRONTIER, BY NATIONALITY, 1889-1908 (continued).

Year	Turkish			Rumanian			Montenegrin		
	Inward	Outward	Balance inward (+) or outward (—)	Inward	Outward	Balance inward (+) or outward (—)	Inward	Outward	Balance inward (+) or outward (—)
1889	11,051	9,941	+ 1,110	1,903	1,334	+ 569	7,363	104	+7,259
1890	10,535	10,260	+ 275	1,880	1,446	+ 434	314	194	+ 120
1891	10,667	10,994	— 327	1,304	1,141	+ 163	594	178	+ 416
1892	12,108	11,568	+ 540	1,226	998	+ 228	445	191	+ 254
1893	11,091	12,888	— 1,797	971	672	+ 299	688	239	+ 449
1894	14,005	14,018	— 13	1,152	874	+ 278	447	332	+ 115
1895	12,993	11,623	+ 1,370	1,150	2,711	—1,561	209	165	+ 44
1896	14,949	14,397	+ 552	1,391	873	+ 518	935	565	+ 370
1897	18,457	16,503	+ 1,594	1,012	458	+ 554	847	541	+ 306
1898	22,413	18,615	+ 3,798	1,195	571	+ 624	768	573	+ 195
1899	23,737	20,417	+ 3,320	1,160	708	+ 452	155	205	— 50
1900	20,131	18,555	+ 1,576	1,567	1,215	+ 352	218	170	+ 48
1901	20,338	19,992	+ 346	1,529	1,303	+ 226	581	203	+ 378
1902	29,238	26,544	+ 2,694	1,290	1,261	+ 29	1,578	494	+1,084
1903	29,632	25,672	+ 3,960	1,572	1,539	+ 33	1,195	352	+ 843
1904	55,541	40,569	+14,972	870	763	+ 107	3,035	725	+2,310
1905	17,421	11,328	+ 6,093	553	474	+ 79	398	207	+ 191
1906	20,918	17,709	+ 3,209	668	584	+ 84	330	236	+ 94
1907	27,265	20,657	+ 6,608	794	661	+ 133	111	116	— 5
1908	23,721	28,052	— 4,331	658	609	+ 49	111	117	— 6

Year	Greek			Other nationalities			Refugees		
	Inward	Outward	Balance inward (+) or outward (—)	Inward	Outward	Balance inward (+) or outward (—)	Inward	Outward	Balance inward (+) or outward (—)
1889	1,175	985	+190	11,017	10,171	+ 846	3,915	13	+3,902
1890	845	743	+102	13,449	12,172	+1,277	4,210	9	+4,201
1891	908	868	+ 40	13,691	10,948	+2,743	1,491	1	+1,490
1892	1,179	1,148	+ 31	32,358	31,169	+1,189	829	35	+ 794
1893	557	533	+ 24	17,509	16,351	+1,158	426	9	+ 417
1894	1,045	931	+114	23,530	24,089	— 559	818	12	+ 806
1895	893	864	+ 29	25,793	25,295	+ 498	805	19	+ 786
1896	767	738	+ 29	28,470	25,907	+2,563	1,410	923	+ 487
1897	849	696	+153	26,914	24,338	+2,576	626	3	+ 623
1898	869	649	+220	29,837	28,122	+1,715	1,561	25	+1,536
1899	724	621	+103	25,215	23,324	+1,891	1,250	37	+1,213
1900	722	544	+178	31,432	28,873	+2,559	1,145	25	+1,120
1901	1,250	1,225	+ 25	23,274	22,681	+ 593	1,149	52	+1,097
1902	1,812	1,760	+ 52	16,651	16,563	+ 88	600	22	+ 578
1903	908	839	+ 69	16,725	15,625	+1,100	486	85	+ 401
1904	538	443	+ 95	24,248	22,018	+2,230	409	33	+ 376
1905	57	49	+ 8	60,247	57,245	+3,002	112	1	+ 111
1906	95	97	— 2	53,321	50,062	+3,259	89	...	+ 89
1907	144	110	+ 34	52,350	44,740	+7,610	398	13	+ 385
1908	201	201	.....	27,983	30,047	—2,064	325	685	— 360

SERB, CROAT AND SLOVENE STATE

TABLE IV.—DISTRIBUTION OF CITIZEN EMIGRANTS TO EXTRA-EUROPEAN COUNTRIES, BY SEX AND AGE, 1919-24.

| Year | Total | Sex | | Age | | | | | | | |
| | | | | Up to 18 years | | 19-30 years | | 31-50 years | | 51 years and over | |
		Males	Females	Males	Females	Males	Females	Males	Females	Males	Females
1919[1]	291	....	....	....	....	....	....	....	....	....	....
1920	5,988	....	....	....	....	....	....	....	....	....	....
1921	12,965	5,102	7,863	1,811	2,400	1,665	3,347	1,439	1,921	187	195
1922	6,086	2,872	3,214	694	734	740	1,247	1,277	1,110	152	132
1923	9,370	5,717	3,653	906	829	2,043	2,016	2,588	747	180	61
1924	17,238	11,587	5,651	2,991	2,231	4,190	1,849	3,968	1,350	438	221

TABLE V.—DISTRIBUTION OF CITIZEN EMIGRANTS TO EXTRA-EUROPEAN COUNTRIES, BY OCCUPATION AND SEX, 1921-24.

| Year | Skilled workers | | Unskilled workers | | Farmers | | Liberal professions | | No occupation, children, women, old persons | |
	Males	Females	Males	Females	Males	Females	Males	Females	Males	Females
1921	356	142	2,477	3,626	837	850	74	7	1,358	3,238
1922	403	41	152	228	1,604	2,045	75	96	680	761
1923	910	86	1,703	1,713	2,053	728	210	347	841	779
1924	645	84	1,424	796	6,866	2,549	177	106	2,475	2,116

For reference notes see page 887.

TABLE VI.—Distribution of Citizen Emigrants to Extra-European Countries, by Race or People, 1921-24.

Year	Serbs, Croats and Slovenes	Bulgarians	Other Slav races	Germans	Hungarians	Rumanians	Albanians	Other races
1921	9,516	..	65	2,594	700	51	..	39
1922	4,880	..	117	760	259	46	..	24
1923	5,698	..	22	2,322	1,169	137	..	22
1924	8,525	..	51	4,239	4,218	149	2	74

TABLE VII.—Intercontinental Emigration of Citizens, by Country of Destination, 1919-24.

Year	Total	United States	Canada	South Africa	Australia	New Zealand	Argentina	Brazil	Chile	Uruguay	Other South American countries	Other countries
1919[1]	291	265	11	15	0				15			
1920	5,988	5,474	189	20	8				317			
1921	12,965	12,461	87	15	10	2	304	...	78	...	8	..
1922	6,086	5,436	179	20	44	12	290	63	7	...	35	3
1923	9,370	4,130	717	7	135	4	2,721	1,535	46	173	72	3
1924	17,238	2,125	1,941	1	1,716	98	3,860	6,862	179	173	274	9

For reference notes see page 887.

TABLE VIII.—Intercontinental immigration of citizens, 1919-24.

Year	Immigrants	Year	Immigrants	Year	Immigrants
1919[1]	7,324	1921	8,163	1923	1,981
1920	18,980	1922	6,588	1924	5,159

TABLE IX.—Distribution of alien emigrants, by sex and age, 1924.

Age	Total	Males	Females
Total...............................	2,337	1,403	934
Up to 18 years...................	747	387	360
19 to 30 years...................	735	456	279
31 to 50 years...................	754	486	268
51 years and over...............	101	74	27

TABLE X.—Distribution of alien emigrants to extra-European countries, by occupation and sex, 1924.

Occupation	Total	Males	Females
Total...............................	2,337	1,403	934
Skilled workers..................	292	237	55
Unskilled workers...............	591	337	254
Farmers.........................	673	435	238
Liberal professions..............	124	74	50
No occupation, children, old persons, women.....................	657	320	337

For reference notes see page 887.

TABLE XI.—Emigration of aliens (mostly ex-nationals), by country of destination, 1923-24.

Year	Total	United States	Canada	Australia	New Zealand	Argentina	Brazil	Chile	Uruguay	Other South American countries	Other countries
1923	2,103										
1924	2,337	1,513	35	20	12	81	599	3	3	61	10

TABLE XII.—Immigration of aliens (mostly ex-nationals), by country of last residence, 1923-24.

Year	Total	United States	British Empire	South America
1923	426			
1924	1,056	1,027	18	11

TABLE XIII.—IMMIGRATION FROM YUGOSLAVIA (OR OF YUGOSLAVS) INTO EXTRA-EUROPEAN COUNTRIES, BY COUNTRY OF DESTINATION, 1899-1924.[2]

Year	Argentina	Brazil	Canada	Cuba		United States[2]			Total	Commonwealth of Australia
				Yugoslavs	from Yugoslavia	Bulgarian, Serbian and Montenegrin	Croatian and Slovenian	Dalmatian, Bosnian and Herzegovinian		
1899	...	...	...	...	...	94	8,632	367	9,093	...
1900	...	...	23	...	...	204	17,184	675	18,063	...
1901	...	...	...	...	...	611	17,928	732	19,271	...
1902	...	...	2	...	...	1,291	30,233	1,004	32,528	...
1903	...	...	10	...	...	6,479	32,907	1,736	41,122	...
1904	...	...	7	...	...	4,577	21,242	2,036	27,855	...
1905	...	...	19	...	...	5,823	35,104	2,639	43,566	...
1906	...	...	4	...	...	11,548	44,272	4,568	60,388	...
1907	...	...	48	...	...	27,174	47,826	7,393	82,393	...
1908	...	...	31	...	...	18,246	20,472	3,747	42,465	...
1909	...	...	76	...	...	6,214	20,181	1,888	28,283	...
1910	...	...	50	...	...	15,130	39,562	4,911	59,603	...
1911	...	...	209	...	...	10,222	18,982	4,400	33,604	...
1912	...	...	366	...	...	10,657	24,366	3,672	38,695	...
1913	...	...	193	...	...	9,087	42,499	4,520	56,106	...
1914	...	...	220	1	...	15,084	37,284	5,149	57,517	...
1915	...	...	6	...	...	3,506	1,942	305	5,753	...
1916	1,753	...	1	7	...	3,146	791	114	4,051	...
1917		...	...	6	7	1,134	305	94	1,533	...
1918		...	1	3	5	150	33	15	198	...
1919		...	12	7	34	205	23	4	232	...
1920	407	37	89	7	3		1,888		...	...
1921	533	22	180[3]	31	5		23,536		...	...
1922	2,598	56	136[3]	43	34		6,047		...	125
1923	3,959	790	1,306[3]	182	5		6,181		...	240
1924		7,889	1,620[3]	365	...		5,835		...	1,933

For reference notes see page 887.

TABLE XIV.—Distribution of emigrants to Yugoslavia (or of Yugoslavs) from
the United States, by race or people, 1908-24.[2]

Year	Total	Bulgarian, Serbian and Montenegrin	Croatian and Slovenian	Dalmatian, Bosnian and Herzegovinian
1908	35,600	5,965	28,589	1,046
1909	11,951	2,422	9,014	515
1910	10,285	2,720	7,133	432
1911	21,142	6,472	13,735	935
1912	22,239	7,349	13,963	927
1913	24,583	13,525	10,209	849
1914	21,098	5,780	14,440	878
1915	4,840	2,354	2,381	105
1916	370	290	76	4
1917	355	325	24	6
1918	962	918	31	13
1919	3,397	3,241	154	2
1920	28,474	. . . . .	. . . . .	. . . . .
1921	13,034	. . . . .	. . . . .	. . . . .
1922	9,733	. . . . .	. . . . .	. . . . .
1923	2,064	. . . . .	. . . . .	. . . . .
1924	1,991	. . . . .	. . . . .	. . . . .

SOURCES

Statistique de la Serbie. Vol. XI. (Published by the Statistical Department of the Ministry of Finance.) Belgrade, 1882.

Table I.

Conférence internationale de l'Emigration et de l'Immigration. (Published by the Italian Commissariat-General of Emigration.) Rome, 1924, vol. I, p. 437.

Tables II, V (years 1919-20).

Information supplied by the Government.

Tables II-XII (years 1921-24).

NOTES

[1]From the constitution of the Kingdom to the end of 1919.
[2]From 1899 to 1919 migrants of Bulgarian, Servian and Montenegrin, likewise of Croatian and Slovenian *race*; from 1920 to 1924 migrants from or to the Serb-Croat-Slovene State.
[3]Fiscal years.

TURKEY

As no direct migration statistics are available for this country, and as the immigration and emigration statistics of other countries to which citizens of Turkey have gone throw some light upon migrations from and back to Turkey, but for this purpose need to be combined, two tables of indirect migration statistics for Turkey have been introduced.

TABLE I.—INDIRECT STATISTICS. IMMIGRATION FROM TURKEY (OR OF TURKS) INTO EXTRA-EUROPEAN COUNTRIES, 1820-1924.

Year	United States Turkey in Europe	Year	United States Turkey in Europe	Year	United States Turkey in Europe	Year	United States Turkey in Europe	Year	United States Turkey in Europe
1820	1	1827	1	1835	3	1842	2	1850	15
1821	..	1828	6	1836	..	1843	5	1851	2
1822	4	1829	1	1837	..	1844	10	1852	3
1823	2	1830	2	1838	..	1845	3	1853	15
1824	2	1831	..	1839	1	1846	4	1854	7
1825	..	1832	..	1840	1	1847	2	1855	9
1826	2	1833	1	1841	6	1848	3		
		1834	1			1849	9		

TABLE I.—INDIRECT STATISTICS. IMMIGRATION FROM TURKEY (OR OF TURKS) INTO EXTRA-EUROPEAN COUNTRIES, 1820-1924. (continued).

Year	Argentina	Brazil	United States		
			Turkey in Europe	Turkey in Asia	All Turkey
1856	...	...	5	...	...
1857	...	...	11	...	...
1858	...	...	17	...	...
1859	...	...	10	...	...
1860	...	...	4	...	...
1861	...	...	5	...	...
1862	...	...	11	...	...
1863	...	...	16	...	...
1864	...	...	11	...	...
1865	...	...	14	...	...
1866	...	...	18	...	...
1867	...	...	26	...	...
1868	...	...	4	...	...
1869	...	...	18	2	20
1870	...	...	6	...	6

Year	Argentina	Brazil	United States		
			Turkey in Europe	Turkey in Asia	All Turkey
1871		2	23	4	27
1872		..	20	...	20
1873		8	53	3	56
1874		21	62	6	68
1875	672	..	27	1	28
1876		15	38	8	46
1877		..	32	3	35
1878		..	29	7	36
1879		..	29	31	60
1880		6	24	4	28
1881		38	72	5	77
1882		..	69	...	69
1883	3,537	6	86	...	86
1884		16	150	...	150
1885		43	138	...	138
1886		...	176	15	191
1887		...	206	208	414
1888		...	207	273	480
1889		...	252	593	845
1890		...	206	1,126	1,332

TABLE 1.—INDIRECT STATISTICS. IMMIGRATION FROM TURKEY (OR OF TURKS) INTO EXTRA-EUROPEAN COUNTRIES, 1820-1924. (concluded).

Year	Argentina	Brazil	Cuba		United States						Canada		
			Turks	From Turkey	Turkey in Europe	Turkey in Asia	All Turkey	Turkish not specified	Arabian	Armenian	Egyptian	Syrian	All Turkish
1891		3			265	2,488	2,753						
1892					1,331	3,172	4,503						
1893	11,583				625	1,829	2,454						
1894					298	1,219	1,517						
1895					245	2,326	2,571						
1896					169	4,139	4,308						
1897		648			152	4,732	4,884						
1898		978			176	4,275	4,451						
1899		1,823			80	4,436	4,516						
1900		874			285	3,962	4,247	37	98	62	1	464	662
1901		781			387	5,782	6,169	17	70	112	3	1,066	1,268
1902		772	23		187	6,223	6,410	43	46	113	1	847	1,050
1903		481	88		1,529	7,118	8,647	29	58	81	3	369	540
1904		1,097	86		4,344	5,235	9,579	30	48	78	2	630	788
1905		1,446	228		4,542	6,157	10,699	357	19	82	18	336	812
1906		1,193	264		9,510	6,354	15,864	232	31	208	10	277	758
1907		1,480	248		20,767	8,053	28,820	489	50	563	8	732	1,842
1908	66,558	3,170	190		11,290	9,753	21,043	236	4	79	2	189	510
1909		4,027	277		9,015	7,506	16,521	517	14	75	2	195	803
1910		5,257	210	90	18,405	15,212	33,617	469	3	20	3	124	619
1911		6,319	223	128	14,438	10,229	24,667	632	2	60		144	838
1912		7,302	320	203	14,481	12,788	27,269	770	10	100	7	232	1,119
1913		10,886	336	439	14,128	23,955	38,083	187	16	139	5	278	625
1914		3,456	205	244	8,199	21,716	29,915	33		36		79	148
1915		514	71	34	1,008	3,543	4,551					3	3
1916	59,272	603	68		313	1,670	1,983	5		3		9	17
1917		259	33		152	393	545			2		2	4
1918		93	13		15	43	58						
1919		504	79	77	10	19	29	1	5	10	364	18[2]	29
1920		4,854	572	566	1,933	5,033	6,966			41			410
1921	162	1,865	159	57	6,391	11,735	18,126	3	13[1]	64		[2]	80
1922	199	2,278	137	109	1,660	1,998	3,658	3	2	59		[2]	64
1923	1,611	4,829	803	42	3,743	2,183	5,926	27	3[1]	486		[2]	516
1924	1,309	4,078	1,148	30	1,481	2,820	4,301	29	3[1]	304		[2]	336

(In the "From Turkey" column the figures are divided into "Asia" and "Europe.")

For reference notes see page 892.

TABLE II.—Indirect statistics.   Emigration to Turkey (or of Turks) from EXTRA-EUROPEAN COUNTRIES, 1891-1924.

Year	Argentina	United States		
		Total	Turkey in Europe	Turkey in Asia
1891-1900	1,011	. . . . .	. . . . .	. . . . .
1901		. . . . .	. . . . .	. . . . .
1902		. . . . .	. . . . .	. . . . .
1903		. . . . .	. . . . .	. . . . .
1904		. . . . .	. . . . .	. . . . .
1905		. . . . .	. . . . .	. . . . .
	31,160			
1906		. . . . .	. . . . .	. . . . .
1907		. . . . .	. . . . .	. . . . .
1908		4,931	3,084	1,847
1909		2,917	1,267	1,650
1910		3,536	1,988	1,548
1911		6,593	4,688	1,905
1912		7,477	5,926	1,551
1913		6,122	4,809	1,313
1914		4,771	2,528	2,243
1915		757	164	593
	20,220			
1916		32	18	14
1917		32	24	8
1918		29	24	5
1919		73	47	26
1920		3,543	1,812	1,731
1921		2,939	405	2,534
1922	1,122	1,932	201	1,731
1923		898	125	773
1924		339	128	211

SOURCE

Indirect statistics only.

NOTES

[1]Including Egyptian.

PALESTINE

The statistics for Palestine begin with the year 1922. The immigration figures are based on the permits issued by the Department of Immigration and Travel to persons intending to reside permanently in the country.

The emigration statistics concern persons leaving the country for permanent residence abroad and relate to two categories: (a) emigrants, that is, natives of Palestine or inhabitants of the country before it became mandated territory (citizens), and (b) "returning immigrants," that is, aliens arrived in Palestine since "the British occupation".

TABLE I.—Distribution of immigrants, by sex, age, and religion, 1922-24.

| Year | Total | | | | | Jews | | | | | Others | | | | |
| | Total | Children | Adults | | Total | Children | Adults | | Total | Children | Adults | |
			Males	Females				Males	Females				Males	Females
1922	8,128	2,173	3,427	2,528	7,844	2,113	3,285	2,446	284	60	142	82
1923	7,991	2,147	3,228	2,616	7,421	2,001	2,965	2,455	570	146	263	161
1924	13,553	3,751	5,502	4,300	12,856	3,579	5,180	4,097	697	172	322	203

TABLE II.—DISTRIBUTION OF IMMIGRANTS, BY RELIGION, SEX AND OCCUPATION, 1922-24.

Occupation	Religion	1922				1923				1924			
		Total	Chil-dren	Adults Males	Adults Fe-males	Total	Chil-dren	Adults Males	Adults Fe-males	Total	Chil-dren	Adults Males	Adults Fe-males
1. Persons of independent means who intend to take up permanent residence in Palestine.	Jews	1,322	444	482	396	967	283	396	288	5,281	1,801	1,953	1,527
	Others	40	8	17	15	36	5	22	9	139	67	47	25
	Total	1,362	452	499	411	1,003	288	418	297	5,420	1,868	2,000	1,552
2. Members of professions who intend to follow their calling.	Jews	115	...	86	29	16	...	11	5	...	...	...	...
	Others	26	...	26	...	1	...	1	...	...	...	...	...
	Total	141	...	112	29	17	...	12	5	...	...	...	...
3. Wives, children and other persons accompanying immigrants classified under category 2.	Jews	44	21	1	22	8	4	...	4	...	...	...	...
	Others	12	4	...	8	...	...	...	...	...	...	...	...
	Total	56	25	1	30	8	4	...	4	...	...	...	...
4. Wives, children and other persons wholly dependent on residents in Palestine.	Jews	3,169	1,106	726	1,337	2,048	629	397	1,022	2,194	637	387	1,170
	Others	81	36	12	33	183	103	6	74	133	46	8	79
	Total	3,250	1,142	738	1,370	2,231	732	403	1,096	2,327	683	395	1,249
5. Persons who have a definite prospect of employment with specified employers or enterprises.	Jews	2,123	...	1,943	180	2,017	...	1,926	91	3,181	1	2,757	423
	Others	65	...	55	10	237	...	192	45	270	1	214	55
	Total	2,188	...	1,998	190	2,254	...	2,118	136	3,451	2	2,971	478
6. Wives, children and other persons accompanying immigrants classified under category 5.	Jews	1,028	536	28	464	2,330	1,084	212	1,034	2,162	1,135	62	965
	Others	20	11	1	8	31	16	1	14	41	20	...	21
	Total	1,048	547	29	472	2,361	1,100	213	1,048	2,203	1,155	62	986
7. Persons of religious occupation who have means of maintenance.	Jews	43	6	19	18	35	1	23	11	38	5	21	12
	Others	40	1	31	8	82	22	41	19	114	38	53	23
	Total	83	7	50	26	117	23	64	30	152	43	74	35
	Jews	7,844	2,113	3,285	2,446	7,421	2,001	2,965	2,455	12,856	3,579	5,180	4,097
	Others	284	60	142	82	570	146	263	161	697	172	322	203
	Total	8,128	2,173	3,427	2,528	7,991	2,147	3,228	2,616	13,553	3,751	5,502	4,300

TABLE III.—Distribution of Jewish wage-earners who entered Palestine, by occupation, in 1924.

Agriculture	1,480
Tailors, cutters, seamstresses, etc.	629
Metal works	417
Wood works	319
Building	235
Textile works	235
Leather works	173
Engineering and electrical trades	164
Printing	44
Various skilled trades (mechanical)	247
Various skilled trades (food)	207
	4,150
Merchants and capitalists	691
Medical	243
Clerks and officials	241
Students	201
Teachers	154
Religious occupation	70
Liberal professions	55
	1,655
Total	5,805

TABLE IV.—DISTRIBUTION OF IMMIGRANTS, BY RELIGION AND COUNTRY OF ORIGIN, 1922-24.

Country	1922 Total	1922 Jews	1922 Christians	1922 Moslems	1923 Total	1923 Jews	1923 Christians	1923 Moslems	1924 Total	1924 Jews	1924 Christians	1924 Moslems
Argentina	[1]				15[3]	15			18	7	11	
Armenia	165	165							5		5	
Austria					144[5]	136	8		129	124	5	
Belgium									16	14	2	
Brazil					305[7]	262	43		3	3		
Bulgaria									358	358		
Canada	28	26	2						12	10	2	
Czechoslovakia	360[1]	307	49	4	19[8]	19			69	69		
China					[3]				4	4		
Cuba									3	3		
Cyprus	[1]								28	12	16	
Danzig									40	40		
Denmark									1		1	
Egypt	225	191	12	22	231	56	30	145	236	65	32	139
Estonia	81[2]	65	16						2	2		
Finland									2		2	
France	78	44	34						35	24	11	
Germany					235[7]	149	86		552	480	72	
Greece									337	311	26	
Holland	33	33							26	20	6	
Hungary	[1]								31	27	4	
Iraq					1		1		101	101		
Italy	[1]				76[6]	34	42		46	10	36	
Japan					[8]				1			
Latvia	281	281			94	92	2		146	146		
Lithuania	223	223			303	303			750	750		
Norway									1		1	
Persia	[1]				568[4]	547	18	3	37	31	2	4
Poland	3,209	3,209			2,252	2,252			5,702	5,695	7	

For reference notes see page 899.

TABLE IV—DISTRIBUTION OF IMMIGRANTS, BY RELIGION AND COUNTRY OF ORIGIN, 1922-24 (continued).

Country	1922				1923				1924			
	Total	Jews	Christians	Moslems	Total	Jews	Christians	Moslems	Total	Jews	Christians	Moslems
Portugal	[1]				[6]				1	1		
Rhodes					[4]				21	19	2	
Rumania	990	990			326	326			593	593		
Russia	727	725	2		1,882	1,876	6		2,157	2,148	9	
San Salvador					[3]				2		2	
South Africa					13[9]	11	2		12	12		
Spain					[6]				6	1	5	
Sweden					[6]				3		3	
Switzerland	37	7	23	7	74	12	48	14	16	13	3	
Syria					46[10]	45	1		159	34	108	17
Tanganyika					180	79	95	6	7		7	
Tripoli	179	143	12	24					2			2
Turkey	1,079	1,079			1,045	1,045			389	325	39	25
Ukraine	38	34	4		46	37	9		504	504		
United Kingdom	175	166	9		136	125	11		166	115	51	
United States	[1]				[4]				361	324	37	
Yemen					[7]				445	445		
Yugoslavia	220	156	61	3					18	16	2	
Other countries												
Total	8,128	7,844	224	60	7,991	7,421	402	168	13,553	12,856	510	187

For reference notes see page 899.

TABLE V.—DISTRIBUTION OF CITIZEN AND ALIEN EMIGRANTS, BY RELIGION, 1922-24 .

Year	"Emigrants" (citizens)				"Returning immigrants" (aliens)			
	Total	Jews	Chris-tians	Mos-lems	Total	Jews	Chris-tians	Mos-lems
1922	1,521	450	559	512	1,418	1,053	157	208
1923	2,165	940	615	610	2,782	2,526	98	158
1924	2,500[11]	...	...	...	....	....	..	...

SOURCES

Report on Palestine Administration, 1922-24. London, 1923-25.

Tables I, II, IV, V.

Appendices to the Report by H. M. British Government on the Administration under Mandate of Palestine and Transjordania for the Year 1924. London, 1925. p. 8.

Table III.

NOTES

[1]The figure for China includes Asiatic immigrants from: China, Japan, Armenia, Cyprus, Persia, Rhodes, Iraq, Yemen.
[2]Immigrants from Estonia are included in the return for Finland.
[3]The figure for Argentina includes immigrants from other countries of Latin America.
[4]The immigrants from Armenia, Cyprus, Persia, Rhodes, Yemen, are included with those from Persia.
[5]Immigrants from Czechoslovakia, Hungary and Switzerland are included in the return for Austria.
[6]The figure for Italy includes immigrants from Belgium, France, Italy, Portugal and Spain.
[7]The figure for Bulgaria includes immigrants from Greece and Yugoslavia.
[8]The figure for China includes immigrants from Japan.
[9]Immigrants from Tanganyika are included in the figure for South Africa.
[10]Immigrants from other parts of North Africa are included in the figure for Tripoli.

SYRIA

Statistics about the number of migrants from Syria to Argentina (1921-24), Canada (1920-24), Cuba (1911-24), United States (1899-1924) and Australia (1902-24) will be found in the national tables for those countries.

BRITISH INDIA

Regular statistical accounts do not begin before 1842. Moreover, detailed emigration regulations were drawn up in order to protect those leaving the country, while the statistical definition of an emigrant varied with the legislation. (See Introduction page 140.) At the start, tables were headed "emigrants," later "coolies" (1871), then "indentured emigrants" (1883). At certain periods, nevertheless, "free" emigrants, not subject to the existing State regulations, were included in the statistical statements.

The figures are furnished by the Protectors of Emigrants who received them from the several Governments and Administrations.

Tables I and IV (years 1842-1870) have been compiled by totalling separately the figures in the original source[1] for "men, women and children emigrating in each year from each of the three British ports, and collectively from the French ports, to each British and foreign colony to which emigration has been, at any time during that period, lawful". The figures for Calcutta cover a fiscal, and those for Bombay and Madras a calendar year.[2]

Between 1856 and 1924 the *Statistical Abstract for British India* published figures for emigration at the ports of embarkation. For the years covered equally by both sources, Geoghegan's figures are generally higher than those of the *Statistical Abstract*. Sometimes the discrepancy is trivial, but at other times the two sources differ by thousands.

It is just possible that the local authorities placed at Geoghegan's disposal fuller details than those utilised by the *Statistical Abstract*. But he expresses doubts regarding the completeness and the homogeneity of his data. Thus he excluded the figures relating to emigration from Pondicherry to French Guiana for the period 1856, 1860 and 1861, because he believed that if British citizens participated in this emigration, they did so illegally.[3] These figures have been inserted in the total column of Table I.

The data published in the *Statistical Abstract* subsequent to 1873 relate expressly to "Coolie Emigrants". From 1878-79 onwards we regard the figures in the *Statistics of British India* as the most reliable ones; but it should be remarked that, with a few exceptions during the earlier years, the figures of the *Statistical Abstract* agree with them.

Concerning the persons included in the statistical statements down to 1922-23, the *Statistics of British India* offers the following information: "The figures in these tables relate to indentured emigration carried on under the Indian Emigration Act (XXI of 1883, repealed by XVII of 1908); and rules framed thereunder relating to the emigration of natives of India. But certain persons who proceed to the colonies or other

[1]Geoghegan, *Note on Emigration from India*, Calcutta, 1873.
[2]Geoghegan states that he "has not thought it worth while to ask the Protector at Calcutta to undertake a readjustment of his figures according to the calendar year." (P. 69.)
[3]Geoghegan, *ibid.*, p. 83.

foreign countries without coming under the operation of the Emigration Act, as for instance, in the capacity of shop assistants or personal domestic servants, are included in the statistics. The figures take no account of the numbers who leave India as passengers under the Native Passenger Ships Act, or of persons who leave India on pilgrimage to the holy places in Arabia under the Pilgrim Ships Act (of whom small but uncertain numbers settle out of India)."[1]

From 1923, under the Indian Emigration Act, 1922, the statistics refer to the emigration of "skilled and unskilled workers and their dependents going to the colonies and various other countries". The Emigration Act (No. VII of 1922) and regulations published under it came into force on March 5, 1923, and, in consequence, emigration to British Malaya and Ceylon, which until then had been unrestricted, was controlled. Emigration to the other colonies (Natal, Fiji, British Guiana, Trinidad, Jamaica, Mauritius) was suspended in 1917. This prohibition is still in force, except for Mauritius, emigration to which was again permitted for one year commencing May 31, 1923, under Notifications Nos. 282 Emi., dated March 22, 1923, and 487 Overseas, dated May 19, 1923, issued by the Government of India. The number to be recruited within the period was limited to 1,500 adult male laborers and dependents.

In regard to returning emigrants, totals are available from 1878-79 onwards, but these contain only particulars about sex. After 1923 it is possible to distinguish the country of last permanent residence and, accordingly, the intercontinental and continental return migrations of unskilled and skilled workers.

Statistics about the number of migrants from British India to South Africa (1879-1912), Mauritius (1834-1910), Canada (1904-15 and 1920-24), United States (1820-1924), Australia (1902-24) and New Zealand (1915-24) will be found in the national tables for those countries. Statistics about the number of migrants returning to British India from Mauritius (1834-1920) and the United States (1908-24) will be found in the national tables for those countries.

[1]*Statistics of British India* for 1911-13 and preceding years, Part V. Calcutta, 1913, p. 217. The same description is repeated in *Statistics* for the year 1922, Vol. IV, while the following definition is added to the above text under Act XVII of the year 1908: "...........nor of persons who go out of, or come out to India by ships as ordinary passengers every year." *Statistics of British India, 1922.* v. IV, p. xiv (Calcutta, 1922).

TABLE I.—DISTRIBUTION OF CITIZEN EMIGRANTS TO EXTRA-ASIATIC COUNTRIES, BY SEX AND AGE, 1842-70.

Year	Total	Men	Women	Children	Year	Total	Men	Women	Children
1842	459	407	49	3	1856	15,080	9,614	3,382	2,084
1843	39,755	33,978	4,380	1,397	1857	20,805	11,682	5,305	3,818
1844	8,242	6,530	1,065	647	1858	45,838	27,992	10,569	7,277
1845	12,511	9,345	1,788	1,378	1859	43,057	26,949	9,377	6,731
1846	16,735	11,810	2,963	1,962	1860	24,062	14,226	6,183	3,653
1847	10,719	8,491	1,313	965	1861	32,026	22,469	6,082	3,475
1848	9,671	7,610	1,236	825	1862	14,766	10,415	2,807	1,544
1849	7,670	6,162	933	575	1863	11,731	7,795	2,374	1,562
1850	9,800	7,521	1,281	998	1864	22,084	14,999	4,692	2,393
1851	14,266	10,917	1,979	1,370	1865	27,589	17,519	5,729	4,341
1852	22,674	16,899	3,312	2,463	1866	21,347	13,066	5,314	2,967
1853	19,781	15,046	2,824	1,911	1867	7,614	5,182	1,804	628
1854	19,327	14,137	2,860	2,330	1868	13,379	8,209	3,358	1,812
1855	16,629	10,954	3,305	2,370	1869	15,827	9,093	4,212	2,522
					1870	12,433	8,082	3,051	1,300

TABLE II.—DISTRIBUTION OF CITIZEN EMIGRANTS TO EXTRA-ASIATIC COUNTRIES, BY SEX, 1870-1923.

Year	Total	Males	Females	Year	Total	Males	Females
1870–71	12,428	....	....	1897–98	13,485	10,122	3,363
				1898–99	19,613	16,502	3,111
1871-72	11,034	....	....	1899–1900	20,438	17,210	3,228
1872–73	20,037	....	....	1900–01	26,508	20,491	6,017
1873–74	29,243	....	....				
1874–75	25,325	....	....	1901–02	22,498	15,457	7,041
1875–76	11,489	....	....	1902–03	15,413	10,895	4,518
				1903–04	13,665	9,524	4,141
1876–77	10,560	....	....	1904–05	15,939	11,087	4,852
1877–78	24,710	....	....	1905–06	21,125	14,741	6,384
1878–79	22,092[1]	13,181	5,802				
1879–80	17,426[1]	10,904	4,530	1906–07	21,003	14,847	6,156
1880–81	16,794[1]	10,873	4,278	1907–08	15,117	10,499	4,618
				1908–09	11,844	8,396	3,448
1881–82	11,509[1]	7,296	3,075	1909–10	11,644	8,218	3,426
1882–83	13,504[1]	8,628	3,528	1910–11	15,439	10,813	4,626
1883–84	17,936[1]	11,269	4,536				
1884–85	22,384[1]	13,667	5,521	1911–12	14,192	10,113	4,079
1885–86	7,979[1]	4,823	2,097	1912–13	12,658	9,063	3,595
				1913–14	7,733	5,600	2,133
1886–87	7,978[1]	4,963	1,982	1914–15	3,285	2,475	810
1887–88	6,559	4,537	2,022	1915–16	7,630	5,504	2,126
1888–89	10,756	7,400	3,356				
1889–90	16,954	11,685	5,269	1916–17	7,682	6,080	1,602
1890–91	20,085	13,741	6,344	1917–18[2]	1,028	1,028	....
				1918–19	381	381	....
1891–92	16,597	11,084	5,513	1919–20	221	221	....
1892–93	12,318	8,314	4,004	1920–21	1,184	1,184	....
1893–94	13,735	9,475	4,260				
1894–95	18,428	12,627	5,801	1921–22	1,047	1,047	....
1895–96	13,022	9,218	3,084	1922–23[3]	204	204	....
				1923–24[3]	1,227	906	321
1896–97	15,572	11,433	4,139				

For reference notes see page 907.

TABLE III.—Distribution of citizen emigrants, by sex and age, 1923 and 1924.

Year	Total	Males	Females	Up to 15 years		15 to 55 years		55 years and over	
				Males	Females	Males	Females	Males	Females
1923	81,502	55,361	26,141	22,201		58,879		422	
1924	149,140	93,509	55,631	25,420	24,229	67,570	30,947	519	385

TABLE IV.—DISTRIBUTION OF INTERCONTINENTAL CITIZEN EMIGRANTS, BY COUNTRY OF FUTURE RESIDENCE, 1842-1924/25.

Year	Total	Mauritius	Natal	British Guiana	Trinidad	Dutch Guiana	Réunion	Jamaica	French West Indies	The minor British West Indian colonies[4] and the Danish colony of Ste.Croix	Other destinations
1842	459	459									
1843	39,755	39,755									
1844	8,242	8,242		1,591	1,332			1,047			
1845	12,511	8,541									
1846	16,735	7,180		4,901	2,264			2,390			
1847	10,719	5,933		2,372	1,236			1,178			
1848	9,671	5,780		3,211	680						
1849	7,670	7,670									
1850	9,800	9,800									
1851	14,266	11,245		1,927	1,094						
1852	22,674	18,594		2,351	1,729						
1853	19,781	15,631		2,653	1,497						
1854	19,337	16,712		2,321	294						
1855	16,629	15,057		949	623				525		
1856	15,080	9,751		2,879	1,561					364	
1857	20,805	17,117		1,855	1,451					382	
1858	45,838	38,735		2,839	3,619			703		645	
1859	43,057	33,927		4,939	2,526			1,709	1,224	962	
1860	24,062	11,603	1,226	5,229	2,710					361	
1861	32,026	14,182	368	5,386	2,030		5,333	2,161	533	2,033	
1862	14,766	8,322		3,326	1,389		864	544		321	
1863	11,731	5,548	1,021	2,643	1,433		1,086		1,178		
1864	22,084	10,607	1,979	3,139	1,450		3,731		807	508	
1865	27,589	19,493	1,320	2,842	1,498		1,121				
1866	21,347	3,549	534	4,509	2,993		1,791	1,705	5,776	490	
1867	7,614	313		3,001	1,840				2,460		
1868	13,379	1,595		4,944	2,248			1,426	2,817	349	
1869	15,827	2,787		6,685	2,935		1,079	924	1,417		
1870	12,433	3,273		3,199	2,087			1,382	1,886	606	
1871–72	11,034	4,321		2,125		410			1,689	2,899	
1872–73	20,037	6,816		6,087		3,523	783		1,312	5,412	
1873–74[6]	29,243	7,725		8,497			1,213		4,540[6]	3,944	
1874–75	25,325	6,800	6,025	3,942			1,047		3,205[6]	4,140	
1875–76	11,489	1,033	393	3,849					2,747[6]	2,420	
1876–77	10,560	1,027	761	3,992			1,177		839	1,601	
1877–78	24,710	3,836	3,510	8,288		324	1,072	1,163	3,593	4,087	
1878–79	22,092	3,647	4,452	6,520	2,632	709	Fiji 498	165	3,248	Mombasa	221
1879–80	17,426	2,137	743	4,496	3,161	320		756	5,534		279
1880–81	16,794	581	2,373	4,416	3,342	965		513	4,283		321
1881–82	11,509		2,229	3,168	2,591	496			3,025		
1882–83	13,504	1,574	1,647	2,984	1,963	451	922	398	3,565		
1883–84	17,936	4,307	2,775	2,731	2,661	1,480	1,514		2,468		
1884–85	22,384	4,109	3,548	6,304	2,191	1,679	2,316	601	495		
1885–86	7,979			4,771	1,656		1,552				1,141

TABLE IV.—DISTRIBUTION OF INTERCONTINENTAL CITIZEN EMIGRANTS, BY COUNTRY OF FUTURE RESIDENCE, 1842-1924/25 (concluded)

Year	Total	Mauritius	Natal	British Guiana	Trinidad	Dutch Guiana	Fiji	Jamaica	French West Indies	Mombasa	Other destinations
1886–87	7,978	1,012	496	3,916	2,291	353					108
1887–88	6,559	110	897	2,777	2,130		537				368
1888–89	10,756	604	1,585	3,572	2,270	1,092	675	590			80
1889–90	16,594	4,544	4,124	3,426	2,897	1,300	583	1,087			556
1890–91	20,085	3,039	4,330	5,218	3,435	1,249	1,171	1,060			
1891–92	16,597	989	3,349	5,231	3,285	698	1,985				
1892–93	12,318		3,119	4,723	2,620	1,075	7,781				157
1893–94	13,735	485	2,612	5,883	1,926	1,104	1,082	486			
1894–95	18,428	1,029	3,592	7,200	3,185	1,279	1,432	711			
1895–96	13,022	1,746	3,337	1,908	2,177	1,696	565	470		1,123	
1896–97	15,572	802	4,038	2,417	3,043	500	1,953			2,819	
1897–98	13,485	426	6,036	1,194	1,851	618	567	623		2,793	
1898–99	19,613		4,958	2,380	1,268	616		670		9,479	289
1899–1900	20,438		1,590	4,959	1,798		1,490			9,931	
1900–01	26,508	3,229	6,312	3,932	2,450		2,553			8,032	
1901–02	22,498	4,251	7,763	4,276	2,542	1,343	2,319			4	
1902–03	15,413	2,571	6,140	1,968	2,341	657	840	663		173	60
1903–04	13,665	510	4,601	2,937	2,449		2,988			25	155
1904–05	15,939	2,067	9,456	1,348	1,844	249	836			97	42
1905–06	21,125	720	8,108	2,737	3,164	175	4,066	1,647		448	60
1906–07	21,003	619	10,049	2,337	2,154	1,270	3,261	606		861	92
1907–08	15,117	587	6,664	1,830	1,868	1,918	1,137	416		383	124
1908–09	11,844		1,722	1,797	2,447	2,435	2,908	1,117		80	39
1909–10	11,644		2,935	2,515	2,480	478	1,947	816		53	119
1910–11	15,439	533	6,257	2,173	3,259		1,898			127	376
1911–12	14,192	[7]	3,401[8]	1,754	3,131	448	4,204	409		384	461
1912–13	12,658			2,201	2,380	768	4,958	1,578		455	318
1913–14	7,733			1,340	1,140	1,773	2,491	294		505	190
1914–15	3,285			806	423	748	721			268	319
1915–16	7,630			2,248	1,905		2,509			187	781
1916–17	7,682			830	1,330	304	1,756	615		234	2,613
1917–18	1,028									239	789
1918–19	381									352	29
1919–20	221									201	20
1920–21	1,184									184	1,000
1921–22	1,047									66	981
1922–23	204										204
1923–24	1,227	1,080									147
1924–25	494	317									177

For reference notes see page 907.

TABLE V.—Distribution of citizen emigrants, by country of future residence, distinguishing also skilled and unskilled, 1923 and 1924.

Country of future residence		1923	1924
Total		81,502	149,140
	Skilled	166	198
	Unskilled	81,336	148,942
Mauritius	Skilled	29	18
	Unskilled	875	504
Continental Africa	Skilled	130[9]	165[9]
Ceylon	Unskilled	49,157	100,250
Straits Settlements and Malaya	Unskilled	31,304	48,188
Persia	Skilled	7[9]	....
Siam	Skilled	..	15

TABLE VI.—Distribution of citizen immigrants, by sex, 1878-79—1921-22.

Year	Total	Males	Females	Year	Total	Males	Females
1878–79	5,586[1]	4,071	1,246	1900–01	7,006	6,008	998
1879–80	7,185[1]	4,989	1,817	1901–02	10,623	9,242	1,381
				1902–03	12,757	10,839	1,918
1880–81	7,061[1]	4,763	1,897	1903–04	11,673	9,803	1,870
1881–82	5,193[1]	3,516	1,356	1904–05	6,341	4,394	1,947
1882–83	5,760[1]	3,850	1,576				
1883–84	4,748[1]	3,245	1,376	1905–06	6,945	4,814	2,131
1884–85	6,647[1]	4,397	1,924	1906–07	8,197	5,653	2,544
				1907–08	6,774	4,713	2,061
1885–86	10,198[1]	6,577	2,987	1908–09	7,918	5,495	2,423
1886–87	8,819[1]	5,610	2,541	1909–10	6,909	5,083	1,826
1887–88	9,665[1]	6,323	2,772				
1888–89	5,242[1]	3,192	1,484	1910–11	5,788	4,093	1,695
1889–90	8,751[1]	5,689	2,851	1911–12	6,299	4,635	1,664
				1912–13	4,641	3,356	1,285
1890–91	6,717	4,547	2,170	1913–14	5,284	3,765	1,519
1891–92	6,451	4,503	1,948	1914–15	6,289	4,602	1,687
1892–93	5,966	4,062	1,904				
1893–94	5,844	4,044	1,800	1915–16	6,047	4,124	1,923
1894–95	5,872	3,949	1,923	1916–17	7,856	5,506	2,350
				1917–18	3,535	2,651	884
1895–96	6,171	4,110	2,061	1918–19	1,741	1,295	446
1896–97	4,794	3,291	1,503	1919–20	3,783	2,616	1,167
1897–98	4,213	3,093	1,120				
1898–99	5,689	4,433	1,256	1920–21	11,575	*	*
1899–1900	9,484[1]	7,808	1,428	1921–22	9,081	*	*

For reference notes see page 907.

TABLE VII.—DISTRIBUTION OF CITIZEN IMMIGRANTS, BY COUNTRY OF LAST RESIDENCE, 1923-24.

Country of last residence	1923	1924
Natal	2,479	1,347
British Guiana	220	392
Jamaica	681	447
Surinam	....	38
Trinidad	1,065	957
Fiji	2,956	....
Ceylon	....	570
Malaya	418	565
Unknown	98	83
Total	7,917	4,399

SOURCES

Statistical Abstract for British India for 1867-68 to 1884-85, Calcutta 1926, and 1914/15-1924/25 in Accounts and Papers.

Tables II and IV (years 1870-71 to 1877-78 and 1920-21 to 1924-25); Table VI (years 1920/21-1921/22).

Statistics of British India for 1906-07 and preceding years. Part IX. Miscellaneous. Calcutta, 1908. For 1911-12 and preceding years. Part V (Area, Population and Public Health). Calcutta, 1913. Volume IV (Administration, Judicial and Local Self-Government). Calcutta, 1922.

Tables II, IV and VI (years 1878/79-1919/20).

Geoghegan. J., (Under-Secretary of the Government of India), Department of Agriculture, Revenue and Commerce. *Note on Emigration from India.* Calcutta, 1873, pp. 77-84.

Tables I and IV (years 1842-70).

Government of Madras. Law (General) Department G. O. No. 1890, June 25, 1924, and G. O. No. 1578, May 12, 1925, Emigration and Immigration Report, 1923 and 1924.

Tables III, V, VII (years 1923 and 1924).

Report on the Working of the Indian Emigration Act, VII of 1922 and the Rules issued thereunder in the Province of Bengal for the Years 1923 and 1924. Calcutta, 1924 and 1925.

Tables III, V, VII (years 1923 and 1924).

Consolidated Annual Report on the Working of the Indian Emigration Act for the Years ending December 31, 1923 and December 31, 1925. Bombay, 1925 and Calcutta, 1925.

Tables III, V, VII (years 1923 and 1924).

NOTES

[1]Including children, the sex of whom is not distinguished in the local statements.
[2]Under the Defence of India (Consolidation) Rules, 1915, in effect from March 12, 1917, emigration was temporarily stopped except in the case of persons permitted to depart by general or special license.
[3]Classification by sex of emigrants from Madras ports not known.
[4]St. Vincent, St. Lucia, Grenada, St. Kitts.
[5]The figures do not total correctly.
[6]Including 1,777, 751 and 427 emigrated in 1873-74, 1874-75 and 1875-76 respectively to French Guiana.
[7]Emigration to Mauritius was prohibited from 1912 to 1922 included.
[8]Represents figures for three months, April, May and June 1911 only, emigration to Natal having been prohibited from July 1, 1911.
[9]According to the headings of the tables in the source whence we quote these figures, they refer to the fiscal years 1922-23 and 1923-24. The Reports as a whole relate to the years ending December 31, 1923 and 1924.

BRITISH MALAYA

1. Portions of the Malay States had separate migration statistics for 1900 (Selangor and Perak) and for 1891-1900 (Negri Sembilan). Chinese and other immigrants were classified by sex.

2. The Labour Department of the Federated Malay States publishes statistics relating to Indian emigrants arriving in the Straits Settlements and in the Federated and non-Federated Malay States.

Immigrants are Indians who have arrived from Southern India at Penang (Straits Settlements), the port of disembarkation for Perak and the first port of call for immigrants to the Federated Malay States. They were of two classes: (a) assisted immigrants (free laborers imported at the expense of the Immigration Fund for work on estates, in mines and elsewhere), and (b) other immigrants (traders, laborers and others who paid their passage). Assisted immigrants are sub-divided into two classes: (a) independent laborers and (b) laborers recruited by kanganies or agents.

The destination of assisted immigrants is given but no definite information is available about the destination of "other immigrants". It is estimated that perhaps one-third of such immigrants proceeded to the Federated Malay States.

All immigrants for the States of Perak, Kedah and Perlis and the Settlement of Penang landed at Penang; those for the States of Selangor, Negri Sembilan, Pahang, Johore, Kelantan, and the Settlement of Malacca landed at Port Swettenham. A considerable proportion of the arriving immigrants had previously lived in the country.

For the years 1923 and 1924 the three groups of arriving immigrants are divided by sex (table V).

3. Emigration statistics concern Indians who leave Penang for Southern India after having worked in the Straits Settlements, the Federated Malay States, or the non-Federated Malay States.

FEDERATED MALAY STATES

a. Negri Sembilan

TABLE I.—DISTRIBUTION OF IMMIGRANTS AND EMIGRANTS, BY NATIONALITY, 1900.

Immigrants			Emigrants		
Total	Chinese	Others	Total	Chinese	Others
15,700	9,598	6,102	8,276	5,442	2,834

b. Perak

TABLE II.—DISTRIBUTION OF IMMIGRANTS AND EMIGRANTS, BY NATIONALITY AND SEX, 1900.

	Immigrants			Emigrants		
	Total	Males	Females	Total	Males	Females
Chinese.....	68,672	61,876	6,796	42,310	36,839	5,471
Others.....	26,056	20,986	5,070	20,594	16,630	3,964
Total....	95,728	82,862	11,866	62,904	53,469	9,435

c. Selangor

TABLE III.—DISTRIBUTION OF CHINESE IMMIGRANTS AND EMIGRANTS, BY SEX, 1891-1900.

Year	Immigrants			Emigrants		
	Total	Males	Females	Total	Males	Females
1891	21,623	20,011	1,612	15,752	14,550	1,202
1892	40,580	38,428	2,152	18,509	17,015	1,494
1893	49,111	45,942	3,169	25,349	23,335	2,014
1894[1]	45,597	43,094	2,503	26,206	24,163	2,043
1895	49,406	46,128	3,278	33,249	30,367	2,882
1896	41,883	38,100	3,783	33,174	29,938	3,216
1897	27,783	24,984	2,799	32,224	29,016	3,208
1898	29,558	26,321	3,237	26,726[2]	23,854	2,874
1899	38,416	34,853	3,563	26,613	23,524	3,089
1900						
Chinese....	50,634	46,300	4,334	33,608	29,859	3,749
Others.....	32,519	26,935	5,584	24,284	19,920	4,364
Total....	83,153	73,235	9,918	57,892	49,779	8,113

For reference notes see page 911.

TABLE IV.—ARRIVALS AT PENANG FROM MADRAS AND NAGAPATAM, BY DESTINATION, 1923-24.

Territory	1923					1924				
	Total	Minors Males	Minors Females	Adults Males	Adults Females	Total	Minors Males	Minors Females	Adults Males	Adults Females
1. Assisted immigrants[3]										
Straits Settlements	4,214	209	177	3,086	742	5,447	384	296	3,688	1,079
Federated Malay States										
Perak	8,371	537	538	5,490	1,806	7,637	629	552	4,736	1,720
Selangor	8,732	464	356	6,294	1,618	14,562	1,129	840	9,552	3,041
Negri Sembilan	2,527	125	96	1,901	405	4,599	228	245	3,262	864
Pahang	523	24	15	398	86	806	64	65	497	180
Total, Federated Malay States	20,153	1,150	1,005	14,083	3,915	27,604	2,050	1,702	18,047	5,805
Other Malay States										
Johore	2,340	131	120	1,639	450	3,292	205	197	2,266	624
Kedah	3,040	269	205	1,895	671	6,191	597	520	3,517	1,557
Perlis	....	....	....	....	....	....	....	....	426	....
Kelantan	487	61	39	263	124	613	43	44	....	100
Total, other Malay States	5,867	461	364	3,797	1,245	10,096	845	761	6,209	2,281
Total assisted	30,234	1,820	1,546	20,966	5,902	43,147	3,279	2,759	27,944	9,165
2. Other immigrants—i.e., ordinary passengers.	19,268	1,104	471	15,952	1,741	18,905	1,133	504	15,613	1,655
Grand total	49,502	2,924	2,017	36,918	7,643	62,052	4,412	3,263	43,557	10,820

For reference notes see page 911.

TABLE V.—ARRIVALS AT PENANG OF INDIANS FROM MADRAS AND NEGAPATAM, BY SEX AND AGE, 1923-24.

Description	Year	Total	Adults		Minors	
			Males	Females	Males	Females
Independent laborers........	1923	7,462	5,522	1,246	397	297
	1924	9,641	7,002	1,632	553	454
Laborers recruited by kanganis................	1923	22,772	15,444	4,656	1,423	1,249
	1924	33,506	20,942	7,533	2,726	2,305
Other immigrants, i. e., ordinary passengers.......	1923	19,268	15,952	1,741	1,575	
	1924	18,905	15,613	1,655	1,133	504
Total..............	1923	49,502	36,918	7,643	4,941	
	1924	62,052	43,557	10,820	4,412	3,263

TABLE VI.—DEPARTURES FROM PENANG FOR SOUTHERN INDIA, BY AGE, 1923-24.

Year	Total	Age	
		Minors	Adults
1923	42,778	2,533	40,245
1924	37,326	2,370	34,956

SOURCES

Statistical Tables relating to the Colonial and other Possessions of the United Kingdom. London, Parts XXII, XXIV and XXV.

Tables I, II and III.

Federated Malay States. *Report on the Working of the Labor Department* for the **Year 1923 and** for the Year 1924. Kuala Lumpur, 1925.

Tables IV, V, VI (years 1923 and 1924).

NOTES

[1]Immigration from all ports of the southeast of China was prohibited from June 18, 1894 to September 21, 1894, on account of an outbreak of bubonic plague.
[2]The sum of the distribution by sex does not correspond exactly with the total.
[3]Independent laborers and laborers recruited by kanganis.

STRAITS SETTLEMENTS

1.   The first table records the arrival and departure of Indian and Chinese passengers from 1900 to 1924 and of East Indian indentured laborers shown separately from 1900 to 1910.   After 1910 their emigration was suspended.

2.   Since 1920, the Controller of Labour of the Straits Settlements and the Federated Malay States has prepared the statistics of Indian immigrants and emigrants.   Their destination is given as the Straits Settlements, the Federated Malay States, or the non-Federated Malay States.

The annual report of the Labour Department of the Federated Malay States (Kuala Lumpur) is published both under the title of the Federated Malay States and that of the Straits Settlements.   The table dealing with the statistics of the Straits Settlements has been placed in this volume under Malay States as table IV.

3.   Chinese immigrate through the three ports of Singapore, Penang and Malacca.   Immigrants whose passage was unpaid at the time of their departure (styled "unpaid" or "credit ticket" passengers) are distinguished from 1877 onward from other, or free, immigrants.   The figures given in the *Journal of the Indian Archipelago* (1854) for the total annual immigration of Chinese, free and indebted, increased from 5,063 during 1840-41 to 11,484 during 1852-3.

In 1877, 16,688 Chinese immigrants were examined in the Straits Settlements.   Of the 9,776 immigrants landed in Singapore in that year, 2,653 were "unpaid" or "credit ticket" passengers.   This ratio of "unpaid" to free immigrants may perhaps be taken for the total immigration into the Straits Settlements in 1877.   Of the earlier years there is no sufficient record.[1]

The figures for Singapore and Penang begin with 1881 (table II) and those for Malacca with 1891 (table III).

The unpaid passengers sometimes occasioned considerable embarrassment, as not infrequently they were detained on the boats until they had found a purchaser, and the master of the vessel had received the passage money.   These passengers also sign labor contracts before their departure.[2]

[1]Crawford, Campbell, *Chinese Coolie Emigration*, London, 1923, p. 8
[2]Ta Chen, *loc. cit.*, p. 86.

TABLE I.—Immigration and emigration of aliens, 1900-24.

Year	Immigrants. East Indian indentured	Chinese and Indians	Emigrants Indian coolies from Penang	Year	Immigrants. East Indian indentured	Chinese and Indians	Emigrants Indian coolies from Penang
1900	7,615	297,423	11,251	1913	....	426,381[1]	70,090
1901	2,785	254,919	16,204	1914	....	237,010[1]	63,073
1902	2,430	266,706	18,183	1915	....	197,629[1]	50,320
1903	572	284,079	17,832	1916	....	331,196[1]	54,479
1904	2,721	280,657	19,550	1917	....	284,123[1]	57,583
1905	4,823	262,356	19,750	1918	....	140,843[1]	52,132
1906	3,674	278,861	21,879	1919	....	183,489[1]	46,767
1907	5,499	357,298	30,500	1920	....	221,297[1]	55,481
1908	5,456	255,573	30,920	1921	....	236,716[1]	61,551
1909	4,119	245,018	31,394	1922	....	191,560[1]	45,733
1910	2,523	360,243	39,080	1923	....	208,651[2]	120,899[3]
1911	....	460,374	48,103	1924	....	243,482[4]	125,075[5]
1912	....	436,264	63,885				

TABLE II.—Chinese immigrants and emigrants to and from Singapore and Penang, 1881-1915.

Year	SINGAPORE Immigrants Total	Passage unpaid	Females	Emigrants	PENANG Immigrants Total	Passage unpaid	Females	Emigrants	Labor contracts
1881	47,747	*	2,053	*	42,056	17,000	1,068	*	32,473
1882	55,887	11,404	1,534	*	45,122	17,011	1,115	*	33,601
1883	61,206	10,249	1,701	*	47,930	16,197	2,272	*	31,663
1884	68,517	9,690	2,089	*	38,231	15,181	1,431	*	29,088
1885	69,314	9,357	2,014	*	42,142	17,034	1,354	*	32,180
1886	87,331	15,733	2,345	*	57,186	23,459	1,733	*	45,717
1887	101,094	19,496	3,037	*	65,348	22,904	2,784	*	51,859
1888	103,541	18,421	3,164	60,759	62,812	16,186	2,176	11,818	44,451
1889	102,429	11,962	3,837	*	44,441	9,251	1,980	*	32,666
1890	96,230	8,152	3,820	31,706	36,044	6,813	1,726	5,921	26,204
1891	93,843	6,229	4,710	32,245	49,066	8,416	2,416	383	17,538
1892	93,339	9,118	4,804	*	45,227	6,281	2,529	*	*
1893	144,558	18,973	6,387	*	68,251	9,967	3,868	*	38,326
1894	106,612	8,983	5,007	31,083	46,230	6,083	2,425	371	22,302
1895	150,157	14,518	6,997	*	60,559	8,731	3,653	*	*
1896	142,358	15,089	6,451	*	57,055	9,531	3,216	*	29,825
1897	90,828	8,859	5,427	24,150	41,124	4,916	3,224	2,333	17,268
1898	106,983	10,978	6,192	26,575	44,811	5,004	3,301	1,890	20,459
1899	117,794	14,198	5,514	31,903	51,299	4,371	2,764	2,764	22,233
1900	159,571	18,056	8,482	41,376	72,821	7,239	3,847	4,026	27,033
1901	157,657	15,012	11,822	39,512	66,411	5,395	4,128	4,594	22,408
1902		....		....		....		....	
1903	172,770	13,870	14,539	47,551	75,401	4,582	5,346	4,450	18,768
1904	163,079	16,930	10,163	41,717	39,215	357	4,156	1,260	17,045
1905	136,001	12,144	13,714	37,130	35,645	1,942	4,833	1,475	14,864
1906	*	*	*	*	*	*	*	*	18,675
1907	179,756	20,206	13,785	47,580	44,495	2,079	5,682	1,809	24,089
1908	121,639	12,416	11,147	31,813	29,387	812	4,295	2,296	13,604
1909	120,954	12,875	9,602	30,798	27,529	233	3,901	3,540	13,379
1910	173,423	22,990	14,121	42,898	37,955	140	5,333	867	23,935
1911	215,036	23,522	19,754	54,818	49,875	400	7,302	4,516	24,345
1912	203,124	13,394	21,779	48,520	44,284	103	6,384	4,236	13,600
1913	240,979	14,198	28,547	41,018	37,161	17	5,611	3,862	14,198
1914	124,032	2,648	13,096	13,118	41,988	*	2,714	3,345	2,648
1915	80,352	*	10,632	15,382	26,698	*	4,123	1,743	*
Total	4,088,141	419,670	278,266	781,652[6]	1,573,799	247,635	112,520	67,499	776,444
Average..	123,883	13,538	8,432	37,221	47,691	7,988	3,409	3,214	25,047

For reference notes see page 914.

TABLE III.—Indirect statistics. Chinese immigrants to Malacca, 1891-1912.

Year	Immigrants to Malacca		Year	Immigrants to Malacca	
	Total	Unpaid passengers		Total	Unpaid passengers
1891	1,355	491	1902	....	....
1892	882	311	1903	271	271
1893	908	194	1904	357	357
1894	1,112	478	1905	187	187
1895	2,060	922	1906	....	....
1896	1,325	680	1907	467	467
1897	328	233	1908	134	134
1898	625	608	1909	96	96
1899	1,323	1,288	1910	790	790
1900	537	494	1911	427	427
1901	....	347	1912	103	103

SOURCES

Statistical Abstract for the several British Overseas Dominions and Protectorates. London, 1914 and 1924.

Table I (years 1900-21).

Annual Report of the Labor Department of the Straits Settlements, 1923, p. 13.

Table I (year 1922).

Colonial Reports (Annual). No. 1264. *Straits Settlements, Report for 1924.* London, 1925, p. 43.

Table I (years 1923 and 1924).

Information supplied by the British Government (Ministry of Labor).

Table IV (year 1923).

Annual Departmental Reports of Straits Settlements. Quoted in "Chinese Migrations with Special Reference to Labor Conditions", by Ta Chen. *Bulletin of the United States Bureau of Labor Statistics,* Washington, 1923, pp. 84-85.

Tables II-III.

NOTES

[1]Except Malacca, for which no returns are available.
[2]49,502 from Southern India, 159,149 from China.
[3]78,121 to China, 42,778 to Southern India.
[4]62,052 from Southern India, 181,430 from China.
[5]37,326 to Southern India. 87,749 to China.
[6]The yearly figures total 771,652.

TABLE I.—IMMIGRATION FROM AND EMIGRATION TO INDIA[1], 1878-1900.

Year	Immi-grants	Year	Immi-grants	Year	Emigrants	Year	Emigrants
1878	105,862	1890	52,769	1878	91,744	1890	46,085
1879	82,669			1879	81,093		
1880	45,343	1891	76,728	1880	73,533	1891	39,138
		1892	113,379			1892	20,344
1881	54,204	1893	100,152	1881	61,415	1893	22,663
1882	51,640	1894	94,489	1882	58,356	1894	17,439[2]
1883	39,055	1895	72,556	1883	51,205	1895	15,802[2]
1884	45,962			1884	50,128		
1885	46,665	1896	72,267	1885	48,525	1896	15,434[2]
		1897	84,830			1897	14,123[2]
1886	39,907	1898	80,238	1886	45,250	1898	16,347[2]
1887	72,660	1899	57,736	1887	55,121	1899	884[2]
1888	81,710	1900	86,055	1888	55,380	1900	52,607
1889	64,459			1889	52,016		

TABLE II.—IMMIGRATION FROM AND EMIGRATION TO INDIA, 1911-24.[3]

Year	Immigrants	Emigrants	Year	Immigrants	Emigrants
1911	137,115	106,123	1918	103,928	116,227
1912	188,273	137,275	1919	191,128	147,465
1913	188,428	148,978	1920	136,699	146,247
1914	174,032	160,161	1921	106,598	127,107
1915	176,237	160,028	1922	174,569	145,737
1916	200,146	172,702	1923	169,607[4]	130,406[5]
1917	105,916	130,117	1924	. . . . . .	156,523

TABLE III.—IMMIGRATION FROM AND EMIGRATION TO INDIA (INDIAN COOLIES ONLY), 1900-24.

Year	Immigrants	Emigrants	Year	Immigrants	Emigrants
1900	207,994	112,936	1913	120,354	90,374
1901	120,603	118,343	1914	78,662	49,031
1902	87,763	63,917	1915	94,828	38,298
1903	63,446	47,715	1916	115,713	47,588
1904	77,302	56,246	1917	47,296	32,119
1905	160,080	65,513	1918	43,184	23,161
1906	88,945	59,659	1919	112,391	34,268
1907	55,724	63,671	1920	45,912[6]	. . . . .
1908	86,401	78,740	1921	22,365[6]	. . . . .
1909	79,845	61,287	1922	77,636[6]	. . . . .
1910	118,613	64,660	1923	89,859[6]	. . . . .
1911	97,536	58,916	1924	153,989[6]	. . . . .
1912	117,475	77,840			

For reference notes see page 916.

SOURCES

Statistical Tables relating to the Colonial and other Possessions of the United Kingdom, London. Parts XVII to XXV.

Table I (years 1878-1900).

Statistical Abstract for the several British Overseas Dominions .and Protectorates. Statistical Department, Board of Trade, London, 1914, 1922, 1924.

Tables II (years 1911-21); III (years 1900-19).

Ceylon Administration Reports for 1924. Immigration and Quarantine. Galle, 1925

Table III (year 1920).

Information supplied by the Ceylon Government: *Ceylon Administration Reports for 1924.* "Indian Immigrant Labor", p. 1519.

Table III (years 1921-24).

Information supplied by the British Government (Foreign Office).

Table II (year 1922).

Information supplied by the British Government (Ministry of Labor).

Table II (years 1923-24).

(Emigration figures for 1924 taken from the Ceylon Blue-Book for 1925.)

NOTES

[1]It is not certain whether coolies are included or not. The figures given in table III for 1900 concerning coolies are higher than the'figures indicated in table I. The British Government (Ministry of Labor) in a communication dated July 26, 1926, gives the following explanation:

"The migration statistics for 1900 published in the Statistical Tables relating to the Colonies and Protectorates were extracted from the Ceylon Blue-Book. The figures supplied by the Ceylon authorities for use in the *Statistical Abstract for the Dominions and Protectorates* for the year 1906 contained a revision of the 1900 and also of the 1905 figures. These revised figures were accepted and were published in place of the original Blue-Book figures ".

The difference in the description of migrants in the two publications does not seem to account for the revision, as in subsequent years.

[2]Exclusive of the emigration from the Province of Sabaragamuwa, the particulars of which are not known.

[3]The figures 1911-21 represent the total number of immigrants and emigrants from and to India. (*Statistical Abstract*, 1907-21. London, 1924, p. 10, note *e.*) The same note refers to the figures for 1922, which were communicated by the Foreign Office.

The emigration figures from the Ceylon Blue-Book for 1925 and communicated by the Ministry of Labor (Emigration from Ceylon, 1920-24) correspond in 1920-22 with the figures indicating emigration to India, but the figure for 1923 agrees with the *total* emigration (147,860) of which about one-eighth only was emigration to India (see note 5). It is impossible to tell whether the other figures also include a certain number of immigrants and emigrants from and to other countries than India.

[4]The total number of arrivals in 1923 was 190,512, of which number 169,607 were from India. The number of Europeans was 5,665.

[5]Total departures in 1923 numbered 147,860, of whom 130,406 were bound for India. There were 3,501 departures of Europeans during the year.

[6]Indian Estate Laborers.

DUTCH EAST INDIES

Table I appears to refer to immigrants proper, including citizens and aliens of all nationalities and races.

Table II records the number of landing permits issued.

In conformity with the Royal Decree of October 15, 1915, the following classes of persons arriving from a country other than the Dutch Indies are required to have a written permit to land: (a) Dutch citizens not born of parents settled in the Dutch Indies nor themselves domiciled in the Dutch Indies, (b) aliens not domiciled in the Dutch Indies.

These landing permits are obtainable on board upon payment of 100 gulden, the amount being returned if the person leaves within a period specified by the Governor-General.

The permits are valid for two years and may be extended twice for a maximum period of one year.

Table III relates to the migrations of native coolies.

TABLE I.—DISTRIBUTION OF IMMIGRANTS, BY NATIONALITY, 1923

Netherlanders	2,268
Other Europeans, Americans, Africans and Australians	906
Japanese	668
Chinese	21,169
Arabs	675
Other oriental aliens	2,224
Total	27,910

TABLE II.—NUMBER OF PERMITS FOR ADMITTANCE, 1915-24.[2]

Year	Total	Europeans	Chinese	Arab	Other alien Asiatics
1915	30,504	3,350	25,163	422	1,569
1919	35,180	6,638	25,279	378	2,885
1920	42,046	9,229	28,653	719	3,445
1921	63,011	7,427	49,844	839	4,903
1922	48,867	4,621	39,623	969	3,654
1923	41,617	4,140	34,015	702	2,760
1924	37,812	4,374	30,232	494	2,712

For reference notes see page 918.

TABLE III.—Emigration and immigration of coolies, by country of future or last residence, 1923-24.

Country of future or last residence	Emigrants		Immigrants	
	1923	1924	1923	1924
New Caledonia	....	650	133	298
British North Borneo	353	92	224[1]	79[1]
Sarawak	....	299	8[1]	....
Federated Malay States and Straits Settlements	145	156	19[1]	30[1]
Cochin-China	....	....	27	14
Dutch Guiana	633	1,089	198	....
Total	1,131	2,286	609	421

SOURCE

Information supplied by the Government (Colonial Department).

Tables I, II, III.

NOTES

[1]These statistics include only returning workmen who reported themselves on their arrival in Java to the Commissary for Labor Recruitment.
[2]Citizen and alien officials, crews, and transients are not required to have permits.

Cochin China
TABLE I.—DISTRIBUTION OF EUROPEAN IMMIGRANTS AND REPATRIATED PERSONS[1], BY
NATIONALITY, 1879-83.

Nationality	1879							
	Immigrants				Repatriated			
	Total	Males	Fe-males	Chil-dren	Total	Males	Fe-males	Chil-dren
French.................	130	89	35	6	109	82	24	3
English.................	14	12	2	..	7	6	1	...
German.................	12	5	1	6	5	5	..	...
Italian.................	6	5	1	...	1	1	...	...
Austrian................	1	1	...	...	1	..	1	...
Spanish................	1	1	...	...	1	1	...	...
Swiss..................	1	1	...	...	1	1	...	...
Belgian................	...	...	...	...	...	...	...	...
Russian................	...	...	...	...	...	...	...	...
Portuguese.............	9	4	1	4	8	4	2	2
Netherlander...........	1	1	...	...	1	1	...	...
Greek..................	2	2	...	...	...	...	...	...
Turkish................	...	...	...	...	...	...	...	...
Swedish................	...	...	...	...	...	...	...	...
	1880							
French.................	161	94	42	15	139	101	30	8
English.................	19	17	2	...	12	11	1	...
German.................	17	15	2	...	6	5	1	...
Italian.................	7	2	5	...	4	2	2	...
Austrian................	..	...	..	...	1	1	...	...
Spanish................	2	...	2	...	...	...	...	...
Swiss..................	3	3	...	...	1	1	...	...
Belgian................	2	1	1	...	1	1	...	...
Russian................	1	...	1	...	...	...	...	...
Portuguese.............	2	1	1	...	1	1	...	...
Netherlander...........	2	2	...	...	1	1	...	...
Greek..................	1	1	...	...	3	3	...	...
Turkish................	...	...	...	...	...	...	...	...
Swedish................	...	...	...	...	...	...	...	...
	1881							
French.................	170	115	37	18	147	95	29	23
English.................	30	16	5	9	18	12	1	5
German.................	12	9	3	...	5	5	...	...
Italian.................	2	1	1	...	1	1	...	...
Austrian................	1	1	...	...	...	...	...	...
Spanish................	...	...	...	...	...	...	...	...
Swiss..................	...	...	...	...	2	2	...	...
Belgian................	...	...	...	...	...	...	...	...
Russian................	...	..	...	...	3	1	2	...
Portuguese.............	2	1	1	..	...	...	...	...
Netherlander...........	2	2	...	..	1	1	...	...
Greek..................	...	...	...	...	...	...	...	...
Turkish................	...	...	...	...	...	...	...	...
Swedish................	...	...	...	...	...	...	...	...

For reference notes see page 920.

TABLE I.—DISTRIBUTION OF EUROPEAN IMMIGRANTS AND REPATRIATED PERSONS,[1] BY NATIONALITY, 1879-83 (continued).

Nationality	1882							
	Immigrants				Repatriated			
	Total	Males	Fe-males	Chil-dren	Total	Males	Fe-males	Chil-dren
French.................	206	145	45	16	140	110	22	8
English................	30	27	2	1	16	13	3	...
German................	10	10	...	...	4	4	...	...
Italian................	3	3	...	...	2	1	1	...
Austrian...............	...	...	...	...	...	...	...	...
Spanish................	1	1	...	...	...	...	...	...
Swiss.................	1	1	...	...	1	1	...	...
Belgian................	...	...	...	...	1	1	...	...
Russian................	1	1	...	...	1	1	...	...
Portuguese.............	1	1	...	...	1	1	...	...
Netherlander...........	1	1	...	...	4	3	1	...
Greek.................	1	1	...	...	...	...	...	...
Turkish................	2	2	...	...	...	...	...	...
Swedish................	1	1	...	...	...	...	...	...
	1883							
French.................	254	187	48	19	208	147	39	22
English................	45	37	4	4	28	9	7	12
German................	5	4	1	...	5	4	1	...
Italian................	4	4	...	...	3	3	...	...
Austrian...............	7	3	3	1	6	5	1	...
Spanish................	...	...	...	...	2	2	...	...
Swiss.................	2	1	1	...	...	...	...	...
Belgian................	2	2	...	...	2	2	...	...
Russian................	2	...	2	...	4	1	2	1
Portuguese.............	2	2	...	...	1	1	...	...
Netherlander...........	2	2	...	...	...	...	...	...
Greek.................	1	1	...	...	...	...	...	...
Turkish................	1	1	...	...	3	2	1	...
Swedish................	...	...	...	...	...	...	...	...

TABLE II.—CHINESE IMMIGRATION AND EMIGRATION, 1879-83.

Year	Immigrants	Emigrants	Year	Immigrants	Emigrants
1879	15,236	9,042	1882	8,414	7,848
1880	15,073	9,734	1883	10,989	6,992
1881	7,497	8,499			

SOURCE

Notices Coloniales. Paris, 1885, pp. 410-13.

NOTE

[1]Members of the administrative staff are not included.

TABLE I.—DISTRIBUTION OF ENGLISH AND FRENCH PASSENGERS EMBARKED AND DISEMBARKED, BY SEX AND NATIONALITY, 1913-24.

Year	Disembarked from the Straits Settlements (Singapore, Rangoon, Penang), or from Ceylon								Embarked for the Straits Settlements (Singapore, Rangoon, Penang, etc.)							
	French				English				French				English			
	Total	Chil-dren	Men	Women	Total	Chil-dren	Men	Women	Total	Chil-dren	Men	Women	Total	Chil-dren	Men	Women
1913	617	19	564	34	533	16	493	24	682	49	570	63	1,099	57	981	61
1914	534	51	428	55	817	41	720	56	418	25	352	41	763	28	683	52
1915	314	22	273	19	367	17	323	27	653	68	554	31	1,564	118	1,404	42
1916	281	23	239	19	350	23	300	27	709	58	607	44	1,450	86	1,299	65
1917	290	19	255	16	432	24	373	35	424	41	358	25	527	48	460	19
1918	102	8	88	6	236	31	180	25	341	19	315	7	453	42	414	7
1919	119	16	98	5	179	21	139	19	757	65	653	39	1,233	155	1,067	11
1920	250	22	210	18	258	24	215	19	607	55	513	39	1,798	194	1,560	44
1921	261	20	222	19	186	10	156	20	404	43	339	22	3,212	339	2,778	95
1922	164	23	133	8	164	21	125	18	162	27	128	7	2,150	198	1,849	103
1923	230	14	204	12	454	13	420	21	97	7	74	16	2,299	160	2,023	116
1924	135	5	129	1	203	14	173	16	142	18	119	5	2,654	200	2,347	107

SOURCE

Information supplied by the French Government (Etablissements français de l'Inde. Public Works).

PONDICHERRY

TABLE I.—Distribution of passengers disembarked from the packet-boats of the Messageries Maritimes shipping company, by nationality, 1916-24.

Year	Total	Nationality	Place of embarkation
1916	13	12 French and 1 English.	
1919	23	Including 9 French and 12 Hindus.	
1920	35	17 French, the remainder Hindus or English.	Saigon, Haiphong or Marseilles.
1921	5		Marseilles, Colombo or India.
1922	44	Chiefly Hindus.	Indo-China or India.
1923	7		Mostly from Saigon.
1924	18		

TABLE II.—Distribution of passengers embarked on the packet-boats of the Messageries Maritimes shipping company, by nationality, 1916-1924.

Year	Total	Nationality	Destination
1916	11	French.	Mostly for Saigon or Jibuti.
1918	6	French or English.	
1919	18	Chifly English or Hindus.	Mostly for Saigon or Haiphong.
1920	62	Chiefly French, a few Hindus.	Mostly for Marseilles or Saigon.
1921	14	Including a few French.	For Saigon or Colombo.
1922	2	1 English and 1 French.	
1923	10	9 French and 1 Pole.	For Marseilles, Saigon or Colombo.
1924	3	2 French and 1 Persian.	For Colombo.

SOURCE

Information supplied by the French Government (Colonial Ministry).

Tables I and II.

TABLE I.—Distribution of immigrant aliens, by sex and age, 1910-24.

Year[1]	Total	Males	Females	Under 16 years	16-44 years	45 years and over
1910	2,308	1,984	324	440[2]	1,768[3]	100
1911	2,946	2,456	490	625[2]	2,195[3]	126
1912	2,536	2,098	438	547[2]	1,912[3]	77
1913	4,408	3,865	543	964[2]	3,323[3]	121
1914	4,049	3,550	499	816[2]	3,086[3]	147
1915	3,926	3,463	463	1,113[2]	2,729[3]	84
1916	4,122	3,553	569	1,038[2]	2,861[3]	223
1917	5,797	5,236	561	1,243[2]	4,374[3]	180
1918	7,698	6,985	713	1,203	6,313	182
1919	9,872	8,260	1,612	2,646	6,936	290
1920	10,009	8,357	1,652	2,713	6,884	412
1921	10,652	8,978	1,674	2,844	7,346	462
1922	6,537	5,641	896	1,780	4,582	175
1923	6,689	5,588	1,101	2,146	4,365	178
1924	7,139	5,485	1,654	2,205	4,633	301

TABLE II.—Distribution of immigrant aliens, by occupation, 1910-24.

Year	Total	Agriculture	Industry and mining	Transport and commerce	Domestic service and general labor	Liberal professions and public services	Other occupations, none or unknown
1910	2,308	26	324	581	283	181	913
1911	2,946	405	331	471	64	164	1,511
1912	2,536	407	208	423	64	131	1,303
1913	4,408	874	309	626	154	191	2,254
1914	4,049	683	348	729	120	175	1,994
1915	3,926	434	286	219	43	100	2,844
1916	4,122	534	235	527	42	157	2,627
1917	5,797	1,886	53	424	17	197	3,220
1918	7,698	3,685	73	395	11	107	3,427
1919	9,872	1,483	83	864	204	106	7,132
1920	10,009	322	66	802	65	165	8,589
1921	10,652	275	54	776	19	134	9,394
1922	6,537	154	26	368	12	104	5,873
1923	6,689	191	19	301	12	39	6,127
1924	7,139	331	31	441	9	93	6,234

For reference notes see page 924.

TABLE III.—DISTRIBUTION OF EMIGRANT ALIENS, BY SEX AND AGE, 1910-24.

Year[1]	Total	Males	Females	Under 16 years	16-44 years	45 years and over
1910	1,010	900	110	41[2]	558[3]	411
1911	896	747	149	94[2]	668[3]	134
1912	729	557	172	108[2]	522[2]	99
1913	768	566	202	107[2]	539[3]	122
1914	1,782	1,459	323	195[2]	1,324[3]	263
1915	1,120	884	236	112[2]	880[3]	128
1916	850	646	204	80[2]	646[3]	124
1917	807	604	203	84[2]	606[3]	117
1918	795	629	166	43	682	70
1919	1,215	951	264	99	1,023	93
1920	1,509	1,203	306	201	1,106	202
1921	1,724	1,377	347	283	1,181	260
1922	1,105	941	164	69	959	77
1923	1,077	900	177	85	904	88
1924	938	707	231	138	628	172

TABLE IV.—DISTRIBUTION OF EMIGRANT ALIENS, BY OCCUPATION, 1910-24.

Year[1]	Total	Agriculture	Industry and mining	Transport amd commerce	Domestic service and general labor	Liberal professions and public services	Other occupations, none or unknown
1910	1,010	12	54	378	282	57	227
1911	896	18	81	359	116	46	276
1912	729	15	91	277	46	47	253
1913	768	17	63	299	52	66	271
1914	1,782	48	166	492	522	86	468
1915	1,120	44	174	315	197	77	313
1916	850	69	137	263	66	51	264
1917	807	55	104	214	56	84	294
1918	795	209	124	135	68	48	211
1919	1,215	347	115	202	152	44	355
1920	1,509	470	48	300	141	67	483
1921	1,724	285	36	536	33	62	772
1922	1,105	580	90	111	23	62	239
1923	1,077	537	71	125	48	47	249
1924	938	275	49	165	29	70	350

SOURCE

Annual Report of the Commissioner-General of Immigration to the Secretary of Commerce and Labor for the fiscal year ended June 30. Washington, 1910 to 1924.

Tables I-IV.

NOTES

[1]Fiscal years ended June 30.
[2]Under 14 years.
[3]From 14 to 44 years.

TABLE I.—ARRIVALS AND DEPARTURES, PORT OF BANGKOK AND SOUTHERN FRONTIER, 1918/19—1923/24.

Year[1]	Arrivals	Departures	Excess of arrivals	Year[1]	Arrivals	Departures	Excess of arrivals
1918–19	80,233	52,989	27,244	1921–22	104,570	75,797	28,773
1919–20	88,117	74,669	13,448	1922–23	126,557	99,876	26,681
1920–21	96,670	68,746	27,924	1923–24	158,863	103,607	55,256

TABLE II.—ARRIVALS AND DEPARTURES AT THE PORT OF BANGKOK, BY SEX, 1922/23—1923/24.

Year[1]	Arrivals			Departures		
	Total	Males	Females	Total	Males	Females
1922–23	91,669	77,539	14,130	63,701	54,043	9,658
1923–24	110,546	89,100	21,446	63,342	52,484	10,858

TABLE III.—ARRIVALS AND DEPARTURES AT THE PORT OF BANGKOK, BY NATIONALITY, 1922/23—1923/24.

Nationality	Arrivals		Departures	
	1922-23[1]	1923-24[1]	1922-23[1]	1923-24[1]
Siamese	406	501	1,246	819
Chinese	89,329	107,987	60,162	60,342
British	406	401	407	366
French	69	103	75	129
Danish	80	59	67	55
American	162	126	156	115
Indian	478	585	566	528
Malay	378	344	597	554
Japanese	64	110	141	91
Others	297	330	284	343
Total	91,669	110,546	63,701	63,342

TABLE IV.—ARRIVALS AND DEPARTURES ACROSS THE SOUTHERN FRONTIER, 1922/23—1923/24.

Year[1]	Arrivals	Departures	Excess of departures (—) or arrivals (+)
1922–23	34,888	36,175	—1,287
1923–24	48,317	40,265	+8,052

SOURCE

Statistical Year-Book of the Kingdom of Siam, 1924. Published by the Department of Commerce and Statistics, Ministry of Finance. English Edition, Bangkok, 1924, pp. 28-32.

All tables.

NOTE

[1]Years ending March 31st.

CHINA

Chinese emigration, notably of industrial laborers, started at different ports in different years. Diverse authorities were responsible for the collection of the statistics relating thereto.

1. For the first decade (1845-55) port statistics, based on consular reports, were laid before the British Parliament. These data have been taken from the official Portuguese report of 1874 which declares that the earliest data published in the English sources are not entirely correct and convey the impression that the exportation of indentured laborers increased more rapidly than it did. (*Relatorio e Documentos. . .*, p. 4).

In addition to the earliest figures for Amoy, data relating to four ports in the Province of Canton, the most important emigration centre, are available for the period 1848-52. Later Hongkong and Macao alone play a noteworthy part. The figures for emigration from Canton to Peru are derived from the reports of the Peruvian consul at Canton and are not included in the emigration statistics of the four ports. According to an English statement, 2,025 emigrants left the four ports in 1852 for South America, Peru (1,350) presumably included.

The data for Hongkong from English sources, and for Macao from a Portuguese source, are available until 1873, but not for every year. We have not been able to ascertain whether no coolies were exported during those years or whether no data were collected.

2. From 1876 onward figures are available relating to Chinese emigration or passenger traffic via Amoy (1876-1917, tables V and VI) and also Kungchow and Swatow (1901-07, table VII). These figures relate mainly to continental emigration, *e. g.*, to the Straits Settlements, Siam, Cochin China, Java, Sumatra, and Philippines, and to coastwise traffic with Hongkong. They were collected by the Customs authorities of the several ports. (China. Inspectorate General of Customs. *Annual Statistical Series.* Data for certain years are not available.) For Amoy the classification, until 1901, differs from that of later dates (compare the *Bulletin* by Ta Chen), and accordingly two tables are given.

3. For the period 1870-1900 no figures were found for Hongkong. From 1900 onward they reappear in British colonial statistics. It is a question of aggregate figures of Chinese emigrants and immigrants proceeding to and from countries outside China (more especially to and from the Straits Settlements).

Immigrants or emigrants who are not resident in Hongkong but in other parts of China and who use Hongkong as their port of arrival or departure appear in the statistics only when they disembark from, or embark for, places outside of China.

Statistics about the number of migrants from China to Cochin China (1879-83), Straits Settlements (1881-1915), Brazil (1908-24), Canada, Cuba, Indo-China, Mexico (1909-24), United States (1820-1924), Hawaii (1911-24), New South Wales (1859-1901), Victoria (1886-1901),

Queensland (1875-1901), Australia (1902-24) and New Zealand (1871-1919) will be found in the national tables for those countries. Statistics about the number of migrants returning to China from Cochin China (1879-83), Straits Settlements (1888-1915), Mexico (1911-24), United States (1908-24), Hawaii (1911-24), New South Wales (1859-1919), Victoria (1866-1919), Queensland (1875-1919), Australia (1920-24) and New Zealand (1872-1919) will be found in the national tables for those countries.

TABLE I.—EMIGRATION OF INDENTURED LABORERS (CITIZENS), BY PORTS OF EMBARKATION, 1845-73.

| Year | From Amoy[1] | From Canton | | | | Total of available figures |
		From Wampu, coming Macao and Hong-kong[2]	To Peru	From Hongkong	From Macao	
1845	180	....	....	....	....	180
1846	200	....	....	....	....	200
1847	....	....	....	....	....	....
1848	120	10	....	....	....	130
1849	280	900	75	....	....	1,255
1850	1,000	3,118	1,465	....	....	5,583
1851	2,069	3,508	1,163	....	....	6,740
1852	1,739[3]	15,000	1,350	....	....	18,089
1853	....	....	2,070	....	....	2,070
1854	....	....	1,233	....	....	1,233
1855	....	....	....	14,991[4]	....	14,991
1856	....	....	....	14,466	2,493	16,959
1857	....	....	....	25,980	7,383	33,363
1858	....	....	....	15,810	10,034	25,844
1859	....	....	....	10,217	8,969	19,186
1860	....	....	....	15,183	8,119	23,302
1861	....	....	....	12,840	*	12,840
1862	....	....	....	*	2,536	2,536
1863	....	....	....	*	6,660	6,660
1864	....	....	....	*	10,712	10,712
1868	....	....	....	8,877[5]	12,206	21,083
1869	....	....	....	18,285[5]	9,000	27,285
1870	....	....	....	12,992[5]	13,407	26,399
1871	....	....	....	*	17,083	17,083
1872	....	....	....	*	21,854	21,854
1873	....	....	....	*	13,016	13,016

For reference notes see page 932.

TABLE II.—Distribution of intercontinental emigrants from Hongkong, by sex and country of destination, 1859-61.

Year	Country of destination	Total	Adults			Children		
			Total	Males	Females	Total	Males	Females
1859	Australia......	5,316	5,316	5,316	...	..	..	...
	Demerara......	821	798	742	56	23	15	8
	California......	4,080	4,054	3,543	511	26	8	18
	Total........	10,217	10,168	9,601	567	49	23	26
1860	Australia......	6,564	6,564	6,564	...	..	..	..
	India..........	66	66	66	...	..	..	..
	Demerara......	1,313	1,221	902	319	92	59	33
	California......	7,240	7,240	6,799	441	..	..	..
	Total........	15,183	15,091	14,331	760	92	59	33
1861	Australia......	2,809	2,799	2,799	...	10	10	..
	Demerara......	2,297	2,269	1,921	348	28	16	12
	California......	7,734	7,718	7,096	622	16	5	11
	Total........	12,840	12,786	11,816	970	54	31	23

TABLE III.—Emigration and immigration through Hongkong[6], 1900-24.

Year	Emigrants	Immigrants	Year	Emigrants	Immigrants
1900	83,643	121,322	1912	122,657	163,248
			1913	142,759	166,921
1901	69,774	129,030	1914	76,296	168,827
1902	71,711	129,812	1915	68,275	109,753
1903	83,384	140,551			
1904	76,304	149,195	1916	117,653	72,405
1905	64,341	140,483	1917	96,298	98,232
			1918	43,830	74,109
1906	76,725	134,912	1919	59,969	136,020
1907	105,976	145,822	1920	105,258	122,438
1908	71,081	157,809			
1909	77,430	144,821	1921	156,011	159,064
1910	111,058	149,564	1922	98,393	143,547
			1923	120,227	121,102
1911	135,565	149,894	1924	129,859	.....

TABLE IV.—Intercontinental emigration through Macao, by country of destination, 1856-73.

Year	Total	Havana	Peru	Other countries	Year	Total	Havana	Peru	Other countries
1856	2,493	2,253	....	240	1864	10,712	4,469	6,243	325
1857	7,383	6,753	450	180	1868	12,206	8,835	3,371	...
1858	10,034	8,913	300	821	1869	9,000	4,124	4,876	...
1859	8,969	7,695	321	953	1870	13,407	1,064	12,343	,...
1860	8,119	5,773	2,098	248	1871	17,083	5,706	11,377	...
1861	....	.....	....	...	1872	21,854	8,045	13,809	...
1862	2,536	752	1,459	325	1873	13,016	6,307	6,709	...
1863	6,660	2,922	3,738	325					

For reference notes see page 932.

TABLE V.—PASSENGERS INWARD TO AND OUTWARD FROM AMOY, 1876-1901.

Year	Total		Hongkong		Straits Settlements		Saigon		Manila		Java		Other places	
	To	From	To	From	To	From	To	From	To	From	To	From	To	From
1876	26,546	18,338	1,528	5,206	15,115	4,931	1,039	370	6,675	4,876	974	216	2,254	2,739
1877	26,496	23,279	1,002	6,107	13,804	6,750	.....	675	5,362	5,736	1,975	169	3,314	3,842
1878	30,281	24,524	1,579	6,241	15,734	6,539	980	21	7,170	7,914	1,474	215	3,344	3,594
1879	22,336	20,764	1,353	3,919	10,903	7,499	539	180	5,210	6,679	995	258	3,336	2,229
1880	22,037	24,318	831	2,471	13,563	13,628	195	.....	4,104	6,031	722	268	2,622	1,920
1881	39,991	33,475	1,344	4,785	21,003	9,821	5	62	9,472	9,295	575	1	7,592	9,511
1882	52,835	35,270	2,697	3,684	32,511	12,933	80	.....	8,572	8,080	.....	.....	8,975	10,573
1883	48,963	53,998	4,157	4,516	24,977	24,191	.....	202	11,098	10,599	.....	.....	8,721	14,490
1884	58,272	45,309	2,421	4,811	34,471	17,756	13	.....	12,871	11,583	.....	.....	8,496	11,159
1885	49,737	43,613	2,594	4,375	28,818	21,221	.....	.....	8,726	10,437	.....	.....	9,599	7,580
1886	65,292	50,872	2,019	6,396	42,785	20,494	.....	.....	8,365	9,714	.....	.....	12,123	14,268
1887	51,436	66,624	5,791	7,970	21,810	46,119	.....	.....	11,761	7,409	.....	.....	12,074	11,126
1888	73,663	54,714	2,585	6,267	47,908	23,849	.....	23	13,269	11,540	416	.....	9,485	13,035
1889	73,500	49,538	3,162	4,879	43,417	23,997	.....	.....	12,029	8,873	.....	.....	14,892	11,789
1890	70,697	54,288	3,233	6,190	42,896	27,969	.....	.....	11,559	7,995	.....	.....	13,409	12,134
1891	78,012	55,194	4,294	7,147	47,922	23,372	.....	.....	9,836	6,938	.....	.....	15,960	13,737
1892	69,478	50,217	1,928	7,398	46,638	20,545	.....	.....	9,702	10,060	.....	.....	11,210	12,214
1893	83,581	78,311	4,048	8,296	48,071	36,479	1,022	17	8,855	9,842	.....	.....	22,607	23,677
1894	85,961	60,204	2,885	14,634	52,627	23,685	1,637	617	7,633	2,973	.....	.....	21,794	18,295
1895	113,600	74,012	6,066	25,498	69,159	17,992	971	25	5,874	953	.....	.....	30,964	29,544
1896	70,896	54,844	2,469	12,845	52,811	29,244	375	34	4,461	2,438	.....	.....	10,194	10,283
1897	58,556	66,560	3,246	23,297	35,130	26,582	1,124	.....	7,201	1,143	.....	.....	12,604	15,538
1898	75,287	61,217	7,609	23,660	47,115	23,511	2,021	80	9,364	2,839	.....	.....	10,075	11,207
1899	81,607	70,335	4,306	26,646	54,711	27,046	1,050	.....	9,544	1,520	.....	.....	11,025	15,043
1900	105,416	67,711	4,855	26,860	79,263	24,893	1,033	346	10,044	985	.....	.....	10,204	14,627
1901	95,481	72,258	5,523	24,430	68,829	32,794	.....	640	9,537	1,335	.....	.....	10,559	13,059

TABLE VI.—CHINESE PASSENGERS OUTWARD FROM AMOY, 1902-17 (SCATTERED YEARS).

Year	Total	To Singapore, etc.	To Manila, etc.	To Formosa, Hongkong, etc.
1902	102,516	78,232	7,431	16,853
1908	79,243	46,937	5,184	27,122
1912	126,008	91,807	5,720	28,481
1915	66,907	29,465	7,272	30,170
1917	77,781	48,139	4,042	25,600

TABLE VII.—Passengers (Chinese) inward to and outward from Kiungchow, 1876-1901.

Year	Total		Hongkong		Cochin-China		Straits Settlements		Bangkok		Other places	
	To	From	To	From	To	From	To	From	To	From	To	From
1876	1,097	1,827	1,078	799	8	19		737			11	292
1877	1,452	1,824	1,397	1,808	40	9					6	7
1878	2,031	2,245	1,981	2,204	29	38			30	3		
1879	3,051	3,307	2,982	2,645	31	44					38	618
1880	2,382	3,431	2,150	3,254	13	15					219	162
1881	3,142	5,022	2,963	4,360	29	99				270	150	293
1882	4,187	6,732	3,761	4,999	93	136		519		183	333	895
1883	3,921	8,921	3,600	5,624	124	623	63	1,590		687	134	397
1884	5,333	8,725	5,237	5,567		146		2,124		808	96	140
1885	10,500	13,607	7,402	8,811	23	225	1,370	2,686	841	867	864	1,218
1886	9,879	12,488	5,062	7,248	103	335	3,461	2,708	906	849	347	1,348
1887	12,325	14,807	6,252	8,457	55	184	4,499	3,940	875	927	644	1,299
1888	15,521	15,150	6,727	9,577	184	141	5,973	3,684	2,415	1,039	222	709
1889	17,477	16,112	5,771	7,071	113	183	8,638	6,900	2,703	1,506	252	452
1890	15,422	15,197	4,075	8,122	84	143	9,123	5,486	1,874	1,167	266	279
1891	14,492	15,005	5,074	8,991	86	70	6,975	3,655	1,895	1,499	462	790
1892	10,988	12,320	3,970	7,720	154	109	5,172	3,193	1,538	1,119	154	179
1893	17,892	16,372	6,097	10,499	110	77	7,829	4,042	3,612	1,506	244	248
1894	20,396	14,813	6,173	10,879	91	110	7,531	2,037	6,255	1,596	346	191
1895	18,969	11,975	4,146	7,971	73	110	10,154	2,072	4,361	1,684	235	138
1896	16,680	16,761	5,126	8,506	98	81	6,782	5,003	4,393	2,935	281	236
1897	17,203	16,601	7,046	12,049	29	90	4,517	1,811	5,429	2,482	182	169
1898	20,356	14,685	5,783	9,234	140	98	6,954	2,699	7,329	2,382	150	182
1899	21,836	15,624	4,291	10,025	50	108	10,466	1,949	6,646	3,233	383	309
1900	15,254	15,844	4,438	11,748	47	50	7,610	1,142	2,947	2,610	212	294
1901	16,986	16,838	4,109	11,531	341	208	9,280	2,165	2,809	2,802	447	132
	298,772	296,233	116,691	189,709	2,148	3,251	116,397	60,142	56,858	32,154	6,678	10,977

TABLE VIII.—PASSENGERS (CHINESE) INWARD TO AND OUTWARD FROM SWATOW, 1876-1901.

Year	Total		Hongkong		Siam		Cochin-China		Straits Settlements		Sumatra		Coastal places	
	To	From	To	From	To	From	To	From	To	From	To	From	To	From
1876	40,259	25,202	11,639	21,302	942	257	138	142	24,675	35			2,865	3,466
1877	37,362	25,921	12,608	23,244	795	31	622	164	20,014	42			3,323	2,440
1878	40,889	29,044	15,626	26,507	876	231	337	33	20,948				3,102	2,273
1879	38,799	30,739	18,967	27,607	535	66	467	25	16,274	284			2,556	2,757
1880	40,735	30,734	20,986	27,762	219		147	153	16,547	15			2,836	2,804
1881	49,356	28,533	17,333	25,512	838	7		76	28,066	30			3,119	2,908
1882	71,301	40,042	16,983	34,603	10,480	26	18	312	40,087				3,733	5,101
1883	77,071	44,773	16,417	40,775	10,533		536	24	45,733				3,852	3,974
1884	68,246	44,586	12,566	37,447	5,347	207		118	44,351	3,446			5,982	3,368
1885	65,167	54,147	15,415	41,194	6,541	20	95	22	37,446	3,555			5,670	9,356
1886	71,311	48,499	13,777	44,587	6,333		1,366	30	46,710	300			3,125	3,582
1887	72,018	52,590	12,983	49,159	8,736		429	103	46,667				3,203	3,328
1888	68,747	58,040	16,311	46,291	6,129	2,499	1,600	115	40,066	5,516	1,222	73	3,419	3,619
1889	77,377	57,462	16,394	53,277	9,171		368	25	44,208	152	3,825	44	3,301	3,935
1890	68,573	53,553	13,358	49,486	10,844		505	115	35,570	265	5,066	32	3,230	3,643
1891	62,618	58,652	18,542	53,574	8,430	25	435	25	27,742	262	3,912		3,257	4,738
1892	62,465	50,261	14,521	46,043	9,652		1,211		30,728	97	2,991		3,362	4,121
1893	93,095	56,217	17,370	51,797	15,509		2,137	57	48,601		5,930	466	3,548	4,363
1894	78,747	54,173	15,302	46,995	17,109	887	4,016	230	33,146	1,420	5,882	1,054	3,202	4,175
1895	91,100	51,717	10,506	45,511	15,754		4,496		45,915	894	8,342	629	6,087	4,258
1896	91,487	62,424	12,639	48,729	15,259	5,783	2,922	8	49,918	322	7,194	1,054	3,555	6,953
1897	71,248	62,038	17,147	46,915	17,122	8,345	3,026		24,752	1,149	5,302	1,161	3,899	4,468
1898	73,995	58,557	14,580	44,417	17,754	8,649	3,780		28,070	355	6,360	827	3,451	4,309
1899	89,794	70,011	16,629	54,440	20,581	10,052	4,962		34,775		8,916	669	3,931	4,850
1900	98,201	80,107	21,719	61,971	16,678	8,843	5,863		40,420	225	8,699	637	4,822	8,431
1901	94,344†	79,718	18,052	62,345	20,059	10,711	7,491		36,888		6,110	942	5,467	5,720
	794,298	1,307,744	408,424	1,111,490	252,226	56,639	47,267	1,777	908,367	18,364	79,750	6,534	97,987	112,940

For reference notes see page 932.

SOURCES

Relatorio e Documentos sobre a Aboliçao da emigraçao de chinas contratados e Macau. Apresentado as côrtes na sessâo legislativa de 1874 pelo Ministro e Secretario d'Estado dos negocios de Merinha e Ultramar. Lisbon, 1874.

Tables I (except Hongkong, 1859-61) and IV.

Bulletin of the United States, Bureau of Labor Statistics, No. 340. *Chinese Migration with special Reference to Labor Conditons,* by Ta Chen, Washington, 1923, p. 15.

Table VI.

Statistical Tables relating to the Colonial and other Possessions of the United Kingdom. Parts VI, VII, IX, London, 1862.

Table I (Hongkong, 1859-61) and II.

Statistical Abstract for the several British Overseas Dominions and Protectorates, London, 1914, 1922, 1924.

Table III (years 1900-21).

Information supplied by the British Government (Foreign Office and Ministry of Labour).

Table III (years 1922-24).

H. Gottwaldt, *Die überseeische Auswanderung der Chinesen,* Bremen, 1903, pp. 39-41.

Tables V, VII and VIII.

NOTES

[1] These coolie emigrants were bound for the following places: "990 for Havana, 469 for Demerara, 380 for the Island of Bourbon, 2,666 for Australia, 380 for the Sandwich Islands, 600 for Batanes in the Philippine Group, 350 for California, or more probably for Peru, and 420 for Peru." *Relatorio e Documentos,* p. 5. The difference between the annual figures of table I and the figures referring to countries of destination derive from the original source.

[2] To California only.

[3] 8 months.

[4] From December 1, 1854 to September 30, 1855. This figure refers to free ór spontaneous and non-indentured emigrants; of them 10,467 sailed for Australia, 3,042 for California, 1,375 for Chinese ports, 11 for the Philippines, 50 for Siam, and 46 for Singapore.

[5] Principally non-indentured emigrants.

[6] The figures given represent the movements of Chinese through Hongkong from and to ports outside of China (principally in the Straits Settlements).

[7] Including 277 to German New Guinea.

JAPAN

I PASSENGER STATISTICS

(Tables I-II)

Table I indicates the total number of passports issued to Japanese passengers from 1868 to 1924 and classifies the passengers according to the country of destination. Table II, which gives the occupations of the outward bound passengers, is compiled on the same basis. The figures contained in the last column represent, however, emigrants proper. (See explanation which follows.)

II STATISTICS OF MIGRANTS

(Tables III-V)

Emigration statistics are available from 1898 (table III), immigration figures from 1908 (table V).

The term "emigrant" is defined as follows: "By an emigrant is meant a person who departs for abroad except China and Corea, with a view to earning his living there, and includes the members of his family who accompany him or who proceed to join him in his new domicile." The term "labor" in Article 1 of the Regulations relating to the Emigrant Protection Act includes the following classes of labor: farm laborers, fishermen, miners, mechanics, transport workers, builders, cooks, laundry workers, tailors, hairdressers, waiters, nurses and others.

These emigrants are also given in the last column of table II (1899-1924). The two groups "laborers" and "persons in the employ of aliens" are, according to the Japanese delegation at the League of Nations, to be considered—so far as the period 1884-98 is in question—as corresponding to the category "emigrants". Migrants given in the tables under other headings than those mentioned are nonemigrants.

The immigration statistics (table V) cover third class passengers returning to Japan from the United States, Hawaii and Canada (1908-24).

Statistics about the number of migrants from Japan to Brazil (1908-24), Canada (1900-24), Cuba (1911-24), Mexico (1911-24), United States (1861-1924), Hawaii (1911-24), Australia (1902-24) and New Caledonia (1897-1924) will be found in the national tables for those countries. Statistics about the number of migrants returning to Japan from the United States (1908-24), Hawaii (1911-24), Mexico (1911-24), Australia (1920-24), and New Caledonia (1897-1924), will be found in the national tables for those countries.

TABLE I.—DISTRIBUTION OF PASSENGER CITIZENS OUTWARD, BY COUNTRY OF DESTINATION, 1868-1924.

Year	Total	United States	Hawaii	Canada	Mexico	Other North American countries	Brazil	Peru	Argentina
1868–1875	4,637	596	. . . .	. . . .	. . .	. . .	. . . .	. . . .	. .
1876	709	128	. . . .	. . . .	. . .	. . .	. . . .	. . . .	. . .
1877	1,002	35	. . . .	. . . .	. . .	. . .	. . . .	. . . .	. . .
1878	1,140	57	. . . .	. . . .	. . .	. . .	. . . .	. . . .	. . .
1879	1,133	37	. . . .	. . . .	. . .	. . .	. . . .	. . . .	. . .
1880	1,510	48	. . . .	. . . .	. . .	. . .	. . . .	. . . .	. . .
1881	1,067	55	. . . .	. . . .	. . .	. . .	. . . .	. . .	. . .
1882	1,274	60	5	. . . .	. . .	. . .	. . . .	. . .	. . .
1883	1,390	59	. . . .	. . . .	. . .	. . .	. . . .	. . . .	. . .
1884	1,554	284	. . . .	. . . .	. . .	. . .	. . . .	. . . .	. . .
1885	3,461	312	1,959	. . . .	. . .	. . .	. . . .	. . . .	. . .
1886	3,007	332	971	. . . .	. . .	. . .	. . . .	. . . .	. . .
1887	4,735	461	1,893	. . . .	. . .	. . .	. . . .	. . . .	. . .
1888	6,552	757	3,308	. . . .	. . .	. . .	. . . .	. . . .	. .
1889	7,772	599	4,244	. . . .	. . .	. . .	. . . .	. . . .	. . .
1890	8,166	611	4,540	. . . .	. . .	. . .	. . . .	. . . .	. . .
1891	13,618	1,461	7,171	181	. . .	. . .	. . . .	. . . .	. . .
1892	10,218	2,344	2,413	112	39	. . .	. . . .	. . . .	. . .
1893	13,669	1,978	4,764	1,135	35	. . .	. . . .	. . . .	. . .
1894	16,726	1,497	4,036	779	6	. . .	. . . .	. . . .	. . .
1895	22,411	1,049	2,445	454	3	. . .	. . . .	. . . .	. . .
1896	27,565	1,764	9,486	549	15	. . .	. . . .	. . . .	. . .
1897	23,857	1,945	5,913	206	21	. . .	. . . .	. . . .	. . .
1898	33,297	2,936	12,952	1,039	. . .	. . .	. . . .	. . . .	. . .
1899	51,057	6,942	27,155	. . . .	. . .	. . .	. . . .	. . . .	. . .
1900	41,339	10,562	4,760	. . . .	. . .	. . .	. . . .	. . . .	. . .
1901	24,034	1,986	2,982	69	152	. . .	. . . .	. . . .	. . .
1902	32,900	5,096	11,457	490	187	. . .	. . . .	. . . .	. . .
1903	34,202	5,215	86	455	159	. . .	. . . .	. . . .	. . .
1904	27,375	3,490	12,621	341	201	. . .	. . . .	. . . .	. . .
1905	19,466	3,124	7,146	. . . .	374	. . .	. . . .	. . . .	. . .
1906	58,851	8,466	30,393	1,100	5,322	. . .	19	1,000	6
1907	44,619	9,618	15,757	3,603	3,945	4	15	108	13
1908	21,354	3,214	3,621	738	18	. . .	709	3,026	6
1909	15,502	1,766	1,273	342	13	. . .	16	1,277	10
1910	21,982	2,900	1,919	629	37	23	847	492	9
1911	29,950	3,895	2,950	865	60	. . .	9	411	14
1912	20,782	6,021	5,243	1,125	74	. . .	1,244	713	30
1913	44,084	6,460	4,872	1,432	106	28	2,703	1,147	123
1914	43,570	8,398	3,558	1,423	102	53	1,595	1,118	71
1915	43,692	8,537	3,474	887	61	80	80	1,386	62
1916	45,765	8,659	4,321	1,205	72	521	63	1,518	185
1917	60,377	9,962	4,856	1,368	103	283	3,941	2,021	154
1918	62,571	10,716	3,578	1,994	215	364	5,532	1,844	188
1919	60,187	11,305	3,759	1,883	137	290	1,362	1,605	231
1920	55,607	11,142	3,497	1,534	107	313	1,008	1,029	68
1921	35,640	8,557	3,939	1,378	143	269	1,011	800	94
1922	30,411	7,454	3,553	1,160	142	250	1,091	295	81
1923[1]	24,847	6,289	2,661	765	136	269	844	443	102
1924	26,932	8,723	2,760	1,250	276	447	3,858	751	123

For reference notes see page 941.

TABLE I.—Distribution of passenger citizens outward, by country of destination 1868-1924 (continued).

Year	Chile	Other South American countries	Africa	England	France	Germany	Other European countries	Australia	Federated Malay States, etc.	Philippines
1868–1875	..	4	..	225	96	73	153	3	....	....
1876	..	2	..	28	14	2	9	....	....	....
1877	..	..	..	32	40	5	3	9	....	....
1878	..	76	..	47	66	4	9	3	....	....
1879	..	..	..	25	12	8	4	....	....	....
1880	..	..	..	16	18	22	36	7	....	....
1881	..	..	..	15	12	3	9	2	....	....
1882	..	..	..	26	24	17	27	....	....	....
1883	..	2	..	15	21	13	8	41	....	....
1884	..	..	..	83	32	49	11	6	....	....
1885	..	..	..	250	11	27	23	21	....	....
1886	..	..	..	56	31	56	8	49	....	....
1887	..	..	..	107	38	46	30	11	....	....
1888	..	4	..	241	40	34	196	8	....	....
1889	..	21	..	300	31	38	16	14	....	....
1890	..	10	..	219	43	52	28	14	....	....
1891	..	3	..	92	296	25	17	53	40	4
1892	..	1	..	69	201	26	10	834	132	6
1893	..	1	1	299	15	29	6	1,242	86	26
1894	..	4	3	177	10	26	8	963	88	5
1895	..	..	..	173	10	23	4	169	106	13
1896	..	..	..	779	23	29	10	843	144	4
1897	..	..	..	100	16	56	..	351	153	....
1898	..	..	..	1,217	32	42	..	1,128	96	..
1899	..	..	..	701	93	84	13	258	154	12
1900	..	..	..	1,188	395	269	..	314	278	61
1901	..	..	..	553	29	76	..	427	173	42
1902	..	..	..	98	17	76	..	255	118	47
1903	..	97	..	50	25	81	24	220	68	271
1904	..	21	2	78	6	43	16	222	44	646
1905	..	28	5	116	27	53	22	60	125	542
1906	6	14	11	154	33	110	29	36	161	225
1907	16	15	2	223	34	98	51	48	194	271
1908	7	30	4	195	34	115	17	40	160	197
1909	3	13	..	278	39	89	29	26	140	227
1910	5	15	..	537	20	96	40	1,053	235	396
1911	5	4	..	265	22	90	37	386	392	657
1912	10	4	..	206	27	141	31	52	673	923
1913	39	13	..	208	33	115	233	84	704	1,092
1914	38	11	..	194	76	65	136	63	543	922
1915	37	13	1	651	34	..	77	87	587	741
1916	31	29	6	535	38	..	394	83	1,065	1,281
1917	43	43	25	148	32	..	124	71	1,634	3,599
1918	52	44	23	220	95	..	371	126	1,706	3,738
1919	40	36	10	246	91	..	340	211	1,339	1,497
1920	41	17	13	189	110	14	306	152	1,066	901
1921	35	50	38	194	112	50	274	164	707	799
1922	24	50	23	190	102	102	300	299	594	575
1923[1]	14	16	9	184	106	116	422	164	566	746
1924	16	14	11	....	..	..	769	297	591	857

For reference notes see page 941.

TABLE I.—Distribution of passenger citizens outward, by country of destination, 1868-1924 (concluded).

Year	Other islands of the Pacific	India	Siam	Indo-China	China	Hong-Kong	Russia and Territories	Korea	Other Asiatic countries	Various countries
1868–1875	....	....	..	..	1,214	....	90	1,965	...	218
1876	....	....	..	..	284	....	100	80	...	62
1877	....	....	..	..	299	....	71	505	...	3
1878	....	....	..	..	271	....	62	545	...	....
1879	....	....	..	..	319	....	50	660	...	18
1880	....	....	..	..	277	....	122	934	...	30
1881	....	2	..	..	219	....	306	434	...	10
1882	....	....	..	..	397	....	247	448	...	23
1883	....	12	..	3	392	....	246	559	...	19
1884	....	3	..	3	460	....	106	457	...	60
1885	....	1	..	2	307	....	118	407	...	23
1886	....	4	..	3	365	....	184	842	...	106
1887	....	1	..	..	517	....	250	1,118	...	263
1888	....	1	1	..	317	....	31	1,432	...	172
1889	....	3	1	1	373	....	260	1,713	...	158
1890	....	4	1	2	390	....	273	1,791	...	188
1891	7	11	4	8	378	135	582	3,100	...	50
1892	14	12	5	14	592	270	941	2,165	...	18
1893	79	32	..	..	627	319	1,097	1,776	...	122
1894	653	29	48	16	402	192	1,418	6,065	...	301
1895	104	47	79	18	1,510	206	4,721	10,391	...	886
1896	24	....	34	28	880	184	7,177	4,745	...	847
1897	....	66	30	..	4,588	295	4,899	4,547	...	671
1898	23	50	22	19	2,929	293	3,375	4,987	...	2,157
1899	66	34	35	36	1,973	324	4,001	4,701	...	4,475
1900	926	49	47	44	7,539	385	5,819	4,327	...	4,376
1901	180	42	16	24	5,686	371	4,903	4,843	...	1,480
1902	101	60	49	17	5,457	392	4,354	3,026	...	1,603
1903	102	60	61	28	6,005	436	3,881	4,258	...	12,620
1904	55	28	27	10	3,302	309	....	5,113	...	800
1905	740	30	31	..	5,256	142	230	523	...	892
1906	155	72	71	45	5,186	216	5,237	49	...	735
1907	125	103	41	50	3,809	174	5,522	4	...	776
1908	521	47	31	31	2,842	123	5,089	4	...	535
1909	149	64	29	41	2,624	121	6,502	2	...	429
1910	509	133	25	47	2,478	144	8,776	....	...	617
1911	492	80	31	48	2,143	195	16,216	....	...	683
1912	453	66	16	47	2,030	209	680	....	...	764
1913	1,048	89	36	32	1,926	151	20,964	....	131	315
1914	1,867	97	20	33	2,255	120	20,259	....	295	258
1915	499	171	31	33	2,775	143	22,495	....	501	249
1916	871	178	73	43	3,778	376	19,317	....	649	474
1917	1,856	216	49	27	3,568	252	23,523	....	820	1,659
1918	1,334	325	49	87	3,379	300	23,764	....	1,096	1,431
1919	1,045	243	46	61	2,908	705	28,467	....	933	1,397
1920	881	272	30	63	2,174	586	26,747	....	1,373	1,974
1921	706	208	34	47	3,544	647	9,045	....	1,337	1,458
1922	670	263	27	37	2,996	621	7,118	....	997	1,397
1923	676	272	98	76	2,636	452	4,769	....	801	1,215
1924	721	297	63	67	2,814	586	391	....	288	962

For reference notes see page 941.

TABLE II.—DISTRIBUTION OF PASSENGER CITIZENS OUTWARD, BY OCCUPATION, 1884-1924.

Year	Total			Public services		Study		Commerce		Visitors		Agriculture		Fishing		Var. occupations		La-borers	In the employ of aliens
	Total	Males	Females	Males	Fe-males	Males	Fe-males	Males	Fe-males	Males	Females	Males	Females	Males	Females	Males	Females		
1884	1,554	1,282	272	147		414		382		20		....		....		300		51	240
1885	3,461	2,948	513	303		273		394		11		5		....		254		27	2,194
1886	3,007	2,315	692	133		393		715		17		9		....		434		88	1,218
1887	4,736	3,987	749	127		415		855		15		23		....		428		82	2,791
1888	6,552	5,404	1,148	82		379		1,252		14		17		....		548		111	4,149
1889	7,772	6,323	1,449	115		328		1,552		20		72		....		572		159	4,954
1890	8,166	6,477	1,689	140		361		1,558		35		77		....		600		167	5,228
1891	13,618	10,939	2,679	350		362		1,724		14		170		....		2,034		206	8,758
1892	10,209	8,643	1,566	315		334		1,852		32		1,480		....		1,067		865	4,264
1893	13,679	11,629	2,050	324		353		2,180		48		2,592		....		1,435		566	6,181
1894	16,726	14,416	2,310	238		289		4,086		20		5,216		....		1,876		708	4,293
1895	22,411	18,033	4,378	318		374		5,915		12		2,992		....		3,776		1,034	7,990
1896	27,565	24,163	3,402	810		367		3,114		15		3,295		....		1,894		381	17,689
1897	23,857	20,824	3,033	301		445		5,821		33		8,404		....		3,564		458	4,831
1898	33,297	28,618	4,679	1,462		646		5,887		605		746		....		2,625		286[2]	21,040[2]
																		Emigrants	
																		Males	Females
1899	51,057	42,802	8,255	1,277	99	809	10	6,241	666	45	..			8,269	2,287			26,161	5,193
1900	41,339	37,525	3,814	2,105	84	780	11	7,308	378	88	2			11,921	1,904			15,323	1,435
1901	24,034	20,759	3,275	971	116	964	17	4,888	236	76	4			9,465	807			4,395	2,095
1902	32,900	28,990	3,910	450	101	1,798	60	5,288	264	118	2			10,751	.....			10,585	3,483[2]
1903	34,202	30,628	3,574	560	89	1,799	45	6,243	290	71	1			9,814	1,235			12,141	1,914
1904	27,375	24,979	2,396	551	45	1,566	31	5,506	229	35	..			4,060	689			13,261	1,402
1905	19,466	16,833	2,633	757	58	1,095	32	2,487	120	10	2			670	933			11,814	1,488
1906	58,851	53,471	5,380	515	57	3,269	71	5,271	385	24	..			11,410	1,725			32,982	3,142
1907	44,619	36,618	8,001	444	77	3,336	79	3,526	383	15	3			9,810	1,886			19,487	5,573
1908	21,354	17,183	4,171	343	68	645	35	2,151	240	142	11			6,565	707			7,337	3,110
1909	15,502	12,628	2,874	368	66	335	24	1,621	242	28	3			7,867	670			2,409	1,869
1910	21,982	17,362	4,620	446	58	310	18	1,766	347	....	..			10,688	1,398			4,152	2,799
1911	29,950	23,964	5,986	477	34	337	12	1,955	364	....	..			17,027	1,673			4,168	3,903
1912	20,782	13,202	7,580	484	78	400	23	2,030	333	....	..			2,371	149			7,917	6,995
1913	44,084	35,955	8,129	413	69	429	20	2,115	332	....	..			20,987	....			12,011	7,708[2]
1914	43,570	35,449	8,121	398	30	348	38	2,630	342	....	..			21,155	655			10,918	7,056
1915	43,692	35,901	7,791	534	29	340	35	3,780	401	1,250	21			22,694	2,065			7,303	5,240
1916	45,765	36,367	9,398	550	38	415	40	5,312	605	1,515	17			19,345	3,342			9,230	5,356
1917	60,377	47,989	12,388	577	63	208	21	7,333	790	1,682	43			23,387	3,411			14,802	8,060
1918	62,571	49,490	13,080	978	35	238	9	8,210	781	1,834	48			23,427	3,437			14,803	8,771
1919	60,187	48,258	11,929	815	40	336	34	6,994	682	2,741	61			26,339	3,901			11,033	7,211
1920	55,607	43,942	11,665	912	73	241	25	4,955	660	2,402	42			27,800	4,956			7,632	5,909
1921	35,640	25,758	9,882	1,095	114	261	39	4,525	596	2,478	82			10,330	4,243			7,069	4 808
1922	30,411	22,244	8,167	1,214	162	484	42	3,858	500	2,418	81			5,523	3,250			8,747	4,132
1923[1]	24,847	18,117	6,730	967	151	463	53	2,992	506	2,211	155			5,772	2,752			5,712	3,113
1924	26,932	17,737	9,195	807	118	629	61	2,333	380	1,797	260			4,287	3,162			7,884	5,214

For reference notes see page 941.

TABLE III.—Distribution of emigrant citizens, by country of future residence, 1898-1924.

Year	Total	United States	Hawaii	Canada	Mexico	Brazil	Peru	Argentina	Chile	Other South American countries
1898	12,393[2]	170	10,145	1,151[3]	....	....	....	...	..	..
1899	31,354	3,140	22,973	1,726	1	....	790[3]	...	..	..
1900	16,758	7,585	1,529	2,710	1	....	....	...	..	..
1901	6,490	32	3,136[3]	....	95	....	....	...	..	..
1902	15,919[2]	70	14,490	35	83	...:	....	...	..	..
1903	14,055	318	9,091	178	281	....	1,303[3]	...	126	..
1904	14,663	640	9,443	159	1,261	....	....	...	..	..
1905	13,302	714	10,813[3]	196[3]	346	....	....	...	..	..
1906	36,124	1,715	25,752	442	5,068	....	1,257[3]	...	..	..
1907	25,060	2,712	14,397	2,753	3,822	....	85	1	..	..
1908	10,447	1,585	3,455	601	....	799[3]	2,880	...	..	..
1909	4,278	777	1,329[3]	281	2	4	1,138	1	..	..
1910	6,951	926	1,717	538	5	911[3]	483	2	..	..
1911	8,071	1,963	2,595	820	28	....	456[3]	2	8	..
1912	14,912	3,378	4,732	1,025	16	2.859[3]	714[3]	16	1	..
1913	20,966[2]	4,381	4,276	1,270	47	6.947	1,126	103	27	..
1914	17,974	5,553	3,187	1,284	35	3.526	1,132[3]	41	9	..
1915	12,543	5,498	3,055	778	19	39	1,348	33	8	..
1916	14,586	5,761	3,643	1,055	22	35	1,429	135	15	1
1917	22,862	6,457	4,111	1,226	53	3,883	1,948	127	20	5
1918	23,574	6,306	3,024	1,780	128	5,956[3]	1,736	134	18	3
1919	18,244	6,273	3,088	1,764	64	2,732	1,507	174	21	3
1920	13,541	5,959	2,789	1,371	53	970	836	42	16	5
1921	11,877	4,321	3,215	1,163	69	970	717	53	21	5
1922	12,879	3,558	2,960	1,022	77	986	202	52	8	3
1923[1]	8,825	2,617	2,112	648	68	796	333	66	6	2
1924	13,098	4,064	2,163	1,103	76	3,689	651	58	4	..

Year	Africa	Australia	Malay States	Philippines	Other Islands of the Pacific	India	Siam	Indo-China	Russian Territories	Other countries
1898	....	927	....	....	....	..	..	16	....	....
1899	....	14	32	....	36	..	6	..	543	2,077
1900	....	21	48	5	1,032	10	..	..	532	3,285
1901	....	295	28	8	165	4	..	8	782	1,937
1902	....	155	21	77	74	..	4	9	600	301
1903	....	28	36	2,215	22	24	6	16	369	42
1904	....	118	57	2,923	29	1	3	..	8	21
1905	....	27	35	427	692	1	3	..	27	21
1906	2	2	39	71	96	4	1	14	1,642	19
1907	1	5	59	176	95	8	4	19	890	33
1908	....	9	76	143	406	..	..	13	461	19
1909	....	9	58	170	62	2	3	19	389	34
1910	....	8	82	387	1,398	2	1	26	431	34
1911	....	6	170	584	679	13	..	26	678	43
1912	....	6	386	689	281	25	..	21	729	34
1913	....	17	338	927	872	23	2	10	581	19
1914	....	19	250	782	1,548	11	1	12	577	7
1915	1	20	235	468	153	16	2	16	821	33
1916	....	20	334	1,029	218	26	7	12	725	119
1917	1	29	560	3,170	329	46	2	3	841	51
1918	....	41	412	3,046	249	42	5	27	632	35
1919	....	140	343	938	337	45	5	10	682	118
1920	....	105	240	411	200	33	3	10	370	128
1921	....	99	224	415	154	24	4	14	261	148
1922	....	228	171	189	102	10	..	6	3,249	56
1923[1]	....	54	57	449	100	26	..	17	1,450	24
1924	....	112	152	548	81	17	1	5	329	45

For reference notes see page 941.

TABLE IV.—DISTRIBUTION OF EMIGRANT CITIZENS, BY SEX AND BY THE PRINCIPAL COUNTRIES OF FUTURE RESIDENCE, 1898-1924.

Year	United States			Hawaii			Canada			Brazil			Peru		
	Males	Females	Total	Males	Females	Total	Males	Females	Total	Males	Females	Total	Males	Females	Total
1898	168	2	170	8,293	1,852	10,145	1,138	13	1,151[3]	....	....	....	....	....	....
1899	3,072	68	3,140	18,662	4,311	22,973	1,674	52	1,726[3]	....	....	....	790	....	790[3]
1900	7,357	228	7,585	1,175	354	1,529	2,621	89	2,710[3]	....	....	....	....	....	....
1901	29	3	32	1,954	1,182	3,136[3]	....	....	....	....	....	....	....	....	....
1902	50	20	70	9,523	4,967	14,490[1]	29	6	35	....	....	....	1,196	107	1,303[3]
1903	223	95	318	7,656	2,435	9,091[3]	149	29	178	....	....	....	....	....	....
1904	444	196	640	8,416	1,027	9,443	119	40	159	....	....	....	....	....	....
1905	393	321	714	9,859	954	10,813[3]	129	67	196[3]	....	....	....	1,240	17	1,257[3]
1906	1,183	532	1,715	24,093	1,659	25,752	302	140	442	....	....	....	85	....	85
1907	1,829	883	2,712	10,588	3,809	14,397	2,487	266	2,753	....	....	....	2,792	88	2,880
1908	917	668	1,585	1,821	1,634	3,455	425	176	601	612	187	799[3]	1,099	39	1,138
1909	360	417	777	357	972	1,329[3]	168	113	281	3	1	4	466	17	483
1910	382	544	926	500	1,217	1,717	293	245	538	522	389	911[3]	406	50	456[3]
1911	929	1,034	1,963	813	1,782	2,595	472	348	820	....	....	....	574	140	714[3]
1912	1,811	1,567	3,378	1,959	2,773	4,732	583	442	1,025	1,592	1,267	2,859[3]	923	203	1,126
1913	2,473	1,908	4,381	1,785	2,491	4,276	764	506	1,270	3,796	3,151	6,947[3]	836	296	1,132[3]
1914	3,231	2,322	5,553	1,298	1,889	3,187	828	456	1,284	2,082	1,444	3,526[3]	1,138	210	1,348
1915	3,194	2,304	5,498	1,313	1,742	3,055	524	254	778	37	2	39	1,234	195	1,429
1916	3,526	2,235	5,761	1,697	1,946	3,643	731	324	1,055	29	6	35	1,502	446	1,948
1917	3,798	2,659	6,457	1,889	2,222	4,111	828	398	1,226	2,388	1,495	3,883	1,260	476	1,736
1918	3,529	2,777	6,306	1,329	1,695	3,024	1,241	539	1,780	3,453	2,503	5,956[3]	1,281	226	1,507
1919	3,364	2,909	6,273	1,429	1,659	3,088	1,162	602	1,764	1,614	1,118	2,732[3]	692	144	836
1920	3,083	2,876	5,959	1,310	1,479	2,789	940	431	1,371	556	414	970	555	162	717
1921	2,532	1,789	4,321	1,615	1,600	3,215	732	431	1,163	597	373	970	107	95	202
1922	2,086	1,472	3,558	1,450	1,510	2,960	682	340	1,022	549	437	986	212	121	333
1923[1]	1,568	1,049	2,617	995	1,117	2,112	416	232	648	450	346	796	357	294	651
1924	2,435	1,629	4,064	1,116	1,047	2,163	733	370	1,103	2,051	1,638	3,689	....	....	....

For reference notes see page 941.

TABLE V.—Immigrant citizens (third class passengers) from certain countries to Japan, by country of last residence, 1908-24.

Year	Sum of available figures	United States	Hawaii	Canada	Year	Sum of available figures	United States	Hawaii	Canada
1908	9,541	4,641	4,507	393	1917	12,226	6,298	4,047	1,881
1909	7,583	3,773	3,337	473	1918	12,584	6,373	4,556	1,655
1910	8,089	4,257	3,204	628	1919	18,113	11,685	4,611	1,817
1911	8,414	4,599	3,183	632	1920	20,376	12,211	6,096	2,069
1912	8,870	4,440	3,922	508	1921	18,745	11,059	6,259	1,427
1913	9,510	4,860	3,624	1,026	1922	14,412	8,520	4,682	1,210
1914	9,282	4,603	3,435	1,244	1923[1]	10,784	6,256	3,332	1,196
1915	9,731	5,456	3,070	1,205	1924	12,579	8,173	3,014	1,392
1916	10,988	6,613	3,582	793					

TABLE VI.—Immigration and emigration of Japanese, into and from Formosa, 1898-1908.

Year	Immigration	Repatriation	Excess of immigration over emigration	Year	Immigration	Repatriation	Excess of immigration over emigration
1898	13,214	3,078	10,136	1904	11,564	12,155	591
1899	20,743	7,903	12,840	1905	13,427	12,190	1,227
1900	20,995	11,291	9,704	1906	18,278	12,391	5,887
1901	17,841	14,054	3,787	1907	17,966	14,223	3,743
1902	13,821	11,478	2,343	1908	20,360	14,393	5,967
1903	15,892	13,149	2,743				

TABLE VII.—Emigration of citizens from Korea[4], 1911-24.

1911	2,635		1918	4,736
1912	4,266		1919	6,279
1913	3,454		1920	4,232
1914	4,519		1921	3,771
1915	5,063		1922	2,580
1916	5,080		1923	2,841
1917	6,835		1924	210

For reference notes see page 941.

SOURCES

Résumé statistique de l'Empire du Japon. Tokio, 1891, 1897, 1902.

Table II, (years 1884-98).

Information supplied by the Government (compiled from emigration data prepared by the Department of Foreign Affairs).

Tables I, III, VI; II (1899-1924).

Grünefeld, Dr. E. *Die Japanische Auswanderung.* Tokio, 1913, p. 132. (Information supplied by the Department of Foreign Affairs.)

Table VII.

NOTES

[1]Migrants during the month of August 1923 are omitted, the records for that month having been destroyed.

[2]The figures of emigrants given in table II for the years 1898, 1902 and 1913 do not correspond with the totals given in table III for these years.

[3]Although these figures relate to emigrants proper, they are higher than those referring to passengers in table I.

[4]Including Japanese.

THE COMMONWEALTH OF AUSTRALIA AND THE FORMER AUSTRALIAN COLONIES

The statistics of the Australian Colonies, unless otherwise stated, are passenger statistics. They are compiled from lists of all classes of passengers, which lists the ships' captains present to the Customs officials at the arrival or departure of their boats. The statistics are marked by the following circumstances relating to (a) continental migrants and (b) through passengers.

1. The expression "arrivals and departures" does not occur in the sources until the last few decades. Before the sixties of the nineteenth century migration movements are simply entitled "immigration and emigration". Later the phrase "immigration and emigration *by sea*" is occasionally met. This is not identical with migration to overseas countries (Europe, Asia, etc.), but includes migrants by sea arriving from and departing to other States of Australia. The statistics of Victoria, which indicate for the years 1865-1915 the countries of origin and destination, show how large a proportion of the migration by sea is within the Continent. The quinquennial figures show that the proportion of arrivals in Victoria from the other Australian states is between 71 per cent (1866-70) and 90.6 per cent (1906-10) of all arrivals and the proporon of departures to other Australian states between 78.3 per cent (1866-70) and 92.9 per cent (1906-10) of all departures.

In *Australasian Statistics* for 1900 (pp. 8, 10 and 12), in *Votes and Proceedings of Victorian Legislative Assembly*, 1902, statistical tables are found which give for 1873-1900 the number of immigrants and emigrants by sea for all the Australian Colonies. From comparing these figures with those furnished by the several Colonies, it appears that they cover mainly migration by sea, even when the sources do not state it.

2. On the other hand, the figures of arrivals before 1908 are not confined to persons who disembark at the ports mentioned, but include also passengers who do not disembark. Similarly with figures of departures: all passengers leaving a port are counted even if they have previously departed from one or more other ports. This process led to counting passengers twice not only in the several States but for the Commonwealth. In order to remedy this defect, reforms were introduced April 1, 1908, which are described as follows in the report entitled *Shipping and Overseas Migration of the Commonwealth of Australia* for 1909 (pp. 96-97):

> Prior to the 1st April, 1908, all passengers on board overseas vessels were, at the first port of call, counted as "arrivals", and all passengers on board at the last port of clearance within the Commonwealth were counted as "departures". This method was abandoned on the date mentioned, and a new method substituted in its stead, under which only passengers who land at an Australian port are counted as "arrivals" and only passengers who join vessels

at an Australian port are counted as "departures". The previous method unduly augmented Australian migration figures by the inclusion of through passengers who did not join or leave vessels at any Australian port. Passengers who transship in Australia for New Zealand or other countries are recorded both as arrivals and as departures.

The subjoined data show that as a rule the passenger statistics of the several Australian States (New South Wales, Victoria, South Australia, Western Australia, Tasmania), as a guide to the amount of migration, are misleading in both the respects described above.

I.—COMMONWEALTH OF AUSTRALIA

1. *Statistics of Arrivals and Departures.*

Three sources were utilised. The *Statistical Abstract for the several British Overseas Dominions and Protectorates* publishes figures relating to arrivals from and departures to the United Kingdom and all parts. These figures will be found for 1904-17 in table II. Tables III and VI, taken from the *Quarterly Summary of Australian Statistics*, may be regarded as completing the above figures for the later dates. The "expeditionary forces" have been deducted but "crews" included.

The third source is the report entitled *Shipping and Overseas Migration of the Commonwealth of Australia* from which the figures in tables IV and VII are derived. These tables include the military forces. For 1916-24 they were supplemented by data on the sex of the migrants taken from the *Quarterly Summary*. The figures of arrivals in the third source are in substantial agreement with those of the other two, but its figures for departures are lower. They cover only "recorded departures" and these are understated to the extent of 14 ½ per cent for males and 10 per cent for females. (*Shipping*, etc., for 1914-15, pp. 86-87.)

Statistics of arrivals and departures for the Commonwealth of Australia are compiled by the Bureau of Census and Statistics from data collected by the Department of Trade and Customs for the purpose of estimating the population of Australia.

The Commonwealth Government has supplied data for totals and sex classes in the annual "net immigration" of the whole Commonwealth and the several States, covering the years 1860-1919. These figures are contained in the *Year Book*, but only for quinquennial periods.

For 1904-19 these Commonwealth figures agree with the differences between the arrivals and departures. But for the earlier years there is nothing to suggest the basis of the statistical data. The statistics for the several States, most of which were collected at the Library of the British Museum in London (see Victoria, Queensland, etc.), yielded in every instance examined different "net immigration" figures. In the *Statistics of the State of Tasmania* for 1919-20 and 1922-23 the figures for "net immigration" are not consistent with those supplied to us.

In reply to an enquiry on our part the Commonwealth Government furnished the following explanation: Prior to 1904, the Migration re-

turns for each State were prepared by the statisticians of the individual States, each State being considered as a separate entity. There was no co-ordination in this matter between the States. After the census of Australia for 1911, which was the first census to be taken for the whole of Australia under the supervision of a Commonwealth Department (Commonwealth Bureau of Census and Statistics), it was found necessary to adjust the migration figures in order to build up from the results of the census of 1901 to those of the census of 1911.

Interpretation of methods and of state returns offered special difficulties.

Chinese. The first trace of Chinese immigration in Australia dates from 1849, when 270 Chinese were introduced into New South Wales. They appear in 1859 for the first time in the statistics of this Colony. Most of the States soon passed restrictive laws.[1] After that was done, only Chinese admitted under the law have been recorded in the statistics.

2. *Statistics of Immigrants admitted.* (Table V, p. 952).

By the Commonwealth Constitution, the Parliament of the Commonwealth is empowered to make laws with respect to immigration and emigration and since 1901 several laws have been enacted. These regulate immigration mainly by discriminating between entrants.

The Commonwealth Statistics commenced in 1902 and are compiled by the Department of Home and Territories in accordance with the provisions of the Immigration Act, 1901-25. According to the *Official Year Book of the Commonwealth of Australia* (No. 18, 1925, p. 946) they relate to "Australian citizens who have been abroad, and other persons landing in Australia irrespective of the length of time which they propose to stay. Certain persons, who are permitted to land (under security for their subsequent departure) pending transshipment to another country, are not included. The majority of the persons of Asiatic or other non-European nationality shown in the table are former residents of Australia who have returned from visits abroad, or are persons who have been admitted temporarily under exemption certificates, for business, educational, or other purposes".

The Immigration Act, 1901-1925, does not require any statistical record being kept of departures from Australia. Accordingly, the *Year Book* contains no data about emigration, apart from "departures of persons of non-European races" for 1920-24.

3. *Assisted Immigration.*

All available statistical data upon state-assisted immigration, a form of particular importance in Australia, have been assembled for the present volume. This form of immigration is explained as follows in the *Official Year Book of the Commonwealth of Australia* (No. 18, 1925, p. 944.)

[1]First, Victoria: *An Act to make Provisions for certain Immigrants*, 1855, then, *New South Wales Chinese Immigration Restriction Act*, 1867. The other Colonies followed (Queensland, 1876; South Australia, 1886). In 1881, uniform restrictive legislation was introduced, save in Tasmania, where an Act was passed in 1887. This Act is still in force. In the other Colonies, the legislation became more and more restrictive. The Commonwealth Immigration Act of 1901 excluded all colored peoples.

"In the earlier days of settlement in Australia, State-assisted immigration played an important part. Such assistance ceased for the time being in Victoria in 1873, in South Australia in 1886, and in Tasmania in 1891. In New South Wales, general State-aided immigration was discontinued in the year 1887, but those who arrived under that system and were still residing in New South Wales, might, under special regulations, send for their wives and families. A certain amount of passage money, graduated according to the age of the immigrant, had to be paid in each case. Under the provisions of these regulations, immigrants to the number of 1,994, received State assistance during the years 1888 to 1899 inclusive. From 1900 to 1905 no assistance of any kind was given, but from 1906 onwards assistance has again been granted. In Queensland and Western Australia, such assistance, although varying considerably in volume from year to year, has been accorded for many years past. Assistance to immigrants, which in the case of Victoria had practically ceased in 1873, has recently been again afforded. In South Australia the principle of State assistance was again introduced in 1911, and in Tasmania in 1912."

For Victoria figures upon State-aided immigration have been found down to 1882, and for South Australia to 1885. After the temporary suspension of assisted passages, statistics on the subject once more began to appear in 1906 for New South Wales, in 1911 for South Australia, and in 1913 for all Australian States. For the Commonwealth, as a whole, the annual figures began with 1908.

II New South Wales

All these migration figures refer to immigrants and emigrants by sea. For the earlier years, to be sure, there is no statement to that effect, but from 1863 onwards the figures indicate the number of immigrants and emigrants who arrived and departed *seaward*. Attached to the figures for 1869-84 is a note to the effect that no account was kept of the number of persons who arrived or departed overland. Nevertheless, the figures for 1881-90 are somewhat lower than those published in the Australian statistics for all Australian States.

The emigration figures for 1843-68 are taken from official returns published by the Colonial Secretary's Office, Sydney, relating to increase and decrease of population. They appear in our source under the head of "Departures" from New South Wales, including the district of Port Philip. After 1850 returns of this district are no longer included. For 1858 and 1860-68 the following note appears: "There is no means of ascertaining the overland migration between New South Wales and Victoria, or South Australia."

III. Victoria

All figures refer to immigration and emigration by sea. In addition to the above-cited passage, the one which follows, and in which figures for immigration and emigration for 1886-1896 are given, relates to the problem of continental emigration statistics:

In consequence of the migration returns being inflated by the inclusion of persons passing through Victorian ports en route to

other countries, the figures are misleading as a guide to the movement of population between Victoria and other colonies and countries. The *net* emigration balance of emigration over immigration to Western Australia, for example, consists not only of Victorians, but also of emigrants bound for that Colony from New South Wales, Queensland, Tasmania and New Zealand, in vessels which happen to call in on their way at the Port of Melbourne. Hence this number may be regarded as practically the net emigration from the whole of Eastern Australia, including Tasmania and New Zealand. (*Statistical Register of Victoria*, 1896, "Population," p.9.)

Again: In the (*Statistical Register*, 1911 "Population," p. 29) we find the following explanation:

From the beginning of 1903 the migration returns have been amended and do not now include persons who merely call at the port of the State on their way to other places.

IV. QUEENSLAND

The source from which table I has been taken declares that the figures refer to the total number of immigrants arriving in Queensland "since the commencement of immigration *direct* from Europe".

Table III and the following tables up to 1877 concern arrivals and departures by sea. Figures in tables IV-VII include also migration by train across the border from 1888. From 1909 onward the figures are not as recorded, but are the result of adjustments by the Commonwealth statistician.

V. SOUTH AUSTRALIA

Table I, as well as the other tables up to 1887, gives arrivals and departures by sea. The figures in tables II-V refer to passengers by rail and by sea in 1888 to 1890; to passengers by sea, rail and River Murray in 1891 to 1907; and to the total recorded immigration and emigration from 1908, which means that continental migrations are included. In some years, allowance is made for unrecorded departures (explanatory note 2). The figures for 1882 to 1907 represent immigration and emigration to and from South Australia exclusive of the Northern Territory.

VI. WESTERN AUSTRALIA

Our source (*Western Australia Year Book* for 1902-04, published 1906, p. 1152) states that "from the first settlement of the Colony up to the year 1837, there were no Blue Books issued, and the figures relating to *arrivals* and *departures* were taken either from the reports of the Harbour Master at Fremantle or from the Perth newspapers of that period", and that the Blue Books for 1838-59 give only net immigration. There is every reason to think that these statistics were based on the same principle of arrivals and departures as in the other Colonies.

VII. TASMANIA

An examination of the statistical tables of this State conveys a similar impression to that recorded in connection with the preceding States.

TABLE I.—Net Immigration (excess of arrivals over departures) of the Commonwealth, by sex and states, 1860-1919.

Year	Commonwealth			New South Wales			Victoria		
	Total	Males	Females	Total	Males	Females	Total	Males	Females
1860	23,949	13,483	10,466	13,416	10,169	3,247	6,360	332	6,028
1861	—6,283	—12,390	6,107	—522	—798	276	—11,409	—15,310	3,901
1862	8,299	99	8,200	—173	—1,428	1,255	2,687	—5,243	2,556
1863	22,321	7,022	15,299	1,958	—658	2,616	2,114	—4,158	6,272
1864	31,550	19,951	11,599	2,710	873	1,837	13,304	8,332	4,972
1865	30,259	16,948	13,311	7,589	4,995	2,594	4,334	508	3,826
1866	23,945	13,846	10,099	10,072	7,413	2,659	3,087	386	2,701
1867	7,552	3,739	3,813	6,206	3,770	2,436	825	—1,125	1,950
1868	17,962	12,717	5,245	7,210	5,579	1,631	5,846	2,978	2,868
1869	15,044	,8571	6,473	5,703	3,985	1,718	10,028	5,595	4,433
1870	15,916	8,841	7,075	4,118	2,634	1,484	10,432	5,682	4,750
1871	11,682	7,031	4,651	4,976	3,585	1,391	5,061	2,243	2,818
1872	3,037	933	2,104	4,708	3,370	1,338	—3,552	—4,124	572
1873	11.368	7,008	4,360	4,809	3,065	1,744	—2,219	—1,940	—279
1874	17,121	11,020	6,101	7,617	5,183	2,434	—2,278	—2,220	—58
1875	18,454	1,4334	4,120	7,631	5,143	2,488	—2,607	—2,052	—555
1876	25,082	17,349	7,733	7,816	5,196	2,620	—2,718	—2,069	—649
1877	34,384	23,728	10,656	15,575	10,438	5,137	277	—393	670
1878	21,602	12,109	9,493	13,653	8,543	5,110	—2,896	—2,273	—623
1879	25,300	15,859	9,441	20,870	13,584	7,286	—2,880	—2,072	—808
1880	23,774	14,824	8,950	15,545	10,617	4,928	2,352	1,111	1,241
1881	28,528	20,901	7,627	18,426	13,843	4,583	517	345	172
1882	37,856	23,633	14,223	15,492	9,714	5,778	5,687	3,294	2,393
1883	69,865	45,761	24,104	26,963	17,255	9,708	5,153	4,184	969
1884	51,067	32,945	18,122	24,079	14,924	9,155	7,979	5,426	2,553
1885	36,724	25,127	11,597	24,903	15,260	9,643	8,450	6,676	1,774
1886	38,702	25,478	13,224	17,954	9,479	8,475	18,007	12,589	5,418
1887	33,822	20,864	12,958	7,301	3,675	3,626	14,721	9,689	5,032
1888	38,927	23,417	15,510	5,566	4,026	1,540	35,385	21,977	13,408
1889	22,606	11,754	10,852	7,351	3,594	3,757	8,894	3,598	5,296
1890	24,644	14,404	10,240	14,393	8,571	5,822	9,224	4,041	5,183
1891	26,873	15,107	11,766	16,723	8,991	7,732	4,770	1,944	2,826
1892	—3,122	—1,445	—1,677	4,356	1,765	2,591	—11,605	—8,036	—3,569
1893	—7,379	—4,421	—2,958	—980	—1,074	94	—12,621	—8,438	—4,183
1894	3,163	3,757	—594	1,477	340	1,137	—12,843	—8,725	—4,118
1895	2,857	2,662	195	—112	—1,35!	1,239	—14,549	—9,937	—4,612
1896	6,545	6,935	—390	—3,806	—1,787	—2,019	—22,290	—15,994	—6,296
1897	6,995	4,116	2,879	242	1,434	—1,192	—13,928	—7,355	—6,573
1898	—507	—950	443	2,295	956	1,339	—11,302	—6,191	—5,111
1899	—1,736	—2,492	756	1,209	—327	1,536	—8,170	—5,066	—3,104
1900	—8,810	—8,554	—256	—937	—1,130	193	—7,892	—5,199	—2,693
1901	2,959	2,478	481	—6,704	—5,029	—1,675	—1,417	—178	—1,239
1902	—4,293	—1,568	—2,725	5,299	5,515	—216	—15,953	—10,549	—5,404
1903	—9,876	—6,058	—3,818	3,771	3,730	41	—17,463	—10,857	—6,606
1904	—2,983	—780	—2,203	6,968	5,768	1,200	—14,504	—9,654	—4,850
1905	—2,600	—1,249	—1,351	7,903	5,687	2,216	—10,618	—6,733	—3,885
1906	—5,049	—3,528	—1,521	7,761	5,572	2,189	—6,196	—4,652	—1,544
1907	5,195	2,933	2,262	14,164	10,433	3,731	—3,851	—3,090	—761
1908	5,437	3,287	2,150	—4,052	—3,301	—751	2,311	1,907	404
1909	21,783	15,266	6,517	2,004	—471	2,475	9,465	8,058	1,407
1910	29,912	20,041	9,871	670	—1,076	1,746	7,681	7,177	504
1911	74,379	51,001	23,372	26,775	18,956	7,819	20,675	13,757	6,918
1912	91,892	58,266	33,633	53,037	35,547	17,490	23,453	12,084	11,369
1913	63,227	37,124	26,101	26,828	16,421	10,407	12,367	7,449	4,918
1914[2]	—8,226	—18,125	9,898	593	—7,038	7,631	53	—3,665	3,718
1915[2]	—84,410	—87,898	3,485	—20,138	—25,403	5,265	—29,929	—28,057	—1,872
1916[2]	—128,737	—127,214	—1,519	—40,632	—41,775	1,143	—37,528	—36,687	—841
1917[2]	—17,822	—17,689	—138	485	—2,259	2,744	—6,081	—4,438	—1,643
1918[2]	23,359	21,713	1,640	10,031	9,305	726	3,765	5,075	—1,310
1919[2]	166,303	156,559	9,750	54,593	47,916	6,677	53,541	49,996	3,545

For reference notes see page 959.

TABLE I.—NET IMMIGRATION (EXCESS OF ARRIVALS OVER DEPARTURES) OF THE COMMONWEALTH, BY SEX AND STATES, 1860-1919 (continued).

Year	Queensland			South Australia[1]			Western Australia		
	Total	Males	Females	Total	Males	Females	Total	Males	Females
1860	3,778	2,638	1,140	—385	409	—794	130	—78	208
1861	5,388	3,612	1,176	1,641	1,296	345	262	248	14
1862	9,805	5,988	3,817	1,593	1,043	550	1,340	1,015	325
1863	15,444	9,943	5,501	2,477	1,499	978	1,385	1,021	364
1864	10,674	7,433	3,241	4,327	2,679	1,648	517	402	115
1865	11,544	7,055	4,489	6,225	3,753	2,472	661	527	134
1866	6,334	3,329	3,005	3,401	1,836	1,565	606	499	107
1867	971	1,354	—383	—134	—263	129	383	273	110
1868	4,718	4,276	442	—1,038	—896	—142	759	575	184
1869	167	—422	589	274	145	129	—56	—161	105
1870	2,851	1,653	1,198	—1,538	—1,064	—474	7	—4	11
1871	3,051	1,818	1,233	—606	—218	—388	—116	—63	—53
1872	3,435	2,299	1,136	—1,025	—390	—635	—61	—34	—27
1873	7,951	4,652	3,299	1,381	1,113	268	—295	—216	—79
1874	10,826	7,275	3,551	2,299	1,512	787	114	76	38
1875	12.160	10,192	1,968	2,558	1,816	742	260	157	103
1876	9,644	7,766	1,878	9,810	6,037	3,773	136	68	68
1877	9,813	7,633	2,180	8,190	5,573	2,617	90	26	64
1878	1,508	—424	1,932	8,411	5,625	2,786	—107	—68	—39
1879	78	—509	587	6,634	4,233	2,401	—39	—11	—28
1880	641	—574	1,215	4,988	3,588	1,400	—129	—194	65
1881	5,909	3,980	1,929	2,882	1,716	1,166	—1	81	—82
1882	16,236	10,812	5,424	—330	—691	361	201	163	38
1883	33,437	22,245	11,192	3.077	1,432	1.645	572	426	146
1884	17,154	11,232	5,922	—18	263	—281	1,073	705	368
1885	9,657	6,598	3,059	—7,693	—4,702	—2,991	1,813	1,326	487
1886	8,623	5,070	3,553	—9,546	—4,973	—4,573	3,985	3,029	956
1887	11,222	6,468	4,754	—3,559	—1,870	—1,689	2,361	1,722	639
1888	6,568	3,543	3,025	—7,336	—5,287	—2,049	—851	—535	—316
1889	6,054	3,100	2,954	—1,681	286	—1,967	863	646	217
1890	858	333	525	—2,083	—1,051	—1,032	1,821	1,549	272
1891	—1,266	—655	—611	—738	—436	—302	3,758	2,964	794
1892	—356	25	—381	3,842	2,863	979	4,475	3,534	941
1893	618	1,035	— 417	3,377	2,036	1,341	5,187	4,532	655
1894	2,319	2,090	229	—2,600	—2,811	211	15,614	13,726	1,888
1895	3,351	2,593	758	—3,410	—3,145	—265	18,167	14,687	3,480
1896	1,269	735	534	—5,866	—4,236	—1,630	35,539	27,281	8,258
1897	1,699	1,756	—57	—5,248	—3,261	—1,987	22,301	10,445	11,856
1898	3,877	3,670	207	—1,762	—484	—1,278	4,131	—843	4,974
1899	3,699	3,062	637	—459	812	—1,271	530	1,900	2,430
1900	—1,522	—1,128	—394	—2,531	—1,070	—1,461	6,495	1,970	4,525
1901	4,578	4,164	414	—3,025	—2,368	—657	10,435	6,504	3,931
1902	—2,493	—1,431	—1,062	—7,014	—5,158	—1,856	14,963	9,076	5,887
1903	—787	180	—967	—4,576	—3,282	—1,294	8,864	4,166	4,698
1904	—1,625	— 961	—664	—3,046	—693	—2,353	10,301	5,711	4,590
1905	—1,576	—1,457	—119	—1,818	470	—2,288	5,857	2,670	3,187
1906	—1,433	—1,812	379	—1,157	784	—1,941	319	—602	921
1907	—2,110	—1,362	—748	1,675	543	1,132	—5,414	—3,893	—1,521
1908	2,144	1,523	621	6,246	3,985	2,261	255	—10	265
1909	10,724	7,576	3,148	784	672	112	1,106	665	441
1910	10,746	6,366	4,380	7,445	4,606	2,839	6,312	4,551	1,761
1911	13,6 67	8,813	4,854	5,511	4,070	1,441	11,923	7,821	4,102
1912	3,813	2,271	1,542	5,812	4,086	1,726	6,344	3,645	2,699
1913	12,110	7,976	4,134	3,692	965	2,727	8,030	3,779	4,251
1914[2]	4,837	3,376	1,461	—4,868	—3,181	—1,687	—4,007	—4,277	270
1915[2]	—9,336	—9,399	63	—9,015	—10,201	1,186	—11,451	—10,779	—672
1916[2]	—19,439	—18,796	—643	—10,927	—11,861	934	—15,261	—14,111	—1,150
1917[2]	—3,754	—3,805	51	—2,092	—2,278	186	—5,155	—3,961	—1,194
1918[2]	5,362	2,936	2,426	3,878	2,673	1,205	—928	492	—1,420
1919[2]	22,044	22,559	—515	18,326	17,653	673	14,330	13,979	351

For reference notes see page 959.

TABLE I.—Net Immigration (excess of arrivals over departures) of the Commonwealth, by sex and states, 1860-1919 (concluded).

Year	Tasmania			Northern Territory[1]			Federal Capital Territory		
	Total	Males	Females	Total	Males	Females	Total	Males	Females
1860	650	13	637	...	...	...	...	...	...
1861	—1,643	—1,438	—205	...	...	...	...	...	...
1862	—1,579	—1,276	—303	...	...	...	...	...	...
1863	—1,057	—625	—432	...	...	...	...	...	...
1864	18	232	—214	...	...	...	...	...	...
1865	—94	110	—204	...	...	...	...	...	...
1866	445	383	62	...	...	...	...	...	...
1867	—699	—270	—429	...	...	...	...	...	...
1868	467	205	262	...	...	...	...	...	...
1869	—1,072	—571	—501	...	...	...	...	...	...
1870	46	—60	106	...	...	...	...	...	...
1871	—684	—334	—350	...	...	...	...	...	...
1872	—468	—188	—280	...	...	...	...	...	...
1873	—259	334	—593	...	...	...	...	...	...
1874	—1,457	—806	—651	...	...	...	...	...	...
1875	—1,548	—922	—626	...	...	...	...	...	...
1876	394	351	43	...	...	...	...	...	...
1877	439	451	—12	...	...	...	...	...	...
1878	1,033	706	327	...	...	...	...	...	...
1879	637	634	3	...	...	...	...	...	...
1880	377	276	101	...	...	...	...	...	...
1881	795	936	—141	...	...	...	...	...	...
1882	570	341	229	...	...	...	...	...	...
1883	663	219	444	...	...	...	...	...	...
1884	800	395	405	...	...	...	...	...	...
1885	—406	—31	—375	...	...	...	...	...	...
1886	—321	284	—605	...	...	...	...	...	...
1877	1,776	1,180	596	...	...	...	...	...	...
1888	—405	—307	—98	...	...	...	...	...	...
1889	1,125	530	595	...	...	...	...	...	...
1890	431	961	—530	...	...	...	...	...	...
1891	3,626	2,299	1,327	...	...	...	...	...	...
1892	—3,834	—1,596	—2,238	...	...	...	...	...	...
1893	—2,960	—2,512	—448	...	...	...	...	...	...
1894	—804	—863	59	...	...	...	...	...	...
1895	—590	—185	—405	...	...	...	...	...	...
1896	1,699	936	763	...	...	...	...	...	...
1897	1,929	1,097	832	...	...	...	...	...	...
1898	2,254	1,942	312	...	...	...	...	...	...
1899	1,455	927	528	...	...	...	...	...	...
1900	—2,423	—1,997	—426	...	...	...	...	...	...
1901	—783	—387	—396	—125	—228	103	...	...	...
1902	1,046	1,066	—20	—141	—87	—54	...	...	...
1903	510	219	291	—195	—214	'19	...	...	...
1904	—1,075	—914	—161	—2	—37	35	...	...	...
1905	—2,195	—1,755	—440	—153	—131	—22	...	...	...
1906	—4,235	—2,742	—1,493	—108	—76	—32	...	...	...
1907	833	380	453	—102	—78	—24	...	...	...
1908	—1,351	—737	—614	—116	—80	—36	...	...	...
1909	—2,272	—1,247	—1,025	—28	13	—41	...	...	...
1910	—2,782	—1.438	—1,344	—160	—145	—15	...	...	...
1911	—4,388	—2,444	—1,944	—40	—53	13	256	87	169
1912	—794	436	—1,230	237	202	35	—10	—10	...
1913	—7	390	—397	192	145	47	15	1	14
1914[2]	—5,071	—3,555	—1,516	310	277	33	—73	—61	—12
1915[2]	—4,997	—4,426	—571	616	477	139	—160	—107	—53
1916[2]	—5,519	—4,383	—1,136	230	190	40	339[3]	205[3]	134[3]
1917[2]	—1,206	—861	—345	131	46	85	—150	—128	—22
1918[2]	1,360	1,403	—43	—194	—242	48	85	77	8
1919[2]	3,906	4,720	—814	—115	—96	—19	—322	—174	—148

For reference notes see page 959.

TABLE II.—Arrivals from and departures to the United Kingdom and all
ports, 1904-17.

Year	Arrivals		Departures	
	From the United Kingdom	From all countries	To the United Kingdom	To all countries
1904	9,811	47,808	9,848	50,791
1905	10,594	47,904	9,633	50,504
1906	12,674	50,887	10,885	55,936
1907	17,194	68,638	11,796	63,443
1908	21,416	72,208	13,608	66,771
1909	29,959	83,609	14,076	61,826
1910	39,902	95,692	16,371	65,780
1911	71,650	141,909	19,172	67,448
1912	90,882	166,958	21,490	74,936
1913	76,082	141,906	25,775	78,533
1914[4]	45,700	111,086	25,759	84,620
1915[4]	16,737	62,436	11,915	59,571
1916[4]	6,422	47,393	6,353	47,948
1917[4]	2,049	36,640	3,478	36,376

TABLE III.—Distribution of arrivals, by country of last residence, 1918-24.

Country	1918[4]	1919[4]	1920[4]	1921	1922	1923	1924
United Kingdom	1,535	21,024	41,149	37,937	45,538	46,528	47,955
Canada	1,407	1,586	1,712	1,475	1,835	1,414	2,062
Fiji	1,120	1,111	1,440	1,490	1,200	1,040	1,024
Hongkong	2,279	2,507	1,986	2,411	3,114	3,241	3,473
India and Ceylon	915	699	1,406	1,509	1,789	2,006	2,120
New Zealand	10,308	12,228	23,471	22,005	21,963	22,899	23,670
Norfolk Island	78	64	76	126	254	273	229
Papua	684	508	735	916	917	823	1,293
Solomon Islands	*	*	*	*	*	355	436
South African Union	332	307	1,416	1,928	1,871	1,977	1,994
Straits Settlements	1,650	1,535	1,737	1,457	1,135	1,069	1,168
Territory of New Guinea	*	*	*	*	*	846	830
Other British Possessions	591	833	1,167	1,761	2,412	729	360
Total, British countries	20,899	42,402	76,295	73,015	82,028	83,200	86,614
China	173	140	1,269	760	259	267	5
Egypt[5]	*	*	*	*	*	1,444	2,895
France	18	264	902	889	1,240	1,649	3,367
Germany	....	....	....	1	5	27	25
Italy	....	34	642	1,447	4,100	2,232	5,902
Japan	506	515	611	495	662	532	823
Dutch East Indies	*	*	*	*	*	529	978
New Caledonia	696	920	841	489	458	342	477
Philippine Islands	*	*	*	*	*	180	167
South Sea Islands	432	352	121	188	164	170	144
United States	1,015	2,384	2,239	1,726	1,685	1,724	1,897
Other Foreign countries	1,085	1,984	2,316	1,306	1,453	563	373
Total Foreign countries	3,925	6,593	8,941	7,301	10,026	9,659	17,053
Crews discharged	9,950	10,205	12,327	7,622	1,459[6]	*	*
Grand total	34,774	59,200	97,563	87,938	93,513	92,859	103,667

For reference notes see page 959.

TABLE IV.—Distribution of arrivals, by sex and age, 1904-24.

Year	Total			Males			Females		
	Total	Under 12 years	Over 12 years	Total	Under 12 years	Over 12 years	Total	Under 12 years	Over 12 years
1904	46,336	3,698	42,638	32,414	1,985	30,429	13,922	1,713	12,209
1905	48,836	4,200	44,636	33,146	2,062	31,084	15,690	2,138	13,552
1906	54,164	5,511	48,653	36,312	2,809	33,503	17,852	2,702	15,150
1907	68,638	7,450	61,188	45,755	3,660	42,095	22,883	3,790	19,093
1908	72,208	7,475	64,733	48,677	3,732	44,945	23,531	3,743	19,788
1909	83,609	9,275	74,334	57,487	4,717	52,770	26,122	4,558	21,564
1910	95,692	11,232	84,460	65,745	5,665	60,080	29,947	5,567	24,380
1911	141,909	18,844	123,065	96,964	9,703	87,261	44,945	9,141	35,804
1912	166,958	24,171	142,787	110,387	12,368	98,019	56,571	11,803	44,768
1913	141,906	21,098	120,808	90,680	10,742	79,938	51,226	10,356	40,870
1914[2]	111,086	12,811	98,275	74,277	6,681	67,596	36,819	6,130	30,679
1915[2]	70,981	6,118	64,863	50,639	3,090	47,549	20,342	3,028	17,314
1916[2]	63,405	. . . .	. . . .	48,911	. . . .	. . . .	14,494	. . . .	. . . .
1917[2]	65,089	. . . .	. . . .	55,264	. . . .	. . . .	9,825	. . . .	. . . .
1918[2]	78,925	. . . .	. . . .	69,530	. . . .	. . . .	9,395	. . . .	. . . .
1919[2]	222,956	. . . .	. . . .	197,721	. . . .	. . . .	25,235	. . . .	. . . .
1920[2]	109,109	. . . .	. . . .	67,294	. . . .	. . . .	41,815	. . . .	. . . .
1921	87,938	. . . .	. . . .	53,221	. . . .	. . . .	34,717	. . . .	. . . .
1922	93,513	. . . .	. . . .	58,057	. . . .	. . . .	35,456	. . . .	. . . .
1923	92,859	. . . .	. . . .	56,415	. . . .	. . . .	36,444	. . . .	. . . .
1924	103,667	. . . .	. . . .	62,400	. . . .	. . . .	41,267	. . . .	. . . .

For reference notes see page 959.

TABLE V. DISTRIBUTION OF ARRIVALS, BY NATIONALITY, 1902-24.

Nationality	1902	1903	1904	1905	1906	1907	1908	1909
European:								
Austrian............	647	809	930	683	691	651	736	895
Belgian.............	14	20	20	25	33	64	45	35
British.............	35,330	35,061	39,026	39,975	47,396	60,172	64,374	71,201
Danish.............	52	94	103	125	259	280	227	272
Dutch..............	45	30	26	43	91	94	120	187
French.............	1,011	1,390	2,076	1,402	1,866	1,685	1,546	1,347
German.............	1,162	1,028	823	926	1,339	1,909	1,911	2,109
Greek..............	268	210	194	121	240	202	296	327
Italian.............	1,181	793	814	734	839	992	902	1,078
Maltese............	...	...	...	...	...	...	...	...
Polish.............	9	8	8	13	5	6	22	24
Portuguese.........	4	5	...	2	3	6	5	10
Rumanian	10	...	...	...	...	...	12	11
Russian............	100	148	122	157	293	388	349	466
Scandinavian	221	382	320	281	776	1,173	825	891
Spanish............	32	53	27	35	32	86	57	56
Swiss..............	55	20	79	63	68	78	78	131
Turkish............	12	13	...	3	8	6	4	14
Other European.....	1,121	...	7	17	18	29	112	16
American:								
North American.....	471	561	563	603	867	889	687	692
South American.....	6	6	...	...	12	15	10	14
American Indian....	...	...	...	...	...	...	...	...
French Creole.....	1	...	...	...	...	...	...	...
Negro..............	7	10	13	16	4	9	4	6
West Indian........	8	10	6	4	...	13	23	6
Asiatic:								
Arab...............	1	...	...	3	...	8	3	1
Afghan.............	9	...	...	7	3	9	15	3
Chinese............	1,336	986	847	1,269	1,134	1,424	1,771	1,729
Burmese............	1	...	...	...	...	...	...	1
Cingales	15	10	9	15	6	12	10	10
Eurasian...........	2	2	...	...	...	...	...	6
Filipino............	99	37	54	75	120	57	27	37
Chaldean...........	2	...	...	...	...	...	...	...
Hindu..............	72	50	461	146	75	129	74	130
East Indian.........	...	1	...	...	...	...	...	...
Japanese............	521	559	461	251	356	521	555	509
Kurd	3	...	...	...	...	...	...	...
Javanese............	3	...	75	62	52	1	...	52
Malay..............	321	526	469	289	436	370	230	309
Syrian..............	47	44	39	51	66	58	45	73
Timorese............	...	...	...	...	...	...	...	...
Other Races:								
Maori..............	...	1	...	1	2	8	48	108
Mauritian...........	6	...	...	...	...	...	3	3
Pacific Islander......	1,177	1,098	193	98	156	121	89	94
Papuan.............	93	145	552	415	368	493	430	439
St. Helena Black.....	1	...	...	...	...	...	1	1
Unspecified.........	25	20	20	33	32	30	14	31
Total...........	45,501	44,130	48,337	47,943	57,646	71,988	75,660	83,324

TABLE V.—DISTRIBUTION OF ARRIVALS, BY NATIONALITY, 1910-24 (continued).

Nationality	1910	1911	1912	1913	1914	1915[4]	1916[4]	1917[4]
European:								
Austrian.............	816	1,184	855	794	676	277[7]	107[7]	....
Belgian.............	50	84	95	63	63	105	69	35
British.............	81,457	124,061	146,602	122,443	93,136	60,505	50,489	45,988
Danish.............	269	393	371	444	478	305	173	137
Dutch.............	175	307	435	288	287	182	156	194
French.............	1,160	1,166	1,238	1,491	1,187	595	516	676
German.............	2,449	2,517	3,501	3,155	3,395	890[7]	452[7]	58[7]
Greek.............	380	583	736	480	772	361	160	265
Italian.............	883	1,365	1,632	1,963	1,642	645	179	93
Maltese.............	....	41	122	193	464	57	173	212
Polish.............	11	34	17	7	12	2	....	1
Portuguese..........	3	6	9	25	12	1	....	7
Rumanian..........	3	13	24	9	34	6	8	13
Russian.............	735	994	1,159	1,334	1,446	716	497	341
Scandinavian........	1,210	1,384	1,303	1,285	1,489	1,202	786	552
Spanish.............	49	128	118	116	169	206	51	37
Swiss.............	109	130	209	202	220	64	40	21
Turkish.............	10	10	6	5	19	1	1	....
Other European......	22	27	57[8]	5	165[9]	13	7	1
American:								
North American......	746	914	1,386	1,713	1,529	1,066	1,050	870
South American......	13	17	37	14	31	5	16	24
American Indian......	....	31	9	....	1	1	...	....
French Creole.......	....	....	....	....	....	....	...	....
Negro.............	14	13	47	7	23	9	8	9
West Indian.........	13	11	8	1	3	2	9	1
Asiatic:								
Arab.............	1	1	18	14	19	2	6	....
Afghan.............	2	14	17	7	2	3	....	....
Chinese.............	1,817	2,009	2,250	2,286	1,975	2,287	2,289	2,016
Burmese.............	....	....	....	1	1	1	...	....
Cingalese...........	14	4	17	8	9	6	18	11
Eurasian.............	14	7	13	2	....	....	...	....
Filipino.............	66	17	13	12	4	15	15	15
Chaldean............	....	....	....	....	....	....	...	....
Hindu.............	156	188	157	187	305	144	133	111
East Indian.........	....	....	....	....	....	....	...	....
Japanese.............	610	459	698	822	387	423	1,089	888
Kurd.............	....	....	....	....	....	....	...	....
Javanese.............	4	12	6	3	20	3	4	20
Malay.............	304	479	326	303	291	285	254	190
Syrian.............	95	104	75	31	19	5	14	13
Timorese.............	....	....	....	....	....	....	...	....
Other Races:								
Maori.............	62	31	32	41	21	16	6	2
Mauritian............	4	9	2	7	1	....	...	....
Pacific Islander.......	54	69	92	105	101	37	59	40
Papuan.............	622	139	196	171	189	185	178	132
St. Helena Black.....	....	....	....	....	....	....	...	....
Unspecified..........	141	65[10]	102[10]	214[10]	104[10]	58[10]	225[10]	63
Total..............	94,543	139,020	163,990	140,251	110,701	70,436	59,140	53,036

For reference notes see page 959.

TABLE V.—Distribution of arrivals, by nationality, 1910-1924 (concluded).

Nationality	1918[4]	1919[4]	1920[4]	1921	1922	1923	1924
European:							
Austrian	3[7]	22[7]	3	5	8	2	9
Belgian	35	31	90	73	72	84	69
British	27,614	53,281	84,333	76,518	84,263	85,440	88,335
Danish	110	124	189	201	179	172	189
Dutch	163	526	699	321	233	219	248
French	571	815	785	529	525	378	660
German	36[7]	54[7]	115	76	86	130	195
Greek	288	93	131	258	472	922	2,028
Italian	24	116	631	1,278	3,367	1,739	4,540
Maltese	14	47	88	132	373	323	418
Polish	3	2	27	51	45	58	111
Portuguese	8	9	9	8	2	4	...
Rumanian	9	6	10	9	14	14	23
Russian	199	142	121	100	116	256	312
Scandinavian	493	448	437	487	361	491	383
Spanish	23	37	37	83	51	85	108
Swiss	39	30	90	149	169	160	277
Turkish	...	1[7]	...	...	4	2	...
Other European	...	106	197	344	339[11]	587[12]	2,735[13]
American:							
North American	749	1,102	1,698	1,577	1,372	1,470	1,400
South American	12	8	16	35	14	13	27
American Indian	...	...	6	...	...	...	...
French Creole	...	...	...	...	...	...	...
Negro	2	5	5	6	5	13	11
West Indian	3	5	...	7	3	6	2
Asiatic:							
Arab	...	...	...	...	...	...	...
Afghan	...	...	2	4	5	3	16
Chinese	1,723	1,495	1,753	1,833	1,964	1,974	1,917
Burmese	...	...	...	...	...	...	...
Cingalese	2	7	12	19	12	12	5
Eurasian	...	...	...	...	...	...	...
Filipino	10	18	10	13	10	25	15
Chaldean	...	...	...	...	...	...	...
Hindu	102	203	241	163	213	129	169
East Indian	...	...	...	...	...	...	...
Japanese	431	521	345	282	390	222	240
Kurd	...	...	...	...	...	...	...
Javanese	21	27	12	6	8	4	1
Malay	65	320	207	44	39	29	23
Syrian	1	6	56	39	79	147	288
Timorese	...	...	282	34	371	243	316
Other Races:							
Maori	1	...	1	...	...	...	...
Mauritian	...	...	5	...	...	...	...
Pacific Islander	43	24	47	46	47	43	50
Papuan	133	135	30	170	368	282	365
St. Helena Black	...	...	...	...	...	...	...
Unspecified	88[10]	214[10]	85	44	39	44	86
Total	33,018	59,980	92,805	84,944	95,618	95,725	105,571

For reference notes see page 959.

TABLE VI.—DISTRIBUTION OF DEPARTURES, BY COUNTRY OF FUTURE RESIDENCE, 1918-24.

Country	1918[4]	1919[4]	1920[4]	1921	1922	1923	1924
United Kingdom	751	15,152	18,442	15,989	15,776	16,122	18,697
Canada	1,246	1,312	2,133	1,636	1,417	1,413	1,262
Fiji	1,145	1,417	1,823	1,809	1,078	919	823
Hongkong	2,271	2,463	2,598	3,265	3,017	3,512	3,032
India and Ceylon	450	1,078	1,435	1,290	1,327	1,676	1,778
New Zealand	8,049	12,480	26,995	23,750	18,920	18,882	20,765
Norfolk Island	104	89	84	144	245	232	242
Papua	682	546	990	731	615	966	1,114
Solomon Islands	*	*	*	*	*	399	386
South African Union	383	898	1,760	2,113	1,621	1,555	1,261
Straits Settlements	1,836	1,549	1,570	1,603	1,108	1,385	1,475
Territory of New Guinea	*	*	*	*	*	893	882
Other British Possessions	319	676	1,734	2,534	1,802	261	365
Total British countries	17,236	37,660	59,564	54,864	46,926	48,215	52,082
China	103	140	429	516	318	107	4
Egypt[5]	*	*	*	*	*	179	233
France	1	130	791	1,041	751	860	1,397
Germany	....	....	....	2	6	32	15
Italy	....	616	617	255	788	599	931
Japan	732	711	930	909	640	647	519
Dutch East Indies	*	*	*	*	*	319	790
New Caledonia	117	445	348	221	249	296	346
Philippine Islands	*	*	*	*	*	132	95
South Sea Islands	213	210	187	310	277	225	231
United States	1,238	2,074	2,345	1,722	1,645	1,671	1,422
Other Foreign countries	820	992	1,538	1,795	1,161	659	386
Total Foreign countries	3,224	5,318	7,185	6,771	5,835	5,726	6,369
Crews shipped	11,034	11,227	12,749	9,044	1,389[6]	*	*
Allowance for unrecorded departures	4,248	7,191	1,624	1,470	1,340	1,378	1,467
Grand total	35,742	61,396	81,122	72,149	55,490	55,319	59,918

For reference notes see page 959.

TABLE VII.—Distribution of departures, by sex and age[14], 1904-24.

Year	Total			Males			Females		
	Total	Under 12 years	Over 12 years	Total	Under 12 years	Over 12 years	Total	Under 12 years	Over 12 years
1904	44,947	3,786	41,161	30,363	2,135	28,228	14,584	1,651	12,933
1905	46,686	3,952	42,734	30,965	2,089	28,876	15,721	1,863	13,858
1906	51,299	4,080	47,219	34,088	2,124	31,964	17,211	1,956	15,255
1907	56,124	4,398	51,726	37,370	2,188	35,182	18,754	2,210	16,544
1908	59,058	4,088	54,970	39,611	2,123	37,488	19,447	1,965	17,482
1909	54,676	3,504	51,172	36,845	1,835	35,010	17,831	1,669	16,162
1910	58,145	3,795	54,350	39,885	1,941	37,944	18,260	1,854	16,406
1911	64,206	3,899	60,307	43,894	1,954	41,940	20,312	1,945	18,367
1912	73,541	4,547	68,994	51,595	2,475	49,120	21,946	2,072	19,874
1913	77,043	5,003	72,040	53,008	2,581	50,427	24,035	2,422	21,613
1914[2]	117,568	5,332	112,236	91,813	2,712	89,101	25,755	2,620	23,135
1915[2]	154,230	3,561	150,669	138,075	1,885	136,190	16,155	1,676	14,479
1916[2]	192,056	.....	....	176,139	.....	.....	15,917	.....	.....
1917[2]	82,864	.....	....	72,954	.....	.....	9,910	.....	.....
1918[2]	55,529	.....	....	47,820	.....	.....	7,709	.....	.....
1919[2]	56,572	.....	....	41,180	.....	.....	15,392	.....	.....
1920	81,503	.....	....	52,145	.....	.....	29,358	.....	.....
1921	72,284	.....	....	45,611	.....	.....	26,673	.....	.....
1922	55,490	.....	....	31,660	.....	.....	23,830	.....	.....
1923	55,319	.....	....	30,317	.....	.....	25,002	.....	.....
1924	59,918	.....	....	33,551	.....	.....	26,367	.....	.....

EXPEDITIONARY FORCES

	Males	Females	Total
July to Dec. 1914	34,355	186	34,541
Jan. to June 1915	34,273 } 95,097	268 } 615	34,541 } 95,712
July to Dec. 1915	60,824 }	347 }	61,171 }
Jan. to June 1916	73,943	124	74,067

TABLE VIII.—Departures of persons of non-European race, 1920-24.

Nationality	1920	1921	1922	1923	1924
American Negro	11	7	4	4	7
West Indian	10	2	2	7	1
Afghan	....	....	....	1	2
Arab	5	4	6	3	3
Chinese	2,115	2,912	2,189	2,310	1,898
Cingalese	11	20	5	10	7
Filipino	53	19	25	23	14
Hindu	227	338	194	157	149
Japanese	554	626	359	436	366
Javanese	24	8	4	2	3
Malay	144	209	79	92	43
Pacific Islander	51	43	46	38	57
Papuan	178	82	146	359	282
Other	128	330	154	214	488
Total	3,511	4,600	3,213	3,656	3,321

For reference notes see page 959.

TABLE IX.—Assisted immigrants arriving in each state, 1913-24.

Year	Total Common- wealth	New South Wales	Victoria	Queens- land	South Australia	Western Aus- tralia	Tas- mania
1913	37,445	9,860	12,146	4,757	2,759	7,708	215
1914	20,805	6,655	7,496	4,096	644	1,729	185
1915	5,796	1,695	1,724	1,599	79	635	64
1916	1,397	649	327	300	....	103	18
1917	504	239	146	91	....	26	2
1918	426	199	101	100	....	26	....
1919	245	67	139	39	....	....	....
1920	9,059	3,211	2,763	1,272	....	1,499	314
1921	14,682	4,980	3,987	1,147	572	3,381	615
1922	24,258	7,087	9,145	1,711	1,531	4,373	411
1923	26,645	5,005	9,504	2,377	1,711	7,654	394
1924	25,036	6,211	8,721	1,788	1,375	6,715	226
Total to end of 1924....	939,472	298,495	221,014	222,481	107,896	65,443	24,143

TABLE X.—Distribution of assisted immigrants, by sex and age, 1907-24.

Year	Total	Males	Females	Children included in previous columns	
				Males	Females
to the end of 1907	653,698	.....	.....	.....	.....
1908	6,367	.....	.....	.....	.....
1909	9,820	.....	.....	.....	.....
1910	16,781	.....	.....	.....	.....
1911	39,796	.....	.....	.....	.....
1912	46,712	.....	.....	.....	.....
1913	37,445	18,715	18,730	5,856	6,199
1914	20,805	11,449	9,356	2,717	2,529
1915	5,796	2,134	3,672	895	814
1916	1,397	421	976	217	240
1917	504	145	359	92	87
1918	426	79	347	55	73
1919	245	84	161	24	36
1920	9,059	4,614	4,445	1,050	1,008
1921	14,682	8,216	6,466	1,812	1,645
1922	24,258	9,330[15]	5,783[15]	1,515[15]	1,417[15]
1923	26,645	17,901	8,744	2,344	2,092
1924	25,036	14,958	10,078	2,745	2,607

For reference notes see page 959.

TABLE XI.—DISTRIBUTION OF ASSISTED IMMIGRANTS, BY OCCUPATION, 1913-24.

Occupation		1913	1914	1915	1916	1917	1918	1919	1920	1921	1922	1923	1924
Wood, furniture, etc.	selected	92	8	2	..	..	..	..	5	32	6	44	40
	nominated	238	84	11	3	..	..	..	47	65	130	170	183
Engineering, metals, etc.	selected	327	28	3	1	..	..	1	19	89	4	1	3
	nominated	623	247	41	12	2	1	5	336	558	717	749	773
Food, drink, tobacco, etc.	selected	138	13	..	..	..	..	..	2	31	1	..	..
	nominated	246	140	35	9	2	2	..	102	130	103	69	95
Clothing, hats, boots, etc.	selected	171	15	..	..	..	..	..	4	25	2	1	..
	nominated	588	325	88	50	14	14	8	205	197	181	353	387
Books, printing, binding, etc.	selected	64	3	..	..	..	..	..	1	6	..	..	..
	nominated	105	45	10	3	..	2	..	24	36	28	41	69
Other manufacturing	selected	65	6	..	..	..	..	..	4	27	3	..	..
	nominated	285	120	34	7	1	1	1	52	83	103	146	147
Building	selected	161	18	2	..	..	..	..	11	39	..	89	78
	nominated	698	188	33	8	3	1	..	102	152	168	137	232
Mining	selected	56	10	..	..	..	..	..	2	13	..	..	..
	nominated	214	100	31	5	..	..	..	80	141	422	347	319
Rail and tramway transport	selected	45	4	..	..	..	..	..	..	7	1	..	..
	nominated	117	42	7	1	1	..	..	54	80	79	45	51
Other land transport	selected	113	10	1	..	..	..	..	4	10	2	2	..
	nominated	151	74	13	1	..	..	1	65	78	107	89	87
Shipping, wharf labor, etc.	selected	17	2	..	..	..	..	..	1	5	1	1	..
	nominated	21	7	3	2	..	..	..	18	22	47	37	35
Agricultural, pastoral, etc.	selected	4,364	5,740	501	58	17	..	25	1,320	1,430	3,812	11,525	7,844
	nominated	978	482	97	10	7	2	10	263	1,769	751	535	516
Domestic, hotels, etc.	selected	2,425	1,791	994	168	34	..	..	473	572	500	1,077	1,405
	nominated	1,747	871	367	105	56	33	9	604	1,346	1,072	1,274	1,115
General labor and miscellaneous	selected	1,118	105	15	4	..	..	3	74	160	18	70	3
	nominated	1,729	963	311	97	33	10	18	844	1,132	1,093	1,255	1,370
Dependents, adults	selected	1,062	725	199	16	7	..	7	652	722	311	1,168	1,310
	nominated	7,432	3,393	1,289	380	148	232	97	1,633	2,268	2,519	2,985	3,622
Dependents, children under 12 years	selected	1,368	718	234	16	8	..	6	500	690	157	1,390	1,928
	nominated	10,687	4,528	1,475	441	171	128	54	1,558	2,767	2,775	3,046	3,424
Total	selected	11,586	9,196	1,951	263	66	..	42	3,072	3,858	4,818	15,367	12,611
	nominated	25,859	11,609	3,845	1,134	438	426	203	5,987	10,824	10,295	11,278	12,425

SOURCES

Official Year-Book of the Commonwealth of Australia. Melbourne, 1908-25.

Tables V and VIII.

Quarterly Summary of Australian Statistics, (Commonwealth Bureau of Census and Statistics.) Melbourne, 1920-25.

Tables III and VI, IV and VII (years 1916-24).

Shipping and Overseas Migration of the Commonwealth of Australia for 1909 to 1915-16, Melbourne.

Tables IV and VII (years 1904-15).

Statistical Abstract for the several British Overseas Dominions and Protectorates. London, 1914, 1922, 1924.

Table II.

Information supplied by the Commonwealth Bureau of Census and Statistics. Melbourne.

Table I.

Labor Report of the Commonwealth Bureau of Census and Statistics, Melbourne, 1913-14, 1914-15, and 1916-24.

Tables IX, X, XI.

NOTES

[1]Northern Territory figures prior to 1901 included with South Australia.
[2]Expeditionary forces included.
[3]Jervis Bay transferred to Federal Capital Territory in 1916.
[4]Expeditionary forces excluded.
[5]Prior to 1923 included with "Other British Possessions".
[6]First six months only. The practice of recording crews has been discontinued since July 1, 1922.
[7]Principally prisoners of war and their families.
[8]Bulgarians.
[9]Including 162 Bulgarians.
[10]A large percentage of these immigrants were Timorese.
[11]Including 110 Finns and 125 Yugoslavs.
[12]Including 154 Finns and 240 Yugoslavs.
[13]Including 374 Finns and 1,933 Yugoslavs.
[14]Recorded departures only.
[15]Exclusive of Victoria.

NEW SOUTH WALES

TABLE I.—ARRIVALS BY SEA, CLASSIFIED BY SEX AND AGE, 1825-28 AND 1829-97.

Year	Total	Children[1]			Adults		
		Total	Males	Females	Total	Males	Females
Nov.1,1825 to Nov. 1, 1828²	4,673²	547	285	262	4,126	2,561	1,565
1829	564	145	*	*	419	306	113
1830	309	73	*	*	236	166	70
1831	457	174	*	*	283	185	98
1832	2,006	481	*	*	1,525	819	706
1833	2,685	701	*	*	1,984	838	1,146
1834	1,564	397	*	*	1,167	571	596
1835	1,428	233	*	*	1,195	551	644
1836	1,721	290	*	*	1,331	624	807
1837	3,477	1,312	*	*	2,165	1,125	1,040
1838	7,430	2,627	*	*	4,803	2,692	2,111
1839	9,835	2,528	*	*	7,307	3,981	3,326
1840	6,522	1,313	*	*	5,209	2,859	2,350
1841	13,786	3,190	*	*	10,596	5,393	5,203
1842	6,605	1,622	*	*	4,983	2,737	2,246
1843	967	145	*	*	822	559	263
1844	3,211	1,004	*	*	2,207	1,186	1,021
1845	958	274	*	*	684	381	303
1846	402	75	33	42	327	210	117
1847	515	103	56	47	412	258	154
1848	5,027	1,353	735	618	3,674	1,898	1,776
1849	9,801	2,603	1,332	1,271	7,198	3,316	3,882
1850	4,637	781	382	399	3,856	1,453	2,403
1851	2,602	559	288	271	2,043	1,131	912
1852	8,762	2,015	1,049	966	6,747	4,112	2,635
1853	13,767	3,823	1,777	2,046	9,944	4,402	5,542
1854	10,002	2,495	1,199	1,296	7,507	4,125	3,382
1855	17,683	4,553	2,285	2,268	13,130	6,750	6,380
1856	16,001	4,651	2,445	2,206	11,350	5,691	5,659
1857	15,578	2,628	1,347	1,281	12,950	8,538	4,412
1858	24,739	3,452	1,686	1,766	21,287³	14,418	6,869
1859⁴	15,496	1,786	1,008	778	10,688	7,169	3,519
1860⁴	23,031	1,638	915	723	14,435	11,090	3,345
1861⁴	13,421	1,106	617	489	9,741	7,261	2,480
1862⁴	15,205	1,682	912	770	12,493	9,289	3,204
1863⁵	5,636	997	494	503	4,639	2,461	2,178
1864⁵	5,176	781	382	399	4,395	2,429	1,966
1865⁵	3,358	527	266	261	2,831	1,435	1,396
1866⁵	1,852	257	143	114	1,595	833	762
1867⁵	2,179	319	183	136	1,860	932	928
1868⁵	1,223	179	92	87	1,044	576	468
1869⁴	19,756	2,185	1,136	1,049	17,283	13,581	3,702
1870⁴	18,621	2,270	1,184	1,086	16,321	12,531	3,790
1871⁴	19,820	2,291	1,125	1,166	17,103	13,205	3,898
1872⁴	24,107	2,483	1,320	1,163	21,395	17,001	4,394
1873⁴	24,022	3,122	1,603	1,519	20,494	15,623	4,871
1874⁴	29,756	3,450	1,847	1,603	25,441	19,669	5,772
1875⁴	30,967	3,894	2,168	1,726	26,448	20,210	6,238
1876⁴	32,942	4,216	2,364	1,852	28,030	21,256	6,774
1877⁴	38,628	5,459	2,895	2,564	32,285	23,638	8,647
1878⁴	39,879	5,353	2,872	2,481	32,041	22,860	9,181
1879⁴	44,501	6,115	3,137	2,978	36,407	25,738	10,669
1880⁴	45,870	5,535	2,932	2,603	37,393	26,894	10,499
1881⁴	47,723	5,776	3,016	2,760	37,482	26,712	10,770
1882⁴	47,289	6,333	3,264	3,069	39,949	28,416	11,533
1883⁴	67,206	9,194	4,661	4,533	56,076	39,946	16,130
1884	69,145	6,899	.....	.....	62,246	44,667	17,579
1885	72,807	7,885	.....	.....	64,922	46,570	18,352
1886	68,904	5,535	.....	.....	63,369	45,035	18,334
1887	63,418	4,413	.....	.....	59,005	43,769	15,236
1888	60,176	4,435	.....	.....	55,741	40,295	15,446
1889	60,782	4,855	.....	.....	55,927	39,208	16,719
1890	67,516	5,285	.....	.....	62,231	43,124	19,107
1891	69,919	6,082	.....	.....	63,837	44,519	19,318
1892	62,197	4,902	.....	.....	57,295	39,538	17,757
1893	66,909	5,770	.....	.....	61,139	42,536	18,603
1894	75,588	6,848	2,815	4,033	68,740	46,917	21,823
1895	76,051	6,994	2,875	4,119	69,057	46,338	22,719
1896	62,633	6,127	2,519	3,608	56,506	38,164	18,342
1897	67,016	6,105	2,510	3,595	60,911	42,270	18,641

For reference notes see page 969.

TABLE II.—ARRIVALS BY SEA, CLASSIFIED BY SEX, 1898-1920.

Year	Total	Males	Females	Year	Total	Males	Females
1898	75,526	49,186	26,340	1910	111,525	72,421	39,104
1899	77,634	49,960	27,674				
1900	68,783	45,585	23,198	1911	141,667	92,269	49,398
				1912	163,788	106,187	57,601
1901	76,139	50,234	25,905	1913	146,749	92,925	53,824
1902	81,191	54,942	26,249	1914	143,143	91,413	51,730
1903	70,570	46,121	24,449	1915[6]	111,675	72,163	39,512
1904	72,978	48,700	24,278				
1905	74,165	47,871	26,294	1916[6]	104,777	68,579	36,198
				1917[6]	75,158	48,824	26,334
1906	79,465	50,257	29,208	1918[6]	67,612	46,851	20,761
1907	101,125	65,684	35,441	1919[6]	112,774	88,100	24,674
1908	101,589	66,156	35,433	1920[6]	113,649	67,378	46,271
1909	106,310	69,330	36,980	....	......	......	......

For reference notes see page 969.

TABLE III.—ARRIVALS BY SEA, CLASSIFIED BY COUNTRY OF ORIGIN, 1900–23.

Year	Australian States	New Zealand	United Kingdom	Canada	India	South Africa	Other British Possessions	China and Japan[7]	United States	Other countries	Crews[8]	Total
1900	45,962	9,770	4,857	....	....	....	1,384	1,646	....	5,164	....	68,783
1901	46,982	13,706	4,579	....	....	....	2,252	1,191	....	7,429	....	76,139
1902	46,899	13,161	4,864	....	....	....	6,080	1,410	....	8,777	....	81,191
1903	42,529	12,868	4,249	....	....	....	2,313	1,755	....	6,856	....	70,570
1904	42,910	14,314	4,842	....	....	....	3,172	1,197	....	6,543	....	72,978
1905	44,310	15,093	4,859	571	....	722	2,197	956	....	5,457	....	74,165
1906	48,294	16,525	5,641	752	....	1,475	1,598	805	620	3,755	....	79,465
1907	58,734	21,588	8,464	1,266	....	2,821	2,494	936	237	4,585	....	101,125
1908	56,582	20,612	10,537	2,328	....	2,073	3,011	771	170	5,505	....	101,589
1909	55,285	23,040	15,057	1,641	....	922	1,933	1,434	358	6,640	....	106,310
1910	58,146	22,410	16,537	2,286	....	452	2,851	1,113	390	7,340	....	111,525
1911	71,262	27,008	24,217	2,878	....	610	3,789	1,515	550	9,838	....	141,667
1912	75,872	26,696	36,925	3,459	....	774	4,813	1,093	1,900	12,256	....	163,788
1913	71,490	23,284	30,318	2,958	....	1,052	4,991	765	2,601	9,290	....	146,749
1914	75,875	25,290	19,936	2,465	931	1,225	6,264	416	2,561	8,180	....	143,143
1915	65,736	18,037	7,299	1,896	1,106	653	6,883	492	2,695	3,251	....	108,048[6]
1916	55,423	15,065	2,721	1,221	578	94	5,615	424	1,726	2,534	....	88,894[6]
1917	40,095	10,682	382	802	553	257	3,446	419	1,059	2,272	3,493	67,092[6]
1918	28,868	9,682	494	1,407	194	78	1,661	374	1,015	4,418	7,125	55,113[6]
1919	19,498	11,062	10,297	1,586	280	105	4,236	449	2,380	2,489	6,922	59,902[6]
1920	41,134	21,238	20,197	1,711	518	643	4,470	1,528	2,230	3,056	7,520	107,333[6]
1921	37,238	19,808	17,493	1,475	610	953	5,758	996	1,698	2,416	10,608	94,428
1922	36,740	19,771	17,699	1,832	709	934	6,407	538	1,668	3,184	5,983	90,066
1923	40,390	19,571	13,617	1,409	834	1,025	6,494	499	1,705	2,930	....	88,474

For reference notes see page 969.

TABLE IV.—DEPARTURES BY SEA, CLASSIFIED BY SEX, 1843-1920.[9]

Year	Total	Males	Females	Year	Total	Males	Females
1843	4,730	3,485	1,245	1881[4]	24,825	16,525	7,371
1844	5,052	3,936	1,116	1882[4]	27,972	19,230	7,858
1845	4,183	3,266	917	1883[4]	34,396	22,884	10,110
				1884	43,595	*	*
1846	4,514	3,467	747	1885	46,275	*	*
1847	4,474	3,312	1,162				
1848	4,751	3,534	1,217	1886	49,030	*	*
1849	*	.....	.....	1887	54,220	*	*
1850	5,257	3,699	1,558	1888	54,901	*	*
				1889	50,318	*	*
1851	*	.....	.....	1890	53,880	*	*
1852	16,393	14,277	2,116				
1853	*	.....	.....	1891	52,073	*	*
1854	*	.....	.....	1892	52,687	*	*
1855	10,212	7,546	2,666	1893	58,850	*	*
				1894	71,773	48,492	23,281
1856	6,500	4,694	1,806	1895	72,128	48,331	23,797
1857	.....	.....	.....				
1858	8,889	7,294	1,595	1896	67,887	44,429	23,458
1895	6,309	4,693	1,616	1897	65,611	43,039	22,572
1860	6,847	5,368	1,479	1898	71,398	46,945	24,453
				1899	71,563	47,817	23,746
1861[10]	9,900	7,794	2,106	1900	67,190	45,259	21,931
1862	15,079	11,965	3,114				
1863	13,796	11,033	2,763	1901	69,500	44,332	25,168
1864	17,448	13,582	3,866	1902	67,400	43,431	23,969
1865	18,154	14,096	4,058	1903	63,626	39,529	24,097
				1904	67,549	44,240	23,309
1866	15,093	11,312	3,781	1905	69,606	44,739	24,867
1867	13,450	10,038	3,412				
1868	18,679	15,279	3,400	1906	75,421	47,797	27,624
1869[4]	13,717	9,740	3,403	1907	90,748	59,731	31,017
1870[4]	14,206	9,874	3,807	1908	93,521	60,474	33,047
				1909	92,504	59,729	32,775
1871[4]	12,974	8,939	3,572	1910	96,514	62,093	34,421
1872[4]	16,881	12,258	4,026				
1873[4]	16,770	11,936	4,434	1911	108,011	68,638	39,373
1874[4]	19,279	13,631	4,715	1912	119,496	77,147	42,349
1875[4]	20,350	13,915	5,226	1913	119,485	76,443	43,042
				1914[6]	139,645	93,513	46,132
1876[4]	21,923	15,251	5,732	1915[6]	137,179	100,945	36,234
1877[4]	20,174	13,888	5,796				
1878[4]	22,913	15,100	6,253	1916[6]	145,420	109,544	35,876
1879[4]	20,695	14,068	6,070	1917[6]	85,761	60,800	24,961
1880[4]	26,559	17,882	7,801	1918[6]	65,289	47,513	17,776
....	.....	.....	.....	1919[6]	60,695	42,017	18,678
....	.....	.....	.....	1920	96,136	58,478	37,658

For reference notes see page 969.

TABLE V.—Departures by sea, classified by sex and age, 1843, 1869-97.

Year	Total	Children			Adults		
		Total	Males	Females	Total	Males	Females
1843	4,730	632	327	305	4,098	3,158	940
1869	13,717	1,334	791	543	11,809	8,949	2,860
1870	14,206	1,690	961	729	11,991	8,913	3,078
1871	12,974	1,515	867	648	10,996	8,072	2,924
1872	16,881	1,485	851	634	14,799	11,407	3,392
1873	16,770	1,734	1,051	683	14,636	10,885	3,751
1874	19,279	1,841	1,123	718	16,505	12,508	3,997
1875	20,350	1,992	1,167	825	17,149	12,748	4,401
1876	21,923	1,949	1,162	787	19,034	14,089	4,945
1877	20,174	1,626	980	646	18,058	12,908	5,150
1878	22,913	2,269	1,409	860	19,084	13,691	5,393
1879	20,695	1,870	1,215	655	18,268	12,853	5,415
1880	26,559	2,359	1,612	747	23,324	16,270	7,054
1881	24,825	2,091	1,424	667	21,805	15,101	6,704
1882	27,972	2,325	1,547	778	24.763	16,783	7,080
1883	34,396	3,110	1.845	1,265	29,884	21,039	8,845
1884	43,595	3,599	*	*	39,996	29,311	10,685
1885	46,275	3,707	*	*	42,568	31,060	11,508
1886	49,030	2,736	*	*	46,294	34,453	11,841
1887	54,220	3,619	*	*	50,601	38,162	12,439
1888	54,901	4,070	*	*	50,831	36,278	14,553
1889	50,318	3,753	*	*	46,565	32,535	14,030
1890	53,880	4,043	*	*	49,837	34,302	15,535
1891	52,073	3,684	*	*	48,389	33,877	14,512
1892	52,687	4,020	*	*	48,667	33,839	14,828
1893	58,850	4,548	*	*	54,302	37,923	16,379
1894	65,976	5,624	*	*	60,352	41,060	19,292
1895	66,334	6,038	*	*	60,296	40,747	19,549
1896	62,516	6,809	*	*	55,707	36,941	18,766
1897	60,410	6,244	*	*	54,166	35,931	18,235

TABLE VI.—DEPARTURES BY SEA, CLASSIFIED BY COUNTRY OF DESTINATION, 1900-23.

Year	Australian States	New Zealand	United Kingdom	Canada	India	South Africa	Other British Possessions	China and Japan[7]	United States	Other countries	Crews[8]	Total
1900	42,863	9,477	5,798	....	....	....	2,733	1,325	....	4,994	....	67,190
1901	43,426	12,159	5,221	....	....	....	2,983	1,290	....	4,421	....	69,500
1902	36,540	12,803	5,956	....	....	....	6,386	1,461	....	4,254	....	67,400
1903	34,909	13,204	5,136	....	....	....	4,293	2,007	....	4,077	....	63,626
1904	38,844	13,245	6,049	....	....	....	4,125	1,382	....	3,904	....	67,549
1905	41,738	12,747	5,696	1,022	....	722	2,686	967	1,059	2,969	....	69,606
1906	45,060	15,994	4,789	1,444	....	814	2,409	1,284	1,148	2,479	....	75,421
1907	53,333	21,201	5,176	2,422	....	736	2,304	1,501	789	3,286	....	90,748
1908	51,590	22,141	7,467	1,603	....	764	3,330	1,367	459	4,800	....	93,521
1909	54,756	17,812	6,766	1,616	....	1,071	3,177	1,401	430	5,475	....	92,504
1910	56,722	17,247	7,834	1,623	....	1,247	3,734	1,339	829	5,939	....	96,514
1911	66,922	18,593	8,837	2,469	....	923	4,729	1,437	593	6,792	....	111,295
1912	71,179	19,691	11,647	2,861	....	927	7,329	219	3,232	7,925	....	125,010
1913	68,923	20,767	13,002	3,779	....	987	6,625	406	3,484	7,211	....	125,184
1914	71,758	20,978	13,883	2,188	801	843	6,635	497	3,699	6,434	....	127,716[6]
1915	58,728	16,178	5,842	1,998	576	544	8,455	1,023	3,375	3,571	....	100,290[6]
1916	51,550	14,436	3,186	1,409	735	420	6,484	781	1,789	2,762	3,849	87,401[6]
1917	36,530	9,277	3,209	819	410	253	3,822	380	1,233	1,527	7,761	65,221[6]
1918	25,447	7,418	432	1,270	197	238	3,964	394	1,256	948	7,620	49,184[6]
1919	17,104	12,013	10,517	1,339	546	467	4,628	403	2,106	1,598	8,652	59,373[6]
1920	35,780	24,861	9,104	2,157	618	829	5,803	808	2,385	2,254	11,212	95,811
1921	36,888	22,423	7,834	1,675	640	1,053	7,149	692	1,758	2,118	6,738	88,968
1922	36,414	17,598	7,768	1,453	663	858	5,693	443	1,676	1,965	622	75,153
1923	41,092	16,644	7,372	1,451	795	739	5,992	354	1,712	1,856	....	78,007

For reference notes see page 969.

TABLE VII.—Chinese[11] IMMIGRATION AND EMIGRATION, 1859-1919.

Year	Immigrants	Emigrants	Year	Immigrants	Emigrants
1859	3,022	450	1890	15	637
1860	6,958	1,098			
			1891	17	581
1861	2,574	893	1892	21	755
1862	1,030	1,118	1893	34	558
1863	....	633	1894	76	627
1864	....	1,044	1895	94	413
1865	....	832			
			1896	99	450
1866	....	913	1897	34	428
1867	....	852	1898	32	419
1868	123	548	1899	36	449
1869	288	574	1900	75	379
1870	30	525			
			1901	71	342
1871	426	463	1902	56	425
1872	229	597	1903	62	676
1873	406	400	1904	176	702
1874	865	933	1905	392	948
1875	625	1,209			
			1906	364	818
1876	696	940	1907	375	928
1877	884	490	1908	497	883
1878	2,485	1,560	1909	562	900
1879	1,979	557	1910	502	807
1880	2,942	876			
			1911	753	844
1881	4,465	929	1912	887	1,052
1882	1,007	884	1913	1,000	1,131
1883	1,936	1,402	1914	957	1,096
1884	2,191	1,038	1915	1,135	1,235
1885	2,929	1,726			
			1916	1,141	1,203
1886	3,092	1,883	1917	923	797
1887	4,436	2,773	1918	883	704
1888[12]	1,848	1,562	1919	786	791
1889	7	941	....	....	....

For reference notes see page 969.

TABLE VIII.—IMMIGRANTS AT THE PUBLIC EXPENSE AND ASSISTED IMMIGRANTS, BY SEX AND AGE, 1832-99.

Year	Total	Children			Adults		
		Males	Females	Total	Males	Females	Total
1832	792	....	....	197	140	455	595
1833	1,253	....	...	348	177	728	905
1834	484	....	....	133	52	299	351
1835	545	....	....	86	33	426	459
1836	808	....	....	140	73	595	668
1837	2,664	....	....	1,136	688	840	1,528
1838	6,102	....	....	2,501	1,928	1,673	3,601
1839	7,852	1,134	1,043	2,177	2,911	2,764	5,675
1840	5,216	561	589	1,150	2,029	2,037	4,066
1841	12,188	1,462	1,374	2,836	4,552	4,800	9,352
1842	5,071	633	620	1,253	1,931	1,887	3,818
1843	.....	.....	.....	.....	.....	.....	.....
1844	2,726	469	467	936	891	899	1,790
1845	497	69	77	146	173	178	351
1846	.....	.....	.....	.....	.....	.....	.....
1847	.....	.....	.....	.....	.....	.....	.....
1848	4,376	671	578	1,249	1,514	1,613	3,127
1849	8,309	1,110	1,071	2,181	2,637	3,491	6,128
1850	4,078	331	342	673	1,182	2,223	3,405
1851	1,846	207	210	417	742	687	1,429
1852	4,981	763	673	1,436	1,635	1,910	3,545
1853	10,412	1,373	1,629	3,002	2,706	4,704	7,410
1854	7,309	863	913	1,776	2,816	2,717	5,533
1855	14,567	1,837	1,800	3,637	5,441	5,489	10,930
1856	7,210	785	770	1,555	2,884	2,771	5,655
1857	10,205	1,128	1,075	2,203	4,415	3,587	8,002
1858	6,916	641	682	1,323	2,860	2,733	5,593
1859	5,114	467	426	893	2,122	2,099	4,221
1860	3,089	245	258	503	1,351	1,235	2,586
1861	1,589	101	99	200	794	595	1,389
1862	2,631	214	198	412	1,172	1,047	2,219
1863	4,633	391	404	795	1,966	1,872	3,838
1864	3,977	289	315	604	1,701	1,672	3,373
1865	2,717	213	217	430	1,073	1,214	2,287
1866	1,204	92	68	160	501	543	1,044
1867	944	66	58	124	385	435	820
1868	470	41	31	72	183	215	398
1869	†47	.....	.....	.....	22	25	47
1870	.....	.....	.....	.....	.....	....	.....
1871	357	15	15	30	28	299	327
1872	326	16	14	30	25	271	296
1873	140	3	5	8	13	119	132
1874	1,080	109	133	242	427	411	838
1875	973	135	119	254	395	324	719

TABLE VIII.—Immigrants at the public expense and assisted immigrants, by sex and age, 1832-99 (continued).

Year	Total	Children			Adults		
		Males	Females	Total	Males	Females	Total
1876	1,463	208	184	392	642	429	1,071
1877	6,018	743	756	1,499	2,892	1,627	4,519
1878	5,190	699	646	1,345	2,091	1,754	3,845
1879	5,731	840	844	1,684	1,906	2,141	4,047
1880	3,134	414	375	789	1,150	1,195	2,345
1881	2,577	327	292	619	929	1,029	1,958
1882	3,233	509	524	1,033	1,209	991	2,200
1883	8,369	1,154	1,127	2,281	3,370	2,718	6,088
1884	7,568	1,095	1,082	2,177	2,785	2,606	5,391
1885	5,554	736	736	1,472	1,871	2,211	4,082
1886	4,081	572	560	1,132	1,044	1,905	2,949
1887	1,362	286	258	544	131	687	818
1888	528	149	131	280	58	190	248
1889	431	104	115	219	44	168	212
1890	376	110	79	189	55	132	187
1891	190	45	38	83	26	81	107
1892	179	40	41	81	25	73	98
1893	120	23	31	54	19	47	66
1894	67	18	8	26	13	28	41
1895	37	12	7	19	2	16	18
1896	17	3	3	6	8	3	11
1897	35	8	10	18	6	11	17
1898	5	2	. . . . .	2	1	2	3
1899	9	1	1	2	3	4	7

TABLE IX.— Assisted immigrants, by sex, 1906-23.

Year	Total Assisted Immigrants	Males	Females	Year	Total Assisted Immigrants	Males	Females
1906	590	. . . .	. . . .	1915	1,696	535	1,161
1907	2,917	. . . .	. . . .	1916	655	185	470
1908	3,048	. . . .	. . . .	1917	256	68	188
1909	4,308	. . . .	. . . .	1918	199	31	168
				1919	68	16	52
1910	5,058	3,039	2,019				
1911	9,922	5,880	4,042	1920	3,269	1,526	1,743
1912	14,956	8,361	6,595	1921	4,981	2,491	2,490
1913	9,860	4,180	5,680	1922	7,087	4,009	3,078
1914	5,624	2,463	3,161	1923	5,042	2,661	2,381

New South Wales 1828, pp. 146-9.

Table I (years 1826-28).

Accounts and Papers, 1839 (10), XXXIX, p. 381, London. (Figures extracted from Blue-Book for 1837.)

Table I (years 1829-31).

Votes and Proceedings of Legislative Council of New South Wales, 1844 to 1869.

Tables I (years 1832-52); IV, V and VII (years 1843-68).

Statistical Register for New South Wales for 1861 to 1923-24, Sydney.

Tables I (years 1852-97); VIII (years 1852-99); IV, V and VII (years 1869-1920); II, III, VI, and IX.

NOTES

[1]The sources do not make it possible to indicate the age limit with any certainty. For the period 1825-58 children under 12 are recorded and for 1832-52 children under 14. For the succeeding years there are decennial divisions. As occasionally the years overlap in the tables we learn that the figures are continuations of those for 1832-52. No age limit is indicated for children; but in a later tabulation of Assisted Immigrants for 1860 we find the description "Children under 12 years". (Statistical Register for New South Wales for 1889, p. 189.)

[2]Not including immigration of convicts, which was from Nov 1, 1825-Nov. 1, 1828, as follows:

	Males	Females	Total
1825	175	58	233
1826	1,715	100	1,815
1827	2,085	502	2,587
1828	2,156	293	2,449
Total	6,131	953	7,084

[3]In this number are included immigrants from the adjacent Colonies and Port Curtis.
The Chinese migrants are always included in the totals, but for 1859-62 (immigration) and 1869-83 (immigration and emigration) they are not included in the figures indicating sex and age. See also table VII (Chinese immigration and emigration).

[4]The figures for 1863-68 are for immigrants from the United Kingdom. The total number of persons arriving in the colony was in 1867 19,972 and in 1868, 26,564 (21,903 males including Chinese and 4,661 females). These numbers include intercolonial as well as foreign arrivals.

[5]Expeditionary forces (A. I. F.) departed and arrived by sea numbered:

1914	11,812	
1915	36,806	3,627
1916	57,945	15,883
1917	20,483	8,066
1918	16,089	12,499
1919	1,235	52,872
1920		6,316

[6]These figures are included in tables II and IV (immigration and emigration by sex), but not in table III and VI (immigration and emigration by countries).

[7]For 1900-13, China and India.

[8]"Crews" prior to 1916 were included as immigrants. After June 30, 1922, crews were not recorded separately.

[9]After 1894, includes allowances for those unrecorded.

[10]Undetected departures 9,874 as revealed by census taken April 7, 1861.

[11]Chinese by race but not necessarily by nationality.

[12]See Introducton.

QUEENSLAND

TABLE I.—Distribution of immigrants from extra-Australasian countries, by sex and age, 1860-63.

Year	Total	Adults		Children	
		Males	Females	Males	Females
1860	298	134	115	19	30
1861	1,040	473	390	93	84
1862	8,081	3,705	2,492	993	891
1863 to June 30	4,528	2,256	1,226	542	504

TABLE II.—Distribution of immigrants from Europe, by sex, age and nationality, from the census of 1864 to 17 May 1871.

Year	Nationality	Total	Males	Females	Adults		Children 1-12 years		Infants	
					Males	Females	Males	Females	Males	Females
1864	English..........	6,059	3,667	2,392	3,150	1,946	394	341	123	105
	German..........	858	587	271	486	172	91	83	10	16
	Total........	6,917	4,254	2,663	3,636	2,118	485	424	133	121
1865	English..........	10,979	6,700	4,279	5,619	3,269	868	799	213	211
	German..........	1,771	1,091	680	848	437	214	198	29	45
	Total........	12,750	7,791	4,959	6,467	3,706	1,082	997	242	256
1866	English..........	8,542	5,059	3,483	4,114	2,578	773	744	172	161
	German..........	1,309	737	572	543	386	166	159	28	27
	Total...,......	9,851	5,796	4,055	4,657	2,964	939	903	200	188
1867	English..........	1,075	632	443	496	339	119	90	17	16
1868	English..........	566	350	216	309	169	30	43	11	4
1869	English..........	1,913	1,091	822	939	678	127	108	25	36
1870	English..........	2,413	1,362	1,051	1,178	830	176	136	55	37
	German..........	339	214	125	184	93	28	25	2	7
	Total........	2,752	1,576	1,176	1,362	923	204	161	57	44
1871	English..........	705	389	316	309	261	57	49	23	6
	German..........	223	166	57	141	39	22	13	3	5
	Total........	928	555	373	450	300	79	62	26	11

TABLE III.—Arrivals and departures by sea, 1860-1900.

Year	Arrivals	Departures	Year	Arrivals	Departures
1860	1,815[1]	*	1881	16,223	9,209
			1882	27,000	9,957
1861	6,178	1,809	1883	46,330	11,959
1862	12,252	2,447	1884	36,883	18,263
1863	17,450	3,761	1885	34,334	22,768
1864	17,009	6,050			
1865	22,855	10,886	1886	34,101	20,911
			1887	32,393	16,414
1866	16,389	9,757	1888	30,392	18,030
1867	917[1]	*	1889	27,834	16,778
1868	13,382	9,095	1890	24,464	18,817
1869	6,701	7,124			
1870	7,997	5,587	1891	18,769	16,892
			1892	14,646	13,566
1871	9,238	5,879	1893	15,351	13,628
1872	10,335	5,257	1894	18,900	14,992
1873	15,141	5,474	1895	23,591	18,653
1874	20,951	7,713			
1875	24,809	9,640	1896	19,541	16,096
			1897	19,615	15,760
1876	21,831	9,695	1898	23,713	18,083
1877	22,596	10,408	1899	27,217	21,271
1878	16,139	11,890	1900	22,083	19,949
1879	13,828	11,150	....	.....	.....
1880	13,396	10,349	....	.....	.....

For reference notes see page 978.

TABLE IV.—Distribution of arrivals, by sex and age, 1862-1907.

Year	Total	Males	Females	Infants		Children[2]		Adults[3]	
				Males	Females	Males	Females	Males	Females
1862	12,252	8,015	4,237	...	...	1,253	1,087	6,762	3,150
1863	17,450	11,602	5,848	...	...	1,910	1,635	9,692	4,213
1864	17,009	12,291	4,718	...	...	998	879	11,293	3,839
1865	22,855	15,919	6,936	...	...	1,754	1,532	14,165	5,404
1866	16,389	*	*	...	...	*	*	*	*
1867	917[1]	1,342[1]	425[1]	...	...	*	*	*	*
1868	13,382	12,022	1,360	...	...	*	*	*	*
1869	6,701	4,954	1,747	...	...	348	281	4,606	1,466
1870	7,997	5,947	2,050	...	...	472	340	5,475	1,710
1871	9,238	6,880	2,358	...	...	....	....	....	....
1872	10,335	7,883	2,452	...	...	....	....	....	....
1873	15,141	10,216	4,925	...	...	....	....	....	....
1874	20,951	15,458	5,493	...	...	1,549	1,254	13,909	4,239
1875	24,809	20,631	4,178	...	...	962	712	19,669	3,466
1876	21,831	17,700	4,131	110	93	978	658	16,612	3,380
1877	22,596	18,223	4,373	111	114	920	684	17,192	3,575
1878	16,139	11,307	4,832	127	128	995	841	10,185	3,863
1879	13,828	10,102	3,726	40	57	597	486	9,465	3,183
1880	13,396	9,361	4,035	58	47	597	426	8,706	3,562
1881	16,223	11,554	4,669	57	55	792	630	10,705	3,984
1882	27,000	18,622	8,378	237	207	1,594	1,273	16,791	6,898
1883	46,330	31,827	14,503	546	508	3,395	3,002	27,886	10,993
1884	36,883	25,638	11,245	407	317	2,267	1,935	22,964	8,993
1885	34,334	24,087	10,247	195	161	1,779	1,452	22,113	8,634
1886	34,101	24,555	9,546	253	196	1,760	1,441	22,542	7,909
1887	32,393	22,385	10,008	297	278	1,900	1,612	20,188	8,118
1888	34,864	24,330	10,534	288	227	1,712	1,542	22,330	8,765
1889	35,606	24,713	10,893	238	199	1,505	1,301	22,970	9,393
1890	33,005	23,334	9,671	185	131	1,405	1,052	21,744	8,488
1891	28,082	19,536	8,546	162	109	1,075	871	18,299	7,566
1892	23,611	16,391	7,220	196	129	907	804	15,288	6,287
1893	22,007	15,771	6,236	184	99	905	741	14,682	5,396
1894	25,247	17,749	7,498	189	132	1,094	960	16,466	6,406
1895	30,066	20,694	9,372	221	146	1,392	1,284	19,081	7,942
1896	27,723	18,765	8,958	171	101	1,384	1,114	17,210	7,743
1897	29,110	20,536	8,574	169	126	1,167	991	19,200	7,457
1898	34,243	23,999	10,244	232	164	1,520	1,325	22,247	8,755
1899	39,916	27,751	12,165	287	334	1,893	1,691	25,571	10,140
1900	36,348	25,053	11,295	207	278	1,723	1,707	23,123	9,310
1901	41,998	29,641	12,357	190	247	1,721	1,886	27,730	10,224
1902	34,082	23,817	10,265	81	89	1,343	1,499	22,393	8,677
1903	34,329	24,289	10,040	67	35	1,093	1,087	23,129	8,918
1904	39,873	28,093	11,780	64	59	1,236	1,379	26,793	10,342
1905	40,232	27,480	12,752	81	56	1,645	1,708	25,754	10,988
1906	47,677	31,649	16,028	190	131	2,179	2,304	29,280	13,593
1907	61,927	42,120	19,807	336	182	2,903	2,877	38,881	16,748

TABLE V.—Distribution of arrivals, by sex, 1908-23.

Year	Total	Males	Females	Year	Total	Males	Females
1908	70,804	47,785	23,019	1916[4]	130,528	81,334	49,194
1909	79,540	53,816	25,724	1917[4]	123,243	75,123	48,120
1910	86,264	57,284	28,980	1918[4]	110,878	69,040	41,838
1911	109,720	73,240	36,480	1919[4]	79,005	56,786	22,219
1912	102,436	67,374	35,062	1920	89,299	52,050	37,249
1913	109,310	72,354	36,776	1921	84,364	49,090	35,274
1914	120,544	78,178	42,366	1922	85,533	51,022	34,511
1915	131,003	82,784	48,219	1923	89,237	54,040	35,197

For reference notes see page 978.

TABLE VI.—ARRIVALS, BY COUNTRY OF LAST RESIDENCE, 1870-1924.

Year	Total	United Kingdom	Germany	Australasian Colonies (States)	New Zealand	South Sea (Pacific) Islands	Hongkong	India and other British Possessions in Asia	British New Guinea (Papua)	Java	Japan	Other countries
1870	7,997	2,499	337	4,103	..	656	..	..	..	..	..	402
1871	9,238	1,637	1,916	3,642	..	1,428	..	..	..	..	..	615
1872	10,335	1,311	1,433	7,123	..	468	..	..	..	..	..	...
1873	15,141	5,097	2,502	6,291	..	1,023	..	..	..	..	..	228
1874	20,951	8,854	727	9,210	..	1,503	..	..	..	..	..	657
1875	24,809	5,871	....	8,511	..	2,734	7,254	..	..	..	..	439
1876	21,831	5,540	287	7,615	..	1,726	6,555	..	..	..	..	108
1877	22,596	4,834	1,378	6,942	..	1,926	7,460	..	..	..	..	56
1878	16,139	6,105	1,053	7,178	..	1,442	130	..	..	..	..	231
1879	13,828	3,150	936	6,896	..	2,197	481	..	..	..	..	168
1880	13,396	3,404	....	7,656	..	2,044	168	..	..	..	..	124
1881	16,223	4,289	..	8,844	..	2,686	246	..	..	..	..	158
1882	27,000	12,656	..	9,605	..	3,179	949	..	..	..	..	611
1883	46,330	26,725	..	10,770	..	5,343	2,951	..	..	..	..	541
1884	36,883	16,486	..	15,324	..	3,365	1,489	..	..	..	..	219
1885	34,334	10,907	..	20,184	..	2,012	673	..	81	..	..	477
1886	34,101	12,084	..	18,708	..	1,625	501	384	127	577	..	95
1887	32,393	10,680	..	19,120	..	2,029	307	5	91	96	..	65
1888	34,864	9,312	..	22,683	..	2,328	45	43	336	2	..	115
1889	35,606	7,355	..	25,017	..	2,086	282	..	794	42	..	30
1890	33,005	3,785	..	25,888	..	2,513	263	..	193	352	..	11
1891	28,082	2,815	..	23,132	..	1,070	303	..	92	313	..	357
1892	23,611	1,348	..	21,013	..	474	449	9	65	163	..	90
1893	22,007	524	..	18,882	..	1,232	543	16	82	157	..	571
1894	25,247	293	..	22,010	..	1,907	429	6	101	116	370	15
1895	30,066	375	..	27,527	..	1,337	547	10	98	133	5	34
1896	27,723	610	..	24,852	..	803	368	161	173	71	627	58
1897	29,110	756	..	24,966	..	947	506	158	793	94	862	28
1898	34,243	895	..	30,036	..	1,195	..	123[4]	274	39	875[4]	17
1899	39,916	1,415	..	35,371	..	1,542	523	26	489	48	189	313
1900	36,348	2,386	..	30,464	3	1,768	891	19	424	..	92	301
1901	41,998	1,202	..	35,504	2	1,752	1,777	159	571	..	535	496
1902	34,082	769	..	29,929	1	1,158	660	28	428	..	275	834

For reference notes see page 978.

TABLE VI.—ARRIVALS, BY COUNTRY OF LAST RESIDENCE, 1870-1924 (continued).

Year	Total	United Kingdom	Germany	Australasian Colonies (States)	New Zealand	South Sea (Pacific) Islands	Hongkong	India and other British Possessions in Asia	British New Guinea (Papua)	Java	Japan	Other countries
1903	34,329	172	...	31,983	...	1,051	297	74	382	...	128	242
1904	39,873	227	...	38,181	...	85	212	87	790	...	86	205
1905	40,232	357	...	38,440	...	19	299	97	627	...	71	322
1906	47,677	734	...	45,601	...	22	236	54	595	...	68	367
1907	61,927	1,710	...	58,434	1	39	351	45	721	...	74	552
1908	70,804	2,674	...	66,206	7	47	457	23	764	...	75	551
1909	79,540	4,684	...	72,641	6	21	584	74	715	...	121	694
1910	86,264	7,932	...	75,353	6	26	696	84	1,111	...	320	736
1911	109,720	14,949	...	91,592	28	25	665	227	676	...	561	997
1912	102,436	8,660	...	90,385	6	24	835	145	728	...	434	1,219
1913	109,310	7,335	...	98,726	6	13	846	96	730	...	678	880
1914	120,544	5,350	...	111,945	4	10	788	76	805	...	651	915
1915	131,003	2,162	...	126,866	13	...	560	63	636	...	143	560
1916[4]	130,528	708	...	127,985	10	17	868	91	411	...	102	336
1917[4]	123,243	165	...	121,367	...	1	753	83	397	...	82	395
1918[4]	110,878	5	...	109,384	...	5	463	141	344	...	100	436
1919[4]	79,005	565	...	72,866	1	14	486	127	251	...	115	4,580
1920	89,299	2,425	...	85,210	...	...	419	154	220	...	156	715
1921	84,364	2,415	...	79,910	2	...	441	149	371	...	158	918
1922	85,533	2,869	...	79,507	...	...	547	108	433	...	273	1,796
1923	89,237	3,603	...	83,560	2	56	555	75	495	...	152	739
1924	92,871	3,462	...	86,342	...	...	...	...	...	...	...	3,067

For reference notes see page 978.

TABLE VII.—Distribution of departures, by sex, 1908-23.

Year	Total	Males	Females	Year	Total	Males	Females
1908	67,528	45,740	21,788	1916[4]	151,860	102,102	49,758
1909	69,441	46,906	22,535	1917[4]	118,138	74,771	43,367
1910	76,058	51,506	24,552	1918[4]	104,749	66,455	38,294
1911	97,560	66,024	31,536	1919	58,862	36,202	22,660
1912	100,594	67,118	33,476	1920	89,099	53,406	35,693
1913	99,063	66,518	32,545	1921	81,802	48,936	32,866
1914[4]	117,555	76,754	40,801	1922	80,176	47,980	32,196
1915[4]	140,447	92,373	48,074	1923	80,304	48,953	31,351

TABLE VIII.—Distribution of departures, by sex and age, 1862-1907.

Year	Total	Males	Females	Infants		Children[2]		Adults[3]	
				Males	Females	Males	Females	Males	Females
1862	2,447	2,027	420	...	...	99	56	1,928	364
1863	3,761	3,068	693	...	...	138	108	2,930	585
1864	6,050	4,926	1,124	...	...	111	152	4,815	972
1865	10,886	8,928	1,958	...	...	197	203	8,731	1,755
1866	9,757	*	*	...	...	*	*	*	*
1867	*	*	*		...	*	*	*	*
1868	9,095	7,887	1,208	...		*	*	*	*
1869	7,124	5,489	1,635	...	...	396	290	5,093	1,345
1870	5,587	4,384	1,203	...	...	297	191	4,087	1,012
1871	5,879	4,650	1,229	...	...	....	....	.. ..	...
1872	5,257	4,269	988	...	...	....	....	....	...
1873	5,474	4,253	1,221	...	...	....	....	....	....
1874	7,713	6,255	1,458	...	...	324	245	5,931	1,213
1875	9,640	7,980	1,660	..	...	344	203	7,636	1,457
1876	9,695	7,980	1,715	5	9	363	230	7,612	1,476
1877	10,408	8,728	1,680	7	6	337	229	8,384	1,445
1878	11,890	9,668	2,222	3	5	475	326	9,190	1,891
1879	11,150	8,745	2,405	7	3	508	290	8,230	2,112
1880	10,349	8,188	2,161	1	4	407	231	7,780	1,926
1881	9,209	7,000	2,209	3	2	433	266	6,564	1,941
1882	9,957	7,531	2,426	12	10	428	255	7,091	2,161
1883	11,959	9,240	2,719	37	23	488	300	8,715	2,396
1884	18,263	13,892	4,371	90	50	659	467	13,143	3,854
1885	22,768	16,865	5,903	72	58	825	588	15,968	5,257
1886	20,911	16,287	4,624	96	75	698	400	15,493	4,149
1887	16,414	12,478	3,936	114	67	627	462	11,737	3,407
1888	23,059	17,063	5,996	170	110	725	547	16,168	5,339
1889	24,680	18,141	6,539	146	112	877	710	17,118	5,717
1890	26,656	19,237	7,419	201	87	1,211	853	17,825	6,479
1891	26,512	18,414	8,098	264	179	1,422	1,082	16,728	6,837
1892	22,281	15,367	6,914	250	183	1,123	963	13,994	5,768
1893	19,704	13,716	5,988	178	103	951	747	12,587	5,138
1894	21,070	14,548	6,522	263	199.	971	849	13,314	5,474
1895	24,393	16,735	7,658	244	193	1,110	869	15,381	6,596
1896	24,466	16,824	7,642	246	117	1,191	941	15,387	6,584
1897	25,479	17,571	7,908	218	153	1,164	993	16,189	6,762
1898	28,110	19,013	9,097	232	169	1,246	1,125	17,535	7,803
1899	33,590	23,094	10,496	231	234	1,349	1,263	21,514	8,999
1900	35,433	24,634	10,799	246	279	1,719	1,598	22,669	8,922
1901	36,524	24,966	11,558	213	253	1,604	1,789	23,149	9,516
1902	35,288	24,334	10,954	111	108	1,580	1,602	22,643	9,244
1903	34,286	23,600	10,686	78	36	1,478	1,186	22,044	9,464
1904	40,980	28,423	12,557	105	69	1,387	1,432	26,931	11,056
1905	40,424	27,516	12,908	100	84	1,751	1,643	25,665	11,181
1906	47,713	32,052	15,661	178	123	2,193	2,067	29,681	13,471
1907	57,504	39,216	18,288	263	144	2,664	2,358	36,289	15,786

For reference notes see page 978.

TABLE IX.—DEPARTURES, BY COUNTRY OF DESTINATION, 1870-1924.

Year	Total	United Kingdom	Australasian Colonies (States)	New Zealand	South Sea (Pacific) Islands	Hongkong	India and other British Possessions in Asia	British New Guinea (Papua)	Java	Japan	Other countries
1870	5,587	240	4,899	...	447	...	...	...	...	...	1
1871	5,879	214	4,847	...	806	...	...	...	...	...	12
1872	5,257	150	4,618	...	488	...	...	...	...	...	1
1873	5,474	78	5,090	...	288	...	...	...	...	...	18
1874	7,713	219	6,153	...	1,060	...	...	...	...	...	281
1875	9,640	71	6,720	...	475	2,016	...	...	...	...	358
1876	9,695	114	6,436	...	752	2,241	...	...	...	...	152
1877	10,408	133	6,094	...	984	2,894	...	...	...	...	303
1878	11,890	117	7,565	...	1,614	2,266	...	...	...	...	328
1879	11,150	88	8,134	...	1,371	1,389	...	...	...	...	168
1880	10,349	51	7,509	...	1,586	969	...	...	...	...	234
1881	9,209	110	7,158	...	1,073	741	...	...	...	...	127
1882	9,957	350	7,326	...	1,244	941	...	...	...	...	96
1883	11,959	217	9,260	...	1,205	1,114	...	...	...	...	163
1884	18,263	231	14,675	...	2,102	1,164	...	...	...	...	91
1885	22,768	625	18,617	...	1,949	1,238	...	135	...	...	204
1886	20,911	833	15,779	...	2,820	1,223	19	138	62	...	37
1887	16,414	513	12,640	...	2,120	821	37	107	38	...	138
1888	23,059	612	18,998	...	1,385	873	5	657	405	...	124
1889	24,680	851	21,076	...	1,268	695	1	666	107	...	16
1890	26,656	786	23,511	...	1,482	570	...	43	238	...	26
1891	26,512	911	23,755	...	1,012	575	11	81	140	...	38
1892	22,281	1,018	19,511	...	867	493	29	75	269	...	37
1893	19,704	779	16,670	...	864	526	12	86	191	...	56
1894	21,070	466	19,006	...	801	467	8	106	125	3	21
1895	24,393	400	22,238	...	...	493	...	188	209	1	55
1896	24,466	491	21,718	...	672	380	48	465	132	506	54
1897	25,479	444	22,365	...	938	444	148	721	80	327	12
1898	28,110	477	25,751	...	744	500	62	211	60	2,584	47
1899	33,590	535	29,988	4	981	679	83	444	138	2,544	488
1900	35,433	456	31,122	...	1,025	668	77	401	...	363	1,317
1901	36,524	275	32,265	5	928	640	102	421	...	453	1,435
1902	35,288	335	30,645	25	1,837	421	191	392	...	394	1,048

For reference notes see page 978.

TABLE IX.—DEPARTURES, BY COUNTRY OF DESTINATION, 1870-1924 (continued).

Year	Total	United Kingdom	Australasian Colonies (States)	New Zealand	South Sea (Pacific) Islands	Hongkong	India and other British Possessions in Asia	British New Guinea (Papua)	Java	Japan	Other countries
1903	34,286	60	31,635	7	1,111	411	101	254	...	233	474
1904	40,980	210	38,289		665	522	179	568	...	168	379
1905	40,424	306	37,037	3	998	510	171	751	...	112	536
1906	47,713	450	43,395	1	2,058	537	144	387	...	175	567
1907	57,504	474	52,774	...	1,838	395	197	625	...	173	1,027
1908	67,528	680	64,378	...	40	617	203	636	...	185	789
1909	69,441	635	66,564	...	41	549	142	673	...	183	654
1910	76,058	718	72,579	...	13	582	165	1,111	...	197	693
1911	97,560	1,154	93,925	7	12	550	211	845	...	197	659
1912	100,594	958	97,167	5	13	824	228	657	...	261	481
1913	99,063	1,165	95,634		23	597	192	669	...	298	485
1914[5]	117,555	1,451	110,203	12	4	793	228	821	...	464	3,579
1915[5]	140,447	693	128,627	1	14	818	206	461	...	486	9,141
1916[5]	151,860	323	138,590	1	3	612	134	413	...	205	11,579
1917[5]	118,138	24	116,473	1	2	480	125	369	...	302	364
1918[5]	104,749	...	103,056	5	...	579	163	295	...	220	434
1919	58,862	339	57,348	5	...	528	63	78	...	191	310
1920	89,099	1,335	85,706	4	...	575	126	374	...	295	684
1921	81,802	1,052	78,421	...	9	678	167	275	...	387	813
1922	80,176	1,050	77,491	6	57	577	89	142	...	153	674
1923	80,304	1,031	77,195		...	624	158	528	...	232	473
1924	83,376	1,402	79,910	...	...	....	...	...	...	...	2,064

For reference notes see page 978.

SOURCES

Queensland Legislative Council Journals 1863 to 1865.

Tables I (years 1860-63) III; (years 1861-63); IV, VI (years 1862-64).

Return to an Order made by the Legislative Assembly of Queensland on the 4th May, 1871 (Immigration Office, Brisbane, May 17, 1871. *Queensland Votes and Proceedings,* 1871, first session, p. 873).

Table II (years 1864-70).

Queensland Legislative Assembly Votes and Proceedings 1866 to 1871-72.

Tables III (year 1866); IV, VI (years 1865-70).

Statistics of the State of Queensland, Population 1874 to 1923.
Tables III (years 1860, 1864, 1865, 1867-87); IV, VI (years 1874-1907);

V, VII (years 1870-1923).

Australasian Statistics, 1900, p. 10 (in *Votes and Proceedings of Victorian Legislative Assembly,* 1902 (2)).

Table III (years 1873-1900).

A B C of Queensland Statistics, 1926, Brisbane, 1926.

Tables V, VII (year 1924).

NOTES

[1]Excess of arrivals over departures. Complete figures not available.
[2]1862-70 under 14 years; 1874 and 1875, under 12 years; 1876 onwards, 1-12 years.
[3]1862-70 over 14 years, 1874 onwards over 12 years.
[5]Including members of expeditionary forces, destination not stated.
[4]Including respectively Chinese, Japanese, other Asiatics and Pacific Islanders **arriving** from, or departing to, other than their native countries.

SOUTH AUSTRALIA

TABLE I.—Arrivals and departures by sea, 1836-1900.

Year	Arrivals	Departures	Year	Arrivals	Departures
1836	546	. . . . .	1869	2,807	2,724
1837	1,279	. . . . .	1870	2,302	4,128
1838	3,154	. . . . .			
1839	5,320	. . . . .	1871	2,532	3,182
1840	3,148	. . . . .	1872	2,401	3,405
			1873	4,548	3,172
1841	776	. . . . .	1874	5,557	3,271
1842	. . . . .	. . . . .	1875	6,566	4,019
1843	1,213	1,477			
1844	1,114	436	1876	13,841	4,995
1845	2,336	449	1877	15,016	9,008
			1878	14,572	8,174
1846	4,458	863	1879	13,480	9,137
1847	5,645	885	1880	14,765	13,002
1848	7,664	1,042			
1849	16,166	2,694	1881	19,552	16,800
1850	10,358	4,221	1882	14,870	14,136
			1883	19,830	15,562
1851	8,464	6,025	1884	17,290	16,082
1852	20,789	16,425	1885	14,500	20,596
1853	20,128	11,648			
1854	17,258	5,467	1886	17,626	25,231
1855	17,211	4,501	1887	15,468	17,667
			1888	12,637	12,750
1856	9,525	7,278	1889	9,230	8,736
1857	8,138	4,909	1890	9,904	7,114
1858	7,855	3,609			
1859	4,869	3,651	1891	16,684	12,807
1860	4,374	4,902	1892	17,906	15,005
			1893	18,966	19,261
1861	3,127	2,077	1894	34,692	36,993
1862	3,230	2,685	1895	37,193	40,838
1863	4,234	2,892			
1864	5,958	2,676	1896	56,963	59,805
1865	8,469	3,703	1897	58,473	59,359
			1898	55,465	54,636
1866	6,955	4,135	1899	34,095	31,368
1867	3,651	4,046	1900	31,460	30,809
1868	2,900	4,193	. . . .	. . . . .	. . . . . .

TABLE II.—Distribution of arrivals, by sex and age 1851-1924.

Year	Total	Sex		Sex and age			
		Males	Females	Adults		Children	
				Males	Females	Males	Females
1851	8,464	5,176	3,288	4,022	2,349	1,154	939
1852	20,789	16,795	3,994	15,294	2,810	1,501	1,184
1853	20,128	15,102	5,026	13,514	3,613	1,588	1,413
1854	17,258	10,036	7,222	8,254	5,451	1,782	1,771
1855	17,211	8,497	8,714	6,923	7,016	1,574	1,698
1856	9,525	5,769	3,756	4,648	2,845	1,121	911
1857	8,138	5,262	2,876	4,437	2,150	825	726
1858	7,855	4,826	3,029	4,081	2,365	745	664
1859	4,869	2,910	1,959	2,522	1,557	388	402
1860	4,374	3,109	1,265	2,806	952	303	313
1861	3,127	2,181	946	1,979	757	202	189
1862	3,230	2,091	1,139	1,919	923	172	216
1863	4,234	2,685	1,549	2,338	1,199	347	350
1864	5,958	3,720	2,238	3,219	1,781	501	457
1865	8,469	5,318	3,151	4,518	2,335	800	816
1866	6,955	4,400	2,555	3,800	1,995	600	560
1867	3,651	2,482	1,169	2,215	931	267	238
1868	2,900	2,069	831	1,856	642	213	189
1869	2,807	1,879	928	1,694	744	185	184
1870	2,302	1,574	728	1,458	596	116	132
1871	2,532	1,681	851	1,552	698	129	153
1872	2,401	1,604	797	1,431	661	173	136
1873	4,548	3,064	1,484	2,676	1,155	388	329
1874	5,557	3,555	2,002	3,027	1,525	528	477
1875	6,566	4,311	2,255	3,828	1,816	483	439
1876	13,841	8,750	5,091	7,332	3,759	1,418	1,332
1877	15,016	9,934	5,082	8,797	4,082	1,137	1,000
1878	14,572	9,715	4,857	8,553	3,871	1,162	986
1879	13,480	8,962	4,518	7,965	3,587	997	931
1880	14,765	10,180	4,585	9,106	3,861	1,074	724
1881	19,552	13,438	6,114	12,340	5,404	1,098	710
1882	14,870	9,966	4,904	9,124	4,306	842	598
1883	19,830	12,879	6,951	11,386	5,703	1,493	1,248
1884	17,290	12,155	5,135	11,221	4,290	934	845
1885	14,500	10,152	4,348	9,394	3,643	758	705
1886	17,623	13,485	4,138	12,750	3,510	735	628
1887	15,468	11,006	4,462	10,201	3,778	805	684
1888	60,850	44,545	16,305	41,766	14,027	2,779	2,278
1889	46,086	33,625	12,461	31,249	10,589	2,376	1,872
1890	47,835	34,832	13,003	32,466	11,089	2,366	1,914
1891	58,706	41,993	16,713	39,130	14,036	2,863	2,677
1892	57,583	41,895	15,688	38,805	13,091	3,090	2,597
1893	50,556	35,710	14,846	32,783	12,171	2,927	2,675
1894	62,399	47,242	15,157	44,334	12,481	2,908	2,676
1895	65,944	48,150	17,794	44,728	14,873	3,422	2,921
1896	92,591	68,151	24,440	63,160	20,018	4,991	4,422
1897	96,827	67,292	29,535	62,129	24,510	5,163	5,025
1898	94,060	63,682	30,378	58,136	25,690	5,546	4,688
1899	73,557	48,269	25,288	43,668	21,355	4,601	3,933
1900	77,789	48,940	28,849	43,663	23,933	5,277	4,916
1901	83,780	52,037	31,743	46,967	26,924	5,070	4,819
1902	71,896	44,202	27,694	39,545	23,320	4,657	4,374
1903	70,465	41,869	28,596	37,436	24,408	4,433	4,188
1904	44,022	29,134	14,888	.....	.....	.....	.....
1905	53,389	35,086	18,303	.....	.....	.....	.....
1906	58,797	36,927	21,870	.....	.....	.....	.....
1907	76,112	48,894	27,218	.....	.....	.....	.....
1908	74,302	46,741	27,561	.....	.....	.....	.....
1909	62,824	40,443	22,381	.....	.....	.....	.....
1910	74,940	48,045	26,895	.....	.....	.....	.....
1911	95,847	63,118	32,729	.....	.....	.....	.....
1912	109,035	70,035	39,000	.....	.....	.....	.....
1913	115,464	75,861	39,603	.....	.....	.....	.....
1914	105,007	70,524	34,483	.....	.....	.....	.....
1915[1]	82,428	54,316	28,112	.....	.....	.....	.....
1916[1]	82,974	54,060	28,914	.....	.....	.....	.....
1917[1]	88,162	55,523	32,639	.....	.....	.....	.....
1918[1]	124,631	79,356	45,275	.....	.....	.....	.....
1919[1]	101,849	70,698	31,151	.....	.....	.....	.....
1920[1]	122,197	75,702	46,495	.....	.....	.....	.....
1921[1]	112,632	70,267	42,365	.....	.....	.....	.....
1922[1]	113,166	70,296	42,870	.....	.....	.....	.....
1923	121,049	76,829	44,220	.....	.....	.....	.....
1924	128,671	81,017	47,654	.....	.....	.....	.....

For reference notes see page 987.

TABLE III.—DISTRIBUTION OF ARRIVALS, BY SEX, AGE AND COUNTRY OF LAST RESIDENCE, 1851-1924.

Year	Total	Great Britain				British Colonies				Foreign States			
		Adults		Children		Adults		Children		Adults		Children	
		Males	Females	Males	Females	Males	Females	Males	Females	Males	Females	Males	Females
1851	8,464	2,789	1,881	862	706	1,011	305	171	146	222	163	121	87
1852	20,789	3,717	2,189	1,127	993	11,435	560	345	163	142	61	29	28
1853	20,128	3,003	2,511	1,086	1,137	10,204	985	464	247	307	117	38	29
1854	17,258	3,281	4,210	1,274	1,346	4,400	939	396	321	573	302	112	104
1855	17,211	3,581	5,875	1,193	1,353	2,623	659	227	224	719	482	154	121
1856	9,525	2,261	1,906	609	632	2,049	671	388	158	338	268	124	121
1857	8,138	1,910	1,250	536	482	2,298	713	224	195	329	187	65	49
1858	7,855	1,681	1,424	427	358	2,071	722	207	195	137	219	111	111
1859	4,869	865	985	220	250	1,520	468	123	110	66	104	45	42
1860	4,374	503	434	157	145	2,237	482	135	153	84	36	11	15
1861	3,127	169	96	32	37	1,728	600	139	131	25	61	31	21
1862	3,230	448	393	58	73	1,387	496	103	125	52	34	11	18
1863	4,234	770	628	194	173	1,543	553	149	172	57	18	4	5
1864	5,958	1,306	1,020	272	261	1,861	729	213	180	92	32	16	16
1865	8,469	1,810	1,515	534	524	1,898	774	241	270	61	46	25	22
1866	6,955		1,276	336	304	1,626	650	234	226	70	69	30	30
1867	3,651	528	367	87	73	1,596	520	167	149	52	44	13	16
1868	2,900	190	115	44	33	1,449	488	156	132	27	39	13	24
1869	2,807	193	114	31	30	1,289	608	143	141	19	22	11	13
1870	2,302	142	107	35	33	1,398	473	74	93	12	16	7	6
1871	2,532	154	112	41	39	1,319	586	94	114	..	..	..	..
1872	2,401	93	101	64	44	2,413	550	130	88	..	10	2	4
1873	4,548	251	208		67	1,953	937	321	262	3	10	3	..
1874	5,557	1,071	721	352	322	2,610	802	174	152	..	2	2	3
1875	6,566	1,208	851	234	246	3,406	962	243	191	10	3	6	2
1876	13,841	3,853	2,283	988	953	6,069	1,443	405	364	73	33	25	15
1877	15,016	2,272	1,546	496	454	6,001	2,316	516	428	456	220	125	118
1878	14,572	2,384	1,391	518	492	5,519	2,359	549	416	168	121	95	78
1879	13,480	2,357	1,369	530	513	7,831	2,181	455	395	89	37	12	23
1880	14,765	1,201	866	244	202	11,020	2,975	827	519	74	20	3	3
1881	19,552	1,220	692	284	192	7,888	4,660	588	495	100	52	17	23
1882	14,870	1,068	909	232	231	8,393	3,328	596	351	168	69	22	16
1883	19,830	2,688	2,236	804	730	9,476	3,316	560	436	305	151	93	82
1884	17,290	1,428	929	271	268	8,226	3,188	533	493	317	173	103	84
1885	14,500	1,009	623	209	192		2,956	650	502	159	64	16	11
1886	17,623	548	319	76	53	12,066	3,147	726	570	136	44	9	5
1887	15,468	784	319	67	66		3,393		606	223	66	12	12
1888	60,850	685	294	64	48	40,880	13,652	2,698	2,214	199	81	17	16
1889	46,086	636	329	89	64	30,403	10,188	2,265	1,777	210	72	22	31
1890	47,835	596	333	66	55	31,712	10,687	2,274	1,849	158	69	26	10
1891	58,076		445	81	95	38,065	13,488	2,756	2,559	281	103	26	23
1892	57,583	671	403	95	67	37,878	12,573	2,961	2,515	256	115	34	15

TABLE III.—DISTRIBUTION OF ARRIVALS, BY SEX, AGE AND COUNTRY OF LAST RESIDENCE, 1851-1924 (continued).

Year	Total	Great Britain				British Colonies				Foreign States			
		Adults		Children		Adults		Children		Adults		Children	
		Males	Females	Males	Females	Males	Females	Males	Females	Males	Females	Males	Females
1893	50,556	466	250	51	42	32,123	11,835	2,859	2,621	194	86	17	12
1894	62,399	482	223	28	24	43,622	12,155	2,841	2,624	230	103	39	28
1895	65,944	490	260	62	37	44,053	14,542	3,346	2,871	185	71	14	13
1896	92,591	577	278	51	31	62,347	19,675	4,921	4,375	236	65	19	16
1897	96,827	531	296	63	46	61,375	24,109	5,079	4,956	223	105	21	23
1898	94,060	430	273	56	45	57,504	25,333	5,458	4,621	202	84	32	22
1899	73,557	494	277	78	54	42,964	20,988	4,501	3,861	210	90	22	18
1900	77,789	620	373	67	62	42,780	23,457	5,190	4,844	263	103	20	10
1901	83,780	510	350	41	36	46,217	26,461	5,005	4,761	240	113	24	22
1902	71,896	474	308	41	43	38,790	22,907	4,598	4,319	281	105	18	12
1903	70,465	365	275	35	33	36,836	24,033	4,385	4,149	235	100	13	6
			Males	Females			Males	Females			Males	Females	
1904	44,022		330	258			28,518	14,536			286	94	
1905	53,389		377	255			34,407	17,916			302	132	
1906	58,797		389	255			36,239	21,486			299	129	
1907	76,112		465	332			48,022	26,715			407	171	
1908	74,302		1,002	462			45,232	26,927			507	172	
1909	62,824		1,249	523			38,443	21,635			751	223	
1910	74,940		1,699	681			45,293	26,051			1,053	163	
1911	95,847		3,293	1,403			58,116	30,967			1,709	359	
1912	109,035		4,600	3,100			63,986	35,597			1,449	303	
1913	115,464		3,190	2,788			71,257	36,532			1,414	283	
1914	105,007		1,592	1,176			67,834	33,167			1,098	140	
						Commonwealth States		Other British Possessions					
						Males	Females	Males	Females				
1915	82,428[1]		489	412		52,800	27,560	304	116		238	24	
1916	82,974[1]		217	132		53,189	28,648	210	105		202	29	
1917	88,162[1]		29	27		53,984	32,542	120	58		13	5	
1918	124,631[1]		40	1		77,247	45,230	67	33		1	...	
1919	101,849[1]		926	1,291		55,833	29,647	185	111		34	20	
1920	122,197[1]		1,176	1,638		73,104	44,646	224	137		105	53	
1921	112,632[1]		2,248			109,327		403			221		
1922	113,166[1]		2,966			109,330		354			367		
1923	121,049		3,012			117,224		506			307		
1924	128,671		3,150			123,455		440			1,626		

For reference notes see page 987.

TABLE IV.—DISTRIBUTION OF DEPARTURES, BY SEX AND AGE, 1851-1920.

Year	Total	Sex		Sex and age			
		Males	Females	Adults		Children	
				Males	Females	Males	Females
1851	6,025	4,677	1,348	4,242	957	435	391
1852	16,475	14,123	2,352	13,420	1,911	703	441
1853	11,648	9,286	2,362	8,374	1,809	912	553
1854	5,467	3,773	1,694	3,305	1,319	468	375
1855	4,501	3,025	1,476	2,655	1,187	370	289
1856	7,278	5,252	2,026	4,826	1,657	426	369
1857	4,909	3,205	1,704	2,830	1,356	375	348
1858	3,609	2,499	1,110	2,274	919	225	191
1859	3,651	2,271	1,380	1,961	1,090	310	290
1860	4,902	3,444	1,458	3,042	1,098	402	360
1861	2,077	1,243	834	1,050	638	193	196
1862	2,685	1,787	898	1,546	657	241	241
1863	2,892	2,022	870	1,767	651	255	219
1864	2,676	1,776	900	1,575	702	201	198
1865	3,703	2,669	1,034	2,431	781	238	253
1866	4,135	2,899	1,236	2,630	999	269	237
1867	4,046	2,815	1,231	2,483	925	332	306
1868	4,193	3,041	1,152	2,749	911	292	241
1869	2,724	1,778	946	1,550	748	228	198
1870	4,128	2,705	1,423	2,336	1,071	369	352
1871	3,182	2,037	1,145	1,765	869	272	276
1872	3,405	2,173	1,232	1,887	964	286	268
1873	3,172	2,126	1,046	1,940	850	186	196
1874	3,271	2,226	1,045	2,079	898	147	147
1875	4,019	2,718	1,301	2,491	1,114	227	187
1876	4,995	3,605	1,390	3,387	1,205	218	185
1877	9,008	6,213	2,795	5,755	2,433	458	362
1878	8,174	5,826	2,348	5,434	2,072	392	276
1879	9,137	6,737	2,400	6,374	2,108	363	292
1880	13,002	9,391	3,611	8,874	3,240	517	371
1881	16,800	12,154	4,646	11,516	4,151	638	495
1882	14,136	10,108	4,028	9,458	3,521	650	507
1883	15,562	10,858	4,704	10,020	4,035	838	669
1884	16,082	11,280	4,802	10,421	4,065	859	737
1885	20,596	14,089	6,507	12,451	5,074	1,638	1,433
1886	25,231	17,508	7,723	15,447	5,888	2,061	1,835
1887	17,667	12,213	5,454	10,878	4,360	1,335	1,094
1888	66,739	48,998	17,741	45,407	14,950	3,591	2,791
1889	46,727	32,781	13,946	30,112	11,765	2,669	2,181
1890	48,849	35,283	13,566	32,708	11,589	2,575	1,977
1891	58,300	41,589	16,711	38,664	14,152	2,925	2,559
1892	52,677	38,178	14,499	35,543	12,179	2,635	2,320
1893	45,816	32,587	13,229	30,276	11,090	2,311	2,139
1894	62,285	47,715	14,570	44,878	12,183	2,837	2,387
1895	66,677	49,107	17,570	45,709	14,682	3,398	2,888
1896	94,620	69,331	25,289	63,982	20,626	5,349	4,663
1897	98,037	67,504	30,533	61,281	24,866	6,223	5,667
1898	92,306	61,657	30,649	55,696	25,682	5,961	4,967
1899	71,966	46,071	25,895	41,583	22,191	4,488	3,704
1900	78,264	48,622	29,642	43,234	24,720	5,388	4,922
1901	82,880	51,548	31,332	46,478	26,499	5,070	4,833

TABLE IV.—DISTRIBUTION OF DEPARTURES, BY SEX AND AGE, 1851-1920 (continued).

| Year | Total | Sex | | Sex and age | | | |
| | | Males | Females | Adults | | Children | |
				Males	Females	Males	Females
1902	72,810	44,454	28,356	39,882	23,953	4,572	4,403
1903	70,115	41,229	28,886	36,608	24,688	4,621	4,198
1904	44,416	27,018	17,398	.....	.....	.....	.....
1905	51,797	30,931	20,866	.....	.....	.....	.....
1906	57,018	32,923	24,095	.....	.....	.....	.....
1907	68,631	42,402	26,229	.....	.....	.....	.....
1908	66,353	41,281	25,072	.....	.....	.....	.....
1909	60,188	38,149	22,039	.....	.....	.....	.....
1910	65,710	41,907	23,803	.....	.....	.....	.....
1911	89,544	58,723	30,821	.....	.....	.....	.....
1912	102,866	66,120	36,746	.....	.....	.....	.....
1913[2]	113,441	76,811	36,630	.....	.....	.....	.....
1914[2][3]	111,556	75,626	35,930	.....	....	.....	.....
1915[2][3]	91,562	64,900	26,662	.....	.....	.....	.....
1916[2][3]	95,330	67,621	27,709	.....	.....	.....	.....
1917[2][3]	91,618	59,452	32,166	.....	.....	.....	.....
1918[2][3]	122,104	78,323	43,781	.....	.....	.....	.....
1919[2][3]	84,948	54,739	30,209	.....	.....	.....	.....
1920[4][3]	119,254	74,150	45,104	.....	.....	.....	.....

For reference notes see page 987.

TABLE V.—DISTRIBUTION OF DEPARTURES, BY SEX, AGE AND COUNTRY OF FUTURE RESIDENCE, 1851-1924[1]

Year	Total	Great Britain				British Colonies				Foreign States			
		Adults		Children		Adults		Children		Adults		Children	
		Males	Females	Males	Females	Males	Females	Males	Females	Males	Females	Males	Females
1851	6,025	106	49	22	15	4,124	901	411	376	12	7	2	..
1852	16,475	245	57	25	18	13,173	1,853	678	423	2	1	..	..
1853	11,648	322	136	56	63	8,048	1,671	853	490	4	2	3	7
1854	5,467	264	123	50	47	3,033	1,190	411	321	8	6	7	5
1855	4,501	65	63	27	28	2,587	1,121	338	256	3	3	5	..
1856	7,278	92	107	41	29	4,728	1,549	385	340	6	1	..	2
1857	4,909	82	63	23	32	2,746	1,286	349	314	2	7	3	..
1858	3,609	37	52	26	29	2,232	861	199	162	5	6	..	..
1859	3,651	72	64	26	28	1,878	1,026	284	262	11	..	..	..
1860	4,902	127	99	50	48	2,915	999	352	312	..	..	..	..
1861	2,077	83	88	34	39	967	550	159	157	..	..	2	2
1862	2,685	107	83	29	37	1,438	571	210	202	1	3	..	..
1863	2,892	51	53	17	27	1,716	598	238	192	..	..	1	3
1864	2,676	52	44	13	19	1,517	653	187	176	6	5	1	1
1865	3,703	96	81	26	36	2,332	697	211	216	3	3	..	..
1866	4,135	179	146	68	54	2,447	851	201	183	4	2	1	..
1867	4,046	120	92	36	39	2,354	831	295	267	9	2	..	..
1868	4,193	127	107	42	36	2,621	804	250	205	1	..	4	6
1869	2,724	138	98	45	34	1,409	647	179	158	3	3	24	15
1870	4,128	131	102	43	45	2,131	923	302	292	74	46	..	..
1871	3,182	163	137	60	56	1,599	729	212	220	1	3	..	..
1872	3,405	120	111	45	47	1,766	852	241	221	..	1	..	..
1873	3,172	122	110	39	46	1,815	738	147	150	3	2	3	1
1874	3,271	84	93	26	25	1,972	801	118	121	23	4	1	..
1875	4,019	110	116	34	35	2,370	997	192	151	11	1	1	3
1876	4,995	143	107	34	24	3,217	1,096	183	161	27	2	..	1
1877	9,008	217	162	49	50	5,455	2,262	408	309	83	9	1	..
1878	8,174	338	168	48	35	5,070	1,891	344	240	26	13	..	2
1879	9,137	404	187	41	57	5,901	1,906	322	235	69	15	1	4
1880	13,002	495	247	72	53	8,323	2,988	444	316	56	5	7	5
1881	16,800	550	209	74	45	10,939	3,931	557	446	27	11	4	4
1882	14,136	649	287	96	76	8,771	3,208	550	426	38	26	9	5
1883	15,562	512	234	73	66	9,429	3,768	756	599	79	33	3	4
1884	16,082	499	283	83	67	9,864	3,761	773	665	58	21	3	5
1885	20,596	418	240	71	55	11,984	4,813	1,562	1,376	49	21	5	2
1886	25,231	425	196	56	50	14,938	5,646	1,988	1,775	84	46	17	10
1887	17,667	414	230	57	55	10,366	4,088	1,262	1,025	98	42	16	14
1888	46,739	402	230	39	34	44,920	14,692	3,543	2,752	85	28	9	5
1889	46,727	390	194	48	39	29,616	11,536	2,608	2,139	106	35	13	3
1890	48,849	447	234	48	30	32,153	11,318	2,519	1,939	108	37	8	8
1891	58,300	497	305	49	43	38,040	13,803	2,871	2,509	127	44	5	7

For reference notes see page 987.

TABLE V.—DISTRIBUTION OF DEPARTURES, BY SEX, AGE AND COUNTRY OF FUTURE RESIDENCE, 1851-1924[1] (continued).

Year	Total	Great Britain Adults Males	Adults Females	Children Males	Children Females	British Colonies Adults Males	Adults Females	Children Males	Children Females	Foreign States Adults Males	Adults Females	Children Males	Children Females
1892	52,677	462	262	59	40	34,960	11,869	2,560	2,271	121	48	16	9
1893	45,816	503	299	78	73	29,525	10,735	2,209	2,033	248	56	24	33
1894	62,285	395	249	64	52	44,327	11,889	2,756	2,326	156	45	17	0
1895	66,677	449	263	78	50	45,119	14,390	3,315	2,834	141	29	5	4
1896	94,620	395	267	66	42	63,463	20,312	5,268	4,612	124	47	15	9
1897	98,037	568	335	99	71	60,550	24,471	6,113	5,582	163	60	11	14
1898	92,306	488	300	89	64	55,089	25,330	5,854	4,891	119	52	18	12
1899	71,966	478	343	107	83	41,006	21,800	4,377	3,615	99	48	4	6
1900	78,264	606	416	60	63	42,493	24,237	5,324	4,851	135	67	4	8
1901	82,880	314	242	37	52	46,074	26,212	5,020	4,777	90	45	13	4
1902	72,810	422	282	29	35	39,331	23,613	4,526	4,354	129	58	17	14
1903	70,115	304	222	22	22	36,210	24,415	4,587	4,170	94	51	12	6

Year	Total	Great Britain Males	Females	Children Males	Children Females	British Colonies Males	Females	Children Males	Children Females	Foreign States Males	Females
1904	44,416	277	170			26,597	17,181			144	47
1905	51,797	266	169			30,343	20,581			322	116
1906	57,018	328	287			32,400	23,747			195	61
1907	68,631	293	214			41,891	25,918			218	97
1908	66,353	460	239			40,478	24,695			343	138
1909	60,188	670	285			37,065	21,615			414	139
1910	65,710	919	266			40,397	23,407			591	130
1911	89,544	1,400	412			56,667	30,225			656	184
1912	102,866	1,187	535			64,274	36,063			659	148

Year	Total	United Kingdom Males	Females	Children Males	Children Females	Commonwealth States Males	Females	Other British Posessions Males	Females	Foreign Countries Males	Females
1913[2]	113,441	1,471	652			74,078	35,709	410	119	852	150
1914[2]	111,556[3]	1,524	703			71,637	34,909	437	142	822	148
1915[3]	91,562[3]	769	359			55,899	26,086	345	156	279	38
1916[2]	95,330[3]	362	245			55,343	27,315	257	117	148	28
1917[3]	91,618[3]	20	19			57,175	32,073	115	26	26	1
1918[3]	122,104[3]	18	12			75,976	43,726	44	26	3	··
1919[3]	84,948[3]	353	392			53,881	29,761	46	43	33	5
1920[3]	119,254[3]	579	603			72,968	44,328	176	135	114	33
1921[4]	107,878[3]	1,009				106,038		290		118	
1922[4]	109,439[3]	858				107,999		228		180	
1923[4]	115,872[3]	1,350				114,017		351		154	
1924[4]	121,287	1,270				119,528		237		252	

For reference notes see page 987.

TABLE VI.—Immigrants at public expense and assisted immigrants, by sex, 1851-85 and 1911-15.

Year	Total	Males	Females	Year	Total	Males	Females
1851	3,670	2,030	1,640	1871	....	....	....
1852	5,279	2,779	2,500	1872	....	....	....
1853	4,583	1,949	2,634	1873	226	104	122
1854	8,824	3,609	5,215	1874	2,152	1,192	960
1855	11,871	4,514	7,357	1875	2,067	1,156	911
1856	4,177	2,335	1,842	1876	7,730	4,663	3,067
1857	3,965	2,422	1,543	1877	4,947	2,866	2,081
1858	3,553	1,894	1,659	1878	4,250	2,459	1,791
1859	2,011	913	1,098	1879	3,235	1,706	1,529
1860	972	492	480	1880	808	345	463
1861	21	18	3	1881	783	418	365
1862	611	281	330	1882	1,122	471	651
1863	1,499	811	688	1883	4,132	1,959	2,173
1864	2,647	1,459	1,188	1884	968	427	541
1865	4,625	2,692	1,933	1885	293	130	163
1866	3,891	2,252	1,639	1911	665	315	350
1867	349	198	151	1912	3,212	1,464	1,748
1868	....	....	....	1913	2,759	1,110	1,649
1869	87	47	40	1914	644	240	404
1870	....	....	....	1915	79	22	57

SOURCES

Statistical Register of South Australia for 1860 to 1924-25, Adelaide, 1926.

Tables I (years 1836-87); II-VI (years 1851-1924).

Australasian Statistics, 1800, p. 10.

(In *Votes and Proceedings of Victorian Legislative Assembly*, 1902 (2)).

Table I (years 1873-1900).

NOTES

[1]In these figures are included expeditionary forces overseas and crews:

	Expeditionary Forces Overseas		Crews shipped	
	M	F	M	F
1915	485	—		
1916	107	—	135	—
1917	986	7	391	—
1918	1,728	11	273	—
1919	13,302	79	418	3
	M. and F.		M. and F.	
1920	827		287	
1921	—		433	
1922	—		149	

[2]Figures including allowances.

[3]In these figures are included expeditionary forces overseas and crews.

	Expeditionary Forces Overseas		Crews discharged	
	M	F	M	F
1914	1,206	28	—	—
1915	7,608	23	—	—
1916	11,378	4	133	—
1917	1,795	44	321	—
1918	1,965	17	317	—
1919	7	—	419	8
			M. and F.	
1920			318	
1921			423	
1922			174	

[4]Allowances for unrecorded migration (345 in 1920, 341 in 1921, 337 in 1922, 354 in 1923 and 348 in 1924) not included.

TASMANIA

TABLE I.—Arrivals and departures by sea, 1833, 1847-1919

Year	Arrivals	Departures	Year	Arrivals	Departures
1833[1]	2,345	. . . . .	1886	15,399	14,630
1847	5,538	4,787	1887	14,980	12,288
1848	4,410	3,799	1888	18,866	17,936
1849	4,191	3,617	1889	23,443	20,771
1850	. . . . .	4,612	1890	20,517	27,070
1851	3,930	7,463	1891	27,315	21,233
1852	12,632	21,920	1892	23,744	21,407
1853	14,997	12,684	1893	18,089	18,649
1854	9,525	11,280	1894	17,009	15,786
1855	10,887	7,055	1895	18,767	17,168
1856	4,956	7,636	1896	19,076	15,419
1857	6,063	5,231	1897	20,735	16,697
1858	4,003	4,496	1898	24,074	19,323
1859	2,975	2,921	1899	24,959	20,805
1860	3,432	3,114	1900	23,056	22,574
1861	3,684	4,861	1901	25,084	23,751
1862	3,174	4,444	1902	27,550	24,572
1863	3,621	4,410	1903	25,163	23,205
1864	3,711	3,521	1904	25,432	24,922
1865	3,597	3,509	1905	31,116	29,887
1866	4,679	4,079	1906	30,540	30,938
1867	3,559	4,025	1907	34,803	32,557
1868	5,043	4,320	1908	35,188	36,838
1869	6,521	7,159	1909	33,297	35,919
1870	5,982	5,888	1910	35,377	38,508
1871	4,648	5,326	1911	41,503	45,664
1872	5,665	6,127	1912	46,669	46,739
1873	6,787	7,039	1913	45,883	45,168
1874	6,265	7,714	1914	42,647	47,327[2]
1875	6,535	8,075	1915	39,767	44,488
1876	8,571	8,169	1916	41,361	46,047
1877	9,717	9,270	1917	35,924	36,780
1878	9,524	8,483	1918	37,639	35,921
1879	10,578	9,932	1919	23,804	19,544
1880	10,411	10,025	. . . .	. . . . .	. . . . .
1881	12,579	11,163	. . . .	. . . . .	. . . . .
1882	12,822	11,403	. . . .	. . . . .	. . . . .
1883	14,240	12,636	. . . .	. . . . .	. . . . .
1884	14,257	12,524	. . . .	. . . . .	. . . . .
1885	14,822	14,173	. . . .	. . . . .	. . . . .

For reference notes see page 989.

TABLE II.—Arrivals and departures by sea, classified by sex, 1909-19.

Year	Arrivals			Departures		
	Total	Males	Females	Total	Males	Females
1909	33,297	20,036	13,261	35,919	21,639	14,280
1910	35,377	. . . . .	. . . . .	38,508	. . . . .	. . . .
1911	41,503	24,895	16,608	45,664	27,218	18,446
1912	46,669	28,100	18,569	46,239[3]	27,519	19,720
1913	45,883	27,214	18,669	45,668[3]	26,681	18,987
1914	42,647	24,426	18,221	47,327[2]	27,719	19,608
1915	39,767	22,519	17,248	44,488	26,756	17,732
1916	41,361	23,191	18,170	46,547[3]	27,338	19,209
1917	35,924	19,460	16,464	36,780	20,073	16,707
1918	37,639	21,054	16,585	35,921	19,398	16,523
1919	23,804	15,637	8,167	19,544	10,666	8,878

SOURCES

Accounts and Papers (Published by order of the Parliament, London) 1835, vol. XXXIX, p. 732.

Table I (year 1833).

Tasmanian Parliamentary Papers, vol. LXXXIII 1920-21, *Statistics of Tasmania*, Appendix A, p. 7.

Table I (years 1847-1919).

Tasmanian Parliamentary Papers, 1910 to 1919-20, *Statistics of Tasmania*.

Table II (years 1909-19).

NOTES

[1] Of which number 1,638 adults (850 males and 788 females) and 707 children.

[2] 47,327 is the *recorded* emigration. The *total emigration* in the Tasmanian Parliamentary Papers, Vol. LXXIII 1915-16, *Statistics of Tasmania*, p. 90, is given as: Total=47,505; Males=27,843; Females=19,662. The figure for males includes 1,133 males and 19 females Expeditionary Force. In later years the figures given in Table I are the figures of total emigration, including a certain number of unrecorded cases.

[3] These figures do not agree with the totals given in table I.

VICTORIA

TABLE I.—ARRIVALS BY SEA, CLASSIFIED BY SEX, 1837-1924.

Year	Total	Males	Females	Year	Total	Males	Females
1837	740	. . . . .	. . . . .	1881	59,066	41,579	17,487
1838	1,260	. . . . .	. . . . .	1882	59,404	41,218	18,186
1839	3,221	. . . . .	. . . . .	1883	66,592	46,391	20,201
1840	4,080	. . . . .	. . . . .	1884	72,202	49,901	22,301
				1885	76,976	53,291	23,685
1841	6,908	. . . . .	. . . . .				
1842	4,136	2,584	1,552	1886	93,404	65,946	27,458
1843	1,264	925	339	1887	90,147	63,219	26,928
1844	2,648	1,830	818	1888	102,032	68,575	33,457
1845	4,335	3,317	1,018	1889	84,582	56,163	28,419
				1890	79,777	52,171	27,606
1846	3,676	2,798	878				
1847	4,568	3,893	675	1891	62,448	41,537	20,911
1848	8,235	5,042	3,193	1892	62,951	42,849	20,102
1849[1]	13,618	7,503	6,115	1893	74,047	50,674	23,373
1850	10,760	6,479	4,281	1894	84,261	58,688	25,573
				1895	81,199	55,481	25,718
1851	15,433	11,656	3,777				
1852	94,664	74,872	19,792	1896	84,872	59,137	25,735
1853	92,312	66,025	26,287	1897	90,847	63,123	27,724
1854	83,410	57,369	26,041	1898	94,436	64,026	30,410
1855	66,571	47,889	18,682	1899	85,384	55,799	29,585
				1900	82,157	53,559	28,598
1856	41,594	28,335	13,259				
1857	74,255	51,951	22,304	1901	93,107	61,118	31,989
1858	56,168	43,006	13,162	1902	87,557	56,984	30,573
1859	32,735	21,961	10,774	1903	52,756	33,275	19,481
1860	29,037	19,566	9,471	1904	55,049	34,339	20,710
				1905	62,798	38,875	23,923
1861	26,912	18,491	8,421				
1862	37,836	28,434	9,402	1906	60,282	42,274	27,008
1863	38,983	26,141	12,842	1907	75,784	46,277	29,507
1864	36,156	25,427	10,729	1908	76,863	47,507	29,356
1865	30,976	21,234	9,742	1909	78,744	48,404	30,340
				1910	82,594	49,544	33,050
1866	32,178	22,920	9,258				
1867	27,242	18,914	8,328	1911	106,349	60,239	41,990
1868	32,805	24,283	8,522	1912	124,527	73,766	50,761
1869	33,570	23,355	10,215	1913	114,586	68,592	45,994
1870	32,554	22,202	10,352	1914	109,149	65,749	43,400
				1915[2]	85,977	51,016	34,961
1871	28,333	19,289	9,044				
1872	27,047	19,056	7,991	1916[2]	80,458	46,526	43,932
1873	29,460	20,805	8,655	1917[2]	58,976	. . . . .	. . . . .
1874	30,732	21,876	8,856	1918[2]	48,566	. . . . .	. . . . .
1875	32,744	23,326	9,418	1919[2]	33,621	. . . . .	. . . . .
				1920[2]	65,595	. . . . .	. . . . .
1876	35,797	25,477	10,320				
1877	41,196	29,229	11,967	1921	66,537	. . . . .	. . . . .
1878	42,268	30,087	12,181	1922	81,903	. . . . .	. . . . .
1879	44,384	32,072	12,312	1923	87,248	. . . . .	. . . . .
1880	56,955	40,631	16,324	1924	88,467	. . . . .	. . . . .

For reference notes see page 997.

TABLE II.—Arrivals by sea, classified by country of last residence, 1865-1916.

Year	Total	Australia	New Zealand and South Seas	United Kingdom	South Africa	Other British Dominions	Foreign ports and crews	United States
1865	30,976	14,291	4,114	10,862	....	1,709		...
1866	32,178	15,908	6,087	8,514	....	1,669		...
1867	27,242	14,687	5,217	6,522	....	816		...
1868	32,805	18,734	6,614	6,748	....	709		...
1879	33,570	17,722	5,323	8,733	....	1,792		...
1870	32,554	17,681	4,460	9,187	....	1,226		...
1871	28,333	15,533	4,635	7,152	....	1,013		...
1872	27,047	16,975	4,350	4,818	....	904		...
1873	29,460	18,913	3,869	5,515	....	1,163		...
1874	30,732	20,361	4,348	4,645	....	1,378		...
1875	32,744	21,824	4,397	5,363	....	1,160		...
1876	35,797	24,107	4,710	5,688	....	1,292		...
1877	41,196	28,792	4,469	6,376	....	1,559		...
1878	42,268	28,623	4,054	8,121	....	1,470		...
1879	44,384	27,003	3,539	11,939	....	1,903		...
1880	56,955	39,014	6,177	9,674	....	2,090		...
1881	59,066	40,962	5,586	9,073	....	3,445		...
1882	59,404	39,563	4,523	13,036	....	2,282		...
1883	66,592	43,072	4,075	17,011	....	2,434		...
1884	72,202	47,784	4,562	17,226	....	2,630		...
1885	76,976	54,225	5,070	15,168	....	2,513		...
1886	93,404	64,077	6,147	18,586	....	4,594		...
1887	90,147	60,631	5,191	16,761	....	7,564		...
1888	102,032	67,188	12,364	18,406	....	4,074		...
1889	84,582	55,203	5,288	19,282	....	4,809		...
1890	79,777	57,144	5,613	11,715	....	5,305		...
1891	62,448	50,044	4,028	5,846	....	2,530		...
1892	62,951	53,469	3,334	4,091	....	2,057		...
1893	74,047	59,364	5,112	5,571	....	4,000		...
1894	84,261	70,038	3,489	7,155	....	3,579		...
1895	81,199	66,202	3,395	6,467	136	4,999		...
1896	84,872	70,185	3,416	6,066	333	4,872		...
1897	90,847	72,960	3,539	7,177	824	6,347		...
1898	94,436	78,325	3,167	6,560	740	5,644		...
1899	85,384	68,715	3,534	7,325	994	1,341	3,475	...
1900	82,157	61,650	3,669	9,295	1,878	1,810	3,855	...
1901	93,107	66,847	3,889	11,180	4,785	2,209	4,197	...
1902	87,557	64,699	4,258	8,392	4,215	1,490	4,503	...
1903	52,756	44,677	3,122	2,459	794	796	908	...
1904	55,049	46,273	3,509	2,337	1,325	899	706	...
1905	62,798	53,656	3,697	2,437	1,186	918	904	...
1906	69,382	59,372	4,095	2,606	1,382	1,041	886	...
1907	75,784	63,322	5,207	2,998	2,162	1,029	1,066	...
1908	76,863	65,554	4,204	3,583	1,163	1,154	1,205	...
1909	78,744	66,693	4,830	3,970	665	1,273	1,313	...
1910	82,594	69,750	4,317	5,757	483	1,146	1,141	...
1911	102,229	82,252	5,163	11,315	551	1,201	1,747	...
1912	124,527	88,879	5,030	24,022	872	1,665	3,965	94
1913	114,586	84,984	3,664	20,086	1,159	1,913	2,709	71
1914	109,149	87,967	3,502	13,212	930	1,430	2,054	54
1915[2]	85,977	77,517	1,922	3,867	291	1,751	508	121
1916[2]	90,458	84,492	1,841	1,233	124	1,655	922	191

For reference notes see page 997.

TABLE III.—Arrivals and departures, classified by age, 1844-50, 1873, 1896.

Year	Arrivals			Year	Departures		
	Total	Children[3]	Adults[3]		Total	Children[3]	Adults[3]
1844	2,648	811	1,837	1844	1,423	191	1,232
1845	4,335	483	3,852	1845	1,519	199	1,320
1846	3,676	405	3,271	1846	1,775	227	1,548
1847	4,568	1,056	3,512	1847	1,540	140	1,400
1848	8,235	1,719	6,516	1848	1,669	150	1,519
1849[1]	13,618	3,316	10,302	1849	1,992	308	1,684
1850	10,760	1,998	8,762	....	.....	....	.....
1873	29,460	3,416	26,044	1873	26,294	3,876	22,418
1896	84,872	7,580	77,292	1896	99,419	9,369	90,050

For reference notes see page 997.

TABLE IV.—Departures by sea, classified by sex, 1841-1924.

Year	Total	Males	Females	Year	Total	Males	Females
1841	939	.....	.....	1883	55,562	37,481	18,081
1842	1,964	1,337	627	1884	58,061	39,495	18,566
1843	2,000	1,395	605	1885	61,994	41,395	20,599
1844	1,423	1,042	381				
1845	1,519	1,095	424	1886	68,102	47,382	20,720
				1887	68,121	47,536	20,585
1846	1,775	1,319	456	1888	60,229	41,380	18,849
1847	1,540	1,180	360	1889	68,418	46,679	21,739
1848	1,669	1,264	405	1890	63,820	42,740	21,080
1849	1,992	1,364	628				
1850	3,304	2,300	1,004	1891	53,172	36,033	17,139
				1892	69,214	46,718	22,496
1851	3,706	2,854	852	1893	80,460	54,271	26,189
1852	31,038	28,620	2,418	1894	90,110	61,892	28,218
1853	42,443	36,532	5,911	1895	88,886	60,061	28,825
1854	34,975	28,669	6,306				
1855	26,395	20,585	5,810	1896	99,419	68,978	30,441
				1897	97,301	64,706	32,595
1856	21,187	17,362	3,825	1898	98,225	64,467	33,758
1857	20,471	16,752	3,719	1899	86,947	55,880	31,067
1858	25,882	21,691	4,191	1900	83,684	53,946	29,738
1859	19,615	15,349	4,266				
1860	21,689	17,220	4,469	1901	90,126	58,182	31,944
				1902	97,933	62,963	34,970
1861	35,898	30,914	4,984	1903	66,159	40,803	25,356
1862	38,203	31,043	7,160	1904	65,831	40,318	25,513
1863	34,800	27,929	6,871	1905	65,404	39,199	26,205
1864	21,779	15,758	6,021				
1865	25,292	19,105	6,187	1906	67,348	40,383	26,965
				1907	73,045	44,063	28,982
1866	27,629	20,772	6,857	1908	78,614	47,198	31,416
1867	25,142	18,472	6,670	1909	73,768	44,275	29,493
1868	25,552	19,639	5,913	1910	77,951	46,196	31,755
1869	22,418	16,371	6,047				
1870	21,087	15,228	5,859	1911	85,329	50,190	35,139
				1912	99,933	60,028	39,905
1871	19,951	14,189	5,762	1913	101,718	61,838	39,880
1872	25,295	18,685	6,610	1914[2]	99,043	59,395	39,648
1873	26,294	18,335	7,959	1915[2]	82,189	48,397	33,792
1874	27,365	19,424	7,941				
1875	29,342	20,457	8,885	1916[2]	76,687	43,604	33,083
				1917[2]	58,774	.....	.....
1876	31,977	22,205	9,772	1918[2]	51,631	.....	.....
1877	33,943	23,878	10,065	1919[2]	37,099	.....	.....
1878	37,492	26,085	11,407	1920	59,956	.....	.....
1879	39,212	27,523	11,689				
1880	45,294	31,857	13,437	1921	63,944	.....	.....
				1922	66,355	.....	.....
1881	51,744	35,692	16,052	1923	69,986	.....	.....
1882	48,524	33,677	14,847	1924	72,458	.....	.....

For reference notes see page 997.

TABLE V.—Departures by sea, classified by country of future residence, 1865-1916.

Year	Total	Australia	New Zealand and South Seas	United Kingdom	South Africa	Other British Dominions	Foreign ports	United States
1865	25,292	12,486	6,277	4,789	....	....	1,740	...
1866	27,629	12,594	9,618	4,302	....	....	1,115	...
1867	25,142	11,911	7,717	4,338	....	....	1,176	...
1868	25,552	14,992	5,176	3,909	....	....	1,475	...
1869	22,418	12,081	5,048	3,674	....	....	1,615	...
1870	21,087	12,165	4,119	3,553	....	....	1,250	...
1871	19,951	12,753	2,960	2,949	....	....	1,289	...
1872	25,295	17,807	2,675	3,183	....	....	1,630	...
1873	26,294	18,216	3,329	3,433	....	....	1,316	...
1874	27,365	18,683	4,182	3,230	....	....	1,270	...
1875	29,342	20,683	4,312	3,244	....	....	1,103	...
1876	31,977	23,886	4,236	2,873	....	....	982	...
1877	33,943	25,802	3,685	3,372	....	....	1,084	...
1878	37,492	27,461	4,317	4,413	....	....	1,301	...
1879	39,212	28,472	5,407	4,308	....	....	1,025	...
1880	45,294	33,769	4,463	5,362	....	....	1,700	...
1881	51,744	39,826	4,314	5,113	....	....	2,491	...
1882	48,524	36,157	4,358	6,334	....	....	1,675	...
1883	55,562	43,651	3,668	6,735	....	....	1,508	...
1884	58,061	45,331	3,766	7,363	....	....	1,601	...
1885	61,994	50,505	3,442	6,293	....	....	1,754	...
1886	68,102	55,752	3,453	6,864	....	....	2,033	...
1887	68,121	52,595	3,653	7,948	....	....	3,925	...
1888	60,229	44,620	3,889	8,512	....	....	3,208	...
1889	68,418	49,696	4,927	8,995	....	....	4,800	...
1890	63,820	47,584	4,314	8,213	....	....	3,709	...
1891	53,172	42,997	3,313	4,853	....	....	2,009	...
1892	69,214	59,427	4,181	3,917	....	....	1,689	...
1893	80,460	60,391	8,321	7,187	....	....	4,561	...
1894	90,110	72,684	4,828	8,223	....	....	4,375	...
1895	88,886	71,069	4,958	6,248	1,524	....	5,087	...
1896	99,419	80,480	4,008	6,550	3,214	....	5,167	...
1897	97,301	79,599	4,905	7,132	1,570	....	4,095	...
1898	98,225	81,970	4,591	7,509	870	....	3,285	...
1899	86,947	69,454	5,056	7,603	1,192	1,188	2,454	...
1900	83,684	61,069	4,733	9,853	3,645	1,185	3,199	...
1901	90,126	69,998	4,453	8,097	3,715	1,108	2,755	...
1902	97,933	72,401	6,853	8,645	5,460	1,365	3,209	...
1903	66,159	52,498	5,952	2,637	3,511	983	578	...
1904	65,831	54,576	5,823	2,769	1,125	984	554	...
1905	65,404	54,847	5,278	2,422	1,068	949	840	...
1906	67,348	55,548	6,427	2,580	878	1,103	812	...
1907	73,045	62,063	5,781	2,627	644	1,043	887	...
1908	78,614	67,463	5,992	2,728	596	954	881	...
1909	73,768	63,928	4,547	2,551	777	1,112	853	...
1910	77,951	68,522	4,143	2,540	814	1,047	885	...
1911	85,329	75,296	4,268	2,752	883	1,068	1,062	...
1912	99,933	86,820	4,743	4,473	940	1,472	1,476	9
1913	101,718	87,729	4,455	5,633	838	1,343	1,708	12
1914[2]	99,043	85,999	3,732	5,664	666	1,374	1,560	48
1915[2]	82,189	73,853	2,397	2,914	314	1,977	564	170
1916[2]	76,687	70,514	1,813	1,448	254	1,505	1,066	87

For reference notes see page 997.

TABLE VI.—Colored immigration and emigration, 1861, 1866, 1873-75, 1886-1923.

Year	Immigrants			Year	Emigrants		
	Total	Chinese	Other		Total	Chinese	Other
1861	154	154	. . .				
1866	974	974	. . .	1866	1,043	1,043	. . .
1873	269	269	. . .	1873	523	523	. . .
1874	386	386	. . .	1874	386	386	. . .
1875	299	299	. . .	1875	521	521	. . .
1886	1,108	1,108	. . .	1886	492	492	. . .
1887	2,049	2,049	. . .	1887	902	902	. . .
1888	372	372	. . .	1888	582	582	. . .
1889	124	124	. . .	1889	655	655	. . .
1890	232	232	. . .	1890	593	593	. . .
1891	293	293	. . .	1891	604	604	. . .
1892	584	584	. . .	1892	709	709	. . .
1893	1,094	1,094	. . .	1893	507	507	. . .
1894	416	416	. . .	1894	415	415	. . .
1895	569	569	. . .	1895	416	416	. . .
1896	709	709	. . .	1896	512	512	. . .
1897	762	762	. . .	1897	435	435	. . .
1898	711	711	. . .	1898	341	341	. . .
1899	636	636	. . .	1899	417	417	. . .
1900	569	569	. . .	1900	385	385	. . .
1901	1,473	864	609[4]	1901	954	471	483[4]
1902	921	614	307	1902	959	434	525
1903	504	408	96	1903	595	503	92
1904	420	372	48	1904	516	441	75
1905	564	506	58	1905	645	509	136
1906	447	376	71	1906	655	526	129
1907	505	464	41	1907	498	419	79
1908	630	566	64	1908	510	448	62
1909	592	523	69	1909	625	556	69
1910	561	424	137	1910	574	418	156
1911	539	435	104	1911	531	454	77
1912	678	545	133	1912	630	556	74
1913	592	475	117	1913	670	579	91
1914	381	323	58	1914	568	501	67
1915	609	530	79	1915	689	592	97
1916	561	481	80	1916	489	397	92
1917	67	. . .	67	1917	208	. . .	208
1918	402	350	52	1918	316	270	46
1919	233	187	46	1919	559	408	151
1920	359	300	59	1920	496	410	86
1921	385	315	70	1921	655	591	64
1922	411	346	65	1922	556	509	47
1923	538	462	76	1923	551	487	64

For reference notes see page 997.

TABLE VII.—Assisted immigrants, by sex, 1838-60.

Year	Total	Males	Females	Year	Total	Males	Females
1838	297	200	97	1850	2,248	852	1,396
1839	601	313	288	1851	2,551	1,382	1,169
1840	1,538	736	802	1852	15,477	7,762	7,715
1841	8,000⁵	4,008	3,992	1853	14,578	5,236	9,342
1842	1,787	932	855	1854	16,318	5,456	10,862
1843	13	8	5	1855	9,245	3,149	6,096
1844	1,430	764	666	1856	4,679	1,763	2,916
1845	177	177	.....	1857	14,369	5,429	8,940
1846	342	342	.....	1858	5,859	2,320	3,539
1847	537	537	.....	1859	3,151	552	2,599
1848	3,993	2,210	1,783	1860	1,736	185	1,551
1849	7,669	3,823	3,846	....	.....	.....	.....

TABLE VIII.—Assisted immigrants, 1861-85.

Year	Assisted	Year	Assisted	Year	Assisted
1861	1,534	1869	3,716	1877	17
1862	1,502	1870	4,341	1878	18
1863	2,583	1871	3,212	1879	15
1864	576	1872	1,093	1880	5
1865	5,104	1873	863	1881	..
1866	4,194	1874	149	1882	2
1867	3,202	1875	102	1883	..
1868	2,871	1876	71	1884	..
....	....	....	....	1885	..

For reference notes see page 997.

SOURCES

Statistical Register of Victoria, Part IX. Social Conditions. Statistical Summary of Victoria, from 1836 to 1900 inclusive, in *Votes and Proceedings of Victorian Legislative Assembly.* Melbourne, 1902, vol. 2. Melbourne.

Tables I (years 1837-1900) (totals); IV (years 1841-1900) (totals).

Idem, 1867 and 1876.

Tables I (years 1857-64); IV (years 1857-64).

Statistical Register of Victoria. Melbourne, 1854, pp. 232-8.

Tables I (years 1843-50); III (years 1844-50).

Idem, 1875 to 1917.

Tables I, II, IV and V (years 1865-1916); III (year 1896); VI (years 1866-1916).

Statistical Notes on Progress of Victoria, 1835-60, Melbourne. Vol. I, pp. 5-8

Tables I (years 1842-43, 1851-56); IV (years 1842-56).

Victorian Year-Book, 1873-75, 1922-23, 1924-25.

Tables I, IV and VI (years 1873-75, 1916-24); III (year 1873).

Victoria. Report of immigration and emigration in 1861. (In *Accounts and Papers,* 1861-63 (19) pp. 13-21.)

Table VI (year 1861).

Victoria. *Immigration Returns* for 1862, 1863 and 1864.

Table VIII (years 1862-64).

NOTES

[1] In 1849 the figures referring to sex and age (*Statistical Register,* 1854) total 13,618 instead of 14,618 as given in other sources in later years.
[2] Excluding Australian Expeditionary Forces departed from and arrived in Victoria.
[3] For 1844 and 1845 are specified "above 14 years" and "under 14 years".
[4] From April 1 to December 31, 1901.

WESTERN AUSTRALIA

TABLE I.—ARRIVALS AND DEPARTURES BY SEA, 1829-1920.

Year	Arrivals	Departures	Year	Arrivals	Departures
1829	652	. . .	1886	5,615	1,877
1830	1,125	. . .	1887	4,450	2,400
1835	96	68	1888	1,598	2,794
1840[1]	123	. . .	1889	2,850	2,272
1845[1]	. . .	129	1890	3,567	1,996
1850[1]	203	. . .	1891	6,346	2,667
1855[1]	537	. . .	1892	7,440	2,978
1856[1]	294	. . .	1893	8,928	3,716
1857[1]	. . .	92	1894	25,858	9,923
1858[1]	848	. . .	1895	29,523	11,163
1859[1]	. . .	261	1896	55,215	19,324
1860	461	450	1897	49,387	26,867
1861	560	424	1898	32,709	28,845
1862	1,808	653	1899	20,278	20,287
1863	1,920	737	1900	24,921	19,078
1864	1,173	916	1901	32,762	20,780
1865	1,268	836	1902	37,860	21,001
1866	1,069	647	1903	30,943	20,216
1867	721	467	1904	31,517	19,563
1868	1,038	404	1905	28,791	22,934
1869	503	752	1906	25,396	25,077
1870	268	303	1907	22,326	27,740
1871	320	479	1908	24,594	24,339
1872	320	419	1909	24,643	23,537
1873	285	639	1910	31,403	25,091
1874	660	601	1911	41,359	29,178
1875	733	520	1912	38,326	31,732
1876	727	650	1913	37,637	29,366
1877	613	575	1914	27,270	31,097
1878	322	471	1915	20,734	31,761
1879	214	278	1916	19,322	34,010
1880	577	777	1917	17,822	22,318
1881	611	690	1918	24,262	24,511
1882	932	838	1919	32,561	17,695
1883	1,507	1,071	1920	30,351	30,106
1884	2,434	1,563	. . . .	. . . . .	. . . . .
1885	3,047	1,419	. . . .	. . . . .	. . . . .

SOURCES

Western Australia Year-Book for 1902-04 (13th ed., 1906), p. 1152. "Statistical View of the Progress of Western Australia, 1829 to 1904".

Table I (years 1829-90).

Statistical Register of Western Australia, 1919-20. "Statistical View of the Progress of Western Australia, 1829 to 1919-20", p. 2.

Table I (years 1890-1914).

Idem, 1924-25.

Table I (years 1915-25).

NOTE

[1]From 1838 to 1859, inclusive, the figures give only the excess of arrivals over departures or vice versa

NEW ZEALAND

Prior to April 1, 1921, the statistics of migration were compiled from statements furnished monthly by Collectors of Customs showing the totals, by sex, of arrivals from and departures to various countries, with information about the birthplaces of arriving and departing "race aliens". (Tables I-VI and XIII.) These tables have been continued as far as possible up to 1924. Notes 1 and 3 show that the figures for earlier years are defective. Their source for the period 1853-60 (tables II and V) states that "generally the figures are to be regarded as only the closest approximation to accuracy that can be obtained from the returns". (*Statistics of New Zealand for 1869*, Wellington, 1870, Table III.) The source also contained data for the earlier period relating to passenger traffic between New Zealand ports. These have been ignored because our interest centres in international migrations.

2. After April 1, 1921, a new system of statistics was introduced which requires each person arriving or departing to fill in a form which records statistical particulars and also in the case of arrivals discloses whether the person is a new immigrant intending permanent residence, a returned New Zealander or a visitor on business or pleasure. Similarly in the case of departures, a distinction is made between those temporarily and those permanently leaving the Dominion. Under the new system, statistics enable us thus to distinguish *real immigrants and emigrants* from other passengers. (Tables VII-XII.)

Concerning assisted immigrants, see p. 103,f of the text.

TABLE I.—Distribution of immigrants, by sex and age, 1853-1924.

Year	Total	Sex		Age			
				Children		Adults	
		Males	Females	Males	Females	Males	Females
1853[1]	3,154[2]	....	....	319[3]		1,729	635
1854[1]	4,041[2]	....	....	430[3]		2,367	912
1855	7,220	....	....	1,042[3]		4,406	1,772
1856[1]	4,851	....	....	600[3]		2,876	1,375
1857	5,927	....	....	970[3]		3,485	1,472
						3,601	1,995
1858	7,678[2]	4,641	2,961	1,040	966	5,036	2,631
1859	10,203	6,340	3,863	1,304	1,232	4,338	2,400
1860	8,935	5,460	3,475	1,122	1,075	19,099	1,736
1861[4]	22,339	19,896	2,443	797	707	25,072	5,571
1862[4]	34,290	27,005	7,285	1,933	1,714	31,395	8,240
1863	45,730	34,516	11,214	3,121	2,974	10,140	5,578
1864	20,931	12,882	8,049	2,742	2,471	11,776	4,270
1865	18,916	13,227	5,689	1,451	1,419	10,059	3,102
1866	14,893	10,979	3,914	920	812	6,757	2,869
1867	11,126	7,581	3,545	824	676	5,425	2,211
1868	8,723	6,045	2,678	620	467	5,784	2,181
1869	8,903	6,302	2,601	518	420	5,508	2,400
1870	9,124	6,178	2,946	670	546	6,892	2,066
1871	10,083	7,526	2,557	634	491	5,684	3,017
1872	10,725	6,775	3,950	1,091	933	6,362	4,272
1873	13,572	7,871	5,701	1,509	1,429	19,488	12,215
1874	43,965	25,830	18,135	6,342	5,920	15,730	8,629
1875	31,737	19,558	12,179	3,828	3,550	9,577	5,152
1876	18,414	11,524	6,890	1,947	1,738	6,980	3,812
1877	12,987	8,104	4,883	1,124	1,071	9,421	4,477
1878	16,263	10,671	5,592	1,250	1,115	12,841	6,638
1879	23,957	15,186	8,771	2,345	2,133	8,092	4,389
1880	15,154	9,564	5,590	1,472	1,201	5,803	2,389
1881	9,688	6,643	3,045	840	656	6,129	3,150
1882	10,945	7,042	3,903	913	753	9,562	6,426
1883	19,215	11,218	7,997	1,656	1,571	10,862	6,085
1884	20,021	12,475	7,546	1,613	1,461	9,461	4,273
1885	16,199	10,766	5,433	1,305	1,160	9,966	3,998
1886	16,101	11,068	5,033	1,102	1,035	8,380	3,607
1887	13,689	9,224	4,465	844	858	8,363	3,782
1888	13,606	9,112	4,494	749	712	9,230	4,386
1889	15,392	10,158	5,234	928	848	8,858	4,461
1890	15,028	9,753	5,275	895	814	8,649	4,238
1891	14,431	9,427	5,004	778	766	11,076	4,947
1892	18,122	12,131	5,991	1,055	1,044	15,577	7,019
1893	26,135	17,385	8,750	1,808	1,731	14,829	7,367
1894	25,237	16,375	8,862	1,546	1,495	12,973	6,588
1895	21,862	14,181	7,681	1,208	1,093	10,192	5,128
1896	17,236	11,145	6,091	953	963	11,095	5,381
1897	18,592	12,153	6,439	1,058	1,058	11,504	5,438
1898	18,855	12,524	6,331	1,020	893	10,822	5,707
1899	18,506	11,862	6,644	1,040	937	10,997	5,206
1900	18,074	11,966	6,108	969	902	15,724	6,942
1901	25,086	16,968	8,118	1,244	1,176	20,029	7,406
1902	30,293	21,522	8,771	1,493	1,365	18,628	8,603
1903	30,883	20,479	10,404	1,851	1,801		

For reference notes see page 1014.

TABLE I.—DISTRIBUTION OF IMMIGRANTS, BY SEX AND AGE, 1853-1924 (concluded).

Year	Total	Sex		Age			
				Children		Adults	
		Males	Females	Males	Females	Males	Females
1904	32,632	21,980	10,652	1,862	1,644	20,118	9,008
1905	32,685	21,344	11,341	1,803	1,735	19,541	9,606
1906	39,233	25,607	13,626	2,233	1,975	23,374	11,651
1907	36,108	23,228	12,880	1,962	1,800	21,266	11,080
1908	44,970	29,342	15,628	2,678	2,359	26,664	13,269
1909	38,650	24,065	14,585	2,302	2,105	21,763	12,480
1910	35,769	22,135	13,634	1,974	1,802	20,161	11,832
1911	41,389	25,333	16,056	2,452	2,103	22,881	13,953
1912	44,660	26,775	17,885	2,749	2,443	24,026	15,442
1913	44,588	25,891	18,697	3,019	2,896	22,872	15,801
1914	37,646	22,526	15,120	2,166	2,100	20,360	13,020
1915	25,551	14,487	11,064	1,494	1,475	12,993	9,589
1916	21,799	11,959	9,840	1,302	1,434	10,657	8,406
1917	15,649	9,159	6,490	825	907	8,334	5,583
1918	11,906	6,356	5,550	671	708	5,685	4,842
1919	20,931	10,772	10,159	1,431	1,337	9,341	8,822
1920	44,062	23,687	20,375	. . . . .	. . . . .	. . . . .	. . . . .
1921	41,882	22,446	19,436	6,001[5]		35,881[5]	
1922	35,233	18,811	16,422	5,154[5]		30,079[5]	
1923	36,488	19,445	17,043	5,022[5]		31,466[5]	
1924	39,815	21,719	18,096	5,727[5]		34,088[5]	

For reference notes see page 1014.

TABLE II.—Distribution of immigrants, by sex and country of origin, 1853-1919.

Year	Total	United Kingdom			British Possessions			Hawaii, South Sea Isles and other places		
		Males	Females	Sex not stated	Males	Females	Sex not stated	Males	Females	Sex not stated
1853	2,768[2]	510	313	177	1,157	302	141	62	20	86
1854	4,041[2]	461	330	339	1,570	458	325	336	124	98
1855	7,220[2]	938	655	422	2,118	739	644	1,156	305	243
1856	4,851[2]	870	576	563	1,117	426	344	595	207	153
1857	[6]5,927[2]	1,287	763	610	1,660	365	187	89	64	13
1858	7,678[2]	3,387	2,501	24	1,179	458	52	75	2	. . .
1859	10,203	4,625	3,166	. . .	1,662	695	. . .	53	2	. . .
1860	8,935	4,109	2,820	. . .	1,329	651	. . .	22	4	. . .
1861	22,339	2,350	1,597	. . .	17,454	829	. . .	92	17	. . .
1862	34,290	5,318	3,429	. . .	21,598	3,845	. . .	89	11	. . .
1863	45,730	8,247	6,131	. . .	26,164	5,069	. . .	105	14	. . .
1864	20,931	6,187	4,455	. . .	6,570	3,574	. . .	125	20	. . .
1865	18,916	5,473	4,368	. . .	7,647	1,315	. . .	107	6	. . .
1866	14,893	2,404	1,878	. . .	8,464	2,003	. . .	111	33	. . .
1867	11,126	2,372	2,088	. . .	4,936	1,348	. . .	273	109	. . .
1868	8,723	1,742	1,280	. . .	3,909	1,230	. . .	394	168	. . .
1869	8,903	1,587	1,190	. . .	4,518	1,351	. . .	197	60	. . .
1870	9,124	2,266	1,749	. . .	3,526	1,127	. . .	386	70	. . .
1871	10,083	1,768	1,368	. . .	5,313	1,111	. . .	445	78	. . .
1872	10,725	3,067	2,324	. . .	2,842	1,028	. . .	866	598	. . .
1873	13,572	4,682	4,240	. . .	2,744	1,224	. . .	445	237	. . .
1874	43,965	20,197	16,203	. . .	5,002	1,625	. . .	631	307	. . .
1875	31,737	12,547	9,311	. . .	4,428	1,900	. . .	2,673	968	. . .
1876	18,414	6,433	4,699	. . .	3,963	1,566	. . .	1,128	625	. . .
1877	12,987	4,308	3,327	. . .	3,414	1,441	. . .	382	115	. . .
1878	16,263	5,216	3,993	. . .	5,045	1,469	. . .	410	130	. . .
1879	23,957	9,863	6,872	. . .	4,878	1,759	. . .	445	140	. . .
1880	15,154	4,675	3,839	. . .	4,492	1,639	. . .	397	112	. . .
1881	9,688	1,988	1,519	. . .	4,378	1,425	. . .	277	101	. . .
1882	10,945	1,764	1,441	. . .	4,939	2,334	. . .	339	128	. . .
1883	19,215	5,060	5,338	. . .	5,831	2,567	. . .	327	92	. . .
1884	20,021	5,307	4,553	. . .	6,657	2,839	. . .	511	154	. . .
1885	16,199	4,385	2,856	. . .	5,922	2,450	. . .	459	127	. . .
1886	16,101	4,412	2,481	. . .	6,148	2,417	. . .	508	135	. . .
1887	13,689	2,972	1,934	. . .	5,958	2,429	. . .	294	102	. . .
1888	13,606	2,562	1,576	. . .	6,249	2,801	. . .	301	117	. . .
1889	15,392	1,971	1,304	. . .	7,735	3,771	. . .	452	159	. . .
1890	15,028	1,685	1,127	. . .	7,736	4,019	. . .	332	129	. . .
1891	14,431	1,485	950	. . .	7,153	3,898	. . .	429	156	. . .
1892	18,122	1,512	1,043	. . .	10,162	4,769	. . .	457	179	. . .
1893	26,135	1,760	1,169	. . .	15,229	7,446	. . .	396	135	. . .
1894	25,237	1,723	1,123	. . .	14,194	7,536	. . .	458	203	. . .
1895	21,862	1,506	859	. . .	12,278	6,657	. . .	397	165	. . .
1896	17,236	1,202	754	. . .	9,467	5,160	. . .	476	177	. . .
1897	18,592	1,714	1,010	. . .	10,075	5,258	. . .	364	171	. . .
1898	18,855	1,677	921	. . .	10,411	5,215	. . .	436	195	. . .
1899	18,506	1,164	754	. . .	10,203	5,681	. . .	495	209	. . .
1900	18,074	1,473	841	. . .	9,942	5,116	. . .	551	151	. . .
1901	25,086	1,595	968	. . .	14,702	6,867	. . .	671	283	. . .
1902	30,293	2,245	1,229	. . .	18,677	7,291	. . .	600	251	. . .
1903	30,883	2,108	1,439	. . .	17,801	8,679	. . .	570	286	. . .

For reference notes see page 1014.

TABLE II.—Distribution of immigrants, by sex and country of origin, 1853-1919, (concluded).

Year	Total	United Kingdom			British Possessions			Hawaii, South Sea Isles and other places		
		Males	Females	Sex not stated	Males	Females	Sex not stated	Males	Females	Sex not stated
1904	32,632	2,863	1,791	...	18,470	8,610	...	647	251	...
1905	32,685	3,418	2,135	...	17,271	8,889	...	655	317	...
1906	39,233	5,280	3,013	...	19,691	10,328	...	636	285	...
1907	36,108	4,463	2,986	...	18,391	9,741	...	374	153	...
1908	44,970	6,907	4,441	...	29,863	3,044	...	530	185	...
1909	38,650	6,492	4,692	...	17,029	9,660	...	544	233	...
1910	35,769	5,36⊁	4,003	...	16,111	9,323	...	660	308	...
1911	41,389	6,390	4,989	...	17,925	10,604	...	1,018	463	...
1912	44,660	6,764	6,148	...	19,193	11,401	...	818	336	...
1913	44,588	7,493	7,214	...	17,629	11,103	...	769	380	...
1914	37,646	4,374	4,205	...	17,295	10,587	...	857	328	...
1915	25,551	1,512	2,019	...	12,252	8,764	...	723	281	...
1916	21,799	1,890	1,504	...	8,636	8,006	...	1,433	330	...
1917	15,649	2,350	581	...	6,086	5,612	...	723	297	...
1918	11,906	418	758	...	5,408	4,578	...	530	214	...
1919	20,931	957	3,711	...	8,937	5,925	...	878	523	...

Year	Total		United Kingdom			Austra-lian Common mon-wealth	Other places	
	All im-migrants	Chinese included in fore-going column	Total	As-sisted	Unas-sisted		Total	Govt. immi-grants in-cluded in fore-going column
1870	9,124	.....	4,015	.....	4,015	4,643	466	.....
1871	10,083	1,596	3,136	303	2,833	4,036	2,911	.....
1872	10,725	.....	5,391	4,736	655	3,390	1,944	.....
1873	13,572	.....	8,922	8,754	168	3,769	881	.....
1874	43,965	1,123	36,400	31,774	4,626	5,504	2,061	344
1875	31,737	776	21,768	18,324	3,444	6,328	3,641	2,046
1876	18,414	112	11,132	8,242	2,890	4,956	2,326	1,435
1877	12,987	162	7,635	5,298	2,337	4,500	852	46
1878	16,263	1,025	9,209	6,580	2,629	6,348	706	38
1879	23,957	329	16,735	10,311	6,424	6,413	809	.....
1880	15,154	296	8,514	2,689	5,825	5,899	741	.....
1881	9,688	1,029	3,507	103	3,404	5,579	602	.....
1882	10,945	23	3,205	726	2,479	6,975	765	.....
1883	19,215	44	10,398	5,902	4,496	8,056	761	.....
1884	20,021	84	9,860	3,888	5,972	9,064	1,097	.....
1885	16,199	94	7,241	1,072	6,169	7,899	1,059	.....
1886	16,101	239	6,893	917	5,976	8,133	1,075	.....
1887	13,689	354	4,906	1,286	3,620	8,035	748	.....
1888	13,606	308	4,138	485	3,653	8,784	684	.....
1889	15,392	16	3,275	91	3,184	11,212	905	.....
1890	15,028	18	2,812	144	2,668	11,539	677	.....
1891	14,431	5	2,435	44	2,391	11,144	852	.....
1892	18,122	58	2,555	.....	2,555	14,674	893	.....
1893	26,135	116	2,929	.....	2,929	22,351	855	.....
1894	25,237	278	2,846	.....	2,846	21,291	1,100	.....
1895	21,862	214	2,365	.....	2,365	18,573	924	.....
1896	17,236	173	1,956	.....	1,956	14,125	1,155	.....
1897	18,592	13	2,724	.....	2,724	14,799	1,069	.....
1898	18,855	20	2,598	.....	2,598	14,969	1,288	.....
1899	18,506	26	1,918	.....	1,918	15,529	1,059	.....
1900	18,074	27	2,314	.....	2,314	14,565	1,195	.....
1901	25,086	75	2,563	.....	2,563	19,923	2,600	.....
1902	30,293	69	3,474	.....	3,474	22,526	4,293	.....
1903	30,883	132	3,547	.....	3,547	25,888	1,448	.....
1904	32,632	235	4,654	1,058	3,596	26,110	1,868	.....
1905	32,685	239	5,553	2,191	3,362	25,132	2,000	.....
1906	39,233	260	8,293	3,880	4,413	28,699	2,241	.....
1907	36,108	255	7,449	2,510	4,939	26,916	1,743	.....
1908	44,970	538	11,348	4,466	6,882	31,769	1,853	.....
1909	38,650	171	11,184	3,990	7,194	25,548	1,918	.....
1910	35,769	209	9,367	2,179	7,188	24,502	1,900	.....
1911	41,389	546	11,379	2,839	8,540	26,909	3,101	.....
1912	44,660	348	12,912	3,772	9,140	28,522	3,226	.....
1913	44,588	325	14,707	5,148	9,559	26,764	3,117	.....
1914	37,646	511	8,579	3,716	4,863	25,967	3,100	.....
1915	25,551	265	3,531	1,300	2,231	19,499	2,521	.....
1916	21,799	327	3,394	580	2,814	15,321	3,084	.....
1917	15,649	272	2,931	231	2,700	10,146	2,572	.....
1918	11,906	256	1,176	419	757	8,282	2,448	.....
1919	20,931	418	4,668	3,638	1,030	11,568	4,695	.....
1920	.....	.....	.....	4,075	.....	.....	.....	.....
1921	.....	.....	.....	7,501	.....	.....	.....	.....

TABLE IV.—Distribution of emigrants, by sex and age, 1853-1924.

Year	Total	Sex		Age			
				Children		Adults	
		Males	Females	Males	Females	Males	Females
1853[1]	1,677[2]	.....	.....	306[3]		1,063	280
1854[1]	1,984[2]	.....	.....	233[3]		1,175	389
1855	3,283	.....	.....	392[3]		2,187	704
1856[1]	2,326	.....	.....	141[3]		1,611	574
1857	2,885	.....	.....	223[3]		2,165	497
						1,009	304
1858	1,548[2]	1,116	425	107	121	985	293
1859	1,566	1,134	432	149	139	1,913	501
1860	2,871	2,149	722	236	221	5,559	319
1861[4]	6,117	5,687	430	128	111	12,525	478
1862[4]	13,299	12,695	604	170	126	9,392	747
1863	10,610	9,654	956	262	209	10,455	1,142
1864	12,404	10,879	1,525	424	383	4,949	986
1865	6,607	5,326	1,281	377	295	5,611	976
1866	7,294	5,992	1,302	381	326	4,680	896
1867	6,267	5,075	1,192	395	296	6,233	925
1868	7,863	6,647	1,216	414	291	3,615	960
1869	5,262	4,001	1,261	386	301	3,838	1,040
1870	5,547	4,203	1,344	365	304	3,650	938
1871	5,297	4,041	1,256	391	318	4,036	1,001
1872	5,752	4,417	1,135	381	334	3,117	939
1873	4,761	3,507	1,254	390	315	3,945	1,103
1874	5,859	4,367	1,492	422	389	4,227	1,357
1875	6,467	4,727	1,740	500	383	4,121	1,352
1876	6,459	4,677	1,782	556	430	4,146	1,448
1877	6,611	4,696	1,915	550	467	3,673	1,231
1878	5,761	4,138	1,623	465	392	3,582	1,181
1879	5,234	3,852	1,382	270	201	5,319	1,682
1880	7,923	5,816	2,107	497	425	4,961	1,697
1881	8,072	5,705	2,367	744	670	4,561	1,890
1882	7,456	5,082	2,374	521	484	5,551	2,380
1883	9,186	6,230	2,956	679	576	6,521	2,750
1884	10,700	7,303	3,397	782	647	7,047	3,043
1885	11,695	7,866	3,829	819	786	9,287	3,566
1886	15,037	10,442	4,595	1,155	1,029	7,412	3,358
1887	12,712	8,434	4,278	1,022	920	13,018	5,858
1888	22,781	15,048	7,733	2,030	1,875	8,204	4,371
1889	15,178	9,493	5,685	1,289	1,314	9,702	4,961
1890	16,810	10,809	6,001	1,107	1,040	10,098	5,023
1891	17,629	11,396	6,233	1,298	1,210	7,680	3,947
1892	13,164	8,469	4,695	789	748	9,457	4,693
1893	15,723	10,263	5,460	806	767	14,508	6,229
1894	22,984	15,708	7,276	1,200	1,047	12,685	6,292
1895	20,967	13,746	7,221	1,061	929	9,212	4,932
1896	15,764	10,032	5,732	820	800	9,501	4,896
1897	15,840	10,250	5,590	749	694	9,653	4,969
1898	16,159	10,438	5,721	785	752	9,749	5,294
1899	16,619	10,567	6,052	818	758	10,382	4,559
1900	16,243	11,043	5,200	661	641	11,646	5,477
1901	18,564	12,426	6,138	780	661	14,752	5,969
1902	22,301	15,600	6,701	848	732	12,120	5,969
1903	19,608	12,983	6,625	863	656		

TABLE IV.—Distribution of emigrants, by sex and age, 1853-1924 (concluded).

Year	Total	Sex		Age			
				Children		Adults	
		Males	Females	Males	Females	Males	Females
1904	22,277	14,671	7,606	889	678	13,782	6,928
1905	23,383	15,390	7,993	922	829	14,468	7,164
1906	26,385	17,211	9,174	1,188	1,092	16,023	8,082
1907	30,378	19,310	11,608	1,342	1,245	17,968	9,823
1908	30,709	19,707	11,002	1,343	1,223	18,364	9,779
1909	33,931	22,244	11,687	1,472	1,314	20,772	10,373
1910	32,361	20,451	11,910	1,419	1,281	19,032	10,629
1911	37,189	23,539	13,650	1,809	1,460	21,730	12,190
1912	35,733	21,914	13,819	1,763	1,541	20,151	12,278
1913	30,369	18,560	11,809	1,372	1,291	17,188	10,518
1914	32,506	20,025	12,481	1,565	1,254	18,460	11,227
1915	22,476	13,318	9,158	1,090	907	12,228	8,251
1916	21,163	11,932	9,231	1,215	958	10,717	8,273
1917	13,869	7,597	6,272	701	600	6,896	5,672
1918	11,660	6,097	5,563	620	534	5,477	5,029
1919	19,877	11,377	8,500	1,291	1,060	10,086	7,440
1920	32,924	17,951	14,973	. . . . . .		. . . . . .	
1921	28,559	16,019	12,540	3,383[5]		25,176[5]	
1922	28,389	15,643	12,746	3,315[5]		25,074[5]	
1923	29,668	16,037	13,631	3,354[5]		26,314[5]	
1924	30,593	16,489	14,104	3,179[5]		27,414[5]	

For reference notes see page 1014.

TABLE V.—Distribution of emigrants, by sex and country of destination, 1853-1919.

Year	Total	United Kingdom			British Possessions			Hawaii, South Sea Islands and other places		
		Males	Females	Sex not stated	Males	Females	Sex not stated	Males	Females	Sex not stated
1853	1,677[2]	30	17	15	960	238	294	73	25	25
1854	1,984[2]	15	7	10	763	224	245	397	158	165
1855	3,283[2]	18	8	2	851	255	235	1,239	419	256
1856	2,326[2]	34	13	21	987	343	71	520	192	145
1857	2,885[6]	46	29	10	1,925	410	170	56	11	8
1858	1,548[2]	109	71	..	1,004	353	7	3	1	...
1859	1,566	75	71	..	1,027	353	...	32	8	..
1860	2,871	184	122	..	1,886	568	...	79	32	...
1861	6,117	140	113	..	5,490	311	...	57	6	...
1862	13,299	238	133	..	12,394	458	...	63	13	...
1863	10,610	316	141	..	9,268	787	...	70	28	...
1864	12,404	418	168	..	10,363	1,337	...	98	20	...
1865	6,607	309	200	..	4,861	1,032	...	156	49	...
1866	7,294	313	187	..	5,373	1,018	...	306	97	...
1867	6,267	417	221	..	4,224	814	...	434	157	...
1868	7,863	302	198	..	5,865	852	...	480	166	...
1869	5,262	451	289	..	3,423	910	...	127	62	...
1870	5,547	384	212	..	3,275	1,012	...	544	120	...
1871	5,297	413	264	..	3,108	815	...	520	177	...
1872	5,752	371	257	..	3,470	873	...	576	205	...
1873	4,761	272	184	..	2,831	929	...	404	141	...
1874	5,859	555	312	..	3,538	1,070	..	274	110	...
1875	6,467	443	356	..	3,255	1,085	...	1,029	299	...
1876	6,459	645	465	..	3,865	1,264	..	167	53	...
1877	6,611	585	407	..	3,876	1,412	..	235	96	...
1878	5,761	504	334	..	3,289	1,154	...	345	135	...
1879	5,234	423	234	..	3,195	1,053	...	234	95	...
1880	7,923	383	300	..	5,083	1,686	...	350	121	...
1881	8,072	352	317	..	5,030	1,910	...	323	140	...
1882	7,456	269	195	..	4,432	2,064	...	381	115	...
1883	9,186	521	391	..	5,363	2,424	...	346	141	...
1884	10,700	901	556	..	5,984	2,686	...	418	155	...
1885	11,695	1,139	718	..	6,308	2,973	..	419	138	...
1886	15,037	1,448	937	..	8,484	3,475	...	510	183	...
1887	12,712	1,250	836	..	6,643	3,225	...	541	217	...
1888	22,781	1,223	741	..	13,239	6,730	..	586	262	...
1889	15,178	1,249	790	..	7,738	4,694	..	506	201	...
1890	16,810	1,119	744	..	9,107	5,011	...	583	246	...
1891	17,629	985	720	..	9,948	5,282	...	463	231	...
1892	13,164	952	660	..	7,051	3,853	...	466	182	...
1893	15,723	945	638	..	8,843	4,632	..	475	190	...
1894	22,984	1,001	668	..	14,282	6,449	...	425	159	...
1895	20,967	1,037	666	..	12,261	6,377	...	448	178	...
1896	15,764	977	601	..	8,628	4,915	...	427	216	...
1897	15,840	951	641	..	8,873	4,778	...	426	171	...
1898	16,159	706	493	..	9,347	5,051	...	385	177	...
1899	16,619	763	561	..	9,355	5,281	...	449	210	...
1900	16,243	711	543	..	9,766	4,429	...	566	228	...
1901	18,564	668	484	..	11,276	5,417	...	482	237	...

For reference notes see page 1014.

TABLE V.—Distribution of emigrants, by sex and country of destination, 1853-1919 (concluded).

Year	Total	United Kingdom			British Possessions			Hawaii, South Sea Islands and other places		
		Males	Females	Sex not stated	Males	Females	Sex not stated	Males	Females	Sex not stated
1902	22,301	901	596	..	14,074	5,808	...	625	297	...
1903	19,608	1,124	667	..	11,019	5,613	...	840	345	...
1904	22,277	1,115	819	..	12,618	6,379	....	938	408	...
1905	23,383	1,128	726	..	13,259	6,863	...	1,003	404	...
1906	26,385	1,508	987	..	14,726	7,841	...	977	346	...
1907	30,378	1,427	1,019	..	17,276	9,816	...	607	233	...
1908	30,709	1,507	1,128	..	17,888	9,773	...	312	101	...
1909	33,931	1,624	1,052	..	19,966	10,355	...	654	280	...
1910	32,361	1,383	1,126	..	18,099	10,397	...	969	387	...
1911	37,189	1,514	1,241	..	20,575	11,883	...	1,450	526	...
1912	35,733	1,444	1,161	..	19,352	12,215	...	1,118	443	...
1913	30,369	1,448	1,201	..	16.258	10,199	...	854	409	...
1914	32,506	1,538	1,036	..	17,449	11,054	...	1,038	391	...
1915	22,476	1,222	841	..	11,294	7,979	...	802	338	...
1916	21,163	1,196	1,412	..	9,442	7,456	...	670	363	...
1917	13,869	1,009	492	..	6,076	5,514	...	512	266	...
1918	11,660	241	204	..	5,377	5,149	...	479	210	...
1919	19,877	1,913	1,646	..	8,655	6,288	...	809	566	...

TABLE VI.—Emigration, by country of destination, distinguishing Chinese, 1870-1919.

Year	Total of all emigrants	Chinese included in foregoing column	United Kingdom	Australia	Other places
1870	5,547	. . .	596	4,274	677
1871	5,297	. . .	677	3,802	818
1872	5,752	190	628	4,148	976
1873	4,761	. . .	456	3,457	848
1874	5,859	355	867	4,225	767
1875	6,467	384	799	4,340	1,328
1876	6,459	453	1,110	4,256	1,093
1877	6,611	443	992	4,946	673
1878	5,761	299	838	4,316	607
1879	5,234	396	657	4,152	425
1880	7,923	386	683	6,506	734
1881	8,072	371	669	6,757	646
1882	7,456	168	464	6,297	695
1883	9,186	297	912	7,434	840
1884	10,700	306	1,457	8,171	1,072
1885	11,695	164	1,857	9,103	735
1886	15,037	181	2,385	11,686	966
1887	12,712	246	2,086	9,600	1,026
1888	22,781	211	1,964	19,649	1,168
1889	15,178	104	2,039	12,144	995
1890	16,810	169	1,863	13,862	1,085
1891	17,629	160	1,705	15,016	908
1892	13,164	197	1,612	10,669	883
1893	15,723	134	1,583	13,277	863
1894	22,984	143	1,669	20,488	827
1895	20,967	170	1,703	18,377	887
1896	15,764	122	1,578	13,208	978
1897	15,840	123	1,592	13,293	955
1898	16,159	93	1,199	13,619	1,341
1899	16,619	184	1,324	14,184	1,111
1900	16,243	181	1,254	12,392	2,597
1901	18,564	145	1,152	5,218	2,194
1902	22,301	87	1,497	15,670	5,134
1903	19,608	124	1,791	15,939	1,878
1904	22,277	128	1,934	18,340	2,003
1905	23,383	187	1,854	19,367	2,162
1906	26,385	133	2,495	21,722	2,168
1907	30,378	182	2,446	25,848	2,084
1908	30,709	248	2,635	26,468	1,606
1909	33,931	335	2,676	28,995	2,260
1910	32,361	298	2,509	27,100	2,752
1911	37,189	579	2,755	30,918	3,516
1912	35,733	412	2,605	30,141	2,987
1913	30,369	323	2,649	24,961	2,759
1914	32,506	537	2,574	26,693	3,239
1915	22,476	237	2,063	17,793	2,620
1916	21,163	216	2,608	16,390	2,165
1917	13,869	313	1,501	10,499	1,869
1918	11,660	214	445	9,477	1,738
1919	19,877	238	3,559	12,722	3,596

TABLE VII.—New arrivals of settlers, by sex and age, 1921-24.

Year	Total	Sex		Age			
				Under 15 years		15 years and over	
		Males	Females	Males	Females	Males	Females
1921[7]	11,135	5,929	5,206	1,134	1,106	4,795	4,100
1922	13,845	7,315	6,530	1,602	1,508	5,713	5,022
1923	11,762	.6,145	5,617	1,367	1,359	4,778	4,258
1924	14,314	7,957	6,357	1,760	1,635	6,197	4,722

TABLE VIII.—New arrivals of settlers, by occupation, 1921-24.

Year	Total	Agri-culture	Industry and mining	Transport and commerce	Domestic service and general labor	Liberal professions and public services	Other or unknown occupa-tions
1921[7]	11,135	1,038	2,101	873	1,387	810	4,926
1922	13,845	1,193	2,650	976	1,546	1,028	6,452
1923	11,762	1,086	2,035	840	1,501	743	5,557
1924	14,314	1,664	2,413	1,120	4,365	839	3,913

For reference notes see page 1014.

TABLE IX.—NEW ARRIVALS OF SETTLERS, BY SEX AND COUNTRY OF LAST RESIDENCE, 1921-24.

Country	1921[7]			1922			1923			1924		
	Total	Males	Females	Total	Males	Females	Total	Males	Females	Total	Males	Females
British Possessions:												
British Isles............	8,008	4,016	3,992	11,079	5,611	5,468	9,142	4,548	4,594	11,082	5,819	5,263
Australia..............	2,128	1,256	872	1,669	968	701	1,586	907	679	1,576	954	622
Other British possessions in Oceania...........	97	65	32	90	51	39	86	40	46	97	55	42
Canada..............	375	234	141	281	202	79	270	170	100	361	229	132
Other British possessions..	205	147	58	210	125	85	225	158	67	270	175	95
Foreign countries:												
European.............	105	70	35	160	100	60	203	146	57	650	529	121
China................	48	38	10	175	152	23	107	90	17	112	96	16
Other Asiatic countries...	17	8	9	11	7	4	12	6	6	43	24	19
Africa...............	3	3	...	3	3	...	5	3	2	1	1	...
United States.........	120	80	40	94	62	32	70	40	30	86	55	31
Other American countries.	17	8	9	19	10	9	10	8	2	3	3	...
Oceania.............	12	4	8	14	8	6	6	6	...	5	13	1
Not stated...........	...	...	...	40	16	24	40	23	17	28		15
Total..............	11,135	5,929	5,206	13,845	7,315	6,530	11,762	6,145	5,617	14,314	7,957	6,357

For reference notes see page 1014.

TABLE X.—PERMANENT DEPARTURE OF NEW ZEALAND RESIDENTS, BY SEX AND AGE, 1921-24.

Year	Total	Males	Females	Under 15 years		15 years and over	
				Males	Females	Males	Females
1921[7]	1,446	753	693	215	186	538	507
1922	2,150	1,134	1,016	262	245	872	771
1923	2,474	1,204	1,270	306	347	898	923
1924	2,256	1,130	1,126	275	283	855	843

TABLE XI.—PERMANENT DEPARTURE OF RESIDENTS, BY OCCUPATION, 1921-24.

Year	Total	Agri-culture	Industry and mining	Transport and commerce	Domestic service and general labor	Liberal professions and public services	Other or unknown occupations
1921[7]	1,446	92	147	111	99	151	846
1922	2,150	117	305	161	171	272	1,124
1923	2,474	131	342	206	218	211	1,366
1924	2,256	116	289	211	197	230	1,213

For reference notes see page 1014.

TABLE XII.—PERMANENT DEPARTURE OF RESIDENTS, BY SEX AND COUNTRY OF FUTURE RESIDENCE, 1921-24.

Country	1921[7]			1922			1923			1924		
	Total	Males	Females	Total	Males	Females	Total	Males	Females	Total	Males	Females
British Possessions:												
British Isles............	268	135	133	552	276	276	492	214	278	470	221	249
Australia............	920	478	442	1,348	713	635	1,656	803	853	1,470	730	740
Other British Possessions in Oceania.........	36	22	14	31	20	11	43	22	21	47	27	20
Canada.............	61	28	33	47	26	21	100	59	41	120	64	56
Other British Possessions.	50	23	27	45	28	17	35	19	16	32	15	17
Foreign countries:												
European............	12	9	3	24	18	6	10	8	2	24	19	5
China..............	20	19	1	15	14	1	20	14	6	19	17	2
Other Asiatic countries..	4	1	3	6	1	5	...	...	...	2	1	1
Africa.............	...	...	...	...	...	...	...	...	...	...	...	...
United States........	60	·30	·30	68	32	36	98	58	40	53	22	31
Other American countries.	7	4	3	8	4	4	15	6	9	16	14	2
Oceania............	8	4	4	6	2	4	5	1	4	3	...	3
Total..........	·1,446	753	693	2,150	1,134	1,016	2,474	1,204	1,270	2,256	1,130	1,126

For reference notes see page 1014.

TABLE XIII.—Arrivals and departures of persons of extra-European race, by race, 1912-24.

Year	Arrivals				Departures			
	Total	Chinese	Indians	Others	Total	Chinese	Indians	Others
1912	803	348	325	130	...	...	...	...
1913	589	325	133	131	...	...	...	...
1914	823	511	257	55	...	...	...	...
1915	322	265	13	44	329	237	68	24
1916	1,013	327	92	594	569	216	39	314
1917	724	272	92	360	708	313	12	383
1918	917	256	138	523	404	214	19	171
1919	708	418	193	97	322	238	18	66
1920	1,734	1,477	225	32	443	380	54	9
1921	641	255	137	249	707	368	100	239
1922	549	345	32	172	700	362	125	213
1923	729	365	115	249	632	378	66	188
1924	1,017	548	128	341	911	451	128	332

SOURCES

Statistics of New Zealand for 1853-56, 1857, 1858-69 (Auckland 1858 to 1870).

Tables I, II, IV, V (years 1853-69).

Statistics of the Dominion of New Zealand for the year 1919, vol. I, Wellington, 1920.

Tables I-VI (years 1870-1919).

Statistical Report on the External Migration of the Dominion of New Zealand for the years 1921 to 1924, Wellington, 1922 to 1925.

Tables I and IV, (years 1920-24); VII-XII (years 1921-24).

New Zealand Official Year-Book, Wellington, 1922 and 1925, 1923 and 1926.

Table XIII.

NOTES

[1]The Returns for New Plymouth and Canterbury for 1853 and 1854 are wanting; also those for Canterbury for 1856.
[2]Include immigrants whose sex and age were not stated.
[3]The Returns for children are wanting and defective for: New Plymouth, Nelson and Canterbury for 1853 and 1854, for Nelson for 1855, Auckland, Nelson and Canterbury for 1866, and Auckland and Nelson for 1857.
[4]The figures for these years relating to Australia and included in the totals are defective.
[5]After 1921, the classification is: "under 15 years" and "15 years and over"
[6]The totals for 1857 do not represent the correct addition of the preceding figures, there having been 889 immigrants and 220 emigrants with regard to whom the countries whence they arrived or to which they departed were not stated.
[7]Only for the last 9 months of the year.

TABLE I.—Distribution of Polynesian and Indian laborers introduced into Fiji, by sex and nationality, 1879-1900.

Year	Total	Males	Females	Polynesians	Indian laborers
1879[1]	2,386	2,098	288	. . . .	. . . .
1880[1]	2,534	2,500	34	. . . .	. . . .
1881[1]	1,158	1,100	58	. . . .	. . . .
1882[1]	3,072	. . . .	. . . .	2,171	901
1883[1]	Return not received.			. . . .	. . . .
1884[1]	3,272	. . . .	. . . .	1,294	1,978
1885[1]	1,546	. . . .	. . . .	300	1,246
1886[1]	1,273	. . . .	. . . .	278	995
1887[1]	276	. . . .	. . . .	276	. . . .
1888[1]	817	. . . .	. . . .	278	539
1889[1]	788	. . . .	. . . .	111	677
1890[1]	1,361	. . . .	. . . .	200	1,161
1891[1]	1,409	. . . .	. . . .	369	1,040
1892[1]	1,748	. . . .	. . . .	214	1,534
1893[1]	777	. . . .	. . . .	. . . .	. . . .
1894[1]	1,419[2]	. . . .	. . . .	. . . .	. . . .
1895	1,636	. . . .	. . . .	. . . .	. . . .
1896	1,273	. . . .	. . . .	. . . .	. . . .
1897	1,331	. . . .	. . . .	. . . .	1,331
1898	670	. . . .	. . . .	. . . .	. . . .
1899	1,029	. . . .	. . . .	. . . .	. . . .
1900	2,275	. . . .	. . . .	. . . .	. . . .

TABLE II.—Distribution of Polynesian and Indian laborers sent away from Fiji, by sex or nationality, 1879-1900

Year	Total	Males	Females	Polynesians	Indian laborers
1879[1]	345	313	32	. . . .	. . . .
1880[1]	188	170	18	. . . .	. . . .
1881[1]	884	860	24	. . . .	. . . .
1882[1]	1,139	. . . .	. . . .	1,137	2
1883[1]	Return not received.			. . . .	. . . .
1884[1]	753	. . . .	. . . .	753	. . . .
1885[1]	1,180	. . . .	. . . .	1,169	11
1886[1]	1,351	. . . .	. . . .	1,343	8
1887[1]	989	. . . .	. . . .	898	91
1888[1]	298	. . . .	. . . .	193	105
1889[1]	570	. . . .	. . . .	37	533
1890[1]	268	. . . .	. . . .	119	149
1891[1]	573	. . . .	. . . .	146	427
1892[1]	643	. . . .	. . . .	147	496
1893[1]	593	. . . .	. . . .	. . . .	. . . .
1894[1]	1,184	. . . .	. . . .	. . . .	. . . .
1895	964[2]	. . . .	. . . .	. . . .	. . . .
1896	683	. . . .	. . . .	. . . .	. . . .
1897	34	. . . .	. . . .	. . . .	. . . .
1898	669	. . . .	. . . .	. . . .	. . . .
1899	547	. . . .	. . . .	. . . .	. . . .
1900	412	. . . .	. . . .	. . . .	. . . .

For reference notes see page 1016.

TABLE III.—IMMIGRATION AND EMIGRATION, 1900-24.

	Immigrants		Emigrants		Immigrants		Emigrants
Year	East Indian indentured	Indian and Polynesian laborers	Indian and Polynesian laborers	Year	East Indian indentured	Indian and Polynesian laborers	Indian and Polynesian laborers
1900	2,275		412	1910	3,847	3,926	586
1901	2,521		561	1911	4,328	4,340	804
1902	1,585		545	1912	3,402	3,402	939
1903	1,972	Cannot	579	1913	3,289	3,289	802
1904	1,291	be	430	1914	1,572	1,572	1,465
1905	3,255	stated	381	1915	2,583	2,583	510
1906	2,760		438	1916	1,756	1,756	678
1907	3,038		711	1920	. . . . .	. . .	4,741
1908	2,468		782	1921	. . . . .	1,844	3,168
1909	2,197	2,256	507	1924	. . . . .	. . . . .	1,022

SOURCES

Statistical Tables relating to the Colonial and other Possessions of the United Kingdom. Parts XVII to XXV, London.

Tables I-II (years 1879-1900).

Statistical Abstract for the several British Overseas Dominions and Protectorates Statistical Department, Board of Trade, London, 1914, 1922, 1924.

Table III (years 1900-21).

Colonial Reports (Annual), Fiji, for 1924, p. 23.

Table III (year 1924).

NOTES

[1]Years ending June 30.
[2]Inclusive of Japanese.

NEW CALEDONIA

TABLE I.—EUROPEAN IMMIGRATION, BY NATIONALITY, AND REPATRIATION, 1879-83.

Year	Total	French	English	Other nationalities	Repatriated
1879	154	65	82	7	23
1880	111	53	53	5	32
1881	151	73	67	11	19
1882	177	76	94	7	21
1883	158	63	86	9	16
Total.........	751	330	382	39	111

TABLE II.—DISTRIBUTION OF IMMIGRANTS, BY SEX, AGE, RACE AND NATIONALITY, 1897-1924.

Year	Total			White race									Other races						Natives and others		
				French			English			Other nationalities			Chinese and Indo-Chinese			Japanese and Javanese					
	Total	Males	Females and Children	Total	Males	Females and Children	Total	Males	Females and Children	Total	Males	Females and Children	Total	Males	Females and Children	Total	Males	Females and Children	Total	Males	Females and Children
1897	390	240	150	272	134	138	33	26	7	8	4	4				63	63		14	13	1
1898	345	198	147	263	131	132	35	28	7	9	4	5							38	35	3
1899	371	176	195	319	148	171	25	15	10	13	5	8	3	2	1				11	6	5
1900	615	447	168	321	171	150	48	39	9	72	66	6	3	2	1	166	166		5	3	2
1901	753	535	218	330	168	162	56	41	15	178	176	2	1	1		4	4		184	145	39
1902	1,502	1,265	237	473	300	173	43	32	11	195	188	7	450	450					341	295	46
1903	352	208	144	270	150	120	53	35	18	18	16	2				3	2	1	8	5	3
1904	393	231	162	247	117	130	49	29	20	23	12	11	1	1					73	73	
1905	343	181	162	241	103	138	48	32	16	24	16	8							30	30	
1906	323	218	105	161	88	73	68	47	21	19	9	10	4	4					71	70	1
1907	234	127	107	170	84	86	47	33	14	10	3	7							7	7	
1908	224	119	105	160	71	89	47	34	13	7	4	3	8	8					2	2	
1909	408	307	101	162	76	86	27	19	8	15	8	7	2	2		200	200		2	2	
1910	227	114	113	193	87	106	28	21	7	6	4	2									
1911	1,262	1,140	122	171	85	86	66	37	29	57	53	4	55	55		963	960	3	5	5	
1912	615	514	101	188	97	91	25	21	4	10	4	6				270	270		67	67	
1913	469	337	132	219	102	117	38	28	10	15	10	5	191	191		188	188		9	9	
1914	726	609	117	205	93	112	39	37	2	11	10	1				256	256		20	20	
1915	292	188	104	171	86	85	58	40	18	12	10	2				47	47		5	5	
1916	438	266	172	221	67	154	52	36	16	10	5	5	3	3		142	142		11	11	
1917	295	164	131	160	48	112	51	37	14	15	14	1				74	74				
1918	298	180	118	184	80	104	77	64	13	23	10	13	7	7		11	11		8	8	
1919	430	246	184	224	73	151	69	50	19	9	3	6	7	7		114	113	1			
1920	460	216	244	355	153	202	79	44	35	13	8	5							2	2	
1921	379	154	225	326	115	211	27	19	8	8	3	5	7	7		4	4	1	2	2	
1922	285	138	147	239	105	134	30	22	8	37	10	5	2	2		2	2		4	1	
1923	946	634	312	238	106	132	64	38	26	26	14	27	607	480	127						
1924	1,638	1,515	123	175	96	79	45	25	20			12	1,392	1,380	12						

TABLE III.—DISTRIBUTION OF EMIGRANTS, BY SEX, AGE, RACE AND NATIONALITY, 1897-1924.

Year	Total			White race									Other races						Natives and others		
				French			English			Other nationalities			Chinese and Indo-Chinese			Japanese and Javanese					
	Total	Males	Females and Children	Total	Males	Females and Children	Total	Males	Females and Children	Total	Males	Females and Children	Total	Males	Females and Children	Total	Males	Females and Children	Total Males	Males	Females and Children
1897	317	211	106	196	97	99	35	33	2	4	2	2	61	60	1	1	1		20	18	2
1898	244	131	113	189	92	97	28	22	6	15	8	7	3	3					9	6	3
1899	238	136	102	161	85	76	25	15	10	29	15	14							22	20	2
1900	257	157	100	183	96	87	27	18	9	12	10	2				3	3		22	20	2
1901	423	323	100	157	88	69	49	33	16	28	25	3	10	10		53	53		37	33	4
1902	780	670	110	179	96	83	48	31	17	128	121	7	99	91	8	79	79		75	73	2
1903	456	309	147	249	131	118	35	18	17	109	103	6	271	270	1	4	4		22	16	6
1904	535	390	145	231	117	114	41	24	17	77	66	11	37	37		5	5		146	143	3
1905	499	380	119	212	111	101	48	35	13	63	58	5	35	35		10	10		86	86	
1906	499	308	191	247	109	138	62	43	19	35	24	11	80	80		33	33		97	79	18
1907	641	462	179	253	119	134	60	41	19	15	8	7	25	20	5	125	122	3	140	124	16
1908	478	339	139	210	96	114	41	26	15	8	4	4	48	48		97	97		26	25	1
1909	295	178	117	188	83	105	31	24	7	9	5	4	96	91	5	11	11		15	14	1
1910	440	227	213	212	92	120	33	21	12	12	7	5	41	41		50	35	15	95	41	54
1911	532	349	183	242	107	135	60	41	19	41	29	12	38	31	7	101	96	5	39	30	9
1912	526	366	160	244	113	131	42	28	14	23	19	4	49	46	3	141	137	4	33	29	4
1913	448	265	183	275	118	157	41	28	13	17	7	10	43	40	3	67	67		11	8	3
1914	689	509	180	272	110	162	42	37	5	3		3	37	37		252	251	1	20	11	9
1915		557		180	70	110	45	36	9	15	10	5	100	100		423	419	4	3	1	2
1916	559	372	187	238	69	169	48	35	13	7	4	3	21	21		229	227	2	33	33	
1917	647	467	180	214	73	141	63	41	22	34	20	14	4	4		116	116		218	215	3
1918	491	327	164	215	67	148	76	61	15	15	14	1	2	2		183	183		1	1	
1919	574	393	181	262	105	157	68	54	14	24	18	6	1	1		160	157	3	60	59	1
1920	548	336	212	309	135	174	74	38	36	7	5	2				149	149		9	9	
1921	580	354	226	333	126	207	20	17	3	20	8	12	3	1	2	186	184	2	18	18	
1922	499	251	248	325	113	212	44	24	20	15	5	10	2	2		104	104		9	3	6
1923	721	539	182	278	133	145	42	21	21	41	27	14	322	322		26	26		12	10	2
1924	885	564	321	379	143	236	73	38	35	22	17	5	371	328	43	24	23	1	16	15	1

TABLE IV.—Distribution of immigrants, by occupation, 1897-1924.

Year	Total	Agriculture	Transport and commerce	Domestic service and general labor	Other occupations, none or unknown
1897	390	62	78	134	116
1898	345	58	81	98	108
1899	371	79	89	74	129
1900	615	77	86	315	137
1901	753	115	95	435	108
1902	1,502	213	127	1,051	111
1903	352	45	98	89	120
1904	393	55	82	140	116
1905	343	62	99	79	103
1906	323	36	81	129	77
1907	234	13	63	53	105
1908	224	8	69	60	87
1909	408	11	75	236	86
1910	227	29	67	49	82
1911	1,262	13	78	717	454
1912	615	20	74	361	160
1913	469	14	91	232	132
1914	726	17	80	418	211
1915	292	14	63	92	123
1916	438	18	73	191	156
1917	295	9	47	104	135
1918	298	7	77	55	159
1919	430	3	58	111	258
1920	460	24	54	89	293
1921	379	36	58	74	211
1922	285	21	29	40	195
1923	946	16	29	662	239
1924	1,638	13	19	1,449	157

TABLE V.—DISTRIBUTION OF EMIGRANTS, BY OCCUPATION, 1897-1924.

Year	Total	Agriculture	Transport and commerce	Domestic service and general labor	Other occupations, none or unknown
1897	317	14	73	130	100
1898	244	15	75	61	93
1899	238	18	61	64	95
1900	257	16	66	75	100
1901	423	13	67	243	100
1902	780	14	80	589	97
1903	456	20	98	210	128
1904	535	28	93	288	126
1905	499	29	88	233	149
1906	499	29	109	121	240
1907	641	23	107	169	342
1908	478	15	70	174	219
1909	295	16	75	99	105
1910	440	14	83	213	130
1911	532	20	104	211	197
1912	526	24	96	202	204
1913	448	23	92	184	149
1914	689	19	85	269	316
1915	687	11	52	234	390
1916	559	10	74	145	330
1917	647	10	62	308	267
1918	491	5	85	86	315
1919	574	6	74	199	295
1920	548	15	43	77	413
1921	580	22	61	80	417
1922	499	14	25	53	407
1923	721	20	32	372	297
1924	885	22	36	441	386

SOURCES

Notices Coloniales, Paris, 1885.   Vol. III, p. 170.

Table I.

Information supplied by the French Government.

Tables II, III, IV, V.

HAWAII

TABLE I.—DISTRIBUTION OF IMMIGRANTS, BY SEX, AGE AND NATIONALITY (FISCAL YEARS ENDED 30 JUNE) 1907 and 1910-24.

Year	Total	Sex and age			Nationality										
		Adults		Children	Por-tuguese	Spanish	Porto-Rican	Russian	Hindu	Other Caucasian races	Chinese	Japanese	Corean	Filipino	Other
		Males	Females												
1907	4,684[1]	1,400	1,143	2,141	2,438[3]	2,246[3]	….	….	….	….	….	….	….	….	….
1910	5,379[1]	3,702	801	876	868[3]	….	….	1,790[2]	….	….	….	….	….	2,721[3]	….
1911	6,765	….	….	….	601	908	1	270	7	10	583	2,248	14	2,209[3]	206
1912	9,837	5,632	2,892	1,313	862	911	….	96	….	170	512	3,500	26	3,038	722
1913	15,086	8,723	4,346	2,017	362	2,422	….	38	13	….	586	5,015	50	5,749	830
1914	9,342	5,475	3,174	693	208	25	….	….	….	….	552	4,562	….	3,199	695
1915	5,760	3,066	2,180	514	112	24	7	….	….	103	385	3,180	….	1,244	705
1916	7,441	4,631	2,315	495	180	4	….	18	1	17	563	4,195	….	1,752	577
1917	8,343	5,288	2,430	625	159	15	….	4	1	….	471	4,029	8	2,932	720
1918	7,321	4,353	2,355	613	35	1	….	4	1	….	306	3,886	….	2,676	390
1919	7,435	4,413	2,376	646	17	….	….	3	1	….	288	3,952	….	2,727	447
1920	8,127	5,230	2,281	616	8	….	….	….	….	….	426	3,631	6	3,504	547
1921	8,224	5,369	2,193	662	46	4	….	2	….	….	563	3,753	16	3,304	538
1922	15,766	11,497	3,031	1,238	105	….	684	12	….	….	1,333	4,491	38	8,713	395
1923	12,686	8,608	2,842	1,236	90	15	2	17	….	….	1,342	3,501	24	7,348	367
1924	12,609	7,255	3,889	1,465	54	….	51	….	….	….	1,129	4,373	70	6,440	460

For reference notes see **page 1023**.

TABLE II.—DISTRIBUTION OF EMIGRANTS, BY SEX, AGE AND NATIONALITY (FISCAL YEARS ENDED 30 JUNE) 1911-24.

Year	Total	Sex and age			Nationality										
		Adults		Children	Por-tuguese	Spanish	Porto-Rican	Russian	Hindu	Other Caucasian races	Chinese	Japanese	Corean	Filipino	Other
		Males	Females												
1911	6,786	....	....	....	624	....	232	....	....	651	927	3,491	....	462	399
1912	6,356	3,712	1,170	1,474	539	534	13	150	6	....	747	3,490	65	156	656
1913	7,783	4,485	1,421	1,877	989	1,079	33	127	8	....	813	3,545	41	344	804
1914	8,050	4,807	1,418	1,825	819	754	105	239	10	....	728	3,778	41	693	883
1915	6,697	3,914	1,202	1,581	469	447	50	....	....	171	645	3,449	....	678	788
1916	6,211	3,691	1,198	1,322	474	496	210	....	....	10	604	3,068	....	697	652
1917	7,202	4,309	1,241	1,652	367	1,003	41	....	4	61	419	3,448	....	1,130	733
1918	8,885	4,982	1,444	2,459	844	838	57	47	1	....	389	4,737	....	1,470	538
1919	7,939	4,066	1,707	2,166	226	283	43	127	....	....	495	5,199	14	994	485
1920	8,709	4,657	1,880	2,172	111	136	14	13	2	....	650	5,931	33	1,300	512
1921	11,966	6,686	2,446	2,834	236	86	16	49	3	....	1,549	6,869	66	2,434	659
1922	10,464	5,625	2,317	2,522	103	82	22	22	....	....	1,393	6,140	84	2,172	443
1923	8,335	5,023	1,656	1,656	398	137	151	36	....	....	831	4,002	61	2,146	573
1924	10,231	6,403	1,979	1,849	368	242	307	25	....	....	812	4,027	26	3,769	655

SOURCE

(1) *Report of the Governor of Hawaii to the Secretary of the Interior* (for fiscal years ended June). Washington, 1911 to 1924.

All tables.

NOTES

[1] Does not include persons assisted from continental United States.
[2] Immigration assisted by Territorial Government.
[3] Introduced by the Hawaiian Sugar Planters' Association.

NAURU

TABLE I.—Distribution of immigrants (arrivals), by race or nationality, 1922-24.

Year	Total	Europeans	Chinese	Kanakas[1]	Nauruans
1922	427	70	288	68	1
1923	479	169	303	7	..
1924	461	135	325	1	..

TABLE II.—Distribution of emigrants (departures), by race or nationality, 1922-24.

Year	Total	Europeans	Chinese	Kanakas[1]	Nauruans
1922	459	62	216	175	6
1923	657	180	322	148[2]	7
1924	363	124	137	100	2

SOURCE

Report of the Administration of Nauru during the years 1922, 1923, 1924. Prepared by the Administrator for submission to the League of Nations. Printed and published for the Government of the Commonwealth of Australia by the Government Printer for the State of Victoria, 1923, 1924, 1925.

Tables I and II (years 1922-24).

NOTES

[1]These figures refer to South Sea Islanders other than Nauruans.
[2]Including 30 New Guinea natives.

NEW GUINEA

(Australian Mandate)

TABLE I.—DISTRIBUTION OF EMIGRANTS, BY SEX, NATIONALITY, RACE AND COUNTRY OF FUTURE RESIDENCE, 1923-24.

Nationality and race	Country of future residence								
	Total			Australia		Papua		British Solomon Islands	
	Total	Males	Females	Males	Females	Males	Females	Males	Females
European:									
British.........	803	556	247	525	238	4	1	27	8
American.......	3	2	1	2	1	..	..	..	..
Austrian........	1	1	...	1	...	..	.:	..	..
Belgian.........	2	2	...	2	..	..	..	..	..
Finnish.........	4	2	2	2	2	..	..	..	..
French.........	6	6	...	5	..	..	..	1	..
German........	23	15	8	15	8	..	..	..	..
Italian.........	1	1	...	1	..	..	..	..	..
Polish..........	1	1	...	1	..	..	..	..	..
Spanish.........	3	3	...	3	..	..	..	..	..
Swedish........	2	2	...	2	..	..	..	..	..
Asiatic:									
Chinese.........	348	325	23	308	23	..	..	17	..
Japanese........	12	8	4	8	4	..	..	..	..
Malay..........	18	13	5	3	..	..	..	10	5
Other:									
Melanesian......	59	59	...	59	..	..	..	..	..
Total.........	1,286	996	290	937	276	4	1	55	13

TABLE II.—Distribution of immigrants, by sex, nationality and country of last residence, 1923-24.

Nationality and race	Total			Australia		Papua		Caroline Islands		China	
	Total	Males	Females	Males	Females	Males	Females	Males	Females	Males	Females
European:											
British.....	794	552	242	542	236	9	5	..	..	1	1
American...	6	5	1	5	1	..	..	..	..	..	..
Czecho-slovakian.	1	1	...	1	...	..	..	..	..	..	..
Danish.....	1	1	...	1	...	..	..	..	..	..	..
Dutch......	10	6	4	6	4	..	..	..	..	...	..
French.....	7	5	2	5	2	..	..	..	..	...	..
German....	27	18	9	18	9	..	..	..	..	..	..
Italian......	1	1	...	1	...	..	..	..	..	..	..
Swedish....	2	2	...	2	...	..	..	..	..	..	..
Asiatic:											
Chinese.....	307	284	23	51	...	..	..	..	..	233	23
Japanese....	4	3	1	2	1	..	..	1	..	...	..
Javanese....	1	...	1	..	1	..	..	..	..	...	..
Other:											
Melanesian..	109	104	5	104	5	..	..	..	..	...	..
Polynesian..	3	1	2	1	2	..	..	..	..	...	..
Total.....	1,273	983	290	739	261	9	5	1	..	234	24

SOURCE

Report to the League of Nations on the Administration of the Territory of New Guinea from July 1, 1923 to June 30, 1924. Printed and published for the Government of the Commonwealth of Australia by H. J. Green, Government Printer for the State of Victoria.

Tables I, II.

WESTERN SAMOA
(New Zealand Mandate)

TABLE I.—DISTRIBUTION OF IMMIGRANTS, BY RACE OR PEOPLE, 1920, 1922-24.

Year	Total	Native Samoans	Europeans and half-castes	Chinese laborers	Melanesian laborers
1920	500[1]	....	...	500	..
1922[2]	1,342	807	517	18	..
1923[2]	1,242	794	448	...	..
1924[3]	1,556	1,156	399	1	..

TABLE II.—DISTRIBUTION OF EMIGRANTS, BY RACE OR PEOPLE, 1920, 1922-24.

Year	Total	Native Samoans	Europeans and half-castes	Chinese laborers	Melanesian laborers
1920	13[1]	....	...	...	..
1922[2]	1,873	1,194	414	261	4
1923[2]	1,921	982	505	434	..
1924[3]	2,012	1,273	496	207	36

SOURCE

First to Fifth Report of the Government of the Dominion of New Zealand on the Administration of the Mandated Territory of Western Samoa. Wellington, 1921 to 1925.

Tables I, II (years 1920 and 1922-24).

NOTES

[1]500 laborers recruited with the assistance of the Hongkong Government arrived in August 1920. A few men (thirteen) were repatriated on this occasion.
[2]1922 and 1923: fiscal years ended March 31 of the following year.
[3]Calendar year 1924 (migrants from January to March 1924 are evidently also included in the figures for 1923).

ALGERIA

TABLE I.—Passengers inward by sea, by country, 1893-1924.

Year	Coming from								
	Total	France	Spain	Eng-land	Italy	Mo-rocco	Tunis	Ger-many	Other countries
1893	68,999	49,385	18,354	577	503	.....	....	...	...
1894	73,675	50,468	18,127	566	425	1,439	2,255	...	395
1895	76,716	49,385	18,534	577	503	6,009	322	...	1,386
1896	89,300	56,124	21,064	349	695	10,519	265	...	284
1897	84,753	59,424	17,276	251	440	7,083	172	...	107
1898	81,787	57,791	14,922	210	350	7,656	793	...	65
1899	85,492	56,826	18,665	210	867	8,014	853	...	57
1900	97,534	68,931	18,207	254	608	8,034	1,423	...	77
1901	84,508	58,398	16,055	318	1,118	6,690	1,716	...	213
1902	111,170	73,042	21,727	407	2,648	11,642	1,353	...	351
1903	116,852	71,216	22,710	205	1,486	18,927	1,976	...	332
1904	120,695	66,594	27,788	703	1,153	21,862	2,055	...	540
1905	143,883	83,368	32,544	56	1,683	21,937	3,531	...	764
1906	142,349	85,680	25,738	139	2,126	21,936	3,232	...	3,498
1907	127,444	79,444	21,466	86	1,695	18,838	2,948	...	2,967
1908	137,138	80,633	31,115	41	1,438	21,145	1,990	..	776
1909	136,703	87,352	25,168	21	2,100	17,111	1,673	...	3,278
1910	146,376	87,465	30,268	84	1,806	21,548	1,996	...	3,214
1911	161,964	111,075	30,206	200	2,501	14,024	1,478	...	2,480
1912	178,309	115,634	35,940	563	2,327	20,103	562	...	3,180
1913	195,253	131,384	34,904	670	2,519	22,388	835	262	2,291
1914	166,598	118,671	23,727	481	1,453	17,546	477	...	4,243
1915	144,279	114,331	16,512	50	237	11,472	45	...	1,632
1916	173,979	150,275	9,974	48	165	10,341	79	...	3,097
1917	211,047	201,547	1,654	12	102	4,859	1,645	...	1,228
1918	179,706	147,145	54	5	....	7,717	106	...	24,679
1919	281,629	262,434	6,559	...	3	11,922	53	...	658
1920	193,934	170,945	10,145	7	25	8,354	4	...	4,454
1921	179,764	159,012	9,326	17	68	7,792	....	...	3,549
1922	167,462	146,932	8,720	9	208	8,061	1,315	...	2,217
1923	209,945	180,897	9,431	374	466	16,178	57	...	2,542
1924	218,941	201,157	7,988	522	382	5,049	18	...	3,825

TABLE II.—Passengers outward by sea, by country, 1893-1924.

Year	Proceeding to							
	Total	France	Spain	Eng-land	Italy	Morocco	Tunis	Other countries
1893	63,569	45,886	17,059	366	258	.....	....	....
1894	77,912	46,687	20,693	167	285	7,741	2,153	186
1895	78,814	45,886	17,059	366	258	8,455	177	6,613
1896	80,417	48,327	16,523	229	334	14,011	252	741
1897	71,112	49,345	13,483	145	327	7,524	232	56
1898	75,739	54,390	9,506	168	274	10,338	1,040	23
1899	79,755	54,243	13,245	202	557	10,102	1,398	8
1900	87,555	61,728	13,687	239	237	10,055	1,553	56
1901	87,665	51,869	16,114	289	537	14,360	2,063	2,433
1902	110,920	70,682	19,040	306	2,413	14,207	2,212	2,060
1903	105,985	66,804	18,443	95	1,233	17,075	1,845	490
1904	119,548	64,711	22,869	453	786	27,447	2,605	677
1905	135,283	83,597	24,475	11	726	21,905	3,365	1,204
1906	133,124	84,230	23,135	19	1,000	20,194	3,438	1,108
1907	131,882	88,359	19,385	18	925	17,267	2,767	3,161
1908	131,509	77,786	22,076	17	1,522	26,171	2,070	1,867
1909	126,866	83,957	24,177	16	2,290	13,091	1,560	1,775
1910	143,635	81,322	25,203	253	2,351	32,192	1,085	1,229
1911	163,264	101,100	26,977	124	3,091	29,121	1,311	1,540
1912	162,732	99,287	30,208	465	3,023	27,439	471	1,839
1913	192,499	126,190	30,854	531	2,919	28,747	308	2,950
1914	220,479	149,571	46,652	527	3,061	18,846	732	1,090
1915	153,211	124,186	17,885	62	416	10,310	36	316
1916	198,088	175,402	12,890	69	321	7,367	104	1,935
1917	217,832	204,596	2,334	27	264	5,745	2,445	2,421
1918	192,243	186,215	19	...	...	5,332	3	674
1919	221,498	196,197	5,720	...	3	17,738	29	1,811
1920	195,237	160,945	11,947	...	5	13,844	1	8,495
1921	174,130	145,616	6,865	4	274	15,662	23	5,686
1922	188,141	168,955	8,458	9	293	6,719	177	3,530
1923	217,351	198,859	9,089	271	740	4,322	46	4,024
1924	220,209	202,712	8,187	51	533	4,293	....	4,433

TABLE III.—Natives embarked for and returned from France, 1923-24.

Year	Departed	Returned	Year	Departed	Returned
1923	58,586	36,990	1924	71,028	57,467

SOURCES

Information supplied by the General Government of Algeria.

Tables I and II.

Bulletin du Ministère du Travail et de l'Hygiène Publique (formerly *Bulletin de l'Office du Travail*). Paris, Nos. 4, 5, 6, April, May, June, 1926, p. 248.

Table III.

TUNIS

The statistics are based on the provisions of a Decree of April 13, 1898, regulating the registration of aliens. Every alien intending to reside in Tunis is required within five days of his arrival to make a declaration to this effect to the local police. A separate form must be filled in for every member of a family, with the exception of children who are not able to earn their own living. Should the place of residence be changed, notice must be given within two days to the local police.

The Decree of July 24, 1916, extended the above requirement of compulsory notification to all aliens born in Tunis and 16 years of age as well as to aliens who subsequently become residents.

TABLE I.—DISTRIBUTION OF IMMIGRANT ALIENS, BY NATIONALITY, 1903-24.

Nationality	1903	1904	1905	1906	1907	1908	1909	1910	1911	1912	1913	1914	1915	1916	1917	1918	1919	1920	1921	1922	1923¹	1924¹
German	25	48	60	54	48	75	71	59	44	63	49	66				2			4	7	9	12
American	1	2	4	2	3		5	2	4	5	5	1	2	2	4	2		7	13	25	17	15
Anglo-Maltese	66	218	212	183	164	205	213	211	307	445	733	477	309	246	275	286	375	329	275	345	216	117
English																	45	13	70	58	42	49
Austrian	29	23	33	19	93	79	19	15	41	12	11	17	1	19	41	29	40	25	29	7	15	15
Belgian	22	32	32	19	17	27	22	15	18	11	25	17	33			1			2	4	38	24
Bulgarian																			2	1	1	5
Chinese																						2
Chilian					2	1	2					3	2	1	2	1	2	1				
Danish	2	2	4	14	2	1	2		3	2				1		1	4	1	1	3	2	1
Egyptian																	3	2	48	64	27	3
Spanish	53	92	69	69	59	51	63	72	43	25	33	32	69	46	51	34	68	39	76	59	62	25
Greek	20	44	61	31	40	45	33	23	30	32	24	43	25	17	28	6	39	27	14	18	15	39
Netherlander		10	13	7	8	3	6	4	2	3	14	4	11	4	4	4	4	14	4	4		15
Italian	4,631	11,882	7,986	7,714	8,918	10,539	6,197	5,258	4,097	3,521	4,424	3,874	2,646	2,674	2,948	2,449	2,795	3,954	3,560	3,498	2,121	1,992
Japanese													4							2	2	3
Luxemburger							3										3	2	7	9	4	
Mexican											1	1			1						3	
Norwegian	1	2	2	2	1	2	3	4			1	1		2		2	1	1	4	4	1	6
Persian	2			1	1	1	1	6		2		7	2	2	2		4	4	9	13	1	1
Portuguese	3	1	1	1	6	8	2	7	9	4	3	6	5	1	4	4	117	14	7	4	3	10
Rumanian	5	6	12	8	19	8	6	1	7	47	4	2	2		2	5	8	4	450	570	109	53
Russian	5	16	7	2	4	1	1			34	24	48	59	19	31	46	39	54	9	4	4	8
Swedish																			84	78	71	89
Swiss		48	39	32	36	34	42	37	44	34	24	48	59	19	31	46	39	54				
Czechoslovak																			4	4	13	20
Turkish	52	125	230	193	124	78	12	12	2	4	2	3	14	2		4	6	6	45	1	32	21
Finnish														2	2			1	1	1		1
Syrian																						1
Serb, Croat and Slovene¹																	13	25	21	5	5	7
Total	4,918	12,541	8,766	8,351	9,549	11,160	6,698	5,729	4,652	4,213	5,351	4,605	3,189	3,039	3,387	2,875	3,479	4,506	4,740	4,830	2,718	2,534

For reference notes see page 1032.

TABLE II.—DISTRIBUTION OF EMIGRANT ALIENS, BY NATIONALITY, 1903-24.

Nationality	1903	1904	1905	1906	1907	1908	1909	1910	1911	1912	1913	1914	1915	1916	1917	1918	1919	1920	1921	1922	1923²	1924³
German		25	49	36	46	39	46	40	24	17	27	47	20	3	5	1			3	4	4	10
American		3	1	2		1	2		2		2	2	4					5	19	19	12	12
Anglo-Maltese		193	175	155	212	128	167	161	155	88	141	187	219	325	349	275	241	186	189	250	118	55
English																		18	64	29	36	31
Austrian		27	17	12	30	67	101	10	10	8	6	8	6	29	25	19	19		4	4	11	9
Belgian		31	8	25	7	8	18	8	4	1	4	7							14	17	14	14
Bulgarian																			1			4
Chinese																			1		3	2
Chilian																						
Danish		1					1				2	4		2		2	1	1	1		1	1
Egyptian			2	10	1		1											2	4	1	1	2
Spanish		59	35	42	32	27	29	20	21	7	7		13	64	21	39	35	28	54	29	14	17
Greek		41	45	28	36	20	22	22	13	13	8	8	10	14	14	17	18	16	39	48	41	11
Netherlander	1	6	3	2	2	3	5	2	1	1	1	3	3	8	3		4	2	6	11	8	7
Italian		6,131	4,836	5,112	4,465	4,219	3,398	3,037	2,859	2,016	2,090	3,047	1,910	2,149	1,850	2,130	2,859	2,469	1,854	2,475	782	873
Japanese											2		1	2	1	1	1					1
Luxemburger																			4	5	3	
Mexican		2		1					2			2		1			1			2		2
Norwegian							1					1				1			1		1	
Persian									1	1	1	1	1	1	1	1		1	2	4	1	
Portuguese		3	3		4	1	2	4	1	1		3	1	2	1		2	2	8	7	2	4
Rumanian		5	12	3	11	3	2	1	1	3	1	5	3		3	3	4	7		1	88	24
Russian		2	2		2	2	9	9	1	1	1	5		10	8	10	4	4	120	140		7
Swedish		23	6	26	21	19	34	42	19	13	20	34	22	25	17	34	21	29	59	34	51	74
Swiss		23	25	26	21	19	34	42	19	13	20	34	22	25	17	34	29	29	59	34	51	74
Czechoslovak																			2		8	16
Turkish		75	142	129	89	48	17	12	6	13	13		3	4	3	5	4	3	24	14	12	9
Finnish																						
Serb, Croat and Slovene¹																	7	15	14	31	2	5
Total	1	6,627	5,359	5,583	4,960	4,587	3,846	3,372	3,119	2,181	2,312	3,367	2,216	2,640	2,302	2,537³	3,257	2,805	2,483	3,126	1,217	1,192

SOURCE

Information supplied by the French Government (City of Tunis, Police Commissioner of Immigration).

NOTES

¹Serbs and Yugoslavs were given separately in the source, but have been combined here.
²In the years 1923 and 1924 the figures do not include the children but only the declarations of residence (men and women).
³The figures given for the different nationalities total 2,538.

EGYPT

According to the explanations in the *Statistique de l'Egypte* for 1873, p. xii, the first two columns of table I refer to passengers arriving from or departing to Europe or the Levant from Alexandria and Port Said mainly. Inasmuch as the transmigrants are shown separately, the difference between the annual arrivals and departures represents the number of aliens who have stayed for some time in Egypt, including residents who return from a journey.

The caravans naturally proceed by land routes.

TABLE I.—ARRIVALS, 1873-77.

Year	By ocean-going shipping (civilians)		By coastal shipping (civilians)	By caravan (by the El Arich route)
	For Egypt	In transit		
1873	54,834	44,470	4,401	3,577
1874	39,813	40,433	5,838	4,157
1875	34,361	42,447	5,842	2,146
1876	24,626	41,943	5,590	2,903
1877	20,992	46,092	6,213	6,543
Total...	174,626	215,385	26,884	19,325

TABLE II.—DEPARTURES, 1873-77.

Year	By ocean-going shipping (civilians)		By coastal shipping (civilians)	By caravan (by the El Arich route)
	For Egypt	In transit		
1873	41,550	46,199	4,072	2,697
1874	29,970	40,750	4,763	2,503
1875	20,996	41,051	3,739	387
1876	18,143	40,366	4,088	491
1877	21,482	43,920	3,860	632
Total.....	132,141	212,286	20,522	6,710

SOURCE

Essai de Statistique Générale de l'Egypte, 1873-77.   Cairo, 1879, vol. I. p. 37-41.

Tables I and II.

MOROCCO

The Inspectorate of Immigration and Emigration in Morocco was instituted by a Decree of the Vizier of June 8, 1915.

The statistics are based on the embarking and landing tickets which every passenger is required to deliver to the Port Commissioner. The latter tickets distinguish at present between travellers residing in Morocco and those who arrive there for the first time. A distinction is also made between immigrants and tourists.

Until 1923, all persons arriving in Morocco for the first time were counted as immigrants. Most of them were unable to make a definite declaration, as they did not know whether they would stay for long or permanently. Tourists proper thus far have been few.

Emigrants are all those who leave the country without intending to return. The embarking ticket requires information on this point.

TABLE I.—DISTRIBUTION OF ALIEN IMMIGRANTS THROUGH CASABLANCA, BY NATIONALITY, 1916-24.

Nationality	1916	1917	1918	1919	1920	1921	1922	1923	1924
French	1,980	1,714	1,994	6,688	7,062	8,731	5,306	3,682	2,739
Spanish	697	565	630	1,640	1,613	1,966	1,056	532	337
Italian	423	183	90	621	1,027	1,571	737	382	206
English	99	41	55	193	383	284	199	63	46
Algerian	57	11	21	56	48	73	55	46	13
Tunisian	36	10	6	19	30	40	30	15	4
Belgian	17	13	13	100	122	124	111	57	92
Swiss	73	51	35	75	146	194	112	106	87
Portuguese	29	31	35	142	516	241	95	48	25
Greek	48	34	24	35	52	61	29	33	35
Egyptian	1	1	5	2	2	9	...	2	1
Lebanese	1	...	...	...	6	3	3	9	4
Netherlander	1	5	3	4	8	23	22	7	5
Montenegrin	1	...	...	...	...	...	...	...	...
Norwegian	1	...	1	2	3	7	1	1	2
Syrian	2	6	2	...	34	14	9	11	13
Rumanian	4	...	1	7	5	8	3	3	1
Alsatian	5	...	5	1	...	...	...	...	...
Senegalese	12	5	4	19	8	22	7	19	17
Ottoman	16	20	7	4	2	7	7	27	11
Russian	6	2	6	5	19	18	120	10	19
Bulgarian	2	3	...	1	1	3	...	...	...
Armenian	2	...	1	2	4	6	9	2	...
Argentinian	5	1	...	...	9	5	3	1	6
American	4	3	3	10	58	70	81	11	8
Luxemburger	2	2	1	3	2	4	5	5	2
Austrian	...	1	...	...	1	...	...	2	2
Cuban	...	3	...	...	3	...	1	...	1
Danish	...	1	2	17	11	15	8	2	4
Swedish	...	1	...	9	14	19	2	2	5
Venezuelan	...	1	...	...	...	...	...	...	...
Chilian	...	4	...	...	1	1	1	...	...
Serbian	...	2	2	2	4	11	14	4	4
Monegasque	...	1	...	...	...	1	...	...	...
Mexican	...	1	...	...	...	...	2	...	...
Brazilian	...	...	3	6	9	6	5	4	2
Peruvian	...	...	2	...	...	1	...	...	...
Polish	...	...	1	5	11	13	14	6	16
Rhode Islander	...	...	1	2	5	2	1	4	4
Albanian	...	...	...	1	...	5	...	...	...
German	...	...	...	2	2	4	3	1	1
Special protégés	...	...	...	18	...	...	...	...	...
Czechoslovak	...	...	...	1	4	8	5	10	5
Hindu	...	...	...	2	...	...	...	...	...
Japanese	...	...	...	1	...	...	...	...	...
Persian	...	...	...	...	4	3	...	...	...
Andorran	...	...	...	...	2	3	...	...	...
Indian	...	...	...	...	1	15	24	14	4
Uruguyan	...	...	...	...	1	...	2	...	1
Lithuanian	...	...	...	...	1	...	...	...	...
Ukrainian	...	...	...	...	1	...	...	...	...
Finnish	...	...	...	...	2	...	...	...	...

TABLE I.—DISTRIBUTION OF ALIEN IMMIGRANTS THROUGH CASABLANCA, BY NATIONALITY, 1916-24 (concluded).

Nationality	1916	1917	1918	1919	1920	1921	1922	1923	1924
Estonian	...	...	...	...	...	2	...	4	...
Madagascan	...	...	...	...	...	1	...	...	...
Bolivian	...	...	...	...	...	2	...	...	...
Chinese	...	...	...	...	...	1	6	2	...
Irish	...	...	...	...	...	1	...	1	...
Dominican	...	...	...	...	...	...	2	...	...
Arab	...	...	...	...	...	...	1	...	...
Tripolitan	...	...	...	...	...	...	...	8	...
Canadian	...	...	...	...	...	...	...	1	1
Hungarian	...	...	...	...	...	...	...	3	1
Anglo-Maltese	...	...	...	...	...	...	...	8	4
Serb,Croat and Slovene	...	...	...	...	...	...	...	1	...
Martinique	...	...	...	...	...	...	...	2	...
Liechtensteiner	...	...	...	...	...	...	...	2	...
Sudanese	...	...	...	...	...	...	...	...	1
Gambian	...	...	...	...	...	...	...	...	1
Palestinian	...	...	...	...	...	...	...	...	1
Colombian	...	...	...	...	...	...	...	...	1
Saarese	...	...	...	...	...	...	...	...	1
Cyprian	...	...	...	...	...	...	...	...	1

TABLE II.—DISTRIBUTION OF EMIGRANTS THROUGH CASABLANCA, BY NATIONALITY, 1916-24.

Year	Total	French	Spanish	Italian	Other nationalities
1916[1]	667	*	*	*•	*
1917	1,677	*	*	*	*
1918	1,342	*	*	*	*
1919	3,202	*	*	*	*
1920	3,769	2,400	675	281	413
1921	5,078	2,977	989	422	690
1922	5,505	3,371	904	523	707
1923	5,391	3,500	620	675	596
1924	4,444	3,056	428	524	436

SOURCE

Information supplied by the French Government (Ministry of Labor. Resident General of Morocco).

NOTE

[1]Seven months (June-December) only.

TABLE III.—Distribution of alien emigrants, by nationality, 1920-24.

Nationality	1920	1921	1922	1923	1924
French	2,400	2,977	3,371	3,500	3,056
Spanish	675	989	904	620	428
Italian	281	422	523	675	524
English	113	171	145	84	38
Portuguese	50	163	166	95	39
Swiss	34	61	73	81	63
Algerian	37	39	35	38	36
Tunisian	11	27	19	18	6
Belgian	40	54	64	39	66
Netherlander	5	14	16	9	7
Norwegian	1	3	..	..	1
Danish	6	8	3	1	1
Greek	43	31	35	36	37
Russian	3	5	10	13	14
American	19	28	53	22	4
Persian	1	2	..	3	..
Polish	4	2	9	10	10
Lebanese	2	..	1	2	4
Syrian	11	16	11	17	12
Swedish	5	10	3	3	..
Senegalese	6	3	10	17	31
Brazilian	4	3	2	7	3
German	1	4	1	..	1
Serbian	2	4	2	11	1
Armenian	1	7	3	6	.
Luxemburger	2	1	3	1	4
Ottoman	3	2	10	11	6
Ukranian	1	..	..	..	..
Finnish	2	..	..	1	..
Egyptian	5	5	3	2	3
Japanese	1	..	..	..	..
Indian	..	7	16	16	6
Rumanian	..	4	3	2	1
Czechoslovak	..	4	1	7	8
Chilian	..	1	2	..	..
Bolivian	..	1	..	..	..
Peruvian	..	3	..	2	..
Argentinian	..	1	2	1	6
Chinese	..	1	4	4	..
Rhode Islander	..	1	..	9	..
Austrian	..	2	1	3	3
Lithuanian	..	1	..	..	..
Cuban	..	1	..	2	..
Mexican	..	..	..	..	2
Venezuelan	..	..	1	..	..
Hungarian	..	..	..	3	1
Anglo-Maltese	..	..	..	11	15
Serb, Croat and Slovene	..	..	..	4	..
Bulgarian	..	..	..	1	1
Somali	..	..	..	1	..
Uruguayan	..	..	..	1	..
Dominican	..	..	..	2	..
Sudanese	..	..	..	..	1
Palestinian	..	..	..	..	2
Colombian	..	..	..	..	..
San Marino	..	..	..	..	2
Albanian	..	..	..	..	1

BASUTOLAND

TABLE I.—EMIGRATION OF NATIVES, 1907-24.

Year[1]	With labor passes	With visiting passes, miscellaneous[2]	Total	Year	With labor passes	With visiting passes, miscellaneous[2]	Total
1907–8	78,863	51,463	130,326	1914–15	29,523[3]	. . . . . .	. . . . . .
1908–9	68,870	43,723	112,593	1920	58,305	103,999	162,304
1909–10	82,000	55,300	137,300	1921	67,829	50,442	118,271
1910–11	84,600	51,100	135,700	1922	57,663	59,529	117,192
1911–12	66,900	41,754	108,654	1923	76,202	33,194	109,396
1912–13	77,244	59,422	136,666	1924	88,627	41,841	130,468
1913–14	90,816	53,184	144,000	. . . .	. . . . . .	. . . . . .	. . . . . .

TABLE II.—DISTRIBUTION OF EMIGRANT NATIVES WITH LABOR PASSES, BY COUNTRY OF DESTINATION, 1907-08 AND 1908-09.

Year[1]	Total	Country of destination			Occupation		
		Orange River Colony	Cape Colony	Transvaal	Farm and domestic	Miscellaneous	Railway construction
1907–08	78,863	3,943	2,898	15,593	15,523	33,948	6,958
1908–09	68,870	5,406	1,659	15,489	12,046	28,783	5,487

SOURCES

Colonial Reports (Annual). Basutoland. London, 1910-25.

Tables I (years 1907/08-1914/15 and 1922/24); II (years 1907/08-1908/09).

Information supplied by the British Government (Ministry of Labor).

Table I (years 1920, 1921).

NOTES

[1]1907/08-1910/11, years ended June 30, 1911-12, 9 months ended March 31, 1912/13-1914/15, years ended March 31.
[2]For visiting purposes and passes issued to men on their own affairs.
[3]Native laborers who proceeded to work on the gold mines only.

A. EAST AFRICA PROTECTORATE
TABLE I.—PASSENGERS INWARD AND OUTWARD, BY RACE, 1908-09—1913-14.

Year[1]	Inward			Outward		
	Total	Europeans	Natives	Total	Europeans	Natives
1908–09	8,225	2,418	5,807	7,582	1,508	6,074
1909–10	10,287	1,882	8,405	8,516	1,389	7,127
1910–11	7,861	2,016	5,845	6,642	1,572	5,070
1911–12	11,250	2,794	8,456	7,636	1,889	5,747
1912–13	12,738	3,608	9,130	8,326	2,081	6,245
1913–14	15,040	3,897	11,143	8,581	2,359	6,222

B. COLONY AND PROTECTORATE OF KENYA
TABLE II.—DISTRIBUTION OF IMMIGRANTS, BY SEX AND RACE, 1920-24.

Year	Total	Europeans, Americans, and Eurasians		Indians	Goans	Arabs	Others, viz., Seychelloises, Cingalese, natives of Africa, Chinese, etc.	
		Males	Females	Males		Females	Males	Females
1920	15,879	3,020	1,685	8,237		1,698	1,005	234
1921	12,125	2,635	1,663	5,275		1,215	1,098	239
1922	10,491	3,088		5,966			1,437	
1923	10,504	2,845		4,406	583	2,670	.....	
1924	12,636	3,412		5,775	739	970	1,740	

C.—KENYA, UGANDA AND TANGANYIKA TERRITORY COMBINED
TABLE III.—DISTRIBUTION OF IMMIGRANTS AND EMIGRANTS, BY RACE, 1923-24.

Race	Immigrants		Emigrants[2]	
	1923	1924	1923	1924
European..................	3,430	4,079	3,374	3,236
Indian....................	6,075	7,973	4,433	4,380
Goan.....................	688	890	582	628
Arab.....................	867	1,044	...	491
Others...................	2,014	1,871	...	1,589
Total.................	13,074	·15,857	8,389[3]	10,324

SOURCES

Colonial Reports (Annual). East Africa Protectorate. London, 1910-15.
Table I (years 1908/09-1913/14).
Colonial Reports (Annual). Colony and Protectorate of Kenya. London, 1923-26.
Table II (years 1920-24); III (years 1923-24).

NOTES

[1]Years ending March 31.
[2]There is at present no machinery for the collection of emigration statistics, but shipping figures show that 3,260 Europeans, and 7,184 non-Europeans left Mombasa Port during the year 1922. It is not known what proportion of these emigrants were from Kenya, as opposed to persons proceeding to Uganda and Tanganyika via Mombasa. No information available in respect of the years 1920 and 1921. (Information supplied by the British Government.)
[3]Sum of available figures.

MAURITIUS

TABLE I.—IMMIGRANTS INTO MAURITIUS SINCE THE ABOLITION OF SLAVERY,
BY COUNTRY OF ORIGIN, 1834-75.

Year	Total	East Indies	Ibo, East Coast of Africa	Mada-gascar	Reunion	Aden	China	Direct from cap-tured slavers
1834 to 1839	25,468	25,468	...	...	...	...	...	...
1843	32,096	31,258	...	...	...	...	838	...
1844	14,152	14,152	...	...	...	...	...	...
1845	10,290	10,285	...	...	...	..	5	...
1846	6,789	6,789	...	...	...	...	...	...
1847	5,729	5,729	...	...	...	...	...	...
1848	5,303	5,303	...	...	...	...	...	...
1849	7,282	7,282	...	...	...	...	...	...
1850	9,823	9,823	...	...	...	...	...	...
1851	9,334	9,295	...	39	...	...	...	...
1852	16,796	16,796	...	...	. .	...	...	...
1853	12,144	12,144	...	...	...	...	...	...
1854	18,516	18,516	...	...	...	...	...	...
1855	12,915	12,915	...	...	...	...	...	...
1856	13,811	12,854	325	...	...	632	...	...
1857	12,725	12,725	...	...	...	...	...	...
1858	29,946	29,946	...	...	...	...	...	...
1859	44,397	44,397	...	...	...	...	...	...
1860	14,016	13,286	...	...	...	...	...	730
1861	14,553	13,985	...	...	...	...	...	568[1]
1862	10,092	9,893	...	...	...	...	...	199[2]
1863	5,254	5,254	...	...	...	...	...	...
1864	7,575	7,575	...	...	...	...	...	...
1865	20,402	20,278	...	...	...	...	...	124
1866	5,647	5,596	...	...	...	...	...	51
1867	483	....	...	...	350	...	...	133
1868	3,077	1,886	...	17	722	...	...	452[2]
1869	1,828	1,682	...	146	...	...	...	...
1870	4,076	4,076	...	...	...	...	...	...
1871	3,292	3,292	...	...	...	...	236[2]	...
1872	6,009	5,773	...	...	...	...	...	...
1873	7,614	7,614	...	...	...	...	...	...
1874	6,984	6,984	...	...	...	...	...	...
1875	2,928	2,928	...	...	...	...	...	...

For reference notes see page 1047.

TABLE II.—Distribution of Indian immigrants arrived and departed, by sex, 1834-1920.

Year	Arrivals			Departures		
	Total	Males	Females	Total	Males	Females
1834	75	75	..	4	4	...
1835	1,254	1,182	72	26	25	1
1836	3,823	3,639	184	190	187	3
1837	7,292	6,939	353	134	114	20
1838	11,808	11,567	241	154	148	6
1839	1,035	933	102	173	170	3
1840	116	107	9	422	394	28
1841	542	499	43	1,089	995	94
1842	83	73	10	2,115	2,021	94
1843	34,525	30,218	4,307	2,992	2,884	108
1844	11,549	9,709	1,840	2,461	2,312	149
1845	10,971	8,918	2,053	2,662	2,492	170
1846	7,339	5,718	1,621	2,760	2,556	204
1847	5,830	5,174	656	1,784	1,651	133
1848	5,395	4,739	656	3,015	2,639	376
1849	7,425	6,378	1,047	4,892	4,298	594
1850	10,030	8,436	1,594	3,725	3,283	442
1851	10,020	8,257	1,763	3,269	2,895	374
1852	17,485	13,671	3,814	2,426	2,034	392
1853	12,144	9,877	2,267	2,028	1,767	261
1854	18,484	14,995	3,489	3,675	3,166	509
1855	12,915	9,645	3,270	4,267	3,702	565
1856	12,653	9,130	3,523	4,897	4,220	677
1857	12,725	8,640	4,085	4,603	3,794	809
1858	29,946	20,932	9,014	8,165	6,707	1,458
1859	44,397	31,643	12,754	5,117	4,146	971
1860	13,286	9,070	4,216	2,833	2,290	543
1861	13,985	10,232	3,753	2,257	1,786	471
1862	9,893	7,440	2,453	2,212	1,752	460
1863	5,254	3,667	1,587	3,220	2,553	667
1864	7,552	5,626	1,926	3,413	2,692	721
1865	20,283	14,910	5,373	3,521	2,854	667
1866	5,596	3,702	1,894	3,815	2,925	890
1867	350	317	33	3,398	2,571	827
1868	2,608	1,968	640	2,544	1,880	664
1869	1,772	1,182	590	2,320	1,684	636
1870	4,076	2,831	1,245	2,842	2,172	670
1871	3,292	2,318	974	3,074	2,369	705
1872	5,774	4,015	1,759	3,819	2,788	1,031
1873	7,614	5,226	2,388	3,035	2,160	875
1874	7,052	4,818	2,234	4,075	2,874	1,201
1875	2,919	1,996	923	3,423	2,368	1,055

TABLE II.—Distribution of Indian immigrants arrived and departed, by sex, 1834-1920 (concluded).

Year	Arrivals			Departures		
	Total	Males	Females	Total	Males	Females
1876	502	330	172	3,271	2,354	917
1877	2,187	1,528	659	2,417	1,794	623
1878	4,826	3,203	1,623	2,352	1,825	527
1879	3,079	2,013	1,066	2,555	1,926	629
1880	742	371	371	2,345	1,731	614
1881[3]	....	....	....	1,551	1,180	371
1882	1,241	805	436	1,863	1,466	397
1883	1,915	1,283	632	2,406	1,766	640
1884	6,389	4,450	1,939	1,853	1,362	491
1885	358	246	112	4,001	2,891	1,110
1886	746	511	235	2,320	1,649	671
1887	264	191	73	2,350	1,707	643
1888	713	482	231	1,731	1,283	448
1889	4,532	3,244	1,298	1,319	990	329
1890	3,025	2,152	873	1,055	827	228
1891	991	713	278	900	716	184
1892[3]	....	....	....	1,478	1,129	349
1893	485	353	132	1,654	1,197	457
1894	1,026	758	268	968	754	214
1895	1,734	1,249	485	1,135	860	275
1896	801	593	208	1,155	858	297
1897	426	314	112	919	671	248
1898[3]	....	....	....	1,106	842	264
1899[3]	....	....	....	746	564	182
1900	2,890	2,094	796	1,151	858	293
1901	4,574	3,265	1,309	631	469	162
1902	2,565	1,875	690	648	462	186
1903	508	374	134	523	383	140
1904	2,057	1,513	544	561	413	148
1905	720	534	186	419	314	105
1906	618	463	155	615	435	180
1907	586	439	147	511	366	145
1908[3]	....	....	....	1,041	775	266
1909[3]	....	....	....	686	512	174
1910	532	397	135	585	403	182
1911[3]	....	....	....	491	364	127
1912[3]	....	....	....	457	338	119
1913[3]	....	....	....	353	264	89
1914[3]	....	....	....	381	277	104
1915[3]	....	....	....	353	240	113
1916[3]	....	....	....	495	343	152
1917[3]	....	....	....	2	1	1
1918[3]	....	....	....	....	....	...
1919[3]	....	....	....	6	6	...
1920[3]	....	....	....	36	27	9

For reference notes see page 1047.

TABLE III.—TOTAL AND INDIAN INDENTURED IMMIGRATION AND TOTAL EMIGRATION, BY COUNTRY, 1900-24.

Year	Immigrants			Emigrants	
	East Indian indentured	From the United Kingdom	From all countries	To the United Kingdom	To all countries
1900	1,975[4]	Cannot be stated	6,869	107	4,242
1901	2,909	"	....	50	4,338
1902	1,743	"	8,676	8	6,239
1903	355	"	5,587	2	5,780
1904	1,456	"	2,065[5]	69	4,017
1905	520	..	4,262	449	4,850
1906	440	184	4,405	162	3,402
1907	429	106	3,618	631	3,607
1908	....	155	3,504	440	3,670
1909	....		3,884	244	3,175
1910	387		3,292	148	3,341
1911	....	Cannot be stated	4,281	197	3,111
1912	....	"	3,691	226	4,282
1913	....	"	3,812	324	5,071
1914	....	"	3,714	237	4,146
1915	....	36	2,799	140	3,093
1916	....	16	3,027	101	2,518
1917	....	..	1,295	8	3,134
1918	....	..	1,008	5	3,714
1919	....	10	1,648	45	4,329
1920	....	9	3,523	383	3,621
1921	....	33	4,809	192	3,243
1922	....	..	4,821	....	4,529
1923	....	..	2,593[6]	....	1,515[7]
1924	....	..	1,261[8]	....	2,123[7]

For reference notes see page 1047.

TABLE IV.—DISTRIBUTION OF INDIAN IMMIGRANTS, BY SEX AND AGE, 1860-1910.

Year	Total[9]	Infants		Children		Adults	
		Males	Females	Males	Females	Males	Females
1860	13,286	168	195	890	683	8,014	3,336
1861	13,196	181	187	740	606	9,311	2,171
1862	9,893	109	107	527	413	6,804	1,933
1863	5,254	57	76	388	332	3,222	1,179
1864	7,575	88	93	416	305	5,145	1,528
1865	20,283	168	174	1,410	1,114	13,332	4,085
1866	5,596	57	64	592	516	3,053	1,314
1867	350	1	2	6	9	310	22
1868	2,608	30	9	137	107	1,801	524
1869	1,682	15	20	122	83	1,045	397
1870	4,076	50	41	240	176	2,541	1,028
1871	3,292	31	47	160	98	2,127	829
1872	5,774	99	93	356	266	3,560	1,400
1873	7,614	163	136	430	311	4,633	1,941
1874	7,052	206	175	456	341	4,156	1,718
1875	2,914	78	72	185	146	1,733	700
1876	502	13	15	16	16	301	141
1877	2,187	35	54	130	95	1,363	510
1878	4,826	137	140	316	245	2,750	1,238
1879	3,079	35	33	215	186	1,758	852
1880	580	3	7	41	47	313	159
1881[3]	....	...	...	...	...	....	....
1882	1,241	12	24	103	81	690	331
1883	1,915	31	30	118	101	1,134	501
1884	6,389	74	91	337	299	4,039	1,549
1885	355	3	5	31	21	212	83
1886	736	4	10	31	51	466	74
1887	274	2	1	10	14	89	58
1888	707	2	12	41	41	433	178
1889	4,547	64	81	349	264	2,833	956
1890	3,025	36	24	212	169	1,904	680
1891	977	13	14	56	52	630	212
1892[3]	....	...	...	..	...	....	...
1893	485	10	10	11	11	332	111
1894	1,026	14	9	26	25	718	234
1895	1,734	42	29	67	58	1,153	385
1896	742	7	1	19	16	508	191
1897	426	8	...	19	16	287	96
1898[3]	....	...	...	...	...	....	....
1899[3]	....	...	...	...	...	....	....
1900	3,038	75	84	113	118	1,976	672
1901	4,593	135	112	222	182	2,909	1,023
1902	2,570	41	28	91	84	1,743	583
1903	508	5	8	14	9	355	117
1904	2,055	20	24	37	35	1,454	485
1905	720	3	4	11	11	520	171
1906	618	7	4	16	7	440	144
1907	586	1	3	9	2	429	142
1908[3]	....	...	...	...	...	....	....
1909[3]	....	...	...	...	...	....	....
1910	....	...	...	...	...	....	....

For reference notes see page 1047.

TABLE V.—Distribution of Indian emigrants, by sex and age, 1860-1909.

Year	Total[9]	Infants		Children		Adults	
		Males	Females	Males	Females	Males	Females
1860	2,833	32	24	160	141	2,098	378
1861	2,257	18	17	129	131	1,639	323
1862	2,212	21	21	114	123	1,617	316
1863	3,220	22	20	177	162	2,354	485
1864	3,413	38	26	227	188	2,427	507
1865	3,621	27	29	186	188	2,641	550
1866	3,815	38	35	256	256	2,631	599
1867	3,398	28	23	218	241	2,325	563
1868	2,544	17	15	223	166	1,640	483
1869	2,320	9	14	136	150	1,539	472
1870	2,842	18	12	225	180	1,929	478
1871	3,074	15	16	197	204	2,157	485
1872	3,819	27	23	307	284	2,454	724
1873	3,035	21	14	174	230	1,965	631
1874	4,075	34	46	331	315	2,509	840
1875	3,473	48	54	311	345	2,009	706
1876	3,271	33	24	239	233	2,082	660
1877	2,417	23	19	175	177	1,596	427
1878	2,352	15	18	147	128	1,663	381
1879	2,583	28	17	183	183	1,715	457
1880	2,345	26	11	162	167	1,543	436
1881	1,551	9	9	90	96	1,081	266
1882	1,863	...	...	11	14	1,455	383
1883	2,406	14	17	160	154	1,592	469
1884	1,863	4	12	104	102	1,254	387
1885	4,021	29	31	296	280	2,566	819
1886	2,320	7	9	147	141	1,495	521
1887	2,353	9	12	166	149	1,535	482
1888	1,731	4	8	91	56	1,188	384
1889	1,329	5	6	61	55	936	266
1890	1,055	3	...	25	29	799	199
1891	902	2	3	42	26	674	155
1892	1,478	7	4	70	69	1,052	276
1893	1,635	4	14	117	96	1,058	346
1894	969	7	1	52	31	696	182
1895	1,135	4	4	72	52	784	219
1896	1,196	3	3	115	74	781	220
1897	....	...	...	...	...	....	....
1898	1,068	4	3	58	49	733	221
1899	746	3	4	49	38	512	140
1900	1,142	4	6	79	63	768	222
1901	178	...	...	...	...	143	35
1902	109	...	...	...	1	90	18
1903	541	21	5	29	22	352	112
1904	654	6	5	46	21	416	160
1905	441	3	1	31	25	294	87
1906	535	3	2	14	15	379	122
1907	511	3	4	26	23	337	118
1908	933	3	10	45	41	640	194
1909	686	7	3	45	35	460	136

For reference notes see page 1047.

TABLE VI.—Distribution of immigration and emigration, by sex and race, 1923-24.

Year	Total	Males	Females	Indian population exclusive of immigrants[10]			Immigrant population[11]			Indo-Mauritians			Chinese		
				Total	Males	Females	Total	Males	Females	Total	Males	Females	Total	Males	Females
IMMIGRANTS															
1923	2,593	2,126	467	631	538	93	559	394	165	356	282	74	1,047	912	135
1924	1,261[8]	841	420	...	...	...	...	...	...	...	...	...	...	...	...
EMIGRANTS															
1923	1,515	1,263	252	425	343	82	21	5	6	292	231	61	777	674	103
1924	2,123	1,691	432	584	477	107	533	361	172	226	175	51	780	678	102

For reference notes see page 1047.

SOURCES

General Reports of the Emigration Commissioners for the years 1850, 1861, and 1873. London.

Table I (years 1834-72).

Colonisation Circular, No. 34, issued by Her Majesty's Colonial Land and Emigration Commissioners, London, 1877.

Table I (years 1873-75).

Statistical Abstract for the several British Overseas Dominions and Protectorates, London, 1914, 1921, 1924.

Table III (years 1900-21).

Mauritius Almanack, 1886 to 1920, St. Louis.

Table II (years 1834-1920); IV and V (years 1875-1909).

Mauritius Blue-Book for 1860 to 1874. Report on Immigration.

Tables IV and V (years 1860-74).

Colonial Reports (Annual). Mauritius, 1924. London, 1925.

Table III (year 1924) (immigration).

Information supplied by the British Government (Ministry of Labor).

Tables II and VI (years 1923, 1924).

NOTES

General Note.—The figures published in the various sources do not agree in every year. No precise explanation can be given of these differences. (See Introduction.)

[1] 202 of these were landed in the Seychelles.
[2] Landed in the Seychelles.
[3] No Indian immigrants were introduced into the Colony in these years.
[4] Excluding the number of women and children.
[5] Indian coolies only.
[6] Immigrants by nationality and sex, see table IV.
[7] Emigrants by nationality and sex, see table V.
[8] "New Immigrants", no other description given in the source.
[9] In the source, figures for men, women, boys, girls, male and female infants are given for each port separately. The yearly totals have been obtained by adding all these figures.
[10] This term is intended to mean all persons except Indo-Mauritions.
[11] Persons of any nationality, who, having arrived in the colony, left during the same year, and who—as immigrants—are included in the figures for the other categories.

NYASALAND.

TABLE I.—DISTRIBUTION OF EMIGRANTS AND IMMIGRANTS (NATIVES[1] AND ALIENS[2]),
BY RACE, 1912-24.

Year	Emigrants				Immigrants			
	Total	Euro-peans	Natives	Hindus	Total	Euro-peans	Natives	Hindus
1912–13	1,831	274	1,390	167	4,271	362	3,740	169
1913–14	2,248	309	1,835	104	3,020	357	2,538	125
1920	6,642	506	6,099	37	4,479	913	3,533	33
1921	7,774	377	7,194	203	7,217	521	6,419	277
1922	5,562	484	4,758	320	6,549	515	5,607	427
1923	4,074[3]	491	....	170	....	451	....	227
1924	6,548[3]	566	....	147	....	599	....	252

TABLE II.—ALIENS IN TRANSIT, OUTWARD AND INWARD, 1923-24.

Year	Outward		Inward	
	Europeans	Hindus	Europeans	Hindus
1923	145	92	124	100
1924	129	42	95	55

Sources

Colonial Reports (Annual). Nyasaland, London, 1915-25.

Table I (years 1912/13-1924); II (1923-24).

Communication of the British Government (Ministry of Labor).

Table I (years 1923-24).

NOTES

[1]Natives leaving the country for work in Rhodesia or elsewhere. Largely a seasonal movement.
[2]Exclusive of persons merely passing through the country.
[3]These figures refer to persons emigrating but whether they relate to the total or to natives only is not stated.

ST. HELENA

TABLE I.—Immigration and emigration, 1900–24.

Year	Immigrants[1]		Emigrants		Year	Immigrants[1]		Emigrants	
	From the United Kingdom	From all countries	To the United Kingdom	To all countries		From the United Kingdom	From all countries	To the United Kingdom	To all countries
1900	..	.....	..	697	1912	22	72	13	90
					1913	15	40	29	95
1901	..	...	..	748	1914	44	64	41	70
1902	..	1,164	..	6,174[2]	1915	23	60	16	63
1903	..	66	..	129					
1904	..	81	..	83	1916	..	58	..	54
1905	36	69	30	85	1917	..	38	..	54
					1918	..	23	..	79
1906	19	38	46	97	1919	..	33	..	163
1907	35	72	36	183	1920	..	101	..	83
1908	29	55	27	72					
1909	22	43	14	79	1921	..	67	..	144
1910	12	27	25	203	1922	..	102	..	174
					1923	..	101	..	191
1911	74	122	30	186	1924	..	130	..	149

SOURCES

Statistical Abstract for the several British Overseas Dominions and Protectorates. Statistical Department, Board of Trade, London, 1914, 1922, 1924.

Table I (years 1900-21).

Colonial Reports (Annual). St. Helena. Report for 1924, p. 7.

Table I (years 1923, 1924).

Information supplied by the British Government (Ministry of Labor).

Table I (year 1922).

NOTES

[1]Excluding visitors.
[2]Including prisoners of war.

SEYCHELLES

TABLE I.—Arrivals and departures[1], 1900-24.

Year	Arrivals	Departures	Year	Arrivals	Departures
1900	900	593	1912	183	160
			1913	311	456
1901	606	537	1914	394	367
1902	491	434	1915	339	325
1903	171	175			
1904	418	348	1916	265	941
1905	284	259	1917	587	381
			1918	101	280
1906	295	446	1919	305	429
1907	373	227	1920	213	427
1908	384	225			
1909	350	329	1921	252	305
1910	350	329	1922	380	318
			1923	304	254
1911	471	359	1924	278	476

SOURCES

Statistical Abstract for the several British Overseas Dominions and Protectorates.
Statistical Department, Board of Trade, London, 1914, 1922, 1924.

Table I (years 1900-21).

Information supplied by the British Government (Foreign Office).

Table I (year 1922).

Information supplied by the British Government (Ministry of Labor).

Table I (years 1923, 1924).

NOTE

[1]Travellers from and to all countries.

SOMALILAND PROTECTORATE

TABLE I.—Distribution of emigrants and immigrants, by race, 1908-12.

Year	Emigrants		Immigrants		
	Europeans and whites	Somalis	Europeans and whites	Somalis	Indians
1908	..	3,209	8	3,753	...
1909	10	2,824	1	3,488	...
1910	..	3,013	0	2,853	...
1911	4	....	3	....	...
1912	16	2,583	37	2,783	340

SOURCE

Colonial Reports (Annual). Somaliland Protectorate. London, 1909-13.

Table I (years 1908-12).

SOUTH AFRICA

I. STATISTICS OF CAPE OF GOOD HOPE, ORANGE FREE STATE AND NATAL
(Tables I-IV)

The figures for the migrants from and to the United Kingdom and from and to all countries for the years since 1900 (tables II and III) generally give the total number of persons that arrived at, and departed from, Port Natal and Cape ports by sea. In consequence of the formation of the Union of South Africa, however, the figures from 1910 onwards do not include passengers from one Union port to another. Further, figures for the Cape prior to 1906 give the number of *adults* (*i. e.* including children calculated at the ordinary scale as adults.)[1]

II. UNION STATISTICS OF ARRIVALS AND DEPARTURES
(Tables V-VIII)

The *Official Year Book of the Union of South Africa* publishes for 1910-23 statistics of arrivals and departures by sea. New arrivals and permanent departures after 1913 (including visitors, transit passengers, and others) are given separately. (The figures for 1924 have been calculated; see Notes 6 and 9.) Tables VI-XIII since 1918 include migrants passing the land frontiers. These relate to Europeans, Asiatics and colored persons of mixed race, the aboriginal natives of the Bantu race being excluded.[2]

III. UNION STATISTICS OF IMMIGRATION AND EMIGRATION
(Tables VIII-XX)

A more detailed and improved questionnaire for the collection of migration statistics in the Union was introduced by the South African Government in 1924, which makes it possible now to distinguish immigrants intending permanent residence and emigrants relinquishing domicile from "holiday visitors" and travellers "in transit". In table XVIII, emigrants relinquishing domicile are described as "South Africans". A comparison of their distribution according to British and other nationalities in the same table with the preceding table shows that the figures are for emigrants of European origin who had settled permanently in South Africa.

At the Union seaports permanent immigration officers undertake the enumeration and collection of particulars, while the agents of shipping companies assist in the issue of statistical forms to passengers leaving the

[1]*Statistical Abstract for the several British Overseas Dominions and Protectorates*, London, 1914, pp. 12 and 13.
[2]*Official Year Book of the Union of South Africa*, No. 6. 1910-22, Pretoria, 1924, p. 165.

Union by sea.   At the continental border stations officials of the Railway Administration or of the frontier police issue forms to, and collect forms from, all passengers travelling on single journey tickets crossing the border by train.

The data, however, cannot be considered flawless.   In fact, the working of the new system in its earlier years was less satisfactory than was expected.   The details collected from railway passengers are especially incomplete.[1]

[1]See Union of South Africa. *Statistics of Migration to and from the Union*, 1920 to March 1925, pp. 1 and 2.

NATAL

TABLE I.—NATAL IMMIGRATION (EUROPEAN AND COOLIE) AND EMIGRATION, 1880-1900.

Year[1]	Immigrants					Emigrants
	Total	European			Coolies	Total
		Total	Free	Assisted		
1880	1,403	287	. . .	. . .	1,116	*
1881	2,547	874	596	278	1,673	*
1882	3,447	835	360	475	2,612	*
1883	3,074	1,448	. . .	. . .	1,626	*
1884	3,098	694	. . .	. . .	2,404	*
1885	3,287	324	123	201	2,963	*
1886	1,313	74	. . .	. . .	1,239	1,062
1887	232	5	. . .	. . .	227	1,119
1888	967	26	. . .	. . .	941	2,004
1889	1,154	212	. . .	. . .	942	1,860
1890	4,124	755	. . .	. . .	3,369	1,665
1891	4,883	475	. . .	. . .	4,408	1,453
1892	3,764	581	. . .	. . .	3,183	930
1893	3,216	339	. . .	. . .	2,877	1,069
1894	2,633	not stated	. . .	. . .	2,633	724
1895	3,450	not stated	. . .	. . .	3,450	764
1896	4,105	154[2]	. . .	154	3,951	1,788
1897	6,312	261	. . .	261	6,051	1,497
1898[3]	6,153	214	. . .	214	5,939	929
1899[3]	1,530	230	. . .	230	1,300	912
1900[3]	5,607	172	. . .	172	5,435	665

For reference notes see page 1066.

TABLE II.—Natal arrivals from and departures to the United Kingdom and all countries, 1900-12.

Year	Immigrants			Emigrants	
	East Indian indentured	Total		To the United Kingdom	To all countries
		From the United Kingdom	From all countries		
1900	5,435		24,125		16,857
1901	7,345		26,867		15,120
1902	6,528		35,382		24,308
1903	4,965	Cannot	36,093	Cannot	18,042
1904	7,692		50,681		22,207
1905	7,917	be	58,592	be	21,470
1906	11,641		41,609		24,460
1907	6,486	stated	21,964	stated	40,055
1908	3,174		18,403		46,026
1909	2,487		22.378		29,961
1910	7,935		17,867		14,676
1911	7,722	6,233	17,583	5,576	13,325
1912	1,673	6,037	11,424	7,872	14,433

CAPE OF GOOD HOPE

TABLE III.—Arrivals from and departures to the United Kingdom and all countries, 1900-12.

Year	Immigrants		Emigrants	
	From the United Kingdom	From all countries	To the United Kingdom	To all countries
1900	18,435	29,848	11,760	21,163
1901	19,980	30,852	11,831	20,984
1902	34,778	59,060	12,196	22,151
1903	47,573	61,870	18,969	29,615
1904	23,876	32,282	22,050	33,651
1905	22,946	33,775	19,353	34,533
1906	21,598	34,041	22,409	40,180
1907	19,250	29,767	23,054	39,550
1908	17,525	27,498	19,517	32,929
1909	19,550	30,445	15,961	29,697
1910	23,814	31,281	16,095	26,913
1911	27,656	37,544	23,324	32,875
1912	24,811	30,602	21,320	27,764

ORANGE FREE STATE AND TRANSVAAL

TABLE IV.—IMMIGRATION INTO ORANGE FREE STATE AND THE TRANSVAAL, 1903-07.

Year	Orange Free State (British immigrants under assisted passage scheme)	Transvaal (Chinese indentured immigrants)
1903	189	. . . . . .
1904	255	. . . . . .
1905	182	43,296[4]
1906	. . .	10,642[4]
1907	. . .	5,358[4]

UNION OF SOUTH AFRICA

TABLE V.—ARRIVALS AND DEPARTURES AND NEW ARRIVALS, 1910-22.

Year	Immigrants disembarked	Emigrants embarked	Immigrants by sea arrived for the first time	Year	Immigrants disembarked	Emigrants embarked	Immigrants by sea arrived for the first time
1910	49,123	41,575	*	1917	6,858	11,988	2,079
1911	55,127	46,200	*	1918	6,579	8,474	3,044
1912	42,026	42,197	*	1919	23,801	21,279	9,038
1913	39,827	42,741	14,251	1920	47,913	29,945	22,816
1914	34,027	42,631	9,047	1921	42,926	33,618	20,933
1915	17,487	27,220	5,158	1922	32,518	32,429	13,235
1916	13,096	23,167	3,846				

TABLE VI.—DISTRIBUTION OF NEW ARRIVALS, BY SEX AND AGE, 1913–24.

Year	Total	Sex		Sex and age					
		Males	Females	Minors (under 16 years)			Adults		
				Total	Males	Females	Total	Males	Females
1913	14,251	7,990	6,261	2,065	. . .	. . .	12,186	. . . .	. . . .
1914	9,047	4,958	4,089	1,189	. . .	. . .	7,858	. . . .	. . . .
1915	5,158	2,675	2,483	945	486	459	4,213	2,189	2,024
1916	3,846	1,792	2,054	657	354	303	3,189	1,438	1,751
1917	2,079	1,180	899	395	245	150	1,684	935	749
1918	4,565	2,959	1,606	. . . .	. . .	. . .	. . . .	. . . .	. . . .
1919	9,608	5,006	4,602	. . . .	. . .	. . .	. . . .	. . . .	. . . .
1920	22,095[5]	11,795	10,300	. . . .	. . .	. . .	. . . .	. . . .	. . . .
1921	20,933[5]	10,911	10,022	. . . .	. . .	. . .	. . . .	. . . .	. . . .
1922	13,235[5]	6,890	6,345	. . . .	. . .	. . .	. . . .	. . . .	. . . .
1923	11,641[5]	6,161	5,480	. . . .	. . .	. . .	. . . .	. . . .	. . . .
1924	16,409[6]	. . . .	. . . .	. . . .	. . .	. . .	. . . .	. . . .	. . . .

For reference notes see page 1066.

TABLE VII.—DISTRIBUTION OF NEW ARRIVALS, BY OCCUPATION AND SEX; (a) BY SEA, 1913-17; (b) BY LAND AND BY SEA, 1918-23.

Year	Total	Leisured, professional, and business classes			Mechanics and skilled artisans			Laborers and unskilled workers		
		Total	Males	Females	Total	Males	Females	Total	Males	Females
1913	14,251	3,442	...	...	1,786	...	...	774	...	...
1914	9,047	2,548	...	...	1,023	...	...	550	...	...
1915	5,158	1,424	926	498	661	629	32	236	235	1
1916	3,846	1,197	649	548	332	310	22	212	212	..
1917	2,079	893	567	326	202	195	7	50	50	..

Year	Shop assistants and clerks			Hawkers and petty traders			Domestic servants			Unclassified (including minors)		
	Total	Males	Females	Total	Males	Females	Total	Males	Females	Total	Males	Females
1913	1,453	...	...	877	...	...	749	...	...	5,170	...	...
1914	959	...	...	364	...	...	462	...	...	3,141	...	...
1915	441	298	143	61	44	17	234	40	194	2,101	503	1,598
1916	379	205	174	25	10	15	218	19	199	1,483	387	1,096
1917	135	105	30	6	3	3	65	7	58	728	253	475

TABLE VII.—DISTRIBUTION OF NEW ARRIVALS, BY OCCUPATION AND SEX; (a) BY SEA, 1913-17; (b) BY LAND AND BY SEA, 1918-23 (concluded).

Year	Total	Professional			Domestic			Commercial			Transport and communications			Industrial		
		T.	M.	F.	T.	M.	F.	T.	M.	F.	T.	M.	F.	T.	M.	F.
1918	4,565	968	756	212	268	44	224	431	404	27	278	269	9	417	409	8
1919	9,608	1,360	1,034	326	2,483	59	2,424	715	671	44	365	359	6	789	753	36
1920	22,816	3,555	2,313	1,242	5,100	172	4,928	2,463	1,905	558	685	653	32	2,840	2,524	316
1921	21,880	3,167	1,897	1,270	5,045	168	4,877	2,276	1,825	451	691	664	27	2,946	2,626	320
1922	14,003	1,642	960	622	358	125	233	1,229	940	289	232	230	2	1,175	987	188
1923[7]	12,604	1,152	629	523	251	72	179	864	670	194	171	169	2	742	644	98

Year	Agricultural			Mining			Independent or indefinite			Dependents			Unspecified		
	T.	M.	F.	T.	M.	F.	T.	M.	F.	T.	M.	F.	T.	M.	F.
1918	159	152	7	104	103	1	554	100	454	1,097	647	450	289	75	214
1919	498	492	6	145	144	1	680	157	523	2,302	1,292	1,010	271	45	226
1920	1,135	1,095	40	367	367		1,477	574	903	4,385	2,363	2,022	809	283	526
1921	785	759	26	351	349	2	937	523	414	4,527	2,416	2,111	1,155	281	874
1922	463	446	17	78	78	·	2,705	1,713	992	4,946	1,552	3,394	1,175	356	819
1923[7]	349	342	7	31	31	·	4,282	2,741	1,541	3,901	1,261	2,640	861	212	649

For reference notes see page 1066.

TABLE VIII.—DISTRIBUTION OF NEW ARRIVALS, BY NATIONALITY, 1913-23.

Nationality	1913	1914	1915	1916	1917	1918	1919	1920	1921	1922	1923
British subjects:											
United Kingdom and British Colonies	9,855	6,443	4,029	2,671	....	....	....	....	....	....	....
British Asiatic	87	56	115	139	....	....	....	....	....	....	....
Other	67	24	29	29	....	....	....	....	....	....	....
Total British	10,009	6,523	4,173	2,839	1,467	3,280	8,330	19,109	16,782	10,968	9,712
African (non-British)	....	....	....	....	....	4	....	2	2	....	....
American (South)	10	7	8	....	3	17	15	12	31	118	26
American (United States)	293	203	146	182	191	206	219	400	394	199	326
Austro-Hungarian	74	41	....	2	....	1	1	1	7	5	17
Belgian	318 [8]	256 [8]	186 [8]	207 [8]	189 [8]	300	427	999	941	579	990
Chinese	225	117	48	100	26	21	18	11	63	20	51
Dutch (Holland)	98	57	37	21	21	89	16	378	431	160	174
French	....	....	13	....	....	45	55	149	152	110	82
German	724	411	....	....	....	18	78	257	277	285	315
Greek	133 [8]	97 [8]	43 [8]	46 [8]	21 [8]	19	20	56	74	37	53
Italian						22	22	156	194	134	139
Japanese	....	....	8 [8]	....	....	9	24	10	5	6	2
Spanish	57	56 [8]	73	41	63 [8]	4	14	17	10	3	6
Portuguese	....	....	8 [8]	....	....	223	127	105	149	139	75
Rumanian						27	113	37	14	13	5
Russian	1,737	815	176	96	29 [8]	46	4	513	1,416	200	86
Norwegian	447	376	221	267	56	86	49	215	101	153	193
Danish						23	7	47	38	29	25
Swedish						26	37	76	70	46	26
Swiss	67	51	18	30	6	22	23	111	120	68	49
Turkish (Ottoman)	12	9	4	1	....	....	....	....	9	3	3
Lithuanian	....	....	....	....	....	....	....	....	....	477	190
Polish	....	....	....	....	....	....	....	....	....	124	31
Other	47	28	12	14	7	77	9	155	600	127	28
Total foreign	4,242	2,524	995	1,007	612	1,285	1,278	3,707	5,098	3,035	2,892
Grand total	14,251	9,047	5,158	3,846	2,079	4,565	9,608	22,816	21,880	14,003	12,604

For reference notes see page 1066.

TABLE IX.—Distribution of new arrivals, by race, 1913-23.

Year	Total	European	Hebrew	Asiatic	African	Mixed and other races
1913	14,251	12,231	1,804	131	38	47
1914	9,047	8,080	872	65	13	17
1915	5,158	4,806	193	120	15	24
1916	3,846	3,547	122	143	8	26
1917	2,079	1,868		191	20	
1918	4,565	4,045		520		
1919	9,608	8,871		737		
1920	22,816	22,135		681		
1921	21,880	21,107		773		
1922	14,003	13,411		592		
1923	12,604	12,027		577		

TABLE X.—DISTRIBUTION OF NEW ARRIVALS, BY OCCUPATION AND COUNTRY OF LAST RESIDENCE, 1918-23.

Country	Year	Total	Professional	Domestic	Commercial	Transport and communications	Industrial	Agricultural	Mining	Independent or indefinite	Dependents	Unspecified
Total	1918	4,565	968	268	431	278	417	159	104	554	1,097	289
	1919	9,608	1,360	2,483	715	365	789	498	145	680	2,302	271
	1920	22,816	3,555	5,100	2,463	685	2,840	1,135	367	1,477	4,385	809
	1921	21,880	3,167	5,045	2,276	691	2,946	785	351	937	4,527	1,155
	1922	14,003	1,641	357	1,222	232	1,177	466	78	2,690	4,964	1,176
	1923	12,604	1,152	251	864	171	742	349	31	4,282	3,901	861
United Kingdom	1918	906	276	62	68	95	74	45	19	112	103	52
	1919	6,188	875	1,839	361	183	370	314	69	521	1,483	173
	1920	16,036	2,633	3,706	1,797	391	2,078	659	251	1,069	2,904	548
	1921	14,136	2,164	3,356	1,387	363	2,112	511	238	643	2,657	705
	1922	8,569	1,080	238	759	140	819	306	55	1,478	2,928	766
Rhodesia	1918	613	82	8	59	11	45	20	20	71	250	47
	1919	145	24	21	13	1	16	15	7	5	37	6
	1920	300	63	71	38	10	22	19	11	13	51	2
	1921	220	29	52	22	13	18	10	15	9	49	3
	1922	388	25	4	23	2	15	8	8	173	122	8
Africa, British	1918	904	200	58	93	52	106	35	10	97	192	61
	1919	677	147	122	48	25	106	34	2	22	140	31
	1920	989	166	192	90	34	104	86	5	62	225	25
	1921	683	133	143	50	46	46	48	3	35	146	33
	1922	600	65	28	29	19	13	20	.....	204	187	35
Africa, non-British	1918	513	115	31	58	27	66	9	7	55	114	31
	1919	323	40	73	40	31	42	25	11	4	45	12
	1920	627	110	114	76	51	63	23	13	41	120	16
	1921	901	98	191	120	54	150	26	12	48	159	43
	1922	565	54	19	74	15	26	9	5	179	156	28

TABLE X.—Distribution of new arrivals, by occupation and country of last residence, 1918-23 (concluded).

Country	Year	Total	Professional	Domestic	Commercial	Transport and communications	Industrial	Agricultural	Mining	Independent or indefinite	Dependents	Unspecified
Australia........	1918	192	62	20	11	5	13	1	2	15	43	20
	1919	365	73	74	48	18	35	14	7	18	70	8
	1920	874	112	192	95	18	116	55	16	50	197	23
	1921	906	141	230	93	16	109	43	14	45	158	57
	1922	654	73	16	51	4	54	28	2	119	264	43
New Zealand.....	1918	6	..	1	3	1	..	..	..	..	1	..
	1919	56	15	3	9	1	6	8	2	2	8	2
	1920	89	11	20	2	1	5	12	3	6	27	2
	1921	79	11	23	13	1	5	10	..	2	8	6
	1922	60	7	1	4	1	6	1	..	11	21	8
United States....	1918	142	51	7	18	10	8	1	10	3	28	6
	1919	222	45	42	42	3	16	4	7	13	47	3
	1920	381	73	70	58	10	37	9	15	24	78	7
	1921	432	108	85	54	6	42	15	15	17	83	7
	1922	275	45	4	28	..	14	7	1	68	100	8
Europe.........	1918	367	75	12	52	53	59	26	25	40	15	10
	1919	715	76	77	76	82	159	52	38	77	57	21
	1920	2,544	282	498	223	134	370	249	48	171	408	161
	1921	3,617	402	696	435	180	424	93	50	118	933	286
	1922	2,008	194	39	216	41	209	66	6	362	622	253
Asia..........	1918	557	32	60	40	15	16	12	4	98	230	50
	1919	723	36	203	67	8	18	10	1	10	361	9
	1920	769	69	205	66	10	32	12	2	25	324	24
	1921	776	59	235	88	9	25	23	2	17	305	13
	1922	841	91	8	37	9	19	18	1	86	545	27
Other countries....	1918	365	75	9	29	9	30	10	7	63	121	12
	1919	194	29	29	11	13	21	22	1	8	54	6
	1920	207	36	32	18	26	13	11	3	16	51	1
	1921	130	22	34	14	3	15	6	2	3	29	2
	1922	43	7	..	1	1	2	3	..	10	19	..

TABLE XI.—DISTRIBUTION OF PERMANENT DEPARTURES BY SEA, BY SEX, 1918-24.

Year	Total	Sex	
		Males	Females
1918	9,696	6,166	3,530
1919	10,114	5,938	4,176
1920	9,846[5]	5,565	4,281
1921	13,476[5]	7,771	5,705
1922	12,675[5]	7,309	5,366
1923	12,666[5]	7,239	5,427
1924	13,445[9]	.....	.....

TABLE XII.—DISTRIBUTION OF PERMANENT DEPARTURES, BY OCCUPATION AND SEX, 1918-22.

Occupation	Total	1918		1919			1920			1921			1922		
		Males	Females	Total	Males	Females	Total	Males	Females	Total	Males	Females	Total	Males	Females
Total	9,696	.....	.....	10,114	.....	.....	13,032	.....	.....	15,769	.....	.....	14,695	.....	.....
Professional	1,463	1,121	342	1,239	873	366	1,728	1,237	491	1,825	1,251	574	1,139	717	422
Domestic	666	103	563	2,078	86	1,992	2,654	109	2,545	3,120	157	2,963	282	147	135
Commercial	1,020	936	84	880	804	76	1,402	1,256	146	1,433	1,300	133	1,227	1,105	122
Transport and communications	404	380	24	446	438	8	451	438	13	415	401	14	272	271	1
Industrial	1,786	1,622	164	1,568	1,515	53	1,824	1,711	113	3,359	2,771	588	999	936	63
Agricultural	398	382	16	488	474	14	775	757	18	697	681	16	403	396	7
Mining	263	261	2	234	232	2	345	241	104	237	235	2	221	221	
Independent or indefinite	969	150	819	341	134	207	682	365	317	618	409	209	4,281	2,994	1,287
Dependents	1,995	1,070	925	2,517	1,298	1,219	2,770	1,367	1,403	3,062	1,526	1,536	4,781	1,292	3,489
Unspecified	732	141	591	323	84	239	401	179	222	1,003	467	536	1,090	466	624

For reference notes see page 1066.

TABLE XIII.—DISTRIBUTION OF PERMANENT DEPARTURES, BY OCCUPATION AND COUNTRY OF FUTURE RESIDENCE, 1918-22.

Country	Year	Total	Professional	Domestic	Commercial	Transport and communications	Industrial	Agricultural	Mining	Independent or indefinite	Dependents	Unspecified
Total	1918	9,696	1,463	666	1,020	404	1,786	398	263	969	1,995	732
	1919	10,114	1,239	2,078	880	446	1,568	488	234	341	2,517	323
	1920	13,032	1,728	2,654	1,402	451	1,824	775	345	682	2,770	401
	1921	15,769	1,825	3,120	1,433	415	3,359	697	237	618	3,062	1,003
	1922	14,695	1,139	282	1,227	272	999	403	221	4,281	4,781	1,090
United Kingdom	1918	594	136	26	52	78	77	25	36	52	47	65
	1919	3,732	524	862	272	175	326	70	129	197	1,011	166
	1920	4,687	761	1,133	446	173	401	91	116	373	990	203
	1921	5,995	899	1,505	578	179	613	135	113	355	980	638
	1922	6,460	689	138	563	159	575	101	112	991	2,394	738
Rhodesia	1918	3,031	406	148	327	83	325	152	129	444	749	268
	1919	475	58	123	46	8	69	36	27	3	94	11
	1920	743	134	153	76	14	130	100	30	23	61	22
	1921	826	125	199	100	20	121	77	32	40	91	21
	1922	843	79	34	88	15	98	60	22	200	210	37
Africa, British	1918	1,696	440	103	160	97	125	143	10	175	299	144
	1919	2,388	413	507	223	74	148	311	25	72	536	79
	1920	2,784	444	622	209	85	155	411	21	102	664	71
	1921	2,034	388	453	177	69	113	242	10	62	402	118
	1922	1,047	99	20	78	25	36	92	1	224	383	89
Africa, non-British	1918	1,503	218	72	333	51	214	35	60	190	177	153
	1919	696	85	119	146	24	116	25	30	23	106	22
	1920	1,258	180	239	283	84	180	27	45	77	117	26
	1921	1,313	150	298	226	56	181	48	36	73	164	81
	1922	1,083	79	36	199	16	93	34	25	271	282	48

TABLE XIII.—DISTRIBUTION OF PERMANENT DEPARTURES, BY OCCUPATION AND COUNTRY OF FUTURE RESIDENCE, 1918-22 (concluded).

Country	Year	Total	Professional	Domestic	Commercial	Transport and communications	Industrial	Agricultural	Mining	Independent or indefinite	Dependents	Unspecified
Australia	1918	177	43	9	8	10	16	3	3	38	29	18
	1919	206	26	46	20	19	23	10	6	10	40	6
	1920	592	78	149	74	14	58	17	13	44	128	17
	1921	1,031	120	264	112	26	126	40	22	41	206	74
	1922	1,078	90	23	112	28	108	37	15	172	403	90
New Zealand	1918	26	6	2	4	2	5	....	....	2	3	2
	1919	11	4	2	1	....	1	....	....	....	3	....
	1920	34	6	8	7	1	4	2	....	4	2	2
	1921	20	1	6	3	....	1	2	....	1	5	1
	1922	60	8	1	4	....	4	2	....	7	32	2
United States	1918	238	84	15	27	21	14	8	5	19	26	19
	1919	117	15	15	19	20	11	3	3	4	23	4
	1920	147	16	8	50	13	9	4	4	8	34	1
	1921	183	27	41	25	11	25	4	3	11	32	2
	1922	176	8	6	25	2	19	4	2	48	55	7
Europe	1918	109	40	3	9	18	8	2	11	8	6	4
	1919	416	77	54	34	72	54	19	11	14	66	15
	1920	551	56	101	60	48	47	103	6	30	69	31
	1921	625	59	94	50	40	103	116	14	21	79	49
	1922	920	46	17	39	18	41	51	42	393	212	61
Asia	1918	2,209	69	285	92	25	979	29	8	31	642	49
	1919	1,904	22	315	98	30	801	9	....	10	606	13
	1920	2,175	48	228	190	8	830	19	108	19	701	24
	1921	3,727	55	256	158	14	2,075	30	4	14	1,102	19
	1922	3,016	39	7	119	9	22	21	2	1,973	806	18
Other countries	1918	113	21	3	8	19	23	1	1	10	17	10
	1919	169	15	35	21	24	19	5	3	8	32	7
	1920	61	5	13	7	11	10	3	2	2	4	4
	1921	15	1	4	4	....	1	3	1	....	1	....
	1922	12	2	....	4	....	3	1	....	2	4	....

TABLE XIV.—Distribution of immigrants by sea and land intending permanent residence, by sex and race, 1924.

	Total	Europeans			Extra-Europeans		
		Total	Males	Females	Total	Asiatics	Other non-Europeans
Total......	5,933	5,265	2,692	2,573	668	632	36
By sea..	5,606	5,149	2,622	2,527	457	430	27
By land.	327	116	70	46	211	202	9

TABLE XV.—Distribution of emigrants by sea and by land relinquishing domicile, by sex and race, 1924.

	Total	Europeans			Extra-Europeans		
		Total	Males	Females	Total	Males	Females
Total......	7,124	5,857	3,147	2,710	1,267	1,231	36
By sea...	5,648	4,419	2,321	2,098	1,229	1,208	21
By land.	1,476	1,438	826	612	38	23	·15

TABLE XVI.—Distribution of Europeans assuming and relinquishing domicile, by sex and age, 1924.

Age	Assuming domicile			Relinquishing domicile		
	Total	Males	Females	Total	Males	Females
Up to 4 years........	457	221	236	378	179	199
5- 9..............	273	133	140	384	176	208
10-14..............	270	144	126	347	188	159
15-19..............	438	277	161	348	179	169
20-29..............	1,768	927	841	1,358	772	586
30-39..............	1,163	552	611	1,240	662	578
40-49..............	534	285	249	987	553	434
50-59..............	220	100	120	475	273	202
60-69..............	94	34	60	248	125	123
70 years and over.....	44	19	25	84	36	48
Unknown...........	4	...	4	8	4	4
Total...........	5,265	2,692	2,573	5,857	3,147	2,710

TABLE XVII.—Distribution of Europeans assuming and relinquishing domicile, by occupation, 1924.

Occupation	Assuming domicile			Relinquishing domicile		
	Total	Males	Females	Total	Males	Females
Primary producers : fishery and agriculture..........	418	410	8	425	421	4
Mining................	30	30	....	109	109	....
Industrial...............	656	581	75	635	599	36
Transport and communications...................	102	99	3	203	201	2
Commercial...............	588	452	136	643	527	116
Professional...............	653	317	336	606	328	278
Personal service...........	227	50	177	163	57	106
Independent..............	53	45	8	106	90	16
Other and unspecified.......	482	118	364	486	170	316
Dependents...............	2,056	590	1,466	2,481	645	1,836
Total.................	5,265	2,692	2,573	5,857	3,147	2,710

TABLE XVIII.—Distribution of European immigrants and emigrants, by nationality, 1924.

Nationality	Immigrants intending permanent residence (assuming domicile)	South Africans relinquishing domicile	Nationality	Immigrants intending permanent residence (assuming domicile)	South Africans relinquishing domicile
British................	3,724	5,275	Hungarian............	1	....
American, South.......	6	1	Russian..............	86	9
American, United States	76	74	Polish...............	69	3
American, Other North.	....	....	Lithuanian............	492	7
Danish...............	19	14	Latvian..............	60	3
Norwegian............	61	137	Rumanian............	1	....
Swedish..............	17	9	Slav (so returned)......	....	1
Netherlander.........	136	42	Turkish..............	9	2
Belgian..............	11	14	Spanish..............	....	1
German..............	326	69	Portuguese...........	18	53
Swiss................	27	18	Italian..............	32	53
French..............	17	34	Greek...............	47	26
Finnish..............	5	....	Hebrew (so returned)...	3	2
Czechoslovak.........	5	2	Syrian...............	....	1
Yugoslav............	10	3	Japanese.............	....	....
Austrian.............	7	4	Unspecified...........	....	....
Total............	4,447	5,696	Total............	818	161

TABLE XIX.—Distribution of extra-Europeans assuming and relinquishing domicile, by sex and age, 1924.

Age	Assuming domicile			Relinquishing domicile		
	Total	Males	Females	Total	Males	Females
Total...............	668	447	221	1,267	890	377
Under 16 years.......	453	391	62	398	218	180
16 years and over.....	215	56	159	869	672	197

TABLE XX.—Distribution of non-Europeans assuming and relinquishing domicile, by birthplace, 1924.

Birthplace	Assuming domicile	Relinquishing domicile
Cape.........	...	46
Natal........	...	426
Bechuanaland........	8	....
Mauritius........	8	7
St. Helena........	12	4
Other British African possessions	6	5
India........	580	756
China........	38	11
Syria........	7	....
Other places........	9	12
	668	1,267

SOURCES

Statistical Tables relating to the Colonial and other Possessions of the United Kingdom. Parts XVII to XXV.   London.

Table I (years 1880-1900).

Statistical Abstract for the several British Overseas Dominions and Protectorates in each year from 1900-12, London, 1914.

Tables II, III and IV (years 1900-12).

Official Year-Book of the Union of South Africa, Nos. 1-7, Pretoria, 1918-25.

Tables V (years 1910-22); VI (years 1913-19); VII, VIII (years 1913-23); IX (years 1918-23); X (years 1918-19); XI, XII (years 1918, 1919, 1921, 1922).

Statistics of Migration to and from the Union, 1920 to March 1925.   (Office of Census and Statistics, Special Report Series, No. 25.)

Tables VI, X (years 1920-24); XIII, XIV, XV (year 1924).

Information supplied by the Office of Census and Statistics, Pretoria.

Tables IX, IX, X and XI (year 1920).

NOTES

[1]From 1880 to 1895 year ended June 30 and since 1896 year ended December 31.
[2]For the six months ended December 31, 1896.
[3]Zululand was annexed to Natal on December 30, 1897.   Figures for 1898-1900 refer to Natal including Zululand.
[4]Year ended June 30.
[5]These figures, taken from the Report for 1920 to March 1925, seem to be revised.   They do not agree exactly with those published earlier in the Year-Book up to 1923.
[6]Total of persons allowed entry, by sea, after the number of residents who return has been deducted.
[7]Figures subject to revision.
[8]Included with "other nationalities"
[9]Total of persons embarked after the number of residents who leave temporarily has been deducted.

SOUTHERN RHODESIA

TABLE I.—DISTRIBUTION OF IMMIGRANTS[1], BY NATIONALITY OR RACE, 1915-24.

Year	Total	British home-born	British South African	Dutch South African	Other British Dominions	European aliens	Asiatics	Other colored races and natives
1915	1,536	821	332	141	42	111	52	37
1916	1,597	722	405	232	42	101	20	75
1917	1,680	609	370	322	20	133	34	192
1918	1,828	670	498	344	25	122	45	124
1919	2,542	1,210	525	428	21	111	75	172
1920	4,093	2,181	625	557	52	227	129	332
1921	3,343	1,543	689	485	70	288	99	169
1922	1,944	1,014	398	227	39	153	56	57
1924	1,645	724	462	166	26	177	60	30

For reference notes see page 1069.

TABLE II.—Distribution of immigrants[1], by sex, age and nationality, 1922 and 1924.

Nationality	1922				1924			
	Total	Males	Females	Minors	Total	Males	Females	Minors
British home-born	1,014	488	388	138	724	380	272	72
South Africans, British	398	170	141	87	462	212	143	107
South Africans, Dutch	227	91	65	71	166	65	49	52
Australasians	21	12	7	2	10	6	3	1
New Zealanders	1	....	1	...	....	...	...	...
Anglo-Indians	2	1	1	....	..	...	...	...
Canadians	....	....	....	....	7	5	2	...
Other British Dominions	....	....	....	....	9	7	2	...
Americans	36	15	13	8	8	4	4	...
French	6	2	4	...	3	2	1	...
Belgians	1	1	....	....	....	....	...	...
Italians	18	11	4	3	6	5	...	1
Rumanians	1	....	1	...	....	...	...	...
Slavs, Yugo- and Czecho-	2	2	....	....	5	4	1	...
Poles	1	1	....	....	1	1	...	...
Netherlanders	2	1	1	...	6	3	2	1
Greeks	22	19	2	1	33	20	9	4
Norwegians	2	2	....	....	....	...	...	...
Danes	1	....	1	...	1	1	...	...
Swiss	6	2	3	1	4	1	2	1
Swedes	1	1	....	...	4	1	3	...
Jews: British	15	8	5	2	15	5	7	3
Italian	10	8	2	....	18	10	6	2
Rumanian	6	3	2	1	....	...	...	...
Lithuanian	2	1	1	...	..	...	...	...
Russian	32	17	8	7	34	20	7	7
South African	....	....	....	....	19	12	...	7
Bulgarian	1	1	....	....	..	...	...	...
Germans	3	2	1	....	15	5	10	....
Serbians	....	....	....	....	3	3	...	...
Latvians	....	....	....	....	1	1	...	...
Spaniards	....	...	....	....	1	...	1	....
British Indians	44	16	13	15	47	17	8	22
Goanese Indians	11	8	1	2	12	4	4	4
Chinese	1	....	....	1	1	...	1	...
Malays	1	....	1	....	2	1	1	...
Mauritians	1	1	....	....	..	...	...	...
Cape, colored	35	17	13	5	16	3	9	4
Natives	20	14	6	....	10	7	3	...
St. Helena	....	....	....	....	2	1	1	...
Total	1,944	915	685	344	1,645	806	551	228

For reference notes see page 1069.

TABLE III.—Distribution of immigrants[1], by occupation and sex, 1922 and 1924.

Occupation	Nature of employment or sex	1922	1924
Mechanics and skilled artisans............	Mines	52	45
	Railways	21	18
	Other	211	126
Laborers and unskilled workers...........	Mines	6	5
	Railways	24	10
	Farms	134	92
	Other	90	65
Medical, clerical and educational..........	Males	55	57
	Females	97	91
Shop assistants and clerks................	Males	173	184
	Females	53	29
Professional...........................	Males	17	39
	Females	3	1
Leisured..............................	Males	1	6
	Females	..	..
Agents, commercial travellers, etc.........	Males	20	24
	Females	2	1
Domestic servants......................	Males	15	11
	Females	98	62
Farm settlers..........................	Males	52	99
	Females	2	3
Hawkers and petty traders...............	Males	4	8
	Females	..	6
Unclassified (wives, fiancees, minors, etc.)...	Males	221	160
	Females	593	503
Total.................................		1,944	1,645

SOURCE

Report of the Commissioner, British South Africa Police, for 1922 and 1924. Salisbury, Rhodesia, 1923 (pp. 11 and 20), 1925 (p. 18).

NOTES

[1]Arriving by sea from overseas countries and from the continent.

SWAZILAND

TABLE I.—EMIGRATION OF NATIVES, 1907-24.

Year[1]	Emigrants[2]	Indentured	Year[1]	Emigrants[2]	Indentured
1907–08	7,906	*	1914–15	12,120	4,651
1908–09	10,320	*	1915–16	12,831	4,571
1909–10	9,580	*	1921	9,985	4,344
1912–13	8,320	4,960	1923	10,449	5,512
1913–14	9,833	3,566	1924	11,067	5,741

SOURCE

Colonial Reports (Annual). Swaziland. London, 1909-25.
Table I (years 1907/08-1924).

NOTES

[1]1907/08 1915/16 years ended March 31.
[2]Mainly natives going to work (principally on the mines in Johannesburg)

TANGANYIKA

British Mandate

TABLE I.—DISTRIBUTION OF IMMIGRANTS, BY RACE, 1920-24.

Year	Total	Europeans, Americans	Asiatics, Goans	Others (including natives of adjoining territories)
1920	4,318	*	*	*
1921	6,278	1,523	867[1]	3,888[2]
1923	2,126	561	1,341	224[3]
1924	2,475[4]	485[5]	809	1,181

SOURCE

Report on Tanganyika Territory. London, 1922-25.

Table I (years 1920-24.)

NOTES

[1]This number includes British Indians and Gôans.
[2]Includes Africans, Cingalese, natives of the Seychelles and China, etc.
[3]This number includes Seychellians, Singalese, Chinese, Arabs and Somalis.
[4]This total does not include visitors or passengers in transit.
[5]Includes Europeans, Americans and Eurasians.

TABLE I.—Distribution of immigrants, by sex, age and nationality, 1921-24.

Nationality	Sex and age	1921	1922	1923	1924
French:					
Citizens..........	Total	330	749	709	810
	Males	153	405[4]	416	360
	Females	95	243	195	226
	Children	82[1]	101	98	224
Somali subjects.....	Total	133	119	23	222[5]
	Males	83	119	22	214[5]
	Females	20	....	1	7[5]
	Children	30	....	....	1[5]
English..............	Total	26	117	91	251
	Males	19	62	54	147
	Females	4	38	21	62
	Children	3[2]	17	16	42
Hindu...............	Total	88	170	126	344
	Males	80	107	97	311
	Females	6	29	15	19
	Children	2	34	14	14
American.............	Total	4	10	6	4
	Males	1	6	3	4
	Females	1	4	3	...
	Children	2	....	....	....
Chinese...............	Total	2	90	16	97
	Males	2	81	13	82
	Females	...	4	2	9
	Children	...	5	1	6
Other nationalities......	Total	13	66	32	40
	Males	9	37	18	20
	Females	2	18	13	10
	Children	2	11	1	10
Total.................		596	1,321[4]	1,003	1,768
	Males	347	817[4]	623	1,138
	Females	128	336	250	333
	Children	121[3]	168	130	297

TABLE II.—Distribution of immigrants, by occupation, 1921-24.

Occupation	1921	1922	1923	1924
Agriculture.........................	6	33	109	208
Industry............................	1	20	5	36
Transport and commerce.............	50	178	186	303
Domestic service and general labor....	83	119	19	188
Liberal professions and public services..	46	201	157	58
Other occupations, none, or unknown...	400	767	527	975
Total.......................	596[3]	1,321[4]	1,003	1,768

For reference notes see page 1073.

TABLE III.—Distribution of emigrants, by sex, age and nationality, 1921-24.

Nationality	Sex and age	1921	1922	1923	1924
French:					
Citizens..........	Total	76	221	183	136
	Males	28	103	85	68
	Females	33	60	60	48
	Children	15	58	38	20
Madagascar subjects	Total	4	23	23	21
	Males	2	16	19	13
	Females	2	7	4	8
	Children	....	....	....	...
Somali subjects.....	Total	....	4	1	33
	Males	....	4	1	33
	Females	....	....	....	....
	Children	....	....	....	....
English..............	Total	2	2	4	12
	Males	1	1	2	12
	Females	1	1	1	....
	Children	....	....	1	....
Hindu...............	Total	....	119	8	12
	Males	....	119	8	11
	Females	....	....	....	1[6]
	Children	....	....	....	....
Greek...............	Total	3	....	3	3
	Males	3	....	2	1
	Females	....	....	1	1
	Children	...	....	....	1
Norwegian...........	Total	....	....	16	....
	Males	....	....	4	....
	Females	....	....	4	....
	Children	....	....	8	....
Swiss................	Total	1	....	1	....
	Males	1	....	1	....
	Females	....	....	....	....
	Children	....	....	....	....
Other nationalities......	Total	....	40	....	....
	Males	....	21	....	....
	Females	....	9	....	....
	Children	....	10	....	....
Total................		86	409	239	217
	Males	35	264	122	138
	Females	36	77	70	58
	Children	15	68	47	21

For reference notes see page 1073.

TABLE IV.—Distribution of emigrants, by occupation, 1921-24.

Occupation	1921	1922	1923	1924
Agriculture..........................	7	37	29	13
Industry:............................	1	13	4	7
Transport and commerce.............	3	70	35	23
Domestic service and general labor....	6	111	22	52
Liberal professions and public services..	8	29	33	12
Other occupations, none, or unknown...	61	149	116	109
Total........................	86	409	239	216[6]

SOURCE

Information supplied by the French Government.

All tables.

NOTES

[1]The sum of the figures by occupations and ports of disembarkation given in the source is 75.
[2]This figure is missing in the return by occupations and ports of disembarkation given in the source.
[3]The total by ports and occupations gives the figure of 111 for children and of 586 for all immigrants.
[4]The total by ports and occupations gives the figure of 402 for males of French nationality, of 814 for all male immigrants and of 1,318 for all immigrants together.
[5]Includes 35 Madagascar subjects of whom 29 are males, 5 females and 1 child.
[6]In the figures supplied by the Government, 1 female Hindu is included for 1924 in table III of whom no trace exists in that year in table IV.

FRENCH SOMALI COAST

TABLE I.—EMIGRATION OF CITIZENS, (LABORERS),[1] 1920-24.

Year	Total	Year	Total
1920	112	1923	761
1921	258	1924	290
1922	403		

TABLE II.—DISTRIBUTION OF IMMIGRANTS DISEMBARKED AT THE PORT OF JIBOUTI WITH INTENTION TO SETTLE, BY NATIONALITY, 1920-24.

Year	Total	French	Other nationalities
1920	40	37	3
1921	7	4	3
1924	5	5	..

TABLE III.—DISTRIBUTION OF PERSONS DEPARTED FROM JIBOUTI, BY NATIONALITY, 1920-24.[2]

Nationality	1920	1921	1922	1923	1924
Citizens:					
French........................	245	40	4	22	23
Aliens:					
German......................	..	..	..	1	2
Austrian......................	..	..	..	..	1
Armenian.....................	26	19	2	2	1
Belgian.......................	3	1	1	1	3
Chinese.......................	..	..	..	1	1
Danish........................	..	..	..	..	1
Egyptian......................	1	1	..	..	..
American......................	..	..	..	..	2
British........................	3	..	..	..	1
Greek.........................	46	32	8	7	10
Hungarian.....................	..	..	1	..	..
Italian........................	18	..	5	3	1
Luxemburger..................	1	..	..	..	..
Netherlander..................	..	..	..	1	1
Russian.......................	..	..	..	..	..
Swiss.........................	3	1	..	..	..
Syrian........................	4	2	2	2	..
Czechoslovak.................	..	..	..	..	3
Total.....................	350	96	23	40	50

SOURCE

Information supplied by the French Government.

NOTES

[1]Workmen departed to work temporarily at sea or in foreign countries.
[2]Persons who were settled for a certain length of time.

ANGOLA

In conformity with the Decree of July 4, 1906, of the Ministry of Shipping, aliens present themselves within a period of three days to the proper administrative authority of the place of entry. Alien travellers in transit, provided their stay does not exceed twenty days, are not required to report.

The statistical account received, however, covers only the years 1923 and 1924.

TABLE I.—DISTRIBUTION OF ARRIVALS (ALIENS), BY NATIONALITY AND SEX, 1923-24.

Nationality	Sex	1923	1924	Nationality	Sex	1923	1924
German..........	Males	73	105	English..........	Males	78	53
	Females	18	28		Females	13	11
Australian........	Males	..	1	Italian..........	Males	1	12
	Females	1	..		Females	3	1
Belgian..........	Males	16	6	North American..	Males	36	27
	Females	3	1		Females	4	6
Brazilian.........	Males	1	..	Norwegian.......	Males	2	3
	Females	..	1		Females	1	1
Danish...........	Males	1	1	Polish..........	Males	..	1
	Females	..	..		Females	..	..
Spanish..........	Males	4	3	Russian..........	Males	..	1
	Females	1	..		Females	..	..
French..........	Males	12	5	Swedish.........	Males	1	1
	Females	2	1		Females	..	..
Greek...........	Males	4	1	Swiss...........	Males	4	..
	Females	..	1		Females	..	..
Dutch..........	Males	8	2	South African....	Males	6	3
	Females	1	1		Females	1	1
Total......	Males	119	124	Total........	Males	128	101
	Females	26	33		Females	22	20
Grand total.......		145	157	Grand total......		150	121

TABLE II.—DISTRIBUTION OF DEPARTURES (ALIENS), BY NATIONALITY AND SEX, 1923-24.

Nationality	Sex	1923	1924	Nationality	Sex	1923	1924
German..........	Males	16	20	Greek..........	Males	..	..
	Females	2	7		Females	..	..
Australian........	Males	..	..	Dutch..........	Males	5	..
	Females	..	..		Females	..	..
Belgian..........	Males	9	7	English.........	Males	35	26
	Females	1	2		Females	9	5
Brazilian.........	Males	..	1	Italian..........	Males	2	1
	Females	..	1		Females	..	..
Danish..........	Males	..	1	North American..	Males	25	9
	Females	..	..		Females	3	..
Spanish..........	Males	5	3	Norwegian.......	Males	1	..
	Females	3	..		Females	..	1
French..........	Males	1	1	Swiss..........	Males	3	..
	Females	2	..		Females	2	1
				South African....	Males	..	2
					Females	..	..
Total........	Males	31	33	Total........	Males	71	38
	Females	8	10		Females	14	7
Grand total......		39	43	Grand total......		85	45

SOURCE

Information supplied by the Portuguese Government.

Tables I and II (years 1923-24.)

TABLE I.—Distribution of emigrant citizens, by sex and age and according to passports issued, 1913-21 and 1923-24.[1]

Year	Total			Children			Over 14 years		
	Total	Males	Females	Total	Males	Females	Total	Males	Females
1913	6,517	3,320	3,197	1,562	794	768	4,955	2,526	2,429
1914	3,812	1,982	1,830	796	383	413	3,016	1,599	1,417
1915	3,938	2,219	1,719	713	339	374	3,225	1,880	1,345
1916	5,036	2,096	2,940	1,362	725	637	3,674	1,371	2,303
1917	2,016	743	1,273	566	314	252	1,450	429	1,021
1918	247	83	164	54	26	28	193	57	136
1919	1,497	726	771	260	127	133	1,237	599	638
1920	8,073	4,571	3,502	1,183	579	604	6,890	3,992	2,898
1921	2,710	1,565	1,145	403	205	198	2,307	1,360	947
1923	1,628	1,039	589	211	...	...	1,417	....	....
1924	789	398	391	153	...	...	636	....	....

TABLE II.—Emigration of citizens, by country of future residence and according to passports issued, 1913-21 and 1923-24.[1]

Year	Total	North America	South America			Oceania	Africa	Asia	Europe
			Argen-tina	Brazil	Other countries				
1913	6,517	6,026	..	433	19	..	3	..	36
1914	3,812	3,547	10	237	..	..	..	..	17
1915	3,938	3,832	1	90	..	..	..	..	15
1916	5,036	4,925	..	66	..	1	14	..	30
1917	2,016	1,959	..	24	1	..	10	..	22
1918	247	197	..	7	..	..	5	..	38
1919	1,497	1,310	..	121	..	..	5	..	61
1920	8,073	7,799	..	213	2	..	3	..	56
1921	2,710	2,465	..	147	..	..	3	11	84
1923	1,628	657	1	682	243	..	3	2	40
1924	789	431	1	217	115	..	1	1	23

TABLE III.—Distribution of third class emigrant and immigrant citizens, by sex, 1924.[2]

Year	Emigrants			Immigrants		
	Total	Males	Females	Total	Males	Females
1924	1,008	630	378	443	292	151

For reference notes see page 1078.

TABLE IV.—Distribution of passengers of all classes (citizens) embarked and disembarked in the Ports of Horta, Ponta Delgada, Heroismo, by sex and destination or place of embarkation, 1924.

		Total	Place of destination or embarkation		
			Brazil	North America	Unknown
Departures:	Total..................	1,165	115	1,046	4
	Males[3]...............	713	68	643	2
	Females..............	452	47	403	2
Arrivals:	Total..................	595	...	588	7
	Males[3]...............	397	...	392	5
	Females..............	198	...	196	2

SOURCES

Portuguese Republic. Ministry of Finance. Statistical Department. *Estatistica Demográfica.* Movements of Population. Lisbon, 1919 to 1926.

Tables I and II (years 1913-21 and 1922-23).

Information supplied by the Portuguese Government Commissioner-General of Emigration.

Table III (year 1924).

NOTES

[1]The figures in both tables I and II for the years 1913-21 are taken from the passport statistics. They are included in the figures given in Tables I, Ia and Ib for Portugal.

[2]The figures for 1924 in table III represent intercontinental emigration and immigration of citizens (third class passengers) by the ports of Heroism, Horta and Ponta Delgada. They contain a certain number of emigrants and immigrants to and from Europe.

[3]415 of the male emigrants and 55 of the male immigrants are described as "workers and day laborers".

TABLE I.—DISTRIBUTION OF EMIGRANTS, BY SEX AND COUNTRY OF DESTINATION (EXCLUDING INDENTURED LABORERS), 1912-20.

	Year	1912	1913	1914	1915	1916	1917	1918	1919	1920
	Total	1,599	2,262	2,353	1,190	2,210	1,747	526	893	2,536
	Males	1,410	1,967	1,900	914	1,715	1,510	396	723	2,133
	Females	189	295	453	276	495	237	130	170	403
Europe	Portugal (Lisbon)	15	6	22	.....	45	27	41	52	66
	England	.....	5	2	.....	11	6	1	9	4
	Other countries: Europe,Gibraltar Genoa,France, Spain, Belgium...	.....	.....	.....	53	5	4	.....	5	2
America	United States	1,066	1,689	1,610	768	1,645	1,500	279	452	1,467
	Brazil	71	150	57	7	9	16	20	73	126
	Argentina	252	147	74	21	19	30	2	70	157
	Uruguay (Montevideo)	10	5	3	4	4	6	.....	1	15
Portuguese and foreign colonies	Angola (Loanda)...	14	6	2	6	24	6	3	2	3
	Other countries....	171	254	583	331	448	152	180	229	696

TABLE II.—DISTRIBUTION OF EMIGRANTS, BY SEX, AGE AND COUNTRY OF DESTINATION (INCLUDING INDENTURED LABORERS), 1912-19.

	Year	1912	1913	1914	1915	1916	1917	1918	1919
	Total	2,393	3,379	3,648	2,049	2,980	2,089	667	1,176
	Males	2,089	2,731	2,851	1,479	2,192	1,734	532	900
	Females	304	648	797	570	788	355	135	276
Over 14 years	Total	2,323	3,334	.....	1,965	2,807	2,016	638	1,098
	Males	2,040	2,699	.....	1,323	2,107	1,696	500	.....
	Females	283	635	.....	642	700	320	138	.....
Under 14 years	Total	70	45	.....	84	173	73	29	78
	Males	49	32	.....	42	79	38	18	.....
	Females	21	13	.....	42	94	35	11	.....
Europe		15	11	24	53	61	37	42	64
America	North America	1,066	1,689	1,610	768	1,645	1,500	223	452
	Brazil	71	150	57	7	9	16	78	56
	Other South American countries	262	156	77	25	23	36	2	88
	Angola	14	.....	.....	10	9	.....	2	2
	Dakar	61	173	76	82	94	41	8	15
Portuguese and foreign colonies	Las Palmas	3	7	1	13	.....	.....	.....	1
	South Georgia	54	.....	.....	16	184	8	47	39
	Guinea	26	9	1	97	115	75	82	144
	St.Thome, Principe...	812	1,138	1,664	888	819	342	167	308
	Fernando Po	.....	36	38	.....	.....	.....	.....	.....
	Loanda	.....	6	2	.....	15	6	4	.....
	Other countries	9	4	98	90	6	28	14	7

TABLE III.—DISTRIBUTION OF EMIGRANT CITIZENS ACCORDING TO SEX, AGE AND COUNTRY OF FUTURE RESIDENCE, 1923-1924.

Year	Total	Sex		Age		Country of future residence				
		Males	Females	Under 14 years	Over 14 years	Europe	America	Asia	Oceania	Africa
1923	25	22	3	..	25	14	3	..	..	8
1924	15	8	7	..	15	7	4	..	.	4

SOURCE

Governor of the Province of Cape Verde.   General Secretariat.   Statistical Section. *Estatistica Geral de Provincia de Cabo Verde.*   Praia, 1915 to 1925.

Tables I (years 1912-20); II (years 1912-19).

Portuguese Republic.   Minister of Finance.   Statistical Department.   *Estatistica Demogràfica.*   Movements of Population.   Lisbon, 1919 to 1924.

Table III (from 1923-24.)

TABLE I.—Distribution of emigrant citizens, by sex and age according to passports issued, 1913-21 and 1923-24.[1]

Year	Total			Children			Over 14 years		
	Total	Males	Females	Total	Males	Females	Total	Males	Females
1913	3,295	2,124	1,171	818	448	370	2,477	1,676	801
1914	992	598	394	169	84	85	823	514	309
1915	1,271	854	417	209	111	98	1,062	743	319
1916	2,323	1,338	985	435	246	189	1,888	1,092	796
1917	611	238	373	193	118	75	418	120	298
1918	104	61	43	42	26	16	62	35	27
1919	1,695	1,062	633	388	212	176	1,307	850	457
1920	6,437	4,211	2,226	1,333	747	586	5,104	3,464	1,640
1921	1,391	834	557	299	156	143	1,092	678	414
1923	2,112	1,420	692	401	...	...	1,711	...	...
1924	1,271	838	433	227	...	...	1,044	...	...

TABLE II.—Emigration of citizens, by country of destination according to passports issued, 1913-21 and 1923-24.[1]

Year	Total	North America	South America			Oceania	Africa	Asia	Europe
			Argen-tina	Brazil	Other countries				
1913	3,295	1,588	..	1,510	62	2	83	..	50
1914	992	705	13	217	19	..	29	..	9
1915	1,271	1,114	2	56	32	1	50	..	16
1916	2,323	2,241	..	39	6	..	11	..	26
1917	611	562	..	11	1	..	1	6	30
1918	104	46	..	16	..	..	8	..	34
1919	1,695	812	..	672	41	..	103	..	67
1920	6,437	3,439	12	2,788	40	..	63	..	95
1921	1,391	321	6	737	67	..	124	..	136
1923	2,112	279	31	779	12	1	48	..	146
1924	1,271	610	22	1,242	43	..	29	..	141

TABLE III.—Distribution of third class emigrant and immigrant citizens, by sex, 1924.[2]

Year	Emigrants			Immigrants		
	Total	Males	Females	Total	Males	Females
1924	923	620	303	802	615	187

For reference notes see page 1082.

TABLE IV.—Distribution of passengers of all classes (citizens), embarked and disembarked in the Port of Funchal, by sex, place of destination or embarkation and occupation, 1924.

	Total	Place of destination or embarkation				Occupation		
		Brazil	Monte-video and Buenos-Aires	North America	Un-known	Arti-sans	General laborers	Total
Departures:								
Total..........	1,098	866	48	...	184	4	418	422
Males..........	730	564	40	...	126	4	418	422
Females........	368	302	8	...	58	0	0	0
Arrivals:								
Total..........	964	326	70	341	227	1	274	275
Males..........	723	228	55	265	175	1	274	275
Females........	241	98	15	76	52	0	0	0

SOURCES

Portuguese Republic. Ministry of Finance. Statistical Department. *Estatistica Demogràfica*. Movements of Population. Lisbon, 1919 to 1924.

Tables I and II (years 1913-21).

Information supplied by the Portuguese Government Commissioner-General of Emigration.

Table III (year 1924).

NOTES

[1]The figures in both tables I and II for the years 1913-21 are taken from the passport statistics. They are included in the figures given in tables I, Ia and Ib for Portugal.

[2]The figures for 1924 in table III represent intercontinental emigration and immigration of citizens (third class passengers) by the port of Funchal. They contain a certain number of emigrants and immigrants to and from Europe.

CAMEROON

French Mandate

TABLE I.—Continental migration of natives and intercontinental migration of Europeans, 1923.

	Interconti-nental (Europeans)[1]	Continental (natives)[2]
Immigration..	570	2,091
Emigration..	466	1,610

SOURCE

Rapport annuel du Gouvernement français sur l'administration sous mandat du Territoire du Cameroun pour l'année 1923, pp. 108-111. Paris, 1924.

Table I.

NOTES

[1]Overseas immigration and emigration of Europeans, mainly officials, soldiers, missionaries, and traders.
[2]Continental emigration and immigration of natives by the sea frontier; agricultural workers going to the Spanish or Portuguese islands with a one or two-year contract, or skilled workers or traders going to other colonies on the African coast to carry on their occupation there.

TOGO

French Mandate

TABLE I.—Continental emigration of natives,[1] 1923-24.

Year	Total
1923	3,000[2]
1924	3,500[3]

SOURCE

Rapport annuel du Gouvernement français sur l'administration sous mandat des territoires du Togo. Paris, 1924, p. 85; Paris, 1925, p. 103.

Table I (years 1923, 1924).

NOTES

[1]Seasonal emigration to the Gold Coast and British Togoland to work on cocoa plantations. By the terms of the Order of December 2, 1922, no native may leave the territory of Togo for more than ten days without a passport bearing his photograph. This formality constitutes a means of controlling emigration and at the same time a safeguard to the natives themselves, as it protects them against unsafe contracts.
[2]The number of natives who expatriate themselves may be estimated at about three thousand.
[3]The number of natives who change their abode may be estimated at between three and four thousand.

BIBLIOGRAPHY

[References in the Introduction not previously cited in full, will be found here. Titles of statistical publications are cited in full under "Sources" of the respective countries—Editor.]

Abbott, Edith, *Immigration*, Select Documents and Case Records, Chicago, 1924.

——————, *Historical Aspects of the Immigration Problem*, Select Documents, Chicago, 1926.

Berne, Pierre, *L'immigration européenne en Argentine*, Paris, 1915.

Blackman, William F., *The Making of Hawaii*, New York, 1899.

Boddy, E. Manchester, *Japanese in America*, Los Angeles, 1921.

Calvo, Charles, *Etude sur l'Emigration et la Colonisation*. Paris, 1875.

Campbell, Persia Crowford, *Chinese Coolie Emigration to countries within the British Empire*, London, 1923.

Canada, *Report of the Department of Immigration and Colonization* for the fiscal year ended 31 March 1924. Ottawa, 1925.

Canstatt, Oskar, *Die deutsche Auswanderung, Auswandererfürsorge und Auswandererziele*. Berlin, 1904.

Ceylon, Administration Reports for 1924. *Indian Immigrant labour.*

Chandèze, Gustave, *L'émigration, Intervention des pouvoirs publics au XIXe siècle*. Paris, 1898.

Clementi, Cecil, *The Chinese in British Guiana*, London 1915.

Cory, G. E., *The Rise of South Africa*. London, 1921.

Duval, Jules, *Histoire de l'émigration*, Paris, 1862.

"Emigrant", *Indian Emigration*, London, 1924.

Emigration Suisse, Enquête auprès de Messieurs les Consuls de la Confédération, suivie des observations de la Commission des Emigrations nommée par la Société d'Utilité publique fédérale, Lausanne, 1845.

Ferenczi, Imre, *Die Arbeitslosigkeit und die internationalen Arbeiterwanderungen*. Report to the International Committee of the International Association on Unemployment, Jena, 1913.

——————, *Die internationalen Wanderungen und die nächste allgemeine Arbeitskonferenz*, in "Soziale Praxis und Archiv für Volkswohlfahrt," Jena, 1922.

——————, *Die internationale Wanderungsfrage und die Statistik*, in "Jahrbücher für Nationalökonomie und Statistik." Band 121, Heft. 3 u. 4, Jena, 1923.

——————, *L'assistenza ai disoccupati ed il problema dell' emigrazione*. Nuova Antologia, Roma, luglio 1923.

——————, *Die internationale Regelung der kontinentalen Arbeiterwanderungen in Europa*, in "Weltwirtschaftliches Archiv," 1924, p. 427 ff.

——————, Article "Migrations" in Encyclopaedia Britannica. Supplement to 13th edition.

Foerster, Robert F. *The Italian Emigration of Our Times*. Cambridge, 1919.

Grünfeld, Ernst, *Die Japanische Auswanderung*, Tokio, 1913.

Guiral, Paul, *L'immigration réglementée aux Antilles françaises et à la Réunion*. Paris, 1911.

Heurtier, M., *Rapport à S. E. le ministre de l'agriculture, du commerce et des travaux publics*, Paris, 1854.

Hotten, John Camden, *Original Lists of Emigrants to America, 1600-1700*, London, 1874.

INTERNATIONAL LABOUR OFFICE, *Migration Movements, 1920-1923,* Genève, 1925.
——————, *Migration Movements, 1920-1924,* Genève, 1926.
IYENAGA, T. AND SATO, KENOSKE, *Japan and the California Problem,* New York, 1921.
JENKS, W. AND LAUCK, JETT., *The immigration Problem,* New York, 1926.
JOHNSON, C. STANLEY, *A History of Emigration from the United Kingdom to North America (1763-1912).* London, 1913.
JOHNSTON, HARRY H., *A History of the Colonization of Africa by Alien Races,* Cambridge, 1913.
KAPP, FRIEDRICH, *European Emigration to the United States,* New York, 1869.
——————, *Geschichte der deutschen Einwanderung in Amerika.*
KARRER, *Das schweizerische Auswanderungswesen und die Revision und Vollziehung des Bundesgesetzes betr. den Geschäftsbetrieb von Auswanderungsagenturen,* Bern, 1886.
LEGOYT, A., *L'Emigration européenne: Son importance, ses causes, ses effects.* Paris, 1861.
LEHMANN, EMIL, *Die deutsche Auswanderung,* Berlin, 1861.
LEROY BEAULIEU, P., *De la colonisation chez les peuples modernes,* Paris, 1902.
LOHER, FRANZ, *Geschichte und Zustände der Deutschen in Amerika.* Leipzig, 1847.
MACLEAN, ANNIE, *Modern Immigration,* London, 1925.
MAKEPEACE, W., *One hundred years of Singapore,* London, 1921.
New Zealand Official Year Book, 1926, Wellington, 1925.
Official Year Books of the Commonwealth of Australia, 1901-1918, 1925, 1926, Melbourne, 1919-1926.
Official Year Book of the Union of South Africa, 1919-1922, 1925. Pretoria, 1922, 1925.
PHILIPPOVICH, DR. E. VON, *Auswanderung und Auswanderungspolitik in Deutschland,* Leipzig, 1892.
——————, Article *"Auswanderung"* in Handwörterbuch der Staatswissenschaften, Jena, 1919.
RATHGEN, K., *Die englische Auswanderung und Auswanderungspolitik im neunzehnten Jahrhundert,* Leipzig, 1896.
RATZEL, F., *Die chinesische Auswanderung.* Breslau, 1876.
REDFORD, ART., *Labour Migration in England, 1800-1850.* Manchester, 1926.
Relatorio e documentos sobre a Aboliçao da Emigraçao de Chinas Contratados en Macao, Lisbon, 1874.
ROBIN, RENÉ, *La question de la main d'oeuvre dans les colonies d'exploitation françaises,* Paris, 1899.
ROY, E., *Notices sur les colonies françaises en 1858.* Extraits de la Revue coloniale (Juillet, 1858), Paris, 1858.
TA CHEN, *Chinese Migrations,* with special reference to labour conditions. In "Bulletin of the United States Bureau of Labor Statistics," No. 340, Washington, 1923.
UNITED STATES OF AMERICA. *Annual Report of the Commissioner-General of Immigration* for the fiscal year ended 30 June 1908, Washington, 1908.
UNITED STATES IMMIGRATION COMMISSION, *Dictionary of Races or Peoples.* Washington, 1911.
WILLCOX, WALTER F., *The Expansion of Europe in Population,* in "American Economic Review" Vol. V, No. 4, Ithaca, N. Y., 1915.
ZIMMERMANN, ALFRED, *Kolonialpolitik,* Leipzig, 1905.
——————, *Die Kolonialpolitik Frankreichs, von den Anfängen bis zur Gegenwart,* Berlin, 1901.
——————, *Die Kolonialpolitik der Niederländer,* Berlin, 1903.

INDEX

(*indicates a diagram)